The register of admissions to Gray.s Inn, 1521-1889

Joseph Foster, Gray.s Inn, Gray.s Inn. Chapel

THE

Register of Admissions

TO

Gray's Inn.

THE

Register of Admissions

TO

Gray's Inn, 1521–1889,

TOGETHER WITH THE

REGISTER OF MARRIAGES IN GRAY'S INN

CHAPEL, 1695—1754

BY

JOSEPH FOSTER,

AUTHOR OF "ALUMNI OXONIENSES," "THE BRITISH PEERAGE," "OUR NOBLE
AND GENTLE FAMILIES OF ROYAL DESCENT," ETC, ETC, ETC

LONDON PRIVATELY PRINTED
BY
THE HANSARD PUBLISHING UNION, LIMITED,
GREAT QUEEN STREET,
1889

CONTENTS.

—— o ——

PREFACE.

———o———

MONG those records of national interest which remain unpublished and comparatively unknown, the Registers of our Inns of Court hold a pre-eminent position As early as the days of Henry VI, we are reminded by Sir John Fortescue "that knights, barons, and the greatest nobility of the Kingdom often " place their children in these Inns of Court, not so much to make the laws " their study, much less to live by their profession, having large patrimonies " of their own, but to form their manners" In the Registers of these Inns we consequently find information which elsewhere we seek in vain, relating to families and individuals in every portion of the realm , the fact, moreover, that this information is contained in a legal register, invests it with an authority superior to that of the treasured Heralds' Visitations, while it enjoys with them the advantage of dealing with the aristocratic classes For, to quote from Ferne's *Glory of Generosity* (London, 1586) —"Nobleness of blood, joyned with virtue, competh the person as "most meet to the enterprizing of any publick service , and for that cause it was, not " for nought, that our antient Governors in this land, did with a special foresight and "Wisdom, provide, that none should be admitted into the Houses of Court, being "Seminaries, sending forth men apt to the Government of Justice, except he were a "gentleman of blood " This being so, it may appear surprising that records covering so extensive a period and of such unrivalled interest, should have remained virtually inaccessible, and consequently little consulted, since Sir William Dugdale drew so largely upon them for the compilation of " Origines Juridiciales," more than two centuries ago. But in this instance, as in some others, the explanation is doubtless to be found in the magnitude of such an undertaking as their transcription and publication

Impressed, however, by the importance of the work, I have myself accomplished the transcription of the whole of these unique Registers, having received special permission from the Benchers for the purpose , but, though it is my hope to see them eventually in print, it should be clearly understood that the permission I have received to transcribe the original records does not carry with it, on the part of the authorities, any responsibility, editorial or otherwise.

Preface.

Of these "Noblest nurseries of humanity and liberty in the Kingdom," as Ben Jonson styled them, Gray's Inn was at the period in which he wrote by far the most important and most numerously frequented   Its Register is, therefore, of special value for that brilliant Elizabethan epoch, in which the Inn may be said indeed to have played a direct part by its famous Masques and Revels   But there is an even more distinctive feature about the Register of Gray's   It was the practice of the Inn that each Treasurer, Bencher, or Reader, introducing a student or honorary member, should enter the admission himself in the Register   The result of this plan was unfortunately the introduction of an endless variety of handwriting, which, however interesting to a lover of autographs, is enough to puzzle a transcriber to distraction. The difficulty of deciphering these scrawling entries of three, or even two, centuries ago, is at times almost insuperable

This leads me to the origin of the transcript from which the present volume is printed   The Register was originally transcribed by G. E. Cokayne, Esq. (now Norroy King-of-Arms), who permitted the late Col. Chester to make a copy of his transcript. This copy has been the basis of my work, but was collated throughout by myself with the original record some years ago, and is now completed to the present time, by permission granted only a few weeks ago   Although, from the nature of the original admission book, it is almost impossible to avoid an occasional misreading, yet, I have been enabled, I trust, with the skilled assistance of Mr J A C Vincent, to reduce them to a minimum ; but even so, it will be easy to examine doubtful names, as I give the reference to each folio in the original register, a point of primary importance for the student.   I have incorporated with the text some variants from the Society's Order Books (o B) and Ledger, together with a few additional names   The entries prior to 1580 are chronologically arranged from Harleian MS 1912, compiled by Simon Segar (see page 274)   A full account of this MS will be found in the valuable work on "Gray's Inn, its History and Associations," by Mr W R Douthwaite (1886), the respected librarian of this Inn, to whom I may here express my thanks for the interest he has taken in this work, and for the very cordial assistance he has at all times afforded me

It is not possible within the limits of a Preface to enumerate the many distinguished individuals whose presence has adorned Gray's Inn   The immortal Bacon, the wise Burleigh, the learned FitzHerbert, the celebrated Gascoigne, Judge Jenkins the Welsh Loyalist, Hall the Chronicler, Camden the Antiquary, Dugdale, Walker, St George, Dethick, and Wriothesley the Heralds, Rymer of the Foedera, and in our own time the poet Barry Waller Proctor (Barry Cornwall), Edward Gibbon Wakefield, the chief founder of the Colonies of New Zealand and South Australia, together with many others, are among those who have contributed to render this Inn illustrious in no ordinary degree   Further familiar names will be recognized on a scrutiny of these pages which invite the delightful task of annotation on a liberal scale

I had at one time hoped to publish the Register in alphabetical form like my other works, and to annotate it myself, but I find myself compelled to abandon the project in default of adequate support   I have yielded, however, to the desire of my subscribers to "Collectanea Genealogica," and printed for them and my later genealogical friends a strictly limited edition of 160 copies, all of which are signed and numbered. I have, however, endeavoured to minimize the disadvantages of the plan I have been compelled to adopt by compiling an elaborate Index to the 16,000 students, of no less than 80 pages, for I feel that a commonplace Index of names to a book of reference such as this would be of little use to the student, who generally desires to bring down his man on the very first reference I have, therefore, added to each name, beside the reference page, the year of admission, and by so simple an arrangement, that I believe it will be universally appreciated. In the arrangement of the 16th and 17th century names, I have generally included the variants of each under its ordinary or best known form. To render the series of Gray's Inn Registers complete, I have included the Chapel Register of Marriages, arranged in alphabetical order

It only remains that I should express my earnest hope that the publication of this Register, which enables me to add yet another volume to my "works of reference" series, should lead eventually to that of the other Registers, so that the whole of this magnificent series may at length see the light of day

JOSEPH FOSTER.

21, BOUNDARY ROAD, LONDON, N W

Memorandum.

This volume is number 113 of the entire Edition of one hundred and sixty copies printed for the subscribers to "Collectanea Genealogica"

THE HANSARD PUBLISHING UNION, Lim , *Printers*

Editor

LIST OF SUBSCRIBERS

TO

COLLECTANEA GENEALOGICA.

THE ROYAL LIBRARY, Berlin
THE ROYAL LIBRARY, Stockholm
THE BRITISH MUSEUM (MS Department)
THE LIBRARY COMMITTEE OF THE CORPORATION OF THE CITY OF LONDON (Guildhall)
GALIGNANI'S LIBRARY, Paris
THE LONDON LIBRARY
THE HONOURABLE SOCIETY OF GRAY'S INN
THE LIBRARY OF THE FACULTY OF ADVOCATES, Edinburgh
THE MITCHELL LIBRARY, Glasgow
THE NATIONAL LIBRARY OF IRELAND
THE ROYAL IRISH ACADEMY
THE BODLEIAN LIBRARY
THE LIBRARY OF BRASENOSE COLLEGE, Oxford
THE LIBRARY OF EXETER COLLEGE, Oxford
UNIVERSITY LIBRARY, Cambridge
TRINITY COLLEGE LIBRARY, Cambridge
THE REFERENCE LIBRARY, ⎫
THE CHETHAM LIBRARY, ⎬ Manchester
THE PORTICO LIBRARY, ⎭
THE LIVERPOOL FREE LIBRARY
THE LEEDS LIBRARY
BIRMINGHAM FREE LIBRARY

STONYHURST LIBRARY
ROCHDALE FREE LIBRARY   [Tyne
THE SOCIETY OF ANTIQUARIES, Newcastle upon-
VIRGINIA STATE LIBRARY
NEW ENGLAND HISTORIC GENEALOGICAL SOCIETY, Boston, U S A
BOSTON ATHENÆUM, Boston, U S A
THE BOSTON PUBLIC LIBRARY, U S A
NEW BEDFORD LIBRARY, Boston, U S A
HARVARD COLLEGE LIBRARY
LIBRARY OF CONGRESS, Washington.
LONG ISLAND HISTORICAL SOCIETY
MARYLAND HISTORICAL SOCIETY
YALE COLLEGE, New Haven, U S A
PEABODY INSTITUTE, Baltimore, U S A
WATKINSON LIBRARY, Hartford, Conn , U S A
FREE PUBLIC LIBRARY, Worc , Mass , U S A.
THE FREE PUBLIC LIBRARY, Sydney, N S W
SIR ALBERT WILLIAM WOODS, Garter King-of-Arms
G E COKAYNE, Norroy King-of-Arms
W H WELDON, Windsor Herald
A SCOTT GATTY, Richmond Herald
J W MITCHELL, Rothesay Herald

AMHERST, M P , W AMHURST T
ASTLEY, JOHN
BARTTELOT, Capt
BAYLEY, His Honour Judge
BEAVAN, Rev A B
DE BERNARDY, Bros
BIDEN, LEWIS
BOASE, GEO C
BOASE, Rev C W
BOSTOCK, R C
BOSWORTH, Mr
BOYD, Miss
BRIDGEMAN, Rev. and Hon JOHN
BROOKE, THOMAS
BRUSHFIELD, Dr
BULWER, Lieut. Col
CHARLTON, THOMAS W
CHORLTON, THOMAS
CLAPP, W W , Boston Journal, U S A
CLARKE and CARRUTH, Boston, U S A
CUPPER, Messrs , Boston, U S A
COLLINS, Dr
CUST, LADY ELIZABETH
DASENT, A I
DERHAM, WALTER
DRURY EDWIN WILMETTE, Cook Co , Illinois, U S A

DUNSTON, F W
CARY-ELWES, D G
EMPSON, C W
ERMERIN, R C Moscow
FALCONER, J E
FOLJAMBE, M P , C J S
FOX, M D , CHARLES H
FULLER, J F
GARSTIN, JOHN R
GIBBS, HENRY H
GIBSON, JAMES, Salem, New York
GRANT, Rev A. T
GRAZEBROOKE, H S
GREEN, Mr., Edinburgh
GREEN, JOSEPH J
GREENFIELD, BENJAMIN W
HAIG, CHARLES E
HANSON, Alderman Sir R , Bart
HEWLETT, W O
HOVENDEN, ROBERT.
HUGHES, H R
KER, J CAMPBELL
KINGSLEY, Mrs HENRY.
KLINCKSIECK, Mr , Paris
LIVINGSTON, E B
MADAN, F
MAHON, T G S
MARSHAM, Hon R

METCALFE, WALTER C
MOENS, W J. C
MONTAGU, Lieut -Col
MULLINS, JOHN
NICHOLLS, S THOMAS
PENFOLD, HUGH C
PENRUDDOCKE, CHAS W
PRIDEAUX, W F
RIDGWAY, Col
ROBINSON, BROOKE
RONKSLEY, J G
ROUND, M A , J H
ROWE, J BROOKING
ROWLEY, Mrs DAWSON
RYE, WALTER
SCULL, G D
STANSFELD, JOHN
STANTON, Capt
SYKES, Dr
SYMONDS, J. A
TRAHERNE, GEO M
KEMEYS-TYNTE, ST. DAVID M
UDAL, J S
HUNTER WESTON, Lieut. Col.
WHATELEY & Co
WILLIAMS & Co , A Boston.

GRAYES INNE.

*** As the writer of this MS, Simon Segar, (see his admission) grandson of Sir William Segar, garter king of arms, manifestly intended to quote the exact words of the several records noticed by him, his extracts have been carefully examined with the originals, and any inaccuracies so found are duly corrected All additions placed between [ ] are reproduced in the actual text of the document, but with the contracted forms extended

This Colledge or Inne of Courte is situate wthin the Manno^r of Purtpole alias Portepole neere Holbourne in the County of Midd. wch said Manno^r of Purtpole alias Portpole & the land thereunto belonginge hath remained hereditary in that honorable familie of ye Grayes the absolute owners thereof from a^o 22 Ed. I^o vntill ye raigne of K. Hen. 7° as by seu'all inquisitions in that behalfe taken remaineth of record.

1294.

Inquisitio capta coram Escaetore domini R^s die lune in crastino clausi Pasche a^o [regni] R^s Edwardi filij R^s Edwardi primo apud Purtepole de terris et Tenementis de quibus Reginaldus Le Grey fuit seisitus die quo obiit in Dominico suo ut de feodo suo in Comit. Midd. p Sacramentum Thome de Meldeburne &c qui dicunt sup sacramentum suum quod dictus Reginaldus Le Grey fuit seisitus apud Purtepole die quo obijt de quodam mesuagio cum Gardinis et cum vno Columbario que valent p ann. vltra reprisam decem solidos. Item dicunt quod sunt ibd triginta acre terr. arrabil. que valent p ann viginti solidos pretium acre viij^d. Item dicunt quod est ibidem de redditu Assise xxij^s solvend ad duos terminos anni Videlicet ad festum Sancti Micha[e]lis xj^s et ad festum Annunciationis beate Marie xj^s Item dicunt quod est ibidem quoddam Molendinum ventriticum quod valet p an. xx^s.

MIDD Escat a^o 1° Ed 2 numb 54 a^o 1308

[Dicunt eciam quod dictus Reginaldus le Grey tenuit omnes predictas terras et tenementa de Decano [et] Capitulo Sancti Pauli Londoniarum in capite per servicium quatraginta duorum solidorum et duorum denariorum solvendorum ad duos anni terminos, videlicet, ad festum sancti Michaelis et ad festum Annunciacionis beate Marie, et sectam curie a tribus septimanis in tres septimanas. Dicunt eciam quod Johannes le

a

Grey propinquior heres est, et est de etate xxx annorum et amplius. In cuius Rei testimonium predicti Jurati sigilla sua apposuerunt]

Escat [ad quod damn-um]a°8 Ed 2 numb. 169

Inquifitio Indentata capta coram Efcaetore Dni R[s] apud Crucem lapideam in p'ochia beate Marie atte Stronde die Jovis px[a] poft feftum Sancti Dunftani Epifcopi a° R. Edwardi filij R[s] Edwardi octave virtute brevis D'ni R[s] Ad quod dampnum p sacramentum &c Qui dicunt quod non eft ad dampnum nec prejudicium D'ni Rg. nec aliorum Si Rex concedat dilecto et fideli suo Johanni filio Reginaldi de Grey Quod ipfe triginta acras terre duas acras prati et x[s] redditus cum ptinentijs in Kentishton iuxta London, et in p'ochia Sancti Andree de Holebourne extra Barram veteris Templi London, dare poffit et affignare dilectis fibi in Chrifto, Priori et Conventui Sancti Bartolomei in Smythefelde, London Habendum et tenendum eifdem Priori et Conventui et Succefforibus suis ad inveniendum quendam capellanum Divina fingulis diebus in Capella Manerij ipfius Joh'is in Pourtepol extra Barram predictam p anima ipfius Joh'is et animabus Antecefforum fuorum et omnium fidelium defunctorum celebraturum inppetu[u]m.

Dicunt etiam Quod predicte xxx acre ter. et due acre prati et decem folid. redditus tenentur de Roberto de Chiggewelle p servitium reddendi eidem Roberto annuatim vnam Rosam.

[Et idem Robertus tenet dicta tenementa simul cum aliis tenementis de Decano et Capitulo Sancti Pauli London Et predicti Decanus et Capitulum ea tenent de Domino Rege in puram et perpetuam elemosinam Dicunt eciam quod predicta terra pratum et redditus valent per annum in omnibus exitibus xxxjs iiijd iuxta verum valorem]

Dicunt etiam Quod predictus Johannes filius Reginaldi de Grey tenet vltra donationem et affignacionem predictas in Kentischeton et in p'ochia Sancti Andree de Holebourne terras et tenementa que valent p an. x[li] et que fufficiunt ad confuetudines et fervitia tam de predictis terris prato et redditu fic datis, quam de alijs terris et tenementis fibi retentis, debita facienda et ad omnia alia onera, que dictus Joh'es de Grey fuftinuit et fuftinere confuevit In cujus rei teftimonium Juratores predicti sigilla fua huic Inquifitioni appofuerunt Dat die anno et loco supradictis.

Rot Pat de anno 8 E 2, pars 2, Memb. 10.

Rex Omnibus ad quos &c Salutem Licet de Communi Confilio Regni noftri [Anglie] ftatutum fit quod non liceat viris Religiofis feu alijs ingredi feodum alicujus Ita quod ad manum mortuam deveniat fine licentia noftra et capitalis d'ni de quo res illa immediate tenetur, per finem tamen quem Dilectus nobis in Chrifto . Prior Sancti Bartholomei in Smethefelde,

London, fecit nobifcum concefsimus et licentiam dedimus p nobis et here-
dibus noftris (quantum in nobis eft) dilecto et fideli noftro Johanni filio
Reginaldi de Grey quod ipfe triginta acras terre, duas acras prati et xˢ
redditus cum ptinentijs in Le Kentisheton iuxta London et p'ochia Sci.
Andree de Holebourne extra Barram veteris Templi, dare pofsit et
afsignare eifdem Priori et Conventui eiufdem loci, Habendum et tenendum eifdem Priori et Conventui et succefsoribus suis ad inveniendum
quendam Capellanum Divina fingulis diebus in Capella Manerii ipfius
Joh'is de Pourtepole extra Barram predictam pro anima ipfius Joh'is. et
animabus antecefsor. fuorum et omnium fidelium defunctorum celebraturum imperpetuum Et eifdem Priori et Conventui quod ipfi predicta
terram pratum et Redditum cum ptinentijs a prefato Joh'e recipere poffint
et tenere fibi et succefforibus suis &c. Nolentes quod predictus Joh'es
vel heredes sui, aut prefati Prior et Conventus feu succefsores fui ratione
statuti predicti p nos vel heredes nostros inde occafionentur in aliquo
feu graventur Salvis tamen capitalibus Dominis feodi illius fervitijs inde
debitis & confuetis In cujus &c T R. apud Westmon 27 die Maij &c

Inquifitio capta coram Efcaetore Domini Regis apud Pourtepole die MIDD Efcat de aᵒ 17 E 2, num 74, Pourtepole.
Sabbati prox poft feftum sancti Hillarij aᵒ regni Regis Edw. filij Regis
Edw. 17ᵒ p sacramentum Galfridi Penninges &c Qui dicunt &c. Quod
Johannes Le Grey defunctus tenuit die quo obiit in dominico suo ut de
feodo quoddam Messuagium cum Gardino et duodecim Shopis annexis Mesuagium.
&c. in Pourtepole extra Barram London &c.

Dicunt etiam Quod Henricus de Grey eft heres ejus propinquior et
ætatis 40ᵃ annorum et amplius. In cujus rei &c.

Touching any office found after the death of yᵉ said Henry yᵉ next
heire of John Le Grey I find none ; but afterwards, yᵗ is to say, divers
yeares after the deceafe of yᵉ said John Le Grey and yᵉ office found thereupon, it is recorded that another Reynold de Grey was owner of
Pourtepole Mannoʳ in fee simple, And of yᵗ eftate about aᵒ 44ᵒ of
Edward 3 died feifed, And left an heire behind him, to inherite his
pofsefsions, whose name was Henry as by yᵉ record itfelfe may appeare.

Inquifitio capta apud Holborne in Comit Midd coram Efcaet. D'ni Rg. MIDD' Efcaet. de anno 44ᵒ Edw. 3, num 30
vicefimo quarto die Junij aᵒ Rg Edw 3. 44ᵒ post mortem Reginaldi de
Gray. Juratores dicunt Quod idem Reginaldus de Gray de Wilton fuper
Wee tenuit die quo obijt in comit predicto quoddam Hospitium in Porte- Hospitium.
pole juxta Holborne &c. in dominico suo ut de feodo. Et quod predicta
Hospitium, Gardinum &c valent p ann in omnibus exitibus vltra reprifas
et redditum resolutum centum solidos. Et fic dimittitur ad firmam &c. Redditus Cᵒ.

Et dicunt vlterius Quod idem Reginaldus obijt vicefimo octavo die Maij vltimo preterito.

Et quod Henricus Grey filius predicti Reginaldi eft filius et heres ipfius Reginaldi propinquior et eft ætatis triginta annor. et amplius. In cujus rei testimonium &c.

MIDD Efcat de anno 20°
H 6

Inquifitio capta apud Westmonafterium in Comit Midd. die veneris prox. poft feftum sancti Leonardi a° regni Regis Henrici sexti vicesimo primo &c. p facramentum &c qui dicunt Quod Ricardus Grey de Wilton miles &c. obijt feifitus in dominico suo ut de feodo de Manerio de Portpole in Holbourne, Vocat. Greys ynne cum ptinentijs [in Comitatu predicto quod valet per annum ultra reprisas quinque marcas et tenetur de Decano et Capitulo ecclesie Sancti Pauli London. set per que servicia Juratores predc̃i penitus ignorant &c.

Et dicunt quod idem Ricardus obijt die lune proximo ante festum assumpcionis beate Marie ultimo preterito Et quod Reginaldus Grey est filius et heres eius propinquior et fuit etatis viginti et unius annorum et amplius vicesimo secundo die Maij ultimo preterito. In cuius &c.]

By all wch feuerall offices it appeares that the faid Manno^r of Portepole now Grayes-Inne or wthin ye wch a parte of Grayes Inne is now fituate was anciently the Inheritance of the Grayes. But I doe not find in any of ye faid former recited inquifitions, that any Gray, Lord or owner of ye said Manno^r and Mefluage did at any time refide there, but were the reputed owners thereof before or about ye time ye same became an *Ostel* for Students and Profeflors of ye Common Lawes, And at what certaine time ye same premifles came to bee demised by Reginald de Grey in y^e

Redd C^s.

44th yeere of ye reigne of Kinge Edw. 3 for ye yearely rent of C^s as is menc̃oned in ye Office then found after his deceafe. And in ye wch office (the same beinge in form^r Inquifitions named *Mesuagium*) is thereby found to be *Hospitium* and on lease, whereby is manifefted y^t y^t house then & yet knowne by ye name of *Grayes-Inne* was demifed to some perfons of fpeciall regard & rancke and not to meane ones or perfons of meane or privat behavio^r, but to such as were vnited into a Society pfeflinge ye lawes that in thofe dayes begunn to congregat and fetle themfelves wthin ye fame, as an aflociated Company entertayning hofpitalitie together. And then this houfe grew to bee off an higher Title in denominac̃on and became to bee totally termed by ye Intitulac̃on of *Hospitium*, and foo thereupon found by inquifition to bee *quoddam Hospitium in Portepole*. And it alfo appeareth That ye faid Reginald De Grey demifed ye same mefluage as aforefaid in ye reigne of King Edw 3. wthin his lifetime and at his

death was held for *Hospitium*. And by the jury before whom yᵉ said ᴬᵒ 1370
Inquifition was taken in yᵉ faid 44ᵗʰ yeare of Ed 3. was found to bee
Hospitium and not *Mesuagium*. Immediatly whereupon yᵉ faid *Hospitium*
is called *Greys-Inne* or *Hospitium Graiorum* for that, that *Ostell* had
been soe longe and by soe many feuerall defcents in yᵗ name. As by yᵉ
faid former Inquifition is apparantly feene, taken in yᵉ 19th yeare of K R.
2ᵈ after yᵉ deceafe of Henry fonne and heire of Reginald de Grey wᶜʰ
name and title it hath not only regained but from time to time retained
as well before as unto this day enterteyning wᵗʰin yᵉ same an honorable
Society by yᵉ name of Treasʳ, Readers, and Students

It appeareth That one Richard Chigwell did enfeoffe yᵉ Deane and
Chapter of St Paul of certaine houfes and rents in yᵗ preband, And
therefore it is apparent that the said Deane and Chapter did before yᵉ
faid 22ᵗʰ yeare of ye reigne of K Ed Iˢᵗ (And before yᵉ makinge of yᵉ
ftatute of *Quia Emptores terrarum*, ordeine[d] in yᵉ 18ᵗʰ yeare of yᵗ Kings
reigne) enfeoffe yᵉ first named Reginald Grey and his heires of yᵉ faid
Mannoʳ of Portpole, who (as by record here recited as other ftronge cir-
cumstances depending upon yᵉ whole) was yᵉ first Gray yᵗ obtained the
faid Mannoʳ from yᵉ Church.

And now to conclude. It alfo appeareth by an other of yᵉ former ᴬᵒ 1570
recited offices found after yᵉ deceafe of yᵉ faid last ment̃oned Reginald
Grey that Edmund Lord Grey of Wilton next heire to yᵉ said Reginald
was feifed of yᵉ said house & appurtenances, And foe feifed by Inden-
ture inrolled in yᵉ 22ᵗʰ yeare of yᵉ reigne of K. H 7ᵗʰ and by fyne levyed
in yᵉ fame yeare did convey & afsure yᵉ p'mifses by yᵉ name of yᵉ
Mannoʳ of Portpole otherwife Grayes Inne unto divers yᵉ Ancients &
Benchers of Grays Inne to yᵉ vfe of them & theire heires (in truft only)
for yᵉ Fellowes & Students there for yᵉ time being, by vertue whereof yᵉ
Inheritance of this Colledge is firmely fetled in this honorable Society

(The statement that Edmund, Lord Grey of Wilton, conveyed the
manor of Purtpole, otherwife Gray's Inn, unto the Ancients and Benchers,
is scarcely accurate, for it was sold by Lord Grey to one Hugh Denys,
to whom, with several other perfons (some, presumably, members of
Gray's Inn), it was conveyed by bargain and sale dated 12 August, 1506,
accompanied by a Recovery, a Fine, and by Deeds of Release, from the
same Edmund, Lord Grey, and his brothers, Richard Grey, clerk, and
John Grey.

In 7 Hen. VIII (1516) the survivors of the persons to whom the
manor was so conveyed obtained the King's licence to alienate to the prior
and convent of Shene "the manor of Portepole" and appurtenances,
estimated at the annual value of £6 13s. 4ᵈ

On the diſſolution of the monaſteries, the poſſeſſions of Shene paſſed to the Crown, and Dugdale ſtates that the manor or inn was granted by the King unto the Society in fee farm, by the yearly payment of the ſum above named, which they continued to pay until the year 1733, when they purchaſed this rent of the perſons deriving title from Sir Philip Matthews.)

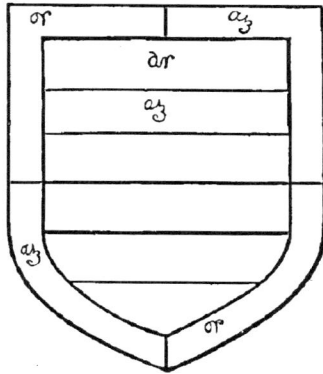

Touchinge yᵉ Auncient Armoriall, not only by tradition received but alſo in Mr. Stowe's Appendix blazoned & authentically deſcried deducted from thoſe of yᵉ Lord Gray of Wilton I have here (not diſcenting from yˡ writers oppinion) ſet forth yᵉ ſame That is to ſay—*Barry of ſix argent and azure a Bordure quarterly or & of the ſecond.*

Of moderne daies This honorable Society neglecting yᵉ one have ſelected yᵉ other wᵗʰ due appropiaçon and no leſſe approbaçon to themſelves, wᶜʰ they entertaine for theire proper HEROIKE & COLLEGIAT

ARMORIALLS before any other blazoned as is in ye margent depicted. The hono^{ble} Colledge of Grayes-Inne doth beare for theire Coat *Azure an Indian Griffon proper Sergreant* wth ye laudable incription invironing the same.

The Griffon is in fashion twofold or byformed or (as it may bee said) double natured. In ye fore partes participatinge wth y^t of ye Eagle, & in ye hinder partes wth those of ye Lion.

This Ayrie fowle, or earthly beaſt as here it appeareth is termed ſergreant not volant or rampant as some hold, for y^t hee seemeth wth his Lionnish loynes to touch ye earth and wth his Eaglish partes advanceth himselfe, as if his flight were towards ye heavens. The Griffon this erected signifieth his prepared purpose to some action of might & force adding thereunto by ye Wings and Talents not only fine force, but Induſtry also. This beaſt, havinge attayned unto his full ſtrength & growth ſomuch disdaineth vaſsalrey and ſubjection That hee will never be ſurpriſed alive Thereby lively sheweinge forth his magnanimous two-fold Kingely ſpirit as well of ye Lion as of ye Eagle.

This ſignall of hono^r diſcovereth ſecretely ye proparty of a generous mind & is very ſignificantly assumed to this hono^{ble} Colledge whose members there (if thereto afsigned by ye Sovereigne) will valourſly both for Prince, Peeres & People attempt ye pformance of noble actions both ingenious, valorous & induſtrious. ffor such generous perſons in ye dayes of peace put in practiſe every commendable acction, y^t may further ye maintenance & continuance thereof, that is ye indifferent diſtribucõn of ye Lawes to all And if contrary should bee offered there is noe doubt, but there hono^{ble} inclinacõn to peace & religion would incite them valorouſly to repreſse the contempⁿ thereof by wch endevo^{rs} nothing cann bee better pleaſing to a Prince & State, or bee accounted more hono^{ble} & commendable.

To this renowned Colledge are appropriat members two Halls or Inns of Chancery—

      STAPLE-INNE   ⎫

          &   ⎬ both ſcituate in Holborne.

      BERNARDS-INNE ⎭

Lib. 1°.		aº	numb	aº	numb	aº	numb
aº	numb	1560 . .	023	1598 . .	088	1637 .	139
1521 . .	021	1561 . .	059	1599 . .	063	1638 . .	152
1522 . .	023	1562 . .	058	1600 . .	093	1639 . .	134
1523 . .	009	1563 . .	034	1601 . .	069	1640 .	133
1524 . .	018	1564 . .	041	1602 . .	085	1641 .	142
1525 . .	017	1565 .	049	1603 . .	021	1642 . .	058
1526 . .	009	1566 .	050	1604 . .	112	1643 . .	024
1527 . .	028	1567 . .	062	1605 . .	114	1644 . .	046
1528 . .	030	1568 . .	059	1606 .	062	1645 .	047
1529 . .	022	1569 . .	020	1607 . .	117	1646 .	102
1530 . .	023	1570 . .	040	1608 . .	120	1647 . .	123
1531 . .	035	1571 . .	069	1609 . .	080	1648 . .	097
1532 . .	024	1572 . .	045	1610 . .	100	1649 . .	087
1533 . .	035	1573 . .	066	1611 . .	112	1650 . .	121
1534 . .	032	1574 . .	038	1612 . .	086	1651 . .	129
1535 . .	024	1575 . .	033	1613 . .	081	1652 . .	132
1536 . .	016	1576 . .	053	1614 . .	123	1653 . .	089
1537 . .	036	1577 .	051	1615 . .	109	1654 . .	156
1538 . .	020	1578 .	052	1616 .	138	1655 . .	178
1539 . .	026	1579 . .	076	1617 . .	152	1656 . .	157
1540 . .	032	1580 . .	082	1618 .	145	1657 . .	117
1541 . .	034	**Lib. 2°.**		1619 .	200	1658 . .	056
1542 . .	026			1620 .	119	1659 . .	046
1543 . .	021	1581 . .	040	1621 . .	115	1660 . .	068
1544 . .	030	1582 . .	052	1622 . .	107	1661 . .	054
1545 . .	027	1583 . .	080	1623 . .	117	1662 .	074
1546 . .	029	1584 .	077	1624 . .	127	1663 .	060
1547 . .	022	1585 . .	047	1625 . .	025	1664 . .	075
1548 . .	017	1586 . .	063	1626 .	098	1665 . .	029
1549 . .	022	1587 . .	095	1627 .	112	1666 . .	059
1550 . .	015	1588 .	047	1628 . .	112	1667 . .	057
1551 . .	035	1589 . .	059	1629 .	083	1668 . .	084
1552 . .	049	1590 . .	078	1630 . .	062	1669 .	092
1553 .	050	1591 . .	069	1631 .	097	1670 . .	083
1554 . .	034	1592 . .	104	1632 . .	098	1671 . .	090
1555 . .	043	1593 . .	050	1633 .	131	1672 . .	054
1556 . .	036	1594 . .	098	1634 . .	073	1673 . .	092
1557 . .	015	1595 . .	098	1635 . .	117	1674 . .	065
1558 . .	024	1596 . .	052	1636 . .	039	1675 . .	
1559 . .	024	1597 . .	084				

BENCHERS, 1889

H R H The Duke of Connaught, K G , K T

The Right Hon John David, Lord Fitzgerald

The Right Hon William, Lord Watson

The Right Hon Edward Gibson, Lord Ashbourne

Hon. Baron Huddleston (Justice, Queen's Bench Division)

Hon Sir Henry Manisty (Justice, Queen's Bench Division)

His Honour Judge Russell.

William Cracroft Fooks, Esq , Q C

Henry Griffith, Esq

Sir Arthur John Hammond Collins, Q C (Chief Justice of Madras)

Sir Benjamin Pine, K C M G

George Francis, Esq (Master of the Supreme Court of Judicature)

Hugh Shield, Esq., Q C

W. Bowen Rowlands, Esq , Q C , M P

James Sheil, Esq (Metropolitan Magistrate)

Arthur Beetham, Esq

Clement Alexander Middleton, Esq

Walter David Jeremy, Esq

Charles Forbes, Esq

Edwyn Jones, Esq

John Rose, Esq

A LIST OF ENGLISH JUDGES
WHO WERE STUDENTS OF GRAY'S INN

RICHARD ALLEBONE, King's Bench	1687	WILLIAM HUSSEY, Chief Just K B	1481
JAMES ALTHAM, Baron of Exchequer	1607	RICHARD HUTTON, Justice Com Pleas	1617
JOHN ARCHER, Common Pleas .	1663	JOHN HYNDE, Justice Common Pleas	1545
NICHOLAS BACON, Lord Keeper	1558	CHARLES INGLEBY, Baron of Exch	1688
FRANCIS BACON, Lord Chancellor	1618	JOHN JEFFREY, Chief Baron of Exch	1577
FRANCIS BACON, King's Bench	1642	RICHARD KEEBLE, Judge	1648-51
ROBERT BALDOCK, King's Bench	1688	THOMAS LEEKE, Cursitor Baron (Exch)	1642
JOHN BANKS, Chief Justice, K B	1641	WILLIAM LEEKE, Baron of Exchequer	1679
JOHN BAYLEY, King's Bench . .	1808	CRESSWELL LEVINZ, Just Com Pleas	1681
THOMAS BEDINGFELD, Common Pleas	1648	JOSEPH LITTLEDALE, Just King's Ben	1824
THOMAS BILLING, Chief justice, K B	1469	SALATHIEL LOVELL, Baron of Exch. .	1708
JOHN BIRCH, Baron of Exchequer	1564	ROBERT LUSH, Justice Queen's Bench	1865
JOHN BIRCH, Cursitor Baron (Exch)	1729	EDWARD LUTWYCHE, Just Com Pleas	1686
THOMAS BRYAN, Chief Justice C P	1471	HENRY MANISTY, Just Queen's Bench	1876
THOMAS BURY, Baron of Exchequer	1701	JOHN MARKHAM, Justice Com Pleas	1408
CHARLES CÆSAR, Master of the Rolls .	1639	JOHN MARKHAM, Chief Just King's B	1461
WILLIAM CARR, Cursitor Baron (Exch)	168⅝	SAMUEL MARTIN, Baron of Exch. .	1850
THOMAS CHAMBERLAYNE, King's Bench	1620	EDMUND MOLYNEUX, Just C Pleas	1550
ALAN CHAMBRE, Common Pleas	1800	RICHARD NEELE, Just King's Bench	1470
WILLIAM CHEYNE, Chief Justice K.B	1424	EDWARD NEVELL, Baron of Exch	1685
THOMAS CLARKE, Master of the Rolls	1754	RICHARD NEWDIGATE, Chief Justice	
WILLIAM COKE, Common Pleas	1552	Upper Bench .	1660
FRANCIS CRAWLEY, Common Pleas	1632	JOHN PARKER, Baron of Exchequer	1655
FRANCIS CRAWLEY, Cursit Baron (Ex)	1679	JOHN PETIT, Baron of Exchequer	1527
THOMAS CROMWELL, Master of the Rolls	1534	PETER PHEASANT, Justice Com Pleas	1643
WILLIAM DALISON, Queen's Bench	1556	THOMAS POWELL, Baron of Exchequer	1687
WILLIAM DANIEL, Common Pleas .	1604	JOHN POWELL, Justice Common Pleas	1686
HUMPH DAVENPORT, Lord Chief Baron	1631	THOMAS RAYMOND, Justice Common	
DUDLEY DIGGES, Master of the Rolls	1635	Pleas	1679
WILLIAM ELLIS, Common Pleas	1672	ROBERT RAYMOND, Chief Just K B	1725
JAMES EYRE { Lord Chief Baron	1787	EDMUND REEVE, Justice Com Pleas	1639
JAMES EYRE { Chief Just Com Pleas	1794	FRANCIS RODES, Justice Com Pleas	1585
GUY FAIRFAX, King's Bench	1477	THOMAS ROKEBY, Justice Com Pleas	1689
WILLIAM FAIRFAX, Common Pleas	1509	JOHN (Lord) ROMILLY, Master of Rolls	1851
JOHN FINCH, Chief Just Com Pleas	1634	JOHN ROTHERAM, Baron of Exchequer	1688
JOHN FINEUX, Chief Justice King's B	1495	WILLIAM SCROGGS, Chief Just K B	1678
JOHN D FITZGERALD, Lord of Appeal	1882	ROBERT SHUTE, Baron of Exchequer	1579
ANTHONY FITZHERBERT, Just C Pleas	1522	JOHN SMITH, Baron of Exchequer	1702
WILLIAM GASCOIGNE, Chief Just K B	1400-13	JOHN SOTHERTON, Baron of Exch	1579
STEPH GASELEE, Justice Com Pleas	1824	NOWELL SOTHERTON, Baron of Exch	1606
GILBERT GERARD, Master of the Rolls	1581	JOHN SPELMAN, Just King's Bench	1532
EDWARD GIBSON, Lord Chan Ireland	1885	CLEMENT SPELMAN, Curs Bar. (Exch.)	1663
JOHN GODBOLD, Justice Com Pleas	1647	WILLIAM STAUNFORD, Just Com. Pleas	1554
WILLIAM GREGORY, Baron of Exch	1679	WILLIAM STEELE { Chief Baron	1655
BERNARD HALE, Baron of Exchequer	1725	WILLIAM STEELE { Lord Chan. Ireland	1656
CHRIST. HALES, Master of the Rolls	1536	THOMAS STRINGER, Just King's Ben	1688
JAMES HALES, Just Common Pleas	1551	FREDERICK THESIGER, Lord Chan.	1858
JOHN HALES, Baron of Exchequer	1522	FRANCIS THORPE, Baron of Exch	1649
EDWARD HENDEN, Baron of Exch	1639	JOHN TURTON, Baron of Exchequer	1689
JOHN HOLKER, Lord Just. of Appeal .	1882	WM. WATSON, Lord of Appeal	1880
GEORGE SOWLEY HOLROYD, Just K B.	1816	RICHARD WESTON, Baron of Exch	1680
JOHN HOLT, Chief Just. King's Bench	1689	WILLIAM YELVERTON, Just K Bench	1443
JOHN W HUDDLESTON, Just Q Bench	1879	CHRIST YELVERTON, Just K Bench	1602
JOHN HULLOCK, Baron of Exchequer .	1823	HENRY YELVERTON, Just Com Pleas	1625

Gray's Inn Admission Register:

1521—1887.

The following distinguished members of Gray's Inn, ancients and readers, prior to the admissions 1521 (page 3) are collected from various parts of the Manuscript compiled by Simon Segar, of Gray's Inn (see page 274), grandson of Sir William Segar, Garter King of Arms

1376 SIR ROBERT DE ASSHETON, Admiral at Sea, Chief Justice of Ireland, and Lord
      Treasurer of England   49 Ed III

1458. SIR OWEN TUDOR

1492. JOHN WIGMORE (*see* Weever's Acts and Monuments ").

    (JOHN ISLIP), Lord Abbot of Westminster.

    (ALEXANDER BACH, or BAUCH), Lord Abbot of Furness

    (LAURENCE CHAMPION), Lord Abbot of Battle

    (HENRY MORE), Abbot of the Blessed Mary of Grays (*i.e*, St Mary Graces), near

    (WILLIAM BOLTON), Prior of St Bartholomew   [London

    (WILLIAM ATTWATER), Bishop of Lincoln, admitted 1520.   f 276

    (THOMAS STANLEY), Earl of Derby, admitted 1520

    (THOMAS WEST), Lord Delawarr

    (THOMAS FIENNES), Lord Dacre of the South

    (THOMAS, or WILLIAM, DACRE), Lord Dacre of the North

    (GEORGE NEVILLE), Lord Abergavenny

    (EDWARD, or THOMAS, STANLEY), Lord Monteagle

    (WILLIAM BROOKE), Lord Cobham.

    (EDWARD), Lord Grey de Powis

    (HENRY), Lord Daubeney

*

B

1518 JOHN PETITT, autumn reader elect
1519 JOHN HIND, autumn reader.
1520 JOHN HARBROWNE, autumn reader
1521. FRANCIS BROWNE, autumn reader.
1522 ROBERT CHALLINOR, autumn reader
1523 ROGER YORKE, autumn reader elect
1524. EDWARD BERESFORD, autumn reader.
  „   HUMPHREY COLES, Lent reader
1525 CHRISTOPHER HALES, Knight, autumn reader.
  „   THOMAS HARLAKENDEN, Lent reader
1526. EDWARD WHITE, autumn reader
1527 GEORGE WHETTENHALL, autumn reader
1528 ROBERT WROTHE, autumn reader
1529 WILLIAM GREY, autumn reader
  „   RICHARD SACKVILLE, Lent reader
      WILLIAM NEVILE, ancient, 1522.
      THOMAS THORNBURGH, ancient, 1522
1530 WILLIAM WALSINGHAM, autumn reader
  „   WALTER HENLEY, autumn reader
      THOMAS PELHAM, ancient, 1522
1531 JOHN COLEPEPER, autumn reader
      EDWARD LEWKNOR, ancient, 1522
      THOMAS HUTTON, ancient, 27 May, 1528
1532 EDMUND MOLLINEUX, Knight, autumn reader
      THOMAS DARRELL, ancient ⎫
      RICHARD BYRD, ancient.   ⎬ 27 May, 1528.
1533 JAMES HALES, Knight, autumn reader
  „   THOMAS MOYLE, Knight, Lent reader
1534. EDWARD HALL, autumn reader
      WILLIAM WYLBYS, ancient, 27 May, 1528
      ROBERT ROWLEIGH, ancient. ⎫
      JOHN BALHAM, ancient   ⎬ 1534
      NICHOLAS WILLOUGHBY, ancient ⎫
      WILLIAM YELVERTON, ancient   ⎬ 1534.
      ROBERT WINGFIELD, ancient, 1534
      ———— URMSTON, ancient ⎫
      ———— WATTON, ancient ⎪
      ———— BUTTON, ancient ⎬ 1536
      ———— SANDFORD, ancient ⎪
      ———— CUTTS, ancient   ⎭

(JOHN), Lord Hussey, ancient, 20 May, 1547

folio 281

1521.	WILLIAM GIRLINGTON
,,	WILLIAM GORING
,,	GEORGE PALMER
,,	JOHN PEYTON
,,	WALTER CARDIFFE
,,	THOMAS HALL (1522, in Segar)
,,	JOHN BOYSE
,,	RICHARD SUTTON
,,	——— UPTON
,,	ANTHONY MISSENDEN
,,	JOHN GUY
,,	JOHN ONBY
,,	RALPH JOHNSON
,,	WILLIAM ERNLEY.
,,	ANTHONY AYLEWORTH
,,	WILLIAM HUDDY

folio 283

,,	RICHARD SKELTON.
,,	WILLIAM SUTTON.
,,	JOHN STAPLE.
,,	THOMAS RUDSTON
,,	FRANCIS WALSINGHAM (Jan. 28)

folio 285.

1522	——— LINDSEY.
,,	——— BARTON
,,	JOHN SENESECLES
,,	EDWARD COBHAM.
,,	WILLIAM EYERARD (1552, in Segar)

folio 286

,,	JOHN ALLEN
,,	WILLIAM KYRTON.
,,	WILLIAM DALLISON
,,	CUTHBERT RICHARDSON
,,	GEORGE LANCASTER
,,	ANTHONY NEVILL
,,	JOHN STAPLETON
,,	JOHN SHIRLEY

folio 288

,,	JOHN DIGGS
,,	JOHN LAURENCE

folio 288—(continued)

1522	JOHN LAMB
,,	WILLIAM BELHOUSE.
,,	GEORGE STANDISH.
,,	NICHOLAS TOWNLEY.
,,	——— WETHERBY
1523	JOHN FREVILL.

folio 290

,,	HENRY ROW
,,	OWEN BRERETON

folio 291

,,	RICHARD SCROOPE
,,	JOHN MARSHALL.
,,	THOMAS RAWSON

folio 293

,,	LEONARD BECKWITH
,,	WILLIAM MILLS
,,	WILLIAM WENTWORTH

folio 296

1524	THOMAS CRYSPSE
,,	JOHN SOUTHWELL
,,	EDMUND GREY
,,	NICHOLAS WONWELL
,,	THOMAS WATSON
,,	GEORGE ALLEN
,,	ROGER RABYTT
,,	——— MUNDAY

folio 298

,,	THOMAS HARDWICKE
,,	THOMAS DODMORE
,.	WILLIAM MARSHALL
,,	MILES GROVER
,,	THOMAS CROMWELL (Earl of Essex)
,,	JOHN STANNEY
,,	CUTHBERT WREN
,,	JOHN ROODES.

folio 400

1525	THOMAS HALSALL
,,	JOHN GODSALVE
,,	EDWARD SCOTT

folio 401

1525	JOHN FINCH (1523?).
,,	JO MARSHALL
,,	JAMES BURY.
,,	GEORGE WALSINGHAM

folio 403

,,	ROBERT KAYER (Hayes?)
,,	GEORGE DANIELL
,,	WILLIAM NAUNTON
,,	CHRISTOPHER PLUNKETT.
,,	THOMAS BOSWELL
,,	ROGER BRADSHAW
,,	WILLIAM SCOTT
,,	GABRIEL THURSBY

folio 404

,	THOMAS MISSENDEN

folio 405

1526	JOHN CHENEY
,,	RICHARD CADDYELL.
,,	CHRISTOPHER LEVYNES

folio 406

,,	JOHN GOSNOLD
,,	JOHN PLUMB

folio 408

,,	GEORGE WOODROFFE
,,	RICHARD WEBB
,,	WILLIAM MANSELL
,,	ROBERT HENEAGE

folio 410

1527	MARTIN NEVILL.
,,	JOHN ASHTON
,,	HENRY MYNE
,	RALPH BUCOCKE
,,	EDWARD BANGHAM
,,	RICHARD SNOW
,,	WILLIAM SKIPWITH

folio 411

,,	THOMAS ASKHAM
,,	WILLIAM OXENBRIDGE

folio 411—(continued)

1527	THOMAS GREENHALL
,,	RICHARD STURGES
,,	JOHN SHIRLEY

folio 413

,,	HENRY HATFIELD
,,	ROBERT ASKE
,,	EDWARD MICHELL
,,	HENRY LINCH
,,	WILLIAM LAMBERT
,,	WILLIAM NEVILL
,,	PETER FABIAN
,,	ROBERT FABIAN
,,	WALTER CLIFTON
,,	THOMAS BERWORTH
,,	ROBERT BROOKES
,,	JAMES BATH
,,	JOHN BASSETT
,,	PATRICK BARNEWALL
,,	JOHN THACKER

folio 415

1528	RICHARD EGERTON
,,	——— THURSBY.
,,	JOHN MARKHAM.
,,	THOMAS PALMER

folio 416

,,	EDWARD CAWOOD (1526, in Segar)
,,	NICHOLAS HARVEY
,,	LAURENCE IRELAND
,,	WILLIAM RYVETT
,,	ROGER PECKHAM
,,	THOMAS POWTRELL.
,,	OSMOND GAY.
,,	JOHN FENNER.
,,	WILLIAM COOKE
,,	GEORGE BROWNE
,,	BALDWIN BRENERS (Berners?)
,,	HENRY STAFFORD (Lord S).
,,	WILLIAM STAMFORD.
,,	JEFFREY TISDALE.
,,	JEFFREY TILDESLEY

folio 416—(continued)

1528	WILLIAM WHIGHT.
,,	WILLIAM SKYRRINGTON.
,,	CHRISTOPHER ROPER.

folio 418

,,	THOMAS HAWERDEN
,,	STEPHEN HOLME.
,,	———— NAUNTON
,,	ROGER PINCHESTER.
,,	JOHN FITZHERBERT (Segar)
,,	JAMES BURTON
,,	ROBERT TILNEY

folio 420

1529	RICHARD WHALLEY
,,	ROBERT WINGFIELD
,,	RICHARD WOOD
,,	JO. BEDINGFELD
,,	———— COURTIS
,,	EDWARD LANCASTER
,,	HUGH LOWTHER
,,	NICHOLAS EVERNBY
,,	FRANCIS NOONE
,,	JAMES PLUNKETT
,,	ANTHONY CLENCOW

folio 421

,,	NICHOLAS STATHAM
,,	WILLIAM CRISPE
,,	CHARLES WRIOTHESLEY
,,	———— TREHERNE
,,	JOHN BOWES
,,	PETER COFFERLEY
,,	FRANCIS GOODYERE

folio 422.

1530	JOHN BREWSE
,,	———— HADDON
,,	GEORGE BLAGGE.
,,	JOHN GILLFORD.

folio 423

,,	JOHN EVERARD.
,,	JO. REYNOLDS
,,	HENRY REVITT

folio 423—(continued).

1530.	JOHN ANKOS.
,,	JOHN DERING
,,	THOMAS MOORE
,,	JOHN GOSTWICKE
,,	GEORGE FANE.
,,	WILLIAM COLPEPER.
,,	WILLIAM HALL.
,,	WILLIAM HURST.
,,	JOHN HALES
,,	PATRICK BARNEWALL.
,,	ROGER SWIFT.
,,	WILLIAM SMITH.
,,	RICHARD WATERTON

folio 424.

,,	THOMAS PAYNELL
,,	ROBERT BOMSTEED
1531	LEONARD RIGBY
,,	CHRISTOPHER NEVILL
,,	CHRISTOPHER GOLDINGHAM
,,	RICHARD WHALLEY
,,	ANTHONY SONDS

folio 425

,,	THOMAS ERNLEY
,,	HENRY GRAY
,,	NICHOLAS POWTRELL
,,	GEORGE ISAAC
,,	JAMES COLES
,,	HUMPHREY CALTON
,,	WILLIAM WOODROFFE
,,	JOHN EGGLEFIELD.
,,	JAMES WELLES

folio 426.

,,	WILLIAM NELSON
,,	CHRISTOPHER PEYTON
,,	GEORGE PAYNE
,,	GEORGE COVERT
,,	CHRISTOPHER STAFFORTON
,,	WILLIAM ROODES
,,	NICHOLAS RUSHTON
,,	JOHN WARD

folio 426—(continued).

1531.	WILLIAM FITZWILLIAM
„	ROBERT FLINT.
„	THOMAS HILL.

folio 428.

„	LIONEL RISBY
„	EDWARD PRICHARD
„	RICHARD HONE
„	FRANCIS FURBISHER
„	ROBERT FRESTON
„	GEORGE FITZWILLIAM
1532	JOHN DOYLEY
„	RICHARD MOLLINEUX.
„	RICHARD LUCAS
„	HENRY LITTLEBURY
„	THOMAS LITTLEBURY
„	JOHN GIBBS.
„	THOMAS CHICHESTER
„	ROBERT CRAINE.
„	JOHN BATTISFORD.
„	FRANCIS BASSETT.
„	JOHN SPELMAN.
„	JEFFREY STYWARD
„	JAMES ANDERTON

folio 429.

„	TRISTRAM LARDER
„	EDWARD GULFORD.
„	RICHARD GOODRICKE
„	JAMES PARGITER
„	RICHARD PEKE.
„	EDWARD HALES.
„	RICHARD IYE
„	EDWARD HALL.
„	ROBERT CHESTER.
„	WILLIAM COPLEY.
„	WILLIAM WOOD.
„	THOMAS WELBY.
„	NICHOLAS BACON

folio 431

| 1533 | JOHN RASTALL |
| „ | JOHN MANYARD (sic) |

folio 431—(continued).

1533.	RALPH PAWLETT
„	ROBERT PECKHAM
„	THOMAS SACHEVERELL
„	HUGH CRESCY (1531, Segar)
„	ROWLAND BOWKELEY (sic)
„	JOHN BUTLER
„	RICHARD BOWLES
„	RICHARD TOWNLEY
„	THOMAS SPELMAN
„	WILLIAM WUTTINE
„	ROBERT WATSON
„	ROBERT ROWLETT.
„	THOMAS SAWKELL
„	BRIAN STAPLETON
„	ADRIAN POYNINGS
„	WILLIAM TALBOT

folio 433.

„	JOHN SMITH
„	WILLIAM WALLER.
„	HUGH WILLOUGHBY.
„	WILLIAM NEDHAM
„	JOHN DRYLAND
„	JOHN MYNE.
„	JOHN GRAY
„	THOMAS FITZHERBERT.
„	WILLIAM CARDINALL
„	ROGER BODENHAM.
„	THOMAS BARNEWALL
„	THOMAS THROWER.

folio 435.

1534	JOHN NEVILL
„	STEPHEN KYRTON
„	ROBERT PRESTON.
„	WILLIAM DALLISON
„	WILLIAM CORDALL
„	ERASMUS HEVENINGHAM
„	RICHARD WELBY.
„	THOMAS SPENCER.
„	WILLIAM HOLES (sic)
„	WILLIAM JACKSON
„	MATTHEW HERBERT

folio 436

1534	JOHN SACHEVERELL
,,	THOMAS WRIOTHESLEY (after Earl of Southampton)
,,	RICHARD WRENCH
,,	ROBERT KIRKE
,,	ROGER DALTON
,,	JOHN LEEKE
,,	GEORGE CHAWORTH
,,	THOMAS PAYNE
,,	ROBERT CHAWSONNETT

folio 437

,,	JOHN BACON.
,,	NICHOLAS BRYTEN.
1535	THOMAS DARRELL
,,	THOMAS MARBURY
,,	BENJAMIN HIDE
,,	CHRISTOPHER HOPTON
,,	JOHN LEVETT
,,	RICHARD KIDDALL
,,	ROBERT ALDERMANUS
,,	HENRY STYERLEY
,,	JOHN WHALLEY

folio 438.

,,	WILLIAM PATCHETT
,,	WILLIAM HILL
,,	EDWARD JERMYN.
,,	JAMES GRINDLE

folio 439

1536	ROGER WATTS
,,	HENRY STOKETH
,,	HUMPHREY SKYRES.
,,	THOMAS WROTH
,,	JOHN WALPOLE.
,,	THOMAS HERBERT.
,,	RALPH HOLDEN
,,	JOHN DREW
::	RICHARD MOORE
,	CHRISTOPHER LEWES
,,	JAMES GUNTHER.
,,	ROBERT PRATT.
::	JOHN FRY.

folio 439—(continued)

1536	RICHARD COVERT
,,	EDMUND COWES
,,	JEFFERY COMOYLD (sic)

folio 440

,,	WILLIAM STYLE
,,	JOHN ROLLES
,,	RICHARD YAXLEY
,,	JAMES WHYTAMES
,,	———— HANCHETT
,,	JAMES LUTTRELL
,,	JOHN GASCOIGNE
,,	JOHN BROMHILT
,,	LEONARD BECKWITH
1537	FRANCIS SOONE

folio 442

,,	JAMES BARNEWALL
,,	WILLIAM WELBORNE
,,	WILLIAM BIGOTT
,,	ROBERT WINGFIELD.
,,	JOHN ROW
,,	GEORGE VERNON
,,	CHARLES ELLIS
,,	WILLIAM WALGRAVE
,,	ROBERT ALDRICH.
,,	GEORGE MILTON.
,,	RICHARD MEW.
,,	HUMPHREY GRESWOLD.
,,	JOHN PRESTON
,,	ROBERT FARTHINGTON.
,,	RICHARD CLERKE
,,	HENRY COTTEN.

folio 443

,,	JOHN FANE
,,	WILLIAM DARCY
,,	JOHN SEYMER

folio 444

,,	THOMAS STANLEY
,,	ANTHONY THOROLD
,,	THOMAS STEVENSON
,,	BAR WARYNER (1538)

folio **444**—*(continued)*

1537	NICHOLAS HUSSEY.
,,	HUMPHREY HALES.
,,	JOHN HOLCROFT.
,,	ROBERT DENYES
,,	RICHARD MEYRICK.
,,	HENRY MANSFIELD
,,	THOMAS LATHWIN
,,	FRANCIS LONGLAND.
,,	FRANCIS GAYLE
,,	GILBERT GERRARD
,,	ANTHONY POPE
,,	WILLIAM, LORD PAGET.
,,	EDWARD FORD
,,	RALPH FITTON.
,,	JOHN BIRCH
,,	ANTHONY BROWNE
,,	WILLIAM BRAMPTON

folio **449.**

,,	EUSTACE WOODFORD
,,	CHARLES WHALLEY.
1539	WILLIAM SWIFT
,,	EDWARD THEVELL
,,	RICHARD SHERBURNE.
,,	JOHN SHERMAN
,,	HENRY VERNON
,,	HENRY WARD
,,	GEORGE HOGARD
,,	JO FITZHERBERT
,,	WILLIAM AUDLEY
,,	RICHARD ALBAN
,,	WILLIAM DAYILE.
,,	ROBERT DEANE
,,	EDMUND DETHICKE.
,,	HENRY GRICE
,,	WILLIAM GREENE.
,,	WILLIAM GRAY.
,,	GAINES FOWLER.
,,	WILLIAM CHARTSEY
,,	GEORGE CHATTERTON
,,	RICHARD BUNNEY
,,	ROBERT BLOMHEAD.
,,	——— BARRYFORD

folio **451.**

1539	THOMAS ROBINSON
,,	THOMAS COKAYNE
,,	JOHN RAMSEY
,,	GEORGE DANVERS
,,	——— DILLON
,,	MARK CHEWYNE
,,	JAMES BARNEWALL

folio **452.**

1540	WILLIAM CROCH

folio **453.**

,,	RICHARD FORSETT.
,,	HENRY HAWES
,,	JOHN HERLEYGH
,,	HENRY OGARD
,,	THOMAS MASSINGBERD
,,	LAWRENCE MEERES.
,,	JOHN LEEKE
,,	WILLIAM PORTER.
,,	RICHARD CHEWINGE
,,	WILLIAM CECIL (Lord Burghley)
,,	THOMAS SECKFORD
,	ROGER SOTHEBY

folio **454.**

,,	RICHARD RAMSEY.
,,	RICHARD NEWTON
,,	CHRISTOPHER DIGHTON
,,	EDWARD DIGHTON.
,,	THOMAS DOCWRA
,,	EDMUND METCALFE
,,	RALPH LEAKE
,,	THOMAS GREENE.
,,	THOMAS COVERT
,,	RICHARD BINGE
,,	NICHOLAS BARHAM
,,	THOMAS THWAYTES.

folio **455.**

,,	GEORGE DARRELL

folio **456.**

1541	JOHN HYLTON
	WALTER HERONDEN

folio 456—(continued).

1541.	WILLIAM HENEAGE
,,	THOMAS EDGAR
,	ANTH TRETSAM.
	———— OGARD.
	RALPH ALLEN.
,,	ROBERT LINDALL
,,	THOMAS LOVELACE
,,	THOMAS GOODRICKE (after Bishop of Ely).
,,	EDWARD GIFFORD.
,,	JOHN PALMER
,,	JOHN COKE
,,	ROBERT BEAMOND
,,	THOMAS BLOMVILE
,,	MICHAEL BABBINGTON.
,,	JAMES SOAMEHURST
,,	LEWES WEST

folio 457.

,,	RICHARD JACKSON
,,	JOHN GREGORY
,,	WILLIAM HALL
,,	GEORGE JACKSON
,,	RICHARD KNIGHT
,,	WILLIAM MIDDLETON.
,,	CHRISTOPHER LANGHOLME.
,,	THOMAS COLPEPER
,,	JOHN WYBURNE.
,,	WILLIAM YERLAND
,,	EDWARD LEIGHTON
,,	GEORGE GELHEARD
,,	SAMUEL PETTITT

folio 460.

1542.	JOHN INCENT (Dean of St. Paul's)
,,	CUTHBERT HUTTON
,,	BAR(THOLOMEW) HALSALL
,,	EDWARD HALSALL (no date)
,,	EDMUND HATLEY.
,,	EDMUND KEMP
,,	GEORGE HARLAKENDEN.
,,	ANTHONY LEWKNOR
,,	HUGH ANDERTON
,,	GRIFF YAXLEY

folio 460—(continued)

1542	JO ASHBURNHAM
,,	RICHARD DEVENISH
,,	EDWARD MAYNE
,,	ARTHUR MAMOZING (Mannering ?)
,,	THOMAS LAWES
,,	RALPH BARTON
,,	CHRISTOPHER CHYVER
,,	RICHARD BEAMOND
,,	HENRY TILNEY
,,	ERASMUS SPELMAN
,,	WILLIAM SHEWRIGHT.
,,	THOMAS WIGMORE
,,	HENRY VESEY
,,	GEORGE VAUGHAN
1543	MATTHEW TUSAKE
,,	JOHN FORSTER

folio 462.

,,	THOMAS ROLFE
,,	RICHARD HAVES
,,	THOMAS ORINGTON
,,	THOMAS LILLY
,,	JOHN COYLER
,,	THOMAS GRAY
,,	RICHARD BRACKYN
,,	FRANCIS WISE

folio 463.

,,	THOMAS HOLCROFT
.,	RICHARD MARDEN
,,	RICHARD LUTTRELL
,,	WILLIAM LLOYD
,,	JOHN GOLDWELL
,,	WILLIAM GERRARD
,,	WILLIAM CAVENDISH
,,	JOHN POOLEY
,,	RICHARD COVERFIELD.
,,	MATTHEW CLIFTON.
,,	HENRY THINGOLD.
,,	P WHITEHAM.

folio 465

1544	JOHN HIND
,,	JOHN KENT.

folio 465—(continued)

1544	THOMAS REVES
,,	WILLIAM NORRIS
,,	WILLIAM MAY (after Archbishop of York)
,,	WALTER MANSELL
,,	JERM PALMER
,,	EDWARD PERCY.
,,	GEORGE CLIFFORD.
,,	SIMON BRODRICK.
,,	ANTHONY BELLASIS.
,,	GILES SEFOWLES
,,	RICHARD TEMPEST
,,	THOMAS RUSSELL
,,	JOHN WASTNEYS
,,	THOMAS WATERTON.

folio 466

,,	JOHN MARKHAM
,,	CHRISTOPHER LOVELL
,,	LORD GILES PAWLETT
,,	ROBERT CADDELL
,,	WILLIAM CLIFTON
,,	WILLIAM BLADWELL
,,	THOMAS BACON
,,	RALPH STANDISH
,,	WILLIAM ROBERTS
,,	EDWARD WELBY

folio 467

,,	JOHN JEFFERY
,,	RICHARD KIRKHEAD
,,	ROBERT NOWELL
,,	CHRISTOPHER DANBY
,,	ABRAHAM MANSFIELD
,,	ROBERT GORING
,,	JOHN FRESTON
,,	WILLIAM FAIRFAX
,,	FRANCIS BOHUN
,,	NICHOLAS CRISPE
,,	JOHN CONSTABLE
,,	ROBERT HARRINGTON
,,	EDWARD BOYSE
,,	CHRISTOPHER BLOWER

folio 467—(continued)

1544	EDWARD TILDESLEY
,,	JOHN WOODHOUSE.
,,	RICHARD WYMOND
,,	JOHN KITCHINGE.
,,	JOHN KEMP
,,	GEORGE CRESSAM

folio 468.

,,	THOMAS PERCY
1546	CHRISTOPHER PLATTER
,,	JOHN HUTTON
,,	HENRY YELVERTON
,,	JO WILLIAMS
,,	JOHN ALLEN
,,	WALTER MILDMAY (Chancellor of the Exchequer, 1577)
,,	PHILIP LYNNE
,,	GILBERT DIGHTON

folio 470

,,	RICHARD HARLAKENDEN (Segar gives 1564)
,,	NICHOLAS HALGHITT
,,	ALEXANDER HUGHES.
,,	HENRY OWEN.
,,	BENJAMIN NICHOLSON
,,	ROBERT ALCOCKE
,,	JOHN GOSLINE
,,	GEORGE PURMORTE
,,	WILLIAM PAWLETT.
,	AUGUST PORTER
,,	EDMUND FLOOD
,	EDWARD CRAYFORD
,,	REYNOLD HEYGATE
,,	WILLIAM KINN
,,	ROBERT NEWMAN
,,	WILLIAM BURTON
,,	THOMAS WISEMAN.
,,	THOMAS WALBUTT
,	THOMAS WHALLEY
,	RICHARD WALLER.
,,	WILLIAM WARRYNE

folio 472

1547	THOMAS BACON
,,	THOMAS FINCHAM.
,,	ROBERT WISE

folio 473.

,,	RALPH HAYMAN
,,	WALTER HENDLEY
,,	THOMAS HONYWOOD
,,	THOMAS LAYTON
,,	ROBERT LAWSON
,,	JAMES LONGWORTH
,,	GEORGE LINDSEY
,,	THOMAS GILLFORD
,,	WILLIAM GODSALVE
,,	JOHN PECKE
,,	FRANCIS BOLDER
,,	RICHARD BROWNE
,,	RICHARD CHESNOLD
,,	HUMPHRY BEDINGFELD
,,	WALTER BARRINGTON
,,	NICHOLAS ROCH
,,	CHRISTOPHER VAWSEY
,,	GEORGE STRINGER
,,	JO THURBARD
,,	JOHN TOWNLEY
,,	WILLIAM WYNCOTT

folio 474

,,	—— SIREETE.
,,	WILLIAM KIRKHAM
1548	STEPHEN AUSTIN
,,	GEORGE FORMA (sic).
,,	JOHN BROWNE
,,	THOMAS CUSACKE
,,	ROBERT VAUGHAN
,,	WILLIAM RUGGE
,,	GEORGE EUSTACE

folio 476.

,,	RICHARD ASHENDEN.
,,	JOHN MANSER
,,	WILLIAM LOVELACE
,,	ROBERT FLETCHER
,,	JOHN BIRD

folio 476—(continued)

1548	FRANCIS BUCKE
,,	JOHN FINGLASSE
,,	ROBERT FRY
,,	RICHARD CLIFFE
,,	GEORGE KENISHAM
,,	THOMAS STAPLE
,,	RICHARD KNYYETT (Segar, 1541)
,,	M TYSDALE
,,	RICHARD TOPCLIFFE
1549	FRANCIS ROODES
,,	ALEXANDER NOWELL
,,	FRANCIS HIND.

folio 477.

,,	EDWARD APPLETON
,,	GEORGE MAY
,,	WILLIAM MOLLINEUX
,,	RANDAL LLOYD
,,	JOHN PEPYS
,,	JOHN CLARKSON

folio 479

,,	CHRISTOPHER MILLER
,,	THOMAS COLBY
,,	GEORGE HARRISON
,,	HUMPHREY BUCKE
,,	JAMES BRAND
,,	JOHN WILDGOOSE
,,	THOMAS WRIGHT

folio 480

,,	FRANCIS FAIRFAX

folio 481

1550	THOMAS COWPER
,,	ERASMUS COPE
,,	EDWARD GREISLEY
,,	RICHARD PEYTON
,,	JO BARNARDISTON
,,	GABRIEL HESKETH
,,	EDWARD ELMES.
,,	JOHN SALISBURY
,,	RALPH DYMOCKE

folio 482

1550	EDWARD MIDDLETON
,,	———— MONTGOMERY
,,	ROBERT SHUTE
,,	ROBERT SHIRBURNE
,,	FRANCIS STRANGMAN.
,,	JOHN NORBURY

folio 483

1551	FRANCIS MOLLINEUX.
,,	NICHOLAS PIGOTT
,,	RICHARD PELLETT
,,	EDWARD FOWLER
,,	RICHARD CRIPPS
,,	ROWLAND SHERRARD
,,	WILLIAM SCOTT

folio 484.

,,	JAMES GLAISER
,,	ROGER CAREW
,,	WILLIAM APSLEY
,,	WILLIAM ALINGTON
,,	THOMAS WISE
,,	FRANCIS THORPE
,,	THOMAS TEMPEST
,,	HUGH TRAYERS.
,,	JOHN HILL
,,	THOMAS KYRLE.

folio 485.

,,	JER REYNOLDS
,,	JO BARKINSDALE.
,,	ROBERT HUTTON
,,	RICHARD AUNGIER
,,	WILLIAM SCOTT
,,	JOHN VAVASOR
,,	EDWARD STAMFORD

folio 486

,,	ROWLAND LAWSON
,,	THOMAS MOYSER
,,	THOMAS NOONE
,,	ANTHONY STAPLE
,,	EDWARD SUTTON

folio 486—(continued)

1551	THOMAS SENHOUSE
,,	THOMAS MICHELBOURNE (1555)
1552	JOHN ROUSE

folio 487.

,,	JOHN PLACE
,,	JO BARNEWALL
,,	RALPH TANKARD
,,	JOHN WEST
,,	WILLIAM WHALLEY
,,	JO REYNOLDS
,,	ROBERT WINGFIELD

folio 488

,,	THOMAS HIND
,,	RICHARD CHARNOCKE
,,	WILLIAM WHISKINS
,,	WILLIAM DALLISON
,,	THOMAS THERLE

folio 490

,,	EDMUND LEIGH
,,	ROBERT LANE
,,	GEORGE CARLTON
,,	WILLIAM CROMER
,,	THOMAS CECIL (Earl of Exeter)
,,	WILLIAM CHAPMAN.
,,	WILLIAM BROMFIELD
,,	EDWARD BASSETT
,,	FRANCIS WALSINGHAM
,,	EDMUND DRIVER
,,	FRANCIS VAUGHAN
,,	ROBERT WHETSTONE
,,	THOMAS REPINGTON
,,	JOHN SOUCH.
,,	JOHN CHEKE (1540, Segar, but query 1552)

folio 491.

,,	GEORGE CARR
,,	JOHN CHERNOCKE
,,	THOMAS PAYNE.
,,	THOMAS BROCKLESBY
,,	MARTIN HARLAKENDEN.

folio 491—(continued)

1552 HENRY NEVILL (probably Lord
         Abergavenny)
  ,,   CHRISTOPHER YELVERTON.
  ,,   EDWARD STEVENSON
  ,,   THOMAS SNAGGE
  ,,   THOMAS STANLEY.
  ,,   THOMAS TURNOR
  ,,   ROBERT WILLIAMS
  ,,   GEORGE IRELAND (1555, Segar)
  ,,   JOHN JERMYN (1555, Segar)

folio 492

  ,,   WILLIAM PLATFOOT
1553 ALEXANDER COLPEPER (1550, Segar)
  ,,   JOHN DUDLEY (Duke of Northumber-
         land)   (Hilary Term)
  ,,   RICHARD PAYTON
  ,,   WILLIAM CARDINALL.
  ,,   ROBERT FALLOWFIELD.
  ,,   THOMAS BERTIE
  ,,   ROBERT HUSSEY
  ,,   ARTHUR WALPOLE
  ,,   JOHN WELDISH
  ,,   MORGAN TYRRELL
  ,,   JOHN HUSSEY
  ,,   WILLIAM KYRTON.

folio 494.

  ,,   CHRISTOPHER LANGTON
  ,,   JOHN GRAY.
  ,,   ROBERT GOSNOLD
  ,,   THOMAS FITTON
  ,,   LEVERIDGE FOSTER
  ,,   JOHN COLPEPER (1550, Segar)
  ,,   WILLIAM COWPER (1550, Segar)
  ,,   THOMAS CECIL
  ,,   GEORGE FLEMINGE
  ,,   RANDLE BRERETON
  ,,   WILLIAM BURNHAM
  ,,   STEPHEN AUSTEN
  ,,   GEORGE AUDLEY
  ,,   RICHARD DERING
  ,,   RICHARD FULLER
  ,,   JOHN WALWYN.

folio 494—(continued).

1553 ROBERT VESEY.
  ,,   RICHARD WYK(E)S.
  ,,   FRANCIS YAXLEY
  ,,   FRANCIS BARNARD
  ,,   JOHN SUTTON.
  ,,   EDMUND HIDER
  ,,   EDMUND HERENDEN
  ,,   WALTER NORTON

folio 496.

  ,,   WILLIAM COOKE
  ,,   EDWARD CARLTON
  ,,   EDWARD COOKE
  ,,   WILLIAM BRADBORNE
  ,,   THOMAS BAKER
  ,,   ROBERT AYRE
  ,,   EDMUND AYRE
  ,,   GEORGE HEIGHAM
  ,,   EDWARD WITHYPOLE
  ,,   JOHN HANMER
  ,,   JOHN THACKER
  ,,   GEORGE SOUCH

folio 498

1554 JOHN LEWES
  ,   CHARLES GRICE
  ,,   ——— VALLANCE (1561, Segar)
  ,,   RICHARD CULPEPER
  ,,   HENRY DARCY
  ,,   HENRY MEGGES
  ,,   JOHN WRIGHT
  ,,   JOHN WINCOLE
  ,,   ROBERT ABELL (1555, Segar)

folio 500.

  ,,   JOHN MARBURY
  ,,   JOHN NEVYSON
  ,,   JAMES NEDHAM
  ,,   WILLIAM AYLMER
  ,,   HENRY GUNVILE
  ,,   ANTHONY GOSNOLD.
  ,,   THOMAS FOWLE.
  ,,   JOHN PARRY
  ,,   STEPHEN GOLDWELL.

folio 500—(continued).

1554	GEORGE CHETTINGE.
,,	REYNOL FAIRELEY
,,	THOMAS FANE.
,,	THOMAS ASHTON
,,	THOMAS BARRINGTON.
,,	THOMAS BOUGHTON.
,,	WILLIAM SYNGLTON
,,	WILLIAM WALPOLE
,,	CHRISTOPHER BARTON
,,	JOHN DUKE
,,	OSWALD METCALFE
,,	WILLIAM HANMER
,,	WILLIAM HOSKINS.
,,	ALEXANDER RIGBY

folio 502

1555	STEPHEN GARDNER (Bishop of Winchester and Chancellor of England)
,,	HENRY GOODYERE
,,	RICHARD PRICE
,,	LEVIN BUFKIN
,,	ROBERT DUNN
,,	EDWARD FOSTER
,,	EDWARD DUKE
,,	RICHARD KNYVETT.
,,	GEORGE GASCOIGNE

folio 503

,,	WILLIAM DEREHAUGH
,,	JOHN HAWES
,,	ARTHUR BELDAUM
,,	JOHN WINGFIELD
,,	GEORGE SOONE
,,	CHARLES WILLIAMS
,,	JOHN BROGRAVE
,,	ROBERT SAMPSON
,,	RICHARD DOUZE
,,	THOMAS TALBOT

folio 505

,,	THOMAS PERSALL
,,	BARTHOLOMEW KENT
,	THOMAS DOYLEY

folio 505—(continued).

1555	CHARLES PAYTON
,,	ROBERT THOROLD (1554).
,,	CHRISTOPHER ENGHAM (1552 Segar)
,,	HENRY GULFORD
,,	ROBERT CLOUGH.
,,	WILLIAM ADYES
,,	WILLIAM BOLMAN
,,	JOHN STEWARD.
,,	GE PENRUDDOCKE.

folio 506

,,	GEORGE HOLCROFT
,,	REYNOLD GRAY (after Earl of Kent)
,,	CHARLES FANE
,,	NICHOLAS THORPE (1555).
,,	ANDREW FOSTER
,,	THOMAS COTTEN
,,	JOHN BINGHAM
,,	PAUL WITHYPOLE
,,	THOMAS MILLER

folio 509

1556	ROBERT LEIGH
,,	RICHARD PRATT
,,	HENRY HUNT
,,	NICHOLAS FRANCKLYN
,,	RICHARD KEMP.
,,	RALPH JACKSON
,,	CHARLES CUTLER
,,	THOMAS TURNEY
,,	HENRY ALWAY
,,	GERARD DANNETT

folio 512

,,	PATRICK PLUNKETT
,,	CHARLES FRAMLINGHAM
,,	THOMAS BROOKS
,,	WILLIAM ASHBY
,,	HUGH SHELTON
,,	JOHN ROLLISLEY
,,	WILLIAM ASHMALL
,,	ARTHUR HALL
,,	ROBERT THORP

folio 513

1556	EDMUND IRBY (1555, Segar)
,,	ROBERT GODFREY
,,	RICHARD JEFFERY
,,	THOMAS ESTCOURTE
,,	EDWARD HOLME
,,	HUMPHREY PUREFOY
,,	CHARLES SCARLETT
,,	GEORGE STANHOPE
,,	JOHN STANHOPE
,,	WILLIAM DANIELL
,,	EDWARD STAMPE
,,	JOHN STAMPE
,,	EDMUND BUTLER
,,	WILLIAM HEWETT
,,	JOHN HUSSEY
,,	LEONARD BAKER
,,	PATRICK SACHEVERELL
1557	ROBERT LEIGH

folio 516.

,,	RICHARD LOVELACE
,,	WILLIAM GROVE
,,	JOHN A'LEIGH
,,	ROBERT STAMFORD.
,,	WALTER HAYDON.
,,	JOHN STRANGE
,,	GEORGE CATLYNE

folio 517.

,,	THOMAS PERCY (Earl of Northumberland). (Trinity Term)
,,	FRANCIS RUSSELL (Earl of Bedford) (Trinity Term)
,,	FRANCIS KENDLEMER
,,	GEORGE JOY
,,	RICHARD TILDESLEY
,,	GEORGE BOOTH
,,	EDWARD NORDEN
,,	ROGER DALTON (1556, Segar)
,,	ROBERT WATSON
,,	RICHARD MOORE

folio 520

1559	CHARLES WENTWORTH
,,	ROGER TWISDEN

folio 520—(continued)

1559	FRANCIS SOUTHWELL
,,	JOHN HUGGINS
,,	JASPER GILPIN
,,	GEORGE FILBY
,,	WILLIAM BUTLER
,,	THOMAS BODENHAM
,,	RICHARD COURTHORP
,,	THOMAS CECIL (after Earl of Exeter) (Jan 20)
,,	ELLIS BRAME.
,,	JOHN SMITH
,,	THOMAS SHIRLEY
,,	JOHN BUTLER
,,	ROBERT WROUTH

folio 521

,,	JOHN COLES
,,	EDWARD GRIMSTON
,,	WILLIAM BOYSE
,,	RICHARD BRADDYLL.
,,	THOMAS BRATHWAY
,,	MICHAEL LEWES.
,,	CLEMENT LEWES.
,,	THOMAS WIGMORE.
,,	CHARLES SANDERS.
,,	RALPH WORSLEY.

folio 523

1560	NORRIS RADNEY.
,,	CHARLES PARRY (May 16)
,,	ROBERT FORTH.
,,	GILBERT SHERRINGTON
,,	JUSTINIAN CHAMPNEYS.
,,	HENRY HORNE
,,	WILLIAM SANISLOW (? St Loe)
,,	ANTHONY STOKES
,,	WILLIAM PARR (Marquis of Northampton)

folio 524

,,	JOHN REVETT

folio 526.

,,	WALTER ARCHER
,,	WALTER DENNYS

folio 526 —(continued)

1560	THOMAS DANIELL
,,	THOMAS DANNETT
,,	JAMES COTGRAVE
,,	JOHN HABDY
,,	RICHARD SEDGRAVE
,,	JOHN ST JOHN

folio 527

,,	THOMAS HAWTAYNE
,,	THOMAS CAMMOCKE
,,	EDWARD WARD
1561	RALPH SADLER

folio 529.

,,	HENRY ASCOUGH
,,	JOHN CUTTS
,,	VINCENT FULNETBY
,,	THOMAS PEYTON
,,	WILLIAM BEVYLE
,,	WALTER VAUGHAN
,,	JASPER HEYWOOD
,,	EDMUND ASHFEILD
,,	ROBERT STAFFORD
,,	FRANCIS WELBORNE
,,	RICHARD SHETH
,,	WALTER WALLER
,,	GEORGE ROTHERHAM

folio 530.

,,	REA OMER & R (1560, Segar)
,,	ROGER NORTH (Sir, after Lord North) (Dec 29)
,,	NICHOLAS PIGOTT
,,	ANTHONY KINDLEMARCH
,,	EDWARD VAUGHAN.
,,	WILLIAM SENTLOW
,	EDMUND BUNNEY
,,	EDMUND BILLETT.
,,	BAR BELLAMY
,,	JOHN HALL
,,	HENRY HERONDEN
,,	HENRY SCROOPE (9th Lord S)
,,	EDMUND THOROLD
,,	JOHN, LORD SHEFFIELD

folio 530 —(continued)

1561	JOHN WATSON
,,	JOHN WALKER
,,	THOMAS HOWARD (Duke of Norfolk) (Dec 28)

folio 531.

,,	HENRY NEVILL (Earl of Westmorland). (Jan 22)
,,	THOMAS RADCLIFFE (Earl of Sussex) (Jan 22)
,,	HENRY STANLEY (Lord Strange) (Jan 24)
,,	EDWARD STANLEY (Earl of Derby) (Jan 28)
,,	FRANCIS CROMWELL
,,	PETER PHEASANT
,,	JASPER LEAKE
,,	AMBROSE BUTTON
,,	WILLIAM ASHTON
,,	CHARLES COOKE
,,	RICHARD KETTON
,,	THOMAS CARTER
,,	THOMAS EDWARDS
,,	HUMPHREY HANMER
,,	LAURENCE BLUNDESTON
,,	WILLIAM HUMINGS
,,	WILLIAM BARKER
,,	WILLIAM BAKER
,,	JOHN TAYLOR
,,	RICHARD SHUTTLEWORTH
1562	JOHN DARCY (Lord D , of Chiche) (Feb 4)
,,	ANTHONY HEYFORD

folio 534.

,,	JAMES CROFTS
,,	JOHN FORTESCUE.
,,	WILLIAM LEYCESTER
,,	WILLIAM HARVEY
,,	ARTHUR HOPTON
,,	PAUL STREETLY

folio 535.

,,	JO PENRUDDOCKE.
,,	JOHN PATCH

	folio 535—(continued).		folio 540.
1562	PETER NOTE.	1562-3	JOHN ROW.
,,	GEORGE QUARLES	,,	RICHARD HARDRES
,,	JOHN GARNISH	,,	THOMAS BARWAYER
,,	JOHN APSLEY	,,	ANTHONY CHESTER

folio 538.

			folio 542
,,	ROWLAND CAREW	,,	HENRY COMPTON (after Lord Compton), (March 1)
,,	THOMAS PALMER		
,,	GEORGE COTTEN	1563	EDWARD NEVILL
,,	RICHARD BELYNG	,,	EDMUND POOLEY
,,	JEFFERY EDMONDSON (folio 83)	,,	COTTON GARGRAYE
,,	EDWARD BROCKETT	,,	EDMUND MATHER
,,	FRANCIS FORTESCUE.	,,	WILLIAM DADE
,,	JOHN LANE.	,,	THOMAS STEWARD
,,	THOMAS TEVY	,,	EDWARD BARWELL
,,	THOMAS WADDINGE.	,,	EDWARD HERBERT
,,	NATHANIEL BACON (Dec 15)	,,	EDWARD BARNES.
,,	NICHOLAS BACON (Dec. 15)	,,	GEORGE BLACKWELL (folio 506)
,,	WILLIAM BENHAM.		
,,	THOMAS HUAHOUSE.		**folio 543.**
1562-3	HENRY CHENEY (Jan. 21)	,,	THOMAS GOLDWELL
,,	HUGH COPSON	,,	HENRY SYDNEY (Sir), (April 19)

folio 539

,,	ROGER EDWARDS (1561, Segar)	,,	HENRY DARRELL
,,	THOMAS FAIRELEY	,,	EDWARD ANDREWES
,,	GABRIEL PULTENEY.	,,	EDMUND PELHAM
,,	RICHARD MILLS.	,,	NICHOLAS FULLER
,,	JAMES ANDERTON	,,	HUMPHREY FERRERS
,,	WILLIAM OXENDEN	,,	ROBERT KINDLEMARCH
,,	FRANCIS SMITH.	,,	THOMAS BROXHOLME
,,	WILLIAM STANLEY	,,	THOMAS BENTLEY
,,	ANTHONY HEREFORD	,,	JOHN HUNT
,,	JOHN HUSSEY	,,	JOHN SOUCH
,,	JOHN HALES	,,	ANTHONY ST LEGER
,,	EDWARD CHESTER.	,,	HENRY STANDISH
,,	JAMES BLUNT (Lord Mountjoy) (Feb 10)	,,	WILLIAM THORPE
,,	PHILOG FORD	,,	ROBERT THOROLD
,,	JOHN SPURLING	,,	ROBERT WOODWARD.
,,	PETER WARBURION	,,	GEORGE ROBERTS
,,	JOHN VAUGHAN	,,	WILLIAM URMSTON
,,	ROBERT WHETTYLL	,,	JOHN ROW
,	RICHARD WORME	,,	JOHN GRENARKE
		,,	WILLIAM VAUGHAN

C

folio 546.

1564 JOHN MIDDLETON.
  ,,   JOHN LANCASTER.
  ,,   HENRY PIERREPOINT.
  ,,   WALTER POWTRELL.
  ,,   RICHARD CAPEL
  ,,   JOHN HARTE
  ,,   FRANCIS HARTE
  ,,   JOHN BARNEWALL.
  ,,   ISAAC RUDSTON.
  ,,   WAR(WICK) WARNER
  ,,   THOMAS SAVILE

folio 547.

  ,,   GEORGE HOWARD
  ,,   CHARLES HOWARD
  ,,   FRANCIS HARVEY
  ,,   THOMAS CATESBY
  ,,   GEORGE BASSETT.
  ,,   ROBERT FYN.
  ,,   THOMAS PROCTER.
  ,,   OLDFE (OWEN ?) PHILLIPS
  ,,   WILFRID LAWSON
  ,,   EDWARD LITTLEBURY
  ,,   ANTHONY MASON
  ,,   EDWARD MORSE
  ,,   HENRY KNOWLES
  ,,   RALPH SMARTE
  ,,   ANTHONY WYKES
  ,,   WILLIAM SNAGGE
  ,,   GEORGE WISEMAN
  ,,   JOHN WILLOUGHBY
  ,,   WILLIAM SMITH
  ,,   JOHN TWYNNE
  ,,   THOMAS BARROW (1565, Segar)
  ,,   THOMAS JEFFERY

folio 548

  ,,   ROBERT HONYWOOD.
  ,,   RALPH EDDOWES
  ,,   ANTHONY WYLLARD
  ,,   ANTHONY MAWHAWD

folio 550

  ,,   FRANCIS NEVILL

folio 550—(continued)

1565 CHARLES GLEMHAM
  ,,   ROBERT PEYTON.
  ,,   WILLIAM FANT
  ,,   WALTER HUSSEY
  ,,   JOHN QUARLES
  ,,   JOHN BAXSTER

folio 551

  ,,   WILLIAM BURMAN
  ,,   EDWARD STANNARD
  ,,   GEORGE CULPEPER
  ,,   WALTER CULPEPER
  ,,   RICHARD PELL
  ,,   ROBERT AYRE

folio 554.

  ,,   JASPER MOORE
  ,,   EDWARD THWAYTES
  ,,   JOHN CUTTS
  ,,   JOHN MICHELL.
  ,,   EDWARD TOWNLEY
  ,,   WILLIAM HUMBERSTON
  ,,   RA HETHERINGTON
  ,,   JAMES HALES
  ,,   THOMAS ASHTON

folio 555.

  ,,   THOMAS GARDENER
  ,,   ASHTON AYLWORTH
  ,,   THOMAS LEEKE
  ,,   RICHARD PROCTER
  ,,   EDWARD FISHER
  ,,   MICHAEL FERRERS
  ,,   PHILIP COURTNEY.
  ,,   ROBERT KEY
  ,,   FRANCIS KNOWLES.
  ,,   HENRY HALL
  ,,   THOMAS VINCENT
  ,,   THOMAS WADE
  ,,   WALTER STRICKLAND.
  ,,   MAURICE ROLL
  ,,   RICHARD THIMBLEBY
  ,,   ROBERT HOWLAND.

folio 555—(continued)

1565   THOMAS HENEAGE
,,   THOMAS HATCHERETT
1565 6   WILLIAM HEWETT 3th (Mar 4)
     (after Lord Mayor of London)

folio 556

1566   ROBERT LE GRICE
,,   HENRY CATLYNE.
,,   NATHANIEL TATTERSALL.

folio 558.

,,   MATHEW WHETNALL (1565)
,,   WILLIAM MEARING
,,   CHARLES MORRISON.
,,   THOMAS PELHAM
,,   WILLIAM YAXLEY
,,   GEORGE VILLIERS.
,,   EDWARD BACON.

folio 559

,,   ROBERT FLINT (1565)
,,   JOHN MEREDYTH
,,   JOHN MANNERS (Earl of Rutland)
,,   CHARLES GODDARD
,,   JEREMIAH BETTENHAM
,,   WILLIAM CASON
,,   CHRISTOPHER CARUS

folio 562

,,   JOHN MAYNE
,,   WALTER MAYNE
,,   HENRY ANDREWES
,,   HENRY ANDERSON
,,   CHRISTOPHER MOLLINEUX
,,   CHARLES NORRIS
,,   NICHOLAS SEDGRAYE
,,   JOHN JEFFERY
,,   WILLIAM JEFFERY
,,   CHARLES HONYWOOD
,,   THOMAS KNEVETT.
,,   ANTHONY CAGE
,,   GEORGE PUREFOY
,,   CHARLES COOKE.
,,   RALPH STRACHEY.
,,   GEORGE SPEKE

folio 563

1566   JER PIERREPOINT
1566-7 EDWARD VERE (Earl of Oxford)
     (Feb. 1).
,,   ROGER BODENHAM.
,,   WILLIAM ALCOCKE
,,   ROBERT MOYLE
,,   FRANCIS BRACKYN
,,   JOHN ELLIS
,,   EDMUND EVENDEN.
,,   THOMAS BUTLER (Earl of Ormond
     and Ossory), (Mar 7)

folio 568

1567   GODFREY BURGOYNE
,,   HUGH OWEN
,,   ROBERT DORMER
,,   MATTHEW ARUNDELL
,,   JO MARKHAM.
,,   JAMES HUSSEY
,,   JOHN LANEY
,,   HENRY BLAKE
,,   NICHOLAS BUCKE
,,   ——— CHATTERTON
,,   JAMES EUSTACE
,,   MICHAEL HENFAGE.
,,   HENRY ROLLES
,,   RICHARD BEALOSSE (1564, Segar)

folio 569

,,   JOHN WARD
,,   JOHN SOUTHALL
,,   JOHN SCARLETT

folio 572

,,   WALTER AYLWORTH.
,,   HENRY MATHEW
,,   THOMAS MERINGE.
,,   RICHARD LYNAM
,,   HENRY GRAY
,,   HENRY POYNINGS.
,,   NICHOLAS POTTS
,,   ROBERT PAYNE
,,   ANTHONY FINCH
,,   CHARLES SECKFORD (1569, Segar)
,,   THOMAS CLEERE

folio 572—(continued)

1567	AMBROSE CHARLTON
,,	HENRY CAVENDISH.
,,	MARTIN BARNHAM.
,,	WALTER COVERT
,,	GEORGE CHAWORTH
,,	HENRY IDEN
,,	GEORGE BASFORD
,,	JOHN BARNEWALL
,,	KENELM BERNEY.
,,	RALPH WOOD
,,	PHILIP SIDNEY (Feb 2)
,,	RICHARD BURTON
,,	THOMAS BURGAINE.
,,	CHARLES SOMERSET
,,	GEORGE CHOWTE
,,	EDWARD TROYELL

folio 573

,,	GEORGE LIGHTFOOT.
,,	JEFFRY NIGHTINGALE
,,	THOMAS DIGHTON
,,	FRANCIS MORDAN
,,	CHARLES LANE
,,	HENRY PATRICKSON.
,,	JOHN CALLOW.
,,	FRANCIS FLETCHER
,,	CHRISTOPHER FORSTER
,,	THOMAS CHAPMAN
,,	CHARLES HALES
,,	ROBERT KEW

folio 574

| ,, | FRANCIS HASLEWOOD |
| ,, | THOMAS LUCAS (folio 483). |

folio 576

1568	EDWARD FITTON
,,	JOHN OWEN
,,	THOMAS ORMLEY
,,	THOMAS GRAY
,,	THOMAS JONES
,,	EDWARD CUSACKE.
,,	ROBERT KYMPTON
,,	HENRY CHETHAM

folio 576—(continued)

1568	OWEN JONES
,,	MICHAEL STANHOPE
,,	ANTHONY ST LEGER
,,	THOMAS SPELMAN
,,	MARK WICOME
,,	STEPHEN WATTERS
,,	AUGUSTIN ELLIS, of Barnard's Inn
,,	THOMAS MARSH, of Staple Inn.
,,	CHARLES TINGLETON
,,	RALPH JOHNSON, of Staple Inn
,,	ANTHONY PICKERING, of Barnard's Inn
,,	RICHARD BAKER, of Staple Inn
,,	JOHN GODBOLD, of Barnard's Inn
,,	——— CHRISTOPHER

folio 578

| ,, | NATHANIEL TATTERSALL |
| ,, | WILLIAM CARR |

folio 579

,,	NICHOLAS FERMOR
,,	JOHN DARRELL
,,	ROBERT ASTON
,,	GEORGE AYLMER
,,	EDWARD ASTON
,,	JOHN DAFFERNE
,,	MOYLE FINCH.
,,	JOHN VERNAY
,,	HENRY SACHEVERELL
,,	JOHN CHICHESTER
,,	WILLIAM CORNWALL
,,	ERASMUS COPE
,,	EDWARD COPE
,,	WILLIAM CHETWYND
,,	WILLIAM SEYMOUR, specially admitted
,,	EDWARD DUNCH

folio 600

,,	RO SHAKERLEY, specially admitted.
,,	ROBERT BAINBRIDGE of Barnard's Inn
,,	RICHARD ERSBY, of Staple Inn
,,	WILLIAM JEPHES, of Barnard's Inn.

folio 600—(continued)

1568   ROBERT PITT, of Staple Inn
,,   ALEXANDER HAMOND.
,,   MICHAEL WARTON
,,   JOHN LASCELLS, of Barnard's Inn
,,   EDWARD HOLLES (called Hales by Segar), of Staple Inn
,,   ——— DOUGHTY
,,   HUMPHREY BOHUN, specially admitted
,,   WILLIAM BOLTON, of Barnard's Inn
,,   HENRY COOKE
,,   ——— BURGOYNE, of Barnard's Inn
,,   LAURENCE LOCKE.
,,   GEORGE CALFIELD
1568-9   REGINALD GREY (after 5th Earl of Kent), specially admitted (Feb 22)
,,   HENRY GREY (after 6th Earl of Kent), specially admitted
,,   ROWLAND BARKER.
,,   NICHOLAS TIRWHITT
,,   WILLIAM ALMON
,,   WILLIAM BOROW (called Barrow by Segar)

folio 603

1569   HENRY HOLCROFT, specially admitted
,,   JOHN CADDELL, specially admitted
,,   JAMES ALINGTON, of Staple Inn
,,   NICHOLAS COOTE
,,   ——— MARYTHE
,,   ——— MAXFIELD
,,   ——— CATESBY.
,,   RICHARD BARKER, of Barnard's Inn
,,   JAMES PLUNCKETT, of Barnard's Inn
,,   FRANCIS DOYLEY
,,   JOHN TALBOT, of Barnard's Inn
,,   HENRY LAWRENCE, of Barnard's Inn
,,   JAMES BUTLER, Lord Dunboyne.

folio 604

,,   ROBERT HATLEY, specially admitted
,,   EDWARD TAVERNER, of Barnard's Inn
,,   ROBERT ROLFE, of Staple Inn
,,   THOMAS KEMP, of Staple Inn
,,   WILLIAM LAURENCE, specially admitted

folio 604—(continued)

1569.   THOMAS CHETTELL
,,   THOMAS LANCASTER.
1569-70.   RALPH ASHTON (12 Elizabeth, Feb 10)

folio 606

1570.   JOHN VESEY
,,   THOMAS DOCWRA
,,   THOMAS WALTON
,,   PETER TAAFE
,,   RICHARD GULDEFORD
,,   JAMES PRESTON, of Staple Inn
,,   RICHARD MISSETT, of Staple Inn
,,   JOHN BYROM (called Biron by Segar).
,,   THOMAS BETAUGH
,,   RICHARD GOLDSBOROUGH, of Staple Inn
,,   JOHN CRIPPES, of Staple Inn (called Crisp by Segar)
,,   ——— LONGE, of Barnard's Inn
,,   THOMAS LEEKE
,,   EDWARD HUNINGS
,,   ALEXANDER FISHER.
,,   WILLIAM FINCHAM
,,   JOHN SOUTHWORTH, of Staple Inn
,,   EDWARD RIGBY
,,   WILLIAM GIBSON

folio 607

,,   THOMAS SELWIN, of Staple Inn.
,,   MATTHEW GROYE, of Staple Inn
,,   WALTER COOPER (called Cope by Segar)
,,   ROGER GRAY, of Barnard's Inn
,,   HENRY WINGFIELD, of Staple Inn
,,   EDWARD MANNING, of Staple Inn
,,   RICHARD LEGH
,,   WILLIAM REITHE, of Staple Inn (called Rowethe by Segar)
,,   HENRY GOODYERE, specially admitted
,,   THOMAS PARKINS, of Staple Inn
,,   ARTHUR BARHAM, of Staple Inn
,,   ——— NOTE, of Barnard's Inn
,,   EDWARD NUGENT, of Staple Inn
,,   JOHN PIGOTT

folio 607—(continued)

1570	CUTHBERT PEPPER.
,,	———— WYLDE.
,,	JOHN PROCTER

folio 608

,,	HENRY VERNON, of Barnard's Inn
,,	ALEXANDER COX
,,	EDWARD WALGRAVE
,,	THOMAS GRAY, specially admitted

folio 609

1571	JOHN POTTS
,,	CHRISTOPHER EGLESFIELD, of Staple Inn
,,	WILLIAM BOWYER
,,	JOHN SALMON, of Staple Inn
,,	EDWARD BRAMPTON
,,	GERVASE WASTENEYS
,,	THOMAS WATTON
,,	WILLIAM LAWSON
,,	CHARLES HEDWORTH
,,	RICHARD ALLETT
,,	LAURENCE WASHINGTON (called Walsingham by Segar)
,,	ROBERT PARGITER
,,	GEORGE WYATE.
,,	THOMAS BURNABY
,,	THOMAS BIRD
,,	THOMAS FLOWER.

folio 611

,	WILLIAM NAPPER, specially admitted
,	THOMAS DALBY
,,	ROBERT DEREHAUGH, of Staple Inn
,	WILLIAM HUNGATE, of Staple Inn
,,	THOMAS LOVELACE (by consent of the reader)
,,	BENJAMIN PURMORTE (called Portmorte in ledger)
,,	WILLIAM HALES, of Staple Inn
,,	WILLIAM BIRD
,,	JOHN TWYNNE, of Staple Inn.
,,	ROWLAND SMARTE
,,	JOHN WESTLAND, of Staple Inn
,,	ROBERT MOORE, of Barnard's Inn
,,	HUGH LYGON, of Staple Inn.

folio 613.

1571.	THOMAS BALL, of Staple Inn
,,	JOHN BIRCHE
,,	JOHN BURMAN, of Barnard's Inn.
,,	GEORGE HOPTON
,,	WILLIAM BIRMINGHAM, of Staple Inn
,,	CHRISTOPHER LINDSEY, of Staple Inn
,,	THOMAS JOHNSON, of Barnard's Inn
,,	———— NOWELL (or Nevill ?)
,,	WILLIAM BRYDGES (or Brigge ?).
,,	THOMAS THOROLD
,,	JOHN CRIPPS (called Crisp by Segar)
,,	THOMAS FITZHERBERT.
,,	PHILIP DRAYCOTT.

folio 614

,,	WILLIAM WALSINGHAM
,,	WILLIAM FLEMING, of Staple Inn
,,	JAMES WALBURNE, of Staple Inn
,,	THOMAS WILSON, specially admitted
,,	RICHARD SHERBURNE, specially admitted
,,	CHARLES MARBURY
,,	WILLIAM WADE
,,	GEORGE BURGOYNE
,,	———— MAINWARING, of Staple Inn
,,	JOHN MEERES, of Barnard's Inn
,,	HENRY SHERBURNE

folio 615

,,	JOHN BEACON (Deacon ?)
,,	HENRY NEVILL (Noell ?, of Barnard's Inn
,,	JOHN NEDHAM.
,.	RICHARD HUMFREY.
,,	JOHN MORGAN.
,,	———— SAUNDERS
,,	JOHN BROWNE (by consent of the reader)
,,	JAMES HILL
,,	BEL RUDSTON
,,	HUGH CARTWRIGHT (called Carteret by Segar)
,,	CHARLES PROWDE, of Staple Inn
,,	THOMAS PLEASANCE, of Staple Inn.
,,	EDWARD POWLTER (or Powtrell)

folio 615—(continued)

1571.   PAUL DAWNEY, of Staple Inn

"   —— TYRWHITT, of Barnard's Inn

"   —— KYTSONE

1571-2.   MR CHARLES STEWART, "absque fine" (after Earl of Lennox) (Jan 9)

"   LAURENCE WASHINGTON, specially admitted.

"   EDWARD SEYMOUR, Earl of Hertford, specially admitted (Feb. 2)

"   NICHOLAS TEMPEST, specially admitted

folio 617.

1572.   JOHN STAFFORD.

"   —— CROMPTON

"   JOHN GARNISH, of Barnard's Inn

"   —— HARVEY

"   ALEXANDER STANDISH

"   ROGER BECKWITH

"   JOHN LEIGH

folio 618

"   WILLIAM GEREY (or Gyrrye) of Barnard's Inn.

"   THOMAS HESKETH.

"   WILLIAM ROTHWELL

"   THOMAS MOUNTNEY, of Staple Inn

"   WILLIAM GEWERSEY, of Staple Inn

"   THOMAS BIRKBECK, of Barnard's Inn.

"   HENRY GOODYERE, of Staple Inn

"   RICHARD CAREY, of Barnard's Inn

"   GILES COTTON, of Barnard's Inn

"   WILLIAM SAUNDERS, of Staple Inn

"   ANTHONY WINGFIELD

"   THOMAS WHETENHALL, of Staple Inn

folio 619

"   THOMAS WATERTON

"   EDWARD FROTHINGHAM

"   ROGER LEIGH

"   —— DARYELL

"   EDWARD BOLDERO, of Staple Inn

"   THOMAS KITCHYNGE.

folio 621

1572.   WILLIAM GERRARD

"   WILLIAM CAVENDISH.

"   WILLIAM LEWIS

"   WILLIAM BLAKISTON.

,   JOHN NORTH

"   GABRIEL POPE, of Barnard's Inn

"   NICHOLAS AYLMER, of Staple Inn.

folio 622.

"   FRANCIS BRACKYN, of Barnard's Inn

"   JOHN BOYLE.

"   RANDLE HANMER, of Barnard's Inn

"   SAMUEL BACKHOUSE

"   THOMAS BUSCALL, of Barnard's Inn

"   JOHN BRADDYLI

"   WILLIAM ANDREWS, of Barnard's Inn

"   WILLIAM LEIGH

"   WILLIAM FORSETT

"   EDWARD SLEGGE (or Sledge), of Barnard's Inn

"   THOMAS COBBE, of Staple Inn

folio 624

1573   ROBERT BARNEWALL, of Staple Inn

"   HENRY WILLOUGHBY, of Staple Inn

"   MICHAEL JOBSON

"   JAMES MEDCALFE, of Staple Inn.

"   —— VERDOME, of Staple Inn

"   —— CONSTABLE.

"   (PATRICK) DROMEGOLDE, of Staple Inn.

"   PATRICK ZOUCHE.

folio 625

"   ROBERT TUNSTALL, specially admitted.

folio 626.

"   JOHN SHEPHEARDE

"   —— READE (Thomas Roods in Segar)

"   RICHARD COURTHOPE

"   THOMAS SALESBURY.

"   RALPH THORNTON, of Barnard's Inn

"   RALPH LAYTON, of Staple Inn

"   WILLIAM BUTTON, of Barnard's Inn

folio 626—(continued)

1573 JOHN STUBBES, of Barnard's Inn.
  ,, THOMAS LAYTON, of Staple Inn
  ,, EDWARD SELWYN, of Staple Inn
  ,, JOHN MATHEW, specially admitted
  ,, RICHARD ALLEN, specially admitted
  ,, JAMES BARHAM, of Staple Inn
  ,, RICHARD DAKYNS, of Staple Inn.

folio 629

  ,, ——— SOUTHEY, of Barnard's Inn
  ,, WALTER MINGAY, of Staple Inn
  ,, THOMAS LENNARD
  ,, JOHN CADDELL, of Staple Inn
  ,, (EDWARD, 11th) Lord ZOUCH, specially admitted (was owing for vacation and commons at this date).
  ,, EDMUND BUTLER
  ,, NICHOLAS BYRON.
  ,, JOHN YAXLEE
  ,, EDWARD STURTON.
  ,, HUMPHREY MILDMAY
  ,, DAVID GREENSMITH, of Staple Inn
  ,, JOHN MARBURY, of Barnard's Inn
  ,, THOMAS TASBOROUGH
  ,, JOHN BAKER, of Staple Inn
  ,, PEREGRINE BERTIE, of Staple Inn
  ,, FRANCIS GUEVARA
  ,, JOHN ROWBOTHAM, of Barnard's Inn
  ,, RALPH BARTON
  ,, ROBERT MITFORD
  ,, GEORGE GWILLIAMS, specially admitted
  ,, THOMAS MARKHAM, specially admitted
  ,, BARTHOLOMEW BENDLOWES, specially mitted
  ,, ROBERT, Lord RICH, specially admitted (Feb 20th).

folio 630.

  ,, JONATHAN CLARKE, of Barnard's Inn
  ,, NEVILLE HASLEWOOD, of Barnard's Inn

folio 630—(continued)

1573 RICHARD FLEMING, of Barnard's Inn
  ,, WILLIAM RAMSAY, of Staple Inn
  ,, NICHOLAS TROTT
  ,, EDWARD MEGGES, of Staple Inn
  ,, EDWARD ENGHAM.
  ,, HUMPHREY HALES (or Halles), of Staple Inn
  ,, RALPH COLSTON, of Barnard's Inn.
  ,, (WM) VAUX, of Barnard's Inn.
  ,, JOHN GYVE (or Jeve), of Staple Inn
  ,, LEONARD CHARLEY, of Barnard's Inn
  ,, ——— JOHNSON, of Staple Inn
  ,, (EDWARD) MORRYSON, of Staple Inn
  ,, FRANCIS BYNGE
  ,, THOMAS HARRISON, of Barnard's Inn.
  ,, CHRISTOPHER FINCH
  ,, HENRY GOLDINGE
  ,, ——— PALMER, of Barnard's Inn
  ,, JOHN FOCH, specially admitted.
  , ——— BALDWIN, specially admitted.
1574 THOMAS HENEAGE

folio 633.

  ,, JAMES HUBBARD, of Barnard's Inn.
  ,, THOMAS SHELLEY, of Staple Inn.
  ,, ——— ALURED
  ,, HENRY MORGAN.
  ,, ——— DANBIE (?)
  ,, FRANCIS HASTINGS, per Yelverton, reader
  ,, THOMAS RANDOLPH, per Walter Mildmay.
  ,, ADRIAN STOKES, per Yelverton, reader
  ,, EDWARD CARY, per Yelverton, reader
  ,, WILLIAM BREWSTER, per Yelverton, reader.

folio 634.

  ,, THOMAS CULPEPER.
  ,, EDWARD ELLIS

folio 634—(*continued*)

1574 WILLIAM ELLIS

„ JOHN LYNNE, specially admitted.

folio 635.

„ WILLIAM HUNYNGE

„ HENRY HUNYNGE

„ RANDOLPH CHRISTOPHER.

„ JOHN HANMER, of Staple Inn (May 19).

„ THOMAS ASH, of Barnard's Inn.

„ CLEMENT GOLDSMITH.

„ FRANCIS GOLDSMITH

folio 638

„ RICHARD ASHTON, of Barnard's Inn

„ THOMAS CLEYBORNE, of Staple Inn

„ ——— CLEYBORNE, of Staple Inn

„ THOMAS MOLYNEUX, ⎱ brothers, of

„ EDWARD MOLYNEUX, ⎰ Barnard's Inn

„ RALPH TREMAYN, of Barnard's Inn

folio 639

„ WILLIAM YELVERTON

„ EDWARD BACON

„ DENIS MAY, of Barnard's Inn

„ SAMUEL BEVERCOTTS, of Staple Inn

„ THOMAS DALISON, of Barnard's Inn

1574-5 HENRY PERCY, Earl of Northumberland, specially admitted (Jan 31)

„ CUTHBERT FORSTER, of Staple Inn

„ THOMAS FITZWILLIAM, of Barnard's Inn

„ THOMAS STOKES, of Barnard's Inn

„ WILLIAM WALGRAVE, of Staple Inn

„ ROBERT CUDDON

„ CHARLES SKIPWITH, specially admitted

„ HENRY PETTITT, specially admitted

1575 FRANCIS DODSWORTH, of Staple Inn

„ WILLIAM FORSETT, specially admitted.

„ THOMAS WINGFIELD

„ JOHN CHAMBERLAYNE

folio 643

„ HENRY KENDAL

„ JOHN CHETWYND, of Staple Inn

folio 643—(*continued*).

1575 RICHARD ASCOUGH, of Barnard's Inn

„ ——— WHETNALL, of Staple Inn.

„ JAMES ALTHAM, specially admitted

„ GILBERT GERRARD, specially admitted

„ WILLIAM COOKE, specially admitted

„ JOHN ROLT, specially admitted

folio 646.

„ AMBROSE COPPINGER, of Barnard's Inn (June 20)

„ WILLIAM HICKMAN

„ ROBERT BASPOLE, of Barnard's Inn

„ THOMAS VAUGHAN, of Staple Inn

„ RALPH EURE

„ THOMAS SHERMAN, of Barnard's Inn

„ RALPH PUDSEY, of Staple Inn

„ THOMAS BYARD

„ ANTHONY WITHAM, of Staple Inn

„ TOBY MATHEW, specially admitted

„ THOMAS CREEKE, specially admitted

folio 647

„ HAMLET ASHTON, of Barnard's Inn

„ WILLIAM GARNET, of Staple Inn

„ JOHN ALLEN

„ ARTHUR DAKYNS, of Staple Inn.

„ FRANCIS MISSENDEN, of Staple Inn, specially admitted

„ WILLIAM SAMUEL, of Barnard's Inn

„ JOHN FOCH, specially admitted

„ LORD ZOUCHE (*O B*, *folio* 47)

folio 649.

1576. JOHN LEVESON

„ NICHOLAS SHARPE, of Barnard's Inn

folio 650

„ GEORGE CLYVE

„ JOHN IRELAND

„ EDWARD SALISBURY, of Staple Inn.

„ CHRISTOPHER THIMBLETHORPE.

„ THOMAS MARTIN (June 27)

„ ANTHONY BACON, ⎱ " de societate

„ FRANCIS BACON, ⎰ magistrorum"

„ WILLIAM BOWES, ⎰ (June 27)

folio 650—*(continued)*

1576	ISAAC WINCOLNT.
,,	JOHN DENNYES
,,	POPE BLOUNT
,,	THOMAS BALGUY, of Barnard's Inn, "de mense clericorum" (June 27)
,,	RICHARD BARKER, specially admitted

folio 651.

,,	THOMAS WALKER
,,	CHRISTOPHER BEAMOND, of Staple Inn
,,	FRANCIS BUTTON, of Staple Inn,
,,	JOHN BUTTON, of Staple Inn, } brothers.
,,	EDWARD BUTTON, of Staple Inn,
,,	ALLEN CHAPMAN, of Barnard's Inn
,,	JOHN LORT, of Barnard's Inn
,,	ROGER WILDRAHAM (June 27),
,,	WALTER ASHTON, of Staple Inn (July 4), } " de mense clericorum "
,,	PETER SHAKERLEV, specially admitted (July 4)

folio 653.

,,	ROBERT LAWRENCE (Nov 7),
,,	LEWIS LAWRENCE (Nov. 7), } " de societate magistrorum "
,,	JOHN EURE (Nov 7)
,,	JOHN RAUNCE (Nov 7),

folio 654.

,,	FRANCIS NEWTON (Nov 7)
,,	ROBERT BRAUNCHE, of Staple Inn (Nov. 7)
,,	HENRY BOLDERO (July in *O B*) (Nov 7)
,,	ROBERT WINGFIELD (Nov. 21).
,,	GEORGE LEIGH (Nov 21)
,,	FRANCIS BULLINGHAM, of Barnard's Inn (Nov 21)
,,	WILLIAM SELBY (Nov 21)
,,	HENRY BARRON, of Staple Inn (Nov 21)

folio 654—*(continued)*

1576	EDWARD VENTRIS (Nov 21).
,,	GEORGE STOCKDALE (Nov 21)
,,	WILLIAM WENTWORTH, specially admitted (Nov 21)
,,	WILLIAM SAXSE, of Staple Inn (Nov 21)
,,	JAMES LUNSFORD, of Staple Inn (Nov 21).
,,	JOHN HAYS, of Staple Inn (Nov 21)
,	RALPH PIGOTT (Nov 21)
1576-7	JOHN SMYTHE (Jan. 30)
,,	RICHARD KIRBY, of Barnard's Inn (Jan 30)
,,	CHRISTOPHER PIGOTT (Jan 30)
,,	ROBERT HEBDEN (Jan 30).
,,	THOMAS COWPER (Jan 30)
,,	JOHN HAGGAR, of Barnard's Inn (Feb 11)

folio 655

,,	ROBERT LANE (Feb 11).
,,	HENRY HEYMAN (Feb 11)
,,	GEORGE GILBVE, of Staple Inn (Feb 11)

folio 656.

1576	THOMAS NEWTON, of Barnard's Inn.
,,	GEORGE CHAWORTH, of Barnard's Inn

folio 657.

1577	THOMAS ST JOHN (May 8).
,,	CHRISTOPHER HOLFORD (May 8)
,,	CHARLES METHAM (May 8)
,,	RICHARD VAUGHAN, specially admitted (May 8)
,,	THOMAS ANDREWS (May 17)
,,	THOMAS DEDYCOTT (May 17).
,,	FRANCIS BOWYER (June 12)
,,	JOHN COXE, son of Richard, Bishop, of Ely (June 17)
,,	FRANCIS SHUTE, elder son of Robert Shute, Serjeant-at-Law (June 16).

folio 658.

,,	THOMAS BARTON, of Barnard's Inn (May 8)
,,	WILLIAM PAGE, of Staple Inn (May 8)
,,	WILLIAM BIRKBECK, of Staple Inn (May 8)

	folio 658—(continued).
1577	WILLIAM GULL, of Staple Inn (May 17)
,,	CHRISTOPHER GOADE, of Staple Inn (June 12)
,,	ROBERT SHEFFIELD, of Barnard's Inn (June 12)
,,	JOHN CLARKE (June 19)
,,	WILLIAM GRESHAM, of Staple Inn (June 19)
,,	RICHARD BEACON, of Barnard's Inn (June 19)

folio 659.

,,	ROBERT MARKHAM.
,,	WILLIAM THOROLD

folio 660.

,,	EDWARD DYMOKE.
,,	JOHN SCAMBLER
	(November 25, 1577.)
,,	WILLIAM KIRKHAM
,,	WILLIAM LEONARD, of Staple Inn.
,,	THOMAS DIGHTON
,,	GEOFFRAY OSBALDESTON.
,,	WILLIAM HYNDE
,,	HENRY FYNCH.
,,	ANTHONY NEVILL
,,	THOMAS ITHEW, specially admitted
,,	JOHN GILBERT
,,	JAMES DALE, specially admitted.
,,	ROGER DALISON
,,	WALTER BARNARD
,,	ROBERT MANSELL, of Staple Inn
,,	FRANCIS AUNGIER, specially admitted
,,	THOMAS CAVENDISH
,,	NICHOLAS SUTTON
,,	THOMAS GERARD, specially admitted
,,	JO ROODES, specially admitted.
,,	FRANCIS ROODES, specially admitted

folio 661

,,	WILLIAM ARMINE
,,	BARTHOLOMEW ARMSTRONG
,,	ROGER ASCOUGH
,,	THOMAS BROGDEN

	folio 661—(continued)
1577.	THOMAS TYLDESLEY, of Staple Inn

folio 664.

1578	RICHARD GOODRICKE
,,	RICHARD ASHTON
,,	WILLIAM THOROLD
,,	WILLIAM FAIRFAX
,,	JOHN STANHOPE
,,	WILLIAM LOCHARD, of Staple Inn
,,	THOMAS SPARKS, of Staple Inn
,,	CHRISTOPHER EGLEFIELD, specially admitted
,,	WILLIAM LISTER (Memo , Jan 26, 21 Elizabeth, 1578-9, was of the Master's Commons, to be allowed as Clerk's Commons)

folio 665.

,,	ELIAS BRANTINGHAM, of Staple Inn
,,	LEONARD SMALLPIECE, Barnard's Inn.
,,	FRANCIS STAFFERTON, of Barnard's Inn
,,	FRANCIS SHEFFIELD, specially admitted
,,	AUGUSTIN SAY, of Barnard's Inn
,,	THOMAS BOWLES, of Staple Inn
,,	CUTHBERT GERRARD
,,	ROBERT GOSNOLD
,,	JOHN HYND, of Barnard's Inn
,,	THOMAS RIGGS
,,	WILLIAM JOHNSON, of Staple Inn
,,	RICHARD WIGHTMAN, of Staple Inn
,,	JOHN BOWYER, of Staple Inn
,,	FRANCIS HELDEN, of Staple Inn

folio 667

,,	FRANCIS BYRNAND, of Staple Inn.

folio 668.
(Nov 17, 1578)

,,	REGINALD LAWSON, of Staple Inn
,,	FRANCIS WHETSTONE
,,	JOHN PEPYS
,,	ARNOLD RERESBY, of Staple Inn
,,	EDMOND MEERE, of Staple Inn
,,	JOHN WALMESLEY
,,	WILLIAM DEREHAUGH

folio 668—(*continued*).

(November 17, 1578.)

1578   ——— DEREHAUGH

,,   PETER DANYELL.

,,   ROBERT THOMPSON

folio 660

,,   THOMAS MOLYNEUX, specially admitted

,,   DANIEL CAGE

folio 661.

,,   THOMAS CHAMBERLAIN.

,,   WILLIAM NORRYS

,,   THOMAS COLSHILL, Easter Term 1578 (see Arms, Dugdale's "Origines Jurid.," page 308).

,,   ROBERT MARKHAM, specially admitted.

,,   JOHN HALFS, specially admitted.

   THOMAS SIANHOPE, specially admitted

folio 669.

,,   ROBERT ROLF

,,   CHRISTOPHER BLAKISTON.

,,   ROBERT RAWNCE, of Staple Inn.

,,   BENJAMIN (BRYAN) TWISLETON

,,   HENRY WALPOLE.

,,   EDMUND CARTWRIGHT.

,,   JOHN TRAVELL, of Staple Inn

,,   THOMAS BAKER, of Barnard's Inn.

,,   GEORGE HENEAGE

,,   WILLIAM HODSON, of Staple Inn.

,,   THOMAS VAUGHAN

folio 671.

1579   WILLIAM BOURCHIER.

,   THOMAS AUDLEY

,,   HENRY APSLEY, of Staple Inn.

,,   ROBERT STOCKDALE.

,,   EDWARD KELLOWAY

,,   WILLIAM ANSELL

,,   ADAM MIDLAM, of Barnard's Inn

,,   THOMAS HAWES (or Hughes).

,,   CONANT PROWSE, of Staple Inn.

,,   RICHARD BRADDYLL.

,,   THOMAS HONYWOOD

folio 671—(*continued*)

1579.   HENRY (LAUR ?) ST. BARBE, of Staple Inn.

,,   BARTYN BURTON, of Barnard's Inn.

,,   WILLIAM JENYSON.

,,   FRANCIS BOWES

,,   TALBOT BOWES

,,   RICHARD HERBERT, of Barnard's Inn

,,   ROBERT DOLMAN, of Staple Inn.

,,   CHRISTOPHER TAMWORTH, of Barnard's Inn

,,   WILLIAM WELCOME, of Staple Inn

,   JOHN MILLS, of Staple Inn.

,,   WILLIAM CARY, of Staple Inn

,,   WILLIAM RICH, of Barnard's Inn.

,,   JOHN SOTHERTON ⎫ No entry of

,,   THOMAS HAWTAYNE ⎪ having paid

,,   JOHN KNEWSTUS ⎪ admission

   (EUSTACE ?) ⎬ dues Query,

,,   WILLIAM DRURY. ⎪ if specially

,,   WILLIAM GRESHAM ⎭ admitted

folio 674

,,   HENRY WENTWORTH, of Barnard's Inn

,,   WILLIAM WELBY

,,   ROWLAND LYTTON

,,   JEROME PEACOCK

,,   CHARLES TILNEY

,,   WILLIAM SEGAR.

,,   WILLIAM JAMES, of Barnard's Inn

,,   EDWARD STANLEY

,,   RICHARD LITTLER, specially admitted

,,   EDWARD STANHOPE

folio 675.

,,   BRYAN DODMORE.

,,   THOMAS FARRYNGTON, of Barnard's Inn

,,   JOHN ROGERS.

,,   JOHN SENHOUSE

,,   CHRISTOPHER THURSBY

,,   SYMON ANDREW.

1579-80   RICHARD BARNES (or Berners), of Staple Inn (Jan 23)

folio 675—*(continued)*.

(January 23, 1579)

1579-80 PATRICK STAFFERTON (called Stafford by Segar)
,,   JOHN TADLEY, of Barnard's Inn
,,   AUGUSTINE EARLE
,,   (JOHN) BLEWETT
,,   JOHN JENISON
,,   THOMAS WALLER, of Barnard's Inn
,,   WILLIAM BODLEY
,,   JOHN BROADBENT, of Staple Inn.
,,   JOHN SHUTE. ⎫
,,   FRANCIS SHELDON   No entry
,,   JOHN HAMOND.   of having
,,   JOHN KYTCHIN   paid admis-
,,   GILBERT PICKERING   sion dues.
,,   ANDREW BARTON   Query if
,,   THOMAS YELVERTON   specially
,,   CHRISTOPHER YELVERTON. ⎭ admitted

folio 676.

,,   THOMAS MAY.
,,   PEXALL BROCAS
,,   LIONEL BAMFORD, of Barnard's Inn
,,   —— WRIGHT, of Staple Inn
,,   WILLIAM HITCHCOCK, of Staple Inn
,,   WILLIAM MANBY, of Barnard's Inn
,,   (EDWARD) SALTER
,,   —— HORRY
,,   BA   WHETSTONE ⎫
,,   WILLIAM WINGATE   No entry
,,   ANTHONY MILDMAY   of having
,,   HENRY HOWARD   paid ad-
,,   GEORGE EURE   mission
,,   THOMAS IRELAND   dues
,,   PHILIP LORD WHARTON   Query if
     (Feb 2)   specially
     ⎭ admitted

folio 679.

1580 JOHN CHAMBERS, of Barnard's Inn
,,   ANTHONY DERINGE (Denny ?)

folio 679—*(continued)*

1580 ANDREW PERNE. ⎫
,,   HENRY CAREY   No entry of
,,   THOMAS CAREY   having paid
,,   EDMUND CAREY   admission
,,   GEORGE CARR   dues Query,
,,   ROBERT BESTNEY   if specially
     ⎭ admitted

folio 680

,,   ANDREW LUTTRELL
,,   ALEXANDER REDDISH
,,   —— GODDARD
,,   JAMES DALE
,,   ROBERT HUGHES (or Hayes).
,,   NATHANIEL FULLER (or Fulware).

,,   JOHN SPENCER. ⎫ No entry of
,,   ROBERT FREVILL   having paid
,,   OWEN HOPTON.   admission
,,   RALPH HORSLEY.   dues Query
     if specially
     ⎭ admitted

folio 681.

,,   WILLIAM HUMBERSTON
,,   JOHN DRYWOOD, of Staple Inn
,,   RUTLAND MOLYNEUX
,,   NICHOLAS ODYERN ⎫
,,   THOMAS ODYERN ⎭
,,   —— MICHELBOURNE
,,   —— WRIGHT, of Barnard's Inn
,,   JAMES BUSCALL.
,,   CHRISTOPHER BENDLOWES
,,   JOHN BLAGRAVE
,,   THOMAS MOYLE, of Staple Inn
,,   SETH COXE
,,   ROBERT TILNEY
,,   JERVASE WOODROFFE
,,   —— GOUGH, of Barnard's Inn.
,,   THOMAS HUGHES (or Hayes), of
     Staple Inn
,,   THOMAS NEDHAM
,,   JO BERRYFORD.
,,   JOHN CRAYFORD, of Staple Inn.
,,   —— BANASTER
,,   JOHN DOLMAN, of Staple Inn

folio 683

1580   WILLIAM LOVELACE, specially admitted

,,   ROBERT SOUTHWELL, specially admitted

,,   ROBERT CECIL, specially admitted

folio 684

,,   RICHARD HUTTON, of Staple Inn (Oct 26).

,,   THOMAS LUTTRELL (Oct 26)

,,   GEORGE LUTTRELL (Oct 26)

,,   THOMAS PEPYS, of Barnard's Inn (Oct 26)

,,   CHRISTOPHER POWELL (Nov. 4)

,,   ROBERT CARR (Nov 4)

,,   WILLIAM HARRYS (Nov 4)

,,   HENRY FLEETWOOD (Nov. 21)

,,   GEORGE ASTLEY, of Staple Inn (Nov 21)

,,   PETER WROTH (Nov 21)

,,   HENRY BERKELEY (Nov 21)

,,   THOMAS LITCHFIELD (Nov 21)

,,   PHILIP BUTLER (Nov 21)

,,   JOHN THOROLD (Nov. 21)

,,   JOHN HUITON (Nov 21)

,,   WILLIAM BLUNT (Nov. 21)

,,   WILLIAM VAUGHAN (Nov 21)

,,   JOHN BASSETT (Nov 21)

No entry of having paid admission dues
Query if specially admitted

folio 684—(continued).

1580-1   RICHARD BELL (or Belt) (Jan 30).

,,   NICHOLAS ROBINSON (Jan 30)

,,   JOHN MOLYNEUX, son of William Molyneux, Esq (Jan. 30)

,,   THOMAS HAYES (Feb 9)

folio 686

1580   WILLIAM SACHEVERELL, of Staple Inn (Oct 26)

,,   THOMAS ATHOW, of Barnard's Inn (Oct. 26).

,,   GEORGE FREVILL (Nov. 21)

,,   JOHN PEES, of Barnard's Inn (Nov 23)

,,   EDWARD CHESNOLD (Nov 23)

1580-1   JOHN SABBE, of Barnard's Inn (Jan. 30)

,,   WILLIAM FITZWILLIAM, Knight, specially admitted (Feb 2)

,,   THOMAS CULCHETH, of Staple Inn (Feb. 9).

,,   HENRY BYROM, of Staple Inn (Feb 9)

,,   JOHN SHAWARDEN (Feb 9)

,,   WILLIAM LYNNE (Feb 9)

,,   HENRY MARTIN (Feb 9).

,,   EDWARD PEPYS (Feb 7)

,,   JAMES DUNBORNE.

,,   GILES BREWSE.

,,   THOMAS PERROTT (Feb. 21)

folio 1.

1580-1   ———— DENNY

1581.

June 7   EDWARD INGLETT (or Englott)

folio 5.

,,   12.   JOHN BINGHAM, gent.

folio 7

April 20.   ALEXANDER RATCLIFFE, of Staple Inn (called Rocliffe in admission book).

,,   ,,   THOMAS WAKLYN, late of Barnard's Inn

,,   ,,   THOMAS SCROPE, son and heir of Lord Scrope.

,,   ,,   ROBERT WARCOP, of Barnard's Inn

May 5.   JOHN WOOD, of Fulborne, co. Camb

,,   ,,   EDWARD BRADDYLL, son of Edward Braddyll, of Whalley, co Lanc.

,,   ,,   EDWARD BARNARDISTON, of Essex, late of Staple Inn

,,   ,,   WILLIAM ROCKYTT, of Bury St. Edmunds, Suffolk, late of Barnard's Inn.

,,   ,,   REGINALD WILLIAMS, of Yerkebye, co Heref, late of Staple Inn

,,   31   ROBERT BARNEWALL, of Staple Inn   [Barnard's Inn.

,,   ,,   RICHARD STACY, son of Francis Stacy, of Castle Bytham, co Linc , late of

June 7   HENRY FLOWER, son of Thomas Flower, of Langar, Notts.

,,   ,,   WILLIAM GRICE, or Le Grice (*O B*, *folio* 367).

,,   ,,   THOMAS LATHAM

,,   ,,   ARTHUR (or AUBREY) BRYAN (*O B*, *folio* 367)

,,   ,,   THOMAS ROBERTS (*O. B*, *folio* 373).

folio 8.

,,   ,,   LANCELOT LOVELACE, of Chawlke, Kent, late of Staple Inn

May 1.   EDWARD MORRIS, of Chirkland, co Denbigh, late of Barnard's Inn

June 12   FIRMYAN TILNEY, of East Tuddenham, Norfolk

,,   ,,   THOMAS ABYNGDON, late of Barnard's Inn

,,   ,,   ROGER GRIFFITH, of Poole, co. Montgomery, late of Barnard's Inn

,,   ,,   JOHN GREGORY, of Kingston-upon-Hull, late of Barnard's Inn

---

,,   ,,   LEONARD CHARLEY (*O B*, *folio* 157).

,,   ,,   ROBERT AUDLEY, of Welbourne ⎫

Oct. 15   T SMALLPAGE   ⎬ (*O B*, *folio*, 373)

Nov 3   WILLIAM VESSYE, gent (*O B*, *folios* 168 & 373)

,,   ,,   HENRY GOSNOLD, of Staple Inn (*O B*, *folio* 373)

,,   ,,   THOMAS HALE, gent (*O. B*, *folio* 373)

,,   ,,   EDWARD RATCLIFFE, gent (*O B*, *folio* 373).

,,   ,,   EDWARD ISAACKE (*O B*, *folio* 373)

,,   ,,   THOMAS BAYNES, gent (*O B*, *folio* 367)

,,   ,,   WILLIAM COLE (*O B.*, *folio* 367)

,,   22.   FRANCIS WORTHINGTON (*O B*, *folio* 367)

,,   ,,   PATRICK ARCHERS (*O B*, *folio* 367)

,,   ,,   JOHN DARVALL (*O B*, *folio* 373)

1581   folio 8—*(continued)*

Nov. 22.   FRANCIS REPPES (*O. B* , *folio* 373)

,,   ,,   HENRY DROWILL (*O B.*, *folio* 373)

,,   25   JOHN LEE (*O B* , *folios* 367 & 373)

folio 13.

,,   23   AWDLEY BAKER, of Terrington, Norfolk, late of Barnard's Inn

,,   ,,   RICHARD ENDERBY, of Metheringham, co Lincoln.

,,   ,,   GEORGE KENRYCK, of town of Northampton, late of Staple Inn.

,,   ,,   JAMES SMITH, of Barnard's Inn, and of Dover, Kent, gent

,,   ,,   JOHN OSBORN, of co Northampton, late of Barnard's Inn

1581-2

Jan 24   JOHN DALBY, son of William Dalby, of London, gent

,,   ,,   JOHN MOYNE, of Barnard's Inn, and of co Linc., gent.

,,   ,,   WILLIAM CLERKE, of Markshall, co Essex

,,   30   WILLIAM QUADRING, of co Lincoln

,,   ,,   THOMAS DOVE, of London, and of Barnard's Inn

Feb   5   JOHN PENNING, of Kettleborough, Suffolk

,,   ,,   ANTHONY FOX, of the City of London.

,,   ,,   EDWARD SNELLYNGE, of Barnard's Inn (erased)

,,   8   DAMYON PECKE, of Calcott, co Cambridge, late of Staple Inn.

folio 14

,,   ,,   THOMAS PERYENT, late of Barnard's Inn.

,,   ,,   ROBERT TIRWHITT, of Rothorne, co. Lincoln.

,,   ,,   TRISTRAM TIRWHITT, of Rothorne, co Lincoln.

,,   ,,   WILLIAM SLINGSBY, of Barnard's Inn, and of Scriven Hall, Yorks

,,   ,,   RICHARD TANKERD, of Barnard's Inn, and of Arden, Yorks.

,,   ,,   EDMUND RICHARDSON, late of Barnard's Inn (born in co. York).

,,   ,,   RICHARD WILLIAMSON, of Barnard's Inn, and of Gainsborough co. Lincoln.

,,   ,,   EDWARD ROLTE, of Bonest, Beds.

O B , folio 373.

Jan.   4   GEORGE SAVER

,,   ,,   GEORGE CARY

,,   ,,   PATRICK LOWE.

,,   ,,   HENRY BILLINGSLEY

,,   ,,   THOMAS CROKE (S.T.D), specially admitted.

Feb.   2   ROBERT CONSTANTINE ⎫

,,   ,,   THOMAS DARCY   ⎪

,,   ,,   GEORGE HORNSEY.   ⎪

,,   ,,   JOHN JACKSON   ⎬   No entry of having paid admission dues

,,   ,,   BARNARD DEWHURST   ⎪   Query if specially admitted

       O. B., folio 367   ⎪

,,   ,,   JOHN LETE.   ⎪

,,   ,,   EDWARD ALCENY   ⎭

1581 2   O B folio 373

Feb   8.   JOHN WHITE, of Tuxford, Notts

,,   ,,   HENRY POYNE (or Poynter), of Staple Inn

,,   ,,   JAMES RITHER

,,   ,,   RICHARD BETTENSON, of Barnard's Inn

,,   ,,   FRANCIS WANDESFORD

,,   ,,   JOHN HANDFORD

,,   ,,   HENRY TOPHAM, of Barnard's Inn

1582   folio 19

May   9   JOHN ZOUCHE, son and heir of John, of Codnor Castle, co Derby, Knight
                            [of the Barons of the Exchequer, and of this Society
,,   ,,   CHRISTOPHER SOTHERTON, son and heir apparent of John Sotherton, Esq, one
,,   ,,   RICHARD VERNEY, of Compton, co Warwick, Esq   [Northampton
,,   ,,   EDWARD KNIGHTLEY, second son of Richard Knightley, of Fawsley, co
,,   ,,   WALTER CHETWYND, of Barnard's Inn (born at Ingestre, co Stafford)
,,   ,,   THOMAS TURNER, of Shiffenhall, Salop, late of Staple Inn
,,   ,,   JOHN REPINGTON, of Amington, co Warwick
,,   ,,   EDMOND MOUNTSTEVYNE, of Paston, co Northampton   [Staple Inn
,,   25   ANTHONY GOSNOLD, son of Robert Gosnold, of Otley, Suffolk, Esq, late of
,,   ,,   RICHARD STAPLETON, son of Brian Stapleton, Esq, of Carleton, co York
June 21   EDWARD PHILLPOTT, of Aspeden, Herts
,,   ,,   CHRISTOPHER IRTON, of Irton, Cumberland, late of Barnard's Inn
,,   27   NICHOLAS BESTNEY (born at Northall, Herts)   [Society
,,   ,,   THOMAS SNAGG, eldest son of Thomas Snagg, Serjeant-at-law late of this
,,   ,,   ROBERT DAY, of Clavering, Essex
                            [Stonham, Suffolk   folio 20
July 2   ROBERT BLOMFYLD, late of Furnival's Inn, son of Nicholas Blomfyld, of

                    folio 22   [readers of this House

May   9   ROBERT KEMP, son and heir apparent of Richard Kemp, Esq, one of the
,,   ,,   EDMOND BARKER, of Barnard's Inn, gent
,,   ,,   CHARLES ASSHETON, of Rochdale, co Lancaster, late of Staple Inn.
,,   ,,   JOHN CONYERS, of Laughton, co York, and of Staple Inn
,   ,,   HASTINGS ASTON, son of Walter Aston, Knight
,,   ,,   RICHARD CONNIE, of Basingthorpe, co Lincoln
,,   25   THOMAS HALL, of Higham, near Norwich, Norfolk

                            folio 23

,,   ,,   RICHARD VINCENT, of Conisborough, co York, late of Staple Inn
,,   ,,   WILLIAM HAMOND, of Kent, son of Ralph Hamond
,,   ,,   LEONARD HOLME, of Barnard's Inn
,,   ,,   JOHN WALTER, of   , and of Barnard's Inn
,,   ,,   ROBERT SHEPPARD, of Staple Inn (born at Tenterden, Kent)   [Society
,,   ,,   RICHARD FORCET, son of Richard Forcet, formerly one of the readers of this

                              D

1582		folio 23—(continued)

1582
May 25   HENRY DAY, of Oxborough, Norfolk ("ex relatione" Christopher Yelverton,
  ,,   ,,   GEORGE BARTON, of Cowton, York, and of Staple Inn   [reader].
  ,,   ,,   THOMAS HYRNE, of city of Norwich, gent
June 20   CHRISTOPHER ESTWIKE, of Milton, Beds
  ,,   27   ROBERT HATLEY, of Goldington, Beds.
  ,,   ,,   HENRY DARNALL, of Middlesex, late of Barnard's Inn, gent
  ,,   ,,   HUGH HILL, gent , of Barnard's Inn (erased, turned out, 1583)
July 2   DAVID HUGHES, of Barnard's Inn (born at Talalyn, co Merioneth)

folio 24

  ,,   ,,   RICHARD HODGSON, of Cherry Burton, co York
  ,,   3   WILLIAM COLMAN, of Barnard's Inn
  ,,   ,,   WILLIAM SQUYER, of Hinxworth, Herts

1582-3		folio 29.

Jan 24   JOHN JAYE (written Daye in *O B*), late of Barnard's Inn
  ,,   ,,   HENRY BLENCOW, late of Barnard's Inn.
  ,,   ,,   THOMAS MONSON, of Carleton, co Linc , son of John Monson, of same, Esq
  ,,   ,,   JUSTINIAN CHAMPNEYS, son and heir of Justinian Champneys, of Bexley, Kent, Esq
  ,,   28   JOHN MARSHALL, of Deeping, co Linc
  ,,   ,,   DAVID HEWES (Hughes), of Magdalen College, Oxford
Feb 2   EDWARD PARKER, Lord Morley   [Knightley, Knight
  ,,   ,,   VALENTINE KNIGHTLEY, of Fawsley, co Northampton, son and heir of Richard
  ,,   6   AMBROSE BAGENALL, third son of Nicholas Bagenall, Knight
  ,,   ,,   EDWARD FLORENS, of King's Norton, co Worcester (vacat, quia admissus et
                                   [postea in suo loco, April 24, 1583) (erased)

folio 32

Jan 28   WILLIAM WYKE, of Staple Inn
  ,,   ,,   THOMAS BURTON, of Deeping, co Lincoln, gent., late of Staple Inn
Feb 6   BARKELEY GARDINER, son of Thomas Gardiner, of Coxford Abbey, Norfolk
  ,,   ,,   THOMAS SCAMBLER, son of the Bishop of Peterburgh (entry erased)
  ,,   ,,   GEORGE BINGHAM, of Staple Inn
  ,,   ,,   JOHN JERMYN, of Debden, Suffolk (see April 24, 1583) (entry erased)

1583		folio 37.

April 24   BAMPTON GURDON, son and heir of John Gurdon, of Asheton, Suffolk, Esq
  ,,   ,,   JOHN JERMYN, of Debden, Suffolk
  ,,   ,,   EDWARD CLERE, son and heir of Edward Clere, Knight, of Blicking, Norfolk
  ,,   ,,   JOHN CROFTS, son and heir of John Crofts, of Saxham, Suffolk, Esq
  ,,   ,,   WILLIAM CADE, son and heir of John Cade, of Aldenham, Herts   [Florence
  ,,   ,,   EDWARD FLORENCE, of King's Norton, co Worc , son and heir of Edward
  ,,   30   ROBERT RATCLIFFE, of Sturmer, Essex
  ,,   ,,   RALPH OKERAM, of London.
  ,,   ,,   MARTIN NEWCOME, son of William Newcome, Esq , of Haddam, Herts

1583.	folio 37—(*continued*)
April 30.	RICHARD FINCHE, of London, gent
May 10.	ROBERT CASTELL, son and heir of William Castell, of Glatton, Hunts
June 5.	ABRAHAM FRAUNCE, of Shrewsbury
,, ,,	JOHN PEROT, of Harvye, co Pembroke, third son of John Perot, Knight
,, ,,	JOHN CROWTHER, son of George Crowther, of London
,, ,,	EDWARD NEWPORT, of Sandon, Herts
,, ,,	CHRISTOPHER FARFURTH, of Lincoln folio 38.

folio 39

April 24	ROBERT LACY, son and heir of William Lacy, of Stamford, co Lincoln
,, ,,	JOHN HYND, of Tedford Hall, co Lincoln
,, ,,	THOMAS CRIMES, of Antingham, Norfolk
,, ,,	FRANCIS CLARKE, of Stevenage, Herts
,, 30	THOMAS BRYERTON, of town of Norwich, late of Staple Inn
,, ,,	ROBERT HANSLOP, of Solihull, co Warwick, son of John Hanslop, Esq
,, ,,	HUGH MORE, of Barnard's Inn, and of Grantham, co Linc
May 10	WILLIAM CATELINE, of Barnard's Inn, and of Gamlingay, co Cambridge
,, ,,	GUY FOSTER, son and heir of Edmund Foster, of Handslopp, Bucks
,, ,,	THOMAS KIRKEHAM, youngest son of Robert Kirkeham, of Fineshead, co
June 4	EDWARD NORRES, of Speke, co Lanc , late of Staple Inn [Northampton

folio 44

Oct 15	THOMAS SHERBURNE, son and heir of Robert Sherburne, Esq (absque fine, [as the said Robert Sherburne was a reader)
,, 30	THOMAS MEADE, son and heir apparent of Thomas Meade, one of the Judges [of the Common Bench , of Wendon Loftes, Essex
Nov 8	WILLIAM ASCOUGHE, of Wisam, co Linc
,, ,,	JOHN HOLLIS (Hales in *O B*), of Houghton, Notts
,, ,,	MICHAEL WENTWORTH, of Leeds, co York
,, ,,	THOMAS DAWNEY, son and heir of John Dawney, Knight [Notts
,, ,,	RICHARD WHALLEY (written also Whale), of Barnard's Inn, and of Screton,
,, ,,	JOHN ALCOCK, son of William Alcock
,, ,,	JOHN MICHELL, son and heir of Thomas Michell, of Anstey, Sussex, Esq
,, ,,	THOMAS SCAMBLER, one of the sons of Edmund, Bishop of Peterborough
,, 13.	THOMAS CHALINER, of Claydon Steeple, Bucks, son and heir of Thomas [Chaliner, Knight
,, 20	THOMAS PERCY, second son of the Earl of Northumberland
1583-4	
Feb 2	HENRY WENTWORTH (Lord Wentworth)

folio 45

,, ,,	FRANCIS CLIFFORD, Esq
,, ,,	THOMAS CONINGSBY, of Hampton Court, co Hereford
,, ,,	EDMUND TILNEY, Esq
,, ,,	WILLIAM GOLDINGHAM, one of the Doctors of Civil Law

1583-4		**folio 45**—(*continued*)
Feb	5	ROBERT SYMONDS, of Wytheford, co. Cambridge.
,,	,,	ISAAC JERMY, eldest son of John Jermy, Esq
,,	,,	JOHN SANKEY, of Sankey, co Lanc
,,	,,	ROGER WOOD, son of Robert Wood, of Islington, Middlesex
,,	,,	FRANCIS DUNSCOMBE, of Brickhill, Bucks , gent , son of Thomas Dunscombe
,,	,,	WILLIAM SNEDE, of Bradwall, co Stafford
,,	,,	FRANCIS TRENTHAM, of Rosciter, in said county (co Stafford)
,,	,,	SYMON MUSKETT, late of Barnard's Inn (erased, but restored at pension,
,,	,,	GEORGE STAPLETON, of Carlton, co York. [8 Feb , 27 Elizabeth)
,,	,,	FRANCIS MANBY, son and heir of [Francis] Manby, of Elsham, co Linc [(erased, because elsewhere "in mensa clericorum").
,,	,,	WILLIAM THOROLD, son of Edmund Thorold, of Hough, co Linc (erased)
,,	,,	CHARLES WREN, of Binchester, co Durham, gent
,,	,,	JO CARDWELL (*O B , folio* 368)
,,	,,	JOHN LEIGH, late of Barnard's Inn (born at Caldwell, Beds)
,	,,	RICHARD HOSE (? illegible) of Lydney, co Glouc , late of Barnard's Inn
1583.		**folio 46**
Nov	8	JOHN CLAXTON (written also Caxton), of Barnard's Inn [Inn
,,	,,	ROGER RAWLINS son of John Rawlins, of London, gent , late of Barnard's
,,	,,	JOHN TUCK, of Staple Inn
,,	13	WILLIAM PRETIMAN, son of William Pretiman, of Bacton, Suffolk
,,	,,	HENRY BALLARD, of Southwell, Notts
,,	,	THOMAS LAMPLUGH, of Dovenby, Cumb , and of Barnard's Inn
,,	,,	THOMAS GREENE, of Grimsby, co Linc
,,	,,	ROBERT BARNEWELL (Robert inserted in lieu of "John" erased)
,,	,,	EDWARD RYVETT, of co Derby
,,	,,	THOMAS COXE, of Cleve, co Glouc , late of Staple Inn.
1583 4		[reader
Jan	31	NICHOLAS BLUNDESTON, gent , son and heir of Lawrence Blundeston, Esq ,
		folio 47
,,	,,	JOHN EDMONDS, of Barnard's Inn (born at Cambridge)
,,	,,	ZACHARY SHEPARDE, son of William Sheparde, of Littlecott, Bucks
,,	,,	WILLIAM THOROLD, son of Edmund Thorold, of Hough, co Lincoln
,,	,,	JOHN SKINNER, of Wiltshire
,,	,,	WILLIAM BENNET, of Berkshire
,,	,,	FRANCIS MANBY, son and heir of Francis Manby, of Elsham, co Lincoln.
Feb	11	WILLIAM WILLOUGHBY, second son of William Willoughby, of Nuneaton, co
,,	,,	GEORGE JACKSON [Warwick, gent.
,,	,,	WILLIAM LYTSTER, son of Thomas Lytster, of Long Kyrkeby, co Linc
		folio 52
Mar	11	RICHARD KNIGHTLEY, of Fawsley, co Northampton, Knight
,,	,,	HUMPHREY DAVENPORT, of Weston, co Warwick

1583-4		**folio 52**—(*continued*)
Mar	11.	HENRY HAWKINS, of St Peter's College, Cambridge
,,	16	GEORGE SCOTTE, Esq , of , Kent
,,	19	THOMAS LENTON, Knight, Governor of Island of Guernsey
,,	,,	GEORGE BELGRAVE, of Belgrave, Esq
1584		
May	13	WILLIAM HAKE, son of Thomas Hake, of Peterborough, Northants, gent
,,	,,	HENRY CHOLMLEY, of Old Windsor, Berks , gent , and of Barnard's Inn.
,,	26	THOMAS HEIGHAM, of Barrow, Suffolk, son of John Heigham, Knight
,,	,,	RICHARD MAY, of London

folio 53

,,	29	PAUL HUNT, of Hylderston, Norfolk
,,	,,	RICHARD COOKE, of Bury St Edmund's
,,	,,	SYLLOWE (ST LOE) KNIVETON, of Mercaston, co Derby
July	1	THOMAS SHEREBURNE of Stonyhurst, co Lanc
Nov	23	CICEL HAWLLE, son of Arthur Hawlle
,,	,,	JOHN BOURCHIER, second son of Ralph Bourchier, of Beningborough, co
,,	,,	JOHN CAVE, of Pickwell, co Leicester [York, Knight
May	29	JOHN FERNLEY, son of Thomas Fernley, of Cretyng, Suffolk.

folio 55

,,	,,	THOMAS COLWEL, late of Barnard's Inn
July	1	MICHAEL STANLEY, of Sutton Bonington, Notts
,,	,,	WILLIAM STAGGE, of Assheton, Dorset
,,	,,	EDMOND HALMAN, of Swaffham, Norfolk
,,	,,	HUMPHREY LEIGH, of Eggington, co Derby
,,	,,	W SHERRINGTON (*O B , folio* 368)
,,	,,	ROBERT BLACKWALL, of Barnard's Inn
,,	5	JOHN EDMONDS, late of Clement's Inn
,,	,,	WILLIAM BUTLER, of Barnard's Inn, Esq **folio 56**

folio 61.

Aug	8	HENRY HOWARD, Viscount Howard, of Bindon.
Oct	21	WILLIAM BORLACE, of Little Marlow, Bucks
,,	,,	PETER GARTON, of London, gent.
,,	28	WILLIAM TWISSENDEN, of East Peckham, Kent
,,	,,	JOHN WILDGOSE, of Iredge, Sussex
Nov	1	EDWARD LEIGH, of Lyme, co Chester
Oct	28	THOMAS LEIGH, of Lyme, co Chester
Nov	6	EDMUND BELLINGHAM, son and heir of John Bellingham, of Hongleton, Sussex.
,,	,,	HENRY CHEKE, Esq , Secretary to the Privy Council in the North
,,	,,	JOHN GWEVARRA, son of ———— Gwevarra, of Stamford, co Linc
,,	23	JASPER HORSEY, of Digwell, Herts, late of Barnard's Inn
,,	,,	CICEL HAWLLE, son of Arthur Hawlle

1584   folio 61—(continued)
Nov 23   JOHN CAYE, of Pickwell, co. Leic
  ,,   ,,   JOHN BOURCHIER, second son of Ralph Bourchier, of Benyngborough, co York

1583-4 (26 Elizabeth)   folio 62   [Beds
Jan 27   EDWARD DUNCOMB, son and heir apparent of William Duncomb, of Battlesden,
  ,,   ,,   WILLIAM HORDEN, of London
Feb 2   PHILIP GERRARD (absque fine)
  ,,   ,,   HENRY, LORD WENTWORTH (see ante)

1584   folio 64
Oct 21   EDMUND BLOMER, of London
  ,,   ,,   MARMION HASILWOOD, of Kirklington, Notts, and of Barnard's Inn
  ,,   28   JOHN CHENEY (of Barnard's Inn) (erased)
  ,,   ,,   CHRISTOPHER CHENEY (of Barnard's Inn) (erased)
  ,,   ,,   THOMAS WALWYN, of Arundel, Sussex, late of Staple Inn, gent
  ,,   6   ROBERT BISHOP, of Mere, Wilts, gent
Nov 23   THOMAS WORLYCHE, son of Charles Worlyche, of Cowling, Suffolk
  ,,   ,,   JOHN ALWAY, of Stretley, Beds, late of Staple Inn, gent (fuit de consortio
  ,,   ,,   JAMES SPURLING, of Barnard's Inn   [illo per duos annos et ultra)

1587-8   folio 64b
Feb 29   HENRY, EARL OF SOUTHAMPTON (per William Cecil, Lord Burleigh)
  ,,   ,,   THOMAS HOLCROFT (Esq) (per William Cecil, Lord Burleigh)
Mar 11   HENRY, EARL OF KILDARE (per Henry, Earl of Southampton)
  ,,   ,,   CHRISTOPHER, BARON OF DELVIN (per William Cecil, Lord Burleigh)
  ,,   ,,   ROBERT SYDNEY, Knight (per William Cecil, Lord Burleigh)   [Burleigh
  ,,   ,,   HENRY BROOKE, son and heir of Lord Cobham (per William Cecil, Lord
  ,,   ,,   ANTHONY COOKE, of Giddy Hall, Essex (per William Cecil, Lord Burghley)
  ,,   ,,   FULKE GREVILL, Esq (per William Cecil, Lord Burghley)
  ,,   ,,   POSTHUMOUS HOBBY (per William Cecil, Lord Burghley)
  ,,   ,,   EDWARD FITTON (per William Cecil, Lord Burghley)
  ,,   ,,   SIMON KILLIGREW, Esq (per William Cecil, Lord Burghley)
  ,,   ,,   ROBERT OGLETHORPE, of Birdsay, co York (per William Cecil, Lord Burghley)

1584   folio 65
Nov 25   WILLIAM FULBECK, of Staple Inn
  ,,   26   JOHN CRADOCK, of co Glamorgan, late of Barnard's Inn (erased)
  ,,   ,,   BAPTIST BASSANO, of London, gent, and of Staple Inn
1584 5
Feb 8   EDWARD GASCOYNE, of Barnham, Suffolk
  ,,   ,,   WILLIAM PLUMMER, of Radmere, Herts, and of Barnard's Inn
  ,,   ,,   JOHN BRYCKETT, of Morton, co Northampton
  ,,   ,,   WILLIAM SOWTHACK, of Hardredge, Cumberland, late of Barnard's Inn,
                                         [and for two years a Fellow of that Inn
  ,,   10   JAMES THURBARNE, of New Romsey, Kent, gent late of Barnard's Inn
  ,,   ,,   PETER DOLMAN, of city of York, gent

1584 5   folio 70.

Feb 28   THOMAS MORISON, arm

Mar 15   WILLIAM, Lord EVERS   (admitted by W Burleigh, Lord Treasurer
  ,,   ,,   GEORGE HENEAGE, Knight   of England).
  ,,   ,,   EDWARD BOUGHTON, arm.
  ,,   ,,   NICHOLAS LUKE, arm
  ,,   ,,   CHARLES HOWARD, son of Thomas Viscount Bindon (admitted by W
                            [Cecil, Lord Burleigh, Lord Treasurer of England)
  ,,   ,,   RICHARD SPENCER, gent   (admitted by W Cecil, Lord Burleigh, Lord
  ,,   ,,   REGINALD SMYTH, gent   Treasurer of England)

                                            folio 71

  ,,   17   LEWES PIGOTT
  ,,   ,,   RICHARD BANKES

1585

May 21   THOMAS MILDMAY, of Ipswich, Suffolk
  ,,   ,,   DUDLEY FITZGARREI
  ,,   ,,   HENRY LINDLEY, of Leathley, co York
  ,,   ,,   ALEXANDER COVERT, of Slaugham (Slaplam), Suffolk, and of Barnard's Inn
  ,,   ,,   RICHARD ARDERNE, of Hawarden, co Chester (? Flints)
  ,,   ,,   THOMAS CREWE, of Namptwich, co Chester
  ,,   ,,   SAMUEL VIRGO, of Chichester, Sussex

1585-6

Feb 9   ALEXANDER CAVE, son and heir of Thomas Cave, of Baggrave, co Leic (erased).

1585.   folio 73.

May 21.   RICHARD AMHERST, of Pembury, Kent, and of Staple Inn
  ,,   ,,   THOMAS CREWE, of Namptwich, co Chester
June 24   THOMAS DOUGHTY, of Houghton, co Nottingham.

                                            folio 80

July 31   HENRY SMYTH, of London
Oct 15   CHRISTOPHER WOODROFFE, of London   [Linc
  ,,   ,,   WILLIAM BERESFORD, son and heir of   Beresford, of Lednam, co
  ,,   ,,   THOMAS MALBY, of London, gent
  ,,   ,,   WILLIAM COOPER (Cowper), of Thurgarton, Notts
  ,,   ,,   EDWARD ROUNSELL, of city of Dublin
  ,,   ,,   JOHN TURNER, of Thaxfield, Herts
  ,,   ,,   RICHARD TYLNEY, son of Robert Tylney, of East Tuddenham, Norfolk, Esq.
  ,,   ,,   THOMAS ROO, of Clopton, Suffolk, late of Barnard's Inn.
Nov 5.   THOMAS WISEMAN, son and heir apparent of Edmond Wiseman, Esq
  ,,   ,,   ROGER HEIGHAM, of Cowling, Suffolk

                                            folio 81

  ,,   ,,   EDWARD ONLEY, of Catesby, co Northampton, Esq   [co Linc.)
  ,,   ,,   DANIEL THOROLD, son and heir of Richard Thorold, of Marston (Muirton)

1585.		folio 81—(*continued*)
Nov	5	EDMUND BURNSTON, of Molton, co Linc
,,	15	HENRY NEVILL, son and heir of John Nevill, Esq , of Burton, Notts
,,	,,	THOMAS MOUNTFORD, of Gainsborough, late of Staple Inn.
,,	,,	WILLIAM NEWTON, of Lewes, Sussex
,,	,,	BARTHOLOMEW LEIGHTON, of Hinckley, co Leicester [Society)
,,	,,	EDWARD CLOUGH, of East Rugton, co York (late one of the butlers of this
,,	24	EDWARD ONLEY, of , co Northampton, son and heir of Thomas
,,	,,	JAMES MAYNE, of Hemel Hempstead, Herts [Onley, Esq
,,	26	WILLIAM JENNISON, of Newcastle-on-Tyne
1585-6		
Jan	31	ROBERT SALUSBURY, of Denbigh

1585		folio 82
Oct	15	ASLACKE LANYE, of Cratfield, Suffolk, late of Barnard's Inn
,,	18	WILLIAM POLEY, of Boxsted, Suffolk
,,	,	HUGH DAVENPORT, of Blackhurst, co Chester, gent , and of Barnard's Inn.
,,	,,	THOMAS SHAKERLY, of Ditton, Surrey, gent , and of Staple Inn
Nov	1	WILLIAM ABNET, of Audley, co Stafford
,,	,,	RICHARD BOLDE, of Lancashire.
,,	,,	ROBERT SHAWE, of Barnard's Inn
,,	22	CHARLES WINGFIELD, of Stamford Barron, co Northampton

		folio 83
,,	5	THOMAS BAKER, of Battle, Sussex, and of Staple Inn
,,	,,	THOMAS GRAVELEY, of Graveley, Herts
,,	,,	RICHARD ALDWYCKE, of Shaftholme, co. York, late of Barnards Inn
,,	15	WILLIAM HARRIS, of Elsworth, co Cambridge, gent , and of Barnard's Inn
,,	,,	ALEXANDER DAVENPORT, of Bromhall, co Chester. late of Barnard's Inn, son [of William Davenport, Esq
,,	,,	HUMPHREY DAVENPORT, of Bromhall, co. Chester, late of Barnard's Inn, son [of William Davenport, Esq
,,	,,	HENRY NEVELL, son and heir of John Nevell, of Burton, Notts (erased)
,,	24	GEOFFREY EDMONDSON, of Sawley, co Derby
,,	,,	GEORGE GERVIS, of Peatling, co Leicester, gent., late of Barnard's Inn
,,	26.	FRANCIS HATTON, late of Staple Inn (two years and more), and of Shrewsbury, [Salop, gent

1585-6		folio 85
Feb	2	THOMAS, LORD BURGHL.
,,	,,	JOHN ROTHERHAM
,,	,,	HENRY CHEEKE (Esq), the Queen's Secretary in the North
,,	9	ROBERT AWDLEY, of Houghton, Beds (*sic*) and of Barnard's Inn.
,,	,,	ALEXANDER CAVE, son and heir of Thomas Cave, of Baggrave, co Leic., Esq

1586		folio 91
April	27	JOHN DABRIDGECOURT, of Ossington, Notts, and of Staple Inn.

1586	folio 91—(*continued*)
April 27	GEORGE PYE, of Colchester
,, ,,	CLEMENT TOKEY, of South Luffenham
,, ,,	ROBERT FAIDOE, of Mailedon, Beds [Esq
,, ,,	GRIFFIN MARKHAM, son and heir of Thomas Markham, of Ollerton, Notts,
,, ,,	ROBERT MARKHAM, son of said Thomas Markham
,, ,,	ADAM CLEYPOLE, of Northborough, co Northampton
,, ,,	ROBERT PILKINGTON, of Rivington, co Lanc, and of Staple Inn, gent
,, ,,	THOMAS CAMPION, of London, gent
May 5	THOMAS TOKFELD (Mr.), of Baldock, Master of Arts
,, ,,	MARMADUKE MATTHEW, of Clement's Inn
,, 9	HENRY ARCHER, son and heir of Archer, of London
,, ,,	ALBAN WAKELIN, of Eydon (Eden), co Northants, and of Staple Inn
,, 13	THOMAS SMITHE, of London

folio 92

,, ,,	RICHARD THACKER, of Repton, co Derby. [of the Earl of Ormond)
June 20.	ROBERT SHEIHE, of Kilkenny, Ireland, and of Barnard's Inn (at the request [Knight)
,, ,,	ANDREW ASHLEY, of London (at the request of Sir Francis Walsingham,

folio 94.

April 27	EDWARD (Edmund in ledger) HENDEN, of Biddenden, Kent, and of Staple Inn
May 12	THOMAS DRIVER, of Barnard's Inn (born at Fulborne, co Cambridge)

folio 102

Oct 12	ROBERT BARKER, son of Christopher Barker, of London, stationer to the
,, ,,	JERVYS GIBBON [Queen
,, ,,	GEORGE PHILIPPS.
,, ,,	THOMAS GOODING, of London [Gilbert Gerard, Knight, Master of the Rolls
,, ,,	RICHARD HOGHTON, of Hoghton, co Lanc, gent At the instance of Sir
,, 19	ROGER YELVERTON, second son of Henry Yelverton, of Sculthorpe, Norfolk, Esq
,, ,,	THOMAS ESTCOURTE, son of Thomas Estcourte, one of this Society
Nov 1	ALEXANDER STANDISH, of Duxbury, co Lanc
,, ,,	ANTHONY BUTLER
,, 4	NICHOLAS STRINGER, of Derby [Lincoln, Esq
,, ,,	WILLIAM HATTECLIFF, son and heir of Thomas Hattecliff, of Hattecliff, co
,, ,,	HENRY BOLDE, son of John Bolde, of Preston, co Lancaster, arm
,, ,,	JOHN LEAVES (written also Lewis), of Molton, co Lincoln

folio 103

,, ,,	RICHARD BANASTER, of Staple Inn [Knight
,, 14	EDMUND BACON, son and heir of Nicholas Bacon, of Redgrave, Suffolk,
,, ,,	JAMES BACON, son and heir of James Bacon, of London, Alderman
,, ,,	GEORGE COPE, son of George Cope, of Cannons Ashby, co Northampton
,, ,,	WILLIAM HALE, of London
,, ,,	ROBERT KENRICKE, of Preston, co Lancaster.

1586   folio 103—(*continued*)
Nov. 16   JOHN JOHNSON, of Staple Inn
  ,,   ,,   JOHN RUSSELL, of Cottingham, co Cambridge   [Barnard's Inn
  ,,   ,,   WILLIAM PYTCHERE (Pychard ?), of Trumpington, co Cambridge, and of
  ,,   ,,   FRANCIS THORNDYKE, of co Lincoln, late of Staple Inn
  ,,   ,,   THOMAS WELCOME, of city of Lincoln (born there), gent, late of Staple Inn
  ,,   ,,   MARMADUKE DAWNEY, of Sessay, co York, gent
  ,,   22   WILLIAM DETHICK, of London, gent
1586-7   [in the city of London)
Feb 2   ROBERT BEALE, Esq, Secretary to the Queen's Council in the North (born

   1586.   folio 104.
Nov 4   SAMUEL BUSSHEYE, of Leverton, co Lincoln, late of Barnard's Inn
  ,,   ,,   JAMES NECTON, of Monks Hadley, Middlesex
  ,,   ,,   THOMAS ESSON, of Ripe (alias Ockington ?), Sussex, late of Staple Inn
  ,,   7   JAMES DOWSON, of city of Chester
  ,,   ,,   NICHOLAS HORNSEY, of Bonby, co Lincoln
  ,,   21.   THOMAS SANDFORTHE, of Howgill, Westmoreland, gent
  ,,   ,,   THOMAS WHALLEY, of Screton, Notts
  ,,   ,,   JOHN STANFORD, of Leicester, gent
  ,,   ,,   THOMAS BURTON, of Branston, co Rutland, gent, late of Staple Inn

                                       folio 105   [of Thimblethorpe
  ,,   22   ROBERT THIMBLETHORPE, of Barnard's Inn, gent, son of George Thimblethorpe,
Feb 6   JOHN MYDDELLTON, late of Staple Inn   [late of this Inn
  ,,   ,,   ANTHONY THOROLD, of Hough (Haghe), co. Linc, son of Robert Thorold,

                                       folio 106
  ,,   ,,   MICHAEL WEIGHMAN (or Wightman), late of Barnard's Inn
  ,,   ,,   WILLIAM HORSPOLE, of Staple Inn, gent.
  ,,   8.   EDMUND BOOTHE, son of Sir William Boothe, Knight, of co Chester
  ,,   ,,   WILLIAM BRERETON, son and heir apparent of William Brereton, of Brereton,
  ,,   ,,   THOMAS HOGAN, son of Thomas Hogan, of London   [co Chester
1587.
May 11.   ROBERT FISHER
  ,,   ,,   GODFREY RHODES, fourth son of Francis Rhodes, one of the Judges of the
                     [Common Bench, "absque fine," as his father was of this Inn

                                       folio 112
  ,,   19.   ROBERT SMYTHE, fifth son of Robert Smythe, of London, arm.
  ,,   ,,   ROBERT LEAKE, of Wymeswold, co Leic.
  ,,   ,,   HENRY LEYGHE, son and heir of Edward Leyghe, of Rushill, co. Stafford
  ,,   26   THOMAS SOUTHWORTH, of Queen's College, Cambridge.
  ,,   ,,   THOMAS COTTON, son of Bartholomew Cotton.   [Bromley, Kent
July 3.   SAMUEL THORNHILL (Thornell), son and heir apparent of Richard Thornhill of
  ,,   ,,   THOMAS DRYWOOD, of Essex

1587   folio 112—(*continued*)
July 3   WILLIAM BIRD, of Ipswich, Suffolk
  ,, ,,   AUGUSTINE WOOD, of city of Norwich
  ,, ,,   JAMES CLERKE, of Ford, co Lancaster

folio 115

May 10   ROBERT PHILLIPSON, of Wyndermere, Westmoreland
  ,, ,,   THOMAS PEPYS, of Cottenham, co Cambridge
  ,, ,,   WILLIAM SPIGER, of Great Drayton, Salop, late of Barnard's Inn
  ,, ,,   JOHN BROWNE, of Furnival's Inn
  ,, ,,   THOMAS HARTOPP
  ,, ,,   ROWLAND BRIGGES, of Lygne, Westmoreland, and of Staple Inn.
  ,, 19   JOHN NEVE, of Ringland, Norfolk, late of Barnard's Inn
  ,, ,,   JAMES MASSEY, of Rixton, co Lancaster   [co. Lincoln, gent
  ,, 26   EDWARD BERESFORD, fifth son of Christopher Beresford, of Long Ledenham,
  ,, ,,   BARNARD ELLIS, of Warnell, in parish of Sebberam, Cumberland, gent
  ,, ,,   ABRAHAM BOWNE, of Trinity parish, city of Coventry, gent , late of Staple Inn
  ,, ,,   RICHARD RANDALL, of Stoke, in town and city of Coventry, late of Staple Inn
  ,, ,,   THOMAS MYLLS, of Harscombe, co Gloucester, and of Staple Inn
  ,, ,,   FRANCIS CLAXTON, of city of Norwich, late of Staple Inn

folio 116

July 3   EDMUND ESTCOURT, of Tetbury, co Gloucester
  ,, ,,   WILLIAM GREGORY, of East Stokwyth, co Lincoln
  ,, ,,   THOMAS DYKE
  ,, ,,   WILLIAM COBBE
  ,, ,,   JOHN HANMER, of Oswestry, Salop

folio 123

Oct 16.   EDWARD BURTON, of Bourne, Sussex, gent
  ,, ,,   NICHOLAS TAILOR (Tailior), son of Richard Tailor
  ,, ,,   OLIVER BUTLER, son of John Butler, Esq
  ,, ,,   EDMOND CALVERLEY (Caverley)
  ,, ,,   WILLIAM BERNERS, of Theckfield, Herts
Nov. 1   JOHN BYRON, of Colwick, Notts
  ,, ,,.   RICHARD HOLLAND, of Denton, co Lancaster, Esq
  ,, ,,   ——— HORSMAN, of Lincoln
  ,, 3.   OWEN GODFREY, eldest son of Richard Godfrey, Esq
  ,, ,,   THOMAS ASTLEY, of Melton, Norfolk
  ,, ,,   JOHN BOLLE, son and heir of Charles Bolle, Esq
  ,, ,,   JOHN FITZWILLIAM, son and heir of Charles Fitzwilliam, Esq , late of Staple Inn
  ,, ,,   JOHN BUTLER, of Cotes, co Lincoln, gent.
  ,, ,,   RICHARD BOWES, of Stretlam, co. Durham.

folio 124.

  ,, 22   EDWARD OWEN

1587		folio 124—(*continued*)
Nov	22	THOMAS BURLES
,,	,,	THOMAS HETLEY, of Brampton, Hunts, late of Staple Inn
,,	,,	ADRIAN FARNEY (Farnham in ledger)
,,	,,	WILLIAM FROST

1587-8   [Knight

Jan	24	JARVIS CLIFTON, son and heir of John Clifton, of Barrington, co Somerset,
,,	,,	JOHN LEPTON, of Kepwyke, co York
,,	,,	JAMES JAVE, of Selston, Notts, late of Barnard's Inn
,,	,,	AMBROSE SMYTH, of Wythycote, co Leicester, late of Staple Inn
Feb	2	WILLIAM ANDERTON, of Euxton, co Lancaster, and of Barnard's Inn
,,	7	NATHANIEL STUDLEY, son of John Studley, of Wimborne Minster, co Dorset,

                                                    [gent, late of Barnard's Inn

1587		folio 126
Nov	1	PETER STARKEY, of Staple Inn (date written 1582)
,	3	WILLIAM WYNNE, of Barnard's Inn, and of Trefford, co Denbigh
,,	,,	CHRISTOPHER PEPPER, of Richmond, co York, and of Barnard's Inn
,,	,,	WILLIAM REDE, of Bromfield, co Hereford (erased)
,,	,,	PHILIP COCK, son and heir of Thomas Cock, of Colchester, Essex
,,	,,	JOHN WOODALL, of Mollington, co Warwick, gent

1587-8

Jan	24	WILLIAM TOOKE, of Hertford, Herts

folio 127.

,	8	NICHOLAS FITZWILLIAM, of Dublin, gent, late of Staple Inn
,,	,,	ANTHONY FOWLE, of Retherfield, Sussex, gent
,,	,,	THOMAS BALLARD, of Lamberhurst, Sussex, gent
,,	,,	GEORGE FISH, of Southall, Beds, gent
,,	,,	WILLIAM KNAPLOCK, of Southampton, gent
,,	,,	RALPH POWELL, of Hanstey, co Denbigh, gent., late of Barnard's Inn
,,	,,	JOHN WRIGHT, son of John Wright, of Wrightbridge, Essex, gent
,,	12.	EDWARD JONES, of London, gent

folio 128

,,	5	EDWARD WOOTTON, of Boughton Malherbe, Kent
,,	,,	JOHN HOTTOMAN (written also Hottman), Esq, a Frenchman
,,	7	WILLIAM PHILLIPP, of London, Esq
,,	,,	THOMAS PHILLIPP, Esq
,,	,,	WILLIAM DETHICK, als Garter, Principal King-of-Arms of England
,,	9	WILLIAM ASHBY, of co Leicester, Esq.
,,	,,	MILES FLEETWOOD, son and heir of William Fleetwood, of Ealing Middx., Esq

folio 135.

,,	,,	RADCLIFFE GERRARD, son of Gilbert Gerrard, Knight, Master of the Rolls.
,,	,,	ROGER BUTLER, gent.
,,	12	THOMAS GREY, son and heir of (Arthur) Grey, Lord de Wilton.
,,	,,	EDWARD VAUGHAN, of the Queen's Exchequer.

1587-8   folio 135—(*continued*)
Jan 12   HENRY SCROOPE, son of Lord Scroope
  ,,   ,,   CHARLES GREY, Esq , brother and heir apparent of Henry, Earl of Kent
  ,,   ,,   BENJAMIN PIGGOT, of Gravenhurst, Beds, Esq
1588   [("Staple" in ledger).
May 1.   WILLIAM FOSBROKE, of Cranford, co Northampton, and of Barnard's Inn
  ,,   ,,   THOMAS STOCKETT, of London, gent
  ,,   ,,   EDWARD LENTON, of Woodford, co Northampton, gent.
  ,,   ,,   WILLIAM HOLT, of Ashworth, co Lancaster, gent

                           folio 136.   [Godsalve, Esq , of same
  ,,   17   ROGER GODSALVE, of Buckenham Ferry, co Norfolk, son and heir of Thomas
  ,,   ,,   THOMAS BEALE, of Stanground, Hunts
  ,,   ,,   JOHN BROCKET, son of Edward Brocket, of Wheathampstead.
  ,,   ,,   RICHARD WOOLBYE ("Wolley" in ledger), of Thorpe, co Linc
  ,,   ,,   GEORGE THIMBELETHORPE, of Barnard's Inn (born at Foulsham, Norfolk)

                           folio 139.
  ,,   1.   HENRY MORRISON, son of Thomas Morrison, Esq
  ,,   17.   EDMUND BRESSY, of Braynfford, Middlesex.   [Lancaster, Esq
June 10   CHRISTOPHER ANDERTON, son of Christopher Anderton, of Lostock, co

                           folio 145.
Aug 13   HENRY BROWN, Esq , of Cowdray, Sussex, son of Anthony, Viscount
  ,,   ,,   FRANCIS LACON, of co Salop, Esq   [Mountague
  ,,   18   STEPHEN EGERTON, of London, clerk   [same, Knight
  ,,   ,,   WILLIAM PELHAM, of Newstead, co Linc , son and heir of William Pelham, of
  ,,   ,,   HERBERT PELHAM, of Michelham, in parish of (? Catsfield), co Sussex
  ,,   ,,   JOHN FINCHE, of Staple Inn, gent, son and heir apparent of Clement Finche,
  ,,   19   JOHN GREENWOOD, of Staple Inn   [of Milton next Sittingbourne, Kent

                           folio 146.
Oct 16   EDWARD GOLDING, of Eye, Suffolk
  ,,   22   THOMAS WRYTINGTON, of London, gent
  ,,   ,,   HENRY WHETENHALL, of East Peckham, Kent
  ,,   27   RICHARD BOLLE, son of Richard Bolle, of Louth, co Linc , Esq
Nov 1   THOMAS MORYSON, junior, of London.
  ,,   ,,   HENRY SHUTTLEWORTHE, of Staple Inn
  ,,   6   WILLIAM DANIELL, son of William Daniell, reader
  ,,   8   ROBERT CASTELL, of East Hatley, co Cambridge
  ,,   21   RICHARD DARLEY, of Buttercrambe, co York.
  ,,   ,,   THOMAS HULME, of Manchester, co Lanc
  ,   26   WILLIAM INGRAM, of London.
  ,,   ,,   JOHN WRIGHT, of Plowland co York.

1588-9   folio 147
Feb 2   THOMAS MOLYNEUX, son of Richard Molyneux, of Sefton, co Lanc , Knight

1588-9   folio 147—(continued)

Feb 7   WILLIAM VAVASOUR, son of Ralph Vavasour, Esq, deceased, and grandson
              [(nepos) and heir apparent of John Vavasour, of Haslewood, co York

,,   ,,   THOMAS PEAKE, of Lutterworth, co Leicester, M A of Cambridge University

,,   ,,   HENRY SCOTT, of Wotton, co Lincoln, gent.

,,   ,,   AMIAS CLIFTON, second son of John Clifton, Knight

,,   ,,   WILLIAM GIFFARDE, late of Staple Inn, gent   [Treasurer)

,,   26   DONOGH, EARL OF THOMOND (admitted by William Burghley, High

,,   ,,   WILLIAM CECIL, Esq. (admitted by his grandfather, William Burghley, High

,,   ,,   RICHARD HATTON, gent   ⎞   [Treasurer).

,,   ,,   GARRETT AYLMER, gent   ⎪   admitted by

,,   ,,   ROBERT WELBY, Esq   ⎬   William Burghley,

,,   ,,   HENRY GOLDSMITH, gent   ⎪   High Treasurer

,,   ,,   EDWARD WARRYN, gent   ⎠

,,   27   THOMAS SEYMOUR, Esq.

,,   ,,   RICHARD BANCROFTE S T D, Archbishop of Canterbury

,,   ,,   WILLIAM LEWIN, Doctor of Civil Law.

,,   ,,   EDWARD DODGE, of Wrotham, Kent, Esq

folio 149

,,   ,,   FRANCIS MARKHAM, of Cotham, Notts, late of Staple Inn

1588

Nov 21. ROBERT DUKE, of Kelsall, Suffolk.   [co Devon, Esq

,,   26   HUMPHREY COURTENAY, son and heir of Philip Courtenay, of Molland,

1588-9

Feb. 2 RICHARD HALSALI, of Barnard's Inn   [Dean of St. Paul's, London)

,,   ,,   ——— HAWORTH, of Staple Inn (at the request of Alexander Nowell,

,,   6. CHRISTOPHER YELVERTON, second son of Christopher Yelverton, Esq, double
                                                          [reader, sine fine

1589   folio 155   [of Lancaster

April 23. SYMEON BROGRAVE, son and heir of John Brograve, Attorney of the Duchy

,,   ,,   THOMAS EDEN, son and heir of Thomas Eden, of Sudbury, Suffolk, Esq.

May 9. FRANCIS PUREFOY, of Barnard's Inn, late of Calcott, co Warwick.

,,   ,,   THOMAS ELLIS, son of Thomas Ellis, of Witham, co. Lincoln, Esq

,,   ,,   ROGER GOWER, of Melsonby, co York

,,   ,,   THOMAS GOTELY, of Staple Inn, late of Molyshe, Kent, gent. (erased)

,,   ,,   RICHARD GREGORY, of Harleston, co Northampton

,,   ,,   PETER LOCKE, of Newport, co Southampton, gent.

June 3   RALPH HOLTE, of Grislehurst, co. Lanc, late of Staple Inn

,,   ,   THOMAS GRAUNGE, of Barnard's Inn, and of East Heilesey co York, gent

,,   9   JOHN BERE, of Minster, Isle of Thanet, Kent, gent

folio 156

,,   ,,   JOHN DANVERS, Knight

Aug. 2. HUGH HALLIWELL, of Wells, co Somerset, gent

1589   **folio 156** —*(continued)*

Aug 4.   GEORGE BONDE, Knight.

,, 7.   MATHEW CAREW, Doctor of Laws, one of the Masters in Chancery.

,, 11   EDWARD STANLEY, Knight

,, ,,   ROGER MARBECK, Doctor of Medicine

,, ,,   ROGER SYDENHAM, gent

,, ,,   EDWARD STAFFORD, son and heir of Robert Stafford, Knight

,, 13   ROBERT CROSSE, Esq

,, ,,   WILLIAM BATHE, Esq , an Irishman

,, ,,   JOHN FINGLASSE (Fyneglass), Esq , an Irishman

,, ,,   GEORGE FULWOOD, gent

folio 158

April 23   WILLIAM KYTTES, of Hillmorton, co Warwick, gent

,, ,,   THOMAS BUTLER, of Staple Inn (born at Orwell, co Cambridge)

May 9   THOMAS GOTELVE, of Staple Inn, late of Molysshe, co Kent

,, ,,   OLIVER BRIGGS, of Earnstree, Salop, gent

,, ,,   JOHN BLACKWOOD, of Halifax, co York, gent   [gent

,, ,,   ROBERT HALL, son and heir of Reginald Hall, of Pinchbeck, co Lincoln,

,, ,,   RICHARD GREGORIE, of ———, co Northampton.

June 3   THOMAS BOWYER (Boyere), of Biddulph, co Stafford, late of Staple Inn

folio 159

,, ,,   ROBERT BEESTON, of Beeston, co York, gent , and of Staple Inn

,, ,,   WILLIAM SMYTH, son of Thomas Smyth, of Burton, co York, gent

folio 165

Oct 23   PETER SEDGRAVE, of Killegton, co Meath, Ireland, gent

,, ,,   THOMAS BUTLER, of Kingston, Surrey, gent.

,, ,,   JOHN NEVILL, of Torksey, co Lincoln, gent

,, ,,   JOHN CURLE, of Enfield, Middlesex, gent.   [Cambridge]

Nov. 1   CHRISTOPHER HATTON, son of John Hatton, Esq. (born at Oakington, co

,, ,,   FRANCIS MILLES.

,, ,,   WILLIAM JOLIPHE.

,, 3.   THOMAS COOK, of Yorkshire, gent.

,, 7   ROBERT ASTON, of Farnham, Surrey ("Asheton" in ledger).

,, ,,   ROBERT WOOLLVERSTON, of Culphoe, Suffolk, Esq   [Esq

,, 20   JAMES CROMER, son and heir apparent of William Cromer, of Tunstall, Kent,

,, 24.   JOHN BOURNE, of London, gent

1589-90   [of same place, Esq

Jan. 30.   EDWARD ENGEHAM, of Goodneston, Kent, son and heir of Thomas Engeham,

folio 166

Feb 2   JOHN JACKSON, of Ruyvell House, in Nederdale, parish of Kirby Malzeard,

,, ,,   RALPH BUSSHE, of Stanstead Abbots, Herts   [co York

,, ,,   ROGER DOWNES, of Staple Inn

,, 4   EDWARD ELDERTON

1589-90		folio **166**—*(continued)*.
Feb	9	ANTHONY MORLEY, son of William Morley, of Glynde, Sussex, Esq
,,	11	SIMYON STEWARD, son and heir of Nicholas Steward, Doctor of Civil Law
,,	,,	THOMAS PENRUDDOCK, son and heir apparent of John Penruddock, Esq, one of [the readers of this Inn
,, ,,		ELIAS FOXTON, son of ———— Foxton, Alderman of the city of Cambridge
1589		
May	21	WILLIAM HOUGHTON, of Houghton Tower, co Lancaster.

folio **168**

Nov.	3	ROBERT HITCHAM, of Levington, Suffolk, gent, late of Barnard's Inn
1589-90		
Jan	28	WILLIAM WORTLEY, of Wortley, co York [Inn
,,	30	ANTHONY STELLING, of Newton Ketton co Durham, gent, late of Barnard's
Feb	9	ROBERT THOROLD, son of Edmund Thorold, of Hough, co Lincoln, Esq
,,	,,	ALEXANDER THOROLD, another son of Edmund Thorold, aforesaid
,,	,,	EDMUND THOROLD, son of Robert Thorold, late of Hough, co Lincoln, Esq

folio **169**

,,	,,	WILLIAM COCKE, of city of Gloucester, gent (born at Newcastle-upon-Tyne, said William Cocke out of Inn, June 21, 44 Elizabeth, restored June 3, 1 James

1590		folio **175**
May	29	THOMAS PALMER, son and heir of Thomas Palmer, of Wingham, Kent, Esq
,,	,,	FRANCIS SMYTH, junior, of Ashby Folville, co Leicester, gent
June	2	THOMAS STEWARD, son and heir apparent of William Steward
,,	,,	NICHOLAS RYVETT, son and heir of John Ryvett, of Barneston, Suffolk
,,	22	MARTIN JAMES (Jones ?), Esq, Registrar of the Court of Chancery

folio **176**

July	2	WILLIAM WALKER, of London
,,	,,	THOMAS POYNTZ, of North Ockendon, Essex
,,	,,	EUBULUS THELWALL, of ———— co Denbigh [Worcester, gent
,,	7	THOMAS HUBAND (Hubard written elsewhere), son of Thomas Huband, of
Aug	1	WILLIAM LEAKE, of Wimeswould, co Leicester
,,	2	HENRY CARY, of Berkhampstead, Herts, son and heir of Edward Cary
,,	6	JOHN AMY, Doctor of Laws, Advocate of the Arches, London
,,	,,	WILLIAM HARLACKENDEN, of Little Chart, Kent
,,	8	JOHN BETTENHAM, son and heir of Daniel Bettenham, of Pluckley, Kent, Esq
,,	,,	JOHN DENNE, of Great Maplestead, Essex, arm
,	,,	EDMUND BUTLER, second son of William Butler, of Tyes, Sussex, gent
,,	,,	NICHOLAS MONYNGE, son and heir of Edward Monynge, of Waldershare
,,	,,	ABRAHAM COPWOOD, of London, gent [Kent, Esq

folio **177.**

May	29	ROBERT GOODHALL, of Hallywell, co Lincoln, gent, late of Barnard's Inn
,,	,,	GEORGE ELLIS, late of Barnard's Inn (" Staple " in ledger)

1590		folio 177—(*continued*)

June 22   ROBERT RYVELL, second son of John Ryvett, of Brandeston, Suffolk

July   2   THOMAS WALGRAVE, of Bures, Suffolk, gent

Aug   8   EDMUND NUGENT, of Tradasse, Ireland, late of Staple Inn

1589-90   **folio 178**   [cellor of the Order of the Garter)

Mar 16   LAUNCELOT ANDREWES, Doctor of Divinity (Bishop of Winchester and Chan-

 ,,   18   ROBERT NEWDIGATE, of Hawnes, Bedfordshire, arm

 ,,   ,,   OLIVER HARVVE, of Thurley, Bedfordshire

1590

May 13   GEORGE CHAWORTH, son and heir of Henry Chaworth, arm

 ,,   ,,   GEORGE RABBET, of Bramfield, Suffolk, gent, late of Barnard's Inn

 ,,   ,,   RALPH ALWAY, of Stretley, Bedfordshire, gent, late of Staple Inn

 ,,   20   GEORGE CONYE, of Bassingthorpe, co Lincoln, gent

 ,,   22   JOHN SUCKLING, of Norwich, gent, second son of Robert Suckling, of same

folio 184

Aug   9   NICHOLAS BROMLEY, of Derfield, co Chester, Esq

 ,,   ,,   ADOLPHUS CARY, second son of Edward Cary, of Berkhampstead, Herts, Esq

 ,,   ,,   PHILIP CARY, third son of said Edward Cary

 ,,   12   JEAN DE LA FINES, "Seigneur de Beauvair et De la Roche, Conseilleirei au Conseil d'État du Roy très chrestienne, Capt de 50ᵗᵉ hommes d'armes et Ambassadeur pres sa Maᵗᵉ notre Souveraine "

 ,,   13   FRANCIS MICHEL, of Old Windsor, Berks, gent (note May 4, 1621, for that this Francis Michel, for misdemeanor, was this day therefore)

 ,,   ,,   RICHARD RIGGE, of Little Strickland, Westmoreland, gent   [York, gent

 ,,   ,,   LEONARD BROUGHE, son and heir of Peter Broughe, of Addlethorpe, co

Oct   14   JOHN PROCTOR, son of ——— Proctor, Citizen of London

 ,,   ,,   GEORGE HIDE, son and heir of William Hide, of Kingston Lisle, Berks, Esq

folio 185

 ,,   ,,   TIMOTHY HUTTON, son and heir of Matthew Hutton, Bishop of Durham

 ,,   ,,   JOHN PALER (Payler), son and heir of William Paler, Esq

 ,,   ,,   RICHARD BOWES, son of Martin Bowes, of Battersey, Surrey, Esq

Nov   1   EDWARD (EDMOND) NEVILL, of High (Peschott?), co York

 ,,   6   RALPH GVLL, of parish of St Peter's ad Vincula, London   [London.

 ,,   18   EDWARD MOSELEY, son of Nicholas Moseley, Alderman and now Sheriff of

 ,,   25   HENRY WIDDRINGTON of Widdrington, Northumberland, gent

 ,,   26   HENRY LACY, of Melton Mowbray, co Leicester, late of Barnard's Inn

1590-1

Feb   2   JOHN PRESTON, of Furness, co Lanc

 ,,   ,,   JOHN GASCOYNE, Esq

 ,,   9   FRANCIS BEALE, son and heir of Robert Beale, Esq

 ,,   ,,   THOMAS BRUCHE, of Bruche, co Lanc   [co Cambridge, Esq

 ,,   3   ROGER HUTTON, cousin and heir apparent of John Hutton, of Dry Drayton,

 ,,   ,,   RICHARD CECIL, son of Thomas Cecil, Knight

E

1590-1		folio 185—(*continued*)
Feb	2	EDWARD CECIL, son of Thomas Cecil, Knight
,,	,,	RICHARD WANDESFORD, of Pickhill, co. York, Esq

folio 186.

,,	22	RICHARD MARTYN, Knight, one of the Aldermen of the City of London
,,	,,	HENRY BYLLYNGSLEY, one of the Aldermen of the City of London
,,	,,	EDWARD GRYMESTON, arm., of co Suffolk
,,	25	WILLIAM BOROUGHE, Esq.
1590		folio 187.
Aug	13	EDWARD TOPHAM, of Aglethorpe, co York, gent
,,	,,	GEOFFREY GALWAY, of Limerick, Ireland, gent
,,	,,	ARTHUR FUTTER, son of William Futter, of East Dereham, Kent (*sic*), gent
Nov	6	THOMAS GIBSON, late of Barnard's Inn
,,	,,	JAMES KITCHAM, son of John Kitcham, late of Islington, Esq
,,	,,	HENRY CHEEKE, son of Henry Cheeke, Esq (erased)
,,	,,	RICHARD FOWLKES (Fooxe), of Bottisham, co Cambridge, and of Barnard's
,,	,,	RICHARD SYDLEY, of Brayborne, Kent [Inn ("Folke" in ledger)
,,	,,	GEORGE STOCKDALE, of Casterton, Westmoreland, and of Barnard's Inn
,,	,,	HENRY WHYSKINS, son of Henry Whyskins, double reader
,,	11	HENRY WOODHOUSE, son of Henry Woodhouse, of Breckell, Norfolk, Esq
,,	18	DAVID SMYTH, of Righam, co Denbigh, gent, late of Barnard's Inn
1590-1		folio 188.
Feb	3	GEORGE DARRELL, son and heir of John Darrell, of Little Chart, Kent, Esq
,,	,,	JOHN MYDLETON, of Mydleton-super-Linton, co York, gent, of Staple Inn
,,	,,	RICHARD ORDE, of Horklye, Northumberland
,,	10	JOHN CLERKE, of Hinderclay, Suffolk, late of Barnard's Inn
,,	25	EDWARD FYTTON
1591 May	14	THEOPHILUS MOUNTGOMERY, of Peterborough, co Northampton **folio 195**

folio 198.

April	28	THOMAS YALE, of Barnard's Inn
,,	29	EDWARD GILPIN, son and heir of John Gilpin, of Highgate, Middlesex, Esq
May	15	WALTER CHARLTON, son and heir of Andrew Charlton, of Apley, Salop, Esq
June	21	MATTHEW CLERKE, of King's Lynn, Norfolk, Esq
,,	,,	JOHN BOLLE, of Louth, co Lincoln, gent

1590-1		folio 201 [aforesaid.
Mar	2	JOHN LANY, eldest son of John Lany, Lent reader of this Inn in the year
,,	3	EDWARD SHERLAND, of Suffolk, and of Staple Inn.
,,	,,	JOHN PERKINS, of Upleadon, co Gloucester, late of Staple Inn
1591 April	28	BARNARD TOWNLEY, of Staple Inn.
May	10	WALTER DAYRELL, of Staple Inn
,,	14	THOMAS SHIRLEY, gent
June	9	RALPH FETHERSTONHAUIGH, of Stanhope, co Durham.

1591		**folio 202**
June	9	FRANCIS SOUTHAKE, gent , of (Netrid ?) land, co Cornwall (erased)
,,	21	FRANCIS SOUTHAKE, of ——— co ———
,,	,,	HUMPHREY WELLINGE, late of Staple Inn, gent

folio 209

Aug	9	RICHARD YONGE, of London, Esq
,,	,,	WILLIAM GETTOR (or Jetter), of Canterbury, Kent, gent.
,,	14	THOMAS BELLAY, of Bugden, Hunts, son and heir of John Bellay
,,	,,	JOHN TOWNLEY, of London
Oct	11	RICHARD BELL, of City of York, gent
,,	,,	JOHN MONSON, son of John Monson, of Carleton, co Lincoln, Knight [Esq
,,	,,	THOMAS BARD, son and heir of Rodolph Bard, of North Kelsey, co Lincoln,
Nov	1	JAMES TOZER, of the town of Southampton, gent
,,	,,	JOHN MACHELL, Junior, of Hackney, Middlesex, son and heir apparent of [John Machell, of Hackney, Esq
,,	,,	THOMAS BAMBURGH, of Howsam, co York
,,	6	GERVASE TEVERY, of Stapleford, Notts, gent ("tortoise" see Gesta Grayorum)
,,	,,	SYMON SMYTH, of London, gent
,,	,,	ROWLAND PERLECT, of Skipwith, co York, gent
,,	,,	PETER BARNEWALL, of Lespopell, co Dublin, gent

folio 210

,,	8.	JOHN DENNE, gent , of Staple Inn
,,	,,	JAYRE FLOWER, son of John Flower, of Edithweston, co Rutland, Esq
,,	,,	JOHN TOMPSON, son and heir of Francis Tompson, of Boothby, co Linc , gent.
,,	24	ROBERT LEGRYCE (called "Grice" in ledger), of Bradisham, Suffolk, gent.
1591-2		
Feb.	2	ROBERT, Lord RICH
,,	,,	JOHN WOLLEY, of the Queen's Council
,,	,,	THOMAS GREY, heir apparent of Lord Grey (de Wilton)
,,	,,	JOHN HERBERT, one of the Masters of Requests.
,,	,,	JOHN PAYTON, Knight
,,	,,	WILLIAM COOKE, Clerk of the Liveries (Gesta Grayorum)
,,	,,	ROBERT LANE, son of William Lane
,,	,,	HENRY DENNY
,,	,,	ROGER MILLISENT, son of Robert Millisent
,,	,,	ROBERT MAIE
,,	,,	ROBERT PENRUDDOCK
,,	,,	CHARLES O'CARROLL, Knight, an Irishman.
,,	,,	HENRY BOYAR (rightly Bowyer), son of John Bowyer, Serjeant-at-Law
,,	,,	CHARLES BUSEY (Bewsey), son of John Busey
,,	,,	FELIX GERRARD
,,	,,	WILLIAM KYDLOWE
,,	,,	HENRY BANYSTER, of Croston, co Lanc

1591-2		**folio 211.**
Feb	2	[GILES, Lord CHANDOS, admitted an Ancient]
,,	7	HENRY GORING, son and heir apparent of William Goring, of Burton, Sussex, Esq
,,	,,	—— BLUNT, son of —— Blunt.
1591		
June 15		GILES DE KILLINGWORTH, of ——, co Cambridge, gent (erased)
,,	,,	ROBERT CODRINGTON, of ——, co Gloucester, gent
,,	,,	MARMADUKE CONSTABLE, of Everingham, co York, gent
1591-2		
Feb	9	ROBERT BEVILL, of Chesterton, Hunts, son and heir of Robert Bevill, Esq
,,	,,	HENRY DIXON, of Stone, Kent, gent
,,	,,	EDWARD JENINSON, of Newark-on-Trent, Notts, gent, late of Staple Inn (erased)
,,	,,	THOMAS PAINE, late of Staple Inn, gent (erased)

1591		**folio 216**
Aug	9	THOMAS DARLEY, of Kilnhurst, co York
,,	14	NICHOLAS STAINES of Barnard's Inn, gent
,,	,,	THOMAS ELLIS, son and heir apparent of John Ellis, reader
Oct	11	JOHN JOSELYN, of Sawbridgeworth, Herts
,,	,,	RALPH STURDY, of Yafford, co York
Nov	5	EDMUND CROFTS, son of Thomas Crofts, of Little Saxham, Suffolk, Esq
,,	6	NICHOLAS (Lane) LOWE, of Denby, co Derby, gent, of Barnard's Inn
,,	,,	GEORGE WRIGHT, son of Thomas Wright, of Debham, Kent, gent
,,	8	FRANCIS FETHERSTONHALGH, of Stanhope, co Durham, gent

		folio 217
,,	22	EDWARD STANLEY, son of Thomas Stanley, of ——, Cumberland, gent
,,	26	FULKE VAUGHAN, of Drumhaglog (Drinheylog), co Denbigh, gent, late of Barnard's Inn (" Staple " in ledger)

1591-2		**folio 224**
Mar	1	EDMUND DEARSLEY, of Dowling, Suffolk
1592		
April 17		THOMAS HOBBES, of London, gent
,,	,,	HAMON CLAXTON, junior, of Norwich late of Barnard's Inn
,,	19	WILLIAM MICHELBORNE, of Newick, Sussex
,,	24	ANTHONY PENNYNGE, of Kettleborough, Suffolk
,,	25	HENRY BYNG, son and heir of Thomas Byng, Doctor of Laws of Cambridge

		folio 225
May	1	EDWARD STAFFORD, Knight
,,	,,	WILLIAM STAFFORD, son and heir of said Edward Stafford, Knight
,,	30	GEORGE ADWYKE, of Arksey, co York [London.
,,	,,	JEROME GARDENER, son of Thomas Gardener, of St Peter's parish, City of
June	5	NICHOLAS MASON, of Egmanton, Notts, gent
,,	,,	EDWARD PAYLER, of City of York, gent, son of William Payler, Esq
,,	,,	ROBERT MONSON, of co Lincoln, son of John Monson, Knight.
,,	12	CHARLES ALINGTON, son of George Alington, Esq
,,	13	RALPH LAWSON, of Nesham, co York

1591-2 folio 234

Mar 1 THOMAS NIGHTINGALE, son and heir apparent of Geoffrey Nightingale, of

,, ,, THOMAS LAMBERT, of Colchester, Essex   [Newport, Essex, reader

1592

April 17 THOMAS PAYNE, late of Staple Inn, gent   [of Earl's Colne, Essex, Esq

,, ,, RICHARD HARLACKENDEN, of Staple Inn, son and heir of Roger Harlackenden,

,, ,, THOMAS HARLACKENDEN, of Staple Inn, second son of said Roger

,, ,, THOMAS FRANCE, of Staple Inn   [Harlackenden

folio 235

,, 24 WILLIAM THOROLD, of Haghe, co Lincoln, late of Barnard's Inn (erased

,, ,, SAMUEL FENTON, of Staple Inn, gent   [Restitutur quiæ se submisit)

May 5 ROBERT COTTON, of West Peckham, Kent, late of Staple Inn, gent.

,, ,, GEORGE WALKER (written also "Waller"), of Harborough, co Leicester,
                     [gent, late of Barnard's Inn

June 7 WILLIAM LEWIS, of Parkesey, co Merioneth, late of Barnard's Inn

,, 12 HUGH ALINGTON, son of George Alington, Esq

,, ,, CHRISTOPHER PARKINSON, son of Thomas Parkinson, of Burneston, co. York

,, 13 LEWIS PICKERING, of Titchmarsh, co Northampton

,, ,, THOMAS BIRCH, of Manchester, co Lanc, now of Barnard's Inn

,, ,, VINCENT CASTELL, of Horsley (Horsell), Surrey, gent

folio 247

Aug 3 HENRY JAYE, citizen of London, cousin of Richard Jaye, Serjeant-at-Law.

,, ,, CORNELIUS FISHE, son of Walter Fishe, "faithful servant of our lady Queen

,, ,, ASCANIUS RIALME, an Italian   [Elizabeth"

,, ,, OWEN SALUSBURY, 'capitaneus militie studiosus."

,, ,, BARTHOLOMEW HALES, cousin to Charles Hales, reader of this Society

,, ,, THOMAS MILLES, gent

,, ,, WILLIAM CAMDEN, "qui Brittanniam nostram doctissime illustravit"

,, 10. WOLSTAN DIXIE, Knight

,, ,, ALEXANDER KING, Esq, one of the ——— of the Queen's Auditors

,, ,, ABRAHAM HARTWELL, gent, Secretary to the Archbishop of Canterbury

,, ,, THOMAS LAKE, Esq, one of the Clerks of the Privy Seal

,, ,, RICHARD KETTERIDGE, gent

,, ,, RICHARD SUTTON, gent

,, ,, GEORGE WODDINGTON, citizen of London

,, ,, NICHOLAS FAUNT, gent.

,, ,, JOHN HAWKESWORTH, gent.

folio 248

,, 12 JOHN HOTHERSALL, of Hothersall, co Lanc

,, , WILLIAM HUMBERSTON, of Yardley, Herts

,, ,, WALTER HAWKSWORTH

1592-3

Jan 29 OWEN VAUGHAN, of Langedwy, co Denbigh, late of Barnard's Inn

,, ,, THOMAS ELWES, of London

1592-3   folio 248—(*continued*).

Jan. 29   ROBERT JOPSON, of Hutton, Westmoreland (erased)

 ,,   ,,   WILLIAM TILDESLEY, of Morleys, co Lanc.   [Lancaster

 ,,   ,,   JOHN BROGRAVE, second son of John Brograve, Attorney of the Duchy of

 ,,   ,,   JOHN BROGRAVE, son of Henry Brograve

 ,,   ,,   EDWARD STANHOPE, son and heir of Edward Stanhope, Esq , of this Society

 ,,   ,,   EDWARD HALES, heir apparent of John Hales, reader of this Inn

 ,,   ,,   SIMON STEWARD, son of Mark Steward, of Berks

 ,,   ,,   THOMAS SISLEY ("Cisley" in ledger), of Barking, Essex

folio 249

 ,,   30   THOMAS POWELL, of (the hundred of) Comot Dichor (Disserth), co Radnor

 ,,   ,,   EDWARD PRICE, of Newton, co Montgomery, late of Barnard's Inn

 ,,   ,,   WILLIAM LLOYD ("Flood" in ledger), of Bettus, Salop

 ,,   31   WALTER NEALE, of Warneford, co Southampton

 ,,   ,,   CHRISTOPHER GRIMSTON, of Grimston in Holderness, co York

Feb 7   NICHOLAS CAGE, citizen of London

 ,,   ,,   ROBERT BLUNDELL, son and heir of Robert Blundell, of Ince Blundell, co Lanc

 ,,   9   ROBERT BROOKE, son and heir of Robert Brooke, Alderman of London

 ,,   ,,   ARTHUR BLEWITT, son and heir of Richard Blewitt, of Holcombe Rogus,
                                                                    [Devon

 ,,   ,,   EDWARD LECHE, son and heir of Robert Leche, of City of Chester

 ,,   ,,   WALTER CHUTE, son and heir of George Chute, of Bradfield, Suffolk

Mar 6   JOHN BRIDGES, S T P , Dean of the Cathedral Church of St Mary, Salisbury

 ,,   ,,   FRANCIS SWANNE, of Wye, Kent

folio 250

 ,,   7   WALTER LONG, of Draycot, Wilts, Knight

 ,,   ,,   EDWARD REVE, of Hounslow, Middlesex, gent

 ,,   8   WILLIAM PARKER, Lord Monteagle

 ,,   ,,   ANTHONY BENNET, gent

 ,,   10   JOHN WHITGIFT, Archbishop of Canterbury

 ,,   ,,   WILLIAM, Lord COMPTON

 ,,   ,,   HUGH ANDERTON, gent

 ,,   ,,   ROGER ANDERTON

 ,,   ,,   WILLIAM MACHELL

 ,,   ,,   RANDAL MANWARING

 ,,   ,,   JOHN BROOKE

 ,,   ,,   EDWARD LEGH

 ,,   ,,   CUTHBERT HALSALL

 ,,   ,,   EDWARD DAVY

 ,,   11. JOHN GREY, of Pirgo, Essex, Esq

 ,,   ,,   NICHOLAS TURWINE, Esq (written also "Turwyne")

folio 251

 ,,   15   HENRY ATSLOWE

1592-3		folio 251—(continued)
Mar	15	JOSEPH THWAITE, of Unerigge, Cumberland
,,	,,	THOMAS BOWER, of Byckerton, co Chester
,,	,,	GABRIEL ARCHER, of Mountnessing, Essex, gent.
Feb	6	THOMAS WYVELL, son of Marmaduke Wyvell, of Constable Burton, co York
,,	,,	RICHARD WILLIAMS, of Rhôdigio, co Anglesey.

1592.		folio 253
Aug	3	STEPHEN HALES, eldest son of Charles Hales, reader
,,	,,	ROBERT HONYWOOD, son of Robert Honywood, Esq , Member of this Society.
,,	,,	GILBERT GERARD, son of William Gerard, Esq

1592-3		folio 254
Jan	29	GEORGE BARDE, of North Kelsey, co Lincoln
,,	31.	JOHN PINCHBECK, of Foulsham, Norfolk
,,	,,	WILLIAM GOOCHE, of Bungay, Suffolk
Mar	7	RICHARD HIGGINS, of Burne, Sussex, late of Staple Inn
,,	8	NATHANIEL FARRER, of Halifax, co York, late of Staple Inn
,,	9	HENRY JENKINSON, of Sywell, co Northampton
,,	15	JOHN THROGMORTON, of Bungay, Suffolk

1593		folio 260
May	7	THOMAS BYCE (Bisse), son and heir of ——— Byce, of Dublin, Ireland, Esq
,,	,,	JOHN POWELL, of City of Shrewsbury, gent
,,	,,	JAMES ELLIS, of Kingston-upon-Hull, co York
,,	,,	ROBERT MARSHALL, of Bickerton (Pickering), co York, Esq
,,	,,	WILLIAM WANDESFORD, of Kirklington, co York, gent
,,	14	FRANCIS DAVISON, of ———, co ———, gent
,,	,,	JAMES ANDERTON, of Clayton, co Lanc
,,	16	JOHN FLEMING, son and heir of William Fleming, of Conyston, co Lanc , Esq
,,	21	EDWARD POYNTZ, of Torkington, co Gloucester, Esq

1593-4		
Jan	28	ROBERT HILL (written also " Hall"), of Staple Inn, gent
,,	,,	THOMAS CRIMES, of London, gent
,,	,,	JOHN JERMY, one of the sons of Francis Jermy, of Brightwell, Suffolk, Esq
,,	,,	THOMAS MILDMAY, son and heir of Thomas Mildmay, of Springfield, co Essex
,,	,,	MICHAEL STANHOPE, second son of Edward Stanhope, Esq., one of the readers

		folio 261.
,,	31	JOHN MORRYS, of Munster, Ireland (erased) [Lincoln, Esq (erased)
Feb	11	THOMAS HARRINGTON, son and heir of Francis Harrington, of Witham, co
,,	,,	THOMAS FITZHUGH, gent , late of Staple Inn (Gesta Grayorum, p 8)
,,	,,	THOMAS MIDDLETON, son of John Middleton, of Carlisle, Cumberland, Esq
,,	,,	WILLIAM BRADLEY, gent , late of Barnard's Inn
,,	20	RICHARD FLETCHER, Bishop of Worcester, Almoner to ye Queen
,,	,,	THOMAS NEVELL, Dean of Peterborough

¹593-4   **folio 261**—(*continued*)

Feb 20   ED IREBYE (Irby), Esq

,,   ,,   BARNE ROBERTS, son of Francis Roberts, Esq, of ————

,,   ,,   NICHOLAS GRIFFITH, of Barnard's Inn

,,   ,,   EDWARD LESTRIDGE, son of George Lestridge, of Iver, Bucks, gent

,,   ,,   THOMAS MYDDELTON, of Weston (?), gent

,,   ,,   ARTHUR BLUETT, Doctor of Civil Law

,,   ,,   HUMPHREY TYNDALL, S T D, Dean of Ely

,,   ,,   HUMPHREY MICHELL, gent

,,   ,,   ———— VINCENT, gent

,,   ,,   GEORGE ALINGTON, Esq

,,   ,,   RICHARD MORISON, gent

folio 262

,,   23   JOHN NIGHTINGALE, gent   [Essex, gent. (erased)

,,   ,,   JOSEPH GODFREY (*alias* Cowper), son of William Godfrey, Esq, of Thackstead,

1594
April 22   THOMAS HARDRES, of Upper Hardres, Kent

,,   ,,   JOHN GIBSON, of York

1593   **folio 267.**

May 9   THOMAS SHEE, gent, an Irishman, from Staple Inn.

,,   ,,   SAMUEL MARTIN, of Bildeston, Suffolk, late of Staple Inn

,,   14.   ROBERT BENDYSHE, of Girton, Kent

1593-4.
Jan 24   JOHN BAKER, of St Edmundsbury, Suffolk, and of Barnard's Inn

,,   ,,   NICHOLAS NOTTE, of Maidstone, Kent

,,   28   WILLIAM LLOYD, of Toowey, Brecon, gent

,,   ,,   STEPHEN PRICE, of Pilleth, co Radnor, gent

,,   29   THOMAS BOWNESSE, of Little Hormead, Herts, gent

,,   31   JOHN MORRES, of Munster, Ireland

Feb 6   WILLIAM DUNCOMBE, of Ivinghoe, Bucks.

folio 268

,,   11   THOMAS HARRINGTON, son of Francis Harrington, of South Witham, co

,,   ,,   RICHARD GRIFFITH, gent, late of Staple Inn   [Lincoln, Esq

,,   ,,   WILLIAM CHESTER, son of ———— Chester, gent

,,   ,,   JOHN SPURLYNGE, son and heir of John Spurlynge

1594
April 22.   THOMAS CARUS, son of Christopher Carus, of Halton, co. Lanc, Esq

,,   ,,   WILLIAM CAPS, son of James Caps, of Ives, co. Somerset, Esq

,,   ,,   MORGAN JONES, of Barnard's Inn

,,   ,,   THOMAS HARDRESS, of Upper Hardress, Kent (erased)

,,   ,,   CHEYNE HARDRESS ("Hales" in MS), of Upper Hardress, Kent (erased)

,,   ,,   JOHN GIBSON, son of John Gibson, of York (erased)

,,   ,,   THOMAS JENKINSON, of Tunstall, Norfolk, gent

,,   ,,   WILLIAM VAUGHAN, of Staple Inn

,,   ,,   HENRY NIGHTINGALE, son of Geoffrey Nightingale, reader of this Inn

1594   folio 269.

April 22   EDWARD BURNELL, of Southwell, Notts

folio 271.

,,   25   JOHN DUDLEY, son of Edmund Dudley, Esq , of Yenwith, Westmoreland
,,   ,,   FRANCIS GREGORY, son of John Gregory, of Hordley, Oxon, gent
,,   ,,   GEORGE DETHICK, son of William Dethick, Principal King of Arms
,,   ,,   PHILIP JONES, of Staple Inn, gent

folio 276.

,,   23   ANTONY DRURY, son and heir of Antony Drury, of Besthorpe, Norfolk, Esq
,,   ,,   TOBIAS TONSTALL, son of Ralph Tonstall, of Croftbridge, Yorks, gent
May   10   JOHN LEEKE, son and heir of Jasper Leeke, of Edmonton, Middlesex.
,,   ,,   JOHN ATHERTON, son and heir of John Atherton, of ———, co Lanc , Esq
,,   ,,   ROGER BRADSHAW, of Wigan, co Lanc , gent
,,   ,,   WILLIAM FITZWILLIAMS, son and heir of William Fitzwilliams, of Milton,
                                            co. Northampton, Esq (erased)
June   5   ROBERT DARRELL, son and heir of John Darrell, of Little Chart, Kent, Esq
,,   ,,   WILLIAM BURNELL, son of William Burnell, of Southwell, Notts, Esq.

folio 276-7.

,,   ,,   JOHN HARDINGE, son of Edmund Hardinge, of Apsley Guise, Beds, gent.

folio 277.

,,   ,,   WILLIAM DANIEL, of Kilnwick, co York, late of Staple Inn
,,   ,,   THOMAS FLEMING, of Rydal, Westmoreland, gent
,,   12   HENRY PAKENHAM, of Tootingbecke, Surrey
,,   17   WILLIAM MORGAN, of Warminster, co Somerset, gent
,,   ,,   EDWARD FLEETWOOD, second son of William Fleetwood, Serjeant-at-Law.
,,   18   MAXIMILIAN DALISON, son of William Dalison.

folio 283.

,,   5   THOMAS PHILIPPS, of Leominster, Hereford, and of Barnard's Inn
,,   17   HENRY HELME, gent , of Rougham (Ruffy), Norfolk (Master of the Revels,
,,   ,,   THOMAS HOPE, of Ireland, and of Staple Inn, gent   {Prince of Purpoole)

folio 292

Aug   8   WILLIAM MOUNSON, of co Linc , Esq , second son of John Mounson, Knight
,,   15   MARK ANTONY GURGES, of Bordeaux
,,   ,,   CHARLES YELVERTON, of Rougham, Norfolk, Esq.
,,   ,,   JAMES BUTLER, of Mountgarret, Ireland, gent
,,   17   THOMAS HILSDEN, of Chalgrave, Beds, gent
,,   ,,   JOHN BOLDE, of Salisbury, gent

folio 293.

,,   ,,   RICHARD BOLDE, of Cranshowe, in Farnworth, co Lanc , gent
,,   ,,   WILLIAM BIRNAND (Byrnand), of Knaresborough, gent

1594.		folio 293—*(continued)*.
Aug	17	ROBERT DE LA FELDE of Paynston, Ireland, late of Staple Inn [Essex, gent
Oct	16	EDWARD GLASCOCK, son and heir of Edward Glascock, of Castle Hedingham,
,,	,,	STEPHEN MONYNS, of City of Canterbury gent
,	,,	ROBERT BARNEWALL, of Gretton, co Northampton, gent
,,	,,	ISAAC WODER, of Luxenam, Suffolk, gent
,,	,,	WILLIAM ROBINSON, of Bangor, co Carnarvon, gent
,,	,,	EDWARD PRICE of Peyver, co Montgomery, gent
,,	23	WALTER DEVEREUX, of Parham Suffolk, Esq
,,	,,	FRANCIS BRACKENBURY, of Sellaby, co Durham, gent

folio 294.

	29	LITTON POULTER, of Cottered, Herts
Nov	1	ROBERT WROTHE, son and heir apparent of Robert Wrothe, Esq
,,	,,	HARBOTTLE GRIMSTON, son and heir apparent of Edward Grimston, Esq
,,	,,	WILLIAM CAVE. of Waterstock, Oxon [Esq
,,	,,	HUGH MAINWARING, son of Henry Mainwaring, of Caringham, co Chester,
,,	,,	WILLIAM COPLEY, of Sprotborough, co York
,,	,,	EDWARD SNELLINGE, of East Horsley, gent
,,	4	THOMAS RANDOLPH, of St Peter's Hill, London
,,	8	FRANCIS BARNHAM, son and heir of Martin Barnham, of Hollingbourne, Kent
,,	,,	WILLIAM GROSVENOR, of Bellaport, Salop, gent
,,	,,	WILLIAM COBBS, son of Thomas Cobbs, of Chilham (erased)
,,	12	ADAM ECCLESTON, of Eccleston, co Lanc , Esq
,.	13	JOHN MARSTON, of Preston, co York, and of Staple Inn ("Marsbury" in ledger)
,,	18.	JOHN ELKYN, of London, gent (Gesta Grayorum, p 6).
,,	25	ALEXANDER COLEPEPER, of Wigsell, co Sussex, gent , late of Staple Inn
,,	,	THOMAS HAWKYNS of Boughton-under-Blean, Oxon, son and heir apparent of [Thomas Hawkyns, of same
,,	,.	HENRY STAPLETON, of Wighill, co York son and heir apparent of Robert [Stapleton, Knight

1594 5		folio 295
Feb	2	EDWARD DEVEREUX, of Castle Bromwich, co Warwick
,,	,,	FRANCIS DETHICK, of Newhall, co Derby
,,	,,	WILLIAM POPE. of Wroxton, Oxon
,,	,,	FRANCIS EAST, of ———, co Cambridge (erased)
,,	4	VINCENT RANDALL, of Albury, Surrey, Esq
,,	,,	GEORGE SMYTHE, second son of George Smythe, the son of Francis Smythe, of Wootton Wawen co Warwick, Esq [Clovell. Esq.
,,	,,	PERCIVAL CLOVELL, of Westhanningfield, Essex son and heir of Eustace
,,	11	GABRIEL LOWE, son and heir apparent of Thomas Lowe, Citizen and Alderman of London [same, gent
,,	,,	THOMAS WILSON, of Willey, Herts, son and heir of ——— Wilson, of
,,	,,	ANTHONY BESSON, of the City of York, gent , one of the Attorneys to the
,	:	WILLIAM EURE, son and heir apparent of Ralph, Lord Eure [Star Chamber

1594		**folio 296.**
Aug	17	THOMAS PUREFOY, son and heir of Humphrey Purefoy, one of the readers of
Oct	16.	EDWARD HERNE, gent., late of Staple Inn ⟩[this Inn
„	23	THOMAS KIRWAN, an Irishman
„	„	JOHN CONWAY, of Borthvatham, co Flint, gent
„	29.	LITTON POULTER, of Cottered, Herts (erased)

folio 297.

Nov	4	ROBERT NUGENT, of Staple Inn, gent. [co Lincoln, Esq
„	„	EDWARD TYRWHIT, son and heir apparent of Philip Tyrwhit, of Stanfield,
„	8	WILLIAM COBBS, son of Thomas Cobbs, of Chilham, Kent, gent.
„	14.	JOHN CRESWELL, of Huggate-on-the-Wold, co York, gent [Esq
„	25	HENRY CLARKE, son and heir of Thomas Clarke, of Arlington, co Southampton,
„	26.	RALPH ELLYS, of Spinkhall, co York, gent
Dec	25	JOHN COOKE, of Westminster
„	„	EDWARD COOKE, of Westminster
„	„	PHILIP WENTWORTH, of Cotton, Suffolk,
„	„	ANTHONY FLETCHER, of Cockermouth, Cumberland,
„	„	THOMAS THOMKINS, of city of London,
„	„	JOHN LILLIE, of city of London,
„	„	THOMAS SMITH, of Framlingham, Suffolk,

admitted by Henry, Prince of Purpoole See his admission, 17 June, 1594, page 85

1594-5		**folio 298.**
Jan	6	JOHN SPENCER, Mayor of London,
„	27	FRANCIS ELRINGTON, of Theydon Bois, Essex
„	„	WILLIAM ELRINGTON, of Theydon Bois, Essex
Feb	4	THOMAS HAWLE, of Staple Inn, son of Henry Hawle, of Costocke, Notts, gent
„	„	LUKE BRADEY, of Isleworth, Middlesex, gent [Esq, late of Barnard's Inn
„	6	CHRISTOPHER HERBERT, second son of Christopher Herbert, of City of York,
„	„	THOMAS SMELTE, son and heir of Robert Smelte, of Richmond, co York
„	11	ARTHUR GOODAY, of Pentlow, Essex
„	„	JOHN HARRISON, of Hindley, co Lanc
„	„	CLEMENT HOO, of Northwold, Norfolk

folio 302.

Mar	13	EDMUND, Lord SHEFFIELD
„	„	JAMES SCUDAMORE, arm
„	„	THOMAS HENEAGE, gent
„	„	THOMAS BULBECKE, gent

1595		**folio 305.**
May	8.	JOHN BOLDES, of South Bercombe, Wilts, gent [gent, of ——— Inn.
„	„	RALPH EWYNS, eldest son of George Ewyns, of South Cawton, co York,
„	„	FRANCIS QUARLES, of Ufford, co Northampton, gent
„	„	THOMAS TASKER, son of Roger Tasker, of London, goldsmith

1595   folio 305—(*continued*)

May	8	THOMAS CHICHELEY, of Wimpole, co Cambridge, gent
,,	,,	CLEMENT PAKENHAM, of Streatham, Surrey, gent [Esq
,,	14	ISAAC APPLETON, son of Thomas Appleton, of Waldingfield Parva, Suffolk,
,,	,,	JOHN HOLT, of Stubley, co Lancaster, Esq
,,	,,	BALDWIN Sr GEORGE, of Hungrie Hatley, co Cambridge.
,,	21	THOMAS MARBURY, son of John Marbury, of ————, co Bedford, arm
,,	30	FRANCIS SPELMAN, of Northborrow, Norfolk, Esq
,,	,,	WILLIAM MASON, of Mongham, Kent, and of Staple Inn
,,	,,	JOHN SKINNER, of Rowington, Warwickshire, gent

folio 306   [Leicester, Esq

June	27	HENRY HASTINGS, son and heir apparent of Walter Hastings, of Kirkby, co
July	1	ROBERT CHAPMAN, of London, gent
,	7	JAMES CULPEPER, of Plumpton, co Northampton, gent
,,	,,	ROBERT ROLFE, of Hadley, Suffolk, gent
,,	8	ANTHONY FOREST, of Morborne, Hunts, gent [Esq
,,	,,	ROBERT TYRINGHAM, of Weston, co Northampton, son of Francis Tynngham,

folio 309.

May	21	GEORGE PRESTON, of Holker, co Lanc, gent
,,	30	LEWIS BOWLES, of Wallington, Herts, gent, formerly of Barnard's Inn
,,	,,	EDWARD MASTER, gent, son of James Master, of East Langland, Kent, gent
,,	,,	HUGH WYRRALL, of Whalley, co York, gent
,,	,,	HENRY HALL, of Wimborne Minster, co Dorset, gent

folio 323.

Aug	8	GEORGE WHARTON, gent, son and heir of Philip, Lord Wharton
,,	15	ROBERT PEPPER, son and heir of Cuthbert Pepper, now reader
Oct	22	EDWARD BERE, son of Nicholas Bere, of Dartford, Kent, Esq
,,	,,	RALPH COWPER, of Slinfold, Sussex, gent
,,	,,	JOHN BRADLEY, son of Thomas Bradley, of Louth, co Lincoln, gent
,,	,,	RICHARD SEDGRAVE, of city of Dublin, gent
,,	,,	JAMES SEDGRAVE, of Kelleglem, co Meath, gent
,,	,,	RICHARD BUTLER, of Mountgarrett, co. Wexford, Ireland, gent
,,	,,	WALTER ARCHER, of Kilkenny, Ireland, gent
,,	,,	MAURICE HURLEY, of Cork, co Cork, gent
,,	,,	THOMAS BOWES, son of George Bowes, of Streatlam, co Durham, Knight
,,	,,	JOHN BOWES, brother of said Thomas Bowes

folio 324.

Nov.	7	WILLIAM SELYOCKE, of " Le Hallowes," co Derby, gent
Oct	29.	WOLSTONE DIXIE, of Catworth, Hunts.
,,	22.	JOHN GYLL, son and heir apparent of Francis Gyll, of Tempsford, Beds, Esq
,,	29	THOMAS LEVETT, of Salehurst, Sussex, gent.
Nov	7	WILLIAM SKEFFINGTON, son and heir apparent of ——— Skeffington, Esq.

1595		**folio 324**—(*continued*)
Nov	7	VALENTINE HARTOPP, of Burton Lazars, co Leicester
,,	11	RICHARD MOORE, son of William Moore, Esq , of Banckhouse, co Lancaster
,,	20	JOHN THOROLD, of Morton, co. Lincoln, son and heir apparent of Richard
,,	,,	NICHOLAS WOODTHORPE, of Abye, co Lincoln, gent [Thorold, gent

1595 6		
Jan	28	THOMAS WILLIAMS, of Haddenham, co. Cambridge, gent
Feb	2	WENCESLAUS LESCINIUS, Baron in Lessno and Golveson, Poland
,,	,,	EDWARD ST BARBE, son and heir of Edward St Barbe, of Whiteparish, Wilts, Esq. [co. Lancaster, gent
,,	,,	EDWARD OSBALDESTON, son and heir of Geoffrey Osbaldeston, of Whalley,
,,	,,	RICHARD JONES, of Monmouth
,,	,,	WILLIAM GIRLING, of Haverham (Havertone), Suffolk, gent
,,	,,	HENRY LEPTON, of Witton, co Somerset, gent

1594 5		**folio 325.**
Feb.	4.	EDWARD FOX, son of Charles Fox, of Ludlow, Salop, Esq , deceased
,,	,,	JAMES HUISHE, son of James Huishe, Citizen of London, deceased
,,	,,	SAMUEL CULVERWELL, S T P , of Cherryburton, co York
,,	9	HENRY MILDMAY, son of Thomas Mildmay, Knight
,,	,,	NICHOLAS BLACKLEECH, of city of Gloucester, gent
,,	,,	ANTHONY MARKHAM, of Sedgebrooke, co Lincoln, gent
,,	11	THOMAS MOLYNEUX, of Darbie, co Lancaster, gent late of Barnard's Inn
,,	,,	REGINALD SOTHERNE, of Fitz, Salop, gent , and now of Clifford's Inn
,,	,,	JOHN DANIEL, of Barnard's Inn, late of Kilnwick, co York

1595		**folio 327**
Oct	22	WILLIAM FISHE, son and heir of William Fishe, of Southoe, Beds, gent
,,	,,	ALEXANDER WYCLIFF, of Stanesbie, co York, gent
Nov	7	CHRISTOPHER HARRYSON, of city of Durham, gent (erased in original) (Mr Christopher Harrison is expelled the house, Mar 9, 1609, for an outrage committed on Mr Steward in his chambers)
,,	13	HENRY GETHIN, of Bottvarre, co Flints
,,	20	THOMAS GOODWIN, of Stoneham Parva, Suffolk, and of Barnard's Inn
,,	,,	JOHN PHILPOTT, of Faversham, Kent, gent , late of Staple Inn

1595 6		
Feb	4	EDWARD WIGHTMAN, of Staple Inn, gent [Society, Feb 6, 1599)
,,	9	ARTHUR LINDLEY, son of John Lindley, of Leathley, co York (put out of the
,,	,,	THOMAS DOWNES
,,	,,	PETER BECONSALL (Beckeonsoll), of London, gent
,,	11	ROBERT BULWER, of Bungay, Suffolk, gent **folio 328.**

		folio 336. [Moravus
Mar	4	"JOHANNES DIONYSIUS," Baron Zerotinus, Namesii et Bronduzii, Dominus [Elizabeth
,,	9	RICHARD BRAKENBURIE, Esq , one of the Gentlemen Ushers of the Queen

1595-6		folio 336—(continued)
Mar	12	JOHN SHEPPARD, of Mendlesham, Suffolk, gent, now of Staple Inn
,,	,,	HENRY PIERCE, gent, now of Barnard's Inn
,,	,,	JAMES TYRRELL, of Suffolk, gent.
,,	,,	THOMAS BRATHWAITE, of co. Lancaster, gent
1596		
May	3	ROBERT HARDIE, son of Robert Hardie, of Manchester, co Lancaster, gent
,,	7	THOMAS SHIRLEY, son and heir of Anthony Shirley, of Preston, Sussex, Esq
,,	12.	JAMES TURVILLE, son of Henry Turville, of Aston Flamville, co Leicester, Esq
,,	18.	EDMUND MILES, of Staple Inn, gent

		folio 337 [Esq
,,	,,	THOMAS LENNARD, son of Sampson Lennard, of Knowle-in-Sevenoaks, Kent,
,,	,,	WILLIAM FRANKLAND, of Pickhouse, co York, gent, late of Barnard's Inn.
June	14	EDWARD TAAFFE, of Cockeston, co Louth, Ireland, gent
,,	,,	JOHN HERBERT, of Poole Castle, co Montgomery [of London
,,	15.	ROBERT CLARKE, son and heir apparent of Roger Clarke, citizen and salter
,,	21.	ROBERT BARNEWALL, son of Alexander Barnewall, of Roberston, co Meath.
,,	,,	WILLIAM DUNCH, son and heir of Edmund Dunch, of Witnam, Berks, Esq
,,	28	CHRISTOPHER MARTIN, of Barton, co Cambridge.

1595-6		folio 342
Mar	12	THOMAS HESKETH, younger son of Cuthbert Hesketh, of Goosenarghe, co
,,	,,	CHRISTOPHER BANASTER, of Barnard's Inn [Lancaster, gent.
,,	,,	ROBERT VERNON, of Barnard's Inn, son and heir of Henry Vernon, Esq, one
1596		[of the Grand Company of this Inn
May	5.	GRIFFIN JOHNES, of Staple Inn, gent
,,	7	ANDREW MARSHE, of Staple Inn, gent
,,	12	JOHN FERROUR, of Barnard's Inn, gent

		folio 343.
,,	17	BARTHOLOMEW BALL, of Staple Inn, gent
,,	18	THOMAS WALLER, of Coleshill, co Hereford, gent
,,	,,	EDWARD CREYKE, of Marton, co York, gent
June	11	EDWARD WARD, of Bixbie, Norfolk, gent
,,	21	ROBERT WRIGHT, of Barnard's Inn, gent
,,	25	THOMAS LOCK, of Barnard's Inn, gent

		folio 352.
Aug	13	THOMAS PROCTOR, of city of York, son of Henry Proctor, of same gent.
,,	,,	ROBERT CALLIS, son of Robert Callis, of Hale Magna, co Lincoln, of same,
		[gent
Oct	20	WILLIAM KILFIN, son and heir of John Kilpin, of Woulson, Bucks, gent
,,	,,	THOMAS STRANGE, of Chesterton, parish of Cirencester, co Gloucester, gent.
,,	,,	HENRY BUFKIN, son and heir of Leven Bufkin, of Otham, Kent, Esq
,,	,,	NATHANIEL CARMARDEN, of Chiselhurst, Kent

| 1596 | folio 353 | [of Lancaster |

1596

Oct 20   CHARLES BROGRAVE, third son of John Brograve, Attorney General of Duchy

,, 26   ROBERT GIFFORD, of Blackladies, co Stafford, gent   [Northampton, Knight

Nov 1   FERDINANDO KNIGHTLEY, fourth son of Richard Knightley, of Fawsley,

,, ,,   MORGAN COLMAN

,, ,,   PETER TORBOCK, of Mytton, co Chester, gent

,, ,,   RICHARD BUCKLEY, son and heir of Richard Buckley, Knight

,, ,,   CHAWORTH CONYE, son of Thomas Conye, of Bassingborne, co Lincoln

,, 3   THOMAS MYDLETON, of Leighton, co Lancaster

,, ,,   ROBERT CANSFIELD, of Roberthall, co Lancaster, gent

,, 4   JOHN FAGAN, of city of Dublin   [Wight

,, ,,   WILLIAM MEUX, son and heir apparent of John Meux, of Kingston, Isle of

,, 5   RICHARD MICHELBOURNE, son and heir apparent of Richard Michelbourne,
         [of Brodehurst, Sussex, Esq

,, ,,   ROBERT BAYLEY, of Barnard's Inn, and of Salisbury, Wilts, gent

,, 25   JOHN SAVAGE, of Frodsham, co Chester gent, son of John Savage, Esq, the
         [son and heir apparent of John Savage, Knight

,, ,,   NICHOLAS HURT, of Staple Inn, late of co Kent

| 1596-7 | folio 354 | |

Jan 26   THOMAS HALES, son and heir of Charles Hales, of City of Canterbury

,, ,,   WILLIAM EVERING, of Staple Inn

Feb 9   THOMAS FULLER, son and heir of William Fuller, of Coggeshall, Essex

,, ,,   AMBROSE WORTLEY, of Aldwark, co York, gent

,, 10   FRANCIS BURDET, of Burthwaite, co York, gent

,, ,,   WILLIAM AMBROSE, of Assheton, co Chester, gent

,, ,,   JOHN PALMER, of Barnard's Inn (born at Moulton, Norfolk)

,, 20   NICHOLAS THEOPHILUS, Ambassador from the King of Denmark   [of Carlisle

,, ,,   CHRISTOPHER PERKYNS, Esq, clerk of the Petition to the Queen, and Dean

,, ,,   MICHAEL RABBET (S T B)   [Canterbury

,, 22   JOHN PARKER, Esq, son and heir of Matthew Parker, late Archbishop of

,, ,,   WILLIAM BEESTON, of Lambeth, Surrey, Esq

,, ,,   WILLIAM HAMOND, gent

Mar 2   STEPHEN BRADWELL, of London, " medicus "

| 1596 | folio 358 | [Francis Brakin, reader |

Aug 7   JOHN BRAKIN, of Shelford Magna, co Camb, son and heir apparent of

,, ,,   ROBERT MORE, of city of York, gent   [request of Earl of Cumberland)

,, 18   DARCYE DAWNE, son of John Dawney, of Sesay, co York, Knight (at

,, ,,   WILLIAM BELL, son of Richard Bell, of city of York, gent (at request of Earl

1596-7   [of Cumberland)

Mar 1   THOMAS CROOKE, son of Thomas Crooke, S T D, and Minister of the Word
         [of God in this Society, sine fine, at the request of the said Father

,, ,,   MATHIAS BACON, of Holborn, London, sine fine

,, ,,   THOMAS GODMAN, of London, gent, sine fine

1596   folio 364
Oct. 20   APOLLO PEPYS, of Impington, co. Cambridge
  „ 26   SAMUEL SHORT, of Tenterden, Kent, gent
Nov 25.   JAMES DREW, of Densworth, near Chichester, Sussex, gent , and of Staple Inn
1596-7
Mar. 2   RICHARD LYE, of Staple Inn

1597   folio 375   [Hon Lord St John, of Bletshoe
April 20   OLIVER ST JOHN, of Bletshoe, Beds, Esq , son and heir apparent of the
  „ 22   WILLIAM ST ANDREWS, of Skeffington, co Leicester, gent.
  „ 24   RALPH BUFKYN, 2nd son of Levin Bufkyn, of Ottham, Kent, Esq
  „ „   THOMAS SHELLEY, son and heir of Henry Shelley, of Worminghurst, Sussex, Esq
  „ „   JOHN LAURANCE, of St Ives, Hunts, gent
  „ 25   ROBERT WELBY, of ——— co Linc (absque fine quod nepos et hæres est),
           grandson and heir of Laurence Meares, double reader of this Inn
  „ 27   ADAM SPRATLING, of St Lawrence, Isle of Thanet, Kent, gent
  „ „   EDMUND WOLFRESTON, late of Barnard's Inn (born at Culfo, Suffolk, gent)

                                 folio 376
Aug 6   THOMAS NEWMAN, son and heir of Thomas Newman, of St Katherine
           Creechurch, alias Christchurch, London, gent   [reader ?)
  „ 19   ALEXANDER CALFILD (Caulfield), son and heir of George Calfield, Esq (now
  „ „   FRANCIS DARLEY, of York, gent
  „ „   HENRY GRIMSTON, gent , son of Edward Grimston, Esq
  „ „   RICHARD HERBERT, of Parke, co Montgomery, gent

                                 folio 386
April 27   HENRY COLLINS, of Shepborne, Kent, gent
June 6   WILLIAM PLEASAUNCE, of Barnard's Inn, son and heir apparent of Thomas
           Pleasaunce, of this Inn, and of Brandonferry, Suffolk, gent
  „ „   MATTHEW LANCASTER, of Little Wratting, Suffolk, gent (Matthew Lancaster
           was one of his " mancupatores ")
  „ „   ERASMUS BRIGGE, of Lowestoffe, Suffolk, gent
  „ „   EDMUND WOLFRESTON, of Barnard's Inn (born at Culpho, Suffolk), (erased)
Aug 6   WILLIAM WISEMAN, of Upminster, Essex, late of Staple Inn, gent

                                 folio 398
Oct 21   HENRY VAUGHAN, of Sutton, co York, Esq   [Barley, co York
  „ 24   CHRISTOPHER TWISELTON, son and heir of George Twiselton, Esq , of
Nov 4   CHRISTOPHER CECILL, son of Thomas Cecill, Knight
  „ „   THOMAS CECILL, son of Thomas Cecill, Knight   [co Lanc , Esq.
  „ „   RICHARD ASSHETON, son and heir apparent of Thomas Asshetor, of Coston,
  „ 21   WILLIAM THREELE, son of John Threele, of Hurstpierpoint, Sussex, Esq

                                 folio 399
  „ 23   JOHN LANGFORD, of co Oxon ,gent
  „ „   THOMAS ELWES, of Leverton, Notts, late of Staple Inn, gent
1597-8   [Esq (Henry Fleetwood, of Gray's Inn, was his " mancupatore ")
Jan 30   ROBERT HESKETH, second son of Robert Hesketh, of Rufford, co Lanc ,

1597-8   folio 399—(continued)

Jan 30   WILLIAM WAILL, of London, gent   [co York, Esq
" "   EDWARD PLUMPION, son and heir apparent of William Plumpton, of Plumpton,
                                                                      [Speaker)
Feb 2   ROGER, Earl of RUTLAND (per Christopher Yelverton, Serjeant at-Law, and
" "   THOMAS, Lord HOWARD, Baron of Walden (per Christopher Yelverton)
" "   WILLIAM, Lord HOWARD, son and heir apparent of Earl of Nottingham (per
                                                          [Christopher Yelverton).
" "   OLIVER, Lord ST JOHN, of Bletshoe (per Christopher Yelverton)
" "   THOMAS BERKELEY, son and heir apparent of Henry, Lord Berkeley (per
                                                          [Christopher Yelverton)
" "   CHARLES HOWARD, second son of the Earl of Nottingham (per Christopher
                                                          [Yelverton)
" "   THOMAS DAVISON, third son of William Davison, of (London?), Esq (per
                                                          [Christopher Yelverton)
" "   W——— COTTON, of the Isle of Wight (per Christopher Yelverton, Serjeant-
                                                          [at-Law, and Speaker)
" "   JOHN KING, S T D (per Christopher Yelverton)

                                        folio 400

" 9   LIONEL GOODERICKE, of East Kirkby, co Lincoln, gent, son and heir apparent
                                                          [of Edward Goodericke, of the same, Esq
" "   WENDESLAUS BLACKWALL, of Dethick, co Derby, gent
" "   JOHN RICHARDSON, of the city of Durham, Esq
" "   RICHARD HALE, of the city of London, gent
" "   FRANCIS PLUMBE, of Fulham, Middlesex, gent
Mar 11   JOHN MORE, now one of the Sheriffs of the city of London
" 14.   EDWARD YORK, Knight
" "   SAMUEL BAGNOLL, Knight
" "   THOMAS GATES (Sir), Knight
" "   THOMAS CONWAY, Esq, of ye Gentlemen Ushers daily attending on ye Queen
" "   CAPTAIN EDWARD RUSSELL, Esq
" 17.   RICHARD, Lord BURKE ("Earl of Clanricarde" Segar)
" "   RICHARD BINGHAM, Knight
" "   FRANCIS BENDLOES, Esq
" "   HENRY, Lord HASTINGS, heir apparent of the Earl of Huntingdon

                                        folio 401

" 21   EDMUND CARY, Knight
" "   ROBERT LOVELL, Knight
" "   VALENTINE MOLINS, Knight
" "   GERATT FITZGERALD, one of the Gentlemen Pensioners of the Queen
" "   JOHN ASTLEY, one of the Gentlemen Pensioners of the Queen
" "   JAMES WINGFIELD, Esq, son and heir apparent of Edward Wingfield, Knight
" "   GEORGE DUTTON, Esq, one of the Serjeants-at-Arms to ye Queen.
" "   JAMES CASEY, son of William Casey, late Bishop of Limerick
" "   RANDLE BELLING, Esq, one of the Queen's shewers.

F

1597-8   folio 401– *(continued)*

Mar 21.   DUDLEY NORTON, Esq

,,   ,,   JOHN DYMMOCK, Esq

,,   ,,   ARTHUR HIDE, gent   [of Wards

,,   ,,   EDWARD MORREYS, Esq, son of James Morreys, late Attorney of the Court

,,   ,,   RALPH WILBRAHAM, gent, brother of the reader, and Solicitor general to the

,,   ,,   JOHN SPRING, of London, gent   [Queen in Ireland

,,   ,,   FRANCIS WROTTE, of Gunton, Suffolk

,,   ,,   THOMAS ROCHE, of Limerick, Ireland, gent

,,   ,,   JAMES BARNEWALL, of Brymore, co Dublin, gent

,,   ,,   THOMAS BATHE, of Athcarne, co Meath, gent.

,,   ,,   THOMAS PUREFOY, son and heir apparent of Humphrey Purefoy, one of the

,,   22   SIMON PARRYE, of Ruthin, co Denbigh, gent   [readers of this Inn (erased)

,,   ,,   WILLIAM FENWICK, gent, son and heir apparent of Richard Fenwick, of
                                 [Stanton, co. Northumberland, Esq (erased)

1597   folio 404.

Nov 21   MICHAEL GRAY, of Langton, co Chester, and of Staple Inn

,,   ,,   ROGER PALMER, gent, late of Staple Inn, second son of Thomas Palmer,
                                   [of Wingham, Kent, Esq

,,   ,,   JOHN PRITCHARD, of Abergavenny, co Monmouth, late of Staple Inn

1597-8   [this Inn

Jan 30   MANWOOD PENRUDDOCK, son of John Penruddock, Esq, double reader of

,,   ,,   EDWARD WRIGHTINGTON, son and heir apparent of John Wrigtington, of
                                   [Wrigtington, co Lancaster, Esq

Feb 9   ROBERT PLEASANCE, of Brandon Ferry, Suffolk, gent   [late of Staple Inn

,,   ,,   ANTHONY SAMMES, second son of John Sammes, of Hatfield Peverill, Essex,

                     folio 405.   [Esq

Mar 21   EDWARD ROBERTS, second son of Francis Roberts, of Willesden, Middlesex,

,,   22   WILLIAM FENWICK, gent, son and heir apparent of Richard Fenwick, of Stanton,
                                   [Northumberland, Esq

1598   folio 422.

May 8   THOMAS HARRYES, of Itchin, co Southampton

,,   ,,   ANTHONY NEWMAN, son and heir apparent of John Newman, of London, Esq

,,   ,,   RICHARD HARFORD, of Bosberne, co Hereford, gent   [Kent, Knight

,,   ,,   LEVYN PALMER, gent, son and heir apparent of Henry Palmer, of Bekesborne,

,,   ,,   THOMAS MAZON, of Egmanton, Notts   [Clothes (Clottes), Notts

,,   ,,   GILBERT ARMSTRONG, son and heir of Gabriel Armstrong, of Thorpe in-le-

,,   ,,   GEORGE LASCELLES, son and heir apparent of John Lascelles, of Elston, Notts

,,   ,,   JOHN WEN(H)AM, son and heir apparent of John Wenham, of Morehall,
                                   [Sussex, gent

,,   17   HENRY WILLOUGHBY, gent, son and heir apparent of John Willoughby, of

,,   ,,   HENRY ARDERNE, of Arderne, co Chester, gent   [Risley, co Derby, Esq

,   ,,   WILLIAM THATCHER, gent, son of James Thatcher, of Priesthawes, Sussex, Esq

,,   26   THOMAS BUTTER, of Rawcliffe, co Lancaster, gent, late of Barnard's Inn

1598   folio 422—(continued).

May 26   PHILIP GREY, of Morpeth, Northumberland, gent

„   „   SAMUEL WROTTE, of Bungay, Suffolk, late of Barnard's Inn

                              folio 423.   [Inn

„   „   RALPH WORMLAIGHTON, of Lutterworth, co Leicester, gent, late of Staple

„   „   WALTER EDULFE, of Adderbury, Oxon, gent   [Kent, gent

July 3   THOMAS BREWER, gent, son and heir apparent of Robert Brewer, of Boxley,

„   „   WILLIAM DUKE, of Cossington, Kent, gent

„   „   RICHARD GIPPS, of London, gent

„   „   ROBERT FILMER, late of Staple Inn, gent   [Esq

„   „   GEORGE MARKHAM, second son of Thomas Markham, of Kirby, co Leicester,

„   „   CUTHBERT BEST, of Barnard's Inn

Aug 8   ROBERT TIRWHITT, of Kettilby, co Lincoln, Esq

„   „   VALENTINE BROWNE, of Croft, co Lincoln, Esq   [deceased

„   „   ROBERT ELLIS, of Cambridge, gent, son and heir of Edward Ellis, Esq,

„   „   WILLIAM WATSON, late of Staple Inn, gent

„   „   MATTHEW JOPHSON ("Jopson" in ledger), late of Staple Inn

                              folio 430

May 8   THOMAS DISNEY, of Carleton-in-Moreland, co Lincoln, gent

„   „   WILLIAM SALTMARSHE, of Strubby, co Lincoln, gent

„   26   ——— SPRATLING, of Isle of Thanet

„   „   FRANCIS CRAWLEY, of Staple Inn   [co Northampton

Aug 16   JOHN LENTON, son and heir apparent of Symon Lenton, Esq, of Aldwinckle,

„   „   JOHN CRANE, of King's Lynn, Norfolk, gent

                              folio 443

Oct 23   JOHN STANHOPE, third son of Edward Stanhope, of Gray's (sic), Esq

„   „   FRANCIS EURE, of Heyford Warren, Oxon, Esq, second son of William,
                                                     [Lord Eure, deceased

„   „   CHARLES EURE, Esq, fourth son of said William, Lord Eure, deceased

„   „   DANIEL POYNES, of the city of London, gent

„   „   OSWALD MOSELEY, of Manchester, co Lancaster, gent

Nov 1   WILLIAM HANCOCK, of Carnefeld, co Lancaster, gent

„   „   ROBERT PURDEY, of Harestane, Norfolk

„   3   JOHN BEVERLEY, late of Barnard's Inn, gent

„   „   ROWLAND THORNBOROUGH, son and heir apparent of William Thornborough,
                                                     [of Hampsfield, co Lancaster, Esq

„   6   HERBERT PELHAM, son and heir apparent of Herbert Pelham, of Mychelham,
                                                     [Sussex, Esq

„   „   LAWRENCE PEARSE, son and heir apparent of Thomas Pearse, of Westfield,
                                                     [Sussex, Esq

                              folio 444

„   „   JOHN WELLES, of Horecrosse, co Stafford, son and heir apparent of
                                                     [Humphrey Welles, Esq, late of Staple Inn

„   15   WILLIAM BELL, of city of York, gent

                              Г 2

1598.		folio **444**—(*continued*)
Nov	15.	OLIVER CHENEY, of Warbleton, Sussex
,,	,,	RICHARD CHETWOOD, gent, son and heir apparent of Richard Chetwood, [Esq, now Sheriff of co. Northampton
,,	22.	HENRY GOODRICKE, son and heir apparent of Richard Goodricke, of [Ribston, co York, Esq
,,	,,	WILLIAM GOODRICKE, second son of said Richard Goodricke (out of the Inn because he struck with his fist a member of this Inn in the presence [of all the members in hall)
,,	,,	ROBERT REVE, late of Staple Inn
1598-9.		
Feb	2	WILLIAM JAMES, D D, and Dean of Durham. [York.
,,	,,	JOHN BENNET, Doctor of Civil Law and Judge of the Prerogative Court of
,,	,,	JOHN KITCHIN, son and heir apparent of John Kitchin, Esq
,,	,,	JOHN BAYLES, of Wilby, Suffolk
,,	,,	HENRY VERNON, second son of Henry Vernon, of this Inn
,,	5	CUTHBERT CLIFTON, of Westby, co Lancaster, Esq
,,	,,	ALEXANDER TOPPE, of Fisherton, Wilts, gent

folio 445.

,,	25	THOMAS BODLEY, of Chart next Sutton Valence, Kent, Esq.
,,	,,	THOMAS TALBOT, third son of John Talbot, of Salwarpe, co. Worcester, Esq.
,,	27	JOHN GIBSON, of London, Esq, Doctor of Laws, Judge of the Prerogative
,,	,,	THOMAS GOLDSMITH, of London, gent. [Court of Canterbury
Mar	1	THOMAS WALSINGHAM, of Chiselhurst, Kent, Knight [tume'
,,	,,	RICHARD CARMARDEN (surveyor of the Customs), "supervisor magne cus-
,,	,,	ROBERT WRIGHT, of Richmond, Surrey, Esq.
,,	,,	EDMUND STILE, of Beckenham, Kent, Esq
,,	,,	CLEMENT BERE, of Dartford, Kent, Esq [Esq
,,	,,	FRANCIS GOLDSMITH, son and heir of Francis Goldsmith, of Crayford, Kent,
,,	,,	RICHARD CHAMPENES, of Bexley, Kent, Esq

folio 446   [Customs, London

,,	4	RICHARD CARMARDEN, son and heir of Richard Carmarden, surveyor of the
,,	,,	NICHOLAS GOLDSMITH, of London, goldsmith
,,	,,	ROBERT ROGERS, son and heir of Francis Rogers, of Dartford, Esq
,,	7	JOHN GARRARD, citizen and Alderman of London
,,	,,	THOMAS LOWE, citizen and Alderman of London.
,,	,,	EDWARD HOLMDEN, citizen, Alderman, and Sheriff of London
,,	9.	RICHARD THEKESTON, of Thekeston, co. York.
,,	,,	WILLIAM ASHBY, gent.
,,	,,	JOHN COWPER, gent
,,	,,	RICHARD TAVERNER, gent
,,	,,	THOMAS LEIVET, gent
,,	,,	JOHN GRIMSDICH, gent

1598.	folio 449
Oct. 23	HUMPHREY HULL, of Windsor, Berks, gent
Nov 15	CHARLES WHIGHT ("Wright" in ledger), of Sturton, Notts, gent.
,, ,,	FRANCIS SYDNOR, gent., late of Staple Inn
,, 22.	WILLIAM DENNY, of Gislam, Suffolk, gent., late of Barnard's Inn
,, ,,	HENRY SANDERS, of Minster, Isle of Thanet, gent

1598-9

[would, co. York, gent

Jan. 31. RALPH DEYVILL ("Daniell" in ledger), son of Christopher Deyvill, of Cuck-

Feb. 8. THOMAS ASCOUGH, of the city of York, gent

1599.	folio 461.	[same, Esq
May 7	JOHN THOROLD, of Hough, co. Lincoln, gent, son of Edmund Thorold, of	
,, 11	HERBERT RANDOLPH, of Ticehurst, Sussex, gent	
,, ,,	EDWARD ESTON, of Tenterden, Kent, gent	[Durham
,, 15.	TOBIAS MATTHEW, gent., son and heir apparent of Tobias Matthew, Bishop of	
,, 18.	DENSE HARTERIDGE, of Mucking, Essex, gent	
June 20.	JOHN UPTON, of Feversham, Kent, gent	
,, ,,	JOHN BURKE, late steward of the Inn, for his good service, sine fine, &c	
,, 22	THOMAS JERVIS, son and heir of Edward Jervis, of Tenterden, Kent, gent	
,, ,,	EDMUND LAWSON, son of Rodolph Lawson, of Burgh, co York, Esq	

	folio 462	[gent
,, 26.	THOMAS WHITTINGHAM, son of Edward Whittingham, of Islington, Middx,	
,, 28.	HARDOLPH WASTNES, son and heir of Jervase Wastnes, of Headon, Notts, Esq	
July 14.	THOMAS JERVIS, of Chatkull, co Stafford, gent	
Aug 9	DANIEL DUNNE, Doctor of Laws	
,, ,,	WILLIAM BLACKWALL, of the city of London, gent	
,, ,,	GEOFFREY CLERKE, of the city of London, gent	
,, ,,	JOHN COOKE, of Milton, co Cambridge, late of Barnard's Inn	
,, ,,	MATTHEW PATTISON, gent	
,, ,,	THOMAS JONES, of Staple Inn, gent	
,, ,,	MARMADUKE DARRELL, of Fulmer, Bucks, Esq	

	folio 463	
,, 14.	THOMAS MAUNSELL, of Chicheley, Bucks, gent, late of Barnard's Inn [Esq	
,, ,,	WILLIAM PUREFOY, son and heir of Francis Purefoy, of Caldecot, co. Warw,	
,, ,,	PHILIP STANHOPE, gent, son and heir of John Stanhope, Esq.	
,, ,,	ROBERT TOWNESEND, younger son of Roger Townesend, Knight, deceased	
,, ,,	GEORGE STANHOPE, one of the sons of Edward Stanhope, Esq	
,, ,,	THOMAS HOLLYS, younger brother of John Hollys, Knight	

	folio 466	
May 7.	RICHARD HUNTER, of Isleworth, Middlesex, gent, late of Staple Inn	
,, 15	RICHARD (called "William" in ledger) WALKER, of the city of York, gent	
June 15	THOMAS GREENE, of Bobbing, Kent, gent	
,, 26	WILLIAM DYER, of Ipswich, gent	

1599   folio 477
Oct 17.   WILLIAM BABTHORPE, son and heir of Ralph Babthorpe, of Osgodbie, co York
  „   24 JOHN BARKER, son and heir of Rowland Barker, of Haughmond, Salop, Esq
  „   „   JOHN FOSTER, son and heir apparent of Augustine Foster, of Massington, co
  „   „   THOMAS CUTLER, of Ipswich, Suffolk, gent   [Northampton, gent
  „   „   PHILIP SHERARD, of co. Leicester, gent
  „   „   JOHN CONSTABLE, son and heir of John Constable, of Lasenby, co York, gent.
  „   „   JOHN BODE, of Catmonden, Essex, gent
Nov. 1   THOMAS HUTTON, second son of Matthew Hutton, Archbishop of York
  „   „   THOMAS SHAWE, of Barnard's Inn, gent
  „   2.   EDWARD DOWDALL, of Athboy, co Meath
  „   9   HERBERT PELHAM, Esq, son and heir of Edmund Pelham, Esq, and reader

                                        folio 478   [Royle, co Lancaster, Esq
  „   „   NICHOLAS TOWNELY, of Barnard's Inn, son and heir of Edward Townely, of
                                                           [ham, co Lincoln, Esq
  „   „   ROBERT THEKESTON, son and heir apparent of William Thekeston, of Nettle-
  „   14 GEORGE JERVISE, of Woodechurch, Kent, gent   [York
  „   „   ARTHUR DAKINS, son and heir apparent of Arthur Dakins, of Longworth, co
  „   26 HENRY GIBSON, of Beeston St Laurence, Norfolk, gent, and of Barnard's Inn
  „   „   GEORGE PALMES, son and heir apparent of John Palmes, of Naburn, co York
1599-1600
Jan 28   JAMES MAYNE, son of ——— Mayne, of Bovingdon, Herts
  „   „   ROBERT PIERREPOINT, son and heir apparent of Henry Pierrepoint, of Holme
                                                           [Pierrepoint, Notts
  „   „   TIMOTHY BRIGHT, gent, son of Dr Bright, of Barwick-in-Elmete, co York
  „   „   RICHARD GERRYE, gent, of Bushmead, Beds

                                        folio 479
Feb 2   ASCOUGH ("Thomas" in Calendar) BROMLEY, of Hampton, co Chester
  „   6   CHRISTOPHER MANN, of Staple Inn, and of the city of Canterbury, Kent, gent
  „   11   THOMAS PEYRS ("Piers" in ledger), late of Staple Inn, gent
  „   „   ROBERT ANDERSON, late of Staple Inn, gent
  „   „   RICHARD SKINNER, of Ledbury, co Hereford, gent
  „   „   JOHN ROTHERAM, of Semors, Bucks, Esq.   [Esq
  „   „   GREVILL VERNEY, son and heir of Richard Verney, of Compton, co Warwick,

1599   folio 480   [March 16, 1608)
Nov. 9   GEORGE TOOKE, of Staple Inn (out of the Inn, June 30, 6 James, restored,
1599-1600.
Feb 11   THOMAS GOTTES, late of Barnard's Inn.

                                        folio 491
  „   19 GEORGE WANDESFORD, of Kirklington (per J Cantuar)
  „   20 ROBERT BOOTH, of Stansted, Herts, Esq
  „   „   JOHN PARRY, of Ruthin, co Denbigh, gent
  „   „   HENRY BETTENHAM, of Pluckley, Kent, gent

1600		**folio 491**—(*continued*).
April	21	THOMAS SECKFORD, of Great Bealings, Suffolk, son of Charles Seckford, Esq
,,	,,	THOMAS CORNWALLIS, son of John Cornwallis, of Earlesham, Suffolk, Esq
,,	,,	WILLIAM DADE, son of Thomas Dade, of Tannington, Suffolk, gent
,,	,,	JOHN AUDLEY, of South Ockenden, Essex, son of John Audley
May	2	GEORGE COGGESHALL, of Fornham St Genevieve, Suffolk, gent
June	2	NICHOLAS PEPYS, of Burnham Westgate, Norfolk, gent
,,	,,	WILLIAM THOMAS, late of Staple Inn

folio 492

,,	9	ROBERT DEWHURST, of Cheshunt, Herts, gent
,,	,,	WHITTINGHAM WOOD, of Bromley, Kent, gent
,,	,,	BARNARD PARKER, of Alkincotes, co Lancaster, late of Barnard's Inn
Aug	2	EDWARD CRAYFORD, gent, late of Staple Inn
,,	3	OTHO NICHOLSON, Esq, one of the Examiners of the Court of Chancery
,,	4	MATTHEW GOAD, son of Roger Goad, S T D
,,	,,	RICHARD KING, son of Edward King, of Ashby, co Leicester, Esq
,,	,,	JAMES ALTHAM, son of Edward Altham, of Latton, Essex, Esq
,,	,,	WILLIAM ASKWITH, of Osgodby, co York, Esq
,,	,,	JAMES ALTHAM, son of James Altham, of Gray's Inn, Esq

folio 493

,,	5	LEONARD HALIDAY, Citizen and Alderman of London
,,	,,	WILLIAM CRAVEN, Citizen and Alderman of London
,,	,,	JOHN TAYLOR, of London, gent
,,	,,	OLIVER SKINNER, of West Ham, Essex, gent
,,	,,	HEWITT STAPER, of London, gent
,,	,,	OTWELL SMITH, of London, gent
,,	7	EDWARD HAWTEN, of London, Esq
,,	,,	CHARLES ADELMARE, *alias* CÆSAR, of London, Esq
,,	8	RALPH HAWTREY, of Rislipp, Middlesex, Esq
,,	10	RICHARD STAPER, of London, gent
,,	,,	ROBERT NAPPER, *alias* SANDYE, of London, gent
,,	,,	WALTER FLETCHER, of London, gent
,,	,,	NICHOLAS LEAT, of London, gent

folio 494

,,	,,	FERDINANDO CLUTTERBUCK, of London, gent
,,	,,	WILLIAM COKAYN, of London, gent
,,	,,	JOHN MORRIS, of London, gent
,,	,,	NICHOLAS FELTON, S T B
,,	12	FRANCIS DARCY, Knight
,,	,,	JOHN BARNES, Esq
,,	,,	FRANCIS ROBERTS, Esq
,,	,,	MARK RIDLEY, M D
,,	,,	THOMAS WEBB, of London, gent

1600.		**folio 494**—(*continued*)
Aug. 12		ROGER HAUGHTON, of the Strand, Middlesex, gent
,, 14		ALBERICUS GENTILIS, Doctor of Civil Law, Regius Professor at Oxford, son [of Matthew Gentilis, M D , by blood " Picenus "
,, ,,		ROBERT TAYLOR, of Muswell Hill, Middlesex, gent

folio 495.

,, ,,		GREGORY GARTH, S T B , and Chancellor of Lincoln Cathedral.
Oct 6		AMBROSE RANDOLFE, second son of Thomas Randolfe, late of the parish of St Peter's-on-the-Hill, London, Esq [Lincoln, gent.
,, ,,		ROBERT CONSTABLE, son and heir of Robert Constable, of Gainsborough, co.
,, ,,		JOHN PARKHURST, son and heir of James Parkhurst, of East Leanham, Kent
Nov 1		PHILIP COCKERAM, of Wigmore, co Hereford, son and heir of William
,, 7.		JOHN FOWLE, of Sandhurst, Kent, gent [Cockerham, of Hampstead
,, ,,		THOMAS SALKELD, son of Lancelot Salkeld, of Whitehall, Cumberland, Esq.
,, ,,		ROBERT WAW, son of Richard Waw, of Weedenbeck, co. Northampton, gent.
,, 25.		NICHOLAS WOOD, of Fulborne, co Cambridge, gent. [Esq., deceased.
,, ,,		GEORGE DARELL, gent , one of the sons of Edward Darell, of Bowley, Sussex,

folio 498. [co Lincoln, gent

April 2 ?		CHARLES WINGFIELD, son and heir apparent of Henry Wingfield, of Hanworth,
,, ,,		WILLIAM PRETYMAN, of Barton, Suffolk, gent , late of Barnard's Inn [gent.
,, ,,		GEORGE HARTOPP, son of William Hartopp, of Burton Lazars, co. Leicester,
,, ,,		EDMUND CHAPLIN, son and heir of Edmund Chaplin, of Linsey, Suffolk, Esq
,, 29		ROBERT LASSELLS, son and heir of Francis Lassells, of Northallerton, co. York, gent [moreland, Esq
May 2.		THOMAS BRATHWAIT, son and heir of Thomas Brathwait, of Burneside, West-
,, ,,		JOHN HALES, son of Charles Hales, of Newland, in the county of the city [of Coventry , one of the readers of this Inn

folio 499. [Queen's Bench.

Nov 21		ROBERT SHUTE, fourth son of Robert Shute, one of the Justices of the
,, ,,		JOHN WILD, of St Martin's, near the city of Canterbury, gent
June 9		RICHARD DAVER, of Great Ellingham, Norfolk, gent , and of Barnard's Inn
Aug 14		HENRY ELWES, son of Thomas Elwes, of London
Oct 16		FRANCIS WILLOUGHBY, second son of John Willoughby, of Risley, co Derby (out of Inn Jan 30, 6 James) [Lancaster, gent
,, 29		THOMAS BARECROFT, son and heir of Robert Barecroft, of Ightwell Park, co
,, ,,		SAMUEL MICHELL, of Windsor, Berks, gent [of same, Esq
Nov 21		WILLIAM DALYSON, of Gretewell, co Lincoln, gent , son of Thomas Dalyson,
,, ,,		EDWARD TOWERS, of Gainsborough, co Lincoln, gent , son and heir of William
,, ,,		THOMAS UNTON, of Drayton, Salop, gent [Towers, gent
1600-1		**folio 510.**
Jan 26		HENRY ALFORD, son and heir of John Alford, late of Fawley, Bucks, Esq
,, 28		MARTIN BARNHAM, of Hollingbourne, Kent, gent
		folio 511
Feb 2		BENJAMIN PUREFOY, of Drayton, co Leicester, gent

1600·1.	folio 511—(continued)
Feb. 2.	JOHN CLOPTON, of Livermere, Suffolk
„ „	WALTER ALLEN, of London, gent　　　　　　　　[terbury, Esq
„ 5.	JOHN FINCH, gent., son and heir apparent of Henry Finch, of the city of Can-
„ 10.	JOHN BYRON, son and heir of John Byron, of Clayton, co Lancaster, Esq
„ „	RALPH ASSHETON, son and heir of Ralph Assheton, of Lever, co Lanc , Esq
„ „	RATCLIFFE ASSHETON, second son of said Ralph Assheton.　　　[Knight
„ „	RICHARD SHERBURNE (Shireburne), son of Richard Sherburne, of co Lanc ,
·, ,	GILES PARKER, son of Nicholas Parker, of Horockford, co Lancaster, gent.
„ „	EDWARD CHUTE, late of Staple Inn, one of the sons of George Chute, Esq ,
Mar 5.	JOHN CARILL, of Warnham, Sussex, Knight　　　　　[of ———.
„ „	JOHN PARKER, of Willingdoe, Sussex, Esq.
„ 7	THOMAS HAWKINS, of Boughton-under-Blean, Esq
, 9.	THOMAS FLUDD, of Millgate, in parish of Bersted, Kent Knight

	folio 512
„ 10	THOMAS DARCY, son and heir of Hon Thomas Darcy, Baron of Chichester
„ „	THOMAS WALLER, of Groomsbridge, Sussex and Kent, Knight
„ „	RALPH HANSBY, of Bishop Burton, co York, Esq.
, „	THOMAS ROKEWOOD, of Fenton, Suffolk, Esq.　　　[Norfolk, Esq
„ „	JOHN WODEHOUSE, son and heir apparent of Francis Wodehouse, of Breccles,
, „	RICHARD VYNER, son and heir apparent of Richard Vyner, of St Lawrence, [Suffolk, Esq
„ 11	THOMAS FLEETWOOD, son of William Fleetwood, of Cranfield, Middlesex Esq
„ ,	JOHN BROWNE, of Furnival's Inn, Middlesex, gent
„	ROGER DOWNTON, of London, gent

1601.	folio 513　　　　[Northampton, Esq
May 22	RICHARD KNIGHTLEY, son of Thomas Knightley, of Preston Capes, co.
June 15	JOHN SEDGRAVE, son of Walter Sedgrave, of Dublin
„ „	ANTHONY GAMAGE, of Burford, Oxon gent
Aug 1	PATRICK DOWDALL, son and heir of Philip Dowdall, of Drogheda, Ireland.
„ „	JAMES PRICE, son of John Price, of Rhandir, co Cardigan.
„ „	CHRISTOPHER FLEMING, son and heir of William Fleming, of Ireland
, 2	JOHN SPENCER, S.T B　　　　　　　　　[Esq
„ 15.	WILLIAM MARKHAM, son of Thomas Markham, of Kirby Belers, co Leicester,
„ „	WILLIAM SINGLETON, son and heir apparent of William Singleton, of London, [Esq

1600·1.	folio 516
Jan 26.	FRANCIS WHITE, of Langley Burnell, Wilts, gent
„ 28.	EDWARD ALTHAM, son of Edward Altham, of Latton, Essex, Esq
Feb 5	THURSTON ANDERTON, of Clayton, co Lanc , gent , late of Barnard's Inn.
„ „	ANTHONY CATLIN, late of Barnard's Inn, gent
,	THOMAS DOLMAN, son of Robert Dolman, of Pocklington, co York, gent.

1600-1   folio 517.
Feb 15 WILLIAM FOGGE, of Staple Inn, gent
 ,,   28, PAUL FLEETWOOD, of Rossall, co Lancaster.
1601.   [Oxon, gent.
May   4 JOHN WHISTLER, son and heir apparent of Hugh Whistler, of Little Milton,
 ,,   22 MICHAEL PVNDER, of Barnard's Inn, gent   [Suffolk, gent
 ,,   ,, WILLIAM MASHAM, son and heir apparent of John Masham, of Bardwell Ash,
June 15 STEPHEN JACKSON, of Newcastle-on-Tyne, gent
 ,,   ,, WILLIAM HUDSON, gent.   [Dublin
 ,,   ,, ROWLAND ARCHBOLD, son and heir of Edward Archbold, of Portmarnock, co
 ,,   22 CHARLES VEYSEY, of Hintlesham, Suffolk, gent
 ,,   ,, JOHN GULSON, of Wymondham, co Leicester, gent
Aug   1 NICHOLAS HOWLAND, of Caistor, co Northampton, gent.
 ,,   ,, BARTHOLOMEW CHAWORTH, son of John Chaworth, of Epperstone, Notts, Esq

                             folio 526
Oct 26 ANTHONY HUTTON, son of William Hutton, of Penrith, Cumberland, Esq
 ,,   ,, FRANCIS TAVERNER, of Hoxton, Herts, gent
 ,,   ,, CHRISTOPHER VIRDEN, of Clanmore, co Louth (?), Ireland, gent
 ,,   ,, JAMES PLUNKETT, of Densoughthe, co Dublin, gent
 ,,   ,, DANIEL LEECH, son of John Leech, of Barking, Essex, gent
 ,,   ,, JOSEPH HOCKELION, of Woderton, Salop, gent
Nov   1 MATTHEW (HUTTON), Archbishop of York
 ,,   ,, HENRY (ROBINSON), Bishop of Carlisle
 ,,   ,, RICHARD MUSGRAVE, of Hartley, Westmoreland
 ,,   ,, JOHN PERCE, of Clifford's Inn, gent
 ,,   ,, PHILIP PERIENT, of Mountfichett, Herts, gent   [Esq
 ,,   6. WALTER BARKER, one of the sons of Rowland Barker, of Haughmond, Salop,

                             folio 527.
 ,,   ,, JONATHAN BOTELER, of Estrye, Kent, gent
 ,,   ,, SAMUEL HARTOPP, of Burton Lazars, co. Leicester, gent.
 ,,   ,, THOMAS READER, of London, gent   [readers of this Inn, absque fine.
 ,,   ,, NICHOLAS FULLER, son and heir apparent of Nicholas Fuller, Esq, one of the
 ,,   9   DREW DRURY, of Rolleston, Norfolk, gent.   [East Riding of York
 ,,   ,, HENRY ALURED, son and heir apparent of John Alured, Esq., of Charterhouse,
 ,,   23 THOMAS PARAMOUR, son of Henry Paramour, of Isle of Thanet, Kent, Esq
 ,,   28 WILLIAM ACCLOM, son and heir of John Acclom, of Moreby, co York, Esq
 ,,   ,, HENRY HAWKER, of Charlcock, co Kent, son and heir of Seilis (?) de
                                               [Hawker, of said County
 ,,   ,, WILLIAM DAVENPORT, son and heir apparent of William Davenport, of Brom-
1601-2   [hall, co Chester, Esq
Feb. 2 PERCIVAL HART, of Lullingston, Kent, Knight   [Middx, gent, deceased
 ,,   ,, JOHN STEPKYN, son and heir of John Stepkyn, late of St Mary, Whitechapel,
 ,,   ,, ROBERT HATTON, of Clynton, Cambridge, son and heir of John Hatton, of
                                               [Long Stanton

1601-2		**folio 527**—(*continued*)
Feb	2	LANCELOT SALKELD, son of Lancelot Salkeld, of Whitehaven, Cumb, Esq
,,	,,	JOHN THORNBOROUGH, Bishop of Limerick, and Dean of York (died, Bishop [of Bristol, about 1641)

folio 528

	11	HENRY ANDERSON, son and heir of Henry Anderson, of Newcastle, Esq
,,	,,	FRANCIS SAUNDERS, gent
,,	,,	GABRIEL DOWSE, gent
,,	,,	THOMAS ROWLAND, gent
,,	20.	DAVID FLOYD, of Llwydyard, Anglesey.
,,	,,	EDWARD SHUTE, of Ockington, Cambridge, gent.
Mar	5	FRANCIS LISLE, of Kingston, Surrey, gent
,,	,,	ROWLAND INGHAM (or Engham), of Gunston, Kent

1601		**folio 532**
Oct	26	ROGER SHERBORNE, of Ribbleton, co. Lancaster, gent
,,	,,	JAMES ARCHER, of Kilkenny, Ireland, gent. [York, Esq
Nov	9.	JOHN ALURED, second son of John Alured, of Charterhouse, East Riding of
,,	18	WILLIAM DEWHURST, son and heir apparent of John Dewhurst, of Dewhurst [Hall, co Lancaster, gent.

1601-2		**folio 533**
Feb	11.	HENRY DEWELL, gent [co. Lancaster, gent
,,	20	SAVAGE HAWARDEN (Howarden ?), son of John Hawarden, of Wydnes,
Mar	5.	ROBERT TOWNSON, of Westmoreland, gent.
,,	,,	WILLIAM POWELL, of London, son of ———— Powell, of London

1602		**folio 540** [co York, Knight
May	3	FERDINANDO FAIRFAX, son and heir apparent of Thomas Fairfax, of Denton,
,,	,,	JOHN CLAPHAM, late servant to Lord Burghley, Treasurer of England
,,	,,	GEORGE KNIGHTON, son of George Knighton, Esq, of Bayford, Herts
,,	,,	SIMON ARCHER, son and heir apparent of Andrew Archer, of Tamworth, co
,,	,,	THOMAS ARCHER, second son of said Andrew Archer [Warwick, Esq
,,	,,	THOMAS BRERETON, of Yearde, co Somerset, gent
,,	,,	NICHOLAS EVERSFIELD, of Uckfield, Sussex, gent
,,	14	JOHN CLARCKE, of Great Dunmow, Essex
,,	,,	WILLIAM CAVENDISH (after Earl of Devonshire), son and heir apparent of [William Cavendish, of Hardwick, co Derby, Esq
,,	,,	JAMES BARKER, son and heir apparent of Richard Barker, Esq, one of the [readers of this Inn, sine fine

folio 541

June	14	EDMUND BRAGGE, of London, gent
July	31	EDWARD AUNGIER, of Cambridge, gent, son of Richard Aungier, Esq, deceased
Aug	3	FRANCIS COPPINGER, of London, gent
,,	,,	THOMAS FITZGERALD, of London, Esq, brother to Gerald, Earl of Kildare
,,	,,	HENRY PLUCKNETT, of Bridgeforth, Dorset
,,	,,	PETER DE LA HYDE, of Belandy, co Meath, gent
,,	,,	WILLIAM BLAKENEY, of Reckinhoe, co Dublin, gent

1602.   folio 541—(*continued*)

Aug. 10   WILLIAM (HERBERT), Earl of Pembroke, Lord Herbert of Cardiff, Lord Parr
                     [and Rosse of Kendal, Baron Marmion and St Quintin

,,   ,,   WILLIAM BROWNE, of Snelston, co Derby, Knight

,,   ,,   WALTER PLUNKETT, of Louth, Ireland

,,   ,,   JOHN PECK, of London, gent

,,   ,,   BENJAMIN BOWYER, of Camberwell, Surrey, gent

,,   ,,   ISAAC BARROW, M D

,,   ,,   EDWARD FITZGERALD, of Ireland, gent

                          folio 542   [co Kildare

,,   13   MAURICE FITZGERALD, son and heir apparent of Thomas Fitzgerald, of Lacah,

,,   ,,   AMBROSE THELWALL, of Ruthin, co Denbigh, gent

Oct 30   JOHN HOWLAND, son of Giles Howland, of Streatham, Surrey, gent

,,   ,,   ROBERT STANLEY, of the city of York, gent

,,   ,,   LAWRENCE ASHBURNHAM, of Bromham, Sussex, gent

,,   ,,   JOHN ASHBURNHAM, of Bromham, Sussex, gent   [late reader of this Inn

,,   26   PETER PHESANT, of Barkworth, co Linc , gent , son and heir of Peter Phesant,

                          folio 543

,,   ,,   WILLIAM SERES, of Barking, Essex, gent

Nov. 5.   ABELL BUCKLEY, of Staple Inn, gent

,,   ,,   WALTER DOBLE, of Falmer, Sussex, gent.

,,   15   RICHARD LEWKYN, of Essex, gent   [co Derby, Esq

,,   22.   GILBERT KNIVETON, son and heir apparent of William Kniveton, of Mercaston,

,,   ,,   RICHARD ALFREY, of Catesfield, Sussex, gent

                          folio 544

,,   25   RALPH CANTRELL, of Bury St. Edmund's, Suffolk, gent

,,   ,,   THOMAS WHIPPLE, of Dickleborough, Norfolk, gent

Dec 1   THOMAS FITZWILLIAMS, of Merrion, co Dublin, Esq

1602-3

Feb 8   THOMAS ASTON, of Aston, co Chester, gent

,,   ,,   JUSTINIAN LEWIN, son and heir of William Lewin, D C L

,,   ,,   JOHN INGLEBY, of Hickin, Notts, son of John Ingleby of Rudby, co York, Esq

,,   ,,   ROBERT BETSON, of the city of Lincoln, gent

,,   ,,   FRANCIS TINDALL, son and heir of John Tindall, of Brotherton, co York, gent

                          folio 545

,,   ,,   EDMOND AVAN, of Lantwit, co. Glamorgan, Esq   [Chester, Esq

,,   11   GEORGE SPURSTOWE, son and heir of George Spurstowe, of Spurstowe, co

,,   ,,   THOMAS CHEYNE, son and heir of William Cheyne, of Kirby-over-Blows, co
                                                                    [York, Esq

Mar. 13.   HENRY LELLO, Esq , Ambassador to the Queen at Constantinople, Turkey

,,   ,,   RICHARD COLTHURST, gent , late Consul at Aleppo (in partibus de Morea in
                                        [Turcia pro mercatoribus Anglie)

,,   ,,   ROWLAND STAPER, gent , son of Richard Staper, senior, of London, gent

1602-3.	**folio 545**—(*continued*)
Mar. 13.	NICHOLAS STAPER, of London, gent
,, ,,	HUMPHREY ROBINSON, of London, gent
,, ,,	HENRY ROBINSON, of London, gent
,, ,,	GEORGE FITZGERALD, of Molenetaght, co Meath, gent
,, 15.	WILLIAM FERRAND, D C L

1602	**folio 546.**
May 3	JOHN OSBALDESTON, son of John Osbaldeston, of Osbaldeston, co Lanc , Esq
,, ,,	THOMAS STOKE, of London, gent
,, ,,	NATHANIEL BIRKHEAD, of Wakefield, co York, gent
,, 14.	JOHN PEPPER, son of Cuthbert Pepper, Esq , surveyor of liveries in the Court [of Wards and Liveries, and one of the readers of this Inn, sine fine
June 17	RICHARD THORPE, of Little Caulden-in-Holderness, co York
,, 23	GAWDY BOLTON, of Garboldisham, co Norfolk

	folio 547. [Bucks, gent
July 31	TIMOTHY EGERTON, son and heir apparent of Thomas Egerton, of Aldstock,
Aug 3	THOMAS EAST, of Swavesey, co Cambridge, gent
Nov 5	RALPH YAXLEY, of Yaxley, Suffolk, gent [Glamorgan, gent
,, ,,	DAVID JENKIN, son of Jenkin Richard, of the parish of Pendilion, co
,, ,,	THOMAS BARRINGTON, of Broad Oak, Essex, gent
,, ,,	HENRY BARRINGTON, of Broad Oak, Essex, gent
,, 11	FRANCIS STACY, gent
,, 21	EDWARD JONES, of Langwarne, co Hereford, gent , late of Staple Inn
,, 25	EDMUND BRERES son of Alexander Breres, of Preston-in-Amunderness, co [Lancaster, gent.

	folio 548. [co. Lincoln, Esq
,, ,,	STEPHEN JEFFREY, of Staple Inn, gent.
Dec 1	GEORGE MARBURY, son and heir of Edward Marbury, of Grimsby (Grisby ?),
,, ,,	WILLIAM MARBURY, second son of said Edward Marbury
1602-3	
Feb 4.	RANDAL EDDOWES, son of Roger Eddowes, of Pibrotune, co Flint, gent.
,, ,,	ANTHONY WILLIAMS, of St Gerry, co Glamorgan, gent.
,, ,,	ROBERT HOLME, son of Seth Holme, of Huntington, co York, gent.
,, ,,	FRANCIS BODENHAM, of Ryall, co Rutland, gent.
,, ,,	WILLIAM HALL, of Barnard's Inn, gent
,, ,,	THOMAS YOUNG, of Staple Inn, gent
,, 11	ROBERT BASSOCK, gent., late of Staple Inn

	folio 549
Mar 12	WILLIAM DRURY, son of Anthony Drury, senior, of Besthorpe, Norfolk, Esq.
,, ,,	JAMES GOODMAN, of Plompton, Northants, gent
,, 17	ROBERT TYRRELL, of Ashdon, Essex, gent
,, ,,	WILLIAM GERVE, of Bushmead, in parish of Eaton, Beds, gent.
,, ,,	JAMES ENYON, of St Mary's, Whitechapel, co Middlesex, gent , and late of
,, ,,	EDWARD JENKINSON, of Tunstall, Norfolk, gent [Barnard's Inn.

1603   **folio 556.**

May 16   WALTER RUMSEY, of Uske, co Monmouth, gent [Lord Treasurer of Scotland

„   22   GEORGE HOME, Knight (Earl of Dunbar), one of the King's Privy Council, and
                                                   [for Scotland.

„   „   JAMES ELPHINSTONE, Knight, one of the King's Privy Council, and Secretary

„   „   THOMAS ERSKINE, Knight (of Gogar Viscount Fenton, Segar), Captain of the
                                                   [King's Guard

„   „   JOHN, Lord ERSKINE, son and heir apparent of John, Earl of Marr

„   „   JOHN BOTHWELL, Lord Holyroodhouse, one of the Privy Council in Scotland

„   „   ROGER ASTON, Knight, one of the gentlemen of the King's Privy Chamber

„   „   DAVID FOULIS, Knight, one of the gentlemen of the King's Privy Chamber

„   „   JAMES HUDSON, Esq, one of the King's Servants   (Servientium)

„   „   GEORGE BLENCOW, one of the King's Servants   (Servientium)

„   „   WILLIAM HUTTON, Esq, of Penrith, Cumberland, one of the King's Servants
                                               (Servientium)

„   „   WILLIAM HUNTER, Esq, one of the King's Servants   (Servientium)

June 3   THOMAS WALKER, of London, gent.

                                       folio 557.

July 12   THOMAS GOLD, son of George Gold, of Cork, Ireland, Esq

1603-4

Jan 31   RALPH HAYMAN, son of Henry Hayman, of Sellinge, Kent, Esq

Feb 7   OWEN OGE McCALLAGHAN, son of Owen McCallaghan, of Carribegg, co Cork

„   „   PHILIP SPURLING, son and heir of John Spurling, Serjeant-at-Law, deceased

„   „   ISAAC ROMNEY, son of William Romney, Knight (in consideration that by
            his industry the greatest part of the house was saved from fire, sine fine)

„   „   THOMAS THEASDALE, of Abingdon, Berks, gent

1604   [Knight

May 7   WILLIAM WHITTINGHAM, son and heir apparent of Timothy Whittingham,

„   „   NICHOLAS CULVERWELL, son and heir apparent of Samuel Culverwell, Clerk

                                       folio 558.

„   „   THOMAS FOLJAMBE, of Walton, co Derby, Esq

„   „   THOMAS ALURED, son of John Alured, of Charterhouse, co York, Esq

„   „   WILLIAM DAVIES, of Epping, Essex, gent

„   „   THOMAS CHUTE, son of George Chute, of Brede, Sussex, Esq

„   18   JOHN KEMPE, son and heir of Thomas Kempe, Esq

„   „   CHRISTOPHER DARCY, son of Edward Darcy, of London, Knight

„   „   THOMAS GOODRICKE, gent, son and heir apparent of Daniel Goodricke, Esq,
                                             [of Ely, co Cambridge

„   „   THOMAS GIBSON, gent, son of John Gibson, of Welborne, co York, Knight

                                       folio 559.

„   „   ANTHONY PELL, gent., son and heir apparent of Richard Pell, of Demblesby
            (Demelbye), co Lincoln, Knight   [principall")

June 18   HENRY HAWTAINE, of Staple Inn ("on certificate of George Wingate,

1604		**folio 559**—*(continued)*
June 18		ANTHONY DUCKETT, Esq., son and heir apparent of Francis Duckett, of [Grayrigg, Westmoreland, Knight
,,	24	JOHN ROUSE, of Henham, Suffolk, being in the King's Custody, son and heir of Thomas Rouse, Knight (at the request of, and his Custody committed to, Sir Christopher Yelverton, a Judge of the Court of King's bench)
,,	26.	RICHARD MILLWARD, of Bentley Heath, co Warwick
,,	,,	THOMAS LUCAS, of Stratford-on-Avon, co. Warwick, gent
,,	,,	GEORGE WHARTON, son of Christopher Wharton, gent, of co Durham

folio 560.   [Dublin, gent

,,	,,	ROBERT BARNEWALL, son and heir of Christopher Barnewall, of Newton, co
Aug	1	ADAM NEWTON, Esq, "a studiis" (? tutor) to Henry, Prince of Wales
,,	,,	THOMAS FRANK, of Hatfield Broadoak, Essex, Esq
,,	,,	THOMAS BIRCHMORE, of St Albans, Herts, Esq
,,	,,	FRANCIS WYAT, son of George Wyat, of Boxley, Kent, Esq
,,	,,	NATHANIEL FINCH, son of Henry Finch, the reader, by whom he is admitted
,,	3	WILLIAM DAVISON, of Stepney (Stebenheath), Middlesex, Esq
,,	,,	WILLIAM DAVISON, son of said William Davison, of Stebenheath
,,	,,	RICHARD BERFORD, son of John Berford, of Kilrow, co Meath
,,	,,	ANTHONY CAGE, of Stow, co Cambridge
,,	,,	HENRY PALMER, Knight, Controller of the King's Fleet

folio 561.

,,	7	THOMAS SOMERSET, Esq., son of the Earl of Worcester, and Master of the
,,	8	RICHARD TALBOT, of Malahide, co Dublin, Esq [Queen's Horse
,,	,,	JOHN GLASIER, of Staple Inn, gent
Oct	24	WILLIAM BOWES, son and heir of Ralph Bowes, of Barnes, co Durham, gent.
,,	,,	GEORGE LAMPLUGH, of Cockermouth, Cumberland, son and heir of Edward [Lamplugh, Esq, deceased.
,,	,,	THOMAS BLECHENDEN, son and heir of John Blechenden, of Monckton, Isle of
,,	,,	GERARD AYLMER, of Dubberston, co Meath [Thanet, Esq
,,	,,	THEOPHILUS ASHTON, of Staple Inn
Nov	1	EDWARD, Lord MORLEY [parts
,,	,,	EDMUND, Lord SHEFFIELD, President of the King's Council in the Northern
,,	,,	JOHN ROUS, of Henham, Suffolk, Esq
,,	,,	PETER DANIEL, of Over Tabley, co Chester, Esq. [London
,,	,,	W BOWES, son and heir apparent of William Bowes, of St John's Street,
,,	,,	ROBERT CRESWELL, of Rochford, Essex, Esq
,,	,,	ROBERT ASKWITH, of York, gent [of this Inn
,,	6	HUMPHREY STEWARD, gent, son of John Steward, Esq, one of the Members
,,	,,	PETER WARBURTON, of Lodge, co Chester, gent, son and heir apparent of George Warburton, Esq [gent
,,	,,	THOMAS RUDDE, son of Thomas Rudde, of Higham Ferrers, co Northampton,

1604		**folio 562.**
Nov	16	WILLIAM WELBY, of Gedney, co Lincoln, gent.
,,	,,	JOHN HEBDEN, son of Goddard Hebden, of Burwashe, Sussex, gent.
,,	,,	THOMAS LEWIS, son and heir of Daniel Lewis, of Giornes, co Cardigan, gent
,,	,,	ROGER MARTIN, son of Richard Martin, of Long Melford, Suffolk, Esq.
,,	,,	JOHN SHERARD, son of William Sherard, of Lobthorpe, co Lincoln, Knight
,,	22	WILLIAM SHERARD, of Stapleford, co Leicester, gent.
1604-5		[Hothleigh, Sussex, Esq
Jan	28.	HERBERT LUNSFORD, son of John Lunsford, of Wiligh, in parish of East

folio 563

,,	,,	ANTHONY NEVILL, of Mattersey, Notts, Esq
,,	,,	JOHN ORRELL, son and heir of William Orrell, of Turton, co Lancaster, Esq
,,	,,	THOMAS BYNG, of Wrotham, Kent, gent
,,	,,	WILLIAM PORDAGE, son of ——— Pordage, of London, gent
Feb	2	ROBERT BERTIE, Knight Lord Willoughby
,,	,,	CHARLES CAREY, second son of Lord Hunsdon [Beds, Knight
,,	,,	THOMAS ROTHERAM, son and heir apparent of John Rotheram, of Luton,
,,	,,	JOHN POTTS, of Chalgrave, Beds, son and heir of Nicholas Potts, one of the
,,	,,	JOHN CURTIS, of Grimley St Mary's, Suffolk. [readers of this Society
,,	,,	W——— HALFORD, of Welham, co Leicester
,,	11	ROGER CHARNOCK, son of Robert Charnock, of Astley, co Lancaster, Esq
,,	16	ROBERT HEWITT, son and heir of William Hewitt, of Millbrook, Beds, Esq
,,	,,	GEORGE CAREW, Knight, Vice-Chamberlain to Ann, Queen of England
,,	21	DUDLEY CARLETON, gent.
,,	23	JOHN POVEY, gent

folio 564

,,	,,	WILLIAM SIDNEY, son and heir of Robert, Lord Sidney
,,	,,	JAMES STEWARD, Esq , son and heir of Lord Blantyre in Scotland
,,	,,	ROBERT MAWDE, of Helthwayte Hill, co York, son and heir of Anthony
,,	,,	WILLIAM DISNEY, of Carleton-in-Moreland, co Lincoln, gent [Mawde, Esq
,,	,,	JOHN HUNT, of Coldnewton, co Leicester, gent
,,	25	JOHN POVY, gent
,,	26.	JOHN OVERHALL, Dean of St Paul's, London
,,	,,	FRANCIS, Lord NORRIS
,,	,,	WILLIAM CECIL, Knight, son and heir of Lord CECIL, VISCOUNT CRANBORNE
,,	,,	THOMAS DUTTON, Knight
,,	,,	THOMAS TUNSTALL, Esq
,,	,,	WILLIAM GOMLETON, gent
,,	,,	THOMAS GARLOND, gent
,,	,,	WILLIAM HAPDON (Hapclon ?), Esq
,,	,,	JOHN FLOWER, gent
,,	,,	PETER FRANK, gent
,,	,,	GEORGE BONWICK, gent

1604-5.   folio 564—(*continued*)
Feb 26   EDWARD LATHAM, gent
  „   „   ANTHONY TUNSTALL, gent

folio 565

  „   „   ROBERT CAREY, of Alwington, Devon
  „   „   JOHN ADDINGTON, gent, of Alwington, Devon
  „   „   ROBERT KEMPE, son and heir of Robert Kempe, of Gissing, Sussex, Esq
  „   „   WINGFIELD HONINGE, gent   [Beds, Esq
  „   27   NICHOLAS PLOMER, son of William Plomer, of Hill, in parish of Warden,
  „   „   CHRISTOPHER CROSSE, of Wolpett, Suffolk, gent
  „   „   THOMAS ROCHE, of Essex, Esq   [Knight
  „   „   WILLIAM WITHIPOLL, son and heir of Edmund Withipoll, of Ipswich, Suffolk,
  „   „   FRANCIS WITHIPOLL, son of said Edmund Withipoll, Knight
1605   [deceased
April 23   ROBERT BOTELER, son and heir of Philip Boteler, of Woodhall, Herts, Knight,
  „   „   JOHN BOTELER, of Woodhall, Herts, gent
  „   „   THOMAS ELIOT, of Ballrest, in Ireland, gent
  „   „   GEORGE WIGFALL, of Long Ridgway, co Derby, gent
  „   „   JOHN BRADSHAW, of Bradshaw, co. Lancaster, gent

folio 566.   [gent

May 10.   WILLIAM CLOPTON, son and heir of William Clopton, of Groton, Suffolk,
  „   „   FRANCIS STEWARD, son of John Steward, late a Member of this Inn
  „   „   JOHN GORTON, of Staple Inn, gent.
  „   „   BARTHOLOMEW FROMONDE, of Cheam, Surrey, and of Barnard's Inn, gent
June 7   RICHARD SHUTTLEWORTH, of Gawthorpe, co Lancaster, gent, grandson
           (nepos) and heir of Richard Shuttleworth, Knight, Serjeant-at-Law to Queen
           Elizabeth ; late Chief Justice of Chester   [Conran, Alderman of Dublin
  „   12.   THOMAS CONRAN, of Wyanstoun, co Dublin, gent, son and heir of Philip
  „   „   JOHN MILL, of Trotton, Sussex, gent, son and heir of Lewknor Mill, Esq
  „   „   WILLIAM JOHNSON, son and heir apparent of William Johnson, of Tunbridge,
                                                              [Kent

folio 567

Aug 3   ROBERT RIGDON, Esq, of Barnard's Inn, son and heir apparent of William
                             [Rigdon, of Dowsbie, co Lincoln, Knight
  „   „   THOMAS HUGHES, gent, son and heir apparent of Thomas Hughes, Esq,
           one of the Grand Company of this Inn.   [ampton, gent
  „   „   WILLIAM MARRIOTTE, gent, son of John Marriotte, of Ashton, co North-
  „   „   WILLIAM ARCHBOLD, gent, son and heir apparent of Walter Archbold, gent,
                                                       [of Naas, co Kildare
  „   „   ROBERT HAGGAR, gent, son and heir apparent of John Haggar, of Bourne,
  „   „   THOMAS RATCLIFFE, of Ordsall, co Lancaster, gent   [co Cambridge, Esq
  „   „   EDMUND WARING, late of Staple Inn, gent
  „   9   DAVID DRUMMOND, of Borland, in Scotland, gent
  „   15   LANCELOT BROWNE, M D
  „   21   SAMUEL WHITE, of Langley, Wiltshire, gent.

G

1605	**folio 568.**
Aug. 23	THOMAS WADDINGTON, of Grindleton, co York, gent, son and heir of [Edward Waddington, gent
,, ,,	JOHN LATHOM, of Dalton, co. Lancaster, gent, late of Barnard's Inn, son of
,, ,,	WILLIAM SHEE, of Kilkenny, Ireland, gent. [Henry Lathom, gent
,, ,,	JOHN EARLE, of Torkesley, co Lincoln, gent

1603 (1 James)   **folio 576**

June 3.	THOMAS PETIT, late of Staple Inn, and of Chilham, Kent, gent.

1603-4

Feb 7.	JOHN JEVE, son and heir apparent of James Jeve, gent, of co. Herts

1604 (2 James)   [gent

May 7	RICHARD OSBALDESTON, son of Edward Osbaldeston, of Altcar, co Lancaster,
,, 18	JOHN RATCLIFFE, of Blanchland, Northumberland (Northants in Reg), gent

folio 577.

,, ,,	RICHARD BANASTER, of Brotherton, co Lancaster, gent [Inn, Esq
June 18	NICHOLAS BESTNEY, son and heir apparent of Nicholas Bestney, of Gray's
,, 26	ROBERT LEWIS, of Barnard's Inn, gent (erased, restored Feb 12, 8 James)
Aug 8	RICHARD CHURCH, son of Edmund Church, of Ardleigh, Essex, Esq
,, ,,	JOHN MICHEL, son of John Michel, of Gray's Inn, Esq
Oct 24	FRANCIS GARDINER, son of Richard Gardiner, of Letherhead, Surrey, Esq
,, ,,	WILLIAM BOWYER, of Staple Inn, gent
Nov 1	CHRISTOPHER SHERLAND, of Easton Mauduit, co Northampton, gent
,, 6	MARTIN CALTHROPPE, of Barnard's Inn, gent
,, 16	JOHN GODBOLDE, of Barnard's Inn (born at Tannington, Suffolk).

folio 578   [Oxford, gent

,, 22	THOMAS STANDDERD, son and heir of Henry Standderd, of Steeple Aston,
,, ,,	ROBERT BRITTON, of Hadleigh, Suffolk, late of Barnard's Inn, gent

1604-5

Feb. 11	THOMAS COLE, of Staple Inn, gent.
,, ,,	THOMAS MOYLE, of Staple Inn, gent
,, 23	THOMAS SEGAR, of Southrepps, Norfolk, gent, late of Barnard's Inn
,, 27	ROBERT DOVER, of Great Ellingham, Norfolk
,, ,,	LAURENCE BLUNDESTON

1605

April 30.	EDMUND DANDY, eldest son of Thomas Dandy, of Combes, Suffolk, Esq
,, ,,	EDMUND POLEY, grandson (nepos) and heir apparent of Edmund Poley, [of Badley, Suffolk, Esq, one of the readers of this Inn
,, ,,	NATHANIEL TAVERNER, of Staple Inn, gent.

folio 579   [Inkpen, Berks, gent

,, ,,	THOMAS BRICKENDEN, son and heir apparent of Thomas Brickenden, of
June 7	JOHN RICHARDSON, son and heir of John Richardson, of the city of Durham, Esq [co Glamorgan, gent
,, 12	MORGAN EVANS, son and heir apparent of John Evans, of Lantwit Major, [co Lincoln, Esq
Aug 23	HENRY SOMERSCALES, gent, son of Robert Somerscales, of Gainsborough,

1605		folio 585
Oct.	18	ADAM FOSTER, of Nassington. co. Northampton, gent
		[Kimbolton, Huntingdon, deceased.
,,	29	EDWARD WINGFIELD, gent, third son of Edward Wingfield, Knight, of
,,	,,	ROBERT DAVENPORT, of Widford, co Chester, gent.
,,	,,	WALTER DUNCH, of Little Wittenham, Berks, gent.
,,	,,	RICHARD BIRBECKE, of Knaresboro', co. York, gent [Southwell, Notts, Esq
Nov	1	GEORGE CHAWORTH, Knight, son and heir apparent of John Chaworth, of
,,	,,	STEPHEN PROCTOR, Knight, of Fountains, co York.
,,	,,	NICHOLAS KNIVETON, of Mercaston, co Derby, Esq [a fine)
,,	,,	FRANCIS RAME, of Hornchurch, Essex (admitted by C Yelverton, without
,,	8.	TOBIAS CHAPMAN, of London, gent
,,	,,	BEALE SAPPERTON, of Langley, Herts, gent

		folio 586. [Essex, Knight
,,	20	ARTHUR HARRIS, Esq, son and heir apparent of William Harris, of Cricksey,
,,	,,	THOMAS POLHILL, of Shoreham, Kent, gent
,,	,,	WILLIAM PENRYN, of Rysnant, co Montgomery, gent
,,	,,	PETER GERING, son and heir of Alexander Gering, of Winterton, co Linc ,gent
,,	25	MARMADUKE TUNSTALL, son and heir of Francis Tunstall, of Scargill, co
—1605-6		[York, gent
Jan	28	EDMUND BREWSTER, of Badley, Suffolk (at the request of Edmund Poley, one
		[of the readers, sine fine)
,,	,,	ALEXANDER RIGBY, gent, son and heir apparent of Edward Rigby, of Brough,
		[co. Leicester (sic)
,,	,,	CHRISTOPHER FULWOOD, son and heir apparent of George Fulwood, of Gray's
		[Inn, gent
,,	,,	FRANCIS SANFORD, son and heir of Arthur Sanford, of Sanford, Salop, Esq

		folio 587.
Feb	2	ROBERT FORSETT, son and heir apparent of Edmund (?) Forsett, of Maryle-bone parish, Esq [this Inn
,,	5	JASPER BUSKELL, gent, son and heir of Thomas Buskell, late Member of
,,	11	JOHN CLERKE, son and heir of William Clerke, of Ford, Kent, Esq
,,	,,	WILLIAM ARTHINGTON, of Arthington, co York, gent
,,	,,	WILLIAM PUREFOY, of Drafton, co Leicester, gent
Mar	8	THOMAS GORE, of Lutterworth, co Leicester
,,	,,	ROBERT BOURCHIER, of Benyngborough, co York, gent
,,	9	HENRY (ROWLANDS), Bishop of Bangor
,,	,,	GEORGE (LLOYD), Bishop of Chester
,,	,,	ROGER FENTON, S T P
,,	,,	JOHN DOYLEY, of Chiselhampton, Oxon, Esq
,,	,,	THEODORE GULSON, M A, Fellow of Merton College, Oxford
,,	,,	HENRY BRERES, Alderman of the city of Coventry
,,	,,	JOHN ROGERSON, Alderman and Burgess of the city of Coventry

1605-6   **folio 588.**

Mar 10   EDWARD TILDESLEY, son and heir apparent of Thurstan Tildesley, of Tanzaker (Stanzaker), co. Lancaster, Esq, "sine fine, quia Edwardus Tildesley, avus suus et meus avunculus admisit me sumptibus suis proprius Thomas Tildesley, lector" [libellorum magister."

" 14   JOHN DUN, son and heir apparent of Daniel Dun, Knight, "a supplicibus [Letherhead, Surrey, Esq

" "   CHARLES BELLINGHAM, son and heir apparent of Thomas Bellingham, of [Penwortham, co Lancaster, Esq

" 15   HENRY FANE, of Hadlow, Kent

" "   EDWARD FLEETWOOD, son and heir apparent of Richard Fleetwood, of

" "   HENRY FLEETWOOD, second son of Richard Fleetwood, of Penwortham, co

" "   GRIFFITH MADDOCKES, of Yale, co Denbigh, Esq [Lancaster, Esq.

" "   THOMAS TILDESLEY, gent, son and heir of Thomas Tildesley, Esq, now reader

" 17   PETER PROBY, of London, Esq [Salisbury

" "   JOHN DELAHEY, of Alterheney, co Hereford, Esq, servant of Robert, Earl of

           folio 589.

" 18   THEOPHILUS, Lord HOWARD DE WALDEN, son and heir apparent of Thomas, [Earl of Suffolk, Lord Chamberlain of the Household

" "   THOMAS HOWARD, K B, second son of said Earl of Suffolk

" "   JAMES ERSKINE, K B

" "   JOHN RATCLIFFE, Knight

" "   GERRARD BOOTH, Knight, sine fine

" "   ROBERT WINGFIELD, son and heir apparent of Robert Wingfield, of Northampton [Blackelege, gent

" "   AUBREY BLACKELEGE (Blackeleech), son and heir apparent of William

" 19   FRANCIS BARRINGTON, of Barrington Hall, Essex, Knight

" "   ANTHONY COPE, of Hanwell, Oxon, Knight

" 20   ROGER PARKER, D D

" "   EDWARD TORBOCK, of Torbock, co Lancaster, Esq

           folio 590

" 22   GEORGE SHILITO, of Houghton, co York, Esq

" "   EDWARD STOCKWITH, son of Humphrey Stockwith, of Stockwith, Notts, gent

" "   NICHOLAS SMYTH, son and heir apparent of Nicholas Smyth, of Theddlethorpe, co Lincoln [of the Household

" 24   EDWARD BALL, Esq, servant to Thomas, Earl of Suffolk, Lord Chamberlain

" "   WALTER WHITE, of Grettenham, in parish of Brinckworth, Wilts

1606

May 21   ALAN ASCOUGH, son of Christopher Ascough, of Richmond, co York [co Hereford

" "   THOMAS BODENHAM, son and heir of Roger Bodenham, Knight, of Rotherwas,

" "   THOMAS ORDE, son and heir of Thomas Orde, of Orde, co Durham, Esq

" "   JOHN GILBEY, son and heir of George Gilbey, of Bole, Notts, Knight

           folio 591.

" "   PAUL CALION, gent, of Melton, Berks

" "   JOHN LAYLR, of London, gent

1606		folio 591—(continued)
May 30		JOHN MOORE, of Holderness, co York, gent. [late Chief Justice of Chester
,,	,,	NICHOLAS SHUTTLEWORTH, grandson (nepos) of Richard Shuttleworth, Knight,
,,	,,	ROBERT SOTHEBY, son of Roger Sotheby, of Pocklington, co. York
,,	,,	HENRY PIGOTT, son and heir apparent of Benjamin Pigott, of Gravenhurst,
,,	,,	THOMAS BRIGGE, of Scremby, co Lincoln, gent. [Beds, Esq
1605		folio 592. [Sutton, Suffolk
Nov. 25.		FRANCIS BURWELL, gent, son and heir apparent of Francis Burwell, of
,,	8	THOMAS LAURENCE, of Quattford, in parish of Ledbury, co Hereford, gent

folio 593.

,,	25.	ROBERT BEVERLEY, of Smeaton, co York, gent.
1605-6		[Esq
Feb	2	EDWARD LOCKE1, second son of Thomas Locket, of Bronesthorpe, Norfolk,
,,	5.	RICHARD MONCKE, late of Staple Inn, gent. [gent
,,	,,	JOHN FALDOE, son and heir apparent of John Faldoe, of Goldington, Beds,
,,	11.	JAMES BALDWER, of Sutton, co. Lincoln, gent., late of Barnard's Inn
Mar	18	GORE LAMBERT, of Barnard's Inn, gent, son of William Lambert, Esq, deceased, late one of the Masters of the Court of Chancery to Queen [Elizabeth
,,	,,	FANE LAMBERT, of Barnard's Inn, gent, another son of said William Lambert
,,	,,	NICHOLAS WARING, of Barnard's Inn [Barnard's Inn
,,	21	THOMAS GOLDESBOROUGH, late of Little Shelford, co Cambridge, and of
1606		
May 21.		RICHARD FOGG, of Staple Inn

folio 594

,,	30	ROBERT BLACKWELL, son of Robert Blackwell, of Bushey, Herts, Esq
,,	,,	WILLIAM WOODMAN, of Betchworth, gent
1606-7		
Feb 4		OLIVER MORRIS, of Staple Inn (erased)
1606		folio 599
July	9	EDWARD CONVERS, of Ashley, co Northampton, gent
Aug	10	FRANCIS JAMES, Doctor of Laws, one of the Masters of Chancery, and [Chancellor of the Diocese of Bath and Wells
,,	,,	ROBERT HYDE, of Hardwell, Berks, Knight
,,	,,	THOMAS SOTHEBY, of Bishop Wilton, co York, gent
,,	,,	JOHN GRAY, of Gosnold, Suffolk, gent

folio 600

,,	16	JOHN ROBARTS, of London, gent
,,	,,	JOHN YOUNG, of Hope, co Flint, gent
,,	,,	ROBERT PARK, of Temple Bryer, co Lincoln, gent
,,	,,	ROGER LANGFORD, of Ruthin, co Denbigh, gent
,,	21	ANTHONY GAWDIE, of Claxton, Norfolk, gent
,,	,,	JAMES BRUCE, of Culross, Scotland, gent [the Bath
,	,,	VINCENT WELBY, son of William Welby, of Gedney, co Lincoln, Knight of

1606.		folio 600—(continued).
Aug. 16.		PHILIP STANHOPE, of Bretbie, co. Derby, Knight.
,,	,,	THOMAS BUTLER, of Kilcash, co Tipperary, gent.
,,	,,	EDWARD MANNING, of St Mary Cray, Kent, gent., now of Staple Inn.
Nov. 24		EDWARD SCROGGS, son and heir of John Scroggs, of Albury, Herts, Esq.

folio 601.

,,	,,	AUGUSTINE PETTUS, Esq, son and heir apparent of John Pettus, Esq
1606-7.		
Feb 2		NOWELL SOTHERTON, one of the Barons of the Exchequer
,,	,,	THOMAS HATTON, of Long Stanton, co Cambridge
,,	,,	EDWARD COOKE, Esq, of Giddy Hall, Essex
,,	,,	HENRY DETHICK, B C L
,,	4	WILLIAM WOODWARD, son of William Woodward, of High Holborn, Middlesex
,,	,,	LAURENCE PARSONS, of Youghall, co Cork
,,	,,	GEORGE SAMMES, son of John Sammes, of Tolleshunt Major, Essex
,,	,,	ANTHONY MAYE, son and heir apparent of Thomas Maye, of Ticehurst, [Sussex, Esq
,,	,,	THOMAS MYDLETON, son and heir of Thomas Mydleton, of London, Knight
,,	,,	OLIVER MORRIS, of Staple Inn, gent [co Durham, Esq
,,	11	JOHN PEMBERTON, son and heir apparent of Michael Pemberton, of Aislabie,
,,	,,	WILLIAM JOHNSON, of Chislett, Kent, Esq [gent, late of Barnard's Inn
,,	,,	DENNIS NORMAN, son and heir of William Norman, of Saxmundham, Suffolk,

folio 602.   [Metheringham, co Lincoln, gent.

,,	21	WILLIAM (?) ENDERBY, son and heir apparent of Richard Enderby, of
,,	,,	THOMAS BRUDENELL, of Stanton, co Leicester, gent.
,,	,,	JAMES ORRELL, of Tottenham High Cross, Middlesex, gent
,,	,,	JOHN ATKINSON, of city of York, gent
,,	27	ROBERT TIPPER, son and heir of William Tipper, Esq
,,	,,	CORDELL SAVILE, of London, gent, sine fine
,,	,,	WILLIAM TIPPER, of London, Esq
,,	28	CHRISTOPHER YELVERTON, son and heir of Henry Yelverton, reader (admitted by Christopher Yelverton, Knight, uncle of Christopher Yelverton, [one of the Justices of the King's Bench)
,,	,,	ROBERT YELVERTON, second son of said Henry Yelverton [co Leicester
Mar 3		GEORGE BELGRAVE, son and heir of George Belgrave, Esq, of Belgrave,

folio 603.   [Lord of Kinloss.

Feb 26		EDWARD BRUCE, son and heir of Edward Bruce, Knight, Master of the Rolls,
,,	,,	ROBERT WOOD, son and heir of Roger Wood, Esq, of Islington, Middlesex.
,,	,,	ROGER WOOD, second son of Roger Wood, Esq, of Islington, Middlesex
,,	,,	BARTHOLOMEW BEALE, Esq, absque fine. [land, Esq.
Mar 3		THOMAS WYBERGH, son and heir of Thomas Wybergh, of Clifton, Westmore-
,,	,,	BEVERLEY NEWCOMEN, of Dublin, gent, son and heir of Robert Newcomen, [Knight.

1606-7		**folio 603**—*(continued)*

Mar 3.   STEPHEN BRADWELL, son and heir of Stephen Bradwell, of London, Esq

,,   ,,   RICHARD LOVELACE, Knight, of Hurley, Berks

,,   8   JOHN STILL, S T D , Bishop of Bath and Wells

,,   ,,   NATHANIEL STILL, son and heir of Bishop John Still   [Lancaster, gent

,,   10.   JOHN BROCKHOLES, son and heir of Thomas Brockholes, of Leighton, co

1607   **folio 604.**   [Lancaster, Esq

May 6.   RICHARD SHERBORNE, second son of Richard Sherborne, of Stonihurst, co

,,   15   JOHN JEFFREY, of Little Bursted, Essex, gent

,,   ,,   ROBERT BRODBRIDGE, of Guildford, Surrey, gent

,,   ,,   RICHARD NORTON, of Norwood, Kent, gent

,,   ,,   THOMAS CAVE, second son of Anthony Cave, of London, gent

June 5.   JOHN LEYBORNE, of Lancaster, gent   [Knight.

,,   17   WILLIAM ANDREWES, son and heir of William Andrewes, of Lathbury, Bucks,

,,   ,,   EMANUEL REYNOLD, of Erddig, co Denbigh, gent , late of Barnard's Inn

,,   ,,   VALENTINE PELL, of Knighton, Norfolk, gent.

Aug 1.   THOMAS DARRELL, son and heir of John Darrell, of Woodhay, Berks

,,   ,,   TOBIAS EWBANCKE, son and heir of Henry Ewbancke, Vice Dean of Durham

,,   ,,   WILLIAM GALLAWAYE, of Kingsale, co Cork.

,,   ,,   JOHN WESTRAYE, of London, gent

                       folio 605.   [Kent, Registrar in Chancery

,,   8   LAURENCE WASHINGTON, son and heir of Laurence Washington, of Maidstone,

,,   12.   BASILL NICOL, of London, gent.

,,   ,,   THOMAS UNDERWOOD, of Hinckley, co Leicester, gent

,,   ,,   ELLIS WYNN, of London, gent   .   [co Northampton

,,   ,,   ROBERT KNIGHTLEY, gent , son of Richard Knightley, Knight, of Fawsley,

Nov 6   EDWARD HUSSEY, son and heir apparent of Charles Hussey, of Honnington,

,,   ,,   GEOFFREY HALL, of Broseley, Salop   [co Lincoln, Knight

,,   ,,   TIMOTHY MYDLETON, son of Thomas Mydleton, of London, Knight

                                                  [Lincoln, Esq

,,   ,,   THOMAS COPLEDIKE, son and heir of Thomas Copledike, of Toynton, co

,,   ,,   LIONEL EDGAR, of Framsden, Suffolk, gent , late of Barnard's Inn

,,   ,,   JOHN GATEFORTH, of Kildwicke, co York, gent   [Knight

,,   27.   ROBERT HYDE, son and heir apparent of Leonard Hyde, of Throcking, Herts,

,,   ,,   JOHN JONES, second son of Walter Jones, of Chastleton, Oxon, Esq

                       folio 606.

,,   ,,   NEVILL CHOWNE, second son of George Chowne, of Oxenhoath, Kent, Knight.

,,   ,,   JOSEPH BRYAN, son of John Bryan, of Northampton, gent   [Mayor of York

,,   ,,   THOMAS HARRISON, son and heir apparent of Robert Harrison, late Lord

,,   ,,   JOHN TAYLLOR the Younger, of London, gent , son of John Tayllor the Elder,

1607 8.   [gent., "Deputy Clerk in the office of First Fruits," &c

Feb 2.   CHRISTOPHER HUTTON, son and heir of Richard Hutton, Serjeant at-Law

,,   ,,   JOHN SKEFFINGTON, of Skeffington, co. Leicester, Esq.

1607-8		folio 606—*(continued)*.

Feb 2   JOHN MEADE, son and heir apparent of Thomas Meade, Knight

,,   ,,   ANTHONY THOROLD, son and heir of John Thorold, of Coryngham, co Lin-
                                        [coln, Knight

,,   ,,   GILBERT ROOS, of Laxton, Notts, gent.

,,   ,,   SAMUEL HODGSON, of Carlisle, gent

,,   ,,   THOMAS EKINS, son and heir of John Ekins, of Great Catworth, Hunts, gent
                                        [Worston, co Lancaster, gent

,,   ,,   JOHN GREENACRES, son and heir apparent of Mr. Richard Greenacres, of

folio 607.

,,   ,,   ROBERT MOLINEUX, of Wood, co Lancaster, Esq.

,,   3   ROBERT CHARLTON, son of Andrew Charlton, of Apley, Salop, Esq

,,   ,,   WILLIAM DIXON, of Ramshaw, co Durham, gent

,,   ,,   JOHN WINGFIELD, of Brantham, Suffolk, gent   [ton, gent

,,   ,,   WILLIAM TAILOR, son and heir of William Tailor, of Brixworth, co Northamp-
                                        [ampton, Esq

,,   ,,   NICHOLAS WOODHALL, son of Nicholas Woodhall, of Thenford, co North-

,,   16 WINGFIELD ATHOW, eldest son of Thomas Athow, Esq, reader

,,   ,,   JOHN ATHOW, second son of Thomas Athow, Esq, reader.

,,   ,,   JOHN HONYWOOD, son and heir apparent of Sir Thomas Honywood, of
         Elmsted, Kent, Knight   [land, Esq, "extra hospitium, Nov 27, 1608"

,,   ,,   EDWARD RATCLIFFE, son and heir of Francis Ratcliffe, of Dilston, Northumber-

,,   ,,   GERRARD LOWTHER, of Penrith, Cumberland, gent

folio 608   [Berkshire, Knight

,,   17 THOMAS BROCAS, son and heir apparent of Sir Pexall Brocas, of Steventon,
                                        [co Northampton, Esq

,,   ,,   JAMES CLEYPOOLE, son and heir apparent of Adam Cleypoole, of North Burrow,

,,   ,,   JOHN EVERINGE, son and heir apparent of John Everinge, of Lymynge, Kent

,,   ,,   ROBERT NOONE, of Staple Inn, gent

,   21   HUGH SAXEY, Esq, one of the Auditors of the King's Exchequer

,,   23 EDWARD BARKHAM, Esq

,,   ,,   RICHARD WELBYE, Esq   [to Spain

,,   25 THOMAS CORNWALLIS, Esq, son of Sir Charles Cornwallis, Knight, Ambassador

,,   26 CHARLES LAMBERT, Esq, son and heir apparent of Sir Thomas Lambert, of
         Pinchbeck, co Lincoln, Knight   [Knight

,,   ,,   THOMAS THOROLD, son of Sir John Thorold, of Coringham, co Lincoln,

,,   ,,   NICHOLAS BACON, son and heir of Edward Bacon, of Shrubland, Suffolk, Esq

,,   ,,   PHILIP BACON, second son of Edward Bacon, of Shrubland, Suffolk, Esq

folio 609   [gent

,,   ,,   RICHARD JONES, one of the sons of Thomas Jones, of Llanvayer, co Denbigh,

1608

May 3   WILLIAM GREEKE, son and heir apparent of William Greeke, of the city of
                                        [Cambridge, Esq.

,,   ,,   ROGER MERES, son and heir of Sir John Meres, of ———, co. Lincoln, Knight

,,   ,,   RICHARD LOWTHER, son of Christopher Lowther, of Lowther, Westmoreland,

,,   ,,   WILLIAM BLAKISTON, of Blackiston, co Durham, gent.   [Knight

1608.   folio 609—(continued)

May 3   EDWARD KELLETT, of parish of Sepulchres, London, gent   [Lancaster, Esq.
,, ,,   EDWARD MOSLEY, son and heir apparent of Rowland Mosley, of Hough, co
,, ,,   WILLIAM LAMBTON, of Lambton, co Durham, gent
,, ,,   RALPH BLAKISTON (Blayxton), of Gibside, co Durham   [Esq
,, ,,   WALTER COVERT, son and heir apparent of William Covert, of Leeds, Kent,
,, ,,   WILLIAM VEYSEY, of Lintlesham, Sussex, gent
,, ,,   THOMAS WENTWORTH, of Elmsall, co. York, gent

folio 610.

,, 6   JOHN BRAND, of Boxford, Suffolk, gent
,, ,,   GILBERT LITTELTON, of Holbech, co Stafford, gent
,, ,,   JOHN LEVENTHORPE, son and heir apparent of John Leventhorpe, Knight
June 3   HENRY HARDWARE, of (Peel), co Chester
,, ,,   ROGER WILBRAHAM, son and heir apparent of Ralph Wilbraham, Esq.
,, ,,   ROBERT ROCKLEY, of Rockley, co York
,, 14. WALTER STRICKLAND, gent, son and heir apparent of Walter Strickland, Esq
,, ,,   EDWARD ROLT, gent, of Bolnehurst, Beds, son and heir apparent of Edward
                                                                [Rolt, gent
folio 611.

,, ,,   EDWARD ASCOUGH, son and heir of Roger Ascough, of Nuthall, Notts, Knight
                                                   [Hay, co Somerset, gent
,, ,,   WILLIAM JACKSON, gent., son and heir apparent of Miles Jackson, of Comb
,, ,,   CHRISTOPHER WASSE, of Cambridge University, gent
,, ,,   ROBERT PERCY, of Settrington, co York, gent
,, 30   THOMAS IRELAND, son and heir apparent of Thomas Ireland, now reader.
,, ,,   ROBERT IRELAND, second son of Thomas Ireland, now reader
,, ,,   ROBERT HARINGTON, son of John Harington, gent
,, ,,   EDWARD SLEGG, son and heir apparent of Edward Slegg, of Cambridge, gent
,, ,,   WILLIAM ROBERTS SMITHE, of Stiffkey, Norfolk, Esq
,, ,,   GEORGE IRELAND, son of Thomas Ireland, now reader   [Lancaster, gent.
,, ,,   HENRY DOUGHTIF, son and heir of Michael Doughtie, of Thorneley, co

folio 612.

Aug 2   GEORGE GREY, son of Henry, Lord Grey of Groby.
,, ,,   JOHN MOLYNEUX, Esq, cousin and heir of Edmund Molyneux, Knight,
                                        [one of the Judges of the Common Pleas
,, 5   ARTHUR AGARD (one of the Knights of the Treasury Chamber?)
,, ,,   HUGH BETHELL, son and heir of Thomas Bethell, of Ellerton, co York, gent
,, 6   THOMAS PARRY, Knight, Chancellor of the Duchy of Lancaster, and P C
                                              [of the Tower of London
,, 9   ARMYGHILD WADE, Esq, son and heir of William Wade, Knight, Lieutenant
,, ,,   THOMAS IRELAND, second son of George Ireland, gent, deceased

folio 613   ["absque fine"

,, 11   EDMUND WALLER, son and heir of Thomas Waller, of Gray's Inn, Esq,
,, ,,   JOHN GAINSFORD, son of William Gainsford, of Ford, Surrey, Knight
,, ,,   RICHARD DAWTREY, of Ipswich Suffolk, gent

1608.   folio **613**—(*continued*).

Aug. 11.   CHARLES HOLT, of Stawell, co. Gloucester, gent.

,, ,,   RICHARD MELLINGE, of Liverpool, gent

,, 12   JAMES, Lord STRANGE, son and heir of William, Earl of Derby

,, ,,   WILLIAM YOWART, of Ashby, co Lincoln, gent

,, ,,   FRANCIS PHILLIPPS, of London, gent.

,, ,,   CHRISTOPHER TRAVERS, of London, gent.   [of the Great Wardrobe

,, ,,   WILLIAM KELLETT, gent , Deputy of Sir Roger Aston, Knight, in the Office

,, ,,   RALPH HEATON, son of Thomas Heaton, gent

,, ,,   FRANCIS IRELAND, son and heir of William Ireland, of London, Deputy of Richard Molineux, Knight, Receiver-general of the Duchy of Lancaster

,, ,,   WILLIAM IRELAND, second son of William Ireland, of London, Deputy of Richard Molineux, Knight, Receiver general of the Duchy of Lancaster

,, ,,   JOHN IRELAND, son and heir of Gilbert Ireland, gent

,, ,,   THOMAS IRELAND, the younger, son of Gilbert Ireland

1606.

July 9   THOMAS BROMLEY, of Norbury, co Chester, gent.   folio **614**

folio 615.

Aug 21   WILLIAM MORRICE, of Creyollwy, co. Monmouth, gent , late of Staple Inn

,,   HENRY RUMSEY, of Crickhowell, co Brecon, gent , late of Staple Inn

Nov 7.   JOHN PARGITER, of Gretworth, co Northampton, gent , late of Barnard's Inn

,, ,,   WILLIAM HUGHES, son of Reginald Hughes, of city of London, gent

1606-7.

Feb 2.   CHRISTOPHER BOWYER, of Sydwaye, co Stafford, "absque fine "

,, 4.   ROBERT WORLECHE, of Ipswich, Suffolk, gent

,, ,,   RICHARD BREAME, son of Richard Breame, of Wasenworth, Surrey, gent

,, ,,   EDMUND NEEDHAM, son of George Needham, of Wymondley, Herts, Esq

,, 11   LEWIS BROOKE, of Barnard's Inn.

Mar. 5   HENRY PINDAR, of Mottesford, Southampton, gent

,, ,,   THOMAS BEERE, son of John Beere, of Gray's Inn, gent

,, 8.   THOMAS STILL, third son of John Still, Bishop of Bath and Wells

folio 616

,, ,,   OLIVER (?) BUCKE, son and heir of John Bucke, late Steward of the Inn, "absque fine "   [Durham, Esq

,, ,,   LUKE PILKINGTON, son and heir of Edward Pilkington, of Stanton, co.

,, ,,   TIMOTHY TURNER, of Staple Inn, gent.

,, 10   HOWARD HOLT, son and heir of William Holt, of Chertsey, Surrey, gent

,, ,,   JOHN MARCH, son and heir apparent of Richard March, of Limehouse,

,, ,,   FRANCIS TYE, of Radford, Notts, gent.   [Middlesex, gent

1607.

May 6   EDMUND ELLIS, son of William Ellis, Esq , one of the readers of this Inn

,, ,,   FRANCIS DORINGTON, of Stafford, gent

,, ,,   RICHARD MARTIN, of Sutton St John, co Lincoln, gent

                                [of Wighton, Norfolk, gent

, 15   EDMUND BEDINGFIELD, son and heir apparent of Christopher Bedingfield,

1607.   folio 616—(continued).
May 15   WILLIAM ACTON, of Maidstone, Kent, late of Staple Inn.
June 17. FRANCIS DOWNE, of Reddiyar (?), co Chester, gent
  ,,   ,,   JOHN BANKE, of Keswick, Cumberland, gent

folio 617.

Aug. 1   PETER KNIGHT, of Staple Inn, late of Sellinge, Kent, gent.
  ,,   ,,   NICHOLAS SWINFORDE, late of Sandwich, Kent, gent., of Staple Inn
  ,,   8.   EDMUND REVE, of Felthorpe, Norfolk, gent, late of Barnard's Inn
1607-8   [Norfolk, Esq, "absque fine "
Feb   2.   EDWARD YELVERTON, son and heir of Edward Yelverton, of Brympston,
  ,,   ,,   JOHN CLARK, son of John Clark, of this Inn, Esq
  ,,   ,,   THOMAS COLE, of Ashdown, Essex, and of Barnard's Inn
  ,,   3   JERMYN BURLES, son and heir of Thomas Burles, of Suffolk, gent.
  ,,   ,,   RALPH WHITFIELD, gent, late of Staple Inn
  ,,   10   WILLIAM MILESON, of Bury St. Edmunds, Suffolk, gent   [Inn.
  ,,   16.   THOMAS ATHOW, third son of Thomas Athow, Esq., now reader of Gray's
  ,,   ,,   CLEMENT ATHOW, fourth son of Thomas Athow, Esq, now reader of Gray's
                                                                 [Inn
  ,,   ,,   FRANCIS BACON, son and heir apparent of John Bacon, Esq, of King's Lynn,
                                          [Norfolk, gent, and of Barnard's Inn
  ,,   ,,   JOHN SPELMAN, son and heir of Sir Henry Spelman, of Norfolk, Knight

folio 618

  ,,   ,,   JOHN ARCHDALE, of Darsham, Suffolk, gent
  ,,   ,,   ISAAC THOMSON, of Kelsall, Suffolk, gent
  ,,   ,,   WILLIAM NORTON, of Whaley, co York, gent, and of Barnard's Inn
  ,,   ,,   JOHN PLATT, of Staple Inn, gent
  ,,   ,,   ROBERT BOWNE, of city of Oxford, gent., and of Barnard's Inn
  ,,   ,,   JOHN BURTON, of Stokerston, co Leicester, gent, and of Barnard's Inn
  ,,   ,,   ROBERT NOONE, of Staple Inn, gent (erased)
  ,,   23   EDWARD LANE, of Fishborne, Sussex, gent
  ,,   26   SYMON HALE, son and heir apparent of Thomas Hale, of this Society, Esq
1608   [Ticehurst, Sussex, gent
June 3   GEORGE COURTHOPE, son and heir of John Courthope, of Wily, parish of

folio 619.   [Thomas E, Esq

  ,,   14   EDWARD EMELEY, of Helmedon, co Northampton, gent, second son of
  ,,   ,,   ROBERT TOCKETTS, of Tocketts, co York, gent ("extra hospitium," May 3, 1611)
July 30.   RICHARD PROCTER, of Barnard's Inn, gent (born in London).
                                                   [Abbots, Essex.
Aug 6.   FRANCIS STONER, gent, son and heir of Clement Stoner, Esq, of Stapleford
  ,,   11.   BARNARD BICKERDICKE, of Barnard's Inn, gent ("extra hospitium," restored
                                  [again March 15, 1608, paying 13s 4d fine)
  ,,   12   JOHN ONBY, of Newton Bargoland, co Leicester, now of Barnard's Inn, gent
  ,,   ,,   EDWARD MIDDLEHAM, of Barnard's Inn, gent.   [co Chester, Esq.
  ,,   ,,   MATTHEW BIRKENHEAD, son and heir of Adam Birkenhead, of Maulay,

1608		**folio 624.**
Oct 17		SAMUEL HASELL, son and heir of Thomas H , of Conysthroppe, co York, gent
,,	,,	WILLIAM GOODMAN, of Blaiston, co Leicester, gent
,,	,,	WILLIAM SKIPWITH, of Cotes, co Leicester, gent
,,	,,	THOMAS COLVILLE, of Newton, co Cambridge, Knight [" sine fine "
,,	,,	WILLIAM YELVERTON, son and heir of William Y , of Rougham, Norfolk, Esq ,

[Leicester, Knight, admitted same day

Nov 1-10 HENRY SKIPWITH, son and heir of William S , Knight, of Cotes, co

[Prerogative Court

,,	,,	JOHN BENNETT, son and heir of John B , Citizen of London, Judge of the
,,	,,	WILLIAM DANIELL, son and heir of William D , of St Margaret, Wilts, Esq
,,	,,	JOHN THELWALL, son and heir of John T , of Bathabarne Park, co Denbigh
,,	,,	MILES DODSON, son and heir of Richard D , of Kirkby-over-Blows, co York

[Suffolk, Esq

,,	,,	HENRY (?) BARNARDISTON, son and heir of Robert B , of Ickwell Bury,
Oct	4	JOHN WORSLEY, of Deeping St James, co Lincoln (Northampton in reg), gent
,,	,,	GEORGE GOODYEAR, of South Cowton, co York, gent
Nov 21.		THOMAS COWPER, son and heir of William C , of Thurgarton, Notts, Esq
,,	,,	RICHARD BOLD, of Farnworth, co Lancaster, gent

folio 625.

| ,, | ,, | WILLIAM PASTON, son of Edward P , of Apleton, Norfolk, Esq |

[Leicester, gent

,,	,,	FRANCIS NOONE, son and heir of Robert N , of Walton-on-the-Wold, co
,,	,,	WILLIAM SCUDAMORE, son and heir of Thomas S , of Overton, co York, Esq
,,	,,	THOMAS GERRARD, son and heir of Miles G , of Ince, co Lancaster, Esq
,,	24.	HENRY NORTH, Esq , son of Henry N , of Wickambrook, Norfolk, Knight
,,	,,	WILLIAM KENNETT, son and heir of William K , of London, gent
,,	,,	JOHN PRESCOTT, son and heir of Hugh P , gent
,,	,,	JOHN JEFFRAYES, son and heir of William J , of Sherford, Norfolk, gent.
1608-9		
Jan.	5	JOHN CHURCHILL, of London, gent
,,	,,	ANTHONY STAPLEY, of East Hoathley, Sussex, gent

folio 626.

,,	25	SAMUEL PEYTON, Knight, son and heir of Thomas P , Knight
,	20	OWEN PRICE, of Llanfair Talhaiarn, co. Denbigh, gent
Feb 10		WALTER MILDMAY, son and heir of Humphrey M., of Danbury, Essex, Esq
,,	,,	THOMAS MAUDISLEY, of Iden, Sussex, gent
,,	,,	JOHN ROBINSON, of the Close, in the city of Lincoln, gent
,,	,,	THOMAS HUTCHINSON, of Owthorpe, Notts, Esq [gent
,,	,,	WILLIAM SMYTH, son and heir of Thomas S , of Great Massingham, Norfolk,
,,	,,	JOHN CORNWALLIS, gent , son of Thomas C , Knight
,,	,,	JOHN BROWNE, of Tollthorpe, co Rutland, Esq , son and heir of Francis B , Esq
,,	,,	JOHN SOUTHBY, gent., son and heir of John S , gent , late of Caswall, Berks
Mar 11		EDWARD, Lord STAFFORD

1608-9   **folio 626**—*(continued)*

Mar. 12   WILLIAM BOWYER, Knight

"   "   ARTHUR FLEETWOOD, Esq, son and heir of Sir George F, of the Vache, Bucks.

folio 627.

"   "   THOMAS RIDLEY, D C L

"   "   RICHARD FUST

"   14.   PHILIP MAINWARING, third son of Randall M, of Peover, Cheshire, Esq

"   "   FRANCIS ROGERS, of London, Esq

"   "   JOHN NEVILL, son of Right Hon Edward N Lord of Burgavenny

"   "   JAMES STURDEY, son and heir of Roger S., of Yafford, co York

"   "   HENRY SHELLEY, son of Henry S, of Worminghurst, Sussex, gent

"   "   ROBERT METHAM, of Bullington, co Lincoln, gent.

"   "   WILLIAM COLLE, of Staple Inn, and of Foy, co Hereford

"   "   JOHN BUTLER, of Staple Inn, and of Standegrove, co York

"   "   ROBERT AUDLEY, of Staple Inn, and of Great Granesden, Hunts, gent

"   "   JAMES PEMBERTON, Knight, Alderman of London

"   "   CLEMENT SCUDAMORE (Sir), Alderman of London, Knight

"   "   GEORGE SMITHES, of London, goldsmith

folio 628.

"   14   WILLIAM FLEETWOOD, son and heir of Henry F, now reader

"   "   HENRY FLEETWOOD, second son of Henry F, now reader

"   "   HARBERT FVERSFIELD, son and heir of Sir Thomas E, of Dene, Sussex, Knight   [Knight

"   "   FRANCIS ASHBYE, son and heir of Sir Robert A., of Harvile, Middlesex,

"   "   ISAACK COTTON, gent   [(erased)

"   "   JOHN VAUGHAN, of Cumber, co Hereford, gent, expelled March 15, 1608

"   "   RALPH KETTELL, D D, Head of Trinity College, Oxford

"   "   (THOMAS) SINGLETON (Dr), Head of Brazenose College

"   "   FRANCIS BRADSHAW, D D, of Magdalen College, Oxford

"   "   (RICHARD) NEYLE, Dean of Westminster and Bishop of Rochester.

"   "   FERDINANDO DOWDESWELL, of Westminster, gent

folio 629

"   "   RALPH YOWART, of London, gent

"   "   JOHN BRVERS (Breares), of Preston, co Lancaster, gent

"   "   JOHN FAIRCLOUGH, of Hoyston, co York, gent

"   "   RICHARD DALLADOWNE, of Holborn, Middlesex, gent

"   "   ANSELME HUNTLEY, of London, Esq

1609

May 11   JOHN EARTON, of Waltham Holy Cross, Essex, gent

"   "   RICHARD BRATHWAITE, son of Thomas B, of Burnside, Westmoreland, Esq

"   "   JOHN MOSELEY, son and heir of Thomas M, Alderman of York

"   "   WILLIAM GOLDINGHAM, of Dedham, Essex, gent

1609.		folio 629—*(continued)*.
May 19.		FRANCIS JERMY, son and heir of William J , of Workingworth, Suffolk, Esq
,,	,,	JOHN STEEDE, son and heir of William S., of Harrietsham, Kent, gent
,,	,,	JOHN JAY, of London, gent
,,	26	THOMAS WHARTON, son and heir of Humphrey W , of Scales, co York, gent

folio 640

,,	,,	JOHN BLENCOWE, son and heir of Henry B , of Blencowe, Cumberland, Esq
,,	,,	WILLIAM GLEGGE, son and heir of William G , of Le Grange, co Chester, gent
June 30		THOMAS HAMPSON, of Oriel College, Oxon, gent.
,,	,,	THOMAS GILBIE, of Bolle, Notts, Esq
,,	,,	JOHN HODGES, of Lufton, co Somerset, gent
,,	,,	JOHN BUNNINGTON, of Barcotte, co Derby, gent
,,	,,	FRANCIS PETYTT, of Boughton under-Blean, Kent, Esq.
,,	,,	WILLIAM GLOVER, of London, gent

folio 641

Aug.	7	FRANCIS LOVELACE, son of Lancelot L , now reader
,,	8	JOHN ELLIOT, son of Thomas E , Esq , and Katharine his wife, daughter and [heir of Nowell Sotherton, one of the Barons of the Exchequer
,,	10.	ROBERT GOODRIGE, of Ipswich, Suffolk, now of Barnard's Inn (erased).
,,	,,	RICHARD KERLE, of Newton, Suffolk, gent
,,	11	JOHN DRURY, of Furnivals (*sic*), gent
,,	,,	EDWARD AMHERST, of Lewes, Sussex, of Clifford's Inn, gent.
,,	,,	ROBERT BOWES, son of Ralph B , of Barnes, in Bishoprick of Durham
,,	,,	JOHN HALES, of Kersley, co Warwick, gent
,,	,,	JAMES LAWSON, son of Ralph L , of Brough, co York, Knight
,,	,,	NATHANIEL GULSTON, Fellow of Trinity College, Oxon
,,	,,	ROBERT BARON, of Worcester, now of Barnard's Inn, gent (erased)
Nov.	3	HENRY FELTON, son and heir of Anthony F , of Playford, Suffolk, Knight
,,	8	JOHN SHADWELL, of Lynedon, co Stafford, gent.

folio 642.

,,	,,	EDWARD CARDINALL, of Furnival's Inn, and East Bergholt, Suffolk, gent
,,	,,	HENRY SWINNERTON, son and heir of John S., Knight
,,	,,	THOMAS MYNOT, gent
,,	27	VINCENT LOWE, son and heir of Patrick L , of Denby, co Derby
,,	,,	GEORGE SCOTT, son and heir of William S , of Conghurst, Kent.
,,	,,	JOHN COOKE, son and heir of Paul C., of North Somercoates, co Lincoln, gent
1609-10		
Jan 24		JOHN CONIERS, of West Brompton, co Northampton
,,	,,	EDMUND ANDERSON, of Manton, co. Lincoln, gent.
,,	,,	JOHN CHOMLEY, gent , son of Henry C., of Burton Coggles, co Lincoln, Knight
Feb	2	THOMAS HOLLAND, S T P , Oxford
,,	,,	NATHANIEL HYDE, gent , son of John H , late of London, deceased, and Helen his wife, now wife of James Altham, Knight, one of the Barons of [the Exchequer, " absque fine "

1609-10.   **folio 643**

Feb   2.   ROBERT HOGAN, Esq , of Bradenham, Norfolk

,,   ,,   NATHANIEL RICH, of Ash, Essex   [reader of this Inn, deceased

,,   ,,   THOMAS GERRARD, of Staple Inn, gent , third son of William G , Esq , late

,,   ,   TIMOTHY ELKS, of Bishopston, Wilts, gent.

Mar. 3.   ROBERT BOWES, son and heir of Thomas B , of Apleton, co York

Feb. 7.   MICHAEL JENISON, of Etwall, co Derby, gent.

,,   ,,   MICHAEL HENEAGE, son of Michael H , of Hogsden, Middlesex, Esq

,,   ,,   RICHARD MADDISON, son and heir of Thomas M , of Trusthorpe, co Lincoln,

,,   ,,   ROBERT MYRES, of the city of York, gent   [gent

,,   ,,   JOHN SEGAR, son and heir of William S , Knight, Garter Principal King of Arms

folio 644.

Mar 4   JOHN THORNEBURGH, Bishop of Bristol

,,   6   HENRY EWBANK, B D , Vice-Dean of Durham

,,   ,,   RICHARD, Earl of CLANRICKARDE

,,   ,,   JAMES, Lord HAY (Haies)

,,   ,,   HENRY, Lord CLIFFORD

,,   ,,   JAMES OUCHTERLONY, Knight

,,   ,,   PATRICK MURRAY, Knight

,,   ,,   WILLIAM ANSTRUTHER, Knight

,,   ,,   JOHN WARREN, Esq , son and heir of Sir Edward W , Knight

,,   ,,   JOHN BOURCHIER, son of William B , Esq , ————, co York

,,   8.   RICHARD SCOTT, of Barneshall, co York

,,   ,,   JOHN DARLEY, of the city of York, third son of Mr. D., of Kilnhurst

,,   ,,   JOHN SMITH, of Bugbrooke, co. Northampton, Esq

,,   ,,   BARNABY GOOCHE, of Alvingham, co Lincoln.

,,   ,,   WILLIAM DARELL, of Iwod, Surrey.

,,   ,,   THOMAS MOUNTENEY, son and heir of Thomas M., Esq.

,,   9.   ROBERT MUSKETT, son and heir of Simon M , Esq.

,,   ,,   GAWYN GROSVENOR, of Sutton Coldfield, co Warwick.   [Lincoln.

,,   ,,   THOMAS DYMOCK, son of John D., of Humelthorpe (? Thimblethorp), co

,,   ,,   JOHN (in Calendar) ATKINS, son of Robert A , of East Greenwich, Kent.

,,   ,,   EDMOND TOPCLIFE, of Horstead, Norfolk.

folio 645.

,,   ,,   CHRISTOPHER WOOD, son of John W , of Ashridge, Devonshire

,,   ,,   JOHN DRURY, son and heir of Robert D., of Docking (?), Norfolk, Esq

,,   ,,   THOMAS WARING, son of William W., of Warrington, co Lancaster

,,   ,,   WILLIAM GERRARD, son of Richard G., B D , of co Chester

,,   ,,   ROBERT BERNERS, of Barnard's Inn, late of London, gent

,,   ,,   JOHN BIRKETT, son and heir of Thomas B , of London

,,   ,,   HENRY SPRINGHAM, son and heir of Matthias S , of London, merchant tailor

,,   ,,   WILLIAM FENTON, son and heir of Sir Geoffrey F , of Thistleworth Court,

,,   18   JOHN PENRUDDOCK, of Compton Chamberlain, Wilts   [Middlesex

1609-10.		folio 645—(*continued*)
Mar	18	ANTHONY ST LEGER, of Leeds Castle, Kent, gent
,,	,,	WILLIAM HALES, son and heir of William H , of the city of Canterbury
,,	,,	JOHN CONEY, of Whissendine, co Rutland, gent
,,	,,	RICHARD CLERKE, of the city of Hereford, gent

1610		folio 646
June	14	GEORGE BALL, of Staple Inn, gent
,,	,,	ANTHONY GIBSON, of Barnard's Inn, and of Anstey, co Leicester.
Aug	7	THOMAS TRICE, of Godmanchester, Hunts, gent
,,	,,	JOHN BALDWIN, of Great Stoughton, Hunts, gent
,,	,,	JOHN LOFTES, of Lutton, co Northampton
,,	,,	JEREMIE THORNTON, of Greenford, Middlesex, gent
,,	,,	MATTHEW HUNDSLEY, of Southall, Middlesex, gent
,,	,,	THOMAS DOYLEY, son and heir of Edward D , of Overbury Hall, Suffolk
,,	,,	WILLIAM THOROLD, of Marston, co Lincoln, gent
,,	,,	ROBERT BOOTHBY, of London, gent
,,	,,	HENRY CORNWALLIS, son of Thomas C , of Portchester, Southampton, Knight.
,,	,,	GEORGE LEWIS, of Staple Inn, gent , and of Manchester, co Worcester (*sic*)
,,	,,	ROBERT BIRCH, son and heir of John B , of Preston, Sussex, Esq

		folio 647.
,,	10	CHRISTOPHER PLUNKETT, Knight, of Dunsoughly, co. Dublin.
,,	,,	JAMES GERRARD, son of William G , Esq , late reader
,,	,,	SAMPSON EURE, son of Francis E , Knight
,,	,,	JOHN DUNCOMBE, of Whitney, Oxon
,,	,,	THOMAS WARROCK, of Hereford, gent
Oct	24	RICHARD THORNES, of Bridgenorth, Salop, gent
,,	,,	TIMOTHY REMINGTON, of Lockington, co York, gent
Nov.	1	ALEXANDER RIGBIE, of Wigan, co Lancaster, gent
,,	,,	JOHN ILES, of London, gent.
,,	,,	JOHN CHARLEWOOD, of Little Burstead, Essex, gent
,,	7	HENRY FARRINGTON, gent , son of Thomas F , of Werden, co Lancaster, Esq

		folio 648
,,	,,	SAMSON DARRELL, son and heir of Marmaduke D , of Fulmer, Bucks, Knight
,,	9	WILLIAM CARDINALL, of Barnard's Inn, gent
,,	,,	THOMAS RIVETT, of Rattlesden, Suffolk, gent [deceased
,,	20.	WILLIAM DICKENSON, of the city of London, gent., son and heir of Daniel D ,
,,	,,	THOMAS DEANE, of the city of London, gent , son of John D , of the same, gent [Knight
,,	,,	RICHARD HARPUR, son and heir of Richard H , of Littleover, co. Derby,
,,	,,	EDMUND MOLYNEUX, son of Edmund M , late of Thorpe, Notts, Esq , deceased
,,	,,	JOHN VAVASOUR, gent , son and heir of Nicholas V , of Waltham Holy Cross,
,,	,,	FRANCIS NEVILL, of Chevet, co York, gent [Essex, Esq

1610.		folio 649
Nov	20	WILLIAM BOYES, gent , son and heir of Samuel B , of Hawkhurst, Kent, Esq
,,	,,	WILLIAM WHITE, of Hawkhurst, Kent, Esq.
,,	,,	HERBERT HAY, of Hurstmonceaux, Sussex, gent
,,	,,	MATTHEW BROOKSBY, of Ashby Magna, co Leicester, gent

1610-11

Feb	2	VIVIAN MOLYNEUX, son of Richard M., Knight
,,	6	WILLIAM DUNCH, of Averie, Wilts, Esq
,,	,,	SAINT-MOUNT (St Amand) WELLS, of Bucksted, Sussex, gent
,,	,,	ROGER GREGORY, son of Roger G , of Stockwith, co. Lincoln, Esq. [ton
,,	,,	THOMAS CHETWODE, son of Richard C., Knight, of Warkworth, co Northamp-
,,	,,	EDWARD CALVERLEY, gent., son of Ralph C , of Saughton, co Chester
,,	,,	FRANCIS APPLEBY, of Clove Lodge, co. York, gent

folio 650.

,,	,,	THOMAS LOVELL, of Skelton, co. York
,,	12	HORATIO EURE, son and heir of Francis E., Knight, of Gray's Inn
,,	,,	WILLIAM EURE, son of Francis E , Knight, of Gray's Inn
,,	,,	EDWARD FINCH, son of Henry F , Esq , reader of this Inn
,,	,,	CHRISTOPHER PHIPP, son and heir of Richard P , of Bould, co Lancaster
,,	,,	FRANCIS THORPE, son and heir of Roger T , of Birdsall, co York, Esq
,,	,,	WALTON POOLE, son of Henry P , Knight
,,	,,	DOMINICK COPINGER, son of Walter C , of Cork, Ireland, Esq
		[Middlesex, Esq
,,	,,	PAINE FISHER, of Chilton, Hants, son and heir of William F , of Pallingswick,
,,	17	LEWIS FOULIS, son and heir of William F , Esq , Secretary to Queen Anne

folio 651

,,	,,	NEVILL POOLE, son and heir of Henry P , Knight, of Okesey, Wilts.
,,	,,	WILLIAM HERVEY, of Ickworth, Suffolk, Knight
,,	,,	HUNTINGDON COLBY, of Beccles, Suffolk, Knight
,,	,,	MORGAN DELAHAY, of Altereyney (Alteryn), co Hereford, Esq.
,,	,,	PHILIP BEDINGFIELD, of Ditchingham, Norfolk, "absque fine "
,,	,,	WILLIAM COX, of Ashton Kenes, Wilts, gent
,,	,,	THOMAS ATHEROLD, of Burgh, Suffolk
,,	,,	ROBERT MEDCALFE, of Staple Inn, and of Ludlow, Salop, gent.
,,	,,	GILBERT NORTH, son of Dudley, Lord North.
,,	,,	GEORGE DUKE, of Wandsworth, Surrey, gent.
,,	,,	GEORGE STANHOPE, of Trinity College, Cambridge

folio 652.

Mar.	22	JOHN SKIDMORE, of Staple Inn, gent. [Henry, Earl of Huntingdon
,,	,,	GEORGE HASTINGS, of Ashby-de-la-Zouch, co Leicester, Esq , brother of
1611.		[Kent, gent
April	24	MICHAEL FAGGE, son and heir of Edward F , of Ewell, parish of Feversham,
,,	,,	EDWARD CLEYPOLE, son of Adam C , of Northburgh, co Northampton, gent

H

1611		folio 652—(*continued*)
April 24		JOHN HALES, of Hales House, in the city of Canterbury, gent.
June 10		THOMAS HEWET, Esq , of London, late of Staple Inn.
,,	,,	JOHN BARNEWALL, of Crickstown, co Meath, gent
,,	,,	THOMAS ROSSETER, son of Richard R , of Somerby, co Lincoln, Esq.
,,	,,	EDWARD HERON, son and heir of Henry H , of Standon, Herts, gent

folio 653.

,,	11	ANDREW BURTON, of Okeham, co Rutland, son of Bartin B , Esq
,,	,,	EDWARD NEWMAN, of Staple Inn, gent , son of Thomas N , formerly of [Handsworth, co. Stafford, gent
,,	,,	HAWTE WYAT, son of George W , of Boxley, Kent, Esq.
,,	,,	HENRY WYAT, son of George W , of Boxley, Kent, Esq.
,,	,,	ROGER PRESTON, son and heir of Henry P , of Upawtrie (Ottery), Devon, Esq
Aug 6		LEWIS OWEN, Esq , one of the King's servants, commonly called Serjeant to [the Larder
,,	,,	PETER BROUGHTON, gent , son of Thomas B., late of Broughton, co Stafford, [Esq , deceased
,,	,,	CUTHBERT OGLE, of the town of Northampton, Esq
,,	,,	WILLIAM GERRARD, son and heir of Philip G., now reader, " sine fine "
,,	,,	PETER HUSSEY, of Galtrim, co Meath.

folio 654.

,,	8	WILLIAM BENNET, one of the sons of John B , Knight, Doctor of Laws, Master [in Chancery, and Chancellor of Anne, the Queen Consort
,,	,,	RICHARD SWINNERTON, one of the sons of John S , Knight, citizen and [Alderman of London.
,,	10	MATTHIAS FOWLE, citizen and merchant of London
,,	,,	RICHARD DIKE, citizen and merchant of London
,,	,,	THOMAS BROWNE, citizen and mercer of London
,,	,,	FRANCIS BRETRIDGE, citizen and merchant tailor of London
,,	,,	NATHANIEL DEARDE, citizen and grocer of London
,,	,,	EDWARD CAMPION, son and heir of Thomas C , of London, gent
,,	,,	JOHN ANDREW TURATO, late of Milan, now of London, gent
,,	11	PAUL GARRAWAY, of Lewes, Sussex, Esq
,,	,,	PHILIP GARRAWAY, son and heir of Paul G , of Lewes, Sussex, Esq

folio 655

,,	13	CHARLES STANHOPE, K B , eldest son and heir of Right Hon John S , Knight, Lord S , Baron Harrington [son of Richard B , Viscount Mountgarret
,,	,,	EDWARD BUTLER, of Monehore, Ireland, Esq , son and heir of Peter B , second
,,	,,	JOHN WOLSTENHOLME, of London, Esq
,,	,,	JOHN WOLSTENHOLME, son and heir of John W , of London.
,,	14	FRANCIS STIDOLPH, of Northbury, Surrey, Knight
,,	,,	CHRISTOPHER MARSHE, of Exeter, Devon, gent.
,,	,,	THOMAS BOURCHIER, son of John B , of Lovedoune, Essex, gent
,,	,,	WILLIAM VAUGHAN, son of William V the younger, late of Walford, co [Hereford, deceased
,,	,,	WILLIAM SHEREMAN, son of Richard S , of Ottery, Devon, Esq

1611   folio 655—(continued).

Aug 14 FRANCIS SMITH, son of Reginald S., of Doncaster, co. York, gent   [Knight.

,, 15   WILLIAM COLEPEPER, Esq., son and heir of Thomas C , of Aylesford, Kent,

folio 656.

,, ,,   FERDINANDO WITHER, son of Richard W., of Manydoune, co Southampton

,, ,,   NICHOLAS BARNEWALL, son and heir of Patrick B , Knight, of Gracedieu,
                                                                      [Ireland

,, ,,   CUTHBERT MARSHALL, son and heir of Richard M , late of Denton, co

,, 16. OWEN SMITH, of Stiffkey, Norfolk, Esq   [Durham, Esq.

,, ,,   FRANCIS ASTLEY, son and heir of Thomas A , of Melton, co Norfolk, Esq

,, ,,   JAMES HOLTE, son of Francis H , of Grislehurst, co Lanc , Esq

,, ,,   WILLIAM HOLTE, another son of Francis H ,of Grislehurst, co Lanc., Esq.

,, ,,   EDWARD ASHTON, son of Edward A , of Clubcliffe, co York, Esq

,, ,,   RICHARD KETERICH, son and heir of Richard K , of South Mimms, Middx ,

,, ,,   ROGER COLE, of London, gent.   [Esq.

folio 657   [Durham (sic).

,, ,,   GREGORY BUTLER, son of Robert Boteler, of Kerklam, in the Bishoprick of

,, ,,   THOMAS GODBOLD, son of Thomas G , of South Holte, Suffolk
                                                    [Southill, Beds, Esq

,, ,,   JOHN ST JOHN, son and heir of Francis St J , of Stanfordbury, in parish of

,, ,,   THOMAS DUNCOMBE, son and heir of John D , of Littlington, Beds, Esq

,, ,,   WILLIAM PAYNTER, son and heir of Anthony P , of Gillingham, Kent, Esq

,, ,,   RICHARD BLOWER, of the city of Westminster, gent   [Middx , gent (erased)

,, ,,   JEREMY THORNTON, son and heir of Thomas T , late of Great Greenford,

,, ,,   THOMAS STAMFORD, son and heir of Thomas S , late of Isleworth, Sion,
                                                    [Middlesex, gent , deceased

,, ,,   EDWARD PEYTON, Knight, son and heir of John P , of Isleham, co. Cam-

1608   folio 658   [bridge, Baronet and Knight

Nov 1   THOMAS BEDINGFELD, second son of Thomas B , of Lincoln's Inn.

folio 659

,, 4.   THOMAS BARNEBY, junior, gent

,, 21. WILLIAM MADOCKE, son and heir of Richard M , gent

,, ,,   PETER ELLIS, of Staple Inn, gent

,, ,,   JOHN BALGUY, of Staple Inn, gent   [readers of this Society

,, 24   GARRET AUNGER (Angier), son and heir of Francis A , Esq, one of the

1608-9

Feb 2   THOMAS LADEMAN, son and heir of Thomas L , of Rougham, Norfolk.

,, ,,   HENRY HALL, son and heir of Henry H , of the city of York, gent   [Beds

,, 10   GEORGE BARNARDISTON, son and heir of Sigismund B , of Over Caldecott,

,, ,,   SAMUEL BARKER, of Staple Inn, gent

folio 660.

Mar. 14. PEDAELL HARLOWE, son and heir of Robert H , of London, Esq

,, ,,   THOMAS SALKELD, son and heir of Thomas S , of Barton, Cumberland

1608-9   folio 660—(continued)

Mar 14   EDWARD TRIPP, of Staple Inn, and of Barton, co Lincoln, gent.

,,   ,,   ROBERT WYNIFFE, of London, gent

,,   ,,   THOMAS TYE, of Tremley, Suffolk, Esq

,,   ,,   HENRY WALLER, second son of Thomas W , of Gray's Inn, Esq

,,   ,,   REYNOLD CLARKE, of Barnard's Inn, and of Bramfield, Suffolk, Esq

,,   ,,   THOMAS LINLEY, eldest son of Francis L , of Skegby, Notts, gent
1609
May   5   GEORGE LUCY, son of Thomas L , Knight, deceased

,,   ,,   WILLIAM WATTON, son and heir of Thomas W , of Addington, Kent, Esq

,,   11   PHILIP CAGE, son of Daniel C , of Harston, Herts

folio 661.

,,   26   JOHN GARDENER (so in Index), of Suffolk, gent   [gent

,,   ,,   NICHOLAS DERLEY (? Denley), of Hollingbourne, Kent, and of Staple Inn,

,,   ,,   ROBERT GOODINGE, of Ipswich, Suffolk, and of Barnard's Inn, gent.

,,   ,,   GILES CROMWELL, of Westerham, Kent, and of Furnival's Inn

Nov   3   FRANCIS MATHEWS, of Blackwell, co Warwick, late of Staple Inn
1609-10
Feb   9   THOMAS CARYE, of Castle Carye, co Somerset   [York

Mar   3   RICHARD BYCKARDIKE, son of Mr Edward B , of Ferneham (Farneham), co
1610 (8 James)
May 18   HENRY DARLEY, son and heir of Richard D , Esq

,,   ,,   MATTHEW HABERGHAM, son and heir of Laurence H , of Habergham
                                                        [(Abram), co Lancaster, Esq

,,   ,,   WILLIAM (or WALTER) ATKINSON, son of John A., late of the city of York.

June 25.   WILLIAM WARD, of Carleton Curlew, co Leicester, gent

Aug 10.   NICHOLAS WOODCOCK, of Staple Inn, gent , born at Clavering, Essex.

folio 662

Nov   7   HENRY EWEN, of Staple Inn, gent   [gent

,,   21   JOHN JACKSON, gent , son and heir of George J , of Grimsthorpe, co York,

,,   ,,   ROBERT LADD, of Staple Inn, gent
1610-11
Feb 13   JOHN PLUMMER, son of William P , of Gray's Inn

,   ,,   RALPH OUTLAW, of Witchingham, Norfolk, gent , and of Barnard's Inn

,,   ,,   JOHN DOUGHTY, son of Robert D , of Hoveton St John, Norfolk

,,   22   HENRY TOLSON, son and heir of Richard T , of Bridekirk, Cumberland
1611
May   3   WILLIAM PYTTMAN, of Woodbridge, Suffolk, and of Staple Inn, gent

,,   ,,   HENRY CORBIN, son and heir of George C., of Hall End, co Warwick, Esq

June 10   RICHARD CRADOCK, gent , son of John C , Archdeacon of Northumberland

,,   ,,   EDWARD GREAVES, son of John G , of Beeley, co Derby, gent

folio 663

Aug   6   LEONARD KEMPE, son and heir of Francis K , of London, gent

,,   16   WILLIAM DRURY, son and heir of Anthony D , Knight, of Besthorpe, Norfolk

,,   ,,   NATHANIEL BACON, third son of Edward B., of Shrubland, Suffolk, Esq

1611   folio 668

Oct 29   WILLIAM STIDOLFE, of Mickleham, Surrey, Esq

„   „   THOMAS MARSH, of London, gent

„   „   WALTER GROSVENOR, of Bushbury, co Stafford.

„   „   FRANCIS FOWKE, of Gunston, Suffolk, son of Roger F , of same, Esq

Nov 8   THOMAS COVERT, son of William C , of Bexley, Kent, Esq

„ 20   ROGER COOPER, third son of William C , of Thurgarton, Notts, Esq

„   „   SYMON PYTTS, of Ashley, Oxon, gent.

„   „   GEORGE METCALFE, of North Allerton, co York, gent , and of Barnard's Inn

„   „   LIONEL MORSE, of Flempton, Suffolk, gent.

„   „   WILLIAM INGLEBY, of Ripley, co York, heir of William I , of same, Knight

                                 folio 669   [Esq

„ 25   MICHAEL WARTON, son and heir of Michael W , of Beverley Park, co York,

„   „   SAMUEL DUNCH, of Little Wittenham, Berks, gent

„   „   ISRAEL DILLAND, son and heir of Henry D , of Himer (Highmore), Oxon, gent

1611-12

Feb 2   HENRY YELVERTON, second son of William Y , of Rougham, Norfolk, Esq

„   „   GEORGE MERLER, of Crayford, Kent, gent

„   „   THOMAS WARD, of Postwick, Norfolk, Esq

„   „   JOHN DAWNEY, son and heir of Thomas D., of co York, Knight

„   5   JOHN SPARROW, gent , son and heir of John S , gent , of Dunton, Beds

„   „   GEORGE RATCLIFFE, of Thornehill, co York, gent

„   „   JOHN WINGFIELD, son of John W , of Tickencote, co Rutland, Esq

„   „   JOHN PALMER, of Carleton Scroope, co. Lincoln, gent

„   „   ROBERT PALMER, of Carleton Scroope, gent   [gent

„   „   WILLIAM GODBOULD, son and heir of William G , of Worlingworth, Suffolk,

                                 folio 670

„   „   FRANCIS HOWARD, son of Right Honourable William, Lord Howard

„   „   ROBERT ABBOT, D D., brother to my Lord's Grace of Canterbury

„   „   WILLIAM STAUNFORD, Esq , son to Judge Staunton.

„ 10.   JOHN HOLLIS, son and heir of Sir John H , Knight

„   „   THOMAS HANMER, of Hanmer, co Flint, Knight

„   „   GEORGE PENNYE, Esq , servant of Henry, Earl of Northampton

„   „   ANTHONY ANDROS, of co Northampton, gent

„ 11   JOHN DAVENPORT, son of William D , Esq , of Henbury, co Chester

„   „   FRANCIS WEEKES, of Broadwood Kelley, co Devon

„   „   THOMAS FOXE, of London, gent

„   „   WILLIAM SELBY, son of Sir Ralph S , of Westwood, Northumberland, Knight

Mar 11   GEFFREY MINSHULL, son of Edward M , of Nantwich, co Chester, gent

„ 12.   JOHN LEVESON (Sir) the younger, Knight

„   „   JAMES MEADOWS, D D

„   „   VALENTINE BROWN, son of Sir Nicholas B , of (the Neale ?), Ireland, Knight

„ 13   CAREW DARCY, son of Sir Edward D

1611-12		folio 670—(*continued*)
Mar 13		JOHN BOROUGH, of Sandwich, Kent, Esq [reader (Thomas Crewe)
,, ,,		THOMAS SOTHERNE, son of George S, of Salop, gent, nephew to the then
1612		**folio 671** ⌐of this Inn
May 8		HENRY FINCH, gent, one of the sons of Henry F, Esq, one of the readers
,, ,,		THOMAS ASTON, son of Robert A, of Farnham, Surrey, gent
,, ,,		HENRY GODDARD, second son of Thomas G, of Kirchenwood, Wilts
,, 14		JOHN RUDSTON, of Horton Kirby, co Kent, gent
		[Attorney-general of Duchy of Lancaster
,, ,,		JOHN BROGRAVE, son and heir of Simon B, son and heir of John B, Knight,
,, ,,		THOMAS HOLMES, son and heir of Christopher H, late of London. gent
,, ,,		THOMAS COTTON, son and heir of William C, of Laughton, co Leicester
,, 22		ROBERT HUSSEY, of Honington, co Lincoln, gent
,, ,,		EDWARD HENSON, of Fordingbridge, co Southampton, gent

folio 672

,, ,,		ANTHONY CROFTS, second son of John C, of Toddington, Beds, Knight
,, ,,		WILLIAM MIDELTON, gent, son of Wm M, of Stockeld, co York, Esq.
June 16		EUBULUS THELWALL, son of John T, of Bathavarne, co Denbigh Esq
,, 18		RICHARD OCKOULD, late steward of the Inn, for his good service
,, 30		WILLIAM LEEKE, gent
Aug 2		EDWARD LYNDESEY, of London, Esq
,, ,,		HENRY SMITH, of London, gent
,, ,,		JOHN COURTHOPE, second son of John C, of Wyley (Whileigh), Sussex, Esq

folio 673.

,, 4		PETER EGERTON, Esq, son of John E, of Egerton, co Chester, Knight
,, ,,		WILLIAM PRIESTLEY, son and heir of Wm. P, citizen and merchant taylor of
,, 9		HERBERT WHITFIELD, of Tenterden, Kent, Esq [London
,, ,,		JOHN WILLIAMS, of London, goldsmith to the King
,, ,,		RICHARD DUKE, of Aylesford, Kent
,, ,,		THOMAS ROBINSON, of London, gent.
,, ,,		ROBERT HOWE, of London, goldsmith.
,, ,,		JOHN GREENE, of London, gent.
,, ,,		RICHARD CROSSRO ("Crofts" in Index), citizen and goldsmith of London
,, ,,		JOHN GRAY, of London, citizen and goldsmith
,, ,,		GEORGE PAYNE, citizen and grocer of London
,, ,,		EDMOND LEVER, citizen and ——— of London.

folio 674.

,, ,,		JOHN AMHERST, citizen and merchant of London
,, ,,		WILLIAM RAYNES, citizen and merchant of London
,, ,,		GEORGE FREVILE, son of Richard F, of Middleham, co Durham Esq
,, ,,		JOHN BINGLEY, of Westminster, Esq
,, ,,		ANDREW HAWES, citizen and fishmonger of London
,, 11		HENRY BROOME, of London, gent

1612.		folio 674—(continued)
Aug	11	WILLIAM BYNG, of Wrotham, Kent, Esq
,,	,,	ROGER MOLINS, of London, Esq
,,	,,	ABRAHAM ALLEN, of London, Esq , chirographer to the King

folio 675

,,	,,	THOMAS BROUNE, eldest son of Thos B , citizen and mercer of London
,,	13	ALEXANDER SERLE, Bachelor of Laws, Procurator-general
,,	,,	EDMUND SCOTT, of London, merchant
,,	14	MORGAN RANDYLL, Esq , son and heir of Edward R , of Albury, Surrey, Knight
,,	,,	NICHOLAS TOKE, son and heir of John T , of Goodinton, parish of Chart, Kent, Esq [Baronet
,,	,,	JOHN HALES, son and heir of Edward H , of Woodchurch, Kent, Knight and [Knight and Baronet
,,	,,	EDWARD HALES, gent , second son of Edward H , of Woodchurch, Kent,
,,	,,	PAUL WADDING, son of Thomas W , of Waterford, Ireland, Esq
,,	,,	WILLIAM ALMON, of Hoo, Norfolk, gent
,,	,,	JOHN LANGFORD, son of Roger L , of Ruthin, co Denbigh, Esq
,,	,,	EDWARD GIBSON, son of John G , Knight, D C L
,,	,,	FRANCIS NEVILLE, of Newark-upon-Trent, Notts, Esq

folio 676

Oct	21	RICHARD CHURCH, of Nantwich, co Chester, gent , son and heir of Randle C , [gent (admitted to the Master's table)
,,	,,	RICHARD CLUTTON, of Nantwich, gent (admitted to the Master's table)
,,	,,	RICHARD KNIGHTLEY, Esq , son and heir of Edward K , Esq , late of this [Inn, deceased (admitted to the Master's table)
Nov	1	CHRISTOPHER WANDESFORD, of Kirklington, co York, Esq , son and heir of [George W , Knight
,,	,,	JOHN THURBARNE, son and heir of James T , Esq [Stafford, Esq
Oct. 6. }		
(? Nov). }		JOHN WHORWOOD, son and heir of Gerrard W , of Sturton Castle, co.
Nov	6	EDMUND VAUGHAN, of Barnard's Inn, gent

folio 677.

,,	26.	PETER WROTHE, of Staple Inn, gent
,,	6.	WALTER ISSONS, of Barnard s Inn, gent.
,,	,,	JOHN WHORWOOD, of Sturton Castle, co Stafford, Esq (erased)
1612-13		
Feb	2	ROBERT BARRINGTON, second son of Francis B , of Barrington Hall, Bart
,,	,,	RICHARD HUTTON, gent , second son of Richard H , Serjeant-at-Law
,,	,,	JOHN WILSON, M A , of Christ Church, Oxford, gent
,,	8	SAMUEL BISPHAM, of London, gent , son and heir of William B
,,	23	MARTIN WHITE, one of the clerks of the Petty Bag of the Court of Chancery
,,	,,	EVAN EDWARDS, of Mold, co Flint, gent
,,	,,	PEREGRINE FOULKES, of Bullock, co Northampton, gent
,,	,,	HENRY ESTDALE of (Fenant ?), Kent, gent
,,	,,	PETER PEAKE, of Sandwich, Kent, gent

1612-13		folio 678

Feb 25   THOMAS RAWLINS, of London, M D.

,,   ,,   JOHN BROOKE, of London, gent

,,   28   ROBERT STANLEY, second son of William, Earl of Derby

,,   ,,   GILBERT GERRARD, Knight, son and heir of Thomas, Lord Gerrard

,,   ,,   RICHARD MOLYNEUX, Esq , son and heir of Richard M , Knight and Baronet

,,   ,,   WILLIAM DAVENPORT, son and heir of Humphrey D , now reader

,,   ,,   CHARLES GERRARD, Esq , son and heir of Ratcliffe G , Esq

,,   ,,   HENRY TRAVERS, gent   [Knight

,,   ,,   JOHN WANDESFORD, second son of George W , of Kirklington, co York,

,,   ,,   MARTIN SMITH, third son of Martin S , of London, gent

,,   ,,   THOMAS MORRIS, son and heir of Oliver M , of co. Denbigh.

folio 679

Mar 1   CHRISTOPHER THACKER, of Clement's Inn, gent.

,,   ,,   HOBYE MORTON, son and heir of George M , of Morton, co Durham, Esq

,,   ,,   WILLIAM READ, son and heir of William R , of Norfolk (Northants?), Knight

,,   ,,   WALTER ROLT, of Clipston, Beds, gent

,,   ,,   THOMAS HUTCHINSON, of London, gent   [Esq

,,   ,,   HUMPHREY MICHELL, son and heir of Francis M , of Old Windsor, Berks,

,,   ,,   RICHARD TILDESLEY, son of Thomas T., of Orford, co. Lancaster, Esq.

1613   [Esq

April 26   HUMPHREY MILDMAY, son and heir of Humphrey M., of Danbury, Essex,

,,   ,,   WILLIAM BANKES, gent , son and heir of James B , Esq

,,   ,,   THOMAS BANKES, gent , second son of James B., Esq

,,   ,,   VALENTINE EVERARD, son and heir of Valentine E , of Canterbury, gent

folio 680.

,,   ,,   OLIVER CAVE, son of Thomas C , of Stanford, co Northampton, Esq

,,   ,,   EDWARD PERROTT (Parrott), of North Leigh, Oxon, Esq.

,,   ,,   WILLIAM GREY (or Gray), son and heir of Ralph G , Knight.

May 5   JOHN BELLOT, son and heir of Edward B., of Morton, co Chester, Esq

,,   ,,   JAMES EVINGTON, son of Francis E., of Enfield, Middlesex, Esq

,,   ,,   ROBERT CHOLMELEY, son of Henry C., of Burton Coggles, co. Lincoln, gent

                                      [York, gent.

,,   13   CHARLES ATKINSON, son and heir of Francis A., of Castle Levington, co

,,   ,,   EDWARD GAMES, son and heir of John G , of Newton, co Brecon, Knight

,,   ,,   THOMAS TUNSTALL, son of Francis T., of Scargill, co York.

folio 681.

June 21   THOMAS APPLETON, brother of Henry A , of Southbenfleet, Essex, Bart

,,   ,,   NATHANIEL HENSHAW, of the city of London, gent

Aug 11   FRANCIS ANDERSON, son of Henry A , of Newcastle-on-Tyne, Esq

,,   ,,   CHRISTOPHER GOODAY, son of Roger G , of Pentlow, Essex, gent   [gent

,,   ,,   WILLIAM STROTHER, son and heir of Clement S , of Newton, Northumberland,

,,   ,,   JENKIN EDMONDS, of Lanthomas, co Monmouth, gent

1613.   folio 681—(*continued*).

Aug 11.   GEORGE MARLER, of Crayford, Kent, gent

,,   ,,   HENRY SHERWOOD, son of Thomas S , of Inisbrocke, co Kilkenny, gent
                                                        [Knight.

,,   13   ROBERT DILLON, Esq , son and heir of James D , of Moymeath, co Meath,

folio 682.

,,   ,,   JOHN LAMBE, of Staple Inn, gent

,,   ,,   GEORGE THEOBALD, second son of John T , of Seale, Kent, Esq

,,   ,,   WILLIAM BLANDE, gent., son of William B , of Tallingstone, Suffolk, Esq

,,   ,,   ROBERT PAMEN, son of Clement P., of Debden, Suffolk, Esq

,,   ,,   FRANCIS KNIGHTLEY, son of Richard K., of co. Northampton, Knight

,,   ,,   SIMON MAYNE, of Dinton, Bucks, Esq.   [Norfolk, Esq

,,   ,,   WILLIAM THURLBYE, gent., son and heir of William T , of Little Dunham,

Oct 25   THOMAS LEAKE, of Wilsland, Salop, gent

folio 683.

,,   ,,   NICHOLAS WINGATE, of Staple Inn, gent

,,   ,,   THOMAS PERIENT, of Colchester, Essex, Esq

,,   ,,   JOHN WINTHROP, son and heir of Adam W , of Groton, Suffolk, Esq

Nov 1   JOHN COPE, son of Sir Anthony C , of Hanwell, Oxon, by his uncle,
                  [Walter C , " that carryed Lytell Law from thys howse "

,,   5   RICHARD TURPIN, son of William T , of Knaptofte, co Leicester, Knight

,,   15   ANTHONY FULWOOD, of Newark-upon-Trent, Notts, Esq

,,   ,,   FRANCIS BACON, son and heir of William B , of Witton, co York, Esq

,,   ,,   JOHN WILLOUGHBY, son and heir of William W , of Aston Rowant, Oxon,
                                                  [Knight

,,   ,,   WILLIAM WILLOUGHBY, son of Sir William W , Knight, of Aston Rowant,
                                                    [Oxon

folio 684

,,   ,,   WILLIAM COLEPEPER, son of Anthony C , of Bedgbury, Kent, Knight

,,   17   ANTONY AUCHER, of Bridge, Kent, Knight

,,   22   GEORGE POCHIN, son and heir of Matthew P , of Barkby, co Leicester, Esq

,,   ,,   GEORGE FLEETWOOD, son of George F , of Chalfont St Giles, Bucks, Knight

1613-14

Feb 2   EDWARD HERBERT, Knight of the Bath, of Castle Montgomery

,,   ,,   WILLIAM TYRRELL, son of Thomas T., of Gipping, Suffolk, Esq   [Esq

,,   3   THOMAS STANDISHE, son and heir of Alexander S , of Duxbury, co Lanc ,

,,   ,,   THOMAS BURTON, son and heir of Edward B , of Bourne, Suffolk, Knight

folio 685.   [of Staple Inn

,,   ,,   ROGER LEMYNGE, son and heir of Simon L , of Audley, co Lincoln, late

,,   ,,   PETER LATHAM, of Brentwood, Essex, Esq   [Suffolk, gent

,,   ,,   OLIVER MOUNDEN, late of Staple Inn, son and heir of Oliver M , of Exning,

,,   ,,   ROBERT LUCKYN, son and heir of Robert L , of East Soham, co Cam-

,,   ,,   JOHN FORDE, of Hackney, Middlesex, gent   [bridge, gent

Mar 15   THOMAS PARKER, son and heir of Nicholas P , of Jevington, Sussex, Knight

1613-14   folio 685—(*continued*).

Mar 15   GEORGE LUTTRELL, son of George L , of Dunster, co Somerset, Esq
                                                                    [Inn, gent
  ,,   ,,   WALTER NURSE (?), of Weston-under-Penyard, co Hereford, late of Staple

folio 686

,,   ,,   EDWARD WRIGHT, son and heir of Richard W , of the city of Durham, gent
,,   ,,   GEORGE BARKER, son of Oswald B , of the city of Durham, gent
,,   ,,   JOHN NYNN (?), gent , late of Staple Inn, Solicitor to Louis, Duke of Lenox,
,,   16   THOMAS WATSON, of Halstead, Kent, Esq   [Earl of Richmond, &c
,,   ,,   WILLIAM FARNWAY, youngest son of William F , of Springthorpe, co Lincoln,
                                                    [gent, late of Staple Inn
,,   ,,   CHARLES DODD, son and heir of Robert D , of Cloverley, Salop, Esq
,,   19   JOHN HARTE, gent

folio 687.

,,   ,,   WILLIAM GRIFFITHS, son of Robert G , of Caernuther, co Anglesey, Esq
,,   ,,   ARCHIBALD PRIMROSE, gent
,,   ,,   ROBERT WILLIAMS, son and heir of Richard W , of Ruthin, co Denbigh, Esq
,,   ,,   FRANCIS SHELDON, son of Francis S , of Bredicot, co Worcester, Esq.
,,   24   JOHN DODSWORTH, son and heir of John D , of Thornton Watlass, co York,
,,   ,,   HENRY PARKER, of Woodford, Essex, Esq   [Esq
,,   ,,   CLEMENT SPELMAN, son of Henry S , of Middleton, Norfolk, Knight

folio 688.

,,   ,,   ROGER TOWNSEND, of Raynham, Norfolk, Esq.
,,   ,,   WILLIAM MORGELL, son of John M , of Mosters, co Leicester, Esq (erased)
1614
May 24   DEVEREUX FERMOR, son of George F , Knight, of co. Northampton, deceased
,,   ,,   RALPH ASHTON, son of Richard A , of Middleton, co Lancaster, Knight
,,   ,,   EDWARD COPLEY, son and heir of Edward C , of Southill, Beds, Esq
,,   ,,   JOHN DUNCOMBE, son of William D , of Ivinghoe, Bucks, gent
                                                    [gent, late of Staple Inn
,,   ,,   RICHARD WOODROFFE, son and heir of Richard W., of Bromlye, co Lancaster,

folio 689   [Middlesex, Esq

,,   ,,   ALEXANDER KETTERICH, son and heir of Richard K , of South Mimms,
,,   ,,   THOMAS HARINGTON, son of Henry H , of Bagworth, co. Leicester, Knight
,,   ,,   JOHN BOOTH, son and heir of William B , of Watton, co. Lincoln, gent
,,   ,,   JOHN PASTON, son of Edmund P., of Appleton, Norfolk, Esq
,,   ,,   ROGER WYNGATE, son and heir of Roger W , of Flamburgh, co York, Esq
,,   ,,   EDMUND WYNGATE, son of Roger W , of Flamburgh, co York, Esq
,,   ,,   NICHOLAS LEACHE, of the city of Exeter, gent
,,   ,,   EDWARD HOBART, late of Barnard's Inn, gent
June 3   RICHARD STRUGGLE, of the city of Canterbury, gent

folio 690.   [York, Esq

,,   ,,   RICHARD ETHERINGTON, son and heir of George E , of Newton Garth, co
July 6   WILLIAM BROWNE, son of Francis B., of Tolthorpe, co Rutland, Esq

1614.   folio 690 — (continued)

July 6   EDMUND WILLIAMSON, son of Richard W , Knight   [Knight, deceased

,,   ,,   EDMUND BUCKE, son of John B, late of Hamby Grange, co Lincoln,

,,   ,,   ROBERT KELKE, son and heir of Robert K , of Barnetby, co Lincoln, Esq
                                                          [and late of Barnard's Inn, gent

,, 12   JOHN BRABYN, son and heir of William B , of Whittington, co Lancaster,

Aug 4   WILLIAM STEWARD, of Marham, Norfolk, gent   [Norfolk, Esq

,,   ,,   ISAAC ASTLEY, gent , one of the sons of Thomas A , of Melton Constable,

,,   ,,   THOMAS PELL, of Dembleby, co Lincoln, gent

,,   ,,   BARTHOLOMEW PELL, gent , brother of Thomas P , of Dembleby, co Lincoln

folio 691

,,   6   HENRY SOUTHWORTH, of Wells, co Somerset, Esq

,,   8. THOMAS BONHAM, M D

,,   ,,   JOHN GRIFFITH, of London, Esq

,,   9   WILLIAM MORGELL, son of John M , of the city of Chester, Esq   [gent

,,   ,,   EDMOND GOODYER, son and heir of William G , of Harborough, co Leicester,

,,   ,,   HENRY BILLINGSLEY, son and heir of William B , late of London, Esq ,
                                                                              [deceased

,,   ,,   FRANCIS JAMES, son and heir of Francis J , Doctor of Laws, and one of the
                                                    [Masters in the Court of Chancery

,,   ,,   JOHN WATTON, second son of Thomas W , of Addington, Kent, Esq

,, 10   THOMAS BILLINGSLEY, second son of William B , late of London, Esq ,
                                                                              [deceased.

,,   ,,   PAUL BASSANO, second son of Arthur B , of Walthamstowe, Essex, Esq.

,,   ,,   JOHN ANTHONY, of Hoggesdoun, Middlesex, gent

folio 692.

,, 12   HENRY DAVIES, of London, Knight.   [Knight

,,   ,,   WILLIAM CHOLMELEY, son of Henry C , of Burton Coggles, co Lincoln,

,,   ,,   RICHARD BENT, son and heir of Ambrose B , deceased, of Cosby, co Leic

,,   ,,   EDMOND TREDWAY, of Ketton, co Rutland, gent

Oct 26   ROBERT OXENBRIDGE, son and heir of Robert O , Knight.

,,   ,,   HENRY DARLEY, eldest son of Richard D., of Buttercrambe, co York, Esq.

,,   ,,   THOMAS SMELT, of Ainderby Myres, co York, late of Barnard's Inn, Esq.

,,   ,,   WILLIAM GIBBON, son of John G , of Bishopsborne, Kent, gent

,,   ,,   JOHN STROTHER, of Newton, Northumberland, Esq.   [Westmoreland

,,   ,,   THOMAS WARD, late of Barnard's Inn, son and heir of John W , of Kirby,

Nov 1   GEORGE BOWES, son and heir of George B , of Stretlam, in Bishoprick of

folio 693   [Durham

,,   4. NICHOLAS POPE, late of Staple Inn, son of John P , Doctor of Laws, of Over,

,,   ,,   CHARLES LE GROS (Groo), of Crostwicke, Norfolk, Esq   [co Cambridge

,,   ,,   WILLIAM SHORT, son and heir of William S , of London, gent   [Esq

,, 11.   THOMAS WALMESLEY, son and heir of Thomas W , of Dunkenhalgh, co. Lanc ,

,, 13   SAMUEL RATCLIFFE, S T B , of Brasenose College, Oxford

,, 16   FRANCIS LASCELLES, son of Francis L , of Northallerton, co York, Esq

Nov 16   JOHN GURDON, son and heir of Bampton G , of Mainesham, Suffolk, Esq

,,   ,,   GILBERT FORTESCUE, son of Francis F , of Salden, Bucks, Knight

,,   24   WILLIAM KEATE, son of Hugh K , of Hodcot, Berks, gent.   [Knight

,,   ,,   JOHN MARKHAM, son and heir of Anthony M , of Sedgebrooke, co Lincoln,

1614-15   folio 694.

Jan 30   JOHN CREWE, son of Thomas C , Esq , one of the readers of this Inn

,,   ,,   HENRY HONYWOOD, son of Robert H., of Markshall, Essex, Esq

,,   ,,   JOHN COLEMAN, son and heir of Walter C , of Cawcke, co Stafford, Esq

,,   ,,   EDWARD PENANT, son and heir of Nicholas P., of Baggitt, co Flint gent

,,   ,,   ROBERT ROKEBY, son and heir of Ralph R , of Marske, co York, Esq

,,   ,,   LAURENCE MILFORD, of Newcastle, gent

Feb 2   GREGORY TURNER, S T P , Rector of Sefton, co Lancaster

,,   ,,   EDWARD GRANL, of Waterford Hall, Herts, gent

,,   ,,   GILES GREGORY, son and heir of Edmund G , of Culham, Oxon, gent

,,   ,,   RICHARD ALTHAM, second son of James A , Knight, one of the Barons of the
                                                                      [Exchequer.

                               folio 695

Feb 8   STEPHEN MILLES, late of Staple Inn, son and heir of Stephen M , of Thornton,
                                                                      [co York, gent.

,,   ,,   WILLIAM ROTHWELL, son and heir of Richard R , of Ewerby, co Lincoln, Esq

,,   ,,   HENRY HUNGATE, son and heir of William H , late of Bradenham, Norfolk,
                                                                      [Esq , deceased

,,   ,,   WILLIAM WEEKES, son and heir of John W , of Honichurch, Devon, Esq

,,   ,,   WILLIAM RISLEY, son and heir of Paul R , of Chetwood, Bucks, Esq

,,   ,,   GEORGE BYNG, son and heir of George B , of Wrotham, Kent, Esq.

Mar 2   RICHARD LUMLEY, Esq , cousin and heir of John, late Lord Lumley

,,   ,,   JAMES CROFTS, Knight.

,,   ,,   ROBERT HOLT, son and heir of William H , reader

,,   3   WILLIAM AMBROSIUS ("Ambrose" in Calendar), late of Staple Inn, gent

,,   ,,   EDWARD BERRY, son and heir of Bradford B., of Eastwood, Essex, gent

,,   ,,   WILLIAM WILSON, son and heir of Thomas W., of the city of York, gent

,,   ,,   JAMES ROBERTS, son of Francis R , of Willesden, Middlesex, Esq

,,   ,,   GEORGE ALLINGTON, son of George A , of Swinhope, co Lincoln, Esq

,,   5   WALTER WALLER, son of Thomas W., Knight, deceased

                               folio 696

,,   ,,   ARTHUR STRANGEWAYS, Alderman Deputy of the Ward of St Sepulchre's

,,   8   ROBERT HOLT, of Ashworth, co Lanc , Esq , brother to William H , reader

,,   ,,   RICHARD HOLT, cousin and heir of Robert H., of Ashworth, co Lanc , Esq

,,   ,,   ROBERT HOLT, brother of Richard H., cousin and heir of Robert H , of
                                                                      [Ashworth, co Lancaster, Esq

,,   ,,   THOMAS WORSLEY, son and heir of Thomas W , Esq

,,   ,,   THOMAS CORBIN, of Westminster, gent

,,   ,,   ALEXANDER PRESCOTT, of London, goldsmith.

1614-15		folio 696—(continued)

Mar	8.	ADLARD WELBY, gent
,,	9	GERRALD AUNGIER, son and heir of Francis A , Knight, Master of the Rolls [in Ireland, and one of the King's Privy Council there
,,	,,	WILLIAM HODGES, son and heir of Owen H , of Langton, Hunts
,,	,,	NICHOLAS ADYE, of Staple Inn, gent
,,	,,	DENZILL HOLLES, second son of John H , of Houghton, Notts, Knight

folio 697

,,	,,	ROBERT JENYSON, son and heir of William J , of Wallworth, co Durham, Esq
,,	,,	HENRY JENYSON, son and heir of William J , of Wynyard, co Durham, Esq
,,	,,	THOMAS SANTYE, of London, gent
,,	,,	RICHARD GREAVES, of Clifford's Inn
,,	,,	JOHN GREAVES, of Beeley, co Derby, gent
,,	,,	GEORGE FREEMAN, of Higham Ferrers, co Northampton, gent

1615		[Sussex, Bart
May	6	THOMAS PELHAM, son and heir of Thomas P , of East Lodely (? East Hoathley),
,,	17	ABRAHAM RUTTER, of Sandwich, Kent, late of Staple Inn
,,	,,	PEREGRINE BUCKE, son of John B , of Hamby Grange, co Lincoln, Knight.
,,	,,	WILLIAM FERNE, of King's Lynn, Norfolk, gent
,,	,,	WILLIAM FLETCHER, son and heir of Henry F , of Morsbie, co. Cambridge, [gent
,,	,,	ROBERT CLEAVER, late of Staple Inn, son and heir of John C , of Salisbury, [Wilts, gent

folio 698.

,,	,,	FRANCIS STORIE, of Donnington, co York, Esq
,,	,,	EDMUND HARDING, gent , son and heir of John H , of Aspley, Beds, Esq
,,	,,	ROBERT STANTON, gent , son and heir of Francis S , of Birchmore, Beds, gent
June	21	WILLIAM FILIOLL, son of John F , of Sandon, Essex, Esq
,,	,,	STANHOPE TOWNESEND, of Heydon, Norfolk, Esq
,,	,,	THOMAS TROLLOPE, son and heir of William T , of Thurlbie, co Lincoln
Aug.	6.	GEORGE HARE, Knight, one of the gentlemen of the King's Privy Chamber.
,,	,,	JOHN JONES, of Ruthin, co Denbigh, gent.
,,	,,	ROGER DOWNES, son and heir of Roger D , Esq , reader of this Inn

folio 699.   [caster, Esq

,,	,,	RICHARD CALVERT, gent , son and heir of John C , of Cockerham, co. Lan-
,,	,,	FRANCIS SHERINGTON, son and heir of John S , citizen of London
,,	,,	THEOBALD PURSELL, late of Barnard's Inn, son and heir of Richard Baron of [Longmore, co. Tipperary
,,	,,	THOMAS MORRIS, son and heir of Oliver M , of Langerwyd, co Denbigh, gent
,,	,,	JONAS WYNDALL, late of Barnard's Inn, son and heir of Jonas W , of Bocking, Essex, gent [co Lincoln, Esq
,,	,,	THOMAS WELCOME, late of Staple Inn, son of William W , of Market Stanton,
,,	,,	THOMAS MAYE, son and heir of Thomas M , of Mayfield, Sussex, Knight
,,	,,	JOHN SOTHERTON, son and heir of John S , one of the Barons of the [Exchequer at Westminster

1615   folio 699—*(continued)*

Aug. 6   EDWARD HUBERT, son and heir of Francis H , of Stansted Mountfichett,

,,   ,,   WILLIAM MOYLE, son of Thomas M , of Buckwell, Oxon, Esq [Essex, Knight

,,   ,,   ROBERT HALL, of Kentish Town, Middlesex, gent.

,,   ,,   THOMAS VALENTINE, clerk, M A

folio 700

,,   10   JOHN, Baron HAYE, of Yester, Scotland

,,   ,,   GEORGE HAY, Esq , son of George H , Knight

,,   ,,   JOHN HOLLYWAY, Comptroller of the King's Customs in London

,,   ,,   JOHN BYDALL, of Wolley, Hunts, gent

,,   ,,   RICHARD LEVER, of Little Lever, co. Lancaster, gent

,,   11   ROBERT VAWDREY, son and heir of Edward V , of Ryddings, Cheshire, gent

,,   ,,   JOHN VAWDREY, of co Chester, gent

,,   ,,   HUGH CARTWRIGHT, son of William C , of Ossington, Notts, gent

,,   ,,   JEROME SPELMAN, son and heir of Alexander S , of Hillingdon, Norfolk, gent

,,   ,,   HENRY BUTLER, of Hackensall, co Lancaster, gent

folio 701.

,,   ,,   ABRAHAM SLACK, of Slackhall, co Derby, gent

,,   ,,   JOHN GREAVES, of Woodhouse, co Derby, gent

,,   ,,   ARTHUR CHAUNCY, of London, gent

,,   ,,   WILLIAM GREAVES, of Brailsford, co. Derby, gent

Oct 25   ANTHONY CHESTER, of Chicheley, Bucks, son and heir of Anthony C , Esq

,,   ,,   JOHN FRANCKLING, of Wilseen, co Westmoreland, Knight

,,   ,,   LAMBERT OSBALDESTONE, son of Lambert O , of London, gent

,,   ,,   ROGER RANT, gent , son and heir of Roger R , Esq.

Nov 1.   JOSEPH HALL, S T D (Bishop of Exeter).

,,   ,,   WILLIAM LAUD, S T D (Archbishop of Canterbury)

,,   ,,   RALPH WESTROPP, of Cornborough, co. York, Esq.   [Esq

,,   ,,   THOMAS SOUTHWORTH, son and heir of John S , of Samlesbury, co Lancaster,

,,   ,,   ALEXANDER NORRIS, son of William N., of Speake, co Lancaster, Knight of
[the Bath.

,,   ,,   WILLIAM STANLEY, son and heir of Richard S , of Thormanby, co. York, gent

,,   ,,   JOHN LEGATT, of Chatham, Kent, gent

folio 702

,,   3   JOHN HAGER, son of John H , of Bourne, co Cambridge, Esq

,,   ,,   TIMOTHY FOTHERGILL, of the city of York, gent

,,   8.   WILLIAM HUNGATE, son of William H , of North Dalton, co York, Esq

,,   ,,   FRANCIS WHITE, of Winchelsea, Sussex

,,   15   EDWARD DAVENPORT, son of Robert D , of Marby, co Lincoln, Esq.

,,   24.   THOMAS INGLEBY, grandson (nepos) of William I , of Ripley, co York, Knight

,,   ,,   RICHARD HALE, son and heir of William H., of King's Walden, Herts, Esq

1615-16   [Burbage, gent

Jan 31   HENRY GREY, of Burbage, co. Leicester, son and heir of Anthony G., of

1615-16		folio **702**—(*continued*)
Feb	19	WILLIAM LANGSTON, of Littleton, co Worcester, son and heir of Anthony L,
,,	21	THOMAS FRENCHE, of Cambridge, gent [of same, Esq
,,	,,	RICHARD ROSSE, son and heir of Richard R, of Norwich, gent
,,	,,	THOMAS FARNELL, of Grays Thurrock, Essex [gent
,,	,,	THOMAS HALL, son and heir of Thomas H, of Priors Marston, co Warwick,

folio 703

,,	,	ROBERT CLENCH, of Witcham, Isle of Ely, co Cambridge, Esq
,,	,,	ANDREW BYNG, S.T P.
,,	,,	WILLIAM ASKWITH, of Osgodby, co York, Esq
,,	,,	PETER MAD (Maude?), of Holme, co York, Esq [Limerick, Ireland, Esq
,,	,,	PATRICK SARSFIELD, late of Barnard's Inn, gent, son and heir of John S, of
,,	,,	GEORGE SIMION (Semion), Knight
,,	,,	THOMAS GOADE, S T P
,,	,,	EDWARD HERBERT, of Redcastle, co. Montgomery, Esq
,,	,,	ROBERT BYNG, of London, Esq
,,	25	ROGER ISAACK, of Exeter, Devon, gent
,,	,,	FULKE GROSVENOR, son of Gawin G, of this Inn, Esq
,,	,,	WILLIAM NEWMAN, son of Edward N, of this Inn, gent
,,	,,	STANLEY FLOWERDEW, son and heir of Anthony F, of Hetherset, Norfolk, Esq
,,	28	JOHN ANTHONY, of Hogesden, Middlesex, gent
,,	,,	GEORGE WITHERS, son and heir of Richard W, of Hastings, Sussex, Esq
,,	,,	THOMAS BYNG, son and heir of Henry B, Esq, reader.
,,	25	VALENTINE BALE, son of George B, of Carleton Curlew, co Leicester, Esq
,,	,,	WILLIAM GOODHALL, son and heir of Robert G, of Haliwell, co Lincoln, Esq

1611		folio **705.**
Oct	29	ROBERT BARWICKE, of Doncaster, co York
,,	,,	NATHANIEL BACON, son and heir of James B, Knight [Esq
,,	,,	JOHN GLOVER, of Barnard's Inn, son and heir of William G, of Ashe, Suffolk,
,,	,,	THOMAS HAMOND, of Ashe, Suffolk, gent.
Nov	1	HENRY TOWNLEY, son and heir of John T, of Gray's Inn, Esq
,,	8	JOHN CASTLE, son and heir of Robert C, of Gray's Inn, Esq
,,	,,	ROBERT VAUGHAN, son of Owen V., of Llwydiarth, co Montgomery, Esq
1611-12.		
Feb	2	WILLIAM BROCKETT, son and heir of John B, of Kimpton, Herts, gent
Mar	13	JOHN PARKER, of Weston Underwood, Bucks

1612		folio **706**
June	15	JOHN SMYTH, son and heir of Thomas S, of Paddington, Middlesex, gent
,,	,,	ANTHONY FARREN, son and heir of Thomas F, of Lutterworth, co Leicester,
,,	30	HENRY WARMOUTH, of Newcastle, gent [gent
,,	,,	CHARLES HALES, gent
,,	,,	ROBERT ANDERSON, gent

1612		folio 706—(continued)
Aug. 14		RICHARD AMHERST, eldest son of Richard A., Esq., reader.
,,	,,	JOHN KING, of Staple Inn, gent
Nov	1	JOHN PECK, son of Paul P , of Reynold, Beds, Esq

folio 707.

,,	27	ALEXANDER RIGBIE the younger son of Alexander R , of Gray's Inn, gent
,,	,,	ROBERT ALDHOUSE, of Ashbocking, Suffolk, son and heir of John A , gent
,,	,,	ROBERT MEESE, of co Oxon, son and heir of John M , gent.
1612-13.		
Feb	3	SAMUEL TITLEY, of Offord (or Orford), Norfolk, gent
,,	27.	ANTHONY RATCLIFFE, son and heir of Edward R , of Gray's Inn, gent
Mar	5	THOMAS BALGAY, of Stamford, co Lincoln, gent
1613		
April 26		HENRY HALE, son and heir of Thomas H , of Gray's Inn, Esq
,,	,,	WILLIAM GOODWYN, son of Humphrey G , of (Hardlow ?), co. Derby, gent
May	5	ROBERT SPENCER, son and heir of Robert S , of West Deeping, cc. Linc , gent

folio 708

,,	10	JOHN JACKSON, son of William J , of Newcastle-upon-Tyne, gent
,,	13	MATTHEW SMELT, son and heir of Leonard S , of Kirby Fletham, co. Richmond, Esq. [Richmond, gent
,,	,,	JOHN WASTELL, son and heir of Leonard W , of Ellerton-on-Swale, co
,,	,,	NICHOLAS CAW, son of Andrew C., of North Repps, Norfolk, gent
June 14		DEVEREUX FERMOR, one of the sons of George F , Knight, deceased
,,	22	JOHN BRETT, son and heir of John B., of Hastings, Sussex, gent
Aug	13	GEOFFREY KEBLE, son of Giles K , gent , of Newton, Suffolk
,,	,,	JOHN CROSTON, of Charnock Heath, Kent, gent
,,	,,	RICHARD NIGHTINGALE, of Charnock Heath, gent

folio 709

Nov	1	EDWARD PALER, son and heir of John P , late of this Inn, Esq
,,	,,	CHRISTOPHER CRANWELL, son of Giles C , of Sevenoaks, gent
,,	,,	RICHARD GULSON, son and heir of John G , of this Inn, Esq
,,	,,	THOMAS FOTHERBY, gent [Middlesex, Esq
,,	,,	ALEXANDER KETERICHE, son and heir of Richard K , of South Mimms,
,,	,,	OLIVER BAKER, son and heir of Leonard B , late of Clifton, Beds, Esq
		[gent
,,	5	WILLIAM COLCLOUGH, son and heir of John C , of (Owercok ?), co Stafford,
,,	,,	FRANCIS CORY, son and heir of Thomas C , of Bramerton, Norfolk, gent
,,	15	MATTHIAS BRAY, of Morley Swanton, Norfolk, late of Barnard's Inn, gent

1613-14		**folio 710**
Feb	3	NATHANIEL HARLOWE, son of Robert H , of London, Esq.
Mar	16	ROBERT KIRKHAM, son and heir of Thomas K , of Cotterstoke, co
1614		[Northampton, Esq
June	3	HUMPHREY RANT, son and heir of William R , of Norwich, M D.

1614		folio 710—(*continued*)

July   6   CHRISTOPHER ABDY, son and heir of Edmund A , of Lincoln's Inn, Esq

„   „   EDMUND HARVYE, of Eye, Suffolk, late of Barnard's Inn, gent

Aug   4   HENRY THURLBYE, son of William T , of Little Dunham, Norfolk, gent

„   „   GREGORY ATHOW, youngest son of Thomas A , now reader, Serjeant elect

Nov   9 ⎰ HUMPHREY GRESWOULD, of Greete, co Worcester, gent   [Oxon, gent.

or 21 ⎱ EDMUND CHAMBERLAYNE, son and heir of Thomas C , of Stratton Audley,

1614-15		folio 711

Mar   8   JOHN GUNTER, gent

„   9   JOHN TOWNLEY, son of John T , Esq.

„   „   ALEXANDER BRERES, son and heir of John B , of Marton, co Lancaster, gent

„   „   JOHN HAYHURST, son of Henry H , of Bayley, co Lancaster, gent

„   „   RICHARD HAWORTH, son of Laurence H , of Thurncroft, co Lancaster, gent

„   „   JAMES PRESCOTT, son and heir of Geoffrey P , of Standish, co Lancaster

1615 (13 James)

May 17   ROBERT GRIX, of Staple Inn, gent

„   „   WILLIAM ELWES (Helwis), of Norfolk, late of Barnard's Inn, gent.

„   „   PETER FRENCH, son and heir of Walter F , of Galway, Ireland, Esq
                                                            [Limerick, gent.

„   „   GARRETT PURSELL, of Barnard's Inn, gent , son of Edmund P , of co

		folio 712.

Aug   6   JOHN LAMBERT, son and heir of Simon L , of Buckingham, gent

„   „   WILLIAM BAYSPOOLE, late of Barnard's Inn, son and heir of John B., of
            Barton, Norfolk, gent   [Oakham, Rutland, gent

„   „   WILLIAM JEP(H)SON, late of Barnard's Inn, son and heir of Roger J , of

„   „   ROGER URMESTON, gent , son of Richard U , of Westleigh, co Lancaster, Esq

„   „   RICHARD CASWELL, of London, Esq

„   11   JOHN BEDINGFIELD, son of Thomas B , of Darson, Suffolk, Esq

„   „   JAMES CATTERALL, late of Staple Inn, gent.

Oct. 25.   ROGER RANT, son of Roger R , of Swaffham, co Cambridge, Esq (erased)

„   „   THOMAS BLOSSE, son and heir of Tobias B , of Ipswich, Suffolk

1615-16

Feb   2.   HUMFREY PERYENT, of Colchester, gent

„   „   JERARD DVOSE, of London, gent.

„   „   PETER HAYMAN, of Sellinge, Kent, Knight (erased).

„   „   TIMOTHY THORNHILL, of Ollantighe, Kent, Knight

		folio 713

„   „   SAMUEL PEYTON, Knight and Baronet, of Kent (*sic*)

„   „   JOHN HEWET, son and heir of John H , of London, Esq.

„   „   HUMPHREY LOWE, of St Alban's, gent.

„   25   JOHN SCARBOROUGH, son of Henry S , of North Walsham, Norfolk, gent
                                                            [Suffolk, gent

1616

Aug 10.   FRANCIS MOSSE, late of Barnard's Inn, son of ——— Mosse, of Wreckham,

1616		folio 713—(*continued*)
Aug	13	TOBIAS ROSE, of Haselgrove, co Somerset, gent [Norfolk, gent
„	„	ROBERT GREENE, son and heir of John G, of Lynn Regis (King's Lynn),
Nov.	1.	HENRY HUTTON, one of the sons of Edmund H, of the city of Durham
„	„	NATHANIEL CHAMBERS, son and heir of George C, of Epping, Essex, gent.
„	18	THOMAS EVANS, third son of John E, of Llwynegrin, co Flint, gent
„	„	CHRISTOPHER JONES, of Uske, co Monmouth, gent
1617		[Suffolk, gent
May	21.	JOHN SAIRE, late of Barnard's Inn, son and heir of John S, of Woodbridge,
		[Athboy, co Meath (erased).
„	30	WILLIAM BROWNE, late of Barnard's Inn, son and heir of Richard E, of

folio 714.

„	„	CHARLES DIXWELL, son and heir of William D, of Coton, in parish of Church-over, co Warwick, Esq [Northampton, clerk
June	30	JOHN LIGHTFOOT, son and heir of Richard L, of Stoke Bruerne, co.
Oct	22.	CHARLES HALES, son and heir of Stephen H, of co Warwick, Esq
„	„	WALTER HALES, brother of Charles H, son and heir of Stephen H, of co.
1617	18.	[Warwick
Feb	6.	WILLIAM MONGER, second son of Benjamin M, of the city of London, gent.
		[of Lambert T., of same, Esc, deceased
„	21.	THOMAS TILDESLEY, of Garret-in-Tildesley, co Lancaster, Esq, son and heir
Mar.	4	WILLIAM KEBLE, second son of Robert K, of Barnetbye, co. Lincoln, Esq
1618		
Aug	10	ROBERT BOURCHIER, third son of John B, of co York, Knight
„	„	HENRY BOURCHIER, fourth son of John B, of co York, Knight
„	„	GEORGE BOURCHIER, fifth son of John B, of co York, Knight.
„	„	JAMES BOURCHIER, sixth son of John B, of co York, Knight
„	„	WILLIAM BOURCHIER, seventh son of John B, of co York, Knight
„	„	VERNEY BOURCHIER, eighth son of John B, of co. York, Knight.

folio 715.

„	„	GEORGE DAWNEY, third son of Thomas D, Knight, of York.
„	„	HENRY MARTIN, son of Henry M, of Blackfriars, London, Esq
„	„	WILLIAM FOSTER, son and heir of Nicholas F, of Tatham, co. Lancaster
„	„	GABRIEL JENINGS, of London, gent.
1619		
Aug	11	THOMAS EDGAR, son of Lionel E., of Ipswich, Suffolk, gent
„	„	JOHN WINTERBORNE, of London, gent
„	„	SIMON THELWALL, son of Richard T, of Llanbeder, co. Denbigh, gent.
1620		[Barley, co York, Esq
July	3	CHRISTOPHER BEVERLEY, late of Staple Inn, son and heir of Thomas B, of
Aug	7	THOMAS JONES, son of Hugh J, of Eastgarstone, Berks, clerk
„	„	RICHARD BARNARDISTON, son of Robert B, of Ickwell Bury, parish of
1621.		[Norrell, Beds, Esq.
Aug	7	JOHN PECK, son of Paul P, of Reynolds, Beds, gent
„	„	WILLIAM CUMBERLAND, of Clifton, Beds, gent.

1621	**folio 716.**
Aug 7.	WILLIAM BROCKETT, son and heir of John B , of Codicote, Herts, gent
1622-3.	[co York, Esq.
Jan. 29	WILLIAM WAISON, son and heir of Peter W , of Austwick, parish of Clapham,
Feb 8	ROBERT WILMOT, late of Staple Inn, son and heir of Robert W , of
1623	[Chaddesden, co. Derby, gent
Oct 20	MICHAEL KEEPIS, of Norwich, gent
1626	[gent
May 10	ROBERT HINDLEY, gent , son and heir of Roger H , of Hindley. co. Lanc ,
,, ,,	JOHN FEILDEN, of Blackburn, co Lancaster, gent
1626-7	[St Sepulchre, London, gent , deceased.
Feb 9	RICHARD BALTHROPP, son and heir of Richard B , late of Smithfield, parish of
1627	
June 12	HUMPHREY IREMONGER, son of John I , of Stanbridge, Beds, gent
1627-8	
Mar 2	THOMAS TYSDAILE, son and heir of (Elias ?) T , of Abingdon, Berks, gent
,, ,,	WALTER HUNGERFORD, late of Staple Inn, son of John H , of Windrush, co
	[Gloucester, Esq.
1628	**folio 717**
May 21	PETER ROGERS, second son of Henry R , of Sherborne, co Warwick, gent
1628-9	
Mar 6	RICHARD RAPER, of the Strand, Middlesex, gent
1629.	
April 28	RICHARD SAVERE, son of John S , of Masworth, Bucks, gent
,, ,,	THOMAS BROOKE, son and heir of Richard B , of Norton, co Chester, gent
,, ,,	JOHN HARLESTON, of South Ockingdon, Essex, gent [gent
,, ,,	THOMAS BATE, son and heir of Nathan B , of Little Chester, co Derby,
	[gent
,, ,,	WILLIAM GILL, second son of Ralph G , of St Giles, Cripplegate, London,
,, ,,	RALPH DAVISON, second son of Alexander D , of Newcastle-on-Tyne, Esq.
May 7	WHITTINGHAM FOGGE, son and heir of Richard F., of Burham, Kent, gent.
,, ,,	WILLIAM CHIPPINGDALE, son and heir of John C , of Blackenwall, co Stafford,
	[Esq.
	folio 718.
Nov 25	EDMUND COBBE, son and heir of Martin C , of Snettisham, Norfolk, gent
May 15	JOHN WALKER, of Fawkham, Kent, son and heir of Robert W., gent , deceased
1616	**folio 725**
May 10	THOMAS WALE, son and heir of Thomas W , of Rudwater, Essex, gent
,, ,,	JOHN ELLIS, son and heir of Barnard E , of Gray's Inn, Esq.
,, ,,	JOHN PIGOTT, son of Benjamin P , of Nether Gravenhurst, Beds, Esq
,, ,,	JOHN BREWSE, of Wenham parva, Suffolk, Esq
,, ,,	RICHARD BEAKE, of Haddenham, Bucks, Esq
,, ,,	WILLIAM LOCKSMITH, of the city of Gloucester, gent
,, ,,	EDWARD WOLLASTON, of Grange, Stafford, gent
,, ,,	BENJAMIN HEWET, of London, gent
,, ,,	JOHN ROGERS, son and heir of Thomas R , of Dartford, Kent, gent

1616.　　　　　　　　　folio 725—*(continued)*

June 3　MAURICE BARROWE, son and heir of William B , of Westrope, Suffolk, Esq
　　　　　　　　　　　　　　　　　　　　　　　　　　　[ampton, gent
July 3　ROWLAND WALKER, son and heir of George W , of East Farndon, co North-

,, ,,　MILES HOBART, son and heir of Miles H , of London, gent , deceased

June 5　GEORGE PUDSEY, son of George P , of Langley, co Warwick, Esq.

,, 10　JOHN DANET, son and heir of Gerrard D , of Elmbridge, co Worcester, Esq

,, 12　EDWARD THOROLD, son of Anthony T , of Hough, co Lincoln, Esq

,, ,,　JEREMIAH ORME, son and heir of Thomas O , of Lee, co Lancaster, gent.

,, ,,　FRANCIS CURLE, Esq , one of the Auditors of the Court of Wards and Liveries

Aug. 10.　MARMADUKE DARELL, son of Marmaduke D , of Fulmer, Bucks, Knight.

folio 726

,, ,,　JOHN WRIGHT, gent , son of John W., one of the Members of this Inn.

,, ,,　ANTHONY PENNING, son and heir of Anthony P , of Kettleborough, Suffolk,

,, ,,　ROBERT WINGFIELD, late of Staple Inn, gent.　　　　　　　[Esq.

,, ,,　RICHARD ETHERINGION, son of Richard E , of Eberston, co York, gent

,, ,,　BENJAMIN BRUGGE, son of Roger B , of Busted, Essex, Esq.　[Barnard's Inn

,, ,,　JAMES SAVILE, son of Simon S , of Cashell, co Tipperary, gent , late of

,, 13　PAUL DAYRRELL, son and heir of Walter D , reader

,, ,,　EDWARD WOODER, of Latham, Suffolk, gent

,, ,,　WILLIAM BRVAN, of Wrotham, Kent, Esq

,, ,,　EDMUND BACON, gent., son of Robert B , of Riborough, Norfolk, Esq.

,, ,,　MARMADUKE MARSHALL, son and heir of John M , late of Moreton-on-Swale,

,, ,,　ROBERT FUTTER, of Tomson, Norfolk, gent.　　　　　　[co York, Esq

,, ,,　HENRY ROLT, son and heir of Thomas R., of (Dartford ?), Kent, gent

,, ,,　THOMAS SWANNE, son and heir of William S , of Southfleet, Kent, Knight

folio 727.

,, ,,　WILLIAM HILTON, of Dublin, Ireland, Esq

,, ,,　FRANCIS THEOBALD, late of Barnard's Inn, gent

,, ,,　THOMAS DAYRRELL, son of Walter D , reader

,, ,,　JOHN GALWAY, son and heir of ——— G , of Limerick, in Ireland, Esq

Oct 17　RICHARD FAGAN, late of Barnard's Inn, son and heir of John F , of Felton, co

,, ,,　HENRY PECKE, son of William P , of Mountnessing, Suffolk, Esq　[Dublin

,, ,,　JOHN MILDMAY, son of Humphrey M , of Danbury, Essex, Esq.

,, ,,　WILLIAM BAYTON, son of William B , of Flitcham, Norfolk, Esq

Nov 1　THOMAS LISTER, son and heir of William L , of Rippingall, co Lincoln, Esq

,, ,,　JOHN BUTLER, son of Henry B , Knight, deceased.

,, ,,　RALPH WORMLEIGHTON, eldest son of Ralph W , Esq , Member of this Society

folio 728　　　　　　　　　[(erased).

,, ,,　THOMAS LISTER, son and heir of William L , of Rippingall, co Lincoln, Esq

,, ,,　HENRY PECK, son and heir of John P., of Winchelsea, Sussex, Esq

,, ,,　HENRY WOLSTENHOLME, son of John W , of London, Esq

,, ,　EURE AIRMINE, second son of William A , of Osgodby, co. Lincoln, Knight

1616	folio 728—(continued)
Nov 1.	RICHARD DOWNTON, son and heir of Thomas D., of Sandhurst, Kent
„ 6.	HENRY PELHAM third son of William P., of Brocklesby, Lincoln, Knight. [berland, Esq
„ 18.	WILFRID IRTON son and heir of Christopher I., of Cockermouth, co Cum-
„ „	FORD BRETT, son and heir of Stephen B., of New Romney, Kent
„ „	JAMES SHORT, of Staple Inn, gent
1616-17 Jan 29	WILLIAM GARDINER, son and heir of William G., of Lagham, Surrey, Knight
1616 Nov 18	JOHN ROBINS, son and heir of William R., of Carmarden, gent
„ „	JOHN DOVLEY, son of Edmund D., of Shottesham, Norfolk, Esq

folio 729.

„ „	VALENTINE BALE, late of Staple Inn, son of George B., of Carlton Curlew, co Leicester, gent [land, Esq
„ „	CHARLES MIDLETON, son and heir of Thomas M., of Belsay, Northumber-
„ „	JOHN JESUP, son and heir of John J., of Revesby, co Lincoln, gent
„ „	BARNARD DORMER, son and heir of William D., of London, Esq
1616-17 Jan. 29.	GILBERT JONES, son of Gilbert J., of Poole, co. Montgomery, Esq
„ „	JOHN CHILDERS, son and heir of Hugh C., of Doncaster, co York, Esq
„ „	ELLIS WYNNE, son of John W., of Gwyddir, co Carnarvon, gent
„ „	ROBERT GOODWYNE, M.A., of Oxford University
Feb. 5	ROBERT BARGRAVE, son and heir of John B., of Patricksbourne, Kent, Esq.
„ „	SAMUEL BARROW, son and heir of Thomas B., of Docking, Norfolk, Esq
„ „	JOHN DRAPER, son and heir of Thomas D., of Flintham, Notts, gent
1617 May 21.	THOMAS BROGRAVE, second son of Simon B., of Braughinge, Herts, Esq
„ „	EDMUND DUDLEY, son and heir of Thomas D., of Yanwith, Cumberland, Esq.
„ „	NATHANIEL THOROLD, son and heir of John T., of Marton, co Lincoln, Esq

folio 730.

„ „	FRANCIS RODES, son of John R., of Barlbrough, co Derby, Knight. [Monmouth, Esq
„ „	ROGER WILLIAMS, son and heir of William W., of Landbadock, co
„ „	WILLIAM CHESTER, second son of Anthony C., of Chicheley, Bucks, Esq
„ „	WILLIAM STRICKLAND, son and heir of Walter S., of Boynton, co. York, Esq
„ „	SAMUEL SELBIE, son and heir of Hugh S., late of Newcastle-on-Tyne, Esq
„ „	EDWARD GERRARD, son and heir of Thomas G., of Burwell, co Camb., Esq
„ „	RICHARD ABRAHAM, son and heir of Richard A., of Quarington, Bucks, gent [Monmouth, Esq
„ „	WILLIAM PRICHARD, son and heir of Charles P., of Landfoyst, co
„ „	JOHN HELWISE (ELWES), of Worlaby, co. Lincoln, gent. [Kent, Esq.
„ „	HENRY PARAMORE, late of Staple Inn, son and heir of Thomas P., of Fordwich,
„ „	ROBERT HUTTON, son and heir of Robert H., of the city of Durham, S T D

1617	folio 730—(*continued*)

May 21	THOMAS WHITTINGHAM, son of Timothy W , of Holmeside, co Durham, Knight
	[Athboy, co Meath, gent
„ „	WILLIAM BROWNE, late of Barnard's Inn, son and heir of Richard B , of

folio 731.

„ „	THOMAS OSBORNE, son and heir of John O , of Chilham, Kent, gent
„ „	JOSEPH LOWE, son of Thomas L , of Highley, Salop, gent	[Esq.
„ „	JOHN HAWTREY, son and heir of Ralph H , of Riselip (Ruislip), Middlesex,
„ „	RICHARD HALFORD, son and heir of Richard H , of Edweston, Rutland, Esq
„ „	RICHARD JENKINSON, son and heir of Thomas J., of Tunstall, Norfolk, Knight.
„ „	PETER WOGAN, son of John W , of Boulston, co. Pembroke, Knight
„ „	RICHARD BELLASYSE, son of Bryan B , of the city of Durham, Esq
„ „	ROBERT COOKE, son of William C , of Highnam, co Gloucester, Knight
„ „	EDMUND HUME, of South Elmham, Suffolk, gent.
„ „	JOHN RISBY, son and heir of William R , of Thorpe (Morcup ?) Suffolk, Esq.
„ „	HUMPHREY WALCOTT, son of William W , of Walcott, co Lincoln, Esq.
„ 26	EDWARD ALDRIDGE, son and heir of George A , of Tottenham High Cross,
	Middlesex, Knight.	[moreland, Esq (erased).
„ „	EDMUND DUDLEY, gent , son and heir of Thomas D , of Yanwith, West-
„ 30.	JOHN SAVILE, son and heir of Thomas S , of Wakefield, co York, Esq

folio 732.

„ „	HENRY KILLEGREW, of London, Esq	[Esq
„ „	RICHARD TOWNLEY, son and heir of Richard T , of Townley, co Lancaster,
	[Baronet
June 26	GILBERT MOLYNEUX, son of Richard M , of Sefton, co Lancaster, Knight and
„ „	WILLIAM WEDDELL, son and heir of Leonard W , of Clifton, co York, gent
	[Moulton, co York, gent
„ „	THOMAS SOTHERTON, late of Staple Inn, son and heir of John S , of New
„ „	RICHARD GERRARD, younger son of William G , Esq , late reader.
July 17	DANIEL THELWELL, son and heir of Simon T , of Woodford, Essex, Esq.
„ „	RICHARD SIBBS, S T P
„ „	HENRY TENVIR (?), (illegible in original), of Bedford, co Lancaster, gent
„ „	AMBROSE APLEBY, son of Thomas A , of Clove Lodge, co York, gent
„ „	ROBERT SHERER, son of ———, of High Bullhawghe, co Lancaster, gent.
„ „	JOHN LOWE, son and heir of Vincent L , of Denby, co Derby, gent.

folio 733.

Aug 7	CHARLES HUTTON, son and heir of Edward H , of the city of Durham, B.C L
„ „	HENRY LAWRENCE, son and heir of Sir John L , of St Ives, Hunts, Knight
„ „	WILLIAM GLOVER, son and heir of Sir Thomas G , of Wilsdon, Middlesex,
„ „	ROBERT ROBERTS, son of Francis R , of Wilsden, Middlesex, gent	[Knight
	[Norfolk, Knight.
„ „	NICHOLAS LE STRANGE, son and heir of Sir Hamon Le S., of Hunstanton,
„ „	GERARD BOOTH, son and heir of Gerard B , of Gray's Inn, gent

| 1617 | folio 733 —(continued) | [Councillor |

Aug 12 RALPH WINWOOD, Knight, Principal Secretary to the King, and a Privy

  ,, ,, THOMAS CONWAY, second son of Edward C , Knight

folio 734.   [and Baronet

  ,, ,, THOMAS MONSON, second son of Thomas M , of Burton, co Lincoln, Knight

  ,, ,, LEWIS MONSON, third son of Thomas M , Knight and Baronet, of Burton.

  ,, ,, WILLIAM MONSON, fourth son of Thomas M , Knight and Baronet, of Burton

  ,, ,, ROGER VAUGHAN, son and heir of William V , of Llowes, co Radnor, Esq

  ,, ,, RICHARD BARD, son and heir of Thomas B , of North Kelsey, co. Lincoln, Esq

  ,, ,, JOHN LEVER, son and heir of Edmund L , citizen and merchant of London

  ,, ,, RICHARD ROSSITER, son and heir of Richard R , of Somerby, co Lincoln, Esq

  ,, ,, JOHN AYSCOUGH, third son of Roger A , of Nuttall, Notts, Knight.   [Esq

  ,, ,, THOMAS BOURCHIER, son of William B , of Beningborough Grange, co. York,

                                                    [Dublin, Esq

  ,, ,, PATRICK BROWNE, late of Barnard's Inn, son and heir of Richard B , of

folio 735

  ,, ,, PETER FOULKES, son of Richard F , of Llanasaph, co Flint, gent.   [Esq.

  ,, ,, EDWARD FENWICK, son and heir of William F , of Stanton, Northumberland,

  ,, ,, WILLIAM LISTER, second son of Wm. L , of Rippingall, co Lincoln, Esq

  ,, ,, FRANCIS HOLLIS, third son of John, Lord Houghton

  ,, ,, WILLIAM LUSHER, son and heir of Nicholas L , of Putney, Surrey, Knight

  ,, ,, WILLIAM LEWYS, S T P

  ,, ,, THOMAS BENNETT, one of the sons of John B , Knight

  ,, ,, RALPH PETTUS, son and heir of William P , of Berles, Essex, Esq , deceased

  ,, ,, WILLIAM LOWTHER, son of Christopher L , of Lowther, co (Bucks ?), sic

                                                 [Knight

  ,, ,, ROBERT MONSHIER (?) (illegible in the original), of Islington, Middlesex, Esq

  ,, ,, SAMUEL MARKHAM, of Islington, Middlesex.

folio 736.

  ,, ,, EDWARD PELHAM, son of William P , of Brockelsley, co Lincoln, Knight

  ,, ,, HAMON LE STRANGE, son of Hamon Le S , of Hunstanton, Norfolk, Knight

  ,, ,, BRAY CHAMBERLAIN, son of Thomas C , of Stratton Audley, Oxon   [Knight

  ,, ,, RALPH BOURCHIER, son and heir of John B , of Hanging Grimston, co Lincoln,

  ,, ,, HENRY CHOLMELY, son and heir of Henry C , Knight   [(Surrey, sic), Esq

  ,, ,, HENRY HERON (?) (doubtful in the original), son of James H , of Eye, Suffolk,

  ,, ,, JAMES HERON (?) (doubtful in the original), son of John H , of Eye, Suffolk,

  ,, ,, WILLIAM (?) STAMPE, of Malmesbury, Wilts, Esq   [Esq

Oct. 22. JOHN PULFORD, son and heir of Thomas P , of London, gent   {gent

  ,, ,, RICHARD MOUNTENEY son and heir of Nicholas M , of Rotheram, co York

folio 737

  ,, ,, EDMUND KNEVITT, second son of Thomas K , of Ashwelthorpe, Norfolk

        Knight   [gent

  ,, ,, ROBERT MORSE, of Barnard's Inn, son of Robert M , of Tittleshall, Norfolk,

1617		folio 737—(*continued*)	[York, Knight

Oct 22   THOMAS MALEVERER, son and heir of Richard M , of Allerton Maleverer, co

,,   ,,   GEORGE POULTON, son and heir of John P., of Desboro, co. Northants, Esq

[Justices of the Court of Common Pleas

Nov 1   THOMAS HUTTON, second son now living of Richard H., Knight, one of the

,,   ,,   WILLIAM GIBBES, son and heir of Wm G., of Elmeston, Kent, Esq

,,   ,,   JOHN WORMLAIGHTON, son of Ralph W., Esq.

,,   ,,   EDWARD BERYE, son and heir of John B., of Canterbury, Esq.   [Hunts, Esq.

,,   ,,   WILLIAM NAYLOR, of Staple Inn, son and heir of Richard N , of Offord Darcy,

,,   ,,   THOMAS AUDIEY, of Staple Inn, gent

folio 738.   [Cumberland

,,   7   WILLIAM PENNINGTON, Esq, son and heir of John P, Esq, of Seaton,

,,   12   CLEMENT FINCH, son and heir of John F , of Grovehurst, Kent, Esq.

,,   ,,   ANTHONY SENIOR, son of Richard S , of Cowley, Devon, gent   [Esq

,,   19   JOHN APPLEYARD, son and heir of Thomas A , of Burstwick Garth, co York,

,,   ,,   THOMAS GOLDING, son and heir of Thos G , of Postlingford, Suffolk, Esq

,,   26   BARTRAM REYELEY, son and heir of George R , of Ancroft, co Durham, Esq

,,   ,,   EDWARD THOMAS, of Astwood, co Worcester, gent.

,,   ,,   ROBERT WILTON, son and heir of Richard W , of Tipcroft, Norfolk

,,   ,,   ROGER TISDALE, of London, gent

,,   ,,   FERNAM (?) SACHEYERELL, of Foxwell, co Derby, gent

,,   ,,   JOHN WHALLEY, of London, gent

folio 739.

Dec 26.   THOMAS WRIGHT, of London, Esq (erased)

,,   ,,   EDWARD ASCHAM, Esq , of Cottam, co [Lincoln

,,   29   SAMUEL TRYON, of London, Knight

,,   ,,   HUNTINGDON CONEY HASTINGS, of Picker- [ing, co York, Esq

,,   30   THOMAS LOWE, of London, Esq

,,   ,,   THOMAS WOODE, Knight, Gentleman of the [King's Chamber

1617-18

Jan 3   EDWARD FILMER, Esq , of East Sutton, [Kent   (admitted by Henry, Prince of Purpole)

,,   ,,   JARVIS ELWISHE (Elwes), of London, Esq

,,   ,,   JOHN (THO. HAN?) SMITH, Knight, of [Leeds, Kent

,,   5.   TOBYAS WRIGHT, son and heir of Richard [W , of Lewknor, Oxon, Esq

,,   ,,   EDWARD YELVERTON, Esq., of London

folio 740.

Feb 2   ESME STEWART, Lord Aubigny

,,   ,,   ARTHUR INGRAM, Knight, Secretary to ye [King's Council in ye North

1617-18   folio 740—(continued).

Feb 2   JOHN BUTLER, Knight, of Woodhall, Herts ⎫
 ,,   ,, WILLIAM BUTTON, Knight, of London   ⎪
 ,,   ,, DUDLEY DIGGS, of Chilham, Kent   ⎪
 ,,   ,, JOHN PACKINGTON, Esq , son and heir of ⎬ (admitted by Henry, Prince of
            John P , Knight   [J   ⎪   Purpole).
 ,,   ,, RICHARD JOHNSON, son and heir of Richard ⎪
 ,,   ,, THOMAS TALBOT, of Risley, Beds   ⎭

 ,,   6   HUGH CHOLMLEY, son and heir of Richard C , of Whitby, co York, Knight
 ,,   ,, VALENTINE BROWNE, son and heir of Valentine B , of Croft, co. Lincoln, Esq
 ,,   ,, THOMAS CHANDLER, son and heir of George C , of Hyde Barton, near Win-
            chester, co Southants, Esq   [of Bristol, gent
 ,,   ,, WILLIAM SANFORD, late of Barnard's Inn, son and heir of John S , of the City
                                                               [Worcester
 ,,   ,, BEVERLEY BRETTON, son and heir of Henry B , Knight, of Aldermaston, co

                                folio 741.
 ,, 21   PETER BLUNDELL, son and heir of Thomas B , of Ince Blundell, co Lancaster,
            [gent , heir male of Robert B , of Ince Blundell, Esq , now reader.
 ,,   ,, CHARLES BROGRAVE, third son of Simon B , of Braughing, Herts, Esq
                                                               [Knight
 ,,   ,, EDWARD RODES, son and heir of Godfrey R , of Great Houghton, Yorks,
 ,,   ,, JOHN SHARPLES, son and heir of Arthur S , of Freckleton, co Lancaster, gent
 ,,   ,, JOSEPH RIGBY, son of Alexander R., of Halton, co Lancaster, Esq
 ,,   ,, GEORGE RIGBY, son of Alexander R , of Halton, co. Lancaster, Esq
 ,,   ,, JOHN HAMOND, son of Henry H , of Pendleton, co Lancaster, gent
 ,,   ,, HENRY SOMERSCALES, son and heir of Robert S , of Eastham, Sussex, Esq
 ,,   ,, THOMAS LAKE, son of William L , of Willeston, Herts, gent
 ,,   ,, THOMAS DUNCOMBE, son of Thomas D , of Berland, Bucks, gent.
 ,,   ,, THOMAS MASSEY, son of Richard M , of Rixton, co Lancaster, Esq
 ,,   ,, THOMAS GUDLAW (Gidlow?), son and heir of Thomas G , of Aspull, co.
            Lancaster, gent   [Lancaster, gent.
 ,,   ,, EDWARD HODGKINSON, son of George H , of Preston in-Amunderness, co.
 ,,   ,, THOMAS LAKE, son of Thomas L , of Willeston, in the parish of Tring, Herts,
 ,,   ,, WILLIAM DUNCOMBE, son of William D , of Ivinghoe, Bucks, gent.   [gent
 ,,   ,, ROBERT BRADSHAW, of Overton, co Lancaster, Esq
 ,,   ,, WILLIAM DICCONSON, son of Edward D , of Eccleston, co. Lancaster, gent
                                                               [Lancaster, Esq
 ,,   ,, RICHARD GREENHALGH, son and heir of John G of Brandesholme, co.
 ,,   ,, JOHN GREENHALGH, son of John G , of Brandlesholme, co Lancaster, Esq

                                folio 742.   [Scotland.
 ,, 25. JAMES, Marquis of HAMILTON, Earl of Arran, Lord Avon, of Avondale,
 ,,   ,, ROBERT SYDNEY, Knight, son and heir of Viscount de Lisle
 ,,   ,, ANTONIO DA COSTA, doliveira da ordem de Christo.
 ,,   ,, RICHARD CARMARDEN, son and heir of Richard C , of London, Esq
 ,, 26   GIDEON CARMARDEN, son and heir of Nathaniel C , of Gray's Inn, Esq

1617		folio 742—(continued)
Feb.	26.	THOMAS HEYES, of Gildon Morton, co Cambridge, Esq
,,	,,	ALEXANDER JOHNSON, son of William J, of London, Esq
,,	,,	LAURENCE LYTLER, of London, gent
Mar	1	GEORGE BLUNDELL, of Cardington, Beds, Knight
,,	,,	WILLIAM SEGAR, Knight, Garter Principal King of Arms
,,	,,	FRANCIS BLUNDELI, Knight, brother of George B, of Cardington, Beds, Knight
,,	,,	GEORGE BLUNDELL, son and heir of George B, of Cardington, Beds, Knight
,,	,,	JOHN ARCHER, son and heir of Henry A, of Theydon Garnons, Essex, Esq.
,,	,,	THOMAS GERRARD, son and heir of Miles G, of Aughton, co Lancaster, gent

folio 743   [gent

,,	2	RICHARD HOLLAND, son and heir of Edward H, of Winwick, co Lancaster, [Esq.
,,	,,	CHARLES SMITH, son and heir of Francis S, of Ashby Folville, co. Leicester,
,,	,,	THOMAS SMITH, second son of Francis S, of Ashby Folville, co. Leicester, Esq
,,	3.	RICHARD ST GEORGE, Knight, Norroy King of Arms. [Arms.
,,	,,	HENRY ST GEORGE, son and heir of Richard St G, Knight, Norroy King of
,,	,,	FRANCIS BEAUMONT, Esq., Master of the King's Hospital, on the foundation
,,	,,	THOMAS DAWSON, of London, gent [of Thomas Sutton, Esq
,,	,,	HENRY BERNEY, of Reedham, Norfolk, Esq
,,	,,	JOHN ASHBURNHAM, son and heir of John A, of Ashburnham, Sussex, Knight
,,	,,	THOMAS EVERSFIELD, son of Thomas E, of Denn, Suffolk, Knight
,,	,,	RICHARD MORE, son and heir of Alexander M, of Grantham, co Lincoln, Esq
,,	,,	RICHARD ANWYLL, son of Lewis A, of Park, co Merioneth, Esq
,,	,,	RICHARD LLOYD, son and heir of Evan L, of Penmachno, co Carnarvon, gent
,,	4.	ROBERT WHICHCOTT, son and heir of Hamon W, of Dunstall, co Lincoln, [Knight.

folio 744   [Knight, (erased)

,,	,,	JOHN WHICHCOTT, third son of Hamon W, of Dunstall (Dunston), co Linc,
,,	,,	WILLIAM BURTON, of Sleaford, co Lincoln, gent
,,	,,	ROBERT WHICHCOTT, sen', of Dunstall, co Lincoln, Knight
,,	,,	JOHN OSBORNE, late of Staple Inn, gent
,,	,,	HENRY MACKWORTH, son and heir of Thomas M, of Normanton, Rutland, Esq.
,,	,,	ROBERT CARPENTER, son of John C, of Middle Temple, gent
,,	,,	HENRY PERCY, of Settrington, co York, gent
,,	,,	CHRISTOPHER LEGARD, son and heir of Robert L, of Anlaby, co York, Esq.
,,	,,	THOMAS CORBIN, second son of George C, of Hall End, co Warwick, Esq
,,	,,	JOHN SAUNDERS, of Wrexham, co Denbigh, gent
,,	,,	JOSEPH THOROLD, second son of John T, of Marton, co. Lincoln.
,,	,,	WILLIAM BLITHE, of Stroxton, co. Lincoln, gent.
,,	,,	GEORGE CONY, son of Richard C, of Whissendine, Rutland, Knight
,,	,,	FRANCIS MORRICE, of Burham, Bucks, gent. [Esq
,,	,,	EDWARD MORRICE, son and heir of David M., of Glankyndeth, co Denbigh,
,,	,,	JOHN SARIS, son of Thomas S., of London, Esq

1618		folio 745

1618

April 27   EDWARD CHETWYND, S T D, Dean of Bristol

,, 29   WILLIAM STILES, son and heir of William S, of Gosbeck, Suffolk, Esq

,, ,,   WALTER CHETWYND, son and heir of Walter C, of Grendon, co Warwick, [Knight

,, ,,   WILLIAM THOMAS, son and heir of William T, of Carnarvon, Knight.

,, ,,   CUTHBERT MORLEY, son of James M, Esq, "Cursitor," of Suffolk

May 15   WILLIAM BEWICKE, son and heir of Robert B, of Newcastle-on-Tyne, gent

,, ,,   THOMAS BROWNE, son and heir of Thomas B, of Walsingham parva, Norfolk, [gent

,, ,,   PHILIP WELBY, son of William W, of Gedney, co Lincoln, Knight of the Bath.

,, ,,   JOHN MARCALL, son and heir of Richard M, of Old Walsingham, Norfolk, [gent

,, ,,   GERVASE EYRE, son and heir of Anthony E, of Rampton, Notts, Esq [Esq.

,, ,,   FRANCIS QUARLES, son and heir of Francis Q, of Ufford, co Northampton,

,, ,,   FRANCIS VENTRIS, son and heir of Francis V, of Compton, Beds, Knight

,, ,,   JOHN DENNY, of Lynn, Norfolk, Esq

,, ,,   JOHN SCUDAMORE, of Kentchurch, co Hereford, Esq

folio 746   [Havering-atte Bower, Essex, gent

,, ,,   WILLIAM WRIGHT, son of John W, of Wrightbridge, in the liberty of

,, ,,   THOMAS CHETWYND, second son of Walter C, of Grendon, co Warwick, Knight   [Esq

,, ,,   WILLIAM SKINNER, son and heir of Anthony S, of Shelfield, co Warwick,

June 10   ROBERT REMINGTON, son of Richard R, of Lockington, co York, Esq

,, ,,   ANTHONY HASLEWOOD, son and heir of Edward H, of Maidwell, co North-

,, ,,   JOHN NORTON, of Cotterstoke, co Northampton, Esq   [ampton, Esq

,, 17   JOHN ROUTH, son and heir of William R, of Walesworth, co York, Esq

Aug 1   EDWARD BASELY, of East Knoyle, Wilts, gent

,, ,,   FRANCIS BACON, son of Edward B, of Shrubland, Suffolk, Esq

,, ,,   WILLIAM THWAYTS, of St Dunstan's, near the city of Canterbury, gent

,, ,,   HUGH PLATT, of Rickmansworth, Herts, Esq

,, ,,   WILLIAM SMITH, son of William S, of London, Knight

folio 747   [reader).

Aug 2   THEOPHILUS FINCH, of Eastwell, Kent, Knight and Bart (per John Finch,

,, ,,   WILLIAM ALABASTER, S T.D, "serenissimœ regie magistati a sacris," (chaplain to the King)   [Chancellor of England

,, ,,   THOMAS CECIL, S T D, chaplain to Francis Bacon, Baron Verulam, High

,, 6   MARCUS ANTONIUS DE DOMINIS, Archbishop of Spalatro (Spalatensis)

,, ,,   EMANUEL, Lord SCROOPE

,, 7   GEORGE WYATT, son of George W, of Boxley Abbey, Kent, Esq

,, ,,   THOMAS WYATT, son of George W, of Boxley Abbey, Kent, Esq

,, ,,   ROBERT CLARKE, of the city of Canterbury, gent.

,, 10   THOMAS BROWNE, second son of Nicholas B., of Molihefe, co Kerry, Ireland.

1618		folio 747—(continued).
Aug	7	FERDINANDO SACHEVERELL, son of Henry S., of Hopewell, co Derby, Esq (erased).
,,	10	THOMAS DAWNEY, son of Thomas D., of Cowick, co York, Knight.

folio 748

,,	,,	RICHARD HUNTER, son of John H., of North Fotheringham, co York, gent.
,,	,,	JOHN DEBNEY, son and heir of Robert D., of Norwich, gent
,,	,,	GABRIEL QUADRING, son of William Q., of Irby, co Lincoln, Esq
,,	,,	ROBERT PERROTT (Parrett), son of Robert P., of Northley, Oxon, Esq.
,,	,,	BERNARD TOWNLEY, son of John T., of Hurstwood, co Lancaster, gent
,,	,,	THOMAS LEAKE, son of Thomas L., of Willestone, parish of Tring, Herts, gent
,,	,,	JOHN HODGSON, son and heir of Christopher H., of Beeston, co York, gent
,,	,,	WILLIAM OWEN, son of John O., of Porkington, Salop, gent
,,	,,	THOMAS GOOTS, son and heir of Thomas G., of Gray's Inn, Esq
,,	,,	WALTER STRICKLAND, son of Walter S., of Boynton, co. York, Esq.

folio 749.

,,	,,	THOMAS STRICKLAND, son of Walter S., of Boynton, co. York, Esq
,,	,,	WATKINSON PAYLER, son and heir of Edward P., of Thoralby, co. York, Esq
,,	,,	MICHAEL WANDESFORD, son of George W., of Kirklington, co York, Knight
,,	,,	RICHARD BOURCHIER, second son of John B., of co York, Knight.
,,	,,	WILLIAM CONY, third son of Richard C., of Hitchin, Herts, Knight
,,	,,	HENRY CHOLMLEY, second son of Richard C., of Whitby, co York, Knight
,,	,,	CAREW STURY, son and heir of Walter S., of Roshall, Salop, Esq
,,	,,	RICHARD CHOLMELY, third son of Richard C., of Whitby, co York, Knight
Oct	21	MATTHEW BENET, a native of York, one of the sons of John B., of London, [Knight, Doctor of Laws, Master in Chancery, and Chancellor to Queen [Anne
,,	,,	FRANCIS MONCKTON, son and heir of Philip M., of Cavill, co York, Knight.
,,	,,	ARTHUR GORING, son of George G., of Lewes, Sussex, Knight

folio 750

,,	,,	THOMAS BAKER, of (Enleasden ?), Sussex, Knight
,,	,,	FRANCIS CURLE, Esq., one of the Auditors of the King's Court of Wards [and Liveries (erased as admitted before June 12, 1614)
Nov	1	CHRISTOPHER BLENCOW, son of Henry B., of Blenco, Cumberland, Knight
,,	,,	EDWARD PERIENT, son of Thomas P., of Colchester, Essex, Esq
,,	,,	RICHARD HARRIS, S T P
,,	,,	ROBERT WILLIAMS, son and heir of John W., of Marnhull, Dorset, Esq
,,	,,	CHARLES GOLDSMITH, son and heir of Henry G., of Gray's Inn

folio 751.

		of St Asaph
,,	16	RICHARD PARRY, of St. Asaph, co Flint, Esq., son and heir of Richard, Bishop
,,	,,	WILLIAM ALLESTRIE, son and heir of Thomas A., of Alvaston, co Derby, gent
,,	23.	CHRISTOPHER PHILIPSON, son and heir of Robert P., of Hollinghall, parish of [Kendall, Westmoreland, Esq.

| 1618 | | folio 751—(*continued*) | [Esq |

1618

Nov 23 THEODORE GOODWYN, son and heir of Thomas G , of Stanton parva, Suffolk,

„ „ FRANCIS POWELL, son and heir of Lewis P , of Greenhill, parish of Pwllcrochan, co Pembroke, Esq   [ampton, gent , deceased

„ „ HENRY HORSLEY, son and heir of Tristram H , of West Sherborne, co South-

„ „ THOMAS ALLINE, son and heir of Edward A , of London, gent

„ „ FRANCIS FEILPLACE, of Swincombe, Oxon, gent

„ „ WILLIAM ROBINS (inserted in lieu of " Robinson " erased), son of Edward R , [of Oxford, gent

„ 26 SELWYN PARKER, son and heir of Thomas P , of Eastbourne, Sussex, gent

„ „ THOMAS STYRROPPE, son and heir of Thomas S , of the Close of Lincoln, gent.

„ „ ROBERT ROBINSON, son of William R , of Worton, co York, Esq

1618-19.   **folio 752**

Jan 27 THOMAS NICCOLS, son and heir of John N , of Shrewsbury, Salop, gent

„ „ RICHARD CANNING, son and heir of Edward C , of Enstone, Oxon, gent [Esq.

„ „ RICHARD A'PUGHE, son and heir of Griffin A , of Llangrin, co Montgomery,

„ „ SAMUEL HERBERT, son of Charles H , of (Stallo ?), co Montgomery, Esq.

„ „ JOHN MUNDY, son and heir of Francis M , of Mackworth, co Derby, Esq.

„ „ EDWARD ATSLOWE, son and heir of Henry A , of Downham, Essex, Esq

„ „ WILLIAM CONSTABLE, son of John C , of Lasenby, co York, Esq [deceased

„ „ BARTHOLOMEW MANFEEIDE, son and heir of John M , of London, gent ,

„ „ JOHN DONCASTELL, of Wellhouse, Berks, gent

„ „ THOMAS WESTROPE, of Cornebrough, co York, Esq

folio 753

Feb 2 JAMES BUTLER, second son of Walter B , Earl of Ormonde and Ossory

„ „ WILLIAM WALGRAVE, Esq , son and heir of William W , Knight, deceased

„ „ WILLIAM CROKE, second son of William C , Knight   [Queen

„ „ THOMAS STAFFORD, Knight, Gentleman Usher of the Privy Chamber to the

„ „ EDMUND SAUNDERS, son and heir of Thomas S , of Charlewood, Surrey, Esq

„ „ THOMAS NORTON, son of William N , of Sharpenhoe, Beds, Esq

folio 754.

„ 10. HOBSON BUTLER, son of Thomas B , of Great Paunton, co Lincoln, Esq

„ 13. RICHARD HIGGONS, son of Richard H , now reader

„ 14 GARRETT KEMPE, Knight, of Slindon, Sussex

„ „ EDMUND ASSHETON, of Chaderton, co Lanc , Esq [Northumberland, gent

„ „ THOMAS WIDDRINGTON, son and heir of Lewis W , of Chesbourne Grange,

„ „ JOHN GILPIN, son of John G , of Croydon, Surrey, gent

„ „ PHILIP KEMPE, son and heir of Garret K , of Slindon, Sussex, Knight

„ „ GEORGE BROWNE, son of William B , of Radford Semele, co Warwick, Knight

„ 13 HENRY BROWNE, son of William B , of Radford Semele, co. Warwick, Knight

folio 755.

Feb 14 WILLIAM RYSTON, son of Robert R , of Almodington, Sussex, gent

„ „ EDWARD HIGGONS, son of Richard H , of Gray's Inn, reader

1618-19		folio 755—(*continued*)
Feb	14	GEORGE HIGGONS, son of Richard H , of Gray's Inn, Reader [gent
,,	,,	RICHARD SANDELL, son and heir of Edward S , late of King's Lyrn, Norfolk,
,,	,,	THOMAS WOOD, son and heir of Thomas W , late of Barnard's Inn, gent
,,	,,	BARTHOLOMEW PIGOTT, of Chichester, Sussex, gent.
,,	22	GEORGE SMYTHE, son of George S , of Louth, co. Lincoln
,,	,,	WILLIAM SALTER, elder son of Edmund S , of Richings, Bucks
,,	,,	BARTHOLOMEW COTTON, son of Thomas C , of Starson, Norfolk
,,	,,	THOMAS COTTON, son of Thomas C , of Starson, Norfolk
,,	,,	WALTER LEE, Esq , one of the King's Serjeants at Arms
,,	,,	EDMUND THOROLD, third son of Richard T , of Marton, co Lincoln, Esq

folio 756.

,,	,,	THOMAS RANT, son of William R , of city of Norwich, M D
,,	,,	WILLIAM THOMPSON, of Easton, Suffolk, gent., late of Barnard's Inn
,,	,,	JOHN SUSAN, of London, gent
,,	,,	MORRICE WALROND, second son of Humphrey W , of Sea, co Somerset, Esq
1619		
April	28	SAMUEL SMITH, son of John S , of Parkfield in Laxfield, Suffolk, gent
,,	,,	ROBERT PAGE, son and heir of William P , of Hemingford, Hunts, gent
,,	,,	HENRY WARD, son and heir of Edward W , of Mendham, Suffolk, gent
,,	,,	JOSIAS ANDROS, son and heir of John A , of Uske, co Monmouth, gent

folio 757.

,,	,,	ROBERT WOOD, son and heir of Robert W , of Thurstone, Norfolk, Esq
,,	,,	RICHARD STOKES, second son of Richard S , Archdeacon of Norfolk [Inn.
,,	,,	HUMPHREY DAVENPORT, second son of Humphrey D , Esq , reader of this
,,	,,	JOHN OWEN, of Porkington, Salop, Esq , son and heir of John O , Esq , decd.
May	7	PATRICK CROSBIE, fourth son of John C , of Ardfert, co Kerry, Ireland,
		[Bishop of Ardfert
,,	,,	JOHN CLEYPOOLE, of Narbrough, co Northampton, gent
,,	,,	JOHN LYNE, son of John L , of Beeston, near Norwich, gent
,,	,,	JOHN ST ANDREW, son and heir of William St A , of Gotham, Notts, Esq
,,	,,	EDWARD GRIMSTON, son and heir of Harbottle G , of Bradfield, Essex, Knight
,,	,,	THOMAS CHARLTON, son of Thomas C., of Sandiacre, co. Derby, gent
June	2	THOMAS BISHOP, son and heir of John B , of Pocklington, co York, Esq
,,	,,	THOMAS MANSELL, son and heir of Robert M , of London, gent
,	,,	ROBERT PAYNELL, son and heir of Henry P , of Bellowe, Norfolk, Esq

folio 758.

,,	9	WILLIAM BYERLEY, son of John B , of Leicester, gent
Aug	1	ROBERT, Lord RICH, son and heir of Robert, Earl of Warwick
,,	,,	JOHN HAYWARD, Doctor of Laws, and one of the Masters in Chancery
,,	,,	WILLIAM OSBASTON, S T D
,,	,,	HUGH ASTON, gent
,,	,,	THOMAS GRIFFITH, of Pantllongdye, co Flint, Esq

1619.		folio 758—(continued)	
Aug.	1.	THOMAS JONES, son and heir of Thomas J , now reader	[clerk
,,	,,	TOBIAS THURSCROSS, son and heir of Henry T , of Kirby Moorside, co York,	
,,	,,	ARTHUR NEWMAN, son and heir of Arthur N., of Rickmansworth, Herts, gent	
,,	,,	JOHN PEARSE, son and heir of John P , of the city of York, Esq.	
,,	,,	EDMUND BUTLER, of Killarney, Queen's Co , Esq	

folio 759.

,,	,,	MATTHEW BILLINGSLEY, son of Henry B , of Syson, co Gloucester, Knight
,,	,,	MICHAEL MOORE, son of Melcher M , of Athboy, co Meath [Esq , deceased.
,,	,,	ROBERT KNAPLOCKE, son and heir of William K , late Member of this Inn,
,,	,,	FRANCIS JONES, son of Thomas J , now reader
,,	,,	RICHARD JONES, son of Thomas J , now reader
,,	,,	CORNELIUS FERMEDON, son and heir of William F Esq , deceased [deceased
,,	,,	WILLIAM SMITHES, son of George S , late Citizen and Alderman of London,
,,	,,	GODHELP COOPER, of Cobham, Surrey, gent.
,,	3	THOMAS BENNET, Knight, Citizen and Alderman of London
,,	,,	EDWARD ROTHERAM, Citizen and Alderman of London
,,	,,	ALEXANDER PRESCOTT, Citizen and Alderman of London.
,,	,,	THOMAS BENNET, Citizen and Alderman of London
,,	,,	ALAN COTTON, Citizen and Alderman of London.
,,	,,	CUTHBERT HACKETT, Citizen and Alderman of London

folio 760.

,,	,,	RICHARD HERNE, Citizen and Alderman of London, and one of the Sheriffs [of the city and co of Middlesex.
,,	,,	HUGH HAMMERSLEY, Citizen and Alderman of London, and one of the [Sheriffs of the city and co. of Middlesex
,,	,,	RICHARD DEANE, citizen and skinner, and one of the Sheriffs elect of the city [of London and co of Middlesex
,,	,,	THOMAS READFERNE, of Bradbury, Wilts, gent.
,,	,,	EDWARD BELL, son and heir of John B , of Pertenhall, Beds, gent
,,	,,	ADRIAN MOORE, son and heir of Adrian M., of Egham, Surrey, Esq
,,	,,	THOMAS ARCHER, son of Walter A , of the city of Kilkenny, in the King's [Privy Council in Ireland.
,,	,,	JOHN WEST, son and heir of William W , of Firbeck, co. York, Esq
,,	,,	MARK SHAFTO, son of Robert S , of Newcastle-on-Tyne.
,,	,,	LEONARD FERBY, son and heir of Edmund F., of Paul's Cray, Kent, Esq
,,	,,	JOHN HALL, son of Robert H., of Gray's Inn, gent.
,,	,	GORE BOND, of London, gent.
,,	,,	LIONEL TITCHBORNE, gent
,,	4	PETER MALLEON, of Fetter Lane, London, gent

		folio 761	[Golborne, co Lancaster, gent
,,	,,	THOMAS TAYLOR, of St Martin's-le-Vintry, London, son of John T , of	
,,	5	EDWARD SHERBURNE, Esq	
,,	,,	THOMAS WESTFIELD, S T D	

1619		folio 761—(*continued*)
Aug	5	ROBERT SHARPEIGH, Esq [Denbigh, gent.
,,	9	EDWARD JONES, son and heir of John J , of Garth Kenan, near Ruthin, co
,,	,,	HUGH HOLLAND, of Denbigh, Esq
,,	,,	HENRY BILLINGSLEY, son and heir of Thomas B , of London, gent
,,	,,	MICHAEL SPENCER, of Great Grimsby, co Lincoln, gent.
,,	,,	JOHN BARD, of North Kelsey, co Lincoln, gent
,,	,,	GEORGE SMITH, sen¹, of Louth, co Lincoln, gent
,,	10.	THEOBALD, Lord BURKE, of Brittas, in Ireland.
·,	,,	DUDLEY NORTH, Knight of the Bath, son and heir of Dudley, Lord N
,,	,,	FRANCIS CRANE, Knight.
,,	11	FRANCIS CLARKE, of Bradgate, Esq

folio 762

,,	,,	EDWARD ASTLEY, son of Thomas A , of Melton Constable, Norfolk, Esq
,,	,,	RICHARD LOWTHER, son and heir of William L , of Ingleton, co York, Esq
,,	,,	THOMAS BOYS, son of Thomas B , of the city of Canterbury, Esq
,,	,,	ROBERT NETTLETON, son and heir of Thomas N , of Thornhill, co York, gent
,,	,,	ROBERT RUDSTON, son of Belknap R , late of Boughton Monchelsea, Kent,
,,	,,	KENELM DIGBY, of Seton, co Rutland, gent [Esq
,,	,,	JOHN PRICE, son and heir of John P , of London, Esq , deceased
,,	,,	ROBERT GILL, gent , son and heir of Ralph G , of London, gent [Esq
,,	,,	THOMAS ARCHER, son and heir of Patrick A , of the city of Kilkenny, Ireland,
,,	,,	JAMES COWLEY, son and heir of Michael C , of Rathdowne, co Kilkenny
,,	,,	THOMAS EDGAR, son of Lionel E , Esq , of Ipswich, Suffolk (erased)
,,	,,	EDWARD LEGGE, Esq.
,,	,,	EVAN EDWARDS, of Mold, co Flint, gent

folio 763

,,	,,	THOMAS BURKE, of Derymaglachna, co Galway, Ireland, Esq
,,	,,	WALTER HENLEY, of Maidstone, Kent, gent.
,,	,,	JOHN HENLEY, son and heir of Walter H , of Maidstone, Kent, gent
,,	,,	JOHN WEBBE, son of John W , of Odstock, Wilts, Knight
,,	,,	THOMAS WEBBE, son of John W , of Odstock, Wilts, Knight
,,	,,	JOHN LLOYD, son and heir of Evan L , of Bodydryst, co Denbigh, Esq
,,	,,	EDWARD BUTLER, of Clare, son of James, Lord B , Baron Dunboyne in Ireland
,,	,,	BEVIS THELWALL, of Easthampstead Park, Beds, Esq
,,	,,	PETER BLAND, Esq
,,	,,	JAMES HODGSON, son of James H , of London, gent
,,	,,	WILLIAM WOOD, son of William W , citizen and goldsmith of London
,,	,,	BACON WALPOOLE, son of Calibut W , of Houghton, Norfolk, Esq.
,,	,,	JOHN HARRIES, son and heir of John H , of Rickmansworth, Herts
Oct	20	ROGER WAFFER, of Dublin, gent

folio 764.   [co ——— (erased),

,,	,,	THOMAS WOOD, late of Barnard's Inn, son and heir of Thomas W , of Wetherby

1619.   folio 764—(continued)

Oct 20   THOMAS TICKERIDGE, late of Barnard's Inn, son and heir of Arnold T , of
                                      [Evesham, co Worcester, gent, deceased

„   „   ROBERT HASELDINE, son and heir of Robert H , of Goldington, Beds, Esq

„   „   JOSHUA RATCLIFFE, son and heir of Savill R., of Todmorden, co Lanc , Esq

„   „   JOHN STONHOUSE, son and heir of William S , of Radley, Berks, Esq.

„   „   GEORGE STONHOUSE, son of William S , of Radley, Berks, Esq

Nov I   WILLIAM MALEVERER, second son of Richard M , Knight, deceased

„   „   JOHN FAGGE, son and heir of John F , of Brensett, Kent

„   „   JOHN HENDON, son and heir of John H , Esq , of Rolvenden, Kent

                        folio 765.   [Esq

„   „   THOMAS HARTOPP, son and heir of William H , of Burton Lazars, co Leicester,

„   „   JOHN SANDERSON, son and heir of John S , of Stanwick, co Northampton, Esq

„   5   ROWLAND HALE, son of William H , of King's Walden, Herts, Esq.

„   ,   JOHN CHESTER, son of Anthony C , of Chicheley, Bucks

„   10   HUMBERSTON MARCH, of Haddenham, Isle of Ely, co Cambridge, gent

„   „   EDWARD BROOME, late of Staple Inn, son and heir of Matthew B , of Aston,
                                      [co Salop, gent

„   15   JOHN NANNEY son of Griffin N , of Nanney, co Merioneth, Esq

„   „   WILLIAM BLOIS, son and heir of William B , of Ipswich, Suffolk, Esq

„   „   THOMAS BUGGS (? Briggs), son of Edward B , of Drinkston, Suffolk, Esq

„   „   JOHN JOSCELYN, son and heir of John J , Esq , late of this Inn

                        folio 766

„   6   JOHN WITHERINGS, of Overton, co Stafford, gent.

„   „   VINCENT CUPPER, son of Thomas C , of Powick, co Worcester, Esq

1619-20
Feb 2   GEORGE FLEETWOOD, second son of Miles F , Knight, Receiver of the Wards

„   „   CHARLES, Lord LAMBERT   .

„   „   THOMAS COOKE, Esq

„   „   FRANCIS HOLLIS, third son of John, Lord Houghton

„   „   FRANCIS BINDLOSSE, son and heir of Robert B , of Borwick, co Lanc Knight

„   „   RANDLE DAVENPORT, younger son of John D , Knight

„   „   WILLIAM LEWIN, son and heir of Gilbert L , of Hardingham, Norfolk

„   „   JAMES KENNEDY (?) (doubtful in the original), Esq of Broucborne, in Scotland

                        folio 767

„   5   THEOPHILUS, Earl of LINCOLN

„   „   THOMAS SMITH, second son of William S , of Theydon, Essex, Knight

„   7   JOHN OLDFIELD, late of Staple Inn, son and heir of Anthony O , of Spalding,
            co Lincoln, gent   [gent , deceased

„   „   HENRY STRATFORD, son and heir of Richard S , of Watling-street, London,

„   „   GARRET RAINSFORD, son of Miles R , of London, Esq

„   „   HENRY BRERETON, son and heir of John B , of London, gent

                        K

1619-20		folio 767—(continued)
Feb	7.	WILLIAM STANTON, son of Francis S , of Burchmore, Beds, Esq
,,	,,	EMANUEL HAYNES, son of John H , of Codicote, Herts, Esq
,,	,,	FRANCIS VERRALL, son and heir of John V , of Sandwich, Kent, Esq
,,	,,	CHARLES DALISON, son of Thomas D , of Greetwell, co Lincoln, Knight.
,,	,,	WILLIAM BROKE, son of Robert B , of Nacton, Suffolk, gent
,,	,,	WILLIAM MORE, son and heir of George M , of Dane Forest, parish of [Cannock, co Gloucester, Esq

folio 768.

Mar	1.	RICHARD OLIVER, of London, Esq
,,	5.	JOHN CLERKE, son and heir of Simon C , Knight and Baronet
,,	9.	THOMAS, Lord WENTWORTH
,,	,,	WALTER STEWARD, Esq , one of the Gentlemen of the Privy Chamber
,,	,,	ENDYMION PORTER, Esq
,,	13	ARTHUR MAINWARING
,,	,,	FRANCIS AYLOFFE
,,	,,	BULLINGE PRANIER (illegible in the original)
,,	,,	HENRY BUTLER, Esq
,,	,,	BARTHOLOMEW INN, Esq
,,	,,	EDWARD SHELDON
,,	,,	JOHN (CROSLER) (illegible in the original).
,,	,,	FREDERICK WINDSOR
,,	,,	THOMAS PORTER
,,	,,	EDMUND WINDSOR
,,	,,	JOHN (JUTTLEISE) (doubtful in the original)
,,	,,	WILLIAM GODBOLD
,,	15	JOHN FARRAR, son and heir of John F , Esq [reader]
,,	,,	EDWARD SHUTE, son and heir of John S., Esq (admitted by Robert Shute,
,,	,,	ROBERT NAPPER, son and heir of Robert N , of Luton Hoo, Beds, Bart.
,,	,,	NATHANIEL TRACY, son of Paul T , of Stanway, co. Gloucester, Bart.
,,	,,	CHRISTOPHER HUDSON, son and heir of William H
,,	,,	WILLIAM HUDSON, second son of William H
,,	,,	THOMAS PEROTT, Esq

folio 769

,,	,,	JOHN BACON, of London, gent
,,	,,	MARK SHAFTOE, son of Robert S , of Northumberland, gent (erased)
,,	,,	GEORGE GRYME, son and heir of George G , Esq
,,	,,	HUMPHREY CLARKE, of London, gent
,,	,,	ALEXANDER MOORE, son and heir of Alex M , of Grantham, co Lincoln, Esq
,,	,,	DAVID COTTON, son of Isaac C , of Stratford Bow, Middlesex.
,,	,,	JOHN UFFLETI, son and heir of John U , of Somerlayton, Suffolk, gent
,,	,,	THOMAS FLETCHER, son and heir of Richard F., of Wreemouth, co Cumber- [land, Knight
,,	,,	PATRICK BROWNE, son and heir of John B , of (Udston ?), co Dublin, gent

1619-20		folio 769—(*continued*)
Mar	15	THOMAS FLOYD, son and heir of Lancelot F, of Queenehope, co Flint.
,,	,,	ROBERT SMITH, gent, son and heir of Robert S., of Horsington, co Lincoln
,,	,,	ROGER WHELLDALE, gent, son and heir of Roger W, of Tydd St Mary, co [Lincoln
,,	,,	MARMADUKE CHOLMLEY, son and heir of Thomas C, of Brandsby, co York,
,,	,,	FRANCIS LANGWORTH, of Ospringe, Kent, son of John L, S T D [gent
,,	,,	GERRARD VERIER, son and heir of Gerrard V., of Canterbury, gent
,,	,,	WILLIAM WORTHINGTON, of Worthington, co. Lancaster, gent.
,,	,,	THOMAS LIDDELL, son and heir of Thomas L, of Ravensworth Castle, co [Durham, Esq
,,	,,	THOMAS HUTTON, gent, of Soame, co Cambridge [Aug. 11, 1619 (erased)
,,	,,	RICHARD LOWTHER, son and heir of William L, of Ingelton, co. York, Esq,
,,	,,	VALENTINE DRICROW (?) (illegible in the original), son and heir of Benjamin [D, of Enfield, Middlesex, gent
,,	,,	HENRY NECO1 (?) (illegible in the original), of Torr, co Devon, gent

folio 770.

,,	18	WILLIAM POTTER, of Bedwell Park, Herts, Esq.
,,	,,	ROGER SCOTT, Esq
,,	,,	RICHARD SCOTT, of London, Esq
,,	,,	THOMAS DIMOCKE, son and heir of Thomas D, Esq
,,	,,	JOHN ANDREWES, son of John A, of Clerkenwell, clerk
,,	,,	JOHN HOLMSTEAD, son of Nicholas H, Esq
,,	,,	WILLIAM DUCKETT, son of Noye D, of Broughton Astley, co Leicester, gent
,,	,,	JOHN BOOTH, son and heir of John B, of South Wheatley, Notts, gent.
,,	,,	JOHN ROOE, late of Staple Inn, son and heir of Roger R, late of Allport, co [Derby, gent, deceased
,,	,,	JOHN GOODMAN, son of James G, of Gray's Inn, Esq
,,	,,	WILLIAM FLOOD, of London, gent
,,	,,	ROBERT YATES, of London, gent
,,	,,	JOHN YATES, of London, gent, younger brother of Robert Y, of London, gent
,,	,,	JEROMY BRETT, of London, Esq
,,	,,	EDMUND ALLEYN, son and heir of Edward A, of Hatfield, Essex, Esq
,,	,,	GEORGE ALLEYN, younger son of Edward A, of Hatfield, Essex, Esq
,,	,,	THOMAS HUTTON, son and heir of Thomas H, of Soame, co Cambridge, gent
,,	,,	JERVASE MALTON, son and heir of Edmund M, of London, gent

folio 771.

,,	,,	CHRISTOPHER HATTON, of Kirby, co Northampton, Esq
,,	,,	RICHARD HATTON, son and heir of Robert H, of Lambeth, Surrey, Knight
,,	,,	RICHARD HOLFORD, son and heir of Henry H, Esq
,,	,	WILLIAM RUDDYER, son of James R, late of Ruddiard, co Stafford, deceased
,,	,,	MATTHEW ERDESWICK, of Sandon, co Stafford, gent
,,	15	HENRY VENTRESSE, son of Francis V, of Compton, Beds, Knight [Inn, Esq
,,	,,	NORRIS LENTON, late of Barnard's Inn, son and heir of Edward L, of Gray's

1620.   folio 771—(continued)

May 26   TOBIAS MORTON, son and heir of William M , of Newcastle, S T P

,,   ,,   JOHN BRADSHAWE, son and heir of Henry B , of Marple, co Chester, gent

,,   ,,   FRANCIS RAINSFORD, son of Henry R , of Clifford Chambers, co Gloucester,

,,   ,,   ROBERT KILBIE, of Ratcliffe-super-Wreke, co. Leicester, gent   [Knight

,,   ,,   WILLIAM INGRAM, son of William I , of the city of York, Knight

,,   ,,   VINCENT BARRY, son and heir of Francis B , of Thame, Oxon, gent , deceased.

,,   ,,   ISHAM PARKYNS, son and heir of George P , of Bunny, Notts, Knight.

folio 772.

,,   ,,   RICHARD TISDALE, son and heir of Richard T , of London, Esq.   [deceased

,,   ,,   HENRY CROMWELL, son and heir of Philip C , of Ramsey, Hunts, Knight,

June 22   RALPH RYMER, son of John R , of Romonby, co York, gent

,,   ,,   ROGER CORBETT, son of Thomas C , of Longnor, Salop, Esq

,,   ,,   PETER BRERETON, fourth son of William B , of Ashley, co Chester, Esq

,,   ,,   TOBIAS WRIGHT, son and heir of Hugh W , of the city of Durham, gent

,,   ,,   THOMAS JOLLEY, son of Thomas J , of Buglawhton, co Chester, gent

,,   ,,   HENRY BLOUNT, son of Thomas Pope B , of Tittenhanger, Herts, Knight

July 3   WILLIAM TAYLOR, son of William T , of Burnham Deepdale, Norfolk, gent

,,   ,,   ROBERT BUSBIE, son and heir of John B , of East Cleydon, Bucks, gent

,,   ,,   RICHARD LOWTHER, son and heir of William L (erased)   [deceased

,,   ,,   JOHN NEWDIGATE, son and heir of John N , of Arbury, co. Warwick, Knight,

,,   ,,   RICHARD NEWDIGATE, son of John N , of Arbury, co Warwick, Knight,
                                                            [deceased

folio 773

,,   ,,   RICHARD SKELTON, son and heir of John S , of Armathwaite, Cumberland,

,,   ,,   ROWLAND TILDESLEY, son of Thomas T , Knight, one of the readers   [Esq.

Aug 5   EDWARD HALL, of Henwick, co Worcester, Esq

,,   ,,   THOMAS CHEYNE, son and heir of Thomas C , of Sandon, Beds, Knight.

,,   ,,   SAINT JOHN (inserted in lieu of "Oliver') THOMPSON, son and heir of John T ,
                                            [of Husband's Crawley, Beds, Knight

,,   ,,   FRANCIS THOMPSON, son of John T , of Husband's Crawley, Beds, Knight

,,   ,,   SAINT JOHN CHERNOCK, son and heir of Robert C , of Holkett, Beds, Knight.

,,   ,,   WILLIAM MASON, son and heir of William M , of Gray's Inn, Esq (extra
                            [hospitium, June 10, 1629 , restitutur, Oct 19, 1629)

,,   ,,   JOHN HARDINGE, son of John H , reader

,,   ,,   CAVENDISH ALSOPP, of Woburn, Beds, Esq

,,   ,,   CHRISTOPHER ROTHERAM, son of John R , of Someres, Beds, Knight

,,   ,,   WILLIAM DOWTHWAYT, of Bridgewater, co. Somerset, gent.

,,   8   ANTHONY FORREST, son and heir of Anthony F., of Morborne, Hunts, Knight

,,   ,,   ROBERT WALLER, third son of Thomas W , of Gray's Inn, Esq

folio 774   [Ireland, Esq

,,   ,,   THOMAS CROOKE, son and heir of Thomas C , late of Gray's Inn, now of

,,   ,,   THOMAS WIDMERPOOLE, late of Staple Inn, son and heir of George W , of
                                            [Widmerpoole, Notts, Esq]

1620		folio 774—(*continued*)
Aug	8	JOHN WORSLEY, second son of Thomas W , of Hovingham, co York, Esq
,,	,,	RICHARD FLOWER, son and heir of Richard F , of Impton, co Radnor, gent
,,	,,	STEPHEN BOVILL, second son of George B , of London, Esq [Esq
,,	,,	THOMAS PARRAMORE, second son of Richard P , of Shankton, co Leicester,
,,	,,	FRANCIS STANTON, son of Francis S , of Birchmore, Esq
,,	,,	EDMUND STANTON, son of Francis S , of Birchmore, Esq [Brickhill, Bucks, gent
,,	,,	SANDES STANTON, son and heir of Anthony S , of Smewnes, in parish of
,,	,,	HENRY KENT, son of Henry K , of London, gent [Conquest, Beds, gent
,,	,,	THOMAS AUDLEY, late of Staple Inn, son and heir of Thomas A , of Houghton
,,	,,	ROBERT LANGFORD, son and heir of John L , of Newton, Bucks, gent

folio 775

,,	,,	EDMUND HARDINGE, of Aspley Guise, Beds, gent (admitted in the grand company by John H , his son and heir, reader of this Inn, and father [of Edmund H , of this Inn)
,,	,,	THOMAS CHEYNE, of Sandon, Beds, Knight
,,	,,	FRANCIS STANTON, of Birchmore, parish of Woburn, Beds, Esq
,,	,,	EDWARD BAKER, of London, gent
,,	,,	GEORGE SMITH, of London, gent
,,	,,	THOMAS TUCKER, of London, gent
,,	,,	JOHN CRAWLEY, son and heir of Francis C , of Gray's Inn, Esq.
,,	,,	TOBIAS FREER, son of Richard F , of Harlston, Norfolk, gent
,,	,,	RICHARD NURSE, son and heir of John N , of Ludgershall, Bucks, gent
,,	,,	WOLSTAN RANDOLPH, son and heir of Wolstan R., of London, gent
,,	,,	JOHN HEATH, son and heir of John H , of Kepier, co Durham, gent

folio 776   [House

,,	,,	HENRY MILDMAY, of Wansted, Essex, Knight, Master of the King's Jewel
,,	,,	WILLIAM (Walter in Calendar) ASHTON, son and heir of William A , of Tin-
,,	,,	RICHARD BENSON, of North Kelsey, co Lincoln, gent [grithe, Beds, gent
,,	9	EDWARD GIBSON, son and heir of Anthony G , of this Inn, Esq
,	,,	THOMAS GIBSON, son of Anthony G , of this Inn, Esq
,,	,,	JOSIAH BERNERS, grandson (nepos) and heir of Robert B , of this Inn, Esq
,,	,,	JOHN RICHARDS, son and heir of Thomas R , of Stanway, Salop, gent
,,	,,	JOHN NEWLOVE, son and heir of Anthony N , of Helpringham, co. Lincoln
,,	,,	JOHN TAPINGE, of Beachampton, Bucks, gent.
,,	,,	JOHN TAPINGE, son and heir of John T , of Beachampton, Bucks, gent
,,	,,	JOHN NICHOLS, of Buckingham, gent
,,	,,	JOHN KINGE, of Woburn, Beds, gent
,,	,,	JOHN KINGE, son and heir of John K , of Woburn, Beds, gent
,,	,,	THOMAS BERNEY, son of Thomas B , of Reedham, Norfolk, Knight

folio 777   [gent

Oct	24	WILLIAM LEVANS, son and heir of Humphrey L , of Evenley, co Northampton,
,,	,,	HENRY RODES, second son of John R , of Barlborough, co Derby, Knight
,,	,,	JAMES COPPINGER, son of Walter C , of Cork, Ireland, Esq

1620.   folio 777—(continued)

Oct 24 JOHN BLITHE, second son of John B , of Denton, co Lincoln, Esq

,,   ,,   TIMOTHY FETHERSTONHAUGH, son and heir of Henry F , of Kirkoswald,

,,   ,,   ROBERT MIDELTON, son of Robert M , of London, Esq   [Cumberland. Esq

,,   ,,   JOHN ATHERTON, gent., son and heir of John A , of Atherton, co Lanc , Esq

,,   ,,   RALPH FREEMAN, son and heir of William F , of Aspeden Hall, Herts , Esq

,,   ,,   GERVASE NEVILL, son and heir of George N , of Haddington, parish of
                                                    Hicham, co Lincoln, Esq
                                     folio 778.

Nov 1   EMANUEL, Lord SCROPE of Bolton, Lord President of the King's most honour-
                                                    [able Council of the North

,,   ,,   EDWARD PHILPOT, son and heir of John P , of Halsham, Kent, Esq

,,   ,,   DRURIE COOPER, son of William C , of Thurgarton, Notts, Esq

,,   ,,   EDMUND SYMONS, son and heir of William S , of Manton, Suffolk, Esq [gent

,,   ,,   DANIEL BATEMAN, son and heir of Thomas B , of Tottenham Court, Middx ,

,,   3   RICHARD WRIGHT, son and heir of Roger W , of Nantwich, co Chester, gent

,, 13   WILLIAM GREGGE, second son of Thomas G , of Bradley, co. Chester, gent

,,   ,,   RALPH CHETWYND, son of Thomas C , of Ridgley, co Stafford, gent

                                     folio 779.

,,   ,,   THOMAS ASTLEY, son and heir of Andrew A , of Writtle, Essex, Knight [gent.

,,   ,,   NICHOLAS REYNOULD, son and heir of William R , of Thaplee, co Cambs ,

,,   ,,   MILES EDGAR, son and heir of Henry E , late of Dynington, Suffolk, gent , dec

,,   ,   THOMAS BUTLER, son of Charles B , of Coates, co Lincoln, Esq

,,   ,,   GEORGE GOODWIN, of Staple Inn, son of William G , late of Wells, co.
                                                    [Somerset, gent , dec

,,   ,,   JAMES COBB, son and heir of William C , of Aldington, Kent , Esq , deceased

,,   ,,   RICHARD KENWRICK, son and heir of Robert K , of King's Sutton, Northampton,
1620-1   Esq (inserted in lieu of "gent.")
Jan 31   ISAACK JOHNSON, son and heir of Abraham J , of South Luffenham, Rutland, Esq

,,   ,,   HENRY GAWDY, son and heir of Robert G , Knight, of Claxton Hall, Norfolk.

,,   ,,   ROBERT EVELYN, son of Robert E , of Godstone, Surrey, Esq , deceased.

,,   ,,   HENRY HOGAN, son and heir of Thomas H , of Castleacre, Norfolk, Knight

                                     folio 780

Feb 2   HENRY HARRINGTON, Esq , of Ridlington, co Rutland

,,   ,,   JOHN JERMYE, Esq , son and heir of Isaac J , Knight

,,   ,,   ASLACK LANYE the younger, son and heir of Aslack L , Esq , of co Norfolk

,,   ,,   THOMAS HUGHES, of Uxbridge, Middlesex, Esq

,,   ,,   THEODORE GULSON, son of John G , Esq , one of the Prothonotaries of the
                                                    [Court of Common Bench

,,   ,   JOHN HUCHINS, son and heir of George H , of Basford, Notts, Esq.

,,   7   JOHN HOO, son and heir of Clement H , of North Creake, Norfolk, Esq.

,,   ,,   EDWARD COTTON, of Cotton, co Chester, gent

,, 17   JAMES WADE, son and heir of William W , of Battleswade, Essex, Knight

,,   ,,   JOHN CREMER, son and heir of George C., of Sechye, Norfolk, gent

1620-1.		folio 781.
Feb 18		HUGH HUGHES, son and heir of Griffin H., of Levenllanvair, co Carnarvon,
,,	,,	JOSEPH OWFIELD, son of Roger O., of London, gent [Esq.
,,	,,	THOMAS GOODWYN, son of Humphrey G , of Hardlow, co Derby, gent
,,	,,	THOMAS BALLARD, son and heir of Thomas B , of Wadhurst, Sussex, Esq.
,,	,,	ROBERT MORLEY, of Glynde, Sussex, Esq , son of William M., Esq
,,	,,	THOMAS BISHOP, son of Richard B , of Hemsewell, co Lincoln, gent.
,,	,,	HENRY FRYER, son of Thomas F , of the city of London, M D
,,	,.	JAMES MONTGOMERY, son of Hugh M , Knight
,,	,	EDWARD GOLDSMITH, son of Francis G , of Craford, Kent, Knight.
,,	,,	EDWARD FITTON, son of Richard F , of London, Esq
,,	,,	JOHN SALVIN, son and heir of James S., of Thorpe Salvin, co York, Esq
,,	,,	JOHN LEGARD, son of Robert L , of Anlaby, co Kingston-upon-Hull, gent ,
		[(erased, restored Feb 4, 1628).
,,	,,	THOMAS COBBES, son and heir of William C , of Chilham, Kent, Esq
,,	,,	DANIEL BATEMAN, of Tottenham, Middlesex, gent.
,,	,,	THOMAS JONES, son of Hugh J , M.A

1621		folio 782 [deceased
April 26		ROBERT LEYNES, son and heir of Christopher L , of Croboy, co Meath, Esq ,
,,	,,	WILLIAM HOBBY, son and heir of William H , of Harels-Barne, co Gloucester,
,,	,,	SAMUEL BLAND, of Whitechapel, London, gent. [Esq , deceased.
,,	,,	WILLIAM GREENE, son of Humphrey G , of Stanningston, Northumberland,
		[clerk.
May 11		WILLIAM BRIGGS, son and heir of David B , of Rickmansworth, Herts, Esq
,,	,,	ROBERT MARKHAM, second son of Anthony M , of Sedgebrook, co Lincoln,
		[Knight, deceased
,,	,,	RICHARD MOSLEY, son and heir of William M , of Carberton, Notts, Esq
June 13		WILLIAM ROBINSON, son and heir of William R , of Rocliffe, near the city of
		[York, Esq
,,	,,	DANIEL WHITE, son of Adam W , of Winchelsea, Sussex, Esq., deceased

		folio 783
,,	,,	THOMAS BRACKIN, Junior, son of Francis B , of Gray's Inn, Esq [Knight.
,,	15	WILLIAM STODDART, son and heir of Nicholas S , of Moddingham, Kent,
,,	18	ASHTON STANSFEELD, son and heir of James S , of Stansfeeld, co. York, Esq
,,	,,	RICHARD TAYLUER, son and heir of John T , of Paternoster Row, London
,,	,,	JOHN KIRTON, of West Camell, co Somerset, son and heir of James K , of the
		[Middle Temple, Esq , deceased
,,	,,	EDWARD PARKER, of Browsholme, co York, son of Thomas P , Esq., of same
,,	,,	PERIAM DOCKEWRAY, of Putteridge, Herts, Esq
,,	,,	WILLIAM BRAGG, son and heir of Robert B., of Bulmer, Essex, gent. [Esq
,,	,,	JOHN GIRLINGTON, second son of John G., of Thurland Castle, co. Lancaster,
,,	,,	JOHN FISHE, "Theologiæ Inceptor," second brother of William F , reader
,,	,,	HUMPHREY FISHE, gent , third brother of William F., reader

1621		folio 783—(*continued*)
June 18		OLIVER FISHE, gent , fourth brother of William F , reader
,,	,,	THOMAS FISHE, gent , fifth brother of William F , reader
,,	,,	HENRY FISHE, gent , sixth brother of William F , reader
,,	,,	RICHARD FISHE, seventh brother of William F , reader

folio 784

Aug. 6		HENRY DENNINGTON, of London, gent
,,	,,	RICHARD BUTTON, gent , son and heir of Richard B , of Wotton, Beds, gent
,,	,,	HENRY RASTELL, of Stamford, co Lincoln, gent [Baronet
,,	,,	WILLIAM WINNE, son of John W , of Gwydyr, co Carnarvon, Knight and
,,	,,	ROBERT RANTE, son of Roger R , of Swaffham, co. Cambridge, Esq.
,,	,,	WILLIAM SMITH, late of Barnard's Inn, son of Henry S , of Withycote, co Leicester, Esq , deceased [Essex, gent
,,	,,	THOMAS TALCOTT, late of Staple Inn, son and heir of Robert T , of Colchester,
,,	,,	JOHN WALCOTT, son and heir of Charles W , of Finsbury, Middlesex, Esq
,,	,,	THOMAS PEAKE, son and heir of Edward P , of Sandwich, Kent, Esq [gent
,,	,,	JOHN SWINFEN, son and heir of Richard S , of Sutton Cheyney, co. Leicester,
,,	,,	NICHOLAS BACON, of London, gent
,,	,,	CORNELIUS SPERINGE, of London, gent
,,	,,	THOMAS STIRROP, of Ross, co Hereford, gent.

folio 785

,,	,,	WOLLMER GOADE, son and heir of Matthew G , of Gray's Inn, Esq
,,	,,	JOHN NORBURY, son and heir of George N , of Holborn, Middlesex, gent
,,	,,	JOHN GREY, of London, gent
,,	,,	THOMAS BOOTH, son of John B , of Thornton, co Lincoln, gent
,,	,,	GEORGE FLUDDE, son and heir of John F , of Hollyroode, co Gloucester, gent
Oct 24		HUMPHREY MACKWORTH, son and heir of Richard M , of Betton Strange, [Salop, Esq , deceased
,,	,,	HENRY GAWDIE, son and heir of Robert G , of Claxton, Norfolk, Knight
,,	,,	REGINALD PECHAM, son and heir of Reginald P , of Yalham, parish of [Wrotham, Kent, Esq
,	,,	FRANCIS NUTTAL, son and heir of Francis N , of Castle Framlingham, Suffolk,
,,	,,	WILLIAM COLLES, of Parkebury, Herts, gent [Esq
,,	,,	TOBY CAGE, Esq , son and heir of Nicholas C , of London, Esq., deceased

folio 786
                                      [Kent,

Nov 1		EDMUND CHAPMAN, gent , son and heir of Edmund C , of East Greenwich,
,,	,,	JOHN WALCOTT, gent , son and heir of Charles W , of Finsbury, Middlesex, [Esq. (see *ante*)
,,	2	WILLIAM DENNY, son of William D , of Bockells, Suffolk, Esq [Knight
,,	,,	EDMUND DUNCH, son and heir of Sir William D , of Little Wittenham, Berks,
,,	,,	JOHN KEYTE, son of Jerome K , of Woodstock, Oxon, gent [Knight
,,	7	GUY CHARLTON, son of Lancelot C., of Wolsingham, co Durham, Esq , dec
,,	,,	HUMPHREY MONOUX, son and heir of Lewis M , of Wotton, Beds, Esq

| 1621. | | folio 786—*(continued)*. | [Esq , deceased |

Nov. 7 MARTIN HASTINGS, son and heir of Thomas H , of Hindringham, Norfolk,

,, ,, ALEXANDER DORRINGTON, late of Barnard's Inn, son and heir of Francis D ,
[of London, Esq , deceased

folio 787 [Esq

,, 21 AMBROSE GOODWIN, son and heir of Thomas G , of Little Stoneham, Suffolk,

,, 26 THOMAS GOWER, son and heir of Thomas G , of Stittenham, co York, Knight

,, ,, DANIEL HECHSTETER, of Keswick, Cumberland, gent. [and Baronet.

1621·2

Jan 29 ROBERT CHARNOCK, son and heir of Thomas C , of Astley, co. Lanc , Esq.

,, ,, RICHARD PEACOCK, son and heir of Richard P , of Abridge, Essex, gent.

,, ,, ADAM MOLINEUX, son of Richard M , of Sefton, co Lancaster, Knight
[and Baronet

,, ,, AUSTIN STEWARD, son and heir of Austin S , of Hogsdon, Middlesex, Esq

,, ,, FRANCIS FREER, son and heir of Israel F , of Godmanchester, Hunts, gent

,, ,, NATHANIEL CREWE, third son of Thomas C., Esq., one of the readers.

, ,, EDWARD DIXON, son and heir of Henry D , of Hilden, Kent, Esq

,, ,, WILLIAM DIXON, second son of Henry D , of Hilden, Kent, Esq.

,, ,, VINCENT DENNE, son and heir of John D , late of Gray's Inn, Esq.

:: ,, EDWARD ASTLEY, son of Andrew A , of Writtle, Essex, Knight

folio 788. [Suffolk, Esq

Feb 2 CLEMENT MARTIN, son and heir of Samuel M , of Wabridge (Weybread),

,, ,, THOMAS HALLEY, son of William H , late of the city of York, gent., deceased

,, 6 JOHN BOSY (? Bewsey or Boosey), son of Edward B., of Springfield, Essex,
[gent

,, 11 FRANCIS BLOIS, second son of William B , late of Ipswich, Suffolk, Esq ,

,, ,, WILLIAM CAWLEY, of the city of Chichester, Sussex, gent [deceased

,, ,, GEORGE FENWICK, son and heir of George F., late of Brinkburne, North
[umberland, gent , deceased.

,, ,, ERASMUS DRYDEN, son of Erasmus D , of Cannons Ashby, co Northampton,

,, ,, THOMAS LEGATE, son of John L , of Chatham, Kent, Esq , deceased [Bart.

,, ,, ANTHONY FOWLE, son of Anthony F , of Redburnfield, Sussex, Esq

folio 789 [deceased

,, ,, JOHN RUTTER, son and heir of John R , of Nantwich, co Chester, gent ,

:: ,, JOHN PECKE, son of William P , of Spixworth, Norfolk, Esq

,, ,, JOHN HARTWELL, of Broxbourne, Herts, gent

,, ,, GEORGE CUMMINGE, of the city of Limerick, Ireland, now of Barnard's Inn

,, ,, VALENCE SACHEVERELL, second son of Henry S , of Morley, co. Derby, Esq ,
[deceased

folio 790

Mar 12. JOHN RAVEN, Esq , M D

,, ,, JOHN WASE, gent.

,, ,, JAMES LOCK, gent , son and heir of Thomas L , Esq , now reader

,, 14 DONALD HASELRIGGE, of Noseley, co Leicester, Esq

,, ,, ALEXANDER BAKER, of Channell Row, Westminster, Middlesex, Esq

,, ,, THOMAS HEYWARD, of Charter House, Middlesex, gent

1621-2   folio 790—(*continued*).

Mar 14.   SAMUEL WINCOP, S.T B., Fellow of St John's, Cambridge.

,,   ,,   JOHN SOANE, of Maldon, Essex, gent

,,   16   SAMPSON PRICE, S T P , Chaplain in ordinary to yᵉ King

,,   17   CHRISTOPHER GOODFELLOW, of Cranford, co Northampton, gent.

folio 791

,,   ,,   WILLIAM BONHAM, gent , son and heir of William B , of London, Esq

,,   ,,   EDWARD FUST, gent , of Hill, co Gloucester

,,   ,,   THOMAS FINCH, gent , son of Henry F , Knight, King's Serjeant-at-Law

,,   18   ALEXANDER PRESCOTT, of Toobie, Essex, gent , son of Alexander P , Citizen
                              [and Alderman of London, deceased

,,   ,,   HUGH INGRAM, son of William I , of the city of York, Knight

,,   ,,   ARTHUR INGRAM, son of William I , of the city of York, Knight

,,   ,,   WILLIAM SUGGOTT, late of Barnard's Inn (extra hospituum, Nov 17, 1628)

,,   ,,   PIERCY NORCOTT, of Ireland, gent

,,   ,,   RICHARD RUDD, gent , Citizen and Haberdasher of London

,,   ,,   NATHANIEL SNAPE, late of Barnard's Inn, of London, gent , son of Edmund
                              [S , late of Northampton, S T D

,,   ,,   JOHN SMITH, second son of John S , late of Ditton, co Cambridge, S T D

,,   ,,   THOMAS HARRINGTON, son and heir of William H , of Witham, co Lincoln,
                              [Esq.

folio 792

,,   ,,   GEORGE SAYIS, of St Mary Axe, London, Esq

,,   ,,   EDMUND (inserted in lieu of "Edward" erased) FORTESCUE, son of Nicholas

,,   ,,   THOMAS HULMES, of London, gent   [F , of Cookhill, co Worcester, Knight

,,   ,,   ROGER PELHAM, son of William P , of Broclesby, co Lincoln, Knight

,,   ,,   CHARLES PENNINGE, son and heir of Edmund P , of Dunmow, Essex, Esq

,,   ,,   THOMAS PENNINGE, brother of Charles P , son and heir of Edmund P , of
                              [Dunmow, Essex, Esq

,,   ,,   ROBERT COOKE, son and heir of Robert C , of Fering, Essex, gent   [Esq

,,   ,,   WILLIAM HARWOOD, son and heir of Walter H , of Odiham, Southampton,

,,   ,,   ANTHONY FILLIALL, son and heir of Anthony F , of Rayne, Essex, Esq

,,   ,,   BENJAMIN HIDE, of London, gent.

1622
May 15   NICHOLAS PLUNKETT, son of Christopher P , Lord of Killeen, co. Meath

folio 793

,,   ,,   HENRY AUDLEY, son and heir of Robert A , of Berechurch, Essex, Esq

,,   ,,   THOMAS ALDERSEY, son and heir of John A , of Spurstowe, co Chester, gent

,,   ,,   STEVEN LENNARD, Esq , son and heir of Samuel L , of West Wickham, Kent,
                              [Esq , deceased

,,   ,,   EDWARD GOULDSMITH, son of Francis G , of Craford, Kent, Knight

,,   22   HENRY CHAPMAN, son and heir of Seth C , of Bury, Suffolk, gent , deceased

,   ,,   HENRY DIXWELL, son and heir of Edward D , of Ponteland, Northumberland,
                              [gent , deceased

1622.   folio 793—(continued).

May 22. WILLIAM BOTELER, son of Oliver B., of Sharnbrook, Beds, Knight

,, ,, GEOFFREY PETTMAN, son and heir of Geoffrey P., of Woodbridge, Suffolk, gent

,, ,, THOMAS ELLYS, son and heir of Thomas E., Knight, one of the King's Council [in the North

,, ,, JOHN BLEWET, son and heir of Thomas B., of Grantham, co. Lincoln, Esq.

,, ,, THOMAS SWINGFIELD, son and heir of Thomas S., of Peckham, Surrey, gent.

folio 794.

,, 24 WILLIAM MAN, son and heir of Christopher M., of Canterbury, Esq

,, ,, ROBERT HOLTE, son and heir of John H., of Stubbley, co. Lancaster, Esq

,, 31. GEORGE MORECROFT, son and heir of George M., of Kingham, Oxon, gent

,, ,, WILLIAM HEWITT, of Dunton, co. Leicester, gent.   [Essex, gent.

,, ,, CHRISTOPHER PURPELL, son and heir of Christopher P., of Little Saling,

July 3. ALEXANDER ROKEBY, second son of William R., of Hotham, co. York, Esq

,, 10 ROBERT CARR, Knight, one of the Gentlemen of the Privy Chamber to Prince [Charles, and Treasurer of the Privy Chamber

,, ,, GEORGE FITZWILLIAM, Esq., son and heir of George F., of Mablethorpe, co. Lincoln, Knight, grandson (nepos) of the present reader, per me, Robert [Callis, reader.

,, ,, THOMAS BROOME, gent., son of Robert B., of Ringewolde, Kent, clerk.

folio 795   [Linc.

,, ,, EDWARD TYRWHIT, Esq., second son of Edward T., Knight, of Stanfield, co

,, ,, JOHN ROWLEY, gent., son and heir of John R., of Barkway, Herts, gent.

Aug 7 WILLIAM ASCOUGH, gent., second son of Roger A., late of Nuthall, Notts, [Knight

,, ,, RICHARD GOWLAND, of the city of Lincoln, gent

,, ,, WILLIAM ROBERTS, gent., son and heir of Barne R., late of Willesden, Mid- [dlesex, Esq

,, ,, ROBERT RAMSEY, gent

,, ,, THOMAS WALLER, gent., son of Thomas W., one of the Prothonotaries of the [Court of Common Bench, Esq

,, ,. RUTLAND TYRWHIT, Esq., third son of Robert T., of Kettleby, co. Linc., Esq

,, ,, RICHARD GAY, of borough of Southwark, Surrey, gent

folio 796.

,, 12 JOHN (WILLIAMS), Bishop of Lincoln, Lord Keeper

,, ,, NICHOLAS RAYNTON, Esq., one of the Sheriffs of London (Lord Mayor, 1632,

,, ,, DAVID DOLBEN, of Denbigh, Wales, Esq   [and a Knight)

,, ,, WILLIAM GROM (?), Esq

,, ,, ARTHUR MAINWARINGE, Esq., "bearer of the Great Seal"

,, ,, RICHARD NAPIER, son of Robert N., of Luton Hoo, Beds, Knight and Bart

,, ,, ALEXANDER NAPIER, son of Robert N., of Luton Hoo, Beds, Knight and Bart

,, ,, GEORGE COTTON, son of Isaac C., of Stratford Bow, Middlesex, gent

folio 797

,, ,, ISAAC COTTON, third son of Isaac C., of Stratford Bow, Middlesex, gent.

,, ,, ROBERT KIRKHAM, one of the clerks of the King's Privy Seal

,, ,, CHARLES PELHAM, second son of William P., of Brocklesby, co. Linc., Knight

1622   folio 797—*(continued)*.

Aug 12   THOMAS PELHAM, fourth son of William P , of Brocklesby, co Lincoln, Knight.

,, ,,   EDWARD BOROUGH, of Stow, co Lincoln, gent

,, ,,   BARNABY HOLBECH, son of William H , of Fillongley, co Warwick, gent

,, ,,   ROBERT CALLIS, son of William C , of the city of Lincoln, gent , grandson [(nepos) of Robert Callis, reader

,, ,,   CHRISTOPHER FARNLEY (?), of Northrop, co Lincoln, gent

,, ,,   ROBERT WHITFIELD, third son of Herbert W , of Tenterden, Kent, Esq

,, ,,   WILLIAM GODBOLD, third son of Thomas G , of Southolt, Suffolk, Esq

,, ,,   EDWARD SWAN, son and heir of Francis S , of Denton, Kent, Knight

folio 798

,, 15.   WALTER KIRKHAM, of Fineshead, co Northampton, Esq

,, ,,   DIXIE HICKMAN, son and heir of Walter H , of Kew, Surrey, Esq., deceased

,, ,,   JOHN BRADSHAW, of the city of Westminster, gent

,, ,,   JOHN GOODALL, son of Thomas G , of Earle Stonham, Suffolk, gent

,, ,,   JOHN NEDHAM, of Ilston, co Leicester, gent

Oct 26   THOMAS BOYS, son and heir of Thomas B , of Mersham, Kent, gent.

,, ,,   JOHN GIBBON, of Oby, Norfolk, gent

,, ,,   EDMUND ELLIS, son of Thomas E , Knight

,, ,,   JOHN PIDGION, gent , son and heir of John P , of the Close, Lincoln, gent

,, ,,   VALLENCE SACHEVERELL, second son of Henry S , of Morley, co Derby, Esq ,

folio 799   [(erased)

,, ,,   GEORGE CARR, son and heir of William C., of Southay, co. York, gent , deceased

,, 30   THOMAS LUNSFORD, son and heir of Thomas L , of East Hadleigh, Essex, Esq

,, ,,   JAMES CARDINALL, son of Charles C , of Great Bromley, Essex, gent

,, ,,   JOHN JEFFERIES, gent , son and heir of John J , Esq , deceased   [gent

,, ,,   NATHANIEL BATE, son and heir of Nathaniel B , of Little Chester, co Derby,

Nov 1   JOHN OGLE, Knight and Colonel

,, ,,   EDWARD FITTON, of Gawsworth, co Chester, Baronet

,, ,,   WILLIAM PESHALL, second son of John P , of Horsley, co Stafford, Baronet.

,, ,,   JOHN FOTHERBIE, Esq , of the city of Canterbury

,, ,,   NATHANIEL STUDLEY, son and heir of Nathaniel S , of this Inn

folio 800   [Esq , deceased

,, 4   HENRY BANASTER, gent , son and heir of Henry B , of Bancke, co Lancaster,

,, ,,   SAMUEL SLEIGHE, son and heir of Gervase S., of Derby, gent

,, 7   WILLIAM BRODNAX, son of Thomas B , of Godmersham, Kent, gent

,, 8   WILLIAM PAYNE, of Bexley, Kent, gent.

,, 13   THOMAS REVELL, son and heir of John R , of Kilgaron, co. Pembroke, Esq

,, 20   THOMAS TILDESLEY, of Morleis, co Lancaster, Esq

,, 25   EDWARD DUKE, of Benhall, Suffolk, Esq   [Knight, deceased

,, ,,   ANTHONY SAINTLEGER, Esq , son and heir of Anthony S , of Wyerton, Kent,

,, ,,   WILLIAM POLEY, second son of William P , of Boxstead, Suffolk, Knight

,, ,,   HENRY PROCTER, son and heir of Thomas P , of Newall, co York, Esq , of [Gray's Inn, and then pensioner

1622-3		**folio 801**

Jan 19 ⎱ PHILIP LANGDALE, son and heir of William L., of Lanthorpe-in-Holderness,
or 29 ⎰ [co York, Esq

,, 29 THOMAS JACKSON, son and heir of Thomas J , of Knaton, co York, gent

,, ,, CHRISTOPHER COPLEY, son and heir of William C , of Wadworth, co. York,

,, ,, JOHN INGLEBIE, of Lawkland, parish of Clapham, co York, Esq [Esq

,, ,, RALPH SULIARD, son of John S , of Hayley, Suffolk, Knight

,, ,, HENRY HALL, son of William H , of Highmedoe, parish of Newland, co
[Gloucester, Esq , deceased

,, ,, CALCOT CHAMBRÉ, son and heir of Calcot C , of Williamscot, Oxon, Esq

,, ,, ROGER ROWLEY, son and heir of William R , of Salop, gent

,, ,, ARTHUR HASELRICE, of Noseley, co Leicester, gent [Esq

,, ,, EDMUND ANDERSON, son and heir of William A , of Broughton, co Lincoln,

folio 802

,, ,, WILLIAM BRERETON, of Handford, co Chester, Esq [Inn

Feb. 2 URIAN BRERETON, of Handford, younger brother of William B , Esq , of this

,, ,, GEORGE, Lord BERKELEY, SEGRAVE and BRAOSE.

,, ,, THOMAS MORTON, Bishop of Coventry and Lichfield

,, ,, ROGER TWISDEN, Knight, son and heir of William T , Knight and Baronet

,, ,, JAMES TIRRELL, son and heir of James T , of Gipping, Suffolk, Esq , an

,, ,, HENRY ASHWOOD, of London, gent [ancient of this Inn.

folio 803

,, 5 KNIGHTLEY CHETWODE, son and heir of Richard C , of Chetwode, Bucks, Esq

,, ,, THOMAS COWPER, son and heir of Ralph C , Esq , reader

,, 7 JOHN WILLIAMSON, second son of Thomas W , late of Grafton, co Chester, gent

,, 10 JOHN WEBBE, son and heir of John W , of Odstock, Wilts, Knight

,, ,, EDWARD COWPER, younger son of Ralph C , Esq , reader.

,, 11 THOMAS WYAT, gent , son of George W , of Boxley Abbey, Kent, Esq

,, ,, ALMOT CLENCH, son and heir of John C., of Great Bealings, Suffolk

,, ,, JOHN LASCELLS, son and heir of George L., of Knyveton, Notts, Esq.

,, ,, JAMES DEREHAUGH, of Redgrave, Suffolk, Esq

1623		**folio 804**

May 7 JOHN PECKE, son of William P , of Spiks(x)worth, Norfolk, Esq (erased, as
[admitted before)

,, ,, ARNOLD CHILDE, son and heir of Arnold C , of Barnes, Surrey, gent , deceased

,, ,, WILLIAM POOLEY, son of William P , of Bury St ——— (erased)

,, ,, JOHN JOWLES, son and heir of John J , of Arkeham, Kent, gent.

,, ,, WILLIAM FOSTER, S T P

,, 12 RICHARD MASTER, son and heir of Edward M , of Ospring, Kent, Esq

,, ,, JOHN DUNGAN, of Castleton, co Kildare, gent

,, 16 JOHN ODINGSELLS, son and heir of John O., of Eperstone, Notts, Esq

,, ,, CHARLES CHAMBER, son of Thomas C , of Cleadon, co Durham, gent.

,, ,, THOMAS BELIALD, son and heir of John B , of Paternoster Row, London, gent.

1623		folio 805

May 16.   RICHARD HARLAKENDEN, son and heir of Richard H , of Earlscolne, Essex, Esq

,,   ,,   EDWARD HARTE, son of Percival H , of Lullingstone, Kent, Knight

,,   ,,   ROBERT MADDISON, son of Henry M , of Newcastle-upon-Tyne

,,   ,,   WILLIAM CODD, of Wateringbury, Kent, gent., late of Staple Inn

,,   23.   WILLIAM DICONSON, son and heir of Thomas D., of Gillingham, Kent, gent.

,,   ,,   JOHN SAMPSON, son and heir of John S , of Carsey, Suffolk, Esq

,,   ,,   GEORGE ELLIS, son and heir of Francis E , of Barnsley, co York, gent.

,,   ,,   JOHN GRIFFITH, son and heir of Richard G , of Bloxham, Oxon, Esq   [gent

,,   ,,   RICHARD GREEN, gent, son and heir of Thomas G , of Congleton, co Chester,

June 16.   PETER BUTLER, son and heir of Edward B , of Lowe Grange, co Kilkenny,
[Knight

,,   ,,   THOMAS BETENSON, son of Richard B , of Layer Delahay, Essex, Esq

folio 806

..   18   CHARLES NODES, son and heir of George N., of Sheppall, Herts, Esq

July   1.   EDMUND POWELL, son and heir of Edmund P , of Sandford, Oxon, Esq

,,   ,,   GEORGE EGHSHAM, Doctor of Medicine to the King

,,   ,,   FRANCIS DOWNES, gent , son of Roger D , Esq , reader.

Aug   7.   JOHN RICHMAN, son and heir of Robert R , of Hedenham, Norfolk, gent

,,   ,,   RANDALL NICOLL, son and heir of Randall N , of London, gent., deceased

,,   ,,   JOHN ROTHERHAM, son and heir of Thomas R , Knight

,,   ,,   ROBERT PAINE, son and heir of Robert P , of Medlow, Hunts, Knight

,,   ,,   FRANCIS HETLEY, son and heir of Thomas H , Serjeant-at-Law elect

folio 807

,,   ,,   FRANCIS CRAWLEY, second son of Francis C , reader

,,   ,,   THOMAS HETLEY, second son of Thomas H , Serjeant-at-Law elect

,,   ,,   NATHANIEL MARSH, second son of Thomas M., of Darkes, Middlesex, Esq

,,   ,,   THOMAS CRAWLEY, third son of Francis C , reader

,,   ,,   NICHOLAS TOWNLEY, son and heir of Francis T , of Littleton, Middlesex, Esq

,,   ,,   JOHN MORRIS, son and heir of Francis M , Principal of Staple Inn

,,   8.   ROBERT NUTTING, son of Robert N., of Hendon, Middlesex, Esq, late of
[Staple Inn

,,   ,,   THOMAS DYKE, son and heir of William D , of Frant, Sussex, Esq

,,   ,,   ROBERT KIPPING, son and heir of Walter K , of Tewdeley, Kent, Esq

folio 808.   [Knight, deceased

,,   ,,   RALPH EURE, son and heir of Peter E , of Washingborough, co Lincoln,

,,   ,,   HENRY STEBBING, son of William S , of Soham Earl, Suffolk, gent

,,   ,,   EDWARD HALDENBY, son of Francis H , of Haldenby, co York, Esq [Knight.

,,   ,,   EDWARD BROOKE, son and heir of Thomas B , of Oakeley co Northants,

,,   ,,   JOHN CAYWORTH (Caperworth ?), gent , son and heir of Edward C , of Warkton,
Northants.   [deceased

,,   ,,   HENRY CALVERLEY, of Calverley, co York, Esq , son and heir of Walter C ,

,,   ,,   JOHN HODGES, of Broadway, co Worcester, gent , son and heir of John H.

,,   ,,   GEORGE ALLESTREY, third son of Thomas A , of Alveston, co Derby, gent.

| 1623 | | folio 809. | [Derby, Esq , deceased |

Oct 20. SAMUEL SLEIGH, son and heir of ———— S, of Ashe, parish of Sutton, co.

,,   ,, JOHN JAQUES, son and heir of John J , of Highgate, Middlesex, Esq.   [gent.

,,   ,, WILLIAM TAWYER, son and heir of Robert T , of Stanwick, co Northampton,

,,   ,, THOMAS FELL, son and heir of George F , of Ulverstone, co Lancaster, gent

,,   ,, ANTHONY KING, gent., son and heir of Richard K., of Ashby-de-la-Laund, co

,,   30 EDWARD NORBURY, gent   [Lincoln, Esq.

Nov 1. GEORGE PENRUDDOCK, son of Thomas P , of Hale, Wilts.

,,   ,, JOHN COOK, son and heir of Isaac C., of Burbridge, co Leicester, Esq   [gent

,,   ,, ROGER JOHNSON, son and heir of Bartholomew J , of Anmer, co. Norfolk,

folio 810.

,,   3 FRANCIS WHETENHALL, son of Henry W , of East Peckham, Kent, Knight

,,   ,, JOHN WARREN, son of Thomas W , late of Bittell, co. Worcester, Esq ,
    deceased   [gent

,,   10 THOMAS WYNN, son and heir of John W , of Corvedwen, co Denbigh,

,,   ,, EDWARD KING, second son of Richard K , of Ashby-de-la Laund, co Lincoln,
    [Esq

,,   12 MAUGER VAVASOUR, son and heir of William V., of Weston, co York, Esq

,,   19 GEORGE BRADLEY, son and heir of John B , of Louth, co Lincoln, Esq

,,   ,, THOMAS KYRLE, late of Staple Inn, son of John K , of Great Marcle, co
    [Hereford, Esq.

,,   24 RUTLAND SNOWDON, son and heir of Robert S , Bishop of Carlisle, deceased.

folio 811

,,   ,, RICHARD TAPPINGE, of Staple Inn, Esq   [Soulbene, Bucks, gent

,,   25 EDWARD MERIDALE, son and heir of Edmund M , of Bragnam, parish of

,,   ,, CHARLES THIMBLETHORPE, son and heir of George T , of Stratton St Mary,

1623 4   [Norfolk, gent
Jan. 26 JAMES USHER, Bishop of Meath, Ireland (see entry, James Tyrrell, 1114)

,,   28 RICHARD POULTENEY, son and heir of Gabriel P , of St Sepulchre's, London,
    gent   [Palatinate

Feb. 2 HORATIO VERE, Knight, Captain-General of the King's army in the

,,   ,, THOMAS HOLKER, of Staple Inn, gent , son of Lancelot H , of Eccles, co Lan-
    [caster, gent

,,   ,, LIONEL EDGAR, son and heir of Lionel E , of Ipswich, Suffolk (at the request
    [of Richard Hutton, Knight, a Justice of the Common Pleas)

folio 812

,,   9 DANIEL BEDINGFELD, son of Christopher B , of Wighton, Norfolk, gent

,,   ,, JOHN DIX, of Wickmer, Norfolk Esq

,,   15 THOMAS HOLLAND, of Quiddenham, Norfolk, Knight

,,   ,, DREW DRURY, of Riddlesworth, Norfolk, Esq

,,   ,, FRAMINGHAM GAWDY, of Harling, Norfolk, Esq

,,   ,, OWEN SHEPPARD, of Kirkby, Norfolk, Esq   [folk, Knight

,,   ,, CLEMENT HIRNE, Esq , son of Thomas H , of Hyveringland (Heverland), Nor-

,,   ,, WILLIAM DENNY, son of William D , now reader.

1623-4   **folio 812**—(*continued*)

Feb 15. THOMAS HIRNE, grandson (nepos) of Thomas H , Knight, of Heverland,

,,   ,,   EDMUND (or Edward) ANGUISH, of the city of Norwich, gent   [Norfolk

,   ,,   RICHARD BASPOOLE, of Bungay, Suffolk, gent

,,   ,,   JOHN WARDE, of the city of Norwich, gent

,,   ,,   HUMPHREY HAGGIT, of London, Esq.

,,   ,,   GEORGE BENFIELD, of Norwich, gent

folio 813

,, 16. GEORGE SMITH, son of John S., of Kirford, Sussex, Esq

,,   ,,   RICHARD BRABONE, son and heir of John B , of Thwaite, Norfolk, gent

,,   ,,   HENRY WARE, of High Holborn, Middlesex, gent

,,   ,,   THOMAS HALMAN, of Swaffham, Norfolk, gent

,   ,,   ROBERT HALMAN, of Swaffham, Norfolk, gent

,,   ,,   RICHARD OAKES, of the city of Norwich, gent

,,   ,,   EDWARD HUNNE, of South Elmham, Suffolk, gent

,,   ,,   THOMAS DENNY, of Thurleton, Norfolk, gent

,,   ,,   THOMAS FLINT, of Yaxley, Suffolk, gent

,,   ,,   ARTHUR BRANTHWAITE, of Hethel, Norfolk

,,   ,,   JOHN DADE, of Beccles, Suffolk, gent

,,   ,,   ROBERT SNELL, of Denton, Norfolk, gent

,,   ,,   JOHN KETTLEBOROUGH, of Heverland, Norfolk, gent

,,   ,,   GREGORY CALNE, of Ditchingham, son and heir of Richard C , of same, gent

folio 814   [Wotton, Esq

,, 17 ROBERT SUCKLING, of Wotton, Norfolk, gent , son and heir of Charles S , of

,,   ,,   RUSSELL ANDREWES, of Evesham, co Worcester, gent.   [the Bath

,, 18 ROBERT BEVILL, son and heir of Robert B , of Chesterton, Hunts, Knight of

,,   ,,   WILLIAM BEVILL, second son of Robert B , of Chesterton, Hunts, Knight of

,, 21. JOHN DENNY, youngest son of William D , now reader.   [the Bath

,,   ,,   ROBERT BIDWELL, gent , son of William B , gent

,,   ,,   THOMAS ALLEN, of Wichingham parva, Norfolk, gent.

,,   ,,   FRANCIS CUDDON, gent

,,   ,,   JOHN DENNY, gent , son of John D , of Gisleham, Suffolk, gent

,, 22 EDWARD RAMSEY, of Hetherset, Norfolk, Esq

,,   ,,   ROGER NORTH, of Mildenhall, Norfolk, Knight

folio 815

,,   ,,   THOMAS BANCROFT, of the city of London, gent

,, 23. WILLIAM HART, of Beeston, Norfolk, gent

,,   ,,   JOHN BROWNE, son of John B , late of Wokingham, Berks, gent , deceased

,,   ,,   JOHN FULWOOD, third son of George F , of Middleton, co Derby, Knight

,,   ,,   ROBERT PLUNCKETT, son of Nicholas P , of Holborn, Middlesex, gent

,,   ,,   WILLIAM SPINCKE, son and heir of William S., gent , late of Driffield, co.
                                           [York, deceased

,,   ,,   THOMAS RUSSELL, second son of Philip R , of North Bashan, Norfolk, gent

1623-4		folio 815—(*continued*)
Feb.	23	ANTHONY WINGFIELD, son and heir of Henry W, of Potter Hanworth, co [Lincoln, gent
,,	,,	THOMAS DICCONSON, son of Edward D, of Eccleston, co Lanc, gent
,,	,,	JOHN MONSON, son and heir of Anthony M, of South Carleton, co Linc, Esq

1624		folio 816.
April	21	NICHOLAS CUMMINE, son and heir of David C, of Limerick, Ireland, Esq
,,	,,	WILLIAM CANNING, son and heir of William C, of Bassingshawe, London, [merchant
,,	,,	JOHN BOYS, son and heir of Edward B, of Fredville, in East Kent, Knight
,,	28	WILLIAM GAMAGE, son and heir of Edward G, of Newcastle, co Glamorgan, Esq [deceased
May	7	WILLIAM FALDOE, son and heir of William F, of Islington, Middlesex, gent,
,,	,,	JOHN COPLEY, of Doncaster, co York, Esq
,,	,,	JOHN LEGARD, son and heir of John L, of Ganton, co York, Esq
,,	,,	STEPHEN HAWARD, of Feversham, Kent, gent
,,	,,	WILLIAM BURROUGH, of Burrough, co Leicester, Esq
,,	,,	RALPH ASSHETON, Esq, son and heir of Ralph A, of Leaver, co Lanc, Bart

folio 817.

,,	,,	AUGUSTINE BROGRAVE, son of Symon B, of Hammills, Herts, Esq, son of [John B, Knight, late Attorney general of the Duchy of Lancaster
,,	,,	JOHN BROGRAVE, son and heir of John B, of Beckenham, Kent, Esq. [Esq.
,,	,,	ROBERT CAWDRON, son and heir of Robert C, of Hale Magna, co. Lincoln,
June	2	WARREN GOUGH, son and heir of William G., of Hewelsfield, co Gloucester, [gent, deceased.
,,	10.	WILLIAM WILLIAMS, son and heir of Richard W, of Llysdylas, co Anglesea, Esq
,,	,,	CHRISTOPHER GRAUNT, son and heir of William G, of Rocksbie in Pickhall, co York, gent [Rutland, Esq
,,	,,	SAMUEL SHEFFIELD, son and heir of Sampson S, late of Seaton, co
,,	,,	EDWARD BROGRAVE, son of Simon B, Esq [Esq
,,	15	THOMAS PRESTWICH, son and heir of Edmund P, of Hulme, co Lancaster,

folio 818.

Aug	1	FRANCIS WORTLEY, of Wortley, co York, Knight and Baronet
,,	,	JOHN STONE, of London, Esq
,,	,,	WILLIAM CLEMENT, M D
,,	,,	JOHN BUNBURY, of Staple Inn, gent.
,,	5	MOUNTJOY (Blount), Lord MOUNTJOY
,,	,,	CHARLES RICH, Knight, one of the sons of Robert, Earl of Warwick, deceased
,,	,,	RICHARD SPENCER second son of Robert, Lord S
,,	,,	EDWARD CONWAY, Knight
,,	,,	WILLIAM RAWLINS, S.T.D
,,	,,	JOHN MILLER, Knight
,,	,,	THOMAS FALDO, son and heir of Robert F, Esq

1624.   folio 818—(*continued*).

Aug. 5   ANTHONY STANTON, son and heir of Renald S , of Stoke, Bucks, Esq , deceased

,, ,,   JOHN GREENE, of London, Esq

,, 9.   STEPHEN PHESANT, eldest son of Peter P , Esq , now reader

,, ,,   ARNOLD MOUNTNEY, son and heir of Thomas M , of Wheatley, co York, Esq.

,, ,,   THOMAS CHINNERY, son of John C , of Isleham, co Cambridge, gent

,, ,,   JOHN ELMES, son of Thomas E., of Greensnorton, co Northampton, Esq

folio 819

,, ,,   ROBERT PARKER, son and heir of Thomas P , of Browsholme, co York, Esq.

,, ,,   JOHN MANSELL, son of Francis M , of M(u)dlescombe, co Carmarthen, Baronet

,, ,,   ROGER WODEHOUSE, son of Philip W , late of Kimberley, Norfolk, Knight [and Baronet, deceased

,, ,,   ELIAS WEICOE, son and heir of William W , of Hilderthorpe, co York.

,, ,,   THOMAS TOWNESEND, son and heir of George T , of Cranworth, Norfolk, Esq

,, ,,   EDWARD BRUCL, son and heir of Edward B , of Walpoole, Suffolk, Esq

,, ,,   PHILIP JENKINSON ("gent " inserted).

,, ,,   JOHN ATTWOOD, second son of John A , of Stanford Rivers, Essex, Esq

,, ,,   RICHARD CLIPSHAM, son and heir of Edmund C , of Otby, co Lincoln, gent.

,, ,,   JAMES WINSTANLEY, of Billing, co. Lancaster, gent

,, ,,   ROBERT BOOTH, son and heir of Humphrey (inserted in lieu of "Robert" [erased] B , of Manchester, co Lancaster, gent

folio 820

Oct 25   BARNARD FARRELL, of Ardanrich, Longford, Ireland, gent

,, ,,   RICHARD TALBOTT, of Baleressen, co Meath, gent

,, ,,   JAMES WHITE, son and heir of John W , of Balregann, co Louth, gent. [Esq.

,, ,,   JAMES WALE, son and heir of William W , of Culummcky(?), co Waterford,

,, ,,   MICHAEL CUSACK, son and heir of Patrick C , of Rathhalron, co Meath, Esq

,, ,,   THOMAS PETITT, son and heir of Thomas P , of London, gent

,, ,,   THOMAS PRESTWICH, son and heir of Edmund P , of Hulme, co Lancaster, Esq (erased)   [hospitium, May 5, 1629 (erased)

,, 27   JOHN PENNINGTON, son and heir of John P , of Chigwell, Essex, Esq , extra

,, ,,   SAMSON SHEFFIELD, of Seaton, co Rutland, Esq , cousin and heir of Robert S , [formerly reader

folio 821.

Nov 1   WILLIAM WILLOUGHBY, of South Muskham, Notts, Esq

,, ,,   EDWARD FINCH, one of the sons of Henry F , Knight, King's Serjeant-at-Law

,, ,,   MATTHEW MILWARD, S T B

,, ,,   JOHN DIXSON, son and heir of William D , of Darenth, Kent, Esq

,, ,,   TOBIAS CRADOCK, son of John C , of the city of Durham, S T P

,, ,,   RICHARD HOVELL, son and heir of Richard H , of Hillington, Norfolk

,, 3   HENRY NORTH, son and heir of Roger N , of Finborough, Suffolk, Knight.

,, ,,   JOHN BERNARD, of Abingdon, co Northampton, Esq

,, ,   GEORGE ROBERTS, son and heir of John R , late of Barnard's Inn, gent

1624	folio 821—(continued)
Nov 10	ROBERT TATTON ("Esq" inserted in lieu of "gent" erased), son and heir of [William T, Esq, deceased.
,, ,,	THOMAS BLOUNT, Esq., son and heir of Edward B., of Wrickelmarsh, Kent, [deceased

folio 822.

,, 17	OLIVER CASHALL, son and heir of John C, of Dundalk, co. Louth, Esq
,, ,,	WILLIAM HOBSON, son and heir of John H, of Boston, co Lincoln, Esq
,, 21.	THOMAS MALLORY, S.T D, Dean of Chester
,, ,,	RICHARD MALLORY, son and heir of Thomas M, Dean of Chester.
,, ,,	EDWARD BRIDGEMAN, son of Thomas B, of Greenway, Devon, Esq
1624-5 Feb. 2.	[co York, Knight, one of the Justices of the Court of Common Pleas HENRY HUTTON, one of the younger sons of Richard H, of Goldesborough,
,, ,,	THOMAS BATEMAN, of London, Esq

folio 823.

,, ,,	ROBERT SYMONS, son of Robert S, of Whittlesford, co Cambridge, Esq
,, ,,	CHRISTOPHER FITZGERALD, son and heir of James F, of Castleton, co Meath
,, ,,	ROGER NOWELL, of Morton, parish of Whalley, co Lancaster, Esq
,, ,,	THOMAS VESEY, son and heir of Charles V, of Hintlesham, Suffolk, Esq
,, ,,	JOHN HARTFLEET, son and heir of William H, of Sandwich, Kent, Esq
,, 9	RICHARD GERRARD, son of Philip G, one of the readers, Esq
,, ,,	JOHN EDWARDS, son and heir of Peter E, of Stepington, *alias* Stebington, co Northampton, gent, deceased [co Lincoln, merchant
,, ,,	WILLIAM PYDDOCK, of Staple Inn, gent, son of Thomas P, of Gainsborough,
,, ,,	THOMAS ROYLLEY, son and heir of James R, of North Hales, parish of [Hartshorne, co Derby, gent

folio 824   [Exeter College, S T P

Mar. 6	JOHN PRIDEAUX, Vice-Chancellor of the University of Oxford, and Rector of
,, ,,	JOHN HARVEY, gent, Serjeant in Ordinary to the King
,, ,,	WILLIAM HARVEY, M D, one of the Physicians to King James
,, ,,	EDWARD GOLDSMITH, eldest son of Clement G, Esq., formerly reader of this [Inn, deceased
,, ,,	DAVID HOLLAND, of Bardre, son and heir of Peter H, of co Denbigh, Esq
,, ,,	SAMUEL CROOKE, son of Thomas C, of Baltymore, co Cork, Knight and Baronet (extra hosp Oct. 13, 1626, stet, for this gent. was mistaken for [his brother Thomas, erased).
,, ,,	EDWARD BOSWELL, son of William B, of the city of Oxford, gent.
,, ,,	JOHN BLADEN, son and heir of Robert B, of Hemsworth, co. York, gent
,, ,,	LEWIS LEWIS, son and heir of William L, of the town of Carmarthen, gent
,, ,,	ALBERT MORTON, Knight, one of the King's Principal Secretaries
,, ,,	HUMPHREY MAY, Knight, Chancellor of the Duchy of Lancaster, and Clerk [of the Council of the Star Chamber

folio 825.

,, 12.	STEVEN MAYE, third son of John M, deceased, late of Lynn, Norfolk, Esq
,, ,,	JAMES CROFT, son of Herbert C, of Croft Castle, co. Hereford, Knight
,, ,,	BAR ALLEYN, of co Leicester, Esq

1624-5		folio 825—(*continued*)
Mar	12	JAMES INGRAM, Esq , Warden of the Fleet
,,	,,	JOHN ST AMAND, Esq , one of the Secretaries to the Lord Keeper
,,	,,	EDWARD PALMER, Esq , one of the Secretaries to the Lord Keeper
,,	,,	WILLIAM HOOKER, of co. Carnarvon, gent
,,	,,	RICHARD REYNOLDS, of co. Oxon, gent
,,	,,	LUMLEY WILLIAMS, of co Denbigh, Esq
,,	,,	CHRISTOPHER GREENE, of London, gent.
,,	,,	JOHN CHOLMELEY, of Highgate, Middlesex
,,	,,	THOMAS OWEN, gent , of co Carmarthen
,,	,,	AMBROSE BROWNE, of Betsworth Castle, Surrey, Esq
,,	,,	HENRY ZINZAN, of Middlesex, gent
,,	,,	HERBERT WHITFIELD, M D , of Tenterden, Kent

folio 826

,,	,	ROBERT WHITFIELD, of Tenterden, Kent, gent
,,	,,	THOMAS WOODWARD, of Throwley, Kent, gent [Knight
,,	14	FRANCIS OSBALDESTONE, son of Edward O , of Osbaldestone, co. Lanc ,
,,	,,	RICHARD SUTTON, son of William S , of Aram, Notts, Knight.
,,	,,	LAURENCE STYRROPE, son of Thomas S , of the Close, in Lincoln, gent.
,,	,,	ALEXANDER OSBALDESTONE, son of Edward O , of Osbaldestone, co Lanc ,
		[Knight
,,	,,	NICHOLAS THORNTON, late of Barnard's Inn, son and heir of Henry T , of
		[Guttlehill, Northumberland, gent
,,	,,	PEREGRINE PALMER, son of Thomas P., late of Fairfield, co Somerset, Knight
,,	,,	RICHARD GRIMSTON, son of Richard G., of Ipswich, Suffolk, Esq [Esq.
,,	,,	RICHARD LEGARD, third son of Robert L , of Anlaby, co Kingston-upon-Hull,
,,	,,	RICHARD LEGARD, second son of John L , of Ganton, co York, Esq
,,	,,	GREGORY CREYKE, of Marton, co York, Esq [gent.
,,	,,	WOLFRAN SMYTH, son and heir of Wolfran S., in Luxfield of Stodow, Suffolk

folio 827.

,,	,,	SAMUEL WALSALL, S T P , Master of Corpus Christi College, Cambridge
,,	,,	THOMAS LEGAT, of Hornchurch Hall, Essex, Esq
,,	,,	JOHN HARVYE, of Kent, gent , Serjeant in Ordinary to King James.
,,	,,	THOMAS TOOKEY, of Kent, gent
,,	,,	EUSTACE CRADOCK, of co Warwick, gent
,	,,	WILLIAM DOBBINS, of co Gloucester, gent
,,	,,	THOMAS BUTLER, of co Worcester, gent
1625		[Ireland, Esq.
May	9	JAMES DILLON, son and heir of Robert D , of Carnaston, co. Westmeath,
,,	,,	HENRY SHARPE, of the city of Carlisle, gent [Lancaster, gent.
,,	,,	ROBERT PARKER, son and heir of John P , of Extwisle, parish of Burnley, co
,,	,	FRANCIS GERARD, son and heir of Gilbert G., of Harrow-on-the-Hill, Middle-sex, Baronet [Baronet
,,	,,	GILBERT GERARD, second son of Gilbert G , of Harrow on-the-Hill, Middlesex,

1625		folio 827—(*continued*)
May	9	SAMUEL PYNDAR, son of Michael P , late of this Society, and grandchild of [Nicholas Fuller, formerly reader, "sine fine "
,,	,,	JOHN WHICHCOTT, second son of Hammond W , of Dunstall, co Lincoln, [Knight

folio 828.

,,	18	THOMAS WILTON, second son of Richard W , of Topcroft, Norfolk, gent
,,	,,	WILLIAM SERGYANT, of Melton Mowbray, co Leicester, gent
,,	,,	LAMBERT GODFREY, son and heir of Thomas G , of Sellenge, Kent, Esq
,,	25	GEORGE QUARLES, son of Francis Q , of Ufford, co Northampton, Esq
,,	,,	ROBERT BROGRAVE, son of Simon B , of Gray's Inn, Esq
,,	27	JOHN WYRLEY, second son of Humphrey W , of Hampsted, co Stafford, Esq
,,	,,	LEWIS LLOYD, late of Barnard's Inn, son and heir of Robert L , of Uronole, [co Radnor, gent
,,	,,	RICHARD MATHEWE, son of Richard (inserted in lieu of " William " erased) [M , of Shields, co Durham, gent

1625-6		**folio 829**
Jan	31	RICHARD HALE, son and heir of Richard H , of Claberrie, Essex, Esq
,,	,,	ROBERT HALE, second son of Richard H , of Claberrie, Essex, Esq
Feb	3	FRANCIS KING, Esq , son of John K , of Dublin, Knight, Privy Councillor [in the Kingdom aforesaid.
,,	8.	THOMAS TRESSE, or Tracy (?), of Tenterden, Kent, gent.
,,	9	ROBERT HARVEY, son and heir of John H , of London, gent ⌊Durham.
,,	,,	HENRY CHATER (Chaytor), son and heir of Thomas C , Esq , of Butterby, co
,,	,,	RICHARD HARDRES, son and heir of Thomas H , of Great Hardress, Kent, [Knight
,,	,,	HENRY HEYMAN, son and heir of Peter H , of Sellinge, Kent, Knight [Esq
,,	,,	ANTHONY THOROLD, son of Anthony T , of Hough-on-the-Hill, co Lincoln,
,,	,,	GEORGE PRATT, son of Henry P , of Paul's Churchyard, London, gent
,,	,,	WILLIAM BRIDON, of Ipswich, Suffolk, gent

folio 830. [Esq

,,	,	THOMAS GREENWOOD, son and heir of Thomas G , of Steple Aston, Oxon,
,,	,,	HUMPHREY COURTNEY, son of Charles C , late of Molland, Devon, Esq
,,	,,	HENRY STICH, son and heir of Thomas S , of Fetter Lane, London, gent

1626.		
May	10	ROBERT HOWARD, son and heir of Robert H , of Tibbingham, Norfolk, gent
,,	,,	WILLIAM MELLISH, son of Edward M , of Allhallows, Bread Street, London, gent [deceased
,,	,,	JOHN BUXTON, son and heir of Robert B , late of Tibbingham, Norfolk, Esq ,
,,	,,	ROWLAND HUNT, son of Richard H , of Shrewsbury, Salop, gent
,,	,,	THOMAS SICKLEMORE, son and heir of John S , of Ipswich, Suffolk, gent.
,,	,,	JOHN COMBES, son of Edward C., of Fetter Lane, London, Esq , deceased
,,	,,	LAURENCE SHAWE, son of Henry S., of Langrodd-by-Colne, co Lancaster, [gent

folio 831

,,	,,	GEORGE ABBOTT, son and heir of George A , of the city of York, Esq

1626		**folio 831**—*(continued)*.
May	10	ROBERT DEREHAM, son of Thomas D , of West Dereham, Norfolk, Knight
,,	15	PHILIP MUSGRAVE, son and heir of Richard M , of Hartley, Westmoreland [Knight and Baronet
,,	,,	ABRAHAM DYKE, son and heir of Thomas D , of Horn, parish of Walderon, [Sussex, Esq
,,	,,	RICHARD ROUTH, second son of William R , of Walesworth, co York, Esq
,,	,,	JOHN VESEY, son and heir of William V , of Brampton, co York, Esq
,,	,,	THOMAS WINGFIELD, son of Humphrey W , of Brantham, Suffolk, Esq
,,	19	GEORGE PUREFOY, son and heir of George P , of Wadley, Berks, Esq
,,	,,	JAMES MAYNE, son and heir of James M , of Bovington, Herts Esq , one [of the readers of this Inn
,,	,,	PETER MAYNE, second son of James M , of Bovington, Herts, Esq , reader

folio 832   [gent

,,	,,	JOHN SHAWEBERY, son and heir of John S , of Bury St Edmunds, Suffolk,
,,	,,	THOMAS TICHBORNE, son and heir of Robert T , of St Michael le Quern,
June	14	THOMAS MEAWTYS, Esq , Clerk of the King's Privy Council [London, gent
,,	16	ROBERT CUTLER, son and heir of Thomas C , of Sprawghton, Suffolk, Esq
,,	,,	SAMUEL HALES, second son of Edward H , of Tenterden, Kent, Knight and [Baronet
,,	21	JOHN STANHOPE, son and heir of Walter S , of Horsforth, co York, gent
,,	,,	PETER BETSWORTH, third son of Peter B , of Sussex, Knight
,,	,,	WILLIAM BERRY, of London, gent
,,	,,	THOMAS PAGE, of Harrow-on-the-Hill, gent , late Steward of the Inn
Aug	3	HENRY DRAPER, son and heir of Timothy D., of Newcastle-on-Tyne, Esq , [deceased
,,	,,	RICHARD ARNOLD, son and heir of Samuel A , of St Martin's parish, London

folio 833

,,	,,	HENRY DUNCH, son of William D , late of Britwell, Berks, Knight
,,	,,	JOHN DANET, of Colchester, Essex, gent , second son of Thomas D , of Chob-[ham, Surrey, Esq
,,	,,	ROBERT HARRISON, son of Robert H , Alderman of York, deceased.
,,	,,	RICHARD LYNE, son of William L , Esq , of Hurlton, co Cambridge, deceased
,,	,,	JOHN BOYLE, of Borris, co Cork, son of John B , Bishop of Cork
,,	,,	JOHN ATKINS, son of John A , of Stanmore, Middlesex, gent
,,	9	EDMUND FLOWERDEW, of Thripton, co. Cambridge, Esq , son of John F , late [of Hethersett, Norfolk, Esq.
,,	,,	PETER DANIEL, son and heir of Peter D , of Tabley, co Chester, Esq.
,,	,,	HENRY SMYTH, son and heir of William S , of co Durham.
,,	,,	HAMON CLAXTON, son and heir of Thomas C , of Booton, Norfolk, gent , deceased. [gent , deceased.
,,	,,	THOMAS WORLICH, son and heir of Thomas W , of Wickhambrooke, Suffolk,
,,	,,	ROBERT COLLINGWOOD, of Brandon, Northumberland, Esq
,	,,	THOMAS DANDIE, son and heir of Edmund D , of Finningham, Suffolk, Esq

1626   folio 834

Aug 9.   NATHANIEL SAMPSON, of borough of Leicester, gent
  ,,   ,,   THOMAS BRIDGMAN, of Exeter, Devon, gent, son and heir of Jasper B, of said
  ,,   ,,   ANDREW FRERE, of Rendham, Suffolk, gent   [co, gent, deceased
  ,,   ,,   RICHARD NEWHOUSE, of Lillinge, co York, gent
  ,,   ,,   JAMES WINSTANLEY, of London, gent, late of the city of York
  ,,   ,,   JOHN PEACOCK, gent (servant to the most serene Prince ——— ?).
Oct 23   JOHN AUBREY, Esq, son and heir of Thomas A, of Lantrythydd, co Gla-
                                        [morgan, Knight.
  ,,   ,,   JOHN WYNNE, son and heir of John W, of Mould, co Flint, gent
  ,,   ,,   EDWARD WHICHCOTE, Esq., son and heir of Hammond W., of Dunstan, co
                                        [Lincoln, Knight
  ,,   ,,   ROBERT WYLD, Esq, son and heir of John W, of Chartham, Kent, Knight
  ,,   ,,   ROBERT SADLIER, son and heir of Richard S, of Sopwell, near St Alban's,
                                        [Herts, Esq, deceased
  ,,   ,,   SAMUEL EBRALL, son and heir of Richard E, of Balsall, co Warwick, gent,
                                        [deceased

                                   folio 835

  ,,   ,,   RICHARD BULKELEY (son and heir of Richard B, Knight) (inserted) of Beau-
                                        [maris, Anglesey, Esq.
  ,, 27   THOMAS COKE, son and heir of Thomas C, of Cley next the Sea, Norfolk,
Nov 1   THOMAS OTWAY, M A   [gent, deceased.
  ,,   ,,   JOHN BOYS, son and heir of Edward B, of Betshanger, Kent, Esq
  ,, 3   JOHN WYNN, son and heir of John Wynne Edwards, of Copperley, Flints, gent
  ,,   ,,   RICHARD LAMPLUGH, son of William L, of Lobberstone, York, gent
  , 8   WALTER DOBELL, son and heir of Walter D., of Lewes, Sussex, Esq   [Esq
  ,,   ,,   BENNET HOBBES, son and heir of Andrew H, of Ardington, Berks (? Beds),
  ,,   ,,   EDMUND BUTLER, son and heir of Beckingham B, of St Giles in the Fields,
                                        [Middlesex, Esq
  ,,   ,,   ANDREW ASTELEY, son of Andrew A, of Writtle, Essex, Knight
  ,, 10.   EDWARD SONDES, son of Richard S, of Throwley, Kent, Knight

                                   folio 836

  ,, 17   RICHARD LECHE, son and heir of William L, of Crewe, near Holt, co
                                        [Chester, gent
  ,,   ,,   ED. (rightly EDWARD) WINGATE, son and heir of Edward W, of Lockley, near
                                        [Welwyn, Herts, gent
  ,, 23.   JOHN BRACKINE, gent., son and heir of John B, Esq, the son and heir of
                                        [Francis B, Esq, one of the readers, "sine fine"
Dec. 1   LAWRENCE OXBURGH, son of Thomas O, of Lynne, Norfolk, Esq
1626-7   [Esq.
Jan 27   RICHARD EARLE, son and heir of Augustine E, of Straglethorpe, co Lincoln,
  ,,   ,,   GEORGE EARLE, second son of Augustine E, of Straglethorpe, co Lincoln, Esq
  ,, 29   JOHN MARSHALL, son of John M, deceased, of Southwark, Surrey, gent
  ,,   ,,   THOMAS CARY, son and heir of Allen C, of Tower Hill, London, Esq   [Esq
  ,,   ,,   MICAIAH NICHOLSON, son and heir of Edmund N, of Edmonton, Middlesex,

　　　　　　　　　　folio 837

Jan 30　JAMES SCAMBLER, gent , grandchild (nepos) and heir of James S., Esq

,, ,,　JOHN WHITE, gent

Feb 2　PHILIP MUSGRAVE, of Hartley, Westmoreland, Baronet, son and heir of
　　　　　　　[Richard M , late Knight of the Bath and Baronet.

,, ,,　JOHN BERYE, gent , son of John B , of Canterbury, Esq

, ,,　HENRY MIDLETON, of Whitby, co Chester, gent

,, 9　WILLIAM THOMAS, son and heir of William T., of West Deane, Sussex, gent.

,, 10　EDWARD PAGE, son and heir of William P , of Barbican, London, Esq

　　　　　　　　　　folio 838.

,, 17.　EDWARD BRAYE, son and heir of Owen B , of Chobham, Surrey, Esq

19　ROBERT GOOCHE, son and heir of Robert G , of Erisham, Norfolk, gent

,, ,,　GILES LONGE, son of Giles L , of Holborn Bridge, London, gent , deceased

,, ,,　MATTHEW PINDER, son of ———— P , of near Bishopsgate, London, gent

,, ,,　THOMAS ST. GEORGE, son of John St G , of Hatley St. George, cc. Cambridge,
　　　　　　　[Esq

,, ,,　JOHN WARRE, son and heir of Edward W , of Chipley, Somerset, Esq

,, ,,　HENRY MORGAN, son and heir of Walter M., of Llangyby, co Monmouth, gent

,, ,,　WALTER JAMES, son and heir of John J , of Trevor, co Monmouth, Esq
　　　　　　　　　　　　　　　　[Kent

,, ,,　JOHN BEST, late of Staple Inn, son of John B , of Allington, near Maidstone,

,, ,,　JAMES ELLIS, late of Staple Inn, son of John E , of St Albans, Herts, gent

,, ,,　JOHN SHEPPARD, son of John S , of Mendlesham, Suffolk, gent

Feb 23　THOMAS PERROCKE, son of Charles P , of Ross, co Hereford, gent　　[gent

,, ,,　EDWARD BRADSHAWE, son and heir of Peter B , of Watling Street, London,
　　　　　　　[Lincoln, Esq , deceased

,, ,,　CHRISTOPHER BERESFORD, son and heir of Christopher B , of Fulbeck, co

　　　　　　　　　　folio 839.

,, ,,　THOMAS HOLMES, son and heir of Thomas H , of Holborn, Middlesex

,, ,,　THOMAS BACON, son of Edward B , of Shrubland, Suffolk, Esq

,, ,,　EDWARD STONHARD, son and heir of Francis S , of Knowls Hall, Essex, Esq

,, ,,　WILLIAM LAMBE, of Fetter Lane, London, gent

,, ,,　JOHN COTTON, son of ———— C , Esq , of London

,, ,,　JOHN VAN, son and heir of Edward V , of Marcrosse, Glamorgan, Esq

,, ,,　JOHN HUGHES, gent , second son of Thomas H , Knight, deceased, of Wells,

,, ,,　RICHARD MANNING, of Henton, co Southampton, gent　　[co Somerset

,, ,,　WILLIAM CARTWRIGHT, son and heir of William C , of Normandy, co Lincoln,
　　　　　　　[gent , deceased

,, ,,　PHILIP ROKEBY, son of William R , of Hotham, co York, Esq

,, ,,　RICHARD BROWNE, son and heir of Christopher B , of Deptford, Kent, Esq

,, ,,　JOHN CALCOTT, son and heir of John C , of Long Itchington, co Warwick,
　　　　　　　[gent

,, ,,　JOHN SUCKLING, son and heir of John S , of Whitton, Middlesex, Knight.

,, ,,　GABRIEL ARMSTRONG, son and heir of Gilbert A., of Widdmerpoole, Notts, Esq

1626-7	folio 840	[York, Esq
Feb 23	EDWARD ROLLESTONE, son and heir of Thomas R , of Hamphall Stubbs, co	
		[gent
,, ,,	JOHN WARDE, son and heir of George W , of Carleton Curliew, co Leicester,	
,, ,,	JOHN HUNT, son and heir of Edmund H., of the city of Cork, Ireland, gent	
,, ,,	THOMAS ELLICE, second son of Griffith E , of Bow Lane, London, merchant	

1627.
April 4   HENRY SANDYS, son and heir of Edwin S , of Northborne, Kent, Knight

,, 10   JOHN PARKER, son of John P , of Norton Lees, co. Derby, Esq , deceased.

                                                                      [Knight
,, 11.   EDWARD CULPEPER, gent., second son of Edward C , of Wakehurst, Sussex,

,, 23   THOMAS WILLIAMSON, son of Robert W., of Great Markham, Notts, Esq

                                                            [Leicester, Knight
,, ,,   WILLIAM QUARLES, Esq , son and heir of George Q , of Enderby, co

,, ,,   THOMAS ROKEBY, son of William R , of Hotham, co. York, Esq , deceased

May 3   THOMAS BROWNE, son and heir of Thomas B , of Weasenham, Norfolk, Esq

                                                                [Lincoln, Esq
,, 10   JOHN HARRINGTON, son and heir of Thomas H., of Boothby Pagnell, co.

folio 841

June 6   EDWARD RUMSEY, son and heir of Walter R , of Llanover, co. Monmouth, Esq

                                                                    [deceased
,, ,,   NEVELL BUTLER, son and heir of Thomas B., of Orwell, co Cambridge, Esq ,

,, ,,   WILLIAM SALUSBURY, son and heir of William S , of Creythyn, co Carnarvon,

,, ,,   JOHN CORBETT, son and heir of Richard C , of Abstone, Salop, Esq   [gent

,, ,,   WILLIAM DEERE, son of Edward D , of Llangu(n)ian, parish of Llanblethyan,
                                                        [co. Glamorgan, gent

,, ,,   WILLIAM GODFREY, son and heir of Joseph G , of Thonock, co Lincoln, Esq

,, ,,   VINCENT CRANFIELD, son and heir of Ranulph C , of London, Knight

,, ,,   WILLIAM SMART, son and heir of Peter S , of Bouldon, co Durham, M A

Aug 10   JOHN ROUS, second son of John R , of Henham, Suffolk, Knight

,, ,,   MICHAEL ROUS, third son of John R , of Henham, Suffolk, Knight

,, ,,   HENRY HENEAGE, third son of Thomas H , of Hainton, co Lincoln, Knight

,, ,,   WILLIAM CAYLEY, son and heir of Edward C , of Brompton, co York, Esq

,, ,,   JOHN WOODWARD, of Bury St Edmunds, Suffolk, gent , "sine fine."

folio 842

,, ,,   THOMAS HUNT, son and heir of Richard H , of Shrewsbury, Salop, gent   [gent

,, ,,   GEOFFREY BURWELL, son and heir of Edward B , of Woodbridge, Suffolk,

,, ,,   PATRICK TYRRELL, son and heir of Peter T., of Athboy, co. Meath, gent
                                                                        [gent

,, ,,   THOMAS TYRRELL, son and heir of Richard T , of Kilbride, co Westmeath,

,, ,,   EDWARD WOODWARD, son and heir of Edward W , of Leigh, Bucks, Esq

,, ,,   RICHARD STACY, son of Richard S., of co. Durham.

,, ,,   CHRISTOPHER STACY, son of Richard S , of co Durham

,, ,,   RICHARD BELLASIS, son and heir of William B , Knight, of co. Durham.

,, ,,   THOMAS KING, of Durham, gent

1627   folio 842—(*continued*)

Aug 10   THOMAS HENSLOW, of Henton, co Southampton, Esq

,,   ,,   THOMAS LOTCHERD, of Willerton, Salop, son and heir of Hugh L , late of
                    [Stanton-super-Arrowe, co Hereford, gent, deceased

folio 843

,,   ,,   ROBERT ELLICE, son and heir of Griffin E , of London, gent

,,   ,,   RICHARD COLCHESTER, of London, gent.   [deceased

,,   ,,   JOHN GODBOLD, son and heir of Richard G , late of Fincham, Norfolk, gent ,

,,   ,,   AUGUSTINE REEVE, of the city of Norwich, gent

,,   ,,   EDWARD BARTON, son and heir of Edward B , of Thethorpe, co York, gent

,,   ,,   SCIPIO LE SQUIRE, of St. Martin-in-the-Fields, London, gent , Deputy
                    [Chamberlain of the Exchequer.

,,   ,,   JOHN GREENE, son and heir of John G , of Hornton, Oxon, gent

,,   ,,   JOSEPH WALL, son and heir of William W , of Hoggesden, Middlesex, Esq

,,   ,,   ANDREW WALL, second son of William W , of Hoggesden, Middlesex, Esq

,,   ,,   THOMAS TAYLOR, son and heir of Thomas T , gent , Member of this Inn

,,   ,,   PHILIP TAYLOR, second son of Thomas T., gent , Member of this Inn

,,   ,,   THOMAS GARDNER, second son of Thomas G , of Thorpe Mandeville, co
                    Northampton.   [deceased.

,,   ,,   WILLIAM PEAD, fourth son of Thomas P , of Bury St Edmunds, Suffolk, gent ,

,,   ,,   ROBERT CUTHBERT, son of Henry C , of Levington, Suffolk, gent

,,   ,,   ROBERT FREVILL, son of Richard F., of Bishop Middleham, co Durham, gent

folio 844

,,   ,,   ROBERT SMYTH, second son of William S , Esq , of co Durham

,,   ,,   WILLIAM BROCK, son and heir of Bartholomew B , late of Southold, Suffolk,
                    [gent , deceased

,,   ,,   RICHARD HARWARD, son and heir of Vincent H , of East Sutton, Kent, gent.

Oct 9   JOHN COOKE, Esq , son and heir of John C , Knight, one of the King's
                    [Principal Secretaries

,, 24   THOMAS ROTHERAM, son of George R , of Farley, parish of Luton, Beds, Esq

,,   ,,   CHARLES GRIFFITH, son and heir of Walter G , of Llannvechan, co Monmouth,
                    [gent

,,   ,,   RICHARD DERHAM (Dereham), son of Thomas D , of West Der(e)ham,

,,   ,,   JOHN HEILIN, son and heir of Peter H , of London, gent   [Norfolk, Knight

,,   ,,   JOHN CASSON, son of John C , of ———, Herts, gent.

,, 27   FRANCIS PEACOCK, son and heir of John P , of Cumnor, Berks, gent

folio 845

Nov 1   ROBERT ASKWITH, son and heir of George A., of the city of York, gent

,,   ,,   GEORGE ROSSE, son of John R , of London, merchant   [Serjeants-at-Law

,,   ,,   JAMES DAVENPORT, second son of Humphrey D , Knight, one of the King's

,,   ,,   FRANCIS WETHERED, son of Francis W , of Ashlings, parish of Berkhampstead,
                    [Herts, Esq

,,   ,,   THOMAS BOSVILLE, son and heir of Gervase B , of Warmsworth, co York,

,,   ,,   GEORGE MALLORY, fourth son of Thomas M , Dean of Chester   [gent

1627		folio 845—*(continued)*
Nov	6	WILLIAM ELLIS, second son of Thomas E , of Grantham, co Lincoln, Knight, deceased [Iselham, co Cambridge
,,	,,	JOHN PEYTON, Esq , son and heir of Edward P , Knight and Baronet of
,,	,,	WILLIAM WARREN, son and heir of Thomas W , of Crayford, Kent, gent [gent
,,	9	JOHN BELLEW, son and heir of Patrick B , of Grafostone, co Louth, Ireland,
,,	,,	WALTER WARING, son and heir of Edmund W , of Lea, co Stafford, Esq

folio 846.

,,	17	DOVE BRIDGEMAN, second son of John B , Bishop of Chester
,,	,,	SAMUEL SALTONSTALL, second son of Samuel S , of London, Knight
,,	21	JOHN PLUMMER, son and heir of John P , late of London, Esq , deceased
,,	,,	THOMAS HICKMAN, second son of William H , of Gainsborough, co Lincoln, [Knight
,,	,,	HENRY ATKINSON, son and heir of Charles A , of Tolestone, co York, Esq
,,	,,	EDWARD WINGFIELD, son of John W , of Tickencourt, co Rutland, Esq
,,	,,	HENRY BROMEFIELD, son and heir of Arthur B , of Tichfield, Hants, Esq
,,	,,	RICHARD CRACKENTHORPE, son and heir of Christopher C , of Newbiggin, [Westmoreland, Esq , deceased
,,	,,	GEORGE BUCKE, second son of John B , of Croydon, Surrey, gent , deceased.
,,	,,	JOHN BASPOOLE, son and heir of John B , of Hadscoe, Norfolk, gent , deceased
,,	,,	WILLIAM HILL, son and heir of William H , of Hales, Norfolk, gent
,,	,,	GEORGE GIRLING, son and heir of William G , late of Stradbrook, Suffolk, [Esq , deceased
,,	,,	THOMAS MEERES, son and heir of William M , of Alciston, Sussex, gent

folio 847   [Hall, Norfolk, deceased

,,	29	THOMAS GAWDY, Esq , son and heir of Clipsby G , Knight, late of Gawdy
,,	,,	JOHN SKERNE, gent , son of Robert S , of Bonby, co Lincoln, Esq
,,	,,	RICHARD BUCKLEY, Esq , son and heir of Richard B , deceased, who was son
1627-8		[and heir of Richard B , late of Cheadle, co Chester, Knight deceased
Feb	2	JOHN HACKET, S T B., Rector of St Andrew, Holborn
,,	,,	WILLIAM HATCHER, son of Thomas H., of Careby, co Lincoln, Esq
,,	,,	WILLIAM BELL, of London, Esq.
,,	,,	EDWARD BELL, of London, Esq.
,,	,,	JOHN HOCKENHALL, of Aldersgate Street, London, gent
,,	6.	WILLIAM PARRY, late of Barnard's Inn, son of Simon P , of Nantlwyd, co [Denbigh, Esq , deceased
,,	,,	WILLIAM GREENWELL, son and heir of William G , of near Leadenhall, Lon-
,,	,	DUDLEY NORTH, son of Roger N., of Mildenhall, Suffolk, Knight. [don, gent
Feb.	6.	JOHN LUKYN, son and heir of Samuel L., of Roxwell, Essex, gent
,,	,,	HENRY PARKER, third son of Calthrop P., of Arwarton, Suffolk, Knight.

folio 848.

,,	21	WILLIAM BURWELL, third son of Edmund B , of Woodbridge, Suffolk, gent.
,,	,,	JOHN HARVIE, son and heir of Oliver H , of Thurley, Beds, Esq
,,	26	ANTHONY LIGHTFOOT, son and heir of Anthony L , of Gloreston, co Leicester.

1627-8   folio 848—(continued).

Mar 6   WILLIAM CLOPTON, son and heir of William C , Esq., reader

„ „   GERVASE SLEIGH, second son of Gervase S , of Ash, co. Derby, Esq , deceased

„ „   HUGH SLEIGH, third son of Gervase S , Esq , of Ash, co. Derby deceased.

„ „   WILLIAM BRYERS, of Pulloxhill, Beds, Knight

„ „   ROGER HARLAKENDEN, second son of Richard H., of Earls Colne, Essex, Esq.

„ „   GEORGE GARL, second son of John G , of Hadleigh, Suffolk, gent.

, „   JOHN BRAND, son and heir of Benjamin B , of Edwardstone, Suffolk, Esq

„ „   DENNER STRUTT, son and heir of John S , of Hadleigh, Suffolk gent

                          folio 849.   [of London

„ 13   JOHN RAVEN, son and heir of John R., M.D , of the Royal Medical College

„ „   EDMUND CREMER, second son of George C , of Sieche, Norfolk, gent.

„ „   JOHN TANCRED, second son of Thomas T , of Burroughbridge, co. York, gent ,
              deceased   [Lincoln, Esq , deceased

„ 14   SAMUEL WENTWORTH, son and heir of Walter W , of Castle Bytham, co

„ „   WILLIAM HUGHES, son and heir of William H , of Gray's Inn, Esq

„ „   ROBERT PRICE, son and heir of Thomas P , of Spytty, co. Denbigh, Esq

„ „   HENRY MASON, younger son of William M , of Barningham, Suffolk Esq ,
              deceased   [deceased

„ „   MATTHEW CLARK, son and heir of Matthew C , of Lynn, Norfolk, gent ,

„ „   JOHN CLARK, younger son of Matthew C , of Lynn, Norfolk, gent , deceased.

„ „   EDWARD SHAWBERRY, second son of John S , of Bury, Suffolk, gent.

„ „   LAURENCE FARCLOTH, of Holborn, Middlesex, gent.

„ „   THOMAS HULME, son and heir of Thomas H , of Holborn, Middlesex, gent

                          folio 850

„ „   HENRY GOODRICKE, son and heir of Henry G , of Ribstone, co York, Knight
1628.   [and Baronet
April 12   JOHN HOTHAM, son and heir of John H , of Scorborough, co. York, Knight,
                                                   [fine ”
May 9   GEORGE MORTON, son and heir of Robert M , of Eaststure, Kent, Esq , “absque

„ „   HENRY ALINGTON, son and heir of Medcalfe A., of Hodgsdon, Middlesex,
              gent   [deceased

„ „   GEORGE SWAN, second son of William S , of Southfleet, co Lanc , Knight,

„ 16   JOHN GIBBS, second son of Daniel G , of Meath, co Glamorgan, gent.

„ „   EDWARD HOBSON, late of Barnard's Inn, son of William H , of Horsley,
              Essex, gent.   [Knight

„ „   ARTHUR HEVENINGHAM, second son of John H , of Ketteringham, Norfolk,

„ „   HENRY MIDDLETON, son of Hugh M., of St Michael Bassishaw (inserted),
                                       [London, Baronet.

„ „   ROBERT OFFLEY, son of Robert O , of London, Knight.

„ 21   JOHN DIXIE, son of Wolstan D , of Market Bosworth, co Leicester, Knight

                          folio 851

„ 22.   THOMAS GILL, son and heir of Christopher G , of Barton, co York, gent

„ „   THOMAS RUDSTONE, son of Samuel R , of ———, co. York, Esq

1628		folio 851—(continued)

May 22   RICHARD WATSON, son of Richard W., of Ravensworth, co Durham, gent

,,   ,,   JOHN WILSON, of the city of Chester, gent

,,   26   THOMAS FAIRFAX, Esq , son and heir of Ferdinand F , of (Denton), co York, [Knight, who was son and heir of Thomas, Lord F , of (Denton)

,,   27   FULLER MEADE, son and heir of Fuller M , of Foxton, co Cambridge, gent

,,   ,,   PEIER ALSTON, son and heir of Peter A , of Bramford, Suffolk, gent , deceased

June 23   WILLIAM DAVENPORI, gent , son and heir of William D , Esq , who was son [and heir of William D , of Bramhall Hall, co Chester, Knight

,,   ,,   ROGER POWER, son and heir of Peirce P , of Ballygannon, co Waterford, Esq

,,   ,,   NATHANIEL HARTLEY, son of Richard H , of Gilkirke, co York, Esq

,,   ,,   RICHARD OSBORNE, son and heir of Richard O , of Capagh, co Waterford, Esq

,,   ,,   RICHARD BARON, son and heir of John B , of Trumpington, co Cambridge,

,,   ,,   ARTHUR JONES, son and heir of Henry J , of Chastleton, Oxon, Esq   [gent

July 4   ARTHUR GRYMES, second son of Thomas G , of Peckham, Surrey, Knight

folio 852

,,   5.   THOMAS PROCTER, son and heir of Robert P , of Cullmullen co Meath, gent

,,   ,   RALPH BALDWIN, son and heir of Henry B , of Hale, parish of Windsor,

Aug 5   JOHN FRIER, son and heir of Thomas F , of London, M D   [Bucks, gent.

,,   ,,   ROBERT BATEMAN, gent , of London   [Dublin, Knight

,,   ,,   RICHARD FITZWILLIAMS, gent , son and heir of Thomas F , of Merion, co.

,,   ,,   OLIVER FITZWILLIAMS, gent , son of Thomas F , of Merion, co. Dublin,

,,   ,,   JOHN MILLER, gent , son and heir of Richard M , of Liston, Middx   [Knight

folio 853
                                                               [Esq , now reader.

,,   11   GEORGE FULWOOD, son and heir of Christopher F., of Midleton, co Derby, [Esq., now reader

,,   ,,   AUDLEY FULWOOD, second son of Christopher F , of Midleton, co Derby,

,,   ,,   JOHN ALURED, son and heir of Henry A , of Charterhouse, near Hull, co [York, Esq

,,   ,,   WILLIAM BACON, son of William B , of Otterhampton, co Somerset, gent

,,   ,,   JOHN REYNOLDS, son and heir of Richard R , of Exeter, gent.

,,   ,,   WILLIAM NICOLSON, son of Richard N., of London, Esq.

,   12   JAMES, Duke of LENOX

,,   ,,   WILLIAM ANSTRUTHER, Knight and Baronet

,,   ,,   WILLIAM HOWARD, Knight of the Bath   [co Derby

,   13   PETER BRADSHAW, of London, gent , fourth son of Godfrey B , of Bradshaw,

folio 854

,,   15   THOMAS LEWIS, son and heir of Thomas L , of Marr, co. York, Esq

,,   ,,   THOMAS MASSIE, son and heir of John M , of Coddington, co Chester, Esq

,,   ,,   HENRY GOODRICKE, son of Henry G., of Rowlie, co. York, Esq

,,   ,,   PEIRSE SHERLOCK, son of James S., of Gracedieu, co Waterford, gent.

,,   ,,   JOHN BUCKLEY, son and heir of Abel B , of Buckley, co Lancaster, Esq.

1628   folio 854—(continued).

Aug 15   GEORGE DODDINGE, son and heir of Miles D , of Conishead, co Lanc , Esq

"   "   EDMUND WAYTE, second son of Thomas W., of St John's-street, Middx , Esq

"   "   RICHARD PRICE, son and heir of John P , of Gorgarthen, co. Cardigan, Knight.

"   "   JOHN APSLEY, late of Staple Inn, gent.

"   "   JAMES WOOD, late of Staple Inn, gent.

"   "   THOMAS GARDNER, son of Roger G , of St Giles, Cripplegate, gent

                              folio 855.

Oct 29.   EDMUND BRAY, son and heir of Peter B , of Clonmell, co. Tipperary, Esq

"   "   EDWARD HUSSEY, son and heir of Thomas H , of Moyle Hussey, co Meath,
          Esq   [Esq

"   "   HENRY BARKLEY, son and heir of Henry B., of Ballycahan, co Limerick,

"   "   PATRICK BOYTON, son and heir of Edward B., of Cashel, co Tipperary, Esq

"   "   JOHN TYNTE, son of Robert T , of Ballycreenan, province of Munster, Knight

"   "   EDWARD HARBY, son and heir of Daniel H., of Evedon, co Lincoln, Esq.

"   "   FRANCIS AUNGIER, Esq , son of Francis Lord A , Baron of Longford, and
          [Master of the Rolls in Ireland, "absque fine"

"   "   DANIEL SHETTERDEN, of Great Chart, Kent, gent

"   "   THOMAS REMINGTON, son and heir of Richard R , of Iounde, co York, Esq

Nov 1   WILLIAM SAVILL, of Thornhill, co York, Baronet, son and heir of George S ,

"   "   FROXMER COCKET, of the city of Westminster, gent   [Knight

                              folio 856

"   7   FRANCIS CHERRY, of Greenstreet, Essex, gent

"   "   EDWARD HOLT, son of Francis H , of Grislehurst, co Lancaster, Esq.

"   "   JOHN WILFORD, son and heir of William W , of Hadlow, Middlesex, Esq

"   12   JOHN NAYLOR, son and heir of Thomas N , of Sturry, Kent, gent

"   17. JOHN SMITH, son of Roger S , of Edmondthorpe, co Leicester, Esq

"   "   ALEXANDER HALL, son and heir of William H , of Newcastle-on-Tyne, Esq

"   "   THOMAS DAVISON, son and heir of Alexander D , of Newcastle-on-Tyne, Esq

"   19. CHARLES TASBURGH, son and heir of John T , of Flixton, Suffolk, Knight

"   "   CRESSY TASBURGH, second son of John T , of Flixton, Suffolk, Knight [gent

"   "   WILLIAM TOWRY, son and heir of George T , of Kirby Grindalyth, co York,

                              folio 857.

"   25   HENRY FRANCKLAND, son and heir of William F , of Thirkleby, co York, Esq
1628-9   [caster, "sine fine"
Feb 2   EDWARD MOSELEY, son and heir of Rowland M , Esq , of Hough, co Lan-

"   "   JAMES DAVENPORT, second son of Humphrey D , Knight, one of the King's

"   "   MORGAN JOHNSON, of Staple Inn, gent.   [Serjeants-at-Law (erased).

"   "   RICHARD GIPPS, son and heir of Richard G , of Bury, Suffolk, gent,
                                                          [deceased

"   "   JOHN CASON, son of Edward C , of Furneaux Pelham, Herts, Esq , deceased

"   "   THOMAS KING, second son of Robert K , of Southminster, Essex, gent

"   5   JOHN ROGERS, son and heir of Francis R , of Canterbury, S T D

1628-9		folio 857—(continued).
Feb	9	RICHARD COPE, second son of Richard C , of Hanwell, Oxon, Esq
,,	13	TOBIAS JENKINS, second son of Henry J , of Great Busby, co York, Knight
,,	,,	JOHN ATKINSON, son and heir of Simon A , of Thringtoft, co York, gent

folio 858

Mar	5	HENRY WARDE, son of Thomas W , of Bixley, Norfolk, Esq
,,	,,	JOHN BASSE, son and heir of John B , of Walsingham, Norfolk, gent
,,	,,	FRANCIS TILNEY, son and heir of Richard T , of Rotherwick, Southampton (inserted in lieu of " Norfolk "), Esq
,,	,,	RICHARD SWANNE, son and heir of Andrew S , of London, gent
,,	,,	WILLIAM LISTER, son and heir of William L , of Thornton, co York, Knight.
,,	,,	WILLIAM CHAMPNEYS, son and heir of Richard C , of Bexley, Kent, Esq
,,	,,	EDWARD DARCY, son and heir of Robert D , of Dartford, Kent, Knight
,,	,,	WILLIAM SPENCER, son and heir of Richard S , of Bartholomew Lane, [London, gent.
,,	,,	FRANCIS LASCELLS, son and heir of William L , of Foulton, co York, gent
,,	,,	THOMAS PLOMER, of Mitcham, Surrey, Esq
,,	,,	RICHARD TUFFNELL, of London, gent

folio 859

,,	,,	EDWARD DITCHFIELD, of London, gent
,,	,,	WILLIAM ROBSON, of London, gent
,,	,,	ANTHONY LAMPLUGH, of Little Haseley, Oxon, Esq.
,,	,,	MATTHEW THWAYTES, of London, gent
,,	,,	JOHN ALONSON, of Londo. gent
,,	,,	THOMAS HUDDLESTON, of Little Haseley, Oxon, Esq
,,	6	RALPH WHISLER, of Salterstone, co Londonderry, Esq
,,	,,	HENRY MEDLER, of Isleworth, Middlesex, gent
,,	,,	ANTHONY MASON, of Reading, Berks, gent
,,	,,	WILLIAM WYNNE, son and heir of John W , of Abbey, co Carnarvon, Esq.
,,	,,	JOHN PILKINGTON, son of Richard P , S T D , of Humbleton, Oxon, gent.
,,	,,	JOHN BRETLAND, son of Reginald B , of Thornecliffe, co. Chester, Esq

folio 860

,,	,,	WILLIAM GREENHILL, of King's Langley, Herts, gent.
,,	,,	WILLIAM ELLIS, son and heir of George E , of Wiham, co. Lincoln, gent
,,	,,	ROBERT STILEMAN, son and heir of Robert S , of Fielddalling, Norfolk, gent.
,,	,,	NATHANIEL SHOWELL, son and heir of Nathaniel S , of Morston, Norfolk, gent.
,,	,,	ROBERT BEALES, son and heir of Robert B , of Cley-next-the-sea, Norfolk, gent
,,	,,	JOHN PARSONS, of Sandford, Oxon, gent
1629		[Knight.
May	7	WILLIAM CLARKE, son and heir of John C , of Ford, parish of Wrotham, Kent,
,,	8	STEPHEN PHESANT, eldest son of Peter P , Esq , reader of this Inn
,,	,,	JOHN JAMES, son and heir of William J , of Latham, Suffolk, gent.
,,	14	RALPH BROWNRIGGE, S T.D

1629   folio 860—(continued)

May 14   JOHN FLEETWOOD, of Penwortham, co Lancaster, Esq

  „   „   JOHN LISLEY, son and heir of John L , of Moxhull, co Warwick, Esq

                          folio 861

June 1   HENRY REVE, son and heir of Robert R , of Thwayte, Suffolk, Esq

  „   „   EDWARD SPENCER, late of Staple Inn, gent , son and heir of Robert S , of
                Rendlesham, Suffolk, Esq   [Surrey, gent , deceased

  „   4   JOHN JUXON, son and heir of John J , of East Sheen, parish of Mortlake.

  „   9. STEPHEN JACKSON, son and heir of Thomas J , of Cowling, co York, Esq

  „   „   FRANCIS BOWES, son and heir of Henry B , of Newcastle-on-Tyne, gent ,
                deceased   [Court, Kent, Knight

  „   15   THOMAS HARDRES (late of Staple Inn), son of Thomas H (late) of Hardres

  „   22   EDWARD MORE, son and heir of William M , of Thelwall, co Chester, gent.

  „   29. THOMAS HUNT, second son of Thomas H , of Linden, co Rutland, Esq

Nov 6   BENJAMIN MADDOX, of Boughton Monchelsea, Kent, gent (erased)

                          folio 862.

Aug 3   EDWARD GREY, son of Ralph G , of Chillingham, Northumberland, Knight

  „   „   WILLIAM KINDERSLEY, son of Francis K , deceased, late of London, gent

  „   „   THOMAS HAMERSLEY, son of Hugh H , Knight and Alderman of London

  „   „   EDWARD MARSH, son of Samuel M , of Finchhampstead, Berks, gent

  „   „   JOHN HATT, son of Giles H., of Leckhamsted, Berks, gent

  „   4   JOHN JONES, son of Richard J , of Festiniog, co Merioneth, gent

  „   „   EDWARD PEIRSON, son of Richard P., deceased, late of London, gent

  „   „   THOMAS BRICKENDEN, son of Champion B , deceased, late of Benenden,
                        [Kent, gent (by Thomas Brickenden, reader)

  „   „   THOMAS DYKE, son and heir of Robert D , of Westwicke, co. York, Esq

  „   „   JAMES COOKE, son of Isaac C , of Lutterworth, co Leicester, gent

  „   „   RICHARD STOCKDEN, son and heir of Randolph S , of St Lawrence parish,
                                        [London, gent

                          folio 863.

  „   „   WALTER (BUTLER), Earl of Ormonde and Ossory, in Ireland

  „   „   JAMES (BUTLER), Viscount Thurles, in Ireland

  „   „   THOMAS MORETON, of East Steward, Kent, Knight   [Ireland

  „   „   BARNABY FITZPATRICK, son and heir of Barnaby, Baron of Upper Ossory, in

  „   „   GREGORY NORTON, of Hampdens, Bucks, Knight

  „   7   OSBERT PRATT, son and heir of Osbert P , of Norfolk, gent

  „   „   ANTHONY WILLIAMS, Esq , son and heir of Alexander W , of London, Esq

  „   „   JOHN HAVERS, younger son of Thomas H , of London, Esq

  „   „   CRESSEY DIMMOCK, son of Thomas D , of Gray's Inn, Esq

                          folio 864.

  „   „   WILLIAM DRAKE, of Shardloes, parish of Agmondisham, Esq

  „   „   JOHN TWISLETON, son of John T , of Dartford, Kent, Esq   [Esq.

  „   „   CHARLES (MARIA) CHUTE, son of Charles C , of Wynchelsey Castle, Sussex,

  „   „   FRANCIS YATEMAN, of Staple Inn, gent

1629   **folio 864**— (continued)

Aug. 7   THOMAS BRICKENDEN, son of Thomas B , Esq , now reader

,,   ,,   RICHARD BRICKENDEN, son of Thomas B , Esq , now reader.

,,   ,,   JOHN STAMPE, son and heir of Thomas S , of Peasemore, Berks, gent

,,   ,,   WILLIAM BOLD, son and heir of William B , of Nurrested, parish of Bereton, co Southampton, Esq   [Sussex, gent

,,   ,,   JOHN COOPER, son and heir of —— C, deceased, late of Ditcham,

,,   ,,   CASPAR GOODEMANS, of London, gent   [Esq , deceased

,,   ,,   ROBERT MULSHOE, son and heir of —— M , of Finden, co Northampton,

                                folio 865

Oct 15   JOHN HARRYS, son and heir of Richard H , of Cruckton, Salop, Esq

,,   19   ROBERT CRACROFT, son and heir of Robert C , of Whisby, co Lincoln, Esq

,,   ,,   GARRALD FITZGERALD, son and heir of Redmond F , of Timoge, co Kildare,   [Esq.

,,   27   THOMAS LIDDELL, son and heir of Henry L , of Farnacres, co Durham, Esq

,,   30   JOHN CROPLEY, son and heir of Edward C , of St Michael-le-Quern, London,   [gent

Nov 1   EDWARD WILLIAMS, Esq , one of the gentlemen of the King's Privy Chamber

,,   6   BENJAMIN MADDOX, of Boughton Monchelsea, Kent, gent

,,   ,,   GILBERT PICKERING, son and heir of John P , of Tichmarsh, Notts (sic, error   [for co Northampton), Knight

,,   ,,   THOMAS PORTER, son and heir of John P , of Waterford, Esq

,,   ,,   THOMAS TILDESLEY, of Garret, co Lancaster, Esq

                                folio 866

,,   25   EDWARD SMITH, son and heir of Simon S , of Chart, near Sutton, Kent, Esq.

,,   ,,   WILLIAM HART, late of Barnard's Inn, son and heir of William H , of Beeston, Norfolk, gent   [Denbigh

,,   ,,   JOHN THELWALL, son and heir of John T , Esq , of Bathanarne Park, co

,,   ,,   THOMAS BONHAM, son and heir of William B , of Paternoster Row, London,   [gent , deceased

,,   ,,   WILLIAM BRENT, son of Richard B , of Stoke, co Gloucester, Esq

1629 30.
Feb 2   PHILIP MUSGRAVE, of Hartley, Westmoreland, Baronet

,,   ,,   SOLOMON SWALE, of Staineley, co York, and of Staple Inn, gent

,,   ,,   THOMAS CORYE, son and heir of Thomas C , of the city of Norwich, Esq

,,   ,,   GEORGE LLOYD, son and heir of John L , of Hollwood Campney, co Glouc

,,   ,,   THOMAS STEWARD, gent , of Staple Inn, son and heir of Thomas S , of Barton, Suffolk, Esq   [land, Esq

,,   ,,   THOMAS OGLE, son and heir of Lancelot O , of Durras Hall, Northumber-

                                folio 867

,,   11   RALPH SNEYD, son and heir of Ralph S , of Keel, co Stafford, Esq

,,   ,,   WILLIAM HOLLAND, son of Edward H , of Heaton, co Lanc , Esq   [Knight

,,   ,,   JOHN MEUX, Esq., son and heir of William M , of Kingston, Isle of Wight,

,,   ,,   THOMAS DANDIE, gent , son and heir of Edmund D , of Combes, Suffolk,   [Esq (erased as admitted before)

                                              M

1629-30   folio 867—(continued).

Feb 11   LUKE ROBINSON, son and heir of Arthur R , of Dighton, co York, gent.

,, 25   KNEVITT CLINTON, second son of Thomas, Earl of Lincoln, deceased

,, ,,   EDWARD PERCY, Esq

,, 26   JOHN SWINNERTON, son of Ralph S , of Whitchurch, Salop, gent

,, ,,   FRANCIS FINES (Fiennes), Esq , son and heir of Edward F , of Great Sturton,
                              [co Lincoln, Knight

,, ,,   RALPH MORE, son and heir of John M , Esq , now reader

,, ,   WILLIAM BENDLOWES, second son of Andrew B , late of Brent Hall, in
                              [Finchingfield, Essex, Esq

,, ,,   WILLIAM PLOMER, son and heir of William P , of Radwell, Herts, Esq

,, ,,   FRANCIS FULLWOOD, son and heir of Francis F , late of Dunston, co Derby,
                              [gent, deceased

,, ,,   WILLIAM BRADGATE, son and heir of Thomas B , of Brantirgthorpe, co
                              [Leicester, gent

folio 868

,, ,,   RAVIS EDWARDS, son and heir of ——— E , deceased, Doctor of Spiritual Law

,, ,,   JOHN POWELL, son of Lewis P , of Lanfey, co Pembroke, Esq

,, ,,   ANTHONY STRATFORD, son and heir of Rous S , of Gitinge, co Glouc , gent

,, ,   HOO STEWARD, son and heir of Francis S , of Braughing, Herts, Esq

1630   [King
April 28 THOMAS COKE, second son of John C , Knight, Principal Secretary to the

,, ,,   HENRY HARTFLEET, son and heir of Henry H , of Ashe, Kent, gent.

,, ,,   JOHN FENWICK, son and heir of John F , of Wallington, Northumberland,
         Knight and Baronet   [Lancashire, gent.

,, ,,   WILLIAM LANGTON, son and heir of Roger L , of Preston in Amunderness,

May 1   EDMUND FERNELEY, of West Creting, Suffolk, gent., son of John F , of the same, Esq.

,, 8   RICHARD BENEFIELD ("Richard" inserted in lieu of "Edward"), son and
                              [heir of William B., of Southwark, Surrey, gent

,, ,,   ISAAC APPLETON, of Little Wallingford (Waldingfield), Suffolk, Esq.

,, 11   JOHN WALPOOLE, son and heir of Dymock W., of Pinchbeck, co Lincoln, Esq.

,, 8   JOHN BURTON, son and heir of John B., of Surflect, co. Lincoln, gent   [gent

,, .,   WILLIAM DAVY, gent , second son of Henry D , late of the city of Norwich,

folio 869

,, 14   CUTHBERT OGLE, of Whiston, co Lanc , son and heir of Henry O , of the

,, ,,   EDMUND BRAY, son and heir of John B , of Fifield, Oxon, Esq   [same, Esq.

June 25 NICHOLAS WILLMOTT, fourth son of Robert W , of Chaddesden, co. Derby, gent

,, 26   JOSEPH BENT, son and heir of William B , of Enderby, co. Leicester, gent

,, 28   WILLIAM GRIMSTON, son and heir of Henry G , of Boughton Monchelsea,

Nov 8.   JOHN JEGON, gent , son of John J , S T D , late Bishop of Norwich. [Knight

,, 18   GEORGE BEST, son of Thomas B , of Middleton, co York, Esq   [and Baronet

,, ,,   PATRICK ACHESON, son and heir of Archibald A., of Clancaryie, Ireland, Knight

,, 26   SAMUEL PLOMER, son of John P , late of Romney, Kent, Esq

,, ,,   EDWARD LENNARD, son of Henry L , Lord Dacre

1630   folio 869—(continued)

Nov. 26   WILLIAM NORTON, son and heir of Valentine N , of Fordwich, Kent, Esq.

,,   ,,   WILLIAM GOOCH, gent , son of William G , Member of this Inn

1630-1   folio 870

Jan 25   ANTHONY HICKMAN, gent , only son of Henry H , Doctor of Laws

Feb 2.   DUDLEY DIGGS, of Chilham Castle, Kent, Knight, one of the Masters in
                                                                    [Chancery

,,   ,,   WILLIAM MANNING, son and heir of William M , Esq

,,   ,,   JOHN RIVETT, son and heir of Nicholas R , of Brandeston, Suffolk, Esq

,,   ,,   THOMAS WILLIS, son and heir of Richard W , of St John's, Herts, Esq

,:   ,,   RICHARD WILLIS, second son of Richard W , of St John's, Herts, Esq

,,   3   GEORGE CHUTE, son and heir of Edward C , of Bethersden, Kent, Esq

,,   7   HAMON LEWKNOR, son and heir of Robert L , of Acrise, Kent, Knight

,,   ,,   WILLIAM GLASCOCK, son and heir of Henry G , of Hartisowberrie, Essex, Esq

,,   ,,   THOMAS APLEYARD, son and heir of John A , of Heslington, co York, gent

                              folio 871

,,   ,,   EDWARD DETHE, son and heir of Henry D , of Stanisford, co Lincoln, gent

,,   10   THOMAS MONTFORD, of Gainsborough, co. Lincoln, gent , son and heir of
                                                   [Thomas M , Esq , of the same, deceased.

,,   16   ELLIS EDWARDS, son and heir of Edward E , of Llanaber, co. Merioneth, Esq ,

,,   ,,   HENRY PEYTON, of London, gent   [deceased

Mar 1   ROBERT CARRE, Knight, gent , of the King's Chamber

,,   ,,   WILLIAM BALFOUR, Knight, Lieutenant of the Tower of London

,,   ,,   GEORGE KIRKE, Esq , Master of the Robes of the King

,,   ,,   JAMES PALMER, Knight

,,   ,,   HENRY TUNSTALL, son and heir of John T , Knight

,,   ,,   PAUL PINDAR, Knight
                              folio 872

,,   ,,   WILLIAM RUSSELL, Knight, Treasurer of the King

,,   ,,   JAMES MAXWELL, Esq , ——— of the King's Bedchamber

,,   ,,   JAMES BAGG, Knight

,,   ,,   THOMAS PETTS, Esq

,,   ,,   GEORGE ELIOT, Esq

,,   ,,   JOHN EATON, Esq

,,   ,,   PETER APSLEY, Esq

,,   ,,   JOHN JACOB, Esq

,,   ,,   THOMAS DAWES, Esq
                              folio 873

,,   5   RICHARD GRAHAM, Knight and Baronet

,.   ,,   WILLIAM LAKE, Esq

,,   ,,   THOMAS PHILLIPS, Knight

,,   ,,   HENRY KNOWLES, Esq.

,,   ,,   EDWARD DENDY, Esq.

,,   ,,   EDWARD RUSSELL, Esq

1630 1		folio 873—*(continued)*
Mar	5	EUSEBIUS MATTHEWES, Esq
,,	,,	NATHANIEL TOMKINS, Esq
,,	,,	VALENTINE CLARKE, Esq
,,	,,	ROBERT EVANS, Esq

folio 874

,,	10	MATTHEW LISTER, M D
,,	,,	PETER CHAMBERLAYNE, M D
,,	,,	THOMAS RYVES, Doctor of Laws and King's Advocate.
,,	,,	CUTHBERT RADCLIFFE, Esq
,,	,,	CHARLES COTTON, Esq
,,	,,	MATTHEW HOWLAND, Esq
,,	,,	WILLIAM BRAXTON, Esq
,,	,,	RALPH HAWTREY, gent

folio 875

,,	,,	FLORENCE MACCARTE, Esq
,,	,,	JOHN HANIST, Esq
,,	,,	LAMBERT OSBALDESTON, M.A [Knight and Baronet
,,	11	THOMAS HUSSEY, son and heir of Edmund H , of Honington, co. Lincoln,
,,	,,	CHARLES FOTHERBY, son and heir of John F , of Canterbury, Knight.
,,	,,	GEORGE EVELYN, Esq
,,	,,	JOHN BANKES, son and heir of John B , now reader of this Inn, "absque fine "
,,	,,	EDWARD BANKES, second son of John B , now reader [All the admittances in March previous to this were made by the said John Bankes, Esq , reader, as (with the exception of the following three) were all in the subsequent [ones in the said month

folio 876

,,	,,	WILLIAM ATKYNS, son and heir of John A , of Stanmore, Middlesex, gent
,,	,,	ANTHONY LAMPLUGH, son and heir of William L , late of Hampton, Esq
,,	,,	THOMAS BRATHWAITE (from Staple Inn), son and heir of Gawin B , of Amble- [side, Westmoreland, Esq
,,	,,	CARUS PHILIPSON, second son of Robert P , of Hollinghall, Westmoreland, Esq
,,	,,	BARTHOLOMEW FITZGERALD, son and heir of Edward F , of Blackhall, co [Kildare, Esq
,,	,,	ROBERT (inserted in lieu of "Rowland") NELSON, late of Barnard's Inn, son [and heir of Robert N , of the city of London, Esq.
,,	,,	JOHN WELSH, son and heir of David W , of Rathronan, co Tipperary, Esq
,,	,,	THOMAS PURCELL, son and heir of Theobald P , of Clone, co Kilkenny, Esq
,,	,,	WILLIAM MIDELTON, son and heir of Peter M , of Stockheld, co York,
,,	,	CHRISTOPHER HINTON, of Etwall, co Derby, Esq [Knight
,,	,,	DAVID MORGAN, son and heir of Thomas M , of Lanwenarth, co Monmouth, [gent
,,	,,	THOMAS MORGAN, son and heir of Richard M , of Uske, co Monmouth, gent
,,	,,	EDWARD RUMSEY, son and heir of John R , of Eadbrook, co Monmouth, [gent

folio 877

1630-1

Mar 11   JOHN ROCHE, son and heir of Richard R , of Poullelonge, co Cork, Esq

,,   ,,   MATTHEW WEBB, son and heir of Ambrose W , clerk

,,   ,,   GEORGE SKYNER, son and heir of John S , of Southley, Oxon, Esq

,,   ,   JOSEPH GULSTON, Fellow of Trinity College, Cambridge   [Esq

,,   ,   RALPH HAWTREY, son and heir of John H , of Rise(Ruis)lip, Middlesex,

1631

May 2   RICHARD TAVERNER, son and heir of Francis T , of Heyton, Herts, Esq

,,   ,,   ROBERT BARBER, son and heir of William B , of Kensworth, Herts, gent

,,   ,,   JOHN KEMPE, son and heir of Thomas K , of Bewley, co Southampton, Esq ,
        [deceased

,,   ,,   NEALE MACKWORTH, son of Thomas M , of Normanton, Rutland, Baronet,
        deceased   [Knight, deceased

,,   9   THOMAS BUSSEY, son and heir of Rawleigh B , of Margam, co Glamorgan,

,,   ,,   JOHN GWYN, son and heir of Anthony G , of Lansanor, co Glamorgan, Esq

,,   ,,   RICHARD OWEN, son and heir of Richard O , of Penmynydd, co Anglesea,
        [Esq

folio 878

,,   ,,   JAMES (inserted in lieu of "John") HOBARD, late of Barnard's (in lieu of
        ["Staple's") Inn, son and heir of Edward H , of Langley, Norfolk, Esq

,,   ,,   HENRY ATKINSON, late of Staple Inn, son and heir of Charles A , of Beechey
        Grange, co York, Esq   [Wight, co Southampton, Baronet

,   18   ROBERT DILLINGTON, Esq , son and heir of Robert D , of Kingston, Isle of

,,   ,,   THOMAS SANDERS, of Flamstead, Herts, Esq

,,   ,,   WILLIAM BURY, son and heir of William B , of Grantham, co Lincoln, gent

,,   ,,   HENRY PALMER, Esq , son and heir of Henry P , of Howletts, Kent, Knight

,,   ,,   JOHN ANGUISH, son of Edmund A , of Great Melton, Norfolk, Esq

,,   27   THOMAS READ, son of John R , of Wrangle, co Lincoln, Knight, deceased

June 13   WILLIAM STEELE, gent , son and heir of Richard S , of Finchley, Middlesex,

,,   28   JOHN ANLABY, son and heir of Thomas A , of Etton, co York, Esq   [gent

,,   ,,   LEONARD TINDALL, son of Francis T., of Brotherton, co York, Esq

,,   ,,   EDWARD ROBERTS, son and heir of Edward R , of St Dunstan's, near
        [Canterbury, gent

folio 879

Aug 7   ANTHONY HOBARD, of Hales Hall, Norfolk, Esq , cousin and heir of James
        [H , Attorney-general to late King Henry VII

,,   ,,   JAMES HOBARD, son and heir of Anthony H , of Hales Hall, Norfolk, Esq ,
        [cousin and heir of James H , Attorney-general

,,   ,,   ROBERT WELCH, Esq , son and heir of James W , of Ireland, Esq

,,   ,,   JOHN WYTTON, of Isleworth, Middlesex, Esq

,,   ,,   MILES HUMBERSTON, of the city of London, gent

,,   12   HENRY ROOKWOOD, son and heir of Henry R , of Weston, Norfolk, Esq

,,   ,,   GEORGE PROCTOR, son of Thomas P , of Newhall, co York, Esq , one of the
        [Ancients of this Inn

,,   ,,   SIMON HORSPOOLE, son and heir of William H , of London, Esq

,,   ,,   EDWARD WORMELEY, son and heir of John W , of Riccall, co York, gent

1631.		folio 879—(*continued*) [Bucks, Esq
Aug	12	WILLIAM UMFREVILL, son and heir of Thomas U , of Monks Risborough,
,,	,,	NATHANIEL HOOPER, son of Richard H , of St. Andrew's, Holborn, gent
,,	,,	PHILIP KNIVETT, son and heir of Philip K., of Buckenham, Norfolk, Knight [and Baronet
,,	,,	JAMES CHAPLAYNE, son and heir of Thomas C , of Belchamp Otton, Essex, [gent

folio 880

,,	,,	ISMAEL MASON, of Colley Weston, co Northampton, gent [Knight
,,	,,	HENRY MORGAN, son and heir of Edmund M , of Penhowe, Monmouth,
,,	,,	ROGER GARNON, son and heir of Richard G , of Stebenham, co Louth, Esq
,,	,,	PATRICK CHAMBERLAINE, of Islecrathe, co Louth, gent [this Inn, "sine fine "
,,	,,	WILLIAM BYERLEY, son and heir of William B , Esq , one of the Members of
,,	,,	HAMOND CLAXTON, son and heir of Hamon C , of Booton, Norfolk, gent
,,	,,	WILLIAM MEAD, son and heir of Henry M , of Narberrow, co Leicester, gent
,,	,,	HENRY SIMPSON, son and heir of Ralph S , of ———, co Durham, gent
,,	,,	WILLIAM CLARKE, son and heir of John C , of the city of Hereford, gent
,,	,,	EDMUND MORGAN, of Lanwenarth, co Monmouth, gent.
Oct	19	WILLIAM HEYRICK, of Leicester, gent , son and heir of Tobias H , clerk
,,	,,	JOHN LIGHTBORNE, son of James L , of Manchester, co Lancaster, gent

folio 881

,,	,,	JOHN LAMBERT, son and heir of William L , of Buckingham, Esq [gent
,,	,,	ROBERT MALTIWARD, son and heir of Robert M , late of Rougham, Suffolk,
,,	,,	RALPH SMITH, son and heir of George S , of Finchley, Middlesex, Esq
Nov	1	THOMAS DENTON, of Warnell, Cumberland, Esq. [land, Knight
,,	,,	JOHN DALSTON, son and heir of Christopher D , of Acornbanck, Westmore-
,,	,,	BERNARD WELLS, son and heir of Bernard W., of Hulme, co Derby, Esq
,,	,,	NICHOLAS WALLER, son and heir of Nicholas W , of Beverley, co York, Esq.
,,	,,	ROBERT OVERTON, son and heir of John O , of Essington, co York
,,	,,	FRANCIS LUTTRELL (of Staple Inn), second son of John L , late of Stanton
,,	,,	RICHARD WILLIAMS, of Denton, co Lincoln, gent [Court, Devon, Esq.

folio 882.

,,	4	ABRAHAM HARSENET, of the city of Norwich, gent
,,	,,	VINCENT RANDYLL, son of Edward R , of Albury, Surrey, Knight
,,	,,	WILLIAM BERNARD, of Abingdon, co Northampton, gent [Esq
,,	,,	ROBERT WILD, son and heir of Marmaduke W , of East Coulton, co. York,
,,	,,	GEORGE TIRREY, son and heir of William T , of St Mary Wolnoth, London, gent. [deceased
,,	,,	HENRY MOTT, son and heir of Mark M , (late) of Rayne, Essex, gent,
,,	,,	MARK MOTT, second son of Mark M , late of Rayne, Essex, gent., deceased.
,,	20	JOHN HARPUR, son and heir of Henry H , of Calke, co Derby, Baronet.
,,	,,	HENRY HARPUR, second son of Henry H , of Calke, co Derby, Baronet.
,,	23	THOMAS DIGGES, son and heir of Dudley D , of Chilham Castle, Kent, Knight, "sine fine " [and Baronet
.	,	THOMAS ROBERTS, son and heir of Walter R , of Glassenbury, Kent, Knight

1631   folio 882—(continued)

Nov 25   WILLIAM POWELL, son and heir of Thomas P., of Hampton, Middlesex, gent

„   „   HENRY SPENCER, son of Robert S., of Rendlesham, Suffolk, Esq

„   „   WILLIAM MADDOX, of Boughton Monchelsea, Kent, gent

folio 883

„   „   PETER PRESTON, of ———, Suffolk, late of Barnard's Inn, gent   [Knight

Dec 7   WILLIAM DALSTON, Esq, son and heir of George D., of Dalston, Cumberland,

„   „   GEORGE BRATHWAITE, son and heir of Thomas B., Knight, of Warcop,
                                                              [Westmoreland

„   „   THOMAS DIMOCKE, son and heir of Thomas D., of Gray's Inn, Esq

„   „   HUMPHREY MATHEW, son and heir of Thomas M., of Castlemenich, co Glamor-

1631-2   gan, Esq   [Knight

Jan 28   WILLIAM BOWYER, son and heir of William B. of Knipersley, co Stafford,

Feb 2   RALPH PUDSEY, son and heir of Thomas P., of Stapleton, co York, Esq

„   „   ROBERT BAINES, son and heir of John B., of Sellet (sic), co Lancaster, Esq

„   „   THOMAS FLINT, son and heir of William F., of Allesley, co Warwick, Esq

„   3   JOHN ALLEN ("John" inserted in lieu of "William"), son and heir of William
                                                   [A., of Cheapside, London, gent

folio 884

„   „   EDMUND WILSON, son and heir of Thomas W., of Willian, Herts, Esq

„   „   WILLIAM SPENCER, son and heir of William S., of Attercliffe, co York, gent

„   18   JOHN BOOTH, third son of George B., of Dunham Massey, co Chester, Knight
              and Baronet.   [Radnor, Esq

„   21.   PIERCY MADOCKES (Maddock?), son and heir of John M., of Llangoulle, co

„   „   TIMOTHY TOURNEUR, son and heir of Timothy T., Esq, now reader

„   „   HUGH POWELL, son and heir of John P., late of Stretton, Salop, gent

„   „   WILLIAM ROBINS, son and heir of John R., of Castell May, co Carnarvon, Esq

„   22   HENRY MILDMAY, son of Henry M., of Moulsham, Essex, Knight

„   „   JOHN SMITH, son and heir of Nicholas S., of Thedelthorpe, co Lincoln, Esq

„   „   GEORGE BARNEWALL, of Crickstoun, co Meath, second son of Patrick B.,
              Baronet   [King, of the Parish of St Andrew Undershaft, London.

Mar 2   JOHN PHELIPS, second son of Francis P., Esq, one of the Auditors of the

„   „   JOHN THELWALL, son and heir of Edward T., of Llanbedr, co Denbigh, gent

„   „   WILLIAM WINNE, son and heir of Edward W., of Llanwith, co Denbigh, gent

folio 885.   [co Denbigh, gent

„   „   PETER MOYLE (late of Staple Inn), son and heir of Geoffrey M., of Ruthin,
                                                              [Leicester, gent

„   „   ROBERT RICHARDSON, son and heir of John R., of Frisby on-Wreke, co

„   „   LYON PILKINGTON, son and heir of Arthur P., of Stanley, co York, Esq

„   „   GEORGE STARLING (late of Staple Inn), son and heir of George S., of Chast-
                                          [field, Suffolk, Esq, deceased

„   „   ALEXANDER RIGBY, son and heir of Alexander R., of Middleton in-Amunder-
                                                   [ness, co Lancaster, Esq

„   „   HERBERT WHITFIELD, son and heir of Ralph W., of Tenterden, Kent, Esq
                                          [("absque fine," as son of a reader)

1631-2   folio 885—(*continued*)

Mar   2   HUGH HINDLEY, son of Roger H , of Hindley, co Lancaster, gent.

,,   ,,   EDWARD LUTTRELL, third son of John L , of Stanton Court, Devon, Esq

,,   ,,   RICHARD SPITTY son and heir of Richard S , of Bremfield, Essex, gent

,,   ,,   WILLIAM KILBURNE, of Huntingdon, gent , son of Isaac K , of London, gent.

,,   ,,   ROBERT CORBETT son and heir of Reginald C , of Edgmond, Salop, Esq

                                   [Great, London, merchant, deceased.

,,   27   CHARLES RUGGLE, son and heir of Roger R , late of St Bartholomew the

,,   ,,   JAMES HAYWARD, of Fletherhill, co Pembroke, gent

,,   ,,   HENRY BROWNE, son of William B , of Radford, co Warwick, Knight

1632   folio 886   [deceased

April 14   SAMUEL SANDYS, son and heir of Edward S , of Estwicke, Westmoreland, Esq

                                   [Knight, deceased

,,   ,,   RICHARD HUTTON, Esq , son and heir of Thomas H , of Poppleton, co York,

,,   ,,   JOHN HILL, son and heir of Edward H , of Cosby, co Leicester, gent

,,   ,,   EDWARD CHUTE, son of Edward C , of Bethersden, Kent, Esq

,,   ,,   JOHN GIBBON, son and heir of Robert G , of Bethersden, Kent, Esq.

,,   ,,   THOMAS DADE, son and heir of William D , of Tannington, Suffolk, Esq

                                   [deceased

,,   ,,   GEORGE ROSE, son and heir of William R , late of Eastergate, Sussex, gent ,

May   4   EDWARD ESTCOURT, son of John E , of Tetbury, co Gloucester, Esq.

,,   8   THOMAS MORE, of Agharren, co Cork, Esq

,,   ,,   THOMAS CUTLER, son and heir of Thomas C , of Spratton, Suffolk, Esq

,,   ,,   JOHN SMITH, son and heir of James S , of Burlington (Bridlington), co York,

,,   11   PETER BINDLEY, son of John B , of Louth, co Lincoln, Esq   [gent

                           folio 887.   [gent

,,   ,,   JOHN BRADSHAWE, son and heir of John B , of Darcy Lever, co Lancaster,

June 7.   WILLIAM WAKELYN, of Assington, Essex, gent., son and heir of Thomas W , Esq , deceased, formerly of this Inn   [gent , deceased

,,   ,,   ANTHONY HAWKRIDE, son and heir of Anthony H , of Boston co Lincoln,

,,   ,,   HENRY OXENDON, son and heir of Richard O , late of Berhan, Kent, gent , deceased   [deceased

,,   ,,   JOHN BOSTOCK, son and heir of Richard B , of Tattenhall, co Chester, Esq ,

,,   ,,   RICHARD BALDWER, son and heir of James B , of Sutton, co Lincoln, gent

,,   20   OWEN SALUSBURY, son and heir of William S , of Rug, co Merioneth, Esq

,,   ,,   JOHN THOMPSON, of Beardon, Essex, Esq.

,,   ,   WILLIAM GOODWYN, son and heir of John G , of Hasketon, Suffolk, gent

                                   [gent , deceased

,,   ,,   EDWARD LOWDEN, son and heir of John L , late of Stratford Bow, Middlesex,

,,   ,,   JOHN HEADLAM, son and heir of Leonard H , of the city of York, gent

                           folio 888

,,   22   JOHN ASHTON, son and heir of Radcliffe A , of Cuerdale, co Lancaster, Esq

,,   ,,   ROBERT ROBOTHAM, son and heir of John R , of St Albans, Herts, Esq

July   4   WILLIAM NEWBY, son and heir of Richard N , of Draughton, co York, gent

1632   folio 888—(continued)

July 5   PETER WILLIAMS, son and heir of Hugh W , of Halkin, co Flint, gent
                                              [in the city of London, merchant

Aug 4   WILLIAM WEBB, son and heir of William W , of (St Catharine Cree Church),

„   5   HENRY, Earl of STAMFORD, and Lord GREY of Groby

„   „   THOMAS LE GROS, Esq , son and heir of Charles Le G , Knight

„   „   THOMAS ANGUISH, gent

„   „   ARTHUR KNYVETT, Esq

„   9   JAMES, Earl of BUCHAN.

„   „   JAMES LAYSTLYE (Leslie), Knight

„   „   ROBERT LAYSTLYE (Leslie), Knight

folio 889

,   „   WILLIAM CARNE (or Carew), Esq

„   „   HENRY MOODY, Baronet

„   „   SAMUEL BLENNERHASSETT, Esq

„   „   JOHN PELLEW

„   „   THOMAS BALLARD, Esq

„   „   JOHN THOROUGHGOOD, Esq

„   „   RICHARD SMYTH, gent ("Esq" erased)

„   „   HENRY CHETWYND, of Islington, Middlesex, Esq

„   13   HENRY WHITFIELD, gent , second son of Ralph W , of this Inn, "absque fine"

„   „   AUGUSTUS MILDMAY, son of Henry M , of Danbury, Essex, Knight

„   „   ROBERT COMPTON, of London, Esq

„   17   ROBERT MANSELL, Knight and Vice-admiral

„   „   ESAIAS LADKYN, of Chancery-lane, London, gent

folio 890.   [Esq

„   „   ROBERT DALLYSON, son and heir of William D , of Greetewell, co Lincoln,

„   „   GEORGE DALLYSON, son of William D , of Greetewell, co Lincoln, Esq

„   20   PETER LEYCESTER, son and heir of Peter L , of Tabley, co Chester, Esq

Sept 20   THOMAS SCOTT son and heir of Robert S , of Sandgate, Kent, Esq

„   „   RALPH DARNALL, of the city of London, gent

„   „   ROBERT SHAWE, son and heir of Robert S , of St Peter's, Cornhill, London

Oct 30.   THOMAS SOUTHLAND, Esq , son and heir of William S , of Kent, Knight,

Nov 1.   FRANCIS GOODWIN, of Winchendon, Bucks, Knight   [London
                   [George R , Esq , Attorney-general to the King in the North

„   „   THOMAS RADCLIFFE, son and heir of George R , who is son and heir of

„   „   JOHN COGHILL, son and heir of Thomas C , of Coghill Hall, co York, gent

folio 891

„   „   HENRY BING, son and heir of Henry B , Serjeant at-Law.

„   „   ALBERT MORTON, second son of Robert M , of Eastremead (?), Kent, Knight

„   „   JOHN MASON, son of William M , late of this Inn

„   „   THOMAS CREMER, son and heir of John C , of Snettisham, Norfolk, gent

„   „   JOHN VAUGHAN, second son of John V , of Trawscoed, co. Merioneth, gent

1632   folio 891—(*continued*)

Nov 9   JOHN LYNNE, son and heir of George L., of Southwick, co Northampton, Esq
                                                              [Leicester, clerk
„   „   EUSEBIUS PELSAINT, gent , son of William P , of Market Bosworth, co
„   „   JOHN TAYLOUR, son and heir of Michael T , of Swords, co Dublin, Esq
                                                              [Esq , deceased
„   „   JAMES RUDYARD, son of Laurence R , (late) of Winchfield, Southampton,
„   „   RALPH STARKEY, son and heir of Richard S , of Newton, co Chester, gent
„   „   THOMAS LUCAS, son of William L , of Great Horningheath, Suffolk, Esq

                                 folio 892.

„   21 WILLIAM WALLER, Knight, son and heir of Thomas W , Knight, formerly
                              [Lieutenant of the Castle and territory of Dover
„   „   GEORGE STROUD, of Westerham, Kent, Esq   [deceased
„   „   JOHN WILLESBY, son and heir of William W , late of Spalding, co Lincoln, gent ,
„   „   GEORGE SEWSTER, son and heir of Edward S , late of Cheapside, London, Esq
Dec 3   JAMES GOUGHE, son of Warren G , of St Briarwells, co Gloucester, Esq
1632-3   [Treasurer of the Navy
Jan 31 WILLIAM RUSSELL, gent, second son of William R , Knight and Baronet,
„   „   JOHN CREMER, of Snettisham, Norfolk, gent   [deceased
„   „   EDWARD SEWSTER, son of Edward S , late of Cheapside, London, gent ,
„   „   JOHN READE, son of William R , late of Canterbury, Esq , deceased
„   „   THOMAS MASON, son and heir of Thomas M , of St Sepulchre's, London, gent.
„   „   JOHN LECHE, son and heir of John L , of Cawarden, co Chester, Esq
„   „   FRANCIS FISHER, son and heir of William F , late of Threckingham, co.
                                 folio 893   [Lincoln, Esq., deceased

Feb. 2   JOHN WHELPDALE, son and heir of William W , of Penrith, Cumberland, gent
„   „   DAVID OFFLEY, of Aldermanbury, London, gent , one of the sons of Robert O ,
                                                   [of the same, gent , deceased.
„   8   FRANCIS ROWDON, of St Clement's, Temple Bar, Middlesex, gent   [Esq
„   11 ROBERT TYRRELL, of Gipping, Suffolk, gent , son of James T , of Gray's Inn,
„   „   WILLIAM GIRLING, of Stradbroke, Suffolk, son of William G , of Gray's Inn,
             Esq.   [deceased
„   „   JOHN PROCTER, son and heir of John P , of Alderchurch, co. Lincoln, gent ,
„   „   JAMES AISCOUGH, son and heir of Allan A , of Middleton-one-Rowe, co
„   „   ROBERT BUTLER, of Southwell, Notts, gent   [Durham, Esq.

                                 folio 894

„   „   TIMOTHY WHITTINGHAM, son and heir of Timothy W , late of Holmeside,
             co. Durham, Esq , deceased   [Esq
„   „   ROBERT MITFORD, son and heir of Michael M , of Seghill, Northumberland,
Mar. 9. THOMAS ADDERLEY, of Dundrum, co Cork, gent.   [ampton, Esq
„   „   LAURENCE MANLEY, son and heir of Laurence M., of Sprattor, co North-
„   „   JOHN MANLEY, son of Laurence M , Esq , of Spratton, co Northampton, Esq
„   14 RALPH FREEMAN, citizen and Alderman of London
„   „   MAURICE ABBOTT, Knight, and Alderman of London

1632-3		folio 894 — (*continued*)
Mar	14	ANTHONY BROWNE, Knight
,,	,,	GEORGE CLERK, citizen and merchant of London
,	,,	ROBERT HICKES, Esq
,,	18	HENRY BULL, son of William B , of the city of Wells, co Somerset, gent
,,	,,	WILLIAM WILSON, son of Gawin W , of Epping, Essex, gent
,,	,,	ROBERT BOSTOCKE, gent
,,	19	ROBERT PEYTON, son and heir of John P , of Donnington, Isle of Ely, Knight.

folio 895.

,,	,,	MICHAEL JERMYN, S T D
,,	,,	SAMUEL GOTT, son and heir of Samuel G., citizen and merchant of London
,,	,,	GEORGE PAYNE, son of Robert P., late of Southoe, Hunts, Knight, deceased
,,	,,	EDWARD VAUGHAN, son and heir of William V , of Terrycoed, co Carmarthen, Knight [marthen, gent
,,	,,	HENRY MORGAN, second son of Morgan M , of Llanarth Bleddry, co Car-
,	,,	EDMUND SHAA, son of Edmund S , of Tarlinghall, Essex, gent
,,	,,	SPENCER POTTS, of Charlgrave, Beds, gent

folio 896

,,	21	SPENCER, Earl of NORTHAMPTON
,,	,,	THOMAS CLAYTON, M D , Regius Professor at Oxford
,,	,,	JOHN SPEED, M D
,,	,,	WILLIAM TRESHAM, Esq
,,	,,	HUMPHREY EDWARDS, son of Thomas E, of Shrewsbury, Salop
1633		
Mar	25	WILLIAM PECOCKE, son of Richard P , of Fenchurch street, London, merchant
,,	,,	RICHARD MUSGRAVE, son and heir of Thomas M , of Ashby Puerorum, co Lincoln, Knight, deceased [Esq
May	17	RICHARD KNIGHTLEY, son and heir of Richard K,, of Burghall, co Stafford,
,,	,,	EDWARD VAUGHAN, son and heir of William V , of Llangandiron, co Carmarthen, Knight
,,	,,	GEORGE POLHILL, son and heir of Thomas P , of Shoreham, Kent, Knight
,,	,,	THOMAS POLHILL, second son of Thomas P , of Shoreham, Kent, Knight
,,	,,	MARMADUKE TOMLIN, son and heir of Thomas T , of Cotnesse, co. York, gent

folio 897

,,	29	THOMAS LEIGH, gent , son and heir of Thomas L , of Adlington, Cheshire, Esq
,,	,,	JOHN LEIGH, gent., second son of Thomas L., of Adlington, Cheshire, Esq
,,	,,	JOHN FINCH, son of John F., of Milton, Kent, Esq.
,,	,,	WHITTINGHAM MAN, of the city of Canterbury, gent [deceased
,,	31	THOMAS ALSTON, third son of Peter A , late of Bramford, Suffolk, gent ,
,,	,,	ESSEX DEVEREUX, son and heir of Walter D., of Leigh Court, co Worcester, [Knight and Baronet
,,	,,	WILLIAM PENTLOW, son and heir of William P , of Wilbie, Northumberland,
June	25	ROBERT EGERTON, gent , son of Richard E , Knight, of co Chester [gent
,,	,,	JOHN THOMPSON, of London, Esq , " absque fine " [deceased
July	5	ARTHUR REDHEAD, son and heir of Robert R , of Holden, co York, Esq ,

1633　　　　　　　　　　folio 897—(*continued*)

July　6　JOHN FARRINGTON, son and heir of Thomas F, of Chichester, Sussex, Esq

,,　,,　GEORGE STARKEY, son and heir of George S, of New Windsor, Berks, gent

folio 898

,,　9　CHARLES HOWARD, Knight, son of Charles, Earl of Nottingham, deceased

,,　,,　JOHN APPLEWHAYTE, late of Barnard's Inn, son and heir of John A, of Stoke
　　　　　　　　　　　　　　　　　　　　　　　[Ash, Suffolk, gent

,,　20　RALPH WHITFIELD, third son of Ralph W, Esq, reader of this Inn

,,　,,　WILLIAM WHITFIELD, son and heir of William W, of Snodland, Kent, Esq

,,　,,　THOMAS ALFRAY, son and heir of Richard A, of Catsfield, Sussex, Esq

,,　,,　WALTER ROBERTS, second son of Walter R, of Glassenbury, Kent, Knight
　　　　and Baronet　　　　　　　　　　　　　　　　　[Knight

,,　,,　WILLIAM LE HUNT, son and heir of John Le H, of Middleton, co Warwick,

,,　,,　JOHN LE HUNT, second son of John Le H, of Middleton, co Warwick, Knight

,,　,,　EDWARD FINCH, son and heir of William F, of Tenterden, Kent, gent

,,　,,　WILLIAM WOODWARD, of Throwleigh, Kent, gent

,,　,　ROBERT RAWORTH, of Dover, Kent, gent

folio 899.

,,　,,　CHARLES READE, of Rushaume, co York, gent

,,　,,　HOWELL VAUGHAN, second son of John V, of Glanllin, co Merioneth, Esq

Aug　3　SAMUEL SHORT, son of Samuel S, of Tenterden, Kent, gent

,,　,,　RALPH BOVEY, son and heir of Ralph B, Esq, deceased

,,　4　ROGER NORTH, Esq

,,　,,　HENRY CHITINGE, Esq

,,　,,　GEORGE OWEN, Esq

,,　,,　THOMAS BROWNE, of Hoe, co Southampton, gent

,,　7.　JAMES HEATH, of London, gent　　　　　　　　[bridge, Esq, deceased

,,　,,　THOMAS WENDY, son and heir of Francis W, late of Haslingfield, co Cam-

,,　,,　RICHARD MERIDALE, of London, gent

,,　,,　WILLIAM MARWOOD, son of Henry M, late of Ayton, co York, gent

,,　8　RALPH WARD, son and heir of Ralph W, of Suffield, Norfolk, Esq

folio 900

,,　,,　WILLIAM CURTEENE, Knight

,,　,,　WILLIAM TRESHAM, Esq, son and heir of Lewis T, Knight and Baronet

,　,,　AURELIAN TOWNESHEND, Esq

,,　,,　WILLIAM FULLER, S T D

,,　,,　ROBERT (inserted in lieu of "William") CURSON, Esq

,,　,,　WILLIAM PAGE, of Barbican, London, Esq (in lieu of "gent")

,,　,,　THOMAS (inserted in lieu of "William") HERBERT, Esq.

,,　,,　WILLIAM GWYN, Esq

,,　,,　PETER DE LIX, gent

,,　,,　FRANCIS (inserted in lieu of "Edmund") MOSSES, gent

,,　,,　ROBERT DAVIES, of London, gent

1633   **folio 901.**

Aug 8   CECIL, Lord BALTIMORE.

„   „   LEONARD CALVERT, Esq , second son of George, Lord Baltimore, deceased

„   „   GEORGE KEMPE, Knight (and Baronet)

„   10   WILLIAM CURTEEN, Esq , son and heir of William C , of London, Knight

„   „   PHILIP DE LA ROCHE, second son of Richard Roche, of Foullertonge, co
                                                            [Cork, Esq

„   „   PETER TURNER, second son of William T , of the city of Dublin, Alderman

„   „   THOMAS SHAWBERRY, son of John S , of St Edmundsbury, Suffolk, gent

„   „   HUGH LEWIS, son of Morgan L , of Abergavenny, co Monmouth, gent

„   „   EUBULUS THELWALL, second son of John T , of Plasclough, co Denbigh, Esq

„   „   RICHARD COKERAM, of ——bye, Sussex, gent

„   „   BARNABY FERRALL, son and heir of John F , of Tennelick, co Longford, Esq

„   „   THOMAS DABRIDGECOURT, son and heir of Thomas D , of Hammersmith,
                                                            [Middlesex, Esq

„   „   THOMAS MAWDESLEY, son and heir of Thomas M , of Gray's Inn, Esq ,
                                                            [deceased

                                       folio 902

„   12   JOHN, Viscount BRACKLEY, son and heir of John, Earl of Bridgewater

„   „   PHILIP, Viscount LISLE, son and heir of Robert, Earl of Leicester.

„   „   THOMAS EGERTON, Esq , second son of John, Earl of Bridgewater

„   „   ALGERNON SYDNEY, Esq , second son of Robert, Earl of Leicester

„   „   GEORGE CAREY, Esq , son of Henry, Earl of Dover

„   „   RICHARD LENNARD, third son of Richard, Lord Dacre, deceased

„   „   FRANCIS NEWPORT, Esq , son and heir of Richard N , of Eyton, Salop, Knight

„   „   THOMAS FOWLER, M A

„   „   GEORGE BINGLEY, of St Giles, Cripplegate, gent

„   „   JOHN BILLINGSLEY, of London, gent

„   „   ROGER SPELMAN, gent , son and heir of John S , of Haydon, Norfolk, Esq

                                       folio 903

„   13   WILLIAM, Viscount MONSON, of Castlemayne

„   „   HENRY BOURCHIER, of London, Knight

„   „   JOHN CASPAR DE WOLLFEN, Esq , Resident for the King of Denmark

„   „   AMADIS DE WOLLFEN, Esq , son of John Caspar de W , Esq , Resident for the

„   14. ROBERT MASON, of Greenwich, Kent, Esq   [King of Denmark

„   „   JOHN LEVER, of Cheshunt, Herts, gent   [Treasurer of the Royal Fleet.

„   15   FRANCIS RUSSELL, Esq , son and heir of William R , Knight and Baronet,

„   16   JOHN CARRILL, son and heir of Simon C , late of Tangley, Surrey, Esq ,
                                                            [deceased

„   „   JOHN WINNE, son and heir of Thomas W , of Llandurnocke, co Denbigh, Esq

„   „   JOHN WINCHCOMBE, son and heir of John W , of Henwick, Berks, Esq

„   „   LUKE CLAPHAM, son and heir of John C , late of Willenhall, co Warwick,

„   „   WILLIAM PILL, son and heir of William P , of London, gent   [gent , deceased

„   „   MARTIN SCURLEGE, son of Patrick S , of Rathcreden, co Dublin, Esq

1633.   folio 903—(*continued*)

Aug 16   ROGER WHITFIELD, fourth son of Ralph W , Esq , now reader of this Inn

,,   ,,   CHARLES SPELMAN, second son of John S , of Haydon, Norfolk, Esq

,,   ,,   HENRY MARWOOD, of Ayton, co. York, gent

,,   ,,   CHARLES WILSON, son and heir of John W , of Warden, Beds, Esq , deceased
                                                    [Durham, Esq , deceased

Oct 9   ROWLAND PLACE, Esq , son and heir of Christopher P , of Dinsdale, co

,, 14   JAMES HUXLEY, third son of George H , Esq , late of Edmonton, Middlesex,
        deceased   [Burton, co York, Knight and Baronet

,,   ,,   CHRISTOPHER WYVELL, Esq , son and heir of Marmaduke W , of Constable
                                  [Knight (inserted in lieu of " Esq ").

,,   ,,   THOMAS CHATER (Chaytor), son and heir of William C , of Croft co York,

,,   ,,   THOMAS SALTMARSHE, son and heir of William S , of Strubby, co Lincoln, Esq

,,   ,,   JOHN SICKLEMORE, gent , second son of John S , of Ipswich, Suffolk

,,   ,,   WILLIAM FOSTER, son and heir of William F , of Cardington, Beds, gent

,,   ,,   ROBERT CLENCH, son and heir of John C , of Creting All Saints, Suffolk, Esq

folio 905

,, 23   NICHOLAS FISHER, son and heir of Edward F , of Kendall, Westmoreland, Esq.

,,   ,,   HENRY MORGAN, son of Edward M , of Llanternam, co. Monmouth, Esq
                                         [Knight

,, 25   THOMAS DIXIE, third son of Wolstan D , of Market Bosworth, co Leicester,

,, 31   EDWARD NUGENT, son and heir of Thomas N , of Tradath, Ireland, Esq

Nov 1.   THOMAS POVEY, gent , second son of Justinian P , one of the Auditors of the
      King's Exchequer   [Worcester, gent (erased)

,,   4   RICHARD BALLARD, son of John B , of St John's-in-Bedwardine, co

,,   ,,   JOHN TURVILLE, son and heir of Henry T , of Newhall Park, co Leicester,
      Esq   [Knight.

,,   ,,   WILLIAM OGLANDER, son and heir of John O , of Newport, Isle of Wight,

,,   7   JOHN RICHARDSON, son and heir of John R , of the city of Durham, gent ,
      deceased   [deceased

,,   ,,   HENRY HARDWARE, son and heir of Henry H , of Peele, co Chester, Esq ,
                     [Knight, Comptroller of His Majesty's household.

,, 19   HENRY (inserted in lieu of " Francis ") FANE, son and heir of Henry F ,

,, 21   CUTHBERT NORRIS, son and heir of Thomas N., of Anmer, Norfolk, gent

,,   ,,   FRANCIS LOW, son and heir of Humphrey L , of St. Albans, Herts, gent

folio 906.

,, 25   JOHN VAUGHAN, son and heir of Henry V , of Derwith, co Carmarthen, Esq

,, 26   WILLIAM MARKENFIELD, of Markinton, co York, gent   [and Baronet

,, 27   RICHARD ASHTON, second son of Ralph A , of Whalley, co Lancaster, Knight

Dec 7   WILLIAM GWINN, son and heir of Rowland G , of ——— Esq

1633-4
Jan 17   NATHANIEL PARSELL, son and heir of William P., of Tower Hill, London, Esq
             [Chamber of Queen Henrietta Maria, " absque fine."

,, 23   JAMES SHIRLEY, of High Holborn, Middlesex, gent , one of the Valets of the

,,   ,,   ROBERT KELWAY, of Salisbury, Wilts, gent., " absque fine."

,, 24   LEONARD SPRACKLING, of the city of Canterbury, gent

folio 907.

1633-4

Feb 2   THOMAS STOCKTON, son and heir of John S , of Kiddington, Cheshire, Esq

,, ,,   LUKE CLAPHAM, son and heir of John C , late of Willenhall, co Warwick,
                                                                  [gent (erased)

,, 10   JAMES ALTHAM, of Mark Hall, Essex, Esq

,, ,,   THOMAS FOSTER, second son of William F , of Cardington, Beds, gent

,, ,,   THOMAS PIERCE, son and heir of Laurence P , of Westfield, Sussex, Esq
                                                               [and Baronet

,, 16   WALTER ROBERTS, son and heir of Walter R , of Glassenbury, Kent, Knight

,, ,,   ELKIN WYMONDESOLD, son and heir of William W , of Putney, Surrey, gent
                                                        [County Palatine of Chester

,, 21   WILLIAM MAINWARING, son and heir of Edward M , Esq , Chancellor of the

,, ,,   JOHN VINCENT, son and heir of Thomas V , late of Wooton, Kent, gent
                                                         [Lancaster, gent

,, ,,   WILLIAM CAWTHORNE, son of Christopher C , of Nether Wyersdale, co

,, ,,   BARNARD HARRISON, son and heir of Gilbert H , of the city of London, mercer.

,, ,,   THOMAS CROFT, of the county and borough of Carmarthen, gent

folio 908.

,, 23   THOMAS SOMERSET, Esq , son of Henry, Earl of Worcester.

,, ,,   GEOFFREY JEFFREYS, Esq , of Abercunncke, co Brecon.

,, ,,   EDWARD RUMSEY, Esq , of Crickhowell, co Brecon   [(erased)

,, ,,   HOWELL VAUGHAN, second son of John V., of Glanyllin, co Merioneth, Esq

,, 25.   GEORGE DOVE, sergeant-major.

,, ,,   JAMES PRAGER, gent , son of Peter P , gent.

,, ,,   MILES BUTTON, Esq., son of Thomas B., Knight

,, ,,   NICHOLAS JONES, of Matherne, co Monmouth, gent

,, ,,   THOMAS DABRIDGECOURT, of Hammersmith, Middlesex, Esq   [Esq

,, ,,   EDWARD RAWSTORNE, son and heir of Edward R , of Newhall, co Lancaster,

,, 26.   THOMAS JOHNSON, gent., son of William J., gent.

,, ,,   GEORGE PROBERT, gent , son of Henry P , of Pantyglass, co Monmouth, Esq

,, ,,   PETER DALTON, son and heir of Henry D , of Brigham, Cumberland, gent.

Mar 3   TREVOR WILLIAMS, son of Charles W , of Langibby, co Monmouth, Esq

,, ,,   JOHN WILLIAMS, gent , son of Charles W , of Langibby, co Monmouth, Esq

,, ,,   RICHARD GIBBES the younger, son and heir of Richard G , of Harlesden,
                                                          [Middlesex, Esq

,, ,,   JOHN CARTWRIGHT, of Bole, co Northampton, gent

,, ,,   EDWARD WISEMAN, gent , son of Richard W , of London, merchant   [gent

,, ,,   CHRISTOPHER WEBB, son and heir of Giles W , of Lyddiard Millicent, Wilts,

,, ,,   ROGER HASSALL, of Alkington, Salop, gent

,, ,,   THOMAS DANET, of Pinner, Middlesex, gent

,, ,,   THOMAS EDWARDS the younger, son of Thomas E , of Shrewsbury, gent.

,, ,,   DAVID EVANS, son of William E , of Neath, co Glamorgan, gent

,, ,,   MORGAN AUBREY, son of Morgan A , of Inyskedwyn, co Brecon, Esq

,, ,,   JOHN COLEMAN, of Llanover, co Monmouth, gent.

,, 5   ROBERT JOHNSON, of St. Martin's, London, gent.

1633-4.   folio 908—(continued)

Mar. 5   EDWARD REYNOLDS, of Llantrissent, co Monmouth, gent.

  ,,   ,,   WILLIAM ALEN, gent , son of William A , of Cheapside, London, gent.

folio 909.

  ,,   ,,   BRUNO RYVES, Pastor of the Church of St Martin's le Vintry, London.   (The
          celebrated author of the " Mercurius Rusticus," afterwards Dean of
          [Chichester, and Dean of Windsor, died 16 July, 1671, æt 81)

  ,,   ,,   THOMAS LEWIS, of the borough of Carmarthen, gent   [Esq.

  ,,   ,,   CHARLES KEMYS, son and heir of Nicholas K., of Lanvayre, co Monmouth,

  ,,   ,,   ROBERT JONES, M A , Rector of Tixall, co. Stafford.

  ,,   ,,   JOHN ARTHUR, gent

  ,,   ,,   JAMES CROFT, Esq , son of Herbert C , Knight, of Croft, co Hereford

  ,,   ,,   NICHOLAS LANGFORD, son of John L., of Newton, Bucks, gent , deceased

  ,,   ,,   EDMUND SAWYER, Knight   [deceased

  ,,   ,,   RICHARD CLUITON, son and heir of Thomas C., of Nantwich, Cheshire, gent ,

  ,,   ,,   THOMAS PARKINSON, son of Dennis (Dionysius) P , of co York, gent.

  ,,   ,,   HOPKINS THOMAS, son of Walter T , of Swansea, co Glamorgan, gent

  ,,   ,,   EVAN EVANS, son and heir of John E , of Neath, co Glamorgan, gent

  ,,   ,,   WILLIAM SMVGREGILL, gent

  ,,   7   RICHARD BRFAME, of Windsor, Berks, gent

  ,,   ,,   THOMAS WOOLSENDEN, son of Thomas W , of Bamford, co Lancaster, gent

  ,,   ,,   STEPHEN TERRY, of the city of Cork, Ireland, gent

  ,,   ,,   JOHN CLARKE, of Abridge, Essex, gent

  ,,   ,,   HENRY RUMSEY, son of Henry R , of Uske, co Monmouth, gent

  ,,   ,,   JOHN RUMSEY, son of Henry R , of Uske, co Monmouth, gent

  ,,   ,,   HENRY JONES, son of John J , of Hardwicke, co Monmouth, gent

  ,,   ,,   THOMAS WAITE, son of Henry W , of Wymondham, co Leicester, gent

folio 910

  ,,   ,,   JOHN BROWNE, of Nantwich, co Chester, late of Barnard's Inn, gent

  ,,   26   ROBERT MITFORD, of Mitford, Northumberland, Esq
1634
Apr 16.   ROBERT GARDINER, son and heir of Jeremy G , of the city of London

  ,,   25   FRANCIS GOLDSMITH, son and heir of Francis G , of St Giles in the Fields,
                                                            [Middlesex, Esq

  ,,   ,,   JOHN MELTON, of the city of York, Knight, one of the King's Council in the
                                          [North, and Secretary of the same

  ,,   ,,   THOMAS FOCHE, son and heir of Thomas F , of Sutton, near Dover, Kent,

  ,,   ,,   THOMAS HOLT, of Stokelyne, Oxon, Esq   [gent

May 1   GEORGE CHAMBERLAYNE, second son of Thomas C , Knight, late Chief Justice
          of Chester, and one of the Judges of the King's Bench   [Chester, &c

  ,,   ,,   JAMES CHAMBERLAYNE, third son of Thomas C , Knight, late Chief Justice of

  ,,   9.   WILLIAM SNEYDE, gent , second son of Ralph S , of Keele, co Stafford, Esq

  ,,   10   THOMAS COKE, gent , third son of George C , Bishop of Bristol

  ,,   ,,   EDWARD PACKER, son and heir of Humphrey P , of Ware, Herts, gent   [Knight

  ,,   ,,   RICHARD NORTON, second son of Daniel N , of Southwicke, Southampton,

1634.		folio 910—(continued)
May	10	ROBERT RAWLINSON, of Carke, co Lancaster, gent, late of Staple Inn
,,	,,	JOHN WHELPDALL, son and heir of William W, of Penrith, Cumberland, Esq.

folio 911.

[land, Esq

		FRANCIS ANDERSON, son and heir of Roger A, of Jesmond, co Northumber-
,,	,,	ROBERT CARRE, son and heir of James C, of Newcastle-on-Tyne, Esq
,,	,,	SAMUEL DAVISON, third son of Alexander D, of Newcastle-on-Tyne, Esq
,,	,,	HENRY BIGG, son and heir of William B, of Sharford, Essex, gent, deceased
,,	,,	THOMAS OWENS (inserted in lieu of " Price "), son and heir of Richard O, of [Mothevay, co Carmarthen, gent
,,	,,	JOHN (inserted in lieu of "George") WARREN, of Backerings Bark, Beds, late [of Staple Inn
,,	,,	GEORGE FOX, late of Staple Inn, gent
,,	,,	JOHN BREWER, of Waterford, Ireland, gent.
June	3	THOMAS HOLLOWAY, of Woolwich, Kent, gent. [(erased)
,,	13	GEORGE STERLING, son and heir of George S, of Charsfield, Suffolk, gent.
,,	,,	PETER BUCKE, son and heir of Peter B, of Rochester, Kent, Esq.
,,	,,	JOHN FORCER, son and heir of Peter F, of Harborhouse, co Durham, Esq, [late deceased.
,,	,,	EDWARD NELTHORPE, son and heir of Edward N, of Beverley, co. York, Esq, [deceased.
Aug	12	RICHARD COMPTON, Esq, son and heir of Henry C, of Brambletye, Sussex, Knight of the Bath. [Esq
,	,,	CLEMENT PASTON, Esq, son and heir of Thomas P, of Thorpe by Norwich,
,,	,	FRANCIS BACON, son and heir of Francis B, now reader, " sine fine "
,,	,,	THOMAS BACON, second son of Francis B, now reader, " sine fine "

folio 912.

,,	,,	GEORGE (?) CROFTON, son and heir of John C, of King's county
,,	15	EDMUND WELD, son of Matthew W, of Bracon Ash, Norfolk, gent
,,	,,	ISAAC METHAM, son and heir of Isaac M, of Onehouse, Suffolk, gent
,,	,,	ROBERT FORREST, Esq, son and heir of Anthony F, of King's Langley, co [Hereford (Herts ?), Knight, late deceased
,,	,,	ERASMUS COPE, of Cannons Ashby, co Northampton, Esq [L, Knight
,,	,,	THOMAS LAMBARD, of East Greenwich, Kent, Esq, son and heir of Multon
,,	,,	ELDRED CURWEN, of Rottington, Cumberland, Esq
,,	,,	JOHN JERMY (son of Clement J, late), of Marlingford, Norfolk, gent, deceased
,,	,,	JOHN BUTTOLFE, of the city of Norwich, gent
,,	,,	JOHN PALGRAVE, son of Thomas P, of Pulham, Norfolk, gent
,,	,,	THOMAS JENKINS, son of John J, of Llandwgwyn, co Cardigan, Esq
,,	,,	WILLIAM HATTON, son of Robert H, of Lymme, co Chester, gent
,,	,,	RICHARD FITZGERALD, son of Edward F, of Ballinamartyr, co Cork, Esq
,,	,,	WILLIAM MANSELL, third son of William M, of Foulkestown, co Tipperary,
,,	,,	RICHARD CARTER, son of Richard C, of Northwold, Norfolk, gent [gent
Oct	2	STEPHEN MASON, second son of Stephen M, of the city of Lincoln, gent

N

1634   folio 913.

Oct 2   GEORGE NEVLE, second son of William N , of Stoke Fleming, Devon, gent

,, 10   JOHN POTTS, son and heir of John P , of Mannington, Norfolk, Esq

,, ,,   HENRY HUDSON, son of Robert H , of the city of London, gent   [gent

,, ,,   THOMAS WHITE, son and heir of John W , of Saltwood-juxta-Hythe, Kent,

,, ,,   GEORGE DANVELL, son and heir of Ingleby D , of Beswicke, co York, Knight

,, ,,   JOHN PICKERING, second son of John P , of Tichmarsh, Notts (co North-
                                    [ampton), Knight

,, ,,   ROBERT DOUGHTY, son and heir of William D , of Hamworth, Norfolk, Esq

,, ,,   LEWIS MORGAN, son of James M , of Llangeney, co Brecon, gent   [Baronet

,, ,,   ANDREW KNIVELON, son and heir of Gilbert K , of Bradley, co Derby,

,, ,,   JOHN DAYRELL, son and heir of Robert D , of Calehill, parish of Little Chart,
                     [Kent, Knight (inserted in lieu of " Esq ")

,, ,,   THOMAS EURE, late of Tewkesbury, co Gloucester, gent

Nov 1   THOMAS DAWNEY, Esq , son and heir of John D , deceased, and heir of
                    [Thomas D , of Cowick, co York, Knight

,, ,,   EDWARD HUTCHINSON, son and heir of Stephen H , of Wickham, co York,

,, ,,   JOHN JOHNSON, son of Bartholomew J , of Anmer, Norfolk, gent   [Esq

                                folio 914.

,, 12.   ROBERT FRANK, of Bradford, co York

,, ,,   WILLIAM LEWIS, son and heir of David L , of Llanmellen, co. Monmouth, Esq

,, ,,   ARTHUR CAYLEY, second son of Edward C , of Brompton-in-Pickering Lythe,
                                 [co. York, Esq

,, ,,   ROBERT HORSMAN, son and heir of Robert H , of Shetton (? Seaton), co Rut-

, ,,   RICHARD FOWLE, son of Anthony F , of Rotherfield, Sussex, Esq   [land, Esq.

,, ,,   EDWARD GWYNNE, son of Thomas G , of London, Esq

,, ,,   HENRY WARREN, of Broxton, Herts, gent

,, 19   PETER GODFREY, second son of Thomas G , of Sellinge, Kent, Esq   [Esq

,, ,,   JOHN NELTHORPE, second son of Richard N , of Glanfordbridge, co Lincoln,

,, ,,   JOHN NELTHORPE, of Beverley, co York, Esq

,, ,,   WILLIAM CLEGATE, son and heir of George C , of the city of Canterbury, gent
                                     [Herts, Esq

,, ,,   WILLIAM COLE, son and heir of Richard C , of Salisbury, parish of Shenley,

,, 21   JAMES BANKES, son and heir of William B , of Winstanley, co. Lancaster, Esq

,, ,,   JOHN HALE, son of William H., of King's Walden, Herts, Esq

,, ,,   JOHN NEEDLER, son and heir of John N , of Horley, Surrey, Esq.

                                 folio 915

,, 29   THOMAS ASSHETON, second son of Thomas A , of Penketh, co Lancaster, Esq.

,, ,,   JOHN CONYERS, son and heir of Robert C , of Charroton (Sheraton), co
                                     [Durham, Esq

,, ,,   JOHN (inserted in lieu of " George ") HERON, son and heir of ——— H., of
                                 [Chipchase, Northumberland, Esq

,, ,,   GEORGE HERON, second son of ——— H , of Chipchase, Northumberland, Esq

,, ,,   JOHN COCKSHUTT, of (Sarrett ?), Herts, gent

1634-5		**folio 915**—*(continued)*
Jan	22	EDWARD FREEMAN, son of William F , of Blockley, co Worcester, Esq
,,	26	NATHANIEL PACKHURST, son and heir of Henry P , of St Lawrence, Old Jewry, London, Esq [Northampton, Esq
,,	30	HENRY SHUCKBURGH, son and heir of Henry S , of Naseby (Nevasbee), co [Leicester, clerk
,,	,,	ROBERT PELSAINT, second son of William P , of Market Bosworth, co
Feb	2	ANTHONY FOTHERBYE, son of John F , of the city of Canterbury, Knight
,,	,,	RICHARD BARNEWALL, second son of Patrick B , of Kilbrew, co Meath, gent
,,	,,	ROGER CALCOTT, of London, gent

folio 916

,,	9	PETER KING, son of Robert K , S T D , Rector of Tilston, Cheshire
,,	,,	EDWARD JONES, son and heir of Gilbert J , of Gyngrog, co Montgomery, Esq
,,	27.	ANDREW WHEATLEY, son and heir of Andrew W , of Woolley, co York, gent
,,	,,	WILLIAM ADAM, son and heir of William A , of London, gent
,,	,,	WILLIAM SAXBIE, son and heir of Edmund S , of Brenchley, Kent, gent
,,	,,	THOMAS ATKINSON, son and heir of Richard A , of London, gent
,,	,,	ROBERT READE, of St Margaret's, Westminster, gent
,,	,,	JOHN MILWARD, son and heir of Thomas M , of London, gent
,,	,,	THOMAS CHARLTON, son and heir of Edward C , of co Derby, gent
,,	,,	PIERS BUTLER, son of James B , of Ballynehensy, co Tipperary, gent
,,	,,	EDMUND KEALY, son and heir of Piers K , of Gowran, co Kilkenny, gent [Cork, gent
,,	,,	CALLAGHAN MAC'KARIY, son and heir of Florence M , of Doon Daroil, co

folio 917.

,,	,,	RICHARD PITTS, son and heir of Richard P , of Okesey, Wilts, Esq
,,	,,	JOHN WATERS, son and heir of Hugh W , of Charlton, Wilts, gent
,,	,,	WILLIAM PARRY, son of John William P , of Penryclaure, co Monmouth, Esq
,,	,,	JOHN POOLE, son of John P , of Painswick, co Gloucester, gent
1635		
April	3	HENRY DYNHAM, second son of John D , of Okeley, Bucks, gent , deceased
,,	29	PETER STEADMAN, son of Edmund S , of the city of London, gent , deceased [Lancaster, gent
May	1	JOHN ABBOT, son and heir of William A , of Preston-in-Amunderness, co
,,	,,	ROGER KYNASTON, son of Edward K , of Hordeley, Salop, Esq , deceased
,,	,,	THOMAS BARNARDISTON, son and heir of Nathaniel B , of Keddington Suffolk, Knight [deceased
,,	,,	NATHANIEL PARKER, son of Calthrop P , late of Arwarton, Suffolk, Knight,
,,	,,	ARTHUR BECKWITH, son of Roger B , of Aldboro, co York, Esq
,,	,,	ROBERT BENNETT, son and heir of Robert B , of New Windsor, Berks, Knight
,,	8	GEORGE PROCTER, son of Thomas P , of Newhall, co York, Esq
,,	,,	MARMADUKE CONSTABLE, son and heir of Philip C , of Wassand, co York, Esq
,,	,,	EDWARD WILFORD, son of William W , late of Hadley, Middlesex, Esq
,,	,,	GEORGE GREAVES, son of John G , of Woodhouse, co Derby, Esq
,,	,,	JOHN ROBINSON, son of Arthur R , of Dighton, co York, Knight.

1635　　　　　　　　　　　　folio 918.

May 8　JASPER SHARPE, son and heir of Jasper S , of Bury St Edmunds, Suffolk, gent

,, ,,　WILLIAM PHILIPPS, son and heir of John P , of Fynnongaynge, co. Pembroke,

,, ,,　ROBERT DORMER, son and heir of the Hon Robert D　　　　　[Esq

,, ,,　JOHN LANY, son and heir of John L , of Gray's Inn, Esq , "sine fine "

,, ,,　CHARLES TUCKE, son and heir of Thomas T , of East Beere, Kent, Esq

,, ,,　HENRY WARNER, son and heir of Thomas W , of Balsham, Cumberland,
　　　　　　　　　　　　　　　　　　　　　　　　　　[S T D

,, ,,　EDMUND PAGE, second son of Edmund P , of the city of London, citizen

,, ,,　MOUNTAGUE CHOLMLEY, of ———, co Lincoln, Esq

June 3.　HENRY MEWTIS, son and heir of Henry M , of Hertford, Esq

,, ,,　THOMAS ROCKLEY, son and heir of Robert R , of Rockley, co York, Esq.

,, ,,　THOMAS LORAINE, son and heir of Robert L , late of Kirkharle, Northum-
　　　　berland, Esq , deceased　　　　　　　　　[merchant

,, ,,　JOSEPH SPURSTOW, son of William S , of St Stephen's, Coleman, London,

,, 12　HENRY GREENWOOD, son and heir of Thomas G , of North Parrott, co

,, ,,　THOMAS HOLLAND, of Bridgnorth, Salop, gent　　　[Somerset, Esq , deceased.

,, ,,　THOMAS HARRISON, son and heir of Thomas H , of Cayton, co. York, Esq

,, ,,　CUTHBERT CARRE, second son of James C , of Newcastle-on-Tyne, Esq

,, ,,　JOHN ADDISON, son and heir of Anthony A , gent , of Egleston, co Durham

,, ,,　RICHARD GOODWIN, son and heir of Geoffrey G , of the city of Norwich, gent

　　　　　　　　　　　　folio 919.

Aug 6　FRANCIS BIONDI, of London, Knight

,, ,,　CASSEY BOROUGH, son and heir of John B , of London, Knight

,, ,,　RICHARD (inserted in lieu of " John ") PAGE, second son of Richard P , of
　　　　London, gent　　　　　　　　　　　　　[co Warwick, gent

,, ,,　JOHN BRIDGES, late of Clifford's Inn, son and heir of John B , of Alcester,
　　　　　　　　　　　　　　　　　　　　　　　[co Carmarthen, Esq.

,, ,,　JOHN LLOYD, second son of Griffin L , of Forrest, parish of Llanvihangell

,, ,,　WILLIAM WATTON, son and heir of William W , of Addington, Kent, Esq

,, ,,　JOHN PAGE, of Finchley, Middlesex, gent

,, 14　GEORGE TUKE, son and heir of George T , of Frayting, Essex, Esq

, ,,　SAMUEL TUKE, third son of George T , of Frayting Essex, Esq

,, ,,　HUGH WHITE, of South Petherton, co Somerset, gent

,, ,,　JOHN GIBES, son of ——— G , late of Thurston, Suffolk, gent , deceased

,, ,,　JOHN BOURNE, son and heir of John B , of Ufford, co Northampton, Esq.

,, ,,　WILLIAM LINGWOOD, son and heir of William L , of Braintree, Essex, gent

,, ,,　JOHN BUSHELL, son and heir of Thomas B , of Enston, Oxon, Esq

,, ,,　STEPHEN LAKE, son and heir of Thomas L , of Fetter lane, London, Esq

,, ,,　JOHN WILLIAMS, second son of Richard W , of Lyghillas, co Anglesey, Esq

　　　　　　　　　　　　folio 920　　　　　　　　[gate, Esq

,, ,,　THOMAS SPARROW, son and heir of Thomas S , of St. Botolph's, near Alders-

,, ,,　PEER WILLIAMS, son and heir of Anthony W., of St James', Clerkenwell, Esq

,, ,,　STEPHEN BAXTER, son of Stephen B , of Mendham, Suffolk, gent , deceased

1635		folio 920—*(continued)*
Aug	14.	WILLIAM BRAGG, son and heir of John B , of co Stafford, gent
,,	,,	JOHN CLARKE, son and heir of Humphrey C , of Edmonton, Middlesex, gent
,.	,,	WILLIAM SAVILL, son of William S , of Oxton, Notts, Esq , deceased
,,	,,	ROBERT GORTON, son of Robert G , of Middleton, co Worcester, gent
Nov	1.	THOMAS MORTON, Knight, brother-german to the Right Hon Albert M , [Knight, Secretary to Kings James and Charles, Privy Councillor, &c
,,	,,	THOMAS MORTON, Esq , son and heir of Thomas M , Knight
,,	,,	JOHN MEAUTYS, of North Mimms, Herts, Esq [Common Pleas
,,	,,	GEORGE GULSTON, one of the sons of John G , one of the Prothonotaries of the
,,	,,	ROBERT CLARKE, son and heir of Robert C of Canterbury, gent

folio 921

,,	,,	EDMUND STUBBS, of Huntingfield, Suffolk, S T D [gent.
,,	,,	PATRICK MOORE, son and heir of Bartholomew M , of Dowanstowne, co Meath,
,,	,,	EDWARD HUSSEY, son and heir of Peter H of Cullmullin, co Meath, gent
,,	,,	EDWARD WARD, son and heir of Thomas W , of Bixley, Norfolk, Esq
,,	5	JAMES KENT, of Thames-street, parish of St Martin's, London, gent
,,	,,	JOHN SIBSON, second son of Henry S , of Bewcastle, Cumberland, S T D.
,,	6.	THOMAS BRATHWAITE, son and heir of Richard B , of Burneshead, West-[moreland, Esq
,,	,,	RICHARD SIMONS, son and heir of Samuel S , of Topsfield, Essex, gent
,,	,,	JOHN BARRINGTON, son and heir of Thomas B , of Hatfield, Essex, Knight [and Baronet.
,,	,,	WINGFIELD BODENHAM, son and heir of Francis B , of Ryhall, Rutland, [Knight
,,	,,	WILLIAM KNIPE, son and heir of Anthony K , of Fairbanck, Westmoreland, [gent

folio 922.

,,	,,	GEORGE PENRUDDOCK, son and heir of John P , of Compton Chamberlain, Wilts, Esq [Esq
,,	,,	BALTHAZAR WOODLOCKE, son and heir of James W., of Waterford, Ireland,
,,	,,	HERBERT PERROT, son and heir of Robert P , of Moreton-on-the-Lugg, [co Hereford, gent
,,	,,	DANIEL FOXE, son and heir of Thomas F , of St Andrew's, Holborn, citizen
,,	,,	COMPTON EURE, son of Francis E., late one of the readers of this Inn, [Knight, deceased
,,	,,	JOHN GREENE, son and heir of John G , of the city of Norwich, Esq
,,	,,	JOHN EGERTON, third son of Richard E , of Rydley, co Chester, Knight, deceased [Esq , deceased
,,	.,,	EDWARD CHISNOLL, son and heir of Edward C , of Chisnoll, co Lancaster,
,	,,	THOMAS DRIWOOD, son and heir of Thomas D , of Orsett, Essex, gent, [deceased
,,	,,	JOHN DOWNES, second son of Roger D , Esq , one of the readers of this [Inn, "sine fine"
,,	13	JOHN HAWKINS, son and heir of Richard H , of Selinge, Kent, Esq
,,	,,	THOMAS PHILPOTT, son of John H , late of Thruxton, Hants, Knight.

1635   **folio 923.**

Nov 13   JOHN BENCE, son and heir of John B , late of Benhall, Suffolk, gent

,,   ,,   THOMAS MORLEY, son and heir of Francis M , of Wennington, co Lancaster,
          Esq   [Stephen's, Kent, Esq

,,   ,,   HENRY WHITE, son and heir of John W., late of Hackington, *alias* St

,   ,   CHARLES SHRUBSOLL, son and heir of Richard S , late of Canterbury, gent ,
                                                          [deceased

,,   ,,   NICHOLAS STYLEMAN, second son of Robert S., of Field Dalling, Norfolk,

,,   ,,   JOHN LOWEN, of North Hall, Herts, gent   [gent

,,   26   RICHARD HICKES, of Dynder, Somerset, gent.

,,   ,,   ROBERT DICKONSON, son and heir of George D , of Lincoln, gent

Dec 15   EDMUND BELL, son and heir of Robert B , of Beaupré Hall, Norfolk, Knight

,,   ,,   ROBERT BELL, second son of Robert B , of Beaupré Hall, Norfolk, Knight

1635-6
Jan 29   JERRARD SALVIN, son and heir of Jerrard S , of Croxdale, co Durham, Esq

,,   ,,   JOHN MATHIAS, of Llwynegwarren, co Pembroke, gent

,,   ,,   JOHN HARVIE, son and heir of John H , of Bedingfield, Suffolk, gent

,,   ,,   JOHN GLEGG, son of William G , of Geyton, co Chester, Esq

                                folio 924

Feb 2   JOHN MARTIN, son and heir of George M , of the city of Durham, Esq

,,   ,,   PATRICK BRIAN, son and heir of James B , of co Kilkenny, Esq

,,   10   GEORGE GERRY, second son of Richard G , of Bushmead Abbey, Beds ("co
          Northumberland " erased), Esq   [(erased)

,,   ,,   RICHARD SIMONS, son and heir of Samuel S , of Topesfield, Essex, gent

,,   ,,   WILLIAM FENWICK, second son of John F , of Wallington, co Northumber-
                                              [land, Knight and Baronet

,,   ,,   JOHN BENNETT, son and heir of John B , of Dawley, Middlesex, Knight

,,   ,   JOHN HOLLED son and heir of John H , of Sempringham, co Lincoln

,,   ,,   BENJAMIN GARFIELD, son and heir of Benjamin G , of St James's, Clerken-
                                                          [well, gent

,,   23   THOMAS BLUNT, of the city of Bristol, gent , late of Barnard's Inn ("He

,,   ,,   THOMAS WEBBE, of Cowledge, Suffolk, gent   [would not be admitted ")

,,   ,,   HENRY LLOYD, son and heir of Fulke L , late of Havodunnes, co Denbigh,
          Esq , deceased   [(erased)

,   ,,   EDWARD MASTER, fifth son of Edward M , of Ospringe, Kent, Knight

,,   ,,   THOMAS MARBURIE, son of ———M , of Chester, Esq

                                folio 925

Mar 15   ROBERT CORDELL, son and heir of John C , Alderman of London

,,   ,,   JOHN BROWNE, of Nantwich, co Chester, gent , late of Barnard's Inn,
                                                          [admitted before.

,,   ,,   MATHIAS BECKWITH, second son of Roger B., of Aldboro', co York, Esq

,,   ,,   JAMES ANDERTON, son and heir of Roger A., of Byrchley, co Lancaster, Esq

,,   ,,   JOHN HARRISON, son and heir of William H , of (Uper ?), parish of Wood-
          nesborough, co. Kent, gent   [Esq

,,   ,,   EDWARD WELCOME, son of John W , late of Market Stainton, co. Lincoln,

1635-6.   folio 925—(continued).

Mar. 17.   LEWIS BOYLE, Knight, Lord Boyle, Baron of Bandon Bridge, and Viscount

"   "   ROGER BOYLE, Knight, Lord Boyle, Baron of Broghill [Boyle, of Kynalmeahy

"   "   THOMAS BEDINGFIELD, son and heir of Philip B , of Ditchingham, Norfolk,
           Esq   [reader

"   "   THOMAS BEDINGFIELD, son and heir of Thomas B , of Gray's Inn, Esq , now

"   "   THOMAS HOSKINS, son and heir of Charles H , of the city of London, Esq

"   "   BERNARD LYFORD, of Peasemore, Berks, gent   [Elmham, Suffolk, gent

"   "   VINCENT SELLINGE, son and heir of John S , late of All Saints', in South

"   "   JOHN BOLD, son of Arthur B , of Petersfield, co. Southampton, gent

                                          folio 926

"   18   JOHN MARCH, (late) of Barnard's Inn, gent

"   "   GEORGE CROSTON, son and heir of John C , of Bury, co Lancaster, gent.

"   "   JOHN WINNE, of Evenechtid, co Denbigh, son and heir of Hugh W , gent ,
                                                                           [deceased

"   "   JOHN WINNE, son and heir of Robert W , of Kenegard, co. Westmeath, gent

"   "   THOMAS DIMMOCK, son and heir of Humphrey D , of Willington, co Flint, Esq

"   "   THOMAS PARAMORE, son and heir of Thomas P , of St Nicholas, Isle of
                                                             [Thanet, Kent, Esq

"   "   STEPHEN BECKINGHAM, son and heir of Stephen B , of Tolleshunt, Essex, Esq

"   "   EDWARD MASTERS, son of Edward M , of Ospringe, Kent, Esq

"   "   HENRY KELSEY, late of Barnard's Inn, gent

"   "   JOHN ROSSE, son of John R , late of London, merchant.

1636
May 2   WILLIAM JUXON, Bishop of London, and Lord Treasurer of England

"   5   JOHN EYTON, gent., son of John E., of Layth, or Lythewood, Flint, Esq

"   13   EDWARD MOSELEY, second son of Oswald M , Esq   [Esq

"   14   BEVERCOTES CORNWALLIS, son and heir of Thomas C , of the city of Lincoln,

"   "   WILLIAM COOKE, son and heir of Robert C , of Highnam, co. Gloucester, Knight

                                          folio 927.   [deceased

"   "   RALPH BROWNE, son and heir of Ralph B , late of Ince, co Lancaster, gent ,

"   "   JOHN PENRUDDOCK, second son of John P , of Compton Chamberlain, Wilts,
           Esq   [Knight

"   "   JOHN AILWARD, son and heir of Peter A , of Faithlegh, co Waterford,

"   "   EDWARD STANFORD, son and heir of William S , of Pury (Perry) Hall, co
           Stafford, Esq   [Esq , deceased

"   "   HENRY HUNLOKE, son and heir of Henry H , of Wingerworth, co Derby,

"   "   RICHARD SANDYS, second son of Edwin S , of Ombersley, co Worcester,
           Knight   [Lincoln, gent

"   23   RICHARD SANDWITH, son and heir of Henry S , of Burton-on-Humber, co

"   "   EDWARD CORBETT, son and heir of Edward C , of Longnor, Salop, Esq

"   "   ANTHONY DUNCOMBE, son and heir of John D , Esq , one of the Members of

"   "   LANCELOT LADE, son and heir of Robert L , of Canterbury, Esq   [this Inn

"   27   RICHARD HOBDAY, son of Stephen H , of Cheriton, Kent, gent , late of

"   "   JOHN VINCENT, son of Thomas V , of the city of London, gent   [Staple Inn

1636   folio 927—(*continued*)

May 27   LEWIS LEWYNS, son and heir of Thomas L , of Rusholme, co York, Esq.

,,   ,,   JOHN SALKELD, son and heir of John S., of Rocke, Northumberland, Esq.

,,   ,,   ROBERT BLACKWELL, Junior , of Bushey, Herts, gent   [gent

June 1   WILLIAM HALSALL, son and heir of Richard H , of Harleton, co Lancaster,

,,   ,,   HENSON BROOME, late of Staple Inn, son and heir of Thomas B of the town of
                                                            [Nottingham, Esq

1636-7   folio 928

Feb 3   JAMES LEMYNG, son and heir of John L , of Colchester, Essex   [Esq.

,,   ,,   FRANCIS HATCHER, son and heir of William H , late of Sutterton, co Lincoln,

,,   6   ROGER LE STRANGE, son of Hamon, of Hunstanton, Norfolk, Knight.

,,   ,,   EDWARD DA(V)RELL, second son of Robert D , of Calehill, Kent, Knight.

,,   ,,   CLINTON MILNER, son and heir of Henry M , of Whickenby, co Lincoln, Esq

,,   ,,   EDWARD TORKSEY, of the city of Coventry   [Suffolk, gent

,,   ,,   THOMAS DADE, son and heir of Thomas D , of (Tannington), Framshed,

,,   ,,   DANIEL WATSON, second son of Henry W , late of Burton-on-Trent, co
                    Stafford, gent , deceased.   [Glamorgan, gent

,,   7   ROBERT THOMAS, son of Thomas James (*sic*), of St Brides Major, co

,,   10   MARK PARKER, son and heir of John P , Esq , one of the Members of this Inn

,,   ,,   RALPH TUFTON, son of Joseph T , of Lee, Surrey, late of Staple inn, gent

,,   ,,   OWEN ANDREW, late of Staple Inn, eldest son of William A , late of Carnarvon,
                    gent , deceased   [Essex, gent , deceased.

,,   ,   THOMAS ROBERTS, son and heir of Thomas R , (late) of Little Braxted,

,,   ,,   HERBERT LLOYD, son of Thomas L., of Kylkyteth, co Pembroke, Esq , deceased

,,   ,,   JAMES OAKES, son and heir of Richard O , of the city of Norwich, gent

                                   folio 929

,,   13   JOHN BUTTS, third son of Thomas B , of the city of Worcester, gent.

,,   ,,   ANTHONY EMERY, late of Staple Inn, son of Thomas E , late of Little Baddow,
                                                            [Essex, gent , deceased.

,,   ,,   WILLIAM BURTON, son and heir of John B , late of Purleigh, Essex, gent ,
                    deceased.   [Esq

,,   ,,   CHARLES WILSON, son and heir of Charles W , of Sheepwash, co Lincoln,

,,   ,,   PETER BLAND, son and heir of William B , of Lewes, Sussex (duplicate)

,,   ,,   WILLIAM WATTS, son and heir of John W , of Burnham Ulph, Norfolk, gent

1637.   [gent

May 5   WILLIAM CLAYTON, son and heir of Thomas C , of Fulwood, co Lancaster,

,,   ,,   ROBERT HESKETH, of Dunderdale, co Lancaster, gent.   [Lancaster, Esq

,,   12   URIAN RIGBY, gent , son of Alexander R , of Rigby-in-Amunderness, co

,,   ,,   THOMAS HOWE, son of William H , of South Ockendon, Essex, Esq

,,   13   WILLIAM PARLET, of Downham Market, Norfolk, gent.

,,   ,,   JOHN SOTHERBY, son and heir of Thomas S , of Combe, Suffolk, clerk

,,   ,,   GEORGE REVE, second son of Robert R , of Thawke, Suffolk, Esq

,,   ,,   THOMAS BERKELEY, son and heir of Francis B , of Ewdnes, Salop, Esq

,,   ,,   GEORGE HEARNE, of the city of Oxford, gent.

1637		folio 929—(*continued*)

May 13   WILLIAM ROBINSON, son and heir of Piers R , of Fillybrooke, co Stafford, Esq

,,   ,,   PETER ELLISION, son of Matthew E , of Castle Headingham, Essex, gent

folio 930.

,,   19   EDWARD DIGGS, son of Dudley D , Knight, Master of the Rolls

,,   ,,   LEONARD DIGGS, son of Dudley D , Knight, Master of the Rolls

,,   ,,   DUDLEY PALMER, son and heir of Anthony P , of Kent, Knight, deceased

,,   ,,   MATHEW BUNCE, son and heir of Stephen B , late of Throwleigh, Kent, [gent , deceased

,,   ,,   WILLIAM BARNES, son and heir of William B , of Ely, co Cambridge, Esq.

,,   ,,   JOHN STRONGHILL, son and heir of JOHN S , late of Lydd, Kent, gent , [(deceased)

,,   ,,   ROBERT SANDYS, son of Edwin S , of Northborne, Kent, Knight

,,   ,,   RUDOLPH DOD, son of John D , of Tandridge, Surrey, gent   [gent

,,   ,,   JOHN DODSWORTH, son and heir of John D , of Thornton Watlass, co York,

,,   ,,   RICHARD SION, son and heir of John S , of Tower Street, London, merchant

,,   ,,   THOMAS CHASE, son and heir of Thomas C , of Empshott, Southampton, gent.

June 16   ROBERT WIGMORE, son and heir of John W , of Luckton, co Hereford, Esq

,,   ,,   TAMBERLANE BOWDLER, son and heir of William B , of Ludlow, Salop, gent

,,   ,,   WILLIAM WEST, of Lancaster, gent   [Knight and Baronet.

,,   22   EDWARD NIGHTINGALE, third son of Thomas N , of Clavering Park, Essex,

folio 931.   [gent

,,   ,,   AMBROSE THELWALL, second son of Edward T , of Llanbedei, co. Denbigh,

,,   23   WALTER CARWARDINE, son and heir of Abel C , of Carwardine Green, parish of Madeley, co Hereford, gent   [Esq , late of Staple Inn

,,   ,,   THOMAS MORE, son of John M., of Paynes Farm, parish of Teynton, Oxon,

,,   ,,   ALEXANDER NORWOOD, son and heir of Richard N , of Boughton Malherbe, [Kent, Esq.

,,   ,,   NICHOLAS BURWELL, son of Edmund B , of Woodbridge, Suffolk, Esq

,,   ,,   OWEN BARNES, second son of William B , of Isle of Ely, co Cambridge, Esq

,,   ,,   ROBERT DALYSON, son and heir of William D , of Greenwell, co Lincoln, Esq (duplicate)   (duplicate)

,,   ,,   GEORGE DALYSON, second son of William D , of Greenwell, co Lincoln, Esq

,,   ,,   THOMAS CHARLTON, eldest son of Nicholas C , of Chilwell, Notts, Esq

,,   ,,   JOHN BROWNELL, of Derby, gent

,,   ,,   EDWARD ANDREWS, son of John A , of Muchfalley, co Hereford, gent

,,   ,,   EDWARD OGLE, of Cunsey Park, Northumberland, Esq

,,   ,,   GEOFFREY FAVERING, of Glengall, co Tipperary, gent   [gent

Oct 13   EDWARD STRADLING, son and heir of John S , of Kellgare, co Glamorgan,

,,   ,,   ROBERT HUSSEY, third son of Patrick H , of Galtrim, co. Meath, Esq   [Esq.

,,   ,,   WILLIAM HARRISON, second son of John H , of St Olave's parish, London,

folio 932

,,   18.   RICHARD CHAMPION, son of Richard C., of Stanford-le-Hope, Essex, gent

1637   folio **932**—(continued)
Oct. 18.   PHILIP GAMAGE, son and heir of Edward G , late of Newcastle, co Gla-
                                                        [morgan, Esq , deceased.
,,   ,,   JOHN ALTHAM, second son of Edward A , of Markhall, Essex, Knight
,,   ,,   RICHARD SHAA, son and heir of Mark S , of co Kilkenny, gent.
,,   28   HUGH OVER, son of Hugh O , late of London, merchant
Nov   1.   JOHN BRADSHAWE, son and heir of William B., of Middlesex, Esq
,,   ,,   HANNIBAL POTTER, S T D.
,,   ,,   HUMPHREY WARREN, son and heir of John W , of this Inn, Esq
,,   ,,   RICHARD KYNNESMAN, Esq , one of the Auditors of the Exchequer
,,   ,,   DAVID LLOYD, son of Edward L., of Llanyfydd, co. Denbigh, gent.
,,   3   JOHN WINTER, son and heir of Edward W , of Amberley, co. Monmouth, Esq

folio 933

,,   ,,   GEORGE GOODDAY, son of William G , of St Andrew's, Holborn, gent
,   ,,   FRANCIS THEOBALD, son and heir of Francis T , of this Inn, Esq
,,   ,,   THOMAS GARDINER, son and heir of John G , of Shrewsbury, gent
                                                        [Staple Inn
,,   ,,   EDMUND JONES, son of John J , of Landeney, co Monmouth, gent , late of
,,   ,,   RICHARD WISEMAN, second son of Henry W , of Elsenham, Essex, Esq
,,   ,,   PETER PEAKE, son of Edward P , of Sandwich, Kent, gent
,,   ,,   SAMUEL WINGFIELD, son and heir of Thomas W , of Shrewsbury, gent
,,   ,,   JOHN LOWE, son and heir of Vincent L , of Denbie, co Derby, Esq
                                                        [gent , deceased
,,   ,,   THOMAS GOODALL, son and heir of Thomas G , late of Earls Stonham, Suffolk,
,,   ,,   ROGER WHITLEY, son of Thomas W , of Ashton, co Flint, Esq
,,   ,,   ROBERT DUKENFIELD, son and heir of Robert D , of Dukenfield, parish of
                                                        [Stockport, co Chester, Esq., deceased
,,   ,,   PETER DORMER, son of Fleetwood D , of the Grange, parish of Quainton,
                                                        [Bucks, Knight.
,,   ,,   JOHN COOKE, son and heir of Lambert C , of London, Esq.
,,   ,,   THOMAS PARADINE, son of Peter P , of the town of Bedford, Esq
,,   17   ROBERT HEYMAN, son of Peter H , of Selling, Kent, Knight.

folio 934

,,   ,,   JOHN ACTON, son and heir of John A , of Bramford, Suffolk, Esq
,,   ,,   GILES BINCKES, son and heir of Giles B , of London, gent
,,   24.   JOHN WAYTE, son of Thomas W , of Keythorpe, co Leicester, Esq
,,   ,,   WILLIAM JACKSON, son and heir of Philip G , of Stanhope, co Stafford, gent
                                                        [Northampton, Esq
,,   ,,   CHRISTOPHER PICKERING, son and heir of Robert P , of Titchmarsh, co
,,   ,,   JOHN LOWE, son of Humphrey L , of Southmills, Beds, Esq.
,,   27.   JOHN ANGELL, second son of Robert A , late of London, merchant, deceased
,,   ,,   JOHN AMHERST, son of Geoffrey A , of Horsmonden, Kent, clerk
,,   ,,   EDWARD COTTON, son and heir of Thomas C , of Lawton, co Leicester, Esq
,,   ,,   EDWARD SKIPWITH, son and heir of Edward S., of Grantham, co Lincoln, Esq

| 1637 | | folio 934—(continued) | [deceased |

Nov 27. GEORGE VENNARD, son of Charles V , of Goorley, co Southampton, gent ,

,, ,, THOMAS BERNEY, son and heir of John B , of Bishop's Thornton, co York,
[gent

,, ,, WILLIAM WHICHCOTT, son of of Hamon W , of Dunstan, co Lincoln, Knight.

,, ,, THOMAS ROCKE, son and heir of Richard R of Shrewsbury, Esq , deceased

,, ,, THOMAS OWEN, second son of Edward O , of Shrewsbury, Esq

folio 935. [gent

Dec 20 RALPH ASHTON, son and heir of John A , of Ashton under-Line, co Lancaster,

,, ,, ROBERT WILDBORE, son of Laurence W , of Balne, co York, gent

,, 23 THOMAS STRICKLAND, eldest son of Robert S , of Sizergh, Westmoreland, Esq

,, ,, JOHN ROBINSON, son and heir of William R , of Gwersilt, co Denbigh, Esq

,, ,, JOHN WRIGHT, son and heir of Richard W , of Pulford, co Chester, gent
[of Staple Inn

,, ,, PAUL NICCOLL, son and heir of William N of Hendon, Middlesex, gent , late

,, ,, WILLIAM CARDINALL, son and heir of William C , of East Bergholt, Sussex, Esq
[Spelhurst, Kent, clerk

,, ,, HENRY WESTON, son and heir of Edward (inserted in lieu of " John ") W , of

,, ,, THOMAS ROLAND, son and heir of John R , of Egham, Surrey, Esq [Baronet

,, ,, THOMAS BERNEY, son and heir of Richard B , of Parkhall-in-Reedham, Norfolk,

,, ,, KENNET FREEMAN, son and heir of John F , of Bewley, co Worcester, gent

1637-8 [deceased, " sine fine "

Feb 2 WILLIAM HETLEY, gent , son of Thomas H., King's Serjeant-at-Law, late

,, ,, ROBERT BLOWER, son and heir of Christopher B , late of Weston-on-the-Green,

,, ,, SOLOMON ROBINSON, son of Thomas R., gent., " sine fine " [Oxon

folio 936 [deceased

,, ,, RICHARD GAMMON, gent., son and heir of John G , late of Thetchworth, Herts,
[Knight, deceased

,, 12 THOMAS PRYSE, second son of John P., of Aberbetham, co Montgomery,

,, ,, EDWARD WALPOOLE, late of Staple Inn, son of Dimock W , of Spalding, co
Lincoln, Esq. [Lancaster, gent

,, ,, MATHEW RICHARDSON, son and heir of Mathew R , of Ravenheads, co

,, ,, HENRY PORTER, son of Henry P , of Egleston, co Worcester, gent., deceased

,, ,, SAMUEL BARKER, son and heir of Samuel B , of South Luffenham, co Rutland,
Esq [Baronet

,, ,, RICHARD CONVERS, son and heir of John C , of the Bishoprick of Durham,

,, ,, CHRISTOPHER CONYERS, son of John C , of the Bishoprick of Durham, Baronet

,, ,, WILLIAM MAULEVERER, son of James M , of Arnecliffe, co York, Esq

,, ,, PHILIP WARWICK, of the city of London, Esq

,, ,, THOMAS RATCLIFFE, of the city of London, Esq

,, ,, WILLIAM GREENE, of the city of London, Esq.

,, ,, JOHN POVEY, son and heir of John P , of Woodnesse, Salop, gent

folio 937. [" sine fine."

,, 15 JOHN EURE, son and heir of Sampson E , of Gray's Inn, Esq , now reader,

1637-8   folio 937—(continued)

Feb. 15   RICHARD (VAUGHAN), Earl of CARBERY

 ,,   ,,   WILLIAM CROFT, of Croft, co Hereford, Knight

 ,,   ,,   ALEXANDER THISTLETHWAYTE, of Danbury, Essex, Esq

 ,,   ,,   THOMAS CRUMP, of Ludlow, Salop, gent , son and heir of Thomas C , of same,

 ,,   ,,   EDWARD MORRIS, of Llansillin, co Denbigh, Esq   [gent.

 ,,   ,,   WILLIAM WASHBOURNE, of Withingford, co Worcester, Esq

 ,,   ,,   ROBERT LLOYD, M D

 ,,   ,,   GABRIEL IPSLEY (? Hippisley), of Marlow, Bucks, Esq

folio 938.

 ,,   ,,   JOHN BRICKENDEN, S T D

 ,,   ,,   JOHN LITTLETON, S T.D

 ,,   ,,   JOHN PIRTON, of the city of London, M D

 ,,   ,,   WILLIAM BRINKER, of Brinker, co Carnarvon, gent

 ,,   ,,   JAMES BRUIERE, son and heir of James B , of Cullen, co. Waterford, Esq

 ,,   ,,   THOMAS MORT, son and heir of Richard M , of Blackrode, co Lancaster, gent

 ,,   ,,   JOHN BRIDGES, of Bosbury, co Hereford, gent, son of William B , of same,

 ,,   ,,   EDWARD POLEY, of Badley, co. Suffolk, gent   [deceased.

folio 939

 ,   ,,   EDWARD EDWARDS, of Colfrin, co Montgomery, gent

 ,,   ,,   EDWARD WINWOOD, of Ludlow, Salop, gent

 ,,   ,,   RICHARD BLAYNEY, of Gateley Park, co. Hereford, gent.

 ,,   ,,   GEORGE RODES, son of George R , of Lotherton, co York, gent.

 ,,   ,,   PETER WALLEY, son and heir of Ralph W , of Middlewich, Cheshire, gent

 ,,   ,,   HENRY RICHES, son and heir of Henry R , late of Aylsham, Norfolk, Esq ,

 ,,   ,,   JOHN HARBORNE, son and heir of John H , of Tackley, Oxon, Esq   [deceased

 ,,   ,,   EDWARD HARBORNE, second son of John H , of Tackley, Oxon, Esq

folio 940

 ,,   ,,   RANDOLPH MANWARING, son and heir of Philip M , of Peover, Cheshire, Esq

 ,,   ,,   THOMAS MANWARING, second son of Philip M , of Peover, Cheshire, Esq

 ,,   ,,   THOMAS GREGORY, son and heir of Francis G , of Gray's Inn, Esq

 ,,   ,,   RALPH EURE, Esq , son and heir of William, Lord Eure, Baron of Malton

 ,,   ,,   WILLIAM EURE, Esq , second son of William, Lord Eure, Baron of Malton.

 ,,   ,,   FULLER MEADE, son and heir of Fuller M , of Foxton, co Cambridge, gent

 ,,   ,,   ROBERT FAIRBEARD, of Holborn, Middlesex, gent

folio 941.

 ,,   23   JOHN WINNE, son and heir of Peter W of Tythin, co Flint, Esq

 ,,   ,,   EMANUEL PALMER, of Tydd St Mary, co Lincoln, gent   [Esq

 ,,   ,,   GERALD FITZGERALD, son and heir of William F , of Castle Roe, co. Kildare,
                                                                              [Esq

 ,,   ,,   THOMAS FITZGERALD, son and heir of Gerald F , of Welsh Town, co. Carlow,

 ,,   ,,   THOMAS ALLEN, son and heir of Matthew A , of Palmerston, co. Dublin, Esq

 ,,   ,,   JOHN ALLEN, second son of Matthew A , of Palmerston, co Dublin, Esq

1637-8	folio 941—*(continued)*
Feb 23	EDWARD MAN, son and heir of Edward M , of Ipswich, Suffolk, gent
,, ,,	JOHN ST JOHN, son and heir of John St J , of Cold Overton, co Leicester, Esq
,, ,,	RICHARD AMOYLD, son and heir of Richard A , of Penmachno, co Carnarvon, gent [co Derby, gent
,, ,,	HUGH BATEMAN, late of Staple Inn, son and heir of Richard B , of Hartington,
,, ,,	GEORGE HARRIS, son and heir of Richard H , of Bakewell, co Derby, gent
,, ,,	JOHN ROGERSON, late of Staple Inn, son and heir of William R , of Stockton, [Salop, clerk

folio 942

Mar 24	JAMES BUTLER, son and heir of Peter, Viscount Ikerrin, in Ireland
,, ,,	ASHTON NUTTALL, son and heir of Francis N , of Roecliffe, co York, gent
,, ,,	THOMAS ST. QUINTIN, son of William St Q , of Foulton, co York, Esq
,, ,,	JOHN HENDEN, son and heir of Simon H , of Benenden, Kent, gent.
1638	
April 20	JOHN BOROUGH, second son of John B , Knight, Garter Principal King of Arms
,, ,,	EDMUND HULL, son and heir of William H , Esq , of Tolepuddle, Dorset
,, ,,	FRANCIS WHITE, son of Francis W , of Broughton, co Leicester, Esq , deceased
,, ,,	JOHN WILDBORE, son and heir of Thomas W , of Knottingley, co York, Esq
,, ,,	EZEKIEL SPALDING, son and heir of John S , late of (Roughton ?) Suffolk, [clerk, deceased
,, ,,	WILLIAM LAURENCE, son and heir of Robert L , of Brockdish, Norfolk, Esq
,, ,,	WILLIAM VELE, son and heir of Thomas V , of Alveston, co Gloucester, Esq
,, ,,	SAMUEL STERLING, son and heir of Samuel S , of St Mary's, Whitechapel, gent

folio 943

,, 30	THOMAS SKIPWITH, second son of Edward S , of Grantham, co Lincoln, Esq [deceased
,, ,,	CHRISTOPHER BROWNE, son and heir of John B , of Tolthorpe, Rutland, Esq ,
,, ,,	THOMAS SEGAR, fifth son of William S , Knight, Garter Principal King of Arms
,, ,,	JAMES CLAVERING, son and heir of John C , of Newcastle-on-Tyne, Esq
,, ,,	HENRY ANDREWS, son and heir of William A , of Lathbury, Bucks, Knight
,, ,,	SAMUEL PINDER, son of Nicholas P , late of this Society, and grandchild of Nicholas Fuller, formerly Reader
,, ,,	HENRY GOODERE, son and heir of Henry G , of Baggington, co Warwick, gent.
May 4	WILLIAM ELLIS, son and heir of Edmund E , of Wellingore, co Lincoln, Esq [Knight
,, ,,	RICHARD INGOLDESBY, son and heir of Richard I , of Lethenborough, Bucks,
,, ,,	THOMAS SADLEIR, son and heir of Thomas Lee S , of Apsley Guise, Beds, Esq
,, ,,	LEONARD BECKWITH, son and heir of Newark B , of Handale Abbey, co York,
,, ,,	PHILIP SMYTH, son and heir of Philip S , of Pewsey, Wilts, Esq [Esq
,, ,,	JOHN HILTON, son and heir of John H , of Hilton, co Durham, Esq
,, ,,	GEORGE GREENWOOD, son and heir of George G , of Chastleton, Oxon, gent

folio 944

,, ,,	HENRY MILDMAY, son and heir of Henry M , of Grays, Essex, Knight
,, ,,	THOMAS WALLER, son of Nicholas W , of Bentley, co York, Esq

1638   folio 944—(*continued*)

May 4   JAMES BUTLER, son and heir of Peter B , of Bellerdrotie, co Tipperary, Esq

,, ,,   WALTER KIRKHAM, son and heir of Robert K , of Fineshead, co Northampton,

,, ,,   JOHN GRACE, son and heir of James G , of Rath, co Tipperary, gent   [Esq

,, ,,   THOMAS POCHIN, son and heir of George P , of Barkley, co Leicester, Esq

,, ,,   EDWARD EMPSON, son and heir of Francis E , of Boston, co Lincoln, gent.

,, 31.   PHILIP MORSE (late of Barnard's Inn), son and heir of Robert M , of Stuston, Suffolk, gent   [Esq

June 2   TIMOTHY REMINGTON, son of Richard R , of Launde on-the-Wolds, co York,

,, ,,   THOMAS WEBB, son and heir of Russell W , of Berkhamstead, St Mary's, *alias* North Church, Herts, gent   [S T P

,, ,,   ROBERT ADDAMS, son and heir of Robert A , of Kimpton, co Southampton,

,, 6   EDWARD TURPIN, son and heir of John T , of Bassingborne co Cambridge,

,, 8   JOHN PAGE, son of William P , of Harrow-on-the-hill, Middlesex, Esq   [gent

folio 945

,, ,,   JOHN LANGFORD (late of Staple Inn), son and heir of Robert L , late of [Constantine, co Cornwall, gent , deceased

,, ,,   THOMAS PILFORD, son of William P , late of Hadley, Middlesex, Esq , deceased.

,, ,,   FRANCIS CARY, son and heir of George C , of Redcastle, co Donegal, Esq
                                                   [York, gent

,, 12   THOMAS APPELBY, son and heir of Ambrose A , of Linton-on-the-Ouse, co

,, ,,   FRANCIS APPELBY, son of Ambrose A , of Linton-on-the-Ouse, co. York, gent

,, ,,   THOMAS RODE, son and heir of Thomas R , late of St Leonard's, Foster-lane, [city of London, gent , deceased

,, ,,   JOHN BURMAN, son and heir of John B , late of the city of Norwich, Doctor of

,, 14   THOMAS COLE, son of Robert C , of Haverhill, Suffolk, gent.   [Laws

,, 16   JOHN GLEGG, son of William G , of Geyton, co Chester, Esq (duplicate)

,, ,,   HENRY PASLEW, son and heir of Henry P , of Glemham, Suffolk, gent.

folio 946

, 19   THOMAS SOUTHWELL, son and heir of Dunsany S , of Morton, Norfolk, Esq

,, ,,   ABRAHAM BOUN, son and heir of Ralph B , of Coundon, co Warwick, gent

,, ,,   FRANCIS MICHELL, son and heir of Robert M , of Arthington, co York, gent

,, ,,   MORRIS ROCHE, son and heir of Richard R , of Dondorow, co Cork, Esq

,, ,,   PETER COOPER, son of Christopher C , late of Yakesley, Hunts, Esq , deceased.

,, ,,   THOMAS SKIPTON, son and heir of ——— S , late of Londonderry, Ireland,

,, ,,   WILLIAM LANE, son and heir of William L , of Canterbury, gent.   [Esq
                                                   [deceased

,, ,,   MATTHEW BIGG, son of Richard B , of St Giles-in-the-Fields, Middlesex, gent ,

,, ,,   BRACKENBURY BOTELER, son of Edward B., of Danbury, Essex, Knight
                                                   [Esq , deceased.

,, ,,   EDWARD MUSGRAVE, son and heir of William M , late of Hayton, Cumberland,

Aug 6.   HENRY HUGHES, gent , son and heir of Thomas H , Esq , now reader

,, ,,   WILLIAM WEEKES, son and heir of Edward W , of Wells, co Somerset, Esq

1638		folio 947
Aug 13		JOHN COLETON, Doctor of Physic, born in France
,,	,,	GREGORY FENNER, Knight
,,	,,	THOMAS BRAY, Esq , Gentleman of the Prince's Chamber
,,	,,	JOHN HOWE, gent
,,	,,	PHILIP PROGER, Esq , of the King's Privy Chamber
,,	,,	WILLIAM MASON, gent , son and heir of William M , Esq , Fellow of this Inn
,,	,,	HENRY MANNINGE, gent., son and heir of Richard M , of Detton, Salop, Esq
,,	,,	THOMAS COOKE, gent , eldest son of Thomas C , of Coate, Wilts, Esq
,,	,,	EDWARD MANNING, gent , son and heir of Edward M , of St Mary's Cray, [Kent, Esq
,,	,,	THOMAS MANNING, gent , son and heir of James M , of London, Esq

folio 948.

,,	,,	THOMAS NAPPER, gent , son and heir of Thomas N , of Cowley, Oxon, Esq
,.	,,	EDMUND WILLIAMS, gent , son and heir of Ed. W , of Kevenforest, co Glamorgan, gent. [co Gloucester, gent
,,	,,	JOHN CLUTTERBUCK, gent , second son of John C , of Standley St Leonards, [Holborn, gent
,,	,,	CIPRIAN MORSE, gent , son and heir of Ciprian M , late of St Andrews,
,,	,,	BENJAMIN KENT, gent , son of Robert K , of the city of York, gent
,,	,,	NICHOLAS RIVET, gent., son of Nicholas R , of Bramston, Suffolk, Esq
,,	,,	ROBERT WYNN, gent , son and heir of Henry W , of Panteg, co Carnarvon, [Esq
,,	,,	RICE VAUGHAN, son and heir of Henry V , of Machenlleth, co Montgomery, [Esq

folio 949.

,,	,,	JOHN MOORE, son and heir of Edward M , late of E(a)ling, Middlesex, gent
,,	,,	EDWARD TOPHAM, son and heir of Francis T , of the city of York, gent
,,	,,	PETER DODSON, son and heir of Miles D , of Kirkby Overblows, co York, Esq
,,	,,	JOHN WILCOCKE, son of William W , of Wichling, Kent, clerk
,,	,,	WILLIAM TOUCHET, son and heir of Robert T , of Whitly, co Chester, Esq
,,	,,	WILLIAM DYMOCKE, son of Humphrey D , of Willington, co Flint, Esq
.,	,,	JOHN WINNE, son and heir of Peter W , of Leeswood, co Flint, Esq
,,	,,	ROBERT LLOYD, son of David L., of Leeswood, co Flint, Esq
,,	,,	JOHN TREVOR, son and heir of Matthew T , of Trevor, co Denbigh, Esq [deceased
,,	,,	ITHEL BYTHELL, son and heir of Edward B , of Cwmgrin, co Flint, Esq ,
,,	,,	THOMAS CORRY, son and heir of John C , of Clonmell, co Tipperary, gent

folio 950

,,	,,	JOHN EVANS, son and heir of Edward E , of Leeswood, co Flint, Esq
,,	,,	ALEXANDER WINNE, son of David W , of Towyn, co Flint, Esq , deceased
,,	,,	JOHN PETIT, son and heir of William P , of Colquns, parish of Boughton,
,,	,,	FRANCIS WOTTON, son of Thomas W , of Tradath, co Meath, Esq [Kent, Esq.
,,	,,	GERALD NUGENT, son of Edward N , of Bracklyn, co Westmeath, Esq
,,	,,	ROBERT NUGENT, son of James N , of Drimory, co Westmeath, Esq

1638   folio 950—(continued)

Aug 13   ROBERT NETTERVILLE, son of Nicholas, Viscount of Dowth, co Meath

,, ,,   PATRICK WALSH, son of Robert W , of Kenmure, co Dublin, gen

,, ,,   ARTHUR BELLEW, son of James B , of the city of Dublin, gent   [Esq.

,, ,,   THOMAS RYAN, son and heir of William R , of Drumgruanach, co Limerick,

,, ,,   JOHN BAGOT, son and heir of John B , of Gormanstoun, co Limerick, Esq.

                                       folio 951   [deceased

,, ,,   WILLIAM BAKER, son and heir of William B , of Tunstall, Suffolk, gent ,

Sept 22 NICHOLAS HALLY, son and heir of Richard H., of Coghall, co Tipperary, Esq

,, ,,   MICHAEL BELLEW, son and heir of Patrick B , of Verdonston, co. Louth, Esq.

,, ,,   MICHAEL DORMER, son of Matthew D , of New Ross, co Wexford, gent
                                                            [gent , deceased.
,, ,,   THOMAS JENKINS, son of Richard J , late of Myghrin, parish of Llantrissant,

,, ,,   THOMAS CROFT, son and heir of Christopher C , of the city of York, Esq

,, ,,   GEORGE TOWNSEND, son and heir of Charles T , of Foord, co Gloucester, gent

Oct 24   THOMAS BEDELL, second son of Matthew B , of Paul's Churchyard, London

,, ,,   HENRY TEMPEST, son and heir of John T , of Tong, co York, Esq

,, ,,   EDWARD SHORTE, gent , son and heir of Samuel S , one of the Fellows of this

,, ,,   MATTHEW GILLY, gent , son and heir of William G , of London   [Inn
                                                   [parish of Nowell, Beds, Esq
,, ,,   ROBERT BARNARDISTON, gent , son and heir of Henry B , of Ickwelbury,

,, ,,   HENRY MILDMAY, son and heir of Thomas M , of Barnes, Essex, Knight

,, ,,   JOHN RUMBALD, son and heir of John R , late of Manuden, Essex, gent

                                       folio 952.

Nov 1   JOHN OTWAY, son of Roger O , of Midleton, Westmoreland, gen

,, ,,   HENRY GRIGSON, fourth son of Henry G , of Turnditch, co Derby, gent
                                                                [bridge, Esq
,, 2   EDWARD VENTRIS, son and heir of Edward V , of Great Shelford, co Cam-

,, 13   ROBERT APLETON, son and heir of John A , of Chilton, Suffolk, Esq , deceased

,, ,,   RICHARD NORTON, son and heir of Anthony N , of Rye, Sussex, gent

,, ,,   FRANCIS HILDESLEY, son and heir of William H , of Little Stoke, Oxon, Esq.

,, ,,   LEONARD EGERTON, son and heir of Peter E , of Shaw, co Lancaster, Esq

,, ,,   NATHANIEL ROBINSON, son and heir of Robert R , of Mobberley, co Chester,
            gent   [Stafford, gent
,, ,,   JOHN SMITH, son and heir of Thomas S , of Handley, parish of Stoke, co

,, ,,   EDWARD OSBORNE, second son of William O , of Sutton in-Ashfield, Notts,
                                                                [gent
                                       folio 953.

,, 30   WILLIAM NORWOOD, second son of Richard N , of Boughton Malherbe, Kent,
1638 9   [Esq
Jan 16   EDWARD POLHILL, son and heir of Edward P , of Burwash, Sussex, clerk

,, ,,   CHARLES FLEETWOOD, son of Miles F , of Wood-street, London, Knight

,, ,,   HENRY HALL, son and heir of Henry H , of Lillinge, co York, gent

,, ,,   EDWARD HODSON, son and heir of Phineas H , of the city of York, S T D

1638-9 folio 953—(continued)

Jan 16   EDMUND POWER, second son of Alexander P , of Powerstown, co Tipperary, Esq   [Esq

,,   ,,   WILLIAM GLOVER, son and heir of William G , of Campsey, Ash, Suffolk,

,,   26.   ANTHONY SHARDELOW, son and heir of Edmund S , late of Mettfield, Suffolk,   [Esq , deceased.

,,   ,,   CHRISTOPHER WORMELEY, second son of Henry W , of Riccall, co York, gent

,,   ,,   RICHARD WAKEMAN, son and heir of Edward W , of Beckford, co Gloucester,   [arm

folio 954

Feb   2   EDWARD HENDEN, son and heir of John H , of Biddenden, Kent, Esq

,,   ,,   GEORGE PROCTER, son and heir of Richard P , Esq , reader

,,   4   ROBERT AUDLEY, Esq , second son of Robert A , of Berechurch, Essex, Esq.

,,   ,,   HENRY AUDLEY, gent , son and heir of Robert A , of Danbury, Essex, Esq

,,   ,,   BENJAMIN GROOME, son and heir of Edmund G , of Woodbridge, Suffolk, gent.

,,   ,,   NATHANIEL THOROLD, son of Edmund T , of Easthampstead, Berks, gent.

,,   ,,   THOMAS HEBER, son and heir of Thomas H., of Marton, co York, Esq.

,,   ,,   THOMAS BEAUMONT, third son of Thomas, Viscount of Swords, in Ireland

,,   ,,   ROBERT SANDFORD, son and heir of John S , of High Ashes, co Lancaster, gent

folio 955

,,   ,,   NICHOLAS CHUTE, third son of Edward C , of Bethersden, Kent, Esq

,,   ,,   JOHN HEWLEY, son and heir of John H , of Wistow, co York, gent

,,   ,,   JOHN BRADSHAW, son of Laurence B , of Hope, co Lancaster, gent

Mar 15   JUSTINIAN PAGITT, of Holborn, Middlesex, Esq

,,   ,,   JOHN KEBLE, son and heir of Richard K , now reader

,,   ,,   RICHARD KEBLE, second son of Richard K , now reader

,,   ,,   JOHN DEANE, son of John D , late of Deane Hall, Essex, Knight

,,   ,,   BENJAMIN CUTLER, son and heir of Thomas C , of Ipswich, Suffolk, Esq

,,   ,,   JONATHAN SICKLEMORE, son of John S , of Ipswich, Suffolk, gent

,,   ,,   ABRAHAM GREGG, second son of Michael G , of Paul's Churchyard, London,   [Esq

,,   ,,   WILLIAM DADE, son of William D , of Tannington, Suffolk, Esq

,,   ,,   WILLIAM ASTON, son and heir of John A., of Tixall, co Stafford, gent

,,   ,,   LEWIS EVANS, son and heir of Evan ap Howell ap Rythech, of Plasedvon, co. Montgomery, gent   [gent.

,,   ,,   MORGAN EVANS, son and heir of Lewis E , of Plasedvon, co Montgomery,

folio 956

,,   ,,   JOHN FENWICK, second son of William F , of Stanton, Northumberland, Esq

,,   ,,   THOMAS SANDYS, son of Edmund S , of Northborne, Kent, Knight

,,   ,,   FRANCIS BIRCH, son and heir of Francis B , of Todham, Sussex, Esq

,,   ,,   JOHN ROCHE, second son of Richard R , of Dundrum, co Cork, Esq

,,   ,,   RICHARD BIRKBECK, son of Richard B , late of Morton Tynemouth, co   [Durham, Esq

,,   ,,   SAMUEL BENHAM, son of Robert B , late of Ipswich, Suffolk, gent , deceased

,,   ,,   RICHARD POWER, son of Alexander P , of Powerstown, co Tipperary, gent

O

1638-9		folio 956—(*continued*)
Mar	15	JOHN SALVIN, son and heir of Francis S , of Hurworth, co Durham, gent
,,	,,	ROBERT HALL, son and heir of Robert H , of the city of London, gent
,,	,,	ROBERT WYNN, second son of Robert W , of Drumin, co Longford, gent
,,	,,	JAMES ASCOUGH, son and heir of Edward A , of Hempsall, Notts, Esq
,,	,,	JOHN HARPER, son and heir of John H , of Friday-street, London, gent
,,	,,	NATHANIEL TAYLOR, son of John T , late of Eastcheap, London, gent
,,	,,	JAMES KELK, of Hollesworth, Suffolk, gent

1639		folio 957
May	8	RICHARD BALLARD, son and heir of Richard B , of Lamberhurst, Sussex, gent
,,	,,	EDWARD MORRIS, son and heir of Daniel M , late of Lloran, co Denbigh, Esq , deceased [gent
,,	,,	ROGER WILLIAMS, son and heir of William W , of St Nicholas, co Glamorgan,
,,	,,	JOHN RICHARDSON, son and heir of Thomas R , of Canterbury, gent
,,	,,	WILLIAM INGE, son and heir of Richard I , of the town of Leicester, gent
,,	,,	EDWARD FILMER, son and heir of Robert F , of East Sutton, Kent, Knight
,,	,,	WALTER JONES, son of Henry J , of Chastleton, Oxon, Esq
,,	,,	NETHERMILL GARRARD, son of John G , Knight and Baronet, of Lammer, parish of Wheathampstead, Herts. [Knight
,,	,,	FRANCIS TRENTHAM, son and heir of Thomas T., of Rocester, co Stafford, [Esq
,,	,,	FRANCIS KIRKHAM, second son of Robert K , of Fineshead, co Northampton,
,,	,,	EDWARD KNATCHBULL, son of John K., of Mersham, Kent, arm , deceased

		folio 958
,,	14	LEONARD SMELT, son and heir of Matthew S., of Kirby Fletham, co York, Esq
,,	,,	LEONARD ROBINSON, son and heir of John R , of Applegarth, co York, gent
,,	,,	GEORGE HARTPOOLE, son and heir of Robert H , of Shrowle, in Queen's co , Ireland, Esq [Esq
,,	,,	WILLIAM LEWIS, son and heir of David L , of Abergavenny, co Monmouth,
,,	,,	CECIL AYSCOUGH, second son of Edward A , of South Kelsey, co Lincoln, [Knight
,,	,,	SAMUEL RIDLEY, son and heir of Christopher R , of Beverley, co York, Esq.
,,	,,	EDWARD MAN, son and heir of Edward M , of Ipswich, Suffolk, Esq
,,	,,	WILLIAM BOLD (*alias* Wine), of Trevilim Meyricke, co Anglesey, gent.
,,	,,	THOMAS SNAWSELL, son and heir of Hugh S , of Bilton, co York, Esq
,,	,,	RICHARD PIOTT, son and heir of Richard P , of Streethay, co Suffolk, Esq
,,	,,	NICHOLAS BACON, son and heir of Nicholas B , Esq , one of the Fellows of this (erased; then " stet ")
,,	,,	JOHN COLLINS, son of Samuel C , of Cambridge (? Canterbury), S T D

		folio 959.
June	18	JONAS THOMPSON, son of Richard T , of Scarborough, co. York. gent
,,	,,	GEORGE NAPER, of Holiwell, Oxon, son of Edward N , of the same, Esq
,,	,,	NICHOLAS BACON, son and heir of Nicholas B , Esq [co. Durham, Esq.
,,	,,	ROBERT BYERLEY, son of Richard (rightly Christopher) B , of Midridge Grange,

1639		folio 959—(*continued*)
June 18		JOHN BRIGHT, son and heir of Stephen B, of Carbrook, co York, Esq
,,	,,	WILLIAM THOROLD, son and heir of William T, of Arborfield, Berks, Esq
,,	,,	THOMAS BAWDEWYN, son and heir of Edward B, of Didlebury, Salop, Esq
,,	,,	THOMAS COOTE, son of Charles C, of Castle Coote, Queen's co, Knight and
,,	,,	BARTHOLOMEW BEALE, son of Bartholomew B, of Gray's Inn, Esq. [Baronet
,,	,,	JOHN HARRISON, son and heir of John H, of Scarborough, co York, gent
,,	,,	WILLIAM DRYVER, son and heir of Richard D, late of Wonton, co Hereford, gent, deceased [Derby, gent
,,	,,	ROBERT HARDIE (*alias* Harding), son of Nicholas H, of King's Newton, co

folio 960.

July 23.		RICHARD ADDAMS, second son of Thomas A, of St Leonards, Eastcheap, Esq
Aug 13.		Captain JOHN BOND
,,	,,	EDWARD MERIDALE, of London, gent
,,	,,	HENRY JENKINS, son of Henry J, late of Grimston, co. York, Knight [Middlesex
,,	,,	JOHN PULFORD, second son of Richard P, Esq, of Tottenham High Cross,
,,	,,	VALENTINE BROWNE, son and heir of John B, of East Kirby, co Lincoln, Knight [Lincoln, gent
,,	,,	ROBERT BROXHOLME, son and heir of William B, of Reepham, co
,,	,,	JAMES ASHTON, son and heir of Peter A, of Grantham, co Lincoln, Esq
,,	,,	JOHN BRITTEN, son and heir of Thomas B, of Hadley, Suffolk, gent
,,	,,	SANDFORD NEVILLE, son and heir of Francis N, of Chevet, co York, Esq [this Inn
,,	,,	CORNELIUS BURTON, son and heir of Andrew B, Esq, one of the Fellows of

folio 961.

,,	,,	EDWARD SHEE, son and heir of Peter S, of Kilkenny, Esq
,,	,,	THOMAS BUTTON, son and heir of Robert B, of Worlton, co Glamorgan, Esq
,,	,,	HUMPHREY LOWE, son of Humphrey L, of South Mills, Beds, Esq
,,	,,	RALPH ASHTON, son and heir of Ralph A, of Midleton, co Lancaster, Esq.
,,	,,	WILLIAM QUADRING, son and heir of William Q., of Burgh-in-le-Marsh, co Lincoln, Knight [(Monoquell), co Tipperary, Esq
,,	,,	THERLOGH (Terence) MAGRATH, son and heir of John M, of Mocoil
,,	,,	WALTER PRINCE, son and heir of Richard P, of Shrewsbury, Knight
,,	,,	NATHAN RICH, son and heir of Robert R., late of Felstead, Essex, Esq, deceased [Knight.
,,	,,	CHRISTOPHER LISTER, son of William L., of Thornton-in-Craven, co York,
,,	,,	ROBERT LEGARD, fourth son of Robert L, of Anlaby, co Kingston-upon-Hull,
,,	,,	GEORGE NORBURY, son and heir of John N, of Gray's Inn, Esq. [Esq.

folio 962

Nov 2		EDMUND GODDARD, son of Thomas G, of Swindon, Wilts. [Leicester, Esq
,,	,,	THOMAS DISNEY, son and heir of Thomas D, of Wykin, parish of Hinckley, co
,,	,	WILLIAM WINBON, son and heir of Robert W, of the city of Bristol, gent

1639   folio 962—(continued)

Nov 2   CHRISTOPHER DAWNEY, son and heir of John D , late of Wormsley, co York,
            Esq , deceased   [Chelmsford, Essex, gent.

,,   ,,   ANTHONY KNIGHTBRIDGE, from Staple Inn, son and heir of John K , of

,,   ,,   MARK WISEMAN, from Staple Inn, son and heir of Richard W , of Wig-
                                                        [borough, Essex, gent.

,,   ,,   EDWARD BEWSEY, son and heir of Edward B , of Braintree, Essex, S.T P.

,,   ,,   ROBERT PICKERING, son and heir of John P., of Walford, co Chester, gent

,,   ,,   EDWARD KELKE, son and heir of Edward K , of Sandwich, Kent gent

,,   ,,   EDMUND GAMAGE, second son of Edward G , of Newcastle, co Glamorgan,
                                                        [gent , deceased.

,,   ,,   WILLIAM INGILBY, son and heir of William I , of Ripley, co. York, Esq

                                   folio 963
                                                        [perary, Esq
,,   18   RICHARD PURSELL, son and heir of Theobald P., of Loughmcugh, co Tip-

,,   ,,   JOHN RASHLEIGH, son and heir of Robert R., of Combe, co Cornwall, Esq.

,,   ,,   WILLIAM ARMINE, son and heir of William A , of Osgodby, co Lincoln, Esq

,,   ,,   THEOPHILUS ARMINE, second son of William A , Esq

,,   ,,   MICHAEL ARMINE, third son of William A , Esq   [Lincoln, Esq , deceased

,,   ,,   BRAMPTON FEARNE, son and heir of Thomas F , late of South Reston, co

,,   ,,   WILLIAM PERCIVAL, third son of Thomas P , of Halton, co Chester, gent.

,,   ,,   RICHARD BLACKWELL, son of Robert B , of Bushey, Herts, Esq   [ton, Esq

,,   ,,   RICHARD WALKER, son and heir of Rowland W , of Hoothorpe, co Northamp-

,,   ,,   JOHN FRANK, son and heir of Richard F , of Campsall, co York, gent

,,   ,,   FRANCIS BERKELEY, son and heir of William B , of Wormley, Salop.

,,   ,,   HENRY LITTLE, second son of Thomas L., of the city of Dublin, Esq

,,   ,,   JOHN SKRYMSHER, son and heir of John S , of Norbury, co Stafford, Esq.

,,   ,,   ROBERT FILMER, second son of Robert F , of East Sutton, Kent, Knight

1639-40   folio 964.

Jan 23   ROGER GARDNER, son and heir of Roger G , of St Giles, Cripplegate, Esq

,,   ,,   HUGH O'RORKE, son and heir of Bryan O'R , of Munterchenny, co Leitrim

,,   ,,   RICHARD BERNEY, second son of Richard B , of Parkhall-in-Redham, Norfolk,
                                                        [Baronet

,,   ,,   MICHAEL WARTON, son and heir of Michael W , of Beverley, co (York), Esq.

,,   ,,   TIMOTHY DODSWORTH, son of John D , of Thornton Watlass, co. York, gent.

,,   ,,   ANTHONY BYERLEY, son and heir of Christopher B , of Middridge Grange, co
                                                        [Durham, Esq

Feb 5   JOHN HEWORTH, son of Richard H , late of Hensam, co York, gent , deceased

,,   ,,   HATTON COURTNEY, son of Edward C , late of Trethurffe, co. Cornwall, Esq ,
            deceased.   [lingham Suffolk, gent.

,,   ,,   THOMAS ALEXANDER, from Staple Inn, son and heir of Thomas A , of Fram-

,,   ,,   EDWARD BORRETT, son and heir of Edward B , of Stradbrook, Suffolk, gent

                                   folio 965.

,,   27   CHARLES (WEST), Lord LE WARR

,,   ,,   ROBERT THORNES, son and heir of Richard T , now reader

1639-40.		**folio 965—**(*continued*).
Feb. 27.		RICHARD RIDLEY, son and heir of Richard R., of Bowldings, Salop, gent.
„	„	THOMAS WISE, son of Thomas W., late of Bardsey, co York, gent , deceased
„	„	WILLIAM SMITH, son and heir of Edward S , of Snape, co Lancaster, gent.
„	„	MICHAEL WOOLVERSTON, son of Sampson W , late of Woodbridge, Suffolk, Esq , deceased. [Wilts, gent , deceased.
„	„	ROBERT PARHAM, son and heir of ——— P , late of Stratford-on-the-Oldcastle,
„	„	THOMAS LAWRENCE, son and heir of Thomas L., of the city of Lincoln, gent.
„	„	THOMAS MORTON, son and heir of Thomas M , of Wimbledon, Surrey, Knight.
„	„	LUKE WYVILL, son of John W., of Laybourne, co York, Esq. [gent.
„	„	CHARLES COLEMAN, son and heir of Charles C, of Fetter Lane, Holborn,
„	„	FRANCIS GOLDSMITH, son and heir of Francis G., of Coldharbor, London, gent

		folio 966 [Esq
„	„	WALTER RUMSEY, son and heir of Edward R , of Llanover, co Monmouth,
„	„	RICHARD LEWIS, of Llangattock, Crickhowell, co Brecon, Esq [Esq
„	„	RICHARD LEWIS, son and heir of Richard L , of Llangattock, Esq
„	„	JOHN DELHAY, of Alterynis, co Hereford, Esq
„	„	WILLIAM MORGAN, of Llanelly, co Brecon, gent
„	„	WILLIAM JONES, son and heir of John J , of Hardwicke, co Monmouth, gent
„	„	WILLIAM LLOYD, of Abergavenny, co Monmouth, gent
„	„	HENRY POWELL, of Crickhowell, co Brecon, gent
„	„	GEORGE PAYNE, son and heir of George P , of Brenchley, Kent, gent
„	„	EDWARD STANSBY, son of Robert S , of Michelldever, co Southampton, Esq
„	„	EDWARD FREEMAN, son and heir of Coningsby F , of Neene Sollers, Salop, Esq.
„	„	JOSEPH EVERARD, son and heir of Gabriel E , of ———, co Waterford
„	„	EDWARD SEDGWICKE, late of Barnard's Inn, son and heir of James S , of [Ongar, Essex, gent.

		folio 967. [gent.
„	„	THOMAS HUSBAND, son and heir of Thomas H., of East Somerton, Norfolk,
„	„	CHARLES HASTINGS, son and heir of George H , of St Bartholomew's, London, [Knight
„	„	BENJAMIN BILLINGSLEY, son of Francis B , of Abbot Ashley, Salop, Esq
„	„	MAURICE LEWIS, son and heir of John L , of Festiniog, co Merioneth, Esq
„	„	THOMAS PURCELL, son and heir of Pierce P , of Cwgh, co Limerick, Esq
„	„	WILLIAM JONES, son of Richard J , of Wimborne, Dorset, gent
„	„	WILLIAM BERMINGHAM, son of Walter B , of ———, co Kildare, Esq
„	„	ROBERT MICHELL, son and heir of Robert M , Deputy Town-clerk of London
„	„	PETER NUGENT, son of Thomas N , of Tredarth, co Meath, Esq.
„	„	WILLIAM FREEMAN, son and heir of Wm. F , of Blockley, co. Worcester, Esq
„	„	WALTER MORGAN, son and heir of James M , of Llangeney, co Brecon, gent
„	„	WILLIAM MORGAN, another son of James M , of Llangeney, co Brecon, gent
„	„	WILLIAM ALEE, son and heir of William A , of East Lexham, Norfolk, gent

		folio 968
„	„	BENJAMIN BILLINGSLEY, of Clifford's Inn, London, gent

1639-40		folio 968—(*continued*).
Feb	27	CHARLES MORGAN, son and heir of Edward M , of Llangattock Collening, [co Monmouth, gent
Mar	18	THOMAS HALFORD, second son of William H , of Welham, co Leicester, Esq
,,	,,	JOHN ANDERSON, son of Richard A , of Penley, Herts, Knight
,,	,,	THOMAS LEICESTER, son and heir of Peter L , of Tabley, Cheshire, Esq
,,	,,	THOMAS PAINE, from Barnard's Inn, son and heir of Thomas P , of Charlfield, Suffolk, gent [gent
,,	,,	EDMUND COTTON, son and heir of Edmund C , of St Mary's Bothaw, London,
,,	,,	ZOUCH BROCKMAN, second son of Henry B , of Birchborough, Kent, Esq
,,	,,	RICHARD HARMAN, son and heir of Richard H , of the city of Norwich, Esq
,,	,,	HENRY WILSON, son and heir of Thomas W , of Underley, Westmoreland, Esq
1640		folio 969.
April	4	WILLIAM SMITH, son and heir of Robert S , of Grisham, Norfolk, gent.
,,	,,	RICHARD POYNTZ, son and heir of James P , of ———, Essex, Knight
,,	5	CONYERS DARCY, son and heir of Conyers D , of Swillington, co York, Esq
,,	,,	THOMAS TURNER, from Barnard's Inn, son and heir of William T , late of [Thaxted, Essex, gent., deceased.
,,	,,	FRANCIS LOWE, son and heir of John L , of Hasland, co Derby, gent
May	7	EDWARD DEWE, son and heir of Richard D , of Harwell, Berks, gent
,,	,,	EDWARD PALMER, son and heir of Edward P., late of St. Lawrence-lane, [London, gent
,,	,,	THOMAS LISTER, son of Thomas L , late of Westby, co York, Esq , deceased
,,	,,	NORTON CURTIES, son and heir of George C., of Chart, by Sutton Valence, [Kent, Esq
,,	,,	JOHN WARD, son and heir of Henry W., of Rigmaden, Westmoreland, gent
,,	,,	JAMES BELLINGHAM, son and heir of Henry B , of Levins, Westmoreland, [Knight and Baronet
,,	,,	JOHN CONSTABLE, son and heir of John C., of Catfoss, co York, Esq
,,	,,	EDWARD SIMEONS, of St. Andrews, Holborn, gent
		folio 970
,,	13	THOMAS BACON, son and heir of Nathaniel B , of Friston, Suffolk, Esq
,,	,,	ALEXANDER BANASTER, son and heir of Richard B , of Okenbotham, co. Lancaster, gent [gent (admitted before)
,,	,,	WILLIAM KNIPE, son and heir of Anthony K , of Fairbanck, Westmoreland,
,,	,,	GEORGE WITHER, of Staple Inn, son of Henry W , of Hall, co Southampton,
,,	,,	WILLIAM TAINTER, son and heir of William T , of Rochford, Essex, gent [Esq
,,	,,	RANDLE WILBRAHAM, son and heir of Roger W , of Dorfold, Cheshire, Esq
,,	,,	RICHARD SHEE, son and heir of Richard S., of the city of Kilkenny, Esq
,,	,,	JOHN BROWNE, son and heir of Edmund B , of Stanford, co. Lincoln, gent
,,	,,	JOHN WOLSTENHOLME, son and heir of John W , of Nostell, co York, Knight
,,	,,	EDWARD LEGGE, son and heir of Edward L , late of St. Andrews, Holborn, [gent.
		folio 971
June	13	THOMAS SAVAGE, of Elmley Castle, co Worcester, Esq

1640   folio 971—(continued)

June 13   RICHARD ROBSON, son and heir of John R , clerk, one of the Prebendaries of
                                                                    [Durham

,,   ,,   RICHARD KIRKBY, son and heir of Roger K., of Kirkby, co Lancaster, Esq

,,   ,,   THOMAS CATERALL, son and heir of Peter C., of Crooke, co Lancaster, gent.

,,   ,,   JOHN SANDERS, son and heir of Thomas S , of Beechwood, parish of Flamsted,

,,   ,,   JOHN LEGATE, son and heir of John L., of Rampton, Notts, gent [Herts, Esq

,,   ,,   JAMES HAWKINS, son of James H , late of Clifford's Inn, gent

,,   ,,   WILLIAM JONES, son and heir of John J , of Hardwick, co Monmouth, gent

,,   26. WALTER ROBERTS, of Glassenbury, Knight and Baronet

,,   ,,   WILLIAM SOAME, son and heir of Thomas S , Esq , Alderman of London.

,,   ,,   THOMAS GIBBON, son and heir of Thomas G , of Westcliff, Dover, Kent, gent

,,   ,,   WILLIAM ORFEUR, son and heir of William O , of High Close, Cumberland,
                                                                    [Esq

                                 folio 972.   [deceased

July 15. GEORGE BERTRAM, son of Robert B , late of Newcastle-on-Tyne, gent ,

,,   ,,   THOMAS CHAMBERLAINE, of Broadway, co Worcester, gent

,,   ,,   ANTHONY AUCHER, son and heir of Edwin A , of Wilesby, Kent, Esq

,,   ,,   ARTHUR RYTHE, of St Martins-in-the-Fields, gent

,,   ,,   ANTHONY PALMER, son of Anthony P , of Antonines, Kent, Knight, deceased.

,,   31   FRANCIS FARNHAM, of Quorndon, co Leicester, son of Adrian F , late of
             Quorndon, Esq., deceased   [Cork, Esq , deceased.

Aug 5   RANDOLPH (Randal?) CLAYTON, son of Laurence C , late of Mallow, co

,,   ,,   CHARLES BYERLEY, second son of William B., of Belgrave, co Leicester, Esq

,,   ,,   JOHN CLAXTON, son and heir of John C , of Livermere Magna, Suffolk, Esq

,,   ,,   HAMOND CLAXTON, second son of John C , Esq   [gent.

,,   ,,   RICHARD BROWNE, second son of Richard B , late of St Andrews, Holborn,

,,   ,,   ARTHUR KNIGHT, son and heir of Arthur K , of Covent Garden, Esq

                                 folio 973

,,   14   JOHN HINDMARSH, son and heir of Richard H , of Walsend, co Durham, gent

,,   ,,   GEOFFREY SHAKERLEY, of Shakerley, co Lancaster, Esq   [gent

,,   ,,   FRANCIS BAINBRIDGE, son and heir of Francis B , of Newcastle-on-Tyne,

,,   ,,   THOMAS BELLOT, third son of John B , of Morton, Cheshire, Esq   [Knight.

,,   ,,   CHARLES LANDEN, son and heir of Philip L , late of Hundleby, co. Lincoln,

,,   ,,   AUDLEY LADD (alias Baker), son and heir of Robert L , of Terrington,
             Norfolk, Esq   [Baronet, deceased

,,   ,,   HENRY BAKER, second son of Henry B , late of Sissinghurst, Kent, Knight and

,,   ,,   JAMES APSLEY, late of Staple Inn, gent

,,   ,,   JOHN BARKER, son of John B , late of St. Michaels, Cornhill, gent.

,,   ,,   THOMAS BARGRAVE, son and heir of Isaac B , of Eythorn, Kent, S T P ,
                                                          [Dean of Canterbury

,,   ,,   ROBERT BARGRAVE, another son of Isaac B , Dean of Canterbury.

,,   ,,   RICHARD GLYD, son and heir of Richard G., of Blechingley, Surrey, gent

,,   ,,   JOHN SALUSBURY, son and heir of John S., of Bochegraige, co Flint, Esq.

1640		folio 973—(continued)
Aug	14.	FRANCIS BICKLEY, son and heir of Francis B , of the city of London, Esq
,,	,,	FRANCIS LADE, son of Robert L , Esq , now reader, " sine fine."

folio 974.

,,	,,	ROBERT TIGHE, son of William T , of Deeping, co Northampton, gent
,,	,,	THOMAS GOODERE, son and heir of Henry G , of Collingham, Notts, Esq , [deceased
Sept	5	HENRY CUST, son and heir of John C , of Pinchbecke, co Lincoln, gent
,,	,,	EDWARD BARHAM, son and heir of Robert B , of St Andrews, Holborn, Esq
,,	,,	RICHARD ANDERTON, son and heir of Richard A , of Hawton, co Lancaster,
,,	,,	WALTER HARRIS, son of Richard H , of Cruckton, Salop, Esq [gent
Oct	2	THOMAS MANWARING, son and heir of Roger, Bishop of St David s
,,	,,	PATRICK KEARNEY, son and heir of James K , of the city of Cork, Esq [gent
,,	,,	PATRICK KEARNEY, son and heir of Nicholas K , of Kilmallock, co Limerick,
,,	,,	JOHN COTTON, son and heir of John C , of St Andrews, Holborn, Knight
,,	,,	ABRAHAM SIMON, son of Peter S , of Downe, Kent

folio 975. [deceased

,,	20	TOBIAS MATTHEWS, son of George M , of Thurleigh, co. Tipperary, Esq ,
,,	,,	WILLIAM GREGORY, of Fownhope, co. Hereford (in lieu of " Salop," erased), gent
,,	,,	HENRY WYAT, son and heir of Francis W., of Boxley Abbey, Kent, Knight
Nov	1	JOHN OSBALDESTON, of Whalley, co Lancaster, gent.
,,	,,	THOMAS WEAVER, of Staple Inn, son and heir of Edmund W , late of London, deceased [gent , deceased
,,	,,	ISAAC SMITH, son and heir of Isaac S , late of Padleyfield Hall, co. Derby,
,,	,,	ROBERT BUTLER, son and heir of Robert B , of Southwell, Notts, gent
,,	,,	JOHN BINGE, son of Henry B , of Granchester, co Cambridge, Serjeant-at-Law
,,	,,	PHILIP TURNOR, son of John T , late of Garton, co York, gent , deceased
,,	,,	THOMAS HOLLYMAN, gent , of Cuddington, Bucks, son of Francis H., Esq , [of same

folio 976. [gent, deceased.

,,	14	JULIUS WESTWOOD, son of Humphrey W , late of St Botolphs, Aldersgate,
,,	,,	GODFREY CLARKE, son and heir of Gilbert C , of Somersall, co Derby, Esq
,,	20	LANCELOT LOVELACE, son and heir of Francis L , of this Inn, Esq
Dec	3	HENRY HARRINGTON, son of William H , late of Witham-on-the-hill, co [Lincoln, Esq
,,	,,	WILLIAM MORGAN, son of Thomas M , of Ruperra, co Glamorgan, Knight
,,	,,	EDMUND BERRY GODFREY, son of Thomas G , of Sellinge, near Monk's [Horton, Kent, Esq.
1640-1		
Jan	29.	JOHN SADLIER, of Warwick, gent
,,	,,	THOMAS PURY, son and heir of Thomas P , of the city of Gloucester, gent
,,	,,	THOMAS GOODWYN, son and heir of Ambrose G , of Stoneham, Suffolk, Esq
,,	,,	JOHN CLENCH, son and heir of Almet C , of Great Beling, Suffolk, Esq
,,	,,	WILLIAM HARRINGTON, son and heir of Henry H , of St Giles-in-the-Fields, [Esq , deceased

1640-1		folio 977

Jan 29 JOHN HOLLAND, son and heir of Ralph H , of Tarvine, Cheshire, gent

,, ,, RICHARD SALTONSTALL, son and heir of Richard S , of South Ockendon, Essex, Knight   [Suffolk

Feb 2 JOHN GODBOLD, son and heir of John G , Serjeant-at-Law, of Southland,

,, ,, THOMAS GODBOLD, second son of John G , Serjeant-at-Law, of Southland, Suffolk   [deceased

,, ,, WILLIAM GODBOLD, son and heir of Thomas G , of Mendham, Suffolk, gent ,

,, ,, THOMAS COALE, son and heir of Thomas C , of Liss, co Southampton, Esq

,, ,, PHILIP PARKER, son and heir of Philip P , of Erwarton, Suffolk, Knight

,, 10 WILLIAM TROLLOPE, son and heir of Thomas T , of Caswicke, co Lincoln, Esq.

,, ,, WILLIAM BLAKISTONE, of ———, co Durham, Esq

,, ,, GEORGE WATSON, son of Richard W , of St Andrews, Holborn, gent

,, ,, GEORGE CROXTON, son of Thomas C , of Ravenscroft, Cheshire, Esq

folio 978.

,, 20 JAMES RUSSELL, son of Paul R , of Hereford, gent

,, ,, RICHARD WARSE, of Whickenby, co Lincoln, gent

,, ,, FRANCIS LECHE, son of John L , late of the city of Chester, gent

,, ,, SAMUEL HANCH, son and heir of Robert H , of Allhallows Wall, London, gent

,, 22 JOHN BOURNE, son of John B., late of Streat, co Somerset, Esq., deceased.

,, ,, JOHN BROUGHTON, son and heir of John B , of Broughton, co Flint, Esq

,, ,, ROWLAND WHITEHALL, son and heir of Rowland W , of Whitchurch, Salop,

,, ,, JOHN JEFFERY, son and heir of Simon J , of Bedfield, Suffolk, gent   [Esq

,, ,, GEORGE BEESLOW, son and heir of Peter B , of Gravesend, Kent, Esq

,, ,, JOHN RUSSELL, son and heir of Robert R , of Blackney, Norfolk, gent

,, ,, WILLIAM SCROGGS, of Stifford, Essex, gent

,, ,, ROBERT FISHBORNE, son and heir of John F , of Winesword, Berks, gent.

,, ,, SAMUEL CALCOTT, son and heir of Roger C , of London, gent

folio 979.

Mar. 16 THOMAS, Lord GREY, of Groby, son and heir of Henry, Earl of Stamford.

,, ,, JOHN BELLASIS, Esq , second son of Thomas, Lord Falconbridge, Baron of Yarm

,, ,, ARTHUR JONES, son and heir of Viscount Ranelagh, in Ireland   [Knight

,, ,, MICHAEL WENTWORTH, son and heir of George W , of Woolley, co York,

,, ,, WILLIAM BELT, son and heir of William B , of the city of York, Knight.

,, ,, LEONARD BELT, Esq , son and heir of Robert B , of the city of York, Knight.

,, ,, GEORGE BROCKES, son of Thomas B , of the city of Oxford, gent.

,, ,, WILLIAM WIDDRINGTON son and heir of William W., of Widdrington, North-
[umberland, Knight.

,, ,, RALPH WIDDRINGTON, son and heir of Henry W , late of Colwell, North-
[umberland, gent , deceased.

,, ,, THOMAS WIDDRINGTON, son and heir of Henry W , of Blackheddon, North-
[umberland, gent., who is brother to William W , now reader

,, ,, RALPH WIDDRINGTON, Fellow of Christ's College, Cambridge, and brother to
[William W , now reader

1640-1   folio 979—(continued)

Mar 16   CUTHBERT PEPPER, son and heir of Cuthbert P , of Farrington Hall, co.
  ,,   ,, JOHN SMITH, of the city of Oxford, gent   [Durham, Esq

                                      folio 980

  ,,   ,, THOMAS HARRISON, son and heir of Thomas H , of the city of York, Knight
  ,,   ,, RICHARD HUTTON, son and heir of Richard H , of Gouldsborough, co York,
           Knight, the son and heir of Richard H , Knight, one of the Judges of the
           Court of King's Bench.   [land, Baronet.
  ,,   ,, RICHARD MUSGRAVE, son and heir of Philip M , of Hartley Castle, Westmore-
  ,,   ,, CHRISTOPHER NEVILE, son and heir of Gervase N , of Awber, co. Lincoln,
                                                                    [Knight.
  ,,   ,, JOHN DAWNAY, second son of John D., late of Cowick, co York, deceased
  ,,   ,, ROBERT SHAFTO, son and heir of Mark S , of Gray's Inn, Esq
  ,,   ,, CHARLES PELHAM, son of William P , of Brockelsby, co Lincoln, Knight
  ,,   ,, HENRY FAIRFAX, son and heir of Henry F , of Newton Kyme, co York, clerk
  ,,   ,, THOMAS FAIRFAX, son and heir of Charles F , of Menston, co York, Esq
  ,,   ,, THOMAS WIDDRINGTON, son and heir of Thomas W , Knight, now reader.
  ,,   ,, LEONARD WASTELL, son and heir of John W , of Scorton, co York, Esq [Esq
  ,,   ,, FRANCIS BRATHWAYTE, fifth son of Gawin B , of Ambleside, Westmoreland,
  ,,   18 CHARLES (CAVENDISH), Lord MANSFIELD, son and heir of William, Earl of
                                                                    [Newcastle
  ,,   ,, FRANCIS BURWELL, son and heir of Francis B , of Sudborne, Suffolk, Esq

                                      folio 981

  ,,   ,, JOHN SLEIGH, Alderman of Berwick-upon-Tweed.
  ,,   ,, DUDLEY DIGGS, son of Dudley D , Knight, Master of the Rolls, deceased
  ,,   ,, JOHN DAVVES, son and heir of John D , of Middleton, Salop, Esq
  ,,   ,, HENRY STEBBING, son and heir of Henry S , of Brandeston, Suffolk, gent
  ,,   ,, MARMADUKE PECKET, second son of Marmaduke P , of London, gent.
  ,,   ,, FRANCIS CARNABY, son of William C , of Farnham, Northumberland, Esq ,
  ,,   ,, HENRY GRIFFITH, of Agnes Burton, co York, Baronet   [deceased
  ,,   ,, FRANCIS WORTLEY, Esq , son and heir of Francis W , of Wortley, co. York,
           Knight and Baronet   [co York, Knight
  ,,   ,, BARRINGTON BOURCHIER, son and heir of John B , of Benningtboro' Grange,
  ,,   ,, WILLIAM BOURCHIER, second son of John B , Knight, of Benningboro' Grange,
           co York   [Knight
  ,,   ,, JOHN BOURCHIER, third son of John B , of Benningboro' Grange, co York,
  ,,   ,, FRANCIS STANTON, son and heir of Robert S , of Birchmore, Beds, Esq.
  ,,   ,, EDWARD REPINGTON, son and heir of John R , of Amington, co Warwick,
  ,,   ,, ROBERT STRICKLAND, of Thornton Briggs, co York, Esq   [Knight
  ,,   ,, RICHARD BARWIS, of Islekirk, Cumberland, Esq.
  ,,   ,, EDWARD CROFTES, of Kirklington, co York, gent
  ,,   ,, WALTER STRICKLAND, of Sizergh, Westmoreland, Esq

                                      folio 982   [land, Esq , deceased

  ,,   21 ROBERT MIDLETON, son and heir of Charles M , of Belsay Castle, Westmore-

1640-1.   folio 982—(*continued*).

Mar. 21.   CHARLES FAIRFAX, son of Ferdinand, Lord Fairfax, Baron of Cameron

,,   ,,   ROGER DODSWORTH, of Longton, co. Lancaster, Esq

,,   ,,   RICHARD DARLEY, son and heir of Henry D , of Buttercrambe, co. York, Esq

,,   ,,   THOMAS CREW, son and heir of John C , of Steyne, co Northampton, Esq

,,   ,,   GODFREY RHODES, son and heir of Edward R , of Houghton, co. York, Knight

,,   ,,   WILLIAM INGRAM, son and heir of Arthur I , of the county of York, gent

,,   ,,   WILLIAM MASON, son and heir of William M , of Gray's Inn, Esq

,,   ,,   ROBERT GRIFFITH, fourth son of George William G , of Beny Benlegge, co.

,,   ,,   JOHN BROWNE, of St. Martins-in-the-Fields, Middlesex, gent   [Pembroke, gent.

,,   ,,   WILLIAM HOWARD (Most Hon), of Naworth Castle, Knight

,,   ,,   EDWARD WILSON, son and heir of (Dionysius) Denis W , late of Pegsworth, Northumberland, gent   [London, gent

,,   ,,   ROBERT YOWARD, son and heir of Robert Y , of St. Dunstans in Fleet Street,

folio 983

,,   ,,   ABRAHAM NELSON, son and heir of William N , of St Dunstans-in-the-West,

,,   ,,   THOMAS PINDAR, of St Dunstans-in-the-West, gent   [gent

,,   ,,   —————— METCALFE, son and heir of Mark M , of the city of York, Esq

,,   ,,   ROBERT BARWICK, son and heir of Robert B , of the city of York, Esq

,,   ,,   JOSEPH SLINGER, of the city of York, gent

,,   ,,   WILLIAM BRAYNE, son and heir of Thomas B , of Whixall, Salop, gent.   [gent

,,   ,,   OLIVER PAMPLIN, gent , son and heir of Thomas P , of Ely, co Cambridge,

,,   ,,   EDWARD PROGER, son and heir of Lewis P , of Guernevalde, co Brecon, Esq

,,   ,,   JOHN JEFFEREY, son and heir of Geoffrey J , of Albercunricke, co Brecon, Esq.   [Canterbury, Kent, gent

,,   ,,   HUMPHREY ROSE, from Barnard's Inn, son and heir of Christopher R , of

,,   ,,   JOHN SAUTHEY, second son of Robert S , of Burton, co Denbigh, gent

,,   ,,   SIMON VAUGHAN, son and heir of Robert V , of Ludlow, Salop, gent

,,   ,,   GEORGE NEVILLE, second son of George N , of Awber, co Lincoln, Esq

,,   ,,   CHARLES ALLANSON, son and heir of William A , of the city of York, Knight

folio 984.

,,   ,,   THOMAS CROFT, son and heir of Christopher C , Lord Mayor of York

,,   ,,   THOMAS IBSON, son and heir of John I , of the city of York, gent

,,   ,,   THOMAS MYERS, Junior, of Allerthorpe, co York, gent

,,   ,,   ROGER JAQUES, son and heir of Roger J , of the city of York, Knight

,,   ,,   (WILLIAM) HEDLAM, second son of Leonard H , of the city of York, gent

,,   ,,   JOHN JACKSON, of St Martins in-the-Fields, Middlesex, clerk

,,   ,,   ROBERT ROBOTHAM, of Skipton, co York, Esq   [co. Stafford, gent

,,   ,,   CAWARDEN CHADWICK, son and heir of Lewis C , of Mareyson Ridware,

,,   ,,   ROBERT HILTON, son and heir of Thomas H , of Marton, Westmoreland, gent

,,   ,,   THOMAS HILTON, second son of Thomas H , of Marton, Westmoreland, gent

,,   ,,   RICHARD HUTTON, son and heir of Thomas H , of Gray's Inn, Esq

,,   ,,   JAMES SHAWE, son of James S., of Tregare, co Monmouth, gent

,,   ,,   JOHN WARDELL, son and heir of John W , of Cottingham, co York, gent

1640-1.   folio 984—(continued)
Mar 21   LEONARD PINCKNEY, of St Clement Danes, Middlesex, gent.
  „   „   THOMAS ROWE, son and heir of Francis R , of London, gent.

                              folio 985   [berland, Knight.
  „   „   HENRY WIDDRINGTON, second son of William W , of Widdrington, Northum-
1641
May 14   PHILIP TURNER, son of John T , of Garton, co York, gent , deceased
                                                            [deceased
  „   „   EDWARD WIFFIN, son and heir of David W., of Haverall, Suffolk, gent ,
  „   22   GASCOYNE WELDE, son of Mathew W., of Tasborough, Norfolk, gent
                                                       [Esq , deceased
  „   „   THOMAS BROWNE, son and heir of Gamaliel B , of Boston, co Lincoln,
  „   „   GEORGE STANHOPE, third son of Philip, Earl of Chesterfield, of Bretby, co Derby
  „   26.   THOMAS EUEN, son and heir of Henry E , of Marlsford, Suffolk
  „   „   ROWLAND ST JOHN, son of John St. J , of Cole Orton, co Leicester, Esq.
                                                       [Esq , deceased
June 2.   JOHN FINGLASSE, son and heir of Richard F , of West Spelston, co Dublin,
  „   „   JOHN ARTHUR, son and heir of Robert A , of Skinner-rowe, city of Dublin, Esq
  „   „   GEORGE WHITE, son and heir of Rowland W , of Newry, co Down, gent
                              folio 986
  „   „   JOHN CUSACKE, son and heir of Richard C., of Trevott, co Meath, Esq.
  „   „   JOHN CHARLETT, son of John C , of Hill, co Worcester, Esq deceased. [Esq
  „   „   CHRISTOPHER EARLE, son and heir of Christopher E , of ———, co Dorset,
  „   „   EDWARD NEWMAN, son of Edward N , of Frank(s)worth, Hunts, gent , deceased
  „   „   JOHN RAVEN, son of William R , of Elworth, co Chester, gent
  „   28   GILBERT DETHICKE, son of Henry D , of Poplar, Middlesex, Esq , deceased
                                                            [gent
  „   „   EDWARD WILSON, son and heir of Thomas W , of Heversham, Westmoreland,
  „   „   ROGER FENWICK, third son of William F , of Stanton, Northumberland, Esq
  „   „   THOMAS WINSTON, son and heir of John W , of Cannons Ashby, co North-
           ampton, Esq.   [Esq
July 1   THOMAS SNAGGE, son and heir of Thomas S , of Marston Mortayne, Beds,
  „   „   JOHN HAWES, son and heir of Edward H , of Stoke Albany, co Northampton,
  „   „   CLINTON FYNES, son of Henry F , of ———, co Lincoln, Knight   [gent
                              folio 987.
  „   7   RICHARD SANDYS, son of Edward S., of Northborne, Kent, Knight.
  „   „   FRANCIS NICCOLSON, son of Francis N , of Chappell, Essex, gent.
  „   „   ROBERT WATERS, son and heir of Christopher W., of Cundall, co York, gent
  „   „   WILLIAM SMITH, son and heir of Henry S., of Perivale, Middlesex, gent
  „   „   WILLIAM BETTENHAM, son of John B., of Pluckley, Kent, Esq
  „   „   LEWIS STOCKETT, son and heir of Thomas S , of Beaksbourne, Kent, Esq
  „   „   THOMAS FLETCHER, son and heir of Thomas F , of Winder, co Lanc , gent.
  „   „   RICHARD FRERE, son and heir of Anthony F., of Mulbarton, Norfolk, clerk
  „   „   RICHARD LEEKE, son and heir of William L., of this Inn, Esq

1641		folio 987—(continued) [land, Esq
July	7	JOHN PICKERING, son and heir of Thomas P., of Ravensthwaite, Westmore-
,,	12	RICHARD BOYLE, son of Richard B., Archbishop of Tuam, in Connaught
,,	,,	DAVID MORGAN, son of Morgan Lewis, of Abergwilly, co Carmarthen, gent

folio 988.   [co. York, Esq.

,,	,,	RICHARD MALEVERER, son and heir of Thomas M., of Allerton Maleverer,
		[merchant
,,	,,	CORNELIUS HOOKER, son and heir of Edward H., of St Mary-at-Hill, London,
Aug	11	THOMAS DENION, son and heir of Thomas D., of Warnell, Cumberland
,,	,,	WILLIAM WISE, youngest son of Thomas W., of Bardsey, co York, gent
,,	,,	PHILIP TUBBING, son of William T., gent., of Hindringham, Norfolk
,,	,,	RICHARD BOSTOCK, son of John B., of Tatnall, co. Chester, Esq
,,	,,	ROBERT BIRD, son and heir of John B., of Luton, Beds, clerk. [Esq
,,	,,	NICHOLAS TERRELL, son and heir of George T., of St Edmundsbury, Suffolk,
,,	,,	THOMAS YONGE, son of George Y., late of North Petherton, co Somerset,
		[gent., deceased
,,	,,	GEORGE WALKER, son of Matthew W., of Doncaster, co York, gent
,,	,,	EDWARD PERRY, son of Richard P., of Minehead, co Somerset, gent
,,	,,	THOMAS FOWLER, of Staple Inn, son of Robert F., of Fowler Hill, parish of
		[Garstang, co Lancaster, gent

folio 989.

,,	,,	JOHN BRITTON, son of James B., of Kellosty, co. Tipperary, gent
,,	,,	THOMAS HOLDER, son of ——— H., of Southwell, Notts, gent., deceased.
,,	,,	THOMAS WATTS, son of John W., of Burnam, Notts, gent., deceased [Esq
,,	,,	WILLIAM BASSETT, son and heir of Richard B., of Fishward, co Glamorgan,
,,	,,	RALPH MORRIS, son and heir of Thomas M., of Woodford, Essex, Esq.
,,	,,	THOMAS LLOYD, son of Edward L., of Treyn-Bridd, co Flint, gent
,,	,,	ROBERT NEAVE, son of William N., of Burnham Norton, Norfolk, gent
,,	,,	GEORGE RUMSEY, son of Walter R., Esq., of this Inn
,,	,,	WILLIAM WILLIAMS, son of William W., of St. Nicholas, co Glamorgan, gent
,,	,,	EDWARD DRAKE, son of Thomas D., of Ingoldsthorpe, Norfolk, gent
,,	,,	THOMAS BUTLER, son of John B., of Hockerton, Notts, gent.
,,	,,	CHARLES MORGAN, son and heir of Edward M., of Llangattock Glenning, co
		[Monmouth, gent

folio 990

,,	,,	ANTHONY HINTON, son and heir of Anthony H., Knight
,,	14	JOHN BEARCROFT, son and heir of Philip B., of Hanbury, co Worcester, Esq
,,	,,	EDMOND TOOKE, son and heir of Nicholas T., of Dartford, Kent, Esq
,,	,,	THOMAS YARBURGH, son of Harsey Y., late of Willoughby, Notts, gent,
,,	,,	THOMAS MILWARD, of St Martins-in-the-Fields, Middlesex, gent [deceased
,,	,,	THOMAS KEBLE, son and heir of Thomas K., of Newton, Suffolk, gent
Nov	1.	EDWARD DICCONSON, son of William D., of Eccleston-by-Crofton, co Lan-
,,	,,	SAMUEL KELLO, clerk [caster, gent
,,	,,	EDWARD GULSTON, son of John G., Esq

1641		folio 990—*(continued)*
Nov	2	WILLIAM HARBORNE, son of John H , of Tackley, Oxon, Esq
,,	,,	SAMPSON HARBORNE, another son of John H , of Tackley, Oxon, Esq
,,	,,	PATRICK AILWARD, son and heir of Patrick A , of Waterford, Esq

folio 991.

,,	15	RICHARD LANGLIE, son and heir of Richard L , of Millington, co York, Esq.
,,	,,	THOMAS GLYN, *(sic)* son of Thomas Glyd, *(sic)* of Nantley, co. Carnarvon
,,	18	HENRY LEMING, second son of John L , of Colchester, Essex, gent.
,,	,,	DOW HODGES, second son of Anthony H , of Brodwell, co Gloucester, gent
,,	,,	JUSTINIAN LEWIN, D C L , one of the Masters in Chancery
,,	26	RICHARD ANWYLL, son and heir of Richard A , of Hanodwryd, parish of [Penmachno, co Carnarvon, gent
,,	,,	ROBERT HEWETT, son of John H , of Waresley, Hunts, Knight and Baronet.
,,	25	EDWARD RIGBY, son of Alexander R , of Preston, co Lancaster, Esq. [gent
,,	,,	ALEXANDER MAUDISLEY, son and heir of Robert M , of Maudisley, co Lancaster,
,,	,,	WILLIAM PARKER, son and heir of ——— P., of the city of York, gent
,,	,,	THOMAS KECK, son of Nicholas K., of Bredmarston, co Gloucester, gent
Dec.	4	STEPHEN SOAMES, son and heir of Thomas S , Knight and Alderman of London
,,	,,	THOMAS EDWARDS, son and heir of Evan E , of Rywell, co Flint, Esq

folio 992

,,	,,	THOMAS SYMONDS, son and heir of Thomas S , of the city of Winchester, gent
,,	,,	GEORGE HALFIELD, of Maydbury, Beds, gent
,,	,,	THOMAS BOLD, second son of William B , of Nurrested, co Southampton, Esq
,,	,,	JAMES MOYSER, son and heir of Thomas M , of Lockington, co York, Esq
,,	,,	FRANCIS MOYSER, second son of Thomas M , of Lockington, co York, Esq
,,	,,	JOHN SNEYD, of Longdon, co Stafford, gent
1641-2		
Jan	29	JOHN ALLEYN, son of Giles A , of Waltham Parva, Essex, clerk [co York
Feb	2	ROBERT BAYNES, son and heir of Ralph B , of Mewith, parish of Bentham,
,,	9	WILLIAM WILFORD, son of Thomas W , of Ilding, Kent, Knight
,,	,,	THOMAS TALBOTT, son of Clere T , D C L , of Dunstone, Norfolk, Esq

folio 993.

,,	,,	THOMAS MORSE, son and heir of Francis M , of Wrentham, Suffolk, gent
,,	,,	THOMAS ATKINSON, late of Staple Inn, son of Charles A , of Beckhay, co York, Esq [deceased.
,,	,,	JOHN LOCKTON, son and heir of Francis L , of Swinstead, co Lincoln, Esq ,
,,	,,	JOHN LAMPLUGH, of Lamplugh, Cumberland, Esq
,,	,,	ROBERT WOOD, of Kingston-on-Thames, Surrey, Esq
,,	,,	JOHN FOWLE, son and heir of John F , of ———, Kent, Knight
,,	,,	HENRY FIENNES, son of Edward F , *alias* Clinton, of Sturton, co Lincoln, Knight [gent , deceased
,	,,	THOMAS ROSENDALE, son and heir of Thomas R , of Ashton Grange, Cheshire,
,,	12	HENRY FETHERSTONHAULGH, son and heir of Timothy F , of Kirkoswold, [Cumberland, Knight

1641-2.   folio 993—(*continued*)

Feb 12   JOHN BUCKE, son and heir of John B , of Fyley, co York, Knight   [Esq

„   „   WILLIAM CO(U)RTHOPE, gent , son and heir of Thomas C , of Studworth, Kent,

folio 994.
                                                                          [Esq

„   14   JAMES BELLINGHAM, son and heir of Alan B , of Gaythorne, Westmoreland,

„   „   RICHARD EGERTON, son and heir of ——— E , of Allerston, co York, Esq

„   18   THOMAS HUMPHREY, of Furnival's Inn, gent, son and heir of Charles H , of
                                              [Harleston, Suffolk, gent , " sine fine "

„   „   HENRY BRERETON, son and heir of ——— B., of Eglestone, Cheshire, Esq ,
                                                                          [deceased

„   „   WILLIAM COWLEY, son and heir of Thomas C , of ———, co. Chester, Esq

„   „   MICHAEL PENDLETON, son of Francis P , of St Peter's, city of London, Esq ,

„   „   CHARLES DOYLEY, son of Cope D , of Chiselhampton, Oxon, Knight [deceased

„   „   FRANCIS COCKE, son of ——— C , of Catherine Hall, co Cambridge, gent

„   „   JOHN CRAYNE, son of John C , of King's Lynn, Norfolk, Esq

„   „   WILLIAM BLOISE, son and heir of William B , of Grundisbury, Suffolk, Esq

„   „   JOHN NICHOLAS, LL D , son and heir of David N , of Llansamlet, co
                                                                     [Glamorgan, gent

folio 995

„   „   WILLIAM MORGAN, son and heir of Turberville M , of Lannaugh, co Mon-

„   „   FRANCIS MANLEY, of Wrexham, co. Denbigh, gent [mouth, gent , " sine fine "

„   „   THOMAS TOLL, son and heir of Thomas T , of King's Lynn, Norfolk, gent

„   „   JOHN VAUGHAN, son and heir of Richard V , of Court Deales, co Carmarthen,

„   „   THOMAS SHELLEY, son and heir of Thomas S , of Barton, Suffolk, D D   [Esq

„   „   EDWARD THAYER, son of Anthony T , of Stepney, Essex, Esq

„   „   JOHN LIGHTFOOT, eldest son of John L , one of the Fellows of this Inn

„   „   WILLIAM JONES, son and heir of Wythen J , of Trewythin, co Monmouth,

„   „   EDWARD JONES, son and heir of Gilbert J , of Gray's Inn, Esq   [Esq

„   „   GILBERT JONES, second son of Gilbert J , of Gray's Inn, Esq

„   „   LITTLETON JONES, third son of Gilbert J , of Gray's Inn, Esq

„   „   JOHN PURCELL, son and heir of James P , of Clone, co. Kilkenny, Esq

folio 996.

„   „   WILLIAM ELLIS, son and heir of William E., of Stradbroke, Suffolk, gent.

„   „   ROBERT BOOTH, son of Robert B , of Salford, co Lancaster, gent

„   „   PAUL PYNDAR, son and heir of Paul P., of London, Esq

„   „   GEORGE PUREFOY, son and heir of George P , of Belgrave, co Leicester, Esq.

„   „   ROBERT GOSTELOE, son and heir of Edmund G , of Hemingford Grays,
                                                                     [Hunts, gent

„   „   ROBERT PESCODE, son of John P., of Silksteed, co Southampton gent.

„   „   GEORGE METCALFE, son of Richard M , of North Allerton, co York, gent ,
                                                                          [deceased

„   „   GRIFFIN GLIN (Glyn), son of Thomas G , of Nantley, co Carnarvon, Esq

„   „   WILLIAM ADAMS, son and heir of William A , late of Owston, co York, Esq

1641-2		folio 997.
Feb 18		ARTHUR ROBERTS, son and heir of Hugh R , of St. Asaph, co Flint, gent.
,,	,,	LANCELOT LEWIS, son of James L , of Gwersilt, co Denbigh, gent
,,	,,	GRIFFIN OWEN, son of Edward O , of Greigwen, co Anglesey, gent
,,	,,	BENJAMIN NORCLIFFE, second son of Thomas N , of Nunnington, co York, [Knight
,,	,,	HENRY BELLINGHAM, second son of Allan B , of Gaythorne, Westmoreland,
1642.		[Esq
May 4.		JAMES RUMSEY, son of Walter R , Esq , one of the readers of this Inn
,,	,,	RICHARD CREEDE, son of Richard C , of Llanover, co Monmouth, gent
,,	5	EDWARD GLASCOCK, son of Henry G , of Farnham, Essex, Esq
,,	,,	THOMAS GAWDY, son and heir of Edward G , of Barney, Norfolk, Esq
,,	13	FERDINAND(o) HASTINGS, second son of George H , of St Giles, Cripplegate,
,,	,,	JOHN WORMELEY, son of Henry W , of Riccall, co York, gent [Knight
,,	,,	GEORGE BURD, son and heir of John B , of Wichingham, Norfolk, gent
,,	,,	THOMAS BREWER, son of Richard B , of West Farleigh, Kent, gent
		folio 998.
,,	,,	THOMAS BARNFIELD, son of Robert B , of Wolverhampton, co Stafford, gent
,,	,,	WILLIAM BEVERSHAM, son and heir of Robert B , of Wilby, Suffolk, gent , deceased, late of Barnard's Inn [Esq
,,	,,	ROBERT PALMER, son and heir of Robert P , of Carlton Scroop, co Lincoln,
,,	16	ROBERT BATTESON, son and heir of William B , of Bourton-on-the-Hill, co Gloucester, gent [Leicester, Esq
,,	,,	FERDINANDO SACHEVERELL, son and heir of Ferdinando S , of Old Hayes, co
,,	17	GEORGE GIFFORD, son of John G , of St Leonards, Shoreditch, & T P.
		[deceased
,,	19	RICHARD THORNTON, son and heir of Tempest T , of Tyersall, co York, Esq ,
,,	20	THOMAS DALE, second son of Anthony D , of Gyldfield, co York, Esq
,,	,,	ARTHUR STANHOPE, fourth son of Philip, Earl of Chesterfield
,,	,,	JOHN CLARKE, second son of Gilbert C , of Somersall, co Derby, Esq
		folio 999 [Esq
,,	24	THOMAS CORBETT, second son of Edward C , of Leighton, co. Montgomery,
,,	26	WILLIAM LUCAS, of Wolverton, Bucks, gent
,,	,,	HENRY RILEY, of Wakefield, co York, gent [Esq
,,	,,	FRANCIS RADCLIFFE, son and heir of Roger R , of Mulgrave Castle, co York, [Knight, deceased
,	,,	ALLEN BRODRICK, son and heir of Thomas B , of Wandsworth, Surrey,
,,	,,	THOMAS HUDSON, son and heir of Thomas H , of Cowfold, Sussex, clerk. [Knight
,	,,	ANTHONY SOUTH, third son of Francis S , late of Kelstern, co Lincoln,
,,	,,	HENRY SMITH, second son of Simon S , of Chart, Sutton, Kent, Esq
June 22		THOMAS WILBRAHAM, son and heir of Thomas W., of Tilstone, Cheshire, Esq
,,	,,	JOHN BENET, son and heir of John B , of London, Esq [gent
,,	,,	EDWARD HAWES, son and heir of Stephen H., of Packenham Cotes, Norfolk,
,,	,,	JOHN HORNYOLD, son of ——— H , of ———, Esq.

1642	folio 1,000.	[berland, Esq

1642
June 22 CUTHBERT BLENNERHASSET, son and heir of Edward B , of Flimby, Cum-
July 8 NICHOLAS TAYLOR, son of Nicholas T , of Presteign, co Radnor, Esq
„   29 ARTHUR WOOLRICH, son and heir of Robert W , of Gray's Inn, reader
              [Worcester, gent , deceased.
„   „ WILLIAM MILLINGTON, second son of Clement M , late of Cropthorne, co.
Aug 1 THOMAS PARKER, son of John P., reader, "sine fine."
„   „ JOHN OUSLEY, son and heir of Richard O , of ———, co Northampton, Esq
„   „ CAVE BECK, second son of John B , of St. James, Clerkenwell, gent
              [don, gent
„   „ HUMPHREY HALY (alias Haling), son and heir of John H (alias H), of Lon-
„   „ HENRY HESKETH, son of Thomas H , of Hestlington, co York, Esq   [Esq
„   „ CHARLES SALUSBURY, third son of William S , of Bachumb(r), co Denbigh,

folio 1,001

„   „ OWEN WYNN, third son of Edward W , of Gertrud, co Denbigh, Esq
„   „ GEORGE CROXTON, son and heir of Thomas C., of Rainscroft, co Chester, Esq
„   „ EDWARD BROMLEY, son and heir of Thomas B , of Hampton, Cheshire, Esq.
„   „ EDWARD COWNLEY (?), son and heir of George C , of Hepopp, co. Radnor,
„ 10 HENRY GOODRICK, of Isle of Ely, co Cambridge, gent   [gent
„   „ SAMUEL GOSSE, son and heir of Walter G , of Wallington, co ———, gent
„   „ RICHARD WESTON, son and heir of Edward W , of Hackney, Middlesex, gent.
              [Baronet
„   „ RAWLEIGH MANSELL, son of Francis M , of Muddelscombe, co Carmarthen,
„   „ JOHN HARRISON, son and heir of John H , of Newcastle-on-Tyne, gent
Sept 2 ANGELO STONOR, of the town of Southampton, gent.
„   „ JAMES DUKINFIELD, fourth son of Robert D , of Dukinfield, Cheshire, Esq

folio 1,002

Nov 8 ABRAHAM SIMONS, son of Peter S , of St Stephens, London, gent
„ 22 GODFREY GIBSON, son of Richard G , of the city of Westminster, gent
1642-3
Jan 23. THOMAS ARTHINGTON, son of Thomas A , of St. Mary Woolchurch, upholster
„   „ WILLIAM POLEY, son of Edmund P , of Badley, Suffolk, Esq
„   „ JOHN HILL, of Jouse-place, co Worcester, gent.
„   „ THOMAS CLARKE, second son of Edward C , of Ardington, Berks, Knight.
Mar 9 JOHN BARBER, second son of Gabriel B , of Hertford, Esq   [deceased
„   „ JOHN TEMPLE, second son of John T , of Franckton, co Warwick, Esq ,
„   „ JOHN COLE, son and heir of Robert C , of Haverhill, Suffolk, gent
„   „ NICHOLAS ASHTON, fourth son of Ralph A , of Whalley, co Lancaster, Baronet

1643	folio 1,003	

June 7 ROBERT PERROTT, son and heir of Edward P , of Northley, Oxon, Esq. [Esq
„   „ JOHN KNYVETT, gent., son and heir of Thomas K , of Ashwellthorpe, Norfolk,
„   „ DAVID MATHEW, late of Ruddiard, co. Glamorgan, gent
„   „ JOHN HARDING, of Shrewsbury, gent
„   „ JAMES NUTLEY, son and heir of William N , of the town of Southampton, gent.

P

1643.		folio 1,003—(continued).
June	7	EDWARD LOMBE, son and heir of John L , Alderman of Norwich
,,	,,	GEORGE NORWOOD, son of Thomas N , of Gray's Inn
,,	,,	JOHN LAMBTON, son of John L , of the city of Durham, Esq , deceased.
,,	,,	ROBERT BRAGG, son and heir of William B , of Gray's Inn, Esq
,,	,,	JOHN HALL, of the city of Durham, gent
,,	,,	JOHN HACKETT, son of George H , of New Inn, Middlesex, gent
Nov.	5.	DANIEL WHITE, son and heir of Daniel W , of Winchelsea, Sussex, Esq
,,	,,	THOMAS TAYLER, son and heir of Thomas T , of Newhall, parish of Linstead, [Kent, Esq

1643-4		folio 1,004
Feb	3	JOHN BRICKENDEN, son of Thomas B , reader.
,,	,,	HERBERT RANDOLPH, of Biddenden, Kent, gent
,,	,,	RICHARD PEIRSON, of Biddenden, Kent, gent
,,	,,	JOHN DUKINFIELD, fifth son of Robert D., of Dukinfield, Cheshire, Esq
,,	,,	JOHN COTTEN, son and heir of Allen C., late of London, Esq , deceased [Esq
,,	,,	LEVINIUS BENNETT, son and heir of Thomas B , of St Andrews, Holborn,
,,	,,	JOHN ELLISTONE, son and heir of John E , of Geslingthorpe, Essex, Esq
,,	,,	SAMUEL ROUSE, son and heir of Anthony R , Esq , deceased
,,	,,	DANIEL WHISTLER, son of William W , of Walthamstow, Essex, gent.

		folio 1,005
,,	,,	PETER PEAKE, son of Matthew P of Sandwich, Kent, gent.
,,	,,	WILLIAM FORSTALL, son of William F , of Gunston, Kent, gent
,,	,,	WILLIAM COLE, son of Thomas C , of Sherborne, co. Dorset, gent
,,	,,	JOHN HATT, son and heir of John H , of London, gent

1644		
July	1	JOHN GOODMAN, son and heir of John G , of Blason, co. Leicester, Esq
,,	,,	NATHANIEL BARKER, son of Samuel B., of Gray's Inn, Esq
,,	,,	JOHN FAGG, son and heir of John F , of Rye, Sussex, Esq
,,	,,	WILLIAM HAVE, son and heir of William H , of Horstead, Sussex, Esq
,,	,,	JOHN SMELT, second son of Mathew S , of Kirby Fletham, co York, Esq
,,	,,	MATHEW SMELT, third son of Mathew S , of Kirby Fletham, co York, Esq
,,	,,	CHRISTOPHER SMELT, fourth son of Mathew S , of Kirby Fletham, co York, [Esq

		folio 1,006.
,,	6	THOMAS TIRRELL, son and heir of Thomas T , of Gipping, Suffolk, Esq
,,	,,	ALEXANDER CHORLEY, of The Field House, parish of Prescott, co Lanc , gent
,,	7	THOMAS MARSH, son and heir of Thomas M , of Hackney, Middlesex, Esq
,,	,,	GEORGE CRESSENER, of London, gent [Beds, Esq
,,	,,	CHRISTOPHER LOWE, son of Humphrey L , of South Mills, parish of Blonham,
,,	,,	HENRY BACON, son of Bacquevill B , of Holkham, Norfolk, Esq
,,	,,	PETER WILBRAHAM, son of Roger W , of Dorfold, co Chester, Esq
,,	,,	ROBERT BALDOCK, son and heir of Samuel B , of Stanway, Essex, gent
,,	,,	JOHN CROSSE, of Halesworth, Suffolk, son and heir of John C , of Heming-
Nov	7	PETER MEERES, of London, gent [ford Abbotts, Hunts, gent

1644   **folio 1,006—(continued).**

Nov 7   CHRISTOPHER SALTER, son of William S., of Richings, parish of Iver, Bucks,
                                                      [Knight

,, ,,   SIMON BRITIFFE, son and heir of Edmund B , of Baconsthorpe, Norfolk, gent

,, ,,   JOHN FOWLE, of Castle Hedingham, Essex, gent

                                       folio 1,007

, ,,   BUTTON WINGATE, son and heir of Edmund W , of Ampthill, Beds, Esq

,, ,,   THEOPHILUS ANDREW, of Offingham, co Worcester, gent

,, ,,   ROGER STOUTEVILLE (Estouteville), of Brinckley, co Cambridge, gent

,, ,,   NICHOLAS BRADLAW (alias Jacob), son and heir of Nicholas B (alias Jacob),
                                             [of Laxfield, Suffolk, gent , deceased

,, ,,   ALEXANDER AKEHURST, son and heir of Ralph A , of Lewes, Sussex, gent

,, ,,   RICHARD NAYLOR, son and heir of William N , of Offord Darcy, Hunts, Esq

1644-5   [Esq.
Feb 6   THOMAS MACKWORTH, son and heir of Humphrey M , of the city of Coventry,

,, ,,   WILLIAM KILBURNE, son of William K , of Gray's Inn, gent

,, ,,   WILLIAM FOSTER, of Hanslope, Bucks, Esq

,, ,,   JOHN MORTON, son and heir of John M , of Sylby, co. Leicester, Esq

,, ,,   ROBERT GILL, son and heir of Robert G , of the Tower of London, Esq

,, ,,   HANNET WARBURTON, son and heir of Thomas W , of Partington, Cheshire,
                                                   [gent

,, ,,   JOSEPH HOBSON, son of William H , of Paternoster-row, London, merchant

                                       folio 1,008

,, ,,   WALTER BLITH, of the city of Coventry, gent

,, ,,   JOHN RAYMOND, of Patricksbourne, Kent, gent   [and Baronet.

,, ,,   THOMAS STRICKLAND, son and heir of William S , of Boynton, co York, Knight

,, ,,   THOMAS BARKER, second son of John B , of Grimston Hall, Suffolk, Baronet

,, ,,   GREVILL WATTS, of Burton Dassett, co Warwick, gent

,, ,,   THOMAS MARKS, son and heir of James M , of Newton, Suffolk, gent

,, ,,   FRANCIS CAPELL, son of Gamaliel C , of Rookwood, Essex, Knight

,, ,,   JOHN MICHELL, son and heir of Robert M , Town Clerk of London

,, ,,   HUGH WELLS, son of Hugh W , of the city of London, Armourer   [deceased

,, ,,   THOMAS RAYMOND, son and heir of Robert R , of Bowes Gifford, Essex,

,, ,,   WILLIAM MARCH, son and heir of Humberston M., of Thetford, Isle of Ely,
           Esq   [deceased

,, ,,   JOHN BARKER, son and heir of John B , late of Mendlesham, Suffolk, gent ,

,, ,,   STEPHEN PANKHURST, son and heir of John Cooper P , the son of Stephen P ,
                                            [of Trodgers-in-Mayfield, Sussex, Esq

,, ,,   ANDREW CORBETT, son and heir of Robert C., of Edgmond, Salop, Esq.

1645   **folio 1,009**

May 10   ROBERT BROWNRIGG, son of Matthew B , of Clopton, Suffolk, clerk
                                                      [deceased.

,, ,,   THOMAS STRINGER, son of Thomas S , late of St. Sepulchres, London, gent ,

,, ,,   CHARLES SKIPWITH, son of Edward S , of Grantham, co Lincoln, Esq

,, ,,   WALTER HARRIS, son of Richard H , of Cru(c)kton, Salop, Esq

1645   folio 1,009—(continued)

July 17   CHARLES GOODHAND, second son of William G , of Kirmond, co Lincoln, gent
  ,,   ,,   TRACY PAUNCEFOTE, son and heir of Grimbald P , of Hasfield, co Gloucester,
  ,,   ,,   GERVASE SLEIGH, son and heir of Samuel S , of Ash, co Derby, Knight [Esq
  ,,   ,,   JOHN ALLEN, son and heir of John A , of Basilden, Berks, gent   [Esq
  ,,   ,,   ROGER RANT, son and heir of Roger R , of Swaffham Prior, co Cambridge,
  ,,   ,,   JOHN RANT, son of Roger R , of Swaffham Prior, co Cambridge, Esq
  ,,   ,,   THOMAS BAYLIE, son and heir of William B , of Foleshill, near Coventry, gent
  ,,   ,,   ARTHUR ROBINSON, son of Arthur R , late of Dighton, co York, Knight,
Nov   3.   WILLIAM THORNTON, of East Newton, co York, Esq   [deceased
  ,,   15.   RICHARD WORSLEY, of Deeping Gate, co Northampton, Esq
  ,,   ,,   WILLIAM VAUGHAN, son of John V , of Pant Glas, co Carnarvor, Esq

                               folio 1,010

  ,,   23   EDMUND REEVE, son and heir of Augustine R., of Thorpe, Norfolk, gent
  ,,   ,,   NICHOLAS CARR, son and heir of Nicholas C., of the city of Norwich, Esq.
  ,,   ,,   DUTTON HILL, son and heir of James H , of High Offley, co Stafford, gent.
  ,,   ,,   JOHN WRENHAM, son and heir of John W , of Calverton, Bucks, gent   [Esq.
  ,,   ,,   WILLIAM HARTOPPE, son and heir of George H , of Dalby Parva, co Leicester,
  ,,   ,,   HENRY DOCWRA, son of Periam D , of Puttridge, parish of Offley, Herts, Esq
  ,,   ,,   RICHARD TROTTER, son of Richard T , of Skelton Castle, co. York, Knight.
  ,,   ,,   JOHN PALGRAVE, son and heir of Edward P , of Reading, Berks, Esq   [Esq
  ,,   ,,   CHARLES HALFORD, son and heir of Richard H , of Edithweston, co Rutland,
  ,,   ,,   EDWARD LEIGH, son and heir of Robert L , of Chingford, Essex, Esq
  ,,   ,,   BARNARD TURNER, son and heir of Barnard T , of Cublington, Bucks, gent

                               folio 1,011

Dec 18   EDWARD BENNET, of Greenford, Middlesex, Esq
  ,,   ,,   DANIEL RHODES, son of ——— R , of Beverley, co York, Esq
  ,,   ,,   GEORGE HALFHYDE, of Maydenbury, Beds, gent.
  ,,   ,,   WILLIAM AMCOTTS, of Estroppe, co. Lincoln, gent.
1645 6   [Oxon, Esq
Jan 21.   FRANK CHAMBERLAYNE, son and heir of Edmund C., of Stratton Audley,
  ,,   ,,   RICHARD BROWNLOW, son and heir of William B , of St Andrews, High
                                                        [Holborn, Baronet
  ,,   ,,   HENRY LAYTON, son and heir of Francis L , of Rawdon, co. York, Esq
  ,,   ,,   EDWARD SWALE, of Hurstpierpoint, Sussex, Esq.
  ,,   ,,   BENET BARBOR, of Cranham Hall, Essex, gent
  ,,   ,,   GEORGE STEPHENS, of Barnard's Inn, gent

                               folio 1,012   [Esq.

Feb 11   RICHARD PENNINGTON, third son of William P., of Muncaster, Cumberland,
  ,,   ,,   NICHOLAS ROBINSON, son and heir of Hugh P., of Seale, Surrey, S.T.D
  ,,   ,,   JOHN ROBINSON, second son of Pierce R , of Fillibrooke, co Stafford, Esq.
  ,,   ,,   WILLIAM MASTERMAN, son and heir of William M , of the city of York, gent.

1645-6	folio 1,012—(*continued*)
Feb 11	THOMAS SNAGG, son and heir of Ralph S , of Kempston, Beds, Esq
,, ,,	JOHN HART, son of William H , of Burton Dasset, co Warwick, gent. [Esq
,, ,,	HENDEN DOWNTON, son and heir of Richard D , of Twickenham, Middlesex,
,, ,,	RICHARD DOWNTON, second son of Richard D , of Twickenham, Middlesex, Esq [of Richmond, co York, Esq.
,, ,,	EDMUND NORTON, son and heir of Maulger N , of St. Nicholas, in the liberty
,, ,,	WALTER HAWKSWORTH, son and heir of Richard H , of Hawksworth, co [York, Knight.
,, ,,	CLEMENT FARNEHAM, son and heir of Peter F , of Hodesdon, Herts, gent.
,, ,,	THOMAS HOLT, son and heir of Rowland H , late of London, gent.
,, ,,	CECIL COOPER, son and heir of Roger C , of Thurgarton, Notts, Knight.

1646	folio 1,013 [Knight
May 2.	THOMAS BATHURST, son and heir of Edward B , of Horton Kirby, Kent,
,, ,,	GEORGE WILD, of Gressinghall, Norfolk, gent
,, ,,	WILLIAM LOVELACE, son of Francis L , of Gray's Inn, Esq
,, ,,	CHARLES BATES, of St Annes Street, Westminster, gent
,, 26.	JOHN SANDFORD, son and heir of William S , of Gray's Inn, Esq
,, ,,	JAMES GOULD, of Dorchester, gent
,, ,,	FRANCIS BREWSTER, son and heir of Robert B , of Wrentham, Suffolk, Esq
,, ,,	JOHN ALDHAM, son and heir of Thomas A , of Sapiston, Suffolk, Esq
,, ,,	HUMPHREY GORE, son and heir of John G., of Gilston, Herts, Knight.
,, ,,	RICHARD LEVETT, of Naburn, co. York, gent.
,, ,,	CHARLES BISHOP, son and heir of Thomas B., of ———, co Lincoln, Knight
,, ,,	WILLIAM ADDAMS, son and heir of John A , of St. Dunstans-in-the-West, gent.
,, ,,	JAMES SYMES, of St Andrews, Holborn, gent.

folio 1,014

,, ,,	WILLIAM BRIGHT, son and heir of John B , of Little Brysett, Suffolk, Esq
,, ,,	EDWARD BYNG, of Granchester, co. Cambridge, gent
,, ,,	ROBERT COLLINGWOOD, son of Robert C , of the city of Durham, Esq
,, ,,	ANSLETT FOWLE, of Sedlerskam, Suffolk, gent
,, ,,	ROBERT SOTHEBY, son and heir of Robert S , of Birdsall, co York, Esq
,, ,,	CHARLES PERROTT, second son of Edmund P , of Northey, Oxon, Esq
,, ,,	HENRY ATKINSON, of Killinghall, co York, gent
,, ,,	RICHARD COMBE, son and heir of Toby C , of Hempsted, co York, Esq
,, ,,	RICHARD MORE, son and heir of Samuel M , of Lyndley, Salop, Esq
,, ,,	CHARLES SMITH, son and heir of Charles S , of Ipswich, Esq
,, ,,	PETER PIERS, son of Peter Thomas, of St Asaph, co Flint, gent
,, ,,	WILLIAM STANTON, of the city of Norwich, gent
,, ,,	THOMAS BIRCH, son and heir of Thomas B., of Birch, co Lancaster, Esq

folio 1,015.

June 29	ROWLAND HUNT, son and heir of Thomas H , of Shrewsbury, Esq
,, 24	CHARLES STUART, Baron of Newberry and Aubigny.

1646.   folio 1,015—(continued)
June 24   JOHN ELWES, of the city of London, Esq   [York, clerk, deceased.
,,   27   WILLIAM DRAKE, son and heir of Thomas D , of Thornton-in-Craven, co.
July 27   CHARLES SMITH, second son of John S , of Sutton, Kent, Knight
June 29   COURTHOPE WOOD, of Harbledown, Kent, gent
Aug   8   WILLIAM MASSEY, of London, gent   [gent
,,   10. THOMAS WOOLHOUSE, son and heir of Thomas W , of Glapwell, co Derby,
,,   ,,   FRANCIS HALL, second son of Henry H , late of East Lilling, co York, gent ,
              deceased   [deceased
,,   ,,   RICHARD WARD, second son of Thomas W , late of Sheene, co Stafford, gent ,
Sept 22   JAMES HALES, third son of John H , of the city of Coventry (sic) (Canter-
              bury?), Esq   [deceased.
,,   26   JOHN LOWDER, son and heir of Robert L , late of Harwell, Berks, gent ,
,,   ,,   THOMAS MARSH, son and heir of Gabriel M , late of Upton Court, parish of
                                          [Shepardswold, Kent, deceased.

folio 1,016
,,   ,,   WILLIAM PENNYMAN, third son of James P , of Ormsby, co. York, Esq
Oct 23   ROBERT HARRYSON, son and heir of Thomas H., late of Cayton Grange, co
,,   ,,   HENRY SNAPE, son and heir of Nathaniel S., of Gray's Inn, Esq. [York, Esq.
,,   ,,   JOHN REDMAN, son and heir of John R., of Bread Street, London, merchant.
,,   ,,   JOHN LOWTHER, son and heir of John L , of Lowther, Westmoreland, Knight
                                                              [and Baronet.
,,   ,,   JOHN WEST, son and heir of John W , Esq , Lieutenant of the Tower of London
,,   ,,   SAMUEL WHITE, of Milk Street, London, gent
,,   ,,   RICHARD TOLSON, son and heir of Henry T , of Bridekirk, Cumberland
,,   ,,   ROBERT BACON, son and heir of Robert B , of the city of Norwich, Esq
,,   31   WILLIAM RANT, son and heir of Humphrey R , of Yelverton, Norfolk, Esq
,,   ,,   RICHARD HIGGINS, son of Edward H , of this Inn, Esq
,,   ,,   CHARLES HUSSEY, son of Edward H , late of Honington, co Lincoln, Knight
                                                  [and Baronet, deceased.
,,   ,,   JOSEPH AYLOFFE, of Brittayns, Essex, gent

folio 1,017.
Nov   4   SAMUEL BEDFORD, late of Barnard's Inn, gent
,,   ,,   RICHARD SOUTHBY, son and heir of John S , of Karswell, Beds, Esq
,,   ,,   FRANCIS SMALEPEECE, son and heir of Thomas S , deceased   [Knight.
,,   13   ROBERT ROUTH, son and heir of John R , of Boughton under-Blean, Kent,
,,   ,,   GERRARD CARPENTER, of London, gent.
,,   ,,   MATTHEW BARKER, of London, gent
,,   18   RICHARD ILES, son of Thomas Iles, S T.D
,,   20. JOHN PAGE, son of Anthony P., of Ely, Isle of Ely, Esq.
Dec 21   WILLIAM MOTHAM, son of Thomas M , late of Lincoln's Inn, gent , deceased.
1646-7
Jan 22   JOHN MORRIS, of Isleworth, Middlesex, Esq
,,   ,,   GEORGE JACKSON, of Ware, Herts, gent.
,,   ,,   MATTHEW HALL, of the city of York, gent

1646-7		**folio 1,018.**
Feb	1	HENRY BOKENHAM, son of Wiseman B , of Thorneham, Suffolk, Esq
,,	,,	WILLIAM GOLDINGHAM, son of William G , of this Inn, Esq
,,	,,	JOHN NUTHALL, of Chelmsford, Essex, late of Staple Inn, Esq
,,	,,	JOHN BURWELL, son of Edmund B , of Rougham, Suffolk, Esq
,,	,,	JAMES WEBSTER, son and heir of James W , of Alverthorpe, co. York, gent
,,	,,	FRANCIS DOWNES, of ———, co Northampton, Esq
,,	,,	WILLIAM HORTON, son and heir of Christopher W , of Cotton, co Derby, Esq
,,	,,	NICHOLAS HARDY (*alias* Hardinge), son of Nicholas H , of Kings Newton, co. [Derby, gent , deceased
,,	,,	JOHN BRETLAND, son of John B , of Thorncliffe, Cheshire, gent
,,	,,	EDWARD SCOTT, of Smeeth, Kent, gent
,,	,,	STEPHEN SANDFORD, late of Staple Inn, gent

folio 1,019

,,	4	THOMAS BRISTOWE, son and heir of William B , of Elston, Notts, gent.
,,	,,	NICHOLAS BACON, son and heir of Nicholas B , of Shrubland Hall, Suffolk, Esq (see also fo 959) [ceased
,,	,,	WILLIAM KNIGHT, son and heir of John K , late of Heath, Kent, gent , de-
,,	,,	TIMOTHY KETTLEWELL, late of Barnard's Inn, son and heir of John K , late of [New Alresford, co Southampton, gent.
,,	17	RALPH GORE, of St. Andrews, Holborn, Esq.
,,	,,	ROBERT MARSHALL, son and heir of Robert M., of the city of Lincoln, Esq.
,,	,,	EDMOND TYRELL, second son of Thomas T , of Gipping, Suffolk, Esq
,,	,,	GERMAN POLE, son and heir of German P., late of Radborne, co Derby,
,,	,,	HENRY BIGLAND, of Queen's College, Cambridge, A M. [Knight, deceased

folio 1,020

Mar.	1	HUMPHREY WHARTON, of Gillingwood, co. York, Esq.
,,	,,	RICHARD OATLEY, son and heir of Francis O , of Pitchford, Salop, Knight
,,	,,	JAMES GERRARD, son and heir of Miles G , late of Ince, co Lancaster, Esq , [deceased
,,	,,	THOMAS JOPSON, son and heir of Thomas J , of Cudworth, co York, Esq
,,	,,	TOBIAS HUMPHREY, of the city of York, gent
,,	,,	JOHN BRETT, son and heir of John B , of Hawkhurst, Kent, gent.
,,	,,	CHRISTOPHER WASE, son of John W , of the town of Cambridge, gent.
,,	,,	CLIFFORD CLIFTON, second son of Gervase C., of the town of Nottingham, [Knight and Baronet
,,	,,	HENRY TROTTER, son and heir of George T , of Skelton Castle, co York, Esq
,,	,	ROBERT BUCK, second son of John B., of Filey, co. York, Knight
,,	,,	JOSEPH PARKER, son of John P , of Gray's Inn, Esq., reader.

folio 1,021

,,	,,	IMMANUEL HALTON, son of Miles H , of Graystock, Cumberland, Esq
,,	,,	THOMAS SOUTHWELL, son of Ralph S , of the city of London, Esq
,,	,,	RICHARD BAYLEY, son and heir of Lionel B , of Woodford, Essex, Esq
,,	,,	EDWARD MINSHULL, son and heir of Geoffrey M , of Stoake, Cheshire, Esq

1646-7		folio 1,021—(continued)

Mar 1   JOHN WARREN, son and heir of Thomas W , of St Andrews, Holborn, gent

,,   ,,   EDMUND ANDERSON, son of Edmund A , of Broughton, co Lincoln, Esq

,,   ,,   THOMAS CALDECOTT, of Calthorpe, co Leicester, Esq

,,   ,,   JAMES MOYSES, of Appleton, co York, Esq

1647

April 24   THOMAS ARSCOTT, second son of Tristram A , of Cornwall, Esq

May 6   WILLIAM OSBALDESTON, son and heir of Richard O , Knight, late Attorney-
                                                    [General of Ireland, deceased.

,,   ,,   THOMAS RAYNER, son and heir of William R , of co Derby, gent

,,   ,,   GEORGE SHERMAN, son and heir of George S , of Wooburn, Beds Esq

folio 1,022.   [Cumberland, Knight

,,   ,,   FERDINAND(O) HUDDLESTON, son and heir of William H., of Millum Castle,

,,   ,,   ANTHONY OLDFIELD, son and heir of John O , of Spalding, co Lincoln, Esq

,,   ,,   RICHARD FLOWRE, of Norton, co. Radnor, gent

,,   ,,   OTTWELL MEVERELL, son and heir of Ottwell M , of St Lawrence Jewry, gent

,,   ,,   THOMAS BLOSSE, son and heir of Thomas B , of Belstred Hall, Suffolk, Esq

,,   ,,   JAMES LENNARTES, son and heir of Peter L , of Walthamstow, Essex, gent

,,   ,,   EDWARD HONYWOOD, son and heir of John H , of Elmsted, Kent, Knight

,,   ,,   THOMAS KEBLE, third son of Richard K , reader, "sine fine "

,,   ,,   JOSEPH KEBLE, fourth son of Richard K , reader, "sine fine "

,,   ,,   ANTHONY STAPLEY, son and heir of Anthony S , of Sussex, Esq

,,   ,,   ROBERT GARRARD, son and heir of William G , of Inckpen, Berks, gent

,,   ,,   WILLIAM JONES, son of Richard J , of Stowey, co Somerset, Esq

folio 1,023

,,   28   ADOLPHUS Oughton, son and heir of Thomas O , of Fillongley, co Warwick,

,,   ,,   RICHARD WARING, of Woodcott, Salop, gent   [Knight

,,   ,,   EDMUND HARCOCK, son and heir of Gregory H , of Worstead, Norfolk, gent

,,   ,,   HENRY BERNEY, of Norfolk, gent

,,   ,,   WILLIAM AVERY, son of Samuel A , citizen and alderman of London

,,   ,,   CHARLES EGERTON, son of Rowland E , late of Farthinghoe, co Northampton,
                                                    [Knight and Baronet

,,   ,,   THOMAS SMITH, son and heir of Thomas S , of Bynderton, Sussex, Esq

,,   ,,   WILLIAM HEADLAM, of the city of York, gent

,,   ,,   ARTHUR HODSON, of the city of York, gent

,,   ,,   WILLIAM DUNSTON, son and heir of William D , of Bramfield, Suffolk, gent

folio 1,024

,,   ,,   JOHN KEBLE, son and heir of James K , of Halesworth, Suffolk, gent

,,   ,,   JOHN HENDEN, second son of John H., of Biddenden, Kent, Knight

,,   ,,   SIMON HENDEN, third son of John H , of Biddenden, Kent, Knight   [Esq

,,   ,,   WILLIAM KINGSLEY, son of William K , of the city of Canterbury (Cambridge ?),

,,   ,,   SEABRIGHT NASH, son of Richard N , of King's Swinford, co Stafford, gent

,,   ,,   WILLIAM BRADSHAW, of Richards Castle, co Hereford, Esq

1647		folio 1,024—(continued).

May 28 JOHN RICHMAN, son and heir of John R , of Hedenham, Norfolk, gent

„ „ EDWARD BEDDINGFIELD, third son of Philip B , of Ditchingham, Norfolk, Esq

„ „ TIMOTHY NEALE, second son of John N., of Nether Dean, Beds, Esq [Esq.

„ „ STEPHEN HALES, son and heir of Charles H , late of Newland, near Coventry,

„ „ WILLIAM AVERY, son of ——— A , late of Bishops Itchington, co Warwick,
[gent

folio 1,025.

„ 29 THOMAS TRAUNTER, son and heir of Richard T , late of Bilbrook, co Stafford,

„ „ GILES POCOCK, son and heir of John P , of Chadlow, Berks. [gent , deceased

„ „ GEORGE BILLINGHURST, of London, gent

„ „ JOHN ROBINS, of Staple Inn, gent

June 1 JOHN DARNTON, son and heir of Richard D , of Tanfield, co York, clerk

„ „ THOMAS BENDLOWES, son and heir of Thomas B , of Sutton Holgrave, co
[York, gent

„ „ GEORGE BOWER, son and heir of George B , of Allhallows, London, Esq

„ „ THOMAS LASCELLES, son and heir of Thomas L , of Northallerton, co York,
Esq   [Esq

„ „ ROBERT SHAFTOE, son and heir of Robert S , of Benwell, Northumberland,

„ „ JOHN BUNCE, son and heir of James B , citizen and Alderman of London

„ „ CHRISTOPHER BOYS, son and heir of Edward B , of Uffington, parish of
[Goodneston, Kent, gent

folio 1,026

„ „ CHARLES WILFORD, of Weston Underwood, Bucks, gent

„ „ LEONARD GOOCH, son and heir of Robert G., of Eartham, Norfolk, Esq

„ „ ROBERT GOOCH, another son of Robert G , Esq , of Eartham, Norfolk

„ „ HENRY BRESSEY, son and heir of Edmund B , late of Wooton, Beds, Esq

„ „ TOBIAS WICKHAM, of the city of York, gent

„ „ EDWARD SULIARD, of Runwell, Essex, Esq.

„ „ RALPH FETHERSTONHAULGH, of Stanhope, co. Durham, Esq

„ „ HENRY PIGOTT, of Abingdon Pigotts, co Cambridge, gent

„ „ THOMAS SMITH, son and heir of Alexander S , of Stutton, Suffolk, gent

„ „ RICHARD MEADE, son of Richard M , late of Braggnum, parish of Soulbury,

„ „ HUMPHREY FISHE, of Hunsdon, Herts, gent   [Bucks, gent , deceased.

„ „ JOSIAS PEERS, son and heir of John P , of Fulham, Middlesex, gent

folio 1,027   [ton, Esq

Aug 2 FRANCIS CUPPER, son and heir of Vincent C , of Paulers Pury, co Northamp-

„ „ JOHN ROTHERAM, son and heir of Thomas Atwood R , Clerk, of Tring, Herts

„ „ ADAM OATLEY, son of Francis O , of Pitchford, Salop, Knight

„ „ ROBERT HAWYS, son of Gregory H , of Badwell Ash, Suffolk, gent

„ „ THOMAS BURTON, son and heir of Richard B , of Westmoreland, Esq

„ „ MATTHEW WHITFIELD, son and heir of Mathew W , of Appleby, Westmore-

„ „ WILLIAM BRIDGES, gent , son of John B , of London, Esq   [land, gent

„ „ THOMAS BROGRAVE, son and heir of John B , of Beckenham, Kent, Esq

„ „ SAMUEL TRELAWNY, of Plymouth, Devon, Esq

1647		folio 1,027—(*continued*).
Aug	2	PETER STANLEY, son of Thomas S , of Alderley, Cheshire, Esq
,,	,,	HENRY LOANE, son and heir of John L , of Ellough, Suffolk, gent
,,	,,	EDWARD FIELDINGE, of London, gent

folio 1,028

,,	,,	EDWARD BIGLAND, second son of Edward B , of Little Leake, Notts, clerk
,,	,,	JOHN HODGES, of Kensington, Middlesex, gent
,,	,,	JOHN ASHTON, son and heir of Robert A , of Shepley, co Lancaster, Esq
,,	,,	FRANCIS KING, of Hempsted, Herts, gent
,,	,,	JOHN KING, of ———, co ——— [Baronet
,,	,,	BARRINGTON EVERARD, second son of Richard E , of Waltham Magna, Essex,
,,	,,	JOHN REDMAN, of Newcastle-on-Tyne
,,	,,	ARTHUR HARRIS, of Coytie, co Glamorgan, gent
,,	,,	RICHARD BEARD, of Frimley, Surrey
,,	,,	THOMAS WISEMAN, son and heir of Ralph W , of Rivenhall, Essex, Esq
		[Esq , deceased
Nov	6	THOMAS SANDFORD, son and heir of John S., late of Askham, Westmoreland,
,,	,,	HENRY NORTH, son and heir of Henry N , of Laxfield, Suffolk, Esq
,,	,,	SUMMERFIELD OLDFIELD, of Summerfield, co Chester, Esq

folio 1,029.

,,	,,	ROBERT FAIRBEARD, son and heir of Robert F., of this Inn, Esq
,,	,,	DAVID MORGAN, son and heir of Maurice M., of Clidey, co Pembroke, gent
,,	,,	RALPH MADYSON, son and heir of Humphrey M , of Coningsby, co. Lincoln,
,,	,,	PETER HEYMAN, of Selling, Kent, gent [gent
,,	,,	GERVASE FULLER, son and heir of William F , D D , of Cambridge, Esq (*sic*),
,,	,,	WILLIAM JACKSON, of Wittington, co Lancaster, gent.
,,	,,	WILLIAM FERMOR, son and heir of Alexander F , of Rotherfield, Sussex, Esq
,,	,,	HENRY ST JOHN, son of John St J , of Lydiard Tregoz, Wilts, Knight and
,,	,,	THOMAS GERRY, of Bushmead Abbey, Beds, gent. [Baronet
,,	,,	JOHN CORNWALLIS, son and heir of John C , of Ashfield, Suffolk, Esq
,,	,,	SYMON PEACOCK, of Topcliffe Manor, co York, gent
,,	,,	WILLIAM GREGORY, of Staple Inn, gent
,,	,,	WILLIAM GREENE, of Burnham Market, Norfolk, gent
,,	,,	JOSEPH SEDGWICK, son and heir of Joshua S , of Cambridge, gent

folio 1,030

Dec	7	FRANCIS WINGFIELD, son of John W., of Tickencote, co Rutland, Knight
,,	,,	THOMAS TOWNSEND, second son of Roger T., of Horsted, Norfolk, Esq
,,	,,	JOHN ROOPE, of Tounstole, Devon, gent
,,	,,	THOMAS RICHARD, son of Peter R , of Ailsford, Kent, Knight
,,	,,	RICHARD WATTS, son and heir of Richard W , of Gt Munden, Herts, Esq
,,	,,	WILLIAM WIMBERLY, son of John W , of Pinchbeck, co. Lincoln, Esq
,,	,,	WILLIAM MORDANT, son of Charles M , of Hampstead, Middlesex, Esq

1647-8.   folio 1,030—(continued)

Feb 4   PETER LANCASTER, son of Nathaniel L , of Imperley, Cheshire, clerk   [Law
,,   ,,   ROBERT GRIFFITH, son and heir of Hugh G , of Denbigh, Professor of Civil
,,   ,,   MOYSES KEELING, son and heir of John K , of Hackney, Middlesex, Esq.
,,   ,,   THOMAS SHENTON, son of John S , of Burland, co. Leicester, Esq

                                 folio 1,031.

,,   8   THOMAS BOUGHTON, son and heir of Thomas B., of Bilton, co Warwick, Esq
,,   ,,   RICHARD BOUGHTON, second son of Thomas B , of Bilton, co Warwick, Esq.
,,   ,,   RALPH ADEANE, son and heir of Thomas A , of Chalgrove, Oxon, gent
,,   ,,   LAURENCE TIRRELL, son and heir of John T , of East Thorneton, Essex, gent
,,   ,,   HENRY EDGAR, son and heir of Miles E , of Eye, Suffolk, gent
,,   ,,   JOHN BARRAGE, son of John B , of London, gent
,,   ,,   DANIEL RHODES, son of ——— R , of Beverley, co York, Esq
,,   ,,   VINCENT BARRY, son and heir of Vincent B , of Thame, Oxon, Esq
,,   ,,   EDWARD GALLARD, son of Joseph G , of London, gent
,,   ,,   HENRY SPELMAN, eldest son of Clement S , of this Society, Esq   [ton, Esq
,,   ,,   WILLIAM ANDREWS, son and heir of William A , of Appletree, co Northamp-

                                 folio 1,032

,,   ,,   THOMAS EYRE, of Rowter Hall, co Derby, gent.
,,   ,,   RALPH SPELMAN, second son of Clement S , of this Inn, Esq
,,   ,,   THOMAS WHARTON, son of Humphrey W , of Warcopp, Westmoreland, gent
,,   ,,   WILLIAM CULPEPER, son of William C , of Aisleford, Kent, Knight
,,   ,,   THOMAS HASELL, son and heir of Samuel H , of Sutton-on-Derwent co
                                                                    [York, Esq
,,   ,,   WILLIAM BROWNLOW, son of William B , of St Andrews, Holborn, Knight.
,,   ,,   JAMES MASTER, son and heir of Richard M , of East Langdon, Kent , Esq
,,   ,,   RICHARD FERRES, of ———, co Derby, Esq
,,   ,,   RICHARD NELTHORPE, son and heir of Edward N , of ———, co York, Esq
Mar 16   WILLIAM BURY, son and heir of William B , of Grantham, co Lincoln, Knight
,,   ,,   DANIEL WALDOE, son and heir of Daniel W , citizen and mercer of London

1648   folio 1,033

April 19   JOHN DUNCH, son and heir of Samuel D , of Pewsey, Berks, Esq
,,   ,,   JOHN COMBES, son of Edward C , late of Backton, Suffolk, gent
,,   ,,   REGINALD RABBETT, son and heir of Lambert R , of Kelsall, Suffolk, Esq
,,   ,,   GILBERT MARSHALL, son of Thomas M , of Denton, co Durham, Esq
,,   ,,   GEORGE HOLEMAN, son of Philip H , of Warkworth, Northumberland, Esq
,,   ,,   ROBERT MARSHE, of Staple Inn, gent
,,   ,,   ROBERT PEIRSON, of Norfolk, gent
,,   ,,   VINCENT DENNE, son and heir of Thomas D , of St. Alphage, Canterbury, gent
,,   ,,   JOHN RAYMOND, of ———, Kent, gent
,,   ,,   HENRY HARVEY, son and heir of Edmund H., of this Inn, Esq
,,   ,,   WILLIAM SATTERTHWAITE, son of John S , of Hornsey, co York, S T P

1648   folio 1,034.

May 5   WILLIAM BREWER, son and heir of William B , of Dighton, Kent, Esq
 ,,   ,,   JASPER SCOLES, son and heir of Robert S., of Wateringbury, Kent, Esq
 ,,   ,,   ROGER PALMER, second son of Thomas P , Baronet, of Wingham Kent
 ,,   ,,   THEODORE WYNNE, of Llanwthyn, co. Montgomery, gent
 ,,   ,,   RICHARD MIDDLETON, of Plasnewth, co Denbigh, gent.
 ,,   ,,   GEORGE BROWNE, of Overpeover, co Chester. gent   [Esq
 ,,   ,,   VINCENT AMCOTTS, son and heir of Vincent A , of Nettleham, co. Lincoln,
 ,,   ,,   NICHOLAS KEMYSS, of Llanederne, co Glamorgan, Esq
 ,,   ,,   HUMPHREY BETHELL, of the city of Durham, Esq   [deceased
 ,,   ,,   EDMUND ESTERFORD, son and heir of Edmund E., of Ovington, Essex, gent ,

                                       folio 1,035

 ,,   24   WILLIAM PAYNE, of St Martins-in-the-Fields, Middlesex, gent
 ,,   ,,   ROBERT MAYDESTONE, son and heir of Robert M , of Felsted, Essex, gent
 ,,   ,,   GEORGE MANWARING, son and heir of Arthur M , of Slepe, Salop, gent
 ,,   ,,   ROBERT GLAPTHORNE, son and heir of George G , of Whittlesea, co Cam-
 ,,   ,,   SAMUEL NICHOLS, of Whickham, co. Leicester, gent.   [bridge, Esq
 ,,   ,,   FRANCIS WRIGHT, son and heir of Francis W , of Bolton-on-Swale, co York,
 ,,   ,,   AMBROSE BENNET, son of John B , of London, Esq.   [Esq
 ,,   ,,   RICHARD PENNINGTON, third son of William P , of Seaton, Cumberland, Esq

                                       folio 1,036   [Knight, deceased
June 23   RICHARD FRANCKLYN, son and heir of John F , of Willesden, Middlesex,
 ,,   ,,   ROBERT SLOWE, of Barnard's Inn, gent
 ,,   ,,   JOHN LLOYD, son and heir of Edward L , of Measbury, Salop, gent
 ,,   ,,   THOMAS LEE, third son of Richard L , of Langley, Salop, Baronet
 ,,   ,,   EDWARD DOMVILLE, son of Richard D , of Lymm, co Chester, Esq
 ,,   ,,   MILES FLEETWOOD, son and heir of William F , of Aldwinckle, Northants,
                                                                  [Knight
 ,,   ,,   THOMAS OXENDEN, son and heir of Henry O , of Barkham, Kent, Esq
 ,,   ,,   WILLIAM AUSTIN, son of William A , of St Mary's Over, Surrey, gent
 ,,   ,,   WILLIAM THOMAS, son and heir of George T , of Savernake, Wilts, Esq.

                                       folio 1,037

 ,,   26   JAMES COLEBY, son and heir of Thomas C, of Caston, Norfolk, S T P.
 ,,   ,,   TOBY CAGE, son and heir of Toby C., of Woodford, Essex, Knight
 ,,   ,,   EDWARD CHOLMLEY, son of John C., of Kirkby Underwood, co Lincoln, Esq ,
 ,,   ,,   EDWARD BIGLAND, of East Lecke, Notts, gent   [deceased.
 ,,   ,,   THOMAS GARDINER, son and heir of Francis G , of Tollesbury, Essex, Esq.
 ,,   ,,   LEWIS ROBERTS, son of Lewis R , of Wooton, co. Gloucester, gent.
 ,,   ,,   HUMPHREY BUTLER, son of Robert B , of Southwell, Notts, gent.
 ,,   ,,   EDWARD FAWKENOR, late of Staple Inn, son and heir of Kenelm F., of
                                                   [Uppingham, co Rutland, gent
 ,,   ,,   THOMAS TRESHAM, son of Thomas T., of Pilketon, co Northampton, Esq

1648   folio 1,037—(*continued*)

June 26   JOHN NORWICH, son and heir of Ascariah N , of Bigstock, Northants, gent

"   "   SALATHIEL LOVELL, son of Benjamin L , of Lapworth, co Warwick, clerk

folio 1,038   [Knight

Oct 26   WILLIAM RICHARDSON, second son of Thomas R , of Honingham, Norfolk,

"   "   EDWARD BARNARD, eldest son of Henry B , Alderman of Kingston upon-Hull

"   "   SAMUEL ENNOS, son and heir of Nicholas E , of London, merchant

"   "   EDWARD GORGES, son and heir of Samuel G , of Charleton, co Somerset, Esq

"   "   PHILIP HARRIS, of Mulbrowe, Devon, gent

"   "   WILLIAM COBB, son and heir of Francis C , of Ottringham, co York, Knight

"   "   THOMAS BOWYER, second son of William B , of Knypersley, co Stafford, Knight

Nov 3   EDMOND ASHTON, fourth son of Ralph A , of Whalley, co Lanc , Baronet

"   "   JOHN AILEYN, of Stone, Kent, gent

folio 10,39   [Baronet

"   6   WILLIAM WOLRYCHE, son of Thomas W , of Dudmaston, Salop, Knight and

"   "   THOMAS WOLRYCHE, son of Thomas W , of Dudmaston, Salop, Knight and

"   "   JOHN FENWICK, son and heir of John F , of Newcastle-on-Tyne, Esq [Baronet

"   "   RICHARD TEMPLE, son and heir of Peter T , of Stowe, Bucks, Knight and

"   24   HENRY GUY, son of Henry G , of Tring, Herts, Esq   [Baronet

"   "   HENRY PUREFOY, second son of George P , of Wadley, Berks, Esq

folio 1,040

"   "   ALEXANDER BROME, son of John B , of Milton, Dorset, gent

"   "   HUGH STRODE, son of John S , of Parnham, Dorset, Knight, deceased

"   "   JAMES OGLE, son of Henry O , of Whiston, co Lancaster, Esq

"   "   ST JOHN GUYLLIAMS, son and heir of Abel G., of London, merchant.

"   "   EDWARD SHORTE, son and heir of Edward S , of Mayford, co Stafford, gent

"   "   ROBERT SHEPHERD, son of Robert S , of Stanton, Suffolk, clerk.

"   "   THOMAS GALLOWAY, Esq , son of James G , Knight, Lord Dunkeld, in Scotland

"   "   WILLIAM ATHERTON, of Atherton, co Lancaster, gent

"   "   ROWLAND NICCOLLS, of Boycott, Salop, Esq

"   "   WILLIAM BURLEIGH, son and heir of Thomas B , of Lycham, Norfolk, gent

"   "   THOMAS MARSHALL, son and heir of Richard M , of Newark-on-Trent, Notts,

"   "   WILLIAM DENTON, son of John D , of Fawler, Oxon, Esq   [gent

"   "   WILLIAM COOKE, son and heir of William C , of Bromehall, Norfolk, Esq

"   "   RALPH KENRICK, son of ——— K , of co Northampton, Esq

folio 1,041

"   29   RICHARD CLEVER, son and heir of Richard C , of Norton Bury, Herts, gent

"   "   JOHN DAUBENEY, of Woolmiston, parish of Crewkerne, co Somerset, gent

"   "   WILLIAM TAYLOR, second son of Nicholas T , of Presteign, co. Radnor,

"   "   NATHANIEL STIRROPP, of Wood Street, London, gent   [Esq., deceased.

"   "   RICHARD CARRILL, son and heir of Richard C , of Thorpe, Surrey, Esq

"   "   BIASE CARRILL, third son of Richard C , of Thorpe, Surrey, Esq

1648		folio 1,041—(*continued*)
Nov	29	PETER JOHNSON, son of Henry J , of the Isle of Thanet, Kent, gent
,,	,,	GEORGE LANGTON, of Stanswick, Berks, gent
,,	,,	JAMES BALE, of Seaburrow, parish of Crewkerne, co. Somerset, Esq.
,,	,,	HENRY SWALE, gent , son and heir of Solomon S., Esq , of this Inn.
,,	,,	JOHN GIBSON, Esq , son and heir of John G , of Welborne, co York, Knight

folio 1,042.

,,	,,	THOMAS SIMPSON, of Ryton, co York, gent
1648-9		[deceased
Mar	10	JOHN CRISPE, son and heir of Nicholas C , late of Seaton, co. Rutland, Esq,
,,	,,	JOHN HUMPHREY, son of Christopher H , of Pinchbeck, co Lincoln, gent
,,	,,	JOHN STEWARD, son and heir of Humphrey S , of Trotton, Sussex, Esq
,,	,,	EDWARD STORY, of Barnard's Inn, second son of Thomas S , of Chesterton, [co, Cambridge, Esq.
,,	,,	THOMAS PRYSE, son and heir of Robert P , of Geeler, co Denbigh, Esq
,,	,,	WILLIAM WALLER, son and heir of Hardres W , Knight, of Dublin.
,,	,,	WALTER WALLER, second son of Hardres W , Knight, of Dublin. [Baronet
,,	,,	RICHARD MEREDITH, second son of William M , of Leeds Abbey, Kent,
,,	,,	THOMAS PEGGE, son and heir of Thomas P , of Yeldersley, co Derby, Esq [deceased
,,	,,	CONSTABLE BRADSHAW, son and heir of James B., of Durham, Esq.
,,	,,	——— DANYELL, of Ruddham, Norfolk, gent

		folio 1,043 [gent
,,	,,	WILLIAM PARKINSON, son and heir of Edward P , of Haggurst, co Durham,
,,	,,	FRANCIS TOPHAM, second son of Francis T , of Aglethorpe, co York, Esq ,
,,	,,	WILLIAM HERBERT, of Kilybebill, co Glamorgan [deceased.
,,	,,	ROWLAND PRICE, of Bodgwyn, co Anglesea
,,	,,	THEODORE WYNNE, of Llanvair, co Denbigh [Esq
,,	,,	OWEN HUGHES, son and heir of Francis H , of Cambridge University,
,,	,,	HENRY BISHOP, of Staple Inn, gent [deceased
,,	,,	EDWARD TOPHAM, son and heir of Francis T , of Aglethorpe, co York, Esq ,
,,	,,	RICHARD MILNER, son of John M , late of Sutton-in-Holderness, co York, [gent , deceased
,,	,,	ROBERT NEWTON, son and heir of Edward N., of Mickleover, co Derby, gent
,,	,,	JOHN FAWKES, son of Thomas F , of Leamington Priors, co Warwick, gent
,,	,,	SAMUEL CLARKSON, son and heir of John C , of Langham, Essex, gent
,,	,,	JOHN FULTHORPE, son and heir of Clement F , of Tunstall, co Durham, Esq

1649		folio 1,044
May	29.	SYMON RUDGLEY, of Knighthorpe, co Leicester, Esq [Esq
,,	,,	WALSINGHAM BOKENHAM, second son of Wiseman B , of Thornham, Suffolk,
,,	,,	THOMAS TURNER, son of John T , of Blechingley, Surrey, Esq
,,	,,	WILLIAM DALYSON, second son of Charles D , of Gray's Inn, Knight
June	6	RICHARD HARLACKENDEN, gent , son and heir of Richard H , of Earls Colne, [Essex, Esq

1649.		**folio 1,044**—*(continued)*.
June	6	WILLIAM FENNE, son and heir of Edward F , of Harrow-on-the-Hill, Middlesex,
,,	,,	JOHN BAKER, son and heir of John B , of Sissinghurst, Kent, Baronet [gent
,,	,,	FRANCIS FARNABY, son of Thomas F , of Sevenoaks, Kent, Esq
,,	,,	JOHN WHITFIELD, son of Thomas W , of Biddenden, Kent, gent
,,	,,	GILBERT HAVERS, second son of Gilbert H., of Turnham, Suffolk, Esq.

folio 1,045   [Esq.

,,	15	WILLIAM BLANCHARD, son and heir of William B , of Cathorne, co Somerset,
,,	,,	JOHN HATHORNE, eldest son of Nathaniel H , of Cookham, Berks, Esq
,,	,,	WILLIAM SWAN, son of William S , of Heugh, Northumberland, gent.
,,	,,	SAMUEL ROWE, son and heir of Christopher R , late of Maxfield, Cheshire, gent
,,	,,	FRANCIS WOODCOCK, third son of Thomas W , of Newtimber, Sussex, Esq
,,	,,	JOHN SWINBURNE, son and heir of Thomas S , of Butterby, co Durham, Esq
,,	,,	JOHN GAYRE, son of John G., of London, Knight
,,	,,	ROBERT GAYRE, son of John G , of London, Knight
,,	,,	THOMAS CALVERLEY, son and heir of John C , of Eryholme, co York, Esq
Sept	2	SAMUEL HARVEY, eldest son of Edmund H , of Fulham, Middlesex, Esq
,,	,,	WILLIAM COPLEY, son and heir of Christopher C , of Wadworth, co York,

                                                          [Esq

folio 1,046

,,	3	ROBERT LUKYN, son of John L , of Isleham, co Cambridge, Esq
,,	,,	HUMPHREY DOVE, of Brixton-causeway, Surrey, son and heir of John D , S T D , deceased [Cheshire, gent , deceased
,,	,,	THOMAS WHITTINGHAM, son and heir of Thomas W , late of Middlewich,
,,	,,	THOMAS BAINBRIGGE, son and heir of Thomas B , of Cambridge, deceased
,,	,,	WILLIAM NORTON, son of Maulger N , of Richmond, co York, Esq
,,	,,	WELBERY NORTON, son of William N , of Welton, co York, Esq
,,	,,	WILLIAM RAVEN, son and heir of William R , of Elworth, co Leicester, gent
,,	,,	JOHN STRATFORD, of Nuneaton, co Warwick, gent
,,	,,	WILLIAM PARGITER, of Gretworth, co Northampton, gent [deceased
,,	,,	WILLIAM WISEMAN, son and heir of William W , late of Gray's Inn, Esq ,
,,	,,	EDWARD ELLIS, son of John E , of Milton, co Cambridge, Esq
,,	,,	HENRY WHALEY, third son of Richard W , late of Gray's Inn, Esq , deceased.

folio 1,047.

Nov	6	BARTHOLOMEW LAMBE, son of Bartholomew L , of London, gent
,,	,,	RICHARD WALMESLEY, of Dunkenhalgh, co Lancaster, Esq
,,	,,	WILLIAM GOOCH, son and heir of William G , of Mettingham, Suffolk, Esq
,,	,,	JONATHAN BARTHROPP, of Shrewsbury, gent [bridge, gent
,,	,,	JOHN JENKINSON, of Barnard's Inn, gent , son and heir of John J , of Cam-
,,	,,	JAMES HEYWARD, son and heir of Thomas H , late of Rudbackston, co Pem-
,,	,,	[broke, gent , deceased
,,	,,	WILLIAM WILKINSON, of Staple Inn, gent , son and heir of Thomas W , late
,,	,,	[of Pontefract, co York, gent , deceased
,,	,,	JOHN BATT, son and heir of John B , of Okewell, co York, Esq

1649   folio 1,047—*(continued)*.

Nov 6   EDWARD FLETCHER, son and heir of Anthony F., of the city of York, gent

Dec 28   DANIEL THELWALL, son and heir of Daniel T , Esq

                    folio 1,048   [Judges of the Admiralty

"   "   THOMAS EXTON, son and heir of John E , Doctor of Laws, and one of the

"   "   JOHN CASTELL, son and heir of Robert C , of Glatton, Hunts, gent

"   "   ROBERT PELHAM, son and heir of Thomas P , of Compton Valence, Dorset,

"   "   JOHN NEWBURGH, of Worth Frances, Dorset, Esq   [Esq

"   "   SAMUEL VINCENT, of London, gent

"   "   ROBERT FOWLE, of Seddlescumbe, Sussex, gent   [deceased

"   "   THOMAS PARKER, son and heir of Thomas P., of Anglesey, co. Cambridge,

"   "   RICHARD EDWARDS, of Nanhoron, co. Carnarvon, gent.

"   "   GEORGE FAIRFAX, son and heir of William F , of London, S.T.D

                    folio 1,049

"   "   JONATHAN JENINGS, son of Jonathan J , late of Ripon, co York, deceased

"   "   HENRY PAWLETT, Esq , son and heir of Henry, Lord P , of the Grange, co
          Southampton   [Carmarthen, Esq

"   "   ROWLAND GWYNNE, son and heir of Howel G , of Glanbrane, co

"   "   WILLIAM EDWARDS, son of Evan E , of Rhuall, co Flint, Esq

"   "   JOHN WARREN, son and heir of Edward W , of Poynton, Cheshire, Esq

"   "   FRANCIS BERESFORD, son and heir of Francis B , of Newton Grange, co
                                   [Derby, Esq

"   "   RICHARD FRANK, son and heir of Richard F , of Campsall, co York, Esq

"   "   CHRISTOPHER HODGSON, son of John H , of Newhall in Beeston Park, co
                                  [York, Esq

"   "   ZACHARY COOKE, son and heir of Thomas C , of ———, co Cornwall, Esq

"   "   HENRY JENKINSON, eldest son of Robert J., of Wickham, co Lincoln, Esq

"   "   WILLIAM DICKINS, son of William D , late of Fleet Street, London, Esq
                                  [deceased

1649-50   folio 1,050.

Mar 20   HENRY DEERHAM, son and heir of Henry D , of London, Esq

"   "   JAMES WILMOTT, son of Simon W., of St. Peters, Cornhill, Esq   [deceased

"   "   JOHN BLAKISTON, son and heir of John B , of Newton, co Durham, Esq ,

"   "   FRANCIS MOYSER, son of Thomas M , late of Appleton, co York, Esq

"   "   FRANCIS BRIDGES, son of John B , of Hackney, Middlesex, Esq   [gent

"   "   WILLIAM GREENHILL, son and heir of William G , of Blackfriars, London,

"   "   JOHN CARPENTER, son and heir of Robert C , Deputy Registrar of Chancery

"   "   GEORGE DARCY, son and heir of William D , of Witton Castle co Durham,
                                  [Knight

"   "   THOMAS PRESTWICH, son and heir of Thomas P , of Hulme, co Lancaster.

"   "   HUMPHREY MITFORD, son and heir of Robert M , of Mitford, Northumber-

"   "   EDWARD MOORE, of Bankhall, co Lancaster, Esq   [land, Esq

1650.   folio 1,051.

May 8   ROBERT CONSTABLE, son of Robert C , of Blackfriars, London

1650		folio 1,051—(*continued*)
May	8	ROBERT GABIN, son and heir of Roger G , of Woodalling, Norfolk, gent
,,	,,	JOHN LLOYD, second son of Pierce L , of Lligny, co Anglesea, Esq
,,	,,	MICHAEL BERKELEY, of Roy Court, Kent, Esq
,,	,,	WILLIAM ACTON, second son of John A , of Bramford, Suffolk, Esq
,,	,,	MAXIMILIAN DALYSON, of Halinge, Kent, Esq
,,	,,	ROBERT DOUGHTY, son and heir of John D , of Hoveton St Johns, Norfolk,
,,	,,	FRANCIS RAWORTH, son and heir of Francis R , of Dover, Kent, gent [Esq
,,	17	CHARLES ROBERTS, son of Thomas R , of Brecon, gent
,,	,,	WILLIAM BALLETT, son and heir of William B , of Woodthorpe, parish of [Strubby, co Lincoln, Esq
,,	,,	CHARLES BROGRAVE, son and heir of Edward B , of Braughing, Herts, Esq

folio 1,052.

,,	,,	WILLIAM HULME, of Hulme, co Lancaster, gent [Esq , deceased
,,	,,	WILLIAM DALTON, son and heir of John D , late of Hawkswell, co York ,
,,	,,	THOMAS DALTON, son of John D , late of Hawkswell, co York, Esq , deceased
,,	,,	WILLIAM TAYLER, son of Marmaduke T , late of Crome, parish of Sledmere, [co York, gent , deceased
,,	,,	WILLIAM THOMAS, of Christioneth, co Denbigh, gent
,,	,,	WILLIAM ANDREWS, son and heir of Owen A , of Gray's Inn, Esq [gent
,,	,,	GEORGE HAWARD, son and heir of George H , of Fletherhill, co Pembroke,
,,	,,	JAMES HAWARD, son of George H , of Fletherhill, co Pembroke, gent [Esq
,,	,,	JOHN BEILBY, second son of William B , of Mickelthwaite Grange, co York,
,,	,,	THOMAS ROKEBY, second son of Thomas R., of Burnby, co York, Esq [Esq
,,	,,	BRIDSTOCK HARFORD, son and heir of Bridstock H , of the city of Here- [ford, M D

folio 1,053.

,,	21	ROBERT COLES, son of Robert C , of Beamondcote, co Lancaster, gent
,,	,,	HENRY WARD, son of William W , late of Gray's Inn, Esq , deceased
,,	,,	JOHN HAWTREY, second son of John H , of Riselip, Middlesex, Esq
,,	,,	THOMAS PARKER, son and heir of Edward P , of Browsholme, co York, Esq
,,	,,	THOMAS HAWORTH, son of Peter H , of Thurcroft, co Lancaster, gent
,,	,,	ROBERT PURLAND, son and heir of Robert P , of Warham, Norfolk, gent
,,	,,	THOMAS HUMPHREY, son of Christopher H , of Pinchbeck, co Lincoln, gent
,,	,,	JOHN JOLLY, son and heir of Philip J , of Spalding, co Lincoln, gent
,,	,,	FRANCIS EMPSON, of Boston, co Lincoln, gent , son of Francis E , late of [Boston, gent , deceased
,,	,,	JOHN WYBUNBURY, son and heir of John W , of Atherley, Salop, Esq
,,	,,	WILLIAM KETCHFORTH, son of John K , of Greddington, co Northampton, [Esq , deceased

folio 1,054

,,	29	THOMAS ELLIS, of Wrexham, co Denbigh, gent
,,	,,	EDWARD NUTT, son and heir of John N , of Nackington, Kent, Esq
,,	,,	WILLIAM JOHNSON, son and heir of William J , late of East Barnet, Herts, [Esq , deceased

Q

1650.   folio 1,054—(continued)

May 29   JOHN NORCLIFFE, son of Thomas N , late of Nunnington, co York, Knight,

,,   ,,   ANDREW LYDDALL, son of Richard L , of Sunning, Berks, Knight [deceased

,,   ,,   JOHN RADCLIFFE, son and heir of Alexander R , of Ordsall, cc Lancaster,

,,   ,,   GEORGE HEWETT, of Charlwood, Surrey   [Knight of the Bath

,,   ,,   AMBROSE PHILLIPPS, late of Staple Inn, son and heir of Ambrose P , of
                                 [Wolverhampton, co Stafford, gent

,,   ,,   JOHN THOMAS, son of Anthony T , of ———, Surrey, Knight

June 21   ANDREW SORRELL, eldest son of Manuel S , of Ipswich, Suffolk, gent

,,   ,,   DANIEL COLLINGWOOD, son and heir of Robert C , of Branton, Northumber-
                                 [land, Knight

folio 1,055.   [Knight

,,   24   THOMAS CARR, son and heir of William C , late of Ford, Northumberland,

,,   ,,   THOMAS WHITCOMBE, son and heir of John W , late of St Margaret Moses,
                                 [London, deceased

,,   ,,   JOHN TIRREL, second son of John T , of East Horndon, Essex, Knight

,,   ,,   DANIEL FLEMING, son of William F , of Connistone, co Lancaster, Knight

,,   ,,   ROBERT SADLIER, son and heir of Robert S , of Sopwell St Albans, Herts, Esq

,,   ,,   THOMAS PRICHARD, son and heir of Walter P , of Trevryn, co Monmouth, gent

,,   ,,   WILLIAM PRICHARD, second son of Walter P., of Trevryn, co Monmouth, gent

,,   ,,   GEORGE STARKEY, son of George S , of Gray's Inn, Esq.

,,   ,,   JAMES HALFORD, son and heir of Peter H , of Newbrooke, co Cheshire, Esq

,,   ,,   JAMES MARKS, son of James M , of Newton, Suffolk, gent.

,,   ,,   GEORGE HARCOURT, son of William H , of Winsham, co Chester, Esq.

,,   ,,   HENRY PECKE, son and heir of Henry P , of Lewes, Sussex, Esq.

folio 1,056.

July 6   ROBERT WILTSHIRE, son of Richard W , of Little Rowden, Northants, gent

,,   ,,   WILLIAM GILBERT, of Barnard's Inn, son and heir of Robert G , of Melton
                                 [Mowbray, co Leicester, gent

,,   ,,   ANTHONY THOMAS, son of Anthony T , of Chobham Park, Surrey, Knight

,,   ,,   ANDREW POPE, of London, gent

,,   ,,   FRANCIS SITWEIL, son and heir of George S , of Renishaw, co Derby, Esq

,,   ,,   JOHN STANHOPE, son and heir of John S , of Horseforth, co York, Esq

,,   ,,   FRANCIS MOUNTENEY, son and heir of Richard M , of Rotheram, co York, Esq

,,   ,,   JOHN WRIGHT, son and heir of John W , of Wrightsbridge, Essex, gent

,,   ,,   WILLIAM ANDREWS, son and heir of William A , of Appletree, Northants, Esq

,,   ,,   HENEAGE FFTHERSTONE, of Blackfriars, London, Esq

,,   ,,   JOHN HITCHINGE, son of Thomas H , late of Pontefract, co York, gent [Esq

,,   ,,   NATHANIEL HUMPHRIES, second son of John H , of Westminster, Middlesex,

,,   ,,   JOSEPH GARRARD, late of Clement's Inn, Middlesex, gent

folio 1,057

Oct 21   JOHN HARDINGE, son and heir of John H , of Long Bredy, co Dorset, Esq

,,   ,,   FRANCIS SWAINE, son and heir of Francis S , of the city of York, gent.

,,   ,,   JOHN BROOKES, son and heir of James B , of the city of York, Esq

1650		folio 1,057—(continued)

Oct 2 1   CHRISTOPHER BEDINGFIELD, son and heir of Humphrey B , of Wyton, Norfolk,

,,   ,,   FRANCIS NEILOR, of St Giles-in-the-Fields, gent   [Esq

,,   ,,   WILLIAM LILBOURNE, son of George L , of Sunderland, co Durham, Esq

,,   ,,   EDWARD NEVILL, second son of Henry N , of Bathwick, co Somerset, Esq

,,   ,,   JOHN BARRINGTON, of Bentley, co Suffolk, gent

,,   ,,   MICHAEL HARVEY, son of Michael H , late of London, merchant, deceased

,,   ,,   RICHARD STEELE, eldest son of William S , Esq , of this Society, Recorder of
                                                                [the city of London

,,   ,,   WILLIAM LISTER, son of William L , of Colby, co Lincoln, Esq

,,   ,,   THOMAS HORD, son and heir of Thomas H , of Cote, Oxon, Knight

,,   ,,   RICHARD LAMPLUGH, son and heir of Thomas L , of Ribton, Cumberland, Esq

folio 1,058

Nov 12   JOHN TAVERNER, son of John T., of Soundes, Oxon, Esq.

,,   ,,   EDWARD RANDOLPH, son of Edmund R , late of Canterbury, Doctor of Physic

,,   ,,   THOMAS CRADOCK, of Harperley Hall, co Durham, gent

,,   ,,   WILLIAM WILLIAMS, son of Hugh W , of Llantrissaint, co Anglesey, S T D

,,   ,,   RICHARD SHALLCROSSE, son and heir of John S , of Shallcrosse, co Derby, Esq

,,   ,,   ISAAC READE, son of John R , of the city of London, merchant

,,   ,,   JOHN JOHNSON, son and heir of Robert J , of Baynton, co York, clerk

,,   ,   JOHN JONES, of Exeter, Devon, gent

,,   ,,   PAUL BARRETT, son and heir of Paul B , of Chislett, Kent, gent

,,   ,,   JOHN ROBERTS, son and heir of John R , of Canterbury, Knight

,,   ,,   JOHN LLOYD, son and heir of Edward L , of Kelligynan, co Denbigh, gent

,,   ,,   JOHN WILLIAMS, second son of Griffin W , of Nerquies, co Flint, gent

folio 1,059

,,   ,,   RICHARD HUNT, son of Richard H , of London, Esq

,,   ,,   THOMAS HUNT, son of Richard H , of London, Esq

,,   ,,   EDWARD FREEMAN, son of Edward F , of Gray's Inn, Esq

,,   ,,   GODWIN SWIFT, son of Thomas S , of Goodrich, co Hereford, gent

,,   ,,   JOHN POWELL, son of John P , of Llanvard, co Carmarthen, Esq

,,   ,,   THOMAS WORSLEY, son of John W , of Gatcombe, Isle of Wight, Esq   [gent

,,   ,,   THOMAS OWENS, son and heir of Francis O , of Little Brampton, co Hereford,

,,   ,,   JOHN BRIDGES, son and heir of William B , of Bosbury, co Hereford, gent

,,   ,,   ALLAN PRICKETT, son and heir of William P , of Natland, Westmoreland, gent

,,   ,,   EDWARD NEWTON, son of Edward N , of Mickleover, co Derby, gent

,,   ,,   JOSEPH HATCHER, son and heir of Thomas H , of Careby, co Lincoln, Esq

folio 1,060

Dec 10   CHARLES ROGERS, son and heir of John R , of Crowan, Cornwall, gent.

,,   ,,   CHRISTOPHER DRIFFIELD, of Easingwold, co York, gent

,,   ,,   RALPH MILBANKE, son and heir of Mark M , of Newcastle-on-Tyne, Esq

,,   ,,   WILLIAM STISTED, son and heir of William S , of Fulham, Middlesex, gent

,,   ,,   EDWARD WEEDON, son of Edward W , of Harefield, Middlesex, gent , deceased

1650   folio 1,060 – (*continued*)

Dec 10   JOHN BRIGGS, son and heir of William B , of Rickmansworth, Herts, Esq

,,   ,,   HENRY RUMSEY, son and heir of Edward R , of Crickhowell, Brecon, Esq

,,   ,,   EDWARD RUMSEY, second son of Edward R , of Crickhowell, Brecon, Esq

,,   ,   CHARLES CREMER, son and heir of Edmund C , of Snetisham, Norfolk, Esq

,.   ,,   ALEXANDER NOWELL, son and heir of Roger N , of Rede, co Lancaster, Esq

,,   ,,   THOMAS WYNNE, of Glydlom, co Flint, second son of John W , of same, gent

,,   ,,   WILLIAM HERBERT, of Swansea, co. Glamorgan, Esq

               folio 1,061   [Cornelius V Knight

,,   31   CORNELIUS VERMUYDEN, of East Greenwich, Kent, Esq , son and heir of

,,   ,,   JOHN CLARKE, of Pinchbeck, co Lincoln, gent

,,   ,,   HENRY CHAMBRE, son and heir of Arthur C , of Petton, Salop, Esq

,,   ,,   PHILIP KINNERSLEY, son and heir of Clement K , of Richmond, Surrey, Esq

,,   ,,   THOMAS BRAND, son and heir of Mathew B , of West Moulsey, Surrey, Knight

,   ,,   WILLIAM HILTON, son and heir of Adam H , of Hilton, co Lancaster, Esq

,,   ,,   ROGER KENYON, of Parkhead, co. Lancaster   [gent

,,   ,,   BENJAMIN WALLINGER, son and heir of Benjamin W , of Great Warley, Essex,

,,   ,,   PETER FABIAN, son and heir of Thomas F., of Straddish Hill, Suffolk, gent

                                           [fawen, co Denbigh, gent

,,   ,,   ROBERT TURBRIDGE, late of Barnards Inn, son and heir of John T , of Caer-

,,   ,,   JOHN LEWIS, son and heir of David L , of Geyrnos, co Cardigan gent

,,   ,,   RICHARD BETENSON, son and heir of Richard B , of Layer de la hay, Essex,

                                               [Knight

,.   ,,   WILLIAM JOHNSON, son and heir of Alexander J , of Rushton Grange, co

,,   ,,   THOMAS DANIEL, son and heir of Roger D , of London, gent   [York, Esq

,,   ,,   RANDLE DOD, son and heir of Thomas D , of Edge, Cheshire, Esq

,,   ,,   THOMAS MILLARD, of Staple Inn, gent

1651   folio 1,062

April 12   JOHN MILLWARD, son and heir of John M , of Snitterton, co Derby, Esq

,,   ,,   WILLIAM BURROUGH, son and heir of William B , of Woodford, Essex, Esq

,,   ,,   THOMAS BRADDYLL, son and heir of John B , of Portfield, co Lancaster, Esq

,,   22   RICHARD LEWIS, gent , son of Lewis Thomas, of Langeney, Brecon, gent

,,   ,,   THOMAS HOSIER, of the town of Brecon, gent   [Inn

,,   ,,   THOMAS TOURNEUR, son and heir of Timothy T , one of the readers of this

,,   ,,   DRYDEN SWIFT second son of Thomas S , of Goodrich, co Hereford, clerk

,   ,,   ——— PICKERING, of London, gent

,,   23   GEORGE BIRCH, second son of Thomas B , of Birch, co Lancaster, Esq

,,   ,,   MATHEW BIRCH, third son of Thomas B , of Birch, co Lancaster, Esq

,,   ,,   THOMAS KINNERSLEY, of Loxley, co Stafford gent   [gent

,,   ,,   THOMAS CHORLEY, second son of Alexander C , of Prescott, co Lancaster,

               folio 1,063   [gent

,,   29   SIMON RUGELEY, son and heir of Benjamin R , of Barton Park, co Stafford,

May 3   ROBERT COPLEY, son and heir of John C , of Doncaster, co York, Esq

1651		folio 1,063—(continued)

May 3   NATHANIEL BAYNE, son and heir of Francis B , of Wes———, in Nitherdale, [co York, gent

,, ,,   THOMAS BURTON, son and heir of Francis B , of Longnor, Salop, Esq

,, ,,   FRANCIS LINDLEY, son and heir of William L , late of Kingston on-Hull, gent ,

,, ,,   SAMUEL GOODAY, son and heir of Forth G , of Preston, Suffolk   [deceased

,, ,,   JOHN BAKER, of Rotherfield, Kent, Esq

,, ,,   HIGGINS JAMES, son and heir of John J., of Trippleton, co Hereford, gent [Middlesex, Esq

,, ,,   HENRY LOVELL, son and heir of Henry L , of Tottenham High Cross,

,, ,,   NATHANIEL BACON, elder son of Nathaniel B , one of the readers of this Inn

,, ,,   SAMUEL BRANDLING, elder son of John B , of Ipswich, Suffolk

,, ,,   JOSEPH VAUGHAN, son and heir of Joseph V , of the city of London, gent

,, ,,   WILLIAM HALE, son and heir of Rowland H , of Kingswalden, Herts, Esq

,, ,,   RALPH WARTON, of Beverley, co York, gent

,, ,,   HENRY HAWTEN, of Barnard's Inn, gent

folio 1,064

,, 6   HENRY CROMPTON, son of William C , late of Bedford, co Lancaster, gent

,, ,,   ALEXANDER VINCUM (or VINCOMBE), of Staple Inn, third son of Andrew V , of [Cranbrooke, Kent, gent.

,, ,,   THOMAS MOSTYN, son and heir of Samuel M , of Holywell, co Flint, gent

,, ,,   HENRY DAVISON, son of Henry D., of London, gent

,, ,,   JOHN SALUSBURY, of Bachegraig, co Flint, Esq

,, ,,   THOMAS STILLINGTON, son and heir of John S , of Kelfield, co York, Esq

,, ,,   RICHARD CHAMBERLAYNE, son and heir of William C , of London, gent

,, ,,   SAMUEL LONT, son and heir of Thomas L , of Godmanchester, Hunts, gent

,, ,,   MATTHEW WHITTINGHAM, of St Martins-in-the-Fields, gent

,, ,,   ROBERT PARKER, second son of Edward P , of Browsholme, co York, Esq.

,, ,,   JOHN COMPTON, son of William C , of Paxton, Hunts, gent

,, ,,   RICHARD BRIDGER, fourth son of George B , of Godalming, Surrey, gent

,, ,,   HENRY ROOTES, son and heir of James R , of Hastings, Sussex, gent

,, ,,   THOMAS HARRIS, of Fladbury, son and heir of Edward H , Esq of co [Worcester.

,, ,,   JOHN KINERSLEY, second son of Clement K , of Richmond, Surrey, Esq

folio 1,065.

June 14   ASHFIELD OGLE, son and heir of Thomas O , of Badwell, Suffolk, Esq

,, ,,   CLIFTON HILTON, son and heir of Nicholas H , late of Bilby, parish of Blyth, [Notts, gent

,, ,,   SAMUEL WARD, son and heir of Isaac W , of Fairfield, Kent, gent

,, ,,   RICHARD BOOKER, son and heir of Richard B , of Horso ——— , Sussex, gent

,, ,,   MILDMAY DOWMAN, son of William D , of Uffington, co Lincoln, Esq

,, ,,   THOMAS COPPIN, son and heir of Thomas C , of Caddington, Herts, Esq.

,, ,,   JOHN COPPIN, second son of Thomas C , of Caddington, Herts, Esq

,, ,,   WILLIAM LEIGH, of Newent, co Gloucester, gent , eldest son of William L , [of same, gent

1651   folio 1,065—(continued)

June 14   JOHN ONEBYE, gent, son and heir of John O, of Hinckley, co. Leicester, Esq

,,   ,,   ANDREW SMALLWOOD, son of William S, of Perry Barr, co Stafford, gent.

,,   ,,   JAMES PILKINGTON, son and heir of William P, of Wigan, co Lanc, gent.

,,   ,,   WILLIAM MORGAN, son of Henry M, of Rubiney, co Glamorgan, gent

,,   ,,   CHARLES RUSHWORTH, of Boston, co. Lincoln, gent

,,   ,,   EDWARD SADLIER, second son of Robert S, of Sopwell, Herts, gent

,,   ,,   JOHN UNDERHILL, second son of Thomas U, of Loxley, co Warwick, Esq

folio 1,066.

,,   28   JOHN LEVER, of Alkrington, co Lancaster, gent

,,   ,,   JOHN CHORLEY, son of William C, of Walton, co Lancaster, gent

,,   ,,   OWEN OWENS, son and heir of Thomas O., of Rheydoes, co Montgomery, gent

,,   ,,   EDMUND WARCUP, son of Samuel W, of Southwark, Surrey, Esq   [Baronet

,,   ,,   PETER HARDRES, son and heir of Richard H, of Hardres Court, Kent,

,,   ,,   RICHARD MARSHALL, son and heir of Thomas M, of Denton, co Durham,
                                                              [Esq

,,   ,,   ALEXANDER WESTLAKE, son of Nicholas W, of Inwardleigh, Devon, gent

,,   ,,   HENRY BELL, son and heir of Edward B, of Pertenhall, Beds, Esq

,,   ,,   ROBERT BARWICK, son and heir of Robert B, of Tolston, co York, Knight
                                                              [(erased)

,,   18   WILLIAM WIDDRINGTON, son and heir of Henry W, of Blackheddon, North-

,,   ,,   JOHN STOUGHTON, of the city of Dublin, gent   [umberland, gent.

,,   HENRY WEEKLY, second son of Henry W., of Attilborough, co North-
                                                              [ampton, gent

,,   ,,   DANIEL OSBORNE, son of Thomas O, of Hollyland, parish of Horley,
folio 1,067.   [Surrey, gent

,,   30   HENRY PIERREPOINT, Marquess of Dorset and Earl of Kingston-upon-Hull

,,   ,,   ALEXANDER RADCLIFFE, of Foxdenton, co Lancaster, Esq

,,   ,,   ROBERT HARRINGTON, of Leytonstone, Essex, Esq

,,   ,,   HENRY HARRISON, second son of Thomas H., of Copgrave, co York, Knight

,,   ,,   GABRIEL MORE, of Grantham, co Lincoln, Esq

,,   ,,   GEORGE WESTBY, son and heir of Thomas W., of Ranfield, co York, Esq

,,   ,,   THOMAS NEWARKE, son and heir of Thomas N, of Aton, co York, Esq

,,   ,,   JOHN GOLLOP, son and heir of John G., of Northboward, Dorset, Esq.

,,   ,,   JOHN CLEYPOLE, son and heir of John C, of Northborough, co Northampton,

,,   ,,   JOHN HERON, of Beverley, co York, Esq   [Esq

,,   ,,   JOHN BLUNT, of Beverley, co York, Esq

,,   ,,   JOHN THURBARNE, son and heir of James T, of Sandwich, Kent, gent, son
                                           [of James T, late of Gray's Inn, Esq

,,   ,,   ROBERT CUTLER, son and heir of Robert C, of Farnham, co Radnor, gent

,,   ,,   THOMAS HOLCROFT, son and heir of John H., of Holcroft, co Lancaster, Esq

,,   ,,   RICHARD ADDERLEY, son of Ralph A, of Coton, co Stafford, Esq

folio 1,068.

Nov 6   THOMAS KNIGHT, son of Isaac K, Bachelor of Divinity

1651		folio 1,068—(continued).
Nov	6	EDWARD MANWARING, third son of Henry M , of Kirmincham, Cheshire, Esq
,,	,	ROBERT WHICHCOTT, gent , second son of Hamond W , late of Dunston, co Lincoln, Knight, deceased [ham, Northumberland, Esq , deceased
,,	,,	GEORGE HESLOP, son and heir of William H , late of Hermitage, near Hex-
,,	,,	JOHN JAY, son and heir of Christopher J , of the city of Norwich, gent
,,	,,	ISAAC COOK, son and heir of James C , of Little Bowden, Northants, gent
,,	,,	GEORGE HEWYT, second son of William H , of Dutton Bassett, co Leicester, Esq [of Falkham, Kent, gent
,,	,,	JOHN WALTER, junior, late of Staple Inn, son and heir of John W , senior,
,	,,	RANDAL BRERETON, son and heir of Randal B , of St Andrews parish, [Middlesex, Esq
,,	,,	GEORGE POLE, son and heir of George P , of Heage, co Derby, Esq
,,	,,	ANTHONY MAYNE, Esq , son and heir of John M , of Linton, Kent, Knight [and Baronet
,,	,,	WALTER MAYNE, second son of John M , of Linton, Kent, Knight and Baronet
,,	,,	PETER MAYNE, third son of John M , of Linton, Kent, Knight and Baronet
,,		RICHARD LOWE, junior, son of Richard L , senior, of Harbridge, Bucks, Esq.
,,	,,	HENRY BEESTON, eldest son of William B , of Postbrooke, Hunts, Esq
,,	,,	THOMAS WALLER, son and heir of Thomas W , of this Inn, Esq

folio 1,069

,,	26	EDWARD BARRETT, eldest son of Thomas B , of Sylerscott, Salop, gent
,,	,,	FRANCIS EWER, of Yexham, Norfolk, Esq
,,	,,	ROBERT LASCELLS, son and heir of Cuthbert L , of Sowerby, co York, gent
,,	,,	PAUL HARRIS, son of Paul H , of Boreatton, Salop, Knight and Baronet.
,,	,,	JOHN WHITFIELD, son and heir of Thomas W , of Biddenden, Kent, gent
,,	,,	SAMUEL HOLDEN, third son of Robert H , of Ashton-on-Trent, co Derby, gent
,,	,,	JOHN-AYTON, son of Robert A , of Herrington, co Durham, gent
,,	,,	JOHN JEFFERSON, son and heir of John J , late of the city of Durham, gent
Dec	23	WILLIAM LEE, eldest son of William L , late of Oswestry, Salop, gent , [deceased
1651-2		
Jan	10	JOHN NEWTON, of Chirbury, Salop, gent , son and heir of Peter N , of the [same, Esq
,,	30	CHARLES FOSTER, second son of Sir Humphrey F , of Aldermaston, Berks,
,,	,,	ROBERT WILLIAMS, of London, gent. [Baronet
,,	,,	WILLIAM GORE, gent , third son of Sir John G , of Gilston, Herts, Knight
,,	,,	EDWARD HALES, of Norton, Kent, Esq , son and heir of Samuel H , late of [Donington, Kent, Esq
,,	,,	EDWARD HERLE, son and heir of Charles H , of Winwick, co Lancaster, gent.
,,	,,	JOHN THROWER, son and heir of John T , of Eye, Suffolk, gent [Knight
,,	,,	GERVAS NEVILL, second son of Sir Gervas N , of Awburne, co Lincoln,

folio 1,070

Feb	2	LEMUEL SHULDHAM, gent
,,	,,	DUTTON SEAMAN, son of Thomas S , of London, gent
,	,,	JOHN WILLIS, second son of John W , late of the city of Winchester, gent

1651-2		folio 1,070—(continued)

Feb 2   NATHANIEL CREW, fourth son of John C , Esq , eldest son of Mr Serjeant
     Sir Thomas C , of Steyne, co. Northampton   [Herts, Esq

,,   ,,   EDWARD SADLIER, second son of Robert S , of Sopwell, near St Albans,

,,   ,,   JOHN BARRINGTON, son of Henry B , of Colchester, Essex, gent   [Northants

,,   ,,   EDWARD BAGSHAW, of Staple Inn, son of Edward B , Esq , of Morton,

,,   12   RICHARD GRAHAME, second son of Sir Richard G , of Norton Conyers, co
     York, Knight and Baronet   [deceased

,,   ,   THOMAS DARCY, son and heir of Thomas D , late of Patteswick, Essex, Esq ,

,,   ,,   JOHN TRICE, gent , second son of Thomas T , late of Godmanchester, Hunts,
     gent   [co York, Knight (admitted before March 21, 1640)

,,   ,,   GODFREY RHODES, Esq , son and heir of Sir Edward R , of Great Haughton,

,,   14   WILLIAM JERMY, eldest son of John J , of Sutton, Suffolk, Esq   [gent

,,   ,,   THOMAS LAMPLUGH, son and heir of George L , of Papcastle, Cumberland,

,,   ,,   RALPH CONINGSBY, son and heir of Ralph C , of Aston, Herts, Esq

		folio 1,071 [Revenue

,,   ,,   HUGH POWELL, of Barnard's Inn, Esq , one of the Auditors of the Public

,,   ,,   WILLIAM BURNET, of Staple Inn, gent.

,,   ,,   JOHN BLUMLEY, eldest son of Lawrence B , of Aldersgate Street, gent

Mar 23   WATKINSON PAYLER, of Thoraldby, co York, Esq

,,   ,,   GEORGE PAYLER, of Nun Monkton, co. York, Esq.

,,   ,,   GEORGE SOUTHCOTT, gent , second son of George S , of Buckland, Devon, Esq.

,,   ,,   JAMES BRYAN, eldest son of John B , of Dale, co Pembroke, Esq

,,   ,,   WILLIAM ROKEBY, son and heir of Alexander R , of Sandall, co. York, Esq

,,   ,,   HUMPHREY BORLASE, son and heir of Nicholas B , of Borlase, co Cornwall,
     Esq   [Esq

,,   ,,   THOMAS HUSSEY, son and heir of Thomas H , of Hungerford Park, Berks,

,,   ,,   WILLIAM HUSSEY, second son of Thomas H , of Hungerford Park, Berks,
     Esq   [York, Doctor of Divinity, deceased

,,   ,,   HENRY WICKHAM, of the city of York, gent , one of the sons of Henry W , of

,   ,   WILLIAM WOGAN, of Rickardstone, co Pembroke, gent

,,   ,,   JOHN SHAWE, son and heir of John S , of Ferry-on-the-Hill, co Durham, gent

,,   ,,   PAUL RYCHAUT (Ricaut), son of Sir Peter R , of Aylesford, Kent, Knight

,,   ,,   RALPH DAWSON, son of Marmaduke D , of Suncliffe, co York, gent

,,   ,,   SAMUEL BUCK, son of John B , of Cambridge University, Esq

1652		folio 1,072

May 12   CHRISTOPHER BAYNE, eldest son of Christopher B , of Kilburne, co York, gent

,,   ,,   SAMUEL BYFIELD, eldest son of Richard B , Rector of Long Ditton, Surrey

,,   ,,   JOHN YOUNG, eldest son of John Y , of Colbrook, Devon, Esq

,,   ,,   WILLIAM DANIEL, eldest son of Thomas D , of Silsoe, Beds, Esq

,,   ,,   GEORGE JERMY, son of Sir Arthur J , of Knoddishall, Suffolk, Knight.

,,   ,,   SIEWARD LEWKNOR, of Rochester, Kent, Esq   [gent

,,   ,,   JOHN LLOYD, son and heir of Thomas L , of Llanhavon, co. Montgomery,

,,   ,,   NORTON BRYAN, of Bullingbroke, co Lincoln, Esq

1652		**folio 1,072**—(*continued*)
May	12	EDWARD THELWALL, eldest son of Edward T , of Llanbeder, co. Denbigh,
,,	,,	JOHN RAWSON, son and heir of John R , of Fithnge, co York, Esq [Esq
,,	,,	EDWARD LUTWICHE, son and heir of William L , of Salop Esq , deceased.
,,	,,	JOHN BAILEY, eldest son of John B , of Hodsden, Herts, Esq
,,	,,	ALINGTON PAINTER, son and heir of William P , of Gellingham, Kent, Esq
,,	,,	JOHN MAPLETOFT, of Margaretting, Essex, gent [Knight, deceased
,,	,	CHARLES LE GROS, second son of Sir Charles Le G , of Crostwick, Norfolk,
,,	,,	THOMAS CRADOCK, son and heir of Joseph C , of Harperley Hall co Durham, [Doctor of Laws

folio 1,073

,,	27	JOHN JOHNSON, eldest son of John J , of Lingfield, Surrey, Esq
,,	,,	GERVASE DEANE, eldest son of Francis D , of Long Eaton, co Derby, gent
,,	,,	THOMAS SLATER, of Great St Bartholomews, London, gent
,,	,,	RICHARD EYNES, son and heir of Richard E., of Charlboro', Oxon, Esq
,,	,,	JOHN LAW, eldest son of John L , of Blackburn, co. Lancaster, gent
,,	,,	WILLIAM AMHERST, eldest son of Richard A , of Bayhall, parish of Pepingbury, [alias Pembury, Kent, Esq.
,,	,,	ROBERT LEGARD, son and heir of John L., of New Malton co. York, Esq , [deceased
,,	,,	HENRY KING, son of Sir Robert K , of Whitaker, co Warwick, Knight
,,	,,	EDMUND EYRE-ADDERLEY, son of William A , of East Burnham, Bucks, gent
,,	,,	THOMAS HANSON, of the city of Westminster, gent [H , Doctor of Physic
,,	,,	BRADDOCKE HARFORD, of the city of Hereford, gent , eldest son of Braddocke
,,	,,	GEORGE SMITH, son of Thomas S , of Buscott, Berks, gent
,,	,,	THOMAS SANDERS, eldest son of Francis S , of Hadnam, Bucks, Esq
,,	,,	WILLIAM IREMONGER, son of Humphrey I , of Ampthill, Beds, gent

folio 1,074   [Herts, Esq

July	7	EDWARD WINGATE, son and heir of Edward W , of Lockleys, parish of Welwyn,
,,	,,	WILLIAM BARNARD, of West Heslerton, co York, gent
,,	,,	THOMAS GULSTON, of Witham, Essex, gent , son of John G , Esq , late of [Gray's Inn, deceased (at the request of Mr Justice Atkins)
,,	,,	JOHN GULSTON, of Witham, son of John G , Esq , late of Gray's Inn, deceased
,,	,,	SAMUEL JEPP, of Chew Magna, co Somerset, gent
,,	,,	JOHN STRACHEY, of Chew Magna, co Somerset, gent.
,,	,,	RICHARD HALSALL, son of John H , of Meriden, co Warwick, Esq
,,	,,	THOMAS BROCK, eldest son of William B , of ———, Suffolk, Esq
,,	,,	ROBERT BROCK, second son of William B , of ———, Suffolk, Esq
,,	,,	ISAAC PEDDER, son of Toby P , of Hunstanton, Norfolk, Esq
,,	,,	JOHN GUN, of Clanville, Oxon, gent , formerly of Staple Inn
,,	,,	WILLIAM LANGHORNE, son and heir of William L , of Hitchin, Herts, gent
,,	,,	EDWARD GRAY, son and heir of Edward G , of Beverley, co York, gent
,,	,,	JOSEPH HILL, of Bramley, co York, gent
,,	,,	MARCHMONT NEDHAM, of the city of Westminster, gent

1652.   **folio 1,075**

Aug 2   ANTHONY SMITHSON, son of Hugh S , of Richmond, co York, Esq

,, ,,   JAMES DILLON, eldest son of Luke D , of Trim, co Meath, Esq   [gent

,, ,,   JOHN SMITH, of Clerkenwell, gent , son and heir of John S , of Laycock, Wilts,

,, ,,   THOMAS BROWNE, son of John B , late of Bromley, Kent, Esq

,, ,,   JOHN DONCASTER, of St Mary Bothaw, London, gent

,, ,,   ROBERT BRATHWAITE, of Bewley Castle, Westmoreland   [Esq

,, ,,   GEORGE EVELYN, son and heir of George E , of Hammersmith, Middlesex,

Oct 21.   GEORGE SACHEVERELL, son and heir of Valence S , of Sutton Coldfield, co
                                             [Warwick, Esq

,, ,,   WILLIAM LILBURNE, son of George L , of Sunderland, co Durham, Esq

,, ,,   MAURICE DIGGS, son and heir of Thomas D , of Chilham Castle, Kent, Esq

,, ,,   WILLIAM HUDSON, son and heir of William H , of Tottenham High Cross,
                                     [Middlesex, Esq , deceased.

,, ,,   GEORGE VINCENT, son and heir of George V , of Stow Bardolph, Norfolk, gent

,, ,,   JOHN CULPEPPER, second son of Sir Thomas C , of Folkington, Kent, Knight,

,, ,,   WILLIAM MORTON, of Staple Inn, London, gent (erased)   [deceased

,, ,,   ROBERT REDMAYNE, son and heir of John R , late of Fonforth, co York, Esq

                            folio 1,076.

,, ,,   WICKSTED WELD, late of Barnard's Inn, gent

,, ,,   SIMEON BROGRAVE, son and heir of Edward B., of Gray's Inn, Esq

,, ,,   JOHN PORTER, son and heir of Richard P , of Halesworth, Suffolk, gent

,, ,,   WILLIAM WHITTINGHAM, gent , son of John W , gent , of the city of Chester

,, ,,   THOMAS WRIGHT, son and heir of Thomas W , of Lexham, Norfolk, Esq
                                           [Chester

,, ,,   JOHN SHENTON, gent , son and heir of William S , late of Rotherstone, co.

Nov 16   THOMAS OWEN, eldest son of Edward O , of Dint Hill, Salop gent

,, ,,   EDWARD HOPTON, son and heir of Morgan H , of St Andrews, Holborn, Esq

,, 19   ARTHUR BORRON, son of Arthur B , of Warrington, co Lancaster, gent

,, ,,   HUMPHREY MACKWORTH, son of Humphrey M , of Gray's Inn, Esq

,, ,,   MORGAN WYNNE, eldest son of Richard W , of Pentre Morgan, Salop, Esq
                                        [Knight, deceased

,, ,,   RICHARD LUCY, Esq , third son of Thomas L , late of Charlcote, co Warwick,

,, ,,   JOHN HOLT, son of Thomas H , of Gray's Inn, Esq

                            folio 1,077.

,, 20   JOHN WILLOUGHBY, Esq , son of Philip W , late of Grendon co North
                                       [ampton, Esq , deceased

,, ,,   EDMUND STAFFORD, son and heir of Thomas S , of ———, co Bucks, Esq

               [co Kent, Esq , deceased (presented by William Dixon, an antient)

,, ,,   CHARLES DIXON, gent , son of Henry D , late of Hilden, parish of Tunbridge,
                                       [Baronet.

,, ,,   THOMAS HASLERIG, eldest son of Sir Arthur H , of Noseley, co Leicester,

,, ,,   ROBERT NEWCOMEN, son of Robert N , of Raseby, co Lincoln, gent.

,, ,,   DORINGTON CLARK, son and heir of Valentine C , of Marlborough, Wilts, gent

,   THOMAS MILFORD, of St. Martins in-the-Fields, Middlesex, gent

1652   folio 1,077—(*continued*).

Nov 20   WILLIAM CARR, eldest son of Robert C , of Etall, Northumberland, Esq

,,   ,,   WILLIAM NEWBOLD, son of William N , of London, gent.

,,   ,,   THOMAS JOHNSON, son and heir of William J , of Oldney, Bucks, Esq

,,   ,,   WILLIAM BODING (*alias* Pudding), son and heir of William B (*alias* P), late
                           [of Saxlingham, Norfolk, clerk, deceased

,,   ,,   RICHARD ASHEBY, of Stratton Audley, Oxon, gent

,,   ,,   THOMAS PIERSON, of St Andrews, Holborn, Middlesex

,,   ,,   JOHN FISHER, of Staple Inn, gent.

folio 1,078

,,   26   ALEXANDER RIGBY, Esq , son and heir of Edward R , late of Burgh co
          Lancaster, Esq , deceased   [Lancaster, Esq , deceased

,,   ,,   THOMAS GRENEHALGH, son and heir of Richard G , late of Brandlesome, co

,,   ,,   WILLIAM PENNINGTON, son of William P , of Muncaster, Cumberland, Esq

,,   ,,   LAURENCE IRELAND, Esq , son and heir of Edward I , late of Lydyeate, co
                            [Lancaster, Esq , deceased

,,   ,,   GEORGE HALFHYDE, son and heir of George H , of Maydbury, Beds, gent

,,   ,,   JAMES MICKELTON, son of Christopher M , of the city of Durham, gent

,,   ,,   JOHN KINASTON, of Lee, Salop, gent.   [Baronet

,,   ,,   JOHN EYERY, gent , second son of Sir Symon E., of Eggington, co Derby,

,,   ,,   BENJAMIN AYLOFFE, son and heir of Thomas A , of Brittons, Essex, Esq

,,   ,,   RICHARD WILLOUGHBY, eldest son of Thomas W , of Sutton Coldfield, co.
                            [Warwick, Esq

,,   ,,   MICHAEL HENEAGE, son of Thomas H , of Minchall (Ninghall), Essex, Esq

,,   ,,   HENRY BIRCHINHEAD, son and heir of Henry B , of Walthamstow, Bucks,
                              [gent

1652-3   folio 1,079

Jan. 24   JAMES BOULTON, son and heir of George B , late of Bardney, co Lincoln, gent

,,   ,,   JEDIDIAH HODSON, son of Benjamin H , of Earsbye, co Lincoln, gent

,,   ,,   PHILIP EYTON, eldest son and heir of Sir Thomas E , of Eyton, Salop, Knight

,,   ,,   THOMAS EYTON, second son of Sir Thomas E , of Eyton, Salop, Knight.

,,   ,,   WILLIAM EYTON, fourth son of Sir Thomas E , of Eyton, Salop, Knight.

,,   ,,   RICHARD LUCY, second son of Sir Francis L , of Preston Capes, Northants,
          Esq   [of Divinity

,,   ,,   GEORGE LUCY, son of William L , of Burghclere, co Southampton, Doctor

,,   ,,   THOMAS BROGRAVE, son of John B., of Albury, Herts, Esq

,,   ,,   JAMES HEIRDSON, of Leck, co Lancaster   [Doctor of Divinity.

,,   ,,   ANDREW HACKET, gent , son and heir of John H , of Cheyne, Surrey,

,,   23   JOHN HOBSON, son and heir of William H , of Siceston, co Lincoln, Esq
                              [Knight

,,   ,,   WILLIAM DOYLY, son and heir of Sir William D , of Shottisham, Norfolk,

,,   ,,   EDMUND DOYLY, third son of Sir William D , of Shottisham, Norfolk, Knight

,,   ,,   EDWARD DOYLY, son of Bartholomew D , of Sutton, Norfolk, Esq

folio 1,080.

Feb. 9   JOHN PRESCOT, son and heir of Alexander P , of Thoby, Essex, Esq

1652-3   folio 1,080—(continued)

Feb 9   HUGH POCOCK, of Woodley Farm, Berks, gent

,, ,,   JOHN RICARDS, son and heir of Francis R , of Presteigne, co Radnor, gent

,, ,,   THOMAS CHAMBERLAYNE, son and heir of Thomas C, of Oddington,

,, ,,   JOSEPH HARVEY, gent, of Merton College, Oxford   [co Gloucester, Esq

,, ,,   RICHARD LAMBERT, of Newcastle-upon-Tyne, gent   [land, Esq

,, ,,   RICHARD HIGHMORE, son and heir of Robert H, of Armathwayte, Cumber-

,, ,,   FRANCIS HEWET, of Ampthill Grange, Beds, Esq   [ampton, gent

,, ,,   THOMAS COX, gent, son and heir of Thomas C, of Meares Ashby, co North-

,, ,,   THOMAS SHORT, son and heir of Peter S, of Tenterden, Kent, Esq

,, ,,   GEORGE FELL, eldest son of Thomas F, of Swarthmore, co Lancaster, Esq

,, ,,   WILLIAM PARKER, eldest son of William P, of the Strand, Middlesex, Doctor
                                                              ... [of Physic.

1653   folio 1,801.   [gent

April 27   ROBERT WEST, son of John W, of Lanston, near Horncastle, co Lincoln,

,, ,,   THOMAS REYE, son and heir of Thomas R, of Blo Norton, Norfolk, Esq

,, ,,   ROBERT BUXTON, Esq, son and heir of John B, of Tibbenham, Norfolk, Esq

,, ,,   ANDREW AGAR, second son of John A., of Stockton, co York, Esq.

,, ,,   NATHANIEL WALKER, of Harborough, co Leicester, Esq

,, ,,   HENRY REPPS, son and heir of John R, of Mattishall, Norfolk, Esq.

,, ,,   WILLIAM FINCH, eldest son of William F, of Southill, Beds, gent

,, ,,   CHRISTOPHER NEVILLE, Esq, eldest son of Sir Gervase N, of Awburne, co
              Lincoln, Knight   [barrister)

,, ,,   JOHN SPICER, of Standon, Herts, gent (presented by Mr Hoo Steward,

,, ,,   JOHN SHEFFIELD, son of Sampson S, of Navestock, Essex, Esq

,, ,,   WILLIAM KING, of Harnsworth, Middlesex, gent

,, ,,   ROBERT LEECH, gent, second son of Sir Edward L, Knight, late one of
              the Masters in Chancery, deceased.   [Common Pleas.

,, ,,   JEROM BANKES, third son of John, Lord B, late Lord Chief Justice of the

                             folio 1,082   [Harwood, co. York, Esq

May 23   CHRISTOPHER DRIFFIELD, of Staple Inn, gent., son of William D, late of

,, ,,   EDWARD MASTERS, son of Richard M, of East Langdon, Kent, Esq

,, ,,   MARMADUKE WYVELL, Esq, son and heir of Sir Christopher W, of Constable
              Burton, co York, Baronet   [Doctor of Physic

,, ,,   RICHARD SMITH, eldest son of Thomas S, of St Giles-in the Fields, Middlesex,

,, ,,   ROBERT YALLOP, eldest son of Robert Y, of Thorpe next Norwich, gent

,, ,,   THOMAS GREY, eldest son of Henry G, of Enville, co Stafford, Esq

,, ,,   RICHARD LEIGH, of Lyme, co Chester, Esq   [deceased

,, ,,   ROBERT CROMPTON, gent, son of Robert C, of Great Driffield, co York, Esq,

,, ,,   MAURICE WOGAN, eldest son of Thomas W, of Llanstylan, co. Pembroke,
              Esq   [Esq

,, ,,   WILLIAM WOGAN, second son of Thomas W, of Llanstylan, co Pembroke,

,,   WILLIAM FORSTER, son and heir of Nicholas F, of Bamborough, Northumber-
                                                     [land, Esq, deceased

1653.   folio 1,082—(continued).   [gent

May 23   THOMAS BROWNE, eldest son of Edmund B , of Hungry Bentley, co. Derby,

,, 25   RICHARD ZOUCH, son and heir of Richard S , D C L , of Oxford University

folio 1,083.   [deceased

June 23   WALTER CALVERLEY, son and heir of Henry C , late of Calverley, co York,

,, ,,   WILLIAM LEAKE, eldest son of William L , of Wymeswold, co Leicester, Esq

,, ,,   WILLIAM FRANCKLYN, son and heir of George F , late of London, merchant,
       [deceased

, ,,   ALEXIUS EDEN, third son of Robert E , of Windleston, co Durham, Esq

,, ,,   EDMUND GREGORY, son of Edmund G , of Cuxham, Oxon, Esq

, ,,   JOHN WASTELL, second son of John W , of Scorton, co York, Esq

,, ,,   PATRICK ROCHE, eldest son of Philip R , of Kinsale, co Cork.   [deceased

, ,,   GEORGE CAREW, son and heir of George C , late of Hitcham, Suffolk, Esq ,

,, ,,   JAMES HOLME, son and heir of Thomas H , of Rochdale co Lancaster, gent

,, ,,   THOMAS GUNTER, son and heir of John G , of Hungerford, Berks, gent

, ,,   HENRY (or Thomas) THOMSON, son and heir of John T , late of the city of
       [York, gent , deceased

,, ,,   RICHARD PIERSE, son and heir of John P , of Bedall, co York, Esq

,, ,,   EDMOND DETHICK, Esq , eldest son of John D , Esq , Alderman of London

,, ,,   HENRY MARWOOD, eldest son and heir of George M , of Little Busby, co
       [York, Esq

folio 1,084

Oct 24   JOHN FINCHAM, son and heir of John F , of Outwell, Norfolk, gent

,, ,,   WILLIAM DANBY, son and heir of James D , of the city of York, gent

,, ,,   WILLIAM LIGHTFOOT, son of John L , late of Gray's Inn, Esq , deceased

,, ,,   ROBERT CONNEY, son and heir of William C , of Walpoole, Norfolk, Esq

,, ,,   ROBERT PUDSEY, son and heir of George P , of Langley Hall, co Warwick,
       [Esq.

,,   HENRY PUDSEY, second son of George P , of Langley Hall, co Warwick, Esq.

,, ,,   CHARLES HARDRES, eldest son of Thomas H , of this House, Esq

,, ,,   THOMAS TYRRELL, second son of Sir John T , of Herne, parish of East
       [Horndon, Essex, Knight

,, ,,   RICHARD WELBY, son and heir of William W , of Denton, co Lincoln, Esq

Nov 14   HERBERT AUBREY, son and heir of Herbert A , Esq., of Clayhonger, co

,, ,,   HERBERT WESTFALING, of Mansell, co Hereford, Esq   [Hereford

,, ,,   THOMAS BRADSHAW, son and heir of Henry B , of Wybersley, co Chester, Esq

,, ,,   JOHN PICKERING, son and heir of Robert P , of Walford, co Chester, Esq

,, ,,   RICHARD LIGHTFOOT, son of John L , Esq , late deceased, an antient of this

,, ,,   JOHN JOWLES, of Biddenden, Kent, Esq   [Society

,, 28   SYMON MIDDLETON, of Middlesex, Esq , son of Sir Hugh M., deceased

folio 1,085

,, ,,   JOHN CORNEWALL, of London, gent . son of John C , of the same, deceased.

,, ,,   GEORGE COLLOP, of Staple Inn, gent

,, ,,   JOHN ORLEBAR, son of George O , of Podington, Beds, gent

1653   folio 1,085—(continued)

Nov 28   NICHOLAS NUTLEY, second son of William N , late of the town of Southamp-
[ton, gent , deceased

,,   ,,   ROBERT FISH, second son of Robert F , of Adington, co Northampton, gent

1653-4

Jan 10   THOMAS LYTCOTT, son and heir of Thomas L , of Ealing, Middlesex, Esq

,,   ,,   PIERSE LEIGH, of Bruche, co. Lancaster, gent

,,   ,,   GEORGE RIDER, of Shrewsbury, gent   [certified to be a gent of Staple Inn

,,   ,,   MICHAEL PICKERING, eldest son of Mark P , of Ackworth, co York, gent,

,,   ,,   CHARLES CÆSAR, second son of Sir Charles C , Knight, late Master of the
[Rolls, deceased

,,   ,,   WILLIAM WISEMAN, eldest son of Ralph W , Esq , late of West Malling, Kent

,,   ,,   RICHARD HOBLYN, fourth son of Edward H , late of Nanswhiddon, co Cornwall,
[Esq , deceased

,,   ,,   JOHN BUSBY, son and heir of Robert B , late of Gray's Inn, Esq , deceased

,   ,,   WILLIAM LAMPLUGH, son and heir of Richard L , late of Leverston, co York,

,,   ,,   MARTIN CARTER, of Shalford, Essex, gent   [Esq

folio 1,086   [deceased

,   23   WILLIAM BALL, Esq , son and heir of William B , of the city of London, Esq ,

Feb. 7   RICHARD NEWDIGATE, son and heir of Richard N , of Gray's Inn, Esq

,,   ,,   ROBERT WITHER, son of William W , of Manydoune, co Southampton, Esq
[Knight

,,   ,,   CHRISTOPHER HILDYARD, son and heir of Sir Robert H , of Lynton, co York,

,,   ,,   WILFRID LAWSON, second son of Sir Wilfrid L , of Isell, Cumberland, Knight

,,   ,,   WILLIAM RANDOLPH, of Biddenden, Kent, gent

,,   ,,   ROBERT PHILIPPS, of Wisprington, co Lincoln, Esq   [Baronet

,,   ,,   PAYTON CHESTER, one of the sons of Sir Anthony C of Chicheley, Bucks,

,,   10   GEORGE LYNNEY, of St Giles-in-the-Fields, Middlesex, gent

,,   ,,   FRANCIS WILLOUGHBY, of Colshall, Notts, gent   [Esq

,,   ,,   EDMUND SWETTENHAM, eldest son of Edmund S , of Somerford, co Chester,

,,   ,,   THOMAS BARRINGTON, son and heir of Robert B , late of Hatfield Broad Oak,
[Essex, Esq , deceased

,,   ,,   JOHN BARRINGTON, second son of Robert B , late of Hatfield Broad Oak,
[Essex, Esq , deceased

folio 1,087

,,   11   ALEXANDER FITTON, son of William F., of Gawsworth, co Chester, Esq.

,,   ,,   NATHANIEL JAMES, of Niccolshen, Devon, Esq

,,   ,,   HOWLAND ROBERTS, Esq , son and heir of Thomas R., Esq., deceased, son
[and heir of Sir Walter R., of Glassenbury, Kent, Knight and Baronet

,,   22   Lord HENRIE CROMWELL, second son of His Highness Oliver C , Lord Pro-
[tector of England, Scotland and Ireland

,,   ,,   GEORGE PELHAM, of Brockelsby, co Lincoln, Esq , one of the sons of Sir
1654.   [William P , Knight, deceased

April 15   WILLIAM SWAYNE, of Sarson, co Southampton, gent.

,,   12   THOMAS ADAMS, second son of William A , of Owston, co York, Esq

| 1654 | | folio 1,087—*(continued)* | [Esq |

1654

April 12   THOMAS ASHURST, Esq , eldest son of William A , of Ashurst, co Lancaster,

,,   ,,   JOHN (or Joseph) BRAME, eldest son of John B , of Campsie Ash, Suffolk, Esq

,,   ,,   THOMAS BISHOP, son and heir of ——— ., of Midleton-cum-Fordley,
                                        [Suffolk, gent

,,   ,,   THOMAS BULKLEY, son of Thomas B , of Barronhill, co Anglesey, Esq

,,   ,,   HENRY BULKLEY, son of Thomas B , of Barronhill, co Anglesey, Esq

,,   ,,   EDWARD GODDARD, Esq , son and heir of Francis G , late of Standon Hussey,
                                        [Wilts, Esq , deceased

folio 1,088

,,   25   FRANCIS TUFTON, of ye Mote, Kent, Esq , one of the sons of Sir Humphrey T ,

,,   ,,   JOHN GOODAY, of Pentlow, Essex, gent   [Knight and Baronet

,,   ,,   WILLIAM BRANTHWAYTE, of Hethel, Norfolk, Esq

,,   ,,   SAMUEL BUCK, son of John B , of Cambridge, gent

,,   ,,   FRANCIS CARLYLE, second son of Lawrence C , of Bishop's Norton, co
           Lincoln, Esq   [gent

,,   ,,   THOMAS MOORE, son and heir of Thomas M , of Sewsterne, co Leicester

May 1   ROBERT MARRIOT, of Bradfield, Suffolk, Esq , son of Robert M , gent , one of
                             [the Antients of Barnard's Inn

,,   ,,   ROBERT HOWARTH, son of ———, co Lancaster, gent   [gent

,,   ,,   JOHN PHILLIPS, son and heir of Robert P , of Langdon-upon-Teigne, Salop,

,,   10   BRIAN FAIRFAX, second son of Henry F , of Bolton Percy, co York, clerk

,,   ,,   WILLIAM HAMMOND, son and heir of Anthony H , of St Albans, East Kent,
                                        [Esq

,,   ,,   EDMUND KENN, son and heir of George K , of Quedgley, co Glouc , Esq

,,   24   WILLIAM WALCOTT, son of Humphrey W , Esq , of Walcott, Salop

,,   ,,   NATHANIEL BROWNE, of Henley, co Worcester, Esq

folio 1,089
                                        [clerk

,,   27   THEOPHILUS EVANS, son and heir of Walter E , of St Clere, co Carmarthen,

,,   30   JOHN WALLER, second son of Thomas W , Esq , an Antient of this Society

June 9   RALPH SMITH, son and heir of Ralph S , of Middleton, *alias* Milton Keynes,

,,   ,,   HENRY MELLOR, son and heir of Robert M , of Derby, gent   [Bucks

,,   ,,   HENRY BEST, of Middleton, co York, Esq

,,   ,,   JOHN WHITE, Esq , son and heir of Thomas W , late of Tuxford, Notts, Esq

,,   ,,   ROBERT SNELL, gent , son and heir of Robert S , late of Denton, Norfolk, gent ,

,,   ,,   RICHARD LLOYD, eldest son of Richard L , of Escluse, co Denbigh [deceased

,,   ,,   WALTER PIGOT, eldest son of Thomas P , of Chetwynd, Salop, Esq

,,   16   LUCIUS GWILLIM, son and heir of Thomas G , of High Holborn, Midd , Esq

,,   17   WILLIAM RIMES, of Staple Inn, gent

,,   19   CHARLES BRADSHAW, son of Charles B , of Holt, co Denbigh, gent

,,   ,,   TUDOR MONSSEY, son and heir of Antony M , late of Cotton, Suffolk, gent

folio 1,090

,,   ,,   CORNELIUS JACKSON, son and heir of John J , of Bubnell, co Derby, gent

,,   21   JOHN PEABLES, son and heir of John P , of Dewsbury, co York, gent

1654		folio 1,090—(continued)
June 21		HUMFRY STEWARD, second son of Humfry S , of Trotton, Sussex, Esq [Knight
,,	,,	WILLIAM RODES, second son of Sir Edward R , of Long Haughton, co York,
,,	,,	JOHN HATFEILD, son and heir of Anthony H , of Laughton in le Morthen, co [York, gent
,,	,,	JOHN WITHAM, son and heir of William W , of Methley, co York
,,	23	ROBERT READ, son of William R , of Thorneham, Norfolk, gent
,,	,,	THOMAS BASKERVILL, son and heir of John B., of Blackden, co. Chester, Esq.
,,	,,	ALEXANDER RIGBY, eldest son of Joseph R , of Aspul, co Lancaster, gent [presented by Mr. Edward Rigby, Barrister of this House)
,,	,,	ROBERT BLANEY, of St Martins-in-the-Fields, Middlesex, gent
,,	26	JASPER PECK, second son of John P , of Trevallin, co Denbigh, Esq
,,	27	WILLIAM FELTHAM, son and heir of Robert F , of Sculthorpe, Norfolk, gent
,,	,,	JOHN GRYFFITH, son and heir of William G , of Llanwaythley, co Anglesey, [Doctor of Civil Law

folio 1,091

,,	,,	OWEN FELTHAM, second son of Robert F , of Sculthorpe, Norfolk, gent
,,	,,	BELLINGHAM WEST, son of Thomas W , of Woodmancote, Sussex, gent
,,	29	ROBERT LEWKNOR, son and heir of Hamon L , of Acrise, Kent, Esq , deceased
July 15		ROBERT BARRINGTON, second son of Thomas B , of Westchester, gent , deceased
,,	20	THOMAS SANDFORD, eldest son of William S , of White Rodding, Essex, clerk
Oct 16		JOHN STANHOPE, son and heir of Richard S , of Eccleshill, co York, gent
,,	18	WILLIAM BURROUGH, son and heir of James B , of the town of Burrough, in [the co of Leicester, gent
,,	,,	CHRISTOPHER MUSGRAVE, second son of Sir Philip M , Baronet, of Edenhall, [Westmoreland
,,	,,	THOMAS LEGH, of Blakeley, co Lancaster, gent.
,,	,,	WILLIAM LAURENCE, son of Anthony L , of Hackney, Midd , gent (erased)
,,	26	JOHN COOCHMAN, son and heir of John C , of Canterbury, gent.
,,	,,	ROBERT DOUGLASS, Esq , eldest son of Sir Robert D , of Blakerstone, Scotland, Knight [gent , deceased
,,	29	RICHARD JESSUPP, son and heir of Richard J , late of Brickford, Suffolk,
,,	31.	JOHN BARGRAVE, son and heir of Robert B., of Patricksbourne, Kent, Esq

folio 1,092

Nov 1		CHARLES CLEAVER, gent , son of Francis C , of Bygrave, Herts, Esq
,,	4	THEOPHILUS HALLIWELL, son of James H , of Pikehouse, parish of Rochdale, co Lancaster, Esq [gent
,,	,,	BRERETON ANKETEIL, son and heir of Francis A , of Shaftesbury, Dorset,
,,	,,	ROBERT DILLINGTON, son and heir of Robert D , of Motteston, Isle of Wight,
,,	7	ABELL RICHARDSON, of Pershore, co Worcester, Esq [gent
,,	,,	JOHN HOLME, eldest son of Robert H , of Netherton, co Gloucester, Esq
,,	8	WILLIAM CLOPTON, son and heir of Thomas C , of Liston, Essex, Esq
,,	,,	WILLIAM GLEW, of Belton, Isle of Axholm, co Lincoln, gent , second son of [James G , late of Belton, gent , deceased
,,	11	ROGER HACKET, son of Roger H , of North Crawley, Bucks, Esq

1654.   folio 1,092—(continued)
Nov 11   STEPHEN KNIGHT, gent, only son of Stephen K, of Norwich, Esq
 ,,   ,,   KENELM DIGBY, gent, Fellow of All Souls College, Oxford
 ,,   14 THOMAS FRERE, second son of Anthony F, of Mulbarton, Norfolk, clerk

                                        folio 1,093   [Esq
 ,,   ,,   HENRY HALLOWAY, gent, son and heir of Thomas H, of Woolwich, Kent,
 ,,   17 WILLIAM MAN, Esq, son and heir of Sir William M, of Canterbury, Knight
 ,,   18 THOMAS COOKE, son of Thomas C, of Melbourne, co Derby, Esq
 ,,   20 WILLIAM BRERETON, of Staple Inn, London, gent
 ,,   ,,   PETER WILLIAMS, of Mold, co Flint, gent   [deceased
 ,,   21 TOBIAS BLAKISTON, son of Tobias B, late of Newton, co Durham, Esq,
 ,,   22 ROBERT JENKIN, son and heir of Godman J, of Harpeden alias Hardinge,
                                                               [Herts, gent
 ,,   ,,   RALPH CARRE, son and heir of William C, of Newcastle-on-Tyne, gent
 ,,   23. HENRY JAMES, son and heir of Henry J, of Redmarley Adam (D'Abitot),
                                                               [co Worcester, gent
 ,,   25 JOHN DAND, son and heir of Rowland D, of Mansfield Woodhouse, Notts,
Dec   1   GUY LEAKE, gent, son of William L, of Newark, Notts, Esq   [Esq
 ,,   ,,   MATTHIAS SOUTHERTON, gent, son and heir of Thomas S of Hellesdon, in
                                                    [the county of the city of Norwich, Esq
 ,,   ,,   RICHARD GILDON, son and heir of Richard G, of Motcombe, co Dorset, gent

                                        folio 1,094   [Northampton, Esq
 ,,   ,,   HAROLD KINNESMAN, gent, son and heir of Richard K, of Broughton, co
 ,,   ,,   WALTER LEIGHTONHOUSE, of Alford, co Lincoln, son of Richard L,
                                                    [Parson of Desford, co Leicester
 ,,   ,,   FRANCIS TAYLOR, of the parish of Quatt, Salop, gent   [gent
 ,,   2   EDWARD COLLINGWOOD, son of Ralph C, of Ditchbourne, Northumberland,
 ,,   6   OWEN GRIFFITH, son of Alexander G, of Glasbury, co Radnor, gent [gent
 ,,   12 THOMAS LYNCH, eldest son of Theophilus L, of Great Sankey, co Lancaster,
 ,,   13 THOMAS HUXLEY, second son of John H, of Edmonton, Middlesex, Esq
 ,,   ,,   JAMES HUXLEY, third son of John H, of Edmonton, Middlesex, Esq
 ,,   16 HENRY HUNLOKE, Baronet, son and heir of Henry H, Knight and Baronet,
            of Wingerworth, co Derby, deceased   [Esq, deceased
 ,,   18 JOHN CALVERLEY, second son of Henry C, of Calverley, West Riding of York,
 ,,   22 WILLIAM PERSHALL, eldest son of Sir William P, of Cannall, co Stafford,
                                                               [Knight

                                        folio 1,095
 ,,   ,,   THOMAS ALDERSEY, son and heir of Thomas A, of Spurstow, co Chester, Esq
 ,,   ,,   JOHN EDISBURY, son and heir of John E, of Pentre-yr-Clawdd, co Denbigh,
            Esq   [Knight
 ,,   ,,   HENRY DACRES, son and heir of Sir Thomas D, of Lanercost, Cumberland,
 ,,   ,,   WILLIAM BUTTERWORTH, son and heir of ——— B., of Belfield, co Lancaster,
1654-5.   [Esq, deceased
Jan. 22 ANTHONY BRADSHAW, of Stifford Clayes, Essex, gent
 ,,   24 JOHN MELLERSH, of Farncomb, parish of Godalming, Surrey, gent

                                        R

ᴠ 1654-5.   folio 1,095—(*continued*).

Jan 26   WILLIAM HOVELL, son and heir of Sir Richard H , of Hillingdon, Norfolk,
                                        [deceased

,,   ,,   WILLIAM HEBBS, son of Thomas H , late of Billerley, Essex, gent , deceased

,,   ,,   ROGER CHALKHILL, only son of Roger C , late of London, gent , deceased

,,   ,,   JOHN TRYE, only son of James T , late of the city of Westminster, gent ,
                                        [deceased

,,   ,,   JOHN THORNICROFT, eldest son of Edward T , of Siddington, co Chester, gent

,,   ,,   JOHN VAUGHAN, eldest son of Richard V , of Courtfield, co Monmouth, Esq

,,   29.   MATHEW BLUCKE, son of William B , of the city of London, Esq

,,   ,,   RALPH GARDNER, of Barnard's Inn, gent , only son of Devereux G , of
                                      [Hunsdon, Herts, Esq.

folio 1,096

,,   ,,   ROBERT CHOPPYNE, of Coddenham, Suffolk, gent

,,   ,,   ANTHONY STURGEON, son and heir of Anthony S , of Chelmsford, Essex, gent

Feb. 2.   JOHN   RIVERS, youngest son of Sir John R , of Chafford, parish of
                                      [Penshurst, Kent, Baronet

,,   ,,   ROBERT SEAMAN, son of William S , of the city of Gloucester, gent

,,   5   SAMUEL LAWSON, eldest son of Samuel L , of Beverley, co. York, gent

,,   6   ALEXANDER WALTHALL, son and heir of Alexander W , of Eggington, co
         Derby, gent   [Notts, Baronet

,,   7.   THOMAS WILLIAMSON, Esq , son and heir of Sir Thomas W., of East Markham,

,,   ,,   HENRY ROOKES, son of John R , of Wickhambrook, Suffolk, gent

,,   ,,   SAMUEL MAWDE, son and heir of John M , of Sowerby, co York, Esq

,,   9   FRANCIS ONGE, eldest son of Francis O , of Peldon, Essex, clerk.

,,   10   RICHARD LILBURNE, son of George L , of Sunderland, co Durham, Esq

,,   ,,   THOMAS HANMER, son of Humphrey H , of Hanmer, co Flint, gent

folio 1,097

,,   12   JOHN SHAN, gent , eldest son of Francis S . of Methley, co York, Esq

,,   ,,   ROBERT ROGERS, gent , eldest son of William R , of the city of York, gent

,,   13   WILLIAM TODD, of Staple Inn, gent , eldest son and heir of Anthony T , of
                                      [Addlethorpe, co Lincoln, gent.

,,   ,,   NICHOLAS ROTHERAM, son of Thomas Atwood R , of Boreham, Essex, gent.

,,   ,,   GEORGE LACOCK, son and heir of Philip L , of East Stoke, Notts, Esq

,,   ,,   THOMAS FOSSAN, gent , son of Thomas F , citizen and skinner of London, gent.

,,   14   WILLIAM ADAMS, gent , eldest son and heir of William A , of Longdon, Salop,

,,   ,,   ROBERT IRTON, third son of Wilfrid I , of Throlcott, Cumberland, Esq   [Esq

,,   ,,   WARNER SOUTH, gent , son and heir of Warner S , late of Altor, Wilts, gent.

,,   16   MARMADUKE URLWIN, son of John U , of Stoke Pogis, Bucks, gent

,,   ,,   ROBERT WILLIMOT, gent , son and heir of Edward W , late of Derby, Doctor
         of Divinity   [of Divinity.

,,   ,,   EDWARD WILLIMOT, gent , second son of Edward W , late of Derby, Doctor

·,   ,,   THOMAS VAUGHAN, eldest son of Henry V , of Pantglas, co Carnarvon, Esq.,
                                      [deceased

1654-5   folio 1,098

Feb 16   ROBERT WILLIMOT, gent, eldest son of Nicholas W, of Gray's Inn, Esq

,,   ,,   NICHOLAS WILLIMOT, second son of Nicholas W, of Gray's Inn, Esq

,,   ,,   JOHN WILLIMOT, third son of Nicholas W, of Gray's Inn, Esq

,,   ,,   MARTIN HEADLEY, gent, eldest son of Charles H, of Snayth, co York, gent

,,   17   JOHN TAYLOR, son and heir of Samuel T, of Norton, co Derby, gent

,,   ,,   THOMAS UMFREVILE, eldest son and heir of William U, of Stoke by
                                              [Nayland, Suffolk, Esq

,,   ,,   ARTHUR HATTON, only son of William H, of Derby, Doctor of Physic

,,   20. THOMAS BIRKBECK, son and heir of George B, of Orton, Westmoreland, gent.

,,   ,,   WILLIAM MIDGLEY, second son of John M, late of Headley, in Bradfordale,
                                              [co York, gent

,,   21   WILLIAM LASCELLES, son and heir of Francis L, of Stanke, co York, Esq

,,   ,,   RICHARD COWSE, second son of Richard C, of Romsey, co Southampton, Esq

,,   ,,   HENRY STEVENSON, eldest son of Christopher S, late of Hulcot, Northants,
                                              [gent, deceased

folio 1,099.

,,   ,,   THOMAS HANBURY, son of John H, of Preston, co Gloucester, Esq

,,   ,,   GEORGE POWELL, of Taunton, co Somerset, gent

,,   ,,   NATHAN DONBARVIN, of the city of Oxford, gent   [gent

,,   ,,   GEORGE VINCENT, son and heir of William V, of Bitteswell, co Leicester,

,,   24   EDWARD PARKER, third son of Edward P, of Browsholme, co York, Esq

,,   ,,   HENRY MARSH, second son of Henry M, of Edgworth, co Gloucester, Esq.

Mar 1   ISAAC MORGAN, gent, son of Henry M, Rector of Kilken, co Flint

,,   5   HENRY WOODWARD, son and heir of Hugh W, of St Martin-in-the-Fields, gent

,,   ,,   ANDREW HILTON, youngest son of Ciprian H, of Arneside, Westmoreland,
1655   [Esq

Mar 27   CUTHBERT ELLISON, son and heir of Robert E, of Newcastle-on-Tyne, Esq

April 6. PETER MANWARING, fourth son of Henry M, of Carnincham, co Chester,
          Esq   [gent

,,   ,,   JOHN HEATHCOTT, younger son of George H, of Culthorpe Hall, co Derby,

,,   ,,   THOMAS SEDGWICK, son and heir of Edward S, of Gray's Inn, Esq

,,   13   JOSEPH SAUNDERS, son and heir of Robert S, of Bow-lane, London, Esq

,,   ,,   ROBERT THORNTON, of Baythorpe, co. Northampton, gent

folio 1,100.

,   23   EDMUND LEWES, son of Sir Thomas L, of Penmarke, co Glamorgan, Knight

,,   ,,   ROBERT BELT, son and heir of Sir William B, late of the city of York,
                                              [Knight, deceased

,,   30   ARTHUR KETTELSBY, son and heir of Arthur K, of London, gent

May 2   JOHN HAGER, of Bourne, co Cambridge, Esq

,,   4   SAMUEL PAWSON, youngest son of Samuel P, of the city of York, gent

,,   7   WISTON BROWNE, fourth son of John B, of Wildhall, Essex, Esq

,,   8   PHILIP STORY, son and heir of Philip S, of Chesterton, co Cambridge, Esq

,,   10   JOHN PAYNELL, son and heir of Robert P, of Gray's Inn, Esq

1655.

May 11   CHARLES ASHBY, of Rickmansworth, Herts, Esq

,,   ,,   EDWARD NEDHAM, son and heir of John N , of Ilston, co Leicester, Esq

folio 1,101 (omitted in pagination)

folio 1,102

,,   17   GEORGE HITCHCOCK, son of John H , of Preshot, Wilts, Esq.

,,   ,,   HENRY DIXON, only son of Edward D , of Hilden, parish of Tunbridge,
                                                    [Kent , Esq

,,   ,,   MILES FINCHAM, son and heir of Thomas F , of Outwell, co , Cambridge, Esq

,,   ,,   CHRISTOPHER SMELT, son of Mathew S , late of Kirkby Fleatham, co York,

,,   ,,   JOHN RISLEY, son of Thomas R., of Chetwode, Bucks, Esq   [Esq

,,   ,,   WILLIAM LEAKE, son and heir of ——— L , of Wymswould, co Leicester,
                                                [Esq (admitted before)

,,   18   JAMES BATE, eldest son and heir of Richard B , of Lydd, Kent, Esq

,,   ,,   THOMAS BARKER, of Churchill, co. Worcester, gent

,,   20   MARK SHAFTOE, second son of Mark S , Esq., a Bencher of this House.

,,   ,,   MARK SHAFTOE, third son of Robert S , of Newcastle-on-Tyne, gent.

,,   ,,   NATHANIEL MIDDLETON, son and heir of John M , of Darlington, co Dur-
                                                    [ham, gent

,,   ,,   CHARLES MORGAN, son and heir of Thomas M., of Lansore, co Monmouth,
                                                    [Esq

folio 1,103

,,   22   JOHN ANDREWES, son of Edward A , of Oxton, Notts, Esq

,,   ,,   THOMAS SHEPPARD, of Hilton, Hunts, gent

,,   ,,   ROBERT CONSTABLE, Esq , son of Francis C , of Clyffe, co York, Esq

,,   25   SAMUEL WARD, son and heir of Samuel W , of Lidgate, Suffolk, Esq

,,   ,,   WILLIAM INGLEBIE, son and heir of William I , late of Pallenthorpe, co
                                                  [York, Esq , deceased

,,   26   ROBERT WOLLEY, of Stortford, Herts, gent (admitted of Staple Inn, 23 May,

,,   25   GREGORY BAKER, of Stortford, Herts, gent   [1645)

,,   26   THOMAS PARKYNS, son of Isham P , of Bunny, Notts, Esq

,,   ,,   RICHARD WILLOUGHBY, son of Robert W , of Lenton, Notts, Esq.

,,   28   WILLIAM BASSETT, Esq , son and heir of Sir Richard B , of Beaupré, co
                                                 [Glamorgan, Knight

folio 1,104

,,   ,,   JOHN GUISE, gent son and heir of John G , of the city of Gloucester, Esq

,,   ,,   THOMAS HORTON, Doctor of Divinity, Master of Queen's College, Cambridge,
         and late Preacher of this Society   [co Rutland, Knight

,,   ,,   BEAUMONT BODENHAM, Esq , son and heir of Sir Wingfield B , of Ryhall,

,,   ,,   ANTHONY MAWDE, son and heir of Robert M , of Ripon, co York, Esq

,,   ,,   HENRY MARSDEN, of Gisborne, co. York, gent., but now of Staple Inn

,,   ,,   CHARLES HERLE, son of Thomas H., late of Prideaux, co Cornwall, Esq ,
         deceased   [minster, Middlesex, Esq , deceased.

June 2   HENRY FAULCONBERGE, third son of John F , of St Anne's-street, city of West-

1655   folio 1,104—*(continued)*.

June 2   RALPH BRADFORD, son and heir of Thomas B , late of Fletham, Northumber-
          land, Esq , deceased.   [co York, Esq

  „   6   WILLIAM DARLEY, gent , son and heir of Richard D , of Bishops Wilton,

  „   „   JAMES CHAPMAN, of Markes Hall, Essex, gent   [umberland, Esq

  „   „   WILLIAM WIDDRINGTON, gent , son and heir of Robert W , of Hauxeley, North-

  „   „   JOHN COGHILL, gent , son of Sir Thomas C , of Blechington, Oxon, Knight

                                folio 1,105

  „   14 NICHOLAS BERNARD, Doctor of Divinity, and Preacher of this Society.

  „   „   RICHARD STREETE, only son of Leonard S , of St Andrews, Holborn, gent

  „   „   JOHN TANAT, son of Rice T , of Aber-Tanat, Salop, Esq

  „   20 JOHN BERNEY, gent , son and heir of Thomas B , of Sewardston, Norfolk, Esq.
                                                                [Esq
  „   „   RICHARD BERNEY, gent , second son of Thomas B , of Sewardston, Norfolk,

  „   „   THOMAS CHURCH, son of Thomas C , of High Holborn, Middlesex, gent.

  „   22 THOMAS FARRINGTON, son and heir of John F , of Chichester, Sussex, gent.

  „   23 JOHN HEATHCOTE, second son of George H , of Culthorpe, co Derby, gent

  „   „   JOHN COREN, third son of John C , of St Stephens, in Braynall, Cornwall,
          gent.   [co Cornwall, gent

  „   25 HUMPHREY LANGFORD, son and heir of William L , of Marham Church,
                                                   [of Great Kimble, Bucks
  „   „   CHRISTOPHER TEMPLE, second son of Christopher T , of Marsh, in the parish

                                folio 1,106.

  „   26 JOHN LEMAN, of Charsfield, Suffolk, gent

  „   28 NATHANIEL BENNETT, gent , son and heir of Gervas B , of Derby, Esq.

  „   „   ANDREW HUDDLESTON, gent , son and heir of Andrew H , of Hutton John,
          Cumberland, Esq   [ampton, gent.

  „   „   JOHN BROGRAVE, gent , second son of John B , of Wappenham, co North-

  „   29 JOHN LITTLETON, gent , son and heir of James L , of Aston, co Hereford,
                                                       [Doctor of Laws

July 2   GEORGE BERNARD, younger son of John B , of Laceby, co Lincoln, Esq

  „   3   NICHOLAS CHAMBERLAINE, of Hunsdon, Herts, gent

  „   „   WILLIAM PHILLIPS, son and heir of Philip Williams, of Darynock, co. Breck-
                                                       [nock, gent.

  „   „   JONATHAN OAKELEY, son of George O., late of the town of Carmarthen, gent ,

  „   4   THOMAS PAGE, son of Thomas P , of Beccles, Suffolk, Esq   [deceased.

  „   „   JOHN OWEN, of Brodelho, co Anglesey, gent.

                                folio 1,107   [Oxford

  „   „   RICHARD KING, of ———, gent , now Master of Arts in Brazenose College,

  „   7   GEORGE DOWNINGE, of Axe-yard, in the city of Westminster, Middlesex, Esq

  „   „   CHARLES GOWER, Esq , son and heir of Sir Thomas G , of Stitnam, co York,
          Knight and Baronet   [Esq

  „   „   LEWIS WATKINS, gent , eldest son of James W , of Llanigon, co Brecon,

  „   10 HUGH AISCOUGH, of Great Carlton, co Lincoln, gent , son and heir of
                                                   [Henry A , of Great Steeping, co. Lincoln, gent

1655   **folio 1,107**—(*continued*).

July 12   WILLIAM PHILLIPPS, gent, son and heir of Rowland P, late of the town of
[Carmarthen, Esq, deceased.

,,   ,,   JAMES WILLIMOTT, son and heir of James W, of Kelsall, Herts, gent.

,,   13   THOMAS ALURED, second son of John A, of Charter House, near Kingston-
[on-Hull, co York, Esq

,,   ,,   SAMUEL BILLINGSLEY, gent, son and heir of Robert B., of St Sepulchres,
[Middlesex, Esq

,,   ,,   EDWARD THELWALL, eldest son of Edward T, of Llanbedr, co. Denbigh, gent

                folio 1,108   [ford, co Durham, Esq

,,   ,,   HENRY BRACKENBURY, gent, third son of John B, of Sellaby, parish of Gain-

,,   14   FRANCIS LEEKE, son and heir of Francis L, of Balderton, Notts, gent.

,,   16   GEORGE FELL, gent, son and heir of Thomas F, Esq, one of the Benchers of
[this Society (*see* also folio 1,080)

,,   20   ARTHUR MATHEWES, son and heir of Edward M, of Burrington, co Hereford
gent   [Knight, deceased

,,   21   JAMES FRANCKLYN, fourth son of Sir John F, late of Willesden, Middlesex,
Knight, deceased   [Sussex, Knight, deceased

,,   30   THOMAS CULPEPER, Esq, son and heir of Sir Thomas C, late of Folkington,

Aug 17   MILES BRANTHWAYTE, second son of Arthur B, of Hether, Norfolk, Esq
[(presented by his brother, Mr William B, of this House)

,,   ,,   THOMAS SERGEANT, eldest son of William S, of the city of Gloucester, gent

Sept 12   RALPH LAWSON, eldest son of James L, of Brough, co York, Esq, deceased

,,   ,,   HENRY LAWSON, second son of James L, of Brough, co York, Esq, deceased

,,   ,,   ROBERT WYNNE, eldest son of John W, of Ystedd, co Denbigh, gent.

,,   22   CHRISTOPHER ROBINSON, son and heir of Adam R, of Penrith, Cumberland,
gent   [Esq (erased)

,,   ,,   SIMON SEGAR, son and heir of Thomas S, of St Giles-in-the-Fields, Middlesex,

,,   ,,   WILLIAM LAWRENCE, son of Anthony L, of Hackney, Middlesex, gent

                folio 1,109   [Knight

Oct 24   ROBERT ANDERSON, son and heir of Sir Francis A, of Bradley, co Durham,

,,   25   THOMAS BRAND, eldest son of Thomas B, of Wandsworth, Surrey, gent

,,   ,,   JAMES OAST, gent, son and heir of Derick O, citizen and merchant of London

Nov 1   FREDERICK BACCHAR (BAKER), of Christ Church College, Oxford

,,   ,,   THOMAS DENTON, son and heir of Thomas D, of Warnall, Cumberland, Esq

,,   2   JOHN BENET, gent, second son of Sir Humphrey B., of Shaldon, co. South-

,,   3   THOMAS LAZONBY, of Escrick, co York, gent   [ampton, Knight.

,,   5,   NATHANIEL FINES, Esq, son and heir of Right Hon Nathaniel F, one of the
[Lords Commissioners of the Great Seal of England

,,   9   CRESWELL LEVINZ, gent, son of William L, of Evenley, co Northampton,
Esq   [Esq

,,   14   DUDLEY DIGGES, gent, second son of Thomas D, of Chilham Castle, Kent,

,,   ,,   RICHARD WINE, son and heir of Richard W, of St. Ives, Hunts, Esq

                folio 1,110   [London

,,   15   JOHN MELLISH, second son of John M, citizen and merchant taylor of

1655   folio 1,110—(continued)

Nov 15   RICHARD LLOYD, third son of Andrew L , of Aston, Salop, Esq   [Hull

,, 17   ROBERT LEGARD, third son of Christopher L , of Anlaby, in the county of

,, 18.   FRANCIS FANE, Esq , son and heir of Sir Francis F , of Aston, co York,
                         [Knight of the Bath

,, 20   SAMUEL DAVIES, son and heir of Nicholas D , of Pentre-y-Coyd (Pentrecoed),
                         [parish of Oswestry, Salop, gent

,, ,,   GEORGE STANLEY, son and heir of William S , of the town of Southampton, Esq

,, ,,   SAMUEL SLEIGH, Esq , son and heir of Sir Samuel S , of Ash, co Derby, Knight

,, ,,   EDWARD SLEIGH, second son of Sir Samuel S , of Ash, co Derby, Knight

,, ,,   WILLIAM WIDDRINGTON, son and heir of Robert W , of Hauxley, North-
                         [umberland, Esq

,, 22   THOMAS PITTS, son and heir of Thomas P., of Niton, Isle of Wight, gent.

folio 1,111.   [Suffolk, Esq

,, ,,   NATHANIEL BACON, one of the younger sons of Nicholas B , of Shrubland,

,, ,,   HENRY BROOKE, second son of Henry B , of Norton, co Chester, Esq

,, 26.   THOMAS TOLSON, gent , son and heir of Lancelot T , of Windsor, Berks, Esq

,, ,,   WILLIAM SALTER, of Richings, Bucks, Esq   [Esq

,, ,,   ALEXANDER COLEBY, eldest son and heir of John C , of Ashkridge, co York,

,, ,,   HENRY THOMPSON, son and heir of George T , of Burford, Salop, gent.

,, ,,   NATHAN ROGERS, son and heir of Wrouth R , of the city of Hereford, Esq

,, ,,   JOHN MINGAY, of Gymingham, Norfolk, gent

folio 1,112.

,, 27   RICHARD ENTWISLE, gent , son and heir of John E , of Foxholes, parish of
       [Rochdale co Lancaster, Esq (presented by John Entwistle, Esq ,
                      [Barrister of the Middle Temple)

,, ,,   JAMES HELLIWELL, eldest son and heir of John H , of Rochdale, co Lanc.

,, ,,   WILLIAM JOHNSON, second son of William J , of Olney, Bucks, Esq   [gent

,, ,,   ROBERT BAKER, son and heir of Anthony B , late of Wrentham, Suffolk, gent

,, 28   RICHARD LISTER, son and heir of Thomas L , of Rowton, Salop, Esq

,, ,,   ROBERT AYTON, of West Herrington, co Durham, gent

,, ,,   ANTHONY MEABURNE, of Pontop, co Durham, gent

,, ,,   HUGH WILLIAMS, son and heir of John W , of Llwayn, co Anglesey, gent

,, ,,   THOMAS GORE, son and heir of William G , of Tooting, Surrey, Esq

,, ,,   WILLIAM GORE, second son of William G , of Tooting, Surrey, Esq (presented
                      [by Mr Thomas Gower, of this House)

folio 1,113.

,, ,,   HUMFREY CLERKE, son and heir of Felix C , of Edmonton, Middlesex, Esq

,, ,,   WILLIAM LOWTHER, son and heir of Wm L , of Swillington, co York, Esq

Dec. 3   ABRAHAM BOURCHIER, of St Clement Danes, Middlesex, gent.

,, 6   JOHN WOLRICH, gent , one of the sons of Sir Thomas W , of Dudmaston,
      Salop, Knight and Baronet.   [John Bynge, Barrister of this House

,, ,,   HENRY BYNGE, son and heir of Henry B , of Hitcham, Suffolk, Esq (by Mr

,, 10   THOMAS HESKETH, of Heslington, co York, Esq

,, ,,   WILLIAM JONES, son of Wm J , of Nashe, parish of Lydney, co. Glouc , Esq

1655.		folio 1,113—(*continued*)
Dec	12	SAMUEL THEED, of Wingrave, Bucks, gent [co York, gent.
,,	14	THOMAS GLEDHILL, son and heir of John G , of the town of Barkisland,
,,	15	WILLIAM CARR, of Newington, Middlesex, Esq
,,	,,	FRANCIS HORTON, third son of Christopher H , of Catton, co Derby, Esq

1655-6		folio 1,114
Jan	2	GEORGE TATTERSHALL, son and heir of George T , of Stapleford, Wilts, Esq
,,	7	JAMES TYRRELL, Esq , son and heir of Sir Timothy T , of Oakeley, Bucks, Knight, being the grandson of Right Hon James (Usher), Archbishop of Armagh, formerly admitted of this Society [Gisburne, co York, Esq.
,,	19	THOMAS LISTER, son and heir of Thomas L , late of Arnold's Biggin, parish of
,,	26	GEORGE HALL, son and heir of Thos. H , of Donnington, co Lanc (*sic*), Esq
,,	,,	WALTER CARNABY, of the city of Westminster, Middlesex, Esq
,,	,,	HUMPHREY RANT, second son of Humphrey R , of Yelverton, Norfolk, Esq. [(by Mr John Rant, Barrister of this House)
,,	,,	LATIMER CROSSE, of Oxford University, gent [Crawley, Beds, Esq
Feb	6	ST JOHN TOMSON, son and heir of St John Thomson (*sic*), of Husband's
,,	9	JOHN BARTON, of Billing, co Lancaster, gent
,,	,,	THOMAS CARPENTER, of Tillington, co Hereford, gent
,,	,,	ROBERT RODD, son and heir of Thomas R , of Foxley, co Hereford, gent

		folio 1,115. [co Cardigan, Esq
,,	12	DAVID EVANS, son and heir of Thomas E , of Peterwell, parish of Llanbedr,
,,	,,	CHARLES TREVANION, second son of Hugh T , of Gerrans, Cornwall, Esq
,,	,,	BRABASON AYLMERE, son and heir of John A , late of Utting, Essex, Esq , [deceased
,,	,,	RICHARD GODBOLD, third son of John G , of Hatfield Peverill, Essex, gent
,,	,,	LUKE CLAPHAM, son and heir of Luke C , of Willenhall, co Warwick, Esq
,,	13	JOHN ONLBY, son and heir of John O , of Hinckley, co Lincoln, Esq , one of [the Antients of this House
,,	,,	DANIEL LLOYD, second son of Daniel L., of Llanon, co Carmarthen, Esq
,,	14	EDWARD FLEETWOOD, son and heir of John F , of Penwortham, co Lanc , Esq
,,	20.	DAVID THOMAS, son of ———— T., of Savernake, Wilts, Esq.
,,	,,	JOHN LLOYD, son and heir of Oliver L , of Lledrod, co Cardigan, Esq
,,	,,	RALPH SWINNERTON, son of John S , of Gray's Inn, Esq

		folio 1,116.
,,	22	LUKE SKIPPON, eldest son and heir of Right Hon Maj gen Phil p S [Esq
,,	,,	TILSTON BRUEN, son and heir of Jonathan B , of Stapleford Bruen, co Chester,
,,	26	JOHN WYNNE, son and heir of William W., of Ty Gwyn, co Carnarvon, gent
Mar	1	WILLIAM SAVILE, son and heir of Thomas S , of Copley, co York, Esq
,,	4	PHILIP LANGDALE, son of Sir Marmaduke L., of Northdalton, co York, Knight
,,	,,	JOHN SALKELD, son and heir of John S , of Threpland, Cumberland, Esq
,,	,,	JOHN AGLIONBY, son and heir of John A , of Carlisle, Cumberland, Esq.
,,	11	FRANCIS JESSOP, of Broom Hall, co York, Esq , son and heir of William J , [late of Broom Hall, Esq , deceased

1655-6		**folio 1,116**—(continued)
Mar	17	ERNEST BYRON, son and heir of Nicholas B , Knight, of Gaynes Park, Essex.
,,	18	THOMAS POWELL, of Staple Inn, London, gent
,,	,,	ROBERT JASON, son and heir of Robert J , of Broad Somerford, Wilts, Esq
,,	,,	HENRY JASON, second son of Robert J , of Broad Somerford, Wilts, Esq

folio 1,117.

,,	19	WILLIAM RADCLIFFE, son and heir of Richard R , of Manchester, co Lanc , Esq
,,	,,	THOMAS BISPHAM, gent , son and heir of Samuel B , of co Lanc , Doctor of [Physic
1656		
April	2	RICHARD SENHOUSE, second son of John S , of Alnbrough Hall, Cumberland,
,,	,,	LANCELOT WHARTON, of Shildon, co Durham, gent [Esq
,,	24	JOHN BROWNELL, son and heir of Richard B , of Stilton, Hunts, gent
,,	26	PHILIP MAINWARING, son and heir of George M , of Sleape, Salop, gent
,,	,,	HENRY SHELLEY, son and heir of Henry S , late of Lewes, Sussex, Esq , deceased
,,	,,	HENRY MILDMAY, gent., second son of Sir Henry M , of Wanstead, Essex
,,	,,	THOMAS WOOD, son and heir of Thomas W , of Orchard, co Devon, Esq

folio 1,118

,,	29	THOMAS WARNE, of the town of Cambridge, gent
,,	30	WILLIAM MELHAM, of Bullington, co Lincoln, Esq
May	1	WILLIAM DAVISON, son and heir of Ralph D , of Wynyard, co Durham, Esq
,,	,,	GEORGE LEA, son and heir of Michael L , of Basingshaw Street, London, gent
,,	2	RALPH BANKES, Esq , son and heir of Sir John B , Knight, late Lord Chief [Justice of the Court of Common Pleas
,,	6	JOHN JOWER, son and heir of Luke J , of Ipswich, Suffolk, gent
,,	,,	WILLIAM CONSTABLE, of Holme in-Spaldingmore, co York, Esq
,,	7	JOHN VENTRIS, of Kempton, Beds, Esq
,,	,,	MARMADUKE BECKWITH, of Aldborough, co York, Esq
,,	,,	WILLIAM SANDERS, son and heir of John S , of Maidstone, Kent, gent
,,	9	JOHN BALGUY, gent , son and heir of John B., Esq , an Antient of this House
,,	,,	St LEGER CODD, son and heir of William C , late of Wateringbury, Kent, Esq.

folio 1,119.

,,	10	WILLIAM BRERETON, of Burras, co Denbigh, Esq
,,	12	ESSEX MEYRICK, Esq , son and heir of Sir John M , late of Mouncton, co [Pembroke, Knight, deceased
,,	,,	JOHN COLLINS, son and heir of John C , late of Priston, co Somerset, gent
,,	14	WILLIAM CARTWRIGHT, son and heir of William C , of Ossington, Notts, Esq
,,	,,	EDWARD WIDDRINGTON, Esq , third son of William, Lord Widdrington, of Widdrington, Northumberland [Winchester
,,	15	THOMAS MUSPRATT, son and heir of Mr Thomas M , Alderman of the city of
,,	,,	WILLIAM HODGES, third son of Thomas H , late of London, Esq , deceased
,,	,,	WILLIAM BIX, gent., son and heir of John B , late of Babchild, Kent, Esq , deceased [Honnington, Kent, Esq
,,	,,	DUDLEY HAMMOND, gent , son of Anthony H , of St Albones, parish of
,,	,,	PIERCE BRACKENBURY, second son of John B , of Sellaby, co Durham, Esq

1656		folio 1,120
May	15	ROBERT SCOTT, son and heir of Thomas S , of Canterbury, Kent, Esq
,,	,,	MICHAELL LEA, of London, gent. [Bramston, co Rutland, gent
,,	16	THOMAS SHUTTLEWORTH (*alias* Shuttlewood), son and heir of Kenelm S , of [wall, Esq , deceased
,,	17	FRANCIS BOND, gent , son and heir of Francis B , late of Bodmin, co Corn-
,,	19	RICHARD GRESWOLD, son of Humphrey G , of Yardley, co Worcester, gent
,,	20	JOHN WILDBORE, son and heir of John W , of Glynton, co Northampton, gent
,,	,,	CHARLES PIDGEON, son of Henry P , of St Edmundsbury, Suffolk, gent
,.	21	JOHN ARDERNE, of Harden, parish of Stockport, co Chester, Esq
,,	22	JOHN IRONS, second son of John I , of Noake, Oxon, gent
,,	,,	THOMAS FRANCKLIN, son and heir of Walter F , of Maidstone, Kent, Esq
,,	,,	THOMAS OCLE, Esq , son and heir of Thomas O , of Pinchbeck, co Lincoln, Esq [Esq
,,	31.	RALPH READ, son and heir of Ralph R , late of East Clinton, Northumberland,

folio 1,121
                                           [Esq , deceased

June	2	THOMAS STUTEVILLE, son and heir of Thomas S., late of Dalham, Suffolk,
,,	5	JOHN TAYLOR, son and heir of John T , of Brimstage Wirrall, co. Chester, gent
,,	9.	JOHN PENRICE, son and heir of John P , of Lincoln's Inn, Esq
,,	,,	EDWARD PENRICE, third son of John P , of Lincoln's Inn, Esq
,,	,,	THOMAS THROWER, of Ipswich, Suffolk, gent [House.
,,	,,	FRANCIS BACON, gent , son and heir of Francis B , Esq , Bencher of this
,,	12	THOMAS BROWNE, of Netherleigh, co Chester, gent [merchant, deceased
,,	,,	ROBERT HOLLIS, son and heir of Maccabeus H , late of Kingston-upon-Hull,
,,	13	ALEXANDER DAVISON, son and heir of Thomas D , of Blakiston, co Durham, Esq [Esq
,,	14.	THOMAS JONES, son and heir of Thomas J , of Dole Cothye, co Carmarthen,
,,	,,	ROBERT DOVE, son and heir of Robert D , late of East Bergholt, Suffolk, gent
,,	,,	THOMAS LLOYD, of Castell Howell, co Cardigan, gent

folio 1,122

,,	15	GEORGE PRICKET, son of Marmaduke P , late of Allerthorpe, co York, gent [Chester, Knight and Baronet
,,	16	THOMAS BRERETON, Esq , son and heir of Sir William B , of Handford, co
,,	19	EDMUND SHUTTLEWORTH, of Barnard's Inn, gent
,,	,,	ROBERT EYRE, son and heir of Robert E , of Highlowe, co Derby, Esq
,,	,,	THOMAS EYRE, second son of Robert E , of Highlowe, co Derby, Esq
,,	,,	RICHARD EYRE, third son of Robert E , of Highlowe, co Derby, Esq
,,	,,	EDWARD KENYON, son of Roger K , of Parkhead, co Lancaster, gent, [deceased
,,	20	ANTHONY RANT third son of Humphrey R , of Yelverton, Norfolk, Esq
,,	,,	JAMES CODD, son and heir of William C , late of Wateringbury, Kent, gent , deceased [Esq
,,	,,	WILLIAM BOWES, son and heir of Robert B , late of Bedwick, co Durham,
,,	,,	JOHN FARNWORTH, son and heir of Edward F , of Euxton, co Lancaster, gent
,,	,,	BENJAMIN GVIES, son of George G., of East Coker, co Somerset, Esq

1656   folio 1,123

June 24   THOMAS BROMFIELD, son and heir of Thomas B , of Udimere, Sussex, Esq

,,   26   JOHN ALLEN, son and heir of Francis A , of Frodley, co Stafford, gent

,,   27.   WILLIAM REMINGTON, gent , second son of Sir Thomas R , of Lund, co York, Knight   [Durham, gent

,,   28   ANTHONY DODSWORTH, son and heir of Anthony D., of Stranton, co

,,   30   JOSEPH CRADDOCK, second son of Joseph C , of Harperley Hall, co. Durham, Doctor of Laws (presented by his brother, Mr Thomas C , of this Inn)

July   2.   RICHARD MIDDLETON, son and heir of Francis M , of Offerton, co Durham, [gent

,,   3   EVAN GWYNNE, third son of Evan G , of Moellyvor, co Cardigan, Esq

,,   ,,   JOHN BELGRAVE, eldest son of William B , of North Kilworth, co Leicester, [gent

,,   ,,   ROBERT ATKINSON, eldest son of Thomas A , of the town of Cambridge

,,   ,,   WILLIAM STYLE, of Hunningstone, Suffolk, gent

,,   8   JOSEPH CLARKE, youngest son of Thomas C , of Mellis, Suffolk, gent.

,,   ,,   MATTHEW POWELL, of Penrose, co Monmouth, gent

                   folio 1,124   [ton, Esq

,,   13   JOHN WHITEHEAD, youngest son of Richard W , of Tytherley, co Southamp-

,,   ,,   EDMUND RYVES, youngest son of Edmund R , of Drayton, co Southampton, [gent

,,   14   ROBERT BEALE, son and heir of Thomas B , of Garford, co Hereford, gent

Aug   7   MATTHEW TREVOR, son and heir of John T , of Trevor, co Denbigh, Esq

,,   26   WILLIAM GROSVENOR, eldest son of William G , deceased, of ye Brand, [Salop, Esq

Oct 20   EDWARD NORTON, third son of John N , of Welton, co York, gent , deceased

,,   21   RALPH WILBRAHAM, third son of Sir Thomas W , of Woodhay, co Chester, [Baronet

,,   23   GEORGE RIDLEY, eldest son of John R , of Alnwick, Northumberland, gent

,,   ,,   JOHN ROBINSON, son and heir of Edward R , of Buckshaw, co Lancaster, Esq

,,   ,,   EDWARD ROBINSON, second son of Edward R , of Buckshaw, co Lancaster, Esq   [Esq , deceased

,   27   THOMAS HUTTON, son and heir of Richard H , late of Poppleton, co York,

,,   31   RICHARD WILKINSON, son and heir of Christopher W , of the Parkhouse in [Burnsall in Craven, co York, gent , deceased

                   folio 1,126.

Nov   2.   WALTER COPE, eldest son of Walter C , of ———, in Ireland, Esq

,,   ,,   ANTHONY COPE, eldest son of Anthony C , of ———, in Ireland, Esq

,,   ,,   CHARLES BUSBIE, son and heir of John B , of the city of London, gent , deceased   [deceased

,,   4   JAMES FULLWOOD, son and heir of ———, F , of Stapenhill, co Derby, gent ,

,,   5.   WILLIAM KILLINGHALL, son and heir of John K , late of Middleton St [George, co Durham, Esq , deceased

,,   7   KNIGHTLEY PUREFOY, third son of George P , of Wadley, Berks, Esq

,,   ,,   JOHN ALDWORTH, of Staple Inn, gent   [gent , deceased.

,,   8   WILLIAM STANE, son and heir of William S , late of Norton Mandevill, Essex,

1656   folio 1,126—(continued).

Nov 10   JOHN SALUSBURY, son and heir of John S , of Bachegreg, co Flint, Esq
  „   „   NATHANIEL NEECH, late of Corpus Christi College, Cambridge Master of
                                                                [Arts
                                                                [Esq

                            folio 1,127.

  „   12   JOHN WIGHT, son and heir of John W , of the parish of St Nicholas, Surrey,
  „   18   EDWARD GREVILL, Esq , son and heir of Sir Fulk G , of White Rodding,
             Essex, Knight   [of this House
  „   19   ROBERT PAVNELL, second son of Robert P , of Gray's Inn, Esq , and a Bencher
  „   20   TYMOTHIE SLADER, of the city of Westminster, Middlesex, Esq.
  „   24   GEORGE MILBURNE, of Chirton, Northumberland, gent
  „   „   JOHN MAN, son and heir of John M , of the city of Norwich, Esq   [Esq
  „   26   HUMPHREY DAVENPORT, son and heir of James D , of Sutton, co Chester,
  „   27   LEWIS THOMAS, third son of Sir Edward T , of Llanvihangel, co Glamorgan,
  „   „   FRANCIS SOUTH, of Kelsterne, co Lincoln, Esq.   [Baronet
  „   28   GEORGE ELPHICK, son and heir of ——— E., of Worth, Sussex, gent.

                            folio 1,128

  „   „   JOHN STONHOUSE, second son of George S , of Radley, Berks, Knight
Dec 4   JOHN CARY, second son of Nathaniel C , of Yeovil, co Somerset, gent.
  „   „   JOHN HULSE, son and heir of Stephen H , of Westwell, Kent, gent
  „   10   GEORGE SKYPP, son and heir of John S , of Ledbury, co Hereford, Esq
  „   „   EDWARD OVERAND, son and heir of George O., of Kirkby Lonsdall, West-
                                                            [moreland, gent
  „   „   JOHN LOCK, son and heir of John L , of Pensford, co Somerset, gent
  „   „   ROBERT CHUTE, son of Robert C , of Welles, co Somerset, gent
  „   26   DAVID MORGAN, son and heir of Morgan David, of Llantrissant, co Gla-
1656-7   [morgan, gent.
Jan 2   JOSEPH PHILLIPPS, of Ledbury, co Hereford, gent   [gent
  „   5   THOMAS HOLBECH, son and heir of Amillian H , of Fillongley, co. Warwick,
                                                            [umberland, Esq
  „   10   GEORGE REVELEY, son and heir of Edward R , of Newton Underwood, North-

                            folio 1,129   [York, Knight of the Bath.

  „   „   HENRY FANE, gent , third son of the Right Hon Sir Francis F , of Aston, co
  „   „   ROBERT HOLCOTT, of Stoughton, co Leicester, gent
  „   „   GEORGE LEIGH, son and heir of John L , of Oughtrington, co Chester, gent
  „   21   JAMES LEWES, son and heir of James L , of Coedmore, co Cardigan, Esq
  „   24   THOMAS SALUSBURY, third son of John S , of Bachegreg, co Flint, Esq
  „   26   BASILL NICOLL, of Isleworth, Middlesex, gent
  „   „   PHILIP HODGSON, of Stixwold, co Lincoln, Esq   [Esq , deceased
  „   27   TIMOTHY STOUGHTON, second son of Anthony S , of St Johns in Warwick,
  „   „   RALPH COOKE, gent., son and heir of Ralph C , of Burstowe, Surrey, clerk.
  „   29   ARTHUR INGRAM, son of Arthur I , of Knottingley, co York, Esq
  „   31   THOMAS WODEHOUSE, son and heir of Philip W , of Downham Lodge, parish
             of Wymondham, Norfolk, Esq   [of Wymondham, Norfolk, Esq
  „   „   EDMUND WODEHOUSE, second son of Philip W , of Downham Lodge, parish

1656-7.   folio 1,129—(continued)

Feb. 4   EDWARD SMITH, son of Thomas S., of Hill Hall, Essex, Esq

  „   „   ROBERT GREENE, son and heir of Robert G., late of Fornecett, Northumber-
                                                                    [land, gent

                                     folio 1130.

  „   2 (sic) THOMAS THOROLD, son of Sir William T., of Marston, co Lincoln, Knight
  „   „   JOHN MORLEY, of Chichester, Sussex, Esq.   [and Baronet
  „   5. NICHOLAS SUGAR, son and heir of George S., of Ashby cum-Tenby, co
  „   „   LAUNCELOT STONOR, of Stonor, co Oxon, gent   [Lincoln
  „   9. RALPH ALLANSON, of the city of Durham, gent.
  „   „   WILLIAM KIRBY, of Cripplegate, Middlesex, gent.
  „   „   SAMUEL WARDE, son and heir of Nathaniel W., of Stapleford Toney, Essex,
  „   10 THOMAS LORAINE, of Kirkharle, Northumberland, Esq   [clerk
  „   11 JOHN LANCASTER, of Cornworthy, co Devon, Esq
  „   „   EDWARD HARFELL, eldest son and heir of John H., of Winchester, co
  „   12 JOHN COGHILL, of Coghill Hall, co. York, gent   [Southampton, gent
  „   „   WILLIAM WALL, son and heir of Joseph W., late of Crondall, co Southampton,
                                                                          [Esq

                                     folio 1,131

  „   „   ROGER CROFT, son and heir of Edward C., of Newby, co York, gent
  „   „   THOMAS NEWMAN, of Chelford, co. Stafford, gent
  „   13 EDWARD ROBERTS, gent, son and heir of Joseph R., of St. Dunstans, Kent, gent
  „   20 WILLIAM RAWLINSON, son of William R., of Graithwayte, co Lancaster, gent
  „   24 PERCIVALL FERBY, son and heir of Sir Leonard F., of Paulscray, Kent, Knight
  „   26 THOMAS IRELAND, of Staple Inn, gent.
  „   27 BENJAMAN PENKEVELL, son and heir of Thomas P., of Tregaire, co Cornwall,
  „   28 THOMAS PIGGE, of Wisbech, Isle of Ely, co Cambridge, gent   [gent
  „   „   THOMAS ANLABY, son and heir of John A., of Etton, near Hull, co York,
Mar   5   HENRY BLUNDELL, of Ince Blundell, co Lancaster, Esq   [Esq
  „   „   WILLIAM WALL, son and heir of the said (sic) Andrew W., now of Ludshott,
                                                              [co. Southampton, Esq

                                     folio 1,132

  „   „   WILLIAM BOARD, of Board Hill, Sussex, Esq
  „   10 JOHN BREWER, son and heir of John B., of St Bartholomews Exchange,
                                                                 [London, grocer
  „   „   WILLIAM GREENWOOD, son and heir of Edmund G., of Skipton-in-Craven, co
1657   [York, gent
April 6   CHRISTOPHER BARRET, son and heir of William B., of Bradwell, Suffolk, gent
  „   11 PHILIP NEVILL, son and heir of ——— N., a merchant of London, deceased,
                                                          [late dwelling in Ivy Lane
  „   13 ROBERT AVERY, son and heir of Robert A., of Witheridge, co Devon, gent
  „   „   WILLIAM PETTY, gent, son and heir of William P., of Storris, co York, gent
  „   17 WILLIAM SYDENHAM, son and heir of Col William S., of Winford Eagle, co
          Dorset, Esq   [Seale, Kent, Baronet
  „   „   THOMAS PEIRS, Esq, son and heir of Sir Thomas P., of Stonepit, parish of

1657   folio 1,132—(continued)

April 18   RICHARD FARMER, son and heir of Richard F , of Daventry, co North-
            ampton, Esq.   [gent.

  ,,   ,, FRANCIS WARDE, son and heir of Francis W., of South Walsham, Norfolk,

                                 folio 1,133.

  ,,   ,, ROBERT STAPLETON, second son of Sir Philip S , of Warter, co York.

  ,,   20 ARTHUR INGRAM, son and heir of Arthur I , of Knottingley, co York, Esq
                                                    [(admitted before).

  ,,   ,, ARTHUR CAYLEY, second son of Sir William C , of Brompton, co York, Knight

  ,,   22. FRANCIS WORTLEY (Sir), of Carlton, co. York, Baronet

  ,,   27. JOHN DAVYES, son and heir of Priam D , of Coxhall, co Hereford, Esq

  ,,   ,, THOMAS CLARK, second son of Sir William C , late of Wrotham, Kent,
                                                    [Knight, deceased

  ,,   29 JOHN BOOTH, son of Mathew B , of Knaresborough, co York, gent.

  ,,   30 SAMUEL SMITH, son and heir of Samuel S , of Colkirke, Norfolk, Esq , a
                                                    [Bencher of this House

  ,,   ,, MATHEW WARD, son of Francis W., of South Walsham, Norfolk, gent

  ,,   ,, PETER BEILBY, second son of William B , of Wetherby Grange, co York, Esq.

May   1   ROBERT SANDFORD, son and heir of George S , of Colchester, Essex, gent

  ,,   ,, JOHN BOOTH, son and heir of John B , of Peasborough, co York, Esq

  ,,   ,, CYRILL WYCH, second son of Sir Peter W , Knight, late of London, deceased

                                 folio 1,134.

  ,,   4   NICHOLAS RIVETT, son and heir of John R , of Brandeston, Suffolk, Esq.

  ,,   ,, CHRISTOPHER WADE, son and heir of Cuthbert W , of Kilnsea, co York,
            Knight.   [deceased

  ,,   ,, THOMAS LUKINE, of Fordwich, Kent, gent , son and heir of John L , Esq , late

  ,,   5. THOMAS BENET, second son of Thomas B , of Babraham, co Cambridge, Esq

  ,,   6   HERBERT PALMER, of Wingham, Kent, gent , second son of Sir Thomas P ,
            Baronet, deceased [parish of Heckfield, co. Southampton, Esq , deceased

  ,,   ,, THOMAS CROMPTON, of London, gent., eldest son of John C , late of Holshot,

  ,,   8   CHARLES VERMUYDEN, gent., son of Sir Charles V , of the city of West-
                                                    [minster, Knight

  ,,   ,, WILLIAM MOORHEAD, son and heir of William M , of Farnham, Surrey, Esq

  ,,   ,, JOHN PENNANT, second son of David P , of Bighton, co Flint, Esq.   [Esq.

  ,,   ,, JOHN MATTHEWES, son and heir of John M , of Trefnanney, co Montgomery

  ,,   6   JAMES PALMER, of Wingham, co Kent, gent , third son of Sir Thomas P
                                                    [Baronet, deceased

  ,,   11 PHILIP BACON, son and heir of Nathaniel B , of Ipswich, Suffolk, Esq.

  ,,   ,, HERBERT ROBERTS, of Abergavenny, co. Monmouth, gent , youngest son of
                                                    [John R., gent , deceased.

                                 folio 1,135.

  ,,   ,, RICHARD JONES, son of Richard J , of Wimborne Minster, co Dorset, gent

  ,,   ,, WALGRAVE CREWE, sixth son of John C , of Stene, co Northampton, Esq

  ,,   ,, CLEMENT HOBSON, of (St) Saviours, Southwark, gent , son and heir of William
                                                    [H , gent , deceased

1657   folio 1,135—(continued)

May 11   THOMAS WILLIAMSON, of Beckingham, co Lincoln, gent, son and heir
                        [of Thomas W , Doctor of Divinity, deceased

,,   ,,   BENJAMAN BROWNLOW, third son of Sir William B., of Humby, co Lincoln,
,,   ,,   JOHN VIGURES, of Parkham, co Devon, gent   [Baronet
,,   ,,   EDWARD BARRY, son and heir of Christopher B , of Hampton Gay, co Oxon,
,,   ,,   EDWARD AYLMER, of Claydon Hall, Suffolk, Esq   [gent
,,   18   CHRISTOPHER CROW, son and heir of Brome C , of East Bilney, Norfolk, gent
,,   21   FRANCIS WILLOUGHBY, Esq., son and heir of Sir Francis W , of Midleton
                        Park, co Warwick, Knight.   [Esq

,,   ,,   EDWARD CLEYPOOLE, eldest son of John C., of Northborough, co Northampton,
,,   ,,   THOMAS GOODING, third son of Henry G., of Wanborough, Wilts, gent
,,   30   WILLIAM BROOKES, of Yoxford, Suffolk, Esq.   [(erased)
June 4   HASELLWOOD PILKINGTON, son and heir of George P , of Stanton juxta Dale,
                        [co Derby

,,   ,,   THOMAS ROOKBY, eldest son of Francis R , of Mortham, co York, Esq
                        [deceased

folio 1,136   [Divinity

,,   8.   JAMES JOHNSON, fifth son of Robert J , of Baynton, co York, Doctor of
                        [and Baronet
,,   9   GEORGE WOLRYCH, sixth son of Sir Thomas W , of Dudmaston, Salop, Knight
,,   15   THEOPHILUS PARKYNS, son and heir of Isham P , of Bunney, Notts, Esq
,,   ,,   ROBERT HARDINGE, son and heir of Robert H , of Gray's Inn, Esq
,,   ,,   FRANCIS STRINGER, of Sutton-upon-Lound, Notts, Esq
,,   ,,   GEORGE TOULSON, son and heir of Clement T , of Lancaster, Esq   [Esq
,,   16   FRANCIS CORNEWALLIS, son and heir of Charles C , of Rock, co Worcester,
                        [Esq
,,   ,,   WILLIAM RAVENSCROFT, son and heir of Thomas R , of Bangor, co Denbigh
,,   ,,   CLEMENT HERNE, son and heir of Thomas H , of Heveringland, Norfolk, Esq
,,   18   MATTHEW WELD, of Barnard's Inn, gent, son of Matthew W , of Bracon-
                        ashe, Norfolk, Esq , deceased   [gent
,,   ,,   WILLIAM BLUNDELL, son and heir of William B , of Prescott, co Lancaster,
,,   ,,   WILLIAM COLE, son and heir of Anthony C , of Horne, Suffolk, gent.

folio 1,137.   [chant.

,,   23.   WILLIAM BROOKES, second son of James B., of Aldermanbury, London, mer-
,,   25.   GEORGE SAYER, second son of Thomas S , of Yarm, co York, Esq
July 1.   WILLIAM FERRERS, eldest son of William F , of Barnes, Surrey, Esq ,
                        deceased   [College, Oxford
,,   2   RUGELEY FERRERS, of Burton-on-Trent, co Stafford, gent , now of Lincoln
,,   7.   THOMAS METCALFE, eldest son of Robert M , of Sowerby, near Allerton, co
                        York, gent.   [Esq
,,   ,,   OSWALD MOSLEY, son and heir of Nicholas M , of Ancoate, co Lancaster,
,,   13.   BENJAMIN CROSSE, fourth son of Thomas C , of Chester, gent , deceased
,,   17   JOHN BOORD, son and heir of John B , of Batcombe, co Somerset, gent
,,   23   ARTHUR INGRAM, son and heir of John I , of Insworth, co Cornwall, gent

1657   folio 1,137 — (*continued*).

July 28   THOMAS LLOYD, gent, son of Thomas L, late of Pentrehobin, co Flint, clerk,
          deceased   [gent

,,   ,,   RICHARD MILWARD, son and heir of Thomas M, of Aldermaston, co. Worcester,

Sept 1   JOHN PETRE, son and heir of John P, Esq, of Fidlers, Essex

                                  folio 1,138.   [Esq.

,,   ,,   ROWLAND GWYNNE, son and heir of William G, of Talliare, co Carmarthen,

Oct. 14   FLEETWOOD SHEPPARD, son of William S, of Rollwright, co. Oxon, Esq.

,,   21   EDWARD TROTTER, of Skelton Castle, co York, Esq

,,   ,,   CHARLES LAYTON, son of Sir Thomas L, of Layton, co York, Knight, deceased

,,   ,,   JAMES RAVEN, of Donnington, co Lincoln, gent, second son of John R, late
                                  [of London, Doctor of Physic, deceased

,,   23. JOHN AUSTEN, son and heir of Robert A, of Hallhand, Kent, Esq

,,   ,,   ROBERT AUSTEN, second son of Robert A, Esq, of Hallhand, Kent, Esq

,,   26. HENRY PORTER, gent, son and heir of Henry P, of Lancaster, Esq

,,   ,,   JOHN WILCOCKE, gent, son and heir of John W, of this Society, barrister

,,   ,,   MICHAEL BEVNON, of Redborne, Herts, gent   [wall, Esq

,,   ,,   JOHN MORTH, gent., son and heir of Edward M., of Talland, co Corn-

,,   ,,   RICHARD BOURNE, of Ufford, co Northampton, gent.

                                  folio 1,139   [Protector's Privy Council

,,   29   SAMUEL JONES, son and heir of the Right Hon Philip J, one of the Lord

,,   ,,   PHILIP JONES, second son of the Right Hon Philip J, one of the Lord Pro-
          tector's Privy Council   [Protector's Privy Council

,,   ,,   JOHN JONES, youngest son of the Right Hon Philip J, one of the Lord
                                                                          [gent

,,   31   THOMAS GILL, son of Thomas G, of Great Bowton, parish of Crepredy, Oxon,

,,   ,,   RICHARD MARSH, gent, son and heir of John M, of St Albans, Herts, Esq

Nov 3   FRANCIS CLEVER, gent, son and heir of Charles C, of Richings Bucks, Esq.

,,   12   WILLIAM ASKEW, gent, son and heir of Hugh A, of Graymayres, Cumber-
          land, Esq   [gent, deceased

,,   14   WILLIAM GWILLIN, gent, son and heir of John G, of Walthamstow, Essex,

,,   18   GEORGE GILBERT TORKINGTON, of London, gent, third son of Lawrence T,
          of Great Stukeley, Hunts, Esq, deceased   [Esq

,,   19. JOHN THOMAS, son and heir of Arnold T, of Lampeter, co Pembroke,
                                                                          [gent

,,   20   WILLIAM WALKER, son and heir of William W, of Kirkham, co Lancaster,

                                  folio 1,140.

,,   21. THOMAS HALFHEID, second son of George H, of Maydburye, Beds, gent

,,   ,,   SILVANUS TOMKINS, second son of John T, late of the city of Worcester, gent

,,   ,,   WILLIAM TOMKINS, third son of John T, late of the city of Worcester, gent.

,,   27. THOMAS MATHEW, of Monk's Castle, co Glamorgan, Esq

,,   ,,   WILLIAM SPRIGGE, of Lincoln College, Oxford, gent

,,   28   EDWARD DOBSON, of Liverpool, co Lancaster, gent

,,   ,,   GEORGE NEVILE, of Thorney, Notts, gent.

1657		folio 1,140—(continued)	[Esq
Nov	28	JOHN BRADSHAWE, son and heir of Richard B , of West Chester, co Chester,	
,,	,,	SUTTON OGLETHORPE, son and heir of Sutton O , of the city of York, Esq	
,,	,,	WILLIAM HOWES, son and heir of John H , of Greenham, Berks, gent	
,,	,,	SAMUEL GREGG, son of Ralph G , of Hammersmith, Middlesex, gent	

folio 1,141.   [Kent, Esq

,,	,,	JAMES OXENDEN, son and heir of Henry O., of Deane, parish of Wingham,
,,	,,	SAMUEL LEECH, of Brentwood, Essex, gent [co. Northampton, gent.
Dec	3	ROBERT STUBBS, of Barnard's Inn, son and heir of John S , of Nassington,
,,	,,	THOMAS FERRAND, of Barnard's Inn, son of Francis F , of Haverhill, Suffolk,
,,	4	JOHN PHILLIPS, son of John P , of Aylsham, Norfolk, clerk [gent
,,	15	ROBERT WYNNE, son of Robert W , of Garthewgen, co. Denbigh, gent [gent
,,	22.	ALEXANDER HAYES, gent , son and heir of Thomas H , of Chertsey, Surrey,

1657-8   [Itchingham, Sussex, Esq ,
Jan 22.   JOHN BUSBRIDGE, gent , son and heir of John B , of Haremo(a)re, parish of

folio 1,142.

,,	,,	THOMAS BEWLY, gent , son and heir of Thomas B , of London, Esq
,,	,,	NATHANIEL STERRY, son of Anthony S , of Southwark, Surrey, gent.
,,	26	BENJAMIN GLADMAN, son of Thomas G , of South Mimms, Herts, clerk
,,	29	ROBERT COLE, third son of Sir Nicholas C , of Kepyer, co. Durham, Baronet
Feb	3	THOMAS SERGEANT, son and heir of Peter S., of Pilkington Strand, co
	5	ROBERT CARR, of Staple Inn, gent. [Lancaster, Esq
,	,,	JOHN PEYTON, of Doddington, Isle of Ely, co Cambridge, gent , son and heir

[of Algernon P , of same, clerk

folio 1,143

,,	6	CLEMENT WINSTANLEY, son and heir of James W , of Gray's Inn, Esq
,,	,,	RICHARD HILL, son and heir of Rowland H , of Soulton, Salop, Esq
,,	10	WILLIAM YEO, son and heir of Robert Y , of Shebbeare, co Devon, Esq
,,	,	JOHN CALVERLEY, son and heir of John C , of Eryholme, co York, Esq
,,	,,	HENRY CALVERLEY, second son of John C , of Eryholme, co York, Esq
,,	,,	LAWRENCE BATHURST, son and heir of Sir Edward B , of Lechlade, co Glou-

                        cester, Baronet   [Kent, Esq.

,,	,,	WILLIAM KENRICKE, son and heir of William K , of Boughton-under-Blean,
,,	12	PHILIP FLANNER, second son of Thomas F , of Withersfield, Suffolk, gent

folio 1,144.

	,,	ROBERT HOW, of Little Waltham, Essex, gent [Kent, Esq.
,,	,,	PETER PETT, son and heir of Peter P , late of Deptford, alias West Greenwich,
,,	,,	TIMOTHY PULLER, son and heir of Isaac P , of Hertford, Esq
,,	26	THOMAS AGAR, son and heir of John A , of Barnes, Surrey, gent [deceased
,,	,,	JOHN VERNON, gent , third son of Sir Edward V , late of Sudbury, co Derby,
,,	,,	JOHN MOORE, son of John M , late of the city of Westminster, gent , deceased
,,	,,	JOHN DONCASTELL, son of John D , of Binfield, Berks, gent
Mar	10	HENRY NORTON (Sir), of Richmond, Surrey, Baronet

1658.   [Esq
April 27   WILLIAM MORGAN, son and heir of Thomas M , of Machen, co Monmouth,

s

1658   **folio 1,146.**

April 27   THOMAS MORGAN, second son of Thomas M , of Machen, co Monmouth, Esq

,,   ,,   THOMAS BUTTON, son and heir of Miles B , of Cottrell, co Glamorgan, Esq

,,   28   JOHN ALURED, son and heir of Christopher A , of Martin, Notts, Esq

,,   ,,   WILLIAM MALIBY, son and heir of Robert M , of Bawtry, co York, gent

,,   ,,   JOHN POLLEN, eldest son of John P , late of London, merchant.   [Esq

,,   ,,   PRICE DEVEREUX, son and heir of George D , of Veynor, co. Montgomery,
                                                          [Standon, Herts, Esq

May 7   EDWARD BROGRAVE, second son of Edward B , of Oldhall Greene, parish of

,,   11   LEONARD WEDDELL, second son of William W , of Earswick, co York, Esq.

                                   folio 1,147.

,,   12.   JOHN JAVE, son and heir of Suckling J , of Holneston, Norfolk, Esq

,,   ,,   JOHN DARRELL, son and heir of Edward D , of Gray's Inn, Esq

,,   ,,   CHRISTOPHER DARRELL, second son of Edward D , Esq , of Gray's Inn

,,   ,,   JAMES ASTYN, son and heir of Edward A , of the city of Oxford, gent.

,,   18   GEORGE CHUTE, second son of George C , late of Bethersden, Kent, Esq
                                                    [Esq , deceased

,,   ,,   RICHARD FOSTER, son and heir of Richard F , of Newham, Northumberland,

,,   ,,   JOHN GARLAND, son and heir of John G , of Todwicke, co York, gent.

,,   ,,   THOMAS MORTON, son and heir of Francis M , of Spouthouse, parish of Brad-
          field, co York, gent   [Gloucester, Esq , deceased

,,   ,,   THOMAS BRIDGES, son and heir of Thomas B , late of Little Colesbourne, co

,,   ,,   WILLIAM SALUSBURY, son and heir of Owen S , late of Rug, co Merioneth,
                                                  [Esq , deceased

,,   ,,   HATTON AUCHER, second son of Sir Anthony A , of Bishopsbourne, Kent,
                          folio 1,148   [Knight

,,   24   WILLIAM PARKER, youngest son of Sir Thomas P , of Willington, Sussex,

,,   ,,   SAMPSON EYTON, of the Moore, near Ludlow, Salop, gent   [Knight.

June 2   RICHARD ALLFRAY, son of Richard A , late of Potmans, parish of Catsfield,
                                              [Sussex, gent , deceased.

,,   ,,   CHARLES BAKER, son of Sir Thomas B , of Aston, co Oxon, Knight

,,   ,,   GEORGE COTTINGHAM, gent , son of George C , of Middle Trafford, co
         Chester, clerk   [Southampton, Esq , deceased

,,   12   RICHARD KNIGHT, son and heir of Richard K , late of Chawton, co

,,   ,,   JOHN BUXTON, scholar of Jesus College, Cambridge, son and heir of Michael
                          [B , of Manchester, co Lancaster, gent

,,   ,,   THOMAS TANNER, of Godmanchester, Hunts, gent

,,   ,,   JOHN SHILLINGFORD (alias Izard), son and heir of John S (alias I) late of
         Beckley, co Oxon, Esq , deceased.   [Glamorgan, Knight, deceased

,,   21   ARTHUR MANSELL, third son of Sir Anthony M , late of Briton Ferry, co

,,   ,,   JOHN DARLEY, son and heir of Richard D , of Bishop Wilton, co York, Esq.

,,   ,,   BENJAMIN DARLEY, second son of Richard D , of Bishop Wilton, co York,

,,   ,,   BARNARD COLE, son and heir of William C., Esq , of this House   [Esq.

                              folio 1,149   [Middlesex

,,   22   CHARLES CLARE, third son of Andrew C , doctor of divinity, of Cranford,

1658   folio 1,149 — (continued)

July 8   JAMES DESBOROWE, second son of Right Honourable John, Lord Desborowe

Sept 16   JOHN STOW, eldest son of William S , of Lutton-next-Trent, co Lincoln, gent.

Nov 1   ROBERT HASILRIGG, second son of Sir Arthur H , of Noseley, co Leicester,
           Baronet   [Esq.

   ,, 13   THOMAS WALL (Walls ?), son and heir of Evan W , of Preston, co Lancaster,

   ,, 17   GEORGE MORRICE, son of Richard M , late of Burbage, co Leicester, gent ,
                                                                            [deceased

   ,, 19   THOMAS MONINS, son and heir of Sir Edward M , of Waldershare, Kent,

   ,, ,,   JOHN ATWOOD, son and heir of John A , of this House, Esq   [Baronet

   ,, ,,   THOMAS EDGAR, son and heir of Thomas E , of Gray's Inn, Esq

   ,, 25   ANTHONY GILEY, son and heir of Anthony G , of Everton, Notts, Esq

                                     folio 1,150.

   ,, 26   ROBERT DAVIES, second son of Robert D , of Gwysanney, co Flint, Esq

   ,, 27   EDWARD LEE, youngest son of Gervase L , of Norwell, Notts, Esq

   ,, ,,   JAMES NASH, son and heir of James N , of Martley, co Worcester, gent

Dec 6   JOHN HAMBY, son and heir of Francis H , late of Tathwell, co Lincoln, Esq

Nov 20 (sic) FRANCIS HUETT, son and heir of Francis H., of Ampthill, Beds, Esq

1658-9
Feb 4   JOHN POOLEY, son and heir of Sir William P , of Boxsted, Suffolk, Knight

   ,, 5   WILLIAM RIVETT, son and heir of William R , late of Bildeston, Suffolk, Esq ,
           deceased   [Esq , deceased

   ,, ,,   WILLIAM COOPER, son and heir of John C , late of Ratling Court, Kent,

   ,, 9   MICHAEL WRIGHT, son and heir of John W , of Brixworth, co Northampton,
                                                                              [gent

                                     folio 1,151.

   ,, ,,   THOMAS PATRICKSON, son of Joseph P , of the How, Cumberland, gent

   ,, ,,   EDMOND TREHARNE, of Munks Castle, alias Castle Menich, co Glamorgan,

   ,, 21   THOMAS BULWER, of Whitgift, co York, gent   [gent

   ,, ,,   CHARLES REEVE, son and heir of John R , late of the city of Westminster,
                                                                           [deceased

   ,, 26   ALLAN SWANWICKE, son and heir of Samuel S , of Oswestry, Salop, gent

1659
Mar 31.   ROBERT PLUM, second son of Samuel P , of Great Yeldham, Essex, gent

April 18   JOHN LAWSON, son and heir of John L , late of Cramlington, Northumber-
                                                                  [land, Esq , deceased

   ,, 22   MARK MILBANKE, son and heir of Mark M , of Newcastle-upon-Tyne

   ,, ,,   ROBERT MARRIOT, son and heir of Robert M , of Lenham, Kent, gent

                      folio 1,152   [late of London, Esq , deceased

   ,, ,,   FRANCIS OFFLEY, of Bermondsey, Surrey, Esq , son and heir of Thomas O ,

   ,, 29   GEORGE VYNER, son and heir of Sir Thomas V , of London, Knight (being
           allowed from his admission at Lincoln's Inn, April 24, 1656, and paying
           half fine)   [Esq

May 3   CHRISTOPHER BERESFORD, son of Christopher B , late of Fulbeck, co. Lincoln,

   ,, ,,   PETER MANWARING, son and heir of Henry M , late of Kerminchan, co
                                                              [Chester, Esq , deceased.

                                        S 2

1659   folio 1,152—(*continued*)

May   4   EDMOND WEBB, son and heir of Edmond W , late of Rodborne, Wilts, Esq

,,   11   WILLIAM ALLESTREY, son and heir of Roger A , of Derby, gent

,,   ,,   THOMAS LAW, of Ocley, son and heir of Thomas L , late of Whaddon,
                                               [Bucks, gent , deceased

,,   18   AUGUSTINE REEVE, son of Augustine R , of Bracondale, Norfolk, gent

folio 1,153

May 30   DANIEL POPLER, of Southwark, Surrey, gent

June 3   EDWARD MASTER, son and heir of Edward M , of Canterbury, Esq

,,   9   EDMUND STEDE, son and heir of Edmund S , of Biddenden, Kent, gent

,,   ,,   EDMUND DRAYNER, son and heir of Robert D , of Biddenden, Kent, gent.

,,   18   JOHN STUFFIN, son and heir of John S , of Shyrbrooke, co Derby, gent.

,,   21   WILLIAM STOW, son and heir of William S , of Swinthorpe, co. Lincoln, gent ,
                deceased   [Salop, Esq , deceased.

,,   23   PONTSBURY OWEN, son and heir of Pontsbury O , late of Eaton Mascott,

,,   ,,   [DANIEL BEDINGFIELD, O B. ii. f 13 (Trin Term)]

,,   21   HENRY SCLATER, son and heir of Henry S , of Lightoakes, co Lancaster, Esq.

July 4   RICHARD BRADSHAW, of Staple Inn, gent

,,   13   JOHN JACKSON, son and heir of Robert J , of Ash, Salop, gent

,,   ,,   EDMOND ASSHTON, of Chadderton, co Lancaster, Esq

,,   ,,   ANTHONY CAICOT, of Pickering, co York, gent

folio 1,154.

,,   ,,   JAMES CHEETHAM, son and heir of Edward C , of Smedley, parish of Man-
            chester, co. Lancaster, gent

Aug 1   ROBERT DUKENFEILD, son and heir of Robert D , of Dukenfeild co Chester,

Oct 20.   RALPH WIDDRINGTON, third son of William, Lord Widdrington   [Esq.

,,   24   THOMAS FAWKES, son and heir of Michael F , late of Farneley, co York, Esq ,
            deceased.   [deceased

,,   31.   APSLEY NEWTON, son and heir of William N , late of Lewes, Sussex, Esq ,

,,   ,,   THOMAS HART, son of George H , late of the city of Bristol, gent., deceased

Nov 1   JAMES MURGATROYD, son and heir of John M , of Ridlesden, co York, gent

,,   3   CHRISTOPHER WILKINSON, son and heir of Francis W , of Oxenefeild, co.
                                               [Durham, gent

,,   14.   THOMAS BRETT, son of Thomas B , of Snave in Romney Marsh, Kent, gent

folio 1,155   [deceased

,,   16.   WILLIAM SAVILE, son of William S , late of Pontefract, co York, Esq ,

,,   18   HENRY BROMFEILD, son and heir of Henry B., of Haywood, in the New
                               [Forest, co Southampton, Esq

,,   26   DAVID WILLIAMS, son and heir of Thomas W , of Llethercadfen, co.
                                          [Carmarthen, Esq

,,   29   JOHN SPENCER, son and heir of Edward S , of Rendlesham, Suffolk, Esq

Dec 12   JOHN SOTHERION son and heir of John S , late of this Society, Esq , deceased

1659-60.

Jan 27   FRANCIS NEAVE, son of Henry N , late of Witchingham, Norfolk, gent

1659-60		folio **1,155**—(continued)

Feb 13 JOHN BUXTON, second son of John B., of Tibenham, Norfolk, Esq

,, ,, FRANCIS BRADBURY, son of Francis B., late of Wickin, Essex, Esq., deceased

,, 21 EDMOND BLACKBORNE, son and heir of Henry B., of Wymondham, Norfolk,
[gent

folio **1,157**   [deceased

,, 27 JOHN HOYLE, son and heir of Thomas H., late of the city of York, Esq.,

,, ,, ROBERT HOPWOOD, younger son of Edmond H., of Middleton, co Lanc., Esq

Mar 24 BENJAMIN HOLLY, son and heir of Benjamin H., of Lynn, Norfolk, Esq

,, ,, WILLIAM BLUNT, third son of William B., of Beverley, co York, gent

1660

Mar 26 JAMES TENNANT, son and heir of James T., of Roughton, Norfolk, gent

April 2 WILLIAM TALCOTT, son and heir of William T., of New Windsor, Berks, Esq

,, 5 LEWES MEYRICK, son of Edmund M., of Ulcheldrei, co Merioneth, Esq

,, 11 GRIFFITH LLOYD, son and heir of William L., late of Lanarthney, co Car-
[marthen, Esq., deceased

,, 12 WILLIAM SAVILE, son of Thomas S., of Copley-in-Skircoate, co York, gent

folio **1,158**

May 12 JOHN SEDGWICKE, son of William S., late of the city of Durham, gent

,, 14 JAMES BRIAN, son of Patrick B., of Ludenham, Kent, Esq

,, 15 WILLIAM BUTCHER, son of John B., of Staplehurst, Kent, Esq.   [gent

,, 18 NICHOLAS CUNLIFFE, son and heir of John C., of Woodhead, co Lancaster,

,, 31 JOHN ANTHONY VAN VOLKENBURGH, Baronet, son of Sir Mathew V., late of
[Middlings, co York, Baronet, deceased

June 16 ELLIS YOUNG, son and heir of Richard Y., of Bringwin, co Flint, Esq

,, 19 GEORGE KNIPE, son of William K., of Semley, Wilts, gent   [deceased

,, 25 THOMAS SPENCER, son and heir of Mathew S., late of Canterbury, gent,

,, ,, WILLIAM SPENCER, son of Mathew S., late of Canterbury, gent, deceased.

May 15 (sic) JAMES COCKS, son of James C., of Bromsgrove, co Worcester, gent

folio **1,159**   [before)

June 30 THOMAS HUXLEY, son of John H., of Edmonton, Middlesex, Esq (admitted

July 2 RICE WILLIAMS, son and heir of Nicholas W., of Rhyd Odgvyan, co
[Carmarthen, Esq

,, 3 ROGER OATS, son and heir of Roger O., of Landenny, co Monmouth, Esq

,, 4 RICHARD SWYNFEN, son and heir of John S., of Swynfen, co Stafford, Esq

,, 5 ROBERT CROKE, Knight, son and heir of Henry C., late of Chequers, Bucks,
Knight, deceased   [deceased

,, ,, WILLIAM DIXON, son and heir of William D., late a Fellow of this Society,

,, 6 THOMAS CHOWNE, son and heir of Henry C., of Slinfold, Sussex, Esq.

,, 7 JUSTINIAN CHAMPNEYS, son of John C., of Wrotham, Kent, clerk.

,, 9 THOMAS FANSHAWE (Sir), specially admitted

,, ,, JOHN MATTHEW, son and heir of Brian M., late of Hoddington, co South-
[ampton, gent, deceased

folio **1,160**.

,, ,, GEORGE CANNING, son and heir of William C., of Akgany, co. Londonderry.

1660   folio 1,160—(continued)

July 10   St John Jones, son and heir of William J , late of Bridgewater, co Somerset,
                                                              [Esq., deceased

„ 12   John Salesbury, second son of Owen S , of Rug, co. Merioneth, Esq

„ „   Gabriel Salesbury, third son of Owen S , of Rug, co. Merioneth, Esq.

„ 14   William Thelwall, son of Edward T , of Llanbedr, co Denbigh, gent

„ 25   William Welby, son of William W , late of Denton, co. Lincoln, Esq ,
                deceased.   [Suffolk, gent.

Oct 6   Stephen Blomfeild, son and heir of Stephen B , of Stonham Aspall,

„ 12   Humphrey Monoux, son and heir of Humphrey M , of Wotton, Beds, Esq

„ 22   Edward Walker, Knight, Principal King of Arms and Garter , one of the
                                              [Clerks of the King's Privy Council.

                                    folio 1,161

„ „   William Dugdale, Esq , Norroy King of Arms.

„ 23   Charles Amherst, second son of Richard A , of Bayhall, parish of Peping-
                bury, alias Pembury, Kent, Esq   [Norfolk, gent

„ 27   Henry Reve, son and heir of Augustine R , of Barkendell (Bracondale),

Nov 1   John Moyle, Esq , son and heir of Robert M , of Buckwell, Kent, Knight,
                " anno fælicissimo 1660, anno 12 optime regis Caroli Secundi "

„ „   Richard Hutton, second son of Richard H , of Poppleton, co York, Esq

„ 2   John Porter, son of Thomas P., late of this Inn, Esq , deceased

„ 7   Roger Moore, son and heir of James M , of Brandsbancke-in-Middleton,
                                                              [Westmoreland, gent

„ 9   Henry Chapman, eldest son of Henry C , a Bencher, specially admitted (O B)

, 10   Richard Davenport, son and heir of Richard D , of Oswestry, Salop, gent

                                    folio 1,162   [gent

„ 14   Thomas Carter, son and heir of Thomas C , of Northweston co Oxon,

„ „   James, Marquess of Ormonde, Earl of Ormonde, Ossory and Brecon ,
                Viscount Thurles, Lord Seaton of Arklow and Lanthony, Lord of the
                royalties and liberties of the county of Tipperary, Chancellor of the
                Academy of Dublin, Lord Steward of the King's Household, of the Privy
                Council of both England and Ireland, Gentleman of the King's bed-
                                              [chamber, and Knight of the Garter

„ „   Thomas, Earl of Ossory, eldest son of James, Marquess of Ormonde

„ „   Lord Richard Butler, second son of James, Marquess of Ormonde

„ „   Lord John Butler, third son of James, Marquess of Ormonde

„ 17   Justinian Pagett, son and heir of Justinian P , of this Inn, Esq

„ 21   Richard Mayne, son of John M , of Elmedon, co Warwick, gent

                                    folio 1,163   [Baronet, deceased

, 24   Richard Colbrond, Baronet, son and heir of James C , late of Lewes, Sussex,

„ „   Edward Ward, son and heir of Edward W , of Bixley, Norfolk, Esq

„ 26   William Busby, son of Robert B , of Addington, Bucks, Esq , deceased

„ 27   John Greenfield, son and heir of John G , late of London, gent , deceased

„ 28   Thomas Southouse, son and heir of Thomas S , of Faversham, Kent, gent.

„ „   Richard Crashaw, son and heir of Joshua C , of Woolley, co York, gent

1660-1.   folio 1,163 —(*continued*)   [erased)
Jan 20. THOMAS GOODING, son of Henry G , of Wanborough, Wilts, gent. (This entry
 ,, 23   JOHN CLAVERING, son and heir of James C , of Axwell, co Durham, Esq
 ,, 25   WILLIAM ELLISON, son of John E , of Silkston, co. York, gent

                          folio 1,164.   [Esq , deceased
 ,, 26   NICHOLAS MAULEVERER, son and heir of John M., late of Letwell, co York,
 ,, ,,   SAMUEL SALTONSTALL, son of Samuel S , late of Rogerthorpe, co York, Esq
 ,, ,,   CHRISTOPHER COE, son of Stephen C , of Ordsall, Notts, gent
 ,, 28   WILLIAM WOODROFFE, son of John W , of Yarmouth, Norfolk, gent
 ,, 31   THOMAS ROWE, son and heir of Thomas R., of Hornsey, Middlesex, Knight.
Feb 2.   DANIEL O'NEALE, Esq , one of the Gentlemen of the King's Bedchamber
 ,, ,,   ROBERT ASKWITH, son of Robert A , of Newton-on-Derwent, co York, gent.
 ,, ,,   ROGER TIRWHITT, son and heir of Cecil T , of Cameringham, co Lincoln,
                                            [Esq

                          folio 1,165.
 ,, 5.   ROBERT BARKHAM, second son of Robert B , of Wainfleet, co Lincoln, Knight
 ,, ,,   ROBERT MORETON, son and heir of William M , of Hulme Walfeild, co
        Chester, gent   [Sussex, gent
 ,, 6   EDWARD LUXFORD, son and heir of John L , of Ockley, parish of Kymer,
 ,, 12   WILLIAM FISHER, son and heir of Francis F , late of Threckington, co
1661   [Lincoln, Esq
May 1   WILLIAM SPENCER, son of William S , of Attercliffe, co York, Esq
 ,, 2   JOHN COCKSHOTT, son of John C , late Fellow of this Inn, deceased
 ,, 4   DANIEL WIGMORE, son of Gilbert W , of Shelford, co Cambridge, S T P

                          folio 1,166.
 ,, 6   THOMAS VACHELL, son and heir of Thomas V , of Chertsey, Surrey, Esq
 ,, 8   RICHARD JONES, son of Richard J , late of Wimborne Minster, co Dorset,
                                   [deceased (erased)
 ,, ,,   JAMES HOLLINGWORTH, son of Arthur H , of St. Andrews, Holborn, gent
 ,, 13   HENRY HARPUR, second son of John H , of Caulke, co Derby, Baronet
 ,, 14   FRANCIS EDGCUMBE, son of Piers E , of Mount Edgcumbe, co Devon, Esq
 ,, 15   WILLIAM GRAY, son of William G , late of South Minster, Essex, gent , de-
        ceased   [co Lincoln, Esq ,
 ,, ,,   MARMADUKE DARELL, of Staple Inn, son of Marmaduke D , of Horkstow,
 ,, ,,   THOMAS PAGITT, second son of Justinian P , Fellow of this Inn

                          folio 1,167.   [gent
 ,, 18   MARTIN FO(U)LKES, of Rushbroke, Suffolk, son and heir of Martin F , of same,
 ,, ,,   RICHARD ALEXANDER, son and heir of Richard A , of London, Esq
 ,, ,,   THOMAS STAMP, son and heir of John S , of Speenhamland, Berks, Doctor of
                                      [Medicine
 ,, 21   ELEAZAR DUDLEY, son and heir of William D , of Elstree, Herts, Esq
 ,, 23   THOMAS BROMSALL, son and heir of Owen B , of Biggleswade, Beds, Esq
 ,, 24   REGINALD BRETLAND, son and heir of John B , late of Thorncliff, co Chester,
                                      [Esq , deceased

1661   folio 1,167—(continued)

May 27   HENRY STEBBING, son and heir of Henry S , of Wisset, Suffolk, gent

  ,,   ,,   CHARLES MOREAU, son of Paul M , of Leyland, co Lancaster, Esq

                                   folio 1,168.

  ,,   31   THOMAS HOLT, son and heir of Robert H , of Castleton, parish of Rochdale,
            co Lancaster, Esq   [deceased

June 18   ROBERT WYNN, son of John W , late of Kesselgyfurch, co Carnarvon, Esq ,

  ,,   21   THOMAS LANGFORD, of Staple Inn, son and heir of Charles L , of Sibston
                                        -                 [Castle, Salop, Esq

  ,,   22   JOHN BRIGHT, son of John B , late of Sheffield, co York, gent , deceased.

  ,,   24   THOMAS KING, son of John K , of Coggeshall, Essex, Esq

July 3   MICHAEL LOWE, son and heir of ———— L., late of co Stafford, gent , deceased

  ,,   ,,   WILLIAM MORE, of Loseley, Surrey, Baronet   [deceased

  ,,   15.   WILLIAM DAWSON, son and heir of George D , late of Azerley, co. York, Esq ,

  ,,   16   FRANCIS ROOKES, son of George R , of London, gent.

                                   folio 1,169   [Esq

  ,,   22.   WILLIAM KNIGHT, son and heir of Isaac K , of Brackenbury co Lincoln,

Aug 24   JOHN STEVENS, son and heir of John S., of Colchester, Essex, gent

  ,,   ,,   RICHARD GRIFFITH, son and heir of Richard G , late of Walton, Surrey,
            gent , deceased   [Esq , deceased

Oct 26   PHILIP BABINGTON, son of William B , late of Ogle Castle, Northumberland,

  ,,   28   MONTAGUE CHOLMLEY, son of Montague C , late of Easton, co Lincoln, Esq ,
            deceased   [deceased

  ,,   ,,   MICHAEL GOLD, son and heir of Richard G , late of Cork, Ireland, Esq ,

Nov 1   EDMUND WALLER, son and heir of Thomas W , of Gregories, near Beacons-
                                               [field, Bucks, Esq

  ,,   ,,   CHARLES DALYSON, son of Charles D., Knight, Serjeant-at-Law.

                                   folio 1,170

  ,,   4   WILLIAM DAWGS, son and heir of William D., of Hatfield, Herts, Esq.

  ,,   7   EDMUND SHEFFEILD, son and heir of James S., of Kensington, Middlesex, Esq

  ,,   8   WILLIAM RUDINGE, son and heir of Walter R , of Leicester, Esq

  ,,   11   JOHN OVERTON, of Easington, co. York, Esq   [merchant

  ,,   12   GEORGE ENGLAND, son and heir of George E , of Yarmouth, Norfolk,

  ,,   13   ANTHONY ELCOCKE, son and heir of Anthony E , Subdean of York

  ,,   ,,   JOHN PARKINSON WYKES, son of John W , of Harbridge, co Southampton,
            Esq   [Esq.

  ,,   15   THOMAS IRELAND, son and heir of Robert I , late of Albrighton, Salop,

  ,,   19   HATTON BERNERS, son and heir of Hatton B , of Thavies Inn, London, gent .

                                   folio 1,171

  ,,   21   JOHN TAYLOR, son of William T , of the city of York, Alderman   [Esq

  ,,   ,,   CHRISTOPHER PEPPER, son of Cuthbert P , of Farrington Hall, co. Durham,
            Esq   [deceased

  ,,   28   JOSHUA GREENE, son and heir of Joshua G., late of Lynn Regis, Norfolk, Esq ,

1661		folio 1,171—(continued)
Dec	5	THOMAS COTCHETT, son and heir of Robert C., late of Mickleover, co Derby, [gent, deceased.
1661-2		
Jan	27	THOMAS GRIFFITH, son and heir of George, Bishop of St Asaph.
,,	29	ROBERT KIRKE, son of Matthew K, of Gainsborough, co. Lincoln, gent
Feb.	1	EDWARD PEKE, son and heir of Thomas P, of Canterbury, Esq
,,	7	WALDEGRAVE ALEXANDER, son and heir of Thomas A, late of Framling-[ham, Suffolk, Esq., deceased.
1662		
April	10	GEORGE MORLAND, son and heir of John M, of the city of Durham, gent

folio 1,172   [Manchester, co Lancaster, gent

,,	,,	JAMES LIGHTBOWNE, of Edmund Hall, Oxford, son and heir of James L, of
,,	,,	ROBERT BURDETT, son and heir of Francis B, of Foremark, co Derby, Bart
,,	14	WALTER FITZGERALD, of Ladiestoune, co Kildare, gent
,,	17.	JOHN BROWNE, second son of John B, of Neale, co Mayo, Esq
,,	,,	GEORGE WALTON, son and heir of George W, of Little Burstead, Essex, Esq
,,	23	JAMES BRADLEY, son and heir of Mark B, late of London, gent, deceased
,,	29	ROGER ELLETSON son of Robert E, of Broughton-in-Furness, co Lancaster, gent
May	2	WILLIAM NUTT, son and heir of William N, of Chigwell, Essex, Knight
,,	,,	JOHN CASTLETON, eldest son of John C, of Stuston, Suffolk, Baronet
,,	,,	PHILIP CASTLETON, second son of John C, of Stuston, Suffolk, Baronet

folio 1,173   [deceased

,,	6	WILLIAM VERE, gent, son and heir of John V, late of Henley, Suffolk, gent,
,,	7	THOMAS CHARLTON, son and heir of Thomas C, of Chilwell, Notts, Esq
,,	,,	DANIEL SULLEY, son and heir of Daniel S, of Nottingham, gent
,,	9	ROBERT SUCKLING, son and heir of Robert S, of Wodeston, Norfolk, Esq
,,	12	THOMAS CLARKE, son and heir of John C, of Bury St Edmunds, Suffolk, gent
,,	22	LEFTWICH OLDFEILD, son and heir of Leftwich O, of Leftwich, co Chester, Esq
,,	28	WILLIAM LOVEINGE, of Staple Inn, son and heir of William L, of West-minster, Esq [deceased
,,	31.	FRANCIS WAKEMAN, son of Edward W, late of Middle Temple, Esq,
June	3	HENRY LAMBTON, son of Henry L, of Lambton, co Durham, Esq
,,	7	TEMPLE NELSON, son and heir of Robert N, Esq, Fellow of this Society

folio 1,174

,,	,,	EDMUND POTT, son and heir of Edmund P, of Pott, co Chester, Esq
,,	,,	WILLIAM COO, son and heir of William C, of Cranford, co Northampton, Esq.
,,	12	THOMAS BURGH, son and heir of John B, of Low Layton, Essex, gent
,,	14	MARK MOTT, son and heir of Mark M, of Great Wratting, Suffolk, gent
,,	,,	RATCLIFF SCOFELD, son and heir of James S, of Scofeld, co Lancaster, Esq
,,	16	JOHN LOWE, son and heir of Francis L, Esq, late Fellow of this Inn, deceased.
,,	18	PATRICK PLUNKET, son of William P, of Tullagnog, co Meath, gent
,,	,,	JAMES AYLMER, son of Andrew A, of Donadea, co Kildare, Knight and Baronet.
,,	21	JEROME HANMER, son and heir of James H, of Maesbrook, Salop, gent.
,,	23	GREGORY BYRNE, son of Daniel B, of the city of Dublin, gent

1662   folio 1,174—(continued)

June 26. JOHN WINCHCOMBE, son and heir of John W , of Henwick, Berks, Esq
    ,,   ,,   THOMAS HOGAN, of Great Dunham, Norfolk, Esq

                              folio 1,175.

    ,,   ,,   ROBERT DAVIES, son of Robert D , of the city of Chester, gent., deceased
    ,,   28   ROBERT LLOYD, son of Thomas L , of Llanhavon, co Montgomery, gent
Aug 1   JOHN BYRNE, son of Daniel B , of the city of Dublin, gent
    ,,   ,,   SAMUEL DRAX, of London, Esq   [gent , deceased
    ,,   ,,   EDWARD ALPE, son and heir of Edward A , late of Framlingham, Suffolk,
    ,,   7   Prince GEORGE, Duke of ALBEMARLE, Captain-general of the Army of the
                                                    [King, Privy Councillor, K G.
    ,,   ,,   CHRISTOPHER, Earl TORRINGTON, eldest son of George, Duke of Albemarle
    ,,   ,,   CHARLES, Earl of WARWICK, Baron Rich, of Leighs
    ,,   ,,   CHARLES, Lord RICH, eldest son of Charles, Earl of Warwick
    ,,   ,,   PHILIP HOWARD, Knight, second son of William H , Baron of Naworth

                              folio 1,176

    ,,   ,,   HENRY MONCKE, Esq , Lieutenant of the King's Horse, cousin of George,
    ,,   ,,   THOMAS CLARGES, Knight   [Duke of Albemarle, aforesaid
    ,,   25   WILLIAM JUSSUP, of Clerkenwell, Middlesex, Esq   [gent
    ,,   ,,   EDWARD WALLIS, son and heir of Thomas W , late of Ormsby, co Lincoln,
Sept 30   JOHN SWYNFEN, son of John S , of Swynfen, co Stafford, Esq   [deceased
Oct   1   ADAM WELSH, son of Nicholas W , late of Ballykaroge, co Waterford, Knight,
    ,,   15   GILBERT ORMSBY, second son of Robert O , of Tobernady, co Roscommon,
Nov   1   THOMAS NEWDIGATE, third son of Richard N , Serjeant-at-Law   Esq
    ,,   ,,   WILLIAM WIDDRINGTON, son and heir of Henry W , Knight [of Medicine
    ,,   ,,   SAMUEL SWALLOW, son and heir of William S , of Chelmsford, Essex, Doctor
    ,,   11   SAMUEL CLARKE, son of John C , of Bury St. Edmunds, Suffolk, Esq

                              folio 1,177.

    ,,   14. NATHANIEL JOSCELYNE, son and heir of John J , Fellow of this Society [Esq
    ,,   15   PHILIP SANDERSON, second son of Christopher S , of Eggleston, co Durham,
    ,,   ,,   ROBERT MARKHAM, son and heir of Robert M , late of Grebby, co Lincoln,
                                                            [gent , deceased
    ,,   17   GARDINER HEWYTT, son and heir of William H , of Breccles, Norfolk, Knight
    ,,   18   JOHN WRIGHT, son and heir of John W , late of Brabeiffe, Surrey, Esq , deceased
    ,,   ,,   WILLIAM SAMPSON, son of William S , of South Leverton, Notts, gent
    ,,   24   HENRY HALFORD, second son of William H , of Welham, co Leicester, Esq
    ,,   25   EDWARD ALSTON, son of Edward A , of Strixton, co Northampton, Knight
    ,,   ,,   GEOFFREY BOYS, son of John B , of this Inn, Esq
    ,,   28   JOSHUA LOMAX, of Staple Inn, gent.
    ,,   ,,   RICHARD FANNING, son of Geoffrey F , of Ballingarry, co. Tipperary, Esq
Dec   2   JOHN DARNALL, son and heir of Ralph D , Fellow of this Society

                              folio 1,178.   [gent , deceased

    ,,   3   WILLIAM BOSVILE, eldest son of Edward B , late of Temple Cowley, Oxon,

1662-3   folio 1,178—(continued)

Jan 23   THORESBY HARDRES, son of Richard H , of Upper Hardres, Kent, Baronet
Feb 2   JOHN LEGARD, son and heir of John L , of Ganton, co York, Baronet
 ,, 4   JOSEPH PRIESTLEY, son of John P , of Halifax, co York, deceased
 ,, 5   PHILIP SKIPPON, son of Philip S , late of Acton, Middlesex, Esq , deceased
 ,, 12   WILLIAM WILSBY, son and heir of John W , Fellow of this Society
 ,, 26   MOSES GOODYEARE, son of Moses G , late of London, gent , deceased
Mar 9   GEORGE ENT, son and heir of George E , of near Guildhall, London, Doctor
                                                                    [of Medicine
 ,, 10   THOMAS DALSTON, son of John D , of Acorn Bank, Westmoreland, Esq
1663
April 14 PHILIP BODENHAM, son and heir of John B , of Orpington, Kent, gent
 ,, 27   RICHARD ALLIBOND, son of Job A , of Dagenham, Essex, gent

folio 1,179

 ,, 28   WILLIAM LONG, son and heir of William L , of Barton, co Lincoln, gent
May 9   THOMAS YATE, son of John Y , late of Lyford, Berks, Esq , deceased
 ,, ,,   FRANCIS FOULKE, son and heir of Francis F , of Camphire, co Waterford,
 ,, 12   JOHN BRAGE, son of William B , late Fellow of this Society, deceased [Knight.
 ,, 15   THOMAS GIFFORD, son of George G , Fellow of this Society
 ,, ,,   WILLIAM DADE, son and heir of Thomas D , of this Inn, Esq
 ,, 16   JOHN HALL, son of Nicholas H , of Otterbourne, Northumberland, gent
 ,, ,,   THOMAS LEGH, son of Thomas L , of Adlington, co Chester, Esq
 ,, ,,   HENRY JONES, son and heir of Arthur J , of Chastleton, Oxon, Esq
 ,, 21   GEORGE LANGTON, son and heir of William L , of Stainsweeke, Berks, Esq
 ,, 23   JOHN CLARKSON, son of William C , of Kirton, Notts, Esq

folio 1,180.

May 28   EDWARD RAINEY, son of John R , late of Wrotham, Kent, Baronet, deceased
June 1   JOHN ELLISON, son and heir of James E , of Skircoate, co York, gent
 ,, ,,   SAMUEL BAKER, son of Anthony B , late of Wrentham, Suffolk, gent
 ,, 2   JAMES ARMSTON, son and heir of James A , of Burbage, co Leicester, gent
 ,, 3   SAMUEL SANDERS, son and heir of Thomas S , of Little Ireton, co Derby, Esq
 ,, ,,   STEPHEN MELLICHAP, son and heir of Richard M , of Willeyhall, co Hereford,
 ,, 25   CHARLES INGLEBY, son of John I , of Lawkeland, co York, Esq   [gent
 ,, 26   ROBERT HUNT, son and heir of Robert H , of Hempstead, Norfolk, Esq
 ,, ,,   THOMAS OWEN, son and heir of William O , of Comeog, co Pembroke, Esq
July 1   HENRY PENFOLD, son of ——— P , of Walton-upon-Thames, Surrey, gent
 ,, ,,   EVAN LLOYD, second son of Roger L , late of London, gent , deceased
 ,, 2   RATCLIFF TODD, late of Barnard's Inn, gent

folio 1,181

 ,, 3   HENRY JOWLES, son of John J , late of Newington Butts, Surrey, Esq ,
 ,, 7   THEOPHILUS BEVAN, of Staple Inn, gent.   [deceased
 ,, ,,   ROBERT MARLEY, son of John M , of Newcastle on-Tyne
 ,, 15   BENJAMIN LAWE, son and heir of Richard L , of Woodhouse, co York

1663   folio 1,181—(continued)

July 30 THOMAS RICHARDSON, son and heir of Matthew R, of Rownehead, co Lan-
                                      [caster, Esq.

Aug 3 FRANCIS ALLEN (alias Edgely), son of Thomas A (alias E), of Gretton, co.
                                      [Northampton, gent

Oct 17 ANTHONY VERNATTY (Vernetty), son of Maximilian V, of St Andrews,

,, 23 JOHN JONES, son of Richard J, of Stowey, co Somerset, Esq [Holborn, Esq

,, 24 RICHARD NAGLE, son of James N, of Claner ———, co Cork

Nov 5 CHARNEL MEAD, son of William M, of Narbarrow, co Leicester, Esq.

folio 1,182

,, 9 GILBERT THACKER, son and heir of Gilbert T, of Repington, co Derby, Esq

,, ,, JOHN WILKINSON, Esq, one of the six Clerks in Chancery

,, 10 THOMAS CARLOS, son and heir of William C, of Brewood, co Stafford, Esq

,, 12 ROBERT WARCOP, son of Thomas W, of East Tanfield, York, Esq

,, 18 ROBERT MILDMAY, son of Robert M of Tarling, Essex, Esq

,, ,, RODERICK GWYNNE, son of Howell G, of Glanbrane, co Carmarthen, Esq

,, 19 PETER BRYAN, son of Patrick B, late of this Inn, Esq, deceased

,, 23 HERBERT WOODWARD, son and heir of Edward W, of Ashford, Kent, gent

,, 27 CORNELIUS CAYLEY, son of William C, of Brompton, co York, Knight and

,, ,, ANDREW WHARTON, son and heir of Thomas W, of this Inn, Esq [Baronet

Dec 1 JAMES HODGKINSON, of Preston, co Lancaster, gent

,, 2 GERARD GORE, son of William G, late of London, Alderman, deceased

,, 9 EDMUND BUTLER, son of James B, late of this Inn, Esq, deceased

folio 1,183

,, 11 NATHANIEL PEACOCK, son of Richard P, of the city of York, gent, deceased

,, 19 SAMUEL MANESTEY, son of Nathan M, of Watford, Herts, gent

,, ,, WILLIAM POWELL, of Staple Inn, gent

1663-4

Jan 23 THOMAS POOLEY, son of Thomas P, of Dublin, Esq   [deceased

,, 26 PETER ELLYS, son of Robert E, late of Broughton, co Denbigh, Esq,

,, 29 CHARLES DANBY, son of Thomas D, late of Thorpe Perrove, co York,
          Knight, deceased   [Kinsbury, Berks, Esq

Feb 1 THOMAS HAYNE, son and heir of Daniel H, of Wallington, parish of

,, 2 CHARLES POWELL, son of John P, of Llanurda, co Carmarthen, Esq

,, 9 THOMAS MORGAN, son and heir of William M, of Hurst, co Gloucester, Esq

,, 12 GEORGE MASON, son and heir of Benjamin M, of Pixley Court, co Hereford,
                                            [Esq

,, 13 CHARLES KENRICK, son of William K, of Boughton-under-Bleam, Kent, Esq

,, 18 RICHARD HOLT, son of Robert H, of Castleton, co Lancaster, Esq.

folio 1,184.

Mar 7 GILBERT SHELDON, Archbishop of Canterbury, &c, Privy Councillor

,, ,, GEORGE MORLEY, Bishop of Winchester, Privy Councillor.

,, ,, THOMAS HARDRES, gent, second son of Thomas H, Esq, now reader

1663-4   folio 1,184—(*continued*)

Mar 7   JAMES HARDRES, gent , third son of Thomas H , Esq , now reader

„   22   THOMAS PRESTLEY, son and heir of William P , of Essendine, Herts, Esq

1664

Mar 30   THOMAS LING, son and heir of Thomas L , late of this Society, gent , deceased

April 1. THOMAS DADE, son of Thomas D , of Tannington, co Stafford, Esq

„   13   CHARLES CLIFTON, son of Gervase C , of Clifton, Notts, Knight and Baronet

„   23   THOMAS FRERE, son and heir of Andrew F , of London, gent   [Esq

,,   30   GEOFFREY HOTHAM, son and heir of Durand H , of Winthroppe, co York,

                                folio 1,185

May 7   THOMAS WINGFIELD, son and heir of Samuel W , of Shrewsbury, Esq

„   10   SAMUEL CROSSMAN, son and heir of Samuel C , of Sudbury, Suffolk, S T B

,,   ,,   RICHARD HUTTON, of Queen's College, Oxford, son and heir of Henry H , of
                   [———, Westmoreland, gent , deceased

„   14   RICHARD COOKE, son and heir of Edward C , of Amble, Northumberland, gent

„   16   TOBIAS HUMFREY, son and heir of Tobias H , of Askerne, co York, Esq

1663 (*sic*)   [admission of May 3, 1663

July 3 (*sic*) ROBERT BENSON, gent , of the Inner Temple, half fine, with the date of

1664   [gent

May 19 (*sic*) JOHN DOVER, son and heir of John D , of Barton-on-Heath, co Warwick,

„   „   PETER GREENESTREETE, son of Peter G , of Ospringe, Kent, gent

„   20   JOHN MALTYWARD, son of Robert M , of Rougham, Suffolk, Esq

                                folio 1,186

„   „   WILLIAM WORRALL, son and heir of William W , of Bollen, co Chester, gent

„   „   JOHN ROBINSON, son and heir of James R , of Cowton Grange, co York, gent

„   21   ROBERT MITFORD, Esq , son and heir of Ralph M , late of Seghill, Northum-
              berland, Esq , deceased.   [gent , deceased

„   13   SENHOUSE CLAXTON, second son of Owen C , late of St Paul's, Covent Garden,

„   „   NICHOLAS GRISE, son and heir of Henry G , late citizen and merchant
                              [taylor of London, deceased

June 9   THOMAS SMITH, son of William S., of Hockwold, Norfolk, gent   [land, Esq

„   10   EDWARD FISHER, son and heir of Nicholas F , of Stainebank Green, Westmore-

„   11   WILLIAM LANGTON, son of William L , of Staineswicke, Berks, Esq

„   15   WILLIAM LUCAS, son and heir of Gibson L., of Horningheath, Suffolk, S.T D

„   17   BARNARD ELLYS, son and heir of Robert E , of Greenwich, Kent, gent

                                folio 1,187

„   21   ISAAC BASIRE, second son of Isaac B , Archdeacon of Northumberland, S T P.

„   27   JOHN THORPE, gent , son and heir of Timothy T , late of Halifax, co York,
                                       [gent , deceased

„   30   JOHN COX, son and heir of John C , of Coggeshall, Essex, gent.

„   „   BRIAN O'NEALE, son and heir of Brian, of Dublin, Baronet.   [Baronet

July 2   JAMES CLAVERING, second son of Charles C , of Axwellhouse, co. Durham,

„   „   ALLAN LAMONT, of North Burton, co York, gent

1664.   **folio 1,187—(*continued*)**

July   4   TYRRILL PRETTYMAN, son of George P , of Backton, Suffolk, gent.

,,   9   SAMUEL CLYATT, of Whitgift, co York, gent

,,   18   JOHN KELLY, second son of John K , of Corbecke, co Roscommon, Esq

folio 1,188.

,,   21   JOHN LEECH, son and heir of John L , of Cawardine, co Chester, Esq

Aug   5   JOHN WILKINS, S T P , "sine fine"

,,   ,,   JOHN GODDARD, Doctor of Medicine

,,   8   ZACHARY CRADDOCKE, S T B

,,   ,,   HENRY VAUGHAN, son and heir of Rice V , Esq , of Gray's Inn

,,   9   GEORGE TROTTER, third son of George T , of Dover, Kent, Esq

,,   ,,   FRANCIS MACKWORTH, of Empringham, co Rutland, Knight

Oct   12   SAMUEL STARKEY, son and heir of George S , of New Windsor, Berks, Esq

,,   21   WILLIAM SCRIMSHIRE, son and heir of William S , citizen and "Propalæ" (Shop-
[keeper) of London

folio 1,189

,,   24   NATHANIEL BARD, son of Maximilian B , of London, Esq

,,   28   EDWARD CLUDDE, gent , son and heir of Edward C , of Orleton, Salop, deceased

,,   31   JOHN REYNOLDS, second son of Thomas R , of Colchester, Essex, gent

,,   ,,   EDWARD BURDET, gent., son of Edward B , of Willymontswyk, North-
[umberland, deceased

Nov.   4   THOMAS LAKE, son and heir of Thomas L , of Barking, Essex, gent.

,,   8.   JOHN HOSKINS, son and heir of Peter H , of Sherbourne, Dorset, gent   [Esq

,,   ,,   NICHOLAS JONES, son and heir of William J , of Lantrissint, co Merioneth,

,,   12   EDWARD SMYTH, son and heir of Edward S., of Hornsey, Middlesex, gent

,,   ,,   BENJAMIN WELBY, gent , son of William W , of Denton, co Lincoln, Esq

folio 1,190   [land, deceased

,,   18   MICHAEL WELDEN, Esq , son and heir of Michael W., of Welden, Northumber-

,,   22   NATHANIEL BACON, son and heir of Thomas B , of Friston Hall, Suffolk, Esq

,,   23   JOHN LITCHFIELD, son and heir of John L., of the town of Nottingham, gent

,,   25.   JOHN HAIES, son of Edward H., of Tunstall, Kent, Baronet

Dec   2.   FRANCIS FOLJAMBE, son and heir of Peter F , of Steveton, co York, Esq

,,   ,,   EBENEZER MARKHAM, son and heir of Henry M., of Hertingfordbury, Herts,
Esq   [Womersley, co York, Esq , deceased

,,   5   GEORGE TWISLETON, gent , son and heir of George T , of Woodhall, parish of

,,   8   JERMAN IRETON, son and heir of Jerman I , of London, Esq   [deceased

,,   10.   RICHARD HAWKINS, son and heir of Richard H , of Milton, co Dorset, gent ,

1664-5

Jan   21   THOMAS PRICE, son and heir of Owen P , of Llanclogdach, co Carmarthen, Esq

folio 1,191.

,,   23.   CHARLES CROKE, second son of Robert C , of this Society, Knight

,,   24   ROBERT DICER, son and heir of Robert D , of London, Baronet

,,   27   EDWARD MORGAN, gent , fourth son of Thomas M , late of Tredegar, co
Monmouth, deceased   [co Brecon

,,   ,,   MARMADUKE GWYNNE, gent , son and heir of Rice G , deceased, of Garth,

1664 5.   **folio 1,191**—(*continued*)

Jan. 28   STRAFFORD BRATHWAITE, son and heir of Richard B , of Burnishead, Westmoreland, Esq   [Lincoln (erased)

Feb. 3   CHRISTOPHER CLAPHAM, son and heir of Christopher C , of Stamford, co

,, ,,   CHRISTOPHER CLAPHAM, Esq , of the Inner Temple (by certificate of Inner
Temple, admitted there 12th Feb , 1663, son and heir of Christopher C ,
[of Stamford, co Lincoln, half fine)

,, 9   CORNELIUS HALL, second son of Thomas H , of Donnington-in-Great-

,, 20   THOMAS MORT, of Astley, co Lancaster, gent.   [Holland, co Lincoln, Esq.

,, 25   CÆSAR DUN, eldest son of Daniel D , of Kingsnorton, co Worcester, Esq

,, ,,   JOHN DUGDALE, son of William D , of Blyth Hall, co Warwick

1665
April 15   WILLIAM WILLIAMS, son and heir of William W , of Trevithell, co Brecknock,
                                                       [gent

folio 1,194

,, ,,   THOMAS CHILDERS, son and heir of Francis C , of Carrehouse, parish of
                                 [Doncaster, co York, Esq

,, 22   THOMAS PATRICKSON, son and heir of Thomas P , of Stockhow, Cumberland

,, ,,   THOMAS HOWE, gent , son and heir of Thomas H , late of Abbots Langley,
Herts, Esq , deceased   [gent

,, ,,   ARTHUR PRISCOTT, son and heir of William P , of Darlington, co Durham,

,, 27   THOMAS DICKONSON, son and heir of Peter D , late of Gainsborough. co
Lincoln, Esq , deceased   [Esq

May 4   GEORGE THORNTON, son and heir of William T , of Grantham, co Lincoln,

,, ,,   JOHN OWEN, son and heir of Griffith O , of London, grocer

,, 3   WILLIAM MOSES, Esq , of the Inner Temple (by certificate of the Inner
                            [Temple, admitted July 2, 1661, half fees)

,, 13   LANCELOTT DAWES, son and heir of William D , of Barton, Westmoreland,
                                     [gent

folio 1,195

,, 24   JOHN KNIGHT, son and heir of Ralph K , of Langold, co York, Knight

,, 27   WILLIAM BREAREY, son and heir of Henry B , of the city of York, gent

,, 30   WILLIAM STOPFORD, son and heir of James S , of Dublin, Esq

June 8   HENRY BAGSHAW, son and heir of Thomas B , late of Ridgehall, co Derby,
                                   [gent , deceased

,, 9   JOSEPH HIERON, son and heir of John H , of Little Eaton, co Derby, gent

,, 10   WILLIAM ROWNEY, son of Simon R , of Darlingscott, co Worcester, gent ,
formerly for two years of Staple Inn (admitted by certificate of Richard
Kilburn, Principal of Staple Inn)   [cester, gent., deceased

,, 11   THOMAS BROWNE, gent , son and heir of Thomas B , late of the city of Glou-

June 16   LIONEL VANE, son and heir of George V , of Rogerley, co Durham, Knight

,, ,,   GEORGE VANE, second son of George V , of Rogerley, co Durham, Knight

,, 17   EDWARD ATKINSON, son and heir of Edward A , of Leeds, co York, Esq

,, ,,   FRANCIS WHITE, son and heir of Francis W , of Wakefield, co York, Esq

folio 1,196

July 1   JOHN CRISP, son and heir of John C , of Staple Inn   [S T D.

,, ,,   WILLIAM RAWLEIGH, son and heir of ——— R , of Landbeach, co Camb

1665		folio 1,196—(*continued*).
July	1	MARMADUKE GIBBS, of Neath, co Glamorgan, gent [Baronet
,,	,,	THOMAS EDWARDS, second son of Thomas E, of Shrewsbury, Knight and
1665-6		
Feb	13	PHILIP NISBETT, of St Martins, co York, gent
,,	16	CHARLES SHEPHEARD, son and heir of Thomas S, of Hilton, Hunts, Esq
,,	,,	JAMES MOSELEY, son and heir of James M, of Sheffield, co. York, Esq
1666		[deceased
May	2	THOMAS RYMER, gent, son of Ralph R, of Brafferton, co York, gent,
,,	5	JOHN EDWARDS, gent, son of Francis E, of East Woodhay, co Southampton, [clerk, deceased
,,	8	JOHN NICOLL, son and heir of Paul N, of Hendon, Middlesex, Esq
,,	9	JOHN TWISLETON, son and heir of Philip T, of Drax, co York, Esq
,,	10	RICHARD COLE, son and heir of Thomas C, of Radwill, Herts, gent

folio 1,197.

,,	14	THOMAS DYOSE, son and heir of Thomas D, citizen and vintner of London, [formerly for two and a half years at Staple Inn
,,	15	JOHN HEWYTT, son of William H, of Breccles, Norfolk, Knight
,,	,,	RICHARD WRIGHT, gent, son and heir of Mathew W, late of Nantwich, co [Chester, gent, deceased
,,	17	WILLIAM POLEY, son of William P, of Boxted, Suffolk, Knight
1665-6		
Feb	28	THOMAS ARCHER, son and heir of John A, of London, Esq
Mar	3	STEPHEN CHARLETON, second son of Edward C, of Sandyacre, co Derby,
1666.		[gent (for three years, two months, and 28 days of Staple Inn)
May	19	EDWARD FARNHAM, son and heir of Clement F, of this Inn, Knight (two years [of Staple Inn).
,,	,	GEORGE HUTCHINS, son and heir of Edmund H, of Georgham, Devon, gent
,,	21	JOHN HUNT, son of Thomas H, of Shrewsbury, Esq
,,	22	JOHN WRIGHT, son and heir of John W, of Ipswich, Suffolk, Esq
,,	,,	THOMAS ROBINSON, gent, son of Thomas ——— (erased)

folio 1,198.   [gent., deceased.

,,	29	THOMAS ROBINSON, gent, son of Robert R, late of Whitton, co Lincoln,
April	10	RICHARD VAUGHAN, son and heir of Edward V, of Tarracoed, co Carmarthen,
June	1	JEFFREY AMHERST, son and heir of John A, of this Inn, Esq [Knight
,,	18	ARDEN BAGOT, son and heir of Hervey B, of Pipe Hall, co Warwick, Esq
,,	23	WILLIAM TOWNESEND, son and heir of John T., of Weeton, co Lanc, gent
,,	,,	GEORGE WARBURTON, second son of George W., of Arley, co Chester, Baronet.
,,	28	STEPHEN BECKINGHAM, son and heir of Stephen B, deceased, of Tolleshunt Darcy, Essex, gent [gent.
July	2	THOMAS BENDISH, son and heir of Thomas B, of Great Yarmouth, Norfolk,
,,	3	BARTHOLOMEW RAWLINS, son and heir of William R, of Burleigh Park, in Loughborough, co Leicester, gent [Chester deceased
,	,,	JOHN HAREFINCH, gent, son and heir of John H, late of Chrisleton, co

1666.   folio 1,198—(*continued*)

July 3   WILLIAM WESTFALING, son of William W., of Grafton, co Hereford, gent
,,   4   JOHN CARRE, gent., son and heir of John C., late of Shields, co. Durham,
                                                                    [deceased

folio 1,199.

,,   ,,   JOHN DENNE, son and heir of John D., of Dartford, Kent, S T B.   [gent
,,   ,,   JOHN ATTKINS, son and heir of John A., of Stanwicke, co Northampton,
,,   10   DANIEL BENION, son and heir of Daniel B., of Ash, Salop, gent   [(*sic*), Esq.
Sept 11 WILLIAM LAWRANCE, gent, son and heir of William L., of Wraxall, Dorset
Oct 22. MATTHEW WEBSTER, third son of William W., late of London, merchant,
                                                                    [deceased
,,   25   JOHN, Lord SEYMOUR, son of William, late Duke of Somerset, deceased
,,   27   GEORGE CREMER, sixth son of Edward C., of Lynn Regis, Norfolk, Esq
,,   ,,   THOMAS DOCWRA, son and heir of Thomas D., of Putteridge, parish of Offley,
                                                                    [Herts, Esq
,,   31. WILLIAM HOWE, son and heir of William H., of Windsor, Berks, gent
,,   ,,   EDWARD LLOYD, son and heir of Thomas L., of Pentre Hobin, co Flint, clerk,
          deceased.   [Baronet
Nov. 8. RICHARD NEWTON, son and heir of John N., of Hethersthorpe, co Lincoln,
,,   11   THOMAS PENYSTON, son and heir of Thomas P., of Cornwell, Oxon, Baronet
,,   15. ADAM GOODALL, second son of William G., of Ipswich, gent

folio 1,200.

,   21   RALPH OGLE, son and heir of John O., of Kirkley, Northumberland, Esq.
,,   23   AMBROSE MANNATON, son and heir of Ambrose M., of Trecarell, co Cornwall,
                                                                    [Esq., deceased
,,   27   ROBERT EARLE, gent, son and heir of Christopher E., of Topsfill, Essex, Esq
,,   ,,   JOHN GREEN, son and heir of John G., late of East Bradenham, Norfolk, Esq
Dec   3   EDWARD NEVETT, son and heir of Edward N., of Fryern Barnet, Middlesex,
          Esq   [Lancaster, Esq, deceased.
,,   18   EDWARD ASPINWALL, second son of Edward A., late of Toxteth Park, co
1666-7   [Leicester, Knight
Jan 15   WILLIAM AYSCOUGH, Esq, son and heir of William A., of Buckminster, co
,,   17   WILLIAM RUMNEY, second son of Edward R., late of London, girdler,
          deceased   [taylor
,,   ,,   SAMUEL POYNTER, son and heir of John P., of Shoreditch, Middlesex, merchant
Feb   4   WILLIAM LEWINS, son and heir of Lewis L., of Uske-in-Holderness, co York,
,,   5   STEPHEN LUDLOW (*alias* North), of Dublin, gent   [Esq
,,   6. HENRY RUMSEY, son and heir of John R., of Rydymayne, co Monmouth, gent
,,   ,,   THOMAS JONES, son and heir of William J., of Usk, co Monmouth, gent,
                                                                    [deceased
folio 1,202

Feb   9   RICHARD BROOKE, son of Thomas B., of Norton, Cheshire, gent
,,   ,,   GEORGE HARRIS, third son of Edward H., of Fladbury, co. Worcester, gent
,,   ,,   HENRY HOMBARSTON, second son of Henry H., of Loddon, Norfolk, gent

T

1666-7　　　　　　　　folio 1,202—(*continued*).

Feb 11　CHARLES CARSE, son and heir of John C, of Little Horsley, Essex, S T P.,
　　　　　deceased　　　　　　　　　　　　　　　　　　　　　　　[deceased

　,, 12　WILLIAM LANGTON, son and heir of William L, of Preston, co Lancaster, Esq,

　,, 14　SAMUEL LEWES, son and heir of Daniel L, of London, merchant taylor,
　　　　　　　　　　　　　　　　　　　　　　　　　　　　　　　　[deceased

　,, 16　JEREMIAH PEELE, second son of Richard P, of Gomershall, co York, gent
1667.

April 25　ROBERT ORMESBY, third son of Robert O, of Dublin, Esq

　,, 27　EDWARD BEDINGFEILD, third son of Francis B (? rightly Henry), of Oxburgh,
　　　　　Norfolk, Knight　　　　　　　　　　　　　　　　　　　　[Tyne, merchant

　,, 29　ANTHONY ANDERSON, son and heir of Bartram A., of Newcastle-on-

May 2　WILLIAM LANE, son and heir of William L, of Cowley, Middlesex, Esq

　　　　　　　　　　　　　　　　　　　　　　　[of Burneston, co York, Esq
Mar 29　THOMAS HARRISON, gent, son and heir of Thomas H, of Allerthorpe, parish

　　　　　　　　　　　folio 1,203　　　　　[Lancaster, Doctor of Medicine

May 6　WILLIAM BUTLER FIFE, gent, son and heir of William F, of Wedacre, co

　,,　,,　GEORGE PIGOT, son and heir of George P, of Preston, co Lancaster, gent.

　,, 7　WILLIAM PLAYER, gent, son and heir of Arthur P, of Mangotsfield, co Glou-
　　　　　cester, gent, deceased　　　　　　　　[of Uptonwould, co Worcester, Esq

　,,　,,　EDWARD CARTER, of Couldason, co Gloucester, gent, second son of Edward C,

　　　　　　　　　　　　　　　　　　　　　　　[gent, deceased.
　,, 11　EDWARD WINN, second son of Maurice W, of Langanhavell, co Denbigh,

　,, 13　THOMAS BRAND, second son of Joseph B, of Edwardston, Suffolk, Esq

　　　　　　　　　　　　　　　　　　　　　　　[Baronet
　,, 14　ROBERT WOLSELEY, son and heir of Charles W, of Wolseley, Stafford,

　,, 15　CHARLES WHITEACRE, of the Middle Temple, gent, son and heir of
　　　　　[Charles W., of Windsor, Berks, Esq (admitted there Feb 12, 1665)

　,, 22　GAIMES JONES, second son of Edmund J, of Raglan, co Monmouth, Esq

　　　　　　　　　　　folio 1,204.　　　　　[gent, deceased

　,,　,,　CYPRIAN THORNTON, gent, son of Will... ... ...ate of Grantham, co. Lincoln,
　　　　　　　　　　　　　　　　　　　　　　　[deceased
June ?　Ior... ... ..., son and heir of Samuel N, of Brancaster, Norfolk, gent,

　,, 5　THOMAS JENNEY, gent, fourth son of Arthur J., of Cringleford, Norfolk, Knight

　,,　,,　JOHN HINDMARSH, gent., second son of John H, of Wallsend, Northumber-

　,, 6　BERKELEY SAYER, third son of John S, of London, fishmonger　[land, gent

　,, 10　WALTER LAYCOCK, son and heir of Walter L, of Copmanthorpe, co York, gent

　,, 11.　PETER CLARKE, son and heir of William C, of Clerkenwell, Middlesex, gent

　,, 19.　THOMAS BARNARDISTON, son and heir of Thomas B, of Kedington, Suffolk,
　　　　　　　　　　　　　　　　　　　　　　　[Knight and Baronet

　,,　,,　GEORGE FARINGTON, gent, second son of William F, of Worden, co. Lan-
Aug 10　JOHN DOLBEN, Bishop of Rochester　　　　　　　　　[caster, Esq

　,,　,,　LLUELLIN JENKINS, Doctor of Laws, High Judge of the Admiralty Court

　,, 12　FRANCIS BUTLER, son and heir of Theobald B, of Bottisham Hall, Essex,
　　　　　Esq
　　　　　　　　　　　　　　　　　　　　　　　[deceased
　,,　,,　CHARLES HERBERT, son and heir of Charles H, late of Crickhowell, co Brecon,

1667	folio 1,205	[Esq

Aug 13   JOHN WILLIAMS, son and heir of John W , of the parish of Cwmdu, co Brecon,
                 [co Brecon

,,   ,,   WILLIAM WILLIAMS, second son of John W , Esq , of the parish of Cwmdu,

,,   ,,   EDWARD GAGE, son and heir of George G , of Livden, co Northampton,
           Esq   [deceased

,,   16   JOHN GLYD, son and heir of Richard G , of Blechingley, Surrey, Esq ,

,,   14   EDWARD MORGELL, son and heir of Edward M , of Mossen, co Chester

Oct 23   HENRY HOLME, son and heir of Henry H , of Paulholme, co York, Esq

,,   29   GAWEN AYNSLOE, son and heir of William A , of Highlawes, Northumberland,
           gent   [Esq

Nov 8   WILLIAM WHITAKER, fourth son of Charles W , of New Windsor, Berks,

,,   9   STEPHEN ROBINS, third son of Elisha R , late of London, gent , deceased

,,   ,,   JOSEPH BEAUMONT, son and heir of Joseph B , of Hadley, Suffolk, gent.

,,   12   THOMAS ROBINSON, son and heir of William R , of Rokeby, co York, Esq

,,   15   MICHAEL WARTON, son and heir of Michael W , of Beverley, co York, Esq

,,   26   THOMAS CLAYTON, son and heir of Robert C , of Fullwood, co Lancaster

,,   ,,   THOMAS POULTON, son and heir of Thomas P , of Nottingham, Esq

,,   ,,   THOMAS LUCY, son and heir of Richard L., of Charlecote, co Warwick, Esq

,,   28   THOMAS ADY, son and heir of Thomas A , of Wethersfield, Essex, gent

folio 1,206

Dec 4   ROBERT BLAKE, son and heir of Alexander B , of Ketton, co Rutland, Esq

,,   ,,   SAMUEL LAWSON, son and heir of Richard L , late of London, grocer,
           deceased   [deceased

,,   9   THOMAS DODSWORTH, son and heir of Robert D , of Barton, co. York,

,,   30.   WILLIAM SACHEVERELL, of Morley, co Derby, Esq

1667-8

Jan 26   DANIEL GWINNE, son and heir of Daniel G , of Llannina, co Cardigan, Esq

,,   27   THOMAS GODDARD, son and heir of Richard G , of Swindon, Wilts, Esq

,,   ,,   EDMUND RYANE, second son of John R , of Cashel, co. Tipperary, Esq.

,,   28.   ANDREW MORROGH, son and heir of James M , of Cork, Esq

,,   29   JOHN CRESWELL, son and heir of John C , of Purston, co. Northampton, Esq

,,   28   ALLAN LOCKART, six years a Member of Barnard's Inn, son of James L , of
                                  [St. Martins-in-the Fields

,,   31.   GEORGE NICOLL, second son of John N , of Aldenham, Herts, gent

,,   ,,   EDMUND HARDRES, third son of Thomas H , Esq , now reader

folio 1,207

Feb 7   LEWIS MONOUX, second son of Humphrey M., of Wotton, Beds, Baronet

,,   ,,   JOHN CHADWICKE, son and heir of Jonathan C , of Chadwick, co. Lancaster,
           Professor of Medicine   [Halifax, co York, Esq , deceased.

,,   27.   THOMAS HORTON, son and heir of William H , of Barslam, in Vicarage of

Mar 21   JOHN WILLIAMS, Esq , second son of Trevor W , Baronet, of Llangibby, co.

,,   24   JOHN BATTISHELL, of South Tawton, co Devon, gent   [Monmouth.

1668   folio 1,207—(continued)   [Middlesex, Esq.

April 8   GEORGE MOYSE, son and heir of Erasmus M., of Tottenham High Cross,

,,   11   JOSEPH DEANE, son and heir of Joseph D., of Dublin, Esq

,,   13   ROWLAND NORTON, son and heir of George N., of Disforth, co York, Esq

,,   ,,   ROBERT BOWES, second son of Francis B., of Thornton, co Durham, Knight.

,,   16.   RICHARD BAWDEWIN, son and heir of Thomas B., of Didlebury, Salop, Esq

,,   ,,   ROBERT FULKES, son and heir of Peter F., late of Llanasaph, co. Flint, Esq,
                                                                         [deceased

,,   21   THOMAS BURY, fourth son of William B., of Linwood, co Lincoln, Knight.

,,   23   HENRY BALGUY, son and heir of Henry B., of Rowley, co Derby, gent.

folio 1,208.

,,   ,,   THOMAS LEDGARD, son and heir of Thomas L., of Newcastle on-Tyne, Esq

,,   24   RICHARD WINGFIELD, second son of Samuel W., of St Chads, Salop, Esq.

,,   25   ROBERT FAIREBEARD, son and heir of Robert F., late of this Inn, Esq,
                     deceased   [Professor of Medicine, deceased.

,,   ,,   EDWARD RISHTON, son and heir of Jeffry R., late of Preston, co Lancaster,

,,   ,,   RICHARD ENTWISLE, son and heir of John E., of Ormskirk, co. Lancaster,
                                                                            [Esq.

,,   ,,   JOHN COLLINS, son and heir of John C., of Carleton Colville, Suffolk, gent

,,   24   WILLIAM WALKER, two years of Staple Inn, son and heir of William W., of
                     St Martins-in-the-Fields, goldsmith.   [Westminster, gent, deceased

,,   28   ALEXANDER JOHNSON, son and heir of Archibald J., late of St Margarets,

May 2.   JOHN BOTRY, son and heir of John B., late of Marston, parish of St Lawrence,
                     co Northampton, Esq, deceased   [Esq.

,,   ,,   HENRY CHETHAM, second son of George C., late of Turton, co Lancaster,

,,   ,,   EDWARD MAN, son and heir of Edward M., of this Inn, Esq

,,   7.   RICHARD WATSON, son and heir of Robert W., of Frindsbury, Kent, Esq

,,   11   NEWDIGATE POINTZ, son and heir of Thomas P., of Bradfield, co North-
                                                                     [ampton, Esq

folio 1,209

,,   16.   JOHN GALWAY, son and heir of Edward G., of the city of Cork, Esq

,,   26   JOHN SIMPSON, son and heir of Nicholas S., of Milton, near Canterbury, gent.

,,   27.   WORTLEY WHORWOOD, son and heir of William W., late of Sturton Castle, co
                                                          [Stafford, Knight, deceased.

,,   ,,   EVAN LLOYD, son and heir of Howell L., of Croesgorking, co. Denbigh, Esq

,,   30   RICHARD SPOURE, second son of Henry S., of Northhill, co. Cornwall, Esq

June 1.   RICHARD ATKINSON, son and heir of John A., of Widdington, co York, Esq

,,   9   HENRY POWELL, second son of Henry P., of Worthyn, Salop, Esq

,,   11   JOHN GELL, son and heir of John G., of Hopton, co Derby, Esq

,,   13   LUKE DORMER, second son of George D., late of Stockstown, co Wexford,
                     Esq, deceased   [co York, deceased

,,   16   WILLIAM HORTON, second son of William H., of Barkisland, in Halifax,

,,   18   JOHN POWELL, son and heir of John P. of Besbury, co Hereford, gent

,   27   WILLIAM TREVILL, son and heir of Richard T., of Budshead, Devon, Esq

July 1.   GEOFFREY THACKER, son of Gilbert T., of Repton, co Derby, Esq

1668		folio 1,210

July 1   MICHAEL CHAMBERLAINE, of Dublin

„   „   THOMAS AYLMER, of Dublin

„   „   PERREY PETLEY, son and heir of Thomas P., Esq , of Shoreham, Kent

„   3   EDWARD HAULSEY, son and heir of Francis H , of London, gent   [deceased.

„   14   JOHN NUGENT, son and heir of William N , of Chiven, co Westmeath, Esq ,

Aug 1   NATHANIEL BRENT, second son of Nathaniel B , Knight, late of London,
                                                                        [deceased

„   „   EDWARD CORBET, son and heir of Edward C., S T.D., deceased, late of

,   5   EDWARD PERRY, of Limerick   [Pontesbury, Salop

„   10   WILLIAM RICHARDSON, third son of Thomas, Lord R , Baron of Cramond, in

„   „   JOHN FINES, son and heir of John F , of Great Amwell, Herts   [Scotland

Oct 22   JOHN ROBSON, son of John R., gent, of Waterbeach, co Cambridge

„   „   JOSEPH FECK, third son of Christopher F , clerk, of Croydon, Surrey.

folio 1,211

„   „   ANTHONY SMITH, son of Robert S , citizen and grocer of London

,   „   NATHANIEL MADDISON, son of Humphrey M of Alvingham Abbey, co Lincoln

„   12   EDWARD DYNE, son and heir of John D , of Westfield Sussex

„   22. JOSEPH REA, son and heir of William R , of Camborne, Northumberland, gent.

„   „   JOHN ADY, son and heir of Nicholas A , late of St. Andrews, Holborn, gent ,
              deceased   [Esq , deceased

„   24   WILLIAM BROWNE, gent , son and heir of William B , late of the city of York,

„   „   JOHN OTWAY, son and heir of John O , of Ingmire Hall, co York, Esq.

„   27   DAVID EDWARDS, son and heir of David E., of Rhydgorse, co Carmarthen,

„   „   ROBERT WEST, son and heir of James W , of Banbury, Oxon, Esq   [Esq.

Nov 1   THOMAS WALLER, second son of Edmond W , of Gregories, near Beaconsfield,
                                                                 [Bucks, Esq,

„   2.   GERVASE PIGOTT, son and heir of Gervase P., of Thrumpton, Notts, Esq.

„   7   FRANCIS NEVILE, son and heir of Sandford N , of Chevet, co York, Esq

„   „   RICHARD WITTON, son and heir of John W , of the city of York, clerk

„   „   STEPHEN LAKE, son and heir of Thomas L , of Boston, New England, merchant

„   18. ROBERT MILBOURNE, son and heir of James M , of Great Dunmow, Essex, Esq

„   19   THOMAS NEALE, son and heir of Thomas N , of Bramfield, Suffolk, gent.

„   „   CHARLES LYNN, second son of John L , of Southwick, co Northampton, Esq

folio 1,212.

„   ,.   GERVASE PIERREPOINT, third son of the Right Honourable William P , of St.
              Giles-in-the-Fields, Middlesex, Esq   [Knight

„   21   MARMADUKE DAYRELL, second son of Thomas D , of Camps Castle, Cambs,

„   23   MARMADUKE BULL, son and heir of John B , of Presteign, co Radnor, gent.
              (according to order made May 29, 1663)   [Middlesex, deceased.

„   27   JOHN BOND, son and heir of John B , late Clerk and Master of the Savoy,

1668-9
Jan 22   WILLIAM STREET, third son of Woodall S , of Kidlington, Oxon, gent

„   26. WILLIAM CROMPTON, second son of William C., of the city of Chester, Esq

„   29   RICHARD WEBB, son and heir of William W., of Gray's Inn, Esq

1668-9		folio 1,212—(continued)
Feb	2	EDWARD STILLINGFLEET, S T P.
,,	8	JOHN COWPER, second son of Richard C , of Bubbingworth, Essex, gent
,,	10	HENRY POLEY, Esq , son and heir of Edmund P , of Badley, Suffolk, Knight
,,	,,	ROBERT LYNNE, son and heir of Andrew L , of Waterford, gent
,,	13	JOHN COKE, of Melbourne, co Derby, Esq , son of Thomas C , late of Gray's [Inn, Esq , deceased.

folio 1,213.

,,	16	GERRARD DILLON, son and heir of Theobald D., of Fimore, co Mayo, Esq
,,	18	LANCELOT WOOD, son and heir of Richard W., deceased, late of Kingston-on-
,,	,,	THOMAS VINCENT, son and heir of John V , now reader [Hull.
Mar	1	ROBERT FORSETT, son of Edward F , late of Marylebone, Middlesex, Esq.
,,	6	WILLIAM RISHTON, son and heir of William R , of Farrington, co. Lancaster, gent [Warwick
,,	,,	CHARLES HUGGEFORD, son and heir of Humphrey H , of Samborne, co
,,	,,	SAMUEL IRONSIDE, son and heir of Samuel I , of Reach, parish of Leighton [Buzzard, Beds, Esq
,,	16	EDWARD SCOTT, son of Thomas S , Esq , of the city of Canterbury
,,	24.	EDWARD AUSTEN, third son of Robert A , Knight, of Hayle Place, Kent.
1669		[Norfolk.
Mar	26	HENRY HEVENINGHAM, son and heir of Anthony H., Knight, of Hockwold,
April	19	WILLIAM WRIGHT, second son of William W , deceased, late of Bagby, co. York, gent [gent
,,	23	PETER ROWLANDSON, son and heir of Thomas R , of Langton, Westmoreland,
,,	27	THOMAS BENDLOWES, son and heir of Thomas B , of Sutton Hograve, co [York, Esq

folio 1,214

,,	28	JOHN STEDMAN, son and heir of John S , of Doleygare, co. Brecon Esq
,,	29	FRANCIS BOWES, son and heir of Francis B , of Thornton, co Durham, Knight
May	1	HUMPHREY RANDALL, son and heir of Robert R , of Kintsbury, Devon, Esq
,,	,,	THOMAS SMITH, son and heir of Richard S , of Brandestone, Suffolk, gent
,,	5	SAMUEL MARROW, son and heir of Edward M , late of Berkswell, co Warwick, [Esq , deceased
,,	8	WILLIAM BRIGSTOCK, son and heir of Owen B , of Carmarthen, Esq
,,	13	JOHN HAWTREY, son and heir of Ralph H , of Ruislip, Middlesex, Esq
,,	14	SAMUEL DUNCH, second son of John D , of Pewsey, Berks, Esq
,,	15	THEODORE STRATFORD, sixth son of Edward S , late of Nuneaton, co Warwick, [Esq , deceased
,,	21	ROBERT BAYNES, son and heir of Adam B , of Teeton, co Northampton, Esq
,,	22	THOMAS BARNES, son and heir of William B , of East Winch, Norfolk, Esq
,,	,,	RICHARD HACKER, son and heir of John H , of Flintham, Notts, Esq
,,	25	JOHN GRATWICKE, son and heir of Thomas G , late of Shermanbury, Sussex, [gent , deceased (two years of Staple Inn)

folio 1,215

,,	29	SAMUEL GRIFFITH, son and heir of George G., of London, clerk.
June	14	JOHN MEADE, son and heir of Thomas M , of Wendon Lofts, Essex, Esq

1669   folio 1,215—(continued)

June 14   WILLIAM BURNETT, son and heir of William B, of Newton Morrell, co
                                                        [York, gent.

„   15   JOHN BAINES, son and heir of John B, of Wiston, co York, gent   [Esq

„   17   THOMAS ASHMALL, son and heir of Thomas A, of Amerston, co Durham,

„   19   EDWARD CROFTS, fourth son of Edward C, of East Appleton, co York, Esq

„   21   HENRY BARNARD, son and heir of Edward B, of North Dalton, co York, Esq.

„   26   RICHARD NEVILL, son and heir of Edward N, of Standon, co Stafford, clerk.

„   23   JOHN RUMSEY, gent, of the Inner Temple, (admitted there November 2,
                    1663, and re-admitted February 17, 1684)   [Somerset, Esq

„   30   JOHN BLACKMORE, son and heir of John B., of East Quantockshead,

July   1   JOHN WYNNE, son and heir of John W, of Copperteny, co Flint, Esq

„   5   HENRY BALDOCK, son and heir of Robert B., of Tacolneston, Norfolk, Esq

folio 1,216

„   „   RICHARD HALEY, second son of John H, of Edgware, Middlesex, gent

June 28   CHARLES MOLLOY, of Lincoln's Inn, gent (admitted last day of Trinity Term,
                    1663, but rather August 7, 1667)

July   6.   RICHARD UNIACKE, fourth son of Maurice U, of Youghall, co Cork, Esq

„   „   CORNELIUS MANLEY, of Erbistocke, co Denbigh, gent   [ceased.

„   „   JOHN LINDLEY, son and heir of Thomas L, late of Skegby, Notts, Esq, de-

„   7   ROBERT HORSMAN, son and heir of Edward H., of Stretton, co. Rutland, Esq.

„   8   JOHN POVEY, son and heir of John P, of co Dublin, one of the Barons of

Aug   5   HENRY, Marquess and Earl of WORCESTER   [the Exchequer in Ireland.

„   „   HENRY, third Lord ARUNDELL of Wardour

„   „   ROBERT LLOYD, son and heir of Richard L, Knight   [Monmouth, gent.

„   „   JOHN POWELL, son and heir of Thomas P, of Langattock Linngoed, co

„   „   MOSES JONES, third son of Edmund J, now reader

„   „   EDWARD JONES, fourth son of Edmund J, now reader.

„   „   THOMAS DAVIS, son of John D, of Langharne, co Carmarthen, gent.

folio 1,217.

„   6   JOHN TURTON, of Alrewas, co Stafford, gent

„   7   NEVILL POOLEY, third son of Thomas P, of Dublin, Esq

Oct   22.   LEWIN PAGETT, third son of Justinian P, late of Gray's Inn, Esq, deceased

„   27   WILLIAM MARCH, second son of William M, late of Arundel House, Strand,
                    London, gent   [Knight

„   28   GILBERT GERARD, son and heir of Francis G, of Harrow-on-the-Hill, Middlesex,

„   „   ROBERT GERARD, second son of Francis G, of Harrow-on-the-Hill, Middlesex,
                                                        [Knight

Nov. 12   WILLIAM TOWRY, son and heir of John T, of Kirby Grindalyth, co York

„   „   ADEXANDER RATCLYFF, son and heir of Alexander R, of Hampstead,
                    Middlesex, gent   [Esq, deceased

„   13   OLIVER DEANE, son and heir of Thomas D, of Pulham St Marys, Norfolk,

„   12   WILLIAM CRISPE, son of John C, of Chipping Norton, co Oxford, gent,
                                            [three years and more at Staple Inn

1669		folio 1,217—(*continued*)
Nov	17	HENRY LAWSON, third son of Wilfrid L , of Cumberland, Baronet
,,	16	RICHARD JONES, son and heir of Morgan J , of co Carmarthen, Esq

folio 1,218

,,	,,	CHARLES HUTCHINSON, son and heir of John H , of Pinner Middlesex, Esq.
,,	22	WILLIAM STANDEN, son and heir of William S , of Arborfield, Berks, Esq
,,	25	EDWARD VAUGHAN, son and heir of Thomas V., of Abergwilly, co Carmar-
,,	24	NICHOLAS HARDING, son and heir of Robert H , Esq [then, Esq
,,	25	JAMES GWIN, son and heir of Thomas G , of Pantagored, Brecon, Esq
,,	29	JOHN GIBSON, son and heir of John G , of Welborne, co York, Esq [Esq.
,,	,,	LUKE ROBINSON, son and heir of Luke R , late of Thornton Hall, co York,
,,	,,	WILLIAM BIRD, son of Samuel B , Rector of Claybrooke, co. Leicester [Esq
Dec	6	LAURENCE PARKER, son of Laurence P , of Peterborough, co Northampton,
,	7	HENRY CURRER, son and heir of Hugh C , of Kildwicke, co York, gent
,,	,,	RICHARD NELTHORPE, son of James N , of Charterhouse, Middlesex, Esq

folio 1,219.

,,	11	ISAAC KNIGHT, son of Isaac K , of Louth, co Lincoln, Esq
,,	12	ROBERT HUNTINGDON, son and heir of Robert H , of Hackney, Middlesex, Esq [Lancaster, gent.
,,	13	CHRISTOPHER GREENFIELD, son and heir of William G , of Whalleys, co
,,	14	JAMES WILSON, son and heir of Edward W , of Durham, Doctor of Medicine.
1669-70		
Jan	24	WILLIAM DANIEL, son and heir of William D , of Wigan, co. Lancaster, Esq
,,	29	GOLDWELL HOOPER, son of Richard H , of Saffron Hill, Middlesex, Esq
Feb	2	WILLIAM SCROGGS, son and heir of William S., Knight, King's Serjeant-at-
,,	,,	JOHN FRITH, son of John F , of Bow, Middlesex. [Law
,,	7	LEWIS MORGAN, son and heir of John M , of Llangenny, co Brecon, gent.
,,	9.	WILLIAM DRAKE, son and heir of William D , of Barnaldswicke Coates, co [York, Esq

folio 1,220.

,,	,,	JOHN FRY, son of John F., late of Canterbury, gent
,,	10	STAVELEY STANTON, son and heir of Francis S , late of Burchmore, Beds, Esq
,,	12	HENRY IRETON, son and heir of Henry I , of Notts, gent.
,,	,,	THOMAS SWINBORNE, son and heir of John S , of Gray's Inn, Esq
,,	,,	RICHARD STANES, son and heir of Thomas S , of Thirsk, co York, gent
,,	21	WILLIAM STOWE, son of William S , of Newton, co Lincoln, Esq
,,	25.	JOHN ROBINSON, Knight and Baronet, Alderman of London, King's Lieutenant
,,	,,	THOMAS BLUDWORTH, Knight, Alderman of London [of the Tower.
,,	,,	RICHARD FORD, Knight, Alderman of London.
,,	,,	RICHARD RYVES, Knight, Alderman of London
,,	,,	GEORGE WATERMAN, Knight, Alderman of London.
,,	,,	THOMAS DAVIES, Knight, Alderman of London
,,	,,	FRANCIS CHAPLIN, Knight, Alderman of London
,,	,,	ROBERT VINER, Knight and Baronet, Alderman of London

1669-70   folio 1,221

Feb 26   RICHARD AMHERST, of Staple Inn, son and heir of Richard A , late of
                                              [Southouse, Sussex, clerk.

„   „   HENRY HALL, of Highmeadow, co Gloucester, Esq (son of Benedict ?)

„   „   JOHN HALL, Esq , second son of Benedict H , Esq , deceased, late of High-
                meadow, co Gloucester   [deceased.

Mar 8   EDWARD LLOYD, son and heir of David L , late of Tythin, co Flint, gent ,

„   9   EDWARD BARKER, son and heir of Thomas B., of Wilsthorp, co Lincoln, gent

„   10   HUGH HINDLEY, son and heir of Hugh H , late of Hindley, co Lancaster,
1670.   [Esq , deceased

April 14 EDWARD CHETHAM, third son of Edward C , of Smedley, co Lancaster, gent.

„   19   GILBERT MARSHALL, son and heir of Gilbert M , of Sellaby, co Durham, Esq.

„   20   THOMAS RICHARDSON, second son of Sir Thomas R , Baron of Cramond in
                                              [Scotland

„   30   JOHN CLAVERING, son and heir of Robert C , of Chopwell, co Durham, Esq

May 1   PAUL PULLEYNE, of Middleham, co York, gent

                                folio 1,222.

„   „   JOHN FISHER, son of Nicholas F , of Stonbank Green, Westmoreland, Esq

„   2   AMBROSE MANDEVILL, of Balynrahy, co. Tipperary, gent., son and heir of
                                              [John M , Esq

„   „   JOHN BONNETT, son and heir of John B , late of Gray's Inn, Esq

„   „   ELLIS LLOYD, son and heir of Edward L , of Penylan, co Denbigh, gent

„   6   FRANCIS WETHERED, son and heir of Francis W., of Berkhampstead, Herts,
                Esq.   [Esq

„   7.   GEORGE FAIRFAX, son and heir of Joseph F., late of Moulton, co. Lincoln,

„   „   RICHARD KING, son and heir of Richard K , of Langley, co Derby, Esq

„   9   THOMAS WALLER, second son of Thomas W , of Gregones, Bucks, Esq

„   10. THOMAS COLLEN, son and heir of Thomas C , of Little Laver, Essex, Esq

„   13   THOMAS MOORE, son and heir of Adrian M , of Milton Place, Surrey, Esq

„   16   ARTHUR MEARE, son and heir of William M , of Eastangton (?), co Pembroke,
                Esq.   [Esq

„   „   AURELIUS PERCIE WISEMAN, son and heir of John W , of Broadocks, Essex,

„   26   EDWARD GWIN, son and heir of John G , of Abercrave, Brecon, Esq

                                folio 1,223   [Olaves, Hart-street, London

„   „   BENJAMIN MIDLETON, son and heir of Thomas M , of the parish of St

„   30   EDWARD HOBLYN, son and heir of Robert H , of Nanswhiddon, Cornwall,
                Esq   [Esq

„   „   CHRISTOPHER PERCEHAY, son and heir of William P , of Ryton, co. York,

„   „   RICHARD PARRIE, son and heir of John P , of Pwllhaytog, co Flint, Esq.

June 3   WILLIAM TAYLOR, son and heir of William T , of Holme-near-the-Sea,

„   8   ALTHAM SMITH, son of Thomas S , of Hill Hall, Essex, Baronet [Norfolk, gent

„   „   HUMPHREY SANDFORD, second son of Richard S , late of Upper Rossall,
                                              [Salop, Esq

,   „   JAMES BRYAN, son and heir of John B., of Jenkinstown, co Kilkenny

1670   folio 1,223—(*continued*).

June 11.   EDWARD RIGBY, son and heir of Edward R., of Preston, co. Lancaster, Esq,
                                 [and one of the Ancients of this Inn

,,   13   ISAAC COTTON, son and heir of George C., of Gray's Inn, Esq

,,   ,,   EDWARD THIRKELD, second son of Edward T., of the city of Durham, gent

,,   ,,   CHARLES STANHOPE, son and heir of the Hon Arthur S., of Mansfield Wood-
                                 [house, Notts, Esq.

folio 1,224

,,   17   WILLIAM ATWOOD, gent., of the Inner Temple, son and heir of John A., of
                            [this Inn, Esq. (admitted Sept 29, 1669)

,,   20   JOSHUA IRELAND, fourth son of Robert I., of Albrighton, Salop, Esq.

,,   27   JOHN CLAPHAM, son of Luke C., of Gray's Inn, Esq

,,   28   JOHN GARDINER, son and heir of John G., of Croughton, co Northampton,

,,   29   MORRIS SHELTON, son and heir of Morris S., of Barningham, Suffolk   [Esq

July   4   CHARLES PENRUDDOCK, third son of George P., of Chalk, Wilts, Esq

,,   12   WILLIAM BARKER, son and heir of William B., of St. Andrews, Holborn, Esq.

,,   21   DANIEL WATSON, son and heir of Daniel W., of Gray's Inn, Esq

,,   26   WILLIAM HUGGESSEN, Esq, son and heir of John H., Esq., deceased, the son
                    [and heir (while he lived) of William H., of Linsted, Kent, Knight

Aug   5.   WILLIAM WIDDRINGTON, Baron of Blackney

,,   ,,   WILLIAM CROONE, Doctor of Medicine, of London

,,   ,,   THOMAS SKIPWITH, son and heir of Thomas S., reader.

,,   ,,   ROBERT HANSON, Knight, Alderman of London

folio 1,225

,,   ,,   JAMES EDWARDS, Esq, Sheriff of London   [the Bath

,,   ,,   EDWARD BASH, son and heir of Ralph B., late of Stansted, Herts, Knight of

,,   6.   JOHN VANDEN BEMPDE, son and heir of Abraham V., of St Martins-in-the-
                              [Fields, Middlesex, gent

,,   ,,   THOMAS DINGLEY, son and heir of Thomas D., of Southampton, Esq

,,   12   SAMUEL JOHNSON, son and heir of John J., of co Durham, gent

Sept 15   RANDAL WYNNE, of Gyrianog, co. Carnarvon, gent.

,,   20   EDWARD HAWKESWORTH, son of Joseph H., late of Burwash, Sussex, clerk

,   ,,   JAMES SYMES, son and heir of James S., of Gray's Inn, gent

Oct 22.   LAURENCE STURTEVANT, son and heir of William S., of Norwell, Notts, gent

,,   ,,   WILLIAM POWEL, son and heir of Hugh P., of Castel Madock, Brecon, Esq.

folio 1,226

,,   24   JOHN BEAUMONT TASBURGH, son and heir of John T., of Bodnie, Norfolk, Esq

,,   ,,   JOHN LONGAN, son and heir of David L., of Aarpatrick, co Limerick, Esq

,,   29.   ROBERT FILMER, son and heir of Robert F., of East Sutton, Kent, Esq

Nov   7   MARMADUKE WILLIAMS, son of Nicholas W., of co. Carmarthen, Esq.

,,   11.   ROBERT LILBOURNE, son of Robert L., of Thickley, co Durham, Esq

,,   12   SAMUEL WESTERN, son and heir of Thomas W., of Dike Key, London, Esq

,,   ,,   PETER GOTT, son and heir of Samuel G., of Gray's Inn, Esq.

,,   13   NICHOLAS CUSACK, second son of James C., of Dublin, Esq, deceased

1670 folio 1,226—(*continued*).

Nov. 21. RICHARD GARRARD, son and heir of Richard G., of Mitcham, Berks, Esq.

,, 22 STEPHEN UPMAN, son and heir of Nicholas U., of Westminster, Esq.

folio 1,227. [gent, deceased

,, 26 GEORGE WEAVER, son and heir of George W., late of Yarpole, co. Hereford,

,, ,, FRANCIS THEOBALD, son and heir of Francis T., of Barking, Suffolk, Knight

,, 28 EDWARD LEGH, second son of Thomas L., of Adlington, Cheshire, Esq

Dec 1 THOMAS CLITHEROW, son and heir of Christopher C., late of the city of
London, merchant, deceased [London, merchant, deceased

,, ,, CHRISTOPHER CLITHEROW, second son of Christopher C., late of the city of
1670-1. [Esq

Jan 19 WILLIAM BETHELL, gent, son and heir of William B., of Swindon, co York,

,, 23 NATHAN NICOLS, second son of Francis N., of the city of London, gent

,, 28 ROBERT NEWDEGATE, second son of Richard N., Serjeant-at-Law, of Arbury,
[co Warwick

Feb 2 BENJAMIN LANY, son and heir of John L., of Ely, co Cambridge, Esq

,, 6 JOHN ELWES, son and heir of John E., of Barton, parish of Kintbury, Berks,
Knight [Rutland, gent

,, 7 SAMUEL BARKER, son and heir of Samuel B., of South Luffenham, co.

folio 1,228.

,, 9 JAMES SOTHEBY, son and heir of James S., of Hackney, Middlesex, gent.

,, 10 SAMUEL BLACKERBY, son of ——— B., of Stowmarket, Suffolk, clerk

,, 11 JOHN GOODERE, son and heir of Henry G., of the town of Northampton, Esq.

Mar 1. JOHN NEWTON, son and heir of John N., of Heighley, parish of Cherbury,
[Salop, Esq.

Feb. 15 JOHN SPELMAN, son and heir of Roger S., of Congham, Norfolk, Esq

Mar 10 WILLIAM EAST, gent, son and heir of Gilbert E., of London, gent.

,, 12 STEPHEN PRIMATE, son and heir of John P., deceased (admitted to Barnard's
Inn, December 23, 1661, to Clifford's Inn, May 11, 1666, and to the
[Inner Temple, December 9, 1668)

folio 1,229.

,, 16 JOSEPH SHELTON, Knight, Alderman of London.

,, ,, JOHN SMITH, Knight, Alderman of London.

,, ,, DONAT FORTH, Sheriff and Alderman of London

,, ,, PATIENCE WARD, Sheriff and Alderman of London

,, ,, ADAM WARING, son and heir of Richard W., of Woodcott, Salop, gent

,, 17 HENRY MANNATON, second son of Ambrose M., late of Trecarell, Cornwall,
[Esq, deceased

1671

April 19 CROMWELL FLEETWOOD, second son of Charles F., of Feltwell, Norfolk, Esq

,, 29 EDWARD JEFFREYS, second son of John J., of Acton, co Denbigh, Esq

May 10. EDWARD MINSHULL, son and heir of Edward M., of Stocke, co Chester, Knight

,, ,, HUMPHREY HOWORTH, second son of Humphrey H., of Whitehouse, co Here-
[ford, Esq.

folio 1,230

19 JOHN CRAWLEY, son and heir of Francis C., of Sumeris, Beds, Esq

1671   folio 1,230—(*continued*)

May 19   GODFREY CHYBNALE, son and heir of Thomas C, of Orlingbury, co
[Northampton, Esq

„   „   JOHN BREWER, second son of Thomas B, of Westfalia, Kent, Esq.

„   23.   JOHN EKINS, of Chelveston-cum-Caldecott, co Northampton, son and heir of
[Alexander E, gent.

„   29.   THOMAS FIENNES, second son of Hon. John F., of Great Amwell, Herts.

„   „   GEORGE GUYON, second son of George G, of Coggeshall, Essex, Esq.

„   31.   DANIEL EVANS, of Lampeter, co Cardigan, gent

July 1   CHARLES READ, Esq, son and heir of Thomas R, late of Bardwell, Suffolk, Esq.

„   „   THOMAS READ, second son of Thomas R, late of Bardwell, Suffolk, Esq

June 2   JAMES PARRY, son and heir of James P., of Llandernylogg, co. Brecon, Esq.

folio 1,231.

„   „   EDWARD TAYLER, son and heir of Richard T, of Anstey, co Warwick, Esq

„   „   GEORGE WETHERED, second son of Francis W, of Berkhampstead, Herts, Esq

„   3   JARVIS PEG, son and heir of Edward P, of Beaucheife, co Derby, Esq

„   „   FRANCIS STREET, son and heir of Thomas S, of the city of Worcester, Esq,
one of the Justices of our Lord the King for the great session in cos
[Glamorgan, Brecon and Radnor

„   6   JONATHAN JENNINGS, son and heir of Edmund J, of Ripon, co York, Knight

„   „   BALDWIN ROWCLIFFE, of the city of Exeter, gent   [Esq.

„   „   NATHANIEL PAVLER, son and heir of George P, of Nun Monkton, co York,

„   21   WILLIAM RONAYNE, of the city of Cork, son and heir of Patrick R, Esq

„   „   THOMAS FARREN, son and heir of Thomas F, of the city of Cork, Esq

„   „   GEORGE EVANS, son and heir of George E, of the city of Cork, Esq

„   „   ROBERT HARRISON, third son of Thomas H, of Allerthorpe, co York, Esq

folio 1,232.

„   „   JOHN HENNESSEY, son and heir of Thomas H, of Castletown, co. Cork, Esq.

„   24   GRIFFITH WILLIAMS, son and heir of Peter W, of Placeonn, parish of Mold,
co Flint, gent   [the same, gent.

„   27   WILLIAM GLYN, of Eliernion, co Carnarvon, son and heir of Richard G, of

„   28   ROBERT ARMESTEAD, son and heir of Robert A, of Thurlby, co Lincoln, gent.

„   „   JOHN MILNER, son and heir of Tempest M, of Wistow, co York, Esq

„   „   EDWARD AYSCOUGH, son and heir of Edward A, of South Kelsey, co Lincoln,
Knight   [ter, Esq

July 3   RICHARD SHERBURNE, son and heir of Richard S, of Stonyhurst, co Lancas-

„   „   THOMAS ALESTRYE, son and heir of William A, late of this Inn, Esq

„   7   GEORGE PENNANT, of the Inner Temple, gent, according to his admission
[there, Feb. 9, 1662

folio 1,234.

„   „   JOHN FYFE, third son of William F, of Hackinsall, co Lancaster

„   10   JOHN BORRETT, of Martin, Norfolk, gent, two-and-a-half years of Staple Inn.

„   „   SAMUEL PACKER, of Staple Inn, gent, one year and more

1671.   folio 1,234—(continued)

July 11.   SAMPSON MANNATON, eldest son of Arthur M., of Mannaton, parish of
            Southill, Cornwall, Esq   [Leicester, gent., deceased

„   13   RICHARD WALKER, son and heir of David W., late of Appleby Magna, co.

„   28   JOHN OGLE, second son of John O., of Kirkley, Northumberland, Esq

„   29   RALPH HANSBY, eldest son of Ralph H., of Tickhill, co York, Esq

folio 1,235.

„   31   GEORGE YELVERTON, eldest son of Walter Y., of co Cork, Esq

Aug   1   CHARLES OTWAY, second son of John O., now reader.

„   „   GEORGE MIDLETON, second son of Robert M., of Warton, co Lancaster, gent.

„   4   EDWARD WILSON, eldest son of Edward W., of Dalham Tower, Westmoreland,

„   „   EWAN CHRISTIAN, eldest son of Edward C., of the Isle of Man, Esq   [Esq

„   7   EDWARD BOTELER, of Wennington, Essex, Esq.   [land, gent.

„   8   THOMAS HEBLETHWAYTE, eldest son of Robert H., of Killington, Westmore-
                                                    [dale, Westmoreland

„   „   HENRY WILSON, eldest son of Henry W., of Umberley, near Kirby Lons-

folio 1,236

„   14   GRIFFITH WILLIAMS, of Plason, co Flint, Esq   [Hunts, Esq

„   17   ABRAHAM CORNWALLIS, gent, son and heir of Bevercotes C., of Midlor,
                                                    [Esq, deceased

„   „   RICHARD COX, son and heir of Richard C., late of Bandon Bridge, co Cork,

Oct 21   JOSEPH STEPNEY, of the city of Dublin, son and heir of John S., of same

„   26.   CHARLES BONYTHON, son and heir of John B., of Bonython, Cornwall, Esq

„   „   OLIVER MANDY, of Sundridge, Kent, gent

Nov   1.   GEORGE TOWNSEND, Esq, second Prothonotary of Common Pleas

„   „   LIONEL MADDISON, son and heir of Lionel M., of Saltwell, Durham, Esq

folio 1,237.

„   4   RALPH WINGATE, son and heir of Edward W., of Lockley Bury, Herts, Esq

„   „   JOHN MANLEY, son and heir of John M., of Wrexham, co Denbigh, gent

„   10   MICHAEL GLYD, of Staple Inn, gent, for two-and-a-half years

„   15   DANIEL LLOYD, second son of Lewis L., deceased, late of Buchlaithwen
                                                    [parish of Llangenech, co Carmarthen, gent

„   16   THOMAS PATTEN, of Preston, co Lancaster, gent

„   „   CORNELIUS LEARY, second son of Arthur L., of Munster, Ireland, gent

„   17   THOMAS TURNER, son and heir of Thomas T., of Canterbury, Esq

„   „   JOHN OSBORNE, son and heir of Edward O., of the town of Derby   [Baronet

„   „   RICHARD FRANCKLIN, son and heir of Richard F., of Moore, Herts, Knight and

folio 1,238.

Dec   6   BLUNDY WATERMAN, son and heir of John W., of Holt, Berks, gent.

„   „   FRANCIS HANSON, of London, gent

1671-2
Jan. 20.   EDMUND ROLESTONE, son of Thomas R., of Towton, co Lincoln, gent

„   3   HENRY PLACE, son and heir of Edward P., of Well, co York, gent

1671-2.   folio 1,238—(*continued*).

Jan. 22   ELLIS DUXBURY, son of Laurence D, of Deane, co Lancaster, gent

„   25   JOHN WESTLY, son and heir of John W, of Ethorp, co Warwick, gent

„   29   JOHN CROSS, of the city of Chester.   [deceased

Feb 2   THOMAS ADAMS, one of the sons of William A, of Scawsby, co York, late

„   5   RICHARD LAVALLIN, second son of James L, of Walterstown, co Cork

„   9.   JAMES KYNYIN, gent.

„   10   JAMES GREGORY, gent, son and heir of William G, of Gray's Inn, Esq.

folio 1,239.

„   12   GEORGE STARLING, son and heir of George S, of Chearesfield, Suffolk, Esq

„   14   JOHN ROBINSON, son and heir of Henry R, of Long Whatton, co Leicester,

„   16   EDWARD OSBORNE, second son of Edward O, of Derby, gent   [S T D

„   19   DANIEL BROWNE, son and heir of Daniel B, of Hendon, Middlesex, gent

„   23   JOHN WARNER, son and heir of Simon W, of Knaresborough, co York, gent

„   25   ROBERT CARR, Knight and Baronet, Chancellor of the Duchy and County
                        [Palatine of Lancaster, one of the Privy Council

„   26   THOMAS DONE, son of Ralph D, of Duddon, co Chester, Knight

„   27   CHARLES, Lord GERRARD, Baron of Brandon, Gentleman of the Bedchamber
                        [to the King

„   28   JAMES BEVERSHAM, son and heir of James B, of Kellishall, Suffolk, S T D

folio 1,240

„   29   WILLIAM PEAKE, Knight, Alderman of London

„   „   JONATHAN DAWES, Knight, Sheriff of London

„   „   ROBERT CLAYTON, Knight, Sheriff of London

„   „   WILLIAM MAN, Esq

Mar. 2.   FLORENCE MACNAMARA, third son of John M, of Crenagh, co Clare

„   9   ROBERT FRANCIS, second son of Roger F, of Trewerne, co Montgomery, Esq.

„   „   CHARLES BEST, son and heir of John B, of Emswell, co. York, Esq.

„   „   JOHN WARD, second son of William W., of Preston, co Rutland, gent

1672

April 26.   JOHN YALDEN, son and heir of Robert Y, of the city of London, gent

May 1   JOHN SCROGGS, son and heir of John S, of Albury, Herts, Esq (folio 1242)

„   6   WILLIAM OWEN, son and heir of John O, of Stanham, Oxon, S T D.

folio 1,241

„   8   JOHN NEWTON, son and heir of John N, of Thorpe, co Lincoln, Baronet.

„   10   AMBROSE MOYLE, gent, son of Peter M, gent.   [Esq.

„   13   WILLIAM STROTHER, son and heir of William S, of Fowbery, Northumberland,

„   „   FREDERICK TYLNEY, son and heir of Francis T., of Rotherwick, Southampton,

„   16   JOHN MYHILL, son and heir of George M, of Ballysop, co Wexford, gent [Esq.

„   18   THOMAS BURROUGHS, son and heir of Thomas B, of Ipswich, Suffolk, gent,

„   20   ARTHUR CHARLETT, son and heir of John C, of Gray's Inn, Esq [deceased

„   „   SIMON THOMPSON, youngest son of Simon T, of Manchester, gent

1672.   **folio 1,243**

May 31   EDWARD BARNARD, gent , son of Edward B., of Gray's Inn, Knight

June 3   JAMES WEBSTER, son and heir of James W , of Thrimby, Westmoreland, gent

,, ,,   ALLAN LAMONT, of North Burton, co York, gent   [Durham, Esq , deceased

,, 4   WILLIAM BOWES, gent , second son of Thomas B , of Streatlam Castle, co

,, 6   RICHARD SHUTTLEWORTH, son and heir of Nicholas S , of Clitherow, co

,, 10   POMPEY ALYBOND, son of Job A , of Dagnam, Essex, gent   [Lancaster, Esq

,, 12   WILLIAM ELLIS, son and heir of Sidney E , of Lantilly, co Denbigh, gent

,, 17   EDWARD ROBERTS, junior, son of Edward R., senior, of the city of Dublin, Esq

folio 1,244.

,, 19.   RALPH WHITFIELD, gent , son and heir of Henry W , of Dublin, Esq

,, 22.   WILLIAM MORGAN, son and heir of James M., of the city of Bristol, gent

,, ,,   JOHN FLEETE, son and heir of Thomas F , of Hallowpark, co. Worcester, Esq

,, 28   LEWIS WEST, son of Lewis W , of Salkeld, Cumberland, clerk, deceased

July 1   CHARLES MANN, son and heir of William M , of Thorpe Underwood, co York,

Aug 14   ISAAC WARD, son and heir of Richard W , of Dublin, gent   [gent

,, 15   ROBERT CASIE, son and heir of Robert C , of Dublin, deceased   [London

Sept 17   MAURICE KAYE, son and heir of John K , citizen and merchant taylor of

Oct 15   WALTER HERRIS, son and heir of Walter H , late of Bromfield, Essex, gent.,
                                                           [deceased
folio 1,245   [meath, Esq

,, 26   ROBERT ROCHFORT, second son of Primiron R , of Streamstown, co West-

Nov 1   HENRY WHARTON, third son of Lord Wharton, Baron of Wharton, in West-
         moreland   [Knight and Baronet

,, ,,   BENJAMIN CROPLEY, gent , third son of John C , of Colney Hatch, Middlesex,

,, 8   BARNBY BOWDON, eldest son of Nicholas B , of Bowdon, co Derby

,, ,,   JOHN ARCHDECON, son and heir of William A , of the city of Cork, Esq

,, 11   ROBERT WOOD, son and heir of Thomas W , of Braconash, Norfolk, Esq

folio 1,246.

,, 14   THOMAS FARNABY, son and heir of John F , of Canterbury, gent   [gent

,, 16   THOMAS BROUGHALL, second son of Robert B , of Clonsyllagh, co Dublin,

,, 18   PATRICK CRAUFORD, son and heir of James C , of Edinburgh, gent.

,, 21   ELLIS MEREDITH, son and heir of Hugh M , of Pentrebach, co Denbigh, gent

,, 22   YELVERTON PEYTON, of Rougham, Norfolk, son of Thomas P , Esq

,, 23   JOHN WATKINS, son and heir of William W , of Lanigon, co Brecon, Esq

,, 25   RICHARD BUTLER, of St Brides Major, co Glamorgan, gent

folio 1,247.

,, 27   JOSEPH MICKLETHWAITE, of Swine, co York, Esq

,, 28.   GEORGE WELD, Esq , son and heir of John W , of Willey, Salop, Knight

Dec 3   FRANCIS CHILDERS, son of William C , of Bole, Notts, Esq

,, 4   OLIVER KILLINGWORTH, son and heir of Luke K , of Killingworth, Northum-
         berland, Esq , deceased   [wall, Esq , deceased

,, 21   THOMAS JOHNSON, son and heir of Thomas J , late of Liskard Park, co Corn-

1672-3   **folio 1,247—***(continued)*.

Feb 2.   Roger Bradshaigh, of Haigh, co Lancaster, Knight

,,   ,,   Richard Parker, second son of George P , of Willington, Sussex, Esq.

folio 1,248.

,,   ,   Edward Carr, eldest son of Right Hon Robert C , Knight and Baronet, [Chancellor of the Duchy of Lancaster, &c.

,,   ,,   Peter Legh, eldest son of Richard L , of Lyme, co Chester, Esq

,,   ,,   Beverley Wingfield, eldest son of Francis W., of Stamford, co. Lincoln, Esq.

,,   ,,   Christopher Rose, eldest son of Giles R , of Lynn Regis, Norfolk, gent

,,   3   Benjamin Gaich (of Barnard's Inn, two years, by certificate of Edward Story, [Principal), third son of James G , of Lyme Regis, Dorset, gent

,,   10   Charnock Heron, son of John H , of Godmanchester, Hunts, Esq.

,,   17   Henry Thompson, second son of William T., of Scorborough, co. York, Esq

1673   **folio 1,249.**   [Lincoln, Esq

Mar 28   Thomas Cornwallis, gent , son and heir of Bevercoats C , of the city of [deceased

April 14   Walter Grubb, son and heir of Thomas G , late of Eastwell, Wilts, Esq ,

,,   29   James Weldon, gent , son and heir of George W , of Cookham, Berks, Esq

,,   ,,   Stephen Knight, son and heir of Francis K , of Stoke Prior, co Worcester,

May 1   George Llewellin, son and heir of George L , of Salop, gent   [gent

,,   12   Henry Morgan, second son of Morgan Williams, of Merthyr Tydfil, co   [Glamorgan, gent

,,   16.   Philip Monoux, gent , third son of Humphrey M , of Wotton, Beds, Baronet

folio 1,250

                        [on-Hull, gent , deceased

,,   17   John Wardell, son and heir of Richard W , late of the town of Kingston-

,,   27   William Palmer, son and heir of William P , of the city of Lincoln, Esq

                        [bridge, co Devon, gent

,,   30   John Gilberd, son and heir of Thomas G , of Combe Royal, near Kings-

,,   ,,   John Whiting, son and heir of Joseph W , of Boston, co Lincoln, Esq

                        [gent

,,   ,,   Henry Hodgkinson, son and heir of William H., of Preston, co Lancaster,

June 3   Thomas Beckwith, son and heir of Thomas B., of Lambhill, co. York, gent

,,   4   William Agar, son and heir of John A , of Stockton, co York, gent.

,,   ,,   Richard Uniacke, fourth son of Maurice U , of Youghall, co. Cork, Esq

folio 1,251

,,   5.   John Plummer, son and heir of John P , late of New Windsor, Berks, Esq

,,   10   Arthur Marshall, second son of Samuel M , of Walton, co York, gent

,,   ,,   Peter Nicholls, son and heir of Peter N , of Shenley, Herts, gent

,,   ,,   Edward Nicholls, second son of Peter N , of Shenley, Herts, gent.

                        [Baronet

,,   13   Thomas Stanley, Esq , son and heir of Peter S , of Alderley, co Chester,

,,   ,,   William Ingram, second son of Arthur I , of Knottingley, co York, Esq

2

1673   folio 1,252

June 14   JOHN VAUGHAN, son and heir of John V , of Hergest, co Hereford, Esq

,,   ,,   RICHARD VAUGHAN, son and heir of John V , of Derlhs, co Carmarthen, Esq

,,   17   RICHARD PALFERY, of Dublin, gent   [former admission at Lincoln's Inn)

,,   19   MICHAEL EMERSON, of Barnetby, co Lincoln (allowed two years for his

,,   ,,   JOHN MOORE, son of Nicholas M , of Knowsthrop, co. York, Esq

,,   20   GEORGE BOKENHAM, fifth son of Wyseman B , late of Great Thornham,
          Suffolk, Esq , deceased   [gent.

July 10   FLORENCE MACNAMARA, son and heir of Daniel M , of Doone, co Clare,

,,   11   FRANCIS MOLYNEUX, son and heir of John M , of Tevershall, Notts, Esq

                                             folio 1,253.   [deceased

,,   25   THOMAS WELBY, third son of William W , late of Denton, co Lincoln, gent ,

,,   29   WILLIAM BEVERSHAM, second son of James B , of Kellishall, Suffolk, S T P

Aug 4   FRANCIS RADCLYFFE, of Dilston, Northumberland, Baronet

,,   5   NARCISSUS LUTTRELL, son and heir of Francis L , of Giay's Inn, Esq

,,   ,,   GEORGE ELLISON, son and heir of Benjamin E , of Newcastle-on-Tyne, mer-

,,   6   ROBERT, Lord LEXINGTON, Baron of Aram, Notts   [chant

,,   7   WILLIAM PRITCHARD, Knight, one of the Sheriffs of London and Middlesex

,,   ,,   JAMES SMITH, Knight, one of the Sheriffs of London and Middlesex

,,   8   MARK SHAFIOE, son of Robert S , now reader

                                             folio 1,254.

,,   9   THOMAS TWIGGE, son and heir of ———— T , of the city of Dublin, gent [Esq

Oct. 23   EDMUND FITZGERALD, son and heir of Richard F , of Great Connell, Ireland,

,,   25   DANIEL PHILLIPS, son and heir of Edmund P , of Hampt, parish of Stoke-
          climsland, Cornwall, gent   [land, gent

,,   28.   NATHANIEL TOMPSON, son and heir of John T , of Newham, Northumber-

,,   29   THEOPHILUS LLOYD, son and heir of Thomas L , of Dan-yr alt, co Carmar-
          then, Esq.   [Esq

Nov 1.   ROBERT TIRWHITT, son and heir of Cecil T , of Camringham, co Lincoln,

Oct 31   JOHN HAYES, two years of Staple Inn, gent

,,   ,,   JOHN PLATT, of Westbrooke, parish of Godalming, Surrey, Knight.

Nov 3.   JOHN ODBER, son and heir of John O , of Steeple Court, Southampton, gent.

                                             folio 1,255.

,,   ,,   THOMAS NEWBURGH, son and heir of Thomas N., of Ballihayes, co Cavan, Fsq

,,   19   WATKIN HERBERT, second son of Morgan H , of Rhwbren, co Cardigan, gent

Dec 4   EDWARD ORMSBY, of Shrowle, co Mayo, Knight

,,   15   JOHN LACY, son and heir of Piers L , of Ashlackagh, co Limerick   [Esq

,,   18   WILLIAM ROKEBY, son and heir of William R , of Ackworth Park, co York,

,,   ,,   HENRY SMITH, son and heir of John S , of Snainton, co York, gent

1673-4
Feb 2   WILLIAM WHARTON, Esq , son of Rt Hon Lord Wharton, Baron of Wharton

,,   ,,   EDWARD MIDLETON, of Midleton, Westmoreland, Esq

,,   1   GUICCARDINE WENTWORTH, Esq

                                              U

1673-4　　　　　　　　　　folio 1,256.

Feb　4　JOHN MIDLETON, younger son of ——— M , of the city of Durham, gent

,,　9　WILLIAM ROBINSON, son and heir of Thomas R , of Oldfield, co York, Esq

,,　,,　PAUL PULLEIN, fourth son of John P , of Mounton, co York, gent

,,　,,　TOWERS DRIFFIELD, son and heir of Francis D., of Easingwold, co York, Esq

,,　12　SAMUEL ARMITAGE, second son of Timothy A , of Norwich, clerk, deceased

,,　13　JOSEPH YATES, son and heir of William Y , of Blackburn, co Lancaster, gent

,,　27　JAMES BYRD, of Brougham, Westmoreland, gent

,,　,,　THOMAS CORRY, son and heir of Francis C , Esq , of this Society

Mar　7　JOHN MOLYNEUX, son of John M , of Teversall, Notts, Esq

,,　,,　CHARLES RIGBY, youngest son of Edward R , Esq , now reader

,,　,,　HUGH PENNINGTON, son of Nicholas P , of Wigan, co Lancaster, gent

,,　8　THOMAS CHOLMONDELEY, of Vale Royal, co Chester

folio 1,257

,,　,,　JOHN BARNEBY, of Hull (alias Hill), co Worcester, Knight

,,　,,　GILES STRANGWAYS, of Melbury Sampford, co Dorset, Esq

,,　10　RICHARD, Earl of BURLINGTON and CORK, Viscount Dungarvan and Kynal-
　　　　machy, Baron of Youghall, Bandon, and Clifford, Lord High Treasurer
　　　　of Ireland　　　　　　　　　　　　　[of John, Marquis of Winchester

,,　,,　CHARLES PAWLETT, Earl of Wiltshire, Baron St John of Basing, son and heir

,,　,,　FRANCIS, Lord CARRINGTON, Viscount Bearsford, in Ireland

,,　,,　CHARLES LUCAS, Baron of Shenfield, Essex

,,　,,　FRANCIS, Lord AUNGIER, Baron of Longford, in Ireland

,,　,,　RICHARD, Lord BYRON, Baron of Rochdale, co Lancaster

,,　,,　CHARLES GERRARD, son and heir of Charles, Lord Gerrard, Baron of Brandon

,　,,　GILBERT GERRARD, of Brafferton, co York, Baronet

,,　,,　SAMUEL BARNARDISTON, of Brightwell Hall, Suffolk, Baronet

,,　,,　CHARLES PAWLETT, son and heir of Charles, Earl of Wiltshire

folio 1,258.

,,　,,　THOMAS FYFE, son and heir of William F , late of Hackensall, co Lancaster,

,,　12　WILLIAM HOOKER, Knight, Alderman and Mayor of London　[Esq , deceased

,,　,,　THOMAS ALLEN, Knight and Baronet, Alderman of London.

,,　,,　JOHN FREDERICK, Knight, Alderman of London　　　[victualling the Navy

,,　,,　DENNIS GAWDEN, Knight, Alderman of London, the King's Surveyor for

,,　,,　HENRY TULSE, Knight, Alderman and Sheriff of London

,,　,,　ROBERT JEFFERY, Knight, Sheriff of London

,,　,,　THOMAS LEWIS, of St Olaves, Hart-street, London, Esq

,,　,,　HUNGATE LEWIS, gent , son and heir of Thomas L , of St Olaves, Hart-
　　　　street, London, Esq　　　　　　　　　　[Fellow of this Society

,,　,,　WILLIAM TURTON, son and heir of John T , of Alrewas, co Stafford, gent ,

,,　,,　BENJAMIN HOGHTON second son of Richard H , of Hoghton Tower, co
　　　　　　　　　　　　　　　　　　　[Lancaster, Baronet

,,　19　EDWARD MASSEY, third son of Roger M , of Coddington, co Chester, Esq

,,　21　JOHN LOWNDES, son and heir of Ralph L , of Middlewich, co Chester, gent

1674   folio 1,258—(continued)

Mar 25. HENRY FISH, son and heir of Humphrey F, of Ickwell, Beds, Esq

April 7. DONATUS KARNEY, son and heir of Michael K, of Ballyduagh, co Tipperary,
                                                      [gent

folio 1,259.

,, 10 GEORGE BOOTH, Esq, third son of George, Lord Delamere, of Dunham
                                          [Massey, co Chester

,, 30 JOHN PELHAM, second son of John P, of Haland, Sussex, Baronet [deceased

,, ,, THOMAS COULTHURST, son and heir of Thomas C, late of Chester, gent,

May 11 JAMES HAYES, fourth son of Thomas H, of Rayes, Hants, gent

,, 13 RICHARD LEWIS, son and heir of Nicholas L, of co Cardigan, Esq

,, 16. SAMUEL BARBER, son and heir of Gerald B, late of Uttoxeter, co Stafford,
                                            [gent, deceased

,, 20 THOMAS STORY, of Guilden Morden, co Camb, gent. (two years of Barnard's
                                [Inn, by certificate of Edward Story, principal)

,, ,, ELLIS LLOYD, son and heir of Edward L, of Penylan, co Denbigh, gent

,, 23 JOHN ROBINSON, son and heir of Robert R, of Branston, co Lincoln, Esq

,, 28 HERBERT RANDOLPH, gent, son and heir of Herbert R, of Canterbury, gent

June 1 JAMES CANE, son and heir of Adam C, of the city of London

folio 1,260.   [co Lancaster, Esq

,, 3 ANTHONY PARKER, son and heir of Christopher P, of the parish of Kirkham,

,, 11 JOHN WODEHOUSE, youngest son of Philip W, of Kimberley, Norfolk, Baronet

,, 12 ARTHUR CAYLEY, son and heir of William C, of Brompton, co York, Esq

,, 27 RICHARD GOODEN, son and heir of John G, Esq, late Alderman of London,
            deceased   [Justices of the Common Pleas

,, 29 JOHN ARCHER, Esq, junior, son and heir of John A, Knight, one of the

,, ,, GEORGE ASHBY, of Quenby, co Leicester, Esq

July 7 JOSEPH GREGG, son and heir of Robert G, late of the city of Chester, gent.

,, ,, ANDREW WARNER, son and heir of Francis W., of London, Esq

,, ,, OLIVER GREGORY, son and heir of Oliver G, of Battersea, Surrey, Esq

,, ,, JOHN MASON, third son of Simon M, senior, of Great Gransden, Hunts, gent

,, 15 ADAM COLCLOUGH, second son of ——— C, of Ballysax, co Wexford

,, ,, CHARLES WYNDHAM, son and heir of Charles W, late of Stokesby, Norfolk,
                                            [Esq, deceased

folio 1,261

,, 23 WILLIAM FITZHERBERT, son and heir of John F, of Luckington, Wilts, Esq

,, 30 BENJAMIN CARY, third son of Nicholas C, of St. Andrews, Holborn, Doctor
                                          [of Medicine.

,, ,, WILLIAM PURCELL, son and heir of John P, of Cloghlea, Ireland, Doctor of

,, ,, EDMUND COTTER, of Ballingsperry, co Cork, gent   [Medicine

,, ,, HENRY SQUIRE, third son of Thomas S., of the city of York, gent

,, ,, SAMUEL ACTON, son and heir of Thomas A, of the city of Chester, gent

Oct 28 HENRY LEWIS, son and heir of Andrew L, of Trelegg, co Monmouth, gent

,, 31 WILLIAM WITHAM, second son of George W, of Cliffe, co York, Esq

Nov 10 HENRY KEDDINGTON, gent, second son of Robert K, late of Hickham,
                                        [Norfolk, Esq, deceased.

1674   folio 1,261—*(continued)*

Nov 14   PHILIP HODGES, second son of John H , of Wells, co Somerset, Esq (of
                                             [Barnard's Inn two years)

,,   ,,   HENRY PERROT, second son of Richard P , of Rappahannock River, in
                                             [Virginia, Esq

folio 1,262

,,   18   ROBERT STAFFORD, son and heir of William S , of Bradfield, Berks, Esq.

,,   26   ALEXANDER STANDISH, second son of ——— S , of Duxbury, co Lanc , Esq.

,,   27   WILLIAM MARRIOTT, of the Temple ("Mr Marriott's admittance by pension
                                             [order, Nov 17, 1704")

,,   28   THOMAS WIGHTWICKE, son of Humphrey W , of Ashford, Kent, gent

Dec 1   CHARLES ALLESTRIE, second son of William A , late of Gray's Inn, Esq ,
               deceased
                                               [Esq.

,,   ,,   ROBERT DIMOCKE, son and heir of Edward D , of Tumby, co Lincoln, Esq

,,   5   JOHN PECKE, son and heir of Jasper P , of Trevallyn, co Denbigh, Esq [gent

,,   ,,   JOHN TEASDALE, son and heir of Christopher T , of Knipe, Westmoreland,

,,   21   ROBERT HOOPER, son and heir of Robert H , late of Sarum, Wilts, Esq ,
              deceased
                                                 [Medicine

,,   22   THOMAS WITHERLEY, second son of Thomas W , of London, Doctor of

1674-5

Jan 7   EDWARD FILMER, second son of Robert F , of East Sutton, Kent, Baronet

,,   27   GEORGE ERRINGTON, son of Nicholas E , of Ponteland, Northumberland, Esq

folio 1,263

,,   ,,   JOHN WALCOTT, son and heir of ——— W , of the city of Limerick.

,,   29   ROBERT CONSTABLE, son and heir of Robert C , of Thweng, co York, clerk

Feb 2   CALEB BANKES, son and heir of John B , Baronet   [deceased.

,,   ,,   JOHN BENNET, son and heir of John B , of St Pauls, Covert-garden, Esq ,

,,   3   JOHN HOOKE, son and heir of John H , of Dublin, clerk

,,   4   RALPH WARTON, second son of Michael W , of Beverley, co York, Esq

,,   ,,   CHARLES WARTON, third son of Michael W , of Beverley, co York, Esq

,,   25   RICHARD ATHERTON, Esq , son and heir of John A , of Atherton, co Lan-
                                           [caster, Esq , deceased

,,   ,,   JOHN LE THIEULLIER, Knight, Sheriff of Middlesex

,   ,,   PHILIP JEMMATT, of Berks, Esq

folio 1,264.

,,   26   JOHN ROTHER(H)AM, son and heir of John R , of Gray's Inn, Esq

,,   ,,   JOHN POCOCKE, son and heir of Giles P , of Cheevely, Berks, gent

,,   ,,   HENRY HARRISON, son and heir of Thomas H , of Newcastle-on-Tyne, gent

Mar 2   BARTHOLOMEW MISSETT, of Dowdingtown, co Kildare, gent [Esq , deceased

,,   10   THOMAS DETHICKE, Esq , son and heir of Henry D , of Poplar, Middlesex,

,,   15   HENRY THOMPSON, son and heir of Henry T , of Escrick, co York, Knight

,,   ,,   RICHARD THOMPSON, second son of Henry T , of Escrick, co York, Knight.

,,   16   JEREMY SAWREY, son and heir of Roger S , of Broughton, co Lancaster, Esq

1675

April 27   WILLIAM HILTON, son and heir of William H , of Hilton, co Lancaster, Esq.

,,   ,,   FRANCIS TOOLE, son and heir of Cooley T , of Ballycullin, Ireland.

1675.		folio 1,265.
April	29	JONATHAN SCURLOCK, son and heir of John S., of Carmarthen, Alderman
May	1.	SAMUEL HUGHES, son and heir of Samuel H., late of Alcough, co Cardigan, [gent, deceased
,,	,,	ARTHUR WARD, son and heir of Arthur W., of Hinton, Salop, gent
,,	6	LEONARD SMELT, Esq, son and heir of Leonard S., of Kirby Fleetham, co York, Esq, deceased [deceased
,,	,,	JOHN SMELT, younger son of Leonard S., of Kirby Fleetham, co York, Esq,
,,	,,	RICHARD PINDAR, son and heir of Richard P., of Holmes, Westmoreland, gent
,,	,,	EDWARD FINCH, son and heir of Edward F., of Gray's Inn, Esq
,,	12.	GEORGE WITHER, son and heir of Gilbert W., of Hall, co Southampton, clerk
,,	,,	RICHARD PYLE, son and heir of Richard P., of Easton Town, co Southampton, [gent
,,	17	CHARLES BYERLEY, son and heir of Charles B., of Belgrave, co Leicester, Esq
,,	20	JOHN WETHERID, son and heir of Francis W., of Ashwick, parish of Berk- [hampstead St Peters, Herts, Esq
		folio 1,266　　[Southampton, Esq, deceased
,,	,,	HUMPHREY WESTWOOD, son and heir of Humphrey W., of Eversley, co
,,	28	GEORGE MONSON, third son of John M., late of Broxbourne, Herts, deceased, Knight of the Bath　　[Chester, gent
,,	,,	JOHN COITON, second son of Ralph C., of Birch Hall, Wybunbury, co
,,	31	JOHN BUCKE, son and heir of Robert B., of Kettenby (Rottenby ?), co York, Esq　　[gent
June	3	WILLIAM PERROTT, son and heir of Robert P., of West Alvington, Devon,
,,	4	ROWLAND DORMER, son and heir of Robert D., late of Grove Park, co. Warwick, Esq, deceased　　[gent, deceased
,,	9	STEPHEN CRUD, younger son of John C., late of Ickleton, co Cambridge,
,,	10	NICHOLAS GARRARD, third son of Thomas G., of Greenestreet, Essex, Baronet
,,	15	WILLIAM CASEY, of Whitfield, co Gloucester, gent, son of Thomas C., Esq,
,,	16	ROBERT BUTLER, son and heir of Robert B., of Gray's Inn, Esq　[deceased
,,	,,	ROBERT PEPPARD, of Dublin, gent.　　　　　　　　　　　[gent
,,	17	THOMAS MERITON, son and heir of George M., of Castle Levington, co York,
		folio 1,267.
,,	,,	ALLEN EPES, son and heir of Paul E., of Wye, Kent, gent　　[deceased.
,,	21	JOHN BOWMAN, son and heir of James B., of Beverley, co York, gent,
,,	23.	THOMAS PEERS, son and heir of Thomas P., of Alveston-upon-Avon, co [Warwick, Esq, deceased
,,	,,	SAMUEL STAPLES, son and heir of Samuel S., of the town of Nottingham, gent
,,	,,	THOMAS SOTHEBY, son and heir of Robert S., of Birdsall, co York, Esq
,,	,,	RICHARD THORNTON, gent., son and heir of John T., of Horbury, co York, gent, deceased　　　　　　　　　　　　　　　　　　[Inn)
,,	,,	JONATHAN PERRY, of St Edmundsbury, Suffolk, gent (two years of Barnard's
,,	,,	JOHN CATTERALL, son and heir of John C., of West Witton, co York, Esq
Aug	3.	ROBERT CHAPLIN, citizen and merchant of London

1675		folio 1,267—(*continued*)
Aug	3	JAMES JEFFES, son and heir of John J , of St Martins-in-the-Fields, London
,,	,,	THOMAS ROBINSON, son and heir of William R , late of Wigenhall St Marys, [Norfolk

folio 1,268

,,	,,	NOAH NEALE, son and heir of Noah N , of Upper Deane, Beds, gent
,,	2	HENRY, Earl of LICHFIELD.
,,	,,	CHARLES, Lord CLIFFORD, grandson and heir of Earl of Burlington and Cork
,,	,,	JOHN DARCY (Honourable), son and heir of Conyers D , Esq
,,	4	THOMAS SWIFT, son and heir of Godwin S , of Gray's Inn
,,	,,	WILLIAM CARPENTER, of the Island of Barbados, late of London, gent
,,	10	RICHARD FLOYD, third son of Humphrey F , Bishop of Bangor
Sept	13	FRANCIS HODDER, son and heir of Francis H , of the city of Cork
,,	14	WILLIAM MINSHULL, second son of Edward M , late of Stoke, co Chester, Knight, deceased [Lincoln, Esq , deceased.
Oct	14	RAWSON HART, son and heir of Theophilus H , late of Tumby Woodside, co

folio 1,269

,	15	JAMES EUSTACE, son and heir of Morris E , of Clongonswood, co Kildare [deceased
,,	,,	JOB WALKER, of Wotton, second son of Richard W , late of Wotton, Salop,
Nov	16	JOHN THORNICROFT, son and heir of John T , Esq , Fellow of this Inn [Esq
,,	18	SAMUEL CHAPMAN, son and heir of Benjamin C , of Killua, co Westmeath,
,,	20	RICHARD GIBBS, of Barnard's Inn, gent (allowed two years)
,,	,,	EDWARD TURNER, son and heir of Thomas T., of Gray's Inn, Esq
,,	21	RICHARD AMSON, of Middlewich, co Chester, gent
1675-6.		[Bench (*i e* , a Bencher)
Feb	1.	THOMAS STRINGER, son of Thomas S , Knight, one of the Masters of the
,,	5	RICHARD GIPPS, son and heir of John G , of Great Welnetham, Suffolk, Esq.

folio 1,270.

,,	9	WILLIAM GLASCOCKE, son and heir of William G , of Farnham, Essex, Esq
,,	11	JOHN EVANS, of Philipstown, second son of George E , Esq
,,	12	WILLIAM DAVENANT, second son of William D , of London, Knight
,,	17	GEORGE BARRETT, son and heir of Paul B , of Gray's Inn, Esq
,,	,,	THOMAS GOLD, Knight, Sheriff of London and Middlesex [Esq
,,	,,	JOHN HERBERT, gent , son and heir of Edward H , of Crickhowell, Brecon,
,,	19	JAMES BREWER, third son of Thomas B , of Gray's Inn, Esq
,,	,,	WILLIAM WATTS, son and heir of William W , of Gray's Inn, Esq
,,	,,	EDMUND COSGRAVE, second son of John C , of Bradfield, Essex, gent.
,,	,,	PAUL PEPPER, son and heir of John P , of Dover, Kent, gent

folio 1,271

,,	21	ROBERT WEBSTER, of Ashburne, co Derby, gent
,,	22	ROBERT HOLDEN, of Weston-upon-Trent, co Derby, gent
,	24	LEWIS LLOYD, son and heir of Charles L , of Gwernwett, Brecon, gent

1676   **folio 1,271—(continued)**

Mar 25.   THOMAS COUNDON, son and heir of Thomas C , late of Willerby, co York, Esq

„   „   FRANCIS BROWNE, son and heir of Thomas B , late of Chester, gent

„   „   HARCOURT GOODRICK, son and heir of Henry G , of Ely, co Cambridge, Esq

April 17 THOMAS STRANGWAYS, son and heir of Thomas S , of Pickering, co York, Esq

„   20   WILLIAM MAINWARING, second son of Thomas M , of Baddeley, Cheshire,
                                                              [Baronet

„   21   JOHN TAYLEUR, of Henlow, Beds, gent

„   22   FRANCIS ATTERBURY, of Milton, co Northampton, gent

„   29   SAMUEL GREENE, son and heir of Eliab G , of Dublin, Esq

May 3   JAMES BRAND, son and heir of William B , of Polstead Hall, Suffolk, Esq

„   8   ROBERT HARDING, son of Robert H , of Gray's Inn, Knight

folio 1,272

„   15   THOMAS LAMPLUGH, son and heir of John L , of Lamplugh, Cumberland, Esq

„   26   JOHN EGERTON, son and heir of Philip E , of Oulton, Cheshire, Knight

„   „   ROGER READ, third son of Gabriel R , of Trough End, Northumberland, Esq

June 5   THOMAS BRANTHWAITE, son and heir of William B , of Hethel, Norfolk, Esq

„   „   ARTHUR BRANTHWAITE, second son of William B , of Hethel, Norfolk, Esq

„   6   CHRISTOPHER RICH, second son of John R , of Overstowey, Somerset, gent

„   7   ABRAHAM PARTINGTON, son and heir of Joshua P , of Lancaster, gent

„   10   WILLIAM OXENDEN, son and heir of Henry O , of Breck, parish of Wingham,
                Kent, Esq   [gent , deceased

„   „   EDWARD WHITE, son and heir of Edward W , of Stocke-in-Butsbury, Essex,
                                                              [Esq.

„   12   WILLIAM BANKES, son and heir of William B , of Winstanley, co Lancaster,

„   „   THOMAS BRETHERTON, second son of John B , of Hey, co Lancaster, gent.

folio 1,273

„   13   OWEN MORGAN, of Porthllongdu, co Anglesey, gent

„   15   HENRY HEYMAN, son and heir of Peter H , of Wye, Kent, Esq

„   16   THOMAS DYKE, son of Thomas D , of Sussex, gent

„   „   JOHN TOMLINSON, son and heir of Peter T , of Burne, co York, gent

„   17. JOHN BYROM, of Byrom, co Lancaster, Esq

„   „   ROBERT JENNISON, son and heir of John J , of Wallworth, co Durham, Esq.

„   22   WILLIAM COURTHOPE, son and heir of William C , of Stodmarsh, Kent, Esq.

July 9   WILLIAM STRINGER, son and heir of Thomas S , Knight , one of the Masters
                of the Bench of this Inn (with standing as of Lincoln's Inn, Feb 27, 1671)

„   „   ROBERT BATE, of Billericay, Essex, gent

folio 1,274

„   10   THOMAS MORE, son and heir of Thomas M , of Hackness, co York, Esq.

„   26   HENRY WRIGLEY, son and heir of Henry W., late of Langley, co Lancaster,
                Esq , deceased   [deceased

„   „   HENRY COPPINGER, son and heir of Henry C , late of Buxhall, Suffolk, Esq

Oct 23   CHRISTOPHER BRODKING, son and heir of William B , of co Devon, merchant

„   26   ROBERT FITZGERALD, second son of Gerard F , of Lisquinlane, co Cork, Esq

1676   folio 1,274—(*continued*)
Nov   1   WILLIAM MEREDITH, son and heir of Richard M., of Leeds, Kent, Baronet
                                                          [ampton, gent.
,,   2   EDWARD GOODYER, son and heir of Edward G , of Dogmersfield, co. South-
,,   8   HENRY BARKER, son and heir of Robert B , of Munkewike, Essex, Esq.
,,   14   ROBERT NIGHTINGALE, son and heir of Thomas N , of Langley, Essex,
              Baronet.   [Esq.
,,   27. EDWARD THOMAS, son and heir of Robert T , of Tregrose, co Glamorgan,

                               folio 1,275.
,,   ,,   JOHN WINDER, son and heir of John W , of Lorton, Cumberland, gent
Dec   4   ROGER VAUGHAN, one of the sons of Roger V , of Salisbury, Wilts, Esq.
,,   21   ROGER KENYON, son and heir of Roger K., of Peele, co Lancaster, Esq
1676-7
Jan 22   WILLIAM HALL, of Chattwell, Salop, gent , and of Barnard's Inn, two years
Feb   2   CRESSY PARKYNS, son and heir of Thomas P , of Bunny, Notts, Esq
,,   5   CHARLES BRAMPION, son and heir of William B , of Pulham, Norfolk, gent
,,   8   WALTER MARSHALL, second son of John M , of Broadwas, co Worcester, gent
,,   12   JOHN BOSYER, son and heir of Thomas B , of Over, co Chester, gent
,,   16   DANIEL DISNEY, second son of John D , of the city of Lincoln, Esq

                               folio 1,276.
,,   ,,   ROBERT OTTERBOURNE, son and heir of Robert O., of Sponton, co York, gent
,,   17   RICHARD OXENDEN, son of Henry O , of Deane, parish of Wingham, Kent,
Mar   6   ROGER FINCH, son and heir of Francis F , of Shardake, Salop, gent [Knight
,,   9   EDWARD DONE, son of Edward D , of Duddon, co Chester, Esq
     12. JEREMIAH POWELL, son of Hugh P., of Lomothoyddwr, co. Radnor, gent.
                                                          [gent , deceased
,,   13   THOMAS SMITH, gent., son and heir of Thomas S , late of Malsford, Suffolk,
,,   14   THOMAS PEACHELL, of the city of Lincoln, gent , two years of Barnard's Inn
1677
May   5   JOSEPH LOWNDES, of Middlewich, co Chester, gent.
,,   12   JOHN RAYNER, of Drayton, Notts, Esq , son and heir of John R , Esq ,
              deceased   [deceased.
,,   ,,   JOHN LLOYD, of Berth, co Denbigh, gent , son and heir of Edward, L , Esq

                               folio 1,277.   [deceased.
,,   14   JOSEPH WREN, of Binchester, co. Durham, second son of Charles W , Esq ,
,,   ,,   THOMAS LANT, son and heir of William L , of London merchant [Esq
,,   16   ROBERT MACRATH, one of the sons of Edmond M , of Derrymore, co. Clare,
,,   19   DESPOLINGE (or rather DESPOTINE) POLEY, third son of John P , of Boxted,
                                                  [Suffolk, Knight, deceased
,,   ,,   THOMAS BROOKES, of Middlewich, co. Chester, gent , two years of Staple Inn
,,   22   HENRY LYNN, second son of William L , of Southwicke, co. Northampton.
,,   23   JOHN SHALCROSS, son and heir of Richard S , of Shalcross, co Derby, Esq ,
              deceased   [gent
,,   24   EDWARD GAMES, son and heir of Bartholomew G , of Tregare, co Brecon,

1677.   folio 1,277—(*continued*)

May 24. JOHN HARPUR, son and heir of Joseph H , of Yeevely, co Derby, gent

„   26 THOMAS FRANCKLIN, two years of Staple Inn, gent , second son of Richard F ,
        Knight and Baronet.   [Esq

„   „   EDWARD PARKER, son and heir of Thomas P , of Browsholme, co. York,

„   28 JEREMIAH RHODEAZ, son and heir of Theobald R , of Westminster, gent

„   29 JOHN MAWDE, son and heir of Jonathan M , of Halifax, co York, Esq.

„   31 ELLESTON BARRINGTON, son and heir of Thomas B , of Steeple Bumstead,
                                                            [Essex, Esq

folio 1,278

„   „   WILLIAM HODDER, son and heir of Francis H , of Ringabrow, co Cork, Esq

June 16 HENRY YEAIS, son and heir of Henry Y , late of Warnham, Sussex, Esq ,
        deceased   [of Stockton, co York, gent

„   18 LAURENCE AGAR, late of Staple Inn, gent , third son of John A , deceased, late

„   27 JOHN HODGES, son and heir of Moses H , of Sulgrave, co Northampton, gent

July 2. THOMAS OSBORN, son and heir of Thomas O., of North Fambridge, Essex,

„   3. SAMUEL PALMER, second son of Anthony P , of London, clerk   [Esq

„   7   RICHARD RAINES, Doctor of Laws

„   „   THOMAS WEBSTER, eldest son of Simon W , of Dufton, co. Westmoreland,
        clerk   [of Little Offley, Herts, gent

„   9   RICHARD SPICER (*alias* Helder), son and heir of William S. (*alias* H),

„   11 JOHN MAJOR, son and heir of Richard M , of Leicester, gent (two years
                        [allowed from his admission at Inner Temple).

folio 1,279.

Aug 8   JOHN PEAKE, Knight, Sheriff of the city of London

„   „   THOMAS STAMPE, Knight, Sheriff of the city of London   [Esq

„   „   WILLIAM FREEMAN, son and heir of William F , of Bury St Edmunds, Suffolk,

„   „   JOSEPH MAYNARD, son and heir of John M , Knight, Serjeant-at-Law

„   10 CAVENDISH WEEDON, of Wigginton, Herts, gent

„   11 JOHN LATHOM, son and heir of Thomas L , of Tarporley, co Chester, gent

Oct 23 JOHN BOLLES, of Scampton, co Lincoln, Baronet

„   27 OWEN BOLD, of Treyrddols, co. Anglesey, Esq

„   „   RICHARD LLOYD, son and heir of Hugh L , of Legroth, co Denbigh

Nov 1   JOHN GATAKER, third son of Charles G , of Hoggiston, Bucks, clerk

„   2   FORTESCUE ROWELLS, son and heir of Daniel R , of Dublin, "medici."

folio 1,280

„   6   FRANCIS LLOYD, of Prode, co Carmarthen, gent.

„   10 SAMUEL OGLE, second son of Luke O , of Bowesden, Northumberland, gent

„   16 JOHN BAGGS, second son of Zachary B , of London, Esq

„   „   EDWARD DEANE, son and heir of Joseph D , of Crumlyn, co. Dublin, Esq

„   21. EDWARD PYE, son and heir of John P , of Thrukston, co Hereford, gent.

,   27. JOSEPH AYLOFFE, son and heir of Joseph A , late of Gray's Inn, Esq

„   „   JOHN MIDLETON, son and heir of Nathaniel M , of the city of Durham, gent.
                                            [ford, Knight, deceased

„   „   RICHARD COOMBE, son and heir of Richard C , of Hemel Hempsted, co. Here-

1677   folio 1,280—(continued)

Nov 27   GEORGE FLASKE, son and heir of Robert F , of Linton, co. Cambridge, gent

Dec 6   BRATHWAITE OTWAY, third son of John O , now Treasurer of this Society.

folio 1,281

,, 7   WILLIAM KYFFIN WILLIAMS, son and heir of William W , of this Inr , Esq

                                                   [Derby, Esq

,, 24   WILLIAM POWTRELL, second son of Robert P , of West Halham, co

1677-8   [of Canterbury, Esq

Jan 31   WILLIAM TURNER, gent , son of Thomas T , of this Inn, and of the city

Feb 1   SAMPSON HELE, son and heir of Sampson H , of West Prawle, Devon, Esq

,, ,,   HENRY AUDLEY, son of Henry A , late of Berechurch, Essex, Knight, deceased.   [co York, Esq

,, 9   ROGER TALBOTT, son and heir of Roger T , of Thornton-in-the-Street,

                                               [deceased

,, 11   CONSTANTINE PHIPPS, son of Francis P , late of Reading, Berks, gent,

,, ,,   EDMOND JONES, of Ripon, co York, gent (two years at Staple Inn)   [gent

,, ,,   DYMOKE WALPOLE, son and heir of Dymoke W , of Louth, co Lincoln,

folio 1,282   [Carmarthen, gent

,, 20   JOHN WILLIAMS, son and heir of William W , of Ystradworrall, co

,, ,,   JOHN BACCOT, son and heir of James B , of co Limerick, gent

Mar 4   JOHN ARNOLD, son and heir of Michael A , of Westminster, Esq

1678

April 1   EDWARD BLYTHE, of Straveston, alias Stroxton, co Lincoln, gent

,, 18.   THOMAS LYSTER, of Coleby, co Lincoln, gent

,, ,,   JOHN GILLIAM, son and heir of John G , of Manchester, gent

,, 19   DAVID MORGAN, son and heir of David M , of Coedlloyd, co Pembroke, Esq

,, 20   BRIAN MAGRATH, of Kilb(o)y, co Tipperary

,, 26   RICHARD WOOD, of Dartford, Kent, second son of Richard W , of same, gent

                                               [deceased

May 2   WILLIAM FENWICK, son and heir of John F , of Somerton, Oxon, clerk

,, 7   WILLIAM DICONSON, son of Hugh D , of Wrightington, co Lancaster, Esq

folio 1,283.

,, 8   JOHN STAINTON, of Longbridge, co Warwick, gent

,, 11   WILLIAM MAINSTONE, of Woodberry, co. Cambridge, Esq

,, 16   ROBERT FRANK, son and heir of John F , of Pontefract, co York, gent

June 1   JOHN SMITH, son of Roger S , of Frolesworth, co Leicester, gent

,, 4   JOHN TOWNLEY, second son of Richard T , of Townley, co Lancaster, Esq

,, ,,   HENRY PELHAM, third son of John P , of Lawton, Sussex, Bart

folio 1,284.

,, 10   HENRY ASHLEY, son and heir of Henry A , of Eynsbury, Hunts, gent

,, 13   EDMUND GIBSON, son and heir of Robert G , of Stanck, co Lancaster, gent

,, 15   GEORGE PULLEY, son and heir of Edward P , of Peeton, Salop, gent

,, ,,   JOHN HATFEILD, son and heir of John H , of Hatfield, co York, gent

                                               [Salop, gent

, 17   JOSEPH CROWTHER, son and heir of Joseph C , deceased, late of Wenlock,

1678   folio 1,284—(continued)

June 18   JOHN BRADDYLL, son and heir of Thomas B , of Partfield, co Lancaster, Esq

,,   ,,   JOHN INGLIS, of Edinburgh, gent

,,   ,,   STRELLEY PEGGE, son and heir of Edward P , of Beauchief, co Derby, Esq

,,   19   ROGER SLEDDALL, son and heir of Roger S , of Penrith, Cumberland, gent ,
                             [deceased

folio 1,285

,,   21   RICHARD BERNEY, son and heir of Thomas B , of Norwich, Bart

,,   22   HENRY FAIRFAX, second son of Henry, Lord Fairfax, of Denton, co York

,,   25   ROGER ROGERS, son and heir of Roger R , of Newcroft, co Lancaster, gent

,,   26   BASIL WYVELL, son and heir of Francis W , of Ripon, co. York , Esq

July   5   JOSIAS TOWNSEND, second son of Josias T , of Brain (Brent)ford, Middle
                             [sex, gent

Sept 3   RICHARD LLOYD, son and heir of Richard L , of Allington, co Denbigh

Oct 21   TOMYNS DICKINS, son and heir of Tomyns D , of Enfield, co Stafford

,,   26   THOMAS DALYSON, of Hamptons in Little Peckham, Kent, Esq

folio 1,286.

,,   ,,   CALEB HELE, second son of Sampson H , of East Portlemouth, Devon, Esq

,,   ,,   JOHN COTTON, second son of Ralph C , of Birch Hall, parish of Wyburnbury,
                             [co Chester, gent , deceased

,,   ,,   RICHARD ACTON, son and heir of Richard A., late of the city of Chester, gent ,
                             [deceased

,,   ,,   ROBERT MINSHULL, second son of Thomas M , of Manchester, gent

Nov 21   JOHN FENWICK, son and heir of Robert F , of Nun Ridings, Northumberland,
                             [gent

,,   ,,   ROGER FENWICK, of Stanton, Northumberland, gent

,,   ,,   THOMAS HOWGRAVE, son and heir of Alexander H , of Hornecastle, co

,,   22.   JOHN TOWNELEY, of Hurstwood, co. Lancaster, Esq   [Lincoln, gent

,,   ,,   THOMAS NAPLETON, son and heir of Thomas N , of Feversham, Kent, Esq

Dec 5.   HORATIO SUCKLING, son of Robert S , of Woodeton, Norfolk, Esq

1678-9   folio 1,287.

Jan 9   HUMPHREY STURT, son and heir of Anthony S., of London, Esq

Feb 10   JOHN HOARE, second son of Daniel H , of Kingston on-Hull, Alderman

,,   12.   WILLIAM LATTON, second son of Thomas L , of Kingston, Berks, Esq

,,   14   JOSEPH JORDAN, son and heir of Joseph J , of Hatfield, Herts, Knight

,,   15   THOMAS BELGRAVE, son and heir of William B , of North Kilworth, co

1679.   [Leicester, Esq

April 17   HENRY BOULT, second son of Richard B , of Aldgate, Middlesex, gent

May 26   ROBERT BARKER, second son of William B , of the city of London, Esq

,,   ,,   JOHN WILLIAMS, son of William W , of this Inn, Esq.

,,   ,,   ROBERT MAYDSTONE, son and heir of Robert M , of Akenham, Suffolk, Esq

folio 1,288

,   30   ROWLAND GWYN, of Llanellwey, co Radnor, Esq

1679   folio 1,288—(*continued*)

May 31   ROBERT BARKER, son and heir of Francis B , of Norton Lees Hall, co Derby,

June   2   THOMAS LLOYD, of Dan-y-rallt, co Carmarthen, Esq.   [Esq

,,   13.   CHARLES GREGORY, of Rochdale, co Lancaster, gent

July   1   ANDREW CARD, of Codford, Wilts, gent.

,,   ,,   GERVASE NEWTON, second son of John N , of Thorpe, co Lincoln, Baronet

,,   ,,   WILLIAM DAVIES, of Lampeter Velvrey, co Pembroke, gent , son and heir of
                                       [James D , deceased

,,   ,,   JOHN HARRIS, son and heir of John H., late of Stodbury, Devon, gent

,,   14   NICHOLAS STARKEY, of Huntroyd, co Lancaster, gent

,,   ,,   ROBERT BARKER, of Faulkenham, Suffolk, Esq

folio 1,289.

,,   15.   JOHN LONE, son and heir of John L , of Audley End, Essex, gent , and late of
                           [Staple Inn ; two years allowed, Samuel Ward, principal

,,   ,,   EDMUND EVERARD, of Federdia (Fethard), co Tipperary, Esq   [Baronet

Oct 27   EDWARD WINTER, son and heir of Edward W , of Battersea, Surrey, Knight and

,,   ,,   JOHN WAKE, son and heir of William W , of Piddington, co Northampton,

Nov   1   WALLER BACON, son and heir of Francis B , late of Gray's Inn   [Baronet

,,   5   ROBERT PELHAM, son and heir of Robert P , of Compton Valence, Dorset, Esq

,,   7   JOHN ALLEYN, son and heir of Giles A , of Stibbington, Hunts, S T D

,,   10   ARMYNE BULLINGHAM, son and heir of John B , of Ketton, co Rutland, gent.

,,   11   HENRY CADOGAN, son and heir of William C , of Lyscarton, co Meath, Esq

folio 1,290.

,,   19   WALTER DOBELL, son and heir of Walter D , of Street, Sussex, Esq

,,   26   GEORGE BEALE, son and heir of Henry B , of Darrington, co York, gent

,,   28   SAMUEL LOVELL, son of Salathiel L , one of the Masters of the Bench of this
                                       [Inn, Esq

Dec   3   JOHN WALPOLE, second son of Dymock W , late of Louth, co Lincoln, gent.

,,   6   HENRY TERNE, son and heir of Christopher T , Doctor of Medicine.

1679 80

Jan. 27   HENRY HAYNES, of Netley, Salop, gent.   [ary, Esq.

Feb   5   GEFFREY COMYNS, son and heir of Richard C , of Tallaghmayne, co Tipper-

,,   10   SAMUEL BARNARDISTON, son and heir of Nathaniel B , of Hackney, Middlesex

folio 1,291

,,   12.   GILBERT WALLIS, son and heir of Elstan W , of London, goldsmith

,,   17.   THOMAS PEPYS, son and heir of Thomas P , of Martin Abbey, Surrey, Esq

,,   20.   JAMES FEILD, son and heir of ——— F , of Chertsey, Surrey, gent   [gent

,,   27.   THOMAS WRIGHT, son and heir of William W , of Great Longston, co Derby,

1680   [Esq.

April 24   METCALFE WEDDELL, son and heir of William W , of Earswick, co. York,

,,   28   HUMPHREY RANT, son and heir of William R , of Yelverton, Norfolk, Esq

May   1   ORLANDO NICHOLLS, son and heir of Rowland N., of Boycott, Salop, Esq.

,,   10   WILLIAM BRAGE, son and heir of Francis B , of the city of Norwich, gent

,,   ,,   NEVELL BAGULEY, second son of William B , of Barnsley, co., York, gent

1680		folio 1,292

May 12   JOHN HOPWOOD, son and heir of John H , of Hopwood, co Lancaster, Esq

,,   13   EPHRAIM NEALSON, second son of Edward N , of Berwick-on-Tweed, gent

,,   20   JOHN LANDAUR, son and heir of John L , of Ashton-in-Makerfield co. Lan-

,,   22   JOHN RANT, son and heir of John R , of Gray's Inn, Esq   [caster, gent

,,   ,,   WILLIAM PARKER, son and heir of Edward P , of Brandon, co Lincoln, gent

,,   26   EDWARD WINGFIELD, son and heir of ———— W , of ————, Ireland, Esq

,,   ,,   GEORGE DALE, son and heir of Robert D , of Flag, co Derby, Esq

June 12   WILLIAM HAYES, son and heir of Cornelius H , of Bandon, co Cork, gent

,,   13   JOHN WALDRON, son and heir of George W , of Stapleford Abbotts, Essex, gent

,,   18   HENRY WARREN, second son of Henry W , of Stamford Barron, co North-
[ampton, gent

,,   19   THOMAS BRICKENDEN, son and heir of Richard B , of Inkpen, Berks, Esq

,,   21   RICHARD OLIVER, son and heir of John O , of London, gent

,,   ,,   THOMAS SKIPP, son and heir of Thomas S , of Tuddenham, Norfolk, Esq

folio 1,293.

,,   24   THOMAS CARTER, son and heir of William C , of Gilling, co York, gent

,,   29   ROBERT SNELL, son and heir of Robert S , of Denton, Norfolk, gent

,,   30   ROBERT CUTTLER, son and heir of Robert C , of Gray's Inn, gent

July 7   SAMUEL HANSON, son and heir of Samuel H , of the parish of St George,
[Island of Barbados, gent

,,   9   THOMAS LEGH, son and heir of Thomas L , of Riglehall, co Chester, Esq

,,   10   THOMAS JACKSON, only son and heir of George J , of Merrow, Surrey, Esq

Sept 14   WILLIAM PEER WILLIAMS, son and heir of Peer W , of Gray's Inn, Esq

,,   23   JOHN RAYMOND, son and heir of St Cleere R , of Belchamp Walter, Essex, Esq

Oct 4   JOHN BROWNE, gent , son and heir of George B , late of Hutton, Essex, gent

Nov 1   ROBERT MATTHEWS, of Blodwell, Salop, Esq

,,   ,,   WILLIAM GILBY, of Weald Hall, Essex, gent

folio 1,294.

,,   ,,   WILLIAM GREGORY, gent., son and heir of James G , Esq , the son and heir of
[William G , Knight, one of the Barons of the Exchequer

,,   ,,   JOHN TOPHAM, " serviens Attend Dom Com "

,,   ,,   JOHN PLATT, son and heir of John P , of Westbrooke Place, Surrey, Knight

,,   3   CHARLES WYTHER, of Hall Place, parish of Dean, co Southampton, Esq

,,   ,,   HENRY NEWTON, son and heir of John N , of Highley, Salop, Esq

,,   12   WILLIAM SOTHERON, son and heir of Matthew S , of Holme-super-Spaldingmoor,
[co York, gent.

,,   13   THOMAS GIRLING, son and heir of Thomas G , of Horeham, Suffolk, gent

,,   15   JOHN WALMESLEY, third son of John W , of Blackburn, co Lancaster, Esq ,
formerly of Staple Inn (two years).   [Hereford, gent

,,   22   JOHN RAVENHILL, son and heir of John R , of Hasel, parish of Woolhope, co

,,   24   ANDREW WILKINSON, son and heir of Thomas W , of Boroughbridge, co
York, gent   [Baronet

,,   25   JOHN BOLLES, Esq , son and heir of John B , of Scampton, co Lincoln,

1680   folio 1,295.

Nov 27   JOHN SPARROW, son and heir of John S , of Sible Hedingham, Essex, gent
„   „   HENRY DARLEY, son and heir of Richard D , of Aldby, co York, Esq
„   29   THOMAS JACOB, son and heir of Nicholas J , of Canterbury, Esq
„   „   JOHN OWEN, son and heir of William O , of Berllau, co Pembroke, S.T D
„   „   JOHN BURTON, second son of Thomas B , of Stockerston, co Leicester, Baronet
„   „   WILLIAM HALFORD, son and heir of William H , of Welham, co Leicester,
                                                                   [Baronet
Dec 21   JOHN WASTALL, son and heir of Leonard W , of Bolton, co York, Esq
1680-1   [Chester, Baronet, deceased
Jan 14   JOHN WARBURTON, one of the younger sons of George W , of Arley, co
„   15   CHARLES MARSDEN, son and heir of Henry M , of Gisburne, co York, Esq

                          folio 1,296   [Baronet

„   24   VAUGHAN PRICE, second son of Matthew P , of Newtown, co Montgomery,
„   29   JOHN ASHCROFT, son and heir of Richard A , late of Little Paxton, Hunts,
„   „   JOHN DRURY, of Dublin, gent   [gent
„   „   EDMUND BUTLER, son and heir of Thomas B , of Kirkland, co Lancaster, Esq
Feb 1   ANDREW MILLER, son and heir of Randall M , of St Bartholomew the Great,
          London, gent   [the Common Pleas
„   15   WILLIAM LEVINZ, son and heir of Creswell L , Knight, one of the Judges of
„   „   HALFORD WAINWRIGHT, third son of Jeremy W , of Fennybrigg (Ferrybridge),
                                                                   [co York
Mar 2   THOMAS GUNTER, son and heir of Thomas G , of Gray's Inn, Esq , formerly
„   4   WILFRID LAWSON, of Isell, Cumberland, Esq   [of Staple Inn (two years)
1681   [ampton, gent
April 19   ROWLAND WALKER, son and heir of Nathaniel W , of Hothorpe, co North-
„   25   THOMAS GINDER, son and heir of Richard G , of Canterbury, gent

                          folio 1,297

May 7   JOHN WHITEHALL, son and heir of Rowland W , of Whitchurch, Salop, gent
„   „   JOHN ROOE, son and heir of Roger R , of Normanton Turville, co Leicester,
„   9   RICHARD BULWER, second son of Robert B , of Gray's Inn, Esq   [Esq
„   12   CHARLES YALLOP, son and heir of Robert Y , Knight
„   14   JOHN RISBY, son and heir of John R , of Thorpe Hall, Suffolk, Esq
„   „   WILLIAM MEADOWS, son and heir of William M , of Henley, Suffolk, gent
„   „   MAUREY KENDALL, of Buckenham, Norfolk, gent
„   16   HENRY CONWAY, son of Henry C , Baronet
„   27   THOMAS SOUTHOUSE, son and heir of Thomas S , of Feversham, Kent, Esq
„   30   JOHN BIRCH, son and heir of Francis B , of the Savoy, Middlesex, gent
„   31   PHILIP FORCH, of Cranworth, Norfolk, gent.

                          folio 1,298

June 2   RICHARD PENNINGTON, son and heir of Richard P , late of Gray's Inn, Esq.
„   „   EDWARD DOWNES, son and heir of Edward D , of Shrigley, co Chester, Esq.
„   13   EDWARD COPLEY, of Batley, co York, Esq.
„   17   CHARLES HANSES, son and heir of John H , of the city of York, gent

1681   folio 1,298—(*continued*)

June 17 WILLIAM BIRDS, son and heir of George B , of Stanton Hall, co Derby, gent

,, 20 RECE OWEN, of Colbey, co Pembroke, gent.

,, 23 THOMAS GILL, son and heir of William G , of Ripon, co York, gent

July 8 THOMAS HALFORD, Baronet, of Wistow, co Leicester

,, 12 EDWARD BLOUNT, of Blagdon, co Devon, gent

,, ,, HUGH SMITHSON, son and heir of Anthony S , of this Inn, Esq.

Oct 22 THEOPHILUS EVTON, of Gray's Inn, gent

,, 28 PHILIP MONSON, son of John M , of Burton, co Lincoln, Knight

,, 31 GEORGE ST GEORGE, of Dunmore, co Galway, gent

Nov 1. ROBERT BEAKE, of Canterbury, gent

,, 3 THOMAS BERNEY, son of Thomas B , of Norwich, Baronet.

folio 1,299

,, ,, THOMAS STANLEV, son of Edward S , of Dalegarth, Cumberland, Esq

,, 8 FRANCIS HERBERT, son and heir of William H , of Gray's Inn, Esq

,, 10 RICHARD RICHARDSON, of North Byerley, co York, gent.

,, 15 ROWLAND HALE, son of William H , of King's Walden, Herts, Esq

,, 23 THOMAS BILCLIFFE, of Tathwell, co Lincoln, gent   [gent

,, 24 ANDREW BURTON, brother of Cornelius B , of this Inn, of Exton, co Rutland,

,, 25 ROGER RANT, son and heir of Roger R , of Swaffham Priors, co Cambridge,

,, ,, JOHN RANT, son of Roger R , of Swaffham Priors, co Cambridge, Esq [Esq

,, 28 THOMAS PATTEN, son and heir of Thomas P , of Warrington, co Lancaster,

Dec 2. WILLIAM STREET, of Hallaughton, co Leicester, gent.   [gent

,, 8 WILLIAM GRIFFITH, son and heir of John G , late of Oswestry, Salop, gent ,

1681-2   [deceased

Jan 12 CHARLES BOURCHIER, son and heir of Abraham B , late of London, gent

,, 21 JOHN BALE, son and heir of James B , of Ashford, Kent, gent   [Esq

,, 28 WILLIAM REVELEV, son and heir of George R , of Throple, Northumberland,

Feb 6 THOMAS BROCKE, son and heir of Thomas B , of Darsham, Suffolk, gent

folio 1,300

,, 10 THOMAS FISH POOLE, son of Joseph Fish P , of Billericay, Essex, gent

,, 11 WILLIAM WALLIS, of River Green, Northumberland, gent

,, ,, PHILIP TILNEY, son of Francis T , of Rotherwicke, Southampton, Esq

,, 13. EDWARD HERBERT, of King's Langley, Herts, Esq

,, 21 HENRY SMYTH, son and heir of Matthew S , of Denby, co Derby, gent

,, 25 BENJAMAN PEMBER, son of Thomas P , of Newport, co Hereford, gent

Mar 14. GREGORV GEERING, son and heir of Gregory G , of Denchworth, Berks,

1682   [gent

April 28 CHARLES GARDNER, son and heir of Thomas G., of Southley, co Chester,

May 5 THOMAS JENKIN, son and heir of Thomas J , of Folkstone, gent   [gent

,, 6 THOMAS HAWES, son and heir of Nathaniel H , of London, gent

,, 8 JOHN WALFORD, son and heir of Sturch W , of Wolverton, co. Warwick

,, 9 THOMAS MOLVNEUX, son and heir of Nathaniel M , of West Houghton, co

                                                        [Lancaster, gent

1682	folio 1,300—*(continued)*.	[Esq

May 11	EDWARD BULLOCK, son and heir of Edward B , of Faulkborne Hall, Essex,

,, 18	THOMAS PARKYNS, son and heir of Thomas P , of Bunney, Notts, Baronet

,, 20	GRESHAM PAGE, son and heir of John P , of Saxsthorpe, Norfolk, Esq

,, 23	JOHN SPICER, son and heir of John S , of Standon, Herts, Esq

,, 25	HENRY BAGSHAW, son and heir of Henry B , of Gray's Inn, Esq

,, 27	JOHN BIRCH, son of Thomas B , of Hampton Bishop, co Hereford, clerk.

folio 1,301

,, ,,	HUGH BATEMAN, son and heir of Robert B , of London, gent.	[Berks

,, ,,	RICHARD JENNENS, son and heir of Richard J , Esq , of Long Wittenham,

,, ,,	WILLIAM SHAFTOE, son and heir of John S , of Barrington, Northumberland,

,, 29	THOMAS DRAKE, son and heir of Robert D , of Cambridge, gent	[Esq.

,, ,,	CHARLES KIRKHAM, son and heir of Walter K , of Fineshead, co North-
[ampton, Esq

,, 30	JOHN WHITE, son and heir of John W , of Stanton St John, Oxon, gent

June 7	THOMAS SAWREY, son of Roger S , of Broughton Tower, co Lancaster, Esq

,, 12	GEORGE WESTROPP, son of Edward W , of Newham in Cleveland, co. York,

,, 13	JOHN BUXSTON, son and heir of John B , of the city of York, gent	[Esq

,, 17	ROBERT JONES, son and heir of Thomas J , of Longden-super-Terne, Salop,
[gent

,, 19	DYMMOCK WALPOLE, son and heir of Thomas W , late of Staple Inn, gent

,, 21	EDWARD VAUGHAN, son and heir of Philip V , of Trymcaren, co Carmarthen,
[Esq

,, ,,	CHRISTOPHER DRIFFIELD, son and heir of Christopher D , of Gray's Inn, Esq

,, 23	EUBULUS THELWALL, son and heir of Eubulus T., of Nant Clwyd, co Denbigh,
[Esq

,, 30	WILLIAM NEVILL, son and heir of Gervase N , of Holbech, co York, Esq

,, ,,	JOHN WIGFALL, son and heir of John W , of Renishaw, co. Derby, gent.

July 6.	JAMES FULWOOD, son and heir of Francis F., of Exeter, S T D

,, 8.	THOMAS CHAPPELL, son and heir of Thomas C , of Sheffield, co York, gent

folio 1,302.

,, 17.	ALEXANDER PENDARVES, of Roscrowe, co Cornwall, gent , son of John P., Esq

,, 28	FRANCIS PAYNE, son and heir of William P , of St Dunstan's-in-the-West, gent

,, ,,	THOMAS KILLINGTON, of Kelfield, co York, Esq

,, 30	WILLIAM NEALE, son and heir of Gilbert N , of Ipplepen, Devon, gent

,, ,,	ROBERT ELWES, son of Jeremiah E , of Rokesby, co Lincoln, Esq	[gent

Oct 23.	JOHN CHESHIRE, son of Thomas C , late of Halton (or Hatton), co Cheshire,

,, 26	JONATHAN NEWTON, son and heir of Matthew N., late of Calcott, North-
[umberland, gent.

Nov. 1	WILLIAM MARRIOT, son and heir of Richard M , of Towcester, co. North-
[ampton, gent (see Nov 27, 1674)

,, ,,	ROBERT RAYMOND, only son of Thomas R , Knight, one of the Justices of
[the King's Bench

,, ,,	JAMES GREGORY, son of James G , Esq , one of the Fellows of this Inn

1682   folio 1,302—(continued)

Nov 2   UNTON READ, of Gray's Inn, gent

,, ,,   WILLIAM LEHUNT, son of John L , of this Inn, Esq

,,   6   THOMAS PILLEY, son and heir of John P , of Easby, co York, gent

,,   9   HENRY MARSDEN, son of Henry M , of Gisborne, co York, Esq

,, 14   AMBROSE PUDSEY, of Bolton, co York, Esq

,, 25   CHARLES CORNWALLIS, son and heir of Bevercoats C , of the city of Lincoln,

,, ,,   CHARLES DOBSON, son and heir of Edward D , of this Inn, Esq   [Esq

,, ,,   THOMAS ARAM, of the Weald, Herts, gent , formerly of Clement's Inn, two
                                                                    .   [years

                            folio 1,303.

,, 28   JAMES CORNWALL (or ? Cromwell), of Staple Inn, gent (allowed two years)

,, 29   JOHN LEGARD, son and heir of Robert L , of Kingston-on-Hull, Knight.

Dec 4   JOHN GASCOIGNE, son of George G , late of Barnbow, co York, gent

,,   7   GEORGE BUCHANAN, son and heir of James B , clerk

,, 14   EDWARD PRICE, son and heir of Robert P , of Stoke, co Lincoln, S T P

,, ,,   EDWARD LEIGH, son and heir of Edward L., of London, Esq   [Esq

,, ,,   WILLIAM LOWTHER son and heir of William L , of Swillington Hall, co York,

1682-3

Jan 15   ROBERT THROGMORTON, of Coughton Magna, co Warwick, Baronet

,, 24   JOHN LUTHER, son and heir of Thomas L , of Suttons, Essex, Esq

,, ,,   HENRY STEPHENS, son of Walter S , of Bristol, merchant

,, 25   JONATHAN STANYFORTH, son and heir of John S , of Rotherham, co York, gent

,, 30. THOMAS ASH, of St John, co Meath, Esq

,, 31   JOSEPH CRANMER, son of Robert C , of Mitcham, Surrey, Esq

,, ,,   THOMAS COLE, of Shenfield,, Berks, gent

Feb 2   JOHN BELL, son of Robert B , of Thirsk, co York, gent

,, 20   JOHN HASTINGS, second son of William H , of St Andrew's, Holborn, gent ,
                                                            [two years of Staple Inn

                            folio 1,304

,, ,,   JOHN HUNT, son and heir of John H , of Barroden, co Rutland, gent.

,, ,,   ROBERT WEAVER, only son of Robert W , of Lincoln's Inn, Esq

,, 21   ARTHUR O'KEAFFE, of Bally McGurke, co Cork, gent

1683   [clerk

Mar 28   PEREGRINE PALMER, son and heir of Peregrine P , of Londonderry, Ireland,

April 2 WILLIAM MENHEIRE, of Stanton-upon-Arrow, co Hereford, gent

,, 21   ROBERT LONDON, of Middleton Fordley, Suffolk, gent   [Gray's Inn, Esq

,, 23   SAMUEL AYLMER, son and heir of Brabason A , of Mondon Hall, Essex, late of

,, 24   WILLIAM JESSUP, son and heir of Francis J , of Broomhall, co York, Esq

May 3   JOHN METCALFE, of St Andrew's, Holborn, gent   [Baronet

,,   4   EDMUND ANDERSON, only son of Edmund A , of Gray's Inn, Knight and

,,   8   ALEXANDER ROKEBY, second son of William R , of Skelton, co York, Esq

,, ,,   WILLIAM GYSE (Guise), of St Andrew's, Holborn, gent

,, ,,   EDWARD SHERLOCKE, of Blackhall, barony of Naas, co Kildare, gent

1683   folio 1,304—(*continued*)

May 10   JOHN BATTIE, of Warmsworth, co. York, gent   [Leeds, co York, Esq

,,   11   BENJAMIN WADE, son and heir of Anthony W, of New Grange, parish of

,,   15   JOHN CLENCHE, of Bottesham, co Cambridge, gent

,,   21   HENRY SAXTON, only son of William S, of Harworth, Notts, gent.

,,   ,,   NATHANIEL BOOTH, second son of Nathaniel B, of Mottram, St Andrew, co
                                              [Chester, Esq

folio 1,305.

,,   24   RICHARD HARTLEY, of Warrington, co. Lancaster, gent

,,   28   JOHN BENN, son and heir of John B, of Cleator, Cumberland, gent

June 19   RICHARD SMITH, of Chillington, co Stafford, gent.

,,   20.   SAMUEL REYNOLDS, son and heir of Samuel R, of Colchester, Essex, Esq

,,   25   ARTHUR NEWMAN, son and heir of John N, of Penrhyn, Cornwall gent

,,   ,,   JOHN HEYM, son and heir of John H, of St Kevan's, Cornwall, gent

,,   26   BARNARD TOURNER, fourth son of John T., of Eastbourne, Sussex Esq

,,   28   JAMES ROBERTS, son and heir of Joseph R, of Canterbury, Esq.

,,   29   JOHN BRANDLING, of Ipswich, Suffolk, gent

July   6.   WILLIAM DUNCOMBE, second son of William D, of Ivinghoe, Bucks, gent

.,   31.   WILLIAM WALKER, son and heir of Thomas W, of Iissley, in Connaught,
                                                  [gent

Oct 30   GILBERT RIGBY, second son of Alexander R, of Middleton in Goosnargh, co

Nov   1.   JOHN LEHUNT, second son of John L, Esq.   [Lancaster, Esq

,,   ,,   HENRY BIGLAND, eldest son of Edward B, Serjeant-at-Law

,,   3   EDWARD GOULSTON, of parish of Westphalia, Kent, gent

folio 1,306.

,,   6   ROWLAND BARTLETT, of Hillend, parish of Castle Morton, co Worcester, gent

,,   7   THOMAS CLIFTON, son and heir of Thomas C, of Lytham, co Lancaster,
            Knight and Baronet   [two years of Staple Inn

,,   12   WILLIAM JENNENS, second son of Richard J, of Long Wittenham, Berks, Esq,

,,   ,,   CHRISTOPHER MUSGRAVE, second son of Christopher M, of Little Musgrave,
            Westmoreland, Knight, Lieutenant of the Ordnance, in the Tower of
                           [London, two years of Staple Inn

,,   15   THOMAS PROCTER, of parish of Horton, in Ribblesdale, co. York, gent.

,,   22   THOMAS CLIFTON, of Fairsnapp, co. Lancaster, gent.

,,   ,,   JOHN NEDHAM, son and heir of Edward N, of Ilston, co Leicester, Esq

,,   23   JOHN HUGHES, of the city of Dublin, gent

,,   24   THOMAS SAUNDERSON, third son of George, Viscount Castleton, in Ireland

,,   26   WILLIAM JULIAN, son and heir of James J, late of Melton Mowbray, co
            Leicester, gent, deceased   [gent

,,   ,,   CHARLES TRUBSHAW, third son of James T, of Birmingham, co Warwick,

,,   29   FRANCIS FRASER, only son of Robert F, of St Martin's-in-the-Fields, gent

1683-4

Feb   5   HENRY DAVYF, second son of Alexander D, of Salford, co Lanc, merchant

,,   9   GRIFFIN DAWES, son and heir of Francis D, of Pembroke, gent

,,   11   THOMAS NORTON, second son of Welbury N, of Tanfield, co York, Esq

1683-4.   folio 1,307

Feb 11.   ROBERT HESILRIGE, eldest son of Robert H , of the town of Northampton, Esq

,,   18   GILES THAYER, eldest son of Giles T , of St Margaret's, Westminster, gent

1684
April 19   JOHN CRUMP, eldest son of Thomas C , late of Ludlow, Salop, Esq , deceased

,,   22   JOHN ADDISON, eldest son of Francis A , of Ovingham, Northumberland, Esq

,,   24   THOMAS HARRIS, eldest son of Thomas H , of St Andrew's, Holborn, gent.

,,   25.   GILBERT COSSEIN GERARD, of Brafferton, co York, Esq , son and heir of
                                                       [Gilbert G , Baronet.

,,   26   EDWARD PLACE, second son of Edward P , of Well, co York, gent   [Esq.

,,   28   CHARLES STOUTEVILLE, son and heir of Robert S , of Hunmanby, co York,

May   1   HENRY PARRY, only son of Henry P , senior, of Llanvilling, co Montgomery,
                                                       [gent

,,   7   WILLIAM PHILLIPPS, son and heir of William P , of the town of Brecon, gent

,,   14   ROBERT JEGON, son of Arthur J , late of Lincoln's Inn, Esq , deceased

,,   24.   WILLIAM BARKER, eldest son of William B , of Hammersfield, Suffolk, Esq

                          folio 1,308

June   5   BEAUMONT PARKYNS, youngest son of Thomas P , of Bunney, Notts, Baronet

,,   10.   MAURICE EUSTACE, of Yeomanston, co Kildare, gent

,,   12   GEORGE KENYON, second son of Roger K , of Peel, co Lancaster, Esq

,,   ,,   ROGER KENYON, of Stopford, co Chester, gent

,,   16   FINCH UMFREY (sic), of Fawkham, Kent, gent   (See also page 344)

,,   ,,   BERNARD ELLIS, of Dartford, Kent, gent.

,,   19   HENRY SHAFTOE, second son of Roger S , of Benwell, Northumberland, Esq

,,   22   FRANCIS LINDLEY, son and heir of Francis L , late of this Inn, Esq , deceased

July   3   WILLIAM TURNER, son and heir of Henry T , of Bury St Edmunds, Suffolk,

,,   4   ROWLAND HOLT, second son of Thomas H , Knight, Serjeant-at Law   [Esq

Aug   4   THOMAS CLARKE, eldest son of Richard C , late of Norwich, gent , deceased

Oct   24   PIERS BUTLER, of Ballylinch, co Kilkenny, gent   [gent, deceased

,,   ,,   JAMES PEARSON, son and heir of Luke P , late of Gressingham, co Lancaster,

,,   25   JAMES ARCHBOLD, of Dublin, gent

,,   ,,   GEORGE LAMPLUGH, eldest son of Thomas L , of Gray's Inn, Esq

,,   28   WILLIAM BOND, son and heir of William B , of Hollwood, Cornwall, Esq

                    folio 1,309.   [Baronet

Nov   3   WALTER NEWDEGATE, second son of Richard N , of Arbury, co Warwick,

,,   13   GEORGE NEVILE, son and heir of George N , of Thorney, Notts, Esq

,,   19   VIRTUE RADFORD, gent , two years of Staple Inn

,,   20   THOMAS GLASCOCK, second son of Christopher G , of Felstead, Essex, gent

,,   24   RALPH ASHTON, son and heir of Richard A , of Cuerdale, co Lancaster,
          Esq   [Esq

Dec   4   ANTHONY HAMMOND, son and heir of Anthony H , of Somersham, Hunts,

,,   ,,   BARTON SHUTTLEWORTH, of Carr, co Lancaster, gent
                                              [land, gent, deceased
1684 5
Jan   26   RICHARD WHARTON, son and heir of William W , late of Waitby, Westmore-

,,   27   JAMES ALTHAM, of Barnard's Inn, gent

                          X 2

1684-5   folio 1,310   [Llangonnyd, co Glamorgan, Esq.

Feb   5   JOHN GIBBS, son and heir of William G , late of Hendref Owen, parish of

,,   11   ROBERT ELLISON, son and heir of Cuthbert E , of Jarrow, co Durham, Esq

,,   13.   FRANCIS ALPE, son and heir of Edward A , of Framlingham, Suffolk, gent

,,   16   JOSEPH KEBLE, junior, son and heir of Richard K , of Cold Newton, Suffolk,

,,   ,,   GEORGE POCKLEY, son of George P , of Thurnholme, co York, gent   [Esq

,,   20   HENRY STEBBING, of Brandeston, Suffolk, gent , son and heir of Henry S ,

1685   [late of the same, Esq

May   6   MATTHEW HENRY, gent , son and heir of Philip H , of Iscoed, co Flint, clerk

,,   15   WILLIAM BUTTERWORTH, gent , son and heir of Alexander B , of Bellfielde,
             co Lancaster, Esq   [co Lancaster, Esq

,,   ,,   ALEXANDER BUTTERWORTH, gent , second son of Alexander B , of Bellfielde,

,,   16   PATRICK HURLEY, gent , second son of John H , of Innish, co Clare, gent

,,   ,,   JOSEPH BRAND, of Edwardstone, Suffolk, eldest son of Joseph B , of the same,
                                            [Knight

folio 1,311

,,   29   RALPH BRANDLING, of Alnwick, Northumberland, Esq , son and heir of
             Charles B , late of the same, Esq , deceased   [late of the same, gent

June 29   JAMES WILLINGTON, of the city of Hereford, gent , son and heir of James W ,

July   6   WILLIAM BOOTHBY, gent , son and heir of William B , of Potters Marston, co
             Leicester   [late of the same, Esq

,,   14   EDWARD TONGE, of Luttrington (?), co Durham, Esq , eldest son of John T ,

,,   15   CHARLES WALKLEY, son and heir of John W , of London, gent

,,   ,,   JOHN SPRAGGE, late of Uttoxeter, co Stafford, now of New York, America,
             Secretary to the Governor there   [Esq

,,   21   WILLIAM GRIFFITH, son and heir of John G , of Carregheyd, co Anglesey,

,,   ,,   JAMES BRYNKER, of Brynker, co. Carnarvon, Esq

,,   22   THOMAS WHITE, son and heir of John W., of Cotgrave, Notts, Esq   [Esq

,,   ,,   LEGH BANKES, fourth son of William B., of Winstanley, Wigan, co Lancaster,

Sept 14   CHARLES MORGAN, second son of William M., of Tredegar, Monmouth, Esq.

Oct 30.   CHARLES TYRRELL, gent , son and heir of Charles T., of Sutton, Essex, clerk.

Nov   1   CHEEK GERRARD, Esq

folio 1,312   [same, gent.

,,   5   ROBERT KILLINGBECKE, of Leeds, co. York, gent , third son of John K , of the

,,   7   THOMAS BARTON, of Cawton, co York, gent , son and heir of George B , of
             the same, Esq   [of Horsham, Sussex, gent

,,   9   THOMAS WHITE, gent , son and heir of Thomas W , of Cheeseworth, parish

,,   10   DANIEL WHITE, of Boxley, Kent, gent , son and heir of John W , late of
                    .   [Feversham, Kent, Doctor of Medicine, deceased.

,,   11   THOMAS MEREDYTH, of Dollardstown, co Meath, Esq , second son of Arthur
             M , of the same, Esq   [same, Knight.

,,   12   WALTER STEPHENS, of Warneford, Southampton, son of Richard S , of the
             same, Knight   [the same, Esq

,,   20   SAMUEL BARKER, of Watesfield, Suffolk, gent , son and heir of Samuel B., of

,,   25   SAMUEL ASHTON, of Wiston, co Lancaster, gent , son and heir of Henry A.,
                                           [late of the same, gent

1685	folio 1,312—(continued). [of the same, deceased
Nov 27	WILLIAM COLLARD, of Barneston, Essex, gent, son and heir of William C ,
Dec 1	WILLIAM BELGRAVE, son and heir of William B , of North Kilworth, co
1685-6	[Leicester, Esq
Jan 29	JOHN WALKER, of Priesthall, near Kirkham, co Lancaster, gent, son and [heir of William W , Esq , late of Kirkham
,, ,,	ROBERT WHITE, of Friers, co Anglesey, gent, son and heir of Richard W , [late of the same, Esq

folio 1,313

Feb 2	ANDREW HACKET, of Moxull, co Warwick, gent, second son of Andrew H , of the same, Knight [Birton, co Southampton, Esq , deceased
,, 4	RICHARD PAULET, of Hitchin, Herts, youngest son of William P , late of
,, 9	JOHN WELLES, son and heir of John W , of London, leatherseller
,, 10	JOHN FISHER, gent, of Chawton, co Southampton, second son of William F , of the same, gent [Norfolk, Esq
,, 11.	THOMAS HERNE, gent , son and heir of Clement H , of Heveringland,
,, ,,	JOHN PLAXTON, of Furnival's Inn, gent [same, Esq
,, 16.	WILLIAM LEMAN, of Charsfield, Suffolk, gent, second son of John L , of the
,, ,,	SAMUEL PARKER, gent , third son of Richard P , of Audley, co Stafford, gent
,, 20	CHARLES HILTON, gent , fourth son of William H , of Hilton, co Lancaster,
1686	[Esq
Mar 30	JOHN WALKER, gent , son and heir of John W , of Headingley, near Leeds, [co York, Esq
April 9	CALEB OWEN, gent , son and heir of Thomas O , of Gray's Inn, Esq
, 10	EDMUND HUTCHINS, gent , son and heir of George H , of Gray's Inn, Esq.
,, 15	JAMES SAUNDERSON, fourth son of George, Viscount Castleton, in Ireland
,, 24	LEONARD EGERTON, son and heir of Peter E , of Shaw, co Lancaster, Esq
,, ,,	MURRAY RIDDELL, second son of Thomas R , of Swinburne, Northumberland, Esq [Baronet.
,, 27	HENRY PIERS, second son of Henry P , of Tristernagh, co Westmeath,

folio 1,314   [late of the same, Esq

May 4	SAMUEL ROBINSON, of Cheshunt, Herts, gent., son and heir of William R ,
,, 12	BENJAMIN NELSON, gent , son and heir of Gilbert N , citizen and merchant of London. [of the same, Esq
,, ,,	HENRY BRADSHAW, of Marple, co Chester, gent., son and heir of Henry B ,
June 5	EDWARD LLOYD, gent., son and heir of John L , of Edgware, Middlesex, Esq
July 10	HENRY BERESFORD, son and heir of John B , late of Radbourne, co Derby, clerk [deceased
Sept 1	FRANCIS KING, son and heir of Daniel K , citizen and skinner, of London,
Oct 14	ABEL RAM, son and heir of Abel R , Knight, of the city of Dublin
,, ,,	FRANCIS BARRINGTON, son and heir of Alexander B , of Cullinagh, Ireland
,, 28	WILLIAM FIRTH, son and heir of John F , of Mansfield, Notts, clerk.
,, 30.	ROBERT LEE, second son of Francis L , Esq , of Rathbridge, co. Kildare

folio 1,315.

Nov 1	ELKANA HORTON, second son of ——— H , Esq , of co York [of this Inn
,, ,,	JAMES LOVELL, son and heir of Salathiel L , one of the Masters of the Bench

| 1686 | folio 1,315—*(continued)* | [Pembroke |

Nov. 1   WILLIAM WOGAN, son and heir of Maurice W., Esq., of Larstillon, co.

,, 10   WILLIAM BLUNT, second son of John B., of Beverley, co York, Esq

,, 11   WILLIAM PRIESTLY, son and heir of Thomas P., of Weald Hill, Herts, Esq

,, 18   THOMAS BATCHELER, of Norwich

,, 23   JOHN BOTHOMLY, son and heir of John B., of co York

,, 27   ANDREW WITHER, of Hall, co Southampton

,, ,,   HENRY PINCKE, son and heir of Thomas P., of Winchester

folio 1,316

Dec 14   PEDRO RONQUILLO (Don), " Legatus Extraordinarius Regis Catholici "

,, ,,   CHRISTIAN DE LENIE, " Legatus Regis Denmarke "

,, ,,   FRANCISCUS TERRIESI, " Legatus Illustris Toscaniæ Ducis "

,, 12   WILLIAM ASPIN, third son of William Aspin, S T P

, 13   RATTCLIFF ALEXANDER, second son of John A., of Manchester   [Fairbeard

,, 14   ROBERT RICHARDSON, only son of William R., and heir apparent of Robert

1686-7   ### folio 1,317.

Jan 28   JOHN BREWER, son and heir of Edmund B., Esq., of Benthall, Suffolk

,, ,,   BASIL FITZHERBERT, second son of Basil F., of Swinnerton, co. Stafford, Esq.

Feb 9   ROBERT MEADE, fifth son of Richard M., of Marstry, Bucks, Esq

,, 10   WILLIAM BRANTHWAITE, son of William B., of Hethel, Norfolk, Esq

,, 11   JOHN WOGAN, gent, son and heir of John W., of Gawdy Hall, Norfolk, Esq

,, 14   SAMUEL DIGGLE, second son of John D., of Hernard, Southampton, gent.

Mar 9.   THOMAS BURCH, son and heir of Thomas B., Esq., of this Inn   [gent

,, ,,   JOHN TENCH, second son of John T., of St Giles-in-the-Fields, Middlesex,

1687

April 21   JOHN WALE, son and heir of Charles W., of Saffron Walden, Essex, gent

,, 25   ROBERT WHARTON, third son of Humphrey W., of London, gent

folio 1,318

,, 29   EDWARD WALPOLE, son and heir of Edward W., of Pinchbeck, co Lincoln

,, ,,   JOHN WALPOLE, son and heir of Thomas W., of Dunston, co Lincoln

May 4   WILLIAM HAWTREY, second son of John H., of Pinner, Middlesex, Esq

,, 9   JOHN ROBINSON, youngest son of William R., late of Cheshunt, Herts, Esq.,
[deceased

,, 10   PHILIP MONSON, third son of Anthony M., of Northrop, co Lincoln

,, 13   JOHN FORSTER, second son of Sir William Foster, of Bamborough Castle,

,, ,,   FERDINAND FORSTER, third son of the same   [Northumberland

,, 30   WILLIAM POOLE, second son of James P., of Poole, co Chester, Esq   [Esq

,, ,   EVAN EVANS, son and heir of Walter E., of Eagles-Bush, co Glamorgan,

,, 31   WILLIAM CLARKE, of Cuckfield, Sussex, Esq   [citizen and (haberdasher?)

,, ,,   JAMES DERMER, son and heir of John D., of the city of London, deceased,

folio 1,319.

June 9   JAMES CLAVERING, of Chopwell, co Durham, gent

,, 13   WALSINGHAM BOKENHAM, son and heir of Hugh B., of Norwich

1687   folio 1,319—(continued).   [Esq

June 13   GEORGE GOODINGE, son and heir of George G , deceased, of Wanbrough, Wilts,

,,   14   THOMAS BIRKINHEAD, of the city of Chester, gent   [deceased

,,   ,,   WILLIAM PATTEN, son and heir of Henry P , of Garstang, co Lancaster,

,,   21   HOWEL GWYNNE, son and heir of Lewis G , of Llanvaire, co. Monmouth, Esq

,,   24   JOHN BAGSHAWE, son and heir of Thomas B , of co Derby, gent

July   2   THOMAS HUSBAND, of Somerton, Norfolk, gent

,,   ,,   STEPHEN TEMPEST, of St Andrews, Holborn, gent , six years of Staple Inn

,,   21   WALTER CROSBIE, second son of Thomas C , Knight, of Ardfert, co Kerry

folio 1,320

,,   ,,   JOHN NEWDIGATE, second son of Richard N , of Arbury, co Warwick, Baronet

Sept   7   DONNOUGH MOLLONY, of Thorne, co Clare

,,   22   THOMAS WYNNE, son and heir of Robert W , of Dyffrinaleth, co Denbigh, Esq

Oct   20   EDMOND CLIFFORD, son and heir of Edmond C , of Frampton, co Gloucester, gent (allowed on the certificate of Sir Robert Sawyer, Treasurer of [the Middle Temple)

Nov   1   RICHARD GOULSTON, son and heir of James G , of Wyddial, Herts.

,,   ,,   JOHN POWELL, son and heir of Charles P , of Upland, co Carmarthen

,,   ,,   THOMAS INGLEBY, son and heir of Charles Ingleby, Serjeant-at-Law

,,   ,   JOHN SYMINS, son and heir of Thomas S , late of Martel, co Pembroke, gent

folio 1,321

,,   11   WILLIAM JACKSON, son and heir of William J , of Coleraine, Ireland

,,   12   FRANCIS ROKEBY, son and heir of Thomas R , of Morthem, co York

,,   18   DAVID THOMAS, second son of Henry T , of Pennant, co Montgomery, gent

,,   ,,   FALCALICUS BREN1, son and heir of Robert B , of Gray's Inn, Esq.

,,   ,,   PATRICK JENNINGS, second son of Jonathan J , of Ripon, co York, Knight

,,   22   JOHN TAYLOR, son and heir of John T , of Gate Fulford, co York, Esq

,,   ,,   GRIFFIN DAVIS, youngest son of Griffin D , of Drasleyne, co Carmarthen. gent.

,,   24   JOHN ROBERTS, of Havod-y-bwlch, co Denbigh, Esq

,,   ,,   PETER FLETCHER, fifth son of Thomas F , of Chatham, Kent, gent

,,   26   FRANCIS STEWARD WALDRON, son and heir of George W , of Knowles Hill, [Essex, Esq

1687-8   folio 1,322.

Jan   26   JAMES GOODINGE, fourth son of Henry G , of Wanborough, Wilts, Esq

,,   28   EDMOND MORROUGH, son and heir of John M , of Barres Court, co Cork, gent

,,   30   WILLIAM AYLOFFE, second son of Joseph A , of Gray's Inn, Esq

Feb   3   THOMAS TYRRELL, son and heir of Edmund T , of Gipping, Suffolk, Esq

,,   4   JAMES WINSTANLEY, son and heir of Clement W , co Leicester, Esq , deceased

,,   7   ANTHONY TUCKNEY, son and heir of Jonathan T , of Westminster, gent

,,   ,,   WILLIAM WINFORD, of St Andrew's, Holborn, gent   [deceased

,,   11   ROGER SALUSBURY, second son of William S , of Rug, co Merioneth, Esq ,

,,   27   WILLIAM SHERWIN, of Barnard's Inn, gent

Mar   19   JAMES BIRD (then at the University), son and heir of James B , of this Inn, [and of Brougham, Westmoreland, Esq.

1688	folio 1,322—(*continued*)
April 6	PHILIP TULLY, second son of ———, of the Bishoprick of Durham, gent

folio 1,323   [of Durham, gent

,, 20	WILLIAM TULLY, seventh son of Timothy T , of Middleton, in the Bishoprick
May 1	PETER FROWD, second son of Philip F., Knight, of Kent
,, ,,	BARTHOLOMEW CAUNTER, son and heir of Bartholomew C., late of [Beaworthy, Devon, clerk, deceased.
,, ,,	THOMAS GOODALL, son and heir of Thomas G , of Barnard's Inn, gent.
,, 22	HENRY COLEGRAVE, son and heir of William C., of Middlesex, Esq
,, ,,	EDMUND CLENCHE, son and heir of Andrew C , of Soham, Suffolk, Doctor of [Medicine
,, ,,	JOHN CLENCHE, second son of Andrew C , of Soham, Suffolk, aforesaid
June 4	GRIFFITH DRYSDALE, second son of Hugh D., of ———, Ossory, Ireland.
,, ,,	CLEMENT TOULSON, son and heir of George T , of co York, Esq.

folio 1,324.

,, 21	THOMAS BEANE, son and heir of John B , of Oxton, co York, gent [Inn
,, 27	JOHN ELLIS, second son of Edward E , of Middlesex, gent , six years of Staple
,, 16	THOMAS SHEARSON, son and heir of Richard S , of Ellell, co Lancaster, gent
July 6	MARMADUKE PRICKETT, son and heir of George P , of Gray's Inn, Esq
,, 10	WILLIAM GREENE, of Norwich, gent
,, 21	JOHN SOUTH, second son of John S , of Dinton, Wilts, gent
Aug 14	RICHARD LANE (then at the University), son and heir of William L , late of [Cowley, Middlesex, Esq , deceased
,, ,,	WILLIAM LANE (then at the University), second son of William, aforesaid
,, 20	CHARLES BINGHAM, of Foxford, in Ireland, gent , second son of John B , of [the same, Esq
Sept 10	THOMAS HUTTON, youngest son of Thomas H , of Poppleton, co York, Esq
,, ,,	SAMUEL CROOKE, of Coppul, co Lancaster, gent

folio 1,325.

,, 26	THOMAS PORTER, youngest son of John P , of Waterford, Ireland, Esq
Nov 26. 1688-9	HERBERT RUDDALL WESTPHALING, son and heir of Herbert W , of Ruddall, [co Hereford, Esq
Jan 28	CUTHBERT PEPPER, gent , son of John P , of Long Cowton, co York, gent , [deceased
Feb 16	HUGH OWEN, eldest son of Rice O , of Pwllheli, co Carnarvon, clerk
,, ,,	JOHN ROBINSON, second son of John R , of Gwersillt, co Denbigh, Esq
Mar 4	HUMPHREY FISH, eldest son of Humphrey F , of Ickwell, Beds, Esq
,, 16	THOMAS PEACHELL, son and heir of Thomas P , of this Inn, gent
1689 Mar 29	RICHARD BROOKE, son of Richard B , of Norton, Cheshire, Baronet
April 26	LAWRENCE STOUGHTON, of the Inner Temple, Baronet (according to the date of his admission there, May 6, 1686) [clerk, deceased
May 1	ALEXANDER GRIFFITH, of Brecon, gent., son and heir of Owen G , of Brecon,

folio 1,326   [Esq , deceased

, 2	JOHN HARDRESS, son and heir of Thomas H , late of the city of Canterbury,

1689   folio 1,326—(continued)

May 9   BRADWARDINE JACKSON, Baronet, son and heir of John J , of Hickelton, co
                                                [York, Baronet, deceased

,,   10   JOHN WARD (according to date of his admission at the Inner Temple, June 6,
                                [1683, on the certificate of John Mosyer, Treasurer)

June 10   WILLIAM BRODNAX, of Godmersham, Kent, Esq , son and heir of William B ,
                                                [late of the same, Knight, deceased

,,   15   JENKIN LEWIS, son and heir of Henry L , of Treehure, co Carmarthen, Esq

,,   18   JAMES RANT, youngest son of William R , late of Yelverton, Norfolk, Esq ,
                                                                        [deceased

Aug 17   THOMAS BRIGHT, eldest son of Thomas B , of Nether Hall, in Peckingham,
                                folio 1,327.   [Suffolk, Esq

Oct 18   THOMAS LOWNDES, fourth son of Ralph L , of Newton, co Chester, gent

,,   26   WILLIAM CROSSE, second son of William C , of Upper Darwen, co Lancaster,
                                                                        [Esq

Nov 1   JOHN RAWLINSON, brother of Right Hon William R , Knight, Commissioner

,,   ,,   WILLIAM MORGAN, of London, gent   [of the Great Seal.

,,   19   HUMPHREY DAVENPORT, son of William D , of Bromhall, co Chester, Esq

,,   23   SAMUEL BELGRAVE, second son of William B , of Kilworth, co Leicester, Esq

,,   28   HENRY ATKINSON, son of Henry A , of Leeds, co York, Esq
                                folio 1,328.

,,   29   JOHN FLACKE, eldest son of Robert F , of Linton, co. Cambridge, gent

,,   ,,   ROBERT MALTYWARD, eldest son of Geffrey Maltward (sic), of Hawkington,
                                                                [Suffolk, gent

Dec 14. FREDERICK ALPE, third son of Edward A , of Framlingham, Suffolk, Esq
1689-90
Jan 11   HENRY TOWNELEY, son of John T , of Clitheroe, co Lancaster, merchant

,,   22   THOMAS BROGRAVE, second son of Thomas B , late of Hammels, Herts,
                Baronet, deceased   [gent

,,   ,,   JONATHAN BOLT, fourth son of Richard B , of St Botolph's, Aldgate, Middlesex,

Feb. 11   WILLIAM DAVISON, eldest son of William D , Esq , one of the Fellows of the
                Bench   [Fellows of the Bench

,,   12   DEVEREUX GOODINGE, gent , eldest son of Thomas G , Esq , one of the

,,   ,,   SAMUEL HALLOWS, son and heir of Matthew H , of Rochdale, co Lancaster,
                                                                        [gent
                                folio 1,329.

,,   24   JOHN LIMBREY, eldest son of Henry L , of London, merchant

Mar 21   RICHARD WIN, youngest son of William W , of Llanunda, co Carnarvon, Esq
1690
May 8   JOSEPH HARDISTY, of Furnival's Inn, gent

,,   13   THOMAS WESTBY, son and heir of George W , of Ranfield, co York, Esq

,,   15   ROBERT HITCH, eldest son of Henry H , of Leathley, co York, Esq

,,   ,,   ROBERT GELDART, son and heir of John G , of Wiggenthorpe, parish of
                                                        [Terrington, co York gent

,,   19   EDMUND COLE, youngest son of Thomas C., of Coate, co Lancaster, Esq

,,   24   ELLIS MEWS, eldest son of Ellis M , of Wilton, co Southampton, Esq.

,,   28   WILLIAM BARNARD, second son of Edward B , of Beverley, co York, Knight

1690		**folio 1,330**
May 30		WILLIAM CRADOCK, of Wickhambrook, Suffolk, gent
,, 31		WILLIAM BVRNAND, eldest son of John B , of Padiham, co Lancaster, gent
		[deceased
June 26		CECILL COOPER, son and heir of Cecill C., late of Thurgarton, Notts, Esq,
July 4		CHRISTOPHER GUISE, third son of John G , of Sandhurst, co Gloucester, Esq
,, 8		BENEDICT LEONARD CALVERT, eldest son of Charles, Lord Baltimore
,, ,,		FERDINANDO LATUS, eldest son of John L , of Beck, Cumberland, Esq
Aug 12		PETER DAVENPORT, gent , son and heir of Peter D , of Bramhall, co Chester,
		[Esq
Oct 18		THOMAS GOODINGE, second son of Thomas G , Esq , one of the Fellows of the
		[Bench

folio 1,331

Nov 22		ABRAHAM DUDLEY, gent , third son of Richard D , late of Coventry. co Warwick, deceased (admitted to the Inner Temple, Nov 24 1683 , by [certificate of William Farrer, Treasurer.
Dec 1		JOHN WENTWORTH, son and heir of Henry W., of Brodsworth, co York, Esq
1690 91		
Jan 19		NICHOLAS WILLIAMS, son and heir of John W , of co Carmarthen, Esq
,, 22		ROBERT LEVER, late of Brasenose College, Oxford, son and heir of Robert L , [of Alkrington and Lever, co Lancaster, Esq
,, ,,		JOHN LEVER, late of Brasenose College, Oxford, second son of Robert L , of [Alkrington and Lever, co. Lancaster, Esq
Feb 11		JOHN DAWNEY, son and heir of Thomas D , Esq , late of Selby, co York
,, ,,		LANCELOT LAKE, of Cannons, parish of Stanmore, Middlesex, Esq (admitted [to Lincoln's Inn, Feb 15, 1687 , by certificate of Henry Long, Treasurer

folio 1,332.

,, 17		GEORGE EMPSON, son and heir of George E , late of Goole, co York, gent
,, 20		FRANCIS SCAWEN, second son of Francis S., of Wrexham, co Denbigh, Esq
Mar 10		HUGH FOULKES, eldest son of Robert F , of the city of Chester, gent.
1691		[worker
April 11		THOMAS GOODWIN, eldest son and heir of ——— G , of the town of Derby, cloth-
,, 29		JOHN MORELAND, son and heir of George M , of Windleston, co Durham, Esq
,, ,,		THOMAS MATHEW, son of John M , of the city of Chester, gent
May 7		JOHN JAMES, gent , son and heir of John J , of Felstead, Essex (admitted to the Inner Temple, Oct. 17, 1690, by certificate of John Summers, [Treasurer

folio 1,333

,, 12		CUTHBERT OGLE, son and heir of Ralph O , of Kirkley, Northumberland, Esq
,, 25.		MICHAEL BURTON, son and heir of Thomas B , of Holmesfield, co Derby, Esq
,, 28.		CHARLES WICKS, son and heir of Charles W , of St Sepulchre's, London,
,, 30		JOHN CLARKE, son of Richard C., of the city of London [citizen.
June 6		LEONARD THOMPSON, son and heir of Edward T , of the city of York, Esq.
,, 12		THOMAS LUCK, son and heir of Thomas L , of Hoddesdon, Herts, gent
,, 22.		OSWALD MOSLEY, son and heir of Oswald M , of Ancoats, co Lancaster, Esq.
,, 23.		ROBERT ALDERSEY, son and heir of Thomas A , of Spurstowe, co Chester, Esq
July 2.		DAVID LLOYD, son and heir of David L , of Lwydiarth, co Anglesey, Esq

1691		*folio* 1,334	[bigh, clerk
July	13	PETER WYNNE, second son of Peter W , of Llanverdyffryn Clwyd, co Den- [gent , deceased	
Aug	1	WILLIAM POWELL, gent , third son of Thomas P , of Poole Hall, co Monmouth,	
Oct	21	RICHARD DARBY, gent , son of John D , of Appleby, Westmoreland, gent	
,,	22	JOHN AGAR, son and heir of William A , of Earswick, co York, gent , and nephew by the brother of Laurence A , Esq , one of the Members of this Inn [*alias* Stepney, Middlesex, mariner, deceased.	
Nov	4	ROBERT CONWAY, son and heir of Robert C., of Ratcliffe, parish of Stebenheath,	
,,	6	ST ANDREW THORNHAGH, son and heir of John T , of Fenton, Notts, Esq	
,,	,,	THOMAS SMITHSON, son and heir of Thomas S , of Moulton, co. York, gent	
,,	13	JOHN MICHELL, second son of John M , of Field Place, parish of Warneham, Sussex, Esq [certificate of William Farrer, Treasurer	
,,	,,	ERASMUS CORBETT, of the Inner Temple, gent (admitted Feb 9, 1681, by	

folio 1,335   [minster, gent , "sine fine"

Dec	1	THOMAS BABINGTON, son and heir of Michael B , of St Margarets West-
,,	2	JOHN THORNTON, second son of John T , of Oxcliffe, parish of Lancaster, gent
,,	,,	JOHN HINDLEY, of Hindley, co Lancaster, Esq , son and heir of —— H , Esq
,,	4	MATTHEW SMELT, of St Andrews, Holborn, gent (two years at Staple Inn), [Moses Slade, Principal
,,	12	CHRISTOPHER WILKINSON, gent , son and heir of Christopher W , of Waddon, [co. York, Esq (four years at Barnard's Inn) [ton, Esq
1691-2		
Jan	8	WALGRAVE CREWE, son and heir of Walgrave C , late of Hinton, co Northamp-
Feb	8	ANTHONY DAWSON, Esq , son and heir of William D , of Azerley, co York, Knight
,,	11	HENRY HODGKINSON, son of Thomas H., of Preston, co. Lancaster, gent

folio 1,336

,,	12	WILLIAM DAVISON, son and heir of Timothy D , Esq , of Newcastle-on-Tyne
1692		
April	9	GODFREY BOATE, son and heir of Godfrey B , late of Dublin, Esq , deceased
,,	16.	JOHN VAUGHAN, of Pant-Glas, co Carnarvon, Esq [Esq
,,	,,	THOMAS HILTON, of Hilton, co Lancaster, gent., fourth son of William H ,
,,	20.	RICE THOMAS, son and heir of William T , late of Mydrim, co Carmarthen,
,,	25	JOHN ELWES, of St Andrews, Holborn, gent [gent , deceased
,,	27	JOHN ROWE, son and heir of Hugh R , of St Michaels, Keinton, Wilts, gent
,,	28.	JOHN DALSTON, son and heir of Thomas D , of Milrigg, Westmoreland, Esq
May	3	GEOFFREY AMHERST, son and heir of Geoffrey A , of Gray's Inn, Esq
,,	6	ROBERT GREGGE, son and heir of Edward G , of Chester, gent [deceased
,,	9	LEONARD CHILDERS, son of Thomas C , late of Carrhouse, co York, Esq ,

folio 1,337.

,,	,,	WILLIAM BAGULEY, of Kersley, co Lancaster, gent [Chester, Baronet
,,	14.	CHARLES DUCKENFIELD, son and heir of Robert D , of Duckenfield, co
,,	31	THOMAS WOOD, Fellow of New College, Oxford.
June	1	LEONARD STREATE, son and heir of Richard S , of Bletchingley, Surrey, gent
,,	4	JOHN BIRD, son and heir of James B , of this Inn, and of Brougham, West- [moreland, Esq

1692   folio 1,337—(continued)   [Esq , deceased
June 14   MONCK RAWLINSON, Esq., son and heir of Curwen R , of Carke, co Lancaster,
,,   ,,   WILLIAM POWELL, son and heir of Matthew P , of Whitehouse, parish of
                                                  [Llandillio Grossenny, co Monmouth, Esq
,,   25.   ISAAC BORROW, only son and heir of John B , of Holland, co Derby, Esq
July 2   ORLANDO GREENHALGH, third son of Thomas G , late of Brandelsome, co
                                                  [Lancaster, Esq , deceased.
,,   6   HENRY PRINCE, only son and heir of Philip P , of Mowsby, co York, gent

folio 1,338

Sept 28   SAMUEL SPATEMAN, eldest son of John S , of Rodenook, co Derby, Esq
Oct 28   CHRISTOPHER BUTLER, third son of Walter B , of Kilcash, co. Tipperary, Esq
,,   31   EDWARD BARRON, gent , eldest son of Arthur B , of Warrington, co Lan-
               caster, gent   [minster, Esq , deceased
Nov 7   RICHARD HANWAY, fourth son of William H , late of St Margarets, West-
,,   8   FRANCIS FAWKES, only son and heir of Thomas F , of Farnley, co York, Esq
,,   9   FINCH HUMFREY (sic), gent , only son and heir of Finch H , late of Fawk-
               ham, Kent, Esq , deceased (See page 335)   [co York, Baronet
,,   ,,   MARK BOURCHIER, gent , second son of Barrington B , of Benningbrough,
,,   15   JOHN FINCHAM, only son and heir of John F , of Outwell, Isle of Ely, co
                                                  [Cambridge, Esq
,,   19   ROBERT DUNKIN, gent , son of William D , late of Liscard, co Cornwall, gent ,
               deceased (admitted to Inner Temple, June 20, 1687, by certificate of
                                                  [Thomas Riggs, Under-treasurer)

folio 1,339.   [Sutton, co Lancaster, gent

,,   ,,   PERCIVAL ROUGHLAY, gent , second son of Thomas R , of Costath House,
Sept 30   DAVID JOHNSON, son and heir of George J , of Sherborne, co Durham, gent
Dec 6   NICHOLAS LUTTRELL, of Hartland Abbey, co Devon, Esq
,,   20   STEPHEN WESTON, of Farnborough, Berks, gent.
1692-3.
Jan   5   JOHN BERNEY, of Westwick, Norfolk, Esq   [York, gent
,,   20.   WILLIAM WILSON, eldest son and heir of Thomas W , of Beecroft Hall, co
,.   24   JOHN KNIGHTLEY, second son of Richard K , of Charleton, co Northampton,
Feb. 2   CHRISTOPHER BEDINGFIELD, of Wighton, Norfolk, gent   [clerk.
,,   13   JAMES CLAVERING, only son and heir of James C , of Greencroft, co Durham,
                                                  [Esq.
,,   14   RICHARD HARLAND, eldest son and heir of John H , of Sutton-on-the-Forest-
                                                  [of-Galtresse, co York, gent
1693   folio 1,340.
May   2   JOHN MAYES, son and heir of Nicholas M., late of Fryerage, near Yarm, co
,,   3   HENRY DAVY, of the city of Norwich, gent   [York, gent
,,   5   CHARLES BONYTHON, eldest son and heir of Charles B , Serjeant-at-Law.
,,   23   WILLIAM SALTER, eldest son and heir of William S., of Norwich, gent
,,   27   JOHN WETTENHALL, gent , second son of the Bishop of Cork
,,   29.   WILLIAM NANNEY, gent , youngest son of Hugh N , of Nanney, co Merioneth,
               Esq.   [Doctor of Medicine, deceased
;   ,,   WILLIAM BRIGHT, gent., son and heir of William B , late of Barton, Suffolk,

1693		folio 1,340—(continued)

June 20   GREGORY BYRNE, gent , eldest son of George B , of the city of Dublin

,, 23   NICHOLAS TYRWHITT, Esq , second son of Philip T , late of Stainfield, co [Lincoln, Baronet

,, 24   EDWARD BURDETT, eldest son and heir of Thomas B , of the city of London,

,, 28   THOMAS STONES, of Mosborough, co Derby, Esq   [gent.

folio 1,341

,, 30   THOMAS FAIRFAX, gent , only son and heir of Thomas F , of Menston, co [York, Esq

July 1   WILLIAM BANCKS, son and heir of Adam B , of the city of London, cloth-

,, 6   FRANCIS DICKINS, of Lyndhurst, co Southampton, gent   [worker

, 11   THOMAS WRIGHTSON, second son of Robert W , of Cusworth, co York, gent

,, ,,   GEORGE WARREN, eldest son and heir of Daniel W , of Horsted, Norfolk, clerk.   [Cumberland, Baronet.

,, 17   RICHARD MUSGRAVE, eldest son and heir of Richard M , of Hayton Castle,

Aug 1   JOHN GARDNER, gent , third son of Thomas G , late of London, gent , deceased

,, 8   CHRISTOPHER PHILIPPSON, of Kirby Kendall, Westmoreland, gent , second [son of Robert P , late of Calgarth, Westmoreland, Esq , deceased.

,, 14   WILLIAM BENNETT, gent , only son and heir of William B , late of Tidd St. [Mary, co Lincoln, gent , deceased

Sept 8   MAURICE JONES, of Ddole, co. Merioneth, gent

folio 1,342

,, 22   RICHARD BROOKE, of St Andrews, Holborn, gent   [caster, Esq

Oct 20   THOMAS TOWNLEY, eldest son and heir of Nicholas T , of Royle, co Lan-

,, 25   WILLIAM DAWSON, son and heir of Christopher D , late of Langcliffe, co York, gent , deceased.   [gent

Nov 2   MARTIN KEIGHWIN, eldest son and heir of John K , of Mouseholle, Cornwall,

,, ,,   JOHN STANHOPE, gent , only son and heir of Darcy S , late of High Melwood, [Isle of Axholme, co Lincoln, gent , deceased

,, 6   WILLIAM BUSFEILD, of Ryshworth, co York, gent

,, ,,   JOHN PICKERING, eldest son and heir of John P , of Thelwall, co Chester, gent

,, 14   RICHARD CURTIS, of Reading, Berks, gent

,, 17   ROBERT PETTUS, gent , second son of John P , of Rackheath, Norfolk, Baronet.

,, 27   WARWICK LAKE, gent , only son of Lancelot L , late of Cannons, Middlesex,

,, 28   JOHN FRANCKLYN, of Swansea, co. Glamorgan, gent   [Knight, deceased

folio 1,343

Dec 6   CHARLES ORME, gent , eldest son and heir of Charles O , late of Peterborough, co Northampton, Esq , deceased   [at Staple Inn)

,, 11   JETHRO TULL, only son and heir of Jethro T , of Howberry, Oxon (two years

,, 14   THOMAS HEAMES, gent , son and heir of James H , of St. Martins-in-the-Fields, [Middlesex, gent

,, 21   WILLIAM NORCLIFFE, son and heir of William N , of Nunnington, co York, [gent (two years at Furnival's Inn).

,, 22   BENJAMIN FERRAND, son and heir of Robert F , of Harden Grange, co York, Esq   [Knight and Baronet

,, ,,   JOSEPH MUSGRAVE, third son of Christopher M , of Eden Hall, Cumberland,

1693-4   folio **1,343**—(continued).   [Barone-, deceased

Jan 25   WILLIAM HUNGATE, gent, fourth son of Francis H, of Hudleston, co York,

,, 27.   THOMAS SCLAIER, of Catley (? Hatley), co Cambridge, Esq   [gent

,, 31   HUMPHREY DAVENPORT, son and heir of Edward D, of Stockport, co Chester,

folio 1,344

Feb 9   RICHARD ARNOLD, gent, second son of Thomas A, of Bletchworth, Surrey, gent (one year at Staple Inn)   [bench of this Inn

,, ,,   THOMAS OWEN, second son of Thomas O, Esq, one of the Masters of the

,, 10   RICHARD PALFREYMAN, only son and heir of Richard P, of Boston, co [Lincoln, gent

,, ,,   JOHN DARLEY, youngest son of Richard D, of Aldby, co York, Esq   [Esq

,, 12   WILLIAM WILLIAMS, gent, eldest son of William W, of Pentyr, co Carnarvon,

,, 16   RICHARD MEYRICK, eldest son and heir of William M, of Bodorgan, co Anglesea, Esq   [gent

,, ,,   THOMAS ROBERTS, only son of Humphrey R, of Brynynfodd, co Carnarvon,

,, 22   CHARLES WOOD, youngest son of John W, of Luckham, co Somerset, gent, [(two years at Staple Inn)

1694
Mar. 28.   WILLIAM MEARE, eldest son and heir of George M, of Eastington, co Pem- [broke, Esq

folio 1,345.

April 25.   THOMAS LEVER, of Bolton, co Lancaster, gent   [Durham, gent

,, 30.   RALPH SHIPHERDSON, gent, son of Edward S, of Pittington Hallgarth, co

May 1   WILLIAM RICHARDSON, second son of William R, late of Mearscough, co [Lancaster, Esq, deceased

,, 9   JOHN HATFEILD, son and heir of John H, of Loughton, co York, Esq [gent

, 17.   JOHN KEMPSON, second son of Simon K, of Henley-in-Arden, co Warwick,

,, 21   JOHN COX, eldest son and heir of John C, of Gray's Inn, Esq   [Meath, Esq

June 5.   JOSEPH DEANE, eldest son and heir of Joseph D, junior, of Deanehill, co

,, 25   WILLIAM NORTON, eldest son and heir of William N, of Sawley Hall, co

,, 26.   ROBIE SHERWIN, gent (three years of Staple Inn)   [York, Esq

folio 1,346.

,, 27.   EDWARD WOGAN, son and heir of Lewis W, of Boulston, co Pembroke, Esq.

,, 28.   JOHN CHAWORTH, of Annesley, Notts, gent

folio 1,348

,, 30   WILLIAM HAWARD, gent, of Wakefield, co York, only son of William H, late [of the same, deceased

July 12   JOHN STANHOPE, son of ——— S, of Horsforth, co York, Esq, deceased

Oct 15   HENRY DAVIS, five years of Staple Inn, gent (admitted Feb. 11, 1689-90)

Nov 2   EDWARD MATHEW, third son of John M, of Boyate, parish of Otterbourne, co Southampton, gent.   [Lancaster, Esq.

,, 20   WILLIAM FARINGTON, eldest son of George F., of Shaw Hall, in Leyland, co.

folio 1,349.

,, 21   CÆSAR COOKE, son and heir of Ralph C, Esq, one of the Masters of the [Bench of this Inn, and Treasurer

1694   folio 1,349—(continued)

Nov 27   JOSEPH ROKEBY, only son of Joseph R , of London, Merchant   [land, gent

,,   28   RICHARD WIDDRINGTON third son of Henry W , Esq , of Ryton, Northumber-

1694-5.

Jan 14.   MATTHIAS TUNSTALL, second son of Francis T , of Wickliffe, co York, gent

,,   26   JOHN BROUGHAM, fourth son of Henry B Esq , of Scales, Cumberland, gent
           (three years at Staple Inn ; Edward Dearmer, principal , certificate, July
           16, 1691).   [Esq

,,   30.   GEORGE HILTON, gent , eldest son of Thomas H , of Hilton, Westmoreland,

,,   ,,   RICHARD BERNEY, gent., second son of John B , of Westwick, Norfolk, gent ,
           deceased   [Barony of West Carbery, Ireland, gent

Feb 1   EDMUND O'HANLON, gent., second son of Edmund O'H , of Tourin, in the

folio 1,350.

,,   11.   ROBERT MUCHALL, eldest son of Thomas M , gent , of Muchall, co Stafford

,,   16   RICHARD TAYLER, heir of John T , of Newland, parish of Drax, co York,
           gent   [deceased

,,   21   HENRY THOMPSON, Esq , eldest son of Stephen T , Knight, of the city of York,

,,   23   THOMAS THORNHILL, gent , second son of George T , Esq , of Fixby, parish
           of Eland, co. York   [co Derby, gent

,,   27   ROBERT ASHTON, gent , son and heir of Benjamin A , of Hathersedge,

Mar. 15   JOHN FAWCET, second son of Christopher F , of the city of Durham, gent

1695

April 9   ABRAHAM SPOONER, son and heir of Abraham S , of London, vintner.

,,   ,,   JOHN LYNDLEY, of St Andrew's, Holborn, gent

folio 1,351

May 4   EDWARD SMITH, gent , son and heir of John S , Alderman of Dublin

,,   18   ALEXANDER OSBALDESTON, of co Lancaster

,,   20   JOHN STRINGER, son and heir of Francis S , of Sutton, Notts, gent [deceased

,,   ,,   WILLIAM SACHEVERELL, gent , second son of William S , Esq , of Notts,

,,   30   JOHN HARDESTY, second son of John H , of Furnival's Inn, gent

June 1   VALENTINE FARINGTON, second son of George F , of Shaw Hall in Leyland,
           co Lancaster, gent   [Chester, Esq.

,,   3   EDWARD CORCAR (alias Corker) son and heir of John C , of Hutchfield, co

,,   7   THOMAS STEPHENS, third son of Richard S , of St Margarets, Westminster,
                                                                    [gent

folio 1,352

July 26   GEORGE VANE, heir apparent of George V , of Richmond, co York, Esq

Aug 2.   PATRICK MATHEWS, son and heir of Arnold M , of co Monaghan, gent , deceased

Oct 23.   THOMAS MEREDITH, son of Ellis M , of Wrexham, co. Denbigh, Esq.

Nov 8   RALPH BAYNES, son and heir of William B , of Mewith Head, parish of
                                                       [Bentham, co. York, gent

,,   13.   JOHN BODENHAM, son and heir of Philip B , of Fetcham, Surrey, Esq

,,   18   THOMAS DALY, of Kilclaugh, co Westmeath, gent

,,   22.   GEORGE BUTLER, of Ballyraggett, co Kilkenny, gent

,,   23   WILLIAM BATEMAN, son and heir of William B , of East Hooke, parish of
                                                  [Lambstowne, co Pembroke, gent

1695-6   **folio 1,353.**

Jan   4   MATTHEW PRINCE, son and heir of Matthew P, of Woolley, co York, gent

„   11   STEPHEN HUSBAND, of St Andrews, Holborn, gent, son and heir of Tempest
[H, of Kirkby Lonsdale, Westmoreland, woollen draper

Feb   1   HENRY BERNEY, gent, son of Thomas B, of the city of Norwich, Baronet

Mar   3   FRANCIS BOYNTON, son and heir of Henry B, of Barmston, co York, clerk

1696   [gent

April 21   GEORGE ENGLAND, son and heir of Thomas E, of Great Yarmouth, Norfolk,
[Esq

May   4   PARADIN LIVESAY, son and heir of William L, of Hennwick Hall, Beds,

„   14   EDWARD CLEGG, son and heir of William G, of Grange, co Chester, Esq

folio 1,354.   [Knight

June   8   WILLIAM GREENFIELD, Esq, son and heir of Christopher G, of Gray's Inn,

„   15   THOMAS ASSHETON, of Ashley, co Chester, Esq.

„   29   WORLEY BENYON, eldest son of Worley B, of St Giles-in-the-Fields, gent.

July   8   FRANCIS FORCER, eldest son of Francis F, of St Andrews, Holborn, gent

Oct 29   THOMAS PELHAM, gent, son of Nicholas P, of Catsfield, Sussex, Knight

Aug 14   BENJAMIN MANWARING, gent   [Esq

Sept   6   HENRY EYES, gent, second son of Thomas E, late of Berry's Hall, Norfolk,

Oct 12   DANIEL SULLIVAN, of the city of Dublin, gent

„   13   ROBERT HALEY, of Cork, Esq, son and heir of Robert H., deceased

„   14   BERNARD HALE, of King's Walden, Herts   [ampton, Esq

Nov   5   JOHN RUDYARD, gent, son and heir of Benjamin R, of Winchfield, co South-

folio 1,355

„   13   WILLIAM EYRE, eldest son of William E, of Highlow, co Derby

„   14   LEONARD PINCKNEY, of Mansfield Woodhouse, Notts, gent

„   21   PETER HOET, of Debden, Essex, Esq

„   25   WILLIAM BAMFORD, gent, son of ——— B, of Bamford, co Lancaster, gent

„   23   JOHN BARRY, only son of Edward B, of Gray's Inn, Esq

„   24   ROBERT STRICKLAND, gent, second son of Sir Thomas S, of Sizergh, co
[Westmoreland, Knight, deceased

„   28   JOHN CLARKSON, only son of John C, of Mansfield, Notts, Esq

1696-7

Jan   2   JOSEPH NAGLE, gent, son of David N, of Carriconna, co Cork   [gent

„   25   JOHN HAMILTON, gent, eldest son of Alexander H, of St James, Westminster,

Feb   1   WYRRIOT OWEN, gent, second son of Hugh O, of Orielton, co Pembroke,
Knight   [nephew (nepos) of Lawrence A, Esq, Fellow of this Inn

„   6   JOHN AGAR, eldest son of Thomas A, of the city of York gent, and

„   26   ROBERT BOOTH, gent, son of George B, of Woodford, co Chester, Esq

1697   **folio 1,356**

April 4   JOHN POLEY, Esq, eldest son of John P., of Boxtead, Suffolk, Knight

May   6   SAMUEL RAMSDEN, of Crowston, co York, gent.

1697   folio 1,356—(continued)

May 10.   RICHARD OWEN, gent, third son of Thomas O, Esq, Fellow of this Inn

„ 14.   JOHN ATHERTON, of Atherton, co Lancaster, Esq

June 2   RICHARD WITTON, gent, eldest son of Richard W, of Wakefield, co York,
          Esq   [gent

„   3   ARTHUR TOWERS, gent., eldest son of Henry T., of North Runcton, Norfolk,

„ 11   THOMAS WARBURTON, gent, second son of Peter W, of Arley, co Chester,

„ 28.   RALPH YOWARD, of Stanley, co. York, gent   [Baronet

July 7.   MICHAEL NUGENT, gent, second son of Edmund N., of Carlestown, co West-
                                                              [meath, Esq

„   9   WILLIAM RICE, gent, only son of John R., of Hospitall, co. Limerick, Esq

                              folio 1,357.

„ 14   RICHARD WILSON, gent, son and heir of Thomas W, of Leeds, co York,
          gent.   [Dalton, co. Lancaster, gent

Nov 13.   ROBERT GIBSON, gent, eldest son of Edmund G, of Park House, parish of

„ 18   RALPH ROBINSON, of the city of Durham, gent, eldest son of Richard R, of
          Sunderland-by-the-Sea   [Knight.

Dec 20   GERRARD LOWTHER, gent, youngest son of William L, of Preston, co York,

„   „   WILLIAM ATKINSON, gent, eldest son of Edward A, of Leeds, co York

Nov 9   ALEXANDER RATCLIFF, of Manchester, gent

June 24   WILLIAM CHAMBERS, gent, eldest son of Richard C, of Bawburgh, Norfolk,

1697-8   [gent
Feb 12.   NICHOLAS READ, of Dunboyne, co Meath, Esq

„   „   WILLIAM SWINBORNE, gent, son and heir of Thomas S, of Gray's Inn, Esq

                              folio 1,358   [ford, Esq.

„ 16   GEORGE WIGMORE, gent, third son of Thomas W, of Upton Court, co Here-

„ 17.   CHRISTOPHER ASHTON, gent, second son of Benjamin A., of Stony Midleton,
1698   [co Derby, gent

May 10   THOMAS LISTER, gent, eldest son of John L, of Bawtry, co York, Esq

„   „   THOMAS KINSEY, gent, only son of John K, of Blackden, co Chester, Esq

„ 11.   LEFTWICH OLDFIELD, of Leftwich, co Chester, Esq

, 27   GEORGE REY, of the city of Cork, gent

June 1   CHARLES KENRICK, gent, only son of Charles K, of Feversham, Kent, Esq

July 2   WILLIAM THOMPSON, of Elsham, co Lincoln, Esq   [Chester, Esq

, 13   PETER WILBRAHAM, junior, gent, third son of Ralph W., of Dorfold, co

„   „   THOMAS HULSE, gent, eldest son of Thomas H, of Elworth, co Chester, gent

„   „   ROGER MORE, Esq, son and heir of Roger M, late of this Inn, afterwards
                                          [one of the Serjeants-at-Law, deceased

                              folio 1,360.   [and Baronet, deceased.

Aug 8   EDWARD DERING, Knight, son of Sir Edward D, of Surrenden, Kent, Knight

Oct 8   EDWARD SPENCER, eldest son of John S, of Rendlesham, Suffolk, Esq.

„ 29   WALTER STANHOPE, gent, son of John S, late of Horsforth, co York, Esq,
                                                              [deceased.

Nov 1   THOMAS BEWICKE, eldest son of Thomas B, of Newcastle-on-Tyne, gent

                                  Y

1698   folio 1,360—*(continued)*

Nov 7   CHRISTOPHER PARKER, only son of Anthony P , late of Clitheroe, co
                                                 [Lancaster, Esq , deceased,

" 17   FRANCIS BIDDULPH, second son of Richard B , of Congleton, co Stafford,
                        folio 1,361   Esq

" 18   EDWARD BELLAMY, of St. Andrews, Holborn, gent
1698-9.
Jan 27   ROBERT PESCOD, of Hart Hall, in Oxford University, gent

Feb 11   JOHN LOVEL, of East Harling, Norfolk, gent (ten years of Barnard's Inn)

Mar 2   GEORGE GREY, gent , eldest son of George G., of Burneston, co York, clerk

" 11   RICHARD KIRKBY, second son of Richard K , of Kirkby, co Lancaster, Esq
1699
Mar 29   JOHN JENNISON, of Hurworth, co Durham, gent
                        folio 1,362

April 29 JOHN LORT, gent , eldest son of George L , of Pembroke, Esq

" "   GEORGE LORT, gent , second son of George L , of Pembroke, Esq

May 6   JOHN BRIDGES, eldest son of John B , of the city of Canterbury, gent

" 12   JOHN COOKE, eldest son of John C , of Plymouth, gent

" 13   WILLIAM DRAKE, eldest son of William D , of Coats Hall, parish of Gill-in-
                 Craven, co. York, Esq., deceased   [gent

" 17   THOMAS WILKINS, eldest son of Thomas W., of St Marychurch, co Glamorgan,

" 22   STREYNSHAM MASTER, only son of James M , of East Langdon, Kent , Esq ,
                                                    [and of this Inn
                        folio 1,363.

June 12   JOHN BOND, eldest son of John Bond, of Gray's Inn, Esq , who was eldest son
                 of John Bond, Master of the Savoy, and of the family of Bond of
                                                    [Aerth, co Cornwall

" 21   LUKE KEATING, second son of Robert K , of Knockagh, co Tipperary, Esq

" 29   RICHARD POMEROY, eldest son of William P , of Ballinacree, co Tipperary,

Aug 10   JOHN WATERS, of Brecon, Esq   [gent

Nov 27   EDWARD DOWNES, of Wennington, Essex, gent

" "   CUTHBERT MORLAND, gent , son of George M , of the city of Durham, Esq

" 28   JOHN FLETCHER, second son of James F , of the city of Dublin, merchant
                        folio 1,364

" "   JOHN TOWNLEY, eldest son of John T , of Newhouse, co York, Esq

" "   BENJAMIN GREGG, eldest son of Joseph G , of Manchester, Esq

Dec 4   ROBERT BIGLAND, gent , second son of Edward B , Serjeant-at Law
1699-1700
Jan 29   JAMES SOTHEBY, son and heir of James S , of Gray's Inn, Esq   [Esq

" "   WILLIAM SKYRME, son and heir of William S , of Lawhadden, co Pembroke,

Feb 2   FRANCIS SITWELL, son and heir of George S , of Eckington, co Derby, Esq

" "   GEORGE HALFEHIDE, gent (six years at Clement's Inn)
                        folio 1,365   [Durham, Esq.

" 5   JOHN CARR, gent , only son of John C , of Whitburne, near Sunderland, co

" 10   WILLIAM BELLAMY, of the Inner Temple, gent (admitted there Dec 28, 1692,
                 [by certificate of Arthur Weaver, Treasurer).

1699-1700.   folio 1,365—(continued)

Feb 12.   ROBERT BARTON, of Brigstock, co Northampton, gent.

Mar 16   JAMES UNIACKE, of Kilbrickilbeg, co Clare, gent
1700   [Esq

April 23   HUGH HUGHES, gent., son and heir of Roger H , of Placerock, co Anglesey,

,,   ,,   LAWRENCE COTTON, son and heir of Ralph C , of Birchall, co Chester, gent
                                                                       [York, gent

May 4   JOHN MAUDE, only son of Daniel M , of Alverthorpe, parish of Wakefield, co

folio 1,366

,,   6   RICHARD MUSGRVAE, only son of Edward M , of Ashby, Westmoreland, Esq ,
         deceased   [deceased

,,   7.   PHILIP HENSHAW, son and heir of Thomas H , of Billinghurst, Sussex, Esq ,

,,   13   THOMAS HOWE, eldest son of Thomas H , of Abbots Langley, Herts, Esq

,,   ,,   ALLEN JOHNSON, son and heir of Alexander J , of Rushton Grange, in
                                                        [Bolland, co York, Esq

,,   ,,   JOHN CAYLEY, son and heir of Cornelius C , of the city of York, Esq
                                                                       [Baronet

,   16   FRANCIS NEWDIGATE, fourth son of Richard N , of Arbury, co Warwick,

,,   27   PETER GOTT, second son of Peter G , of Gray's Inn, Esq   [gent

,,   28   THOMAS BUTLER, of Kilvelcagheir, in the Barony of Clanwilliam, co Tipperary,

folio 1,367

June 5   ANTHONY STAFFORD, son and heir of John S , of Shaw, co Derby, Esq

,,   7   JOHN MILOTT, fifth son of Robert M , of Whitehill, co Durham, Esq , deceased.

,,   8   WILLIAM MAHONY, only son of Cornelius M , of the city of Cork, merchant.

,,   11   WILLIAM GALWAY, son and heir of John G , of the city of Cork, Esq

,,   14   HENRY DOTTIN, junior, of Clement's Inn, gent

,,   19   THOMAS SUTTON, eldest son of Thomas S , of Leek, co Stafford, gent

folio 1,368.   [gent

,,   24   EDWARD FISHER, son and heir of Edward F , of Alton, co Southampton,

,,   ,,   ROBERT RAIKES son and heir of Robert R , of North Allerton, co York, gent

July 11   RICHARD BAGENALL, second son of Dudley B , late of St James's, Middlesex,
          Esq   [deceased

,,   12   JOHN TURNER, son of William T , late of Wakefield, co York, gent,

Oct 28   JAMES LIGHTBOURNE, son and heir of James L , of Manchester, Esq

Nov 7   JAMES BUTLER, son and heir of John B , of Barnwell Abbey, co Cambridge,
                                                        [Doctor of Laws.

,,   13   WILLIAM PLAYER, eldest son of William P , of this Inn, Esq

,,   25   GILFRID LAWSON, eldest son of Wilfrid L , of Brayton, Cumberland, Esq

,,   26   WILLIAM PHILLIPPS, son of Charles P , of Sandy Haven, co Pembroke,
                                                                       [Esq.

folio 1,369

,,   28   LEWKNOR L'ESTRANGE, eldest son of Roger L , of How, Norfolk, gent

,,   ,,   ADRIAN METCALFE, eldest son of John M , of this Inn, Esq.

1700-1   folio 1,369 – (continued)

Jan 18   THOMAS STRANGWAYS, eldest son of Thomas S , of Pickering, co York, gent
                                                              [Middlesex, grocer
,,   ,,   WILLIAM WALKTON, eldest son of Robert W , late of St Martins- n-the-Fields,

Feb   4   STEPHEN CROFT, eldest son of Thomas C , of Stillington, co York, Esq
1701
May   3   JOHN EYRE, son of Thomas E , of Hassop, co Derby, Esq

,,   15   FRANCIS LOWE, son of ——— L , late of this Inn, Esq.

,,   21   GEORGE OWEN, Esq , son and heir of George Owen, S T D , of co Pembroke
                             [specially admitted of Middle Temple, Feb 12, 1691)

,,   26   HUGH BRADY, second son of Patrick B , of Toniconally, co Cavan, Esq

                                 folio 1,370

,,   27   WILLIAM YATES, son and heir of Joseph Y , of this Inn, Esq

,.   31   ROBERT EDGAR, son and heir of Devereux E , who was the son of ——— E ,
                 Fellow of this Inn   [gent

June 10   JOHN VAUGHAN, eldest son of Thomas V , late of Farthinghooke, co Pembroke,

,,   23   ROBERT CLARKE, eldest son and heir of Sir Samuel C , Baronet, of Snailwell,
                 co Cambridge   [Edmunds, Suffolk, Esq

,,   24   THOMAS BARNARDISTON, eldest son and heir of Thomas B , of Bury St

July 12   WILLIAM DURRANT, son and heir of Thomas D , of Scottow, Norfolk, gent

Oct 14   ARTHUR NUGENT, of Clancorskoran, co Waterford, gent

,,   22   ELLIS KEY, eldest son of John K , of Long Leddenham, co Lincoln, gent

,,   28.   JOSEPH SLATERY, of Redmondstown, co Tipperary, eldest son of John S , of
                                                          [the same, gent

                                 folio 1,371

Nov   3   JAMES UVEDALE, second son of Robert U , of Enfield, Middlesex, LL D

,,   25   ROBERT BARKER, eldest son of Robert B , of Bredfield, Suffolk, Esq.

Dec 24   CORNELIUS CALLAGHAN, eldest son of Timothy C , of Bantry, co Cork, gent
1701-2
Jan 31   MARKE ROCH, eldest son of John R , of Robinson, co Pembroke, gent

Feb   5   TEMPEST SLINGER, eldest son of Nicholas S , of Dunnow, co York

,,   6   MATTHEW APPLEYARD, son of Matthew A , of Beverley, co York, Esq

,,   9   THOMAS PATE, of Leytonstone, Essex, gent , only son of Thomas P , of
                                                          [London, merchant

,,   14   MAURICE COLBRON, third son of John C , Chaplain of Gray's Inn

,,   18   MARMADUKE TOMLIN, eldest son of William T , of Riby co Lincoln

                                 folio 1,372.   [co Chester

Mar 20   ROBERT LOWE, second son of Samuel L , of Newton, parish of Middlewich,
1702
May   1   ROBERT BLOIS, eldest son of Charles B , of Cockfield, Suffolk, Baronet

,,   4   THOMAS COLTHURST, eldest son of Thomas C , of Gray's Inn, Esq.

,,   5   WALTER PLUMMER, son and heir of John P , of Blacksware, Herts, Esq

,   5   WILLIAM PLUMMER, second son of John P , of Blacksware, Herts, Esq.

.,   6   WILLIAM OLDFIELD, second son of Thomas O , of Bristol, gent

June 4   EDWARD BARNARD, eldest son of Edward B., of Beverley, co York, Esq

1702   folio 1,372—(*continued*)

June 9   NICHOLAS COLE, eldest son of Nicholas C, late of Brancepeth Castle, co [Durham, Esq, deceased

,, 19   JOHN THORNHILL, third son of George T., of Fixby, co York, Esq

,, 22   JOHN SMITH, eldest son of John S, of Wakefield, co York, gent

,, 30   THOMAS HINDMARSH, eldest son of John H, of Newcastle-on-Tyne, Esq

folio 1,373.

Oct. 2.   WILLIAM WELDON, of Knock, co Meath, gent   [of this Inn

Nov 13.   ARTHUR PLAYER, eldest son of William P, one of the Masters of the Bench

,, ,,   BEVERSHAM FILMER, second son of Robert F, of Sutton, Kent, Baronet.

,, 14   EDWARD DAVENPORT, second son of Edward D, of Stockport, co Chester, gent

,, 16   HENRY NEGUS, eldest son of Henry N, of Hoveton St Peter, Norfolk, Esq

,, ,,   RICHARD FULLER, third son of Samuel F, of Great Yarmouth, Norfolk, Esq

,, 25   EDWARD PHILLIPS, eldest son of James P, of Killymaenllwyd, co Carmarthen,

,, 26   ARTHUR JENNY, only son of Edmund J, of Bredfield, Suffolk, Esq   [Esq

folio 1,374

Dec 12   MAURICE WALL, of Limerick, Ireland, Esq

1702-3.
Jan 26.   DENIS CALLAGHAN, of Mountallan, co Clare, gent.

Feb 11   EDWARD WEBB, second son of John W, of St. Andrews, Holborn, Esq

,, 13   WILLIAM PEARSE, of London, gent

1703
Mar 30   ROGER CONINGSBY, eldest son of Roger C, of Potterells, Herts, Esq

April 22   WILLIAM FISHER, eldest son of William F, of St Andrew's Holborn, turner

,, 24   OLIVER CROMWELL, eldest son of Henry C, of St Andrew's Holborn, Esq

May 6   THOMAS WILKINSON, son and heir of Andrew W, of Borroughbriggs, co York,

June 7   JAMES BARRY, second son of Edmund B, of St James's, Middlesex, Esq [Esq

folio 1,375.

,, ,,   JOHN COLEMAN, eldest son of John C, of St James's, Middlesex, Esq

,, ,,   PETER HUGHES, of Lincoln's Inn, gent (admitted there Jan 23, 1693, by [certificate of Robert Dormer, Treasurer)

,, 15   PETER BETTESWORTH, junior, only son of Peter B, of Fytzhall, Sussex, gent.

,, 23   RICHARD WALSH, eldest son of Redmund W, of Culliney, co Cork, gent

,, 26   JOHN DOUGLAS, of Newcastle-on-Tyne, gent (admitted to Barnard's Inn, [Feb 22, 1683, by certificate of Silvester Petyt, Principal)

,, ,,   OLEY DOUGLAS, son and heir of John D, of Newcastle-on-Tyne, gent

Aug 6   ROBERT BAKER, son and heir of Robert B, of Hill Court, parish of Grafton [Flyford, co Worcester, gent

folio 1,376

,, 16   RICHARD BUTLER, gent, son and heir of Colonel John B, of Westcoate, parish of Callen, co Kilkenny   [gent

Oct 26   EDWARD GALE BOLDERO, gent, second son of Daniel B, of the city of York,

Nov 1   JOHN HOLT, eldest son of Rowland H, one of the Masters of the Bench

,, ,,   WILLIAM BURY, eldest son of William B, of Grantham, co Lincoln, Esq

,, ,,   ISHAM BAGGS, eldest son of John B, Esq, one of the Fellows of this Inn

1703	folio 1,376—*(continued)*
Nov 12	ARTHUR BRANTHWAITE, eldest son of Arthur B , of the city of Norwich, Esq
,, 25	WILLIAM BROMFEILD, third son of Thomas B , of St Andrew's, Holborn,
Dec 20	JOHN RAYNER, only son of John R , of Gray's Inn, Esq [apothecary.
,, ,,	WILLIAM SPICER (*alias* Helder), only son of Richard S (*alias* H) of Gray's [Inn, Esq
1703-4	folio 1,377.
Jan 25	JONATHAN DAVISON, fifth son of Timothy D , of Newcastle-on-Tyne [Esq
,, 26	MANNOCK STRICKLAND, second son of Robert S , of Sizergh, Westmoreland,
Feb 11	JAMES PEARSON, eldest son of William P , of St Andrew's, Holborn, gent
,, 21	SAMUEL CLARKE, second son of Samuel C , of Snailwell, co Cambridge, Knight
1704	
April 13	DANIEL CARROLL, eldest son of Anthony C , of Lysomby, co Tipperary, Knight
May 8	JOHN ROGERS, son of ——— R , of Clerkenwell, Middlesex, Doctor of Medicine
,, 9	GEOFFREY RODES, son and heir of William R , of Great Houghton, co York,
,, 10	JOHN ATKINSON, only son of Edward A , late of this Inn, Esq [Esq
	folio 1,378
June 20	JOHN ADAMS, of Camblesforth, co. York, Esq
, 26	WILLIAM LLOYD, eldest son of John L , of Garych, co Denbigh, Esq
July 4	THOMAS PARKYNS, second son of Thomas P., of Bunny, Notts, Baronet
Nov 10	JAMES POWYS, only son of Richard P , of Rochford, co Hereford, gent
,, 27	JOHN BURGH, gent , fourth son of Ulysses B , late Bishop of Ardagh, Ireland, deceased (admitted to Inner Temple Aug 6, 1698, by certificate of George [Wheeler, Under-treasurer)
,, ,,	SAMPSON PARKYNS, of the Middle Temple, Esq (specially admitted Sept 18, [1702, by certificate of Martin Ryder, Treasurer)
	folio 1,379
Dec 19	WASTELL MUSGRAVE, gent , third son of Richard M , of Hayton Castle, Cum- [berland, Baronet
1704 5	
Jan 27.	GUY VANE, second son of George V , of St Andrew's, Holborn, Esq [Baronet
,, 30	HENRY EDEN, gent , sixth son of Robert E , of West Auckland, co Durham,
Feb 1	FRANCIS DAYRELL, eldest son of Marmaduke D , of Shudy Camps, co Camb , Knight [deceased
,, 26	ROBERT BETHELL, son and heir of Robert B., late of Beverley, co York, gent ,
Mar 2	CHARLES WOGAN, eldest son of Patrick W , of Richardstown, co Kildare,
,, 3	IGNATIUS HUSSEY, third son of Walter H., of Donore, co Kildare, gent [gent
,, 19	HENRY BOULT, junior, eldest son of Henry B , of Gray's Inn, senior, Esq
1705	folio 1,380
May 1	ABNEY PARKER, eldest son of John P , of Fermoyle, co Longford, Knight
,, 9	WILLIAM BLUNDEN, only son of ——— B , of Basingstoke, Southampton, Esq
,, 17	RICHARD BONYTHON, gent , eldest son of Charles B , Serjeant at-Law, deceased
,, 19	GEORGE MEREDITH, only son of Richard M , of St Andrew's, Holborn, gent
June 14	JOHN BEAUMONT BYERLEY, eldest son of Charles B , of Belgrave, co Leicester, Esq [Esq
,, 20	GEORGE WALLIS, gent., son and heir of William W , of Wormleybury, Herts,
,. 21	THOMAS CURTIS, gent , only son of Robert C , late of London, gent , deceased

1705   **folio 1,381**

June 23.   LAURENCE AGAR, third son of William A , late of Earswick, co York, gent, deceased, and nephew by (*ex fratre*) the brother of Laurence A , Serjeant-at-Law   [co Derby, Esq

Nov 2   THOMAS SITWELL, third son of George S , of Renishaw, parish of Eckington,

,, 5   THOMAS STILES, son and heir of Thomas S , of Wallton, co Northampton, Esq

,, 17   JAMES DILLON, son and heir of Dominick D , of Bella, co Roscommon, Esq

,, ,,   ROBERT BAYNES, eldest son of Robert B , of Knowsthrope, co York, Esq

,, 28   THOMAS WAINWRIGHT, son and heir of Wayford W , of Gray's Inn, gent

,, ,,   ROBERT FENWICK, son and heir of John F , of Burrowhall, Westmoreland, Esq.

1705 6   [Masters of the Bench of this Inn

Jan 31   WILLIAM BUSBY, second son of William B , Esq , deceased, late one of the

Feb 8   RICHARD SHERLOCK, eldest son of William S , of Ballymore, co West-[meath, Esq

                 folio 1,382

,, 9   THOMAS BREWER, son and heir of James B , of Reading, Berks, Doctor of Medicine   [Knight

,, 11   THOMAS GREENFIELD, third son of Christopher G , of Preston, co Lancaster,

Mar 1   ROWLAND LLOYD, second son of Simon L , of Bally, co Merioneth, Esq
1706

April 15   WILLIAM EUSTACE, son of James E , of the city of Dublin, Esq

,, ,   WILLIAM HENDLEY, eldest son of Bowyer H , of Otham, Kent, Esq

,, 29   THOMAS PLAYER, second son of William P , Esq , one of the Masters of the Bench of this Inn.   [Esq , deceased

May 20   THOMAS YARBURGH, eldest son and heir of Thomas Y , of Campsall, co York, Esq , deceased.   [deceased

,, ,,   EDMUND YARBURGH, second son of Thomas Y , of Campsall, co York, Esq ,

June 3   ROGER WILLIAMS, of the Middle Temple, Esq (admitted there Sept 10, 1703, by certificate of John Whitfield, Treasurer, and to Bar there Hilary [Term, 1704, by certificate of James Buck, Under-treasurer.

                 folio 1,383

,, 8   THOMAS PLACE, son and heir of Edward B , late of Gray's Inn, deceased

,, 14   JOHN CHRISTIAN, son and heir of Evan C , of Unerigg, Cumberland, Esq

,, 22   THOMAS FOTHERGILL, eldest son of Richard F , of the city of York, gent, [deceased

Aug 1   WILLIAM DYOSE, eldest son of Thomas D , Esq , one of the Masters of the Bench of this Inn   [of Medicine

Oct 23   WALTER CRUISE, eldest son of Christopher C , of the city of Dublin, Doctor

Nov 9   HUGH REILLY, eldest son of James R , of co Westmeath, Esq

,, 14   MICHAEL BARSTOW, eldest son of Thomas B , of the city of York, gent

,, 15   ELI ELISHA PHILLIPPS, fourth son of Onia P , of the city of Norwich, gent

,, 28.   THOMAS LYNCH, eldest son of James L , of Lismacanagan, co. Cavan, gent [deceased

                 folio 1,384

Dec 9   THOMAS ROBSON, of the Bishoprick of Durham, gent

1706-7
Feb 25   JOHN FOWLE, eldest son of John F , of Broomhall, Norfolk Esq

1707.	folio 1,384—(continued).
May 2	THOMAS SOTHEBY, second son of James S , Esq , of this Inn
,, 9	ROGER MEREDITH, of Leeds, Kent, Esq (specially admitted to the Middle [Temple May 29, 1694, by certificate of Thomas Lake Treasurer)
,, 21	ROBERT LEGARD, eldest son of John L , of Anlaby, co Kingston-on-Hull, Esq
,, 24	WILLIAM HULTON, son and heir of John H , of the city of Chester, gent.
Nov 5	THOMAS FREEMAN, son and heir of Arthur F., of the city of London, gent
1707-8	
Jan 31	WILLIAM REVELEY, son and heir of William R , of Kirby Wiske, co York, gent (admitted to Lincoln's Inn, Nov 10, 1702, by certificate of James [Montagu, Treasurer)
,, ,,	THOMAS METCALFE, of Nappa, parish of Aysgarth, co York (admitted to the Inner Temple, Oct 10, 1704, by certificate of William Barnsley, Treasurer)

folio 1,385

Feb 2	RICHARD LEVITT, second son of Francis L , of the city of London
,, ,,	FRANCIS BACON, eldest son of Waller B , of this Inn
,, ,,	GEORGE MONSON, second son of George M , of this Inn.
,, 10	WILLIAM JOHNSON, gent (admitted to Barnard's Inn, Feb 4, 1691)
,, 11	ANDREW BURTON, son and heir of Andrew B , of Oakham, co Rutland, gent
1708	
April 20	EDWARD BROME, son and heir of William B , of Farnborough, Kent, Esq
,, 22	RICHARD GARTH (lately called Boevey), of Morden, Surrey, Esq [merchant
,, 27	THOMAS WESTERN, son and heir of Thomas W , junior, late of London,
May 1	JOHN DAVENANT, second son of John D , of Lanford, Wilts, Esq [deceased
,, 6	JOHN REVETT, son and heir of Thomas R , of Brandeston, Suffolk, Esq ,
June 15	WILLIAM TURNER, son and heir of William T , of Gray's Inn, Esq
,, 16	JOSHUA DOUGLAS, second son of John D , of this Inn, Esq
,, 18	EDMUND HOPWOOD, of Hopwood, co Lancaster, Esq [Doctor
Aug 25	THEOBALD GASCOIGNE, eldest son of Joseph G , of Enfield, Middlesex, Theol
Oct 21	WILLIAM BURT, of Gray's Inn, gent
Nov 4	DROPE HALEY, son and heir of John H , late of Stanmore, Middlesex, gent
,, 20	SAMUEL GOWLAND, of Durham, son and heir of Ralph G , gent , of the same

folio 1,386

, ,,	RALPH GOWLAND, second son of Ralph G , of Durham, gent
Dec 10	EDMUND BARSTOW, son and heir of Edmund B , of Hingerskill, co York, Esq
,, 27	EDMUND FLOYD, of Shrewsbury, Esq
1708-9	[Baronet
Feb 3	WILLIAM BLOIS, second son of Charles B , of Cockfield Hall, co Suffolk,
,, 10	CORNELIUS CAYLEY, third son of Cornelius C , of York, Esq
1709	
May 7	EDWARD CHETHAM, son and heir of Edward C , of Manchester, Esq
,, 12	WILLIAM OWEN, of Porkington, Salop, Esq
,, 26	CHARLES USHER, of Carlisle, gent (admitted to the Inner Temple, Feb 10 [1699, by certificate of William Simpson, Treasurer)

1709   **folio 1,387**

June 1   GREGORY GEERING, son and heir of Gregory G , of Denchworth, Berks, Esq

,,   11   SAMUEL CROMWELL, second son of Samuel C , of Mansfield, Notts, Doctor [of Medicine

July 11   JOHN BRACK, second son of William B , of the city of York, gent

,,   12   WILLIAM BOOTH, of Upton, Cheshire, gent

Oct 22   SAMUEL BROWNING, of London, gent   [1702]

Nov 16   GEORGE DASHWOOD, of East Knoyle, Wilts (admitted to Lincoln's Inn, April 3,

,,   17   JOHN HUMPHREYS, second son of John H , of Caerunion, co Menoneth, gent

,,   19   THOMAS STEPHENS, ot Gloucester, gent (specially admitted to the Middle [Temple, June 26, 1683, by certificate of Peter Broughton, Treasurer)

,,   22   JOHN LANCE, son and heir of Nicholas L , of St Martins-in-the-Fields, [Middlesex, gent

,,   27   EDWARD RIGBY, son and heir of Charles R , of the town of Lancaster, Esq

folio 1,388.

,,   28   ROBERT JOCELYN, son and heir of Thomas J , of Sawbridgeworth, Herts, gent

1709-10
Feb   4   MARMADUKE HORSELEY, son and heir of William H , of Carnarvon, gent

,   7   MICHAEL GODFREY SMITHSON, son and heir of Hugh S , of Gray's Inn, Esq

,,   8   THOMAS BROWNE, son and heir of Thomas B , of the city of Dublin, Esq

,,   10   DAVID CAMPBELL, of St James's, Westminster, Esq

,,   11   THOMAS BRANTHWAITE, second son of Arthur B , of Norwich, Esq

1710
April 26   DENIS DALY, of Frenchbrook, co Mayo, gent

May 3   PETER DALY, second son of Denis D , of Carownekelly, co Galway, gent

,,   4   GAMALIEL NIGHTINGALE, eldest son of Edward N , of Kneesworth, co [Cambridge, Esq

,,   16   THOMAS POWNALL, son and heir of Thomas P , of Lincoln, Esq

,,   18   NATHANIEL GYLES, gent (admitted to Clifford's Inn, May 8, 1689)

folio 1,389

June 9   LANGHAM ROKEBY, son and heir of Benjamin R , of London, merchant

.,   10   WILLIAM WYNNE, son of William W , of Beaumaris, Anglesea

,,   11   MEUX RANT, only son of John R , of Drayton, Norfolk, Esq

,,   29   RICHARD BELWARD, only son of William B , of Suffolk, gent , deceased

Oct 20   ANDREW ARCEDECKNE, of Carrowmore, co Galway, gent   [deceased

,,   31.   HUGH FOWLER, eldest son of John F , of Haverfordwest, co Pembroke, Esq ,

Dec 9   BRADSHAW PEIRSON, son and heir of William P., of Stokesley, co York, Esq

1710-11
Jan 20   JAMES CAWLEY, son and heir of Robert C , of Gwersilt, co Denbigh, Esq , deceased (admitted to Lincoln's Inn, May 27, 1703, by certificate of Charles Cox, Treasurer)   [Baronet

Feb 6   ROBERT WILLIAMS, second son ot William W , of Glascoed, co Denbigh,

,,   8   FRANCIS LOGGIN, son and heir of Thomas L , of Butlers Marston, co. Warwick, Esq   [Esq

,,   21   SIMON MOUNTFORT, son and heir of Edward M , of Calmore, co Stafford,

1710-11		folio 1,390.

Feb 28   CHARLES FELIHAM, of St Giles-in-the-Fields, Esq (of full age)

Mar 13   DEVEREUX EDGAR, second son of Devereux E , of Ipswich, Suffolk, Esq
1711

April 17 DAVID DUANE, second son of Thadeus D , of Clonmell, co Tipperary, gent

,,   ,,   THOMAS MACNAMARA, of the city of Annapolis, province of Maryland,
          [America, Esq

May 1.   NICHOLAS LYNDLEY, son and heir of John L , of Gray's Inn, gent

,,   2   RICHARD SHERARD, second son of Richard S , of Lobthorpe, co Lincoln, Esq

,,   10   THOMAS WILLIAMS, third son of Richard W , of Edwinsford, co. Carmarthen,
          [Knight, deceased

,,   15   THOMAS DYER, gent (admitted to Staple Inn, May 27, 1707)

,,   18   SAMUEL FINCH, son and heir of Roger F , of Shadeoak, Salop, Esq.

June 29   RAMSDEN BARNARD, third son of Edward B , of North Dalton, cc. York, Esq.

folio 1,391.

,,   ,,   WILLIAM NELSON, son and heir of Marmaduke N , of Beverley, co York, gent

,,   ,,   ROWLAND HOLT, third son of Rowland H , of Gray's Inn, Esq

July 30   THEOBALD MATHEW, second son of Theobald M , of Thomastown, co
          Tipperary, Esq   [gent

Oct 11   WILLIAM COLLINGWOOD, of Westminster, gent , son of Robert C , of the same,

Nov 14   JOSEPH RICHARDSON, only son of Joseph R , of Dunsfold, Surrey, clerk

,,   23   THOMAS CALDECOTT, of Catthorpe, co Leicester, Esq (specially admitted to
          Middle Temple, Aug 18, 1709, by certificate of Joseph Offley, Treasurer)

,,   24   THOMAS CLENNELL, now of St. John's College, Cambridge, second son of
          [(John) C

folio 1,392   [thwaite, co York, gent

,,   27   CHRISTOPHER KITCHINGMAN, son and heir of William K , of Carleton Hus-

1711-12   [1707, by certificate of William Ettricke Treasurer)
Feb   1   EDWARD SHORT, of Fordwich, Kent (admitted to the Middle Temple, Oct 27,

,,   2   WARDELL GEORGE WESTBY, son and heir of Thomas W , of Ravenfield, co
          [York, Esq

,,   6   JOHN SCOTT, son and heir of John S , of Newbay, co. Wexford, Esq
1712

April 15 CHARLES MOYLNEUX, second son of Francis M , of Teversall, Notts, Baronet.

May   1   WILLIAM PRICE, third son of William P., of Ludlow, Salop, gent.

,,   3   ABRAHAM BARBOUR, of St Andrews, Holborn, gent

,,   ,,   JOHN STARR, of Fryerage-juxta-Yarm, co. York, gent.

folio 1,393.   [Esq

,,   13   BENEDICT ARTHUR, son and heir of John A , of Great Cabragh, co Dublin,

,,   28   JOSEPH STANWIX, son and heir of Lancelot A , of Glanssenby, Cumberland,

,,   ,,   WILLIAM KING, of Ealing, Middlesex, Esq   [gent

,,   29   JOSIAH JAMES HANSES, only son of Charles H , late of Gray's Inn, Esq

,,   30   AMBROSE MANATON, son and heir of Francis M , of Manaton, co Cornwall,
          Esq   [clerk.

June 10   SAMUEL PRIGG, son and heir of Samuel P , of Stanton Drew, co Somerset,

July 12   CHARLES JONES, son of Charles J , of Foord, parish of Lanmartin, co Mon-
          [mouth, Esq.

1712   **folio 1,394**

Aug   1   PETER FRENCH, son and heir of Thomas F , of Muckcullin, co Galway

  „   2.   THOMAS FIELD, son and heir of John F , of Hitchin, Herts, gent

Nov 17   JOSEPH MARTIN, son and heir of John M , of Durham, gent

Oct 23   ROBERT CRANMER, third son of Joseph C , of Gray's Inn, Esq

Nov 28   RICHARD SUPPLE, of Aghadoe, co Cork, Esq

Dec 23   THOMAS CHOLMELEY, son and heir of Thomas C , of Bransby, co York, Esq

1712-13

Jan 22   JOHN SHEPHEARD, son and heir of John S , of Hill-upon-Coate, Salop, gent
           (admitted to the Middle Temple, Jan 20, 1708, by certificate of T
           [Burgh, Treasurer)

                                         folio 1,395

Feb   6   FRANCIS NEALE, gent (admitted to Thavies Inn, ———, 1672)

  „   10   HUGH WILLIAMS, son and heir of John W , of the city of Chester, Esq

  „   11   TIMOTHY LOWE, son and heir of Timothy L , of Newark, co Gloucester, Esq

  „   14   JOHN JOHNSON, of Kingston-on-Hull, gent

  „   17   FRANCIS FOOTE, son and heir of John F , of Verian, co Cornwall, Esq
1713   [deceased

April 10   EDWARD LLOYD, son and heir of Edward L , of Kensington, Middlesex, Esq ,

May   4   WILLIAM HODGSON, of Bascodike, Cumberland, gent

                                         folio 1,396.

  ,   7.   CHARLES MONSON, third son of George M , of Broxbourne, Herts, Esq.

  „   15   JOHN HUGHES, son and heir of Samuel H , of Laugharne, co Carnarvon, Esq

June 3.   THOMAS WILLIS, second son of William W , of Thames Street, London, gent ,

  „   10   WILLIAM ASHTON, of Salford, co Lancaster, gent   [deceased

  „   12. WILLIAM BRIDGES, of Tibberton, co Hereford, Esq , one of the Six Clerks
           in Chancery (Specially admitted to Middle Temple, Nov 19, 1702,
           [by certificate of Joseph Offley, Treasurer)

  „   20   EDMUND WATSON, son and heir of Edmund W , of Hague, co York, Esq

                                         folio 1,397

  „   „   GEORGE MAYFIELD, Esq (admitted to Barnard's Inn, Feb. 14, 1706)

  „   23   DAVID DAVENPORT, son and heir of Monk D , of Woodford, co Chester, gent

  „   24   DANIEL MACNAMARA, son and heir of Florence M , of Ardclony, co. Clare, Esq

Oct. 26   JOHN WISHAW, gent (admitted to Clifford's Inn, May 10, 1700)

Nov   5   WILLIAM BALL, of Queen's College, Oxford

  „   20   THOMAS JONES, of Newcastle, co Glamorgan, gent (admitted to Lincoln's Inn,
           [Feb. 20, 1707, by certificate of John Hungerford, Treasurer)

  „   3   RICHMOND GARNEYS, only son of Clere G , of Heddenham, Norfolk, Esq

  „   23   WILLIAM DERMER, only son of James D , of Gray's Inn, Esq

                                         folio 1,398.

  „   24. WENTWORTH OGLE, only son of Luke O , of Royston, co York, Esq

1713-14.

Jan. 27   ANDREW HAMILTON, of Maryland, America, gent

Feb. 5   JOHN BROWNING, son and heir of Samuel B., of Gray's Inn, Esq

1713-14   folio 1,398—(*continued*)

Feb   6.   TEMPEST THORNTON, son and heir of Richard T, late of Leeds, co York, [Esq, deceased

,,   8   MADDEN FRENCH, son and heir of John F, of Derry, co. Galway, Esq

,,   ,,   JOSEPH BURKE, son and heir of Miles B, of Balleley, co Galway, Esq,

1714   [deceased.

April 22   THOMAS WHITEHEAD, of Preston, co Lancaster (admitted to Lincoln's Inn, [June 29, 1705)

May 11.   RICHARD DRAPER, son and heir of Thomas D, of London, mercer, deceased

,,   25   EDWARD BROWNE, son and heir of Joseph B, of Shepton Mallet, co [Somerset, Esq.

folio 1,399   [gent

,,   26   MICHAEL HOWARD, son and heir of Peter H, of Streamstown, co Westmeath,

June   7   JOHN LEACH, son and heir of John L, of Fulletby, co. Lincoln, gent, deceased   [deceased

,,   10   THOMAS MAYNARD, son and heir of John M, of Yarm, co York, gent,

Oct.   4   RICHARD NEWSTEAD, son and heir of Richard N, of Cavenaghstown, co [Westmeath, Esq.

,,   11.   JOHN TWISLETON, son and heir of Thomas T., of Widdington, Essex, clerk

,,   21   WILLIAM ALSTON, son and heir of Samuel A, of Bramford, Suffolk, Esq.

Nov   9   RICHARD ACKLAM, of London, gent

,,   29   MILES BRANTHWAITE, second son of Arthur B, of Hethel, Norfolk, Esq

,,   ,,   JOHN PRICE, son and heir of Edward P, of Aberknithon, co. Brecon

folio 1,400.   [Somerset, Esq, deceased

Dec   8   CHARLES NEWMAN, fourth son of Francis Holles N, of North Cadbury, co

,,   10   ANTHONY SMITHSON, second son of Hugh S, of Gray's Inn, Esq

1714-15   [of the Masters of the Bench of this Inn

Feb   5   THOMAS BARRETT, son and heir of George B, Esq, deceased, formerly one

,,   ,,   JAMES BRAND, son of James B, of Polstead Hall, Suffolk, Esq

Mar   8   JOHNSON MANWARING, son and heir of James M, of the city of Chester, Esq

,,   14   JOHN TOWNELEY, second son of Charles T, of Towneley, co Lancaster, Esq,

,,   15   WILLIAM LOCKEY, son and heir of ———   [deceased

,,   ,,   THOMAS PEACHELL, son and heir of Thomas P, of Gray's Inn, Esq

1715   folio 1,401

April 30   RICHARD FRANK, son and heir of Matthew F, late of Campsall, co York, Esq, deceased   [of Richard Graham, Principal)

,,   ,,   JOHN WOLFE, gent (admitted to Clifford's Inn, March 24, 1687, by certificate

May 17   JOHN RANDOLPH, of Virginia, gent

,,   20   PATRICK GARDEN, son and heir of James G, of Aberdeen, Scotland, Doctor

,,   26   ABRAHAM GAMAGE, son and heir of Abraham G, of London, gent, deceased

June 29.   THOMAS CASE, son and heir of Jonathan C, of Redhasels, co Lancaster, [Esq

July   1   JOHN HOWES, son and heir of ——— H, of Morningthorpe, Norfolk, Esq.

,,   13   CHRISTOPHER LAYER, son and heir of John L, of Booton, Norfolk, gent, [deceased

1715   folio 1,402

Aug   1   RICHARD BLOWER, son and heir of Richard B, of Wighton, Norfolk, gent

  „   6   GERARD DILLON, of Mount Dillon, *alias* Sleavyne, co Roscommon, Esq,
          son and heir of Richard FitzJames D, of Dunsany, co Westmeath,
                                          [Esq, deceased, formerly of this Society

Sept 1   CHARLES COKER, son and heir of William C, of Winchester, Hants, Doctor
                                                                    [of Medicine

Nov 19   LLOYD KENYON, son and heir of Thomas K, of Manchester, gent

  „ 24   THOMAS EDWARDS, son and heir of Thomas E, of the Society of Lincoln's
1715 16   [Inn Esq (under age)

Jan   8   JAMES MICKLETON, son and heir of Michael M, of Crookehall, co Durham,
          Esq, deceased (admitted to the Inner Temple, Nov 26, 1705, by
                                          [certificate of George Wheeler, Under-treasurer)

Feb   7   JOHN ELLIS, son and heir of John E, of Gray's Inn, Esq

                                       folio 1,403

  „   „   RUMNEY DIGLE, son and heir of Samuel D, of Gray's Inn, gent

  „ 11   JOHN RICHARDSON, son and heir of William R, of High Fearnley, West
                                                          [Riding of York, gent.

  „ 27   JOHN MAIRE, son and heir of Christopher M, of Hart Bushes, co Durham,
          gent   [gent

Mar   9   THOMAS WILLIAMS, son and heir of Maurice W, of Aberdeen (*sic*), co Denbigh,
1716
April 24 THOMAS WILLIAMS, son and heir of Thomas W, of Stoke Neyland, Suffolk,
          Esq (admitted at Lincoln's Inn, Dec 17, 1707, by certificate of Spencer
                                                          [Cowper, Treasurer)

May   4   JOHN DERBYSHIRE BIRKHEAD, son and heir of John B, of Isleworth,
          Middlesex, gent   [co York, clerk, deceased

  „ 28   THOMAS HARDCASTLE, son and heir of Thomas H, of Larton, *alias* Laverton

June 6   WILLIAM LLOYD, son and heir of Thomas L, of Penpedwest, co Pembroke,
          Esq. (admitted to the Inner Temple, May 9, 1705, by certificate of
                                          [Grimbald Pauncefote, treasurer)

  „ 11   WILLIAM WETHERHEAD, son and heir of Christopher W, of Knights Stani-
                                                          [forth, co York, gent

                                       folio 1,404

  „ 15. HENRY EDWARDS, son and heir of John E, of Waltham, Essex, Esq,
          deceased (admitted to Lincoln's Inn, Nov 23, 1711, by certificate of
                                                          [Spencer Cowper, Treasurer)

  „   „   BARTYN BURTON, second son of Andrew B, of Gray's Inn, Esq, deceased

  „   „   THOMAS THURSTON, son and heir of John T, of Bramford, Suffolk, gent

  „ 28. ASHTON WARNER, second son of —— W, of the Isle of Antigua, America (*sic*)

July 3   JOHN CRASTER, son and heir of John C, of Craster, Northumberland, Esq.

  „   7   PETER WESTON, son and heir of Peter W, of the city of Chester, Esq, deceased

Aug 27   JAMES POWELL, son and heir of William P, of Poole Hall, co Monmouth,
          and of this Society, Esq   [marthen, Esq.

  „ 28   RICHARD VAUGHAN, son and heir of John V, of Court Derllys, co Car-

                                       folio 1,405   [Esq

Oct 19   THOMAS DANE, second son of Drue D, of St. Andrews, Holborn, Middlesex,

1716   folio 1,405—(continued)

Oct 26   GEORGE TURNER, son and heir of John T, of Swanwick, co Derby, Esq

„   28   JOHN HEALEY, son and heir of Charles H, of Frodingham, co Lincoln, Esq,
              deceased   [gent, deceased

Nov 6   RICHARD BURDETT, son and heir of William B, of Ugglebarnby, co York,

„   7   THOMAS WILLIAMSON, son and heir of Robert W, of Allington, co Lincoln,
1716-17   [gent

Jan 19   WILLIAM BRISTOW, second son of Thomas B, of Beesthorpe, Notts, Esq

Feb 6.   GEORGE CORBETT, fourth son of Richard C., of Shabree Park, Salop, Esq.

„   „   JOHN FORTESCUE, son and heir of William F., of Cookhill, co Worcester,
                                                      [Esc, deceased.

„   20   JOHN MORRICE, son and heir of Henry M, of the town of Nottingham, gent

„   21   DANIEL DULLANY, of Prince George Co, province of Maryland, America,
                                                              [gent

folio 1,406.

„   22   DENIS L'ISLE, of Cambridge, LL B, son of Maurice L, of Kildale, co York,

„   23   HENRY BLAKE, of Galway, Ireland, Esq   [clerk

1717
May 23   ROBERT BRAGE, son and heir of William B, of Hatfield Peverell, Essex, Esq

June 6   DAVID ATKINSON, gent (admitted to Lincoln's Inn, June 27, 1711, by certifi-
                                        [cate of Laurence Carter, Treasurer)

„   20   WILLIAM FOULKES, second son of Martin F, late of Gray's Inn, Esq, deceased

July 1   WILLIAM SUGER, son of Zachary S, of Feliskirk, co York, clerk

„   4   WILLIAM VAVASOUR, son and heir of William V, of Weston, co York, Esq

„   5.   JAMES LAWES, eldest son of Nicholas L, Governor of Jamaica, Knight

„   6.   JOHN POTTER, of Cranbrooke, Kent, gent.

Oct 23   JOHN HAWLEY, second son of Joseph H, of Harby, co Leicester, gent., deceased

folio 1,407

Dec 23   BRYAN MAC SWEENEY, son and heir of Morrough Mac S, of Dublin, Doctor
1717-18   [of Laws

Jan. 22. HUTCHINS WILLIAMS, son and heir of William Peer W, of Gray's Inn, Esq

„   „   WILLIAM PEER WILLIAMS, second son of William Peer W, of Gray's Inn, Esq

„   23   WILLIAM BONNER, son and heir of William B, of St Andrews, Holborn, gent
1718
April 23 THOMAS SMITH, of Tower Royal, parish of St. Anthonys, London, gent

„   26   EDMUND HOSKINS, second son of John H, of Carshalton, Surrey, Esq,
              deceased (admitted to Middle Temple, Nov 10, 1715, by certificate of
                                          [Edward Jauncy, Treasurer)

May 9   JOHN MOLINS, son and heir of John M, of Covent Garden, gent, deceased

folio 1,408

„   10   NATHANIEL NORBURY, son and heir of John N, of the city of Chester, gent

„   17. WILLIAM HODY, of Spettisbury, co Dorset, gent

„   30   THOMAS DIXON, son and heir of Joseph D, of Islington, Norfolk, gent

June 1.   JAMES COMERFORD, son and heir of Edward C, of Maganstowr, co Tipper-
              ary, gent   [gent, deceased

„   14   FRANCIS BRADSHAW, fifth son of William B, of Abergavenny, co Monmouth,

1718   folio 1,408—(*continued*).

June 16   THOMAS GWYLLIM, son and heir of Thomas G., of Old Court, co Hereford, Esq

,, 23   THOMAS SMITH, gent , second son of Thomas S , late of Brignal, co. York, clerk

July 10   CHARLES ELSLEY, son of William E , of Ryther, co York, clerk

Sept 13   JOSEPH BARNES, son of Joseph B , of Newcastle-on-Tyne, Esq , deceased.

folio 1,409

,, 26   HENRY CARROLL, son and heir of Charles C , of Maryland, America, Esq

Oct 17   JOHN STANHOPE, son of John S , of Horseforth, co York, Esq

Nov 8   EDMUND BARKER, son and heir of Edmund B , of Gleadow, parish of Leeds, [West Riding of York

,, 9   JOHN GORDON, son and heir of John G , of the city of London, gent

,, 18   JOHN WILLIAMS, third son of John W , of the city of Chester, Esq

,, 22   ROGER MANSUER, of Stiffkey, Norfolk, gent

,, ,,   CHARLES BRERETON, of the city of Gloucester, gent

1718-19

Jan 3   ROBERT PAUL, of the city of London, Esq   [Esq , deceased.

,, 23   SAMUEL COTTON, son and heir of Bernard C , of Dadlington, co Leicester,

folio 1,410

,, ,,   GEORGE BOWES, third son of William B , of Streatlam Castle, co Durham,

,, 24   NEWCOMEN WALLIS, of Louth, co Lincoln, gent   [Knight.

,, 25   ROBERT ROBINSON, son and heir of William R , of Scarborough, co. York, Esq ,

,, 26   JOHN SOTHEBY, fourth son of James S., of Gray's Inn, Esq   [deceased.

1719   [gent.

Mar 28   JOHN LOCKER, eldest son of Stephen L., of the parish of St Helens, London,

May 21   THOMAS PENSON, fourth son of Thomas P , of Lilleshall, Salop, gent

,, 23   FLEXMER DAKINS, son and heir of Charles D , of Gray's Inn Lane, gent

June 6   HUMPHREY MONOUX, son and heir of Lewis M , one of the Masters of the

,, 18   CHARLES MEIN, of the city of London, Esq   [Bench of this Inn

folio 1,411

,, 19   BYAM WOOD, gent (admitted to Staple Inn, ——— 1689)   [ary, Esq

July 30   REDMOND BRADSTREET, second son of Simon B , of Port Lahane, co Tipper-

Sept. 3   JOHN CAY, son and heir of John C , of Laygate, co Durham, gent

,, 19   JOHN BEDINGFEILD, of Sturston, Norfolk, gent   [York, gent , deceased

Oct 15   WILLIAM STABLES, gent , son and heir of Leonard S , late of Pontefract, co

,, ,,   THOMAS BARNES, son of Joseph B , of Newcastle-on-Tyne, Esq , deceased

Nov 10   MATTHEW PRICE, second son of Vaughan P , of Newtown, co Montgomery, [Baronet

,, 11   EDWARD COLLINGWOOD, son of Edward C , of Byker, Northumberland, Esq

folio 1,412

,, 12   BROWNLOW SHERARD, son and heir of Brownlow S , of Whitehall, in the

1719-20   [liberty of Westminster, Esq

Jan 15   FRANCIS BISHOP, third son of William B , of Frencham, Surrey, Esq

,, ,,   BENJAMIN PURCHASE, son and heir of Francis B , of Norton, co Durham, Esq

		folio 1,412—(continued)
1719-20		
Feb	2	DANIEL DOLINS, of Lincoln's Inn (admitted there Oct 21, 1713, by certificate [of Sir William Thompson, Knight, Treasurer)
.,	12	JOHN CLARKE, son and heir of John C, of Melles, Suffolk, Esq [Esq
Mar	11	LEONARD DYKES, son and heir of Fretchville D, of Warthall, Cumberland,
1720		[Cambridge, Esq
April	5	EDWARD NIGHTINGALE, gent, second son of Edward N, of Kneesworth, co.

folio 1,413.

May	3	JAMES BURKIN, son and heir of John B, of Burlingham, Norfolk, Esq.
,,	,,	LUKE ROBINSON, third son of Charles R., of Kingston-on-Hull, co York, Esq.
,,	14	THOMAS NICHOLSON, son and heir of John N, of Hawkesdale, Cumberland, Esq
,,	,,	EDWARD ROOME, son and heir of Stephen R, of Fleet Street, London, gent
,,	16	WILLIAM HINTON, of St Margarets, Westminster, gent [Esc, deceased.
,,	,,	RICHARD BENDYSHE, second son of Thomas B, of Barrington, co Cambridge,
June	3	THOMAS WARD, son and heir of Robert W, of Lakenham, Norfolk, gent
,,	18	JOHN WILLIAMS, son of John W, of Ty-fry, co Anglesea, Esq.
July	5	ROGER HOLLAND, son and heir of ——— H, of Chippenham, Wilts, Esq

folio 1,414.

Aug	10	PETER ELWIN, second son of Fountaine E, of Thurning, Norfolk, gent
,,	22.	IGNATIUS KELLY, son and heir of Edmund K, of Castle Ruby, co Ros- [common, Esq
Sept	6	SAMUEL HAYNES, son and heir of Hopton H, of the city of Westminster, gent
,,	21	EGERTON DARBY, son of Thomas D, of the city of York, gent., deceased.
Oct	21	JOSEPH BALL, of Rappahannock, Virginia, gent
.,	25.	BARNABY BACKWELL, second son of Richard B, of the city of London, Esq
,,	31	HENRY CRANMER, gent, of Furnival's Inn
Nov	11.	JOHN OWEN, son of Robert O, of Penrhos, co Anglesey, Esq

folio 1,415

,,	14	JOSEPH CLOWES, fourth son of Samuel C, of Manchester, merchant [clerk.
,,	18	WILLIAM SMITH, gent, eldest son of Thomas S, late of Brignall, co York,
Dec	5	SAMUEL WELLES, son and heir of Samuel W, of Chipping-Wycombe, Bucks, [gent, deceased
1720-1		[tificate of G Dolben, Treasurer)
Jan	25	THOMAS DENISON (of the Inner Temple, admitted Feb 12, 1718, by cer-
Feb	8	WILLIAM CLIFTON, second son of Gervase C, of Notts, Baronet
,,	10	HENRY DODSWORTH, second son of John D, of Thornton Watlass, co York,
,,	13	WILLIAM SPEIDELL, of the city of London, gent [Esq, deceased
Mar	1	JAMES GRIMSTON, son and heir of John G, of Bridlington, co York, gent

folio 1,416.

,,	14	JOHN FREDERICK, son and heir of John F, of Bampton, Oxon, Esq
1721		
May	8.	JOHN BLOIS, fourth son of Charles B, of Cockfield Hall, in Yoxford, Suffolk,
,,	10	PHILIP HARLAND, of Sutton in Galters, co York, Esq [Baronet

1721   folio 1,416—(*continued*)

May 27   ROBERT THOROTON, only son of Thomas T , of the city of Lincoln, Esq

June 21 LUKE THOMPSON, Esq (of the Inner Temple, admitted Nov 17, 1701, by
         certificate of George Wheeler, Vice-Treasurer).   [Norfolk, Esq

„   22   ROBERT CLOUGH, junior, son and heir of Robert C , of Hockwold-cum-Wilton,

„   29   EDWARD PRICE, eldest son of Edward P , of Aberkanithon, co Brecon, gent

July 1 JOHN METCALFE, second son of John M , Esq , one of the Masters of the
         Bench (admitted to the Middle Temple, Nov 21, 1711, by certificate
                                            [of Isaac Jacksone, Vice-Treasurer)

folio 1,417.

Sept 4 EDMUND JENKINS, son and heir of John J , of the Isle of Barbados, Esq

„   11   GEORGE MIDDLETON, son and heir of George M , of South Shields, Durham,
         gent , deceased   [Waterford, Esq

„   20   RICHARD FITZGERALD, son and heir of Nicholas F , of King's Meadow, co

Oct   5 JOHN STAFFORD HOWARD (Hon), of Stafford, Esq

Nov 15   EDWARD EDGWORTH, Esq (had his standing as from Feb 2, 1716)

„   17   WILLIAM VAUGHAN, of Bronhilog, co Denbigh, gent

„   18   WILLIAM HAYTON, junior, of Ivinghoe, Bucks, gent

„   „   NEALE SHELDON, of Thavies Inn, gent

„   „   HENRY MORGAN, of Henbloas, co Anglesey, gent

„   19   JOHN HILL, son and heir of Thomas H , of Tarriers, Bucks, Esq

1721-2   folio 1,418.

Jan 17   EDWARD TAYLOR (of the Middle Temple, admitted there July 18, 1715, by
                                       [certificate of Philip Yorke, Knight, Treasurer)

„   25   MORGAN OWEN, Esq (of the Middle Temple, admitted there June 24, 1698,
                                       [by certificate of R May, Esq , Treasurer)

Feb 22   WALTER LINDLEY, second son of Francis L , of Gray's Inn, Esq

„   23   MICHAEL MACNAMARA, gent , of Annapolis, Maryland, America, son and heir

1722   [of Thomas M , Esq , deceased

April 16 SAMUEL STUART, second son of George S , of Omagh, co Tyrone, Esq

May   2 RALPH FELTHAM, Esq. (admitted to Middle Temple, Nov 21, 1710, by
                                       [certificate of Isaac Jackson, Under-Treasurer)

June 6 THOMAS JETT, Esq (admitted to Middle Temple, April 13, 1705, by
                                       [certificate of Thomas Mulso, Treasurer)

,   8   HENRY BLNDISH, son and heir of Henry B , of Middle Temple, Esq , nephew
                                  [(nepos) of Thomas B , formerly of this Inn, deceased

„   „   FRESTON RANI, son and heir of James R , of Mendham, Suffolk, Esq

folio 1,419

„   27   JOHN DAWSON, of Longwood, parish of Huddersfield, co York, gent

Aug 30   WILLIAM BYAM, of Christ College, Cambridge, gent , son and heir of Wm. B ,
                                                [of Antigua, America, Esq

Oct   6 WILLIAM CORRY, son and heir of Hugh C , of Lincoln's Inn Fields, Esq

„   7.   WILLIAM CORNWALLIS, of Newark, Notts, Esq

Nov 5. ESSEX MEYRICK, son and heir of John M , of Bush, co Pembroke, Esq.

1722   folio 1,419—*(continued)*

Nov 10   THOMAS FAWKES, gent , son and heir of Francis F , of Farnley, co York, Esq ,

,,   17   RICHARDSON PACK, of St Edmundsbury, Suffolk, Esq   [deceased

,,   29.   ANTHONY ANDERSON, son and heir of Anthony A , of Gray's Inn, Esq ,

Dec 3   EDWARD BELL, of the city of York, LL B   [deceased

,,   4   BUSHELL ANNINGSON, son and heir of Joseph A , of Whitby, co. York, gent ,

                              folio 1,420.

,,   12   JOHN TEMPEST BORROW, son and heir of Isaac B , of Castlefield, near Derby,

1722-3   [Esq

Feb 12   WILLIAM SOLEY, senior, third son of George S , of the city of Worcester, Esq ,

,,   ,,   WILLIAM SOLEY, eldest son of William S , of Gray's Inn, Esq   [deceased

1723

May 15   THOMAS ROBINSON, eldest son of John R , of Appleby, Westmoreland, Esq

June 1   BERTRAM CRASTER, third son of John C , of Craster, Northumberland, Esq ,

July 2   JOHN FULLER, son and heir of David F , of Dover, Kent, gent   [deceased

                              folio 1,421   [gent

,,   11   CHRISTOPHER GOULTON, son and heir of Thomas G , of Bessonby, co York,

,,   20   THOMAS SPENCER, son of Thomas S , of Gisborough, co York, gent

,,   25   GILBERT DAWSON, second son of William D , of Azerley, co York, Knight,
                   [deceased (admitted to Middle Temple, August 24, 1698)

Aug 24   THOMAS WARREN, son and heir of John W , of Corduffe, co Dublin, Esq

Oct 14   WYRRIOTT OWEN, of Nash, co Pembroke, Esq   [land, Esq.

,,   23   ANDREW HUDLESTON, son and heir of Wilfrid H , of Hutton John, Cumber-

Nov 12   SIMON BUTTERWICK, son and heir of Matthew B , of Thirsk, co York, gent

,,   16   BENJAMIN MUCHALL, of Muchall, co Stafford, gent.

,,   20   AYSCOUGH FAWKES, second son of Francis F , of Farnley, co York, Esq

                              folio 1,422.

Dec 13   JAMES BURGH, son and heir of John B , of Gray's Inn, Esq

1723-4
Jan 21   EDWARD BERTIE, second son of Hon. James B , of St Margarets, Westminster

,,   ,,   WILLIAM KIRSHAW, son and heir of Richard K , of Ripley, co York, Theol
                                                                             [Professor

Feb 8   HENRY HAWLEY, son and heir of James H , of Isleworth, Middlesex, Esq

,,   11   ROBERT GALLAWAY, son and heir of William G , of Lindridge, co. Worcester,
                                                                             [clerk, deceased

Mar 14.   NICHOLAS BONFOY, son and heir of Nicholas B , of Abbotts Ripton, Hunts,

,,   18   HAWLEY BISHOP, son and heir of Humphrey B , of London, gent   [Esq

1724
April 21   SAMUEL THAYER, son of Samuel T , of London, skinner, deceased

                              folio 1,423

,,   30   ROBERT WILLIS, of the city of London, gent

June 5   JOHN HUSON, gent (admitted to Lincoln's Inn, December 3, 1719, by cer-
                              [tificate of Robert Holford, Treasurer)

,,   30   CHARLES GRAY, of Colchester, Essex, gent

1724   folio 1,423—(continued)

July 15   TREVOR LLOYD, son and heir of Medhop L., of Toma, King's Co, Ireland,
,,   ,,   HENRY JACOMB, of St Andrews, Holborn, gent   [Esq
Sept 22   JUSTINIAN ISHAM, son and heir of John I., of Ormond Street, Middlesex, Esq
Oct 10   THOMAS GARDNER, second son of William G., of the city of London, distiller.

folio 1,424.

Nov 7   RICHARD GIRLINGTON, of London, Esq
,,   10   DRUE DEANE, son and heir of Thomas D., of Gray's Inn, Esq
,,   26   WILLIAM CHURCHILL, of St Annes, Westminster, Esq
Dec 4   JOSEPH STORR, eldest son of Joseph S., of Hilston, co York, Esq
1724-5
Jan 11   CHARLES ROBINSON, brother of Robert R., of Gray's Inn, Esq
,,   20   WILLIAM THOMPSON, son and heir of William T, of Bedford Row, parish of
                             [St Andrews, Holborn, Esq
,,   21   CHAMBERLAIN BECK, of Old Fish Street, London, gent
Feb 1   JAMES ALEXANDER, of New York, America, Esq   [Esq
,,   12   EDMUND LAYCON, son and heir of Edmund L., of Ottley, West Riding of York,

folio 1,425.   [Westminster, Esq

,,   25   RICHARD MORLEY, son and heir of Thomas M., of Pall Mall, in the liberty of
1725
April 17   PHILIP PRIME, son and heir of Philip P., of Ringsfield, Suffolk, clerk
May 7   ROBERT BULMAN, son and heir of George B., of Newcastle-on-Tyne, gent

folio 1,426.

,,   31   JOHN HAMMET, gent (admitted to Lincoln's Inn, June 24, 1720, by certificate
                          [of Philip Yorke, Knight, Treasurer)
June 2   EDMUND HERBERT, of St Margarets, Westminster, gent
,,   11   ROBERT GALE, eldest son of Robert G., of Abbotts Langley, Herts, Esq
,,   25   THOMAS SPEIDELL, eldest son of William S., of Gray's Inn, Esq
Oct 28   THOMAS FANSHAWE, son and heir of Edward F., of Dronfield, co Derby, gent
Nov 8   CHARLES STOURTON, eldest son of Hon Charles S., of Stourton, Wilts
Dec 16   GEORGE STORY, nephew (nepos) of George S., of Bishop Wearmouth, co
1725-6   [Durham
Jan 1   LUCIUS HENRY HIBBINS, of Holbeach, co Lincoln, Esq
Feb 26   ROWLAND HUGHES, only son of Lambroke H., of Brecon, gent, deceased

1726   folio 1,427

April 21   THORNHAGH GURDON, son and heir of Thornhagh G., of Letton, Norfolk, Esq.
,,   28   CHARLES PARRY, of St Andrews, Holborn, gent
May 2   JAMES BOULTON, only son of James B., of Moulton, co Lincoln, Esq.
,,   3   JOHN RYAN, son and heir of Thady R., of Cullen, co. Tipperary, Esq
,,   13   RANDYLL PECK, second son of William P., of Little Sampford, Essex, Esq.
,,   14   MATTHEW DUANE, second son of Thady D., of Clonmell, co Tipperary, Esq
June 25   RICHARD ASSHETON, third son of Richard A., of Gleadow, co. York, Esq.
,,   ,,   CORNELIUS BURTON, third son of Andrew B., of Gray's Inn, Esq, deceased.
Sept 10   RAINES HARRIS, second son of Philip H., of the city of Bristol, Esq.

z 2

1726	folio 1,427—(*continued*)	[gent
Sept 10	THOMAS HOUGHTON, third son of Thomas H, of Killmannock, co Wexford,	
Oct 13	THOMAS SOTHERION, only son of Thomas S, of Taverham, Norfolk, Esq,	
		[deceased
	folio 1,428.	[land, Esq
,, 27	HUMPHREY SENHOUSE, eldest son of Humphrey S, of Nether Hall, Cumber-	
		[Fishe (*sic*), of Gray's Inn, Esq
Nov 2	HENRY FYSHE-PALMER (Fish in the original), second son of Humphrey	
,, 23	THOMAS POTTER, only son of Thomas P, of Fenchurch Street, London, gent.	
Dec 20	WILLIAM PEPPERELL, son of William P, of Kentisbeare, Devon, gent	
1726-7	[certificate of Henry Martyn, Esq, Treasurer)	
Jan 26	RICHARD LEPTON, gent (admitted to Lincoln's Inn, Feb 23, 1721, by	
Mar 8	SAMUEL CLARKE, eldest son of Robert C, of Snailwell, Cambridge, Bart	
,, 10	WILLIAM SMITH, of New York, America, *A M*	
1727		
April 14	JOHN TAYLOR, eldest son of Walter T, of co Galway, Esq	
,, 17	RICHARD LAMPLUGH, only son of Robert L, of Dovenby, Cumberland, Esq	
,, 28	ROBERT ATKINSON, son of William A, of Greystoke, Cumberland gent	

folio 1,429

May 5.	OLIVER MARTON, of Warwick Court, parish of St Andrews, Holborn, Esq	
,, 8	JOHN MAIRE, third son of Thomas M, of Lartington, co York, Esq	[Esq
,, ,,	ZACHARIUS HARNAGE MORE, eldest son of Zacharius M, of Lofthouse, co York,	
,, 13	THOMAS HOIDIP, gent (admitted to Middle Temple, June 2, 1712, by	
		[certificate of Benjamin Wilcock, Under-treasurer)
,, 15	MARTIN BLAKE, third son of Patrick B, of co Galway, Esq	
,, 27	REIMERD WATKINS, of St Andrews, Holborn, gent	
June 9	CHARLES HAMILTON (admitted to Middle Temple, Nov 1, 1717, by certifi-	
	cate of John Raphson, Treasurer) [tificate of Henry Martyn, Treasurer)	
,, 17	WILLIAM SUITON, gent (admitted to Lincoln's Inn, Jan 22, 1723, by cer-	
,, 19	THOMAS BORROW, third son of Isaac B, of Castlefield, co Derby, Esq	
,, ,,	JOHN BORROW, third son of Isaac B, of Castlefield, co Derby, Esq	

folio 1,430

July 31	METCALF PROCTER, only son of Francis P, of Thorpe, co York, Esq, deceased	
Oct 20	THOMAS CLARKE, gent, Fellow of Trinity College, Cambridge	
Nov 8	HUGH CLOUGH, of Plâsclough, co Denbigh, Esq	
,, 28	EDWARD RIDSDALE, eldest son of Edward R, of Ripon, co York, gent	
Dec 2	ROBERT THOMPSON, second son of William T, of Gray's Inn, Esq	
1727-8		
Jan 9	JOHN HUTCHINSON, of Upper Holloway, Middlesex, Esq	
,, 20	JAMES ORD, of Newcastle, Northumberland, Esq	
,, ,,	MATTHEW RIDLEY, son of Richard R, of Newcastle, Northumberland, Esq	
,, ,,	GAWIN AYNSLEY, son of Gawin A, of Little Harle, Northumberland, Esq	
Feb 7	HENRY VANDER ESCH, of the city of London, Esq	
,, ,,	WILLIAM THEED, of the city of London gent	

1727-8.	folio 1,431.
Feb 10	SAMUEL STEPHENS, of St Andrews, Holborn, gent
,, ,,	WILLIAM BRAGE, second son of William, of Hatfield Peverill, Essex, Esq
Mar 20	WIND WILLIAM VANDER ESCH, son of Henry Vander E, of Gray's Inn, Esq

1728	
June 22	MICHAEL ERNLE, gent, son and heir of Edward E, of Brinslade Wilts, Esq (admitted to Middle Temple, March 20, 1724-5, by certificate of R
July 1	KENNETH MACKENZIE, of Portsea, co Southampton, Esq [Agar, Treasurer)
Aug 2	WILLIAM POTTER, son of Wm P, of Hawkwell, Northumberland, Esq
,, 3	EDWARD MARTON, son and heir of Oliver M, of Gray's Inn, Esq
,, 9	THOMAS REYNOLDS, Esq, one of the younger sons of Richard, Bishop of Lincoln
,, 12	ULLICK LYNCH, of Bellwell, co Galway, Esq

	folio 1432. [co York, Esq
Sept 7	AURUNGZEBE HATFEILD, son and heir of John H, of Laughton-en-le Morthen,
,, 8	JOSEPH BUTLER, eldest son of Edward B, of Cappoquin, co Waterford, Esq
	[("colonus"), husbandman
Oct 26	JONATHAN MERCER, eldest son of Samuel M, of Allerton, near Liverpool
Nov 16	HENRY BARKER, brother of Edmund B, of Gray's Inn, Esq [Esq
,, 18	THOMAS RAVENSCROFT, son and heir of Thomas B, of the city of Chester,
	[Andrews, Holborn, gent
,, 25	JOHN OSBALDESTON, eldest son of Roger O, of Southampton Buildings, St
,, 27	CHRISTOPHER FAWCETT, son and heir of John F, of the city of Durham, Esq

1728-9	
Jan 4	EDWARD BYAM, eldest son of William B, of the Isle of Antigua, Esq
,, 14	RICHARD MATTHEWS, youngest son of Isaac M, of Taplow, Bucks ("Hospi-
,, 29	GILBERT HOLKER, of Merton College, Oxford, gent [tium"), innkeeper.
Feb 10	PETER HINDE, eldest son of Richard H, of Hatton Garden, St Andrews,
	[Holborn, Esq, deceased.

1729	folio 1,433.
April 22	WILLIAM HORTON, eldest of Thomas H, of Chadderton, co Lanc, Esq
,, 24.	THOMAS HARRIS, of St Andrews, Holborn, gent
,, 27	JAMES EDWARD OGLETHORPE, of St James, Westminster, Esq
June 24.	ROBERT GRIMSTON, of Bridlington, co York, gent
July 10	PEIRCE GRIFFITH, eldest son of Peirce G, of St Albans, Herts, Esq
,, 20	NICHOLAS CLINTON, only son of John C, of Gragues, co Kildare, Esq
Oct 20	JOHN HODGSON, eldest son of James H, of the parish of Christ Church, city
	[of London, gent

1729-30	[Esq
Jan 22	JOSEPH GROWDON, second son of Joseph G, of Philadelphia, in Pennsylvania,
,, 23	THOMAS WALKER, eldest son of John W, of near Grinstead, Kent, Esq
,, :	OWEN GETHIN, eldest son of Owen G, of Winsford, co Chester, gent

	folio 1,434.
,, 31	RICHARD PATE, eldest son of Robert P, of Longnewtown, Cumberland, gent
Feb 10	STEPHEN BROWN, gent (admitted to Middle Temple, Dec 20, 1716, by cer-
	[tificate of Edward Jauncey, Treasurer)

1729-30   folio 1,434—(continued)

Mar 19   RICHARD BACKWELL, junior, of St. James, Westminster, gent

1730

April 23   GRIFFITH BOYNTON, eldest son of Francis B , of Beverley, co York, Esq

May 8   JOHN METCALFE, eldest son of John M , of Gray's Inn, gent

June 1   JOHN LOWE, only son of Francis L , of Gray's Inn, Esq

July 9   THOMAS WEDDELL, of Earswick, co York, Esq

   ,, 13   DAVID WOOLFE, second son of Henry W , of Bridlington, co York, gent

   ., 14   GILBERT BRYAN, only son of Thomas B , of Carrick-on-Suir, co Tipperary,
                                                                    [gent

Oct 17   WILLIAM STRAHAN, eldest son of William S , of Doctors Commons, LL D

Nov 19   CHRISTOPHER CARLETON, of Warwick-court, St Andrews, Holborn, gent

                                  folio 1,435

   ,, 21   CULPEPER TANNER, of Oakham, Rutland, gent   [Esq

   ,, 27   GEORGE SPEARMAN, son of Gilbert S , of Bishop Midleham, co Durham,

1730-31   [land, Esq

Jan 6   LANCELOT ALLGOOD, only son of Isaac A , of Brandon White, Northumber-

Feb 2   THOMAS WOLLASCOTT, third son of Martin W , of Wollampton, Berks, Esq.

   ,, 3.   THOMAS KING, third son of William K , of Bentworth, Southampton, gent

   ,, 11   RICHARD MACDOWALL, of Navestock, Essex, Esq

   ,, 12   WILLIAM GOOSTRY, of Shear Lane, St Dunstans-in-the-West, Middlesex, gent

   ,, 15   EDWARD BACON, eldest son of Waller B , one of the Masters of the Bench,
              Esq
                                                                    [Esq

   ,, ,,   NATHANIEL BACON, second son of Waller B., one of the Masters of the Bench,

   ,, 23   HENRY LUDLOW COKER, eldest son of Thomas C , of Hill Deverell, Wilts,
              Esq
                                                                    [Esq

   ,, 24   EDWARD TWELLS, only son of Robert T , of Wisbech, Ely, co Cambridge,

1731

April 9   PETER CAMPBELL, of St James, Westminster, Esq

                                  folio 1,436   [Baronet

   ,, 17   ROBERT CLARKE, second son of Robert C , of Snailwell, co Cambridge,

May 7   WILLIAM DIXON, gent , second son of Thomas D , late of Hackney, Middle-
              sex, Esq (admitted to Middle Temple, Nov 18, 1724, by certificate of
                                                          [John Raphson, Treasurer)

   ,, 15   ROBERT BRENT LYTCOTT, only son of John L , Knight, of Stoke, co Gloucester

   ,, ,,   THOMAS WATSON, only son of William W , of Helmsley, co York, gent

July 1   THOMAS GREENE, only son of Thomas G , of St James, Westminster, gent

Aug 14   RICHARD EVERARD, eldest son of Richard E , of Broomfield Green, Essex,

   ,, 27   THOMAS FLOYER, of Pelham, Herts, gent   [Baronet

Nov 10   JAMES COCKERILL, of Scarborough, co York, gent

   ,, 11   THOMAS FITZ GERALD, of Clownings, co Kildare, gent

   ,, 27   JOHN WAPLE, gent , second son of George W , late of Towcester co North
              ampton, gent (admitted to Inner Temple, July 21, 1730, by certificate of
                                                          [Edward Barker, Treasurer)

1731   **folio 1,437.**   [co. Worcester, Esq

Nov 27   WILLIAM BUND, eldest son of Thomas B , late of St. John in Bedwardine,

Dec 1   JOSEPH WILSON, eldest son of William W , of Stiffkey, Norfolk, clerk

1732

May 6   JOHN BALLS, son and heir of James B , of the city of Norwich, Esq

,, 10   PAGGEN HALE, second son of William H , of Kings Walden, Herts, Esq

,, ,,   KINGSMILL EVANS, third son of Thomas E., of Llangattock Vibonavel, co
                                           [Monmouth, Esq

,, 12   WILLIAM CHAPMAN, of Sunderland-near-the-Sea, co Durham, gent.

June 12   RICHARD MARTON, son and heir of Edward M , of Longleat, Wilts, gent

,, 13   ANDREW COLTEE DUCAREL, student of Trinity College, Oxford, gent

1732-3

Jan 20   OSMUND MACDOWALL, brother of Richard M , of Gray's Inn, Esq   [Esq

Feb 3   CHARLES LYMBREY, third son of John L , of Hoddington, co Southampton,

,, 5   THOMAS HOLT, second son of Thomas H , late of St James, Westminster,
                                           [gent., deceased

1733

April 14.   JOHN DEANE, of Bedford-row, parish of St Andrews, Holborn, Esq

                    folio 1,438

,, ,,   LEWIS DEANE, of Bedford-row, parish of St Andrews, Holborn, gent

May 1.   THOMAS BURROWES, gent , Fellow of Trinity College, Cambridge

,, 24   JOHN LISTER, only son of Thomas L , of Bawtry, co York, Esq.

,, 28   EDMUND TYRELL, eldest son of Charles T , of Gray's Inn, Esq

June 5   WILLIAM GINGER, of Hemel Hempstead, Herts, gent , only son of William G ,
                                         [of Edlesborough, Bucks, gent

,, 12   WILLIAM GLANVILE, son and heir of William G., of the Isle of Antigua, Esq

,, 13   STEPHEN COMYN, fourth son of Robert C , late Archdeacon of Salop

,, 15   JOHN CHOLMLEY, eldest son of Hugh C , of Whitby, co York, Esq

,, 29   JOHN SMYTH, Esq , eldest son of Richard S , of Wakefield, co York, Esq

July 6   EDWARD ROOKES, Esq , eldest son of William R , of Royds Hall, West Riding
                                         [of York, Esq , deceased

                    folio 1,439.

,, 31   THOMAS LLOYD, of Hatton Garden, Middlesex, gent , son of Dr William L ,
                              [late Chancellor of the Diocese of Worcester, deceased

Sept 14   JAMES INNES, of Symonds Inn, gent

,, 27   JOHN KING, Esq , Coroner of the city of London and County of Middlesex

Nov 14   JOHN FOOTE, son of John F , of Harwood, co Cornwall, Esq

1733-4

Jan 19   GERY PACKWOOD, only son of Rev Master P , of Coventry, co Warwick

Feb 1   CHRISTOPHER FAWCETT, only son of William F , of Boldon, co Durham, Esq

,, 11   ROEERT WENSLEY, eldest son of Peter W., of Walsoken, Norfolk, Esq [Esq

,, 12   JAMES MAINWARING, eldest son of James M , of Bromborough, co Chester,

Mar 11   WILLIAM COTTON, eldest son of William C , of Crake Marsh, parish of

1734   [Uttoxeter, co Stafford, Esq

April 2   HENRY STEBBING, eldest son of Henry S , Preacher of this Inn, S T P

May 17   RICHARD COMYNS, second son of Richard C , of Dagenham, Essex, Esq

1738.   folio 1,446.

May 12   JOHN ISAACSON, eldest son of John I., late of Newcastle-on-Tyne, Esq

,, 26   THOMAS WILSON, of Caius College, Cambridge, son of Rev ——— W, late of Stiffkey, Norfolk   [(and brother of Thomas)

,, ,,   WILLIAM WILSON, (another) son of Rev ——— W., late of Stiffkey, Norfolk

June 13   HILLIARD HEALY, of Red Lion-street, St. Andrews, Holborn, Esq

,, 24   WILLIAM MACKENZIE, of Gray's Inn Esq

,, ,,   JOHN CARYLL (Hon), of Ladyholt, Sussex, Esq

Oct 18.   STAPLETON DUNBAR, second son of Charles D, of the Isle of Antigua, Esq, Inspector-general of the Leeward Islands (specially admitted to Middle Temple, Nov 26, 1735, by certificate of Charles Worsley, Vice-treasurer)

folio 1,447

Nov 4   JOHN FAWKES, of Furnival's Inn, gent

1738-9
Jan 11   GEORGE RYVES, of Damary Court, Blandford, Dorset, gent.

,, 13   SAMUEL HOPKINS, of Bucknell, Salop, gent.

,, ,,   EDWARD WOODCOCK, gent

,, ,,   JOHN WAINWRIGHT, gent

Feb 1   THOMAS HENZELL, gent

,, ,,   JOSEPH TULLIE, of St Andrews, Holborn, gent

,, 7   WILLIAM UNDERWOOD, of Enfield, Middlesex, Esq.

,, 28   RICHARD PYOTT, of Gray's Inn, Esq

Mar 1   JAMES WALMSLEY, of Jenkins, parish of Barking, Essex, gent

1739
Mar 30   HENRY WILLMOT, late of Furnival's Inn, gent

May 25   DENIS CLARK, second son of John C, of Blakehall, Essex, Esq. (specially admitted to Middle Temple, Sept 24, 1738, by certificate of J Strange, [Treasurer).

folio 1,448   [Esq

June 1   MYDDELION MEREDITH, son of Thomas M, of Pentre-bychan, co Denbigh,

,, ,,   GILBERT BURTON, gent, son and heir of George B, of Hatton Garden, parish of St Andrew, Holborn, Esq (admitted to Inner Temple, Feb 17, 1727, [by certificate of J Finch, Treasurer)

Aug 8   THOMAS BAYNHAM, third son of John B, of the city of Hereford, Esq

Nov 14   WILLIAM CAMELL, only son of Robert C, of Norwich, LL D, deceased.

Dec 11   ROBERT RYDER, of St Andrews, Holborn, gent.

1739-40
Jan 10   THOMAS AMORY, son of Thomas A, late of Brislington, co Somerset, deceased.

,, 30   THOMAS KINSEY, of Chilton, Bucks, gent

,, ,,   THOMAS CANNON, of Westminster, Esq

1740
May 9   GABRIEL HALL, son and heir of Reginald H, of Newbiggin, Northumberland, Esq. (admitted to Inner Temple, Sept. 11, 1734, by certificate of Denis

,, ,,   CHARLES LOWE WHYTELL, of Gilmonby, co York, gent.   [Bond, Esq)

folio 1,449

,, ,,   FRANCIS SMART, of Snotterton Hall, co Durham, gent

1740	folio 1,449—(continued).
Aug 2	SIMON ADOLPHUS SLOPER, of the parish of St Andrews, Holborn, Esq
,, 8	ROBERT MONTGOMERY, second son of Robert M , of Penrith, Cumberland, Esq. [cate of R Brydges, Treasurer)
Oct 24	ARTHUR O'KEEFE, Esq. (admitted to Lincoln's Inn, Oct 20, 1738, by certifi-
,, ,,	WILLIAM ROOKES, second son of William R , late of Royds Hall, co York,
Nov. 7	HENRY NOWELL, of Gray's Inn, gent [Esq., deceased
,, 21	GEORGE WADE, gent
Dec 8	RICHARD KEAN, fourth son of Robert K., of Ross, co Clare, Ireland
	[co York, Esq.
,, 21	PENNYMAN CONSETT, son and heir of Matthew C , of Normanby-in-Cleveland,
1740 41	[ficate of Thomas Owen, Treasurer)
Jan 24	SAMUEL BERKELEY, Esq (admitted to Lincoln's Inn, March 2, 1736, by certi-
	[gent
Feb 18.	POTTER FLEMING, only son and heir of Ambrose F., late of Sedgeford, Norfolk,
Mar 11	CHARLES COLLYER, gent , son and heir of William C , late of the parish of St Giles, Cripplegate, surgeon, deceased (admitted to Inner Temple, [Jan 23, 1739, by certificate of Francis Peters, Under-treasurer)
1741	folio 1,450.
April 20	HUGH BARKER BELL, of Aylesbury, Bucks, gent
May 2	THOMAS D'OYLEY, of Gray's Inn, gent
,, ,,	SAMUEL WEGG, second son of George W , of Colchester, Esq [London, gent
June 4	THOMAS LONGMAN, of the street called Paternoster-row, in the city of
July 11.	THOMAS CORNTHWAITE, of St Martins-in-the-Fields, London, gent
,, 17	EDWARD BANVER, eldest son of Edward B , D D , Vicar of Royston, Herts, and Afternoon Preacher of this Inn [" Albania " (Scotland)
,, 28	PATRICK GUTHRIE, eldest son of David G , Laird of Carsbank, co Angus,
,, ,,	WILLIAM STOURTON, second son of the Right Honourable Charles S., late [of Stourton, Wilts, deceased
,, 29	NATHANIEL GILBERT, eldest son of Nathaniel G , of Antigua, America, Esq
Aug 14	JAMES WRIGHT, of Charlestown, in the province of South Carolina, in America,
	folio 1,451 [gent
Nov 20	HENRY LANGFORD BROWNE, son and heir of Thomas B , late of Gray's Inn,
1741-2	[Esq
Jan 22	TIMOTHY BLENMAN, second son of Jonathan B , Attorney-general of Barbados
,, 23	JAMES MYTTON, of Garth, co Montgomery, Esq
1742	[Esq
April 19	THOMAS WILSON, third son of Daniel W , of Dalham Tower, Westmoreland,
,, ,,	WILLIAM CUMMYN, third son of John C , of the city of Dublin, Esq
May 17	JOHN PENNINGTON, only son of Samuel P , of Bennaventa (? Daventry, Northants), gent [of Chancery
June 16	ROBERT HOLFORD, third son of Robert H , one of the Masters in the Court
,, 30	SACKVILLE AMHERST, son and heir of Jeffrey A , now Treasurer of this Inn (admitted to Inner Temple, Nov 25, 1730, by certificate of M Thurston, [Treasurer)
Aug 27	JOHN WOODLEY, of the Isle of St Christophers (St Kitts), America, Esq

1742	folio 1,451—(continued)

Oct 23   CHARLES BALLARD, eldest son of William B , late of the city of Worcester,
[gent , deceased

Nov 15   JOHN BROUGHAM brother of Henry Richmond B , of this Society Esq

,,   19   ARTHUR BRANTHWAYT, only son of Miles B , one of the Masters of the Bench
[of this Society

folio 1,452

,,   ,,   MILES BRANTHWAYT, eldest son of John B , of Kettlestone, Norfolk, clerk

,,   ,,   THOMAS WRANGHAM, only son of Thomas W , junior, of Newcastle-on-Tyne

1742-3
Jan 29   WILLIAM MARKHAM, student of Christ Church, Oxford

Feb   6   JOHN WORTH, of Aldershot, Hants, gent

,,   26   JOHN ROBINSON, eldest son of William R , of Monckton, co Durham, Esq

1743
May 2   JOHN HOWES, son of John H , of the city of Norwich, Esq

June 21   ROBERT MOXON, of Barnard's Inn, gent

Oct 22   THOMAS LOWES, fifth son of John L , of Ridley Hall, Northumberland, gent

Nov 16   GEORGE PINCKARD, of the parish of St Pancras, co Middlesex, gent

Dec   1   JOHN RUDD, eldest son of Thomas R , of the city of Durham, Esq

1743-4.
Jan 28   HENRY ATKINSON, of Cayley Hall, co York, Esq   [deceased

,,   30   JOHN DAWSON, only son of Robert D , late of Wall, Northumberland, gent ,

1744
April 19   EDWARD GALE BOLDERO, second son of Edward Gale B , of this Society, gent

folio 1,453

May 11   CHRISTOPHER DENTON, of the parish of St Andrews, Holborn, gent

,,   29   CHARLES BARNES, of the Register Office, gent

,,   ,,   JOHN DICKENS, of the Register Office, gent.

Aug 25   HENRY ALLEN, only son of Robert A , of Chappel Plantation, parish of St
[Philip, Island of Barbados, Esq.

1744-5
Jan 28   SIMON STANTON, of the Middle Temple, gent

Feb 28   JAMES COLDHAM, eldest son of John C , of Anmer, Norfolk, Esq

1745
Mar 29   JOHN FENWICK, second son of John F , of Bywell, Northumberland, Esq

Sept 21   RICHARD BOYCE (afterwards Boyse), eldest son of Nathaniel B , late of Graige,
[co Wexford, deceased

Oct 22   WILLIAM BEALE BRAND, eldest son of Jacob B , of Polstead, Suffolk, Esq

Nov 28   JOHN DRAKE, of the city of London, gent

,,   ,,   HENRY METCALFE, second son of John M , of this Society, gent , deceased

folio 1,454

Dec 20   CHARLES MAVERLEY, of Clifford's Inn, gent

1745 6
Feb   5   WILLIAM NEALE, of the parish of St Andrew, Holborn, gent

1746
April 15   WILLIAM WOOD, son of Thomas W , of this Society, Esq , deceased

,,   ,,   WEST HYDE, eldest son of John H , of Charterhouse Square, London, gent

1746   **folio 1,454**—*(continued)*

May 1   JOSEPH CRANMER, son of Joseph C., of the parish of St Andrew, Holborn,

„ 28   WILLIAM BAYNTUN, of the parish of St Andrew, Holborn, gent   [gent

Nov 3   JOHN NOYES, of Staple Inn, gent

1746-7

Jan 26   EDWARD BARNIER, of Gray's Inn, gent

Feb 2   THOMAS PLUMMER BYDE, of Gray's Inn, gent

„ 5   HUGH SMITHSON, son and heir of Hugh S, of Tottenham, Middlesex, Baronet

„ 16   THOMAS DIGGLE, eldest son of Romney D, of this Inn, Esq

Mar 7   RICHARD CROMWELL, of St Andrews, Holborn, gent

folio 1,455

„ „   SAMUEL WHITE, of St Ives, Hunts, gent

1747

Nov 2   WILLIAM ALSTON, son and heir of William A, of Bramford, Suffolk, Esq

, 10   GILBERT GEDDES, of Hopton, Suffolk, Esq

„ 14   TANNAT EATON, of the city of Dublin, Esq

1747-8   [(nepos) of John W, Esq, late Bencher of this Inn, deceased

Jan 12   JOHN WALKER, of Hedingley, parish of Leeds, co York, gent, nephew

„ 28   FRANCIS WYSE, son and heir of Thomas W, of " Manapiæ " (Wexford, or

           Waterford, Ireland, Esq)   [in South Carolina, America

Feb 24   JOHN GARDEN, son and heir of Alexander G, Vicar of the Bishop of London,

Mar 22   JOHN HARDESTY, only son of John H, Esq, late of this Society, deceased

1748

April 7   HENRY SCOTT, son of Henry S, of Leeds, co York, merchant

June 14   GEORGE GOODWIN, of Gray's Inn gent

July 16   WALTER STRICKLAND, eldest son of Thomas S, of Sizergh, Westmoreland, Esq

Nov 14   CHARLES OWEN, son and heir of Morgan O, Esq, late Bencher of this Inn,

                                        [deceased

„ „   JOHN FENTON CLARK, son of John C, late of Hudbeck, Cumberland, deceased

folio 1,456

Dec 15   AMBROSE EDWARDS, son of George E, of Barnard Castle, co Durham, gent

1748-9

Jan 31   ROGER WILSON, only son of Roger W, of Casterton, Westmoreland, Esq

Feb 1   JOSHUA GRIGBY, only son of Joshua G, of St Edmundsbury, Suffolk, gent

„ 3   JOHN GREEN, of Barnard's Inn, gent

1749

April 11   THOMAS HARDCASTLE, nephew (nepos) of Thomas H, of Grays Inn, gent

„ 18   WILLIAM HENRY OGLE, only son of Henry O, of Eglingham, Northumber-

                                        [land, Esq

May 1   HENRY LOWE, Esq, administrator of John L., late of Gray's Inn, Esq, deceased

„ 8   SAMUEL THOMPSON, only son of Samuel T, of Ufford, Suffolk, Esq

July 4   HORATIO PAUL, eldest son of Robert P, of Gray's Inn, Esq

Oct 11   JOHN FELL, of Gray's Inn, gent

Nov 27   HENRY NEGUS, eldest son of Henry N, of Hoveton St Peters, Norfolk, Esq.

folio 1,457

„ 28   GEORGE PORT, of Staple Inn, Esq

1749	folio 1,457—(continued)
Nov 28	EDWARD THOMPSON, of the city of York, gent, nephew of Mr Luke [Thompson (time to be allowed from June 10, 1746)
,, ,,	ENOCH HALL, of Staple Inn, Esq
Dec 22	SELWOOD HEWET, son of Thomas H , of the parish of St James, Middlesex, Esq (admitted to Lincoln's Inn, April 13, 1744, by certificate of I Floyer, [Treasurer)
1749-50 Jan 15	THOMAS LEECH, of Staple Inn, gent
1750 April 26	HENRY CRANMER only son of Joseph C , of the parish of St Andrews, [Holborn, gent
May 1	THOMAS BROGRAVE, second son of Thomas B , of Baddow, Essex, Esq (admitted to the Inner Temple, Oct 31, 1745, by certificate of T Davall, [Vice-treasurer)
,, 25	ROGER JENYNS, junior, son and heir of Roger J , of Windsor, Berks, Esq
Oct 31	VALENTINE NEVILL, of Gray's Inn, gent

folio 1,458

Nov 17	RALPH HODGSON, of Rullington, co York, gent (admitted to the Middle [Temple, Sept 8, 1743, by certificate of Antony Allen, Treasurer)
1750-51 Jan 21	JOHN LEE, of Leeds, co York, gent
,, 29	WILLIAM HENRY RICKETTS, of Gray's Inn, gent
, ,,	WILLIAM DOBINSON, of Gray's Inn, gent
Feb 9	LOUIS RUSSELL, of Gray's Inn, gent
,, 26	WILLIAM LUKE, only son of William L , of Castle Yard, in the parish of St [Andrews, Holborn, gent
1751 April 27	ANDREW HUDLESTON, eldest son of Andrew H , of Huttonjohn, Cumberland, [Esq
May 3	WILLIAM PRUJEAN, of Gray's Inn, gent
,, 11	WALKER DAWSON, eldest son of William D , late of Wakefield, co York, Esq

folio 1,459.

,, ,,	WILLIAM ALVEY DARWIN, second son of Robert D , of Elston, Notts, Esq
,, 13	SAMUEL THOMPSON, of Ufford, Suffolk, Esq [Bencher of this Society
,, 14	JOHN UPTON, nephew (nepos) of Braithwaite Otway, Esq , deceased, late
June 12.	LESLIE HAMILTON, of the city of London, gent.
,, ,,	THOMAS BRANCH, of the parish of St Mary, Islington, London, gent
July 23	JOHN POYNTZ, of Dunster, co Somerset, gent
Nov 1	CHARLES BOOTH, only son of Rev Charles B , of Bradford, co York
,, 2	BARNARD CROSS, of the city of Westminster, gent
Dec 10	DUNCAN CAMPBELL, of South Hall, co ———, Scotland, Esq
,, 13	WILLIAM FLUDYER, eldest son of Henry F , of Wallingford, Berks, gent

1752	folio 1,460
Jan 24	BENJAMIN STEELE, of Furnival's Inn, gent
,, 30	CHARLES MAVERLEY, nephew (nepos) of Charles M , of this Society, gent
,, ,,	WILLIAM TRYE, of Sudgrove, parish of Miserden, co Gloucester, Esq
Feb 26	JOHN BLOFELD, only son of John B., of the city of Norwich, gent.
Mar 10	JOHN LEIGH, son of George L , of Oughtrington, co Chester, Esq
,, 27	HUGH SIMPSON, only son of Thomas S , of Penrith, Cumberland, Esq

1752   **folio 1,460—(continued)**

May 2   EDMUND GARDEN, eldest son of Patrick G , one of the Benchers of this Inn

June 6   RICHARD BAYNES, of Gray's Inn, gent

Nov 4   WILLIAM BUND, eldest son of William B , of this Society, Esq

folio 1,461

„ 25   JAMES BURNET, of Barnard's Inn, gent

„ 27   CHARLES COTTON, only son of Charles C , of Bridewell Hospital, London, gent

Dec 16   SAMUEL MOODY, only son of Hatch M , of Oxhey Lane, parish of Watford,
                                                [Herts, Esq , deceased

1753

Jan 22   JOHN RIGGE, eldest son of William R , of Hawkeshead, co Lancaster, gent

„ 24   RICHARD WILSON, second son of Joshua W , of Pontefract, co York, Esq
         (admitted to Inner Temple, Aug 1, 1752, by certificate of Robert Moreton,

„ „   JOHN WATSON, junior, of Whitchurch, Salop, gent   (Treasurer)

Feb 6   ROBERT WILSON, brother of William W , of this Society, Esq

„ „   HILYARD HELY (? Healy), of the parish of St. George the Martyr, London, Esq

folio 1,462

„ „   WILLIAM BOSLEY, son of William B , late of Bosley's plantation, in the island
         of Jamaica, Esq , deceased   [America, Esq

Mar 28   JEREMIAS BLIZARD, son and heir of Stephen B , of the Isle of Antigua,

April 5   WILLIAM WEDDELL, youngest son of Richard W , of Newby, co York, Esq

May 10   GRANADO PIGOTT, of Horstead Keynes, Sussex, gent

„ „   RALPH LODGE, only son of George L , of the parish of St James, West-
         minster, gent   [S T D , deceased

„ 17   FRANCIS ANNESLEY, eldest son of Martin A , late of Bucklebury, Berks,

„ „   JOHN RICHMOND, second son of Joseph R , of Newcastle-on-Tyne, gent

„ „   WILLIAM TULLIE, of Gray's Inn, Esq   [gent

„ 19   CROMMELIN PIGOU, of the parish of St Mary Somerset, in the city of London,

„ 28   JAMES PETTIT ANDREWS, of Queen's Square, in the parish of St George the
                                         [Martyr, co Middlesex, gent

folio 1,463

June 2   JAMES GUNTER, of Tooley street, Surrey, gent

„ 8   EDWARD AINGE, junior, of Barnard's Inn, gent.   [Esq

„ 28   MAXIMILIAN WESTERN, only son of Maximilian W , of Lincoln's Inn Fields,

„ „   WILLIAM GEE, of Gray's Inn, gent

„ „   EDWARD LONG, of Gray's Inn, gent

July 3   BENJAMIN COLLIER, of Staple Inn, gent

„ 17   WILLIAM COWPER, of the Middle Temple, gent

„ „   LANGHORNE BURTON, of Somerby, co Lincoln, gent

Nov 7   WILLIAM WILSON, third son of John W , of Pontefract, co York, Esq

„ 9   WILLIAM BEACH, of Fittleton, Wilts, Esq

„ 14   LEONARD THOMPSON, eldest son of Leonard T , of Terrington, co York, clerk

„ „   LEVYNS BOLDERO, of Staple Inn, eldest son of Edward Gale B , of this
                                          [Society, gent

folio 1,464   [York, Esq

„ „   CHARLES HARLAND, youngest son of Richard H , of Sutton-in-the-Forest, co

1753   folio 1,464—(*continued*)

Dec 3   DAVID WEBB, of Walbrook, London, gent

,, ,,   ROBERT MOXON, nephew (nepos) of Robert M , of this Society, gent

1754
Jan 24 WILLIAM WARD, of Staple Inn, gent

Feb 1   RALPH BLOISE (Rev), brother of John B , late of Gray's Inn, Esq , deceased.

,, ,,   ROBERT HILTON, son of David H , of the city of Durham, Esq

Mar 27. JOHN LYONS, eldest son of Samuel L , of Antigua, America, gent

April 2 EDMUND BARKER, eldest son and heir of Henry B , late of Potter Newton,

May 3   JOHN HARRIS, of the city of Hereford, gent   [co York, gent , deceased

,, 10 THOMAS GOLDING, nephew (nepos) of Thomas Osborne, bookseller, of Gray's
                                                          ⌐Inn (gate)

folio 1,465

May 24 GEORGE CRASTER, only son of John C , of Craster, Northumberland, Esq

June 8 EDWARD STEPHENSON, eldest son of John S , of the parish of St Andrews,
           Holborn, Esq   [London

,, 14 DUTTON SEAMAN, eldest son of Dutton S , Esq , Comptroller of the city of

July 18 PHILIP MONOUX, son of Humphrey M , one of the Benchers of this Inn

,, 27 JOHN KERRICH, of Topcraft, Norfolk, gent

Nov 14 THOMAS MACGUIRE, youngest son of William M , of Dublin, Esq

, 15   EDWARD WYAT, son of Edward W , of Boswell Court, parish of St Clement
                                              [Danes, co Middlesex, gent

,, 20 RICHARD LLOYD, of the parish of St Clement Danes, co Middlesex, gent
1755   [Andrews, Holborn, gent
Jan 24 HENRY DARBY GARDNER, eldest son of Robert G , late of the parish of St

,, 27. JOSEPH LIDDELL, eldest son of John L , of Moor House, Cumberland, Esq

,, ,,,   BENJAMIN HAMP, of the town of Warwick, gent

folio 1,466.

,, 28 GEORGE WHINFIELD, son of William W , of the city of Durham, Esq

April 15 WILLIAM MILLER, of Ireland, Esq (admitted to Lincoln's Inn, November 29,
                          [1749, by certificate of William Nowell Treasurer)

,, 18 METCALFE RUSSELL, gent , son and heir of Michael R , of Hart Street,
           Bloomsbury (admitted to Lincoln's Inn, April 6, 1754, by certificate of
                                                 [William Nowell, Treasurer)

,, 21 JOHN HYDE, of Charterhouse Square, London, gent

,, 29 THOMAS YEO, of Staple Inn, gent

June 16 WILLIAM GREY, of Gray's Inn, gent

,, ,,   MILES STAVELEY, of North Stainley, co York, Esq

,, 25 THOMAS STRANGWAYES, of the parish of St Andrews, Holborn, gent

July 31 RANDALL KNIPE, eldest son of Edward K , of Epsom, Surrey, Esq

folio 1,467

Nov 3   DAGGE MORE, of Throgmorton Street, city of London, gent

,, 8   JAMES EYRE, gent (admitted to Lincoln's Inn, November 26, 1753, by
                             [certificate of William Nowell, Treasurer)

,, 10 SOLOMON FELL, of Gray's Inn, gent.

1755.   **folio 1,467—(continued)**

Nov. 14   WILLIAM WHITE, of Portsmouth, Hants, gent

1756
Jan 13   MICHAEL SCOTT, fifth son of John S , of King's County, Ireland, gent

,, 29   JOSEPH GIRDLER, gent , son and heir of Joseph G , of the Inner Temple,
           Serjeant-at-Law (admitted to that Society, November 19, 1728, by
           [certificate of John Wright, Treasurer)

Feb 9   ROBERT WARD, of Gray's Inn, Esq

Mar 24   PETER BROUGHAM, only son of John B , of Cockermouth, Cumberland, Esq

,, 31   WILLIAM ROBINSON, of Newcastle-on-Tyne, Esq

                    folio 1,468

April 15   THOMAS SAWER, eldest son of Thomas S , of Leeds, co York, Esq

,, ,,   ALEXANDER CROKE, of Aylesbury, Bucks, gent

May 14   BACON FRANK, of Trinity Hall, Cambridge, gent

June 15   SAMUEL SHEPPARD, of Lincoln's Inn Fields, gent.

,, 25   FRANCIS WRIGHT, of the city of Norwich, gent

Nov. 29   ROGERS JORTIN, of Gray's Inn, gent

Dec 8   OLIVER EDWARDS, of Chancery Lane, gent

1757
Jan 14   JOHN LLOYD, of Gloster, King's County, Ireland, gent

,, ,,   RICHARD STEELE, of the city of Dublin, gent

,, 20   RICHARD WALSH, of the parish of St. Martins-in-the-Fields, London, gent

                    folio 1,469

Feb 4   JOHN STARKIE, of the Exchequer Office, in the Inner Temple, gent

Mar 10   GEORGE WESTBY, of Howorth, co York, Esq

April 1   FORSTER BAINBRIDGE, of St Andrews, Holborn, gent

,, 29   BEVERSHAM FILMER, of Brandon, parish of Cranbrook, Kent, gent

May 5   WILLIAM HAMMOND, only son of Thomas H , of Winchester, gent

,, 6   JOHN HOWARD, eldest son of John H , of Cantshill, Bucks, gent

,, ,,   VALENTINE MORRIS HORNE, only son of Edward H , of Antigua, America

,, 7   NOCKOLD TOMPSON, of Thavies Inn, gent   [Holborn, gent

July 23   THOMAS VAUGHAN, only son of Thomas V , of the parish of St Andrews,

,, ,,   SAMUEL TOOKER, of Rotherham, co York, gent

Oct 1.   JOHN FIELD, eldest son of John F , of Heaton, co York, Esq

Nov 12   DAVID BURTON, eldest son of David B , of Yarm, co York, Esq

                    folio 1,470

,, ,,   ROBERT BURTON, youngest son of David B , of Yarm, co York, Esq

,, 16   JOHN WILKES, eldest son of Nathaniel W , of Wendon Lofts, Essex, Esq

,, 18   CHARLES WOLFRAN CORNWALL, gent (admitted to Lincoln's Inn, Jan 28,
           [1755, by certificate of J Coxe, Treasurer)

1758
Jan 16   HARRY FOCHE SPENCER, eldest son of Harry S , of Great Russell Street, parish
           [of St Georges, Bloomsbury, Esq

,, 28   ANTHONY STOKES, of the parish of St Andrews, Holborn, gent

Feb 10   JOSIAS CAMPBELL, only son of Samuel C , of Mount Campbell, Ireland, Esq

1758   **folio 1,470**—(*continued*)

Feb 10   WILLIAM SCOT, of the city of Durham, Esq

„ 11   JOHN COLMAN, of Gray's Inn, gent

May 30   SAMUEL WEGG, of the parish of St Pancras, London, gent

folio 1,471

„ „   HENRY PALMER WATTS, eldest son of Henry Palmer W , of Horstead, Norfolk, gent (specially admitted to the Middle Temple, Feb 13, 1756, by [certificate of C Taylor, Treasurer)

June 8   JAMES WALLER, of Lincoln's Inn, Esq

„ 22   ROBERT DURLING, of Gray's Inn, gent   [Esq

„ 30   DAVIDSON RICHARD GRIEVE, son of Richard G , of Alnwick, Northumberland,

Nov 4   FREDERICK SMITH of Topcroft, Norfolk, gent

„ 10   ROBERT SUCKLING, of Woodton, Norfolk, Esq

„ 13   WILLIAM MAYHEW, gent (admitted to Lincoln's Inn, Jan 25, 1755, by certi-

„ 16   CORNELIUS GOODWIN, of Gray's Inn, gent   [ficate of C Pratt, Treasurer)

„ 23   CHARLES RIMERD WATKINS, of Gray's Inn, gent.

folio 1,472

„ „   ROBERT GAPPER, of Staple Inn, gent

„ „   JOSEPH GAPE, of the Middle Temple, Esq

„ 28   EDMUND GRIFFITH, of Antigua, America, gent.

1759   [Esq

Feb 1.   JAMES JOHNSON, eldest son of James J , of Tremount, co Down, Ireland,

„ 2   JOHN ROBINSON, of Appleby, Westmoreland, gent.

Mar 30   BENJAMIN LLOYD, son of Rice L , of Killaloe, co Clare, D C L

„ „   HUGH ROBINSON, youngest son of William R , of Gray's Inn, Esq.

„ „   THOMAS CONSETT, son of Peter C., of Brawith, co York, Esq.

„ „   EDWARD MORSE, only son of Edward M , of Vauxhall, Surrey, gent

May 7   ROBERT ANTHONY BROMLEY, eldest son of John B , of Wigan, co Lancaster, [gent

„ 12   WILLIAM HARVEY, of the parish of St Andrews, Holborn, Esq

folio 1,473.

June 25   JOHN HOUGHTON, only son of John H , of Barnerton, Norfolk, gent

Nov 1   JAMES REDMAYNE, of Gray's Inn, gent

1760

Jan. 18   ROGER POCKLINGTON, eldest son of William P , of Newark, Notts, Esq.

„ „   WILLIAM SERJEANTSON, of Wakefield, co York, Esq

„ 21   HUGH BARKER BELI, only son of Hugh Barker B., barrister, of this Society

April 23   JOHN ROMANS, of Staple Inn, gent.

„ „   HENRY STRANGWAYS, only son of John S , of the city of York, gent

„ 25   GEORGE URQUHART, of Gray's Inn, gent

May 7   RICHARD HALE, of Gray's Inn, gent

„ 14   THOMAS BROWNE, of the parish of St. Andrews, Holborn, gent

„ „   GEORGE REAVELY, of Barnard's Inn, gent

1760.   **folio 1,474.**

May 14   EDMUND MASON, of Gray's Inn, Esq.   [Londino," Esq

June 9   JOHN ROBINSON, only son of Christopher R , " de statione generali veredorum

Nov 26   THOMAS MARTIN, of Furnival's Inn, gent.

Dec. 2   BOWLER MILLER, of London, gent

1761

Jan. 23   JOSHUA STEELE, of the parish of St George, Hanover Square, London, Esq

„ 29   MATHIAS HODGSON, of Gray's Inn, gent.

Feb 3.   BENJAMIN COWELL, of the city of London, gent

April 10   PHILIP BURTON, brother of Gilbert B., of this Society, gent

„ 16   CHARLES SKINNER, of the parish of St Clement Danes, Esq

„ „   JAMES MAGHLIN, of the city of Dublin, gent

folio 1,475

„ 18   JAMES DAVENANT, of Pembridge, co Hereford, Esq

„ 30   JOHN MYONNET (Rev)

May 27   GEORGE NEVILLE, of Thorney, Notts, gent

„ 28   PETER CAMPBELL, of the parish of Hanover, Isle of Jamaica, Esq

Nov. 14   THOMAS PITT, of Gray's Inn, gent

1762

Jan 28   NICHOLAS TINDAL, of Greenwich, Kent, gent

April 27   JOHN PRUJEAN, brother of William P , Fellow of this Society

May 4   JOHN MAYER, of Gray's Inn, gent

„ 12   Sir JOHN BLOIS, Baronet.   [ford, co Worcester, gent.

„ 21   ASTON HARRIS, of Trinity College, Oxford, eldest son of John H , of Brad-

„ „   GEORGE SAMUEL WEGG, son of Samuel W , now Treasurer of this Society

June 12   CHARLES ASHMALL, of the parish of St. Andrews, Holborn, gent

folio 1,476.

„ „   ROBERT DYNELEY, of the parish of St Andrews, Holborn, gent

„ „   JOSHUA COX, of the parish of St Andrews, Holborn, gent

July 1   WILLIAM BARTON BORWICK, of Staple Inn, gent

„ 3.   WILLIAM MASTERMAN, of Gray's Inn, gent

Nov 1   ROBERT FELLOWES, youngest son of William F , of Shottisham, Norfolk, Esq

„ 12   JOHN GREENHILL, of Gray's Inn, gent

„ 18   JOHN COTTLE, of Gray's Inn, gent

„ 19   WILLIAM COCHRAN, eldest son of James C , Advocate in Edinburgh

1763

Jan 22   ALEXANDER WHITE, third son of Robert W , of Virginia, Esq (admitted to the Inner Temple, Jan 15, 1762, by certificate of Thomas Tower, Treasurer)

folio 1,477

„ 24   JOHN CRAVEN, of Gray's Inn, gent

„ „   MATTHEW COURT, of Brasenose College, Oxford, gent.

Feb 4   ISAAC JOHN BEAZLEY, of Gray's Inn, gent

April 6   JOHN BYNG, of the parish of St George, Hanover Square, gent

„ 26   EDWARD CANNELL, of the parish of St Andrews, Holborn, gent.

1763   folio 1,477—(*continued*)

Oct 6   ASHTON WARNER BYAM, of Peterhouse College, Cambridge, gent.

Nov 8   THOMAS CHAPMAN, of Staple Inn, gent

„ 14   GEORGE SMYTH, only son of Offley S , of Harleston, Norfolk, gent.

„ „   GEORGE THOMSON, of Maidstone, Kent, gent

„ „   MATTHEW BUTTERWICK, eldest son of Simon B , of Thirsk, co York, Esq

„ 16   ROBERT DIXON, third son of John D , of Virginia, Esq

1764   folio 1,478

Jan 24   RICHARD BRISTOW, of Staple Inn, gent.   [deceased

„ 31   JEREMIAH ROBINSON, son of Charles R , of Appleby, Westmoreland, gent,

Feb 1   ISRAEL RHODES, of Gray's Inn, gent

May 19   FRANCIS HUTTON, of Gray's Inn, gent.

„ „   HENRY BARKER, nephew (nepos) of Edmund B , one of the Benchers.

„ „   FRANCIS RUSSELL, of Gray's Inn, gent

„ 23   JOHN PLATEL, of Staple Inn, gent.

„ „   CHARLES MOLLOY, of the parish of St Anne, Soho, London, Esq.

„ 24.   THOMAS HILL, only son of William H., of Tadcaster, co. York, Esq

June 13   JOHN HOBSON, of the city of Dublin, gent

               folio 1,479   [tificate of G Baker, Treasurer)

July 5   SAMUEL PECHELL, Esq (admitted to the Inner Temple, July 11, 1738, by cer-

„ „   JAMES HERBERT, eldest son of James H , of the Isle of Jamaica, gent,

„ 25   JOHN MINVER, of London, Esq   [deceased

Nov 13   ALAN CHAMBRE, eldest son of Walter C , late of Kirkby Kendal, Westmore-
             land, Esq , deceased (admitted to the Middle Temple, Feb 15, 1758, by

1765   [certificate of Matt Kenrick, Treasurer)

Jan 5   WILLIAM HORNBY, youngest son of Joseph H , of the parish of St Andrews,

„ 3   JAMES PRESTON, of New Malton, co York, Esq   [Holborn, Esq.

„ 26   HENRY BROUGHAM, eldest son of Henry B , who was nephew (nepos) of John

„ 28   JOHN BURKE, of the Island of Antigua, gent   [B , late Bencher of this Inn

May 18   WILLIAM STUKELEY, eldest son of Adlard Squire S , of Holbech co Lincoln,
                                            [Esq

               folio 1,480

June 7   SAMUEL LEIGHTONHOUSE, only son of Samuel L , of St Andrews, Holborn

„ 8   HENRY GABP, of Antigua, America, gent   (" Pictons "), painter

„ 10   ABRAHAM HILTON, of Gray's Inn, gent

„ „   JOHN ELMES, of the Island of Antigua, America, gent

July 2   GEORGE BYNG, brother of John B , late of this Society, deceased

Aug 13   CHARLES WINSTONE, of the Island of Antigua, Esq

Oct 30   RUSSELL HARRIS, of the Island of Jamaica, gent.   [gent.

Nov 21   JOHN LANE, eldest son of John L , of the parish of St. Paul, Covent Garden,

1766

Jan 23   THOMAS MORGAN, of Pendery, co. Glamorgan, Esq.

Feb 1   THOMAS KERRICH, son of Simon K , of Harlston, Norfolk, Esq., deceased

folio 1,481.

1766	
April 16.	JOHN THEAKSTON, of Gray's Inn, gent
June 2.	WILLIAM BLEAMIRE, of Gray's Inn, gent
,, 19	ISAAC MALLISON, of the parish of St Giles-in-the-Fields, co Middlesex, gent.
Nov. 4	JOHN BEARDSLEY, Esq , Clerk of the Peace for Warwick
,, 6.	JOHN MASON, of the Inner Temple, gent
,, ,,	GRATIAN HART, of the Island of Antigua, gent
,, 8	BENJAMIN PARNELL, of Gray's Inn, gent
,, 10	JOHN ASSHETON, second son of Richard A , of Preston, co Lancaster, gent
,, 19	CHRISTOPHER HILL, eldest son of Thomas H., of Blackwell, co Durham, gent
1767 Jan. 15	THEODORE WALROND, eldest son of Maine Swete W , of the Island of Antigua, [Esq
Feb 2	JOHN WILKINSON, youngest son of Andrew W , of Burroughbridge, co York,
,, 27	RICHARD TEMPLER, of Gray's Inn, gent [Esq

folio 1,482

,, ,,	SAMUEL BROOKES, of St Andrews, Holborn, gent
,, ,,	CHARLES SNELL, of Fleet Street, London, gent
Mar 17	JOHN LLOYD, of Berth, co Denbigh, and of the Middle Temple, gent.
May 6	BENJAMIN KEENE, only son of Doctor Edmund K , Bishop of Chester
,, 13	TIMOTHY CUNNINGHAM, of Gray's Inn, gent
,, 20	JOHN LEWIS, of Gray's Inn, gent
,, ,,	SAMUEL EDWARDS, of Sawtrey, Hunts, gent
,, ,,	NICHOLAS RIDLEY, third son of Matthew R , one of the Benchers of this Inn
,, ,,	GEORGE CRAWFORD RICKETTS, of Gray's Inn, gent
June 2	JOHN MARGETSON, of Staple Inn, gent
July 6	WILLIAM SHELDON, second son of William S , of Weston, co Warwick, Esq

folio 1,483

Nov 11	WILLIAM PAUL, only son of William P , of Danesdale, co York, Esq
,, ,,	WILLIAM WITHER BEACH, son of William B , of Gray's Inn, Esq
,, 26	EDWARD CLARKE, of Staple Inn, gent
Dec 3	FLETCHER RIGGE, only son of Roger R , late of Cartmell, co Lancaster, gent , deceased (admitted to the Middle Temple, June 16, 1763, by certificate
1768	[of Francis Keyt Dighton, Treasurer)
Jan 2	GEORGE CRUMP, of the Island of Antigua, gent
,, 23	THOMAS COLLINGWOOD, of Gray's Inn, gent [Martyr, co Middlesex, Esq
May 2	THOMAS LLOYD, youngest son of Richard L , of the parish of St George the
June 16	JOHN BLAGDEN, of Staple Inn, gent
,, ,,	RICHARD BROOME, of Bushton, Wilts, gent

folio 1,484.

,, ,,	JOHN DAWSON, only son of John D., of this Inn, Esq. [Esq.
July 13.	WILLIAM ANTROBUS, only son of William A , of Savannah le Mar, Jamaica,
Nov 11	JOSEPH WRIGHT, of Serjeant's Inn, Chancery Lane, gent.

1769	folio 1,484 —(continued)

Jan 23   JOHN LLOYD, one of the sons of Richard L , of the parish of St George the
[Martyr, co Middlesex, Esq

Feb 1   EDMUND SWYNY, son of Matthias S., of Thurles, co Tipperary, gent

Mar 10   FRANCIS SKYRME, of Lowhaden, co Pembroke, gent.

,, ,,   THOMAS WARNER, nephew (nepos) of Thomas W , of Gray's Inn, Esq

April 12   THOMAS MENDHAM, of Chancery Lane, gent

May 3   HARRY PHILLIPS NICHOLLS, of Gray's Inn, gent

folio 1,485.

Nov 11   OLIVER DIXON, of Stourbridge, co Worcester, Esq

,, 13   DANIEL SUTTON, of Kensington, Middlesex, gent

1770
Jan 23   PETER SYKES, eldest son of Peter S , Fellow of this Society, deceased

Feb 15.   JOHN BARRETT, son of Michael B., of the Inner Temple

April 6   JOHN MUMFORD, second son of John M , of Sutton-at-Hone, Kent, Esq

,, 12.   JOHN GRETTON, of Westcotes Hall, co Leicester, gent.

May 11   WILLIAM HIGGINS, of the Island of Antigua, gent

,, 12   EDWARD MAXWELL, son of Jane M , of Chiswick, Middlesex, gentlewoman

June 27   GEORGE CHALFIELD (Rev), nephew (nepos) of George Sturt, one of the
[Benchers of this Society, deceased

Aug 21   WILLIAM MELLISH, of the Middle Temple, Esq

Nov 8.   HASTINGS ELWIN, fourth son of Peter E , of Booton, Norfolk, Esq

folio 1,486   [terland, gent.

,, ,,   HENRY COLLINGWOOD SELBY, third son of George S , of Alnwick, Northum-

,, ,,   ROBERT PRESTON, second son of Robert P , of Stockton, co Durham, gent

,, ,,   RICHARD MORLAND, of Gray's Inn, gent

,, 14   THOMAS DUCK, of Gray's Inn, gent.

,, 17   WARCOP CONSETT, eldest son of Peter C , of Brawith, co York, Esq

,, ,,   JEREMIAH CHURCH, only son of John C , of Gray's Inn, gent

,, ,,   HENRY STEBBING, only son of Henry S , S T P , preacher of this Society

1771   [Cavan, Esq
Jan 19   FRANCIS SAUNDERSON, eldest son of Alexander S , of Castle Saunderson, co

,, ,,   JOHN FISHER, second son of John F., of Cambridge, linendraper

Feb 1   SAMUEL TURNER, of Nottingham, gent

,, ,,   PETER WOULFE, of West End, Middlesex, gent

folio 1,487.

Mar 8   EDWARD BOUTFLOWER, one of the Clerks in Chancery.

,, ,,   LAWRENCE KIERNAN, second son of William K , of the city of Dublin, gent

,, ,,   THOMAS PLEASANTS, eldest son of William P , of Knockbegg, Queen's County,

,, 18   SAMUEL BOWYER, one of the Clerks in the Exchequer   Ireland, Esq.

,, ,,   JOHN COLBY, of the Island of Grenada, gent.

,, ,,   THOMAS MATTHEW, of the Island of Grenada, gent.

,, ,,   WILLIAM HART, youngest son of John H , of Chard, Somerset, gent

April 15   WILLIAM JOHNSTON, of Hammersmith, Middlesex, gent

1771   folio 1,487—(continued)

June   1   RICHARD BOND, of the parish of St Andrews, Holborn, gent

„   „   JAMES SHANNON, third son of Denis S , of Ibrickan, co. Clare, gent.

„   3   HENRY BELL, eldest son of Henry B , of Stockton-on-Tees, co Durham, gent

„   20. STAFFORD SQUIRE BAXTER, of Furnival's Inn, gent

Nov   6   HENRY HOYLE ODDIE, of Barnard's Inn, gent

                                 folio 1,488.   [gent

„   7   RALPH ALDUS, only son of Robert A , of the parish of St Andrews, Holborn,

„   „   THOMAS HOOD, of Gray's Inn, gent

       1772
Jan   3   WILLIAM CARDALE, youngest son of Ferdinando C , of the city of Worcester,

„   24 Sir THOMAS TANCRED, of Brampton, co York, Baronet   [hop merchant

„   29 SAMUEL STEELE, of St Anns Hill, Surrey, gent

„   „   GEORGE EVANS, of Gray's Inn, gent

Feb   1   THOMAS KIERNAN, of Gray's Inn, gent

„   „   JOSHUA COX, second son of Joshua C , Fellow of this Society

May   6   JOHN HARRISON, of Whitburn, co Durham, Esq

„   8   JAMES CLEATOR, of Gray's Inn, gent

June   6   JAMES SNOWDON, of the parish of St Andrews, Holborn, gent

Sept   2   THOMAS PARES, of Furnival's Inn, gent.   [clerk

„   10 JOHN MATTHEW GRIMWOOD, youngest son of Thomas G , of Dedham, Essex,

Nov   6   KIGGINS PEYTON, of Ipswich, Suffolk, Esq

                                 folio 1,489.

„   „   JOHN DRAGE, eldest son of Thomas D , of Cambridge, grocer

„   10 MEREDITH PRICE, of the parish of St Andrews, Holborn, London, gent

„   „   JOHN KIPLING, of the parish of St George, Bloomsbury, Middlesex, gent

„   „   ANTHONY FAY, of Rotherhithe, Surrey, gent   [gent

„   28 BARNEY REILLY, eldest son of John R , of near Granard, co Longford, Ireland,

„   „   THOMAS BROOKBANK, second son of John B , late Rector of St Matthew,
                                                      [Bethnal Green, deceased
       1773
Jan   23 JAMES PIGOT INCE, only son of Pigot I., late of Hadley, Middlesex, Esq , decd

„   28 ANTHONY AUFRERE, son of Anthony A , of Hoveton St Peter, Norfolk, Esq

May   4   EDWARD MONTAGU, Esq , second son of James M., of Lackham, Wilts,
               Esq (admitted to the Middle Temple, May 3, 1737, by certificate of
                                                   [Thomas Caldecott, Treasurer)

Oct   4   JOHN GAY, only son of John G , of the city of Norwich, Esq.

Nov   3   JAMES READ, eldest son of (Hon) James R , of Savannah, in Georgia

„   „   JAMES Merrifield, second son of James M., of the Isle of St Christophers

„   „   JOHN SKINNER STOCK, of the city of Gloucester, gent   [(Kitts), Esq

„   „   JOHN WILLIAMS WILLIAUME, of St. James, Westminster, Esq.

1774   folio 1,490

Jan   22 THOMAS REILLY, second son of John R., of near Granard, Ireland, Esq

„   26 NICHOLAS WILLIAM LEWIS, of the parish of St Peter le Poer, London, gent (ad-
               mitted to Inner Temple, May 7, 1773, by certificate of C Sayer, Treasurer)

„   26 GERRARD MOORE, eldest son of John M , of Annabegg, co Galway, Esq

1774   folio 1,490—(continued)

Jan 27   JOSEPH HATT TURNER, of Clement's Inn, gent   ]land, Esq

,, 28   THOMAS WHELPDALE, eldest son of John Richardson (sic), of Penrith, Cumber-

April 20   GEORGE SOWLEY HOLROYD, eldest son of George H., of the parish of St Giles
                                              [in the Fields, London, Esq

May 4   WILLIAM BUMPSTEAD, son and heir of William B., of Upton, co Warwick, Esq
                (admitted to the Inner Temple, May 25, 1751, by certificate of C Sayer,
                                                             [Treasurer)

June 1   JOHN HAYNES HARRISON, of St John's College, Cambridge, eldest son of
                                   [John H., of Copford Hall, Essex, clerk,

folio 1,491.

,, 20   JOHN SHERWIN, Esq., son and heir of John S., of the town of Nottingham
                Esq (admitted to the Middle Temple, Dec 26, 1747, by certificate of
                           [William Pagitt, in place of Henry Humphrey, Treasurer)

Aug 26   JOHN NASON, of Trinity College, Dublin, Esq

Nov 1   WILLIAM LAMBE, only son of William L., of Pontefract, co York, gent

,, 2   PETER BARTLETT, youngest son of Thomas B., of the city of Bath, gent

,, 14.   WILLIAM AINGE, second son of Oliver A., of Lincoln's Inn, gent, late deceased

Dec 10   EDWARD KING, fourth son of James K., Canon of Windsor, S T P

,, 20   JAMES MEDDOWCROFT, nephew (nepos) of James Browne, Fellow of this Society,

., 29.   DAVID SCOT, of Scotstarvat, co Fife, Esq   [deceased
1775
Jan 7   WILLIAM COCKELL, eldest son of William C., of Pontefract, co York, Esq

,, 12   CHARLES PHILLIPS, of Monmouth, gent

,, ,,   HENRY BARNES, of Monmouth, gent

,, 23   GERRARD MONTAGU, only son of Edward M., Bencher of this Inn

Mar 7.   WILLIAM SHAKESPEARE KENRICK, son of William K., of the parish of St
                                      [Marylebone, Middlesex, LL D

folio 1,492

,, ,,   RICHARD TROWARD, eldest son of Richard T., of Margate, Kent, gent

,, ,,   RICHARD HEIGHWAY, of Tooks Court, parish of St. Andrews, Holborn, Esq

May 3   RICHARD GRACE, son and heir of William G., of the city of Dublin, Esq

June 8   WILLIAM ATKINSON, only son of William A., of Haverbrack, Westmoreland,

,, 21   JOHN PARRY, of Llangynog, co Montgomery, gent   [gent

,, ,,   MORTO DANIEL SWYNY, son of Matthew S., of Thurles, co. Tipperary, gent

Oct 30   WILLIAM WYLLY, eldest son of Alexander W., of Georgia, in America, Esq

,, ,,   CAMPBELL WYLLY, youngest son of Alexander W., of Georgia, in America, Esq

Nov 6   JOHN DODSWORTH, second son of George D., of Scarborough, co York, clerk

,, 7   CARLOS CONY, of Lynn, Norfolk, Esq
1776
Jan 27   FRANCIS BROOME, brother of Richard B., Fellow of this Inn

folio 1,493.

April 11   JOHN TAYLOR, eldest son of Thomas T., of Manchester, co Lancaster, gent

,, ,,   JOHN CHRICHLOE TURNER, of Huntingdon, youngest son of Rev. James T.,
                                   [late of Wing, co Rutland, clerk, deceased

,, 12   REES DAVIES, second son of Arthur D., of Llandovery, co Carmarthen, gent.

1776	folio 1,493—(continued)

1776
Sept 13   NICHOLAS ALLEN BLAKE, third son of Benjamin B , of the Island of Jamaica,
Nov   2   WILLIAM BENTLEY, of Gray's Inn, gent   [Esq , deceased
,,   6   JOHN LAURENCE, eldest son of John L., of the city of Lincoln, Esq , deceased
,,   8   JOSEPH JAMESON, of Egremont, Cumberland, gent.
,,   20   GEORGE HEALEY, eldest son of George H , of Gainsborough, co Lincoln, gent
1777   [Holborn, gent
Jan 23   WILLIAM DACIE, of Cursitor Street, Chancery Lane, parish of St Andrew,
,,   29   THOMAS BINSTEED, of Portsea, co Southampton, gent
April 16.   JOHN BAYNES, only son of William B , of Middleham, co York, Esq
,,   ,,   CHARLES ARNOLD, second son of Richard A , of Chancery Lane, Esq

folio 1,494

July   1   PETER RORKE, of Gray's Inn, gent
Aug   6   JOHN VENABLES HINDE, son of Robert H , of Preston, Herts, Esq
Nov.   6   RICHARD DAVIES, only son of John D , of Trawsmaui, co. Carmarthen, Esq
,,   17   RICHARD SMART, of Staple Inn, gent
,,   24   JOSEPH FOSTER-BARHAM, eldest son of Joseph Foster-B , of Bedford, Esq
Dec   1   WILLIAM HARDY, of Staple Inn, gent
1778
Jan 23   JOHN NORWOOD, of Gray's Inn, gent.
,,   26   DANIEL ROBINSON, of Staple Inn, gent
,,   ,,   ALBAN PARRY, son of John P , Fellow of this Inn
,,   ,,   JOHN TOWNSON, of Gray's Inn, gent
,,   ,,   MICHAEL MASSEY ROBINSON, of Gray's Inn, gent
,,   ,,   CHARLES GREGORY WADE, of Gray's Inn, gent
,,   27   THOMAS BARRON, of Gray's Inn, gent

folio 1,495.

Mar 10   DAVID FINLEY, son of David F., of the city of Edinburgh, Esq
,,   18.   JAMES MORGAN, of Gray's Inn, gent
April 7   MARMADUKE ALINGTON, eldest son of Henry A , of Aston, Herts, clerk
May   5   SAMUEL ROMILLY, youngest son of Peter R , of the parish of St Marylebone,
     Middlesex, jeweller.   [surgeon
,,   ,,   WILLIAM FITZGERALD, eldest son of Edward F , of Egremont, Cumberland,
,,   20   WILLIAM BERDMORE, son of William B , clerk, Canon Residentiary of the
     [Cathedral Church of York
June 19   JAMES ISAAC MALLISON, son of Isaac M , Fellow of this Inn
July   8   EDWARD ELLIOT, of Stockton-on-Tees, co Durham, gent
Sept. 18   JOHN KNILL, of St Ives, Cornwall, Esq   [deceased
Oct 29.   JOHN KIRTON, only son of Thomas K , late of Newcastle-on-Tyne, merchant,
,,   ,,   JOHN HOWES, eldest son of Thomas H , of Morningthorpe, Norfolk, clerk
Nov 12.   THOMAS MARTIN LANGDALE, youngest son of Marmaduke L , of the parish of
     [St George the Martyr, Middlesex, Esq

folio 1,496   [in Dublin, Esq

,,   ,,   HENRY HAMILTON, one of the sons of James H , of the King's Bench Office,

1778	folio 1,496—(continued).
Nov 12	EBENEZER KING, of Newbury, Berks, gent
,, ,,	HENRY WALKER YEOMAN, of Whitby, co York, Esq
Dec. 3	DAVID HUMPHREYS, of Barnard's Inn, gent [this Inn
,, 4	LEVYNS BOLDERO BARNARD, youngest son of Levyns Boldero B , Fellow of
1779.	[Martyr, Middlesex, gent
Jan 13	FRANCIS DOUCE, youngest son of Francis D , of the parish of St George the
,, 25	GEORGE BROOKS, youngest son of John B., late of Boxford, Sussex, gent, deceased [Andrews, Holborn, co. Middlesex, Esq.
,, ,,	JOSHUA READSHAW, only son of Joshua R , of Hatton Garden, parish of St.
,, 29	GEORGE JOSEPH BROWN, of Kentville, co Galway, Esq , only son of George [B , of Dublin, gent., deceased.
Mar. 1.	THOMAS HAWKINS, son of William H , of Maidstone, Kent., gent.
,, ,,	NATHAN SPRIGG JEFFERY, son of Edmund J , of the city of Exeter, gent.

folio 1.497.

April 20	WILLIAM ROOKES, only son of William R , one of the Benchers of this Inn
May 1	MONTAGUE FARRER AINSLIE, eldest son of James A , of Kendal, Westmoreland, M D [potter
,, 25	DANIEL LEESON, eldest son of Charles L , of Burton-on-Trent, co. Stafford,
July 6	THOMAS BAINBRIGGE HERRICK, of Beau Manor, co Leicester, gent
,, 27	THOMAS BASSETT, of Ropley, Hants, Esq
Nov 5	PETER CONSETT, brother of Warcup C , Barrister of this Inn
,, ,,	JOHN VIVIAN, of Penalewey, co Cornwall, gent
,, 7	THOMAS GREEN, of Slyne, co Lancaster, gent
,, 30	EDWARD ARCHER, M D
1780.	
Mar 27	THOMAS QUIN, only son of Thomas Q , of the city of Dublin, gent
April 12	JOHN WHITE, eldest son of Thomas W , of Cork, gent

folio 1,498.

,, 26	CHARLES SIMPSON, eldest son of James S , of Bruges, in Flanders merchant.
	On April 20, 1785, Charles James, a Member of Gray's Inn, presented a petition stating that he was admitted April 26, 1780, by the name of Charles Simpson, being the name of his uncle, &c , praying that his name might be entered as Charles James, and that his father is John James, of Bruges, in Flanders Petition granted April 22, 1785 —O E. iii 589
,, ,,	GEORGE FREDERICK PARRY, second son of Joshua P , of Cirencester, co. [Gloucester, gent , deceased
May 23	JOHN SMART, brother of Richard S , Fellow of this Inn [Holborn, gent
,, ,,	JOHN BRADLEY REES, eldest son of David R., of the parish of St Andrews,
,, ,,	EDWARD DILLON, eldest son of Francis D., of Carlow, Ireland, Esq [clerk
Nov 3	WILLIAM HARRISON, eldest son of John H , of Bighton, co Southampton,
,, 28	HENRY DOBINSON, son of William D , Fellow of this Inn, deceased.

folio 1,499

Dec 19	ISAAC ESPINASSE, son of Isaac E , of Manfield, co Dublin, Esq
,, 21	RICHARD KING, fourth son of John K , of Ashby, co Lincoln, Esq

1781	folio 1,499—*(continued)*
Jan. 29	ROBERT GRIFFITHS, of Crane Court, Fleet Street, London, gent
,, ,,	STEPHEN GASELEE, son of Stephen G , of Portsmouth, co Southampton, gent
May 2	WILLIAM LYON, son of Edmund L , of Liverpool, merchant
,, ,,	JOSEPH LYON, brother of William L , named above [Esq
,, 9	JOHN LOCK BARGUS, second son of Richard B , of Fareham, co Southampton,
,, ,,	RALPH CLAYTON, Esq , only son of William C , late of Newcastle-on-Tyne, alderman and merchant, deceased (admitted to Lincoln's Inn, May 5, [1775, by certificate of Thomas Grint, Treasurer)
June 26	MOSES GREETHAM, second son of Moses G , of Portsmouth, co Southampton, gent [merchant
July 4	AMBROSE WESTON, eldest son of James W , late of the town of Poole,
,, 30	JAMES CHEETHAM, of the parish of St James, Westminster, co Middlesex, gent [deceased
Nov 13	GEORGE BINSTEAD, second son of Thomas B , of Portsmouth, Hants, gent ,
,, 17	HENRY HOSTY, eldest son of Hubert H , of Galway, Ireland, Esq
,, ,,	JOHN BRADSHAW FLETCHER, second son of Robert F , of Halton Hall, co
1782	[Lancaster, clerk
Feb. 1	CHARLES DOWNES, eldest son of Rev Charles D , of Manchester, co Lancaster [deceased
,, 21	WILLIAM MARSHALL, son of William M , of Newton Kyme, Yorks, Esq ,
Mar 5	JAMES LAINCHBURY, of London, second son of James L , of Ramsden, Oxon, [gent
,, 8	STEPHEN PETER TRIQUET, son of Peter T , of Craven Street, Middlesex, gent
,, ,,	JOHN FELLOWS CLARIDGE, eldest son of John C., of Craven Street, Middlesex,
,, 18	GEORGE PEARSON, of Durham, gent [gent
April 12.	JOHN ROOKE, of Standon, Herts. gent
,, 26	ANTONY PARKIN, of Gray's Inn gent.
July 5	JOHN WEAR, son of George W., of Stockton, co Durham, surgeon
,, ,,	EDWARD CHRISTIAN, of Morland Close, co. Cumberland, gent
Aug 3.	FREDERIC THOMAS SMITH, third son of Joseph Nicholas S , of Staple Inn, gent.
Sept 2	WALTER CRAVEN, of Gray's Inn, gent
Nov. 3	THOMAS LEWIS, second son of William L , of Bristol, gent
,, 5	RALPH HERON, of Newcastle-upon-Tyne, gent
Dec 31	EDMUND SQUIRE, of American Square, London, gent
,, ,,	GEORGE GRAVES, of Bishopsgate Street, London, gent
1783	[S T B
Jan 30	NATHANIEL CLAYTON, son of Rev Nathaniel C , of Newcastle upon Tyne,
Mar. 1	GABRIEL BIZE, of Freemans Court, London, gent
May 7	WILLIAM ROBERT WAKE, only son of Basil W , of the city of Bath, Esq
,, ,,	THOMAS BLAKE, of Norwich, gent
June 29	JOHN WAKEFIELD, of Cheshunt, Herts Esq.
July 1	BENJAMIN DUNN, eldest son of Benjamin D , of Durham, gent.
,, 5	JOHN BRIGHT, of Streatham, Surrey, gent
Nov 8	STIVERD JENKINS, only son of John J , of Stone, co. Gloucester, Esq

1783   [Esq

Nov 10   CALVERLEY JOHN BEWICKE, eldest son of Benjamin B , of Clapham, Surrey,

„ 12   JOHN BAYLEY, second son of John B , of Abbots Ripton, Hunts, Esq

„ 13   WILLIAM HUGHES, only son of William H , of Islington, Middlesex, gent

Feb 17   JOHN SMEATON, of Austhrope, Yorks, gent   [Indies, gent , deceased

Nov 13   CHARLES HERBERT, second son of Charles H , late of Martinique, West

„ 26   JOHN BROWN, son of John B , of the parish of St Andrews, Holborn,

1784   [Middlesex, gent

Feb 10   JOHN BELL, only son of George B , of Berwick-on-Tweed, gent

„ 17   ROBERT CREWE, only son of Robert C , of Fleet Street, London, gent. [land

April 24 CHARLES FIELDING WARD, eldest son of John W , of Bebside, Northumber-

„ 29   EDWARD SWINBURNE, youngest son of Edward S , of Capheaton, Northumber-

May 6   JOSEPH RITSON, son of Joseph R , of Stockton, Durham, gent [land, Barenet

, 19   SEPTIMUS HARDWICKE LUDLOW, son of Daniel L , of Yate, Gloucester, gent

„ 31   JOHN ALLEN, second son of John A , of Wheatley, Oxon, gent.

July 9   BENJAMIN HARGOOD, son of Hezekiah H , late of Deptford, Kent, gent.

Aug. 17   WILLIAM JONES, of Grays Inn, gent.

Oct. 17   JOHN DANIEL MACKINNEN, second son of William M , of Monmouth, Esq

„ 28   GEORGE HASSELL, eldest son of George H , late of Ripon, Yorks, Esq ,
                                                                    [deceased

Nov 17. WILLIAM SWINEY, second son of George S , of Pontefract, Yorks, Esq

„ 20   GEORGE NATHANIEL BEST, second son of the Rev Whittingham B , late
                              [Rector of Sunbury, Middlesex, deceased

„ 23   JOSEPH WRIGHT, only son of John W , late of the parish of St. Luke,

1785   [Middlesex, gent , deceased

Feb 2   ROBERT DENT, second son of Robert D , of Temple Bar, London, Esq

„ 11   THOMAS EAMES, of Staple Inn, London, gent   [London, gent

Mar 26   JOHN WILLING WARREN, only son of Peter W , of Mildred Court, Cornhill,

„ 28   HENRY EDWARD CHURCH, of Gray's Inn, gent.

April 26 GEORGE WATKINS, youngest son of Joseph W , of Kensington, Middlesex,
                                                                    [Esq

„ ,   SAMUEL GRAVES, eldest son of John G , of Gravesend, near Castle Dawson,

July 16   THOMAS RIGGE, of Clifton, Gloucester, Esq.   [Ireland, clerk

June 2   JOHN PARRY, of Broseley, Salop, Esq , second son of Charles P , of Bean-
                              [hall, co Worcester, gent , deceased.

July 20   WILLIAM BULLOCK, of Copthall Court, London, gent.

Dec. 16   JOHN EDGWORTH, eldest son of John E , of Brynigroge, co Denbigh, Esc

„ 17   JOHN ALDRIDGE, only son of John A , late of the parish of St George,
                              [Bloomsbury, Middlesex, gent , deceased

June 9   FOWLER HICKES, only son of Fowler H , of Richmond, Yorks, Esq

Dec 26   THOMAS BEARDMORE, only son of Arthur B., late of Walbrook, London, gent ,

1786   [deceased

Jan 11   JOHN CAYLEY, eldest son of John C , late of Bishopsgate Street, London,
          deceased   [Dinton, Bucks, gent , deceased

„ 26   STEPHEN HOPE, eldest son of Stephen H , late of Upton, in the parish of

1786

Feb 9   JOHN GILPIN COOKSON SAWREY, only son of John Gilpin S , Esq , deceased,
         of Broughton Tower, County Palatine of Lancaster   [Wilts

Mar 7   ROBERT ADDAMS HICKES, of the city of Bath, Rector of Broughton Gifford,

May 9   GEORGE ROWLAND MINSHULL, eldest son of William M , of Aston Clinton,
         Bucks, arm   [Stephen, Coleman Street, London, Esq , deceased

,, 13   BENJAMIN BLACKDEN, eldest son of Benjamin B , late of the parish of St

June 7   BROOKE BAINES HURLOCK, second son of Rev Brooke H , Rector of
         Larmarsh, Essex   [gent , deceased

July 4   JOHN EDWARD BOUFFLOWER, youngest son of Edward B , late of Gray's Inn,

Nov. 6   WILLIAM BRIMAGE, only son of William B , late of Darlington, Durham, gent ,
         deceased.   [Clement Danes, Middlesex, Esq , deceased

,, 8   THOMAS LODINGTON, youngest son of Thomas L , late of the parish of St

,, 15   WILLIAM BENFORD, only son of William B., late of Wanstead, Essex, Esq ,

,, 16   ROBERT BAYLY, second son of John B., of Plymouth, merchant.   [deceased.

1787   [deceased

Jan 8   HENRY PLAYFORD, eldest son of Henry P , late of Northrepps, Norfolk, Esq ,

,, 17   ROBERT BISS, only son of John B , of Deptford, in the parish of Bishop Wear-
         mouth, co. Durham, gent.   [Lodge, Kent, Esq , deceased

,, 20   WILLIAM ALEXANDER MORLAND, eldest son of Thomas M , late of Court

,, 25   WILLIAM LEESON, third son of Charles L , of Burton-upon-Trent, Stafford,
         " Potificis "   [in the city of London, gent

Feb 13   JAMES HAGUE, of Bartletts Buildings, in the parish of St Andrews, Holborn,

Mar 16   WILLIAM ROUTH, eldest son of Richard R , late of the city of York, merchant,
         deceased (admitted to Lincoln's Inn, Nov 6, 1780, per certificate of
         [J Madock, Treasurer)

,, 19   JOHN TOPHAM, arm , third son of Matthew T , of Great Hatfield, Yorks, M A
         (admitted to Lincoln's Inn, Feb 5, 1771, as per certificate of J Madock,
         [Treasurer)

April 24 HARRY EDGELL, eldest son of Hippie E., of Warminster, Wilts, Esq

,, 30   DAVID JENKINS, eldest son of David J , of Presteigne, Radnor, Esq

May 19   ALLATSON BURGH, eldest son of Allatson B , of John Street, in the parish of
         St Andrews, Holborn, Middlesex, gent   [London, merchant

June 23. WILLIAM MALIBY, youngest son of Brough M , of Barge Yard, Bucklersbury,

Aug 24   THOMAS SERMON, third son of John S , late of Wapping, Middlesex, gent , decd

1788

Jan. 23 THOMAS SMITH, only son of John S , of Cirencester, co Gloucester, Esq

,, 29   JAMES COOPER, of Gray's Inn, gent   [Martyr, Middlesex, gent

April 8 EDWARD AINGE, eldest son of Alexander A , of the parish of St George the

,, 19   WILLIAM POPE, eldest son of William P , of Hillingdon, Middlesex, Esq
         [Esq

May 1   ARTHUR DAVIES OWEN, eldest son of Owen O , of Berriew, co. Montgomery,

,, 7   JOHN HULLOCK, only son of Timothy H , of Barnard Castle, co Durham, gent

,, 21   THOMAS COOKE, of University College, Oxford, M A   [the Bench

,, 23   ALAN CHAMBRE, junior, grandson (" nepos ") of Alan C , one of the Masters of

,, 24   JOSEPH LOWTEN, of Gray's Inn, gent   [deceased

,, 28   JOHN STANDFORD GIRDLER, only son of Joseph G., late of Gray's Inn, Esq ,

1788

July 8   JOHN MYERS, youngest son of Rev Thomas M , of Barton, Westmoreland

Aug 26   FRANCIS KINGSTON, fourth son of John K , late of Chesham, Eucks, gent ,
        deceased   [morgan, gent

Nov 5   JOHN HUMPHREYS, eldest son of William H , of Garth-Graban Park, co Gla-

,, 6   CHARLES ELLIOTT ROWAND, eldest son of Robert R , of Edinburgh, Esq

,, 12   WILLIAM WALKER, only son of Thomas W , of Eaglescliffe, co Durham, gent

,, 13   JOSEPH SMITH, eldest son of John S , of Guildford, Surrey, gent

,, 15   WILLIAM DUPPA, second son of William D , of Bromyard, co Hereford, gent

,, 22   EBENEZER GEORGE NICOLAUS BRIAN MUSSELL, only son of Ebenezer M , of
                                [Bethnal Green, Middlesex, Esq

1789   [deceased

Jan 16   WILLIAM BOUTFLOWER, brother of John Edward B , late of this Society,

,, 23   GEORGE DANIEL HARVEY, only son of Daniel H , of Wivenhoe, Essex, Esq

,, ,,   ROBERT LONG, of East Street, in the parish of St George the Martyr, Middle-

,, ,,   JOSEPH EGERTON, of Gray's Inn, gent   [sex, gent

,, 24   CHARLES MURRAY, fifth son of John M , of Norwich, M D

,, 29   WILLIAM DAVID EVANS, of Gray's Inn, gent

,, 30   BASIL MONTAGU, of Christ College, Cambridge, Esq.

Feb. 2   SIMON BRADSTREET, eldest son of Samuel B , Baronet, one of the Justices of
                               [the King's Bench in Ireland

Mar 1   PHILIP DAUNCEY, eldest son of John D , of Wotton-under-Edge, co. Glouces-
        ter, gent. (admitted to the Middle Temple, May 1, 1777, as per certificate
                             [of Jerome Knapp, Treasurer)

,, 21   DUDLEY BAXTER, only son of Dudley B , of Atherstone, co Warwick, gent

,, 27   THOMAS WALKER, only son of John W , of Gray's Inn, Esq

April 29   JOSEPH BILTON, eldest son of Joseph B , late of Healds, Yorks, Esq deceased
                                      [deceased

June 11   FRANCIS MAUDE, eldest son of Francis M., late of Lathley, Yorks, Esq ,

,, 22   GREGOR FARQUHARSON, of the parish of St Clement Danes, Middlesex, gent

,, 23   WILLIAM LAWSON, of Gray's Inn, gent

,, 20   ROBERT SHAFTO HEDLEY, eldest son of Robert H , of Newcastle-upon-Tyne,

July 10   SAMUEL GREATHEAD, of Merstham, Surrey, gent   [Esq

,, 29   NATHANIEL WARNER BROMLEY, of Gray's Inn, gent

Aug 20   JOHN OLIVER, second son of Thomas O , late of Chester, Esq., deceased

Oct 20.   THOMAS THORP, eldest son of Rev Robert T., of Gateshead, co Durham, clerk

,, ,,   JOHN WHISHAW, of Trinity College, Cambridge, gent.

,, 28   WILLIAM DOMVILLE, of St Albans, Herts, gent   [Middlesex, gent , deceased.

Nov 21   WILLIAM WYCHE, only son of William W , late of the parish of St Marylebone,

,, 23   EDWARD O'FARRELL, eldest son of Michael O'F , late of co Limerick, gent.,

1790   [deceased

Jan 14   THOMAS HARRISON, only son of Thomas H , of Kendal, Westmoreland, gent

,, 23   JOHN MARSHALL of Gray's Inn, gent   [gent

,, ,,   HENRY BATEMAN, only son of John B , of the parish of St. Andrew, Holborn,

    28.   RICHARD HUGHES LLOYD, eldest son of Hugh Hughes L., late of Gwerclas,
        co Merioneth, Esq , deceased (admitted to Lincoln's Inn, May 12, 1789,
                            [as per certificate of E Leeds, Treasurer)

1790

Jan 28   GEORGE ALLEN, eldest son of Thomas A , of Bridgewater, co Somerset, Esq

,, 30.   SAMUEL PRYER, of Gray's Inn, gent

Feb. 1   JOHN LEIGH, of Liverpool, co Lancaster, gent.

,, 16   THEOPHILUS WALFORD, of the parish of St George the Martyr, Middlesex, gent

April 23   WILLIAM GREY, of Gray's Inn, gent   [Esq , deceased.

May 1   RICHARD WILSON, second son of George W , late of Hepscot, Northumberland,

,, 2   ROBERT BRADSTREET, only son of Robert B , late of Higham, Suffolk, Esq., deceased (admitted to Lincoln's Inn, July 18, 1782, as per certifi- [cate of Edward Leeds, Treasurer)

,, 6   JAMES CAMPBELL, of the parish of St Martin-in-the-Fields, Middlesex, gent

June 5.   WALTER PRIDEAUX, youngest son of Walter P , of Dartmouth, Devon, gent.

,, 4   JOHN KING, youngest son of Rev. James K , Dean of Raphoe (admitted to [Lincoln's Inn, June 4, 1790, as per certificate of John Soley, Treasurer)

,, 5   GEORGE TENNANT, of Gray's Inn, gent

,, 22   THOMAS SKEPPER, of Gray's Inn, gent.

July 14   RICHARD SPRANGER, second son of John S , of Lincoln's Inn, Esq

,, 26   RICHARD DONOVAN, eldest son of James D , of the Island of Antigua, Esq

Oct 4   JOHN BATEMAN, second son of John B , of Derby, Esq

Nov. 5   MAURICE MAGRATH, third son of Patrick M , of Church Town, co Cork, Esq

,, ,,   COURTNEY KENNY GARNETT, eldest son of John G , late of Warings Town, [co Down, gent , deceased

,, 8   THOMAS WEBB, second son of William W , of Hill Town, co Westmeath, Esq

,, ,,   JOHN BELL, only son of Matthew B , late of Kendal, co Westmoreland, gent. deceased (admitted to the Middle Temple, Nov 10, 1787, as per cer- [tificate of S Brooksbank, Treasurer)

,, ,,   FREDERIC CONINGSBY JONES, eldest son of John J , of Monkland, co. Here- [ford, gent.

,, 13   THOMAS HOPPER, eldest son of Christopher H , of Durham, gent.

,, 16   JAMES TALBOT, second son of Richard T , of Malahide Castle, co Dublin, Esq

,, 18   JOHN WILDE, of the city of Durham, gent

,, 26   BARTHOLOMEW RUDD, son and heir of Bartholomew R , of Gisbrough, Yorks, gent (admitted to the Inner Temple, Aug 11, 1787, as per certificate of [James Mingay, Treasurer)

Dec 10   LOCKHART JOHNSTONE, youngest son of James J , of Worcester, M D

1791   [alderman

Jan 20   RICHARD KIRTON, only son of William K , of the city of Durham, Esq and

,, 24   JOHN MAKEPEACE, of Gray's Inn, gent

,, ,,   HAMLET ALEXANDER CHASE, of Gray's Inn, gent

,, 20   JOHN PINNIGER, eldest son of John P , of Whyr, Wilts, gent

Feb 2   WILLIAM TURBUTT, eldest son of William T , of Ogston Hall, co Derby, Esq

,, 3   WILLIAM HEMPHILL, eldest son of John H , of Rathneny, co Tipperary, Esq

,, 12   JAMES McMICHAEL, of Gray's Inn, gent

,, 21   EDWARD O'SHAUGNUSSEY, of Gray's Inn, gent   [city of Dublin, deceased

,, ,,   JOHN BROWNE, eldest son of Hon Arthur B , an officer in the army, late of the

Mar 18   JOHN BALDWEN, of Ingthorpe, in the parish of Marton-in-Craven, Yorks, gent.

1791

Mar 20   EDWARD STANLEY, eldest son of Arthur S, of Dublin, Esq

„ 31.   ROBERT BRIDE, only son of Patrick B, of Dublin, Esq

April 29   GEORGE BARNES, third son of Thomas B, of Dublin

„ „   JOHN ROBERT GALBRAITH, of Gray's Inn, gent

May 5.   CHARLES ROUND, second son of James R, of Birch Hall, Essex, Esq

April 11   JOHN ATKINSON, fifth son of George A, late of Temple Sowerby, Westmore-
                                                                          [land, Esq, deceased

„ „   JOHN YOUNG, of Kingston-upon-Hull, gent

„ 12   JOSEPH HAY FARQUHARSON, eldest son of Gregor F, Fellow of Gray's Inn

May 20   JOHN DAVIDSON, eldest son of Thomas D, late of Newcastle-upon-Tyne, Esq,
                                                                                 [deceased

„ 21   JOSIAS READSHAW MORLEY, of Richmond, Yorks, gent

„ 24   WILLIAM CHAYTOR, eldest son of William C, of Spennithorne, Yorks, Esq

„ 30   RICHARD ORPEN, eldest son of Richard O, of Ardtully, co Kerry Esq

„ „   THOMAS LLOYD, eldest son of Thomas L, of Prospect, co Limerick, Esq

June 4   JAMES GERAHTY, eldest son of Peter G, of Dublin, Esq

„ „   WILLIAM O'BRIEN LARDNER, eldest son of John L, of Ennis, co. Clare, Esq

„ „   JAMES LYNE, eldest son of Cornelius L, of Dublin, Esq

„ 6   FRANCIS ROBERT SMYTHIE DEVINS, only son of Richard D, of Wimpole
         Street, London, Esq, one of the Examiners (by Letters Patent) "recti-
                                                                     [galium" to the King

July 7   SAMUEL BOWYER, eldest son of Samuel B, late of this Society, deceased.

„ 6   JOHN LONGDEN, grandson (nepos) of John Sherwin, one of the Masters of the
                                                                                  [Bench

June 23   EDWARD CHAPLIN, of Trinity College, Cambridge, only son of Amos C, of
                                                              [Kentish Town, Middlesex, Esq

„ „   THEOBALD BUTLER, eldest son of James B, of Kilcommon, co Tipperary, Esq

„ „   JOHN ARTHUR GOULDSBURY, eldest son of John G., of Aughnagore, co
                                                                       [Longford, Esq.

„ 24   JOHN NEEDHAM, eldest son of Robert N, of Hilston, co Monmouth, Esq.

July 28   JOHN BARBER, of Gray's Inn, gent   [clerk

Aug 1   RICHARD LEIGH SPENCER, second son of Rev. Woolley S, of Upchurch, Kent,

„ 6   GEORGE FRENCH, eldest son of Arthur F., of French Park, co Roscommon,
                                                                                  [Esq

Nov 7   THOMAS CREEVEY, only son of William C, late of Liverpool, merchant,
         deceased (admitted to the Inner Temple, Nov 9, 1789, as per certificate
                                                             [of James Mingay, Treasurer).

„ 8   JOHN BRUMELL, only son of George B, of Newcastle-upon-Tyne Esq

„ 10   THOMAS WILLIAM CARR, of Gray's Inn, gent

„ 12.   RICHARD LEGARD, youngest son of Digby L., of Ganton, Yorks, Baronet

„   GEORGE TISDALL, second son of the Ven Michael T, Archdeacon of Ross,

„ „   JOHN CREAGHE, second son of John C, of co. Limerick, Esq   [Ireland

„ 16   WILLIAM PALMER, of Gray's Inn, Esq.

Dec 8.   JONATHAN TOWNLEY, eldest son of Richard T., of Ambleside, Westmoreland,
1792   [Esq
Jan 4   WILLIAM WILLIAMS, of Gray's Inn, gent

Feb 8   GEORGE CHUBBE PARSONS, eldest son of George P, of Hadley, Suffolk, Esq

1792   [Hants, Esq , deceased

Feb 9   GEORGE JOCELYN ROBINSON, third son of George Jocelyn R , late of Twyford,

„   „   JOHN FENTON CAWTHORNE, of Wyerside, co Lancaster, Esq

„   „   EDMUND BRADSTREET, third son of Samuel B , Baronet, late one of the
                                    [Justices of the King's Bench in Ireland, deceased

„   16   ALEXANDER MACDONELL, of Gray's Inn, gent

„   20   RICHARD PITT, eldest son of George P , late of Worcester, Esq , deceased

Mar 14   JOHN WILLIAMSON, eldest son of William W , of Swinnow Park, Yorkshire,
                  Esq (admitted to the Inner Temple, Jan 20, 1786, as per certificate of
                                                    [John Blencowe, Treasurer)

April 25 SAMUEL DENTON, of Gray's Inn, gent   [the King's Bench in Ireland

May 7   JOHN BRADSTREET, fourth son of Samuel B , Baronet, one of the Justices of

„   „   EDWARD BAYLEY, third son of John B , late of Stukeley, Hunts, Esq , deceased.

„   „   SAMUEL WARD, second son of Benjamin W , of co Dublin, gent

June 13. WILLIAM FRENCH MAJOR, of Market Harborough, co Leicester, Esq

„   18   JAMES WILLIAMS, eldest son of James W , late of Bilmacud, co Dublin, Esq ,
                                                                     [deceased.

„   26   JOHN BENBOW, youngest son of John B , of Ribbesford, co Worcester, gent.

July 4   THOMAS HOWELL ARMSTRONG, eldest son of Robert A , of Dublin, chemist

„   „   JOHN DYNELEY, second son of Robert D , a Fellow of this Society

Nov. 1   GEORGE WAILES, third son of William W , of Northallerton, Yorks, Esq

„   10   HENRY BLACKMAN, only son of Henry B , of Lewes, Sussex, Knight

„   13   WILLIAM SPEAR, of Gray's Inn, gent

„   „   THOMAS HALLWARD, of Gray's Inn, gent

„   15   ROBERT SLOPER, third son of Robert S , Knight of the Bath   [Esq

„   23   ALEXANDER SETON, eldest son of James S , of Perrymount, co Tyrone,

„   24   EYRE EVANS, only son of Eyre E , late of Miltown, co Cork, Esq , deceased

„   „   CHARLES SPREAD, second son of Thomas S , of the city of Cork, Esq

1793

Jan 24   FRANCIS JOHNSON third son of Christopher J , of the city of Durham, Esq ,
                  (admitted to Lincoln's Inn, April 1, 1779, as per certificate, of Francis
                  Burton, Treasurer)   [St Marylebone, Esq

„   28   RICHARD COOKE, only son of John C , of Cavendish Street, in the parish of

„   „   JEFFERY SPRANGER, third son of John S , Master in Chancery

„   29   WILLIAM CARROLL MOONY, eldest son of James Carroll, late of Newlawn, co
                                                    [Tipperary, Esq , deceased

„   „   WILLIAM JACKSON, only son of John J , of Hampton, Middlesex, gent

„   30   ROBERT THORP, eldest son of Rev Robert T , of Gateshead, co Durham,
                  Professor of Theology   [parish of St Pancras, Esq , deceased

Feb. 11   FRANCIS PLAISTOW, only son of Richard P , late of Howland Street, in the

„   „   HORACE TOWNSEND, eldest son of Rev Edward Synge T., of Bridge Mount,

Mar 14. CHARLES JAMES BAILEY, of Gray's Inn, gent.   [co Cork

„   29   ROPER STOTE DONNISON, only son of Rev. Watson Stote D , of Trimdon, co
                                                    [Durham, clerk

April 18 JAMES BOUCHIER, second son of James B , of Baggotshill, co Limerick, Esq ,

1793

April 25.   ROBERT LASCELLES CARR, second son of Samuel C., of Finchley, Middlesex,

,,   29   THOMAS KIERNAN, of Gray's Inn, gent   [Professor of Theology

May   2   JOSHUA LUCOCK WILKINSON, of Gray's Inn, gent   [the Exchequer in Ireland

,,   4   WALTER AGLIONBY YELVERTON, third son of Hon Barry Y., Chief Baron of

,,   ,,   OWEN O'MALLEY, eldest son of George O'M., of Castlebar, co. Mayo, Esq

,,   7   RICHARD NEWTON BENNETT, eldest son of Richard B., of co Wexford, gent

,,   9   PETER RAUGHSEDGE, of Gray's Inn, gent

,,   11   GILBERT FITZGERALD, eldest son of Stephen F., of Ballythomas, Queen's
County   [Dublin, Esq., deceased

,,   12   ANNESLEY HILLAS, eldest son of Wynne H., late of Charlemount Street,

June   5   THOMAS BLACKSTOCK, third son of John B., of Liverpool, merchant.

,,   ,,   JOHN SMYTH, second son of John S., of the city of Dublin, gent

,,   13   THOMAS WHITE, second son of Robert W., of the city of Durham Esq.

,,   ,,   THOMAS HUTCHINSON, second son of Norton H., late of Mardock, near Ware,
Herts, Esq (admitted to the Middle Temple, Nov 3, 1785, as per
[certificate of John Morris, Treasurer)

July   3   JOHN DENNE, of Gray's Inn, gent   [Gloucester, gent

Aug   9   EBENEZER LUDLOW, eldest son of Ebenezer L., of Chipping Sodbury, co

,,   10   WILLIAM WILLIAMS, of the city of Durham, gent

Oct   22   JAMES WILLIAM IRWIN, eldest son of Henry I., of Streamstown, co Sligo, Esq.

Nov   6   WILLIAM MOORE, eldest son of William M., of Cane Wood, Island of Barba-
[dos, Esq

,,   ,,   HENRY KEMMIS, eldest son of Thomas K., of the city of Dublin, Esq

,,   ,,   GEORGE HEALD, eldest son of Richard H., of Horncastle, co Lincoln, Esq

,,   ,,   RICHARD HOLDEN, of Rotherham, Yorks, gent

,,   13   AARON GRAHAM, of Great Russell Street, Bloomsbury, Esq

,,   14   THOMAS POOLE, eldest son of Hewit P., of May Field, co Cork, Esq

,,   ,,   LEONARD RAISBECK, eldest son of John Stapylton R., of Stockton, co Dur-

,,   18   JOHN WILLIAM DAVIS, of Gray's Inn, gent   [ham, gent.

,,   ,,   WILLIAM SMYTH, eldest son of James S., of the city of Dublin, gent

,,   21   FRANCIS PLOWDEN, eighth son of William P., of Plowden, Shropshire, Esq.
(admitted in Middle Temple, July 9, 1791, as per certificate of Edward
[Benson, Treasurer).

,,   22   JOSEPH LITTLEDALE, of St. John's College, Cambridge, gent, eldest son of
Henry L., of Whitehaven, Cumberland, Esq (admitted to Lincoln's Inn,
[March 17, 1786, as per certificate of William Selwyn, Treasurer)

,,   ,,   CHARLES HALL, third son of Charles H., late of the Island of Barbados, Esq.,

,,   26   THOMAS SAUNDERS, only son of Arthur S., of Dublin, M D   [deceased

1794   [Muskerry

Feb   1   ROBERT DEANE (Hon), eldest son of Right Hon Robert Tilson D., Lord

,,   ,,   WILLIAM SMYTH GLENN, eldest son of William G., of the Island of St Vincent, Esq   [Clare, Esq., deceased

,,   8   JOHN WILLIAM HARRISON, eldest son of William H., late of Garrurgh, co

,,   ,,   JOHN SMYTH, second son of John S., late of the city of Dublin, Esq., deceased

,,   11   HENRY BROOKE, eldest son of Gustavus B., of the city of Dublin, Esq

1794

Feb 27 HENRY SOCKEIT, second son of Richard S , late of Worcester, Esq , deceased (admitted to the Inner Temple, Nov 6, 1792, as per certificate of Foster Brown, Treasurer)   [Esq., deceased.

,, ,,   ARTHUR SPARKE, second son of Benjamin S , late of the Inner Temple,

April 12 ROBERT ESPINASSE, son of Isaac E , of Mansfield, co Dublin, Esq

May 2   JOHN WILMER FIELD, eldest son of Joshua F , of Heaton, Yorks, Esq

,, 7   JOHN FRANCIS D'ARCY, eldest son of Christopher D , of Dublin, Esq

,, 13   WILLIAM HAMMOND, only son of John H , of Woodhouse, near Shiffnal,
                                                                [Shropshire, gent.

,, 20   GODFREY SYKES, eldest son of Denis S., of Sheffield, Yorks, gent

,, 31   PETER FLANNAGAN, of Dublin, gent. (admitted to Lincoln's Inn, Nov 15,
                            [1791, as per certificate of Francis Burton, Treasurer)

,, ,,   HERBERT JENNER, second son of Robert J , of Doctors Commons, Esq

June 12 REGNIER BUFFAR, only son of David B , late of Hampstead, Middlesex,
        Esq , deceased.   [Limerick, Esq.

,, 20   WILLIAM JOHNSON WESTROPP, second son of Ralph W , of Attyflin, co

July 1   ARCHIBALD THOMAS ROBINSON, second son of Daniel R , of Gray's Inn, gent.

,, 4   THOMAS TOWNSHEND, fourth son of John T , of Thornhill, co Cork, Esq

,, 8   THOMAS CLIFTON, of Newall-cum-Clifton, Yorks, Esq

,, 9.   WILLIAM FORD DUKE, eldest son of Allured Popple D , late of the Island of
        Barbados, Esq , deceased   [Middlesex, Esq , deceased

Nov 7   WALPOLE EYRE, third son of Walpole E , late of the parish of St. Marylebone,

,, 8   WILLIAM THOMAS, only son of John T , late of county Dublin, Esq , deceased

,, 25   JOHN PRINCE SMITH, only son of Edward S , of Walthamstow, Essex, gent

,, ,,   JOHN SLACKE, only son of Benjamin S , late of Slacke's Grove, co Monaghan,
        Esq , deceased.   [Esq , deceased

,, 29   RICHARD JONES SANKEY, eldest son of Thomas S , late of the city of Dublin,

Dec 3   ROBERRT BLAKENEY, third son of Charles B , of the city of Dublin, Esq

,, 20   EDWARD LLOYD, eldest son of John L , of Berth, co Denbigh, one of the
                                                            [Masters of this Society

1795

Jan. 26. HENRY PLATEL, youngest son of John P , of this Society

,, 30   WILLIAM GRAY, only son of John G , late of Burton-in-Kendal, co West-
        moreland, gent , deceased   [of Birstall, co York, Esq

,, ,,   THOMAS FEARNLEY, eldest son of Benjamin F , of Oakwell Hall, in the parish

Feb. 12 CHARLES HODGSON, third son of Robert H , late of Epsom, co Surrey, Esq ,
        deceased   [Tyne, Esq

April 10 JOHN THEOPHILUS BLAKENEY, second son of William B , of Newcastle-on-

,, 25   ALEXANDER BRUCE, second son of John B , late of Kirkmichael, Scotland,
        Esq , deceased   [land, Esq

,, 29   JOHN PALFREY BURRELL, youngest son of George B , of Alnwick, Northumber-

May 4   RICHARD DAVIS, fourth son of Richard D , of Usk, co Monmouth, gent

,, 12. DANIEL CAMPBELL, second son of Robert C , of the parish of St Anns, Soho,
        Esq   [clerk, deceased

,, 13   JOSEPH BEWSHER, only son of Rev Joseph B , late of Penrith, Cumberland,

June 6   JOHN HUTTON, son and heir of John H , late of Marske, co York (admitted
                                            [to the Inner Temple, May 10, 1795)

1795

June 8   JOHN LYON, eldest son of Edmund L., of Neston, co Cheshire, Esq

,,   9   BRACKLEY KENNETT, third son of Robert K, late of Plymouth Dock, co Devon, Esq, deceased   [bridge, Esq

,,   ,,   HENRY HUDDLESTON, second son of Ferdinand H, of Sawston Hall, co Cam-

,,   ,,   HENRY POTTS, eldest son of Charles P, of the city of Chester, Esq

,,   13   PHILIP ADAMS, only son of Richard A, late of Carlow, Ireland, merchant, [deceased

,,   17   THOMAS PARKER, fourth son of Kenyon P, of Sheffield, co York, gent.

,,   18   ROBERT WHINCOP, eldest son of Edmund W., of Beighton, Norfolk, gent

,,   23   JOHN WHISHAW, fifth son of Richard W, late of Dedham, co Essex, Esq,

,,   ,,   GEORGE JENNER, third son of Robert J, of Doctors Commons, Esq [deceased

July 23   WILLIAM DEANE, eldest son of James D, of Bahama Islands, Esq

Nov 5   THOMAS STRICKLAND, only son of Thomas S, late of Kendal, co Westmore- [land, Esq, deceased

,,   7   THOMAS WALLACE, only son of James W, of the city of Dublin, gent

,,   9   JOHN LEA, eldest son of Edward L, of the city of Dublin, Esq   [deceased

,,   ,,   THOMAS KEATINGE, eldest son of Thomas K, late of the city of Dublin, Esq,

,,   ,,   WILLIAM ELDERTON ALLEN, eldest son of William A, late of Limehouse, co Middlesex, "Carbonari," deceased   [Edinburgh, Esq

,,   ,,   WILLIAM GORDON McCRAE, eldest son of Alexander M, of the city of

,,   21   WILLIAM WHYTEHEAD, eldest son of Rev William W, of Hornsea, co. York,

,,   25   JOHN O'REGAN, eldest son of Matthias O'R, of Grange, co Cork, Esq [clerk

,,   27   HAMILTON MOORE, third son of William M, late of Ramilton, co Donegal, [merchant, deceased.

Dec 4   ROGERS JORTIN, second son of Rogers J, late of this Society, deceased

,,   12   NICHOLAS WILLIAM RIDLEY, second son of Matthew White R, of Blagdon,

1796   [co Northumberland, Baronet

Jan 7   RICHARD WILKINSON, third son of William W, late of Newcastle-on-Tyne, Esq, deceased   [deceased

,,   ,,   JOHN WILKINSON, fifth son of William W, late of Newcastle-on-Tyne, Esq,

,,   27   RICHARD BLEAMIRE, eldest son of William B, barrister, of this Society

Feb 2   WILLIAM TOTTY, third son of John T, late of Holywell, co Flint, gent, deceased   [Esq, deceased

,,   6   WILLIAM COLLES, eldest son of William C, late of Millmount, co Kilkenny,

,,   ,,   CHRISTOPHER JAMES, only son of Christopher J, late of the city of Dublin, merchant, deceased   [merchant

,,   ,,   JOHN KINCHELA, second son of John K, of the city of Kilkenny, Ireland,

,,   8   HENRY BANKES, only son of Rev Thomas B, of the parish of St Martins-in-the-Fields, Middlesex, clerk   [Middlesex, gent

,,   9   WILLIAM ROUGH, only son of William R, of the parish of St James, co

,,   12   CYNRIC LLOYD, fourth son of Bell L, late of Pontryffyd, co Flint, Esq, deceased

Mar 1   WHISTON POWELL, second son of Walter P, of Tooting, co Surrey, Esq.

April 24   HENRY MOORE, eldest son of Richard M, of the city of Dublin, Esq

,   26.   DANIEL O'CONNELL, eldest son of Morgan O'C, of Carhen, co Kerry, Esq (admitted to Lincoln's Inn, January 30, 1794)

1796

April 27   ANTONY WILLS, eldest son of Benjamin W , of the city of Dublin, Esq

,,   28   BUCKNALL McCARTHY, second son of Dalton M , late of the city of Dublin,
                                      [Esq , deceased

,,   30   AMBROSE SMITH, youngest son of Ambrose S , of the city of Dublin, Esq.

,,   ,,   EWER RYAN, second son of George R , of Limerick, Ireland, merchant

May 2   SEDBOROUGH MAYNE, eldest son of Robert M , of the city of Dublin, gent

,,   ,,   JAMES WESTERN, fifth son of Thomas W., late of the city of Bath, Somerset,
      Esq., deceased   [merchant

,,   5   CLEMENT CONOLLY, eldest son of Edward C , of the city of Dublin, Ireland,

,,   ,,   DEANE BAYLY, second son of William B , of the city of Dublin, gent

,,   ,,   JOHN PRUJEAN, only son of John P , formerly of this Society, deceased

,,   30   ROBERT FRY, third son of Robert F , late of Chancery Lane, gent , deceased

June 2   THOMAS SUNDERLAND, second son of Thomas S , of Ulverston, co Lanc , Esq

,,   10   JOHN CALDWELL, eldest son of Colonel Henry C , of Quebec, in the province
      of Canada (admitted to Lincoln's Inn, May 16, 1792).   [Esq , deceased

,,   11   WILLIAM ROSCOE, eldest son of William R , late of Liverpool, co Lancaster,

Dec 24   ALEXANDER DONOVAN, eldest son of James D , of the city of Dublin, Ireland,

Aug 5   JOSEPH BYRNE, eldest son of John B , of the city of Dublin, Esq   [merchant

Nov 8   WILLIAM JOHN McMAHON, eldest son of John McM , late of Arbour Hill, co
                              [Dublin, merchant, deceased

,,   ,,   THOMAS BALL, eldest son of William B , of Rathmines, co Dublin, Esq

,,   ,,   THOMAS RICHARD BABINGTON, eldest son of Richard B , of the city of
                              [Londonderry, Ireland, merchant

,,   23   GILES CROMPE, only son of Giles C , of the city of London, gent

,,   21   DENIS O'BRIEN, eldest son of William O , of Tipperary, co Tipperary, Esq.

,,   25   EDMUND MICHAEL DALY, only son of John Michael D , of the city of Dublin,
1797   M D   [Esq, deceased

Jan 23   RICHARD BOURKE, eldest son of John B , late of Ballyguy, co Limerick,

,,   25   GEORGE ALCOCK, only son of George A , late of the city of Dublin, Alderman,
      deceased   [Yard, in the city of Westminster, Esq

,,   26   GROSVENOR CHARLES BEDFORD, eldest son of Charles B , of New Palace

,,   30   LEWIS THOMAS, second son of Arthur T , of the city of Dublin, gent.

,,   31   HENRY McDOUGALL, eldest son of Andrew M , of the city of Waterford,
      Ireland, merchant   [Holborn, co Middlesex, gent , deceased.

Feb 4   GEORGE LEWES, second son of Philip L , late of the parish of St Andrews,

,,   7   ROBERT SOUTHEY, eldest son of Robert S , of the city of Bristol, gent

,,   9   JOHN STODDART, only son of John S , of the city of Salisbury, Esq.

,,   10   HULTON KING, third son of James K , of the city of Dublin, Ireland, merchant

,,   ,,   JOSEPH DALY, eldest son of Owen D , of the city of Dublin, gent

,,   23   PHILIP STANHOPE, youngest son of Philip S , late of the parish of St James,
      co Middlesex, Esq, deceased   [co Northumberland, Esq

May 6   FRANCIS TWEDDELL, second son of Francis T., of Threepwood, near Hexham,

,,   10   JOHN BARWIS, only son of William B , late of the city of London, M D ,
      deceased   [Esq , deceased

,,   ,,   RICHARD EATON, eldest son of Richard E , late of Richmond, co Dublin,

1799

Nov 7   THOMAS STANLEY, eldest son of Gerard S , of Wallazey, Cheshire, gent.

,, 9   ROBERT GRIFFIN, eldest son of Robert G , of Park Place, in the parish of St. James, co Middlesex, Esq   [Esq

,, 13   WILLIAM MONSELL, eldest son of William Thomas M , of Tervoe, co Limerick,

,, ,,   NORRISON SCATCHERD, eldest son of Watson S , of Morley, co York, Esq

,, ,,   CHARLES JAMES, only son of George J , of Chewmagna, co Somerset, Esq.

,, ,,   WILLIAM TODD, eldest son of William T , of Elstob, co Durham, Esq

,, 18   CHARLES WAPSHARE, son and heir of Charles William W , of Salisbury, co. Wilts, Esq (admitted to the Inner Temple, May 11, 1797)   [Cork, Esq.

,, 22.   THOMAS BARRY, second son of Edmund B , of Kilbolane, near Charleville, co.

Nov 28   JAMES MURE, second son of William M , late one of the Barons of Exchequer [in Scotland, deceased, admitted to Lincoln's Inn, January 30, 1778

Dec 28   JOHN DARBY, eldest son of William D , late of Brough, co Westmoreland,
                                                                    [gent , deceased

1800.   [of Dublin, gent

Jan. 18.   GEORGE CARR, eldest son of Richard Coolan C , of Marlborough Street, city

,, 24   BENJAMIN BURNETT, eldest son of Joseph B , of Christchurch, co Surrey

,, 31.   JOHN WILLSHEN, only son of Daniel W , of Long Acre, co Middlesex, gold-

Feb 7.   JOHN DURDIN, second son of Alexander D , of Dublin, gent   [beater.

Mar 18.   WILLIAM WILSON, youngest son of John W , late of Clapham, co Surrey, Esq , deceased   [deceased

April 22   FOUNTAIN ELWIN, third son of Peter E., late of Booton, co Norfolk, Esq ,

,, 29   RICHARD LAMAR BISSET, only son of Robert B , of London, merchant.

May 2   EATON STANNARD, eldest son of George S , of Priory, co. Cork, Esq

,, 10   JOHN ROSE, second son of Thomas R , of Lower Winchendon, co. Bucking-
                                                                 [ham, gent

,, 9   NICHOLAS PURCELL O'GORMON, second son of James O'G , late of Ennis, co. Clare, Esq , deceased

,, 20   HUGH GEORGE MACKLIN, eldest son of James M., of the city of Londonderry, schoolmaster   [deceased.

June 17   HENRY BARNES, youngest son of John B , late of the Island of Antigua, Esq.,

,, 20   JOHN PENKETH BUÉE, of Cambridge, eldest son of William Urban B , of the [Island of Dominica, Esq

Nov 14   SAMUEL WELLS, eldest son of Samuel W., of Ramsey, co Huntingdon, Esq

,, 17   JOHN ROUND, only son of John R , of Colchester, co. Essex, Esq

,, 21   WILLIAM GRAYDON, eldest son of Robert G., late of Killishee, co Kildare,
                                                                      [Esq , deceased

1801.

Jan 24   JAMES HAMERTON, eldest son of James H , of Peel, near Skipton in Craven, co York, Esq   [deceased

,, 27.   EDWARD VAN HARTHALS, only son of Evert Van H., late of London, merchant,

Feb 10   SAMUEL ROMILLY, eldest son of Thomas Peter R , of Hampstead, Middlesex, Esq   [Esq., deceased

June 9   HENRY WRIXON, eldest son of Edward W , late of Blossom Fort, co. Cork,

Nov 2   JAMES MILES REILLY, youngest son of John R , of Scarva, co Down, Esq

,, 13   THOMAS WILKINSON, eldest son of Matthew W , late of Chester, Esq , deceased.

1802	[Martyr, co Middlesex, gent.
Jan 27	FREDERICK AYRTON, second son of Thomas A, of the parish of St George the
Feb 5	ARTHUR WILLIAM SHAKESPEAR, second son of Arthur S, of Stepney, co Middlesex, Esq [deceased
Mar 9	THOMAS SMITH, only son of Thomas S, late of Walworth, co Surrey, Esq,
April 9	THOMAS NOTTINGHAM, second son of Edward N, late of Heckington Fen, near Sleaford, co Lincoln, Esq., deceased [bone, co Middlesex, Esq, deceased
,, 1	WILLIAM FRANCKLIN, youngest son of John F., late of the parish of St Maryle-
May 18	JAMES KILVINGTON LAMB, only son of James L, of York, gent [deceased
,, ,,	JOHN FRASER, only son of William F., late of Inverness, Scotland, gent,
June 23	GEORGE SHEE, eldest son of Sir George S, of Dunmore, Ireland, Baronet
,, 28	JOHN WYNNE, eldest son of Robert W, of Plasnewydd, co Denbigh, Esq
July 1	JOHN TUBB, eldest son of John T, late of London, gent, deceased [Esq
,, 22	WILLIAM HENRY ROWE, eldest son of William R, of Charmouth, co Dorset,
Nov. 8	ARTHUR DUNN, eldest son of Arthur D, of Ushers Island, co Dublin, gent
,, 9	ROBERT SMITH, third son of Thomas S, of Gedling, co Nottingham, Esq
,, 10	ROBERT PETER DYNELEY, eldest son of Robert D, of this Society [deceased.
,, ,,	BOYCE COMBE, second son of Harvey C, late of Andover, co Hants, gent,
,, 26	EDWARD FOLEY, third son of John F, late of Ridgeway, co Pembroke, Esq [deceased
,, ,,	JAMES JOHN WILKINSON, eldest son of Martin W, of the city of Durham, gent
Dec 11.	SAMUEL COLLINGRIDGE, youngest son of Thomas C, of Theobald's Road, co Middlesex, gent [gent, deceased
1803	
Jan 22.	THOMAS LAMBERT, youngest son of David L, late of New Malton, co York,
Feb. 25	ROBERT ROBBINS, youngest son of George R, late of Fairford, co Gloucester, [gent, deceased,
Mar 19	LUKE PLUNKETT, eldest son of Thomas P, of Portmarnock, co Dublin, Esq
May 2	WILLIAM WALSH, eldest son of John W, of Middleton, co Cork, Esq
,, 9	THOMAS McKANE, youngest son of William M, of Dublin, gent [cary
,, 10	JAMES FALLON, eldest son of Thomas F, of Athlone, co Roscommon, apothe-
,, 17	JOHN WOLFE, eldest son of John W, of Forenaghts, co. Kildare, colonel
,, 22	CHARLES SHEPHARD, eldest son of Rev Thomas S, Rector of Enborne, near Newbury, Berks [schoolmaster
,, ,,	THOMAS THORNTON MACKLIN, second son of James M., of Londonderry,
,, 24	FRANCIS JOHN HASSARD, eldest son of John H, late of the city of Waterford, [Esq, deceased.
,, 25	HENRY COOPER, second son of George C, late of Dublin, Esq, deceased
July 1	Sir RICHARD HANKEY, Knight, eldest son of Joseph Chaplin H, late of London, Esq, deceased. [master
,, 2	GEORGE WRIGHT, eldest son of George W, of Richmond, co Surrey, school-
Nov 11	WILLIAM FITZGERALD, eldest son of David F., late of Adrivale, co Kerry, Esq, deceased [folk, deceased
,, 22	EDWARD HIBGAME, eldest son of Rev Edward H, late of Tasburgh, Nor-
1804	
Jan 28	JOHN ABBOTT, second son of Christopher A, of Dublin, Esq [gent, deceased
Feb 7	CHRISTOPHER BROOME, second son of Francis B, late of Bushten, co Wilts

1804

Feb 8   JOHN BURKE, third son of Ulysses B , of Cork, Esq.

„ 16   PHILIP RAINE, eldest son of Richard R , of Barnard Castle, co Durham, gent

April 24.   JAMES BESSONNET, eldest son of Francis B , late of Dublin, Professor of
[Theology, deceased

May 22   JAMES BLAKE, third son of Charles B , of Innis, co Clare, Ireland, merchant

June 5   FREDERICK CHAMBERLAINE, second son of John C , of Brompton, co
[Middlesex, Esq

„ „   NATHANIEL BARRETT BROMLEY, eldest son of Nathaniel Warner B , of this
Society.   [Esq , deceased

„ 18.   RICHARD SARGENT FOWLER, third son of John F., late of Cote, co Gloucester,

„ 23.   PATRICK ARTHUR, only son of Francis A , of Manchester Square, co
Middlesex, Esq   [Clement Danes, co Middlesex, gent , deceased

July 21   CHRISTOPHER JOHNSON, second son of Robert J , late of the parish of St

„ „   MATTHEW TOPHAM, fourth son of Matthew T , formerly of Great Hatfield,
co York, Master of Arts, deceased   [Southwark, Esq , deceased

Aug 4   EDWARD CLARKE, eldest son of Edward C , late of the parish of St Saviours,

„ 11   WILLIAM YOUNG, eldest son of William Y , of Chancery Lane, co Middlesex,
gent.   [gent , deceased

„ 20   BENJAMIN WINGROVE, second son of John W , late of the city of Bath,

„ „   JAMES STALLARD, only son of James S , of Bath Easton, co Somerset, gent

„ „   JOHN PHYSIC, eldest son of John P , of Tamar, co. Devon

„ „   RICHARD ELSE, ninth son of Rees E , of Bristol, gent   [gent , deceased

„ „   GEORGE ROSS, only son of John R , late of Stoke Newington, Middlesex,

Sept. 6   GEORGE MERRYFIELD, second son of Thomas M , late of the Exchequer
Office, Temple, gent , deceased   [gent , deceased

„ 10   JOHN HOUCHEN, only son of John H , late of Saxlingham Thorpe, Norfolk,

„ 18   JOHN CRISP, eldest son of William C , of Brinton, near East Dereham,
[Norfolk, gent

„ 27   JOHN BEADNELL, eldest son of Christopher B , of Chesterfield, co Derby, gent.

Oct 1   WILLIAM WITHAM, second son of Thomas W., late of the city of Durham,
Esq , deceased   [Middlesex, gent , deceased

„ 4   JOHN WATKINS WILLIAMS, second son of John W., late of Clerkenwell, co.

„ 5   RICHARD STEPHENS TAYLOR, eldest son of William T., of Ebrington, near
[Campden, co Gloucester, gent.

„ „   WILLIAM LEGG, eldest son of William L., of Ely, co. Cambridge, gent

„ 6   WILLIAM DAWSON, only son of Thomas D., late of the city of Lincoln, gent ,
deceased   [gent , deceased.

„ 8   JOHN MITCHINSON, only son of John M , late of Rickergate, near Carlisle,

„ „   THOMAS DOGHERTY, youngest son of Patrick D , late of Edenderry, King's
County, gent , deceased   [gent , deceased

„ „   RICHARD GELDARD, only son of James G., late of Staple Inn, co Middlesex,

„ „   JOHN HINCKLEY, second son of Henry H , late of London, M D , deceased

„ „   THOMAS HAYES LYON, second son of Joseph L , Esq , Barrister of this Society

„ 17   JOHN SQUIRE, son of William S , of Fulstow, co Lincoln, yeoman (" pagani ")

„ 22   EDWARD HOWARD, eldest son of Richard H , late of Oxford University, gent ,

„ 26   JAMES FLORANCE, third son of John F , of Chichester, gent   [deceased

1804   [mouth, gent , deceased

Oct 26.   ROBERT MORGAN KINSEY, eldest son of Robert K , late of Usk, co Mon-

Nov. 2   JOHN COBLEY, eldest son of John C , of Edmonton, co Middlesex, gent

,, 13   WILLIAM BIRT, only son of Thomas B , late of Painswick, co Gloucester,
          gent , deceased   [gent

,, 20   JAMES JAMES, third son of John J , of St Clement's Parish, co Cornwall,

,, 23   JOHN DAY, second son of John D , of Sculcoates, co. York, gent   [gent

,, ,,   WILLIAM STRANGE, eldest son of John S., late of Shalston, co Bucks, yeoman,
          deceased   [gent

,, 27   JOSEPH MORRIS, only son of Joseph M , of Mount Pleasant, co Montgomery,

,, 30.   WILLIAM RICKARD, only son of William R , of St Colomb, Cornwall, gent

Dec 5   RICHARD GEORGE, eldest son of Nicholas G , of St Colomb Minor, Corn-
                                                                 [wall, gent

,, 21   JOHN BOWER, only son of Nathaniel B , of Huddersfield, co York, gent

,, ,,   RICHARD HUTCHINSON, son of Robert H , late of North Wingfield, co Derby
1805   [gent., deceased

Jan 4   GEORGE GOSLING, second son of John G , late of Chesterfield, co Derby,
          yeoman, deceased   [Essex, S T.P.

,, 25   JOHN SWARBRECK GREGORY, eldest son of the Rev George G , of Westham,

,, 21   RICHARD CURGENVEN, second son of William C , of Tregothnan, co Corn-
          wall, Esq   [gent , deceased

,, 23   JOHN SYKES, eldest son of Matthew S , late of East Ardelcy, co York,

,, 24   THOMAS DYNELEY SHORT, second son of Charles S , late of Calcutta, East
          Indies, Esq , deceased.   [co Durham, Esq

Feb 8   JOHN WILLSON, eldest son of William W., of Picktree, near Chester-le-Street,

,, 28   NICHOLAS PEARCE, third son of Richard P , of the parish of St Veep, Corn-
          wall, gent   [" Cultellarii "

Mar 6   JOSEPH HARRIS, eldest son of Edward Masters H , of Huntington,

,, 28.   JOHN YOLLAND, eldest son of John Y , late of Moreton Hampsted, Devon,
                                                            [gent , deceased

,, ,,   MATTHEW ELLISON, eldest son of Michael E., late of the city of Durham,
          gent , deceased   [Worcester, deceased

April 13 THOMAS JAMES, eldest son of the Rev. Thomas J , D D , late Prebendary of

,, 18   JAMES JOHN BAGOT, second son of John B , late of Castle Bagot, co Dublin,
          Esq , deceased   [deceased

,, 30   JAMES DOHERTY, eldest son of John D , late of the city of Dublin, gent ,

May 8   THOMAS RICHARD NEEDHAM, eldest son of Thomas N , of Merrion Street,
          Dublin, Esq   [gent , deceased

,, ,,   THOMAS FLIGHT, second son of Thomas F , late of Hackney, co Middlesex,

,, 10   GEORGE LYNDON, only son of James L., late of Dublin, Esq , deceased

,, 13   WILLIAM BEARD, eldest son of John B , late of Bodmin, Cornwall, gent ,
          deceased   [gent , deceased

,, 14   CHARLES SCOTT, second son of John S , late of High Beckington, Devon,

,, 21   JOHN HELM, eldest son of Richard H , of Kensington, Middlesex, Esq

,, ,,   GEORGE JENKINS, eldest son of William J., late of the parish of Prendergast,
          co Pembroke, yeoman, deceased   [deceased

,, 21   HENRY HAKE SEWARD, eldest son of Henry S , late of Bromley, Kent, gent

1805

June 5   GEORGE WILLIAM WYE, second son of George W., of Mortlake, co Surrey,
      Esq   [Wilts, gent

,, 8   JOHN WHIFFEN HOOPER, only son of Joseph H , of near Warminster,

,, 14   CHARLES HENRY BARBER, only son of John B , a Member of this Society

,, 19   JOHN DAVIES, eldest son of John D , late of Staple Inn, co Middlesex, gent,
       deceased   [Sligo, co Sligo. Ireland, Esq

,, 29   RICHARD HIGGINS EVERARD, B A, aged 21, second son of Ignatius E , of

July 11   JOHN TYSON, aged 52, of Woolwich Dockyard, eldest son of Thomas T , late
                             [of Ulverstone, Lancashire, Esq , deceased

,, 12   THOMAS ALFRED SIMMONS, aged 24, of Northleach, co Gloucester, land
       steward to Viscount Courtenay, only son of Thomas S , of Northleach,
       co Gloucester, Esq   [Hilary, co Cornwall, gent , deceased

Aug 8   FRANCIS JAMES, aged 47, second son of John J , late of the parish of St

,, 22   JOHN WELLS, aged 44, of St Neots, Hunts, only son of Edmund W , of Market
       Rasen, co Lincoln, gent   [St Mary, Devon, gent , deceased

,, 26   GILBERT HELE CHILCOTT aged 40, only son of Joseph C , late of Ottery

,, 28   FRANCIS BAILY, aged 31, third son of Richard B , of Newbury, Berks, gent

Sept 3   JOHN EVSTON, aged 45, of Welford, Northants, second son of John E , late
       of Hendred, Berks, Esq , deceased   [Devon, gent , deceased

,, 15.   ROBERT BINT, aged 54, only son of Robert B , late of Mount Edgcumbe,

Oct. 30.   ALEXANDER LAW, aged 50, of Littleham, Devon, ninth son of John S , late of
       the city of Aberdeen, gent , deceased   [Cork, gent , deceased

Nov 21.   CORNELIUS O'LEARY, aged 36, eldest son of Arthur O , late of Raleigh, co

,, ,,   ROBERT PHIPPS, LL D., aged 38, eldest son of Matthew P , late of Sligo,
       Ireland, Esq , deceased   [Highgate, Middlesex, gent

Dec 19.   CHARLES HODGES WARE, aged 35, an attorney, second son of Samuel W., of

,, 29.   JOHN LEACOCK, merchant, aged 45, eldest son of John L , late of the Island of
1806   [Madeira, merchant, deceased

Jan. 6.   GEORGE SIMMONS, aged 47, the elder, of Trevella, Cornwall, eldest son of
               [George S , late of Treventham, co. Cornwall, gent , deceased.

,, 24.   JOHN JOPE (Rev), only son of Robert J , late of Callington, co. Cornwall,
       gent , deceased   [Chichester, Sussex, gent , deceased

Feb. 6   GEORGE LONG, aged 26, second son of Joseph L , late of Shopwick, near

,, 8   JOHN DAW, aged 45, of East Budleigh, gent , fourth son of John D., late
                      [of Black Torrington, co Devon, yeoman, deceased

,, 12   PETER PAIGE, aged 38, eldest son of Peter P , late of Black Torrington,
                      [co Devon, yeoman, deceased

April 7   GEORGE HILL, aged 43, of Launceston, third son of Roger H , late of the
               [parish of St. Peter, city of Exeter, serge maker, deceased

,, ,,   RICHARD DEWES, aged 40, of Coventry, only son of Richard D., late of
               [Kenilworth, co Warwick, seedsman, deceased

May 9.   WILLIAM CARTWRIGHT, aged 37, land steward to William, Viscount Courtenay,
       eldest son of William C , late of the parish of Exminster, co Devon,
                                 [gent , deceased

,, 15   OLIVER CROMWELL, aged 63, of Cheshunt Park, Herts, clerk of St Thomas
       Hospital, Southwark, second son of Thomas C , late of Enfield, co
                            [Middlesex, Esq , deceased

1806		[city of Dublin, Esq

1806   [city of Dublin, Esq

May 17   WILLIAM FRANKLAND, aged 29, of Clifford's Inn, second son of John F, of the

„ 23   JOSEPH BENNICKE, aged 60, of Brixton, Devon, gent, eldest son of Thomas B,
                         [late of Liskeard, co. Cornwall, gent, deceased.

„ 24   CUTHBERT ROMILLY, aged 17, third son of Thomas Peter R, of Warren Street,
       Fitzroy Square, co Middlesex, Esq   [Ireland, Esq

June 2.   WILLIAM BRIEN, aged 30, eldest son of Henry B, of Gargadis, co Tyrone,

„ 7   WILLIAM CROOTE, aged 30, land surveyor, only son of John C, of Chumleigh,
                               [co Devon, land surveyor

„ 9   EDWARD GREENHILL, aged 24, of Girdlers Hall, City, only son of James G,
       formerly of Lincoln's Inn, and late of Greville Street, Holborn, co
       Middlesex, gent, deceased   [gent

„ 14   WILLIAM HARVEY, aged 39, only son of John H, of Donnington, co Lincoln,

„ „   THOMAS FOSTER, aged 36, second son of William F, late of Stamford, co
       Lincoln, Esq, deceased   [P, of Cullompton, co Devon, gent

„ 16   HENRY PANNELL, aged 44, of Cullompton, land steward, eldest son of Thomas

„ 19   JAMES STAVELY, aged 21, fourth son of Luke S, of Halifax, Yorks, merchant

„ 10   JOHN HONEY, aged 41, of Redruth, schoolmaster, eldest son of John H, late
                         [of Redruth, co Cornwall, schoolmaster, deceased

Aug 14   WILLIAM CALDWELL, aged 35, of Frodsham, Cheshire, only son of Joseph C,
                               [of Moore, co Chester, gent

„ 15   FRANCIS DYNELEY, aged 21, fifth son of Robert D, of Bloomsbury Square,
             [Middlesex, gent, deceased, late a Member of this Society

„ 16   WILLIAM EDWARD WARD, aged 54, clerk of the Mercers Company, only son
           [of William W, late of Greenwich, co Kent, gent, deceased

Sept 20   GEORGE JEFFERYS, aged 23, of Magdalen Hall, Oxford, third son of John
         [Latoysonere J, late of the Island of Nevis, Esq, deceased.

Nov 8   HUGH DELAP, aged 28, third son of Rev Hugh D, late of Stranfield, co
                               [Tyrone, Ireland, deceased

„ „   JOHN CLARK, aged 20, eldest son of John C, of the city of Dublin, Esq

„ 10   PATRICK KIERNAN, eldest son of Francis K, of the Custom House, Dublin,
       Esq   [Ireland, Esq, deceased

„ 15   JOHN BERNARD, aged 21, eldest son of John B, late of Ballynegar, co Kerry,

„ „   JAMES O'DOGHERTY, aged 33, second son of George O, late of Clones, co
                       [Monaghan, Ireland, merchant, deceased

„ 19   JACOB STORDY, aged 45, of Carlisle, youngest son of Thomas S, late of
       Thurstonfield, Cumberland, gent, deceased   [gent

Dec 6   JOHN MARTIN BLIGH, aged 26, only son of James B, of St Mabyn, Cornwall,

„ 26   JOHN SPRINGALL, aged 29, only son of John S, of the city of Canterbury,

1807   gent   [W, late of the city of Dublin, Esq, deceased.

Jan 28   CHAMBERLEN RICHARD WALKER, aged 22, eldest son of Maynard Chamberlen

„ 30.   THOMAS WARE, aged 50, of Beaminster, Dorset, third son of Richard W,
       late of Sherborne, Dorset, gent, deceased.   [gent, deceased

Feb 20   JAMES BROWN, aged 47, eldest son of Thomas B, late of Dulverton, Somerset,

Mar 2   JOSEPH HONE, aged 24, second son of William H, of Hammersmith, Middle-
                               [sex, lime merchant

„ 24   THOMAS LEADBITTER, aged 54, of Hexham, sixth son of Matthew L, late of
             [Nether-Warden, Northumberland, gent, deceased

1807

April 16   THOMAS HOLMES, aged 16, eldest son of Rev Thomas H , of Bungay, Suffolk,
            Rector of Woodton, Norfolk   [Ireland, Esq

May 6   THOMAS FORDE, aged 18, third son of Matthew F , of Seaford, co Down,

,,   2   JOHN BOOTH BARTON, aged 20, of Trinity College, Dublin, eldest son of
            [Colonel John B , late of the Hon E I C S , deceased

,,   20   ROBERT PEACOCK, aged 35, of Winchester, only son of Francis P , late of
            Orange Grove, Bath, gent , deceased   [merchant

June 13   ROBERT LINDSELL, fourth son of John L , of St Ives, co Huntingdon,

July 7   HENRY COLE, aged 60, of Peterborough, eldest son of Henry C , late of
            Melton Mowbray, co Leicester, Esq , deceased   [Derby, gent

Aug 1   WILLIAM WHISTON, of Derby, eldest son of Robert W , of Ashbourne, co

Nov 18   HENRY NORTH, aged 23, only son of Henry N , of Walworth, Surrey, gent.

,,   23   WILLIAM WILLIAMS WILMOT, aged 34, third son of Richard W , of Chichester,
            Esq   [deceased

,,   25   JOHN EVANS, aged 26, eldest son of John E , late of the city of Limerick, gent ,

Dec 26   THOMAS ALEXANDER RAVNSFORD, second son of Richard R , late of Lans-
            down Place, Middlesex, Esq , deceased.   [gent

,,   THOMAS HEATHER, aged 38, eldest son of Thomas H , of Portsmouth, Hants,

1808

Jan 8   SEGRAVE McCORMICK, aged 26, only son of William M , of Wexford, Esq

Feb 8.   JOHN CAMPBELL CAMERON, aged 21, second son of Hugh C , late of Basinghall
            [Street, London, gent , deceased

Mar 11   SAMUEL PONT BUTCHER, aged 34, only son of Thomas B , late of Blackman
            Street, Southwark, gent , deceased.   [Drayton, co Leicester, gent

,,   15.   JOHN ROYLE, aged 35, of the city of Coventry, eldest son of William R , of

April 2   BENJAMIN EAMONSON, aged 19, of Queen's College, Cambridge, eldest son of
            [Benjamin E , late of Bramham, co York, Esq , deceased

May 11   JAMES POPE, aged 33, of Truro, Cornwall, youngest son of Joshua P , late of
            Exeter, gent., deceased.   [co. Cavan, Ireland, Esq , deceased

,,   19   ANDREW NIXON, aged 25, eldest son of George N., late of Lurgan Lodge,

,,   20.   PHILIP CRAMPTON, aged 26, junior fellow, Trinity College, Dublin, fourth son
            [of Rev Cecil C , of Headford co Galway

June 13   ISAAC BARNES, aged 31, third son of Hugh B , of Dalby, co Leicester, gent

,,   14   JOSEPH SMITH, aged 33, eldest son of Charles S., late of Brockham Green,
            co. Surrey, Esq , deceased   [Society

,,   15   WILLIAM JOHN LYON, aged 17, third son of Joseph L , Esq , barrister, of this

,,   21   JAMES HENRY EARLE, aged 20, second son of Sir James E , of Hanover
            Square, co. Middlesex, Knight   [Hospital, London, gent

,,   23.   EDWARD EYRE, aged 35, fourth son of Gillingham E., of St Bartholomews

,   30   STEPHEN CLEMENT WEBB, aged 31, of Bath, only son of Thomas W , late of
            [Worcester, gent , deceased.

Oct 6   ROBERT CARTWRIGHT, of Haldon House, Kenn, Devon, second son of William
            [C , late of the parish of Exminster, co Devon, gent , deceased.

Nov 5   EDWARD LITTON, aged 21, third son of Edward L , late of Holles Street,
            [Dublin, Esq , deceased

,,   7   THOMAS BELL, aged 21, eldest son of Thomas B , of Dublin, M L

1808.

Nov 8 THOMAS LEE, aged 38, third son of George L , late of Queen Street, of the city of London, gent , deceased   [Wexford, gent , deceased

,, 12 PATRICK DOYLE, aged 29, fifth son of James D , late of New Ross, co

,, 21 ROBERT WALMESLEY, aged 32, third son of Thomas W , late of Showley Hall, co. Lancaster, Esq , deceased   [of Leighlin, Ireland.

,, 24 RICHARD MAUNSELL, aged 24, fourth son of the Very Rev George M , Dean

Dec 2 WILLIAM HORWOOD, aged 29, of Ringwood, Southants, eldest son of Thomas [Gee H , late of Gosport, Hants, Yeoman, deceased

1809   [Square, co Middlesex, gent

Jan 25 THOMAS GATTY, aged 22, third son of William G., of East Street, Red Lion

,, 26 ROBERT GREENE BRADLEY, aged 21, only son of Robert B , of Slyne, co Lancaster, gent.   [Esq

Feb 7 WILLIAM FINCH, aged 22, of Nenagh, eldest son of Edward F , of Dublin,

,, ,, GEORGE FIELD HARRIS, aged 24, of Plymouth Dock, Devon, only son of George F , Senior-Lieutenant of Red House Signal Station, Aldborough, [Suffolk, gent

,, 8 JAMES BUSH, aged 30, of Bishops Stortford, Herts, only son of Richard B , [late of Sawbridgeworth, co Hertford, Esq , deceased

,, 14 GEORGE GOSLING, aged 20, eldest son of George G , late of Chesterfield, co Derby, gent., deceased   [gent , deceased.

,, 23 JOHN BERRY, eldest son of Moses B , late of Market Harboro', co Leicester,

Mar 7 JOHN URQUHART, aged 25, eldest of John U , late of Mount Eagle, co Ross, Scotland, Esq , deceased   [of Spilsby, co Lincoln, gent , deceased

,, 25 JOHN ROBINSON, aged 41, of Offord, co Lincoln, eldest son of John R , late

April 3 HENRY WILLIAM LOVETT, eldest son of the Rev Verney L , of Trinity [College, Cambridge, D D , and of Lismore, co Waterford, Ireland

,, ,, WILLIAM SCUDAMORE DACIE, aged 30, only son of William D , late of [Edmonton, Middlesex, and formerly of this Society, deceased

,, 7 ROBERT CLARKE, aged 44, of Bath, eldest son of Arthur C , late a Lieutenant [of H M 's Ship "Edgar," deceased

,, 30 JAMES SHEIL, aged 21, of King's Inns, Dublin, only son of James S , of [Innisrush, co Derry, Ireland, Esq

May 4 THOMAS SMITH WHITE, aged 24, of King's Inns, Dublin, eldest son of James [W , late of the city of Dublin, gent , deceased

,, 6 PERCY GETHIN PAYNE, aged 21, second son of James Theobald P , late of co Cork, Esq , deceased.   [Kerry, merchant, deceased.

,, 12 MAURICE KING, aged 23, second son of Jeremiah K , late of Tralee, co.

,, 13 RICHARD STILEMAN, aged 22, only son of Richard S , late of Winchelsea, [co Sussex, Esq , deceased

,, 29 JOHN RUSSELL ROWNTREE, aged 48, of Stockton-on Tees, Attorney-at-Law, only son of Rev John R , late Rector of Elton, co Durham, deceased.

June 16 JOHN SPURLING, aged 37, of Stratford St. Mary, Suffolk, third son of Stephen [S , late of Dedham, co Essex, gent , deceased

,, 19 CHARLES SHADWELL, aged 27, attorney and solicitor, third son of Lancelot [S., of Gower Street, Bedford Square, co Middlesex, Esq

,, 28 THOMAS RICHARDS, aged 29, eldest son of Thomas R , of Helston, co [Cornwall, gent.

1809

Oct 18.   JACKSON KING HUNT, aged 21, third son of William Hunt Micklefield, of
            [Guildford Street, Middlesex, Esq

Nov 1   GEORGE MORTON, aged 32, of Gray's Inn attorney, second son of William M,
            [late of Swinton, in the parish of Masham, co York, gent, deceased

„ 9.   WILLIAM ORR HAMILTON, aged 28, third son of Robert H, late of Bally-
            [money, co Antrim, gent, deceased

„ 12   HARRY HUMBY, aged 45, of Christchurch, Hants, youngest son of William H,
            of Ringwood, co Southampton, gent   [Hill, co Dublin, Esq

„ 21   DAVID RUTTLEDGE COURTNEY, aged 22, eldest son of David C, of Lion

„ „   DANIEL FREDERICK RYAN, aged 21, eldest son of Daniel Frederick R, late
            of Dublin, Esq, deceased   [Londonderry, Ireland

„ 22   WILLIAM PITT KENNEDY, aged 21, eldest son of John Pitt K of Baltea,

„ 23   JOSEPH HINDE, aged 48, of Arundel, Steward to the Duke of Norfolk, eldest
            [son of Thomas H, late of Aikton, Cumberland, Yeoman, deceased

„ 28   GEORGE BRANEN, aged 29, of New Inn, eldest son of William B, late of
            Dublin, gent, deceased   [Middlesex, gent, deceased

„ 29   JOHN ELLIS, aged 32, third son of James E, late of North Westminster, co

1810   [bridge, gent, deceased
Jan 15   JESSE CLAXTON, aged 34, of Ely, second son of Richard C, late of Cam-

„ 25   WILLIAM FANNING, aged 23, of Dublin, eldest son of Cæsar F, of Cork,
            merchant   [Dublin, gent

„ 26   SAMUEL JOHN PITTAR, aged 32, eldest son of John P, of Cullenswood, co

„ 27   CHARLES EDWARD MOLLOY, aged 22, second son of Tobias M of Dublin,
            Barrister   [Robert M, of Sea Fort, near Kinsale, Ireland, Esq

Feb 6   RICHARD MACDONNELL, aged 22, of Trinity College, Dublin, eldest son of

„ „   NICHOLAS MANSERGH, aged 20, of Trinity College, Dublin, eldest son of
            [Daniel M, of Cashell, Esq

„ 8   JAMES KENNEDY, aged 24, eldest son of Edmund K, of Kilkenny merchant.

„ 9   CHARLES HIRD, only son of Charles H, of Bath, Esq.

Mar 14   THOMAS GREENWOOD, second son of Thomas G, of London, merchant

„ 31   WILLIAM STONE LEWIS, aged 23, only son of William L, of Holborn, Middle-
            [sex, Esq

April 9   AARON CHEVELL, eldest son of Richard C., of Ely, co Cambridge, gent.

„ 13.   RICHARD WEBB, aged 29, of the Close, New Sarum, only son of Thomas W,
            [late of Warminster, Wilts, gent, deceased

„ 26   FRANCIS BERRY, aged 32, of Barnstaple, Devon, Land Steward, second son
            [of Francis B, of Bovey Tracey, co Devon, gent

May 11   CHARLES JAMES, aged 34, only son of Selwyn J, late of Chepstow, co
            Monmouth, Esq, deceased   [Dublin, gent

„ 16   THOMAS HENRY HENLEY, aged 21, eldest son of Michael H, of Henry Street,

„ 18   WILLIAM GUEST, aged 38, only son of Ralph G, late of Manchester, gent,
            deceased   [attorney-at-law, deceased.

„ 23   MICHAEL DOBBYN, aged 21, eldest son of Michael D, late of Waterford,

„ 25   JOHN MATTHEW BOLAND, aged 23, only son of William B, late of Rath-
            [mines, co Dublin, Esq, deceased

1810

May 28　JOHN HUTCHISON, aged 21, of the Custom House, Dublin, eldest son of
　　　　　[Ephraim H., of the Custom House, Dublin, gent

June 2　JOHN FRENCH, son of Arthur F, of French Park, co Ross, Ireland, Esq.

　,,　8　ROBERT BALLMENT, aged 42, of Barnstaple, only son of William B., late of
　　　　　East Down, co. Devon, gent., deceased　　　　　　　　　　[gent

　,,　6　EDWARD WILDES, aged 23, second son of Thomas W of Maidstone, Kent,

　,,　30　ARCHER RYLAND, aged 19, third son of Richard R, of Savage Gardens,
　　　　　near Tower Hill, corn-factor.　　　　　　　　[Wexford, Esq, deceased

July 3　JOHN COLLEY POUNDEN, aged 19, eldest son of John P., late of Daphne, co

　,,　6.　RICHARD VERRALL, aged 44, fourth son of William V, late of Southover, co
　　　　　Sussex, brewer, deceased　　　　　　　　　　[Hereford, gent, deceased

　,,　30　JAMES PEWTRISS, aged 46, youngest son of George P., late of Ledbury, co

Aug 4　JOHN MORRIS FISHER, aged 33, eldest son of Gilbert F, late of Homerton,
　　　　　Middlesex, gent　　　　　　　　　　　　　　　　[Bath, gent

Sept 8　JOSEPH ORCHARD CHAMPION, aged 35, eldest son of Robert Evanes C, of

　,,　,,　WILLIAM RODWELL, aged 18, fifth son of Josiah R, late of Livermere, Suffolk,
　　　　　deceased　　　　　　　　　　　　　　　　　　　[Wexford, Esq

Nov 13　EDWARD COOKMAN, aged 22, eldest son of Nathaniel C, of Besmount, co

　,,　,,　HENRY MAUNSELL, aged 21, third son of Robert M, of the city of Limerick,
　　　　　banker　　　　　　　　　　　　　　　　[co York, gent, deceased

　,,　16　LEONARD HICKS, aged 28, second son of Richard H, late of Terrington,

　,,　19　WILLIAM FENNER, aged 23, eldest son of William F, of Dublin, Esq

　,,　21　HUMPHREY CORNEWALL WOOLRYCH, aged 50, eldest son of Humphrey W,
　　　　　　　　　　　　[late of Evington, co Hereford, Esq, deceased

　,,　23　EDWARD KENYON, aged 25, second son of John K, late of Chenies, co
　　　　　Buckingham, gent, deceased　　　　　　　　　　　[Dublin, merchant

　,,　24　JOHN LEAHY, aged 21, of Trinity College, Dublin, eldest son of David L, of

　,,　27　JOSEPH WILLS, aged 64, of Furnival's Inn, only son of George W, late of
　　　　　[Charles Square, Hoxton, co Middlesex, Esq, deceased

Dec 24　WILLIAM BIRD BLEAMIRE, aged 30, of Portsmouth, Captain, Royal East
　　　　　Middlesex Regiment of Militia, second son of William B, Esq, deceased,
　　　　　　　　　　　　　　　[formerly a Barrister of this Society

1811

Jan 4　GABRIEL FIELDING, aged 18, only son of Gabriel F, of Askew, in the parish
　　　　　　　　　　　　　　　　[of Bedale, co York, Esq

　,,　8　JOSEPH FRANK, aged 40, only son of Robert F, late of Stockton, co Durham,
　　　　　gent, deceased　　　　　　　　　　　　　　　[Ireland, Esq

　,,　21　KEAN MAHONY, aged 21, eldest son of Miles M, of Castlequin, co Kerry,

　,,　24　JOSEPH FREEMAN RATTENBURRY, aged 27, eldest son of Joseph Freeman R,
　　　　　　　　　　　　　　　　[of Plymouth, Devon, Esq

　,,　25　ROBERT FORSTER, aged 31, fourth son of Ralph F, late of Berwick-upon-
　　　　　　　　　　　　　[Tweed, co Northumberland, Esq, deceased

Feb 1　ROBERT BAXTER, aged 51, of Furnival's Inn, fourth son of Michael B, late
　　　　　of Atherstone, co Warwick, gent, deceased.　　　　　　　[Ireland

　,,　2　STANDISH O'GRADY, aged 21, third son of Standish O., of Grange, Limerick,

　,,　14　THOMAS OWEN, aged 59, only son of Evan Lewis, late of King Street, Covent
　　　　　[Garden, co. Middlesex, gent, deceased

1811

Feb 28 JAMES KIBBLEWHITE, aged 39, eldest son of William K , of Liddiard Millicent,
co. Wilts, Esq   [Surrey, gent , deceased.

Mar 21 FRANCIS ADDIS, aged 23, second son of Henry A , late of Southwark, co

,, 28 JOHN O'SULLIVAN, aged 25, third son of John O , late of White House,
Athlone, co Roscommon, Esq , deceased.   [Square, Dublin, surgeon.

April 27 GEORGE WRIGHT CREIGHTON, aged 21, eldest son of John C , of Merrion

May 11. RICHARD WILSON GREENE, aged 19, eldest son of Jonas G , of Dublin, Barrister-

,, 13 DENIS GEORGE LUBÉ, aged 21, eldest son of John L , of Dublin, Esq   [at-Law

,, 16 JOHN PUGH, aged 20, eldest son of John P., of Lamb's Conduit Street, co
Middlesex, gent   [Wicklow, Ireland, Esq , deceased

,, 18 HENRY REVELL, aged 20, fourth son of John R., late of Ballymony, co

,, 20. JAMES HOGG, aged 20, graduate, Trinity College, Dublin, eldest son of
William H , of Belmont, co Antrim, Esq   [Devon, Esq

,, 21 JOHN GODFREY TEED, aged 17, second son of John T , of Plymouth, co.

,, ,, ANDRE ALLEN MURRAY, aged 20, A B , Trinity College, Dublin, second son
[of James M., of the town of Monaghan, Esq

,, 22 WALTER STEELE, aged 21, only son of Norman S , late of Carrickmackross,
co. Monaghan, Esq , deceased   [field, co York, gent

,, 23 JOHN BERRY, aged 25, of Wakefield, eldest son of N——— B , of Hudders-

June 21. RICHARD EATON, aged 33, of Nottingham, merchant, second son of Michael
[E , of Sittingbourne, co Kent , Esq

July 6 GEORGE WILLIAM LEMON, aged 42, of Downham Market, only son of George
[William L , clerk, deceased, late Vicar of East Walton, Norfolk.

Oct 5 WILLIAM KING, aged 30, second son of John K., late of Newberry, co
[Buckingham, gent , deceased.

,, 23 ROBERT OLDERSHAW, aged 33, of Islington, vestry clerk, eldest son of Robert
[O , late of Islington, Middlesex, gent , deceased

Nov 4 JOHN WALPOLE WILLIS, aged 19, of Newark-upon-Trent, second son of
William W., late of Badsworth, co York, and formerly Captain of the
[13th Light Dragoons, deceased.

,, 8 SAMUEL TAGERT, aged 20, of Trinity College, Dublin, eldest son of John T ,
[late of Woodbrook, co Tyrone, Ireland, Esq , deceased

,, 13 WILLIAM DERBY, aged 41, third son of William Booker D , late of Horton,
near Colnbrook, co Bucks, Esq , deceased   [Dublin, Esq

,, 15 WILLIAM DEEY, aged 20, eldest son of Robert D , of Merrion Square,

,, 21. JOHN WILLIAM WILLIAMSON, aged 22, second son of Robert Hopper W , of
Newcastle-upon-Tyne, Barrister-at-Law   [Member of this Society.

,, 30 THOMAS GREENE, aged 18, only son of Thomas G , gent , deceased, late a

,, ., HENRY TENNANT, aged 17, eldest son of George T , gent , of Gray's Inn

Dec. 6 GEORGE KING, aged 28, of New Inn, second son of Samuel K , late of
[Beccles, co Suffolk, gent , deceased.

,, 15 JAMES JOHN MALLETT, aged 28, Chief Clerk at the Public Office, Shadwell,
[eldest son of William M , of Kent Road, co Surrey, gent

,, 20. ROBERT EVANS, aged 44, of Duffield, co. Derby, second son of Joseph E ,
1812   [late of Derby, co Derby, sculptor, deceased.

Jan 11. JACOB JACOBS, aged 42, attorney of His Majesty's Court of King's Bench, only
[son of Michael J , late of Goodman's Fields, co Middlesex, gent , deceased

1812

Jan 27   PATRICK MACABE, aged 27, third son of Matthias M , late of Ushers Quay,
                                                    [city of Dublin, Esq , deceased

" 30   NASH CROSIER HILLIARD, aged 22, third son of Edward H , of Cowley House,
                                                    [near Uxbridge, co Middlesex, Esq

Feb 11   JAMES ESPINASSE, eldest son of Isaac E , one of the Masters of the Bench, and
            Treasurer of this Society.   [Essex, Esq , deceased

" 15   EDWARD WRIGHT, aged 29, third son of John W , late of Kelvedon Hall,

April 6   HENRY PILKINGTON, aged 24, eldest son of William P , of Whitehall, city of
            Westminster, architect   [Esq , deceased.

" 16   SAMUEL TURNER, aged 22, second son of John T , late of Brill, co Bucks,

" "   ROBERT MORGAN, aged 23, third son of Robert M , late of Dublin, Esq ,
            deceased.   [Hall, Wickhambrook, Suffolk, a Member of this Society

" 31.   WILLIAM BROMLEY, aged 24, second son of Nathaniel Warner B , of Baresfield

" 23.   JACOB GOGERLY, aged 39, second son of John G , late of Ulverstone, co.
            Lancaster, Esq , deceased   [Surrey, Esq , deceased

" 24   ROWLAND YALLOP, aged 22, second son of Rowland Y , late of Reigate, co

" 29   WILLIAM MEDDOWCROFT, aged 16, third son of William M , of Liscard, co
            Chester, gent   [son of William M , of Little Glemham, Suffolk, gent

May 2   WILLIAM NATHAN MARKIN, aged 26, of Aston, near Birmingham, second

" 7   JOHN SCOTT VANDELEUR, aged 21, eldest son of Boyle V., of Rahine, co
            Clare, Esq   [of the Island of Barbados, Esq , deceased

" 27   JOHN DAYRELL MARTIN, aged 46, of Furnival's Inn, only son of John M , late

June 11   RICHARD FRASER LEWIS, second son of Michael L , of Dublin, Esq.

" 24   JESSE BERRIDGE, aged 40, fourth son of William B , of Syston, co. Leicester,
            gent   [Kibworth, co Leicester, deceased.

Aug 3   HENRY EDWARD BASELEY, aged 40, second son of Rev Henry B , late of

Sept 11   WILLIAM HICKS, aged 40, second son of Thomas H , late of Bodenham, co.
            Hereford, deceased   [late of Kimbolton, Hunts, deceased

Oct 30   JOHN LAWRENCE, aged 40, of Upwell, Isle of Ely, eldest son of Thomas L ,

Nov 4   JOHN UPTON, aged 38, of Stamford, co Lincoln, fourth son of William U ,
                                    [late of Petworth, Sussex, gent , deceased

" "   GEORGE BAKER BALLACHEY, aged 30, son and heir of George B , late of
            Oxford " Colisitor," deceased   [Middlesex, gent , and of this Society

" 9   HUGH PARKIN, aged 20, only son of Anthony P , of Great Ormond Street,

" "   MAURICE LEYNE, aged 21, second son of Maurice L , of Tralee, co Kerry,
            M D   [Willingham, co Lincoln, deceased

" 13.   DYMOKE WELLS, aged 38, eldest son of the Rev Robert W , D D , late of

" 14   URIAH BUTCHER, aged 35, M.A , St John's College, Cambridge, second son
                                    [of Joseph B , of Cambridge, Esq

" 16.   JOHN GEOGHEGAN, aged 20, second son of Edward G , of Dublin, surgeon

" 17   JOHN MACAN, aged 21, of Trinity College, Dublin, second son of Francis M ,
            of Sligo, gent   [Market Harborough, co Leicester, Esq

" "   WILLIAM COLMAN ADAMS, aged 17, eldest son of Poyntz Owsley A , of

" 26.   EDWARD HOLROYD, third son of George Sowley H , Esq , Treasurer, of Gray's
            Inn   [Middlesex, Esq.

Dec 7   JOHN FISHER, eldest son of John Woodcock F , of Upper Thornhaugh Street,

1815

Feb 4 THOMAS MASSINGBERD, eldest son of Thomas M , of Candlesby House, co
         Lincoln, Esq [son of John D , of Manchester Square, Middlesex, Esq

,, ,, ROBERT DALRYMPLE, of the Middle Temple (admitted July 31, 1784), eldest

,, ,, THOMAS HARRISON, second son of George H , of Northampton, Esq

,, 11 WILLIAM HENRY BRACKEN, only son of John B , of Webbsborough, co
         Kilkenny, Esq   [deceased.

April 12 JOHN CUFFE, only son of Joseph C , late of Charlestown, co Kilkenny, Esq.,

,, ,, BINGHAM WALKER HAMILTON, second son of Rev William H , late of Trinity
         College, Dublin, D D , and of Fanet, co Donegal, deceased   [gent

,, 15 THOMAS MCCLELAND, eldest son of Frederick M , of Longford, Ireland,

,, ,, EDMUND GIBSON, of the Middle Temple (admitted June 26, 1802), eldest son
         of Robert G , of Barfield, Cumberland, Esq   [ter in Chancery, Ireland.

,, 29 EDWARD KING, eldest son of Stewart K , of Rutland Square, Dublin, and a Mas-

May 4 JOHN COLTSMAN, only son of John C , of London, Esq

,, 9 JOHN HOUSMAN, only son of James H , late of Catterick, Yorks, gent , deceased

,, 22 JOHN PIERSON, eldest son of Thomas P , late of Bedford, gent , deceased

,, ,, GEORGE SIACY, eldest son of William S , late of Chatteris, co. Cambridge,
         gent , deceased   [Northants, gent , deceased

,, 23 WILLIAM BOWKER, eldest son of Samuel Harris B , late of Peterborough,

,, ,, JOHN ATHAWES, fourth son of Samuel A , of Maidstone, Kent, "sacrista"

,, 24 CHARLES WADE, fourth son of Robert W , of Dublin, Esq

,, 30 JOHN DEVNS, eldest son of John D , of the city of Norwich, gent

June 12 WILLIAM JOPE, only son of the Rev John J , Vicar of St Clear, Carmarthen,
         and Rector of St. Ive, Cornwall   [Middlesex

July 15 WILLIAM CHARLES LEVER KEENE, eldest son of Samuel K , of Grafton Street,
                               ["villica," deceased.

Oct 12 THOMAS PURSELL, eldest son of Thomas P , late of Impington, co Cambridge,

Nov. 3 ROBERT FLEURY, fourth son of George F , of the city of Waterford, gent

,, 4 JOHN THOMAS JUSTICE, eldest son of Francis J , of Abingdon, Berks, Esq.
                               [Armagh, Esq

,, 22 HENRY COOTE BOND, only son of Thomas B , of Bondville Tynan, co

Dec 2 THOMAS TURNER, eldest son of Thomas T., late of London, gent , deceased
                               [deceased

,, ,, JOHN TAMLYN, eldest son of John T , late of Barnstaple, Devon, gent.,

1816   [gent

Jan 25. PIERCE NAGLE, eldest son of Pierce N , of Anakissy, near Mallow, co. Cork,

Feb 28 EDWARD ALLEN, second son of Henry A , of Lodge, co. Brecon Esq

Mar 30. JOHN BONE, second son of James B , of Walworth, Surrey [chequer, Dublin.

April 26. WALLER O'GRADY, second son of Standish O , Knight, Chief Baron of the Ex-

,, 25 JAMES O'HARA, eldest son of James O , of Galway, Esq   [Esq

,, 26 WILLIAM CHAMBERS, eldest son of Joseph Franklin C., of the city of Dublin,

,, ,, WALTER REILLY, eldest son of Hugh R , late of Cavan, Ireland, deceased.

May 5. JAMES CUDDON, fourth son of John C , of Beccles, Suffolk, gent.
                            [Gloucester, deceased.

,, 13 JOSEPH PAGE, second son of William P., late of Wotton-under-Edge, co

1816

May 13   JOHN BROOKE, second son of Hugh B., of Donegal, gent.

,,   ,,   GEORGE DIGGES LATOUCHE, third son of Peter Digges L , of Dublin, gent

,,   15   JOHN PARRY BEST, second son of John B., late of the Island of Barbados,

,,   ,,   ARTHUR PALMER, only son of John Jordan P , of Bristol, gent.   [deceased.

,,   22.   ROBERT HENRY WOOD, eldest son of Robert W , of Richmond, Surrey.

,,   ,,   JOHN SANKEY, second son of John S , of the city of Dublin   [Ireland, Esq

,,   24.   MICHAEL HEAD DROUGHT, second son of John Armstrong D , of Lettybrook,

,,   27   THOMAS HORNCASTLE MARSHALL, third son of Rev Thomas Horncastle M ,
           Vicar of Pontefract, Yorks   [burgh, farmer, deceased.

,,   30   WILLIAM DICKSON, second son of William D., late of Smallholme, co. Rox-

June 14   JOHN PEED, eldest son of John P., of Upwell, Norfolk   [co Stafford, Esq.

,,   29   WILLIAM HERRICK, eldest son of Thomas Bainbrigge H., of Merridale House,

July 5   RICHARD VYSE, eldest son of Andrew V , late of London, gent , deceased
                                                         [deceased.

,,   24   JOHN BROWNE, only son of John B , late of St Mary Major, Exeter, gent ,

Sept 7   THOMAS MARCHANT, second son of John M , of Deptford, Kent, gent
                                                         [deceased

Nov 3   WILLIAM CARDALE, only son of William C , late of Bedford Row, gent ,

,,   ,,   JOHN FREDERICK FIXSEN, eldest son of Fedde F , of London, gent   [Esq

,,   6   JOHN EYKYN HOVENDEN, eldest son of Walter H , of Hemingford Grey, Hants,

,,   7   GEORGE SUTTELL WILSON, third son of Thomas W , of York, Esq

,,   8   JOHN GOOD, fourth son of Thomas G , late of Market Weston, Suffolk, deceased

,,   19   JOHN RAWLING, second son of Joseph R , of Ide, near Exeter, late of Brad-
                                                         [ford, Wilts, deceased

,,   21   SNEYD SANKEY, only son of Henry Gore S , of Dublin   [deceased

,,   25   GEORGE BLAKE HICKSON, eldest son of Robert H , late of Tralee, Ireland,

Dec 24   ANDREW MORION CARR, eldest son of Thomas William C , of Bloomsbury
1817   [Square, Middlesex, Esq

Jan 13   RICHARD GUDE, eldest son of Joseph G , late of Egham, Surrey, deceased

,,   18   EDWARD GEACH, third son of George G , of St Austell, Cornwall, gent

,,   29   WILLIAM HANDLEY, eldest son of Thomas H , of Pentonville, Middlesex, Esq

,,   ,,   THOMAS HANDLEY, second son of Thomas H , of Pentonville, Middlesex, Esq.

Mar 25   WILLIAM GALE THRESHER, only son of John T , late of Poole, "Naupegus,"
                                                         [deceased

,,   ,,   HENRY SOUTHWELL, second son of James S , of Winchester, farmer

April 2   JAMES PULTENEY BARSTOW, eldest son of Nathaniel B , late of Wetherby,
           Yorks, now of St Lucia, West Indies   [Council of Quebec

,,   23   GILBERT AINSLIE YOUNG, second son of John Y , a Member of the Executive

,,   25   NICHOLAS MILL, eldest son of Rev Nicholas M , of Littleham, Devon

,,   29   JOHN GIBSON, only son of Lewis G , of Cloyne, Ireland, Esq

,,   ,,   GEORGE KNOX, eldest son of John K , of Summerhill, Dublin, Esq

,,   ,,   LIONEL NASH, third son of William N , of Cork, Esq   [deceased

May 2   ROBERT ATKINS, third son of Robert A , late of Ninehead, Somerset, gent ,

,,   ,,   MORGAN WILLIAM DONOVAN, eldest son of Morgan D , of the city of Cork, clerk.

1817

May 5   GEORGE SERGEANT, third son of Rev John S , of Callington, Cornwall

,, 8   ABRAHAM BREWSTER, eldest son of William Bagnell B , late of Ballyraghine, [co Wicklow, Esq , deceased

,, ,,   WILLIAM ROUS, second son of Thomas R , of Sunninghill, Berks

,, 9   WILLIAM ROMILLY, eldest son of Samuel R , Knight, King's Counsel, and a Bencher of Gray's Inn   [Henry R , of Bovingdon, Herts, Esq , deceased

,, 17   ROBERT RAY, of the Inner Temple (admitted Feb 9, 1797), only son of

,, ,,   FRANCIS DICKINS, only son of James D , of Rochester, Kent, gent

,, 22   CHARLES BENJAMIN KING, only son of John K , late of Fitzroy Square, [Middlesex, now of Belvedere, Ireland

,, 30   JOHN MUSKETT, third son of John M , late of Thelveton, Norfolk, gent

, ,,   THOMAS CHANDLESS, eldest son of Thomas C , of York Place, Portman Square, [Middlesex, Esq

June 3   PETER HEBBERT, fourth son of John Grant H , late of Birmingham, co Warwick

,, 19   RICHARD HORE, third son of Jeremiah H , of Cork, Esq   [co Cork, Esq

,, 23   HENRY CHINNEY JUSTICE, eldest son of Thomas Henry J , of Annville,

July 8   JOHN GEORGE LOCKET, only son of George L , late of Southampton Place, [Middlesex, Esq , deceased

,, 16   ADAM FITZ ADAM, third son of James A , of Brymbo Hall, co Denbigh, Esq.

,, 22   JOHN STRANGEWAYS DONALDSON, only son of Thomas D , late of Alnwick, Northumberland, Esq , deceased   [gent , deceased.

,, 24   PERCIVAL WILKINSON, fifth son of William W , late of Newcastle-upon-Tyne,

,, 25   JOSEPH ALMOND CROPPER, only son of Henry C , late of Loughborough, co [Leicester, Esq , deceased

Aug 15   WILLIAM WILD, only son of John W , late of Liverpool, Esq , deceased

Oct 30   WILLIAM ARMSTRONG, only son of Robert A , of Dublin, merchant

Nov 3   JOHN EVSAW SCAFE, only surviving son of John S , late of Greenwich, Kent, Esq , deceased   [Essex, D D

,, 4   MORETON JOHN EDWARD FREWEN, only son of Edward F , of Frating,

,, ,,   MATTHEW DONELAN, third son of Malachi D , of Bally Donelan, co Galway, [Ireland

,, 7   ROGER MALLOCK, eldest son of Roger M , of Cockington, Devon, Esq

,, 10   ALGERNON MONTAGU, second son of Basil M , of Lincoln's Inn, Esq

,, 11   JOHN GEORGE SMYLY, eldest son of John S , of Dublin and Ballintyre, co [Dublin, Esq

,, 18   JAMES COLE, only son of James C , late of Thetford, Norfolk, gent , deceased

,, 19   WILLIAM GORMAN, only son of William G , of Dublin, Esq.

,, ,,   EDWARD AMOS CHAPLIN, eldest son of Rev Edward C , of this Inn

,, 24   GEORGE GAME DAY, eldest son of Jonah D , of London

Oct 28   HENRY JOHN WILLIAM COLLINGWOOD, eldest son of Henry C , of Lilburn Tower, Northumberland, Esq.   [Tower, Northumberland, Esq

,, ,,   FREDERICK JOHN WOODLEY COLLINGWOOD, second son of Henry C , of Lilburn

Dec 9   GEORGE WHITEHEAD, second son of Richard W , of Great St Helens, London

,, 15   JOHN ELLIS CLOWES, fourth son of Charles C , of Iver, Bucks, Esq

,, 19   JOSEPH DUNN, only son of Anthony D , of Somers Town, Middlesex, gent

1817

Nov 29 DAVID HARRISON, third son of George H , of Brill Terrace, Somers Town,
        Middlesex, gent   [Edgware Road, London, Esq

Dec 30 JAMES HENRY MANN, only son of James M , of Windsor, Berks, and of
1818

Jan 17 JOHN CARR, second son of Robert C , late of Horbury, Yorks, architect,

  ,, 23. THOMAS JAMES KENNY, third son of William K , of Dublin   [deceased

  ,, 26 JOHN ROMILLY, second son of Samuel R., Knight, King's Counsel and a
        Master of the Bench.

Feb 17. JAMES BRACEY, only son of Richard B , late of Winterbourne, co Gloucester,
        deceased   [Square, and of Edmonton, Middlesex

April 8 HENRY BELWARD RAY, eldest son of Robert R , of Montagu Place, Russell

  ,, ,, THOMAS ABBOTT, eldest son of Thomas A , of Dublin, Esq

  ,, ,, JOHN COLHOUN, eldest son of Thomas C , of Strabane, co Tyrone [deceased.

  ,, ,, FRANCIS BALL, second son of ———— B , Serjeant-at-Law, late of Dublin,

  ,, 9 ROBERT CHARLES ATKINSON, eldest son of Edward A , of Armagh, M D.

  ,, 13 ARTHUR GORE WINTER, second son of John Pratt W., of Agher, co Meath, Esq

  ,, ,, THOMAS WARREN WHITE, eldest son of John W , of Dublin, Esq

  :: ,, JOHN BILLING, eldest son of Augustin B , of Leicester

  ,, 14 FREDERICK FOX, eldest son of William F , of Hackney, Middlesex, Esq

  ,, 20 NATHANIEL CARTWRIGHT, only son of Nathaniel C , late of Leighton Buzzard,
                                    [Beds, deceased

  ,, 27 ROBERT PENTLAND, eldest son of George P , of Dublin, Esq   [meath, Esq

  ,, 29 MICHAEL O'REILLY, second son of Charles O , of Beneson Lodge, West-

May 1 SAMUEL JACOB, third son of ————, of Ireland, M D

  ,, 11 SAMUEL BUTT, only son of Samuel B , formerly of Cirencester, "Lanarius,"
                        [late of Woodchester, near Stroudwater, " Pannifex "

Aug. 10 HENRY BARROW, eldest son of John B , late of Bishop's Taunton, Devon.

  :: 15 JAMES GRIFFITHS, eldest son of Roger G , late of Hereford, deceased

Oct 31 BENJAMIN LANGHORNE, seventh son of Thomas L., of Appleby, Westmore-

Nov 5 THOMAS RAWLINS, eldest son of Joseph R , of Dublin, Esq [land, deceased

  ,, ,, WILLIAM GRANT ALLISON, eldest son of William A , junior, of Louth, co

  :: ,, DOMINICK SARSFIELD, third son of Dominick S , of Ireland Esq [Linc , Esq

  ,, ,, ANDREW CARTERET ARMSTRONG, eldest son of Thomas St George A , of
                        [Langcastle House, Banagher, Ireland

  ,, ,, JAMES DUNN, second son of Patrick D , of Killarney, co Kerry

  ,, 6 ROBERT FLEETWOOD RYND, eldest son (by second wife) of James R , of Rynd-

  , 14 CHARLES OGILVY, of Adam Street, Adelphi   [ville, co Meath, Esq , deceased
                                    [deceased
1819

Jan 4 JAMES WHITEFIELD, eldest of John W , late of Bodmin, Cornwall, gent ,

  ,, 12 JAMES HAMILTON STORY, fourth son of the Rev Joseph S , late of Bingfield
        and Ballyconnell House, co Cavan   [deceased

May 29 ALGERNON, Lord PRUDHOE, second son of [Hugh] Duke of Northumberland,

Feb 1 THOMAS CRONIN, third son of John C , of Brandon, co Cork, gent

  ,, 6 GEORGE FLETCHER MOORE, second son of Joseph M , of Bond's Glen, Ireland,
        Esq   [Middlesex, gent

  ,, ,, JOHN FIELDER, eldest son of John F , of Duke Street, Grosvenor Square,

1819.

Feb   6   WILLIAM JOHN KNOX, eldest son of Samuel K , of Dublin, gent.

,,   12   THOMAS WIGLESWORTH, third son of James W , late of Town Head, near Settle, Yorkshire, Esq , deceased   [Clerkenwell, Middx , deceased

,,   19   WILLIAM MARMADUKE SELLON, eldest son of the Rev William S , late of

,,   ,,   PETER WILLIAM BAKER JOHN SELLON, eldest son of William Marmaduke S , [of Willesden, Middlesex, Esq

Mar 15   JOHN BLAKE, eldest son of Charles B , of Galway, Ireland, Esq [Middx, gent

April 28   JOHN STABLE, third son of Lorenzo S , of Hanover Street, Hanover Square,

,,   ,,   JAMES WILLIAMSON, only son of James W., of Bedale, Yorkshire, gent

May   3   WILLIAM TURTON, eldest son of John T , of Clapham, Surrey, Esq

,,   ,,   ROGER HAYES, eldest son of William H , of Waterford

,,   ,,   THEOBALD McKENNA, eldest son of Theobald M., of Dublin.

,,   10   JAMES CROKE, second son of William C , of Mallow, co Cork

,,   12   THOMAS JAMES DENKIN, second son of John D , late of Kilburn, Middlesex, deceased   [Esq

,,   13   WILLIAM LEGG, eldest son of William L , of Rolls Buildings, Middlesex,

,,   ,,   PATRICK FRANCIS GAHAN, fourth son of Patrick G , of Queen's County,

May 15   JOHN CUMING, eldest son of John C , late of Belfast, Antrim, Esq   [Ireland

Oct 11   GEORGE WAILES, second son of George W , of Potter Newton, Yorks, Barrister-at-Law, of Gray's Inn   [deceased

Nov   4   THOMAS HEWITT, eldest son of Rev Francis H , late Rector in co Cork,

,,   6   JOHN RADCLIFF, third son of Rev. J T R , late Rector in co Meath, deceased

,,   8   WILLIAM THOMAS BARTON, eldest son of William B , of Dublin

,,   ,,   CHARLES OSBORNE, eldest son of Thomas O., of Ballymagary, Ireland

,,   ,,   WILLIAM FENNELL HARVEY, eldest son of Richard H , of Cork,

,,   ,,   ALEXANDER KIRKPATRICK, eldest son of Alexander K , late of Coolemore, [co Dublin, Esq , deceased

,,   10   WILLIAM KEATING, eldest son of Rev William Amboor K , of Madras

,,   12   JEFFREY FRANCIS PRENDERGAST, eldest son of Francis P , of Dublin, Esq

,,   17   JOSHUA FREE, only son of William F , of Dublin, Esq , deceased

,,   18   WILLIAM SHAW, eldest son of John S , late of Calcutta, Esq , deceased

,,   20   JAMES BRYAN, sixth son of Robert B , of Dublin, Esq   [Limerick, Esq

,,   23   NICHOLAS HENRY MAHON, eldest son of Nicholas M , of Castlefield, co

,,   24   WILLIAM JENKINS, eldest son of William J., late of Pentonville, Middlesex, gent , deceased   [common, Esq

,,   ,,   [FITZSTEPHEN] FRENCH, fifth son of Arthur F , of French Park, co Ros-

,,   ,,   JOHN JENKINS, third son of George J., of the parish of St. Mary, Haverford-west, co Pembroke, gent , deceased   [House, co Dublin, Esq

,,   25   MICHAEL KEOGH, eldest son of Michael K , Barrister-at-Law, of Crumlin

,,   ,,   WILLIAM HEMMING, eldest son of Richard H , late of Birmingham,
1820   [co Warwick, gent , deceased.

Jan 14   ANTHONY SINGLETON ATCHESON, second son of Nathaniel A., of Westminster, Esq   [South Pembridge, near Pontefract, Yorks, deceased

,,   19   JAMES FARRER STEADMAN, eldest son of the Rev Miles S , late Rector of

,,   22   JAMES WILLINGTON, only son of John W , of Carisbrooke, Isle of Wight, gent

1820

Jan 24   BARCLAY FARQUHARSON WATSON, second son of Joseph W , " ducis machinæ
              Bellicæ "   [deceased

 "   "   CHARLES CAMBIE, only son of David C , of Brookfield, co. Tipperary, Esq ,

 "   "   WILLIAM ROGERS, only son of Thomas R , of Timsbury, Southants, gent ,

 "   27   JOSEPH O'LEARY, eldest son of Jeremiah O , of Cork, Esq   [deceased.

 "   "   GEORGE BROWN, second son of George B , of Bethnal Green, Middlesex, gent.

 "   31   WILLIAM N ROCHE, eldest son of John R , of Dublin, Esq

 "   "   JOHN HOLLOWAY, only son of Richard H , of St Pancras, Middlesex, gent

Feb 1.   THOMAS LITTLETON HOLT, eldest son of the Rev Ludlow H , D D , late
              [Rector of North Repps, Norfolk, deceased

 "   "   THOMAS BLOOD, third son of Edmund B , Barrister-at-Law, of Dublin

 "   3   THOMAS F KELLY, eldest son of William K , of Dublin, Esq [Esq , deceased

 "   "   GIDEON ACLAND, eldest son of Gideon A , late of Camberwell, Surrey,

 "   4   JOHN CHESNEY, only son of John C , of Kendal, Westmoreland, gent.

 "   10   JOHN WARREN PAGET, second son of Thomas Bradley P , late of Comberford
              Hall, Staffordshire, Esq , deceased   [land, gent , deceased

Mar 4   OSMOTHERLEY LIGHTFOOT, fourth son of Isaac L , late of Wigton, Cumber-

April 26 FRANCIS ROMILLY, fourth son of Thomas Peter R , of Dulwich, Kent, Esq

 "   27   GEORGE CORLETT, third son of George C , of Cork, Esq   [Esq , deceased

 "   28   EDWARD JOHN SHEPHERD, only son of Francis S , late of Beverley, Yorks,

 "   "   CHARLES ELLISON, fourth son of the Rev William E , late of Lintz Green,
              co. Durham, deceased   [Yorks, Esq

May 1   JOHN RALPH MILBANKE, only son of John Peniston M , of Halnaby Hall,

 "   2.   ROBERT DUKE, eldest son of Robert D , of New Park, co Sligo, Esq

 "   4·   JOHN ALEXANDER HAMILTON, eldest son of the Rev. George H., of Hampton,
              Balbriggan, Dublin   [deceased

 "   6   JAMES BRADBY, only son of Blake B , late of Snow Hill, London, Esq ,

 "   8   GEORGE SEYMOUR MARTIN, eldest son of Nicholas M , of the city of Cork,

 "   10   WILLIAM COOLEY, second son of William C , of Dublin, Esq   [Esq

1819 (sic)

May 23   JOSEPH HAYES LYON, eldest son of Joseph L , late of Bloomsbury Square,
              [Middlesex, Esq , deceased

June 23   WILLIAM GREENFIELD, eldest son of William G , late of Romsey, Southants,
              [gent , deceased
1820

May 10   ROBERT WILLIAM JACKSON, eldest son of Robert J., of Armagh, Esq

 "   "   JOHN MIDDLETON MEGGISON, second son of Thomas M., of Whatton,
              [Northumberland, Esq

 "   11   JOHN VICARS COLLINS, second son of James C , late of Dublin, Esq , deceased

 "   12   JOHN ANSTER, only son of John A , of Charleville, co Limerick, Esq

 "   24   FRANCIS DIXON IOHNSON, only son of Francis I , of Aykley Heads, co
              [Durham, Esq

June 1   THOMAS COLLING, third son of Robert C., of Hurworth, co. Durham, Esq

 "   2   THOMAS DISNEY, second son of Thomas D , of Dublin, Esq

 "   13   JOSEPH SHERIDAN LE FANU, second son of Joseph le F , of Dublin

 "   14   JOHN BLAKE KIRBY, eldest son of John K , of Bicester, Oxon, Esq

1820

June 14. JOHN LEWIS, only son of William L., M D , of Ross, co. Hereford

  ,, 17 MICHAEL EATON WILKINSON, second son of John Henry W, of Well Hall,

  ,, 19 GEORGE CONOLLY, third son of John C, of Galway, Esq   [Kent, Esq

  ,, 20 THOMAS SHERLOCK, third son of John S, late of Wimpole Street, Cavendish Square, London, Esq , deceased   [deceased

July 14 JOSEPH BATEMAN, only son of Joseph B, late of Tattenhall, Cheshire, gent,

Oct 24 GEORGE WILLIAM TIREMAN, third son of Thomas T, late of York, gent,   [deceased.

Nov 4 JOHN A GREENE, eldest son of John G, of Court Hill, co. Meath, gent.

  ,, 6 WILLIAM WEST, second son of Charles W, late of the city of Norwich, merchant, deceased   [Hampstead, Middlesex, Esq

  ,, 8 THOMAS WILLIAM CARR, second son of Thomas William C, of Frognal,

  ,, ,, WILLIAM OGLE CARR, third son of Thomas William C, of Frognal, Hamp-   [stead, Middlesex, Esq.

  ,, ,, JAMES BROOKE, second son of John B, of Wincanton, Somerset, gent

  ,, 11 JOHN JENNINGS, third son of William J, late of Dublin, Esq, deceased

  ,, 4 ROBERT H KELLY, second son of Charles K, of Charleville, co Westmeath, gent   [Esq

  ,, 16 CHARLES DEVON, third son of George D, of Clarendon Square, Middlesex,

  ,, ,, RICHARD WOOD, eldest son of Michael W, late of Cork, Esq, deceased

  ,, 21. HUGH R GRAVES, third son of Rev John G, late of Fort William, co. Limerick, deceased   [Justice of the King's Bench

  ,, ,, JAMES JOHN HOLROYD, fifth son of (Hon) George Sowley H Knight, a

  ,, 13 GEORGE WALFORD, only son of Foy W, late of Conduit Street, Middlesex, Esq, deceased   [Esq, deceased

  ,, 21 JOHN BROWNE, second son of John B, late of Leixlip Castle, co Kildare,

  ,, ,, EDWARD SINGLETON, third son of Edward S, late of Quinville, co Clare, Esq,   [deceased

Dec 4 GEORGE EVANS, fourth son of Rev John E, of Islington, Middlesex, D D
1820 (*sic*)

Jan 31 JAMES HAMMOND, fourth son of James H, of Blandford, Dorset, gent

1821

Jan 20 HENRY HOUGHTON, only son of Henry H, of Dublin, Esq   [Esq

  ,, 27 HANS HENRY HAMILTON, fourth son of Henry H, of Ballymacott, co Meath,

  ,, 31 CHARLES MARTIN TEED, fourth son of John T, of Plympton, Devon, Esq

  ,, ,, WILLIAM VINCE BARNARD, only son of William B, late of Beccles, Suffolk, gent, deceased   [Cork, Esq

Feb 6 MICHAEL O'SHAUGHNESSY, eldest son of Patrick O, of Charleville, co

  ,, ,, JOHN BILL, second son of John B, of Farley Hall, co Stafford, Esq

  ,, 8 HENRY COBHAM, eldest son of Elijah C, of Liverpool, Esq, deceased

  ,, 9 JAMES LOCKHART, eldest son of James L, of Haarlem, Holland, Esq

  ,, ,, ANDREW V KIRWAN, eldest son of Thomas K., of Well Park, co Dublin, Esq

  ,, 13 JAMES STARK, eldest son of William S, of the city of Edinburgh, architect

Mar 19 JAMES ROBINSON, third son of Richard R, of Portsmouth, "custodes Gurgustii."   [deceased.

April 12 JAMES ROWLAND, eldest son of Rev James R., of Moreton Hampstead, Devon,

1821

May 5 JOHN EVANS, eldest son of Rev John E , of Islington, Doctor of Laws

„ 8 SAMUEL MARTIN, second son of Samuel M , of Culmore, co. Londonderry, Esq

„ 10 JAMES RICHARD COOKE, second son of James C , of Dublin, Esq

„ 14 WILLIAM HENRY ROSE, eldest son of John R , of Gray's Inn, Esq [sex, gent

„ 16 CHARLES GEORGE THORPE, third son of James T , of Edgeware Road, Middle-

„ „ WALTER HINDES, eldest son of Walter H , of Bruce Hall, co Cavan, Esq

„ „ EBENEZER HORE HATCHELL, second son of Nicholas Christopher Hore H ,
        of the town of Wexford, Esq   [Esq., deceased

„ 18 GEORGE BRUCE, eldest son of Saul B , late of Castle Connell, co Limerick,

„ 26 GEORGE BERESFORD POER, eldest son of Samuel P , of Belleville Park, co

„ 29 THOMAS FORSAYETH, eldest son of Rev J F , of Cork   [Waterford, Esq

„ 30 RICHARD O'GRADY, fourth son of Hon Standish D O., Chief Baron, Ireland

„ 31 JAMES PEEBLES, second son of Robert P , of Dublin, Esq

„ „ ROBERT CASEMENT, sixth son of Roger C , of the city of Dublin, Esq

„ „ HENRY SELWOOD, eldest son of Richard S , late of Beche Manor, Berks, Esq

Nov. 6 JOHN WILSON, eldest son of John Taylor W , of Lancaster, solicitor

„ 9 WILLIAM HENRY BODKIN, only son of Peter B , of Northampton Square,
        Middlesex, Esq   [Esq

„ 15 STEWART DERBISHIRE, fourth son of Philip D , of Berners Street, Middlesex,

„ „ FRANCIS PEARSON WALESBY, eldest son of Francis W , of Louth, co Lincoln,
        gent   [Wilts, Esq

„ 16 EDMUND KIBBLEWHITE, second son of William K , of Lydiard Millicent,

„ 19 EDWARD GRUBB, second son of Edward G , late of Great Queen Street,
        Lincoln's Inn Fields, Middlesex, Esq   [deceased

„ „ JOHN WILLSON JENINGS, third son of George J , late of Tuam, Ireland, Esq ,

„ „ FRANCIS WILLIAM RUSSELL, eldest son of John Norris R , of Limerick, Esq

„ 21 DAVID DAVIS, only son of Edward Davies, late of Langattock, Crickhowell,
        co Brecknock, gent , deceased   [gent , deceased

„ 23 HENRY PARKER, seventh son of Henry P , late of Horningsea, co Cambridge,

„ 24 GEORGE D ORR, second son of Alexander O , of Landmore, co London-
        derry, Esq   [Esq , deceased

„ 26 ROBERT LYONS, eldest son of Charles L , late of Lyonstown, co Roscommon,

„ „ DALKEITH HOLMES, only son of John H , late of Dublin, Esq , deceased

Dec. 5 THOMAS BUTLER, second son of William B , of Ireleth, co Lancaster, gent

1822   [Middlesex, Esq

Jan 17 JOHN L. P TRAPAUD, second son of Francis Plaistow T , of Potters Bar,

„ „ JOHN SMITH, only son of Richard S , of St Albans, Herts, gent , deceased

„ „ EDWARD B LEWIN, third son of Richard L , late of Hollies, near Eltham,
        Kent, Esq , deceased   [Esq

„ 23 WILLIAM MCCARTHY, eldest son of Rodolph M , of Sunday Wells, Cork,

„ 28 HENRY FOLEY, second son of Herbert F , late of Ridgeway House, co
                                                       [Pembroke, Esq , deceased

„ „ THOMAS BUSHE, third son of Charles Kendal B , of Dublin, Esq

Feb 1 THOMAS PARKER, eldest son of Thomas P , of Henrietta Street, Brunswick
                                                       [Square, Middlesex, Esq.

1822   [lateris."

Mar. 14   HENRY BROWN, eldest son of John B, of Skiers Hall, Yorks, "fabricatoris

April 4   JAMES BACON, eldest son of James B, of Exmouth Street, Clerkenwell, Middlesex, Esq   [Africa, Esq, deceased

,, 13   JAMES MOULD, eldest son of James M, late Governor of Cape Coast Castle,

May 2   ANDREW BOURNE, fifth son of Walter B, of Dublin, Esq

,, 4   WILLIAM HENDERSON, second son of William H, of Strabane, co Tyrone, Esq

,, 6   WILLIAM MASSY GREEN, second son of John G, of Green Mount, co

,, 11   STANDISH O'GRADY, eldest son of Edward O, of Dublin, Esq   [Limerick

,, 13   ARTHUR BUSHE, fourth son of Charles Kendal B, Chief Justice, Ireland

,, ,,   ROBERT HARMAN, second son of William M H, of Dublin, Esq   [deceased

,, 14.   "JERONYMUS" DALY, only son of Denis D, late of Rathmines, Dublin, Esq,

,, 17   GEORGE HELY HUTCHINSON, fourth son of Hon Francis Hely H, of Dublin

,, ,,   JAMES MCAULEY, only son of James M, of Dublin, Esq

,, 18   JOHN HUNTER, eldest son of Walter H, of Letterkenny, co Donegal, Esq

June 22   THOMAS COSTELLO, second son of Edmund C, late of Russell Street, [Dublin, Esq, deceased

,, ,,   THOMAS BAILY ROSE, second son of John R, of Gray's Inn

,, 24   JOHN O'DONNOGUE, only son of Cornelius O, late of Cork, Esq, deceased

,, ,,   DANIEL MCDERMOTT, third son of Patrick M, of co Cork, Esq.

,, 26   ANTHONY GOODEVE, third son of Thomas G, late of Museum Street, [Bloomsbury, gent, deceased

,, ,,   SEPTIMUS HODGES, second son of Richard H, of Paddington, Middlesex, Esq

Nov 5.   ALEXANDER DONOVAN, eldest son of James D, late of Clonakilty, co Cork,

,, ,,   JOHN L BRIEN, only son of John B, of Dublin, Esq   [M D, deceased

,, 19   JOHN GEORGE, eldest son of John G, of Dublin, Esq   [Limerick, Esq

,, 20   WILLIAM SCANLAN, eldest son of Michael S, of Ballyknockanes, co

,, 23   WILLIAM TAPRELL, eldest son of William T, of Bristol, Esq   [deceased

,, ,,   DANIEL R KANE, only son of Richard K, late of the city of Limerick, Esq,

,, ,,   JONATHAN WOOD, only son of Jonathan W, late of Pitsford, Northants, gent, [deceased

,, 25   ROGER THERRY, third son of John T, of Dublin, Esq, Barrister-at-Law

,, ,,   FELIX FITZPATRICK, third son of Nicholas F, late of Kilkenny, Esq, deceased

Dec 14   CHARLES PITT, second son of Roger P, of Tiverton, Devon, gent.

,, ,,   JOHN MALLESON, eldest of John Kennedy M, late of Exeter, Esq, deceased

,, 18   JAMES WARREN, second son of Thomas W, late of Hursley, Southants, gent, [deceased

1823   [deceased

Jan 17   AMBROSE CHARLES, eldest son of Thomas C, late of Merton, Surrey, Esq,

,, 27   EDMUND BARKER RAY, second son of Robert R, Barrister-at-Law, of Gray's

,, 30   ROBERT ANDREWS, sixth son of James A, of Comber, co Down   [Inn

Feb 5   WILLIAM HAMILTON ASH, eldest son of William Hamilton A, late of Ashbrook, city of Londonderry, Esq, deceased   [deceased

,, 8.   GEORGE CONDY, eldest son of Richard C, late of Plymouth, Devon, Esq,

,, ,,   MALACHI FALLON, eldest son of Patrick K F, late of Cloona, co Roscommon, [Esq, deceased.

1823   [Middlesex, gent.

Feb 12. ALFRED SEPTIMUS DOWLING, fourth son of Vincent D , of Kentish Town,

  ,,   15   JAMES GEORGE ARTHUR, second son of ——— A , of Glasgow, gent

April 15 THOMAS PEAKE, second son of Thomas P , Serjeant-at-Law, of Bernard Street,
                Russell Square.   [Herts

  ,,   18   SAMUEL GROVE PRICE, only son of Rev Morgan P , Rector of Knebworth,

  ,,   19   WILLIAM PIKE BAYS, third and only surviving son of Thomas B , late of
                Wisbech St Peter, co Cambridge, "nautici," deceased   [common, Esq

  ,,   26   JOHN PLUNKETT, second son of George P , of Mount Plunkett, co Ros-

  ,,   28   JAMES HENRY BLAKE, eldest son of Andrew B , of Galway, Esq   [Meath, Esq.

  ,,   ,,   PATRICK MATTHEW MURPHY, third son of Patrick M , of Boyneavilla, co

  ,,   29   HARRY EDGELL, eldest son of Harry E , Barrister-at-Law, of Gray's Inn

  ,,   ,,   ROBERT NATHANIEL MATHIESON, eldest son of Robert M , of Lambeth, gent ,
                deceased   [Garden, Middlesex, gent

May 3   THOMAS SALOMON, eldest son of William S , of Charles Street, Hatton

  ,,   7   AUGUSTIN THWAITES, eldest son of John Smyth T , of Limerick, Esq

  ,,   ,,   WILLIAM REYNOLDS, eldest son of William R , late of Illogan, Cornwall,
                                                            [Esq , deceased

  ,,   8   MARTIN T LYNCH, eldest son of Antony L , of Lavally, co Galway, Esq

  ,,   ,,   THOMAS GISBORNE BURKE, only son of Edmond B , of Greenfield, co
                Galway, Esq   [deceased

  ,,   16   JOHN MANLEY WOOD, only son of John W , late of Goodneston, Kent, gent ,

  ,,   23   HENRY GORF CHANDLESS, third son of Thomas C , late of Dorset Square,
                Middlesex, Esq , deceased   [city of Dublin.

June 3   GEORGE JOHN GWYNNE, eldest son of Rev. William G , of Castle Knock,

  ,,   5   ARTHUR FRENCH, eldest son of George F , of Dublin, King's Counsel

  ,,   ,,   JOHN HENRY BARROW, third son of Charles B , of Douglas, Isle of Man, Esq

  ,,   7   WALTER BERWICK, second son of Rev Edward B , late of Esher, Surrey,
                deceased |Middlesex, gent

  ,,   9   ARTHUR HANDLEY, second surviving son of Thomas H , of Pentonville,

  ,,   11   WALTER GLASCOCK, eldest son of William G , late of Dublin, gent , deceased

  ,,   12   DANIEL MAUDE, third son of Francis M , of Hatfield Hall, Yorkshire,
                                                            [Barrister-at-Law

  ,,   16   JAMES DWYER, fourth son of Jeremiah D , late of Dublin, Esq , deceased

  ,,   17. FREDERICK BARRY, second son of Robert B , late of the Middle Temple,
                                                      [Barrister-at-Law, deceased

Aug 5   JOHN COOKE, eldest son of James C , of Liverpool, gent

Nov 3   HENRY HOLROYD, 9th but 6th surviving son of George Sowley H , Knight,
                a Justice of the King's Bench   [deceased

  ,,   7   JOSEPH HENRY LYSTER, second son of John Henry L , late of Dublin, Esq.,

  ,,   10   REDMOND CARROLL, eldest son of John C , late of Turlough, co Galway, Esq ,
                deceased |Stafford, Esq , deceased

  ,,   11   JOHN BISHTON, eldest son of William Roger B , late of Shackerley House, co.

  ,,   12. JOHN GETHIN, eldest son of John G , of Sligo, Esq   [deceased.

  ,,   ,,   SAMUEL DALES, second son of Philip D , late of Cottingham, Yorks, gent ,

  ,,   14   MICHAEL ELLISON, eldest son of Matthew E., of Glossop, co Derby, gent

1823

Nov 15   JOHN HODGSON, only son of John H , of Craven Street, City Road, Middlesex,
                                                                          [gent

,,   17   ROBERT HAYMES, eldest son of Robert H , of Great Glenn, co. Leicester, gent.

,,   21   GEORGE RICHARD LEAKE, only son of Richard L , of Rathkeale, co. Limerick,
            gent   [co pal Chester.

,,   26   JOHN CATTLOW, only son of Rev John Stevenson C , Rector of Coppenhall,

,,   14   ECHLIN MOLYNEUX, only son of James M , of Dublin, gent
1824

Jan 14   HENRY GRIFFIN ALSOP, only son of Thomas A , of Calcutta, Esq

,,   ,,   GEORGE BROWNE, fourth son of John B , late of Mount Prospect, co Ros-
            common, Esq., deceased   [London, Esq

,,   21   PHILIP CHARLES MOORE, only son of William M , of Doctor's Commons,

,,   24   JAMES DE GYMINGHAM BURN, eldest son of John Ilderton B , of Bloomsbury,
                                                                  [Middlesex, gent

,,   ,,   PATRICK BRADY LEE, second son of Laurence L , of Shadow, co Cavan, Esq

,,   26   FRANCIS WHITMARSH, eldest son of Francis W , Barrister-at-Law, of Gray's Inn

,,   27   MAURICE DANIEL O'CONNELL, eldest son of Daniel O , of Dublin, Esq

,,   ,,   EDWARD CLEMENTS, second son of Hill C , of Dublin, Esq

,,   28   PHILIP PHILLIPS, eldest son of Richard P , late of Wilston House, co Mon-
                                                          [mouth, Esq , deceased

Feb   4   ALBERT FREDERICK MAXWELL, only son of Albert M , of Dublin, Esq

,,   9   JOHN ROWLAND OTTIWELL, second son of Henry O , late of Belcamp House,
                                                              [co Dublin, Esq

,,   12   WILLIAM MUSKETT, eldest son of David M , of Coleford, co Gloucester, Esq

,,   18   JOHN HIGNETT (formerly Litherland), only son of Nathaniel Litherland, late
                                                  [of Rowton, Cheshire, Esq , deceased

,,   28   JAMES GRIFFITH, second son of John G , of Durham, gent   [Malzeard, York

April27   TOMYNS SCOTT DICKINS, only son of Tomyns D , of Mowbray House, Kirkby

May   5   ASHLEY COWPER CROFT, fourth son of James C., of Greenham Lodge, Berks,
                                                                          [Esq

,,   6   PETER BLAKE MORGAN, fourth son of Charles M , of Monksfield, co. Galway,

,,   7   JOHN SMITH, eldest son of John S , of Great Hatfield, Yorks, Esq   [Esq

,,   11   GEORGE VESEY, only son of George V , of Farmhill, co Mayo, Esq

,,   ,,   JONATHAN MOORE, third son of James M , of Blackheath, Kent, Esq

,,   ,,   JOSEPH KIDD, fifth son of Benjamin K , of Armagh, Ireland, Esq

,,   19   PATRICK SMYTH, second son of John S , of Strabane, co Tyrone, Esq

,,   ,,   WILLIAM DRENNEN, eldest son of Doctor D , late of Belfast.

,,   ,,   ROBERT WILLIAM NUTT, eldest son of Robert William N , late of Greenwich,
            Kent, gent , deceased   [deceased

,,   22   HENRY BALDWIN, only son of Henry B., late of Queen's County, Esq ,

,,   ,,   ADOLPHUS FREDERICK BARRAS, second son of Samuel B , of co. Kildare, Esq

,,   24   THOMAS GROVE GRADY, eldest son of Henry Grove G , of Dublin, Esq

,,   ,,   HENRY GRATTAN CURRAN, second son of the Hon. John Philpot C., late of
            [Rathfarnham at Prior, Master of the Rolls. Ireland, deceased

,,   ,,   BOYLE KELLER, only son of Jeremy K., late of Dublin, Barrister-at-Law,
                                                                      [deceased

1824   [deceased

May 25   JOHN CRESSY HALL, eldest son of Philip H , late of Alfreton, co Derby, gent ,

,, ,,   EDWARD RICHARD COLLES, eldest son of Richard C , late of Dublin, Barrister-

·, ,   ROBERT BELL, second son of Thomas B , of Dublin, Esq   [at-Law, deceased

,, ₂7   LANGFORD ROWLEY SYMES, second son of Richard H S , of Ballybegg, co

,, 28   RICHARD GARDE, eldest son of William G of Dublin, Esq   [Wicklow, Esq.

June 8   STEPHEN GASELEE, eldest son of Stephen G , a Master of the Bench

,, 22   JOHN DUFFY, eldest son of John D , of Balls Bridge, co Dublin, Esq

,, ,,   RICHARD DALY, only son of Daniel D , of Athlone, co Roscommon, Esq

,, 29   JOHN WILLIAMSON, only son of John W , a Master of the Bench

July 5   WILLIAM GEORGE DUNBAR, second son of Major D , of Fermanagh

,, 6   ROBERT BAKEWELL, second son of Robert B , late of Nottingham Esq ,
          deceased   [deceased

,, 11   WILLIAM HIGGON, eldest son of John H , of Tredavy, co Pembroke, gent.,

Aug 5   JAMES COMMIN, second son of John C , of Exeter, salt and cheese merchant

Oct 18   EDWARD TUCKER, second son of Edward T , late of the parish of Kenton,
          Devon, " Ducis nautici," deceased   [Tyne, gent

Nov 6   HENRY STRADFORTH MORTON, second son of Joseph M , of Newcastle-upon-

,, ,,   ALEXANDER McCARTHY, first son of Alexander M , of Cork, Esq

,, 8   MATTHEW J. CONOLLY, third son of Matthew C , late of Shannon Hill, co
                                           [Galway, Esq , deceased

,, 11   JOHN KELLETT, third son of William K , of Gt Clonard, co Wexford, Esq

,, 12   JOSEPH LENTAIGNE, second son of Benjamin L , late of Dublin, M D , deceased

,, 18   JOHN FITZGERALD, fourth son of Robert F , late of New Hall, co Clare, Esq ,

,, ,,   CHARLES CROFTON, fourth son of Hugh C , Baronet, of Dublin   [deceased.

,, 20   EBENEZER WARREN LEWIS, eldest son of Rev John L of Dublin.

,, 24   JOHN HARVEY (Rev), LL B , eldest son of Rev Edward H , late Rector of
                                       [Finningley, Notts, deceased

, ,,   JONATHAN DAVID CLARKE, eldest son of John David C , of Dublin, Esq

,, ,,   JOHN MAHON, second son of John M , of Dublin, Esq

,, 26   JOHN MOSS, only son of John M , late of Nottingham, Esq , deceased

, ,,   PIERCE SOMERSET BUTLER, eldest son of Col the Hon Pierce B., of Kilkenny

,, 27   JOHN HENRY WRIGHT, second son of Francis Bowcher W . of Hinton
                                       [Blewett, Somerset, Esq

,, ,,   MERVYN HAMILTON, second son of Robert H , of Dublin, Esq

Dec 3   THOMAS FITZGERALD, eldest son of Gerald F , late of Bally Donoghue, co
1825   [Limerick, Esq , deceased

Jan 8   JOHN WELCH, third son of George W , late of Leck House, co Lancaster, Esq.

     24   JOHN CAILLARD ERCK, second son of John E , late of Dublin, Esq , deceased

,, ,,   JOHN M MURTON, only son of George M , of Drummond Street, Euston
                                         [Square, Middlesex, Esq

,, ,,   GEORGE FREDERICK BELL, third son of George B , late of Killnan, co Cavan,
                                         [Esq , deceased.

,, 25.   FRANCIS KNIPE, eldest son of Rev Francis K , Rector of Sandon, Essex

,, ,,   JOHN DALY, only son of John D , of London, Esq

1825

Jan 26   ROBERT STEWART KENNEDY, second son of Hugh K , of Cultra, co Down, Esq

,,   31   HENRY GRIFFITH, only son of John G , of the city of Durham, gent

Feb   1   JOHN TYRELL, third son of Peter T , of Clonbrook Cottage, Queen's County, Esq

,,   3   JOHN RADCLIFF, eldest son of Hon John R , of Dublin

,,   5   RICHARD DUNN, youngest son of John D , of Drumsna, co Leitrim, Esq

,,   ,,   JAMES MACAULAY HYNDMAN, fourth son of Robert H , of Dublin, Esq
                                                       [Esq , deceased

,,   7   GEORGE AUGUSTUS JACK, only son of Alexander J , late of the city of Cork,

,,   8   HENRY BALL, only son of Henry B , of Clifton, co Gloucester, Esq

,,   ,,   FREDERICK THOMAS PRATT, third son of John P , of Kennington, Surrey, Esq

,,   10   WILLIAM LELAND, eldest son of John L , of Dublin, Esq

,,   14   JAMES ARTHUR WALL, eldest son of James W , of Knockrigg, co. Wicklow, Esq

,,   22   WILLIAM HENRY WHITE, eldest son of William W , of Artillery Place, Middle-
          sex, Esq , deceased   [deceased

Mar 19   JAMES BARNES, eldest son of James B , late of Shoreditch, Middlesex, gent ,

April 22   EDMUND HAYES, fourth son of William H , of Millmount, Banbridge, co Down,

,,   25   RICHARD BIRD, second son of Richard B , of Birmingham, solicitor   [Esq

,,   30.   WILLIAM PEPPERCORN, eldest son of William Alexander P , of St. Neot's,

May   3   HENRY HASSARD, second son of George H , of Dublin, Esq   [Hunts, Esq

,,   ,,   RANDALL HARVEY PRATT, fifth son of James Butler P , of Mullintra co Cavan

,,   4   SAMUEL WILLIAM BARTON, eldest son of Dunbar B , of Rochestown, co
          Tipperary, Esq   [deceased

,,   7   ROBERT MICHAEL BAXTER, eldest son of Robert B , late of Gray's Inn, gent

,,   ,,   DANIEL HEMING, fourth son of Joseph H , of Banbury, Oxon, gent

,,   9   EDWARD GALWAY, eldest son of William G , of Dublin, Esq

,,   11   JOHN TAYLOR, third son of William T , of Dublin, Esq   [co Waterford, Esq

,,   ,,   JOHN CONGREVE ALCOCK, eldest son of William Congreve A , of Landscape,

,,   12   ROBERT ARMITAGE, second son of Whaley A , of Moriston, co Hereford, Esq

,,   13   THOMAS AYSCOUGH, eldest son of William A , late of London, Esq , deceased.

June   2   WILLIAM WITHAM, second son of William W , late of this Inn, Esq , deceased

,,   7   JOHN O'DONOGHUE, third son of John O , late of Ennis, co Clare, Esq ,
          deceased   [Westmeath, Esq , deceased

,,   9   PETER FITZGERALD NUGENT, second son of Thomas N , late of Donore, co

,,   10   MOUNTIFORT LONGFIELD, second son of Rev Mountifort L , of Desart, co Cork

,,   ,,   FRANK THORPE PORTER, fourth son of William P , of Wilmount, co Dublin,
          Esq   [deceased

,,   14   THOMAS GRIFFITH, eldest son of Henry G , late of Greenhill, Flints, gent ,

,,   17   ARTHUR MOORE, second son of Hon Arthur M , a Justice of the Common
          Pleas, Ireland   [Thomas B , late of Poulton, co Lanc , gent

,,   18   JOSEPH BRIGGS, of the Inner Temple (admitted June 24, 1808), third son of

,,   20   JAMES O'GORMAN MAHON, eldest son of Patrick M , late of New Park, co
          Clare, Esq   [deceased

,,   25   WILLIAM ILLINGWORTH, third son of William I , late of Nottingham, Esq ,

,,   28   GEORGE SHEPHERD (Rev), D D , eldest son of John S , of Feversham, Kent,
          Esq

1825

July 1 GEORGE GOLDSMITH KIRBY, only son of George K , of Kensall Green, Middlesex, gent   [Esq , deceased

,, 8 RICHARD HARRISON, eldest son of William H , late of Poulton, co Lancaster,

,, ,, SAMUEL APPLEBY, eldest son of Thomas A , of Salford, co Lancaster, Esq

,, ,, WILLIAM BRAMLEY, fourth son of Robert B , late of Leeds, Yorks, Esq
deceased   [Devon, Esq , deceased

,, ,, ROBERT GAMLEN, fifth son of William G , late of Geal, parish of Tiverton,

,, 15 WILLIAM MAKEPEACE, eldest son of Robert M , of Lincoln's Inn Fields, Esq

Aug 1 THOMAS CARR, only surviving son of William C , late of the city of Durham,
         [Esq , deceased

Sept 26 GEORGE BLAXLAND ROGERS, eldest son of William R , of London, Esq [Esq

Nov 2 CHARLES COLLINGRIDGE, second son of Samuel C , of Bloomsbury, Middlesex,

,, 3 DAVID LEAHY, only son of Thomas L , late of Newcastle, co Limerick, Esq ,
         [deceased

,, 7 HENRY MARTLEY, fourth son of James Frederick M , of Wells, co Meath, Esq.

,, 8 THOMAS HEDLEY, second son of William H., late of Wylam on-Tyne, Esq ,
deceased   [gent , deceased

,, 9 JAMES WILLIAM SMITH, only son of John S , late of Cirencester, co Gloucester,

,, ,, HENRY BOWES, youngest son of Joseph B , late of Workington, Cumberland,
         [gent , deceased

,, 18 WILLIAM JOHNSTON, eldest son of Alexander J , of Rehsboth, co Dublin, Esq

,, 24 THOMAS CARSON, eldest son of Rev Thomas C , late of Kilmahon Glebe, co.
1826   Cork   [Street, Grosvenor Square, Middlesex, Esq , deceased

Jan 13 WILLIAM FREDERICK AUGUSTUS DELANE, only son of Cavin D , late of Duke

,, 18. GEORGE FRASER, second son of George F , of Nagpoor, East Indies, Esq

,, 19 CHARLES WAKEMAN LONG, eldest son of Wakeman L , late of St Helens, co.
Worcester, gent , deceased   [Esq

,, 21 ARTHUR WILLIAM TOOKE, only son of William T , of Russell Square, London,

,, 23 THOMAS CAYLEY SHADWELL, fifth son of Lancelot S , late of Lincoln's Inn,
         [Esq , deceased

,, 24 EDWARD BULLEN, third son of William B , of city of Cork, M D   [deceased

,, ,, BIGGS MILLS SANKEY, eldest son of Samuel S , late of Eythorne, Kent, gent ,

,, ,, JOHN BURLEY, eldest son of George B , late of Lincoln's Inn, Esq , deceased

,, 25 JOHN LECKY, only son of John L , of Portarlington, Ireland, Esq

,, 27 ALEXANDER DISNEY, only son of Fownes D , of Dublin, Esq

,, 28 HENRY ALEXANDER KENNEDY, seventh son of Rev John Pitt K , late of
Balteagh, co Derry, deceased   [Roscommon, Esq , deceased

Feb 2 GEORGE HUGHES BYRN, second son of Patrick B , late of Corboy, co

,, 3 WILLIAM McKANE, only son of Thomas M , of Dublin, Esq

,, 4 JAMES HENRY MONAHAN, eldest son of Michael M , of Heathlawn, near
         [Portumna, co Galway, Esq

,, ,, JAMES LYNE, second son of James L , of Dublin, Barrister-at-Law

,, ,, JAMES WYNNE, third son of William W of Dublin, Esq   [Esq

,, 7 PATRICK MEAGHER, third son of Thomas M , of Ballycanwin, co. Waterford,

,, 8 RICHARD WALLIS GOOLD ADAMS, eldest son of Michael A , of Jamesbrook,
co Cork, Esq

1826

Feb 9   JOHN PLATTEN, second son of Thomas P , late of Fakenham, Norfolk, gent
[deceased

,, 10   JAMES HAMILTON, only son of Dane H , of Monaghan, Ireland, Esq.

,, ,,   GEORGE KITE, third son of William K , of Stockland, Dorset, gent

,, 24   SMITH SPENCER WIGG, only son of John Smith W , of Carmarthen, Esq

, ,,   WILLIAM MALLETT, fourth son of Humphrey M , of Langtree, Devon, gent

,, 29   FRANCIS WAITES, third son of George W a Bencher of Gray's Inn

April 8   JOHN THOMAS, eldest son of John T , of Penzance, gent

,, 10   ROBERT BRIDE, third son of Robert B , of Broomfield, co Wicklow, Esq

,, 14   JOSEPH NASH eldest son of Joseph N , of Ryegate, Surrey, land surveyor

,, 16   JOSIAS MANLIFFE, only son of Richard M , late of Dublin, Esq , deceased

,, 17   JOHN STONE, second son of William S , late of Withycombe House, Somerset,
[Esq , deceased

,, 18   WILLIAM PATRICK CLARKE, only son of James C late of Keppel Row,
[Middlesex, Esq , deceased

,, 19   GEORGE ABRAHAM WOOD, fourth son of Michael W , late of Cork, Esq

,, ,,   SIMEON HENRY HARDY, eldest son of Simeon H , of Cork, Esq [deceased

,, 22   JOHN ADAMS, fifth son of Samuel A , of Dublin. Esq [Esq

, 26   ROBERT HOBART, eldest son of Robert H , of Prospect Hall co. Waterford,

,, 22   BENJAMIN BAYLY, only son of Richard B , of Finglas Bridge, Dublin, Esq

May 1   WILLIAM HENRY HARDING. second son of Henry H , of Dunville, near
Dublin, Esq [umberland, Esq

,, ,,   WILLIAM BROWN CLARKE, eldest son of William C , of Benton House, North-

,, ,,   FREDERICK McCLINTOCK, third son of John M , of Drumcar, co Louth, Esq

,, 2   JOSEPH MOORE LABARTE, second son of Joseph M L , late of Clonmell, co ,
Tipperary, Esq , deceased [Esq

,, ,,   EDWARD WALLER, eldest son of Thomas W of Borrisokane, co Tipperary,

,, 4   JOHN HAMILTON WHITE, second son of Hamilton W , late of Bantry, co
[Cork, Esq

,, ,,   EDWARD HARTEEN BURROUGHS, third son of William B of Dublin, Esq

,, 5   BRIAN WALLER PROCTOR, eldest son of Nicholas P , late of Gloucester Place,
[Camden Town, Middlesex, Esq , deceased

,, 15   THOMAS LLOYD, only son of Thomas L , of Winchester, Esq

,, 27   ROBERT MORELLET ALLOWAY, eldest son of William Johnson A , of the
[Derries, Emo, Queen's County

June 1   ROBERT JAMES BERKELEY, second son of Richard B , late of Ballinacurra, co
[Cork, Esq , deceased

,, ,,   BENJAMIN ADAIR GAMBLE. second son of Arthur G., of Belfast, Esq

,, 6   JOHN RIALL, second son of Charles R , of Heywood, Clonmel, Ireland, Esq

,, 8   TIMOTHY J McEVOY, second son of Timothy M , late of Dublin, Esq ,
deceased [Esq , deceased

,, 12   GEORGE HOLMES, only son of Charles H , late of Kennington Place, Surrey,

,, 13   WILLIAM FRASER, second son of John F., late of the Six Clerks' Office, Esq ,
deceased [Middlesex, Esq

,, ,,   ROBERT CROOK WALFORD, only son of Thomas Witts W , of Uxbridge,

1826

June 21   JOHN HUNT, eldest son of Thomas H , late of Hinton Blewett, Somerset,
                                         [gent , deceased

,,   30   JAMES CLIFT, eldest son of Jonah C , of Somers Town, Middlesex, Esq

Oct. 12   JAMES GEORGE HAYDEN, eldest son of James H , late of Bath, gent deceased

,,   31   CHARLES DAWSON, eldest son of Thomas D , late of Edwardston Hall, Suffolk,
                                         [Esq , deceased

Nov   7   RICHARD STEVENS TRIPP, eldest son of Robert T , of Ashton, Somerset, Esq

,,   8   MILES HENRY PRANCE, second son of William P , late of Plymouth, Devon,
             merchant, deceased   [Esq , deceased

,,   ,,   SEDLEY BASTARD MARKE, only son of John M , late of Liskeard, Cornwall,

,,   14   GEORGE GARNETT, second son of Rev George Charles G , of Dublin

,,   ,,   JOHN BICKNELL, only son of Joseph B , of Upper Marylebone Street,
                                       [Middlesex, Esq

,,   17   ALFRED MONTAGU, third son of Basil M , Barrister at-Law, of Gray's Inn

,,   ,,   JAMES WOOD, eldest son of John W , late of Castle Grove, co Donegal, Esq ,
             deceased   [sex, Esq , deceased

,,   ,,   JOHN BATE CARDALE, eldest son of William C , late of Bedford Row, Middle-

,,   23   THOMAS O'KEEFFE, fourth son of Daniel O'K , late of Clonakilty, co. Cork,
                                         [Esq , deceased

,,   ,,   THOMAS D'ARCY MAHON, eldest son of D'Arcy M , of Dublin

,,   ,,   FEARGUS O'CONNOR, fourth son of Roger O'C , of Paris, Esq

,,   25   MATTHEW BAKER, eldest son of Robert B , of Dublin, Esq

,,   29   WILLIAM CARVILL, eldest son of George C , of London, merchant, and of
             Hendon, Middlesex, deceased   [deceased

Dec. 6   ROBERT BATE, eldest son of Robert B , late of St Clere, Cornwall, gent ,

,,   13   THOMAS DEASON ROBINSON, second son of George R , of Great Queen Street,
1827   [Lincoln's Inn Fields, " venetitoris "

Jan   18   ROBERT WILTSHIRE, eldest son of Robert W , of Bloomsbury, Esq

,,   20   JAMES MARTIN, only son of Robert M , of Ross House, co Galway, Esq

,,   ,,   PRIDEAUX SELBY, eldest son of Prideaux S , of Hackney, Middlesex, Esq

,,   23   CONSTANTINE O'DONEL, eldest son of Constantine O , of Larkfield, co

,,   ,,   ROBERT BEATTY, fifth son of John B , of Dublin, Esq   [Leitrim, Esq

,,   ,,   JOHN TRAFALGAR BLACK, third son of Rev Richard B , of Hutton Rectory,
                                         [Essex.

Feb   7   WILLIAM MATTHEWSON HINDMARCH, eldest son of William H , of Bishop-
                                [wearmouth, co Durham, Esq

Mar 20   GEORGE JAMES NICHOLSON, third son of John N , of Islington, Middlesex,
             Esq   [Esq , deceased

April 10   JAMES WILLIAM FRESHFIELD, eldest son of James F , late of Chertsey, Surrey,

,,   27   RICHARD CARTER SMITH, fifth son of ———, late of Peckham House, Surrey
                                         [Esq , deceased,

May   2   FREDERICK ALLEN, fourth son of Henry A , of Lodge, near Hay, Brecon , Esq

,,   ,,   ROBERT LONG, second son of John L , late of Coldbath Square, Middlesex,
             gent , deceased   [deceased

,,   3.   MICHAEL SMITH, second son of " vicarii " (Lieut) Michael S , late of Madras,

,,   4   GEORGE GEACH, eldest son of George G , of St Austell, Cornwall, gent

1828   [Esq
May 9 WILLIAM GRACE KELLY, third son of John K , of Stradbally, Queen's County,

„   „   ARTHUR SAUNDERS, only son of John S , of Currans, Castle Island, co Kerry,
         Esq   [Baronet, deceased.

„   10 WILLIAM HUGHES, fourth son of Rev Sir Robert H , late of Southampton,

„   „   JAMES HARDEN, eldest son of Robert H , of Harrybrook, Tandragee, co
                                                            [Armagh, Esq

„   „   ARTHUR DUNN CHAIGNEAU, only son of Peter C , of Dublin, Esq

„   12 THOMAS CHAPMAN, third son of John C , of Hastings, Esq

„   „   THOMAS CROWE, eldest son of Thomas C , of Ennis, co Clare, Esq

„   „   WILLIAM MCDERMOTT, eldest son of Owen M , late of Springfield, co Gal-
                                                            [way, Esq , deceased

„   14 WILLIAM CRAWFORD, eldest son of Stephen C , of Dublin, gent

„   15 DIGBY CAYLEY WRANGHAM, second son of Ven Archdeacon W , of Hunmanby,
         Yorks   [Queen's County

„   „   EDWARD MEADOWS DUNNE, second son of General Edward D , of Brittas,

June 2 ROBERT DRIVER THURGOOD, seventh son of William T , late of Debden, Essex,
         gent , deceased   [deceased

„   6   CHICHESTER BOLTON, third son of John B , late of Maine, co Louth, Esq ,

„   11 JOHN TOLEKEN, eldest son of John T , of Cork, Esq

„   „   JAMES TOLEKEN, second son of John T , of Cork, Esq

„   18 RICHARD BERGOIN BENNETT, only son of Richard Newton B , of Dublin, Esq ,

„   21 JAMES SHERIDAN, second son of Edward S , of Dublin, M D [Barrister-at-Law

,   23 WILLIAM HAMWOOD FRAMPTON, second son of James F , of Frome, Somerset,
         gent   [deceased

„   „   DANIEL NEAL LISTER, only son of Daniel L , of Hackney, Middlesex, gent ,

Nov 6   JAMES FRANCILLON, sixth son of Francis F , late of Harwich, Essex, Esq

„   „   THOMAS ANDREW JAMES, only son of Thomas J , of Burton Crescent, Middle-
                                                            [sex, Esq

„   „   JOSEPH BURKE, son of Peter B , of Elm Hall, Parsons Town, Ireland, Esq

„   „   WILLIAM RATHBONE, only son of John R , of Sandbach, Cheshire, Esq ,
         deceased   [gent

„   8   JOHN RICHARD COOK, second son of Henry C , of Paddington, Middlesex,

„   10 JOHN SAMUEL GRAVES, aged 31, only son of Rear-admiral G , late of Bath,
                                                            [deceased

„   13 ROWLAND GIBSON, aged 35, eldest son of John G , of Monmouth, Esq

„   14 EDWARD O'CONNOR, A B , Trinity College, Dublin, aged 30, eldest son of John
         O'C , of Dublin, Esq   [dufferin, co Down, Esq , deceased

„   13 JAMES BAILIE,] P , co Down, aged 31, eldest son of James B , late of Ring-

„   14 WILLIAM N BARRON, aged 23, fourth son of Pierce B , late of Ballyneil,
         Ireland, Esq   [of Rathmines Castle, co Dublin, Esq

„   15 JONAS GREENE, of Trinity College, Dublin, aged 23, fifth son of ——— G ,

„   „   EYRE BURTON POWELL, of Trinity College, Dublin, aged 33, third son of Eyre
                                              [Burton P , late of Dublin, Barrister-at-Law, deceased

„   17 HAMILTON DOWDALL, of King's Inns, Dublin, aged 22, eldest son of Walter
         D , of Camile, co Meath, Esq , deceased   [Dublin, Esq

„   18 WILLIAM JONES, of Trinity College, Dublin, aged 21, only son of Arthur J , of

1828   [of the Middle Temple, Esq

Nov 20   FRANCIS BACON, B A , Trinity College, Dublin, aged 26, third son of James B ,
                                                 [gent

„ 22   HENRY MORTIMER QUINAN, aged 23, second son of Thomas Q , of Dublin,

„ „   ALBANY CARRINGTON BOND, aged 45, fourth son of John B , late of Hendon,
      Middlesex, Esq , deceased   [London, gent , deceased

Dec 4.   WILLIAM WHITEHEAD, aged 44 (died 1832), eldest son of Richard W , late of

„ 24   SAMUEL OWEN, of Barnard's Inn, aged 31, fourth son of Richard O , late of
      Hackney, Middlesex, gent , deceased   [Jeremiah M , of Dublin, Esq.

„ 25   WILLIAM FRANCIS MARA, of Trinity College, Dublin, aged 21, second son of

„ „   EDWIN HILL HANDLEY, B A , Cambridge, aged 22, second surviving son of
                      [Thomas H , of Gray's Inn Square, Solicitor

„ 27   MICHAEL BELLEW NUGENT, aged 20, second son of William Thomas, Lord

1829   Riverston, of Pallace, Ireland   [Hill, co Armagh

Jan 23   JOSHUA PAUL BARKER, aged 25, eldest son of Joshua Paul B , of Market

„ „   WILLIAM DOWNES GRIFFITH, aged 22, fifth son of Richard G , late of Holy-
      head, Anglesey, Esq., deceased   [Highgate, Middlesex, Esq

„ „   JOHN LAWRENCE TATHAM, aged 22, eldest son of Thomas Trevor T , of

„ 26   THOMAS HUDSON, of New Inn, aged 28, eldest son of Robert H , of Lan-
      caster, gent   [co Westmeath, Esq

„ „   JOHN WILLIAM McKEON, aged 21, fourth son of James M , late of Street,

Feb 2   JOHN BULLAR, of Furnival's Inn, aged 21, eldest son of John B , of South-
      ampton, gent   [son of Joshua M , of Annabeg, co Tipperary, Esq

„ „   JOSHUA ROBERT MINNITT, A B , Trinity College, Dublin, aged 22, eldest

„ 5   THOMAS MULLINS, aged 22, eldest son of Hon E M , of Dingle, co Kerry

„ 23   JAMES STEVENSON BLACKWOOD, of Trinity College, Dublin, aged 23, eldest
                    [son of Pinkstan B , of Killyleagh, co Down, Esq

1827 (sic)   [co Meath, Esq

Nov 24 (sic) SAMUEL JOSHUA FORSTER, eldest son of Samuel F , late of Forster Lodge,

1829   [Peter N , of Athlone, Esq

Feb 5   THOMAS NORTON, of Trinity College, Dublin, aged 22, second son of

„ 7   MICHAEL WHITE, aged 33, only son of Michael W , of Baker Street, Portman
      Square, W., Esq   [T , of Donogue Cottage, co Monaghan, Esq

„ „   BARTHOLOMEW CHARLES TEELING, aged 23, eldest son of Charles Hamilton

„ 9   GEORGE WYSE, aged 35, second son of Thomas W , of Waterford, Esq

„ „   THOMAS STEPHENS, aged 26, fifth son of Thomas S , late of Llechryd, co
      Cardigan, Esq , deceased.   [Esq

May 7   THOMAS JENINGS, aged 21, third son of Ulick J , of Ironpool, co Galway,

„ „   THOMAS ORMSBY, aged 22, eldest son of Lieut -Colonel Antony O , of Ballina-
                    [more House, co Mayo

„ 9   JOHN LAWLESS, aged 45, eldest son of Philip L., late of Dublin, Esq , deceased

„ „   WILLIAM RUSSELL CREED, aged 24, second son of Edward C , late of the city
      of Cork, Esq , deceased.   [Fortfield, Dublin, Baronet

„ 11   WILLIAM JOHN McMAHON, aged 17, second son of Sir William M , of

„ 12   JAMES BOYLE, of Trinity College, Dublin, aged 23, second son of James B ,
      of Ballyshannon, co Donegal, Esq   [co Kerry, Esq

„ 16   MAURICE SANDES, aged 23, fifth son of Thomas William S , of Sallow Glen,

1829

May 20   CHARLES BROWN, late of Barnard's Inn, aged 37, second son of George B,
                                                 [late of Bath, Lieut R N, deceased

,, ,,   JOHN NEWPORT GOULDSBURY, of Trinity College, Dublin, aged 27 eldest son
                                     [of Richard G, of Fortlands, co Longford, Esq

,, 23.   EDWARD ARTHUR LITTON, aged 15, only son of Edward L, of Dublin, Esq

,, 25   ARTHUR ANNESLEY YEO, aged 20, eldest son of Henry Y, of Philipsburgh,
        co Dublin, Esq   [P D, of Chapel Izod House, Dublin, Esq.

,, ,,   JOSEPH DICKSON, of Trinity College, Dublin, aged 22, second son of Samuel

, ,,   CHARLES JAMES GRIFFITH, of Trinity College, Dublin, aged 20, only son of
        Richard G, of Dublin, Esq   [gent

,, 26   THOMAS ELLISON, aged 35, second son of Mathew E, of Glossop, co Derby,

,, ,,   EDWARD SPENCER DIX, Senior Sophister, Trinity College, Dublin, aged 18,
                                   [eldest son of William D, of Dublin, Esq

,, ,,   WILLIAM P LEAHEM, of Trinity College, Dublin, aged 21, second son of
                                  [William L, of Bert, co Derry, Esq

,, ,,   CHARLES JAMES MARTIN, of Trinity College, Dublin, aged 23, only son of
        James Charles M, of Dublin, Esq   [Ireland, Esq

,, ,,   THOMAS L BEHAN, aged 23, only son of Laurence B, of Tullamore,

,, ,,   NATHANIEL HONE, aged 22, eldest son of Joseph H, of Dublin, Esq

,, 28   CHARLES HILL, of Trinity College, Dublin, aged 20, eldest son of Richard
        H, of Dublin, Esq   [Killua Castle, co Westmeath, Knight

,, ,,   MONTAGU LOWTHER CHAPMAN, aged 20, eldest son of Sir Thomas C, of

,, 30   WILLIAM CLEARE BURGES, aged 25, eldest son of John B, of Willhook
        House, co Dublin, Esq   [B, late of Dublin, Esq, deceased

June 19   ROBERT BERNARD, of Trinity College, Dublin, aged 21, eldest son of William

,, ,,   CÆSAR DUDLEY COLCLOUGH, aged 25, eldest son of Rev Dudley C, of
        Enniscorthy, co Wexford   [of Dublin, Esq

,, 20   JAMES BARRETT, of Trinity College, Dublin, aged 22, third son of James B,

,, 22   FRANCIS McDONNELL, of Usk, co Monmouth, aged 39, eldest son of Francis
               [M, late of Abergavenny, co. Monmouth, M D, deceased

,, 23   THOMAS JONES, aged 21, eldest son of Thomas J, of Cork, Esq

,, 27   HENRY FRANK BEASLEY, of Trinity College, Dublin, aged 22, eldest son of
        Thomas B, of Dublin, Esq   [Patrick D, of Dublin, Esq

,, 30   EDWARD DOWLING, of Trinity College, Dublin, aged 26, eldest son of

July 2.   WILLIAM MAWDESLEY BEST, of Trinity College, Dublin, aged 19, eldest son of
               [Thomas B, late Captain 26th Regiment, deceased.

,, ,,   HATTON O'SHEA, aged 21, second son of Luke O, of Cork

,, ,,   GEORGE BOWES MORLAND, aged 21, third son of Benjamin M, of Shepstead,
        Berks, Esq   [O, of Dublin, Esq.

,, 6   DENIS O'CONOR, of Trinity College, Dublin, aged 21, eldest son of Matthew

,, 29   HENRY GOODWIN SELF LONG, aged 21, second son of Wakeman L, late of St
                         [Helens, co Worcester, druggist

Nov 7   RICHARD WEST NASH, aged 21, eldest son of Rev Richard Herbert N, D D.,
             [of Moyle House, co Tyrone, Rector of Ardstragh, co Tyrone

,, ,,   THOMAS MOYLAN, aged 22, third son of Denis M, of Versailles, Esq

,, 17   ARTHUR JONES O'KEEFE, aged 22, eldest son of John Charles O, of Irish-
                                 [town, near Dublin, Esq

1829

Nov 17   WILLIAM ROSE, aged 17, second son of Joseph R , of Aylesbury, Bucks, Esq

,, ,,   HILL HAMILTON, of Trinity College, Dublin, aged 23, only son of Hill H ,
                                                           [of Belfast, Esq

,,   18   WILLIAM MURRAY, aged 24, eldest son of John M , of Dublin, Esq

,,   19   HENRY THUNDER, B A , Trinity College, Dublin, aged 21, fourth son of
             Patrick T , of Lagore, co Meath, Esq   [Dorset, Esq

,,   21   HENRY CHARLES GOODDEN, aged 24, fourth son of Wyndham G , of Compton,

,,   24   PERCEVAL BANKS, A B , Trinity College, Dublin, age 24, eldest son of
                                 [Perceval B , of Rose Bank, co Clare, M D

,,   ,,   HENRY WILLIAMS, aged 35, only son of Henry W , late of Southwark, Solicitor,

1830   [deceased

Jan 27   THOMAS JOSEPH TENISON, late a Student of Trinity College, Dublin, aged 26,
            only son of Rev Joseph T , late of Donoughmore Glebe, co Wicklow,
                 [and late Deputy Governor of the County, deceased

,,   ,.   JOHN EDWARD BYRNE, aged 27, eldest son of Edward B , late of Ballymanus,
                                      [co Wicklow, Esq , deceased

,,   30   GEORGE KEOUGH, of Trinity College, Dublin, aged 25, second son of John
             [K , late of the city of Kilkenny, and late High Sheriff, deceased

Feb   2   THOMAS TEED, of Madras, aged 33, third son of John T , late of Plympton,
                                          [Devon, Esq , deceased

,,   3   FREDERICK LUMB, aged 22, third son of Henry L , of Wakefield, Yorks, gent

,,   6   SKEFFINGTON CONNOR, of Trinity College, Dublin, aged 21, eldest son of
                                        [George C , of Dublin, Esq

,:   ,,   JOHN BROWN TERREWEST, aged 18, fifth son of Reuben T , of Lincoln, Esq

,,   ,,   THOMAS LITTLETON HOLT, of Trinity College, Cambridge, aged 25, eldest
            [son of Thomas Littleton H , of Bedford Place, Middlesex, Esq

,,   ,,   JOHN THOMAS DEVITT, of Trinity College, Dublin, aged 22, only son of
            Thomas D., of Wood Park, co Limerick, Esq   [Essex, Esq , deceased.

Mar 22   CHARLES HODGKINSON, aged 40, third son of Sampson H , late of Upton,

,,   24   FREDERIC READE, aged 44, youngest son of William R , of Camberwell,
            Surrey, Esq   [O , late of Granard, co Longford, Esq , deceased

,,   ,,   JAMES O'BRIEN, of Trinity College, Dublin, aged 25, second son of Daniel

April 26.   WILLIAM PRIOR MOORE, of Trinity College, Dublin, aged 20, fourth son of
                                       [Rev John M , of Cavan, co Cavan

,,   28   CHARLES TUTHILL, graduate of Trinity College, Dublin, aged 20, third son
                                         [of John T , of Dublin, Esq

,,   ,,   OWEN ARMSTONG, aged 21, second son of John A , of Dublin, Esq , deceased

,,   30   SAMUEL ·O'MALLEY, aged 24, eldest son of Sir Samuel O , of Kilboyne,
            Ireland, Baronet   [Town, Middlesex, gent , deceased

,,   ,,   VINCENT GEORGE DOWLING, aged 44, eldest son of Vincent D , late of Kentish

May 7   THOMAS HENRY BAKER, of Trinity College, Dublin, aged 23, only son of
            Thomas B , late of London, gent , deceased   [Esq , deceased.

,,   8   WILLIAM SMITH, aged 17, eldest son of William S , late of Enfield, Middlesex,

,,   ,,   JOHN BENNETT, of Trinity College, Cambridge, aged 21, eldest son of John
                                  [B , of Riverston Nenagh, Ireland, Esq

,,   11   JOHN GALWAY HOLMES, of Trinity College, Dublin, aged 20, eldest son of
                 [Robert H , late of Summer Hill, Dublin, Esq , deceased

1830

                                                        [Peter D., of Dublin, Esq.

May 11   SAMUEL ALLEN DALY, of Trinity College, Dublin, aged 21, eldest son of

,,   12   WILLIAM DONNELLY, A B., Trinity College, Dublin, aged 25, fourth son of
[John D , of Blackwater Town, co Armagh, Esq.

,,   ,,   ROBERT J FEARON, of Trinity College, Dublin, aged 26, third son of Daniel
[F , late of Dublin, Esq , deceased

,,   14   HUGH FAWCETT, of Trinity College, Dublin, aged 18, only son of Hugh F ,
[late of Cavan, Ireland, Esq , deceased.

,,   15   JOHN LYNCH, A B , Trinity College, Dublin, aged 24, eldest son of Henry
[Blosse L , late of Partree, co. Mayo, deceased

,,   ,,   EDMUND KELLY, of Trinity College, Dublin, aged 20, second son of Rev
[Thomas K , of Rathmines Castle, co Dublin

,,   ,,   JAMES KLYNE O'DOWD, of Trinity College, Dublin, aged 27, eldest son of
[Roger O , of Castlebar, co Mayo, Esq

,,   19   GERALD OSBREV, of Trinity College, Dublin, aged 25, seventh son of Gerald
[O , late of Elmville, co Dublin, Esq , deceased

,   ,,   ROBERT S DICKSON, only son of Robert D , of Ballyfree, co Wicklow, Esq

,,   ,,   WILLIAM JOHN JOHNSTON, of Trinity College, Dublin, aged 20, eldest son of
Robert J , of Dublin, Esq   [Julius Cæsar B , of South Mall, Cork, Esq

,,   ,,   JULIUS CÆSAR BESNARD, B.A , Trinity College, Dublin, aged 21, only son of

,,   ,,   JOHN NORTON, of Trinity College, Dublin, aged 24, only son of John N ,
[late of Newtown Park, co. Dublin, Esq , deceased

,,   ,,   JAMES ARUNDEL NIXON, of Trinity College, Dublin, aged 22, second son of
Henry N , of Clour House, co Kilkenny, Esq   [J , of Dublin, Esq

,,   ,,   ROBERT JOHNSTON, of Trinity College, Dublin, aged 18, second son of Robert

,,   21   THOMAS JAMES NORRIS, of Trinity College, Dublin, aged 18½, eldest son of
Berry N , of Mohill, co Leitrim, J P , Esq   [co Dublin, Esq

,,   22   THOMAS KENNEDY, aged 23, eldest son of Macanus John K , of Killester,

,,   ,,   JOHN VIZARD, aged 23, eldest son of John V , late of Dursley, co Gloucester,
[Esq , deceased

,,   ,,   MONTGOMERY DOWNES NIXON, A.B , Trinity College, Dublin, aged 21, eldest
son of Montgomery N , late of Lakeview, co. Fermanagh, M D , deceased

,,   ,,   NORTH PRITCHARD, aged 21, third son of Samuel P , of Norwood, Surrey, Esq

June 11   DAVID LYNCH, of Trinity College, Dublin, aged 21, second son of David L ,
of Dublin, Esq   [mouth, Esq

,,   ,,   THOMAS PHILLIPS, aged 28, eldest son of Thomas P , of Newport, co Mon-

,,   ,,   JOHN McMULLEN, of Trinity College, Dublin, aged 30, eldest son of Patrick
[M , late of Cayaugh, co Tyrone, Esq , deceased

,,   12   THOMAS MORGAN FAIR, aged 28, fourth son of Thomas F , late of Skibbereen,
[co Cork, Esq , deceased

,,   ,,   JOSEPH COOPER WALKER, A.B , Trinity College, Dublin, aged 28, eldest son of
[Samuel W , late of Dublin, Esq , deceased

,,   19   BENJAMIN HARDY, aged 22, third son of Samuel H , of Islington, Esq

,,   23   JOHN MORLAND, of Gainford, co Durham, aged 33, only son of John M ,
late of Natland, formerly of Capplethwaite Hall, Westmoreland, Esq

,,   28   LEWIS PICKERING THOMAS, of Trinity College, Dublin, aged 48, eldest son of
[Richard Baldwin T , late of Dublin, solicitor, deceased

,,   30   CHARLES TURVILE, aged 44, second son of Francis Fortescue T , of Husband's
[Bosworth Hall, co Leicester, Esq

1830   [of Dublin, Esq

June 30   GABRIEL STOKES, of Trinity College, Dublin, aged 22, only son of Gabriel S

July 27   JOHN MEE MATTHEW, aged 24, eldest son of William M , of Ashby de la
        Zouch, co Leicester, architect   [late of Dublin, distiller, deceased

Nov. 6.   JOHN COSTIGIN, of Trinity College, Dublin, aged 22, eldest son of Sylvester C ,

,,   ,,   ANTONY HENRY WILKINSON, aged 31, sixth son of Percival W., late of
                [Gorleston, Suffolk, Esq , deceased.

,,   10   VINCENT SCULLY, of Trinity College, Cambridge, aged 20, second son of
                [Dennis S , late of Dublin, Esq , deceased

,,   11   MONTAGUE EDWARD SMITH, Attorney-at-Law, aged 23, eldest son of Thomas
              [S , late of Bideford, Devon, Esq , deceased

,,   12.   TREVOR ALEXANDER FENTON, B A , Trinity College, Dublin, aged 21, only
        son of John F , of York Street, Middlesex, Esq   [Cork

,   22   RICHARD LLOYD, aged 23, only son of Rev Richard L , of Passage West, co

,,   23   HENRY NICHOLAS CARR, of Trinity College, Dublin, aged 24, second son of
              [John C., late of Dublin, Esq , deceased.

,,   24   JOSHUA KETTLEWELL, A B , Trinity College, Dublin, aged 23, fifth son of
              [Colonel Patrick K , of Clonmel, co. Tipperary

,,   26   WILLIAM HUSTLER, aged 18, second son of William H , late of Bishopwear-
1831   [mouth, co Durham, Esq , deceased

Jan 5   SIDNEY CALDER HORRY, of the University of Edinburgh, aged 24, fourth son
        [of Captain Robert H , master mariner in the Honduras trade

,,   11   GEORGE STEPHEN, aged 36, fourth son of James S , of Kensington Gore,
       Middlesex, Master in Chancery   [D , Vicar of Gulval, Cornwall

,,   13   ROBERT LOGAN DILLON, of Furnivals Inn, aged 27, only son of Rev Robert

,,   17   JOHN WARNER NICHOLLS, aged 32, second son of Samuel N , late of Hatton
            [Garden, Middlesex, Esq , deceased

Feb 8   JOHN GOODSON, aged 66, eldest son of William G , late of West Lydford,
           [Somerset, surgeon and coroner, deceased

,,   19.   WILLIAM BEETHAM, aged 50, eldest son of Edward B , late of Somers Town,
       Middlesex, Esq , deceased   [W , late of Waterford, deceased

,,   20   JAMES WHITE, of Trinity College, Dublin, aged 27, only son of Rev James

Mar 15   THOMAS DAX, aged 42, eldest son of Thomas D , of Brixton, Surrey, Esq

,,   26.   EDMUND WALKER, aged 50, eldest son of Edmund W , late of Chancery Lane,
            [solicitor, deceased

,,   28   JOHN SMITH, aged 16, second son of Thomas S , one of the sworn Clerks in

,,   ,,   F A WALTER   [Chancery

,,   ,,   FRANCIS GODFREY, aged 24, fifth son of Hugh G , of Jersey, Esq

April 15   CHARLES HANDCOCK, of Trinity College, Dublin, aged 22, fifth son of Richard
           [H , of Athlone, co. Westmeath, Esq

,,   16   ARTHUR KNOX OGLE, A B , Trinity College, Dublin, aged 22, eldest son of
           [William O , of Newry, co. Armagh, Esq

,,   18   RICHARD BOLTON McCAUSLAND, A B , Trinity College, Dublin, aged 21,
           [second son of William James McC , of Dublin, Esq

,,   ,,   WILLIAM THOMAS MONSELL, aged 21, eldest son of Ven. Thomas Bewley M ,
           [of Dunboe Parsonage, Coleraine, Archdeacon of Derry.

,,   20   JOHN ADYE CURRAN, A B , Trinity College, Dublin, aged 31, eldest son
           [of John C , of Dundrum, co. Dublin, Esq

1831
          [Miles L , of near Louisburgh, co Mayo, Esq

April 21 PATRICK LAVILLEV, A B , Trinity College, Dublin, aged 29, second son of

,, 22 JOHN JAMES KING, of Coates, Sussex, aged 36, eldest son of John K , late of
          [Grosvenor Place, Middlesex, Esq , deceased

,, 25 RICHARD ROSE, A B , Trinity College, Dublin, aged 21, eldest son of Richard
          [Anderson R , late of Foxhall, Newport, co Tipperary, Esq , deceased

,, 29 BENJAMIN FREND, B A , Trinity College, Dublin, aged 21, only son of Rev
          [W C F , late of co Limerick, deceased

,, 30 GEORGE BRADDELL, A B , Trinity College, Dublin, aged 22, youngest son of
          [Joseph B , late of Ballingate, co Wicklow, Esq , deceased

May 3 EDWARD NORMAN, A B , Trinity College, Dublin, aged 20, third son of John
     N , of Dublin, Esq   [John M , of Dublin, Esq

,, ,, JOHN COOK MEREDITH, A B , Trinity College, Dublin, aged 22, elder son of

,, ,, ALEXANDER NORMAN, A B , Trinity College, Dublin, aged 21, second son of
          [Luke N , of Dublin, Esq

,, 4 JONATHAN CHRISTIAN, of Trinity College, Dublin, aged 22 third son of
          [George C , of Carrick-on-Suir, co Tipperary, Esq

,, 5 ROBERT HENRY HAMILL, A B , Trinity College, Dublin, aged 21, second son of
          [Hugh H , late of Ruskey Clones, co Monaghan, Esq , deceased

,, ,, ROBERT JOHN HILLS, aged 17, eldest son of Charles H , of Mile End, Middle-
    sex, gent   [Ignatius O , of Dublin, Esq

,, ,, ISAAC S O'CALLAGHAN, of Trinity College, Dublin, aged 19, eldest son of

,, ,, WILLIAM BLACK, of Trinity College, Dublin, aged 22, third son of Henderson
          [B , of Larkfield, Belfast, Esq

,, ,, JOHN FRANCIS WALLER, Graduate of Trinity College, Dublin, aged 22, third
          [son of Thomas W , of Finoe House, co Tipperary, Esq

,, 6 CHARLES ROLLESTON, A B , Trinity College, Dublin, aged 23, second son of
          [Charles R , late of Silverhills, Ireland, Esq , deceased

,, ,, JOHN THOMAS LLOYD, A B , aged 23, fourth son of Rev Edward L , late of
          [Abingdon, co Limerick, deceased

,, ,, EDWARD M KELLY, A B , Trinity College, Dublin, aged 21, second son of
     Hubert K , of Parsonstown, Ireland, Esq   [H E.I C S , deceased

,, ,, STEWART BLACKER, A B , aged 22, only son of Captain George B , late

,, ,, JASPAR JOHN BARRY, Senior Sophister, Trinity College, Dublin, aged 25,
    second son of Garret B , late of Ballinachora, co Cork, Esq , deceased

,, ,, DAVID MANIFOLD, A B , aged 20, third son of Daniel M , of Caddenstown
    House, King's County   [eldest son of Joseph M , of Dublin

,, 24. HUMPHREY T MINCHIN, Graduate of Trinity College, Dublin, aged 20,

,, 20 WALTER BUTLER SKELTON, A B., Trinity College, Dublin, aged 20, only son of
          [William S , late of Castle, Kilkenny, Esq , deceased.

,, 25 MAHONY HARTE, B A , Trinity College, Dublin, aged 23, second son of
    William H , of Cooburg, co Limerick, Esq   [Bucks, Esq

,, 30 ABRAHAM KIRKMANN, aged 32, eldest son of Abraham K , of Blackwell Hall,

June 1 WILLIAM SMITH, aged 30, eldest son of Aquila S , of Dublin, Esq

,, 2 ANDREW CASTLE MONTGOMERY, of Trinity College, Dublin, aged 26, second
          [son of Nathaniel M , of Dublin, Esq.

,, 3 ROBERT HENRY WELCH, aged 41, eldest son of George W , late of Leek
          [House, co Lancaster, Esq , deceased

1831		[Brunswick Square, Middlesex, gent
June	6	RICHARD CHAPMAN, aged 20, fifth son of Thomas C, of Henrietta Street,
,,	,,	JOHN FLOOD, A B, Trinity College, Dublin, aged 21, second son of John F, [of View Mount, co. Kilkenny, Esq
,,	9	BENJAMIN CHILLEY PINE, of Trinity College, Cambridge, aged 22, eldest son of Benjamin Chilley P, late of Tunbridge Wells, Kent, Esq, deceased
,,	10	BENJAMIN GRANT, A B, Trinity College, Dublin, aged 25, second son of [Benjamin G, late of Dublin, Esq, deceased
Oct	31	HENRY CAREY, Junior Sophister, Trinity College, Dublin, aged 21, second [son of Henry C., of Dublin, Esq
Nov	1	RICHARD ALBANY NELSON, aged 25, third son of Thomas N, late of Chester-[le-street, co Durham, surgeon, deceased
,,	,,	ROBERT COLE BOWEN, A B, Trinity College, Dublin, aged 22, second son of [Robert Cole B, late of Bowens Court, Ireland, Esq, deceased
,,	,,	ROBERT LUCAS, A B, Trinity College, Dublin, aged 22, eldest son of Colonel [L, of Raconell, co Monaghan, Esq
,,	,,	THOMAS TORRENS ROWLEY MILLER, A B, Trinity College, Dublin, aged 20, [third son of Rowley M, of Moneymore, Ireland, Esq
,,	2	JOHN PRINCE, of Cheltenham, aged 35, eldest son of Richard P, of Beau-régarde, France, gent [Inn Lane, Middlesex, gent, deceased
,,	3	GEORGE WIGG, aged 34, second son of Joseph W, late of North Place, Gray's
,,	,,	MICHAEL BARRY, of Trinity College, Dublin, aged 21, fourth son of Michael B, of Cork, M D, deceased [M D, deceased
,,	,,	FRANCIS ANDREW WALSH, aged 24, only son of Francis W, late of Cork,
,,	4	ROBERT NEITLES, of Trinity College, Dublin, aged 25, only son of Richard Nevill N, of Nettleville Hall, Macroom, Ireland, Esq [gent, deceased
,,	,,	JOSEPH ARDEN, aged 31, eldest son of Joseph A, late of Islington, Middlesex,
,,	6	WILLIAM FOWLE, aged 16, second son of Rev Thomas Hartland F, of North Otterington, co York [John R, of Dublin, Esq
,,	9	THOMAS WHITE REILY, A B, Trinity College, Dublin, aged 20, only son of
,,	10	SIMON ANSLEY FERRALL, aged 27, second son of Simon F, late of Dublin, Esq, deceased [gent
,,	11	JAMES LIGHT, aged 33, eldest son of James L, of Church Stanton, Devon,
,,	12	MICHAEL MURPHY, of Trinity College, Dublin, aged 21, fourth son of Patrick M, of Dublin, Esq [Rev Thomas P, of Banagher, King's County
,,	14	WILLIAM A PUREFOY, A B, Trinity College, Dublin, aged 26, second son of
,	,,	JOHN MANNIN, A B, Trinity College, Dublin, aged 24, only son of Anthony [M, of Lismertagh, co Tipperary, Esq
,,	15	ARTHUR KNOX, A B, Trinity College, Dublin, aged 27, eldest son of Rev [Arthur K, late of Woodlawn, co Dublin, deceased
,,	16	CHARLES GEORGE DARLING, A B, Trinity College, Dublin, aged 22, second [son of George D, of Dublin, Esq
,,	19	JOHN LEALY TOWNSEND, Graduate of Trinity College, Dublin, aged 24, [second son of John T, of Clonakilty, co Cork, Esq
,,	21	ROBERT RUNDELL GUINNESS, aged 40, eldest son of Richard G, late of [Dublin, Esq, deceased
,,	22	ROSS STEVENSON MOORE, A B and Scholar of Trinity College, Dublin, aged 24, eldest son of Hugh M, of North Carlingford, Ireland, Esq

1831   [Lancaster, Esq

Nov 24   JOHN CROSS, aged 24, second son of James C, of Mortfield, Bolton, co.

1832   [Esq

Jan 6   GEORGE WILLIAM JOHNSON, aged 29, second son of William J, of Liverpool

"   "   CUTHBERT WILLIAM JOHNSON, aged 32, eldest son of William J, of Liver-
[pool, Esq

"   "   WILLIAM BUTLER, of Ashfield Hall, co Carlow, aged 28, second son of
[Edmund B, late of E T M Ville, co Tipperary, Esq, deceased

"   11   RICHARD EDWARD ARDEN, aged 27, second son of Joseph A, late of Islington,
Middlesex, gent, deceased   [Baronet, deceased

"   "   WILLIAM DENNY, aged 21, fifth son of Sir Edward D, late of Worcester,

"   "   SAMUEL MILLER, aged 32, eldest son of Samuel M, of Bedford Row, Middlesex, Esq.   [Road, Middlesex, gent

"   14   LAMARE MORISON, aged 18, third son of James M, of Hamilton Place, New

"   16   THOMAS KENNEDY LOWRY, A B, Trinity College, Dublin, aged 21, only son
[of John L, of Killyleagh, co Down, Esq

"   17   JOHN FITZGERALD, A B., Trinity College, Dublin, aged 26, fourth son of
[Gerald F, of Ballydonohue Tarbert, co Limerick, Esq

"   19   BURROWES KELLY, of Trinity College, Dublin, aged 21, fourth son of John
[K, of Stradbally, Queen's County, Esq

"   "   RICHARD DOGHERTY, of Trinity College, Dublin, aged 23, second son of
[Thomas D, of Muff, co Donegal, Esq

"   23   SEPTIMUS HOLMES GODSON, aged 31, sixth son of William G, late of Ten-
bury, co Worcester, gent, deceased   [corthy Castle, Ireland, Esq

"   25   LORENZO NICKSON NUNN, aged 23, third son of John Nickson N, of Ennis-

"   "   GEORGE TOMPSON, late of Wolverhampton, Attorney-at-Law, aged 43, only
son of Charles T, late (died 1801) of Birmingham, co Warwick, gent,
[deceased

"   26   THOMAS JAMES IRELAND, M A, Emmanuel College, Cambridge, aged 39, only
[son of Thomas I, of Verulam Buildings, gent

"   27   WILLIAM PARSONS, of King's Inns, Dublin, aged 40, eldest son of John P,
late of Dublin, King's Counsel, one of the Commissioners for the relief
[of insolvent debtors, deceased

April 16.   ROBERT JEFFERIES SPRANGER, of Exeter College, Oxford, aged 20, eldest son
[of Rev Robert S, of Low Toynton, co Linc, clerk

"   20   EDWARD GERAHTY, of Trinity College, Dublin, aged 22, eldest son of James
G, of Dublin, Esq, re-admitted June 9, 1847, then of King's Inns,
[Dublin, Barrister-at-Law, and A B, Trinity College, Dublin

May 2   GEORGE CAPES, aged 29, second son of Robert C, of Gainsborough, co
Lincoln, Esq   [R R, of Lissglassick, co Longford, Esq

"   3   SAMUEL ROBINSON, of Trinity College, Dublin, aged 22, second son of John

"   "   JOHN FITZHENRY TOWNSEND, of Trinity College, Dublin, aged 21, only son of
[Henry Becher T, of Dublin, Esq

"   4   THOMAS GRAYDON, of Trinity College, Dublin, aged 23, eldest son of Alex-
[ander G, late of Limerick, Esq, deceased

"   5   THOMAS SMYTH, B A, Trinity College, Dublin, aged 23, born Oct 21, 1810,
[eldest son of Carew S, of Dublin, Esq

"   7   JAMES MEADE LOUGHNAN, of Trinity College, Dublin, aged 21, third son of
[James L, of Merino Crescent, Dublin, Esq

1832   [C , of Dundrum, co Dublin, Esq

May 7   WILLIAM CURRAN, of Trinity College, Dublin, aged 20, eldest son of Daniel

„ 9   JOHN O'CONNELL, of Trinity College, Dublin, aged 21, third son of Daniel
O , of Dublin, Esq , M P   [R D , late of Dublin, clerk, deceased

„ „   WILLIAM B DRURY, of Trinity College, Dublin, aged 20, only son of the Rev

„ 10   CHARLES CULLIGAN, Scholar of Trinity College, Dublin, aged 23, eldest son
[of John C , late of Cahirsaghnessy, co Clare, Esq , deceased

„ 11   CHARLES BOWER, aged 25, fourth son of Abraham Abrahams, late of
[Weston Place, St Pancras, Middlesex, gent , deceased

„ 26   HAMPSON WILLIAM WHITMARSH, second son of Francis W , Master of
[the Bench of Gray's Inn, Esq

„ 29   EDWARD GEORGE BARTON, of Trinity College, Dublin, aged 25, second son of
[William B , of Clonelly, co Fermanagh

„ 30   ANDREW JOHN MALEY, aged 32, second son of Michael M , of Dublin, Esq

June 7   W W BURKINYOUNG, aged 21, second son of F H B , of Calcutta, Esq

„ „   JOSEPH WILLIAM O'DONNELL, of Trinity College, Dublin, aged 23, eldest
[son of William O , of Carrick-on Suir, co Tipperary, Esq

„ 9   ROBERT LONGFIELD, A B , Trinity College, Dublin, aged 22, third son of
[Rev Mountefort L , of Church Hill, Bandon, co Cork, Esq

„ „   JAMES STRATHEARNE CLOSE, aged 25, eldest son of William C , of Crumlin,
co Antrim, Esq   [County, Esq

„ „   JOHN DILLON, aged 28, third son of Patrick D , of Maryborough, Queen's

„ 11   HENRY ORPEN PALMER, of King's Inns, and of Trinity College, Dublin, aged
[21, third son of Abraham P , of Dublin, Esq

„ „   HUGH O'CONNOR, of Trinity College, Dublin, aged 22, eldest son of
[Daniel E O , of Castlerea, co Roscommon, Esq

„ 13   RICHARD LEDWITH, aged 32, only son of George L , of Dublin, Esq

„ „   WILLIAM PAYNE, aged 33, second son of William P , late of London, gent ,
deceased   [James H , of Dublin, Esq.

„ 14   HENRY GEORGE HUGHES, of Trinity College, Dublin, aged 21, eldest son of

Oct 13   RICHARD MACHELL BOUSFIELD, of King's Inns, aged 26, eldest son of John B ,
of Dublin, merchant   [Robert F , of Kells, co Meath, Esq

Nov 2   ROBERT FISHER, B A , Trinity College, Dublin, aged 25, eldest son of

„ 3   THOMAS PARSONS, aged 25, second son of Isaac P , of Speen Hill, Berks,
Esq   [Devon, Esq

„ „   FREDERICK TREMLETT SPILLER, aged 28, second son of William S , of Honiton,
[deceased

„ „   WILLIAM SMITH, aged 35, only son of Thomas S , late of Sheffield, gent ,

„ 8   DOMINICK McCAUSLAND, of Trinity College, Dublin, aged 24, third son of
[Marcus M , of Daisy Hill, co Londonderry, Esq , deceased.

„ 12   COWDELL CHAPMAN, B A , of Corpus Christi College, Cambridge, aged 23,
[second son of William C , of Biggleswade, Beds, gent

„ 14   ALBERT WILLIAM BEETHAM, aged 30, eldest son of William B., of Stoke
Newington, Middlesex, Esq   [deceased

„ „   WILLIAM LEAHY, aged 30, sixth son of David L , late of Dublin, merchant,

„ 15   JAMES ROW FLOOD, aged 24, second son of John F , of Leeds, co York,
surgeon   [Leicester, Esq , deceased

„ „   THOMAS KIRK, of Symonds Inn, aged 48, only son of Thomas K , late of

1832
Nov 15   FRANCIS TOWERS STREETEN, aged 19, fifth son of John Mitchell S , of Kempsey,
      co Worcester, Esq   [of Clonbrock, Queen's County Esq

,, 19   JOHN DALLAS EDGE, of Trinity College, Dublin, aged 26, eldest son of John E ,

, ,,   MATTHEW O'DONNELL, of Trinity College, Dublin, aged 22, eldest son of
      Richard O , of Kilkenny, Esq   [of Tritonville, co. Dublin, Esq

,, ,,   J B COLLISON, A B , Trinity College, Dublin, aged 23, second son of Daniel C ,

,, 22   JOHN CURTIS, A B , Trinity College, Dublin, aged 24, eldest son of John C ,
      of the city of Limerick, Esq   [Stowe, Northants

,, 24   GEORGE ABRAHAM CRAWLEY, aged 37, second son of Rev Charles C., of

,, ,,   HENRY BEAUMONT COLES, of Andover, Hants, aged 39, only son of Philip C.,
      [late of Duke Street, Adelphi, Esq , deceased

,, ,,   MICHAEL JOSEPH FAGAN, of Trinity College, Dublin, aged 31, eldest son of
      [Patrick F , of Portrishane, co. Carlow, gent.

1833
Jan 11   HENRY SMITH LAWFORD, aged 17, eldest son of Edward L , of Drapers Hall,
      [London, Esq

,, ,,   JOHN RYALL, A M., Trinity College, Dublin, aged 26, eldest son of Isaac R ,
      Marine Infirmary, Plymouth, surgeon [of Mount Kenny, co Down, Esq

,, 18   ROBERT PARKER, A B , Trinity College, Dublin, aged 25, eldest son of James P ,

,, 19   MATTHEW SHANNON HEALY, of Trinity College, Dublin, aged 22, only son of
      [Luke H , late of Rathmines, co Dublin, Esq , deceased

,, 22   ABRAHAM AUGUSTUS NUNN, of Trinity College, Dublin, aged 23, second son
      [of Joshua N , of Dublin, solicitor

,, 23   NICHOLAS MCCARTHY BARRETT, of Trinity College, Dublin, aged 21, eldest son
      of Nicholas B , late of the city of Dublin, Esq , deceased   [deceased

,, 24   RODOLPHUS HENRY SCULLY, aged 21, third son of Denis S , late of Dublin, Esq ,

,, 25   CALEB HENRY O'CALLAGHAN, A B., Trinity College, Dublin, aged 22, second
      [son of Henry O , late of Dublin, Esq , deceased

, 28   ANDREW LYSAGHT, A.B., Trinity College, Dublin, aged 23, eldest son of John
      [L., of Ballysuda, co Clare, Esq

,, ,,   SAMUEL FRANCIS BILTON, aged 21, second son of John B , of Southampton
      Buildings, Middlesex, Esq   [York, Esq

Mar 26   JOHN HAMERTON, aged 22, second son of James H , of Hellifield Peel, co

April 24   EDWARD THOMAS CARDALE, aged 23, second son of William C , late of Bed-
      ford Row, Middlesex, Esq , deceased.   [Barrister-at-Law, deceased

,, ,,   GEORGE HENRY HOUGHTON, aged 23, only son of Henry H , late of Dublin,

,, 29   RICKARD DEASY, A B , Trinity College, Dublin, aged 20, second son of
      Rickard D , of Clonakilty, co Cork, Esq   [Chester, gent , deceased

,, ,,   JAMES PURCELL, of Frodsham, Cheshire, aged 35, eldest son of John P , late of

May 1   CHARLES MAGINNIS, of Trinity College, Dublin, aged 20, second son of Sir
      [John M , late of Londonderry, Knight, deceased

,, ,,   WILLIAM WESTROP BRERETON, A B , Trinity College, Dublin, aged 23, fourth
      [son of Arthur B , of Cullens Wood Avenue, co Dublin, Esq

,, ,,   JAMES MILO BURKE (signs Milo), a Junior Sophister of Trinity College and of
      King's Inns, Dublin, aged 18, eldest son of Martin B., of Sea Point, co Dub-

,, ,,   RICHARD GARDE, aged 21, only son of Joseph G , of Cork, Esq   [lin, Esq

,, ,,   JOHN ROBERT ECHLIN, A B , Trinity College, Dublin, aged 21, eldest son of
      [John E , of Echinville, co Down, Esq

1833

May 1 WILLIAM SADLEIR, aged 24, eldest son of Clement William S , of Shrone
Hill, co Tipperary, Esq   [Kildare, gent

 ,, 2 THOMAS MACKEY SCULLY, aged 27, eldest son of James S , of Maudlins, co

 ,, ,, MOLYNEUX CECIL JOHN BEIHAM, of Trinity College, Dublin, aged 20, eldest
son of Sir William B , Ulster King of Arms, of Stradbroke House, co
[Dublin, Knight

 ,, 3 ROBERT HEDGES EYRE MAUNSELL, A B , Trinity College, Dublin, aged 21,
[eldest son of Richard M , late of Dublin, Esq , deceased

 ,, 4 MORGAN JOHN O'CONNELL, of Trinity College, Dublin, aged 21, eldest son
of John O , of Grenagh, co Kerry, Esq (re-admitted June 11, 1851, then
B A , Trin Coll , Dublin)   [Charles P A , Lord Mayor of Dublin.

 ,, ,, CHARLES P ARCHER, A B , Trinity College, Dublin, aged 22, eldest son of

 ,, ,, LUKE JOSEPH SHEA, of Trinity College, Dublin, aged 22, only son of Luke
[S , of Bretfieldstown, co Cork, Esq

 ,, ,, JOHN O'DONNOGHOE, of Trinity College, Dublin, aged 20, eldest son of
[Daniel O , of Killarney, co Kerry, Esq

 ,, 8 WILLIAM GEORGE THOMAS BARTER, of Staples Inn, aged 25, only son of
[William B , late of Bombay, Esq , deceased

 ,, 9 Sir WILLIAM DOMVILLE, Baronet, aged 59, eldest son of Sir William D , late
[of St Albans, Herts, Baronet, deceased

 ,, 24 THOMAS CATHER, A B , Trinity College, and of King's Inns, Dublin,
aged 23, second son of David C , of Newtown Limavady, co London-
[derry, Esq

 ,, 28 JOHN EDWARDS MURRAY, aged 19, eldest son of Adam M , of Briton Ferry, co
Glamorgan, Esq   [co Gloucester, Baronet

 ,, 30 THOMAS BASIL TUITE, aged 17, fourth son of Sir George T , of Cheltenham,

June 3 JOHN JOSEPH SKERRETT, of Trinity College and of King's Inns Dublin, aged
21, second son of John D. S., late of Ballinduff, co Galway, Esq , deceased

 ,, 4 STEPHEN BROWNE, A B , Trinity College, Dublin, aged 28, second son of
[James B , of Elphin, co Roscommon, Esq

 ,, 5 JOHN RUTHERFOORD, A B , Trinity College and of King's Inns, Dublin, aged
[22, eldest son of John R , of Dublin, Esq

 ,, 6 WILLIAM MATHEW THISELTON, aged 50, eldest son of William T , late of
[John Street, Fitzroy Square, Middlesex, gent , deceased

 ,, 8 RICHARD O'REILY, of King's Inns, Dublin, aged 22, fifth son of Matthew O'R ,
[late of Thomastown Castle, co Louth, Esq , deceased

 ,, ,, WILLIAM McKAY, of Trinity College, Dublin, aged 20, eldest son of Daniel
M , of Dublin, Esq   [Esq

 ,, 12 HENRY BETHUNE ABBOTT, aged 17, eldest son of William A , of Westminster,
[Baronet

Nov 7 CHARLES JOHN JAMES HAMILTON, aged 23, eldest son of Sir Charles H ,

 ,, ,, MATTHEW FRANKS, second son of John F., of Calcutta, Knight, Puisne Judge

 ,, 8 WILLIAM McHUGH, aged 34, third son of William M , late of Dublin, Esq ,
deceased   [John C , of Sherington, Bucks, M D

 ,, ,, ALEXANDER CHEYNE, A.B , Trinity College, Dublin, aged 20, fifth son of

 ,, 9 MICHAEL DOHENY, aged 27, third son of Michael D , late of Brookhill,
[Ireland, gent , deceased

1833

Nov   9   CORNELIUS FERDINAND PURCELL O'LEARY, of Trinity College, Dublin, aged
            18, eldest son of Cornelius O , Barrister-at-Law, of Mallow, Ireland, Esq

   ,   ,,   WILLIAM HENRY FILGATE, of Trinity College, Dublin, aged 22, eldest son of
            [Townley F , late of Charlestown, co Louth, Esq

   ,,   11   VALERIO MAGAWLY, of Trinity College and King's Inns, Dublin, aged 24,
             eldest son of Count M , of Westmeath   [Devizes, Wilts, M D

   ,,   12   WILLIAM HUGHES BRABANT, aged 24, eldest son of Robert Herbert B , of

   ,,   13   RICHARD BABINGTON RING, of Trinity College, Dublin, aged 21, second son
             of Richard R , of Farra, Mullingar, Ireland, Esq   [Berks, Esq , deceased

   ,,   ,,   JAMES HALL SELBY, aged 17, fifth son of Prideaux S , late of Maidenhead,

   ,   14   DANIEL CONNOLLY, of Trinity College, Dublin, aged 21, only son of James C ,
            [late of Cullenswood, Dublin, Esq , deceased

   ,,   ,,   CHARLES GARDE DURDIN, A B , Trinity College, Dublin, aged 19, third
             [son of Robert D , of Cranemore House, Ireland, Esq

   ,   15   RICHARD BLACKBURNE WEBB, Trinity College, Dublin, aged 25, second
            [son of William W , of Dublin, Esq

   ,,   18   JOHN JOSEPH DEMPSY, of Trinity College, Dublin, aged 24, eldest son of
             [Christopher D , of Dublin, merchant

   ,,   20   GEORGE DE MORGAN, aged 25, second son of Lieut -colonel John de M ,
             H E I S, late of Madras, deceased   [Scotia, Capt R A

   ,,   ,,   JOHN NATHANIEL SPELLEN, aged 19, eldest son of J W S , of Halifax, Nova

   ,,   21   ROBERT NICHOLSON, of Trinity College, Dublin, aged 24, eldest son of William
             [Steel N , of Ballow House, near Bangor, co Down, Esq

   ,,   23   FRANCIS JAMES RIDSDALE, aged 37, second son of Francis R , late of Winsby,
             [near Ripley, Yorks, Esq , deceased

Dec   2   JOHN DEVEREII, aged 33, eldest son of Samuel D , of Winchester, Esq

   ,,   ,,   FOUNTAIN ELWIN, aged 50, Lieutenant-colonel in the Army, eldest son of
             [Fountain E , late of Dulwich, Surrey, Esq , deceased

   ,,   13   EDWARD BRABANT SMITH, of St John's College, Oxon, born July, 1808, second
1834   [son of John S , Barrister-at-Law, of Gray's Inn, Esq

Jan 15   GEORGE WILLIAM FRANCIS COOK, aged 16, second son of Charles John C ,
            [of Sloe Farm, Halstead, Essex, Esq

   ,,   14   JOHN MAUNSELL, M A , Trinity College, Dublin, aged 22, eldest son of Richard
             [M , of Oakley Park, co Kildare, Esq

   ,,   16   WILLIAM VERRALL, aged 35, eldest son of William V , of Lewes, Sussex, Esq

   ,,   21   GEORGE M STACPOOLE, of Trinity College, Dublin, aged 19, eldest son of the
             [Very Rev William Henry S , Dean of Kilfenora, Ennistimon, co Clare

   ,,   ,,   ROBERT KEAN, A B , Trinity College, Dublin, aged 21, third son of Robert K ,
             [late of Hermitage, Ennis, co Clare, Esq , deceased

   ,,   22   THOMAS O'HAGAN, aged 22, only son of Edward O , of Belfast, Esq

   ,,   24   PATRICK ROBERT WEBB, of Trinity College, Dublin, aged 25, eldest son of
             [Robert W , of Dublin, Esq

   ,,   ,,   HORACE TOWNSEND, A B , Trinity College, Dublin, aged 32, second son of
             [Horace T , late of Bridgemount, co Cork, Esq , deceased.

   ,,   15   EDWARD FOACH HILLIER, aged 24, only son of Edward H , of Pentonville,
             Middlesex, gent   [William C , of Dublin, Esq

April 15   HENRY CARLETON, A B , Trinity College, Dublin, aged 20, third son of

1834

April 15   JAMES FREEMAN HUGHES, A B , Trinity College, Dublin, aged 26, eldest son
          of John H , of Stillorgan, Dublin, Esq   [G , of Belfast

  „   24   HENRY GARRETT, of Trinity College, Dublin, aged 21, eldest son of Thomas

  „   „   JOHN DELMEGE, of Trinity College, Dublin, aged 19, eldest son of James D ,
          of Piercetown, Kilcock, Ireland, Esq   [John L , of Dublin, Esq

  „   25   JOHN LALOR, Senior Sophister, Trinity College, Dublin, aged 20, eldest son of

  „   26   WILLIAM CROKER KING, A B , Trinity College, Dublin, aged 23, third son of
                                                [Charles Croker K , of Dublin, Esq

  „   28   IGNATIUS HOUSTON EVERARD, Senior Sophister, Trinity College, Dublin,
                        [aged 23, eldest son of Brian Houston E , of Dublin, Esq

  „   9   ISIDORE JOHN BLAKE, Senior Sophister, Trinity College, Dublin, aged 23,
                        [eldest son of John B , of Weston, co Dublin, Esq

  „   29   FRANCIS SMYTH, of Trinity College, Dublin, aged 28, eldest son of Francis S ,
          late of Brighton, Esq , deceased   [co Southants, Esq

  „   30   CHARLES JOHN SHERBEARE, aged 40, eldest son of Charles S , of Odiham,

May   1   CHARLES DEACON, aged 18, eldest son of Col Charles D , of Manor House,
                                                          [Berkhampstead, Herts

  „   „   VALENTINE FLEMING, A B , Trinity College, Dublin, aged 23, second son of
                        [Capt Duke F , late of Tuam, co Galway, deceased

  „   „   WILLIAM MUSGRAVE, of Belfast College, and of the King's Inns, aged 23, third
          son of Samuel M , late of Lisburn, Ireland, Esq , deceased   [Esq

  „   „   JOHN FITZGERALD, of King's Inns, aged 19, second son of David F , of Dublin

  „   2   MATTHEW ROONEY, A B , Trinity College, Dublin, aged 25, eldest son of
                                           [Henry R , of Trevitte, co Meath, Esq

  „   „   JAMES ROBINSON, Junior Sophister, Trinity College, Dublin, aged 20, eldest
                        [son of James R , of Prust House, co Dublin, Esq

  „   „   ROBERT RUTTLEDGE CRAIG, A B , Trinity College and of King's Inns, Dublin,
                [aged 20 or 22, second son of Rev Robert C , late of Frescati,
                                                          [Ireland, deceased

  „   3   CHRISTOPHER JAMES, of Trinity College and King's Inns, Dublin, aged 21,
                        [eldest son of Christopher J , of Dublin, Barrister-at-Law

  „   „   AQUILLA H KENT, Graduate of Trinity College, Dublin, aged 22, third son of
                        [Aquilla K , late of Dublin, Esq , deceased

  „   „   HENRY LOWTHER ALKER, of Trinity College, Dublin, aged 23, third son of
                        [Samuel A , of Drumcondra Hill, co Dublin, Esq

  „   „   JAMES GILLMOR ACHESON, A B , Trinity College, Dublin, aged 21, only son
                        [of James A , of Ranelagh, Dublin city, Esq

  „   4   JOHN HERBERT ORPEN, A M , Trinity College, Dublin, aged 27, only son of
          Thomas Herbert O , M D , of Dublin   [of Dublin, Esq

  „   5   GEORGE O'HAGAN, of the King's Inns, Dublin, aged 28, eldest son of John O ,

  „   „   BRIAN MCCABE, of Trinity College Dublin, aged 26, eldest son of Edward
                        [M , late of Carrick-upon-Suir, Esq , deceased

  „   „   THOMAS LAURENCE MURPHY, of King's Inns, Dublin, aged 30, only son of
          Luke M , late of Dublin, Esq , deceased   [Brabazon S , of Dublin, Esq

  „   „   WILLIAM ALEXANDER STAFFORD, of King's Inns, Dublin, aged 23, fifth son of

  „   „   EDWARD MORTON, aged 33, second son of George M , late of the city of Bath,
                                                          [Esq , deceased

1835

May 8   James Parkinson Boyle, Resident Master, Trinity College, Dublin, aged 31, fifth son of Colonel James B , late of Newtown Limavady, co London-derry, deceased   [W , late of Dublin, Esq deceased

,,   9.   Thomas Wheeler, of Trinity College, Dublin, aged 23, third son of George

,,   ,,   John Shortt, B A , Trinity College, Dublin, aged 21, eldest son of Jonathan S , late of Dublin, Esq , deceased   [Kilkenny, Esq

,,   ,,   James Dooly, aged 26, second son of Richard D , of Birchwood House, co

,, 21   Daniel Harnett Stack, Scholar Trinity College, Dublin, aged 24, fifth son of Michael S , late of Listowel, co Kerry, Esq , deceased , re-admitted May 21, 1847, then of King's Inns, Barrister-at-law, and A B , Trinity [College, Dublin

,, 21   Arthur Robinson, of Trinity College, Dublin, aged 20, eldest son of Robert [R , of Tinnakelly, Parsonstown, King's County, Esq

,, 26   Henry Fry, A B , Trinity College, Dublin, aged 26, eldest son of Oliver F , late of co Galway, Ireland, Captain R A , deceased   [B , of Dublin, Esq

,, ,,   Joseph Barnes, A B , Trinity College, Dublin, aged 25, fourth son of Thomas

June 1   John Bolger, A B , Trinity College, Dublin, aged 24, eldest son of Joseph [B , late of Liverpool, builder deceased

,,   2   Francis Beamish, A B , Trinity College, Dublin, aged 22, eldest son of John [B , of Bandon, co Cork, M D

,,   6   Robert Ferguson, A B , Trinity College, Dublin, aged 22, fifth son of David [F , of Rathkeale, co Limerick, Esq

,, 10   James Ainge, of Fareham, Hants (born Nov 13 1786), aged 48, brother of [Edward A , late of Hitchin, Herts, Esq , deceased

,, ,,   William Dunn, B A , Balliol College, Oxford, aged 30, eldest son of Rev [James D , of Connaught Square, Middlesex

,, 11   John Amery, of Stourbridge, co Worcester, aged 35, eldest son of John A , [of Doncaster, co York, gent

,, ,,   Edward Slevin, of Trinity College, Dublin, aged 23, sixth son of Anthony S , of Granard, co Longford, Esq   [North Durham, Esq

,, ,,   Anthony Compton, aged 25, third son of Ralf C , of Melhington House,

July 13   Alexander Kennedy, of Belfast College, aged 24, youngest son of Thomas [K , late of Rathfriland, Ireland, Esq , deceased

Nov 2   Alexander Howisson Graydon, aged 21, eldest son of Thomas H G , of Ballinasloe, co Galway, Esq   [Paris, and late of Bath

,,   4   Robert Allen, F S A , aged 34, third son of Samuel A , LL D , F S A , of

,, 10   Edward Jones Brewster, A B , Trinity College, Dublin, aged 22, eldest [son of Edward B , of Dublin, Solicitor.

,, 11   Henry Thomas Vickers, of Trinity College, Dublin, aged 20, only son of Thomas V , late of Dublin, Esq , deceased   [H , of Dublin, M D

,, ,,   William Harty, A B , Trinity College, Dublin, aged 21, only son of William

,, ,,   John William Carleton, A B , Trinity College, Dublin, aged 23, eldest [son of Andrew C , of Mohill, co Leitrim, Esq

,, 17   James O'Flynn, Junior Sophister of Trinity College, Dublin, aged 22, only [son of James O , of Youghal, co Cork.

,, ,,   George Fuller, A B , Trinity College, Dublin, aged 24, eldest son of Thomas F , of Bandon, co Cork, Esq   [Inn, Esq., deceased

,, 18   John Henry Cooke, aged 34, only son of John C , of Cooke's Court, Lincoln's

1835

Nov 18   GEORGE ABBOTT, aged 24, second son of George A, late of the Island of
          Nevis, deceased   [brook S, of Calcutta, Esq

  ,,   ,, CHARLES GARSTIN SUTHERLAND, aged 19, eldest son of James Charles Cole-

  ,,   ,, MAURICE KEATING, of Trinity College, Dublin, aged 20, eldest son of Richard
          K, of Dublin, Esq.   [William W, of Dublin, Esq

  ,,   20 WILLIAM WOODROFFE, A B., Trinity College, Dublin, aged 21, eldest son of

  ,,   21 WILLIAM DWYER FERGUSON, of Trinity College, Dublin, aged 19, only son
                                            [of Francis F, of Dublin, Esq

Dec 18   THOMAS MURDOCK LEACOCK, aged 23, only son of John L, late of Vernon
1836   Villa, Isle of Wight, deceased   [barroch, co Cork, Esq

Jan 13   JAMES RODERICK O'FLANNAGAN, eldest son of John Fitz O, of Fermoy-

  ,,   22 THOMAS CALLAGHAN, student of Trinity College, Dublin, aged 21, second
                                            [son of Malachy C, late of Dublin, merchant, deceased

  ,,   23 RICHARD PARSONS, student of Trinity College, Dublin, aged 22, third son of
                                            [John P., late of Glassnevin, Dublin, lawyer, deceased

  ,,   25 ROBERT COOK, aged 23, fourth son of Henry C, of Wandsworth Road, gent

  ,,   ,, REUBEN NORTON, student of Trinity College, Dublin, aged 20, second son
                                            [of Capt. Theophilus N, of Wainsfort Kimmage, co Dublin

  ,,   25 JAMES HOWORTH, aged 42, third son of John H, late of York Street, St
                                            [James' Square, Esq, deceased

  ,,   ,, WILLIAM HARRIS FALLOON, of King's Inns, Dublin, aged 21, eldest son of
          William F, late of Belfast, Esq, deceased   [surgeon

  ,, -26   GEORGE DUKE, aged 32, eldest son of William D, of Hastings, Sussex,

  ,,   27 GEORGE DEANE, of Trinity College, Dublin, aged 24, second son of John
          Berkeley D, late of Berkeley Forest, New Ross, Ireland, Esq, deceased

  ,,   ,, ROBERT OWEN, A B, Trinity College, Dublin, aged 22, eldest son of William
          O, of Kilkenny, Esq   [Lamerton, Devon

  ,,   ,, ARTHUR MUNTON PRICE, aged 25, third son of Rev Rees P, late Vicar of

  ,,   30 RICHARD CAREY, graduate of Trinity College, Dublin, aged 23, third son of
                                            [Henry C, of Blackrock, co Dublin, Esq

April 15   MATTHEW BELL, of Trinity College, Cambridge, aged 18, only son of John
                                            [B., late Master of the Bench, of Gray's Inn, Esq, deceased

  ,,   ,, JOSEPH JONES, aged 30, third son of William J, late of Shrewsbury, Salop,
          Esq, deceased   [John W, late of Cork, Esq, deceased

  ,,   ,, WILLIAM DOUTHAL WILY, of Trinity College, Dublin, aged 22, only son of

  ,,   18 JOHN WALTER HUDDLESTON, of Trinity College, Dublin, aged 20, eldest son
                                            [of Capt Thomas H, late of Dublin, Esq deceased.

  ,,   19 WILLIAM B CAMPION, of Trinity College, Dublin, aged 22, third son of Rev
                                            [Dr C, of Knockmourne Parsonage, co Cork

  ,,   ,, GEORGE HAMMOND WHALLEY, aged 23, eldest son of James W, late of the
          city of Gloucester, Esq, deceased   [John F, Dean of Elphin.

  ,,   20 JOHN FRENCH, of Trinity College, Dublin, aged 23, only son of Very Rev

  ,,   22 RICHARD ELSE, aged 38, eldest son of Richard E, late of Bath, Esq,
          deceased   [deceased

  ,,   ,, SAMUEL SAUNDERS, aged 40, second son of Samuel S, late of Bath, Esq,

  ,,   23 JAMES ROONEY, aged 23 third son of James R, late of Kinnyad, Ireland,
                                            [Esq deceased.

1836		[late of Hanover Hall, Macroom, co Cork, Esc , deceased
April 25	JOHN HARDING, of Trinity College, Dublin, aged 24, eldest son of John H ,
,,	9	NICHOLAS JAMES O'GORMAN, A B , Trinity College, Dublin, aged 21, eldest [son of N P O , of Ballygallane, Lismore, Esq
,,	29	RICHARD WILLIAMS, of Trinity College, Dublin, aged 23, only son of James W , of Kingstown, co Dublin, Esq [Charter House, London, Esq
,,	9	RICHARD GEORGE STEVENS, aged 24, only son of Richard John Samuel S , of
May	2	GEORGE ROBERT STEWART, A B , Trinity College, Dublin, aged 23, eldest [son of Nathaniel S , of Shellfield, Ramelton, Ireland, Esq
,,	,,	HENRY ROBERT BAYLY, A B , Trinity College, Dublin, aged 23, second son [of Emanuel B , late of Bath, Esc , deceased
,,	3	GEORGE HEPENSTAL A B , Trinity College, Dublin, aged 22, only son of [Rev L W H , of Altadore, co Wicklow
,,	4	JOHN JAGOE, aged 36, only son of John J , of Bantry, co Cork, Esq
,,	,,	WILLIAM MOCKLER, A B , Trinity College, Dublin, aged 23, only son of William M , of Dublin, Esq [R , of 5, Clonliffe, Dublin, Esq
,	5	PATRICK REID, A B , Trinity College, Dublin, aged 24, eldest son of Patrick
,,	23	JAMES GOODLATTE RYND, of Trinity College, Dublin, aged 19, eldest son of [Thomas R , of Guernsey, Esq
,,	24	LEOPOLD NORTON, of Trinity College, Dublin, aged 19, third son of [Theophilus N , of Wainsfort Kimmage, co Dublin, Esq
,,	26	ANDREW SEARLE HART, A B , Trinity College, Dublin, aged 25, fourth son of [Rev George Vaughan H , of Glen Alla, co Donegal
,,	27	JOSIAH HEALE, aged 24, third son of William H , late of Newington Green, Middlesex, Esq , deceased [of Dublin, Esq
,,	30.	HAMILTON GEALE, of Trinity College, Dublin, aged 22, third son of Piers G ,
June	6	JAMES WILLIAMSON, A B , Trinity College, Dublin, aged 22, second son of Richard W , of Dublin, Esq [Tipperary, Esq , deceased
,,	8	WILLIAM MACKEY, aged 27, second son of Thomas M , late of Thurles, co
Nov	1	JAMES OLDHAM, aged 18, only son of Gervase O , of Hackney, Middlesex, [gent
,,	2	CHARLES HENRY MONSELL, of Trinity College, Dublin, aged 21, second son of Venerable Thomas Bewley M , of Dunboe, Ireland, Archdeacon of [Derry
,,	,,	HENRY BROWN, aged 37, third son of George B , late of Bath, Esq , deceased
,,	3	ARTHUR CODD, A B , Trinity College, Dublin, aged 22, third son of John C , [late of Kilbeggan, co. Westmeath, Esq
,,	4	THOMAS BAYLY, of Trinity College, Dublin, aged 28, eldest son of Way B , late of Newtown, co Kilkenny, Esq [Middlesex, Esq , deceased
,	,,	GEORGE FYLER, aged 23, fifth son of Samuel F , late of Twickenham,
,,	12	THOMAS DELANY, aged 20, eldest son of Thomas D , of Roscrea, co Tipperary, M D [Whitley S , of Dublin, M D.
,,	15	WHITLEY STOKES, Student of King's Inns, Dublin, aged 36, eldest son of
,,	,,	JAMES WATT, A B , Trinity College, Dublin, aged 22, eldest son of A A W , of co Londonderry, Esq [Gussage St Michaels, Wilts
,,	16	ROBERT LUSH, aged 27, eldest son of Robert L , of New York, formerly of
,,	,,	WILLIAM PHILIP PINCKNEY, M A , Trinity College, Cambridge, aged 26, third [son of John Hearne P , of East Sheen, Surrey, D D

1836

Nov 17　JOHN HARLOE WORKMAN, of Trinity College. Dublin, aged 19, only son of
　　　　　[Harloe Phibbs W., of Rockbrook, co Sligo, Esq

„　„　CHARLES HUMPHREY, Barrister-at-law, of Lincoln's Inn, aged 30, only son
　　　　　[of Charles H., of Cambridge, banker

„　19　GEORGE HAY, A B., Trinity College, Dublin, aged 21, second son of Rev
　　　　　[George H., of Londonderry, Ireland

„　„　JOHN D CLANCHY, A B., Trinity College, Dublin, aged 23, eldest son of
　　　　　Daniel C., of Charleville, co Cork, Esq　　　　　　　　[Dorset

1837

Jan 11　WILLIAM PETER JOLLIFF, aged 23, only son of Christopher J., late of Tosh,

„　„　WILLIAM BUTLER, A B., Trinity College, Dublin, aged 22, only son of John
　　　　　[B., of Wilton, co Kilkenny, Esq

„　13.　ARTHUR NICHOLAS WRIXON, A B., Trinity College, Dublin, aged 25, fourth
　　　　　[son of John W., of Ballyclough, co Cork, Esq

„　14　JOHN JOHNSTON PERRIER, of King's Inns, Dublin, aged 25, second son of
　　　　　[Sir Anthony P., of Cork.

„　„　EDWARD BULKELEY SWIFT, of King's Inns, Dublin, aged 22, fourth son of
　　　　　[Godwin S., late of Lionsden, co Meath, Esq, deceased

„　„　FRANCIS JOHN GRAHAM, A B., Trinity College, Dublin, aged 21, only son of
　　　　　[Robert G., of Drumgoon, Lisneskea, co Fermanagh, Esq

„　20　FRANCIS SAVAGE, A B., Trinity College, Dublin, aged 36, eldest son of Rev
　　　　　[Henry S., late of Glastry "Kircubbin," co Down, deceased.

„　21　WILLIAM ALFRED HILL, of Worcester College, Oxford, aged 20, second son
　　　　　of George H., of Worcester, Esq　　　　　[Daniel M., of Dublin, Esq

„　26　MANNERS MCKAY, of Trinity College, Dublin, aged 18, second son of

„　„　MICHAEL O'FARRELL, A B., Trinity College, Dublin, aged 22, third son of
　　　　　Michael O., of Shannon Park co Limerick, Esq [formerly of Dublin, Esq

.　27.　MATTHEW MORIARTY, aged 19, eldest son of Christopher M., of London,

„　„　ROBERT FOSTER MULLINS, A B., Scholar, Trinity College, Dublin, aged 24,
　　　　　[eldest son of Patrick M., of Dobrien, co Clare, Esq

„　„　ROBERT GEORGE MOORE, of Trinity College and King's Inns, Dublin, aged 25,
　　　　　[only son of George M., late of Dublin, Esq

April 15　JOHN COURTNEY BLUETT, of Douglas, Isle of Man, aged 45, second son of
　　　　　William B., late of London, Esq, deceased　　　　　[Jamaica, Esq

„　„　ROBERT RUSSELL, aged 28, second son of Alexander Robert R., late of

„　17　ROBERT HART, of Hope Bowdler Hall, Salop, aged 32, eldest son of William
　　　　　[Chacey H., late of same, Barrister-at-Law, deceased

„　22　FRANCIS GARVEY, Junior Sophister, Trinity College, Dublin, aged 21, only
　　　　　[son of Edward Francis G., late of Baymount, co Mayo Esq

„　21　WILLIAM JOHN BRODERIP, eldest son of William B., late of Clifton, co
　　　　　[Gloucester, Esq, deceased

„　27　HENRY KELLET, aged 21, third son of Henry K., of Cork, Esq

„　28　ROBERT ROSS ROWAN MOORE, A B., Trinity College, Dublin, aged 23, eldest
　　　　　[son of William M., of Garden Hill, Mount Brown, Dublin, Esq

„　29　EDWARD O'BRIEN, aged 45, eldest son of Thomas O'B., late of Kingston,
　　　　　Isle of Jamaica, planter, deceased　　　[son of John P., of Dublin, Esq

„　„　WELLINGTON JOHN PEPPER, A B., Trinity College, Dublin, aged 24, second

„　„　THOMAS NEEDHAM, A B., Trinity College, Dublin, aged 26 eldest son of
　　　　　[Thomas Richard N., of Dublin, Esq

1837   [Michael Joseph B , of Cork, Esq

May 1   MICHAEL JOSEPH BARRY, of King's Inns, Dublin, aged 20, eldest son of

 „   2   HENRY AHER, A B , Trinity College, Dublin, aged 25, eldest son of David
                                                [A , of Castle Comer, Ireland, Esq

 „   „   PETER BORROWES, aged 21, eldest son of Peter B , of Dublin, Chief Com-
                                                [missioner of Insolvent Debtors' Court, Ireland

 „   „   ARTHUR KENNEDY FORBES, A B., Trinity College, Dublin, aged 22, eldest son
                                                [of Arthur F , of Craig-a-vad, Ireland, Esq

 „   4   EDWARD C MOONEY, A B , Trinity College, Dublin, and of King's Inns,
                                                [Dublin, aged 20, eldest son of Edward M , of Dublin

 „   „   ROBERT PLAMPIN WALLIS, A B , Trinity College, Dublin, aged 25, eldest son
                                                [of William Douglas W , of Dublin, Esq

 „   6   JOHN ROBERT MINNITT, of Trinity College, Dublin, aged 19, eldest son of
                                                [William M , of Blackfort, Nenagh, co Tipperary, Esq

 „   „   GEORGE WILLIAM KINCHELA, of Trinity College and King's Inns, Dublin,
             aged 22, eldest son of Lewis Chapellin K , of the Green, Kilkenny, Esq

 „   22 RICHARD WESTON MARA, A M , Trinity College, Dublin, aged 24, eldest son
                                                [of James M , of Newtown MtKennedy, co Wicklow, Esq

 „   „   RICHARD CUNNINGHAM INCE, A B , Trinity College, Dublin, aged 25, second
             son of Richard I , of Maryborough, Queen's County, Esq [Esq , deceased

 „   „   ALLEN CHANDLER, aged 20, eldest son of George C , late of Bramley, Surrey,

 „   23 PATRICK SPRIGG, of King's Inns, Dublin, aged 24, fourth son of Samuel S ,
             late of Waterford, Esq , deceased   [Trinidad, Esq , deceased

 „   25 JOHN CHARLES CARR, aged 27, eldest son of John C , late of the island of

 „   27 CAMPBELL BLACK, of Trinity College, aged 19, sixth son of Henderson B , of
                                                [Larkfield, co Antrim, Esq

 „   31 WILLIAM ALLEN, of Royal Belfast College, and of King's Inns, Dublin, aged 21,
             [only son of James A , of Nunsquarter, Kirkcubbin, co Down, Esq

June 2   ROBERT MULLEN, of King's Inns, Dublin, aged 39, eldest son of Thomas M ,
             late of Ardmullen, co Meath, Esq   [Limerick, Esq , deceased

 „   6   JAMES GRIFFIN, aged 41, third son of Patrick G , of Fairy Lawn, co

 „   7   CHARLES P TEULON, A B , Trinity College, Dublin, aged 22, second son of
             John T , of Bandon, co Cork, Esq   [Carnarvon, Esq

 „   8   SAMUEL MANNING, aged 22, eldest son of Samuel M , of Pwllheli, co

July 21 ATHANASE VOLSY HITIE, aged 26, eldest son of Baptiste H , of the island of
             Mauritius, Esq   [Thomas J , of Dublin, Esq

Nov 2   WILLIAM FORBES JOHNSON, of King's Inns, Dublin, aged 24, second son of

 „   „   BENEDICT ARTHURE, junior Sophister, aged 18, only son of Thomas A , late of
             Dublin, M D   [Rev Robert S , of Toynton, co Lincoln

 „   3   WILLIAM FRANCIS SPRANGER, of Exeter College, Oxon, aged 20, third son of

 „   „   GEORGE GODFREY PLACE, A B , Trinity College, Dublin, aged 22, eldest son
                                                [of John P , of Ballyfermots, co. Dublin, Esq.

 „   8   PATRICK McMAHON, A B , Trinity College, Dublin, aged 24, eldest son of James
             [M , late of Lakeview, near Rathkeale, co Limerick, Esq , deceased

 „   11 WILLIAM ROE, A B , Trinity College, Cambridge, aged 27, eldest son of John
             R , of Rockwell, co Tipperary, Esq   [King's County, Esq , deceased.

 „   „   JAMES CUFFE, aged 19, fourth son of Thomas C , late of Thomastown Hall,

 „   18 WILLIAM ALLEN, of Trinity College, Dublin, aged 22, third son of John A ,
                                                [Merchant, late of Portaferry, co Down, deceased

1837   [of Dublin, Barrister-at-Law

Nov 20   JOHN TAGERT, of Trinity College, Dublin, aged 25, eldest son of Samuel T ,

  ,,   21   ANDREW COWAN, A B , Trinity College, Dublin, aged 22, only son of James

1838   [C , late of Ballyhnlogh, co Down, Esq

Jan   1   JOHN VERRALL, aged 32, second son of William V , late of Southover, Sussex,
            Esq , deceased   [William K , of Cork city, Esq

  ,,   13   EDWARD KENFALY, of Trinity College, Dublin, aged 18, eldest son of

  ,,   16   JOHN CLIFFE VIGORS, A B , Trinity College, Dublin, aged 24, eldest son of
            Rev Thomas V , of Burgage, co Carlow   [Esq , J P

  ,,   17   WILLIAM EVANS, aged 28, fourth son of Richard E , of Ross, co Hereford,

  ,,   18   ALEXIS SEVENE, aged 22, third son of Amédée S , late of the Mauritius, mer-
            chant, deceased   [John G , of Clanmorris, co Mayo, Esq

  ,,   19   MOSES WILSON GRAY, A B , Trinity College, Dublin, aged 25, second son of

  ,,   20   JOHN BUTLER GREENE, B A , aged 22, only son of Benjamin G , of Ennis, co
            Clare, Esq   [Richard R , late of Rathcore, co Meath

  ,,   24   WILLIAM RYAN, A B., Trinity College, Dublin, aged 21, only son of Rev

  ,,   ,,   BERNARD WILLIAM BAGOT, of Trinity College, Dublin, aged 21, second son of
                                        [Thomas Neville B , of Ballymore, co Galway, Esq

  ,,   26   THOMAS CARMICHAEL, A B , Trinity College, Dublin, aged 27, eldest son of
                                              [Every C , late of Dublin, Esq , deceased

  ,,   ,,   PETER BORTHWICK, M P , and of Downing College, Cambridge, aged 33,
            only son of Thomas B (by a second marriage), late of Edinburgh, Esq ,
            deceased   [common, Esq

  ,,   27   WILLIAM MULLOY, aged 28, second son of William M , of Oakport, co Ros-

  ,,   29   WILLIAM PHELAN, junior, of King's Inns, Dublin, aged 25, third son of
                                              [William P , of Cashel, co Tipperary, gent

  ,,   10   MAURICE MATHEW GEORGE DOWLING, of Liverpool, aged 45, eldest son of
            Maurice William D , of Fulham, Middlesex, Esq   [of Gray's Inn

Mar 30   MONTAGU HERBERT JENNER, aged 20, sixth son of Sir Herbert J , a Bencher

April 6   RICHARD GREENLAND DENNE, of the Inner Temple, Barrister-at Law, aged
            43, second son of Richard D , late of Winchelsea, Sussex, Esq , admitted
            for Chambers   [Middlesex, Esq

  ,,   21   BENJAMIN BOOTHBY, junior, aged 35, eldest son of Benjamin B , of Holloway,

  ,,   23   THOMAS MCNALLY, of Trinity College, Dublin, aged 23, eldest son of
                                                          [Laurence M , of Dublin, Esq

  ,,   26   ROBERT NATHANIEL TRUMBULL, of Trinity College, Dublin, aged 26, second
                          [son of Nathaniel T , late of Beechwood, co Dublin, Esq , deceased

  ,,   ,,   HENRY PYNE, aged 29, Member of the Inner Temple, eldest son of John P ,
                                              [of Somerton, Somerset, Solicitor

  ,,   ,,   GEORGE FINLAYSON, A B , Trinity College, Dublin, aged 19, third son of John
            F , of Dublin, Esq   [Leamington, co Warwick

  ,,   30   JOHN CORLEY, of the Middle Temple, aged 35, eldest son of Patrick C , of

  ,,   ,,   JAMES DILLON MACNAMARA, of Trinity College, Dublin, aged 20, second son
            of Dillon M , of the city of Dublin, Esq   [K , of the city of Dublin, Esq

May   1   JAMES KERNAN, of Trinity College, Dublin, aged 18, sixth son of George

  ,,   3   JOHN COLLINS, of Trinity College, Dublin, aged 19, third son of James C , of
                                                          [Booterstown, Dublin, Esq

  ,,   4   SAMUEL J KEATINGE, aged 20, second son of Richard K , of Dublin, Esq

1838

May   4   HORACE FIRZGERALD, of Trinity College, Dublin, aged 23, fifth son of Richard
          F , of Muckridge House, Youghall, co Cork, Esq   [deceased

  ,,   5   WILLIAM DANIEL GEARY, aged 32, eldest son of Daniel G , of Limerick, Esq ,

  ,,   7   BRIAN MOLLOY, of King's Inns, Dublin, aged 27, second son of Brian M , of
                                      [Dublin, Esq , and Millicent, co Kildare

  ,, ,,   FRANCIS SOMERS, of Trinity College, Dublin, aged 24, only son of Miles S ,
                                      [of Somerville, Rathfarnham, co Dublin, Esq

  ,, ,,   OLIVER WILLIAM ALLEY, of Trinity College, Dublin, aged 23, eldest son of
                                      [Japhet A , of Ballybrack Grove, co Dublin, Esq

  ,, ,,   JOHN MACARTNEY, A B , Trinity College, Dublin, aged 22, eldest son of John
                                      [M , of Mountgibbon, co Fermanagh, Esq , deceased

  ,, 10   CREMUTIUS CORDUS CALDER, aged 21, eldest son of James C , of Brixton
          Hill, Surrey, Esq   [Lamb Buildings, Temple, Esq

  ,, 23   CHARLES JOHN PLUMTRE, aged 21, eldest son of Edward Hallows P , of

  ,, ,,   THOMAS HARTTREE CORNISH, of Cambridge, a Commoner of New Inn Hall,
          Oxon, aged 40, second son of Thomas C , late of Barnstaple, Devon, Esq

  ,, 24   ABRAHAM BOYD FENTON, Graduate of Trinity College, Dublin, aged 23,
                                      [eldest son of Thomas F , of Castletown, co Sligo, Esq

  ,, 29   O'BRIEN EVANS HENNESSY, of Trinity College, Dublin, aged 31, third son
                                      [of O'Brien H , of the city of Cork, Esq , deceased

June 4   THEOBALD ANDREW PURCELL, Senior Sophister of Trinity College, Dublin,
          aged 20, eldest son of Thomas P , of Dublin, solicitor   [Roscommon

  ,,   5   WILLIAM J MULLOY, aged 22, second son of Conte M , of Hughstown, co

  ,,   6   JOHN CONNELLAN DEANE, of Trinity College, Dublin, aged 23, eldest son
                                      [of Sir Thomas D , of Dundanion, co Cork, Knight, Esq

  ,, ,,   JOHN PITT TAYLOR, of the Middle Temple, aged 26, third son of Thomas T.,
                                      [of Coombe, Croydon, Surrey, Esq

  ,, ,,   SYLVANUS MORIARTY, of Trinity College, Dublin, aged 21, eldest son of
                                      [Merion M., of Clifton, Bristol, Esq

  ,,   8   THOMAS CHARLES McDERMOTT, of Trinity College, Dublin, aged 23, eldest
          son of Mulloy M , of Tubberpatrick, co Roscommon, Esq , J P ,
          deceased   [eldest son of John M , of Dublin, Esq

  ,   9   LUKE JOHN McDONNELL, A B , Trinity College, Dublin, 1838, aged 21,

  ,, ,,   DANIEL NEWTON CROUCH, aged 38, second son of John C , of Edinburgh,
                                      [Esq , deceased

  ,, ,,   GEORGE JOHN CRAWFORD, A B , Trinity College, Dublin, aged 27, second
                                      [son of Rev George C , LL D , of St Ann's, co Longford

  ,, 11   RICHARD HARRIS PURCELL, of Trinity College, Dublin, aged 24, eldest son
                                      [of Richard Harris P , of Annabella, Mallow, Esq

Nov   2   JOHN HARKAN, of Trinity College, Dublin, aged 23, second son of George H.,
                                      [of Ross, Elphin, co Roscommon, Esq

  ,, ,,   JOHN BALDWIN MURPHY, of Trinity College, Dublin, aged 22, second son of
                                      [Michael M , late of Ballymore, Cashel, Esq

  ,, ,,   THOMAS WALLACE, A B , Trinity College, Dublin, aged 22, only son of
                                      [Thomas W , of Dublin, Esq , Queen's Counsel

  ,, ,,   ROBERT PHILIP WHITE, of Trinity College, Dublin, aged 20, eldest son of
                                      [Robert W , of Rathdowney, Queen's County, Esq

1838

Nov 2 JOHN DILLON, of Trinity College, Dublin, aged 24, third son of Luke D , of
          Ballaghadeaine, Ireland, Esq   [near Glasgow, Esq

  „   „ JOHN ARCHIBALD RUSSELL, aged 22, third son of James R , of Rutherglen,

  „   6 MICHAEL EDMOND CORCORAN, of Trinity College, Dublin, aged 19, only son
                                              [of Michael C , of Dublin, Esq

  „   8 JONATHAN PHILLIPS, of Trinity College, Dublin, aged 23, only son of
                              [Thomas P , late of Ranelagh, Dublin, Esq , deceased

  „   9 JAMES ANTHONY LAWSON, of Trinity College, Dublin, aged 21, eldest son of
          James L , of Waterford, Esq   [of Carrickmacross, co Monaghan, Esq

  „   14 HUBERT KERNAN, of Trinity College, Dublin, aged 20, eldest son of J B K ,

  „   20 CHARLES JAMES KILPIN, of Worcester College, Oxford, aged 28, second son
                      [of William Hopkins K , late of Kingsclear, Hants, Esq., deceased

  „   „ EDWARD BYRNE LAWLESS, of Trinity College, Dublin, aged 21, second son
1839   [of Barry Edward L , of Dublin, Esq

Jan 17 MICHAEL JOSEPH FITZGERALD, born Aug 10, 1818, second son of Michael F ,
                              [of Castle Martyr, Ireland, Captain Royal Navy

  „   18 THOMAS SIER, aged 19, second son of Thomas S , late of Dewsall, co Hereford,
          Esq , deceased   [merchant, deceased

  „   22 SAMUEL TILLETT, aged 29, eldest son of Robert T , of Colchester, Essex,

  „   „ JAMES CROOKS BELL, of Trinity College, Dublin, aged 23, second son of
                          [Matthew B , late of Armagh, Ireland, Esq , deceased

  „   24 RICHARD MARTIN, A B , Trinity College, Dublin, aged 29, fifth son of John M ,
          late of the city of Cork, Esq , deceased (called to the Irish Bar, Trinity
                          [term, 1840, and re-admitted to Gray's Inn, Nov 5, 1845)

  „   „ JOHN THOMAS BALL, A B (late scholar), Trinity College, Dublin, aged 23,
          [eldest son of Captain Benjamin Marcus B , of Dundrum, Dublin, Esq

  „   28 SAMUEL SHERIDAN HARPUR, A B , Trinity College, Dublin, aged 26, eldest
                                      [son of Captain H., of Lucan, near Dublin

  „   „ WILLIAM FRANCIS GRAHAM, of Trinity College, Dublin, aged 23, eldest son
          of Captain William G , of Newtown, Kells   [Ireland, Esq , deceased

  „   „ ROOTH LOUGHNAN, aged 22, eldest son of Nicholas L , late of Kilkenny,

April 12 THOMAS CARRIQUE PONSONBY, of King's Inns, Dublin, aged 35, third son of
          [William Carrique P , late of Castle House, co Kerry, Esq , deceased

  „   15 RICHARD LOVELL BROWNE, aged 44, eldest son of William B , late of Ken-
          sington, Esq , deceased   [William McD , of Dublin, Esq

  „   „ TOWNSEND McDERMOTT, of Trinity College, Dublin, aged 20, third son of

  „   „ ALCIDÉ DE ROQUEFEUIL LABISTOUR, aged 19, second son of Ango Alexandre
                              [De Roquefeuil L , of the Mauritius, Esq

  „   20 JAMES MACCULLAGH, LL D , Fellow of Trinity College, Dublin, aged 32,
                              [eldest son of James M , of Strabane, co Tyrone, Esq.

  „   22 FLORENCE McCARTHY, A B , Trinity College, Dublin, aged 22, eldest son
          of Denis M , of Mangrove House, co Youghal, Esq , deceased ,
          re-admitted Jan 19, 1841, then described as a Barrister of King's Inns

  „   „ BENEDICT BUNBURY DILLON, of King's Inns, Dublin, aged 22, second son
                              [of Bartholomew D , of Ballyquin House, co Kilkenny, Esq

  „   24. ALEXANDER DICKSON, A B , Trinity College, Dublin, aged 22, fourth son of
                          [John D , late of Woodville, Bundoran, Ireland, deceased

1839   [Patrick D , of Carlingford, co Louth, Esq

April 30   MATTHEW D'ARCV, of Trinity College, Dublin, aged 21, second son of

May   1   FRANCIS ROBERT DAVIES, A B , Trinity College, Dublin, aged 21, eldest son
            [of Robert D , of Fahy, co Galway, Esq

  ,,   3   JOHN F WALKER, A B , Trinity College, Dublin, aged 23, fourth son of
            [Samuel W , of Dublin, deceased

  ,,   ,,   PETER RICHARD KENRICK, of Trinity College, Dublin, and of King's Inns,
            [Dublin, aged 18, eldest son of Peter K , of Dublin, gent.

  ,,   ,,   WILLIAM HAMILTON MAFFETT, B A , Trinity College, Dublin, aged 22,
            [eldest son of William M , of Dublin, Esq

  ,,   4   WILLIAM MILTON IRELAND, A B , Trinity College, Dublin, aged 22, second
            [son of William I , of Dublin, Esq.

  ,,   ,,   ROBERT RUTTLE, of Trinity College, Dublin, aged 19, youngest son of
            [Henry R , of Tralee, co Kerry, Esq.

  ,,   ,,   WALTER RICHARD BUTLER, of Trinity College, Dublin, aged 20, eldest son
            [of Francis B , of Cregg, Gort, co. Galway, Esq

  ,,   ,.   JAMES BUTLER, of Trinity College, Dublin, aged 22, third son of James B ,
            [of Peak, Templemore, co. Tipperary, Esq.

  ,,   6   EVORY CARMICHAEL, of Trinity College, Dublin, aged 28, second son of
            [Evory Thomas C , late of Dublin, Esq , deceased

  ,,   ,,   JOHN EDWARD NAGHTEN, of Trinity College, Dublin, aged 23, third son
            [of Matthew Barnwall N , of Dublin, Esq , solicitor

  ,:   10   THOMAS DEAN, aged 39, eldest son of James D , late of Islington, Esq ,
            [deceased

  ,,   13   CHARLES THEODORE BEWES, aged 21, fourth surviving son of Thomas B , of
            Plymouth, Esq , M P   [Middlesex, gent

  ,,   22   GEORGE HENRY BARTON, aged 26, eldest son of Henry B , of Camden Town,

  ,,   ,,   JAMES GEORGE YOUNG A B , Trinity College, Dublin, aged 29, second son of
            [George Y , of the city of Cork, Esq

  ,,   25   JOHN MacCULLAGH, A B , Trinity College, Dublin, aged 25, second son of
            James M , of Camarven, Omagh, co Tyrone, Esq   [Esq

June   1   MICHAEL JOSEPH ELLISON, aged 21, eldest son of Michael E , of Sheffield,

  ,,   6   EDWARD ALDAY, of Trinity College, Dublin, aged 21, only son of Paul A ,
            [of the city of Dublin, Esq

  ,,   ,,   OLIVER McCAUSLAND, of Trinity College, Dublin, aged 21, third son of
            [William James M , of Dublin, Esq

Nov   2   DENIS O'CONNOR, of King's Inns, Dublin, aged 33, eldest son of James
            [O , of Ballagh, co Roscommon, Esq

  ,,   ,,   CHRISTOPHER GOOD, of Manchester, Jamaica, aged 33, second son of Godfrey
            [G , late of Dublin, Esq , deceased

  ,,   4   RICHARD SHEIL, of King's Inns, Dublin, aged 18, only son of Right Hon
            Richard Lalor S , of ——— co Tipperary   [deceased

  ,,   6   FREDERICK COSENS, aged 20, third son of Charles C , late of Dorchester, Esq ,

  ,,   7   FRANCIS HARVEY DEVEREUX, of Trinity College, Dublin, aged 20, eldest son
            [of Harvey D , of Kilkenny, Ireland, Esq

  ,   15   WILLIAM ST JAMES WHEELHOUSE, aged 19, eldest son of James W , late of
            [Snaith, co York, Esq , deceased

  ,,   20   HENRY COANE, of King's Inns, Dublin, aged 26, only son of Henry C , late of
            [Phibsboro , Dublin, Esq , deceased

1839	[son of William Marchant A , of Waterford, Esq.
Nov 20.	RICHARD MAUNSELL ARDAGH, of Trinity College, Dublin, aged 23, eldest
,, 22	GEORGE EYSTON, aged 43, third son of Basil E , late of East Hendred, Berks, [Esq , deceased
1840	
Jan 10	ARCHIBALD SWINTON, of Edinburgh, advocate, aged 27, eldest son of John S , of Edinburgh, Esq. [Hyde Park, Middlesex, Esq
,, 13	WILLIAM PATERSON, aged 24, eldest son of William P , of Albion Street,
,, 14	LEWIN TAVERNER, of Lincoln's Inn, Barrister-at-Law, aged 37, eldest son of John T , of Clapton, Middlesex, Esq [marthen, Esq , deceased
, 18	JOHN JONES, aged 53, fourth son of Edward J , late of Llandovery, co Car-
,, 23	THOMAS SOUTHGATE, aged 21, eldest son of Thomas S , of Old North Street, [Red Lion Square, Middlesex, gent
,, 24	HUGH O'LOGHLEN, of Trinity College, Dublin, aged 21, second son of [Hugh O , of Port Ennis, Ireland, Esq
,, 28	JOHN O'MEARA, of Trinity College, Dublin, aged 22, fourth son of Edmond O , of Cahir, co Tipperary, gent [ham, Esq
,, ,,	HENRY JOHN HUNTER, born Jan 29, 1819, only son of John H , of Chelten-
,, ,,	JOHN FITZPATRICK VILLIERS, aged 24, only son of John Fitzpatrick V , late of [Marsham Street, Westminster, Esq , deceased
,, ,,	JOHN MURRAY, Scholar of Trinity College, Dublin, aged 24, eldest son of John [M , late of Cavan, co Cavan, M D
,, ,,	HENRY WILLIS, aged 35, eldest son of Captain Henry W , R.A , of Dagen- [ham, Essex, where he deceased 1828
April 21	MICHAEL FRANCIS McO'BOY, of Trinity College, Dublin, aged 31, eldest son of David M , of the city of Cork, Esq , re-admitted Nov 1846, then a [Barrister of King's Inns
,, 27	BOYCE COMBE, Esq , of Lincoln's Inn, aged 50, third son of Harvey Christian [C , late of Cobham Park, Surrey, Esq , deceased
,, ,,	JAMES ENNIS, of Trinity College, Dublin, aged 20, seventh son of James E , of Nauk, co Meath, Esq [O , of the city of Dublin, Esq
,, ,,	RICHARD O'GORMAN, of Trinity College, Dublin, aged 20, only son of Richard
May 5	JOHN BLACKHAN, of Trinity College, Dublin, aged 22, eldest son of Charles B , of Ballymount, co Dublin, Esq [Limerick, Esq
,, ,,	TOBIAS DELMEGE, aged 21, youngest son of Tobias D , of Rathkeale, co.
,, 6	JOHN POWELL LONGFIELD, A B , Trinity College, Dublin, aged 23½, eldest [son of Henry L , of Waterloo House, co Cork, Esq
,, ,,	NORRIS GODDARD, Senior Sophister of Trinity College, Dublin, aged 21, second [son of William G , of Dublin, Esq
,, 7	GEORGE VAUGHAN CHICHESTER, of Trinity College, Dublin, aged 20, third [son of Rev Edward C , of Kilmore, co Armagh.
,, ,,	RICHARD HODGES CARTER, aged 49, eldest son of Richard C , of Arlingham, co Gloucester, gent [of Balls Grove, co and town of Drogheda.
,, ,,	GEORGE BALL, of Trinity College, Dublin, aged 31, eldest son of George B ,
,, ,,	JOHN WILLIAMS, of Bron Grove, co Monmouth, born June 30, 1799, second [son of David W , late of Saethon, co Carnarvon, Esq , deceased.
,, 8	THOMAS MAJOR, Senior Sophister, Trinity College, Dublin, aged 27, second [son of Thomas M , late of Granard, co Longford, Esq
,, ,,	EDWARD McDONNELL, of Trinity College, Dublin, aged 20, third son of [Edward M , of Galway, Esq.

1840

May 8   THOMAS COLLINS, aged 18, second son of Timothy C , of the city of Cork, Esq

,, 11   MATHEW M CONMEE, of Trinity College, Dublin, aged 19, fourth son of [John C , of Frenchport, Ireland, Esq

June 9   EDWARD THOMAS FRENCH BEYTAGH, of Trinity College, Dublin, aged 23, eldest son of Edward James B , late of Cappagh, co Galway, Esq, deceased   [D , of Well Fort, co. Galway, Esq

,, ,,   DOMINICK D'ARCY, of Trinity College, Dublin, aged 21, second son of Martin

,, ,,   WILLIAM SCULLY, of Trinity College, Dublin, aged 21, eldest son of William [S , late of Cashel, co. Tipperary, M D , deceased

,, ,,   FRANCIS MEAGHER, of Trinity College, Dublin, aged 26, second son of Francis [M , of Nenagh, co. Tipperary, Esq

,, ,,   WILLIAM THOMAS POE, A M , Trinity College, Dublin, aged 26, third [son of Rev James Hill P , Rector of Nenagh, co Tipperary

,, 10   JOSEPH BURNIE, aged 40, fourth son of Joseph B., late of Glasgow, merchant, deceased   [co Stafford, gent

,, 12   CHARLES JOSEPH WADE, aged 23, second son of Charles W , of Hawkshutt,

,, 16   SAMUEL SMITH, aged 25, third son of John S , of Dove Court, city of London, deceased   [Richard E , of the city of Cork, solicitor.

Nov 3   WILLIAM ALLEN EXHAM, of Trinity College, Dublin, aged 20, third son of

,, 5   HENRY MATTOCK BURT, aged 23, eldest son of George B , of Huish Episcopi, Somerset, gent   [dlesex, gent

,, 7   DOUGLASS FINNEY, aged 27, second son of John F , of Welbeck Street, Mid-

,, 11   JOHN BARBER, B A , Worcester College, Oxford, aged 23, eldest son of Stephen [B , of Grimley, co Worcester, Esq

,, ,,   MYLES GERALD KEON, aged 19, only son of Myles Gerald K , late of Keon [Brook, co Leitrim, Barrister-at-Law, deceased

,, 21   CHARLES SKINNER TROUGHTON, aged 19, third son of Richard Foach T , of [Dorset Terrace, Clapham Road, Surrey, Esq

1841   [A , of Dublin, gent

Jan 14   FRANCIS ALBANI, A M , Trinity College, Dublin, aged 35, only son of Lorenzo

,, ,,   THOMAS ELLISON, aged 22, second son of Michael E , of Sheffield, Esq

,, 23   JAMES HENRY BENINGFIELD, aged 30, only son of James B , of St James' [Place, Old Kent Road, gent

,, 27   MICHAEL HENRY WALSH, of Trinity College, Dublin, aged 20, eldest son of [John Hussey W , of Tyrells-pass, Ireland, Esq

,, 29   JOHN SAWYER, aged 30, second son of Richard S , late of Dublin, Esq, deceased   [Inn, Barrister-at-Law

April 14   ALDBOROUGH HENNIKER, aged 20, eldest son of Aldborough H , of Lincoln's

,, 16   EDWARD BENNETT, aged 39, eldest son of Edward B , of Morpeth, Northumberland, gent   [Cross, Esq

,, 26   SAMUEL DARE, aged 47, third son of Samuel D , of Cockspur Street, Charing

,, 28   WILLIAM TYNDALL BARNARD, aged 24, only son of William B , late of [Hackney, Middlesex, Esq , deceased

,, 29   JOHN MOORE, A B , Trinity College, Dublin, aged 21, only son of John M , [late of the city of Dublin, Esq , deceased

May 3   ROBERT TAYLOR, of Trinity College, Dublin, aged 26, eldest son of John Smith [T , of Corballis House, Drogheda, Esq

1841.

May 4 WILLIAM SHAW, aged 25, second son of John S, of Morton-upon Swale, co
York, Esq   [Richard F., of Listowell, co Kerry, Esq.

,, ,, RICHARD FITZGERALD, Senior Sophister, Trinity College, aged 21, only son of

,, ,, THOMAS BOURCHIER, of Trinity College, Dublin, aged 20, third son of Daniel
[Macnamara B, Esq, late Major R A

,, 5 JOHN ROBERT BRERETON, of Trinity College, Dublin, aged 22, eldest son of
John B, of Parsonstown, Ireland, Esq   [of Galway, Esq

,, ,, WILLIAM DUGGAN, of Trinity College, Dublin, aged 21, eldest son of James D,

,, ,, JAMES BURKE, aged 21, fourth son of John Joseph B, late of Dublin, M D,
[deceased

,, ,, FREDERICK L SMYTH, aged 25, sixth son of Thomas S, of Dublin, Esq, deceased

,, ,, MATTHEW JOSEPH MARTYN, of Trinity College, Dublin, aged 23, only son of
Christopher M, late of Low Park House, co Galway, Esq, deceased,
[re-admitted Nov 12, 1845

,, ,, JOHN RUTHERFOORD D'OLIER, A B, Trinity College, Dublin, aged 24, second
[son of Isaac Matthew D, of Collegnes, Booterstown, Dublin

,, ,, GEORGE ORME MALLEY, of Trinity College, Dublin, aged 20, fifth son of John
[M, of Castlebar, Ireland, Esq

,, ,, CHARLES GRAY, aged 20, third son of Rev Joseph G, of Chelmsford, Essex

,, 25 THOMAS G IRWIN, A B, of Trinity College, Dublin, aged 28, eldest son
[of George I, of Plantation, King's Co, Ireland, Esq

,, 31 ROBERT WARREN, junior, of Trinity College, Dublin, aged 21, eldest son of
[Robert W, of the city of Dublin, Esq

June 3 JAMES EDWARD STOPFORD, LL D, Trinity College, Dublin, aged 32, eldest
[son of Edward S, of Belmont, Aughnaclay, Archdeacon of Armagh

,, 7 WILLIAM THOROLD WOOD, aged 25, second son of Charles Thorold W, of
Campsall Hall, near Doncaster, Esq   [co Dublin, Esq

,, ,, HENRY HODGENS, aged 17, eldest son of Robert H, of Beaufort, Rathfarnham,

,, ,, JOHN CONLAN HODGENS, aged 16, second son of Robert H, of Beaufort, Rath-
[farnham, co Dublin, Esq

,, 9 MARCUS WILLIAM MERYWEATHER TURNER, aged 22, second son of William
[Stephens M, of Norton Court, co Gloucester, Esq

Nov 2 BENJAMIN WAY, aged 22, second son of Edward W, of Newport, Isle of
Wight   [Joseph M, of Trim, co Meath, Esq.

,, 16 ALLEN JOSEPH MCCARTHY, of Trinity College, Dublin, aged 25, second son of

,, ,, ROBERT WILLIAM OSBORNE, aged 22, eldest son of Jonathan O, of Dublin, M D

,, 19 CHARLES MONTAGU ORMSBY, aged 30, third son of Rev Henry O, late of
[Galtrim, co Wicklow, deceased

,, 20 ROBERT HENRY FRENCH, aged 20, fourth son of George F, of Dublin, Q C

,, ,, MICHAEL DOWLING, of Trinity College, Dublin, aged 21, second son of Bernard
D, of Dublin, Esq   [Michael B, late of Kilkenny, gent., deceased

,, ,, KYRON THOMAS BUGGY, of King's Inns, Dublin, aged 24, second son of

,, 22 MICHAEL KENNAN, of Trinity College, Dublin, aged 25, second son of Richard
K, of Rathfarnham, co Dublin, Esq   [merchant, deceased.

,, ,, WILLIAM REDFERN, aged 41, eldest son of William R, late of Birmingham,
1842   [Upper Canada, Esq

Jan 11 SAMUEL JOHN PARTRIDGE, aged 23, eldest son of John William P, of Toronto,

1842

Jan 13 PIERSE CREAGH, of Trinity College, Dublin, aged 29, eldest son of Symon C,
                      [of Dangan, co Clare, Esq, deceased

,, 19 HUGH FERGUSON, aged 26, eldest son of Hugh F, of Dublin, Esq

,, 20 GEORGE DUNLEVIE, A B Trinity College, Dublin, aged 40, third son of
        Rev Stephen D, late Rector of Kilmoe, co Cork, and Vicar of Mongan

,, 26 RALPH SMITH CUSACK, of Trinity College, Dublin, aged 20, second son of
                      [James William C, of Dublin, M D

April 5 JAMES HAYWARD, aged 22, only son of Francis H, of Aylesbury, Bucks, Esq

,, 12 WILLIAM HENRY MURRAY, A B, Trinity College, Dublin, aged 21, third
              [son of Thomas M, of Edenderry, King's County, Esq

,, ,, JOHN JOSEPH ANDREW KIRWAN, of Trinity College, Dublin, aged 28, eldest
          [son of Martin K, of Knockdromadough, Dangan, co Donegal, Esq

,, 14 GILES HALL, of Barnard's Inn, aged 22, second son of William H late of
        Bibury, co Gloucester, Esq, deceased   [Dublin, Esq

,, ,, JOHN REILLY, of King's Inns, Dublin, aged 32, second son of Jeremiah R, of

,, ,, THOMAS MATHEW RAY, of King's Inns, Dublin, aged 41, eldest son of Mathew
        R, late of the city of Dublin, Esq, deceased   [Esq

,, 20 WILLIAM FOWLER, aged 22, second son of John F, of Wadsby Hall, Sheffield,

,, ,, HENRY MANISTY, aged 33, second son of Rev James M, late of Edlingham,
        Northumberland   [deceased, re-admitted May 4, 1844

,, 26 JOHN WORSLEY, aged 30, third son of Philip John W, late of Bristol, Esq,

,, 30 BERKELEY WILLIAM KING, aged 19, eldest son of Berkeley K, of Francis
              [Street, Torrington Square, gent

May 2 PERCY WHITESTONE, of Trinity College, Dublin, aged 19, eldest son of Luke
        W W, of Dublin, Esq   [John M, of Dublin, Esq

,, ,, DENIS FLORENCE McCARTHY, of Trinity College, Dublin, aged 24, only son of

,, ,, JOHN WILLINGTON, of Trinity College, Dublin, aged 23, eldest son of James
             [W, of Castle Willington, Nenagh, Ireland, Esq

,, 5 EDMUND JORDAN, of Trinity College and King's Inns, Dublin, aged 23, seventh
        son of Myles J, late of Rossleven, Swinford, co Mayo, Esq, deceased

,, 2 FRANCIS CAHILL, of Trinity College, Dublin, aged 24, only son of Francis C,
        late of Dublin, Esq, deceased   [George P, of Dublin, Esq

,, 23 GEORGE PONDER, of Trinity College, Dublin, aged 21, second son of

,, ,, ROBERT BUCHANAN, of King's Inns, Dublin, aged 25, eldest son of Robert
        [B, late of Prospect, Westport, Ireland, Esq, deceased

June 3 THOMAS SHEARBURN, aged 17, only son of William S, of Snaith, co York, Esq

,, 4 PUREFOY BATEMAN, of King's Inns, Dublin, aged 25, second son of John B.,
        [late of Ballylaken, Edenderry, Ireland, Esq, deceased

,, ,, EDWARD LEDWITH, of Trinity College, Dublin, aged 19, eldest son of William
        [L, of Ledwithstown, Ballymahon, Ireland, Esq

,, ,, SPRINGALL THOMPSON, of St John's College, Cambridge, born Oct 29, 1820,
        [eldest son of Frederick Elijah T, of Raymond Buildings, solicitor

Oct 31 JAMES BROWNLOW HOSKINS, aged 21, eldest son of James H, of Gosport, co
        [Southampton, solicitor, and officiating Judge Advocate

Nov 1 JOHN SHAW, aged 25, fourth son of Samuel S, of Rookhills, co Derby, Esq

,, 2 DANIEL ABRAHAM HUGHES, of Trinity College, Dublin, aged 27, third son of
        [William H, of Pearemount, co Dublin, Esq

1842

Nov 7 WILLIAM FREDERICK BROWNE STAPLES, aged 19, second son of Moses William [S , of Norwood, Surrey, Esq , and of Gray's Inn

„ 4 GEORGE RIBTON CRAMPTON, A B , Trinity College, Dublin, aged 27, second son of Rev Cecil C , of Killucan, Ireland   [Westminster, gent , deceased

„ 17 HENRY BANISTER, aged 26, eldest son of James B , late of St James' Place, [Glanaghen House, co Longford, Esq

„ 21 JOHN LEVY, of King's Inns, Dublin, aged 36, eldest son of Patrick L , late of [27, second son of Dunbar B , of Dublin, Esq

„ „ AUGUSTINE HUGH BARTON, of Trinity College and King's Inns, Dublin, aged [John D , late of Monaghan, Ireland, Esq , deceased

„ 23 CHARLES GAVAN DUFFEY, of King's Inns, Dublin, aged 26, fourth son of

Dec 23 SAMUEL JOYCE, aged 25, third son of James J , late of Chapel Street, Penton- [ville, Esq , deceased

1843

Jan 6 JOHN WARD, of Hampstead, aged 37, eldest son of ——— W , late of Dover, [Kent, Collector of H M Customs

„ 14 RICHARD FRANCIS STACK, A B Trinity College, Dublin, aged 23, eldest son [of William S , late of Dublin, M D , deceased.

„ 27. THOMAS WHEELER, aged 35, eldest son of John W , of Manchester, Esq

Mar 22 GEORGE LANGLEY, aged 38, eldest son of James L , of Walworth, Surrey, gent

May 2 JAMES LEONARD, of King's Inns, Dublin, aged 26, fifth son of John L , of Roscrea, Ireland, gent   [of Rathleasty Castle, co Tipperary, gent

„ 5 MAGRATH CAHILL, of King's Inns, Dublin, aged 21, fifth son of Cornelius C ,

„ „ JAMES WARD, of King's Inns, Dublin, aged 20, second son of James W , [of Strawberry Hill, co Down, Esq

„ „ GEORGE SMYTH, of King's Inns, Dublin, aged 27, youngest son of Captain [Charles S , late of the city of Limerick, deceased

„ „ JOHN DAVID HANLON, of King's Inns, Dublin, aged 19, only son of William H , [of the city of Dublin, gent

„ 6 RICHARD NEWTON KING of Trinity College, Dublin, aged 23, eldest son of [Thomas Newton K , of Harperstown, Taghmon, co Wexford, Esq

„ „ RICHARD PENNEFATHER GOING, of Trinity College, Dublin, aged 20, second [son of Ambrose G , of Ballyphilip, Killnaule, co Tipperary, Esq

„ „ OLIVER JOSEPH BURKE, of Trinity College, Dublin, aged 18, second son of [Joseph B , of Dublin, Solicitor

„ „ THOMAS McMAHON, Junior Sophister, Trinity College Dublin, aged 20, eldest [son of John McM , of the city of Dublin, Esq

„ „ WILLIAM JOSEPH BURKE, of Trinity College, Dublin, aged 19, eldest son of [Joseph B , of the city of Dublin, Solicitor

„ 8 RICHARD CROKER SMYTH, of Trinity College, Dublin, aged 27, only son of [William S , of Ballylin Rathkeale, co Limerick, Esq

„ 20 JOHN FIELD, of London, Stockbroker, aged 35, only son of John F , of [Warneford Court, city of London, Stockbroker

„ 26 PIERS FRANCIS WHITE, A B , Trinity College, Dublin, aged 21, only son of [Francis W , M D , of Dublin

„ 27 JAMES McGOURAN, of Trinity College, Dublin, aged 23, only son of Richard M , late of Comber, co Down, Esq , deceased

„ 30 EDWARD OSBORNE HILLIARD, of King's Inns, Dublin, aged 26, fourth son of [Michael H , late of the city of Limerick, Esq , deceased

1843

May 30   WILLIAM CRACROFT FOOKS, of the Middle Temple, aged 30, third son of
[Thomas Broadley F , late of Dartford, Kent, Esq

June 2   JAMES THOMAS KNOWLES, aged 37, eldest son of James K., late of Reigate,
[Surrey, Esq , deceased

,, 9   TIMMS AUGUSTINE SARGOOD, aged 28, only son of Timms Kight S , of
Greenwich, gent.   [mercial Road, Middlesex, gent

Oct 27   JOHN PENDERGAST, aged 27, eldest son of John P , of Albert Square, Com-

Nov 2   ROBERT ROUIERE PEARCE, aged 30, third son of Robert P , of Dunmanway
co Cork, Esq   [Ignatius O , of the city of Dublin, Esq

,, 3   THOMAS O'CALLAGHAN, of Trinity College, Dublin, aged 19, third son of
[Joseph Manus O , late of Castlebar, Ireland, Esq , deceased

,, 17   CHARLES JOSEPH O'DONEL, of Trinity College, Dublin, aged 24, second son of

,, ,,   WILLIAM HENRY PARTINGTON, aged 19, second son of James Edge P , of
[Manchester, Esq

,, 22   WILLIAM JOHN WARREN, of Trinity College, Dublin, aged 24, only son of
[William W , of Hillsborough, Ballina, co. Sligo, Esq

1844

Jan 11   SAMUEL SIMPSON TOULMIN, aged 41, eldest son of Abraham T , late of Surrey
[Street, Strand, gent

,, 26   SAMUEL ROLLS EWEN, aged 34, only son of the late Benjamin E , Lieutenant
[68th Dragoons

,, 29   RICHARD HORNER MILLS, of Trinity College, Dublin, aged 28, eldest son of
[Francis M , late of the city of Dublin, Esq , deceased

April 15   CHARLES O'MALLEY, of King's Inns, Dublin, aged 22, youngest son of Sir
[Samuel O , of Kilboyne House, co Mayo, Baronet

,, ,,   GEORGE THOMPSON, aged 39, third son of Thomas T , late of Lambeth, bookseller, deceased   [Woodbridge, Suffolk, gent

,, ,,   JOHN STIMSON COLLETT, aged 24, second son of Cornelius C , formerly of

,, ,,   HERBERT VENN SILPHEN, aged 22, eldest son of James S , of the Colonial
[Office, Downing Street, London, Esq

,, 19   EDWARD CRISPE ELLERY, aged 29, eldest surviving son of Peter E , late of
Stonehouse, Devon, Purser, R N   [Sloane Street, Esq

,, ,,   WILLIAM HAWORTH HOLL, aged 20, second son of William H , of Hans Place,

,, 22   WILLIAM FREDERICK HIGGINS, aged 25, eldest son of Colonel Sir J G H ,
[of 34 Chapel Street, Belgrave Square

,, 24   WILLIAM IRVINE, of King's Inns, Dublin, aged 20, eldest son of William I ,
[of Prospect Hill, Enniskillen, co Fermanagh, Ireland, Esq

,, 26   DAVID THOMPSON LAWRENCE, aged 24, eldest son of John L , officer in Her
Majesty's Customs, Dublin   [co Kilkenny, Esq , deceased

,, ,,   JOHN O'DONOVAN, aged 24, third son of Edmond O , late of Attaleemare,

,, ,,   JOHN BAKER, aged 44, eldest son of Harry B , of Shoreham, Sussex, Esq

,, 27   PHILIP GILCREEST, A B , Trinity College, Dublin, aged 22, eldest son of
[George G , of Belmont Avenue, co Dublin, Esq

,, ,,   FREDERICK BOR, A B , Trinity College, Dublin, and of King's Inns, aged 23,
fourth son of Humphrey B , late of Ballindolan, co Kildare, Esq ,
[deceased

,, 29   WILLIAM ROPER, A B , Trinity College, Dublin, and of King's Inns, aged 21,
[fourth son of Edward R , of Dublin, Esq

1844.

April 29.   JOHN HAMILTON WILDER COSBY, A B, Trinity College, Dublin, and of King's Inn, aged 22, only son of Captain John Phillips C, late of 15th Foot, [and of Ballyhamson, co Down, deceased

  ,, ,, JOHN JANE SMITH WHARTON, of St Mary Hall, Oxford (M A, 1850), aged 26, [only son of Antony William W, of Devonport, Devon

  ,, ,, WILLIAM HEMSWORTH, A B, Trinity College, Dublin, aged 25, fourth son of [Thomas H, of Abbeville, Borrisokane, Esq

May 3   ROBERT WALL, Senior Sophister, Trinity College, Dublin, aged 22, only son [of Thomas W., of Milton House, co Dublin, Esq

  ,, 4   GEORGE PERSSE, A.B, Trinity College, Dublin, and of King's Inns, aged 24, second son of Robert Parsons P, of Castleboy, co Galway, Esq, deceased   [John C, late of Dublin, Esq, deceased

  ,, 6   WILLIAM S CHAMNEY, of King's Inns, Dublin, aged 22, second son of

  ,, 6   JAMES McDOWELL WILSON, of King's Inns, Dublin, aged 24, eldest son of [John W., of Drumcondra, co Dublin, Esq

  ,, 23   W ENRAGHT LYONS WALCOTT, of King's Inns, Dublin, aged 22, third [son of E S Walcott-Sympson, late of Clifton, Bristol, Esq, deceased

  ,, 25   HENRY WILLIAM VINCENT, aged 47, eldest son of Henry Dormer V, late of [Bracknell, Berks, Esq, deceased

  ,, 30   MATTHEW COMBE, of Trinity Hall, Cambridge, aged 21, fourth son of Boyce [C, of Gower Street, Bedford Square, Esq

June 1   EDWARD GOODE POWELL, aged 20, eldest son of Edward Joseph P, of Raymond Buildings, Esq   [of Park Place, Essex, Esq

Oct 16   WALTER CHARLES URQUHART, aged 20, eldest son of Walter Alexander U,

  ,, 22   JOSEPH WARNER BROMLEY, aged 52, third son of Nathaniel Warner B, late of Gray's Inn, gent   [set, Esq, deceased

  ,, 26   WILLIAM STOATE, aged 37, second son of William S, late of Selworthy, Somer-

Nov 8   HENRY THOMAS COLES, aged 28, second son of Rev John C, of Ditcham [Park, Hants, and Rector of Silchester, Hants

  ,, 9   HENRY BROCK HOLLINSHEAD, aged 25, eldest son of Lawrence Brock H, [late of Highfield House, co Lancaster, Esq, deceased

  ,, 13   GEORGE JAMES NORMAN D'ARCY, A B, Trinity College, Dublin, aged 25, [eldest son of John D, of Hyde Park, Kinnegad, co Westmeath

  ,, 22   THOMAS SANDS CHAPMAN, of Aston Clinton, Bucks, aged 44, eldest son of Thomas C, of Esher Lodge, Surrey, Esq   [co Sligo, Esq

  ,, ,, WILLIAM KELLY, aged 33, eldest son of Andrew K, of Carryshill, Colloone,
1845   [son of Rev Thomas H, of New Park, Maryborough, Ireland

Jan 20   WILLIAM CHAIGNEAU HARPER, of Trinity College, Dublin, aged 21, second

  ,, 24   MATTHEW, FOX, B A, Trinity College, Dublin, and of King's Inns, aged 32, second son of John F, of Moyally House, King's County, Ireland, Esq, [deceased

April 12   WILLIAM JAMES LUCAS, of Chelmsford, Essex, aged 30, eldest son of William [L, late of Lincoln's Inn, barrister at law, deceased

  ,, 14   ARTHUR RICE JENNER, aged 21, youngest son of the Rt Hon Sir Herbert Jenner-Fust, Bencher of this Society   [Tipperary, Esq

  ,, 15   NICHOLAS LOFTUS, aged 28, only son of James L, of Carrick-on-Suir, co

  ,, 17   OSBORNE MARKHAM, aged 31, only son of Osborne M, late of Rocketts, [Essex, Esq, and of Lincoln's Inn, barrister-at-law, deceased

1845   [co Hereford, Esq

April 19   JOHN STRATFORD COLLINS, aged 29, eldest son of John Stratford C , of Ross,

„   24   MAURICE CHARLES MERTTINS SWABEY, of Christ Church, Oxford, aged 23,
eldest son of Maurice S , of Langley Marish, Bucks, Esq , and of Lincoln's
Inn, Barrister-at-Law   [deceased

„   „   WILLIAM DEVOY, aged 34, eldest son of Patrick D , late of Ireland, Esq ,

May 1   JOHN C KELLY, of Trinity College, Dublin, aged 19, eldest son of Thomas
[K , of Mulyrane Mall, Kingstown, Ireland, Esq.

„   2   JAMES SHEARNAN LOUGHNAN, of King's Inns, Dublin, aged 21, only son of
[Henry James L , of the city of Kilkenny, Esq

„   „   WILLIAM HENRY HARTIGAN, of Trinity College, Dublin, aged 24, eldest son
[of Edward H , of Castletown Glebe, Kilaloe, Ireland, clerk

„   3   JAMES JOHN LYNCH, of Trinity College, Dublin, and of King's Inns, aged 21,
[second son of Lawrence L , of Dublin, Esq

„   „   JOSEPH FOGARTY, of Trinity College, Dublin, aged 19, eldest son of Richard
[F , late of Waterford, Ireland, Esq , deceased

„   „   FRANCIS JOHN HOWARD, of Trinity College, Dublin, aged 24, youngest son of
[Thomas H , of Glasnevin, Ireland, Esq

„   „   EDWARD MULHALLEN MARUM, of King's Inns, Dublin, aged 22, only son of
[Richard M , late of Aharney, Queen's County, Ireland, Esq , deceased

„   5   HUMFREY MINCHIN BOURNE, aged 20, second son of Walter B , of Dublin,
Esq   [H , of the city of Dublin, Esq

„   „   WILLIAM IRVING HARE, of King's Inns, Dublin, aged 25, second son of William

„   „   WILLIAM CAMPBELL, aged 21, fourth son of John C , of the city of Dublin, Esq

,   ,   WILLIAM JAMES SIDNEY, aged 18, fourth son of James Waller S , of the city
of Dublin, Esq   [son of Sandham S , of Dublin, Esq

„   22   ABRAHAM SYMES, of Trinity College and King's Inns, Dublin, aged 21, ninth

„   26   SAMUEL POWELL PURSER, of Trinity College and King's Inns, Dublin, aged 19,
[sixth son of John P , of Rathmines Castle, co Dublin, Esq

„   27   THOMAS WORTHINGTON BARLOW, aged 21, only son of William Worthington
B , of Cranage, co Chester, Esq   [deceased

„   29   LEON ARNAUD, aged 22, son of Aristid(es) A , late of the Mauritius, Esq ,

June 3   CHICHESTER THOMAS SKEFFINGTON (Hon), aged 31, second son of Viscount
Ferrard, late of Collon, co Louth, deceased.   [town, Ireland, Esq

,   7   THOMAS GOGGINS GLOVER, aged 36, second son of William G , of Phillips-

„   „   NICHOLAS BALL, A B , Trinity College, Dublin, aged 20, third son of Rt. Hon
Nicholas B., of Dublin   [Madras Presidency, Esq , deceased

„   „   HENRY JEFFREYS BUSHBY, aged 24, eldest son of Henry Turner B , late of the

Nov 5.   HENRY LOFTUS TOTTENHAM, A B , Trinity College, Dublin, aged 31, fourth
son of Henry Loftus T., late of Mac Murrough, co Wexford, Ireland,
Esq , deceased.   [of Rev Ralph S , of Tenyglass, Borrisokane, Ireland

„   20   THOMAS SADLER SIDNEY, A B , Trinity College, Dublin, aged 23, eldest son

„   22   MONTAGUE MORDAUNT AINSLIE, B A , Christ Church, Oxon, aged 22, eldest
[son of Montague A , of Ambleside, Westmoreland, Esq

„   „   REGINALD ROBERT WALPOLE, A B , Caius College, Cambridge, aged 28, eldest
1846   son of Rev Robert W , of Christ Church, Marylebone.   [Esq

Jan 12.   RICHARD BOLTON BARTON, A B , aged 25, eldest son of John B , of Dublin,

„   22   JEREMIAH GILL, aged 23, second son of John G , of Edgbaston, Birmingham,
[Esq

1846

Jan 22   JOHN HENRY BLENCOWE CHURCHILL, of St Peter's College, Cambridge, and of the Inner Temple, Barrister-at Law, aged 43, only son of Henry C, [late of Bicester, co Oxford, solicitor, deceased

,, 23   CHARLES JOSEPH SMYTH, aged 35, fourth son of John S, late of Clonmel, co [Tipperary Esq, deceased

,, ,,   JAMES FALLON, aged 35, second son of P F, of Kennington, Surrey, Esq

,, 27   RALPH LAWRENSON, aged 33, sixth son of Richard L, of Johnstown, co. Kilkenny, Esq.   [Ireland, Esq.

April 15   JOHN RAYMOND GRACE, aged 28, second son of Gerald G., of Nenagh,

,, 17   MARK CARDIFF, of Trinity College, Dublin, aged 20, second son of Mark C, [of Belmont House, co Dublin, Esq, deceased

May 1   AUGUSTUS FITZGERALD WHITESTONE, A B, Trinity College, Dublin, aged 22, [third son of Thomas W, of Ennis, co Clare, Esq

,, 2   WILLIAM JOSEPH O'NEILL DAUNT, aged 38, eldest son of Joseph D, late of Kilcascan, co Cork   [Dublin, Esq

,, ,,   ST GEORGE KERR, aged 21, second son of James K, of Larch Hill, co

,, ,,   ST JOHN CHINNERY ARMSTRONG, Senior Sophister, Trinity College, Dublin, aged 22, second son of Thomas A, of Temple Michael, Youghal, co Waterford, Esq   [eldest son of Henry Fitz G, of Dublin, Esq

,, ,,   HENRY FITZ GIBBON, Senior Sophister, Trinity College, Dublin, aged 21,

,, 4   JOSEPH NEALE MCKENNA, of Trinity College, Dublin, aged 27, eldest son of [Michael M, of Clontarf, co Dublin, Esq

,, ,,   THOMAS CLARKE LUBY, A B, Trinity College, Dublin, aged 24, only son of [Rev James L, of St James' Terrace

,, ,,   JAMES HENRY O'LOUGHLIN, A B, Trinity College, Dublin, aged 22, second [son of Henry O, of the city of Dublin, Esq

,, ,,   THOMAS HENRY FITZPATRICK, Senior Sophister, Trinity College, Dublin, [aged 24, second son of Samuel F, of Dublin, Solicitor

,, ,,   RICHARD HENRY HORNIDGE, A B, Trinity College, Dublin, aged 24, second [son of George H, late of Burgage, co Wicklow, Esq, deceased

,, ,,   JAMES WILLIAM ALCOCK, aged 26, second son of Stephen A, of Ranelagh

,, 5   JAMES NEWELL ATKINS, of Trinity College Dublin, aged 19, eldest son of [George Newell A, late of Rathfirland, co Down deceased

,, 22   JOHN GEORGE DUFFIELD MAYD, aged 18, eldest son of Rev William M, [rector of Withersfield, near Newmarket, Suffolk

,, 26   WILLIAM DESPARD, of Killaghy Castle, co Tipperary, aged 41, third son of [Joseph Wright, Esq, of Beech Hill, co Dublin

,, 27   THOMAS HUGHES GREENLAND, aged 45, second son of Charles Francis J, [of Bexley Heath, Kent, Esq

June 2   JOHN JAMES FRAZER, A B, Trinity College, Dublin, aged 21, eldest son of [John Whitley F, late of Moate, co Westmeath, M D, deceased

,, 6   RICHARD STRATTON HENDERSON, aged 39, second son of Thomas Stafford H, late of Killyleagh, co Down, Esq, deceased [of Kingstown, Ireland, Esq

,, 8   JOHN JOYES, A B, Trinity College, Dublin, aged 21, eldest son of James J,

Nov 2   RICHARD READER HARRIS aged 32, third son of William H, of Camberwell, Surrey, Esq   [Regent's Park, Middlesex, gent, and also of Bath

,, 3   JOHN DEVEREIL, aged 33, eldest son of John D, of Upper Albany-street,

1846   [James B , late of Carlow, Ireland, Esq , deceased
Nov   7   JOHN ALEXANDER BYRNE, of Trinity College, Dublin, aged 23, third son of
  [Holborn, gent , deceased
,,   10   CHARLES EVANS, aged 29, third son of Thomas E , late of Hatton Garden,
  [Daniel D , late of Clonmel, co Tipperary, Esq , deceased
,,   19   JOHN H DOWLING, A B , Trinity College, Dublin, aged 39, second son of
,,   25   WALLACE HARVEY, aged 25, youngest son of William H., late of the city of
  Glasgow, merchant, deceased   [gent
,,   ,,   JOHN MORGAN, aged 29, eldest son of Christopher M , of Kenstown, co Meath,

1847   [the Mauritius, Esq
Jan   12   FELIX CHARLES FREDERICK GALLET, aged 23, only son of Frederick G , of
,,   16   GEORGE FRANCIS, junior, aged 22, second son of George F , of Maidstone,
  Kent, gent   [Dublin, Esq , deceased.
,,   18   MICHAEL VICTOR DALY, aged 25, eldest son of John D , late of the city of
,,   20   JOHN PARKER GRAHAM, aged 27, second son of Hector G , barrack-master,
  [Chichester, Sussex
,,   21   CHARLES STEELE BOMPAS, aged 23, eldest son of Charles Carpenter B , late
  [of Park Road, Regent's Park, Serjeant-at-Law, deceased
,,   26   GEORGE BARTON, of Trinity College, Dublin, aged 21, only son of James
  [Murray B , late of the city of Dublin, Esq , deceased
,,   ,,   HENRY NICHOLAS REYNOLDS, of Trinity College, Dublin, aged 21, eldest son
  of John R , of Rathmines, co Dublin, Esq   [York, Esq
,   28   SAMUEL SHEPHERD, aged 25, fourth son of William S , of Northallerton, co
Mar   2   ISAAC SOLLY LISTER, aged 51, eldest son of William L , late of Lincoln's Inn
  [Fields, Middlesex, M D , deceased
,,   9   THOMAS TREVETHAN SPICER, aged 32, second and only surviving son of James
  [S , late of May Fair, Middlesex, Esq , deceased
,,   26   STEPHEN CHARLES VENOUR, aged 34, second son of Rev John V , Rector of
  [Bourton, co Warwick, and of Wellesbourne, co Warwick, deceased
April   15   SAMUEL WING, aged 34, fifth son of John W , late of the town of Bedford,
  Esq , deceased   [B , of Bandon, co Cork, Esq
,,   19   GEORGE BENNETT, A B , Trinity College, Dublin, aged 22, only son of Joseph
,,   22   RICHARD EATON, of Trinity College, Dublin, aged 19, eldest son of Richard
  E , of the city of Dublin, Esq   [Road, Middlesex, Esq , deceased
,,   28   GEORGE HORSEY, aged 28, forth son of Charles H , late of St John Street
May   4   DANIEL O'CONNELL RIORDAN, aged 26, eldest son of Timothy J R , of
  Macroom, co Cork, Esq   [Dublin, Esq
,,   ,,   HUGH REILLY, junior, aged 25, eldest son of Hugh R , of Sandymount, co.
,,   ,,   THOMAS PERRY LYNCH, of Trinity College, Dublin, aged 19, only son of
  Thomas L , of Merrion, co Dublin, Esq   [the city of Dublin, Esq.
,,   5   EDWARD WELLESLEY MATHEWS, aged 21, eldest son of William Peter M , of
,,   ,,   JOHN CREIGHTON GRAY, of Trinity College, Dublin, aged 21, eldest son of
  [John G , of Upton House, co Carlow, Esq
,,   6   JAMES FREDERICK NOLAN, of Trinity College, Dublin, aged 20, second son of
  [Daniel N , of the city of Dublin, Esq
,,   ,,   PETER JOHN MCKENNA, of Trinity College, Dublin, aged 19, only son of
  John McK , of the city of Dublin, merchant.   [Somerset, Esq.
,,   22   THOMAS FOLLETT, aged 26, second son of Thomas F , of Uphill Grove,

1847
May 22   EDMUND TONKS, S C L , Queen's College, Oxford, aged 23, eldest son of Wil-
[ham T , of Highgate, near Birmingham, Esq

,,   ,,   ALFRED MCKINNON AITREE, aged 22, fourth son of William A , late of
[Sudbury Park, Middlesex, Esq , deceased

,,   27   CHARLES ALLEN KING, aged 33, eldest and only surviving son of John K , of
[Lower Edmonton, Middlesex, Esq

June 5   WILLIAM DAVID LEWIS, of Lincoln's Inn, Barrister-at-Law, eldest son of Rev
[George William L , of Lambeth, Surrey, clerk

,,   9   JAMES WASHINGTON BROWNE, aged 40, eldest son of James B,, late of
[Croydon, Surrey, Esq , deceased

,,   ,,   WILLIAM PENNEFATHER, of Trinity College, Dublin, aged 24, only son of
William P , late of Ballylanigan, co Tipperary, lieutenant 30th regiment
of foot, deceased   [D , of Loughrea, co Galway, Esq

,,   ,,   ANTHONY RICHARD FRENCH DOLPHIN, aged 19, third son of Henry Joseph

July 13   HUMPHREY WILLIAM WOOLRYCH, of Lincoln's Inn, Barrister-at-Law, aged 51,
only son of Humphrey Cornewall W , late of Rickmansworth, Herts, Esq ,
deceased   [Croydon, Surrey, gent.

,,   21   HENRY GRIFFITH YOUNG, aged 10, eldest son of Thomas Watson Y , of

Nov 4   WILLIAM ARNOLD-BAINBRIGGE (assumed the surname of Bainbrigge on suc-
ceeding to the estates of his maternal grandfather), aged 34, eldest son of
[William Arnold, of Uttoxeter, co Stafford, Esq

,,   20   HENRY BROWNE, aged 19, second son of George B , of Mount Browne, co
[Roscommon, Barrister-at-Law

,,   ,,   JOHN WELSH, A B , Trinity College, Dublin, aged 24, second son of Thomas
[W , of Woodstock Cappoquin, co Waterford, Esq

,,   22   LUKE LOFTUS BUSHE-FOX, aged 25, only son of Michael Charles F , late of
[Dublin, Barrister at-Law, deceased.

1848
Jan 13   THOMAS MARTIN, of Trinity College, Dublin, aged 20, second son of James
[M , late of Cappagh, co Dublin, Esq , deceased

,,   21   CHARLTON STUART RALPH, A.B , late scholar Trinity College, Dublin, aged
[30, eldest son of John R , late of Sligo, Esq , deceased

,,   27   EDWARD HORAN, aged 31, second son of Thomas H , late of the city of Dublin
[Esq , deceased'

,,   ,,   WILLIAM VESEY LANGDALE SIMONS, aged 34, eldest son of William Vesey
[S , of Salt House, co Durham, Esq

Feb 16   JACKSON GILLBANKS, LL B , of St John's College, Cambridge, aged 28, only
[son of Joseph G , of Whitefield House, Cumberland, Esq

,,   19.   ALFRED MATHER, of Brighton, Sussex, aged 27, gent

April 13   JOHN EDWARD THORLEY GRAHAM, aged 19, eldest son of Rev. John Baines
[G , Vicar of Felkirk, near Barnsley, co York.

,,   19   ROBERT FELL, aged 32, only surviving son of Joseph F., late of Newcastle-
[on-Tyne, Esq , deceased

,,   29.   JAMES MARSHALL, Senior Sophister, Trinity College, Dublin, aged 22, fourth
[son of Rev James M , late of Milford, co Donegal, clerk, deceased

,,   ,,   BINSTEED GASELEE, of Lincoln's Inn, Barrister-at-law, aged 35, second son of
[Sir Stephen G , Knight, late a Justice of Common Pleas, deceased

May 4   WILLIAM TURNER, Judge of the County Court of Sussex, aged 57, eldest son
[of John F , late of Brighton, Sussex, Esq , deceased

1848

May 6   JAMES SHEIL, aged 19, eldest son of James S., of the city of Dublin, Esq , Q C

  „   8   JOHN FREKE EVANS, A B , Trinity College, Dublin, aged 31, fifth son of Eyre
           [E , of Ash Hill Towers, co Limerick, Esq . and Miltown Castle, co Cork

  „   9   THOMAS DAWSON, Senior Sophister, Trinity College, aged 22, eldest son of
           [John D , late of Annamartin, co Fermanagh, Ireland, Esq deceased

  „ 17   EDWARD PAUL PACE, aged 27, second son of Captain Henry Edwin P , late
           H E I C S , deceased   [H , late of Dublin, Esq , deceased

  „ 29   TERENCE HUGHES, of Trinity College, Dublin, aged 40, second son of George

June 27   JOHN ADDISON, Civil Engineer, aged 33, only son of David A , late of Inver-
           [ness, North Britain, Esq , deceased

Oct 28   WILLIAM HARTLEY, Solicitor, aged 44, third son of Joseph H , late of Nelson
           Street, City Road, Middlesex, deceased   [Cornwall, Esq , deceased

Nov 1   WILLIAM VOSPER, aged 44, eldest son of Thomas V , late of Alternan,

  „   „   JOSEPH TAYLOR, aged 23, fifth son of Joseph T , of Priestfield, Thornhill. co
           York, Esq   [D , late of the city of Dublin, Esq , deceased

  „   7   AUGUSTIN DUGGAN, A B , Trinity College, Dublin, aged 22, only son of James

  „ 22   ARTHUR HAMILL, aged 33, third son of John H , late of Belfast, co Antrim,
1849   [merchant, deceased

Jan 20.   FREDERICK JAMES FURNIVALL, of Lincoln's Inn (Jan 26, 1846), eldest son of
           [George Frederick F , of Egham, Surrey, surgeon

  „ 25   FRANCIS JOHN GOUGH, aged 53, only son of John G , late of the Strand,
           [city of Westminster, gent , deceased

  „ 27   ANTHONY KEHOE, B A , University College, London, aged 23, youngest son
           [of Anthony K , late of Castle Row, co Kildare, Esq , deceased

  ,   „   NICHOLAS GANNON, of Stonyhurst College, co Lancaster, aged 19, only son of
           John G , late of Lara, co. Kildare, Esq , deceased   [Esq , deceased

Mar 5   EDMUND TAVERNER, aged 42, third son of John T , late of Clapton, Middlesex,

April 17. NEWMAN WARD, aged 26, only son of Thomas Newman W , of Ore, near
           Hastings, Sussex, Esq   [Chester, Esq , deceased

  „ 18   CHARLES CALDWELL, aged 27, fifth son of William C , late of Frodsham, co

  „ 23   HENRY TWYMAN, aged 19, eldest son of George T , of Winchester, Esq

May 3   VINCENT FITZPATRICK EYRE, Senior Sophister, Trinity College, Dublin, aged
           [22, only son of Joseph Considine E , late of Dublin, Esq , deceased

  „   „   PATRICK MARTIN, aged 19, only son of John Henry M , of Dublin, Solicitor

June 1   CHARLES KENNEDY, aged 19, second son of Charles Edward K , late of
           Peamount House, co Kildare, deceased   [Green,. Middlesex, Esq

  „   7   CHARLES JAMES COLEMAN, aged 24, second son of Joseph C , of Turnham

  „   9   HENRY WILLIAMS, aged 45, third son of John W , late of Maida Vale,
           Middlesex, Esq , deceased   [Somerset, gent , deceased

Nov 7   JAMES GOODSON, aged 33, third son of Thomas G , late of Baltonsborough,

  „   „   WILLIAM HENRY TRINDER, aged 41, eldest son of David T , late of Ciren-
           [cester, co Gloucester, Esq , deceased

  „   8   FRANCIS BUCHANAN HOARE, aged 32, only son of John H , late of Cirencester,
           [co Gloucester, Esq , deceased

  „ 10   WILLIAM HOLMES ORR, aged 25, eldest son of John O , late of Innishannon,
           co Cork, Attorney at Law, deceased   [Ryan K , of Dublin, Esq

  „ 12   RICHARD KANE, of Trinity College, Dublin, aged 21, eldest son of Daniel

1850.   [co Stafford, Lieut R N

Jan 23   ROLLO JAMES BULKELEY, aged 18, eldest son of James B , of Huntley Hall,

Mar 15.   CARR WIGG, aged 19, second son of Francis W , of Bedford Row, Middlesex,
              Esq   [Maidenhead, Berks, Esq , deceased

April 15   HENRY COLLINGWOOD SELBY, aged 38, second son of Prideaux S , late of

  ,, ,,   LEONARD HILL GENT, aged 39, eldest son of Thomas G., of Lavendon, Bucks,
              Esq   [C , of Southampton, Esq

  ,, 25   LAWRANCE COUNSEL, of King's Inns, Dublin, aged 25, second son of Loughlin

May 1   HENRY MILFORD, aged 39, third son of William M , of the city of Durham,
              Esq   [Surrey, Esq

  ,, 28   JOHN WILLIAM WHITELOCK, aged 27, second son of Benjamin W , of Putney,

  ,, 29   ISAAC WILSON, of Trinity College, Dublin, aged 18, fifth son of John W , of
                                                       [the city of Dublin, Esq

June 1   JAMES ARCHIBALD MURRAY, aged 53 (Secretary to Lord Langdale, Master of
              the Rolls), second son of Charles M , late of Tellington, near Petworth,
                                                       [Sussex, gent , deceased

  ,, ,,   THOMAS MICKLETHWAITE, aged 35, second son of William M , late of Ashton-
              under-Lyne, co Lancaster, Esq , deceased   [solicitor

  ,, 4   HENRY MACDERMOTT, B A , aged 24, fourth son of William M , of Dublin,

  ,, 7   HYACINTH CHEEVERS PLUNKETT, aged 22, second son of Michael Richard P ,
              of Nenagh, co Tipperary, Esq , Res Magistrate [Chester, Esq , deceased

Nov 6   JOHN GEORGE HARDING, B A , Trinity Hall, Cambridge, aged 25, eldest son
              of John H , of Ringwood, Hants, Esq   [Limerick, merchant

  ,, 7   GEORGE CREE, of Trinity College, Dublin, aged 21, eldest son of James C , of

  ,, 23   JOHN WILSON, aged 33, eldest son of John W , of Kendal, Westmoreland, gent
1851   [Middlesex, gent
Jan 15   FREDERICK DEW, aged 34, eldest son of William D , of Hounslow Heath,

  ,, 27   KENNETH LEITH SUTHERLAND, Paymaster and Purser, Royal Navy, aged 35,
              eldest surviving son of Kenneth S , late Lieutenant 2nd Royal Veteran
              Battalion, deceased   [Andrew Christopher P , of the city of Dublin, Esq

  ,, ,,   CHRISTOPHER PALLES, of Trinity College, Dublin, aged 19, second son of

  ,, ,,   HENRY DEVITT, of Trinity College, Dublin, aged 26, eldest son of Arnold D ,
              late of Dublin, merchant, deceased.   [Southampton, Esq

Feb 25   CHARLES JAMES GUNNER, aged 32, third son of William G , of Winchester, co.

Mar 19   JONAS LEVY, aged 38, eldest son of Lewis L , of Tavistock Square, Middlesex,
              Esq   [of Nicholas C , late of the city of Dublin, merchant, deceased

April 23   NICHOLAS COSTELLO, of Trinity College, Dublin, aged 18, eldest surviving son

  ,, 26   JAMES JOHNSTON, of Trinity College, Dublin, aged 24, eldest son of Arthur J ,
              of Carrick Breda, co. Armagh, M.D   [Galway, Esq , deceased

  ,, 29   ROBERT MAHON ALLEN, aged 32, only son of Theobald A , late of Tuam, co

May 3   JOHN PATRICK O'HARA, of Trinity College, Dublin, and of King's Inns, Dublin,
              aged 20, only surviving son of Martin O , late of Claremorris, co
                                                       [Mayo, merchant, deceased

  ,, 5.   JAMES DUFF MATHEWS, of Trinity College, Dublin, aged 19, eldest son of
                                                [James M , of Mount Hanover, co Meath, Esq

  ,, 6   EDWARD RICHARDS, of Trinity College, Dublin, aged 20, only son of Matthew
                                                [R , late of Ardee, co Louth, merchant, deceased

  ,, 9   WILLIAM GEALE MULVILLE, B A , Trinity College, Dublin, aged 23, eldest
                                                [son of William M , of Gort, co Galway, Esq

1851   [M , of Douay, France, gent
May 14   MORGAN AUGUSTIN MCDONNELL, aged 29, eldest son of Michael Cypryan

,,   27   JOHN GEORGE SMYLY, of Trinity College, Dublin, aged 21, eldest son of
                                           [John George S , of Dublin, Esq , Q C

June 2   ROBERT BAKER JONES, aged 27, eldest son of William J , late of Six-mile
                                           [Bridge, co. Clare, merchant, deceased

Nov 3   WILLIAM LANGFORD, of Magdalen Hall, Oxford, and of Emanuel College,
             Cambridge, aged 29, second son of Joseph L , of Stepney, Middlesex, gent

,,   ,,   JOHN HOLKER, aged 23, second son of Samuel H , late of Bury, co Lancaster,
             merchant, deceased   [Middlesex, solicitor

,,   ,,   CHARLES WRAY LEWIS, aged 19, eldest son of Charles L., of Piccadilly,

,,   5   WILLIAM BARCLAY DAVID DONALD TURNBULL, a Member of the Faculty of
             Advocates, Edinburgh, aged 40, only son of Walter T , late of Kingston,
                                                           [Jamaica, gent , deceased

,,   ,,   WILLIAM ROMILLY, aged 16, eldest son of Rt Hon Sir John R , Knight,
                                                           [Master of the Rolls

,,   12   JOHN MCMAHON, M A , Trinity College, Dublin, aged 36, only son of Hugh
                                 [M , late of Clones, co Monaghan, Esq , deceased

,,   14   EDWARD DUNDAS HOLROYD, B A , Trinity College, Cambridge, aged 23,
             second son of Edward H., of Wimbledon, Surrey, Esq , Barrister of
1852   [Gray's Inn

Jan 6   RICHARD HAMBLY ANDREW, aged 22, eldest son of Christopher Thomas A ,
             of Menkee, Cornwall   [second son of George G , of Stratford, Essex, Esq

,,   10   CHARLES ROBERTSON GRIFFITHS, of University College, London, aged 31,

,,   12   HENRY MILES, aged 57 (admitted to Lincoln's Inn, July 22, 1820, called
             to the Bar there, Nov 28, 1828, and admitted "ad eundem" at the
             Middle Temple, July 6, 1837), second son of John M , late of South-
                                 [ampton Row, Bloomsbury, Middlesex, Esc , deceased

,.   14   WALTER SWEETMAN, B A , University of London, and formerly of Stonyhurst
             College, co Lancaster, aged 20, fourth son of Michael S , of Longtown
                                                           [House, co Kildare

,,   16   EDWARD ALOYSIUS WILLIAMS, of Oscott College, in the University of London,
                       [aged 28, fifth son of John W , of Buckland, Berks, gent

,   20   JOSEPH HERON, aged 43, fourth son of James Holt H , late of Manchester,
                                                           [co Lancaster, Esq , deceased

Mar 24   JOHN RODHAM CARR, LL D , London University, of Carrs Hill, by Gateshead-
             on-Tyne, aged 36, second son of Matthew C , late of Newcastle-on-Tyne,
                                                           [Esq , deceased

April 14   THOMAS MARSHALL, of St John's College, Oxon, aged 20, eldest son of Thomas
             Horncastle M , Esq , Treasurer of Grays Inn, and a Judge of County
             Courts, Leeds   [port, Esq

,,   ,,   RICHARD COGGINS ROGERS, aged 30, second son of Richard R , of Devon-

,,   15   CHARLES HEYWOOD, aged 28, second son of George H , late of Brockmore,
             co Stafford, Esq deceased   [the city of Cork, Esq , deceased

,,   ,,   MARK STEPHEN O'SHAUGHNESSY, aged 28, second son of Mark O , late of

,,   20   ALLAN RALPH, B A Trin Col , Dublin, aged 27, third son of John R , of Sligo, Esq.

,,   29   PHILIP JAMES WINGFIELD, aged 31, third surviving son of Rev John W , D D ,
             late Prebendary of the Cathedral Church of Worcester, and formerly
                                 [Head Master of Westminster School, deceased

1852

May 3   WILLIAM SQUIRE BARKER KAY, of Trinity College, Dublin, aged 21, second son of George K, late of Vera Lodge, co Armagh, Captain 62nd Regiment, deceased   [of Ballyshannon, co Donegal, merchant

,, 4   EDWARD KELLY, of Trinity College, Dublin, aged 21, eldest son of Peter K,

,, 5   WILLIAM ROBERT CUSACK-SMITH, a Student of Trinity College, Dublin, aged [19, only son of Rt Hon. Thomas Berry Cusack-S, Master of the [Rolls, Ireland

,, ,,   JAMES COOPER, aged 22, only son of William C, late of Islington, merchant, deceased   [R, of Regent Square, St Pancras, Middlesex, Solicitor

,, 13   JOHN THOMAS ROUMIEU, of London, Solicitor, aged 39, eldest son of John

Oct. 29   SAMUEL WALKER, of Trinity College, Dublin, aged 21, second son of Alexander [W, of Goreport, co Westmeath, Lieutenant 97th Foot

Nov 1   HENRY JAMES CONINGTON, aged 26, second son of Rev Richard C, of Boston, co Lincoln, clerk   [city of Cork, merchant

,, 3   WILLIAM O'BRIEN, of King's Inns, Dublin, aged 25, son of John O, of the

,, 6   THOMAS KANE, of Trinity College, Dublin, aged 20, second son of Daniel [Ryan K, of the city of Dublin, Barrister-at-Law

, 16   JOHN O'CONNELL O'LEARY, of Trinity College, Dublin, aged 21, only son of [Joseph O, of the city of Dublin, Barrister-at-Law

1853

Jan 10.   THOMAS DUDLEY RYDER, M A, Oriel College, Oxford, aged 37, fifth son of Right Rev Henry R, D D, Bishop of Lichfield and Coventry, deceased

,, 21   EDWARD TYRRELL, Remembrancer of the city of London, aged 60, third son of Timothy T, late of Guildhall, in the city of London, Esq, deceased

April 30   WILLIAM ANDREWS HOLDSWORTH, aged 26, eldest son of William Hickson [H, of Hull, co York, gent

May 2   THADDEUS O'MAHONY, of Trinity College, Dublin aged 28, eldest son of [Cornelius O, late of Ballivalone, co Cork, Esq, deceased.

,, 3   ALEXANDER GEORGE RICHEY, of Trinity College, Dublin, aged 22, only son [of Alexander R, late of Clontay co Dublin, Esq, deceased

,, 5   WILLIAM WOODLOCK, B A, Trinity College, Dublin, aged 21, eldest son of William W, of Blackrock, co Dublin, Solicitor   [Dublin, Surgeon

,, 20   HENRY PARKINSON, aged 24, only son of James Richard P, of Dalkey, co

June 6   JAMES SWANZY, of Trinity College, Dublin, aged 22, fourth son of Samuel [S, of Cavan, co Cavan, Solicitor and Clerk of the Crown

July 6   PETER ALEXANDER MICHAEL STRAPPINI, aged 32 (admitted to the Middle Temple, June 2, 1841, called to the bar there, June 7, 1844), only son [of Cosmo Daniel Michael S, of the city of London, Esq

Oct 17   ADOLPHUS JOHN DALLAIN, aged 20, eldest son of John D, of St Helier, Isle of Jersey, Solicitor   [K, of Dublin, Esq

Nov 2   PHILIP KEOGH, B A, Trinity College, Dublin, aged 21 fourth son of Michael

,, 9   HENRY NICOL, aged 32, third son of William N, of Pall Mall, printer

1854

Jan 24   THOMAS RIDLEY, aged 40, only son of Cuthbert Pigg, late of Newcastle-upon-Tyne, builder, deceased   [B, of Lyme Regis, Dorset, Captain R N

Mar 15   WILLIAM MORGAN BENETT, aged 40, eldest surviving son of Charles Cowper

April 21   CHARLES HENRY PETTER, aged 32, second son of George P, late of Chapman [Street, Cannon Street, merchant, deceased

1854

April 21   HUGH SHIELD, B A , Jesus College, Cambridge, aged 23, second scn of John
        S , of Newcastle-upon-Tyne, Esq.   [O , of Dublin, Esq.

,,   28   RICHARD O'REILLY, of Trinity College, Dublin, aged 20, eldest son of Philip

May   1   CHARLES PRATT, aged 30, second son of James Butler P , late of Mullintra,
        co Cavan, Esq , deceased   [Sussex, Esq

,,   6   WILLIAM DIXON, aged 30, second son of Henry James D , of Brighton,

June 12   FRANK AUSTIN, of Queen's College, Cambridge, aged 24, seventh son of John
           [Drewett A , late of Kennington, Surrey, Esq , deceased

July 14   EDWARD CAVELL, aged 25, fourth son of John C , of Mecklenburg Square,
              [Middlesex, law stationer

Nov 14   MICHAEL MERRIMAN, of the University of London, aged 23, only son of
          [Michael M., late of Rathmines, co Dublin, Esq deceased

,,   16   JOHN JOPP ROGERS, of the Inner Temple, Barrister-at-Law, aged 38, eldest son
1855   [of Rev John R , of Penrose, co Cornwall, clerk

Jan 11   ARTHUR BEETHAM, aged 18, second son of Albert William B , of Rope Hill
          [Lodge, near Lymington, Hants, Barrister-at-Law, Esq

,,   15   TOWNLEY RIGBY KNOWLES, of the Inner Temple, Barrister-at-Law, aged 44,
        eldest son of Joseph K , late of Vellore, in the East Indies, Lieut -col
              [H E.I Co

May 25   JOHN FIELD JOHNSTON, B A , Trinity College, Dublin, and of King's Inns,
        Dublin, aged 21, second son of William J , of Leinster Road, co
        Dublin, gent   [Gallicia, Austria, merchant

,,   31   HERMANN LIEBSTEIN, aged 26, fifth son of David L , of Lemberg, in

Nov 14   FRANK FALCONER WALKER, of King s College, London, aged 23, eldest son
1856   [of William Falconer W , late of Kew, Esq , deceased.

Jan 12.   WILLIAM FREDERICK WRATISLAW BIRD, aged 40, only surviving son of
          [George Ryder B , of Edgbaston, co Warwick, gent

April 7   BEN THOMAS WILLIAMS, M A , aged 23, eldest son of Rev Thomas Rayson
          [W , late of Merryvale, Narberth, co Pembroke, deceased

,,   17   WILLIAM RUSHTON, M A , London University, and a Member of University
        College, aged 33, eldest son of William R , formerly of Liverpool, and
          [late of Bootle-cum-Linacre, co Lancaster, gent , deceased

,,   23   RICHARD LUTHER MARTIN, A B , Trinity College, Dublin, aged 22, second
          [son of Ven John Charles M , D.D , Archdeacon of Ardagh, Ireland

,,   25   EDWARD JOSEPH THACKWELL, aged 28, eldest son of Lieut -general Sir Joseph
        I , of Aghada Hall, co Cork   [Rev John J , of Lampeter, co. Cardigan, clerk

May 21   WALTER DAVID JEREMY, M A , University of London, aged 31, eldest son of

,,   31   THOMAS YOUNG, aged 15, second son of Thomas Watson Y , of Croydon,
            [Surrey, gent

June   2   CHARLES ALEXANDER SMYTH, of Trinity College, Dublin, aged 27, sixth son
        of John S , of Smyth Brook, co Longford, late Lieutenant 27th Regiment

,,   4   WILLIAM HENRY CLARKE, Police Magistrate in Ceylon C S , late of Queen's
        College, Cambridge, S C L , aged 33, eldest son of Rev William C , In-
          [cumbent of St John-the-Less, city of Chester, D D

Nov   1   THOMAS WALKER HODGENS, B A , Trinity College, Dublin, aged 26, only
          [son of Thomas H , of the city of Dublin, LL D

,,   6   ROBERT CECIL AUSTIN, of King's College, London, aged 28, sixth son of John
          [Drewett A , Esq , late of H M Ordnance, deceased

1856   [merchant
Nov 13   JAMES PATRICK SMYTH, aged 32, only son of James S , of Kilmainham, Dublin,
1857   [Street, Bedford Row, Middlesex, gent, deceased
Feb 28   WILLIAM GARLICK COVENTON, aged 48, only son of William C , late of Robert
Mar 2   RICHARD POOLE, of Jesus College, Cambridge, B A , aged 34, eldest son
                                    [of Richard P , late of Gray's Inn, gent , deceased
 ,, 14   JAMES CORNELIUS BROUGH, of King's College, London, aged 20, eldest son of
              Arthur B., of North Brixton, Surrey, gent   [Dublin, merchant
May 1   LIONEL UNIACKE STEELE, aged 22, eldest son of William S , of the city of
 ,, 16   ARTHUR JOHN HAMMOND COLLINS, aged 23, eldest son of John C , of Park-
              stone, Officer in command of H M Coast Guard   [Surrey, gent
July 8   CHARLES JOSEPH SMITH, aged 32, eldest son of Charles Thomas S , of Reigate,
                                                    [Lyne, co Stafford, merchant
Nov 3   JOHN REAVIS BRINDLEY, aged 29, only son of James B , of Newcastle-under-
 ,, ,,   GEORGE HARRY PALMER, M A , of Glasgow University, and of the University
              of London, aged 26, eldest son of Henry P , of Brynbank, co Carmarthen,
                                                                        [gent
 ,, ,,   JOHN EDWARDS, of Owens College, Manchester, and of the University of
              London, aged 22, eldest son of John E , of Lower Broughton, Salford,
1858   [co Lancaster, teacher
Jan 6   ANTHONY WELLINGTON IRWIN, aged 42, third son of John Chambers I., late
                                    [of Ballinlough, co Longford, Esq , deceased.
 ,, 28   TIMOTHY O'BRIEN O'FEELY, LL B , Queen's University of Ireland, aged 26,
                                        [fourth son of Patrick O , of Roscommon, Esq
Feb 10   CAYLEY SHADWELL, of Lincoln's Inn, Barrister-at-Law, aged 59, fourth son of
                            [Lancelot S , late of Lincoln's Inn, Barrister-at-Law, deceased
Mar 25   TOM SMITH, aged 26, second son of William S , of Tavistock Square, Mid-
                                                                [dlesex, Esq
April 14   THOMAS BRADDELL, of George Town, Prince of Wales Island, assistant
              to the resident Councillor there, Magistrate of Police, Commissioner of
              Small Debts Court, and Accountant General, &c , aged 35, eldest sur-
                            [viving son of George William B , of Lisburne, co Down, Esq
Oct 14   JULIAN EMANUEL SOLOMONS, aged 22, only son of Emanuel S , late of Bir-
              mingham, co Warwick, merchant, deceased [Arbroath, co Forfar, Esq.
 ,, 13   SAMUEL KYDD, of Mitcham, Surrey, aged 37, second son of James K , of
Nov 1   BENJAMIN WALTERS LARA, of King's College, London, aged 36, only son of
              Benjamin L , late of Southsea, Hants, a Member of the College of
                                                        [Physicians, deceased
 ,, ,,   WILLIAM BROOK BRIDGES STEVENS, aged 23, only son of Thomas Brook
                            [Bridges S , of Bloomsbury, Middlesex, Solicitor
 ,, 2   WILLIAM WALDY, of Magdalen College, Cambridge, aged 26, second son of
              Edward Garmondsway W , late of Barmpton, near Darlington, co Durham,
                                                                [Esq , deceased
 ,, 12   MARTIN ANDREW O'BRENNAN, of Trinity College, Dublin, aged 48, seventh
                            [son of Martin O , late of Ballyhannis, co Mayo, Esq , deceased.
1859.   [James W , of Belview, Dublin, Esq.
Jan. 11   JAMES LOWRY WHITTLE, of Trinity College, Dublin, aged 19, only son of
 ,, 13   THOMAS GREEN, aged 20, second son of John G , of Mortlake, Surrey, Esq.
 ,, 17   SAMUEL LIVINGSTONE MATTHEWS, aged 21, second son of Samuel M , of the
                                            [city of Dublin, Attorney at-Law.

1859   [gent, deceased.

Jan 18 JOSEPH BURGIN, aged 29, second son of Thomas B, late of Croydon, Surrey,

,, 22 ROBERT EDWARD FRANCILLON, aged 17, eldest son of James F, Esq, of
[Charlton King's, co Gloucester, Judge and Barrister of this Society

,, 26 WILLIAM NICHOLSON, aged 32, third son of Robert N, late of Rotterdam,
Holland, in H M's Service, deceased   [Herts, Esq

,, 28 WILLIAM BARNARD, aged 27, second son of William B, of Sawbridgeworth,

April 23 ISAAC STAMERS HEAZLE, of Trinity College, Dublin, aged 24, eldest son of
[William H, of Cork, Esq

May 10 HUGH COWIE, B A, Trinity College, Cambridge, aged 29, eldest son of
[Alexander C, late of St John's Wood, Middlesex, Esq, deceased

Oct 15 JOHN BRADDICK MONCKTON, of London, Solicitor, aged 27, eldest son of
[John M, of Maidstone, Kent, Solicitor

Nov 7 THOMAS HUDSON JORDAN, aged 29, third son of William J, late of Man-
[chester, a writer to the press, deceased

,, 12 JOHN NICHOL, of Baliol College, Oxford, aged 26, only son of John Pringle N,
[late of Glasgow, "Observator," Professor of Astronomy, deceased

,, 14 WILLIAM HUGHES MOFFATT, of Trinity College, Dublin, aged 21, only son of
[James M, of Drogheda, co Louth, Esq

,, 16 CHARLES RANKEN VICKERMAN, aged 41, eldest son of John V, late of Gray's

1860   [Inn, Solicitor, deceased

Jan 4 JOSEPH BOWVER, aged 33, only son of Matthew B, late of Stamford Hill,
[Middlesex, Esq, deceased

,, ,, HENRY JOHN DAVID, aged 33, only son of John D, of New Orleans, Esq

,, 23 JOHN JAMES DIGGES LA TOUCHE, B A, Trinity College, Dublin, aged 22, fourth
[son of Peter Digges La T, of Dublin, gent

,, 30 NUGENT CHARLES WALSH, aged 20, only son of Charles Robert W, late of
[Piccadilly, Surgeon, deceased

May 22 JAMES CREED MEREDITH, of Trinity College, Dublin, aged 17, eldest son of
Richard Martin M, late of the city of Cork, Major 13th Light Infantry,
[deceased

,, 15 THOMAS NEWTON, of Rangoon, British Burmah (notary public, August 4,
1856, until Aug 15, 1860), aged 36, only son of Major-General Thomas N,
[late of 40th Regiment, Bengal N I, deceased

,, 28 HENRY PALFREY STEPHENSON, aged 34, second son of John S, late Major 6th
[Dragoon Guards (Carabiniers).

Nov 2 CHARLES ARMSTRONG, aged 44, eldest surviving son of William A, late of
[Pentonville Road, Middlesex, Esq, deceased

,, 5 JOHN DEAS MACKENZIE, of the University of Edinburgh, aged 35, youngest son
[of Murdo Deas M, of Spittal Killearnan, Ross-shire, merchant

,, ,, WILLIAM BUSH COOPER, aged 47, only son of William Henderson C, late of
[Gray's Inn, architect, deceased

,, 17 WILLIAM JOHN SMELTER CADMAN, of Trinity Hall, Cambridge, aged 22,
[eldest son of William C, of Handsworth Grange, co York, Esq

1861

Jan 23 FRANCIS FREDERICK PINKETT, Lieutenant Royal Wilts Militia, aged 24,
[son of Edward P, of Barnstaple, Devon, gent

,, 28 WILLIAM LOWES RUSHTON, aged 33, youngest son of Edward R, late of
[Liverpool, Barrister-at-Law, deceased

1861

April 16   EDWARD HENRY HUNT, an Associate of King's College, London, and a clerk in the office of the Masters of Lunacy, aged 41, second son of Edward [H, late of Fareham, Hants, gent.

,, 17   EDWARD ROMILLY, B A, King's Coll, Cambridge, aged 21, second son of Sir John R, Master of the Rolls, and Bencher of Gray's Inn   [Kerry, gent

,, 27   PATRICK O'SULLIVAN, aged 26, eldest son of Patrick O, of Tralee, co

May 3   GEORGE ROBINSON HOLLAND, aged 28, eldest son of George H, late of Poole, Dorsetshire, merchant   [Rissington, co Gloucester, clerk

June 6   WILLIAM FORD, aged 49, eldest son of Rev Richard Wilbraham F, of Little

July 7   SIR JAMES GRAHAM DOMVILLE Baronet aged 48, eldest son of Sir William D, late of Eastbourne, Sussex, Baronet, deceased   [Esq

Oct 18   GEORGE PORTER, aged 31, second son of George P., of Hillingdon, Middlesex,

Nov 2   DENIS MACCARTHY O'LEARY, aged 20, second son of John MacCarthy O, [of Coomlagane, co Cork, Esq

,, 16   FREDERICK WILLIAM CAMPIN, aged 38, youngest son of James Thomas C, [late of Camberwell, Surrey, merchant, deceased

,, 18   JOSEPH HOLMES, of Trinity College, Dublin, aged 29, second son of Samuel [H, of Emo, Queen's County, gentleman farmer

,, 15   NATHANIEL WARNER BROMLEY, of the Middle Temple, Barrister-at-Law, aged 39, eldest son of Joseph Warner B, late of Bansfield Hall, near New-
1862   [market, Suffolk, and of Gray's Inn, deceased

Jan 21   JOHN HAWTREY THWAITES, of Ceylon, and of Trinity College, Dublin, aged 21, [only son of John T, of Ceylon, M D

,, 24   LIONEL HENRY HANBURY-JONES, B A, St Edmund Hall, Oxon, aged 27, [only surviving son of William H J, of Gray's Inn

Mar 17   ALEXANDER EDGELL, aged 47, third son of Harry E, of Cadogan Place, [Sloane Street, Middlesex, Esq., Bencher of Gray's Inn

May 10   ROBERT CARR WOODS, of Singapore, aged 46, third son of William Wylie W, [late of Stepney, Middlesex, Esq, deceased

April 30   ARTHUR PIGOU, of Bengal Civil Service, aged 39, youngest son of Henry [Minchin P, of Banwell Castle, Somersetshire, Esq

June 9   THOMAS HENRY THORNTON, a Judge of Small Cause Court, Lahore, E I C S, B C L, and a Fellow of St John's College, Oxford, aged 28, second son [of Thomas T, of Gloucester Street, South Belgravia, Esq

Aug 19   MICHAEL MADHUSUDANA DAITA, aged 31, only son of Rajnáraina D, late of Calcutta, Esq, deceased   [Esq, deceased

Oct 31   ISAAC SOLLY LISTER, aged 30, eldest son of Isaac Solly L, late of Gray's Inn,

Nov 3   ROWLAND WILKINSON, aged 19, only son of John W, of Brackenhill, Mirfield, co York, Esq   [Brinsden B, of the island of Barbados, clerk

,, 11   WILLIAM COLERIDGE BOVELL, aged 21, eldest son of Rev William Henry

,, 14   JOHN JENKINS, M A, Glasgow University, aged 54, eldest son of David J, [late of Swansea, co Glamorgan, builder, deceased

. 17   HENRY DANBY SEYMOUR, B A, Magdalen College, Oxford, aged 42, eldest
1863   [son of Henry S, late of Knoyle House, Wilts, Esq, deceased

Jan 12.   HENRY ROMILLY, of Trinity College, Cambridge, aged 18, third son of Sir [John R, Master of the Rolls, and Bencher of Gray's Inn.

,, ,,   JOHN ROMILLY, aged 20, eldest son of Charles R, Esq, of Wilton Crescent, [Middlesex, Clerk of the Crown.

1863

Jan 12   CHARLES FORBES, Judge and Sessions Judge at Sholapore, E I C S , aged 43,
eldest son of Major-general David F , c B , late of the 78th Highlanders,
[deceased

,,   24   ROBERT CHRISTOPHER LUSH, of Trinity College, Cambridge, aged 21, eldest
son of Robert L , Esq , Q C , of Upper Avenue Road, Regent's Park,
[Middlesex, a Bencher of Gray's Inn

,,   ,,   JAMES EDMUND BACON PARSONS, Captain Bengal Staff Corps, aged 32, eldest
[surviving son of General P , of Almorah, Bengal

,,   29   THOMAS GRESHAM, of King's College, London, aged 19, only son of William
[G , of Gray's Inn, High Bailiff of Southwark

May 25   JAMES SHEPHERD SCOTT, aged 34, eldest son of Joseph John Monck Mason
[S , of Kensington Park Terrace, Esq

July 13   JOHN LEE, LL D , of Doctors' Commons (ad eundem), aged 80, eldest
[son of John Fiott L , of Totteridge, Herts, Esq

Aug 11   EDWARD HENRY POWER, Major Madras Staff Corps, Deputy Judge Advocate
General, aged 36, youngest son of the late General Sir W G P ,
[K C B and K H

Sept 4   JOHN MILLER, Administrator-General of Madras, an Attorney and Vakeel
of the High Court, and a Notary Public, Madras, aged 32, third son
[of William M , late of Madras, merchant. deceased.

Oct 13   WILLIAM HENRY SPENCER, aged 25, eldest son of Henry Augustus S , of East
Retford, Notts, gent   [R , of Regent's Park, Middlesex, solicitor

Nov 4   HENRY RUTTER, B A London University, aged 25, only son of John Champley,

Oct 30   SIDNEY LAMAN BLANCHARD, author and journalist, aged 36, eldest son of
[Samuel Laman B , deceased, also author and journalist

Nov 7.   CLEMENT ALEXANDER MIDDLETON, aged 25, eldest son of John Charles M ,
[Registrar of Probate Court

,,   11   JOHN SOUTHGATE FORD, aged 30, only son of Richard F , late of King's
Lynn, gent, deceased   [Temple, Esq , Barrister-at-Law, deceased

,,   12   HORACE TOMPSON CHITTY, aged 21, eldest son of Tompson C , late of the

,,   16   JAMES CURRAN, of Trinity College, Dublin, aged 34, eldest son of Waring C ,
of Downpatrick, co Down, Esq   [Lancaster, gent

,,   18   HENRY BOLLAND, aged 31, third son of Thomas Lloyd B , of Liverpool, co

Dec 24   ROBERT PERCIVAL EVANS, aged 33, second son of Robert Mendham E , of
1864   [Orpines, Wateringbury, Kent, Esq.

Jan 9   ARTHUR HENRY HINDMARCH, aged 17, only son of William Matthewson H ,
[Esq , Q C , and Bencher of Gray's Inn

,,   ,,   ROBERT CARR WOODS, jun , aged 21, eldest son of Robert Carr W , Esq , of
[Singapore, East Indies, and Barrister of Gray's Inn

,,   18   HENRY PEAT, B A , Trinity College, Dublin, aged 24, eldest son of Henry P ,
of Rathmines, co Dublin, Esq   [late a Member of Gray's Inn

,,   21   WILLIAM EDWARD HILLIARD, aged 41, third son of Nash Crosier H , Esq ,

April 16   ILLTUDUS THOMAS PRICHARD, aged 58, fifth son of James Cowles P , late of
[Russell Square, Middlesex, M D , deceased

,,   ,,   FRANCISCO EVARISTO PEREIRA, of Singapore, Advocate and Agent of H M 's
Supreme Court of Judicature, at Prince and Coates Island, Singapore,
Malacca, and a Public Notary there, aged 30, only son of Pedro Evaristo
[P , of Malacca, Esq., deceased

1864   [Michael L , of the city of Dublin, Esq
April 14   MICHAEL LAW, B A , Trinity College, Dublin, aged 24, second son of
,, 29   EDWARD MANISTY, of Corpus Christi College, Cambridge, aged 20, second
                [son of Henry M , Esq , Q C , Bencher of Gray's Inn
June 4   WILLIAM GOULDTHORP, aged 24, only son of John G , Esq , of Alderley Edge,
                [Chorley, co Chester,
Nov 2.   EBENEZER DAVID SILVER, of Edinburgh University, Doctor of Medicine, and
                a retired Surgeon of H M 's Indian Army, aged 43, youngest son of
                [Frederick S , Esq , of Camberwell, Surrey
,, ,,   EDWYN JONES, Associate of King's College, London, aged 28, eldest son of
                Henry J , late of Louth, co Louth, Sub-Inspector of Constabulary,
                deceased   [W , Attorney-General for New Zealand.
,, 19   FREDERICK ALEXANDER WHITAKER, aged 17, eldest son of (Hon) Frederick
Dec 17   HENRY GRIFFITHS SEYMOUR COOPER, aged 19, second son of William Bush
                [C , of Harrow, Middlesex, and Gray's Inn, Barrister-at-Law.
,, 31.   WILLIAM MORRIS, of Maidenhead, Bank Manager, aged 39, eldest son of
1865   [Thomas M , of Reading, Berks, Esq
Jan 12   JOHN GIBSON, H B M , Vice-Consul in China, M A , University of Edinburgh,
                [aged 30, third son of Robert G , Esq , of Cullina
,, 23   ALFRED GREATBATCH GOVER, of the University of London, aged 26, fourth
                [son of Thomas G , late of Poplar New Town, Middlesex, Esq , deceased
April 10   JOSEPH TRAVERS SMITH, aged 42, second son of Gustavus S , of Salcombe
                Regis, Devon, Esq , J P   [to the Magistrates
,, 15   JOHN ROSE, aged 23, son of John Randolph R , of Stoke-upon-Trent, Clerk
,, ,,   WILLIAM ARNOLD LEWIS, aged 18, only son of the late William David L ,
                [Esq , Q C , of Lincoln's Inn, Barrister-at-Law
,, 22   CROFT WORGAN DEW, M A , Jesus College, Cambridge, aged 36, second
                son of the late Rev John Worgan D , Curate of St James', Halifax,
                [Yorkshire
May 5   JOHN GEORGE MUSGRAVE, of Andover, Hants, Surveyor of Taxes, aged 27,
                [third son of George M., of Kirkby Malzeard, co. York, builder.
,, 11   FRANCIS HENRY LASCELLES, LL B , Trinity Hall, Cambridge, and of the
                Inner Temple, Barrister-at-Law, aged 40, eldest son of Francis L., Esq ,
                [of the H E I Co
June 11   EDWARD DICEY, B A , Trinity College, Cambridge, aged 38, second son of
                [Thomas Edward D , of Claybrook Hall, co Leicester, Esq , deceased
Nov 2   WILLIAM CHASE WALCOTT, aged 28, only son of William W , of Bridgetown,
                [Island of Barbados, merchant, deceased
,, ,,   HENRY BLAKE GOODALL, Assistant Secretary to the Board of Revenue,
                Allahabad, aged 39, second son of J Alexander G , late of India, gent ,
                deceased   [London, merchant, deceased
,, 15   SIDNEY STRONG, aged 27, only son of Sidney S , late of Watling Street, city of
,, 18   CHARLES BAKER, Superior Clerk, Poor Law Board, aged 20, fourth son of
1866   [Henry B , of Gower Street, Middlesex, architect
Jan 18   ALFRED RHODES BRISTOW, aged 49 , third son of Isaac B , late of Greenwich,
                Kent, Esq , deceased   [son of William S , of Dublin, gent
,, 12   REDMOND UNIACKE STEELE, of St John's College, Cambridge, aged 22, third
May 3   JAMES ACWORTH DAVILS, of King's College, London, aged 20, only son of
                [Rev James D , of Ceylon, clerk

1866   [Middlesex, Esq

May 7   HENRY KEEBLE, aged 25, eldest surviving son of Jabez K , late of Pimlico,

,, 28   ADAM RIVERS STEELE, aged 49, second son of Thomas James S, late of
[Sawbridgeworth Herts, late Capt 25th Regiment, Light Dragoons

July 5   RICHARD WHITE, of Bombay C S , aged 36, eldest son of the late Thomas W ,
[Esq , of the same, deceased

,, 17   JOHN EDWARD DIBB, aged 54, fourth son of Christopher Bolland, D , late of
Leeds, co York, Surgeon in the Army, Acting Registrar of Deeds for the
[West Riding

Oct 8   WALTER GALT GRIBBON, of St John's College, Oxford, aged 21, eldest son of
[the late William G , of King's Road, Middlesex, Esq , deceased

,, 17   ALEXANDER YOUNG ADAMS, Judge of District Court, Negombo, Ceylon, aged
42, eldest son of the late Rev John Alexander A , of Carrick Lea, co
[Tyrone, clerk, deceased

,, 20   ALBERT WILLIAM HUGHES, Deputy Magistrate in Uncovenanted Service,
Bombay, aged 37, eldest son of the late Edmund H , of Stratford-le-Bow,
[Essex, Esq deceased

,, 25   HENRY WILLIAM DENT, aged 32, third son of the late Robert D , of
[Gloucester Terrace, Middlesex, Esq deceased

Nov 2   WILLIAM EDWARD WYNN WILLIAMS, aged 24, eldest son of David W , of
[Dendraeth Castle, co Merioneth, Esq

,, 9   ARTHUR DAVENPORT, of H B M Consular Service, China, aged 30, fourth son
[of the late Rev Charles D , Rector of Welford, co Gloucester, deceased

,, 19   MAXWELL MELVILL, aged 33, second son of the Rev Canon M . Rector of
[Barnes, Surrey

,, 21   GEORGE EDWARDS, Matriculated London University, 1863, aged 26, second
1867.   [son of John E , of Lower Broughton, Manchester, Esq , deceased,

June 11   ROBERT LOW, aged 30, son of Robert L , of Lower Tooting, Surrey, Esq ,
[banker

Nov 14   ERNEST GEORGE BIRCH, of Bengal, C.S , aged 38, fourth son of Rev. Henry
[William Rous B., late of Southwold, Suffolk, clerk

,, ,,   JAMES STOPFORD OWEN, aged 21, A B , second son of George Annesley O ,
of Ramsgate Gorey, co Wexford, Esq   [worth, Surrey, Esq

,, 16   OLIVER LE NEVE FOSTER, aged 23, fourth son of Peter Le Neve F , of Wands-
1868   [Audit Office, Somerset House, Esq , deceased

Jan 20   GEORGE WELBY KING, aged 21, only son of George Seymour K , late of the

,, ,,   GUSTAVUS ADOLPHUS SMITH, late a Civil Engineer, aged 47, eldest son of
[Gustavus S , of Salcombe Regis, Esq , J P

,, 25   JOHN CARR, junior, aged 17, eldest son of John C , of Blackheath, Esq ,
[Barrister of this Society, and late Chief Justice of Sierra Leone

,, 30   ROBERT JARDINE, of Bengal Civil Service, B A , London University, and of
the Middle Temple (admitted Jan 15, 1867), aged 25, second son of
[William J , of Dunstable, Beds, J P

June 9   GEORGE WILLIAM CARTER, M A , Pembroke College, Cambridge, aged 26,
[only son of John C , of Knottingley, co York, Esq

July 28   SAMUEL CLARKE PARTRIDGE, of the University of London, aged 26, second
[son of Samuel P late of Dacca, Bengal, indigo planter

Oct 27.   WILLIAM BOWEN ROWLANDS, M A., Jesus College, Oxon, aged 32, eldest
[son of Thomas R., of Glenover, co. Pembroke Esq

1868

Nov 3 JOHN PROCTER, aged 24, eldest son of John P , late of Long Preston, co
1869   [York, Esq

Mar 4 JAMES FRANCIS OSWALD, of St Edmund Hall, Oxon, and of the Middle
        Temple (admitted Jan 24, 1867), aged 29, third son of William O , of
                                                      [Highbury, Middlesex, gent

April 22 STANLEY BULLOCK, Captain Madras Light Cavalry, aged 27, eldest son of
                          [Major-General B , of Southampton, Hants, deceased

  ,,   ,, HENRY AUGUSTUS STANLEY BULLOCK, aged 23, second son of Major-
        General B , late of Southampton, Hants, deceased   [Clatford, Andover

  ,,   21 RICHARD DAMPIER CHILD, aged 27, second son of Thomas C , rector of Upper

May 6 LEONARD HOPWOOD HICKS, of London, Solicitor, aged 47, eldest son of
              [Leonard H , late of Gray's Inn Square, Middlesex, Solicitor, deceased

  ,,   25 WILLIAM ROBERT STERLING, aged 25, only son of Paul Ivy S , late Judge of
                                                      [the Supreme Court of Ceylon

  ,,   22 ISAAC ESPINASSE, of Hemel Hempstead, Solicitor, aged 39, eldest son of late
                          [James E , of Maidstone, Kent, Barrister-at-Law

June 10 PEIRCE DE LACY HENRY JOHNSTONE of Balliol College, Oxon, aged 21,
        second son of Francis William J , of Lanark, Adjutant 2nd Lanarkshire,
                                                      [and late Captain 27th Foot

  ,,   15 CHARLES TRUWHITT, of London, Solicitor, aged 45, son of George T , late of
                          [Cook's Court, Lincoln's Inn, Solicitor, deceased

Nov 18 CHARLES JAMES FLEMING, of Bombay, aged 29, eldest son of Edmond Lionel
                          [F , of Sale, co Chester, paper manufacturer.

  ,,   30 ROWLAND JONES-BATEMAN, aged 43, of Lincoln's Inn, Barrister at-Law,
        [second son of the late John Jones-B , of Lincoln's Inn, gent , deceased

Dec 6 WILLIAM WEST, aged 53, only son of the late William W , of Gray's Inn,
1870   [Solicitor, deceased.

Jan 17 CHARLES LYTTLETON CHUBB, of Sidney Sussex Coll , Cambridge, aged 19,
        [eldest son of Thomas Henry C , of Malmesbury, Wilts, Solicitor

  ,,   22 ROBERT JOHN PATTEN, Solicitor, aged 27, youngest son of James P , of
                                                      [Gray's Inn, Solicitor

  ,,   24 ROBERT WILLIS, of York Terrace, Regent's Park, Middlesex, Esq Jacksonian
                    [Professor of the University of Cambridge aged 70

  ,,   25 HENRY FITZPATRICK BERRY, aged 22, eldest son of Parsons B , of Mallow,
                                                      [co Cork, surgeon

  ,,   26. RICHARD STEPHEN CHARNOCK, Solicitor, aged 49, son of Richard C , late of
                    [King's Bench Walk, Temple, Barrister-at-Law, deceased.

April 21 JOHN MILES, Attorney and Solicitor, aged 51, eldest son of John M , late of
                                                      [Watford, Herts, Esq , deceased

  ,,   29 DANIEL CHAUNCEY BEALE, of Lincoln's Inn, Barrister-at-Law, only son of
                    [Thomas Barbot B , of Brettenham Park, Suffolk, J P

May 18 THOMAS BOWKER, Attorney and Solicitor, aged 35, second son of Thomas B ,
        of Whittlesey, co Cambridge, Esq   [St Heliers, Jersey, merchant

  ,,   21 WILLIAM LAURENCE DE GRUCHY, aged 31, eldest son of W Philip de G , of

Nov 28 BEDFORD CLAPPERTON TREVELYAN PIM, aged 44, of the Inner Temple
        (admitted April 20, 1870), only son of Edward Bedford P , late of Bide-
                                                      [ford, Devon, Commander, R N
1871

Jan 23 SAMUEL ARNOLD LAWSON, aged 23, second son of Mr Justice L , of Dublin

1871

Feb 1   HENRY GASELEE, aged 28, only son of the late Binsteed G, of Lincoln's Inn,
[Middlesex. Barrister-at-Law

„ 4   THOMAS JOSEPH GREENFIELD, late of the War Office, Pall Mall, aged 35,
eldest son of Thomas Conolly G., of Elizabeth Street, Eaton Square,
[Middlesex, clerk in the War Office

Mar. 23   JOSEPH HARRIS STRETTON, Solicitor, aged 40, third son of William Weston S,
[of Danes Hill House, co. Leicester, Esq.

April 18   BENJAMIN LEWIS MOSELEY, aged 19, fifth son of Ephraim M, late of Dalston,
[Middlesex, Esq, deceased

„ 24   EDWARD POPE, aged 33, youngest son of Rev. Alfred P, of Camden Town,
[Middlesex, retired Independent Minister.

„ 29   ARTHUR ROMILLY (Hon), of Trinity College, Cambridge, aged 22, fourth son
[of Rt Hon. Lord R, Master of the Rolls, Bencher of this Society

May 2.   SAMUEL BARKER BOOTH, Solicitor, aged 48, second son of William B, of
[Dedham, Essex, gent, deceased.

„ 3.   BERTRAM HENRY TALBOT, B A, Queen's University, Dublin, and of King's
Inns, aged 22, eldest son of Marcus T, late of Strasburg, co Clare,
[landed proprietor, deceased

„ 27   WILLIAM LEIGH BERNARD, a chief clerk to the Commissioners of Church
Temporalities, aged 26, eldest son of Michael Charles B, of Dundrum,
co Dublin, M B, Trinity College, Dublin, and L.R Coll. Surg, Ireland

June 21   RICHARD BETTON FOSTER, Attorney and Solicitor, aged 34, only son of Lieut -
[general Thomas F, R E., of Cleveland Terrace, Hyde Park, Middlesex

July 22   FRANCIS CADWALLADER ADAMS, Attorney and Solicitor, aged 25, second son
[of Henry A, of 48, Lincoln's-inn Fields Middlesex, Solicitor

Nov 4   JAMES MULLIGAN, M A, Queen's University, Dublin, and of King's Inns, aged
[23, eldest son of David M, of Annaclone, co Down, Esq

„ 7   WILLIAM TROTMAN STOWER HEWETT, B A, London University, aged 31,
[eldest son of Jesse H, of Tewkesbury, co Gloucester, Dissenting Minister

„ 9   CHARLES RICHARD CRADDOCK, Attorney and Solicitor, aged 58, son of John
[C, deceased, of Tash Court, Middlesex, carpenter.

„ „   FRANCIS PHILLIPS, of the Civil Service, aged 35, only surviving son of the late
[Charles Henry P, of Trafalgar Square, Brompton, Middlesex, F R C S

„ 14   WILLIAM CHUBB, aged 43, youngest son of the late Thomas C, of Malmesbury,
[Wilts, J P

„ 18   UVEDALE CORBETT, of the Middle Temple, Barrister-at-Law, eldest son
of the late Uvedale Corbett Winder, of Cotsbrooke, Shifnal, Salop, Esq.

„ 20   HENRY WILLIAM STUDDY, late a Captain 20th Hussars, aged 36, eldest son of
[Thomas Bradridge S, of Plymouth, Devon, late Major 8th Bengal Cavalry

1872

Jan 18   HENRY DAVIS POOLE, of Lincoln's Inn, aged 47, second son of Richard P,
[deceased, late of Gray's Inn, Middlesex, Solicitor

Aug 8   THOMAS ABBOTT TIBBITTS, Attorney and Solicitor, aged 48, eldest son of
[Thomas Abbott T, late of Longbridge, co Warwick

Nov 13   JOHN FOSTER REED, aged 43, eldest son of John R, of Lewannick, Cornwall,
[gentleman farmer

„ 15   HENRY WILLIAM DYETT, aged 18, only son of Edward Bowman D, of Mont-
[serrat, Police Magistrate, and a Member of Council

1872

Nov 30   JOHN ANDREW SHARP, Solicitor, aged 48, son of W H S, deceased, of the   [City of London, Goldsmith

,, ,,   OSCAR AUGUSTUS ULLITHORNE, aged 41, second son of Charles More U., of
[Red Lion Square, Middlesex, Solicitor, deceased

1873

Jan 13   ARTHUR ELLEY FINCH, Attorney and Solicitor, aged 53, second son of John
[F, of Woburn Place, Middlesex, Esq

Mar 1   RICHARD STEPHENS TAYLOR, the younger, Solicitor, aged 31, only son of
[Richard Stephens T, of Gray's Inn, Solicitor

April 24   JOSEPH AUGUSTUS HELLARD, Solicitor, aged 35, second surviving son of
[Charles Bettesworth H, of Portsmouth, co Southampton, Solicitor

May 3   WILLIAM ARTHUR TOOKE, of the Inner Temple, Barrister-at-Law, aged 29, only
[son of Arthur William T, deceased, of Pinner Hill, Middlesex, Solicitor

,, 26   WILLIAM THOMAS WAITE, Mathematical Teacher, aged 35, second son of
[William W, Esq, of Reading, Berks.

July 22   JOHN HILLYER TOZER, aged 45, second son of John Chappell T, late of
[Teignmouth, Devon, Solicitor

,, 29   BENJAMIN STARLING, Solicitor, aged 60, son of William S, of Camberwell,
Surrey, gent   [Clerk of Bristol

Nov 4   DANIEL TRAVERS BURGES, Solicitor, aged 34, eldest son of Daniel B, Town

,, 7   JOSEPH DALE, the younger, Attorney-at-Law and Solicitor, aged 31, eldest son
[of Joseph Langham D, of Furnival's Inn, Middlesex, Solicitor

,, 8   JOSEPH ST CLAIR MAYNE, of King's Inns, Dublin (Trinity, 1873), and of
Trinity College, Dublin, aged 27, eldest son of James Arthur M, of
[Aughnamallagh, co Monaghan, Solicitor

,, 12   RALPH HERBERT BARNES HOTCHKIN, B A, Trinity College, Cambridge, only
[son of Rev Robert Charles Herbert H, Rector of Thimbleby, co Lincoln

,, 20   JOHN FREDERIC TROTTER, of the Commissariat Department, and late Captain
of the 11th Regiment, aged 33, youngest son of the late Alexander T,
[Esq, of Sydenham Chase, co Gloucester.

Dec 22   WILLIAM TINDAL PERKINS, Attorney and Solicitor, aged 38, third surviving son
[of Rev Benjamin Robert P, of Wotton-under-Edge, co Gloucester, clerk

,, 31   CHARLES LOWE, M A, Edinburgh University, some time Student of Jena,
[aged 25, only son of Charles L, of Brechin, co Forfar, farmer

1874

Jan 10   JOHN JOSEPH FRANCIS, H M Inspector of Irish National Schools, aged 34,
[eldest son of William Francis Aylward, late of the city of Dublin, deceased

,, 17   EDWARD CANT-WALL, aged 24, second surviving son of George Favell Cant,
gent, of Hornsey, Middlesex   [gent.

,, 24   FREDERICK HUXLEY, aged 26, only son of James H, of the city of Manchester,

Feb. 15   JOHN PERRY GODFREY, Attorney and Solicitor, aged 36, eldest son of John G,
[of Liverpool, co Lancaster, retired Solicitor

Mar 14   THOMAS MAXWELL WITHAM, Special Pleader and Conveyancer, and Draftsman
in Equity, under the Middle Temple certificate, aged 37, eldest son of Sir
[Charles W, Knight of Higham, Suffolk, R N.

,, 27   THOMAS HENRY BOLTON, Solicitor, aged 33, son of Thomas B, late of
[Islington, Middlesex, gent

April 18   MILES WALKER MATTINSON, journalist, aged 19, only son of Thomas M, late
[of Newcastle on-Tyne, draper, deceased

May 6   THOMAS HENRY NEAL, Attorney and Solicitor, aged 36, third son of William
[N, of Kingsdon, co Somerset, Esq.

1874

May 7   ERNEST CHESTER THOMAS, of Trinity College, Oxford, late of Lincoln's Inn, aged 23, eldest son of John T., of Medlock Hall, Ashton-under-Lyne, co
[Lancaster, accountant

,, 28   JOHN BURHAM SAFFORD, aged 31, second son of John Burham S., of Long-
[croft Hall, Tring, Herts, gent, deceased

Oct 19   CHARLES MONTAGUE LUSH, of Trinity Hall, Cambridge, aged 20, third surviving son of Hon Mr Justice L., one of the Justices of the Court of Queen's
[Bench

,, 31   FREDERICK COOPER WILLIS, aged 17, eldest son of Edward Cooper W., of 50,
[Chancery Lane, Middlesex, Barrister-at-Law of the Inner Temple.

Nov 6   SAMUEL NEWMAN, Solicitor, aged 49, second surviving son of John N., of
[High Wycombe, Bucks, Esq

,, ,,   JAMES TRAILL CHRISTIE, of the Middle Temple, Barrister-at-Law, son of Jonathan Henry C., of 9, Stanhope Street, Hyde Park Gardens, Middlesex,
[Barrister-at-Law

,, 9   JOHN CHARLES LEWIS COWARD, of Corpus Christi College, Cambridge, aged 22, eldest son of Rev John Henry C., of 86, St. George's Square,
[Middlesex (Clerk in Holy orders).

,, 21   JAMES HANNA, B.A., Queen's University, aged 23, second surviving son of
[William H., of Lisburn, co Antrim, merchant

,, 26   ANDREW THOMAS TURTON PETERSON, of the Middle Temple, Barrister-at-Law, aged 61, only son of Henry P., of Wakefield, co York, Esq,
[deceased

1875   [G., of 3 Gray's Inn Square Middlesex, Solicitor

Jan 5   ROBERT HEALE GAMLEN, Attorney and Solicitor, aged 36, eldest son of Robert

,, 9   WILLIAM EDMUND BALL, LL B., London, Classical and Mathematical Tutor, aged 21, second son of Joseph Lancaster B., of Torquay, Devon,
[Wesleyan Methodist Minister

,, ,,   ARTHUR HENRY BATES, B A., Queen's University, Ireland, aged 21, seventh son
[of John B., deceased, late of Belfast, co Antrim, Solicitor

,, 21   ALFRED HERBERT LUSH, of Trinity Hall, Cambridge, aged 20, elder son of
[John Alfred L., M.D., of Fisherton House, Wilts, M P

Mar 4   HENRY MORGAN NASH, Attorney and Solicitor, aged 22, only son of Henry
[Shuter N., of Clifton, city of Bristol, Esq

April 12   WILLIAM FOOT HUSBAND, aged 30, only son of William Mitchell H., of St Helier, Island of Jersey, Esq   [of Fulnagardy, co Down, Esq

,, 14   JAMES ALEXANDER BOYLE McCONNELL, aged 18, eldest son of Hugh M.,

,, 28   EDWARD CHARLES McCRAW, of King's Inns, Dublin, and of Queen's University, Ireland, aged 40, eldest son of J D M., of Perth, Scot-
[land, deceased

,, 30   HENRY ELLIOTT CHEVALIER KITCHENER, of the Staff College, Farnham, Lieut 46th Regt, aged 28, eldest son of Henry Horatio K., of Dinan,
[Brittany, France, Col late 9th Regt

May 4   WILLIAM PITT COBBETT, of University College, Oxford, aged 21, eldest son
[of Rev Pitt C., of Crofton, Hants, Clerk in Holy Orders

,, 22   PHILIP FOSTER ALDRED, of Hertford College, Oxford, aged 23, eldest son of
[Rev John Thomas Foster A., Vicar of Dore, co Derby.

June 1   JOHN WALTER HUDDLESTON HEATH, aged 22, third surviving son of Nicholas
[William H., F R.C.S Ireland, deceased

1875

June 2   STUART MACASKIE, aged 22, eldest son of Geo M , of Berwick-on Tweed,
newspaper proprietor   [caster, jeweller, deceased.

  „   5   JOSHUA SLATER, aged 34, third son of John S , late of Manchester, co Lan-

  „   12   JASON SMITH, of Lincoln's Inn, Barrister at-Law, aged 39, eldest son of Jason
[S , Esq , deceased

July 2   VINCENT BROWN, aged 19, second son of Joseph B , of Trinidad, West Indies,
[merchants' managing clerk

Oct 29   RICHARD JOHN VILLIERS, Attorney and Solicitor, aged 25, eldest son of John
[Fitzpatrick V., late of Lincoln's Inn, Barrister-at-Law

Oct 30   CHARLES ALFRED RUSSELL, B A , London University, aged 20, second son of
[John Archibald R , Q C , Bencher of this Society

Nov   1   WILLIAM MOUNTFORD KINSEY VALE, aged 42, a Member of Executive Council,
Victoria, formerly a bookseller, eldest son of late John V , of Castlemaine,
[Colony of Victoria, Australia, deceased

  „   3   WILLIAM HENRY SPACKMAN, aged 26, youngest son of John S , late of Brad-
[ford on-Avon, Wilts, gent , deceased

  „   5   HENRY MARMADUKE HEWITT, classical lecturer at New College, London, M A
St John's Cambridge and University of London, aged 32, eldest son of
[Cornelius H , of Kingston-upon-Hull, gent

  „   6   HENRY GEORGE WATTS, of Oriel College, Oxon, aged 23, fifth surviving
[son of William Henry W , of Westbourne Park, Middlesex, journalist

  „   11   WILLIAM TYNDALL BARNARD, aged 20, elder son of William Tyndall B , of
[Islington, Middlesex, Barrister-at-Law

  „   13   JOHN GORDON, B A , Queen's University, Ireland, aged 25, eldest son of Samuel
[G , of Shankhill House, co Down, gent

  „   15   THOMAS SPEECHLY, Registrar of the City of London Court, aged 40, eldest
[son of Thomas Kelful S , of Whittlesey, co Cambridge, Esq

  „   16   GEORGE FRANCIS WATERS, B A , University of Dublin, aged 22, eldest son of
[George W , of Dublin, Q C

  „   18   LIONEL FERNEAUX KNIPE HILL, of New Coll , Oxford, aged 19, second son of
Rev Wm Alfred H , M A , Vicar of Throwley, Kent, and Barrister-at-

1876   [Law

Jan 11   REINHOLD GREGOROWSKI, B A , University of Cape of Good Hope, aged 19,
fifth son of Reinhold G , of Somerset East, Cape of Good Hope, Mis-
[sionary of the London Society

  „   22   GUSTAVUS EDWIN BORN, aged 27, second son of David B , of Berlin, Esq

  „   29   GEORGE HORTON SHEPPARD, of Clare College, Cambridge, fourth son of the late
[John Horton S , of Towcester, co Northampton

Mar   4   JOHN TIMBRELL PIERCE, of the Middle Temple, Barrister-at-Law, aged 44,
eldest son of James Parker P , late of Clifton Lodge, Highgate Road,
[Middlesex, Esq , J P

May 11   WILLIAM SIMON, of St Andrew's University, aged 20, fourth son of James S ,
[of Stirling, gent

  „   15   CHARLES PAGET MOORE, Associate, King's College, aged 18, eldest son of
[Charles William M , of Tewkesbury, co Gloucester, Solicitor

      17   ARTHUR WARREN SAMUELS, B A , Dublin University, Solicitor and Proctor,
aged 23, second son of Arthur S , of Langara, Kingstown, co Dublin,
[Solicitor

1876

May 18   GEORGE THOMAS VAUSTON, LL.B , of Trinity College, Dublin, and a solicitor, aged 22, second son of John Davis V , of Hildon Park, Rathgar, co Dublin, Solicitor   [Calcutta, Ship Builder.

June 12   JAMES CRANSTOUN, aged 21, eldest son of James C , late of Kidderpore,

,, 14   HUGH WILLIAM ELCUM, of the University of London, aged 18, eldest son of [Hugh William E , of Upper Holloway, Middlesex, Solicitor

,, 15   ARTHUR RAYMOND HARDING, Solicitor, aged 39, son of late James Duffield H , of Barnes, Surrey, a member of the Society of Painters in Water [Colours

,, 16   MILES HENRY PRANCE, Solicitor, aged 39, elder son of Miles Hammett P , deceased, late of Hampstead, Middlesex, Barrister-at-Law

,, 28   THOMAS TERRELL, born July 11, 1852, eldest son of Thomas Hull T , of Finchley, Middlesex, County Court Judge.   [Southsea, Hants

Oct 9   ALFRED DUNHAM, aged 23, only son of John D , of Havelock Park,

,, 26   CHARLES ANDREW POPE, of Worcester College, Oxford, aged 19, third son of James P , late of Regent's Park, Middlesex, Colonel Bombay Army, [deceased

Dec 16   WALTER LOVELL, Solicitor, aged 29, eldest surviving son of Charles Henry L ,

1877   [of Gray's Inn Square, Middlesex, Solicitor

Jan 10   COURTENAY CRACROFT SPURRELL FOOKS, aged 16, third son of William [Cracroft F , of Dartford Heath, Kent, Q C , Barrister-at-Law

,, 13   LORENZO FREDERICK PEARSON, eldest son of William P , of Rock Ferry, co Chester, H M Civil Service   [merchant

,, 16   FRANK DODD, aged 19, son of John D , of Rock Ferry, co Chester, glass

,, 22   CHARLES AUGUSTUS VANSITTART CONYBEARE, B A , Christ Church, Oxford, [aged 23, eldest son of John Charles C , of Tonbridge, Kent, Barrister-at-Law

,, 27.   JAMES HENRY MUSSEN CAMPBELL, B A , Trinity College, Dublin, aged 25, [third son of William Mussen C , of Terenure, co Dublin, Esq

,, 31   FREDERIC THOMAS HALL, Solicitor, aged 41, third son of Thomas H , late [of Burslem, co Stafford, earthenware manufacturer.

Mar 28   GODFREY WERGE FARDELL, B A , aged 24, second son of late Charles F , [J P , D L , late of Holbech, co Lincoln

April 9   EDWARD RUNDLE LEVEY, of London University, and a Clerk in the Civil Service, aged 22, fifth surviving son of George L , late of Camberwell, [Surrey, Printer

,, 16   JAMES WALMESLEY, Classical Master, the College, Highbury, aged 23, eldest [son of Thomas W , of Ashton, Newton-le-Willows, co Lancaster, Farmer

,, ,,   WILLIAM HENRY UPJOHN, aged 23, eldest son of William Bellingham Drew U , [of Englefield Road, Middlesex, gent

,, 24   HENRY CECIL DARLINGTON, B A , Solicitor, aged 38, eldest son of John D , [of Bradford, co York, Solicitor

May 1   THEODORE LE GALLAIS, B A , Jesus College, Cambridge, son of the late [John Le G , of La Fevriere, Jersey, Advocate, Royal Court of Jersey

,, ,,   ERNEST SAFFORD, aged 24, fourth surviving son of John Burnham S , of Long-[croft Hall, Tring, Herts, deceased, of H M Civil Service

June 13   ARTHUR WILLIAM A'BECKETT, Journalist and Author, aged 31, third surviving son of the late Gilbert Abbott A , of Hyde Park Gate, Middlesex, [Barrister-at-Law, and Metropolitan Police Magistrate.

1877

June 15. ROBERT HUME GUNION, B A , Lincoln College, Oxford, aged 26, second son
[of Andrew Jeffrey G , late of Greenock, Scotland, Presbyterian Minister

,, ,, JOHN LEOPOLD DOOLEY, B A , Queen's University, Ireland, and of King's
[Inns, Dublin, aged 26, second son of Michael D , of Galway, merchant

July 25 WILLIAM TIMBRELL ELLIOTT, Solicitor, aged 56, only son of William E ,
[deceased, late of Kentish Town, Middlesex.

Oct 25 THOMAS TREVOR WHITE, B A , Dublin, aged 25, only son of Thomas John
[W , of Rathmines, Dublin, Barrister-at-Law

,, 31 ROBERT WEIR BROWN, Junior Examiner in the Exchequer and Audit
Department, aged 22, second son of John B , of Aubrey Road, Middlesex,
[merchant

,, ,, ANDREW GILLMAN, aged 43, only son of John G , of Portsmouth, R N

Nov 2 FREDERICK AWDRY BRABANT, Solicitor, aged 27, sixth son of William Hughes
[B , deceased, late of Hampstead, Middlesex, Solicitor.

Dec 15 REGINALD WARD, Assistant Solicitor to the Metropolitan Board of Works,
youngest son of Rev Robert W , M A , deceased, late of Thetford,
[Norfolk

1878

Jan 14 WILLIAM HENRY WILSON, B A , Dublin University and of King's Inns, Dublin,
[aged 25, younger son of William W , of Dublin, Insurance Agent

,, 19 JOHN LOWRY, aged 32, second son of Michael L , of Killismeestha, Queen's
County, Farmer   [China, Solicitor

,, 26 EDWARD ROBINSON, aged 21, eldest son of Alfred Murray R , of Shanghai,

,, ,, ATHERTON KNOWLES, of St John's College, Cambridge, aged 19, eldest son
[of Rev John K , of Luton, Beds.

May 3 FREDERICK BRIAN DE MALBISSE GIBBONS, B A , Gonville and Caius College,
Cambridge, aged 23, eldest son of Henry Frederick G , of 3, Pump Court,
Temple, Barrister-at-law   [town, Barbados, Shipowner

,, 11 WILLIAM ELLIOTT LEWIS, aged 26, eldest son of Thomas L , late of Bridge-

,, 16 FREDERICK WILLIAM BATCHELOR, B A , Sidney, Sussex College, Cambridge,
aged 22, eldest son of the Rev. Frederick Thomas B , Rector of Jacobstow,
[Cornwall

,, 17 REGINALD EDWIN MORRIS, of Pembroke College, Cambridge, and of the
Inner Temple, aged 23, third surviving son of the Rev L S M , Canon
[of Ripon and Rector of Thornton-in-Craven, co York.

,, 21 WILLIAM JOSEPH HAMILTON, B A , Dublin University, aged 26, second son
[of James H , of Castle Hamilton, co Cavan, Esq , J P , D L

,, 29 HENRY CHARLES RICHARDS, aged 26, second son of Frederick R , of
[Hastings, Sussex, Treasurer's Clerk, County Court

June 28 JOHN ROSS, LL B , Trinity College, Dublin, aged 23, eldest son of the Rev
Robert R , of Ardfoyle, Derry, co Derry   [co Tyrone, gent

July 3 ANDREW TODD, aged 24, fifth surviving son of William T , of Fyfin, Strabane,

Nov 4 HENRY ALBERT ALCAZAR, of the London University, aged 18, second son of
John A , of the port of Spain, Trinidad, Manager in a Merchant's Office

,, ,, DAVID JOUFFROY WATSON, of the London University, aged 19, third surviving
[son of John W , of West Dulwich, Surrey, M D

Nov 5 MICHAEL CHARTRES MACINERNEY, of King's Inns, Dublin, aged 28, second
[son of John M , late of Bleakmount House, co Clare, Esq., deceased

1878
Nov 8   PETER JOHN O'NEILL, B A , Queen's University, Ireland, and of King's Inns,
     [aged 33, fourth son of John O , of Deroran, co Tyrone, farmer

,, 20   ARTHUR EDWARD DESBOROUGH BOURKE, B A , Trinity College, Dublin,
     [aged 26, third son of Rev John B , vicar of Kilmeadon, co Waterford

,, ,,   WILLIAM GEORGE STACK, of Trinity College, Dublin, and Her Majesty's
     Indian Civil Service, aged 19, third surviving son of George Hall S , of
     [Mullaghmore, Omagh, co Tyrone, barrister

,, 21   GEORGE LAWTIE FAGAN, of Dublin University, born Nov 27, 1858, third
     surviving son of George Smoult F , late Judge of Small Cause Court,
1879   [Calcutta
Jan 3   BENJAMIN THOMAS BRADLEY FLOOD, Lieutenant 82nd Regiment of Foot,
     aged 28½, eldest son of Frederick L F , deceased, of the city of Dublin,
     [solicitor

,, 13   JOHN OVEREND EVANS, of London University, aged 34, only surviving son of
     [David Owen E , of Higher Broughton, Manchester, gent

,, 30   WALTER FIELD HOOPER, F.R G S , F Z S , &c , Barrister-at-Law, of the Middle
     Temple and Advocate of the High Court, Madras, at Negapatam, aged 43,
     [eldest son of Samuel Field H , of Great Marlow, Bucks

April 9   WILLIAM GOWLAND FIELD, B A , Corpus Christi Coll , Cambridge, aged 24,
     second son of Charles F , of Liverpool, merchant   [India, Pleader

May 14   HENRY LODER BEDDY, aged 20, eldest son of Leicester Septimus B , of Agra,

Nov 3   FRANCIS WATT, aged 30, eldest son of James W , of Haddington, chemist

,, ,,   GEORGE YEATES DIXON, B A , Trinity College, Dublin, aged 22 second son of
     [George D , late of Dublin, deceased.

,, 11   WILLIAM JOHN REYNOLDS POCHIN, M A , Sydney Sussex College, Cambridge,
     aged 29, eldest son of Rev William Henry P , of Wornall, co Oxford,
     [Clerk in Holy Orders

,, 21   THOMAS HENRY JOHN SHADWELL, of Queen's College, Oxford, aged 30, only
     [son of Cayley S., of Abercorn Place, Middlesex, retired Barrister
1880
Jan 23   WILLIAM FRANCIS MADDEN, Government Clerk, Registrar General's Office,
     [Dublin, aged 33, second son of John M , merchant of the city of Limerick

,, 24   GEORGE GREY BUTLER, aged 27, eldest son of Rev George B , Head Master
     of Liverpool College   [Esq , deceased

,, ,,   EDWARD CLAYTON, aged 23, fifth son of James C , late of Hornsey, Middlesex,

,, 28   JOHN LENTON PULLING, LL D , Univ College, London, aged 44, only son of
     John P , of Blackheath, Kent, gent   [Ashmansworth, Hants, farmer

June 4   CHARLES TURNLEY ELLIS, aged 23, eldest son of Charles Anthony E , of

,, 7   TIMOTHY MICHAEL HEALY, journalist, aged 25, second son of Maurice H ,
     [of Bantry, co Cork, gent

Nov 2   ADALBERT EBENEZER HENDRICKSON, of London University, aged 21, only son
     of William James H , of the Port of Spain, Trinidad, Clerk of the Peace
     for District Courts   [Blackheath, Kent, Barrister-at-Law

,, ,,   REGINALD COOPER WILLIS, aged 17, second son of Edward Cooper W , of

,, 20   JOHN EDWARD REDMOND, aged 24, Clerk in Civil Service eldest son of late
     [William Archer R , J P , of Wexford, deceased

,, ,,   DAVID GRAHAM, aged 26, fourth son of John G , of Airth, co Stirling, farmer

,, 29   RICHARD READER HARRIS, aged 33, Civil Engineer, only son of Richard
     [Reader H , of Gray's Inn, Barrister

1881

Jan 28 ROBERT EVELYN HAY MURRAY, M A , Christ Church, Oxford, aged 29, only surviving son of Robert Hay M , of Godinton Park, Ashford, Kent, Esq   [John W , of Port of Spain, Trinidad, merchant

May 2 LOUIS ANTHONY WHARTON, of London University, aged 19, eldest son of

,,   VALENTINE DENNIS ARCHER, of University of Oxford, aged 36, third sur-
[viving son of Edward Wiltshire A , late of Barbados, gent , deceased

,, 14 JAMES ROBERT VERNAM MARCHANT, M A , Wadham College, Oxford, Assistant Classical Master at St Paul's School, aged 27, second surviving
son of Rev Job M , of Upper Kennington Lane, London, Congregational
[Minister

,, 16 JOHN RICHARD CLARK HALL, of London University, Clerk in the Local
Government Board, aged 26, only son of James John H , of Streatham,
[Surrey, Principal Clerk in the Custom House

,, 17 EUSTACE MEREDITH MARTIN JOHNSTONE, of King's Inns, Dublin, aged 35,
[seventh son of Andrew J , late of Corboy House, co Longford.

June 16 ROBERT BYERLEY PARKES, of the University of London, aged 19, only son of
[Thomas William P , of Hanwell, Middlesex

,, 18 ROBERT HAMILTON SINCLAIR, Civil Service, Ceylon, aged 28, eldest son of
[Allan S , of Kinmore, Perthshire, clergyman

,, 21 WILLIAM HENRY DEVERELL, of Lincoln's Inn, Barrister-at-Law, aged 45,
[eldest son of John D , late of Purbrook Park, Hants, Esq , and of Gray's Inn

,, 24 JOHN WATSON MOSES, aged 31, second son of William M , late of Stockton-
[on-Tees, co Durham, architect, deceased

,, 30 GEORGE KNOWLES PALEY, of Christ's College, Cambridge, aged 20, eldest son
[of Rev Thomas P , of Bournemouth, Hants, Clerk in Holy Orders

July 2 CHARLES PALMER, B A , London University, aged 27, eldest son of Job
Richard P , of Highgate, Middlesex, wholesale stationer

,, 4 **H.R.H. The Duke of Connaught and Strathearn, third son of
H.M. Queen Victoria.**

Nov 1 JAMES MORIARTY, of Trinity College, Dublin, aged 28, eldest son of John M ,
of Mallow, co Cork, Solicitor   [Trinidad, merchant

,, 14 ALBERT INNOCENCIO LACK, aged 20, second son of Albert L , of Port of Spain,

,, 19 CLEMENT BOULTON ROVLANCE KENT, of Trinity College, Oxford, aged 21,
[eldest son of Alfred Clement K , of New Brighton, co Chester, Solicitor

,, 21 WILLIAM TINDAL ROBERTSON, F R.C P L and M D , Edinburgh, aged 57,
[eldest son of Frederick Fowler R , late of Bath, co Somerset

,, 26 ERNEST WILLIAM JORDAN, of Trinity Hall, Cambridge, aged 19, second son of
1882   [Thomas Hudson J , of Manchester, Barrister-at-Law, of Gray's Inn

Jan 12 CHARLES ROSS ALSTON, of University College, London, aged 18, sixth son of
[James Calderhead A , of Glasgow, merchant, deceased

,, 14 JONAS WALLER STUDDERT, B A , Dublin University, aged 24, eldest son of
[Charles Washington S , of Crag Moher, co Clare, J P

,, ,, CLASSON PORTER, B A , Dublin University, aged 24, youngest son of Rev
[Classon P , of Larne, co Antrim

April 26 JOHN JOSEPH HAYDEN, of Trinity College, Dublin, aged 23, only son of
[Thomas Hayden, late of Dublin, deceased

,, 27 JONATHAN ERNEST PIM, B A , Trinity College, Dublin, aged 23, eldest son of
[Thomas P , junior, of Monkstown, merchant, co Dublin

1882	[aged 20, fifth son of Rev John R , of Auchtermuchty, co Fife
April 29	ALEXANDER WOOD RENTON, Law Student, Edinburgh University, M A , 1881,
May 8	GEORGE COFFEY, B.A , Trinity College, Dublin, aged 24, third son of James [Charles C , of Dublin, Q C
June 17.	HENRY EDWARD DUKE, aged 27, second son of William Edward D., of [Princetown, Devon, granite merchant
Oct. 30	SIDNEY WEBB, of the Colonial Office, aged 23, second son of Charles W , of [33, Gerard Street, Soho, public accountant
,, 31	THOMAS HENRY RICHMOND, M A, Lond (Owens), B A Oxon (Ch Ch), [aged 29, eldest son of Thomas R , of Sunny Brow, Kendal.
Nov 4	FERDINAND LEOPOLD MAXIMILIAN PERCY FIRMINGER, clerk in Paymaster-General's Office, aged 23, fourth son of Edward Henry Percy F , of [Ealing, Middlesex
,, ,,	FREDERICK FFOLLIOTT DENNING, Senior Sophister, Trinity College, Dublin, aged 20, fifth son of Frederick Benson D , of Tullamore, King's County, [agent to the Bank of Ireland
,, 10	ALFRED EDWARD CRAWFORD, of Trinity College, Dublin, aged 21, youngest [son of Henry C , of White Abbey, Belfast
,, 11	CHARLES HENRY HARRIS, aged 24, second son of Thomas H of Taunton, [Somerset, clothier, deceased.
,, 16	WILLIAM PATRICK BYRNE, B.A , University College, London, clerk in Civil Service, aged 23, third surviving son of the late John B , of Withington, [co Lancaster, deceased.
,, 17.	SYDNEY OLIVIER, B A , Oxon , clerk in Colonial Office, aged 23, second son [of Rev. Henry Arnold O , Rector of Poulshot, Wilts.
,, 23	EDWARD DARBY VESEY, aged 20, second son of Edward V , of the Grange, [Knockholt, Kent, of H M Paymaster-General's Office.
1883	
Jan. 16	GEORGE ALEXANDER BANBURY, Assistant Colonial Secretary and Treasurer of [Sierra Leone, &c , aged 29, second son of Major William B , deceased
,, 17	EMMANUEL ELLIOTT POLLARD, aged 27, eldest son of the late Thomas P , [of Trinidad, deceased
,, 18	BERTRAM LISLE, of Melbourne University aged 33, only son of William [Beresford Lisle (formerly Orde), of Alnwick, Northumberland, Esq
,, 20	WILLIAM GRIST HAWTIN, aged 26, eldest son of William H , of London, [wholesale stationer
Mar 28	CHARLES EDWARD BRETHERTON, formerly a solicitor, Member of the Bar, Supreme Court, U S , aged 43, eldest son of Edward B , of Birkenhead, [solicitor, deceased
April 3	ARTHUR EDMUND GILL, Scholar of Magdalen College, Cambridge, aged 19, [third surviving son of Charles G , of Ashford, Middlesex, merchant.
,, 17	WILLIAM MACKENZIE, aged 22, fourth son of Robert M , of Langley House, co Perth [of Miltown Malbay, co Clare, solicitor.
,, 18	MATTHEW JOSEPH KENNY, M.P , aged 22, third surviving son of Michael K ,
,, 23	FREDERICK TINDAL ROBERTSON, Fellow of Royal College of Physicians and M D. (Edinburgh), aged 24, eldest son of William Tindal R , of Brighton
,, 27	GERALD CAIRNS WEBB, B A , Trinity College, Dublin, aged 22, eldest surviving son of Thomas W , of Dublin, Barrister-at-Law, Regius Professor [of Law in the University of Dublin
May 29	ROBERT VAUGHAN WYNNE, of London University, aged 30, sixth surviving son [of John W (M R C S , Lond), of Oswestry, Salop

1883

May 30 THOMAS CROSSLEY EASTWOOD, aged 23, eldest son of Wright E, of Man-
[chester, farm agent, deceased

June 2 FREDERICK HENRY HOUSTON, of Trinity College, Dublin, aged 34, second son
[of Thomas H, late of Belfast, deceased

,, 4 JAMES ELDON McCOMBIE SALMON, aged 21, eldest son of John Thomas S,
[of St Lucia, planter

Oct 29 THOMAS DUNCOMBE MANN, of the University of London, aged 26, eldest son of
[Thomas M, of Northampton, deceased

Nov 2 JAMES CHARLES GORDON, aged 24, eldest son of the late Thomas Robert G,
of New Amsterdam, co Berbice, British Guiana, some time Comptroller
[of Customs

,, 3 JOHN HENRY ANDERSON, "army tutor," aged 26, eldest son of John Mills A,
[of Warwick, and of the Civil Service

,, 5 GEORGE PORTIS PRICE, clerk in the Trinity House, aged 25, only son of
[George Hamilton P, of Weymouth, Collector of Customs.

,, 7 WILLIAM CONLAN, of Trinity College, Dublin, and of King's Inns, Dublin,
aged 20, only son of William C, late of Ellershe, co. Lanc, deceased
[Secretary to Pacific Steam Navigation Company

,, 10 MICHAEL MOANE, clerk in Dublin Castle, aged 29, second son of James M,
[late of Crumlin, co Monaghan, deceased

,, ,, DONALD WILLIAM GARDEN COWIE, of Balliol College, Oxford, and a selected
candidate for Indian Civil Service, aged 18, second son of Hugh C,
[Q C, and a Master of the Bench

, 14 JAMES WILLIAM BRADY MURRAY, of Trinity College, Dublin, and of King's
Inns, aged 23, eldest son of Patrick Brady M, of Ballyshannon, co
[Donegal, Solicitor, deceased.

,, 16 ARTHUR PATTON, B A., Trinity College, Dublin, aged 30, eldest son of Rev
[George Augustus Frederick P, of Rathmines, deceased

,, 17 DAVID WILSON, aged 19, of Glasgow University, selected candidate for Indian
[Civil Service, only son of David W, of Glasgow, cabinet-maker

,, ,, ARTHUR EDWIN PRESTON, aged 31, Assistant Overseer of Abingdon, Graduate
of the University of London, second surviving son of John P, of Abingdon,
[Berks, deceased, Assistant Overseer of the Poor

,, ,, THOMAS MOFFITT STEVENS, of Christ Church, Oxford, tutor at St John's
School, Leatherhead, aged 23, only son of Thomas Warner S, late of
[Greenwich, artist, deceased

,, ,, HENRY BRUCE PATMAN, aged 24, only son of Henry P, late of Mecklenburgh
[Square, builder, deceased

1884

Jan 10 JOHN WILLIAM McCARTHY, under-graduate of Dublin University, late Secretary to the Japanese Minister of Foreign Affairs, aged 30, eldest son of
[Jeremiah M, of Cork, merchant

,, 12 FREDERICK ARTHUR GREER, of Aberdeen University, aged 20, second son of
[Arthur G, of Liverpool, metaller

,, 19 ARTHUR BEAUMONT WELLS, aged 20, second son of William W, of Grenada,
[M D, Aberdeen

,, 23 CHARLES RIDGER, M A. Oxon, B A London University, Head Master of Roan
[Schools, Greenwich, aged 37, only son of Joseph R, of London, clerk

,, 24 JOSEPH McGRATH, B A London, and a Student of King's Inns, aged 25, eldest
[surviving son of Pierce M, of Bagnalstown, co Carlow, merchant

2 H

1884.

Jan. 25   PATRICK JAMES NOLAN, of Trinity College, Dublin, and a Student of King's
[Inns, aged 22, third son of James N , of Limerick, merchant

,, 28   HORACE BERTRAM NELSON, B A , Worcester College, Oxford, aged 23
younger son of Sir Thomas James N , of Hampton Wick, Middlesex,
[Solicitor to the Corporation of the city of London

Feb. 27   WILLIAM NAYLOR VALLANCE, aged 17½, only surviving son of William V , of
St John's, co Kent, Clerk of the Whitechapel Union and Superintendent
[Registrar

April 22   SAMUEL GREENIDGE, of St John's College, Cambridge, aged 21, eldest son of
[the Rev Nathaniel Heath G , of Barbados

May 12   JAMES O'DONNELL McLAUGHLIN, of Queen's University, Ireland, aged 32,
[fourth surviving son of William M , of Drimfries, co Donegal

June 16   CHARLES HENRY GLASCODINE, formerly a Solicitor, aged 42, second and only
[surviving son of Richard G , of Swansea, secretary

,, 18   JONATHAN CHRISTIAN, aged 22, second son of the Rt Hon Jonathan C , of
Ravenswell Bray, co Dublin, Privy Councillor and late Lord Justice of
[Appeal

Nov 3   FRANCIS McCARTHY, aged 22, fourth son of Jeremiah M , of Cork, merchant

1885

Jan 23   JAMES EMERSON SCOTT, of King's Inns, Ireland, and B A , Trinity College,
[Dublin, aged 28, eldest son of James Anderson S , of Dublin, journalist

April 14   ROBERT STEWART JOHNSTONE, B A , Trinity College, Dublin, aged 29, second
[son of William John J , of Dunesk, Belfast, co Antrim, J P

,, ,,   CHARLES HERBERT SMITH, sometime a Solicitor, aged 22, fifth son of Thomas
[S , of York city, merchant

,, 16   WILLIAM SCOTT THOMPSON, B A., Queen's College, Oxon, aged 23, eldest son
[of Robert Thompson, of Mere Oaks, Wigan, co Lancaster, J P

,, ,,   MICHAEL MURPHY, Undergraduate of the Royal University, Ireland, Cork,
[aged 20, third son of Michael M , of Cork, wine merchant

June 3   JAMES WILLIAM ROSS BROWN, journalist, aged 28, second son of James B ,
[deceased, of Douglas, Isle of Man, newspaper proprietor.

,, ,,   GEORGE LESLIE BANNERMAN, journalist, aged 28, fifth son of Alexander B , of
[Carnoustie co Forfar, gent

,, 20   SAMUEL JOSEPH GOLDSTON, journalist, aged 23, third surviving son of
[George G , of Clapham Road, Surrey, commercial traveller

,, 18   JAMES KNOTT, shipowner, aged 30, eldest son of Matthew K , of North Shields,
[wine merchant

Aug 25   NEVILLE SKOTTOWE PARKER, undergraduate, St. John's College, Cambridge,
aged 20, elder son of John George Newsome P , of Passage West, co
[Cork

Oct 28   MOSES JONES, aged 28, seventh son of James J , of Bridgend, co. Glamorgan,
[inland revenue officer.

,, 31   WILLIAM HENRY ELDRIDGE, B A , London University, aged 27 (schoolmaster),
[eldest son of John E , of Cheltenham, coachbuilder

Nov 2   WILLIAM HENRY DUMSDAY, Clerk in the Local Government Board Office,
[aged 30, eldest son of Robert D , of Hammersmith, deceased

,, 5   HENRY CHARLES HUGHES, B A , Royal University of Ireland, aged 24½,
[third son of Nicholas H , of Coleraine, co Londonderry

1885

Nov 7. WILFRED KING PORTER, undergraduate of Balliol College, Oxford, aged 20, [ninth son of Robert Tindal P , late of Madras Civil Service, deceased

„ 16 GEORGE VARDEN FITTOCK, journalist, aged 26, second son of William Henry
1886 [F , deceased, late Her Britannic Majesty's Consul in China

Jan 23 JOHN KYRLE FREDERICK CLEAVE, B A , Hertford College, Oxon, aged 24, [eldest son of John James Cleave, of the Inner Temple, Barrister-at-Law

Feb 24 FRANCIS ERNEST BRADLEY, of London University, and Undergraduate of Victoria University (Manchester), aged 23, second son of Nathaniel B , of Hulme, co Lanc , gent., Fellow of the Chemical Society of England

May 4 FREDERICK REDMOND, B A , Trinity College, Dublin, and of King's Inns, aged 24, fourth surviving son of Philip R , of Kilmore Cottage, co [Armagh

„ 7 HENRY WINCH, aged 22, only son of Henry W , of 6 King's Bench Walk, [Temple, Barrister-at-Law

„ 12 WILLIAM JAMES BYRNE, graduate of Trinity College, Dublin, aged 23, eldest [son of William Louis B , of Loughrea, co. Galway, retired magistrate

„ 22 EDMUND FRANCIS VESEY KNOX, of Keble College, Oxford, aged 21, eldest son of Vesey Edmond K , of Shimnah, Newcastle, co Down, late 52nd [Light Infantry

July 5. JAMES DAVIS, aged 33, late a Solicitor, son of Hyman, of London, Artist

Oct 14 COOLS THEODORE LARTIGUE, aged 19, eldest son of Ranald, of Castries, [St Lucia, Notary Public

Nov 3 IVOR BOWEN, aged 24, eldest son of Rev John Bowen Jones, B A , dropped the [name of Jones, Sept , 1883

„ „ MONTAGU SHARPE, aged 30, of the Civil Service and J P , co Middlesex, only [son of Benjamin, of Hanwell Park, Middlesex, J.P , Commander R N

„ 5 CYRUS PRUDHOMME DAVID, aged 19, eldest son of Ernest, of Trinidad, Planter, [deceased

„ „ ERNEST BROWN BOWEN-ROWLANDS, aged 20, eldest son of William, M P , [Q C , and a Bencher

„ 6 ARTHUR EDWARD HUGHES, B A Sidney Sussex College, Cambridge, Senior Mathematical Master, County School, Bedford, aged 29, third son of [Robert, of Tronwell Corris, co Merioneth, gent.

„ 11 EDWARD WILLIAM COX, aged 21, Associate in Arts, University of Oxford, [eldest son of Edward, of Kentish Town, London, Esq

„ 13 CHARLES EDWARD MACDERMOT, B A , Trinity College, Dublin, aged 23, eldest son of The MacDermot, Q C , of Coolnavin, co Sligo, D.L , and a [Bencher of King's Inns, Dublin

„ 15 JAMES SHANKS, aged 27, eldest son of Peter Martin, of London, letter [founder.

„ „ CHARLES WILLIAM SEWELL, of Oxford University, aged 28, only son of William, [of Bideford, Devon, gent

„ 19 WILLIAM CLARKE HALL, Scholar of Christ Church, Oxford, aged 20, eldest son [of William H , of Folkestone, Kent, clerk

1887

Jan 12. ALFRED JAMES SAWYERR, aged 26, eldest son of Thomas John, of Sierra Leone, [merchant.

„ 21 JOHN ERNEST BAGRAM, aged 19, second son of George, of Calcutta, Esq.

2 I

1887.

April 16.   CHARLES EDWARD ERNEST DAMIAN, aged 21, of London University eldest
[surviving son of Francis, of Trinidad, W I

,,   27   EDGAR MACDONALD ROBERTSON, aged 17, fifth son of Henry Finch R., of
[London, Esq.

May 11   JOHN ANDERSON, aged 29, of Aberdeen University, a Clerk in the Colonial
[Office, only son of John A, of Aberdeen, N B, Presbyterian missionary

June 8   HERBERT PARKER REED, Barrister-at-Law, of the Inner Temple, aged 36, only
[son of Herbert Adolphus, of London, Solicitor (ad eundem)

,,   9   FRANCIS STANHOPE HANSON, of Trinity College, Cambridge, aged 18, second son
[of Rt Hon Sir Reginald Hanson, Baronet, the Lord Mayor, 1886-7

,,   14   HAROLD COX, aged 27, second son of Homersham C, of Marlield House,
[Tonbridge, a Judge of County Courts

,,   18   MARK HELMORE, aged 34, eldest son of William H, of Forest Gate, Essex, Esq.

,,   ,,   LANCE BENTLEY, aged 40, Secretary Conservative Registration Association
(Knutsford division), only surviving son of William B, of Eccles, co
[Lancaster

Oct 28   JOHN HENRY BURTON, Civil Engineer, aged 25, eldest son of John Power B,
[late of Monkstown, Land Agent, co Dublin

Nov 3   BERNARD O'CONNOR, B A, D Med, M R C P, London, aged 38, third
[surviving son of William O, of London, D Med

,,   4   LLEWELLYN EVANS OLDING, aged 21, fourth son of William O, late of Brighton,
[schoolmaster, deceased

,,   8   WILLIAM ABRAM WOOLLEY, aged 39, late of Consular service, Japan, retired,
[eldest son of William W, of Bournemouth, Hants, Esq

,,   14   WILLIAM JOSEPH KENNY, of Consular Service, Japan, aged 28, eldest son
[of Patrick Joseph K., of Waterford Ireland, gent

,,   17   WILLIAM MADDEN, aged 34, sometime of Liverpool, solicitor, eldest surviving
[son of William M. (by second marriage), of Liverpool

,,   19   JAMES RICHARD ATKIN, demy of Magdalen College, Oxford, aged 19, eldest
[son of Robert Travers A, of Brisbane, journalist

Dec 20   ALFRED ISAAC TILLYARD, M A, St John's College, Cambridge, aged 35, eldest
[son of Isaac T, late of Norwich, gent, deceased

1888

Jan 14   WILLIAM BLACHE WILSON, aged 20, eldest surviving son of Thomas Bell W, of
[St. Andrews, Grenada, West Indies, planter

,,   ,,   DANIEL THOMAS-TUDOR, aged 21, third son of Timothy (Thomas), of Lampeter,
co Cardigan, merchant, deceased (assumed additional surname of Tudor
[by deed poll 26 July, 1887)

,   ,,   OWEN COOK, of H M. Civil Service, Hereford, aged 29, youngest son of
[John C, of Chesham, Bucks, gent

,   19   WILLIAM DURIE, aged 40, an Undergraduate of London University, and of
H M Customs, Londonderry, Ireland, only surviving son of William
[Shand D, of Arbroath, co Fife, N B, merchant

,,   20   WILLIAM KENDALL, aged 19, only son of Thomas Mitchelson, late of Pickering,
[Yorks, J P, deceased

,,   21   ROGER CHARNOCK RICHARDS, aged 47, fourth son of John R, of Preston,
[co Lanc.

,,   ,,   WILLIAM JOHN GORDON, aged 37, eldest son of Thomas G, of Diamond
[Londonderry, Ireland, merchant

1888

April 4   WILLIAM HENRY CROMIE, aged 34, a lieutenant in the army, eldest surviving
[son of Robert C , of Clough, co Down

,, 12.   ALEXANDER MACDONALD THOMSON, aged 24, M A Aberdeen, and a Hong
Kong Cadet, attached to H M Colonial Office, second son of John T ,
[of Tarriff, co Aberdeen, schoolmaster

,, 28   JOHN ALFRED WYLLIE, aged 33, Captain Madras Staff Corps, eldest son of
[James Shaw W , Examiner of Postal Accounts, Edinburgh

,, 30   WILLIAM RICHARD VALE, aged 20, of the University of Melbourne, second
surviving son of William Mountford Kinsey V , of Melbourne, Australia,
[Barrister-at-Law of this Inn

May 2   FREDERICK WILLIAM LANGSTON, aged 28, of H M Civil Service, eldest son
[of Frederick William L , of London, engraver

,, ,,   SYDNEY GOWER WOODS, aged 28, Chief Clerk of the Treasury, Belize, British
Honduras, eldest son of Sydney Christie Nicholson W , also of Belize,
[deceased

June 9   THOMAS EDWARD MANSFIELD, aged 34, lately a Solicitor of Barrow-in-Furness,
[eldest son of James M , of Donington, co Linc , farmer

Oct 23   THOMAS BAILEY CLEGG, of Victoria, Australia, journalist, aged 30, eldest son
[of Thomas C , of Ballarat, merchant

,, 26   GEORGE EUGENE YARROW, D Med , aged 52, eldest surviving son of George
[Y , late of Shoreditch, London, deceased

Nov 3   SASI BHUSHAN SARDADIICARY, aged 22, only son of Ras Govinda S , of
[Bengal, India

,, 5   HAROLD HARDY, B A Oxford, aged 24, only son of John Brathwaite H , of
Bickley, Kent, Lieut -Col R A (retired), and Secretary of English
[Church Union

,, 6   ANTHONY GORDON DAMIAN, of London University, aged 18, third son of
[Francis D , of Trinidad, Solicitor

,, 8   TOM CUTTER, aged 36, fifth son of John Barclay C , of Knutsford,
[Cheshire, Clerk to the Guardians

,, 9   JAMES RICHARD SEANOR, of London University, and LL B Victoria
University, Manchester, aged 23, second son of Matthias S , of Man-
[chester, Architect

,, 13   FULLARTON JAMES, B A Cantab , aged 24, fifth son of Francis Edward J , late
of Kerelaw, Stevenston, Ayrshire, N B , West India Merchant, deceased

,, 14   WILLIAM HUGH STEVENSON, aged 34, some time an Attorney of the Court of
Queen's Bench and a Solicitor of Supreme Court of Judicature in England,
[son of Rev William Ramson S , of Carrington, Nottingham

,, ,,   GANPAT RAI, aged 25, late of the Law School, Lahore, India, eldest son of
[Dial Mal, Government servant, a reader

,, 17   WILLIAM MUIR, aged 35, M A Queen's University, Ireland, and of Balliol
[College, Oxford, eldest son of William M , of Glasgow, manufacturer

,, 22   CLAUDIUS ERNEST WRIGHT, aged 25, B A Durham University, eldest son of
[Joseph George W , of Sierra Leone, West Coast, Africa

,, 23   JOHN STEWART BAIRD, aged 34, of Queen's College, Oxford, eldest son of
[Hugh B , of Erdington, co Warwick

1889

Jan. 11   CHARLES ERNEST BRANCH, aged 23, B A Durham University, eldest son of
[Rev (Samuel Fitt) B , Hon Canon, St Vincent

make room for Edward Martin whom Palmer had dispossessed), 1660   He had a dispensation to hold the Gresham Professorship, 1660 (Aug. 1), but it was revoked 1661 (May 26)   He was silenced in 1662, but afterwards conformed, and was admitted to the Vicarage of Great St Helen's, London, 1666   Died, 1573. [B A 1626-7   M A 1630   B.D 1637.   D D 1649   D D of Oxford, 1652]

DEAN NICHOLAS BERNARD, June 17, 1651

Pensioner of Emmanuel College, Cambridge, 1617   Dean of Kilmore, 1627   Rector of St Peter's, Drogheda, 1627-8   Chaplain to Abp Ussher   .   Dean of Ardagh, June 22, 1637   Prebendary of Dromore, July 12, 1637   Chaplain to Oliver Cromwell, and one of his Almoners   *Preacher of Gray's Inn,* 1651   Rector of Whitchurch-cum-Marbury, cos Salop and Chester, July 16, 1660   Died October 15th, 1661   [B A 1620-1   M A 1622   M A of Oxford, 1628   D D of Dublin, 16   D D of Cambridge, 1650   D D of Oxford, 1657]

BISHOP JOHN WILKINS, January 28, 1660-1

Commoner of New Inn Hall, 1627, and afterwards of Magdalen Hall, Oxford   Chaplain to Lord Say   Chaplain to the Count Palatine of the Rhine,   Vicar of Fawsley, Northamptonshire, 1637   Took the " Solemn League and Covenant," at the breaking out of the Civil Wars   .   Appointed Warden of Wadham College, Oxford, by " a Committee for reforming the University," 1648   Appointed Master of Trinity College, Cambridge, 1659, by Richard Cromwell, whose aunt—the sister of Oliver Cromwell—he had married   Ejected from the Mastership of Trinity at the Restoration   Prebendary of York, 1660 (Aug 11)   Dean of Ripon, 1660 (August 31)   (He retained this dignity to his death)   *Preacher of Gray's Inn,* 1660-1   Rector of Cranford, Middlesex, 1661   Rector of St Lawrence, Jewry, 1662   One of the Founders of the Royal Society, 1662   Rector of Polebrook, Northamptonshire, 1666   Prebendary of St Paul's, 1667   Bishop of Chester, 1668   Died, 1672   [B A 1631   M A 1634   B D 1648   D D 1649

Mr ABRAHAM CALEY, June 13, 1662

Sizar of St John's College, Cambridge, 1622   Fellow 1629-30   Rector of Rayleigh, Essex, 1643-4   *Preacher of Gray's Inn,* 1662   Ejected from his Rectory in August of that year, and probably ceased at the same time to preach at Gray's Inn, for his successor was elected in November   Died, some time before March 13, 1678 9   [B A 1625-6   M A 1629   B D 1637]

Dr ZACHARY CRADOCK, November 12, 1662

Pensioner of Emmanuel College, Cambridge, 1647   Fellow of Queen's, Cambridge, 1654, and re admitted (as having been appointed during the Commonwealth) at the Restoration in 1660   *Preacher of Gray's Inn,* 1662   Chaplain in Ordinary to the King,   Prebendary of Chichester, and immediately afterwards Canon Residentiary, by Royal Letters Mandatory, 1669-70   Chaplain to the British Residents at Lisbon, 1669-70   Fellow of Eton, 1671   Provost of Eton, 1680-1   Died, 1695   [B.A 1650-1   M A 1654   B D 1661   D D 1666]

Dr WILLIAM CLAGETT, February 7, 1678-9

Pensioner of Emmanuel College, Cambridge, 1660   Lecturer of St Mary's, Bury St Edmund's, 1672   *Preacher of Gray's Inn,* 1678-9   Chaplain in ordinary to the King, 1677   Lecturer of St Michael Bassinghaugh (Basinghall)   Rector of Farnham Royal, Bucks, 1683   Died, 1688   [B A 1663-4   M A 1667   D D 1683]

ARCHBISHOP WILLIAM WAKE, May 7, 1688

Student of Christchurch, Oxford, 1672   *Preacher of Gray's Inn,* 1688   Deputy Clerk of the Closet to the King, 1688.   Canon of Christchurch, 1689   Rector of St James, Westminster, 1693   Dean of Exeter, 1701.   Bishop of Lincoln, 1705

Archbishop of Canterbury, 1715-6   Died 1736-7   [B A 1676   M A 1679. B and D D 1689]

Dr THOMAS RICHARDSON, February 11, 1694-5

Sizar of Pembroke Hall, Cambridge, 1674-5   Fellow of Eton, 1684   *Preacher of Gray's Inn*, 1694-5   Prebendary of Ely, 1697-8   Master of Peterhouse, Cambridge, 1699   Chaplain in Ordinary to the King, 1716   Died 1733   [B A 1678-9   M A , 1682   D D 1698]

DEAN ROBERT MOSS, July 11, 1698

Sizar of Benet or Corpus Christi College, Cambridge, 1682.   Fellow, 1686   One of the University Preachers, 1693.   *Preacher of Gray's Inn*, 1698   Preacher Assistant at St James', Westminster, 1699 1700   Chaplain in Ordinary to the King, 1701   Lecturer of St Lawrence, Jewry, 1708   Dean of Ely, 1713   Rector of Gilston, Herts, 1714   Died, 1729.   [B A 1685-6.   M A 1689   B D 1696   D D 1705]

Dr WILLIAM NORTON, May 13, 1729

Scholar of King's College, Cambridge, 1705   Fellow, 1708   Rector of Walkerne, Herts, 1722   Vicar of Deptford, Kent, 1728   *Preacher of Gray's Inn*, 1729   Died 1731   [B A 1709.   M.A 1713   D.D 1728]

ARCHDEACON HENRY STEBBING, November 2, 1731

Sizar of Catherine Hall, Cambridge, 1705   Fellow, 1710   Rector of Rickinghall Inferior, Suffolk, circa 1714   Rector of Garboldisham, Norfolk, 1726   Lecturer of St Mary-le-Bow, London, 1731   *Preacher of Gray's Inn*, 1731   Chaplain in Ordinary to the King, 1731-2   Archdeacon of Wilts, 1735   Chancellor of the Diocese of Sarum, 1739   Boyle Lecturer, 1747-1749   Died, 1763   [B A 1708-9 M A 1712   D D 1730]

Dr HENRY STEBBING, November 21, 1749

Pensioner of Catherine Hall, Cambridge, 1735   Fellow, 1739   Rector of Coton, co Cambridge, 1744   Rector of Gimmingham and Trunch, Norfolk, 1748   *Preacher of Gray's Inn*, 1749   Chaplain in Ordinary to the King, 1757   Taxor of the University , 1759   F R S , 1765   F S A 1769   Died, 1787   [B A 1738-9 M A 1742   D D 1759]

BISHOP WALKER KING, May 28, 1787

Scholar of Corpus Christi College, Oxford, 1769   Probationary Fellow, 1778   Fellow, 1780   *Preacher of Gray's Inn*, 1787   Prebendary of Peterborough, 1794   (He retained this dignity till his death)   Chaplain to Earl Fitzwilliam, while Lord-Lieutenant of Ireland   Prebendary of Westminster, 1808, but resigned this Prebend on becoming Bishop of Rochester, 1809   Died, 1827   [B.A 1771   M.A 1775 B and D D 1788]

Dr. MATTHEW RAINE, June 7, 1809

Pensioner of Trinity College, Cambridge, 1778   16th Wrangler at B A, 1782.   Members' Prizeman, 1783, and again in 1784   Fellow, 1783   Fourth College Sub-Lecturer, 1785.   Chief Sub-Lecturer, 1787   Head Master of Charterhouse School, 1791   F R.S 1803   *Preacher of Gray's Inn*, 1809   Rector of Little Hallingbury, Essex, 1810   Died, 1811   [B A 1782   M.A. 1785   B D 1794 D D. 1799

Mr. WILLIAM MANSFIELD, November 27, 1811

Pensioner of Queen's College, 1800, and afterwards of Trinity College, Cambridge. 12th Senior Optime at B A., 1804   Travelling Bachelor, 1804   *Preacher of Gray's Inn*, 1811   Rector of Milton Bryant, Bedfordshire, 1811   Rector of Collyweston, Northamptonshire, 1812   Died, 1854   [B A 1804   M A 1807]

Mʀ JOHN HONYWOOD RANDOLPH, June 13, 1815

Student of Christ Church, Oxford, 1809   2nd Class sub lin in Litt Humanior at B A, 1812   *Preacher of Gray's Inn,* 1815   Rector of Burton Coggles, Lincolnshire, 1816   Chaplain of the British Factory at St Petersburg, 1818   Rector of Fobbing, Essex, 1822   Prebendary of St Paul's 1822, and in the same year Rector of Northolt, Middlesex, which in 1835 he exchanged for the Chapel of St Leonard's-on-the Sea   Rector of Mistley with Bradfield and Manningtree, Essex, 1839   Rector of Sanderstead, Surrey, 1845   Proctor in Convocation of Canterbury from 1852 to 1868   Died, 1868   [B A 1812   M.A 1815]

Dʀ GEORGE SHEPHERD, November 12, 1817

Commoner of University College, Oxford, 1784. Scholar, 1788   Fellow, 1794. College Tutor, 1798-1808   Public Examiner in the University, 1803-1804, and also 1807-1808   Select Preacher in the University, 1808, 1814, and 1825   Rector of St Bartholomew-by-the-Exchange, in the City of London, 1807   *Preacher of Gray's Inn,* 1817   Proctor in Convocation of Canterbury from 1833 to 1841   Chaplain to Lord Tenterden   Died, 1849   [B A 1788   M A 1790   B D 1807.   D D 1820

ARCHDEACON JAMES AUGUSTUS HESSEY, January 16, 1850.

Probationary Fellow of St John's College, Oxford, 1832   Fellow 1835   1st Class in Litt Humanior at B A, 1836   Vicar of Helidon, Northamptonshire, 1839, but resigned it in the same year   College Logic Lecturer, 1839-1842   Examiner for the Hertford Latin Scholarship at Oxford in 1842 and 1844   Public Examiner in the University, 1842-1844   Head Master of Merchant Taylors' School, 1845-1870   Select Preacher in the University of Oxford, 1849   *Preacher of Gray's Inn,* 1850   Bampton Lecturer, 1860.   Prebendary of St Paul's, 1860-1875   Grinfield Lecturer in the Septuagint in the University of Oxford (for two years), June, 1865   Reappointed Grinfield Lecturer (for two years), June, 1867   Examining Chaplain to the Bishop of London, 1870   Boyle Lecturer, 1871-1873   Classical Examiner, Indian Civil Service, 1872-1874.   Governor of Repton School, 1874, of Aldenham School, 1875, of St Paul's School, 1876, of Highgate School, 1876   Appointed Examiner in the Honors' Schools of Theology, Oxford, 1875, but resigned without acting   Archdeacon of Middlesex, 1875   Select Preacher in the University of Cambridge, 1878 and 1879. [B.A. 1836   M A 1840.   B D. 1845   B and D C L 1846   D D of the University of the South, Tennessee, 1884]

Dʀ ALFRED THEOPHILUS LEE, November 5, 1879

Pensioner of Christ's College, Cambridge, 1849   Foundation Scholar, 1850   Porteus Gold Medallist, 1853   Vicar of Elson, Gosport, Hants, 1856   Rector of Ahoghill, Diocese of Connor, Ireland, 1858   Rural Dean, 1860   Chaplain to the Duke of Abercorn, the Lord-Lieutenant of Ireland, 1866   Domestic Chaplain to the Marquis of Donegal, 1857   Proctor for the Clergy of Connor in the National Synod, 1869   Clerical Assessor in the Bishop's Court, 1870   Secretary to the Church Defence Institution, and to the Tithe Redemption Trust, 1871   *Preacher of Gray's Inn,* 1879   Died, 1883   [B A 1853   M A 1856, Cambridge   LL D of Dublin, 1866   D C L of Oxford, 1867.]

Dʀ THOMAS HENRY STOKOE, December 21, 1883.

Lord Crewe's Exhibitioner of Lincoln College, Oxford, 1851   1st Class in Litt Humanior at B.A., 1855.   Denyer Theological Prizeman, 1859.   2nd Master of Clifton College, 1861-1863   Head Master of the Grammar School and Perpetual Curate of Holy Trinity Church, Richmond, Yorkshire, 1863-1871   Head Master of Reading School, 1871-1877   Head Master of King's College School, 1880   Preacher at the Foundling Hospital, 1883   *Preacher of Gray's Inn,* 1883   [B A. 1855   M A 1857   B and D D 1871]

INDEX TO ADMISSIONS.

H R H Prince Arthur William Patrick Albert, Duke of Connaught and of Strathearn, and Earl of Sussex, K G , K T , K P , G C S I , G C M.G , the third son of Her Majesty Queen Victoria, was admitted a member, and was called to the bar and to the bench 4 July, 1881, pp ix , 491

Abbott,
1626 George, 177
1835 George, 453
1833 Henry B., 447
1635 John, 207
1804 John, 405
1633 Maurice, 198
1612 Robert, 129
1818 Thomas, 421

Abdy,
1614 Christopher, 141

A'Beckett,
1828 Gilbert A ,435
1877 William A , 488

Abell,
1555 Robert, 24

Abingdon,
1581 Thomas, 59

Abnet,
1585 William, 68

Abraham,
1617 Richard, 145

Acclom,
1601 William, 102

Acheson,
1630 Patrick, 190
1834 James G , 449

Acklam,
1714 Richard, 360

Acland,
1820 Gideon, 423

Acton,
1637 John, 214
1678 Richard, 327
1674 Samuel, 319
1607 William, 119
1650 William 252

Adam,
1635 William, 207
1817 Adam Fitz, 420

Adams,
1866 Alexander Y , 482
1871 Francis C , 484
1704 John, 354
1826 John, 432
1795 Philip, 400
1826 Richard W G , 431
1654 Thomas, 266
1672 Thomas, 314
1642 William, 235
1654 William, 270
1812 William C , 415

Addams,
1639 Richard, 223
1638 Robert, 218

Addams (con),
1646 William, 241

Adderley,
1652 Edmund E , 261
1651 Richard, 258
1633 Thomas, 198

Addington,
1605 John, 109

Addis,
1811 Francis, 414

Addison,
1635 John, 208
1684 John, 335
1848 John, 472

Adeane,
1648 Ralph, 248

Adwyck,
1592 George, 80
1585 Richard, 68

Ady,
1668 John, 305
1667 Thomas, 303
1615 Nicholas, 137

Adyes,
1555 William, 26

Agar,
1653 Andrew, 264
1691 John, 343
1697 John, 348
1677 Lawrence, 325
1705 Lawrence, 355
1658 Thomas, 285
1673 William, 316

Agarde,
1608 Arthur, 117

Aglionby,
1656 John, 276

Aher.
1837 Henry, 456

Ainge,
1753 Edward, 379
1788 Edward, 393
1835 James, 452
1774 William, 388

Ainslie,
1779 Montague F , 390
1845 Montague M , 468

Akehurst,
1644 Alexander, 239

Alabaster,
1618 William, 151

Alban,
1539 Richard, 13

Albani,
1841 Francis, 462

Alcazar,
1878 Henry A , 489

Alceny,
1582 Edward, 60

Alcock,
1797 George, 401
1846 James W , 469
1583 John, 63
1825 John C , 430
1546 Robert, 18
1567 William, 36

Alday,
1839 Edward, 460

Aldermanus,
1535 Robert, 11

Aldersey,
1691 Robert, 342
1622 Thomas, 166
1654 Thomas, 269

Aldham,
1646 John, 241

Aldhouse,
1612 Robert, 140

Aldred,
1875 Philip F , 486

Aldrich,
1537 Robert, 12

Aldridge,
1617 Edward, 146
1785 John, 392

Aldus,
1771 Ralph, 387

Aldworth,
1656 John, 279

Alee,
1557 John, 27
1640 William, 225

Alexander,
1725 James, 367
1686 Ratcliffe, 338
1661 Richard, 291
1640 Thomas, 224
1662 Waldegrave, 293

Alford,
1601 Henry, 100

Alfrey,
1602 Richard, 103
1638 Richard, 286
1633 Thomas, 200

Alibond,
1672 Pompey, 315
1663 Richard, x , 295

Alington,
1592 Charles, 80
1594 George, 84
1615 George, 136

Alington (con),
1628 Henry, 184
1592 Hugh, 81
1569 James, 39
1778 Marmaduke, 389
1551 William, 21

Alker,
1834 Henry L , 449

Allanson,
1641 Charles, 231
1629 John, 187
1657 Ralph, 281

Allen,
1612 Abraham, 131
1816 Edward, 418
1663 Francis, 296
1827 Frederick, 433
1524 George, 4
1790 George, 395
1744 Henry, 376
15-2 John, 3
1546 John, 18
1575 John, 48
1632 John, 195
1638 John, 216
1645 John, 240
1656 John, 279
1784 John, 392
1541 Ralph, 15
1573 Richard, 45
1835 Robert 452
1851 Robert M , 473
1624 Thomas, 172
1638 Thomas, 216
1674 Thomas, 318
1736 Thomas, 372
1601 Walter, 101
1634 William, 204
1837 William, 456
1837 William, 456
1795 William E., 400

Allestree,
1674 Charles, 320
1623 George, 170
1671 Thomas, 312
1618 William, 152
1659 William, 288

Allett,
1571 Richard, 41

Alley,
1838 Oliver W , 458

Alleyn,
1625 Barkeley, 175
1620 Edmund, 159
1620 George, 159
1642 John, 234

Ayscough (*con*),
1655 Hugh, 273
1633 James, 198
1639 James, 222
1617 John, 147
1575 Richard, 48
1577 Roger, 51
1599 Thomas, 97
1825 Thomas, 430
1583 William, 63
1622 William, 167
1657 William, 284
1667 William, 301
Ayton,
1651 John, 259
1655 Robert, 275
Babington,
1541 Michael, 15
1661 Philip, 292
1691 Thomas, 343
1796 Thomas R , 401
Babthorpe,
1599 William, 98
Bach, or Bauch,
— Alexander, 1
Backhouse,
1572 Samuel, 44
Backwell,
1720 Barnaby, 364
1730 Richard, 370
Bacon,
1576 Anthony, 48
1586 Edmund, 69
1616 Edmund, 144
1566 Edward, 35
1574 Edward, 47
1731 Edward, 370
1576 Francis, x , 48
1608 Francis, x , 119
1613 Francis, 133
1618 Francis, 151
1634 Francis, 205
1656 Francis, 278
1708 Francis, 356
1828 Francis, 437
1644 Henry, 238
1586 James, 69
1822 James, 426
1534 John, 11
1620 John, 158
1597 Mathias, 91
1562 Nathaniel, 31
1611 Nathaniel, 128
1611 Nathaniel, 139
1651 Nathaniel, 257
1655 Nathaniel, 275
1664 Nathaniel, 298
1731 Nathaniel, 370
1532 Nicholas, x , 9
1562 Nicholas, 31
1608 Nicholas, 116
1621 Nicholas, 164
1639 Nicholas, 222
1639 Nicholas, 222
1647 Nicholas, 243
1608 Philip, 116
1657 Philip, 282
1646 Robert, 242
1544 Thomas, 17
1547 Thomas, 19

Bacon (*con*),
1627 Thomas, 180
1634 Thomas, 205
1640 Thomas, 226
1679 Walter, 328
1628 William, 185
Bagenall,
1583 Ambrose, 62
1700 Richard, 351
1598 Samuel, Knt , 93
Bagg,
1631 James (Knt), 191
Baggs,
1703 Isham, 353
1677 John, 325
Bagot,
1666 Arden, 300
1838 Bernard W , 457
1805 James J , 407
1638 John, 220
1678 John, 326
Bagram,
1887 John E , 495
Bagshaw,
1652 Edward, 260
1665 Henry, 299
1682 Henry, 332
1687 John, 339
Baguley,
1680 Nevill, 328
1692 William, 343
Bailey,
1793 Charles J , 397
1652 John, 261
Bailie,
1828 James, 436
Baily,
1805 Francis, 408
Bainbridge,
1757 Forster, 381
1640 Francis, 227
1568 Robert, 38
1649 Thomas, 251
Bainbrigge,
1847 William A., 471
Baines,
1669 John, 307
1632 Robert, 195
Baird,
1888 John S , 497
Baker,
1622 Alexander, 165
1581 Audley, 60
1640 Audley, 227
1658 Charles, 286
1865 Charles, 481
1620 Edward, 161
1655 Frederick, 274
1655 Gregory, 272
1640 Henry, 227
1573 John, 45
1594 John, 84
1649 John, 251
1651 John, 257
1844 John, 466
1556 Leonard, 27
1826 Matthew, 433
1613 Oliver, 140
1568 Richard, 38

Baker (*con*),
1655 Robert, 275
1703 Robert, 353
1798 Robert, 402
1663 Samuel, 295
1553 Thomas, 24
1578 Thomas, 53
1585 Thomas, 68
1618 Thomas (Sir), 152
1830 Thomas H , 439
1561 William, 30
1638 William, 220
Bakewell,
1824 Robert, 429
Baldock,
1669 Henry, 307
1644 Robert, 238
Baldwen,
1791 John, x , 395
Baldwer,
1606 James, 113
1632 Richard, 196
Baldwin,
1573 ———, 46
1824 Henry, 428
1610 John 124
1628 Ralph, 185
Bale,
1648 James, 250
1682 John, 331
1629 Thomas, 143
1616 Valentine, 139, 145
Balfour,
1631 William, 191
Balguy,
1668 Henry, 204
1608 John, 127
1656 John, 277
1576 Thomas, 49
1613 Thomas, 140
Balham,
1534 John, 2
Ball,
1596 Bartholomew, 90
1606 Edward, 112
1818 Francis, 421
1610 George, 124
1840 George, 461
1825 Henry, 430
1827 James B 434
1839 John Thomas, 459
1720 Joseph, 364
1845 Nicholas, 468
1571 Thomas, 42
1796 Thomas, 401
1654 William, 266
1713 William, 359
1875 William E , 486
Ballachey,
1812 George B , 415
Ballard,
1742 Charles, 376
1583 Henry, 64
1633 Richard, 202
1639 Richard, 222
1588 Thomas, 72
1621 Thomas, 163
1632 Thomas, 197

Ballett,
1650 William, 253
Ballment,
1810 Robert, 413
Balls,
1732 John, 371
Balthropp,
1627 Richard, 143
Bamburgh,
1591 Thomas, 79
Bamford,
1580 Lionel, 55
1696 William, 348
Banaster,
1580 ———, 56
1640 Alexander, 226
1596 Christopher, 90
1592 Henry, 79
1622 Henry, 168
1586 Richard, 69
1604 Richard, 110
Banbury,
1883 George A , 492
Bancrofte,
1589 Richard, 74
1624 Thomas, 171
Bangham,
1527 Edward, 5
Banister,
1842 Henry, 465
Banke,
1607 John, 119
Bankes,
1675 Caleb, 320
1631 Edward, 192
1796 Henry, 400
1634 James, 206
1653 Jerome, 264
1631 John, x , 192
1685 Leigh, 336
1829 Perceval, 439
1656 Ralph, 277
1585 Richard, 67
1613 Thomas, 132
1613 William, 132
1676 William, 323
1693 William, 345
Bannerman,
1885 George L , 494
Banyer,
1741 Edward, 375
Barber,
1646 Benet, 240
1805 Charles H , 408
1643 John, 237
1791 John, 396
1813 John, 416
1840 John, 462
1631 Robert, 193
1674 Samuel, 319
Barbour,
1712 Abraham, 358
Bard,
1593 George, 82
1619 John, 156
1664 Nathaniel, 298
1617 Richard, 147
1591 Thomas, 79
Barecroft,
1600 Thomas, 100

Conybeare,
1877 Charles A V , 488
Coniers,
1638 Christopher, 215
1606 Edward, 113
1582 John, 61
1610 John, 122
1634 John, 206
1638 Richard, 215
Coo,
1661 Christopher, 291
1662 William, 293
Coochman,
1654 John, 268
Cook,
1834 George W F , 448
1828 John R , 436
1888 Owen, 496
Cooke,
1588 Anthony, 66
1694 Cæsar, 340
1561 Charles, 30
1566 Charles, 35
1553 Edward, 24
1594 Edward, 87
1607 Edward, 114
1568 Henry, 39
1651 Isaac, 259
1629 James, 188
1821 James R , 425
1594 John, 87
1599 John, 97
1609 John, 122
1623 John, 171
1627 John, 182
1637 John, 214
1699 John, 350
1823 John 427
1835 John, 452
1657 Ralph, 280
1584 Richard, 65
1664 Richard, 297
1793 Richard, 397
1617 Robert, 146
1622 Robert, 166
1836 Robert, 453
1589 Thomas, 75
1620 Thomas, 157
1638 Thomas, 219
1654 Thomas, 269
1788 Thomas, 393
1528 William, 6
1553 William, 24
1575 William, 48
1592 William, 79
1636 William, 211
1648 William, 249
1649 Zachary, 252
Cookman,
1810 Edward, 413
Cooley,
1820 William, 423
Cooper,
1646 Cecil, 241
1690 Cecill, 342
1620 Drune, 162
1619 Godhelp, 155
1803 Henry, 405
1864 Henry G S , 481
1788 James, 393

Cooper (con),
1852 James, 475
1629 John, 189
1638 Peter, 218
1611 Roger, 129
1570 Walter, 40
1585 William, 67
1659 William, 287
1860 William B , 478
Coote,
1569 Nicholas, 39
1639 Thomas, 223
Cope,
1606 Anthony, 112
1656 Anthony, 279
1568 Edward, 38
1550 Erasmus, 20
1568 Erasmus, 38
1634 Erasmus, 205
1586 George, 69
1613 John, 133
1629 Richard, 187
1656 Walter, 279
Copledike,
1607 Thomas, 115
Copley,
1623 Christopher, 169
1614 Edward, 134
1681 Edward, 330
1624 John, 173
1651 Robert, 256
1532 William, 9
1594 William, 186
1649 William, 251
Coppin,
1651 John, 257
1651 Thomas, 257
Coppinger,
1575 Ambrose, 48
1611 Dominick, 125
1602 Francis, 103
1676 Henry, 323
1620 James, 161
Copson,
1562 Hugh, 31
Copwood,
1590 Abraham, 76
Corbett,
1645 Andrew, 239
1636 Edward, 211
1668 Edward, 305
1691 Erasmus, 343
1717 George, 362
1627 John, 181
1632 Robert, 196
1620 Roger, 160
1642 Thomas, 236
1871 Uvedale, 484
Corbin,
1611 Henry, 128
1615 Thomas, 136
1618 Thomas, 150
Corcar,
1695 Edward, 347
Corcoran,
1838 Michael E , 459
Cordell,
1636 Robert, 210
1534 William, 10

Coren,
1655 John, 273
Corlett,
1820 George, 423
Corley,
1838 John, 457
Cornewall,
1653 John, 265
Cornish,
1838 Thomas, 458
Cornthwaite,
1741 Thomas, 375
Cornwall,
1757 Charles W , 381
1682 James, 333
1568 William, 38
Cornwallis,
1671 Abraham, 313
1636 Bevercoates, 211
1682 Charles, 333
1657 Francis, 283
1610 Henry, 124
1609 John, 120
1647 John, 246
1600 Thomas, 99
1608 Thomas, 116
1673 Thomas, 316
1722 William, 365
Corry,
1613 Francis, 140
1630 Thomas, 189
1638 Thomas, 219
1674 Thomas, 318
1722 William, 365
Cosby,
1844 John H W , 467
Cosens,
1839 Frederick, 460
Cosgrave,
1676 Edmund, 322
Costa,
1618 Antonio da, 149
Costello,
1851 Nicholas, 473
1822 Thomas, 426
Costigan,
1830 John, 441
Cotchett,
1661 Thomas, 293
Cotgrave,
1560 James, 29
Cotter,
1674 Edmund, 319
Cotterell,
1814 Robert, 416
Cottingham,
1658 George, 286
Cottle,
1762 John, 383
Cotton,
1619 Alan, 155
1619 Bartholomew, 154
1631 Charles, 192
1752 Charles, 379
1620 David, 158
1640 Edmund, 226
1621 Edward, 162
1637 Edward, 214
1562 George, 31
1622 George, 167

Cotton (con.),
1572 Giles, 43
1537 Henry, 12
1609 Isaac, 121
1622 Isaac, 167
1670 Isaac, 310
1627 John 180
1640 John 228
1644 John 238
1675 John 321
1678 John, 327
1700 Lawrence, 351
1592 Robert, 81
1719 Samuel, 363
1555 Thomas, 26
1587 Thomas, 70
1612 Thomas, 130
1619 Thomas, 154
1598 W , 93
1734 William, 371
Coulson,
1813 Walter, 416
Coulthurst,
1603 Richard, 102
1674 Thomas, 319
1702 Thomas, 352
Coundon,
1676 Thomas, 323
Counsel,
1850 Laurance, 473
Court,
1763 Matthew, 383
Courtenay,
1640 Hatton, 224
1588 Humphrey, 74
1626 Humphrey, 177
1565 Philip, 34
Courthope,
1608 George, 119
1612 John, 130
1559 Richard, 28
1573 Richard, 44
1642 William, 235
1676 William, 323
Courtney,
1809 David R , 412
Coventon,
1857 William G , 477
Coverfield,
1543 Richard, 16
Covert,
1585 Alexander, 67
1531 George, 8
1536 Richard, 12
1540 Thomas, 14
1611 Thomas, 129
1567 Walter, 37
1608 Walter, 117
Cowan,
1837 Andrew, 457
Coward,
1874 John C. L , 486
Cowell,
1761 Benjamin 383
Cowie,
1883 Donald W G., 493
1859 Hugh, 478
Cowley,
1619 James, 156
1642 William, 235

Grice (con),
1539 Henry, 13
1664 Nicholas, 297
1566 Robert le, 35
1591 Robert le, 79
1581 William le, 59
Grieve,
1758 Davidson R , 382
Griffin,
1837 James, 456
1834 Nath , 450
1799 Robert, 404
Griffith,
1689 Alexander, 340
1627 Charles, 182
1829 Charles J , 438
1758 Edmund, 382
1641 Henry, 230
1825 Henry, ix , 430
1824 James, 428
1614 John, 135
1623 John, 170
1654 John, 268
1594 Nicholas, 84
1654 Owen, 269
1729 Peirce, 369
1594 Richard, 84
1561 Richard, 292
1641 Robert, 231
1648 Robert, 247
1581 Roger, 59
1669 Samuel, 306
1619 Thomas, 154
1662 Thomas, 293
1825 Thomas, 430
1681 William, 331
1685 William, 336
1829 William D , 437
Griffiths,
1852 Charles R , 474
1818 James, 421
1781 Robert, 391
1614 William, 134
Grigby,
1749 Joshua, 377
Grigson,
1638 Henry, 220
Grimsdich,
1599 John, 96
Grimston,
1593 Christopher, 82
1559 Edward, 28
1591 Edward, 78
1619 Edward, 154
1594 Harbottle, 86
1597 Henry, 92
1721 James, 364
1625 Richard, 176
1729 Robert, 369
1630 William, 190
Grimwood,
1772 John M , 387
Grindle,
1555 James, 11
Grise,
1664 Nicholas, 297
Grix,
1615 Robert, 141
Grom,
1622 William, 167

Groome,
1639 Benjamin, 221
Gros,
1614 Charles le, 135
1652 ——— le, 261
1632 Thomas le, 197
Grosvenor,
1616 Fulke, 139
1610 Gawyn, 123
1611 Walter, 129
1594 William, 86
1656 William, 279
Grove,
1570 Mathew, 40
1557 William, 27
Grover,
1524 Miles, 4
Growdon,
1730 Joseph, 369
Grubb,
1821 Edward, 425
1673 Walter, 316
Gruchy,
1870 William L de, 483
Gryme,
1620 George, 158
Grymes,
1628 Arthur, 185
Gude,
1817 Richard, 419
Guest,
1810 William, 412
Guevara,
1573 Francis, 45
1584 John, 65
Guinness,
1831 Robert R , 443
Guise,
1690 Christopher, 342
1655 John, 272
1683 William, 334
Gulford,
1532 Edward, 9
1555 Henry, 26
1570 Richard, 40
Gull,
1577 William, 51
Gulson,
1601 John, 102
1613 Richard, 140
1687 Richard, 339
1606 Theodore, 111
1621 Theodore, 162
Gulston,
1641 Edward, 233
1683 Edward, 334
1635 George, 209
1652 John, 261
1631 Joseph, 193
1609 Nath , 122
1687 Richard, 339
1652 Thomas, 261
Gun,
1652 John, 261
Gunion,
1877 Robert H , 489
Gunner,
1851 Charles J , 473
Gunter,
1536 James, 11

Gunter (con),
1753 James 379
1615 John, 141
1653 Thomas, 265
1681 Thomas, 330
Gunvile,
1554 Henry, 24
Gurdon,
1583 Bampton, 62
1614 John, 136
1726 Thornhagh, 367
Gurges,
1594 Mark A , 85
Guthrie,
1741 Patrick, 375
Guy,
1648 Henry, 249
1521 John, 3
Guyon,
1671 George, 312
Gwersey,
1572 William, 43
Gwillim,
1573 George, 45
1654 Lucius, 267
1648 St John, 249
1718 Thomas, 363
1657 William, 284
Gwynne,
1668 Daniel, 303
1634 Edward, 206
1670 Edward, 309
1656 Evan, 279
1823 George J , 427
1687 Howel, 339
1669 James, 308
1631 John, 193
1665 Marmaduke, 298
1663 Roderick, 296
1649 Rowland, 252
1657 Rowland, 284
1679 Rowland, 327
1633 William, 200, 202v
Gyll,
1595 John, 88
1590 Ralph, 77
Gyve,
1573 John, 46
Habergham,
1610 Matthew, 128
Hacker,
1669 Richard, 306
Hacket,
1653 Andrew, 263
1686 Andrew, 337
1019 Cuthbert, 155
1628 John, 183
1643 John, 238
1546 Nicholas, 18
1654 Roger, 268
Haddon,
1530 John, 7
1557 Walter, 27
Haggar,
1577 John, 50
1615 John, 138
1655 John, 271
1605 Robert, 109
Haggit,
1624 Humphrey, 172

Haggit (con),
1546 Nicholas, 18
Hague,
1787 James, 393
Hake,
1584 William, 65
Haldenby,
1623 Edward, 170
Hale,
1696 Bernard, x , 348
1613 Henry, 140
1634 John, 206
1827 John (Rev), 435
1732 Paggen, 371
1598 Richard, 93
1615 Richard, 138
1626 Richard, 177
1760 Richard, 381
1626 Robert, 177
1619 Rowland, 157
1681 Rowland, 331
1608 Symon, 119
1581 Thomas, 59
1586 William, 69
1651 William, 257
Hales,
1592 Bartholomew, 81
1567 Charles, 37
1612 Charles, 139
1617 Charles, 142
1536 Christopher, x
1525 Christopher, 2
1532 Edward, 9
1568 Edward, 39
1593 Edward, 82
1612 Edward, 131
1652 Edward, 259
1537 Humphrey, 13
1573 Humphrey, 40
1532 James (reader), 2
1551 James, x
1565 James, 34
1640 James, 242
1522 John, x
1530 John, 8
1563 John, 31
1578 John, 53
1600 John, 100
1609 John, 122
1611 John, 126, 131
1654 John, 298
1626 Samuel, 178
1592 Stephen, 83
1647 Stephen, 245
1597 Thomas, 91
1617 Walter, 142
1534 William, 10
1571 William, 41
1610 William, 124
Haley,
1708 Drope, 356
1669 Richard, 307
Halfhyde,
1641 George, 234
1645 George, 240
1652 George, 263
1700 George, 350
1657 Thomas, 284
Halford,
1645 Charles, 240

Halford (con)
1662 Henry, 294
1650 James, 254
1617 Richard, 146
1640 Thomas, 226
1681 Thomas, 331
1605 W., 108
1680 William, 330
Halghitt,
1546 Nicholas, 18
Haliday,
1600 Leonard, 99
Haling,
1642 Humphrey, 237
Hall,
1628 Alexander, 186
1556 Arthur, 26
1584 Cicel, 65
1793 Charles, 398
1665 Cornelius, 299
1534 Edward (reader), 2
1532 Edward, 9
1620 Edward, 160
1749 Enoch, 378
1646 Francis, 242
1877 Frederick T , 488
1740 Gabriel, 374
1607 Geoffrey, 115
1656 George, 276
1842 Giles, 464
1565 Henry, 34
1595 Henry, 88
1609 Henry, 127
1623 Henry, 169
1639 Henry, 220
1670 Henry, 309
1561 John, 29
1619 John, 155
1643 John, 238
1663 John, 285
1670 John, 309
1824 John C , 429
1881 John R C , 491
1615 Joseph, 138
1647 Mathew, 242
1589 Robert, 75
1615 Robert, 138
1639 Robert, 222
1521 Thomas, 3
1582 Thomas, 61
1616 Thomas, 139
1886 William C , 495
1530 William, 8
1541 William, 15
1603 William, 105
1677 William, 324
Halley,
1622 Thomas, 165
Halliwell,
1589 Hugh, 74
1655 James, 275
1654 Theophilus, 268
Halloway,
1654 Henry, 269
Hallows,
1690 Samuel, 34
Hallward,
1792 Thomas, 397
Haly,
1642 Humphrey, 237
1638 Nicholas, 220

Haly (con),
1696 Robert, 348
Halman,
1584 Edmond, 65
1624 Robert, 172
1624 Thomas, 172
Halsall,
1542 Bartholomew, 15
1593 Cuthbert, 82
1542 Edward, 15
1589 Richard, 74
1652 Richard 261
1525 Thomas, 4
1636 William, 212
Halton,
1647 Immanuel, 243
Hamby,
1658 John, 277
Hamerton,
1801 James, 404
1833 John, 446
Hamill,
1848 Arthur, 472
1831 Robert H , 442
Hamilton,
1714 Andrew, 359
1797 Arthur, 401
1815 Bingham W , 418
1727 Charles, 368
1833 Charles J J , 447
1798 Francis, 403
1821 Hans H , 424
1778 Henry, 389
1819 Hill, 439
1618 James, 149
1826 James, 432
1697 John, 348
1820 John A , 423
1751 Leslie, 378
1824 Mervyn, 429
1809 William O , 412
1878 William J , 489
Hamlyn,
1814 Christopher, 417
Hammersley,
1619 Hugh, 155
1629 Thomas, 180
Hammet,
1725 John, 361
Hammond,
1568 Alexander, 39
1684 Anthony, 335
1656 Dudley, 277
1820 James, 424
1580 John, 55
1618 John, 149
1611 Thomas, 139
1582 William, 61
1597 William, 91
1654 William, 267
1757 William, 381
1794 William, 399
Hamp,
1755 Benjamin, 380
Hampson,
1609 Thomas, 122
Hanbury,
1655 Thomas, 271
Hanby,
1560 John, 29

Hanch,
1641 Samuel, 229
Hanchett,
1536 ———, 12
Handcock,
1831 Charles, 441
1647 Edmund, 244
1598 William, 95
Handford,
1582 John, 61
Handley,
1823 Arthur, 427
1828 Edwin H , 437
1817 Thomas, 419
1817 William, 419
Hanist,
1631 John, 192
Hankey,
1803 Sir Richard, 405
Hanlon,
1843 John D , 461
Hanmer,
1561 Humphrey, 30
1662 Jerome, 293
1553 John, 24
1574 John, 47
1587 John, 71
1572 Randle, 44
1612 Thomas, 129
1655 Thomas, 270
1554 William, 25
Hanna,
1874 James, 486
Hansby,
1601 Ralph, 101
1671 Ralph, 313
Hanses,
1681 Charles, 330
1712 Josiah J , 358
Hanslop,
1583 Robert, 63
Hanson,
1671 Francis, 313
1887 Francis S , 496
1670 Robert, 310
1680 Samuel, 329
1652 Thomas, 261
Hanway,
1692 Richard, 344
Hapdon,
1605 William, 108
Harborne,
1638 Edward, 216
1641 Sampson, 234
1641 William, 234
Harbrowne,
1520 John (reader), 2
1638 John, 216
Harby,
1628 Edward, 186
Harcock,
1647 Edmund, 244
Harcourt,
1650 George, 254
1716 Thomas, 361
1749 Thomas, 377
Harden,
1828 James, 436
Hardestey,
1695 John, 347

Hardestey (con),
1748 John, 377
1690 Joseph, 341
Harding,
1876 Arthur R , 488
1615 Edmund, 137
1620 Edmund, 161
1594 John, 85
1620 John, 160
1643 John, 237
1650 John, 254
1836 John, 454
1850 John G , 473
1647 Nicholas, 243
1669 Nicholas, 308
1639 Robert, 223
1657 Robert, 283
1676 Robert, 323
1827 Thomas, 434
1826 William H , 432
Hardisty,
1690 Joseph, 341
Hardres,
1653 Charles, 265
1594 Cheyne, 84
1668 Edmund, 303
1664 James, 297
1689 John, 340
1651 Peter, 258
1563 Richard, 32
1626 Richard, 177
1594 Thomas, 84
1629 Thomas, 188
1664 Thomas, 296
1663 Thoresby, 295
Hardware,
1608 Henry, 117
1633 Henry, 202
Hardwicke,
1524 Thomas, 4
Hardy,
1830 Benjamin, 440
1888 Harold, 497
1647 Nicholas, 243
1596 Robert, 90
1639 Robert, 223
1826 Simeon H , 432
1777 William, 389
Hare,
1615 George, 137
1845 William 1 , 468
Harefinch,
1666 John, 300
Harfell,
1657 Edward, 281
Harford,
1652 Braddock, 261
1650 Bridstock, 253
1598 Richard, 94
Hargood,
1784 Benjamin, 392
Harkan,
1838 John, 458
Harlakenden,
1542 George, 15
1552 Martin, 22
1546 Richard, 18
1592 Richard, 81
1623 Richard, 170
1649 Richard, 250
1628 Roger, 184

Jenkinson (con),
1649 John, 251
1624 Philip, 174
1617 Richard, 146
1594 Thomas, 84

Jenner,
1845 Arthur R , 467
1795 George, 400
1794 Herbert, 399
1838 Montagu H , 457

Jennison,
1592 Edward, 80
1615 Henry, 137
1580 John, 55
1699 John, 350
1610 Michael, 123
1615 Robert, 137
1676 Robert, 323
1579 William, 54
1585 William, 68

Jenny,
1702 Arthur, 353
1667 Thomas, 302

Jenyns,
1682 Richard, 332
1750 Roger, 378
1683 William, 334

Jephes,
1568 William, 38

Jephson,
1598 Matthew, 95
1615 William, 141

Jepp,
1652 Samuel, 261

Jeremy,
1856 Walter D , ix , 476

Jermy,
1609 Francis, 122
1652 George, 260
1584 Isaac, 64
1594 John, 83
1621 John, 162
1634 John, 205
1652 William, 260

Jermyn,
1535 Edward, 11
1552 John, 23
1583 John, 62
1633 Michael, 199

Jervis,
1585 George, 68
1599 George, 98
1599 Thomas, 97

Jessopp,
1827 James, 434
1656 Francis, 276
1616 John, 145
1654 Richard, 268
1662 William, 294
1683 William, 333

Jett,
1722 Thomas, 365

Jeve,
1573 John, 46
1604 John, 110

Jobson,
1573 Michael, 44

Johnson,
1573 ------, 46
1618 Alexander, 150

Johnson (con),
1668 Alexander, 304
1700 Allen, 351
1804 Christopher, 406
1832 Cuthbert W , 444
1692 David, 344
1793 Francis, 397
1832 George W , 444
1621 Isaack, 162
1657 James, 283
1759 James, 382
1586 John, 70
1634 John, 206
1650 John, 255
1652 John, 261
1713 John, 359
1834 John, 450
1629 Morgan, 186
1648 Peter, 250
1521 Ralph, 3
1568 Ralph, 38
1618 Richard, 149
1634 Robert, 203
1623 Roger, 171
1670 Samuel, 310
1571 Thomas, 42
1634 Thomas 203
1652 Thomas, 263
1672 Thomas, 315
1578 William, 52
1605 William, 109
1607 William, 114
1650 William, 253, 256
1655 William, 275
1708 William, 356
1837 William F , 456

Johnston,
1814 James, 417
1851 James, 473
1855 John F , 476
1827 Robert, 434
1830 Robert, 440
1771 William, 386
1825 William, 431
1830 William J , 440

Johnstone,
1881 Eustace M , 491
1790 Lockhart, 395
1869 Pierce D H , 483
1885 Robert S , 494

Jolliff,
1837 William P , 455
1589 William, 75

Jolly,
1650 John, 253
1620 Thomas, 160

Jones,
1628 Arthur, 185
1641 Arthur, 229
1712 Charles, 358
1616 Christopher, 142
1637 Edmund, 214
1678 Edmond, 326
1588 Edward, 72
1602 Edward, 105
1619 Edward, 156
1635 Edward, 207
1642 Edward, 235
1669 Edward, 307
1864 Edwyn, ix 481

Jones (con),
1619 Francis, 155
1790 Frederick C , 395
1667 Garmes, 302
1617 Gilbert, 145
1642 Gilbert, 235
1596 Griffin, 90
1634 Henry, 204
1663 Henry, 295
1607 John, 115
1615 John, 137
1629 John, 188
1650 John, 255
1657 John, 284
1663 John, 296
1840 John, 461
1836 Joseph, 453
1862 Lionel H H , 479
1642 Littleton, 235
1693 Maurice, 345
1594 Morgan, 84
1669 Moses, 307
1885 Moses, 494
1634 Nicholas, 203
1664 Nicholas, 298
1568 Owen, 38
1594 Philip, 85
1657 Philip, 284
1596 Richard, 89
1608 Richard, 116
1619 Richard, 155
1657 Richard, 282
1661 Richard, 291
1669 Richard, 308
1634 Robert, 204
1682 Robert, 332
1851 Robert B , 474
1660 St John, 290
1657 Samuel, 284
1568 Thomas, 37
1599 Thomas, 97
1619 Thomas, 155
1620 Thomas, 142
1621 Thomas, 163
1656 Thomas, 278
1667 Thomas, 301
1713 Thomas, 359
1829 Thomas, 438
1798 Thomas C , 402
1639 Walter, 222
1640 William, 225
1640 William, 227
1642 William, 235
1647 William, 244
1655 William, 275
1784 William, 392
1828 William, 436
1889 William, 498

Jope,
1806 John, 408
1815 William, 418

Jophson,
1598 Matthew, 95
1593 Robert, 82
1647 Thomas, 243

Jordan,
1842 Edmund, 464
1881 Ernest W , 491
1679 Joseph, 327
1859 Thomas H , 478

Jortin,
1756 Rogers, 381
1795 Rogers, 400

Joscelyn,
1591 John, 80
1619 John, 157
1662 Nath , 294
1709 Robert, 357

Jower,
1656 John, 277

Jowles,
1663 Henry, 295
1623 John, 169
1653 John, 265

Joy,
1557 George, 27

Joyce,
1842 Samuel, 465

Joyes,
1846 John, 469

Julian,
1683 William, 334

Justice,
1815 John T , 418
1817 Henry C , 419

Juttleise,
1620 John, 158

Juxon,
1629 John, 188
1636 William, 211

Kane,
1822 Daniel R , 426
1849 Richard, 472
1852 Thomas, 475

Kay,
1852 Wm S Q B , 475

Kaye,
1672 Maurice, 315

Kayer,
1525 Robert, 5

Kealy,
1635 Edmund, 207

Kean,
1827 Patrick, 434
1740 Richard, 375
1834 Robert, 448

Kearney,
1674 Donatus, 319
1640 Patrick, 228, bis

Keate,
1614 William, 136

Keating,
1699 Luke, 350
1835 Maurice, 453
1819 William, 422

Keatinge,
1838 Samuel, 457
1795 Thomas, 400

Keble,
1613 Geoffrey, 140
1539 John, 221
1647 John, 244
1647 Joseph, 244
1685 Joseph, 336
1609 Richard, x , 122
1639 Richard, 221
1641 Thomas, 233
1647 Thomas, 244
1618 William, 142

O'Dwyer,
1827 Andrew C , 435
Odyearn,
1580 Nicholas, 56
1580 Thomas, 56
O'Farrell,
1789 Edward, 394
1837 Michael 455
O'Feely,
1858 Timothy O , 477
Offley,
1633 David, 198
1659 Francis, 287
1628 Robert, 184
O'Flannagan,
1836 James R , 453
O'Flynn,
1835 James, 452
Ogard,
1541 ——, 15
1540 Henry, 14
Ogilvy,
1818 Charles, 421
Oglander,
1633 William (Sir), 202
Ogle,
1831 Arthur K 441
1651 Ashfield, 257
1611 Cuthbert, 146
1630 Cuthbert, 190
1691 Cuthbert, 342
1637 Edward, 213
1648 James, 249
1622 John (Sir), 168
1671 John, 313
1666 Ralph, 301
1677 Samuel, 325
1630 Thomas, 189
1656 Thomas, 278
1713 Wentworth, 359
1749 William H , 3
Oglethorpe,
1729 James Edwd , 369
1588 Robert, 66
1657 Sutton, 285
O'Gorman,
1836 Nicholas J , 454
1800 Purcell Nich , 404
1840 Richard, 461
O'Grady,
1821 Richard, 425
1811 Standish, 413
1822 Standish, 426
1816 Waller, 418
O'Hagan,
1834 George, 449
1834 Thomas, 448
O'Hanlan
1695 Edmund, 347
O'Hara,
1816 James, 418
1851 John P , 473
O'Hea,
1835 James, 451
O'Keefe,
1683 Arthur, 333
1740 Arthur, 375
1829 Arthur Jones, 438
1826 Thomas, 433

O'Keram,
1583 Ralph, 62
Oldershaw,
1811 Robert, 414
Oldfield,
1647 Arthur, 244
1620 John, 157
1621 Joseph, 163
1662 Leftwich, 293
1698 Leftwich, 349
1647 Summerfield, 246
1702 William, 352
Oldham,
1836 James, 454
Olding,
1887 Llewellyn E , 496
O'Leary,
1805 Cornelius, 408
1833 Cornelius F P ,448
1861 Denis M , 479
1852 John M , 475
1820 Joseph, 423
Oliver,
1789 John, 394
1620 Richard, 158
1680 Richard, 329
Olivier,
1882 Sydney, 492
O Loghlen,
1840 Hugh, 461
O'Loughlin,
1846 James H , 469
O'Mahony,
1853 Thaddeus, 475
O'Malley,
1844 Charles, 466
1793 Owen, 398
1830 Samuel, 439
O'Meara,
1840 John, 461
1560 **Omer,** —, 29
Onby,
1521 John, 3
1608 John, 119
1651 John, 258
1656 John, 276
O'Neale,
1664 Brian, 297
1661 Daniel, 291
O'Neill,
1878 Peter J , 490
Onge,
1655 Francis, 270
Onley,
1585 Edward, 67, 68
Ord,
1728 James, 368
1591 Richard, 78
1606 Thomas, 112
O'Regan,
1795 John, 400
O'Reilly,
1818 Michael, 421
1833 Richard, 447
1854 Richard, 476
Orfeur,
1640 William, 227
Orington,
1543 Thomas, 16

Orlebar,
1653 John, 265
Orme,
1616 Jeremiah, 144
1814 Joseph B , 417
1693 Charles, 345
Ormley,
1568 Thomas, 37
Ormsby,
1841 Charles M , 463
1673 Edward (Sir), 317
1662 Gilbert, 294
1667 Robert, 302
1829 Thomas, 437
O'Rorke,
1640 Hugh, 224
Orpen,
1835 Edward, 451
1834 John H , 449
1791 Richard, 396
Orr,
1821 George D , 425
1849 William H , 472
Orrell,
1607 James, 114
1605 John, 108
Osbaldistone,
1625 Alexander, 176
1695 Alexander, 347
1596 Edward, 89
1625 Francis, 176
1577 Jeffrey, 51
1602 John, 105
1640 John, 228
1728 John, 369
1615 Lambert, 138
1631 Lambert, 192
1604 Richard, 110
1647 William, 244
Osbaston,
1619 William, 154
Osborne,
1819 Charles, 422
1651 Daniel, 258
1638 Edward, 220
1672 Edward, 314
1581 John, 60
1618 John, 150
1671 John, 313
1628 Richard, 185
1841 Robert W , 463
1617 Thomas, 146
1677 Thomas, 325
Osbrey,
1830 Gerald, 440
O'Shaughnessy,
1852 Mark S , 474
1821 Michael, 424
1791 Edward, 395
O'Shea,
1829 Hatton, 438
O'Sullivan,
1811 John, 414
1861 Patrick, 479
Oswald
1869 James F , 483
Otley,
1647 Adam, 245

Otterbourne,
1677 Robert, 324
Ottiwell,
1824 John R , 428
Otway,
1677 Brathwaite, 326
1671 Charles, 313
1638 John, 220
1668 John 305
1626 Thomas, 179
Ouchterlony,
1610 James, 123
Oughton,
1647 Adolphus, 244
Ousley,
1642 John, 237
Outlaw,
1611 Ralph, 128
Over,
1637 Hugh, 214
Overand,
1656 Edward, 280
Overhall,
1605 John, 108
Overton
1661 John, 292
1631 Robert, 194
Owen,
1788 Arthur D , 393
1686 Caleb, 337
1748 Charles, 377
1587 Edward, 71
1633 George, 200
1701 George, 352
1642 Griffin, 236
1546 Henry, 18
1567 Hugh, 36
1689 Hugh, 340
1867 James S , 482
1568 John, 37
1619 John, 154
1655 John, 273
1665 John, 299
1680 John, 330
1720 John, 364
1611 Lewis, 126
1722 Morgan, 365
1659 Pontsbury, 288
1681 Rice, 331
1631 Richard, 193
1697 Richard, 349
1836 Robert, 453
1828 Samuel, 437
1625 Thomas, 176
1637 Thomas, 215
1652 Thomas, 262
1663 Thomas, 295
1694 Thomas, 346
1811 Thomas, 413
1618 William, 152
1672 William, 314
1709 William, 356
1697 Wyrriot, 348
1723 Wyrriot, 366
Owens,
1651 Owen, 258
1634 Thomas, 205
1650 Thomas, 255
Owfield,
1621 Joseph, 163

Rant (*con*),
1646 William, 242
1615 Roger, 138, 141
1645 Roger, 240
1681 Roger, 331
1619 Thomas, 154
Raper,
1629 Richard, 143
Rashleigh,
1639 John, 224
Rastall,
1533 John, 9
1621 Henry, 164
Ratcliffe,
1581 Alexander, 59
1651 Alexander, 258
1669 Alexander, 307
1697 Alexander, 349
1613 Anthony, 140
1631 Cuthbert, 192
1581 Edward, 59
1608 Edward, 116
1642 Francis, 236
1673 Francis, Knt., 317
1612 George, 129
1604 John, 110
1606 John, 112
1650 John, 254
1619 Joshua, 157
1583 Robert, 62
1614 Samuel, 135
1561 Thomas, 30
1605 Thomas, 109
1632 Thomas, 197
1638 Thomas, 215
1656 William, 277
Rathborne,
1828 William, 436
Rattenbury,
1811 Joseph F , 413
Raughsedge,
1793 Peter, 398
Raven,
1657 James, 284
1622 John, 165
1628 John, 184
1641 John, 232
1649 William, 251
Ravenhill,
1680 John, 329
Ravenscroft,
1728 Thomas, 369
1657 William, 283
Rawleigh,
1665 William, 299
Rawling,
1816 John, 419
Rawlins,
1666 Bartholomew, 300
1583 Roger, 64
1613 Thomas, 132
1818 Thomas, 421
1624 William, 173
Rawlinson,
1689 John, 341
1692 Monk, 344
1634 Robert, 205
1657 William, 281
Rawnce,
1576 John, 49

Rawnce (*con*),
1578 Robert, 53
Raworth,
1650 Francis, 253
1633 Robert, 200
Rawson,
1652 John, 261
1523 Thomas, 4
Rawstorn,
1634 Edward, 203
Ray,
1823 Edmund B , 426
1818 Henry B , 421
1817 Robert, 420
1842 Thomas M , 464
Raymond,
1645 John, 239
1648 John, 247
1680 John, 329
1682 Robert, x , 332
1645 Thomas, x., 239
Rayner,
1677 John, 324
1703 John, 354
1647 Thomas, 244
Raynes,
1612 William, 130
Raynsford,
1807 Thomas A , 410
Raynton,
1622 Sir Nicholas, 167
Rea,
1668 Joseph, 305
Read,
1671 Charles, 312
1773 James, 387
1698 Nicholas, 349
1656 Ralph, 278
1654 Robert, 268
1676 Roger, 323
1631 Thomas, 193
1671 Thomas, 312
1682 Unton, 333
1587 William, 72
1613 William, 132
1633 Charles, 200
1830 Frederick, 439
1650 Isaac, 255
1633 John, 198
1635 Robert, 207
1573 Thomas, 44
Reader,
1601 Thomas, 102
Readshaw,
1779 Joshua, 390
Reardon,
1827 Daniel, 435
Reavely,
1760 George, 381
Redferne,
1619 Henry, 155
1841 William, 463
Redhead,
1633 Arthur, 199
Redish,
1580 Alexander, 56
Redman,
1646 John, 242, 246
Redmayne,
1759 James, 382

Redmayne (*con*),
1652 Robert, 262
Redmond,
1880 John E , 490
1886 Frederick, 495
Reed,
1887 Herbert P , 496
1734 John, 372
1872 John F , 484
Rees,
1780 John B , 390
Reeve,
1627 Augustine, 182
1659 Augustine, 288
1659 Charles, 287
1607 Edmund, x , 119
1645 Edmund, 240
1593 Edward, 82
1637 George, 212
1629 Henry, 188
1660 Henry, 290
1598 Robert, 95
1653 Thomas, 264
Reeves,
1544 Thomas, 17
Reid,
1836 Patrick, 454
Reilly,
1772 Barney, 387
1706 Hugh, 355
1847 Hugh, 470
1801 James M , 404
1842 John, 464
1774 Thomas, 387
1816 Walter, 418
Reily,
1831 Thomas W , 443
Reithe,
1570 William, 40
Remington,
1618 Robert, 151
1628 Thomas, 186
1610 Timothy, 124
1638 Timothy, 218
1656 William, 279
Renton,
1882 Alexander W., 492
Repington,
1641 Edward, 230
1582 John, 61
1552 Thomas, 22
Reppes,
1581 Francis, 60
1653 Henry, 264
Reresby,
1578 Arnold, 264
Reveley,
1617 Bartram, 148
1657 George, 280
1760 George, 381
1736 Henry, 369
1682 William, 231
1708 William, 356
Revell,
1811 Henry, 414
1622 Thomas, 168
Revitt,
1530 Henry, 7
Rey,
1698 George, 349

Reynolds,
1607 Emanuel, 115
1634 Edward, 204
1847 Henry N , 470
1551 Jeremiah, 21
1530 Jo , 7
1552 Jo , 22
1628 John, 185
1664 John, 298
1620 Nicholas, 162
1625 Richard, 176
1683 Samuel, 334
1728 Thomas, 369
1823 William, 427
Rhodeaz,
1677 Jeremiah, 325
Rhodes,
1764 Israel, 384
Riall,
1826 John, 432
Rialme,
1592 Ascanius, 81
Ricards,
1653 John, 264
Rice,
1697 William, 349
Rich,
1624 Charles, 173
1662 Charles, Earl, 294
1662 Charles, Lord, 294
1676 Christopher, 323
1610 Nathaniel, 123
1639 Nathaniel, 223
1573 Robert, Lord, 45
1592 Robert, Lord, 79
1619 Robert, Lord, 154
1579 William, 54
Richards,
1851 Edward, 473
1878 Henry C , 489
1620 John, 161
1888 Roger C , 496
1647 Thomas, 246
1809 Thomas, 411
Richardson,
1654 Abel, 268
1522 Cuthbert, 3
1582 Edmund, 60
1598 John, 93
1605 John, 110
1633 John, 202
1639 John, 222
1716 John, 361
1711 Joseph, 358
1638 Matthew, 215
1681 Richard, 331
1632 Robert, 95
1686 Robert, 388
1663 Thomas, 296
1670 Thomas, 309
1695 Thomas, 499
1648 William, 249
1668 William, 305
1694 William, 346
Riches,
1638 Henry, 216
Richey,
1853 Alexander G., 475
Richman,
1623 John, 170

Shepherd,
1666 Charles, 300
1798 Charles, 403
1820 Edward J , 423
1657 Fleetwood, 284
1825 George, 430, 500
1573 John, 44
1596 John, 90
1627 John, 180
1713 John, 359
1624 Owen, 171
1582 Robert, 61
1648 Robert, 249
1847 Samuel, 470
1655 Thomas, 272
1584 Zachary, 64
Sheppard,
1876 George H , 487
1756 Samuel, 381
1835 William, 450
Sherard,
1719 Brownlow, 363
1604 John, 108
1599 Philip, 98
1711 Richard, 358
1551 Rowland, 21
1604 William, 108
Sherburne,
1619 Edward, 155
1571 Henry, 42
1539 Richard, 13
1571 Richard, 42
1601 Richard, 101
1607 Richard, 115
1671 Richard, 312
1550 Robert, 21
1601 Roger, 103
1583 Thomas, 63
1584 Thomas, 65
Shereman,
1611 William, 126
Sherer,
1617 Robert, 146
Sheridan,
1828 James, 436
Sherington,
1615 Francis, 137
1560 Gilbert, 28
1528 William, 7
1584 William, 65
Sherland,
1604 Christopher, 110
1591 Edward, 78
Sherlocke,
1683 Edward, 333
1628 Pierse, 185
1706 Richard, 355
1820 Thomas, 424
Sherman,
1647 George, 244
1539 John, 13
1575 Thomas, 48
Sherwin,
1774 John, 388
1694 Robie, 346
1688 William, 339
Sherwood,
1613 Henry, 133
Sheth,
1561 Richard, 29

Sheth (con),
1586 Robert, 69
Shetterden,
1628 Daniel, 186
Shewright,
1542 William, 16
Shield,
1854 Hugh, ix , 476
Shilito,
1606 George, 112
Shillibeer,
1814 Henry B , 417
Shillingford,
1658 John, 286
Shipperdson,
1694 Ralph, 346
Shirley,
1634 James, 202
1522 John, 3
1527 John, 6
1559 Thomas, 28
1591 Thomas, 78
1596 Thomas, 90
Shorte,
1638 Edward, 220
1648 Edward, 249
1712 Edward, 358
1616 James, 145
1596 Samuel, 92
1633 Samuel, 200
1653 Thomas, 264
1805 Thomas D , 407
1614 William, 135
1835 John, 452
Showell,
1629 Nathaniel, 187
Shrubsolle,
1635 Charles, 210
Shuckburgh,
1635 Henry, 207
Shuldham,
1652 Lemuel, 259
Shute,
1602 Edward, 103
1620 Edward, 158
1577 Francis, 50
1579 John, 55
1550 Robert, x , 21
1600 Robert, 100
Shuttlewood,
1656 Thomas, 278
Shuttleworth,
1684 Barton, 335
1656 Edmund, 278
1588 Henry, 73
1606 Nicholas, 113
1561 Richard, 30
1605 Richard, 109
1672 Richard, 314
1656 Thomas, 278
Sibbs,
1617 Richard, 146, 497
Sibson,
1635 John, 209
Sicklemore,
1633 John, 202
1639 Jonathan, 221
1626 Thomas, 177
Sidley,
1590 Richard, 78

Sidney,
1845 William J , 468
Sier,
1839 Thomas, 459
Silver,
1864 Ebenezer D , 481
Simeons,
1640 Edward, 226
Simion,
1616 George, Knt , 139
Simmons,
1806 George, 108
1805 Thomas A , 408
Simon,
1640 Abraham, 228
1876 William, 487
Simons,
1642 Abraham, 237
1620 Edmund, 162
1635 Richard, 209, 210
1584 Robert, 64
1625 Robert, 175
1641 Thomas, 234
1848 William V L , 471
Simpson,
1780 Charles, 390
1631 Henry, 194
1752 Hugh, 378
1668 John, 304
1648 Thomas, 250
Sinclair,
1881 Robert H , 491
Singleton,
1813 Cuthbert, 416
1820 Edward, 424
1609 Thomas, 121
1554 William, 25
1601 William, 101
Sisley,
1593 Thomas, 82
Sitwell,
1650 Francis, 254
1700 Francis, 350
1705 Thomas, 355
Skeffington,
1845 Chichester T , 468
1608 John, 115
1595 William, 88
Skelton,
1521 Richard, 3
1620 Richard, 160
1831 Walter B , 442
Skepper,
1790 Thomas, 395
Skerne,
1627 John, 183
Skeviett,
1833 John J , 447
Skidmore,
1611 John, 125
Skinner,
1761 Charles, 383
1631 George, 193
1584 John, 64
1595 John, 88
1600 Oliver, 99
1600 Richard, 98
1618 William, 151
Skipp,
1656 George, 280

Skipp (con),
1680 Thomas, 329
Skippon,
1656 Luke, 276
1663 Philip, 295
Skipton,
1638 Thomas, 218
Skipworth,
1575 Charles, 47
1645 Charles, 239
1637 Edward, 214
1608 Henry, 120
1638 Thomas, 217
1670 Thomas, 310
1527 William, 5
1608 William, 120
Skrymsher,
1639 John, 224
Skyres,
1536 Humphrey, 11
Skyrme,
1769 Francis, 386
1700 William, 350
Skyrrington,
1528 William, 7
Slack,
1615 Abraham, 138
1794 John, 399
Slader,
1656 Tymothie, 280
Slater,
1875 Joshua 487
1652 Thomas, 261
Slatery,
1701 Joseph, 352
Sleddall,
1678 Roger, 327
Slegge,
1572 Edward, 44
1608 Edward, 117
Sleigh,
1655 Edward, 275
1628 Gervase, 184
1645 Gervase, 240
1628 Hugh, 184
1641 John, 230
1622 Samuel, 168
1623 Samuel, 171
1655 Samuel, 275
Slevin,
1835 Edward, 452
Slinger,
1641 Joseph, 231
1702 Tempest, 352
Slingsby,
1582 William, 60
Sloper,
1792 Robert, 397
1740 Simon A , 375
Slowe,
1648 Robert, 248
Smalpage,
1581 T , 59
Smallpeece,
1646 Francis, 242
1578 Leonard, 52
Smallwood,
1651 Andrew, 258
Smart,
1740 Francis, 374

Strangeways (*con*),
1676 Thomas, 323
1701 Thomas, 352
1755 Thomas, 380
Strappini,
1853 Peter A M , 475
Stratford,
1630 Anthony, 190
1620 Henry, 157
1649 John, 251
1669 Theodore, 306
Streete,
1547 ——, 90
1671 Francis, 312
1692 Leonard, 343
1655 Richard, 273
1669 William, 305
1681 William, 331
Streeten,
1832 Francis T , 446
Streetly,
1562 Paul, 30
Stretton,
1871 Joseph H , 483
Strickland,
1704 Mannock, 354
1641 Robert, 230
1696 Robert, 348
1618 Thomas, 152
1637 Thomas, 215
1645 Thomas, 239
1795 Thomas, 400
1565 Walter, 34
1608 Walter, 117
1618 Walter, 152
1641 Walter, 232
1748 Walter, 377
1617 William, 145
Stringer,
1657 Francis, 283
1547 George, 19
1695 John, 347
1586 Nicholas, 69
1645 Thomas, x , 239
1676 Thomas, 322
1676 William, 323
Strode,
1648 Hugh, 249
Strong,
1865 Sidney, 481
Stronghill,
1637 John, 213
Strother,
1614 John, 135
1613 William, 132
1672 William, 314
Stroud,
1632 George, 198
Struggle,
1614 Richard, 134
Strutt,
1628 Denner, 184
Stuart,
1646 Charles (Lord) 241
1797 John, 402
1722 Samuel, 365
Stubbs,
1635 Edmund, 289
1573 John, 45
1657 Robert, 285

Studdert,
1882 Jonas W , 491
1835 Lancelot, 451
Studdy,
1871 Henry W , 484
Studley,
1588 Nathaniel, 72
1622 Nathaniel, 168
Stuffin,
1659 John, 288
Stukeley,
1765 William, 384
Sturdey,
1609 James, 121
1591 Ralph, 80
Sturgeon,
1655 Anthony, 270
Sturges,
1527 Richard, 6
Sturry,
1618 Carew, 152
Sturt,
1737 George, 373
1679 Humphrey, 327
Sturtevant,
1670 Lawrence, 310
Stych,
1626 Henry, 177
Stydolph,
1611 Francis, 126
1611 William, 129
Styerley,
1535 Henry, 11
Style,
1599 Edmund, 96
1536 William, 12
1656 William, 279
Styleman,
1635 Nicholas, 210
1629 Robert, 187
Styward,
1532 Jeffrey, 9
Suckling,
1678 Horatio, 327
1590 John, 77
1627 John, 180
1624 Robert, 172
1662 Robert, 293
1758 Robert, 382
Sugar,
1657 Nicholas, 281
Suger,
1717 William, 362
Suggott,
1622 William, 166
Suliard,
1647 Edward, 243
1623 Ralph, 169
Sulley,
1662 Daniel, 293
Sullivan,
1696 Daniel, 348
1799 Edward, 403
1834 Robert, 450
Sunderland,
1796 Thomas, 401
Supple,
1712 Richard, 359
Susan,
1619 John, 154

Sutherland,
1835 Charles G , 453
1851 Kenneth L , 473
Sutton,
1769 Daniel, 386
1551 Edward, 21
1553 John, 24
1577 Nicholas, 51
1521 Richard, 3
1592 Richard, 81
1625 Richard, 176
1617 Robert, 317
1700 Thomas, 351
1521 William, 3
1727 William, 368
Swabey,
1845 Maurice C.M., 468
Swale,
1646 Edward, 240
1648 Henry, 250
1630 Solomon, 189
Swallow,
1662 Samuel, 294
Swan,
1622 Edward, 168
1593 Francis, 82
1628 George, 184
1629 Richard, 187
1616 Thomas, 144
1649 William, 251
Swanwicke,
1659 Allan, 287
Swanzy,
1853 James, 475
Swayne,
1650 Francis, 254
1654 William, 266
Sweetman,
1852 Walter, 474
Swetenham,
1654 Edmund, 264
Swift,
1651 Dryden, 256
1837 Edward B , 455
1650 Godwin, 255
1530 Roger, 8
1675 Thomas, 322
1539 William, 13
Swinburne,
1784 Edward, 392
1649 John, 251
1670 Thomas, 308
1698 William, 349
Swiney,
1784 William, 392
Swinfen,
1621 John, 164
1662 John, 294
1660 Richard, 289
Swinforde,
1607 Nicholas, 119
Swingfield,
1622 Thomas, 167
Swinnerton,
1609 Henery, 122
1630 John, 190
1656 Ralph, 276
1611 Richard, 126
Swinton,
1840 Archibald, 461

Swiny,
1798 Shapland, 403
Swyny,
1769 Edward, 386
1775 Morto Danl., 388
Sydenham,
1589 Roger, 75
1657 William, 281
Sydney,
1633 Algernon, 201
1563 Sir Henry, 32
1567 Philip, 37
1633 Philip, 201
1588 Robert, 66
1618 Sir Robert, 149
1605 William, 108
Sydnor,
1598 Francis, 97
Sykes,
1794 Godfrey, 399
1805 John, 407
1736 Peter, 372
1770 Peter, 385
1738 William, 373
Symes,
1845 Abraham, 468
1646 James, 241
1670 James, 310
1824 Langford R , 429
Symms,
1687 John, 339
Taaffe,
1596 Edward, 90
1570 Peter, 40
Tadley,
1580 John, 55
Tagert,
1837 John, 457
1811 Samuel, 414
Tainter,
1640 William, 226
Talbot,
1871 Bertram H , 484
1790 James, 595
1569 John, 39
1604 Richard, 107
1624 Richard, 174
1678 Roger, 326
1555 Thomas, 25
1599 Thomas, 96
1618 Thomas, 149
1642 Thomas, 234
1533 William, 10
Talcott,
1621 Thomas, 164
1660 William, 289
Tamlyn,
1815 John, 408
Tamworth,
1579 Christopher, 54
Tarat,
1655 John, 273
Tancred,
1628 John, 184
1552 Ralph, 22
1582 Richard, 60
1772 Sir Thomas, 387
Tanner,
1730 Culpeper, 270
1658 Thomas, 285

SUPPLEMENT.

Registers of Marriages

IN

Gray's Inn Chapel,

1695–1774.

ALPHABETICALLY ARRANGED

BY

JOSEPH FOSTER

MARRIAGES

CELEBRATED IN

GRAY'S INN CHAPEL.

Abbitt, Thomas, of the parish of St Andrew. Holborn — 2 Dec 1714 —, Elizabeth [Tomlinson, of same

Abbot, Thomas, widower. of the parish of St Giles, Cripplegate — 5 Dec 1714 [—, Mary Stone, *sing*, of same

Abbott, Ruth, of the parish of St Nicholas Cole Abbey — 1 Aug. 1714 —, John [Poole, of same

Abraham, Armanel, of the parish of St Andrew's, Holborn —24 June, 1704 —, Samuel Rose, cook. in Mutton Lane, [parish of St James, Clerkenwell.

Absalom, Elizabeth — 16 April, 1696 —, Richard Dyer, clothworker in Chancery [Lane.

Abson, John, a butcher in Clare Market — [26 March, 1700-1 —, Mary Frye

Ackers, Jonathan, watchmaker, in the parish of St James, Clerkenwell — 23 Dec [1704 —, Susan Humphreys

Acklon, Bridget, of the parish of St Giles, Cripplegate — 6 Aug 1714 —, John Simons, of parish of St Andrew, Hol- [born

Adam, John, of the parish of St. James, Westminster — 10 July, 1709 —, Ann [Palphrey of same.

Adams, Christian, *sing*, of St Bride's — 23 Dec 1714 —, John Chesmore, [widower, of St. Giles in the Fields

Adams, Elisabeth, of St Mary, Islington — 23 Aug 1744 —, Thomas Adderly, [of St Gregory's, London.

Adams, George, of St. Bride's — 14 Dec 1732 —, Anne Roberts, of St James', [Westminster

Adams, Humphry, of Badgmore. co Oxford — 30 Sept 1752 —, Catherine Cranmer, [of Cheshunt, Herts.

Adams, John, tripeman in St. Clement's parish Clement Danes — 18 Feb. [1699-1700 —, Margaret Late

Adams, Mary, of St Luke's, Old St. — 20 Nov 1748 —, Henry Calvert, of same.

Adams, Nathaniel, of St. Martin's, Ludgate —23 Jan 1727 8—, Mary Vere of same

Adams, Robert, of the parish of St Giles in the Fields. — 9 Feb. 1713-4 —, Sarah [Petit, of same.

Adams, Rose, of the parish of St Andrew's, Holborn — 15 July, 1711 —, Walter [Davis, of parish of St Swithin

Adderley, Samuel, of the parish of St Mary, Abchurch. — 26 Oct 1735 —, Mary [Saunders, of same.

Adderly, Thomas, of St Gregory's, London — 23 Aug 1744 —, Elisabeth Adams, of [St Mary, Islington

Adeane, Mary, of Reading, Berks — 25 July, 1730 —, Abraham Flahan, of St [James', Clerkenwell

Adie, Frances, of Coventry, co Warwick. — 19 Feb 1727-8 —, Thomas Crampe, of [same

Adkins, John, glazier in Hampstead —13 [April, 1697 —, Sarah Fielder.

b

Adshead, Mary, of the parish of St Andrew, Holborn.—License dated May, 1717 —, [John Boote, of same.

Ailey, Matthew, vintner in Milk Street — 21 Jan. 1696-7—, Elizabeth Corllinson [(by Mr. May, curate of Deptford).

Aimy, William, *bat*, of the parish of Shifnall, Salop —29 Sept 1718 —, Margaret Davies, of St Lawrence Jewry, London, [*spin*

Aish, Mary, of St Sepulchre's. —10 Sept 1714 —, Jacob Mellish, of St Margaret's, Westminster.

Albon, Mary, of St Andrew's, Holborn — 26 April, 1736 —, William Olliver, of [same

Alchorne, Susannah, of the parish of Kensington —2 Sept 1715 —, William [Peirson, of same

Alderton (Mr.), of the parish of St Andrew, Holborn — 26 Nov 1714—, Elizabeth [Cutts, of same

Alderton, Joseph, of the parish of St Martin in the Fields — 16 July 1713 —, Elizabeth Martin, of same

Aldridge, Elizabeth, of St. Andrew's Holborn — 28 Jan 1724-5 —, Humphrey [Bartlett, of parish of Bow

Allaire Jane, of St Martin's in the Fields —, 3 May, 1734 —, Rev. Peter Gally, of [St James', Westminster

Allanson, Marmaduke, of Yarm, co York — 11 June, 1733 —, Jane Todd, of [Wickham, Essex.

Allbrooks, Jane, of Shoreditch — 18 April, 1714 —, Samuel Hammond, of St [Katharine's, Coleman St

Allen, Anne, of St Andrew's, Holborn — 14 Feb 1733-4 —, John Harle, of the [Inner Temple

Allen, Benjamin, of St Clement Danes — 23 June, 1751 —, Mary Whetton, of St [Anne's, Soho

Allen, Dorothy — 7 Jan 1696-7 —, William [Pitfield

Allen, Joseph, of St Martin in the Fields, widower — 30 Dec 1719 —, Alice Hammond, of St Anne's, Blackfriars, [widow

Allen, Mary, of the parish of St John's, Wapping — 17 June, 1712 —, John [Rolfe, of same

Allen, Robert, mariner, next the Last Gravelane, Houndsditch — 14 Dec 1699 —, [Sara Baldwin

Allen, Sara, of St Mary, Savoy — 28 May, 1695 — John Parker, of St Mary, [Savoy.

Allen, Sara, — 28 May, 1700 —, Robert Ball, victualler at the Black Lion in [Pall Mall.

Allen, Sarah, of Chelsea — 23 June, 1713 —, William Croocock, of the parish of [St Alban's, Wood St

Allen, Sarah, of Sevenoaks, Kent. — 8 Oct. [1751 —, George Philpot, of same.

Allen-Greenalgh, Thomas, of Gray's Inn, esq — 5 June, 1753 —, Anne Edwards, [of Highgate.

Allin, Anne, *sing*, of the parish of St James, Westminster — 26 Feb, 1714-5 —, Thomas Singleman, *bat*, of same

Allin, Eleanor, of St John's, Clerkenwell — 24 Sept. 1730 —, James Bishop, of St. [Andrews, Holborn

Allington, Elias, salesman, of the parish of St Clement's Danes — 1 Oct 1704 —, [Mary Nash, of same parish.

Allison, Elizabeth, of All Saints', Lombard St — 5 Nov, 1713 —, William Glanvile, gent, of parish of St, Edmund the King, [Lombard St,

Allison, George, of St. Clement's Danes — 26 Jan 1727-8 —, Ann Sherborne of [St Giles in the Fields,

Allison, Tamar, of St Paul's, Covent Garden. — 13 Feb 1734-5 —, Thomas [Topp, of St. Giles in the Fields

Allstroope, Elizabeth, of the parish of St Andrew, Holborn — 27 April, 1714 —, [Richard Layton, of same.

Allwright, Charles, of the parish of St Giles in the Fields — 21 Oct 1714 —, [Mary Deacon, of same

Alsop, Eleanor, of the parish of St James, Westminster — 7 April, 1713 —, John [Smart, of same.

Ambrose, Ann, of the parish of St. Mary Woolnoth, Lombard St. — 10 Aug. 1710 —, Joseph Cooke, of parish of [St. Andrew's, Holborn.

Ambrose, Elizabeth, of the parish of St Mary Woolnoth. — 7 Sept. 1710 —, Francis Underwood, of parish of St. [Michael's, Cornhill.

Ambrose, Thomazina, of the parish of St Giles in the Fields, spin — 17 Aug. 1718 —, William Blathwayt, of parish [of St Martin in the Fields, bat

Amherst, Jefferey, of Sevenoaks, Kent, esq — 10 May, 1753 —, Jane Dalyson, of [Wrotham, Kent

Anderson, Sarah, of Highgate, Middx. — 29 Jan 1727-8 —, Michael Woollaston, [of same

Andress, Alice, of the parish of Hampstead, Middx. — 16 Feb. 1704-5 —, Edward [Applegarth, of same parish, dyer

Andrewes, John, weaver in Bishopsgate St., St. Botolph's. — 18 Aug. 1698 —, Mary [Rawlet.

Andrewes, William, at the Lion and Crown, nr. the New Exchange in the Strand — [4 Feb. 1701-2 —, Elizabeth Blagrave

Andrews, Henry, of the parish of St. Giles in the Fields — 17 Jan 1711-2 —, Elizabeth Carrenden, of parish of St [Martin in the Fields

Andrews, Joseph, silk dyer at Mr. Sharp's, apothecary in Long Acre. — 25 June. [1700 —, Catherine Butler

Anger, Elizabeth, of the parish of St Andrew, Holborn — 4 Feb. 1715-6 —, [Thomas Perry, of same.

Anns, William, of the parish of St Martin's, vintner — 4 Aug 1709 —, Anne Darwin, of parish of St. Faith's, London

Ansell, Sarah, of St. Clement Danes — 2 May, 1743 —, Benjamin Tucker, of St. [Martin's in the Fields.

Appleby, Dorothy, of the parish of St. James, Clerkenwell — 28 Jan 1713-4 [—, Eustance Miles, of same.

Applegarth, Edward, of the parish of Hampstead, Middx., dyer. — 16 Feb. [1704-5 —, Alice Andress, of the same.

Archer, Anne, of St. Clements Danes, — 10 Aug 1727 —, Nicholas Hailstone, of [same.

Archer, John, of the parish of St Botolph's, Billingsgate. — 10 May, 1705 —, Mary Hayward of St. George's, Southwark.

Arkwright, Ann, of St James', Clerkenwell — 26 Aug 1712 —, John Morris, of St [Giles, Cripplegate.

Arlich, Judith. — 30 April, 1700 —, William Childe, twister, near the prison [in Whitechapel

Arlidge, William, of St Andrew's, Holborn — 13 Feb 1734-5 —, Sarah Nicolls, of [Finchley.

Armiger, Gabriel, of the Inner Temple, widower — 24, 25, or 26 May, 1718 —, Judith ye Debuck (sic), of Hamp- [stead

Arnold, Ann, of the parish of St. Martin's, Ironmonger lane — 19 Jan 1713-4 —, Samuel Nash, of the parish of St James, [Westminster.

Arnold, Edward, of the parish of St. Andrew's, Holborn — 31 Oct 1713 —, Elizabeth [Northcutt, of same

Arnold, John, of St Dunstan's in the West. — 6 Feb 1724-5 -, Rebecca Hassell, [of St. Bride's.

Arthington, Dorothy, of Kensington, Middx. — 1 Jan 1753 —, Stephen Pitt, [esq, of same,

Arthington, Frances, of St. Margaret's, Westminster. — 6 March, 1749-50 —, Bodychen Sparrow, of Kensington, esq

Arthur, Robert, of the parish of St Martin in the Fields, bat — 6 July, 1718 —, [Hester Nevile, of same, spin

Ash, Ambrose, taylor at New Inn gate, St. Clement's. — 17 Dec 1696 —, Mary [Havergill

Ash, James, gent, of the Inner Temple. — 29 April, 1703 —, Playdell Tomlinson, [of St. Olave, Southwark

Ash, Joseph, of the Inner Temple, esq. — 8 March, 1710-1 —, Elizabeth James, of the parish of St. Giles in the Fields, ((married, at midnight by Mr Barnes.)

Ashers, Mary, of St Giles, Cripplegate, *spin* — 21 Sept 1721 —, John Butterworth, of St. Katherine Cree Church, [*bat*

Ashes, Sarah, of St Sepulchre's, — 19 Dec [1713 —, Thomas Weston, of same

Ashley, Richard, of St Mary le Strand — 16 May, 1728 —, Sarah Okey, St [Andrew, Holborn

Ashton, Anne, of St George's, Bloomsbury — 24 Dec 1746 —, Robert Gill, of [same

Ashton, Susannah, of St Martins in the Fields. —9 Oct 1716 —, Thomas Draper, of parish of St. Giles in the [Fields

Ashurst, Robert. — 21 May, 1723 —, Judith [Woolley

Ashurst, William, of Friday Street, London — 12 Dec. 1723 —, Elizabeth Hollis, [of Whitechapel.

Ashwell, Jacob, of Eaton Bray, Beds, *bat* — 28 Sept 1721 —, Elizabeth Fox, of [the same, *spin*

Ashworth, Alice, *sing*, of St Giles, Cripplegate — 27 Jan 1714-5 —, Thomas Hollester, *bat*, of parish of St Martin's, [Ludgate

Askew, James, of the parish of St Dunstan's in the West — 8 March, 1712-3 —, Sarah Eaglestone, of parish of St. [Andrew's, Holborn

Aspley, Elizabeth — 24 Feb 1698-9 —, Matthias Perkins, surgeon in Swithin [Lane

Atkins, Anne, of St Andrew's, Holborn — 4 Oct 1716 —, Thomas Barnett, of [parish of St Magnus the Great.

Atkinson, Elizabeth, of the parish of St Andrew's, Holborn — 18 Dec. 1705 —, Thomas Mitchell, of parish of Sunderland, co Durham, mariner, by a licence

Atkinson, George, vintner in St. Martin's le Grand. — 4 Nov. 1697 —, Margaret [Roberts.

Atkinson, Lancelot, of the parish of St Andrew's, Holborn, in Leather lane, coachman — 10 Feb 1703-4 —, Sarah Richardson, of the parish of Wrotham, [Essex

Atkinson, Mary, of St Magnus, near the Bridge — 10 July, 1731 —, Edward [Wilson, of St Andrew's, Holborn

Atkinson, William, of this Inn. — 16 Sept. 1736 —, Dorothy Rutter, of Hackney.

Attey, Marmaduke, chamberlain at the Black Bull, Holborn. — 20 Feb. 1695-6 —, [Elizabeth Dyer.

Attly, Sarah, of the parish of St. Botolph's, Aldersgate — 28 Jan. 1702-3 —, Samuel [Lee, fruiterer, of same parish.

Attwood, John, fruiterer in Thames Street [24 Feb. 1697-8 — Martha Jenkins.

Atwood, John, of St Martin, Vintry, London. — 16 Nov. 1724 — Mary Sunderland, [of St George the Martyr.

Austen, Elizabeth, of Sevenoaks — 14 July, 1722 —, George Hooper, jun., of Ton-[bridge, Kent.

Austen, William, widower, of the parish of St. James, Westminster. — 25 Feb. 1717-[18 —, Margaret May, of same.

Austin, Anne —9 Jan 1695 6 —, John Jennings, a keeper under Sir Basil Fire-[brace, in South Mimms parish.

Austin (Oston), Anne, of the parish of Cheshunt, Herts. — 17 Nov 1714 —, [James Lucke, of same.

Austin, John, *bat*, — 15 April, 1722 —, Mary Stringer, *spin*, of Sevenoaks [(Sennock), Kent.

Austin, Robert, butcher, in St. James' parish, Westminster. — 9 Sept. 1705 —, Sarah [Hall, of the same,

Austin, Susan, of the parish of St. Giles in the Fields. — 10 Jan. 1711-2 —, Joseph [Tale, of same

Axford, Benjamin, of St. Alban's, Wood Street — 10 July, 1753 — Dorothy Dixon, of St. Margaret's, Westminster.

Axtell, Daniel, of St. James, Clerkenwell. — 1 Aug. 1728 —, Mary Emmons, of [same.

Aylworth, George, grocer in Milk Street. [— 5 Dec 1700 —, Elizabeth Hunter.

Ayre, William, at the Blue Ball in Bedford passage. — 4 Nov. 1701 —, Catherine [Cory.

Ayres, Elizabeth, of St Martin's in the Fields. — 17 May, 1730 —, David Dupony, of [St Anne's, Westminster.

Ayres, Mary, of St Martin's in the Fields, *in*". — 25 May, 1721 —, Francis [Goddard, of same, widower.

Ayton, Elisabeth, of West Herrington, Northumberland — 6 Aug 1730 —, [John Thorold, of Lea, co Lincoln

Bach, Elizabeth, of the parish of St Martin's in the Fields — 12 Feb 1708-9 —, [Richard Scrivener, of same

Bacon, Abraham, of St Michael's, Wood St — 29 Oct 1714 —, Esther Ben, of [St Alphage

Bagley, Olivie Margarete, of Enfield, Middx — 15 Dec. 1722 —, William Billinton, [of same

Bailey, Job, victualler, near Temple bar — [3 Sept 1696 —, Catharine Phillips

Baker, Anne, of co Bucks, *spin*. — 8 Feb 1718-9 —, Thomas Meads, esq , widower, [of St Andrew, Holborn.

Baker, Martha, of Covent Garden, *spin* — 28 July, 1720 —, Henry ffaure, of St [Mary Axe, *bat*

Baker, St John, of St Andrew's, Holborn — 20 Aug 1710 —, Magdalene Ingoldesby, of parish of St Giles in the [Fields

Baldwin, Samuel, of the Inner Temple — 3 Aug 1710 — Mary Harman, of the parish of St Andrew's, Holborn (married by Mr Jackson, Reader of the Temple).

Baldwin, Sara — 14 Dec 1699 —, Robert Allen, mariner, next the Last Gravelane, [Houndsditch.

Ball, Robert, victualler at the Black Lion in Pall Mall — 28 May, 1700 —, Sara [Allen

Ball, Robert, of the parish of St. Giles in the fields — 1 April, 1703 —, Bridget Morris, of Camberwell, Surrey, married [by Mr Fettiplace

Ball, William, of the parish of St. Bartholomew the Less — 20 May, 1711 —, [Frances Hall, of same.

Ballard, Isaac, of the parish of St. Mary le Strand — 3 June, 1732 —, Martha [Gillman, of St Giles in the Fields.

Ballet, Henry, of Chelmsford, Essex — 27 Dec 1735 —, Elisabeth Ellard, of St. [George the Martyr, Middx.

Ballinger, James, of St Andrew's, Holborn — 10 April, 1748 —, Mary Cormell, of [same

Bamborough, John, of St Clement Danes — 6 Oct. 1647 —, Sarah Marriot, of [St. Vedast, Foster Lane.

Bambridge, Robert, *bat*, of the parish of St. Clement Danes — 29 Sept 1718 [, Alice Darke, *widow*, of same

Bamford, Catherine — 7 Dec 1701 —, William Thompson, vintner, in Lime [Street.

Bampton, William, of St George's, Bloomsbury. — 5 July, 1744 —, Elizabeth Bew, [of St. Anne's, Westminster

Banbridge, Thomas, of St George's, Queen Sq — 15 Feb 1728-9, Ann Bollington, [of St. Andrew, Holborn

Banbury, Hannah of the parish of St Bennet, Gracechurch St — 1 April, 1711 —, Philip Sheppard, of parish of [St Sepulchre

Bankes, Marlina, of the parish of St. Dunstan's, Stepney — 23 Dec. 1702 —, [Abraham Gboo, seaman, of same.

Banks, Elisabeth, of St. George's, Hanover Sq — 8 Nov. 1744 —, James Hawley, [M D , of St. Paul s, Covent Garden

Banyer, Bellamy, of the parish of St Gregory — 10 April, 1740 —, Jennet [Walker, of St Michael's Bassishaw

Bannister, Thomas, coachmaker in Long Acre. — 20 June, 1697 —, Rebecca [Barnet.

Barber, Elizabeth — 20 Aug 1696 —, John Martin, baker in St. Giles in the [Fields

Barber, Elizabeth, of St Andrew, Holborn. — 23 Nov. 1714 —, Thomas Staple, of [the same.

Barber, Jonathan, victualler in Gray's Inn lane — 20 Jan 1702-3 —, Patronella Cadford, both of the parish of St An-
[drew's, Holborn

Barber, William, of the parish of St James, Westminster — 30 May, 1710 —, Susan Langford, of parish of St Dunstan's in
[the East.

Barker, Ann, of the parish of St James, Clerkenwell — 3 Sept. 1713 —, John
[Hunt, of same

Barker, Benjamin, stationer in Westminster Hall — 14 May, 1702 —, Grace God-
[bould

Barker, George, farrier, St Ann's, Aldersgate — 18 June, 1695—, Ann Holmby.

Barker, James, of St Paul's, Covent Garden — 26 Dec 1737 —, Elizabeth Money,
[of same.

Barker, Margaret, of St. Paul's, Covent Garden — 9 June, 1726 —, John Lan-
[caster, of St James, Westminster

Barkham, Mary, of the Close, near city of Lincoln — 3 July, 1735 —, Tobias
[Rustal, of same

Barlin Rebecca, of the parish of St James —21 May, 1711 —, Thomas Madbury,
[of same.

Barlow, Mary, sing, of the parish of St Andrew's, Holborn — 27 Jan 1714-5
[—, Richard Cooper, bat., of same

Barlow, Robert, of the parish of St Andrew's, Holborn — 19 Jan 1713-4 —,
[Elizabeth Burr, of same

Barmley, Sybil, of the parish of St. Andrew, Holborn. — 17 Oct 1714 —, James
[Robinson, of same

Barnard, John, of Kensington — 17 Feb 1725-6 —, Elizabeth Hiron, of Wands-
[worth, Surrey

Barnardiston, Martha, of the parish of St Andrew's, Holborn — 2 Oct 1712 —, Charles Edwin, esq, of Lincoln's Inn

Barnes, Hannah — 7 Sept. 1700 —, Matthew Green, wine cooper in Budge
[Row

Barnes, John, of St Martin's in the Fields. — 20 June, 1719, Elizabeth Trower, of
[same.

Barnes, Margaret, widow, of St Clement Danes. — 24 Feb 1714-5 —, Francis Playters, widower, of parish of St
[Bride's.

Barnes, Martha, of the parish of Shenley, Herts — 24 Feb 1707-8 —, Daniel
[Nicholls, of same parish

Barnes, Mary, sing, of the parish of St Bride's, London — 17 April, 1715 —,
[William Crosfield, bct, of same

Barnes, Rachel, — 23 April, 1702 —, Hugh Hall, perriwig maker, in Charles St.,
[Covent Garden

Barnet, Rebecca, — 20 June 1697 —, Thomas Bannister, coachmaker in Long
[Acre.

Barnett Thomas, of the parish of St. Magnus the Great — 4 Oct 1716 —, Anne
[Atkins, of St Andrew s, Holborn

Barrabay, Rebecca, — 8 April, 1697 —, Andrew Reed, cook in Abchurch Lane

Barradell, Mary, of the parish of St Paul's, Covent Garden. — 2 Oct 1716 —,
[Samuel Palmer, of same.

Barras, John, of St Clement Danes — 12 May, 1743 —, Elizabeth Hunter, of St.
[Anne's, Soho

Barrett, Frances, — 19 May, 1702 —, William Scrafton, clerk, at Mr Barrett's
[in Doctor's Commons.

Barrett, John, bat., of the parish of St. Giles in the Fields — 17 Dec 1714 —,
[Mary Wells, sing, of same.

Barringer, Richard, coachman to Sir Steinsham Master, in Red Lion sq — 13
[Nov 1705 —, Mary Edlin, (by licence.)

Barrington, Mary, of St Andrew's, Holborn. — 7 Feb. 1735-6 —, John Wiche-
[halse, of same.

Barry, Honor, of the parish of St Andrew's, Holborn. — 17 Feb 1703-4 —, John Speakman, watchmaker, near Hatton
[Wall, in same parish.

Bartlett, Humphrey, of the parish of Bow. — 28 Jan. 1724-5 —, Elizabeth Aldridge,
[of St Andrew, Holborn

Barton, Peter, of St Andrew's, Holborn. — 30 Nov. 1713 —, Sarah Hillay, of
[same.

Barton, Sarah, of St Katherine's, Tower Hill. — 16 Dec. 1713 —, Thomas [Vaughan, of Stepney parish

Barugh, Mary, of the parish of St Bride's, London. — 19 June 1709 —, Thomas [Pusey, of parish of Marcham, Berks

Barwell, Giles, of the parish of St James, Clerkenwell. — 13 May, 1714 —, Katherine Tate, of St. Giles, Cripplegate

Barwick, William, of the parish of St Martin's in the Fields — 9 Nov 1714 [—, Jane Hatton, of same

Bass, Thomas, of the parish of St Martin's in the Fields. — 27 July, 1707 —, Ann [Pusey, of same parish

Basse, Ann, of parish of St. Andrew's, Holborn. — 11 Nov. 1703 —, James Beale, [mariner in Field Lane, same parish.

Bassett, Martha, of Northfleet, Kent. — 30 Oct. 1725 — James Burrus, of St Mary, [Rotherhithe.

Baston, Elisabeth, of St. Andrew's, Holborn — 11 Nov. 1744 —, William Hodgson, of St. Leonard's, Shoreditch

Bastone, Roger, of St. Andrew's, Holborn 24 Oct 1730 —, Elisabeth Evans, of [same

Batchelor, Mary, — 6 July, 1701 —, John Wheeler, tailor, near Drury Lane End, [St Giles

Bates, Mary, of Amersham, Bucks. — 29 Oct 1714 —, John Stallings, of High [Wycombe, Bucks

Bates, Mary, of St Paul's, Covent Garden — 3 May, 1724 —, Josiah Burneby, of [parish of Hampstead, Middx

Bates, Mary, of St George's Queen Sq — 1 Dec 1728 —, Edward Betsworth, of [St Sepulchre's

Bates, Richard, of Chipping Wycomb, Bucks — 16 April, 1741 —, Catherine [Hakewill, of Weston, Bucks.

Batson, Alice, of St Margaret's, widow — 5 March, 1727-8 —, Henry Knowles, of [St. Anne's, Westminster

Batteley, Mary, of St. Dunstan's, Fleet St. — 21 Jan 1730-1 —, John Stacy, of [same.

Battell, Elizabeth, of St Margaret's, Westminster — License dated Jan 1717-8 —, Moses Williams, of Dyfynoly, co [Brecon.

Battershill, Peter, of St Giles, Cripplegate. — 23 June, 1728 —, Margaret Horton, [of same.

Baty, Susanna, of the parish of St Andrew, Holborn. — 21 March, 1750-1 —, Ed- [ward Harte, of same

Bawler, James, baker in Old Street. — 10 [Jan. 1696-7 —, Dorothy Chambers.

Baxter, Matthew, of the parish of St Clement Danes. — 16 May, 1714 —, [Jane Dunbar of same

Baxter, Thomas, of the parish of St Andrew's, Holborn — 12 June, 1709 —, Mary Pounceby, of parish of St Clements [Danes

Baxter, William, of the parish of St Andrew — 21 May, 1738 —, Mary Wilkin, of [same

Bayly, Elizabeth, — 20 Nov 1698 —, James [Smith, brewer's servant

Bayly, Margaret, of the parish of St Dunstan's in the West — 23 May, 1714 [—, Thomas Magew, of same

Bayns, Ann, of the parish of St Paul's, Covent Garden — 3 Feb 1703-4 —, John Gibbons, of Great Marlow, Bucks, [wheelwright.

Bazire, Peter, barber in Dean St, St. Andrew's — 5 June, 1701 —, Hannah [Watts

Beaching, William, of the parish of St Andrew's, Holborn — 4 March, 1710-1 —, Rebecca More, of parish of St Cle- [ment's Danes.

Beakley, Henry, of the parish of St Leonard, Shoreditch — 16 Aug 1713 [—, Mary Eyres, of same

Beakley, John, of the parish of St Bride's, London — 1 Jan 1711-2 —, Mary [Horwood, of same

Beale, James, of the parish of St Andrew's, Holborn, mariner in Field Lane. — 11 Nov 1703 —, Ann Basse, of same [parish.

Berg, Gunder, of the parish of St Magnus, London — 22 March, 1712-3 —, Mary [Dallon, of same

Berkley, Elizabeth, of the parish of St Bride's, London — 14 Feb 1709-10 [—, Thomas Reeve, gent, of same

Bernard, Elizabeth, of the parish of St Bride's, London — 17 Feb 1708-9 —, [Ambrose Dickins, of same

Berners, Mary, of Hampstead — 17 Feb 1749-50 — Durley Wintle, of St James', [Westminster

de Bert, Sarah, of the parish of St. Andrew's, Holborn. — 26 October, 1707 —, James Pember, of the parish of St Clement [Danes, gent (by a licence).

Bertlet, Isaiah, of St Ann's, Westminster, *bat* — 5 Dec 1720 —, Elizabeth Mionet, [of St Bennet Fink, *spin*

Bethel, Mary — 22 July, 1698 —, William Harby, a gentleman of Halton Holgate, [co. Lincoln

Betsworth, Edward, of St Sepulchre's. — 1 Dec 1728 —, Mary Bates, of St. [George's, Queen Square.

Betton, John, of the parish of Mortlake, Surrey. — 28 Jan 1713-4 —, Sarah [Wood, of same.

Betty, Bridget, of the parish of St Pancras — 26 Oct 1714 —, Richard Croucher, [of same

Bety, Bridget, of the parish of St Pancras — 13 April, 1714 —, Richard Croucher, [of same

Bevanck, Mary. — 2 July, 1696 — Benjamin Biddle, shoemaker in Little [Gray's Inn Lane

Beveridge, Ann, of the parish of St Giles in the Fields. — 11 Oct 1705 — Thomas [King, of same parish, soldier

Bew, Elizabeth, of St Anne's, Westminster 5 July, 1744 —, William Bampton, of [St George's, Bloomsbury

Beynon, Eignon, gent, of the parish of Redborn, Herts — 19 June, 1708 —, Mary Ecclestone, of parish of St James, [Clerkenwell.

Bibbee, Theodosia — 28 Jan. 1700-1 —, John Hippisley, apothecary in St Martin's [Lane

Bibbey, William, journeyman tailor at Whit^{e} Hart, in Bloomsbury. — 12 Jan 1698-9 [—, Caroline Wesson.

Bickerton, Edward, of St Stephen's, Coleman Street — 12 April, 1724 — Rachel [Young, of St Martin Vintry

Bickerton, Samuel, of the parish of St. Botolph's, Aldersgate — 20 June, 1710 —, Mary Bedford, of parish of St Dunstan's in the West

Bicks, Mary, of the parish of Heese (Hayes), Middx — 15 April, 1703 —, Nicholas [Spurling, yeoman, of same.

Biddle, Benjamin, shoemaker in Little Gray's Inn Lane. — 2 July, 1696 —, Mary [Bevanck.

Bigg, Martha, of Ross, co. Hereford, — 15 Sept. 1715 —, Richard Underwood, of [same

Bigge, Grace, of the parish of St. Andrew, Holborn — 27 July, 1734 —, Robert Carr, of parish of St. Martin, Ludgate.

Bilbo, Peter, of the parish of St James, Clerkenwell — 13 June, 1714 —, Sarah Potter, of same (the man aged 60, the [woman 34)

Billington, James, gent, of the parish of St Giles in the Fields — 20 Sept 1705 —, Dorothy Gover, of the parish of St Andrew's, Holborn (Married by Mr. Billington, of Dulwich College. The man was aged about 20, the woman 80.)

Billinton, William, of Enfield, Middx — 15 Dec. 1722 —, Olivie Margarete Bagley, [of same.

Bingley, John, a firkin man in Lay-stall Street. — 6 Dec 1696 —, Elizabeth [Peate.

Binnyon, Margaret, of the parish of St. Martin's le Grand. — 21 May, 1713 —, [Thomas Nelson, of same.

Birch Frances, of Writtle, Essex — 26 May, 1748 —, Rev John Taylor, of Swans-[comb, Kent.

Birch, Joseph, of the parish of St Andrew's, Holborn. — 13 April, 1710 —, Judith [Wilds, of same

Birchman, Henry, of the parish of St. Giles in the Fields — 4 May, 1714 —, Katherine Mountsteevens, of parish of [St Martin's in the Fields.

Bird, John, labourer against Chancery Lane, Holborn — 29 Jan 1698-9 —, Mary [Pooley

Bird, John, of the parish of St Sepulchre. — 14 April, 1714 —, Mary Burton, of [same

Bird, Mary, of the parish of St. Andrew's, Holborn — 7 Feb 1711-2 —, John [Young, of same.

Birkhead, Elizabeth, of the parish of St Andrew's, Holborn — 29 Dec 1713 —, [James Bradwin, of same

Bishop, George, of the parish of St Sepulchre, — 6 Dec 1712 —Isabella Whitmore, of [same

Bishop, Henry, of St Clement Danes — 10 Sept. 1714 — Ann Dodge, of St [Margaret's, Westminster

Bishop, James, of St Andrew's, Holborn — 24 Sept 1730 — Eleanor Allin, of St [John's, Clerkenwell

Bishop, Sarah, of Manningtree, Essex — 22 Dec. 1738 —, Richard Williams, esq , [of the Middle Temple

Blabey, Mary — 5 March, 1701-2 —, John [Holbrook, husbandman in Deptford

Black, George, of St. Sepulchre's — 1 March, 1753 —, Betty Bean, of St [Andrew's, Holborn

Black, Hannah, of the parish of St Pancras (where the banns were published) — 22 March, 1710-1 —, Roger Maddox, of [same

Blackbourne, Alice. — 15 Aug 1700 —, William Goode, sword cutler in New [Street.

Blackbourne, John, of St. Clement Danes. — 21 March, 1720-1 —, Susanna Dob- [man, of same, spin

Blackbourn, William, of St Faith's, under St Paul's. London — 24 May, 1714 —, Martha Buckle, of the parish of [Christ Church Hospital

Blackmore, John, broker near St Anne's Church, Soho. — 10 July, 1698 —, [Martha Dickenson.

Blackmore, Raymond, of the parish of Heathfield, Sussex — 29 March 1740 —, Elizabeth Treegood, of St Andrew's, [Holborn.

Blacknoe, Anne, of Christ Church parish, London. — 10 March 1749-50 —, William Parker, of St. Michael's, Corn- [hill.

Blackston, Anne — 12 Dec 1695 —, William Odson, of Arundel St , Strand, [waterman

Blackwell, Elizabeth, of St Dunstan's in the West — 18 Sept. 1712 —, Jonathan [Fryar, of St Giles in the Fields.

Blagrave, Elizabeth. — 4 Feb. 1701-2. — William Andrewes at the Lion and Crown, near the New Exchange in the [Strand

Blake, Ann, of the parish of All Hallows the Great. — 6 Nov 1707 —, Robert Turner, of parish of St Dunstan's in the [East.

Blake, Elizabeth, of St Botolph's, Alders- gate. — 5 March, 1711-2 —, William [Williams, of Finchley, Middx

Blake, Elizabeth, of the parish of All Hallows the Less, — 4 Dec 1716 —, John Eden [Littell, of same

Blake, Hugh, of St. Giles in the Fields — 30 Jan. 1732-3 —, Mary Royse, als. [Rouse, of St Clements in the Strand

Bland, George, of the parish of St Andrew's, Holborn, gentleman's servant — 8 April, 1706 —, Frances Dixon (by a licence)

Bland, Mary, of the parish of St Mary, Whitechapel — 30 April, 1710 —, [Robert Ker.

Bland, Susan, of the parish of St Mary, Whitechapel. — 3 Aug 1710 —, Robert Ker, of parish of St. Stephen, Coleman [Street.

Blare, Elizabeth, of the parish of St Magnus the Martyr — 15 Nov 1707 —, Thomas [Smith, of parish of St Peter's Cheap.

Blathwayt, William, bat, of the parish of St Martin in the Fields — 17 Aug. 1718 —, Thomazina Ambrose, of parish [of St Giles in the Fields, spin.

Blayow, Francis, of the parish of St Mar- tin's in the Fields. — 6 Dec. 1710 —, [Mary Moy, of same.

Bly, Sara — 5 Jan 1696 7 —, Edmund Peat, periwig maker, against St Dun-
[stan's Church

Blyth, John, of the parish of St Dunstan's in the West — 11 Aug 1706 —, Frances
[Honnor, of the same (by a license)

Boan, Ann, of the parish of St Andrew s, Holborn — 2 Nov 1703 —, John Neve, salesman in Monmouth St, parish
[of St Giles in the Fields

Bocker, Elizabeth, of Kentish Town, Pancras parish — 28 Nov 1719 —, Joseph
[Whitehall, of same

Boddington, Elizabeth, of the parish of St. Bartholomew the Less — 26 Aug 1708 —, John Loft, of parish of St Botolph
[without, Aldersgate

Bodges, Alice — 14 Dec 1698 —, Thomas
[Dunn, butcher in Clare market

Boister, William, of the parish of Islington — 2 Nov 1713 —, Susanna Thurkill,
[of St Giles, Cripplegate

Boldock, Edward, of the parish of St. James', Clerkenwell. — 17 July 1707 —, Mary Oliver, of parish of St Andrew's,
[Holborn

Bolland, Mary, of St Botolph's, Bishopsgate — 1 Nov 1744 —, John Page, of
[St Andrew's, Holborn

Bollington, Ann, of St Andrew's, Holborn. — 15 Feb 1728-9 —, Thomas Banbridge, of St George's, Queen Sq

Bolton, Elisabeth, of St. Andrew's, Holborn —30 April, 1737—, John Todd, of same

Boman, Yonchin, of the parish of St Ann's, Blackfriars. — 11 July, 1714 —, George
[Gilson, of same.

Bond, Edward, of St Andrew's, Holborn. — 6 Oct 1709 —, Katherine Salley, of
[parish of St. Giles in the Fields

Bond, William, of St. Paul's, Covent Garden — 6 May, 1732 —, Mary Dorrel, of St
[Andrew's, Holborn

Bone, Honor, of the parish of St Andrew's, Holborn. — 13 July 1711 —, Evan
[Richards, of same.

Bonnivert, Gideon, soldier, in Panton Street. — 29 Sept 1698 —, Anne War-
[dour

Booker, Mary, of the parish of St. Andrew's, Holborn — 29 Nov 1713 —, John
[Richboll, of same

Boone, Elizabeth, of the parish of St Martin's in the Fields — 29 Jan 1707-8 —, Richard Wilkinson, of parish of St Ann's,
[Westminster

Boons, Joan — 20 May, 1701 —, John Stoakes, farmer, of High Ongar, Essex.

Boote, John, of the parish of St Andrew's, Holborn — license dated May, 1717 —,
[Mary Adshead, of same.

Booth, Jane, sing, of the parish of St. George's, Southwark — 31 July, 1715 —,
[Benjamin Hopkins, bat, of same.

Boreman, John, of St. Ann's, Westminster, bat — 6 Jan 1718-9 —, Sara Pierson,
[of same, spin.

Borsley, Richard, turner at the Ditch-side. [— 3 Feb 1699-1700 —, Mary Page.

Bosley, Mary. — 5 June 1723 —, John
[Linter.

Bostock, William, victualler at the George, Piccadilly — 4 March, 1700-1 —, Sara
[Bell.

Boswell, Arrabella, of St Giles in the Fields — 5 Sept 1716 —, William Sudbury,
[of St. Paul's, Covent Garden

Boswell, Edward, of the parish of St. Giles in the fields — 21 Dec 1707 —, Margaret Hale, of same parish.

Boswell, Mary, of the parish of St. Giles in the fields — 25 Nov 1705 —, Thomas Nutling, poulterer in Bloomsbury mar-
[ket.

Boswell, Thomas, of St. Giles in the Fields — 5 Sept. 1716 —, Rachel Vaughan, of
[same

Boswell, Susanna, of the parish of St Andrew, Holborn — 2 Dec. 1712 —,
[Ralph Lodley, of same.

Bosworth, Thomas, of the parish of St Sepulchre's, pewterer near Holborn Conduit — 1 Jan 1703-4 —, Hannah Uphallfence, of the parish of St Andrew's,
[Holborn

Bott, Mary, of St George the Martyr. — 29 Aug 1731 —, Richard Goldsadle, of
[St. Giles in the Fields.

Boughey, Thomas, widower, of the parish
  of St James, Clerkenwell — 27 Dec
  [1714 —, Ann Field, widow, of same

Boulton, Thomas, of Walthamstow, Essex,
  batch — 24 Jan 1720-1 —, Elizabeth
  [Brockly, of same, *spin*

Bourne, Henry, mercer in King's Clere
  parish, co. Southampton — 29 Sept
  [1700 —, Letitia Noak

Bowe, Elisabeth, of St Clement Danes —
  15 May, 1740 —, John Bennet, of same

Bower, Phillis, — 23 Jan 1695-6 —, Bartholomew King, instrument maker in St.
  [Clement's parish

Bowman, Robert, of the parish of St
  Martin's in the Fields — 25 July, 1714
  [—, Elizabeth Forgaron, of same

Bowring, Grace, of Finchley, Middx — 19
  Oct 1744 —, Richard Newsham of
  [same

Bowring, William, of St Michael Bassishaw
  — 19 Oct. 1738 —, Grace Fifield, of
  [St. James, Westminster

van Boxstand, Elena, of the parish of St.
  Ann's, Westminster — 18 April, 1712
  [—, Peter Cavallier, of same

Boycott, Fran — 26 Feb. 1722-3 —,
  [Christian Pearson.

Boydany, Elizabeth, of St. Giles — 25
  Jan 1718-9 —, Tobias Stronovins of
  [same, both single.

Brabben, Mary, of the parish of St. Bride's,
  London — 2 April, 1711 —, John
  [Torver, of same

Brace, Mary, of the parish of St. Martin's
  in the Fields. — 17 April, 1714 —,
  [Joseph Cowel, of same

Bradbury, Mary, of the parish of St. Anne,
  Westminster — 14 Dec. 1708 —,
  [Charles Johnson, of same

Bradhan, William, victualler in St. Cle-
  ment's lane, parish of St Clement's
  Danes — 6 Sept 1705 —, Christian
  [Dixon, of same parish

Bradley, John, of Lamb's Conduit Fields
  — 17 Sept 1696 — Elizabeth Dawson

Bradley, Matthias, of the parish of Hatfield,
  Herts — 25 Aug 1712 —, Martha
  Farrar, of parish of St. Giles in the
  [Fields.

Bradly, John, of the parish of St Andrew,
  Holborn — 24 June, 1714 —, Dina
  [Dorrell, of same.

Bradly, John, of St. Giles in the Fields. —
  8 Jan 1735-6 —, Elisabeth Mallard, of
  [St. Martin's in the Fields.

Bradly, Mary, of the parish of St Bartholomew the Less, in Smithfield — 31 Dec
  [1706 —, Francis Keell.

Bradshaw, Catharine, of St Andrew's, Holborn. — 3 Oct. 1728 —, John Walter,
  [of same.

Bradshaw, Thomas, of St. Mary Magda-
  lene, Bermondsey — 12 June, 1750 —,
  Elizabeth Whitworth, of St John's,
  [Southwark

Bradwin, James, of the parish of St. Andrew's, Holborn — 29 Dec 1713 —,
  [Elizabeth Birkhead, of same.

Brage, William (esq), of Hatfield Peverill,
  Essex — 7 May, 1706 — Elizabeth
  [Player

Brainsby, Katherine, of St Sepulchre's —
  29 Oct 1713 —, Robert Rogers, of
  [same

Bramly, Matthew butcher in Little Lincoln's
  Inn Fields. — 5 Aug 1701 —, Mary
  [Thacker

Bramston, Thomas, — 17 Feb 1701-2 —,
  [Margaret Richards

Brandreth, John, merchant tailor in Fetter
  Lane, parish of St. Andrew's, Holborn.
  — 7 Feb 1703-4 —, Mary Elfie, of
  [same parish, (by license)

Bransbey, John, — 25 Jan 1701-2 —,
  [Susanna Davis.

Brathwaite, Susanna, of St Mary, Islington — 26 Feb. 1739-40 —, William
  [Noble, M A, of Gray's Inn.

Bravill, Mary, of the parish of St Andrew,
  Holborn — 21-26 Oct 1714 —, Ben-
  [jamin Bryant, of same

Bray, Martha, — 4 Sept 1698 —, Richard
  Hatley, a Norwich factor in Abchurch
  [Lane.

Brearey, Henry, clerk, of the parish of
Boxworth, co Cambridge — 13 June,
1711 —, Elizabeth Robinson, of parish
[St. Andrew's, Holborn

Bridgeman, Charles, of the parish of Kensington. — 2 May, 1717 —, Sarah Mist,
[of St. Andrew's, Holborn

Bridges, Thomas, of the parish of St Giles
in the Fields. — 7 Dec. 1712 —, Eliza-
[beth Curwen, of same

Briggs, Jane — 29 Aug 1697 —, William
Carrington, oilman in Bromley St, Hol-
[born

Brightwell, Hanna, of St Andrew, Holborn, widow — 15 Dec 1720 —, Jacob
[Wallis of Edmonton, widower

Brindisdon, Matthias, of the parish of St
Giles in the Fields — 20 Sept 1713 —,
[Margaret Lydford, of same

Brinklett, Elisabeth, of St. George's, Hanover Sq — 10 April, 1748 —, John
[Gibson, of St Andrew, Holborn

Brishow, William, of St Andrew's, Holborn,
widower — 21 Sept 1718 —, Elizabeth
Bucknall, of St Martin's in the Fields,
[widow

Bristow, Anthony, of St Bridget's, widower
— 3 Jan 1720-1 —, Elizabeth Hawkins,
[of same, spin.

Bristow, Margaret, of Reigate, Surrey —
4 Sept 1739 —, Henry Oddie, of St
[Anne's, Soho

Bristow, Martha, of St Andrew's, Holborn
— 5 Feb 1729-30 —, Thomas Shadd,
[of St. James, Clerkenwell.

Broadgate, John, farrier in St. Giles in the
Fields. — 24 Feb. 1697-8 —, Alice
[Smith.

Broadhead, Benjamin, bat, of St Andrew's,
Holborn — 23 April, 1719 —, Grace
[Webel, of St Giles in the Fields, spin

Brocas, Richard, of All Saints' parish,
Bread St. — 8 April, 1716 —, Phebe
[Heneage, of St. Andrew's, Holborn

Brock, Daniel, bat, of the parish of St
James in the Fields — 19 April, 1715
[—, Jane Tumersid, sing, of same

Brockenbury, Elizabeth, of St. Mary le
Bow — 29 April, 1707 —, James Egen,
[of the parish of St Ann, Westminster

Brockly, Elizabeth, of Walthamstow, Essex,
spin — 24 Jan 1720-1 —, Thomas
[Boulton, of same, batch

Brockwell, Elizabeth, of the parish of
Hampstead — 15 Oct. 1713 —, Robert
Bruges, of parish of St Clement Danes

Brodrick, Lawrence, Doctor of Divinity
— 27 April, 1710 —, Ann Humphreys,
[(married by Mr Humphreys).

Broggrove, Sara. — 4 Nov 1701 —, John
Pearson, seaman, near the Ship, in Salis-
[bury Court.

Bromwich, Anne. — 21 May, 1695 —,
John Pace, coachman in St Anne's,
[Westminster.

Brooke, Joseph, servant — 25 Nov 1699
[—, Elizabeth White

Brookes, Elizabeth. — 2 Nov 1699 —,
Samuel Lacey, tallow chandler in Drury
[Lane.

Brookes, Elizabeth, of the parish of St.
Pauls, Covent Garden — 27 April,
1704 —, John Farrer, drysalter, parish
[of St Giles in the Fields.

Brookes, Francis, of the parish of St Giles,
Cripplegate — 12 June, 1712 —, Rebecca Hornblower, of parish of St Leo-
[nard's, Shoreditch.

Brookes, James, of St Andrew's, Holborn
— 1 June, 1732 —, Anne Taylor, of St
[Giles in the Felds

Brooks, Joseph, of the parish of St Giles in
the Fields — 12 May, 1714 —, Katherine
Loudor, of parish of St. Botolph's, Ald-
[gate

Brothers, Richard, wheelwright in Brewer's
St, parish of St James, Westminster.
[— 28 Nov 1704 —, Jane Saunders.

Brotherton, Joseph, of the parish of St.
Giles in the Fields, butcher in Hart St,
Bloomsbury — 9 Dec 1703 —, Ann
[Roberts, of same parish

Brotherton, William, brazier in Fleet Lane,
parish of St Sepulchre's — 30 March,
1703 —, Sarah Gawy, of the parish of St.
[Giles in the Fields.

Broughton, Samuel, of the parish of St
Sepulchre. — 28 Feb 1713-4 —, Sarah
[Morris, of same.

Brown, David, of St Martin's le Grand. — 26 March, 1734 —, Mary Johnson of St [Andrew's, Holborn

Brown, Edward, of Withersfield, co Suffolk — 25 Sept 1715 —, Elizabeth Russett, [of St George's parish, Southwark

Brown, Elizabeth, of the parish of St Ann's, Westminster — 5 Dec 1708 —, William Stevens, of St Katherine Coleman, [London

Brown, Elizabeth, of the parish of St Sepulchre's — 11 Feb 1712-3 —, Morgan Price, of parish of St Olave, South- [wark

Brown, Elisabeth, of St Clement Danes — 1 Aug 1731 —, John Napier, of St [Margaret's, Westminster

Brown, Emblyn, of the parish of Rotherwith, Surrey — 6 March, 1708-9 —, William Young, of parish of St. Michael Basi- [shaw

Brown, Sir George, bart, of Covent Garden — 5 Feb 1721-2 —, Prudence Thorold, [of same, spin

Brown, Grace — 18 Aug 1697 —, William [Edwards, yeoman in East Barnet

Brown, Joan, of Clapham parish, Surrey, widow — 8 Oct 1722 —, William Lane, [of Hampstead, Middx, widower

Brown, Margaret, of St Margaret's, New Fish St — 15 Sept 1747 —, Ynyr Burges, [of St Lawrence Jewry

Brown, Mary, of the parish of St Andrew's, Holborn. — 19 Nov 1713 —, James [Gevett, of same.

Brown, Mary, of St James, Clerkenwell — 11 Oct. 1715 —, John Dean, of parish [of St. Sepulchre's.

Brown, Mary, of Hampstead, Middx, spin — 8 April, 1720 —, Edward Scaife, late [of same, bat

Brown, Richard, of the parish of St. Andrew's, Holborn, organist — 14 March, 1705-6 —, Temperance Guy, of parish of Wimbourne, co Dorset (by [license)

Brown, Samuel, of St. George the Martyr. — 4 Oct 1726 —, Mary Williams, of [same

Brown, Thomas, of the parish of St Antholines. — 7 March, 1710-1 —, Mary Roswell, of parish of St. Giles, [Cripplegate

Browne, Mary — 21 Jan 1700-1 —, William Pearce, upholsterer next the [Dog Tavern in Drury Lane.

Browne, Mary, of St Giles in the Fields — 30 Nov 1752 —, Richard Perry, [esq, of the Inner Temple

Browne, Sara — 20 Jan 1697-8 —, Benjamin Taylor, tailor in Nelson's [Court, Drury Lane.

Browne, Thomas, of St George's, Hanover Sq — 6 June, 1734 —, Sarah Daw- [son, of St. Dunstan's in the West

Brownjohn, Edward, bat, of the parish of St. Michael, Cornhill. — 5 Mar 1717-8 —, Ann Richardson, widow, of parish [of St. Catherine Cree Church

Bruce, Jane — 22 July, 1697 —, Joseph [Paine, apothecary in New Brentford

Brudenell, Edward, gent, of Barton Sea- grave, co Northampton — 19 May, [1698 —, Elizabeth Dilke

Bruges, Robert, of the parish of St. Clement Danes — 15 Oct 1713 —, Elizabeth [Brockwell, of parish of Hampstead

Bryan, Thomas, of St. James, Westminster — 5 Feb 1727-8 —, Mary White, of [Whitefriars, Precinct

Bryan, Thomas, of Whitefriars — 25 Nov 1729 —, Lydia Smith, of Ashton, Salop.

Bryant, Benjamin, of the parish of St. Andrew, Holborn — 21-26 Oct. 1714 [—, Mary Bravill, of same.

Bryon, Elizabeth, of the parish of St. Giles in the Fields — 22 June, 1714 —, Samuel Herbert, of parish of St Andrew's, [Holborn

Buck, Elizabeth, widow, of the parish of St. Sepulchre's. — 9 Jan. 1714-5 —, Augustus [Webb, bat, of same

Buckland, James, carpenter in Castle Yard. — 8 April, 1702 —, Elizabeth Crawley.

Buckle, Anne — 31 March, 1698 —, George Paine, coachman to Squire Middleton in [Soho Square.

Buckle, Martha, of the parish of Christ Church Hospital — 24 May, 1714 —, William Blackbourn, of St. Faith's, under [St. Paul's, London.

Buckley, Lydia, of the parish of All Hallows the Less, Thames Street — 12 July, 1711 [—, Joshua Drake, of same.

Bucknall, Elizabeth, of St Martin's in the Fields, widow. — 21 Sept 1718 —, William Brishow, of St Andrew's, Hol- [born, widower

Bucknall, Hester, of the parish of St. Giles in the Fields. — 20 March, 1710-1 —, Joseph Smith, of parish of St. Andrew's, [Holborn

Budworth, Timothy, coachmaker in High Holborn, parish of St Giles in the Fields — 8 May, 1705 — Anne Linnet, of the [same

Bull, Ann, of the parish of St. James, Clerkenwell — 6 April, 1714 — William Steed, [of same

Bull, John, of the parish of St Clement Danes — 11 July, 1714 —, Jane Curtis, of [same.

Bullock, Samuel, stable groom, in St Anne's parish. — 14 May, 1695 —, Anne Frank- [ling.

Bunce, Matthew, clockmaker in Pearpoole Lane — 3 Feb 1697-8 —, Dennis [Watts

Bundy, Mary, of the parish of St. James, Westminster — 17 June, 1714 —, [William Showwell, of same

Bunes, Elizabeth, — 29 Sept. 1696 —, Harry Gawen Carew, painter in St [Andrew's, Holborn.

Bunfoy, Nicholas, a gent, of Wellington, Herts. — 21 Oct. 1701 —, Elizabeth [Hayle.

Burch, Elisabeth, of St Catherine's, near the Tower. — 26 Aug 1751 —, Richard [Hill, of St George the Martyr

Burchell, Elizabeth. — 31 Aug 1699 —, St. John Wollfrys, farrier without [Bishopsgate.

Burchell, Richard, of the parish of Deptford, Kent — 25 July, 1709 —, Sarah [Chappell, of same.

Burchett, Mary, of St. Mary, Whitechapel. — 19 Dec 1751 —, Thomas Fenwick, [of St. Michael's, Crooked Lane.

Burden, Mary — 16 Feb 1696-7 — Oliver Pervill, mariner in St Peter's Street, [Bloomsbury

Burgen, Margaret. — 14 Sept 1704 —, John Walley, corn chandler in King Street, near Bloomsbury, parish of St [Giles in the Fields (by license)

Burges, Ynyr, of St Lawrence, Jewry — 15 Sept 1747 —, Margaret Brown, [of St Margaret's, New Fish Street

Burgis, Henry, of St. Clement Danes. — 9 May, 1714 —, Mary Jones, of St [James', Westminster.

Burke, Anne — 6 Jan 1696-7 —, Charles [Knapper, tailor in Tuttle Street

Burke, Thomas, an officer under the Lord of Berkley — 8 Nov 1696 —, Judith [ffranklin

Burker, Robert, of Paddington — 2 June, 1739 —, Elisabeth Turst, of St Mary [le bone

Burland, Mary, sing, of the parish of St. Martin's in the Fields — 27 Feb 1714-5 [—, Benjamin Spire, bat, of same

Burneby, Josiah, of the parish of Hampstead, Middx — 3 May, 1724 —, Mary [Bates, of St Paul's, Covent Garden

Burnham, Martha, of St. Andrew's, Holborn — 24 Dec 1749 —, Edward Sells, [of St Saviour's, Southwark.

Buroley, Thomas, of the parish of St Ann's, Westminster — 12 Feb 1709-10 —, [Martha Bennet, of same.

Burr, Elizabeth, of the parish of St Andrew's, Holborn — 19 Jan. 1713-4 —, Robert [Barlow, of same.

Burr, Elisabeth, of Hochff, Beds — 12 Sept. 1734 —, William Thackeray, of St Mary [Monthaw, London.

Burr, John, of St Botolph without, Bishopsgate — 2 Feb 1724-5 —, Mary Hag- [gard, of same.

Burrace, Mary, of the parish of St. Martin in the Fields. — 23 Jan. 1713-4 —, [Joseph Conet, of same.

Burrard, John (esq), of Lunminton (Lymington), co. Southampton. — 22 Oct 1696 [—, Alice Herbert.

Calvert, Henry, of St Luke's, Old St —
20 Nov. 1748 —, Mary Adams, of
[same

Campbell, Ann, of St Clement Danes —
1 Sept. 1711 —, Peter Nightingale, of
[parish of St Mary, Savoy

Campbell, Thomas, of the parish of St
Swithin's, Cannon St — 15 June, 1713
—, Martha Flood, of parish of St John's,
[Hackney

Canby, Mary — 5 Nov 1700 —, Charles
West, gent , in Nagshead Court, Fen-
[church St.

Canham, William, of the parish of St. Giles
in the Fields — 24 May, 1714 —,
[Hannah Hulings.

Canning, Elizabeth — 27 Sept 1696 —,
Henry Paley, a casemaker in Chancery
[Lane

Cape, George, of St Michael's, Wood St —
18 Dec 1740 —, Hannah Noone, of St
[Alban's, Wood St

Carew, Henry Gawen, painter in St Andrew's, Holborn — 29 Sept 1696 —,
[Elizabeth Bunes

Carlile, Robert, of the parish of St Bride's
— 16 Dec. 1716 —, Catherine Lillise,
[of St. Giles in the Fields.

Carpenter, Henry, of the parish of St
Andrew's, Holborn — 27 March, 1712
[—, Margaret Nicolas, of same

Carpenter, Mary, of the parish of St
Edmund the King, Lombard St. — 3
Aug 1707 —, Peter Dry, of same, butler.

Carr, Robert, of the parish of St Martin,
Ludgate — 27 July, 1734 —, Grace
Bigge, of parish of St Andrew, Holborn

Carre, Richard, of St. Sepulchre's parish,
— 26 Jan 1722-3 —, Frances Halstead,
[of St Clements Dane

Carrenden, Elizabeth, of the parish of St
Martin's in the Fields — 17 Jan 1711-2
—, Henry Andrews, of parish of St. Giles
[in the Fields

Carrington, William, an oilman near Bromley St , Holborn — 29 Aug 1697 —,
[Jane Briggs

Carrithers, William, of the parish of St
Andrew, Holborn — 27 Sept 1713 —,
[Elizabeth Quixey, of same

Cart, Robert, of the parish of St. Nicholas,
Rochester, Kent — 18 Feb. 1713-4 —,
Elizabeth Gibbon, of St Gabriel, Fen-
[church St.

Carte, Elizabeth — 25 Aug 1695 —,
Richard Butler, of St Hellens, city of
[Worcester

Carter, Elizabeth — 4 Oct 1698 —, Richard
Langley, a chairman in German St , St
[Anne's parish, Westminster

Carter, Elizabeth, of St Alban's, Herts —
2 Oct 1711 —, John Mist, of parish of
[St Anne, Westminster

Carter, Francis, of Bugden, Hunts — 9
Aug 1742 —, Anne Desborough, of
[Twickenham, Middx

Carter, John, of the parish of St Olave's,
Southwark — 20 April, 1712 —, Elizabeth Langton, of parish of St Giles in
[the Fields

Carter, Jonathan, of the parish of St
Sepulchre — 8 March, 1713-4 —,
[Frances Cobley, of the same

Carter, William, of the parish of St Andrew's, Holborn — licence dated Nov
[1717 —, Jane Williams, of same

Cary, Elizabeth, of the parish of Chiswick.
— 28 Aug 1711 —, Henry Dottin, of
[parish of St. Clements Dane

Case, Babara, of the parish of St. Dunstan's
in the West. — 11 Nov 1713 —, Isaac
Grace, clergyman, of parish of St.
[Martin's in the Fields

Caslon, Thomas, of the parish of St Andrew,
Holborn — 2 June, 1711 —, Sarah
[Chare, of same.

Castell, Philip, clerk, of Little St Bartholomew's, London — 15 Jan 1701-2 —,
[Ann Cole

Catfoss (?), Isabella — 24 May, 1702 —.
Richard Hoggins, victualler in Essex St

Cathrak, Anne, of Christ Church, Spitalfields — 3 Dec. 1751 —, Edward
[Daintree, of St Clements Danes

Cator, Thomas, journeyman baker in Greenwich — 8 Jan. 1695-6 —, Anne John-
[son

Cavallier, Peter, of the parish of St Ann s,
Westminster — 18 April, 1712 —,
[Elena van Boxstand

d

Cave, Robert, of the parish of St. Andrew's, Holborn — 9 April, 1707 —, Mary [Keep, of same

Cavil, Elizabeth, of Poplar, Stepney parish, — 23 Feb 1712-3 —. John Fielding, of [parish of St Giles, Cripplegate

Cawdron, Susanna, of St Margaret, Westminster - 19 Feb 1725-6 —, Abraham [Sharratt, of St Giles in the Fields.

Cawley, Edward, of the parish of St Clements Dane. — 11 July, 1711 —, Mary [Edmunds, of same

Cawley, Edward, of the parish of St Giles in the Fields. — 16 Jan 1713 4 — [Sarah Jordon, of same.

Cawsey, Isabella, of the parish of St James, Westminster — 27 April, 1710 —, William Howard, of parish of St. Andrew, [Holborn

Cawthorne, Elizabeth — 7 Sept 1700 —, Joseph Calcott, tallow chandler near [the Old Bailey

Cawthorne, William, of the parish of Gamlingay, co Cambridge — 14 Oct. 1708 —, Susan Lovell, of parish of St Sepul-[chre, London.

Cawthorp, Joseph, of St Vedast, Foster Lane — 18 Dec. 1729 —, Mary Parfitt, [of Wickham, Bucks

Chadwick, Humphrey, of St. Olave's, Silver St — 23 April, 1730 —, Elizabeth [Millington, of same

Chaigneau, Margaret — 1 March, 1698-9 —, Rene Chantreau, watchmaker in [Monmouth St.

Chamberlain, James, widower, of the parish of Christ Church — 9 Jan 1714-5 —, Sarah Harwood, widow, of [same

Chamberlain, Mary, of the parish of St. Paul's, Covent Garden. — 1 Jan 1711-2 [—, Robert Overston, of same, gent

Chamberlin, Anne, of the parish of St Giles in the Fields — 16 April, 1716 [—, Thomas Cooper, of same

Chambers, Dorothy — 10 Jan 1696-7 —, [James Bawler, baker in Old Street

Chambers, Sarah, of the parish of Islington, Middx. — 23 March, 1702-3 —, Thomas [Greene, yeoman, of same

Chambers, Walter, of Chelsea College. — 4 Oct 1712 —, Elizabeth Robinson, of [parish of St Sepulchre's

Chambre, Edward, silver wire drawer in Maul's Court, near Moorgate — 7 May, [1698 —, Mary Johnson.

Champneys, Simon, barber, against Lincoln's Gate, Chancery Lane — 6 Feb. [1699-1700 —, Anne Davis

Chance, Mary, of Charlton, Ken- — 8 Nov 1729 —, Henry Smith, of St Ethelberg's, [London

Chancller, Elinor — 22 April, 1697 —, [John Pickersgill, a joiner, Pearpolane.

Chandler, Frances, of St Martin's in the Fields — 3 Feb 1740 1 —, Edward [Orpin, of same

Chandler, William, of the parish of St Clement Danes — 25 May, 1718 —, [Mary Sherman, of same

Chantreau, Rene, watchmaker in Monmouth St — 1 March, 1698-9 —, Margaret [Chaigneau.

Chaplyn, Dorothy, of Sutton, Is e of Ely — 10 Jan 1702-3 —, Thomas Soper, of parish of St Clement Dares, woollen [draper

Chapman, Edward, of the parish of Linton, co Cambridge — 28 July, 1711 —, Sarah Halfhide, of parish of St Edmund's, [town of Cambridge

Chapman, Elizabeth — 30 Sept 1695 —, John Pavillard, servant to Squire Popham [in St James' Sq.

Chappell, Jabez, distiller, near Redriff Stairs. — 15 April, 1703 —, Eleanor Dyke (married by Mr Humfreys in Hatton [Garden)

Chappell, Sarah, of the parish of Deptford, Kent — 25 July, 1709 —, Richard [Burchell, of same

Chare, Sarah, of the parish of St Andrew's, Holborn — 2 June, 1711 —, Thomas [Caslon, of same

Charllon, Jonathan, of St Botolph's, Aldgate — 19 Oct 1704 —, Ann Roberts

Chase, Hannah, of St Giles in the Fields.
— licence dated Aug 1717 —, William
[Jephson, of St Paul's, Covent Garden

Chase, William, of St Michael's, Cornhill
— 23 Nov 1718 —, Anne Wingfield, of
[St. Andrew's, Holborn

Chasselup, Mary, of St Andrew's, Holborn
— 8 Aug 1751 —, Gilbert Pond, of
[Christ Church, Newgate St

Chaterton, Ann, of the parish of St James',
Clerkenwell. — 18 Nov 1714 —, John
[Kennell, of same

Chesmore, John, widower, of St Giles in
the Fields — 23 Dec 1714 —, Christian
[Adams, sing, of St Bride's

Chester, Ann, of St Edmundsbury, Suffolk
— 28 April, 1734 —, John Corrance,
[of Rougham, Suffolk

Chester, Edward, of Bygrave, Herts — 9
May, 1734 —, Margaret Long, of Al-
[bury, Herts

Chester, Elizabeth — 30 June, 1696 —,
Thomas White, tallow chandler in White
[Hart Yard, Savoy parish

Child, William, of the parish of St James,
Westminster — 8 Sept 1707 —, Mary
[Makennis, of same

Childe, William, a twister near the prison,
Whitechapel — 30 April, 1700 —,
[Judith Arlich

Chitty, Joseph, bat, of St. Olave's, Heart
St, London — 15 Oct 1720 —, Eliza-
[beth Lewis, spin, of Hackney

Chowse, Anne, of St Bride's, Fleet St —
13 Aug 1752 —, William Merrifield, of
[same

Church, Martha, widow, of the parish of St
Martin's in the Fields. — 22 Sept 1715
[—, John Wright, of same.

Clack, Edward, of parish of St Bride's,
London — 10 Oct. 1713 —, Mary
Pugh, of parish of St Andrew's, Hol-
[born

Claisby. Margaret, of St. Andrew's, Holborn
— 2 Sept 1714 —, Hugh Cotton, of
[parish of St Pancras.

Clark, Edward, bat, of St. Andrew's, Holborn. — 10 Feb 1718 —, Mary Stone,
[spin., of Battersea, Surrey.

Clark, Edward, bat, of the Inner Temple
— 25 April, 1719 —, Catharine Philips,
[spin, of St. Sepulchre's.

Clark, Mary — 21 July 1696 —, John
Garmson, gardener, of East Moulsey,
[Surrey

Clarke, Edward, yeoman in Hog Lane,
near Soho — 30 May 1699 —, Cath
[erine Prichard

Clarke, George, of St Andrew's, Holborn
— 25 June, 1743 —, Sarah Lovelidge,
[of same.

Clarke, James, collier in Clerkenwell —
[4 Oct. 1696 —, Anne Hawksford

Clarke, Philip, of the parish of St. Martin's
in the Fields — 28 June, 1716 —,
Anne Dighton, of St Giles in the Fields

Clarke, Sarah, of the parish of St Botolph's,
Billingsgate — 12 Oct 1707 —, Robert
Smart, of parish of St. Dunstan's in the
[East.

Clarke, Sarah, spin, of the parish of St.
Giles, Cripplegate. — 1 March, 1714-5
[—, James Dryer, bat., of same.

Clarke, William, bat, of the parish of St.
Leonard's, Eastcheap. — 30 Dec. 1714
—, Rebecca Gibbonson, spin., of St
[Mary Botolph.

Clarkson, John. — 16 Oct. 1698 —, Eliza-
[beth Colley.

Clarribus, Cornelius, of Bishopsgate parish.
— 5 Nov. 1710 —, Elizabeth Hook, of
[St. George's, Southwark.

Claxton, Richard, of Finchley, Middx —
23 May, 1734 —, Anne Clewin, of same

Clay, Mary, of St Giles, Cripplegate. — 24
April, 1726 —, James Lapper, of Cather-
[ine Coleman Street.

Clay, Susanna, of Christ Church, Southwark.
— 10 Oct 1714 —, John Henley, of
[St. Leonard's, Shoreditch.

Clayton, Elizabeth, of the parish of St
James', Westminster — 28 Nov 1711
—, Christopher Stackhouse, of parish of
[St. Giles in the Fields.

Clements, John, of St Sepulchre's — 26 Oct 1714 —, Joyce Stedman, of parish [of St Botolph, Aldgate

Clerk, Francis, esq, of North Weston, co Oxford — 28 March, 1713 —, Grace Holbrooke, parish of St Andrew, Holborn

Clewin, Ann, of Finchley, Middx — 23 May, 1734 —, Richard Claxton, of same

Clifford, Elizabeth — 31 March, 1696 —, Walter Beckham, of the parish of St [Andrew's, bricklayer

Clifford, William, of St Giles in the Fields — Licence dated Dec 1717 —, Sarah Walker, of St. Gabriel's, Fenchurch St

Clifton, John, of the parish of St Leonard's, Foster Lane — 22 May, 1708 —, Susan [Dighton, of same

Close, William, a painter in King St, Bloomsbury. — 13 Nov 1698 —, Anne Hop- [kins

Clousedell, Mary, of St Giles in the Fields — Licence dated Dec 1717 —, Henry [Cornwall, of St Andrew's, Holborn.

Cludley, Ann, of the parish of Hampstead, Middx. — 16 Dec 1707 —, Caleb [Hobson, of same

Cluin, Sarah, of Finchley, Middx — 3 Feb 1732-3 —, Thomas Rawlins, of St An- [drew's, Holborn

Cobley, Frances, of the parish of St Sepulchre — 8 March, 1713-4 —, Jonathan [Carter, of same

Cock, John, vintner in Black Bull Court, against Iveybridge in the Strand — 7 [July, 1696 —, Anne Sergant

Cocker, Catherine — 23 May, 1697 —. Andrew Revell, a brewer's clerk near [Cripplegate

Colchester, Caleb, of the parish of St Andrew's, Holborn, bat — 25 March, 1721-2 —, Sarah Prastring, of same, [spin

Cole, Ann — 15 Jan 1701-2 —, Philip Castell, clerk, of Little St Bartholomew's, [London

Cole, Anne — 30 Dec 1706—, Edward [Horn of St Clement Danes

Cole, Eleanor, spin, of St Martin's in the Fields — 19 Jan 1719 — Anthony [Morgan, bat, of same.

Cole, William, butcher in Clare Market — [25 Aug 1695 —, Mary Cook

Coleby, Thomas, of St Luke, Old St. — 9 June, 1745 —, Deborah Sorsby of same

Coleman, Elizabeth, of the parish of Hornchurch, Essex — 8 Oct 1703 —, Samuel Springham, yeoman, of same (by a [licence)

Coleman, Elisabeth, of Paddington — 20 Dec 1733 —, John Lock, of Kensing- [ton.

Coles, Edward, of Richmond, Surrey — 23 April, 1739 —, Anne Micklewright, of [St Andrew's, Holborn.

Coling, Elizabeth, of the parish of St Clement Danes — 10 Sept 1713 —, [Matthew Flemming, of same.

Collet, Martha, of St. Marylebone — (? 12) May, 1749 — John Garne, of St [George the Martyr

Colley, Elizabeth — 16 Oct 1668 —, John [Clarkson

Collier, Ann, of St Giles, Cripplegate. — 14 Feb 1712-3 —, William Side, of the [parish of St Saviour's, Southwark

Collins, Elizabeth, spin, of the parish of St Martin's in the Fields — 28 Feb 1714-5 —, John Wallman, bat, of same

Collins, James, journeyman tallow chandler in the Old Bailey — 19 Oct 1695 —, [Sophia Stephenson

Collins, John, of the parish of St Andrew's, Holborn. — 8 May, 1711 —, Elizabeth [Smith, of same

Collins, Mary, of the parish of St Andrew, Holborn — 16 June, 1708 —, William [Marse, of same.

Collins, Richard, of the parish of St Andrew, Holborn — 7 Dec 1708 —, Ruperha Thorne, of parish of St Stephen, [Walbrook

Colthurst, Mary, of Kensington. — 11 May, 1725 —, George Smith, of St. James, [Westminster

Combe, Ann, of the parish of St Andrew's, Holborn — 4 Feb 1713-4 —, John [Seaborn, of same

Combs, Jane, of the parish of Cheshunt, Herts — 30 Aug 1711 —, Francis [Yexly, of same

Comine, Susanna. — 10 Jan 1698-9 —, Thomas Moulden, journeyman shoe- [maker in Baldwin's Gardens

Compton, William, of Sheevington, co Gloucester — 3 April, 1716 —, Alice Lyne, [of parish of St Giles in the Fields

Conet, Joseph, of the parish of St Martin's in the Fields — 23 Jan 1713-4 —, [Mary Burrace, of same

Cook, Anne — 30 April, 1698 —, Jacob Gerurean, periwig maker in Grafton [St

Cook, Edward, journeyman shoemaker in Middle Row, Holborn — 12 Jan [1695-6 —, Anne Nokes

Cook, Henry, victualler in Bloomsbury, St Giles — 19 Aug 1697 —, Martha [Peart.

Cook, Mary — 25 Aug 1695 —, William [Cole, butcher in Clare market.

Cook, Miles, brazier in Ivy Lane — 29 [Sept 1695 —, Susanna Butler

Cook, Thomas, gent, of Whittingslow, Salop [— 25 Oct 1696 —, Ursula Shaw

Cook, William, of the parish of St Giles in the Fields — 24 Nov 1714 —, Kathrine [Maccoon, of same

Cooke, Ann, of the Poultry, London — 21 Dec 1723 —, George Kinneir, of St [Paul's, Covent Garden

Cooke, Elizabeth, of St. Mary, Islington — 20 May, 1726 —, Thomas Gramer, [of St John Zachary, London

Cooke, James, bat, of the parish of St Paul, Covent Garden — 25 Jan 1718-9 —, Elizabeth Iliff, spin., of St Giles in [the Fields

Cooke, James, of St Dunstan's in the West — 25 Dec 1736 —, Ursula Thomas, of [St Andrew, Holborn

Cooke, Joseph, of the parish of St. Andrew, Holborn — 10 Aug 1710 —, Ann Ambrose, of parish of St Mary Wolnoth, [Lombard St

Cooke, Leonard, of the parish of St. Dunstan in the West. — 2 Nov 1714 —, [Catherine Dixon, of same

Cooke, Mary, of Castle Hedingham, Essex. — 25 Oct 1750 —, John Francis, of same (by Rev Joshua Allen, rector of [St Bride's, Pembroke)

Cooke, Richard, of St Andrew's, Holborn — 10 Jan 1727-8 —, Mary Whitchurch, [of same

Cooke, Robert, of Tottenham High Cross — 21 April, 1712 —, Mary Webb, of [Maidstone, Kent

Cooke, Thomas, bat, of the parish of St Anne's, Westminster. — 14 Dec 1714 [—, Elizabeth Yates, sing, of same.

Coombs, John, of the parish of St Paul's, Shadwell. — 7 Feb 1713 4 —, Mary [Potter, of same

Cooper, Ann, of the parish of St. Sepulchre. — 21 Sept 1714 —, James Everill, of [parish of St Giles, Cripplegate

Cooper, Francis, of All Hallows, Thames St — 30 March, 1730 —, Susanna [Howse, of St James, Clerkenwell

Cooper, Humphrey, bat, of Barnet, Herts — 8 Oct 1719 —, Hannah Yates, of [Charterhouse Yard, London

Cooper, Jacob, of the parish of St Sepulchre — 7 Aug. 1716 —, Constantia [Grinoway, of same

Cooper, Joseph, cheesemonger of the parish of St Stephen's, Colman St — 24 [Jan 1704-5 —, Sarah Wolfrys

Cooper, Mary, of parish of St Vedast, Forster Lane — 18 March, 1717-8 —, Rollinson Evans, of St. Martin's, Lud- [gate

Cooper, Rebecca. — 23 Aug 1696 —, Henry Pinckney, vintner, in Fetter [Lane

Cooper, Richard, bat, of the parish of St Andrew's, Holborn — 27 Jan 1714 5. [—, Mary Barlow, spin, of same.

Cooper, Robert, mercer in Royal Exchange
[— 2 June, 1698 —, Sara Stop.

Cooper, Thomas, of the parish of St Giles
in the Fields — 16 April, 1716—, Anne
[Chamberlin, of same

Coote, Thomas, of Rotherhithe, Surrey. —
21 June, 1734 —, Jane Sutton, of St.
[Andrew's, Holborn

Copen, Jonathan, of St. Andrew's, Holborn — 4 Jan 1735-6 —, Ann Had-
[dock, of St Sepulchre's

Copland, Catharine, of Deptford, Kent. —
8 Jan 1729-30 —, Thomas Hutchins,
[of same.

Corbet, Elizabeth, of St Giles in the Fields
— 16 May, 1714 —, Thomas Lee, of
[St Andrew s, Holborn

Corbin, Mary, of the parish of Allhallows,
Bishopsgate St — 6 Feb 1713-4 —,
[Samuel Man, of same

Cordall, Jane, of the parish of St Giles in
the Fields — 13 Jan. 1707-8 —, Isaac
Lancaster, of parish of St Andrew, Hol-
[born

Corllinson, Elizabeth — 21 Jan 1696-7
—, Matthew Ailey, vintner in Milk St
[(by Mr King, Curate of Deptford)

Cormell, Mary, of St Andrew's, Holborn
— 10 April, 1748 —, James Ballinger,
[of same

Corney, Cordelia, of Bobinger, Essex —
19 July, 1753 —, Thomas Skeeles, of
[St Ives, Hunts

Cornwall, Henry, of St Andrew's, Holborn
— Licence dated Dec. 1717 —, Mary
[Clousedell, of St Giles in the Fields

Cornwall, Margaret, of St George's, Hanover Sq — 13 Jan 1742-3 —,
William Miller, of St James, West-
[minster

Corrance, John, of Rougham, Suffolk. —
28 April, 1734 —, Ann Chester, of St.
[Edmundsbury, Suffolk

Corsen, Robert, of the parish of St Saviour,
Southwark — 14 Oct 1713 —, Sarah
[Glover, of same.

Cory, Catherine — 4 Nov 1701 —, William
Ayre, at the Blue Ball in Bedford Passage

Cotterell, Alice, of St Andrew's, Holborn
— 15 Nov. 1713 —, William Norminger,
[of parish of St Pancras

Cotton, Hugh, of the parish of St. Pancras.
— 2 Sept. 1714 —, Margaret Clasby,
[of St Andrew's, Holborn.

Cotton, John, coachmaker in Chandos St.
[— 23 Feb. 1695-6 —, Mary Fox

Cotton, Katherine, of Madingley, co Cambridge — 9 June, 1710 —, William
Sancroft, esq, of Fressingfield, Suffolk.

Cotton, Mary, spin, of the parish of St
Giles, Cripplegate — 13 March, 1714-5
—, Richard Fallom, widower, of same

Cotton, Mary, of Madingley, co Cambridge.
—31 July, 1735 —, Jacob Houblon,
[esq, of Great Hallingbury, Essex.

Couch, Katherine, of the parish of All Saints,
Broad St — 3 Oct 1713 —, Joseph
[Gynes, of parish of St. Augustine

Courtney, Robert, of St Giles in the Fields
— 9 Sept 1731 —, Jane Philipps, of
[same

Couzins, John, of Bishopsgate —26 May,
[1713 —, Frances Dehore, of Stepney

Cowdall, Margaret, of St. Ann's, Westminster — 27 July, 1725 —, Thomas
[Butler, of St James, Westminster

Cowel, Joseph, of the parish of St Martin's
in the Fields. — 17 April, 1714 —, Mary
[Brace, of same.

Cowell, Thomas Smith, printer in Plumtree
St, parish of St Giles. — 7 Sept. 1703
[—, Alice Winne, of same

Cox, Alice, of the Tower Liberty — 12 May,
[1725 —, John Marlow, of same.

Cox, Jane, of Hampstead parish Middx —
28 June, 1716 —, William Steed, of St
[Giles, Cripplegate

Cox, Mary — 7 Feb 1698-9 —, William
ffurmidge, soldier in the 1st troop of
[guards

Cox, Mary — 9 April, 1702 —, Anthony
Milton, bargeman, in Richmond, Surrey

Cox, Thomas, of Normanton, co Rutland.
— 22 Nov. 1715 —, Letitia Latton, of
[Esher, Surrey

Coxe, Elizabeth, of the parish of St Martin's in the Fields. — 19 May, 1711 —, John Gwinnet, of parish of St. Clements Dane

Coxe, Thomas, of the parish of St Margaret, Westminster — 15 Dec 1716 —, Anne [Petty, of same

Crafford, Mary, of the parish of St Sepulchre — 9 Nov 1714—, John Saunders, [of same.

Craik, John, of St Clements Dane — 21 March, 1750-1 —, Margaret Varden, of [St Andrew's, Holborn

Crampe, Thomas, of Coventry, co Warwick — 19 Feb. 1727-8 —, Frances [Adie, of same

Crane, Judith, of St Martin's, Ludgate — 2 July, 1724 —, John Fuller, of St [Vedast, Foster Lane

Crank, Arthur, of St Stephen's, Coleman St — 3 March, 1716-7 —, Elizabeth [Hillon, of St Sepulchre's parish

Cranmer, Catherine, of Cheshunt, Herts — 30 Sept 1752 —, Humphry Adams, [of Badgmore, co Oxford

Crawley, Elizabeth — 8 April, 1702 —, James Buckland, carpenter in Castle [Yard

Cray, Jane, of St Dunstan's in the West — 9 Sept 1736 —, Thomas Watson, of [this Society

de Creisselle, Ann, of the parish of St Ann's, Westminster — 10 April, 1712 —, [Stephen Desodes, of same

Cresly, Sarah, of St Michael, Wood Street —13 June, 1714 —, Robert Sissons, of [St Giles, Cripplegate

Crew, Henry, of St James', Westminster. — Licence dated July, 1717 —, Mary Howard, of St Martin's in the Fields

Croft, Richard, of St Vedast, als Foster — 20 June, 1725 —, Elizabeth Jackson, [of St Gregory

Crofts, Thomas, upholsterer at the Royal Oak, near Somerset House, Strand — [15 May, 1701 —, Elizabeth Pinfold

Croker, James (Rev), of West Chiltington, Sussex. — 31 March, 1734 —, Ann [Osborne, of Hackney, Middx

Cronk, John, of Bishopsgate parish — 4 Oct 1711 —, Alice Tucker, of Red- [riffe

Crook, Ann, of Henley-upon-Thames — 20 May, 1712 —, Edward Mortimer, of [parish of St Clare, Hart St , London

Crook, John, of St Giles in the Fields. — 2 Jan 1748-9—, Anna Pye, of St Luke's, [Old St

Crosfeild, William, of the parish of St Brides, London, bat — 17 April, 1715 [—, Mary Barnes, spin., of same.

Croshold, Anne, of St Olave, Hart St — 29 Jan 1745-6 — Thomas Robin- [son, of St Andrew, Holborn

Cross, Laurence, widower, of St Giles in the Fields — 27 Oct 1720 —, Mary [Harrison, of same, spin

Cross, Mary, of St. Andrew's, Holborn — 6 May, 1732 —, Jeremiah Pendridge, als Pendred, of St Stephen's, Cole- [man St

Croucher, Richard, of the parish of St. Pancras — 13 April, 1714 —, Bridget [Bety, of same

Croucher, Richard, of the parish of St Pancras. — 26 Oct 1714 —, Bridget [Betty, of same.

Crout, Mary, of St Andrew's, Holborn — 9 Nov 1714 —, John Ewens, of St. [Giles, Cripplegate.

Croutch, Thomas, a tailor lodging in Gray's Inn passage — 26 May, 1696 —, Mary [Wood

Crump, George, surgeon, against Villiers St , Strand — 18 May, 1700 —, Anne [Whiting

Crump, Thomas, apothecary in Shoe Lane [— 22 April, 1701 —, Anne Lasenby

Crundall, Elizabeth, of St Lawrence, Jewry. — Licence dated Dec 1717 —, Phillip Mallory, of St. Bridget, als Bride's [parish

Cuel, John, of St Dunstan's in the West, widower — 15 Sept 1722 —, Mary [Smith, of St Andrew's, Holborn.

Cumber, Edward, of the parish of St Sepulchre's — 1 June, 1712 —, Ann Royston,
[of same

Cumbridge, Francis, of Penshurst, Kent —
22 Jan 1704-5 —, Susan Cumbridge, of
same (married by Mr Wood, of St
[Michael Royal).

Cumbridge, Mary, of the parish of Maidstone, Kent — 2 July, 1707 —, John
[Wren, of same

Cumbridge, Susan, of Penshurst, Kent —
22 Jan 1704-5 —, Francis Cumbridge,
of same (married by Mr. Wood, of
[St Michael Royal)

Cunningham, Ann — 31 Dec 1706 —,
Thomas Love, of parish of St. Andrew's,
[Holborn

Currer, John, of St Mary le Savoy — 7
Jan 1724-5 —, Frances Mills, of same.

Curtis, Jane, of the parish of St. Clements
Dane — 11 July, 1714 —, John Bull,
[of same.

Curwen, Elizabeth, of the parish of St
Giles in the Fields — 7 Dec 1712 —,
[Thomas Bridges, of same

Cutler, Elizabeth, of St Giles in the Fields.
— 27 Oct 1723 —, Lennard Mallard,
[of same.

Cutting, Faith, of St Dunstan's in the West
— 5 March, 1723-4 —, William Hick-
[man, of St Sepulchre's parish

Cuttle, Dinah, of St Giles in the Fields — 28
March, 1713-4 —, Thomas Walker, of
[parish of St Martin, Ludgate

Cutts, Elizabeth, of the parish of St. Andrew's, Holborn — 26 Nov 1714 —,
[Mr Alderton, of same

Dagger, Mary, spin., of St. Andrew's, Holborn — 9 Jan 1714-5 —, William
[Wynde, bat., of St Giles, Cripplegate.

Daintree, Edward, of St. Clement's Danes
— 3 Dec 1751 —, Anne Cathrak,
[of Christ Church, Spitalfields

Dakins, Michal (sic), of St Ann's, Blackfriars — 23 Nov. 1735 —, Thomas
[Fawkener, of St. Clement's Dane.

Dallon, Mary, of the parish of St Magnus, London — 22 March, 1712-3 —,
[Gunder Berg, of same

Dalrsan, Anne — 15 Aug 1695 —, Peter
Ewalt, a soldier in Petit France, Ship
[Yd, Westminster

Dalton, John, of the parish of Bolney,
Sussex — 17 Aug 1714 —, Grace Sale,
[of same

Dalton, Thomas, of the parish of St Magnus. — 20 Sept 1712 —, Elizabeth
[Middleton, of St Giles, Cripplegate.

Dalyson, Jane, of Wrotham, Kent — 10
May, 1753 —, Jefferey Amherst, esq, of
[Sevenoaks, Kent

Dance, Thomas, widower, of St. Paul's,
Covent Garden — 1 Dec 1720 —,
Margaret Salesbury, widow, of Hamp-
[stead

Dancey, Mary, of St. Andrew's Holborn
— 6 March, 1711-2 —, James Gibson,
[of parish of St. Michael, Bassishaw.

Dangerfield, Ann, of St Giles, Cripplegate — 11 June, 1728 —, Edward
[Martin, of Stepney parish

Darby, Joan, of Wimborne Minster, Dorset
— 18 Aug. 1702 —, Samuel White,
[linen draper in Winchester, Hants

Darby, Richard (esq), one of the masters
of this society — 5 Oct 1731 —, Sarah
[March, of Enfield, Middx.

Darby, Sarah, of Enfield, Middx, — 31
Jan 1737-8 —, William Underwood,
[esq, of same

Darby, Simon, of the parish of St. Martin's
in the Fields — 4 May, 1718 —, Diana
[Holding, of same.

Dare, Edward, of St Michael's, Queenhithe — 18 Dec. 1729 —, Jane Mills,
[of same

Darke, Alice, widow, of the parish of St
Clement's Danes — 29 Sept 1718 —,
[Robert Bainbridge, bet, of same.

Darling, Anne, — 20 June, 1697 —, Thomas
[Scholler, hatter in Fetter Lane

Darrell, Mary, of Stepney. — 1 July, 1711
— Henry Hagedorn, of parish of St.
[Martin's in the Fields.

Darwin, Anne, of the parish of St Faith, London — 4 Aug 1709 —, William Anns, of parish of St. Martin, vintner

Dasnett, Mary, of the parish of St Giles, Cripplegate — 22 June, 1714 —, Thomas White, of parish of Stevens, [Coleman St

Davies, Elizabeth, of St Paul's, Covent Garden — 30 Oct 1718 —, Thomas [Hockin, of same

Davies, John, *bat*, of Hillydon — 9 Jan [1720-1 —, Sara Webb, *spin*, of same

Davies, Margaret, *spin*, of St Lawrence Jewry — 29 Sept 1718 - -, William Aimy, *bat*, of parish of Shifnall, Salop

Davies Peter, of St Andrew's, Holborn — [8 Feb 1753 —, Mary West, of same

Davies, Rice, of St Paul's, Deptford, Kent — 22 Sept 1737 —, Elizabeth Rice, of [St George's, Hanover Sq

Davis, Anne — 6 Feb 1699-1700 —, Simon Champncys, barber against Lincoln's [Gate in Chancery Lane

Davis, Bartholomew, of the parish of Christ Church, Southwark — 27 Jan 1712-3 [—, Elizabeth Burton, of same

Davis, Daniel, servant to Mr Littlebury in Hendon — 17 Feb. 1701-2 —, Anne [Wasdell

Davis, Hannah, of the parish of St Andrew's, Holborn — 1 July, 1714 —, Jones Thurston, of parish of St Giles in the [Fields

Davis, Henry, a labourer at the Dolphin in Shoreditch — 12 July, 1697 —, Jane [Horne

Davis, Mary, — 12 Feb 1699-1700 —, George Freeman, barber-surgeon in Bir- [stin Lane

Davis, Mary, of St Anne's, Westminster — 24 June, 1729 —, William Parker, of [St. Faith's

Davis, Richard, of St Clements Dane — 1 [July, 1730 —, Grace Major, of same

Davis, Susanna — 25 Jan 1701-2 —, John [Bransbey

Davis, Walter, of the parish of St Swithin, London — 15 July, 1711 —, Rose Adams, of parish of St Andrew's, Hol- [born

Dawley, Robert, of Highgate parish — 6 May, 1717 —, Dorothy Lawton, of same

Dawson, Elizabeth — 17 Sept 1696 —, John Bradley, of Lamb's Condu't [Fields

Dawson, John, of Islington — 14 Oct 1732 —, Priscilla Kitching, of St An- [drew's, Holborn

Dawson, Sarah, of St Dunstan's in the West — 6 June, 1734 —, Thomas Browne, of St George's, Hanover, [Sq.

Day, Ann, of the Parish of St Giles, Cripple-gate, in Fenton Alley, Little Moorfields — 16 Sept 1714 —, Ralph Harbottle, [of same

Day, Mary, of the parish of St Mary Mag-dalen, Bermondsea — 6 May, 1714 —, John Woodfield, of St Martin's in the [Fields

Day, Mary, *spin*, of the parish of South Mims, Middx — 24 Feb 1714 5 —, [James Wright, *bat.*, of same

Day, Ralph, of Clifford's Inn — 21 Aug [1736 —, Mary Pigeon, of St Bride's

Day, Susanna, of the Tower of London — 23 April, 1750 —, Noah Thomas, of [same, M D

Deacon, Mary, of the parish of St Giles in the Fields — 21 Oct, 1714 —, Charles [Allwright, of same

Deale, Mary, of St Luke's. Old St — 10 Aug 1740 —, Thomas Parrot, of St [Sepulchre's

Dealtry, Frances, of Owston, co Lincoln — 23 April, 1752 —, Godfrey Meynell, [esq, of Bradley, co. Derby

Dean, Job, hatter in Popping Alley, St. Bride's parish. — 3 Dec 1697 —, Mary. [Walden.

Dean, John, of the parish of St Sepulchre — 11 Oct, 1715 —, Mary Brown, of St [James, Clerkenwell

e

Dean, John, of the parish of St Andrew, Holborn — 22 April, 1718 —, Elizabeth Ewen, of St Paul's, Covent Gar-
[den.

De Bert, Sarah, of the parish of St Andrew's, Holborn — 26 Oct 1707 —, James Pember, of parish of St. Clement's
[Dane (by a licence)

Debuck, Judith ye, of Hampstead.—24, 25, or 26 May, 1718 —, Gabriel Armiger,
[of the Inner Temple, *widower*

Deekings, Margaret, *widow*, of the parish of St James, Westminster — 21 Dec 1714 —, Gilbert Manning, *bat*, of same

Dehore, Frances, of Stepney — 26 May, 1713 —, John Couzins, of Bishopsgate

Delafield, Thomas, of St. Giles Without, Cripplegate — 20 Nov 1725 —, Ann
[Goostree, of St Andrew's, Holborn.

Delarus, Mary, *spin*, of the parish of St Giles, Cripplegate — 25 March, 1715
[—, Luke Wells, *widower*, of same

Denew, Elizabeth, of the parish of St James, Westminster — 15 April, 1710 —, John Weeks, of parish of St Ann's, West-
[minster

Denins, John, haberdasher of small wares in Paul's Alley — 9 Feb 1696-7 —,
[Isabella Williamson

Denison, Margaret, of St Dunstan's in the West — 15 Sept 1715 —, Robert Stuart, of parish of St. Andrew's,
[Holborn.

Denn, Mary, *widow*, of the parish of St Andrew's, Holborn — 13 July, 1703 —, George Strut apothecary, of parish of
[Uggly, Essex (by a licence)

Dennis, Agatha, of St. Botolph's, Aldersgate — 6 April, 1731 —, Edward Rabbuts,
[of St Mary Magdalen, Bermondsea

Dennis, Elizabeth, of St Alphage. — 4 Nov. 1714 —, George Windsor, of St.
[Andrew's, Holborn

Dennis, Isabel — 18 April, 1723 —, Ed-
[ward Longdon

Dennis, Katherine, of the parish of Borden, Kent — 28 Oct 1713 —, Edward
[Kirby, of same

Dennis, Mary, of St Botolph's, Aldersgate — 29 June, 1730 —, Daniel Welles, of
[St Clement's, Eastcheap

Dennis Rebecca, of St Botolph's, Aldersgate — 9 May, 1728 —, Thomas Rowe,
[of same

Dennis Sarah, of St Botolph's, Aldersgate. — 6 April, 1731 —, Edward Parr, of
[St. Vedast's, Foster Lane

Dent, Thomas, of St. George's in the East — 31 March, 1751 —, Jane Fawlkener,
[of Battersea

Denton, Andrew, of the parish of St Sepulchre, London — 24 June, 1707 —,
[Sarah Lockwood, of same

Denton, Hannah — 9 Oct 1698 — , Arthur Gardner, a turner without Bishopsgate

Denton, Hannah, of St Paul's, Covent Garden — 20 Sept. 1724 —, Theophilus
[Ward, of same

Denton, Thomas, of Furnival's Inn, *bat* — 19 Oct 1721 —, Sarah Price, of West
[Farnet, *spin*

Desborough, Anne, of Twickenham, Middx. — 9 Aug 1742 —, Francis Carter, of
[Bugden, Hunts

Desodes, Stephen, of the parish of St. Ann's, Westminster — 10 April, 1712 —, Ann
[de Creissele, of same

Detheridge, Joseph, of St John the Evangelist, Westminster — 20 April, 1732 —, Esther Smith, of St. Andrew's, Hol-
[born

Dicken, William, of Shenton, Salop — 26 July, 1716 —, Elizabeth Hooke, of St
[Andrew's, Holborn

Dickenson, Martha — 10 July, 1698 —, John Blackmore, broker near St. Anne's
[Church, Soho

Dickins, Ambrose, of the parish of St. Bride's, London — 17 Feb. 1708-9 —, Elizabeth
[Bernard, of same

Dickinson, Sarah, of the parish of St. Olave's, Silver St — 6 Nov 1712 —, Lionel Wood, of parish of St Giles, Cripplegate

Dighton, Anne, of the parish of St Giles
in the Fields — 28 June, 1716 —,
Philip Clarke, of St. Martin's in the
[Fields.

Dighton, John, Dr , of the parish of St Mary,
in Newmarket, Suffolk — 26 May, 1718
—, Elizabeth Jones, of parish of St
[Margaret's, Westminster

Dighton, Susan, of the parish of St.
Leonard, Foster Lane — 22 May, 1708
[—, John Clifton, of same

Dilke, Elizabeth. — 19 May, 1698 —,
Edward Brudenell, gent., of Barton Sea-
[grave, co. Northampton

Dineley, Mary, of St Dunstan's in the West.
— 29 March, 1725 —, Valentine Scott,
[of same

Dixon, Catherine, of the parish of St
Dunstan's in the West — 2 Nov 1714
[—, Leonard Cooke, of same

Dixon, Christian, of the parish of St.
Clement's Danes — 6 Sept. 1705 —,
William Bradhan, victualler in St
[Clement's Lane, same parish

Dixon, Dorothy, of St Margaret's, Westminster — 10 July, 1753 —, Benjamin
[Axford, of St. Albans, Wood St

Dixon, Frances — 8 April, 1706 —, George
Bland, of the parish of St Andrew's,
Holborn, gentleman's servant (by a
[licence)

Dixon, John, of the parish of Stepney,
Middx. — 17 Feb 1707-8 —, Elizabeth
Robinson, of parish of St Giles in the
[Fields

Dixson, George, of the parish of St Andrew's,
Holborn — 5 July, 1709 —, Frances
[Peters, of parish of St. Mary le Bow

Dobar, William, of the parish of Christ
Church, London. — 5 Oct 1713 —,
Elizabeth Smith, of parish of St
[Katherine Cree Church

Dobbins, Joseph, of the parish of St. An-
drew's, Holborn. — 8 Nov. 1716 —,
Susannah Girdler, of St. Giles in the
[Fields.

Dobbs, William, poulterer next Temple
Bar — 29 Aug 1697 —, Isabella Willi-
[mott.

Dobman, Susanna, spin , of St Clement's
Dane — 21 March, 1720-1 —, John
[Blackbourne, of same.

Dobson, Mary, of the city of Oxford. —
19 May, 1709 —, Thomas Winder, of
parish of Rotherwick, co Southampton.

Dod, Mary, of the parish of Watford, Herts
— 25 May, 1713 —, Giles Groom, of
[same.

Dodd, Thomas, of the parish of St Andrew,
Holborn — 2 March, 1711-2 —, Bridget
[Bell, of same.

Dodge, Anne, of St Margaret's, Westminster
— 10 Sep. 1714 —, Henry Bishop, of
[St Clements Dane.

Doling, Edward, innholder at the Saracen's
Head, in Friday St. — 26 Sept. 1696 —,
[Anne Fauconberge.

Dolphin, Sarah, of the parish of St Andrew,
Holborn. — 1 May, 1714 —, Manasses
[Wadley, of same

Donvile, Margaret, of the parish of ———,
Aldersgate — 31 Dec 1712 —, Thomas
[Greenhill, of St Nicholas Olaves

Dorrel, Mary, of St Andrew's, Holborn —
6 May, 1732 —, William Bond, of St
[Paul's, Covent Garden

Dorrell, Dina, of the parish of St Andrew,
Holborn — 24 June, 1714 —, John
[Bradley, of same.

Dottin, Henry, of the parish of St. Clement's
Dane — 28 Aug 1711 —, Elizabeth
[Cary, of parish of Chiswick

Doughty, Thomas, of St Peter's, Cornhill,
cheesemonger. — 4 March, 1704 - 5 —,
[Rachel Dows.

Douglas, Mary — 3 Jan 1698-9 —, Daniel
Rogers, a soldier at the gentlem porter.

Dovoy, Esther, spin., of the parish of St,
Giles in the Fields. — 13 Jan 1714-5
—, Thomas Gosford, widower, of same

Downer, William, bat , of the parish of
Edgeworth — 16 April, 1715 —, Eliza-
beth Hodge, spin , of Hendon parish,
[Middx.

Dows, Rachel, — 4 March, 1704-5 —,
Thomas Doughty, of St. Peter's, Corn-
[hill, cheesemonger.

D'Oyley, Sibella, of St Paul's, Covent
Garden. — 13 Nov 1729 —, George
[Turner, of same.

Drake Joshua, of the parish of All Hallows
the Less, Thames St — 12 July, 1711
[—, Lydia Buckley, of same

Draper, Jane, of St Michael's Basishaw
— 24 May, 1743 —, Samuel Johnson,
[of St Giles in the Fields

Draper, Thomas, of the parish of St Giles
in the Fields — 9 Oct 1716 —,
Susannah Ashton, of St Martin's in
[the Fields

Drayton, Esther, *sing*, of St Anne's, Westminster — 23 Dec 1714 —, James
Gibbons, *bat*, of St Giles in the Fields
[parish

Drew, Eleanor, of Cheshunt, Herts — 26
May, 1737 —, Henry Richardson, of
[same

Drewett, Mary, of St Olave, Southwark —
26 June, 1732 —, John Knight, of St
[Saviour's, Southwark

Drot (blotted), Ann, of St Olaves, Old
Jewry — 21 Oct 1714 —, John Hassell, of parish of St Giles in the Fields

Droyner, Judith, of the parish of St Mary
Wolnoth — 3 Aug 1713 —, Bartholo-
[mew Sanderson, of same

Drumman, Elizabeth, of the parish of St
Giles in the Fields — 24 April, 1707
—, Josiah German, of same, shoemaker

Dry, Peter, butler, of the parish of St.
Edmund the King, Lombard St — 3
Aug 1707 —, Mary Carpenter, of same

Dryer, James, *bat*, of the parish of St
Giles, Cripplegate — 1 March, 1714-5
[—, Sarah Clarke, *spin*, of same

Duchesne, Theophilus, soldier, in Guillard
St, St Anne's parish, Soho — 2 May,
[1699 —, Bridget Stevens

Duckar, George, of Enfield — 17 Feb
1727-8 —, Mary Lee, of parish of St
[George the Martyr, Queen sq

Ducker, John, of Limber, co Lincoln —
14 Feb. 1733 4 —, Anne Waller, of St
[Hellen's, London

Duckett, Joseph, wine cooper in Elbow
Lane — 3 March, 1697-8 —, Jane
[Kenyon

Duffin, Thomas, of the parish of St Mar-
garet More (?) — 4 Dec 1712 —,
Elizabeth Watkins of parish of St
[Andrew, Holborn.

Dunbar, Jane, of the parish of St Clement's
Dane — 16 May, 1714 —, Matthew
[Baxter, of same

Dunn, Thomas, butcher in Clare Market —
[14 Dec 1698 —, Alice Bodges

Dupony, David, of St Anne's, Westminster
— 17 May, 1730 —, Elisabeth Ayres,
[of St Martin's in the Fields

Dyer, Elizabeth — 20 Feb 1695-6 —,
Marmaduke Attey, chamberlain at the
[Black Bull in Holborn

Dyer, Patrick, of the parish of St Mary,
Whitechapel — 17 Nov 1709 —, Mary
Harrison, of parish of St Botolph,
[Aldgate

Dyer, Rachel, of the parish of St Giles in
the Fields — 24 Aug 1710 —, John
Sumerfield, of parish of St Martin's
[in the Fields.

Dyer, Richard, clothworker in Chancery
Lane — 16 April, 1696 , Elizabeth
[Absalom

Dyke, Eleanor — 15 April, 1703 —, Jabez
Chappell, distiller, near Redriff stairs
(married by Mr. Humfrys in Hatton
[Garden).

Dymmock, Rachel, of St Giles, Cripplegate — 23 July, 1727 —, John Ham-
[mond, of same.

Dyson, John, of the parish of St. Giles in
the Fields — 14 Oct 1714 —, Ester
[Maiden, of same

Dyson, Thomas, of Greenwich, gent —
15 Oct 1696 —, Frances Saunderson

Eaglestone, Sarah, of the parish of St
Andrew's, Holborn — 8 March, 1712-3
—, James Askew, of parish of St
[Dunstan's in the West

East, Elizabeth, of the parish of Hayes,
Middx. — 8 April, 1714 —, George
[Hurlock, of same

East, Mary, of the parish of Drayton,
Middx — 6 June, 1714 —, John
[Hotwes, of same.

Easton, Margaret, of Deptford, Kent —
3 Feb 1729-30 —, Richard Westbrooke,
[of same.

Eaton, John, of St Giles, Cripplegate —
5 Nov 1714 —, Mary Pickford, of St.
[Dunstan's in the West

Eaton, Mary, *sing*, of St. Giles in the
Fields. — 12 Dec 1714 —, James
[Rogers, *bat*, of same

Eccleston, Charles, *bat*, of the parish of
St Giles in the Fields — 12 Dec 1714
—, Cassandra Marjoram, *widow*, of St
[Paul's, Covent Garden

Ecclestone, Mary, of the parish of St
James, Clerkenwell — 19 June, 1708 —,
Eignon Beynon, gent, of parish of
[Redborn, Herts

Eckels, William, of St Giles in the Fields
— 14 Feb 1727-8 —, Anne Morgan
[of St Andrew's, Holborn

Edlin, Mary — 13 Nov 1705 —, Richard
Barringer, coachman to Sir Streinsham
[Master, in Red Lion Sq (by licence)

Edmunds, Mary, of the parish of St. Clements
Danes — 11 July, 1711 —, to Edward
[Cawley, of the same

Edwards, Anne, of Highgate — 5 June,
1753 —, Thomas Allen-Greenalgh, Esq,
[of Gray's Inn

Edwards, Gilbert, a captain at the Nag's
Head, against Short's Garden, Drury
Lane — 23 Dec 1699 —, Mary Herne

Edwards, Hester, of St James', Westminster — 16 Jan 1738-9 —, Thomas
[Wyse, Esq, of this Inn

Edwards, Margaret — 20 Jan 1701-2 —,
William Griffin, haberdasher, of Helmet
[Court, Strand.

Edwards, Mary, of the parish of St Ann's
Westminster — 11 Dec. 1713 —, Peter
Gery, of same (married before, but
"ye world not believing," it was again
[solemnised)

Edwards, Rachel, of St Bartholomew the
Great, Smithfield — 30 Oct 1744 —,
[William Jones, of same

Edwards, Samuel, gent at the Trustee's
office, in Palace yard — 24 Nov. 1699
[—, Rebecca Godolphin.

Edwards, William, a yeoman in East Barnet
[— 18 Aug 1697 —, Grace Brown

Edwin, Charles (Esq.), of Lincoln's Inn
— 2 Oct 1712 —, Martha Barnardiston,
[of parish of St Andrew's, Holborn.

Egen, James, of the parish of St Ann's,
Westminster — 29 April, 1707 —,
Elizabeth Brockenbury, of St. Mary le
[Bow

Egerton, Sarah, of St Dunstan's in the
West — 25 Sept 1733 —, Thomas
[Spicer, of same.

Egleton, Henry, *bat*, of St. Stephen s,
Coleman St — 5 Nov 1720 —, Dorothy
Grey, *spin*, of St Swithin, London Stone

Elbrow, Martha — 5 Oct 1697 —, Isaac
Hall, a cooper against Chancery Lane.

Elfie, Mary, of the parish of St Andrew's,
Holborn — 7 Feb 1703-4 —, John
Brandreth, merchant tailor in Fetter
[Lane, same parish (by licence)

Elham, Susanna — 23 June, 1700 —,
[Richard Green, carpenter

Elland, Mary — 3 Dec 1695 —, Matthias
Elland, of Loworth, co Lincoln, weaver.

Elland, Matthias of Loworth, co Lincoln,
weaver — 3 Dec 1695 —, Mary
[Elland

Ellard, Elizabeth, of St George the Martyr,
Middx — 27 Dec 1735 —, Henry
[Ballett, of Chelmsford, Essex

Ellard, Mary, of St Sepulchre, London —
22 Sept 1734 —, Richard Heart, of
[same

Elley, Richard, of the parish of St James,
Clerkenwell — 19 Jan 1713-4 —, Mary
[Moon, of same

Elliot, George, of the parish of Christ Church
— 19 Nov 1713 —, Martha Hartley, of
[St Martins in the Fields

Ellis, Ann, of the parish of St Anne, Westminster — 15 Jan 1711-2 —, John
[Singleton, of same

Ellis, Catherine, of St Martin's in the Fields.
— 16 April, 1740 —, Richard Lloyd, of
[St George's, Bloomsbury.

Ellis, Elizabeth — 11 June, 1696 —, John
[Jones, barber near Leadenhall

Ellis, James, gent. — 29 May, 1701 —,
[Abigail Lamb

Ellis, John, of the parish of Islington — 9
June, 1710 —, Barbara Beaumont, of
[parish of St. Ann, Westminster

Ellis, William, of Dartford, Kent, surgeon
[— 3 Nov 1695 —, Susanna Monger

Ellon, John, of the parish of Lambourne,
Berks — 15 Oct 1712 —, Ann Green,
[of parish of Great Coxwell, Berks

Ellond, Elizabeth, of the parish of St Giles
in the Fields — 1 June, 1712 —,
Edward Wilson, of parish of St Ann's,
[Blackfriars

Elmes, Henry, of the parish of St Clemen's
Dane — 22 Jan 1712-3 —, Sarah
Stewart, of parish of St Andrew, Hol-
[born

Elmes, Sarah — 13 April, 1697 —, John
[Fowler, shoemaker in Brook Market

Else, Zechariah, brewer's clerk in Hockley
Hole — 19 Oct. 1701 —, Susanna
[Thompson

Emerson, William, servant to squire Strafford, of the parish of St Andrew, Holborn — 18 Feb 1704-5 —, Bridget
[Vanmore, of same parish

Emes, Mary — 4 Aug 1698 —, Edward
Pearles, innholder at the King's Arms
[in St. Martin's Lane

Emley, Sara — 16 June, 1698 —, John
Spencer, servant to Judge Hook in
[Lincoln's Inn Fields.

Emmett, Elizabeth, of St. Andrew's, Holborn. — 1 Oct 1725 —, Roger Ewbanck,
[of same

Emmons, Mary, of St James, Clerkenwell
— 1 Aug 1728 —, Daniel Axtell, of
[same

Engham, Vincent — 14 May, 1699 —,
[Judith Wetherley

England, Thomas, of St Martin's in the
Fields — 2 July, 1739 —, Mary Gibbins,
[of St Giles in the Fields.

Eslon, Edward, of the parish of St Martin,
Ludgate — 20 Jan 1708-9 —, Katherine
Sherlocke, of parish of St Gregory,
[London

Evans, Deborah, of the parish of St An-
drews, Holborn — 24 Feb 1703-4 —,
Thomas Lee, chamberlain at Chequer
[Inn, Holborn

Evans, Eleanor, of St Michael, Cornhill
— 13 Oct 1735 —, William Morgan, of
[St Andrew, Holborn

Evans, Elisabeth, of St Andrew's, Holborn
— 24 Oct 1730 —, Roger Bartone, of
[same.

Evans, Hannah, of Tewin, Herts — 17
June, 1726 —, William Wallis, of Detch-
[worth, Herts

Evans, Margaret — 27 Oct 1698 — Joseph
Huddle, poulterer in St James' Market.

Evans, Mary, of the parish of St Andrew,
Holborn — 31 May, 1713 —, Robert
[Hammond, of same.

Evans, Mary, of the parish of St Giles
Cripplegate — 11 April, 1714 —, Same-
[well Spencer, of same

Evans, Mary, of the parish of St James
Westminster — 29 July, 1714 —, David
Killmain, of parish of St Martin's in
[the Fields.

Evans, Matthew, of Tring, Herts, gent —
18 May, 1703 —, Sarah Harding, of
|same, spin

Evans, Prudentia, of the parish of St Andrew's, Holborn — 22 May, 1708 —,
Anthony Scawen, linen draper of parish
[of St Michael's, Cornhill (by licence)

Evans, Richard, of St Andrew's, Holborn.
— 11 Jan 1731-2 —, Ellen Owen, of St
[Botolph's, Bishopsgate.

Evans, Rollinson, of St Martin's, Ludgate
— 18 March, 1717-8 —, Mary Cooper,
[of parish of St Vedast, Forster lane

Evans, Susanna. — 2 July, 1695 —, Thomas
Sturgeon, of Dean St, St. Ann's, West-
[minster, labourer

Eve, Sarah, of the parish of Watford, Herts.
— 28 Jan 1724-5 —, Henry Wankford,
[of parish of Rickmansworth, Herts

Everet, Mary, of St. Andrew, Holborn. —
5 Feb 1719 —, Daniel Rogers, bat, of
[same.

Everill, James, of the parish of St. Giles, Cripplegate. — 21 Sept 1714 —, Ann [Cooper, of yᵉ parish of St Sepulchre

Everson, Mary. — 4 Jan 1701-2 —, Henry Lasdick, victualler at the Crown in [Burlington Street

Everton, Mary, of the parish of St Giles in the Fields — 31 March, 1706 —, [Robert Furber, gardener at Exeter.

Ewalt, Peter, a soldier in Petit France. Ship Yd., Westminster — 15 Aug 1695 —, [Anne Dalrsan.

Ewbanck, Roger, of St Andrew's, Holborn — 1 Oct 1725 —, Elizabeth Emmett, [of same

Ewen, Elizabeth, of St Paul's, Covent Garden. — 22 April, 1718 —, John Dean, of parish of St. Andrew, Holborn

Ewens, John, of St Giles, Cripplegate — 9 Nov 1714 —, Mary Crout, of St [Andrew's, Holborn

Ewer, Edward, of Luton, Beds — 20 Feb 1730-1 —, Phillis Maccarty, of St [George the Martyr, Middx

Exall, Ruth — 19 May, 1698 —, John Williams, victualler in Newton St, St [Giles.

Eyres, Mary, of the parish of St Leonard, Shoreditch — 16 Aug 1713 —, Henry [Beakley, of same

Fabre, Charles, of St. Paul's, Covent Garden — 8 Jan. 1727-8 —, Margaret Ivie, of St Martin's in the Fields

Faithby, Margaret, of St Giles in the Fields — 3 May, 1714 —, Benjamin Rogers, [of parish of St James, Westminster

Falkener, Elizabeth, of St Leonard's, Shoreditch, widow — 19 May, 1719 —, Robert Jones, bat, of St Bartholomew, [near the Royal Exchange

ffallitt, Thomas, farmer in Chicheley parish, Bucks. — 2 Jan 1699-1700 —, Grace [Watson

Fallom, Richard, widower, of the parish of St Giles, Cripplegate. — 13 March, 1714-5 —, Mary Cotton, spin, of same

ffanch, Mary — 17 June, 1695 —, Edward Leadbetter, of St Clements Danes, [journeyman tailor

Farlie Robert, of the parish of St Andrew, Holborn — 19 Oct 1715 —, Ann [Macgregor, of same

Farmer, Ann, of the parish of St. Andrew, Holborn — 26 May, 1706 —, Thomas Taylour, mason in Red Lion St, same [parish (by licence).

Farrell, Roger, of the parish of St James. Westminster. — licence dated July 1717 [—, Mary Pierce, of same

Farrer, James, of St Mary le Strand — 11 Nov 1729 —, Margaret Prescott, of [St Botolph's, Aldersgate.

Farrer, John, dry salter, of the parish of St Giles in the Fields — 27 April, 1704 —, Elizabeth Brookes, of parish [of St Paul's, Covent Garden.

Farrer, Martha, of the parish of St Giles in the Fields. — 25 Aug 1712 —, Matthias Bradley, of parish of Hatfield, [Herts

Fauconberge, Anne — 26 Sept 1696 —, Edward Doling, innholder at the Sara- [cen's Head in Friday St

Faulkner, Martha, of Ealing, Middx, spin — 22 Dec 1718 —, Richard Peter, of [same, bat

ffaure, Henry, bat, of St Mary Axe. — 28 July, 1720 —, Martha Baker, of [Covent Garden, spin

Fawcett, Elizabeth, of St Ann's, Westminster — 14 Feb 1715-6 —, William Lambton, of St. Dunstan's in the West.

Fawkener, Thomas, of St. Clements Dane, —23 Nov 1735- -, Michael (sic) Dakins, [of St Ann, Blackfriars

Fawkes, Theodosia, of St Luke's parish, Middx. — 12 April, 1743 —, James [Nutter, of same.

Fawlkener, Jane, of Battersea — 31 March, 1751 —, Thomas Dent, of St George's [in the East.

Fendale, Sarah, of Deptford — 12 June, [1729 —, John Webb, of Greenwich.

Fenwick, Samuel, of Stepney parish. — 11 Sept 1714 —, Mary Lowe, of White- [chapel

Fenwick, Thomas, of St Michael's, Crooked Lane — 19 Dec 1751 —, Mary Bur- [chett, of St. Mary, Whitechapel

Fergusson, James, of St Mary le bone. — 4 May, 1728 —, Ursula Goff, of St. [Giles, Cripplegate

Field, Ann, widow, of the parish of St James, Clerkenwell — 27 Dec 1714 —, Thomas Boughey, *widower*, of same.

Field, Benjamin, *bat*, of St Andrew's, Holborn — 5 Feb 1718-9 —, Dorothy Saunderson, of St. Benet's, nr Paul's [ditch

Fielder, Sarah — 13 April, 1697 —, John [Adkins, glazier in Hampstead.

Fielding, John, of the parish of St. Giles, Cripplegate — 23 Feb 1712-3 —, Elizabeth Cavil, of Poplar, Stepney [parish

Fifield, Grace, of St James, Westminster — 19 Oct 1738 —, William Bowring, [of St. Michael Bassishaw

Figgings, John, of the parish of Hillington, Middx. — 3 Dec 1714 —, Ann Grimes, [of same.

Figgins, Henry, periwig maker in Gray's Inn — 8 Dec. 1698 —, Anne Newsom

Finch, Elizabeth, of the parish of St James, Westminster — 26 June, 1711 —, William Pinkney, of parish of St Mar- [garet's

Finch, Jane — 18 Aug 1697 —, Robert Burton, fishmonger in Hungerford [Market.

Finch, Jane of St James', Westminster — 15 Nov 1726 —, Miles Stephenson, of [same

Fish, John, of the parish of St Giles in the Fields — 3 Nov 1714 —, Mary Nichol- [son, of same

Fisher, Antony, of St Nicholas, Deptford. — 28 Feb 1730-1 —, Philippa Slade, [of same

Fisher, Joseph, of the parish of St. Michael's, Cornwall — 16 April, 1713 —, Eliza- beth Styles, of parish of St Andrew, [Holborn

Fisher, Samuel, coal merchant in Red Lion [St — 19 Aug 1699 —, Jane Belcher

Fisher, William, of the parish of St Andrew, Holborn — 23 April, 1713 —, Rebecca [Hodge, of parish of Hendon, Middx

Fitzwater, Richard, of Richmond, Surrey. — 5 March, 1736-7 —, Elisabeth Scar- [bourgh, of same

Flahan, Abraham, of St James' Clerken- well — 25 July, 1730 —, Mary Adeane, [of Reading, Berks

Fleming, James, of St Albans, Wood St — 6 Dec 1750 —, Sarah Parker, of St [George the Martyr, Queen sq

Fleming, William Henry, of St Andrew's, Holborn, *bat* — 3 Jan 1720-1 —, Ann [Samwell, of Watton, Norfolk, *spin*

Flemming, Matthew, of the parish of St Clements Danes — 10 Sept 1713 —, [Elizabeth Coling, of same

Fletcher, John, wire drawer in Distaff, Lane, parish of St Nicholas, Cole Abbey. — 9 Aug 1705 —, Ann Gruban, of [parish of St James, Clerkenwell

Fletcher, William, of St Dunstan's in the West — 26 April, 1739 —, Anne Gandy, [of St Andrew's, Holborn

Flintham, George, of St Andrew's, Holborn — 12 July, 1748 —, Sarah Honour, of [same

Flood, Martha, of the parish of St John, Hackney — 15 June, 1713 —, Thomas Campbell, of parish of St Swithin, [Cannon St

Flower, William — 13 Jan 1697-8 —, [Catherine

Fluellin, Judith — 21 May, 1696 —, George Norket, a saddler near the Greyhound [in the Strand by Charing Cross

Folkes, Edward, of St Giles in the Fields — 17 May, 1714 —, Hannah Morten, [of St Dunstan's in the West

Folwell, Charity, of St Andrew, Holborn — 18 April, 1714 —, George Ryland, of [same

Folwell, Elizabeth, of the Savoy. — 2 April, 1706 —, John Garlick, of parish of St [Clement Dane

Foot, Edward, woolcomber, of the parish of St Martin's, nr Salisbury, Wilts — 23 April, 1704 —, Hannah Whitlow, of [Wycomb, Bucks

Foreel, John, *bat*, of the parish of St Dunstan's in the West — 28 Aug 1715 [—, Sarah Springham, of same

Ford, John, of the parish of Islington — , 2 Nov 1714 —, Ann Lucas, of parish of [St Bride's

Ford, Susanna, of Henley on Thames — 7 May, 1714 —, Thomas Johnson, of [parish of St James, Westminster

Foresyth, James, trader in hair, near the Black Bull, Holborn — 9 Jan 1696-7 [—, Sara Greenaway

Forgaron, Elizabeth, of the parish of St Martin's in the Fields — 25 July, 1714 [—, Robert Bowman, of same

Forrest, Thomas, of St. James', Westminster — 1 Aug 1733 —, Mary [Holmes, of St James', Clerkenwell

Forrester, Dorothy, of St Andrew's, Holborn. — 29 July, 1728 —, James Longworth, of St Stephen's, Coleman St

Foster, Edward, of St Mary le Bow, *bat* — 29 Dec 1720 —, Susanna Littell, of [Stoke upon Aland, Suffolk, *widow*.

Foster, Hannah, of the parish of St. Andrew, Holborn — 27 May, 1707 —, Ambrose Butler. gent, of parish of St [Botolph, Aldgate.

Fountain, Christiana, of the parish of Enfield, Middx, *spin* — 14 March, 1721-2 [—, Benjamin Stephens, of same, *bat*.

Fountain, Robert, of the parish without Bishopsgate — 22 Oct 1713 —, Sarah Graystock, of parish of —— by Sion [College

Fowkes, Honor, of the parish of St Clements Dane — 22 April, 1708 —, [Francis Latham, of same.

Fowler, Elizabeth, of the parish of St Andrew, Holborn — 24 July, 1716 —, [James Hodgson, of same.

Fowler, John, shoemaker in Brook Market — 13 April, 1697 —, Sarah Elmes.

Fowler, Mary — 5 June, 1696 —, Richard Pile, apothecary in Candleford, Cornwall.

Fox, Elizabeth, of Eaton Bray, Beds, *spin*. — 28 Sept 1721 —, Jacob Ashwell, *bat*, [of same

Fox, Mary — 23 Feb 1695-6 —, John [Cotton, coachmaker in Chandos St

Francis, John, *bat*, of North Elmham, Norfolk, clerk — 20 April, 1720 —, [Mary Smith, of Holkham, Norfolk.

Francis, John, of Castle Hedingham, Essex — 25 Oct 1750 —, Mary Cooke, of same (by Rev. Joshua Allen, Rector of [St. Bride's, Pembroke)

Francis, Joyce, of the parish of St. Peter's, nr. Paul's Wharf — 22 June, 1712 —, [Alexander Lamley, of same

Francknell, Thomas, husbandman of Weston on the Green, co Oxford — 25 [Feb. 1700-1 —, Judith Smith

Francomb, Samuel, victualler in Fetter lane, of the parish of St Andrew's, Holborn. — 22 Aug. 1703 —, Penelope Worrall, [of said parish.

Franklin, Anne. — 30 Jan 1699-1700 —, Robert Holland, twister in Allen St., [Clerkenwell parish

Franklin, John, salesman in Cornhill — [31 Jan. 1698-9 —, Honor Burrell

Franklin, Judith — 8 Nov 1696 —, Thomas Burke, an officer under the [Lord of Berkley

Frankling, Anne — 14 May, 1695 —, Samuel Bullock, stable groom in St. [Anne's parish.

Frankling, Anne — 3 May, 1696 —, Edward Griffin, periwig maker near [Ratcliffe Cross

Freeman, George, victualler at the Cross Keys, against the Temple, Fleet St — [11 Feb 1695 6 —, Catharine Harris

Freeman, George, barber's surgeon in Birstim Lane — 12 Feb 1699-1700 —, [Mary Davis

Freeman, John, of St Mary, Aldermanbury, — 13 Sept 1722 —, Susanna Musket, of [Enfield, Middx

f

Freeman, Judith, of St Giles, Cripplegate
— 21 April, 1712 —, James Rewalling,
[of same.

Freeman, Mary — 23 July, 1699 —,
Joseph Males, butcher in Claor Market

Freeman, Mary, of the parish of St James,
Westminster — 15 July, 1713 —, Moses
[Longston, of same

Fretwell, Elizabeth, of Totteridge, Herts
— 16 Sept 1711 —, John Pullin, of
[parish of St Magnus, London

Frewin, Thomas (Esq), of the parish of
Northyam, Sussex — 7 July, 1713 —,
Martha Turner, of parish of St Andrew's
[(married by Mr Frewin).

Friend, John, coachman, of the parish of
St Andrew's, Holborn — 15 June,
1704 —, Grace Miles, of same (by
[licence)

Friend, John, of the parish of Great Stan-
more. — 8 May, 1711 —, Elizabeth
Saers, of parish of Harrow on the Hill,
[Middx

Frist, Ann, of the parish of St James
Westminster — 25 Nov 1711 —,
[Daniell Henn, of same

Frith, Gabriel, of St Giles in the Fields,
bat — 30 Sept 1721 —, Jane Price, of
[St James, Westminster, *spin*

Frith, Henry, of the parish of St James,
Clerkenwell — 25 May, 1742 —, Eliza-
[beth Woollard, of same

Frost, Elisabeth, of St Giles in the Fields
— 19 Feb 1744-5 —, Thomas Place,
[of St Andrew's Holborn

Fry, Mary, of Hornsey — 16 Nov 1728
—, John Lewis, of St Pancras in the
[Fields

Fry, Thomas, glover, near Iveybridge in the
Strand — 2 Dec 1699 —, Anne
[Tyrrill

Fryar, Jonathan, of St Giles in the Fields
— 18 Sept 1712 —, Elizabeth Black-
[well, of St Dunstan's in the West

Fryer, Mary, of St Martin's in the Fields.
— 6 June, 1730 —, Charles Skrymsher,
[of Barnard's Inn

Fuller, John, of the parish of St Giles,
Cripplegate — 8 Aug 1714 —, Hannah
[Linton, of same

Fuller, John, of St Vedast, Foster Lane —
2 July, 1724 —, Judith Crane, of St.
[Martin's, Ludgate.

Fuller, John, of Bushey, Herts — 17 Jan
1727-8 —, Ann Parsons, of St Dunstan's
[in the West

Furber, Robert, gardener at Exeter — 31
March, 1706 —, Mary Everton, of
[parish of St Giles in the Fields

Furley, Mary, of St James', Westminster
— 12 Jan 1701-2 —, Thomas Milner,
gent. of Christ Church parish, London

ffurmidge, William, soldier in the 1st troop
of guards. — 7 Feb 1698-9 —, Mary
[Cox

Furnis, Thomas, of the parish of St Andrew,
Holborn — 17 Jan 1712-3 —, Eliza-
[beth Mills, of same

Futerill, Mary — 3 Aug 1697 —, Hugh
Pugh, gent in Church lane Alley,
[Fetter lane

Gadler, Mary, of St Andrew's, Holborn —
5 Aug 1722 —, Robert Pardee, of St
[Giles in the Fields, widower

Gainsford, Mirabella. — 16 April, 1698 —,
Robert Hill, gent of King St, West-
[minster

Gale, Elisabeth, of St Andrew's Holborn
— 9 Jan 1738-9 —, William Stukeley,
D D, Rector of All Saints Stamford,
[co. Lincoln

Gally, Peter (Rev), of St James, Westminster — 3 May, 1734 —, Jane
[Allaire, of St Martin's in the Fields.

Gamble, Joseph, of the parish of St Giles,
Cripplegate — 13 March, 1711-2 —,
Susanna Hampson, of parish of Christ
[Church, Southwark

Gamble, Luce, of the parish of St James,
Westminster. — 23 July, 1710 —, John
[Linn, of same

Gandy, Anne, of St Andrew's, Holborn — 26 April, 1739 —, William Fletcher, of [St. Dunstan's in the West

Gardiner, Catherine, of St George the Martyr — 10 April, 1731 —, Edward [Kay, of St Andrew's, Holborn

Gardiner, Elizabeth, of the parish of St Andrew, Holborn — 13 Aug 1710 —, [Richard Procter, of same

Gardiner, Mary, of the parish of St Andrew, Holborn — 3 July, 1735 —, Christo-[pher Harris, of same

Gardiner, Robert, of the parish of St Sepulchre. — 3 Nov 1713 —, Mary [Wood, of same

Gardiner, Thomas, carpenter between the turnstiles in Holborn — 19 Aug 1697 [—, Elizabeth Oxley

Gardner, Arthur, turner, without Bishopsgate — 9 Oct 1698 —, Hannah [Denton

Gardon, Elizabeth, of the parish of St Ann's, Westminster — 11 Nov 1713 [—, Tirrill Lindsey, of same.

Garlick, John, of the parish of St Clements Dane — 2 April, 1706 —, Elizabeth [Folwell, of the Savoy

Garmson, John, gardener, of East Moulsey, Surrey — 21 July, 1696 —, Mary [Clark.

Garne, John, of St George the Martyr — (? 12) May, 1749 —, Martha Collet, of St [Mary le bone.

Garraway, Ann, of the parish of St. Botolph, Aldgate. — 20 July, 1708 , William [Keat, of same

Garsden, William, of St James', Westminster — 6 Aug 1724 —, Ann Pemberton, of St Mary Magdalen, Milk St

Gaskell, Elizabeth, of the parish of St. Laurence — 7 Jan 1702-3 —, John Mead, of parish of St Giles in the [Fields, labourer

Gawy, Sarah, of the parish of St Giles in the Fields — 30 March, 1703 —, William Brotherton, brazier in Fleet [lane, parish of St Sepulchre

Gay, Alice — 1 Dec 1698 —, John Lawson, [turner in Jewin St

Gayer, Jacob, of parish of Ottery St. Mary, Devon — 3 Dec 1715 —, Susannah [Beavis, of Farrington, co p'dict

Gboo, Abraham, seaman, of the parish of St Dunstan's, Stepney — 23 Dec 1702 [—, Marlina Bankes, of same

German, Josiah, shoemaker, of the parish of St Giles in the Fields — 24 April, 1707 —, Elizabeth Drumman, of same

Gerrard, Mary, of the parish of St Nicholas Acrons, London — 30 Oct 1711 —, Abraham Pariott, of parish of St Mar-[tin's, Ongars

Gery, Peter, of the parish of St Ann's, Westminster — 11 Dec 1713 —, Mary Edwards, of same (Married before, but " ye world not believing," it was [again solemnised)

Gevett, James, of the parish of St Andrew, Holborn. — 19 Nov 1713 —, Mary [Brown, of same.

Gerurean, Jacob, periwig maker, in Grafton St — 30 April, 1698 —, Anne Cook.

Gibbins, Mary, of St Giles in the Fields — 2 July, 1739 —, Thomas England, of [St Martin's in the Fields

Gibbon, Elizabeth, of the parish of St. Gabriel, Fenchurch St — 18 Feb. 1713-4 —, Robert Cart, of parish of [St Nicholas, Rochester, Kent.

Gibbon, Mary, of St Gabriel, Fenchurch St — 18 Feb 1713-4 —, John Trevor, of parish of St. Nicholas, Rochester, [Kent.

Gibbons, James, bat., of the parish of St Giles in the Fields — 23 Dec. 1714 —, Esther Drayton, spin, of St Ann's, [Westminster

Gibbons, John, of Great Marlow, Bucks, wheelwright — 3 Feb 1703-4 —, Ann Bayns, of parish of St Paul's, Covent [Garden.

Gibbonson, Rebecca, spin, of St Mary Botolph — 3 Dec 1714 —, William Clarke, bat, of parish of St. Leonard's, [East Cheap

Gibbs, Elizabeth, of St. James', Clerkenwell. — 19 Aug 1714 —, Joshua Wills, [of Yeterton, co Northampton

Gibbs, Henrietta, of St James', Clerkenwell — 18 June, 1732 —, Charles Shippey, [of St. Andrew's, Holborn

Gibson, James, of the parish of St Michael, Bassishaw. — 6 March, 1711-2 —, Mary [Dancev, of St Andrew, Holborn.

Gibson. John, of St Andrew's, Holborn — 10 April, 1748 —, Elisabeth Brinklett, [of St George's, Hanover sq

Gibson William, of the parish of St Sepulchre's. — 6 Aug 1709 —, Elizabeth [Holms, of same

Gigg, Rebecca, of St. Gabriel, Fenchurch — 24 July, 1712 —, John Buttan, of [parish of St Ann, Blackfriars

Gilder, Josiah, of the parish of St. Clements Dane — 4 Feb 1713-4 —, Elizabeth [Greenwood, of St Andrew, Holborn

Gill, Anne, of St Giles in the Fields, *spin* — 27 May, 1720 —, John Loyd, *bat*, [ot same

Gill, Richard, of the parish of St Sepulchre — 12 April, 1714 —, Elizabeth Wallis, [of same

Gill, Robert, of St. George's, Bloomsbury. — 24 Dec. 1746 —, Anne Ashton, of [same

Gillman, Mary, of the parish of St James, Westminster — 22 Dec 1716 —, Thomas Hawley, of St Anne's, West- [minster

Gillmar, Martha, of St Giles in the Fields. — 3 June, 1732 —, Isaac Ballard, of [parish of St. Mary le Strand

Gillot, Eleanor of the parish of Leatherhead, Surrey — 7 July, 1709 —, Alexander Millbourn, of parish of Twickenham, [Middx

Gillson, Anna, of the parish of Whitechapel — 26 July, 1713 —, William Lowry, of [Chelsea College

Gilson, George, of the parish of St Ann's, Blackfriars — 11 July, 1714 — Yonchin [Bornan, of same

Girdler, Susannah, of St Giles in the Fields — 8 Nov 1716 —, Joseph Dobbins, of [parish of St Andrew's. Holborn.

Girdler, William (Esq) of the parish of Fulham — 24 Feb 1752 —, Susanna [Ryves, of parish of St Mary le bone

Gisbitzby, Bartholomew, of St Mary Monthaw, London — 23 Aug 1724 —, Elizabeth Platt, of St. Andrew's, Hol- [born

Gitles, Frances, of the parish of St Andrew's, Holborn. — 27 Jan 1703-4 —, Abraham Parkis, of same parish, servant to Mr Shales at the Vine, Lombard St.

Glanvile, William, gent, of the parish of St Edmund the King, Lombard St. — 5 Nov 1713 —, Elizabeth Allison, of [All Saints, Lombard St

Glasford, Ann, of Watford, Herts — 11 Dec 1725 —, William Glasford, of [same

Glasford, William, of Watford, Herts — 11 Dec 1725 —, Ann Glasford, of [same

Gload, Edward, of Putney parish, Surrey — 5 July, 1716 —, Mary Hamond, of [St James', Westminster.

Glover, Sarah, of the parish of St Saviour's, Southwark — 14 Oct 1713 —, Robert [Corsen, of same

Godard, Elizabeth, of the parish of St Martin's in the Fields — 26 Jan 1713-4 —, [David Morris, of same.

Godbould, Grace — 14 May. 1702 —, Benjamin Barker, stationer in West- [minster Hall

Goddard, Francis, of St Martin's in the Fields, *widower* — 25 May, 1721 —, [Mary Ayres, of same, *spin*.

Godfrey, Mary, of Chipping Barnet, Middx. — 4 May, 1741 —, Alexander Simpson, [of Leake, co. Lincoln

Godfry, Anne. — 14 Aug 1701 —, Simon [Parrott, founder in White Cross St

Godolphin, Rebecca — 24 Nov 1699 —, Samuel Edwards, gent at the Trustee's [Office in Palace Yard

Godsalve, Henry, of Baddow, Essex — 16 Aug. 1748 —, Leonora Lannoy, of [same

Goff, Ursula, of St Giles, Cripplegate — 4 May, 1728 —, James Fergusson, of St [Mary le bone

Goldsadle, Richard, of St Giles in the Fields — 29 Aug 1731 —, Mary Bott, [of St George the Martyr

Good, Mary. — 27 April, 1697 —, Stephen Hall, linen draper at Drury Lane End

Goodall, Samuel, of the parish of St Paul's, Covent Garden. — 29 Oct 1713 —, [Mary Lane, of same.

Goodall, Sarah, of the parish of St Paul's, Covent Garden — 9 April, 1713 —, Andrew Slann, of same (married by Mr Goodall, fellow of Peterhouse Coll [Cambridge)

Goode, William, sword cutler in New St —'15 Aug. 1700 —, Alice Blackbourne.

Goodgame, Thomas, of parish of Edmonton, Middx — 28 Jan 1715-6 —, Ruth [Poplewell, of St Andrew, Holborn

Goodwin, Lydia. — 4 March, 1696-7 —, James Perrey, mercer in Chandos St [(by Mr. Elborough of the Fleet)

Goostree, Ann, of St Andrew, Holborn — 20 Nov 1725 —, Thomas Delafield, [of St Giles without Cripplegate

Gorham, William, of the parish of St Paul's, Covent Garden — 2 Dec 1714 —, [Elizabeth Lane, of same

Goring, Dorothy, late of Morpeth, Northumberland — 13 Sept 1715 —, [Cuthbert Wightman, late of same

Gorst, Anne, of St. Martin's in the Fields — 27 Aug 1737 —, James Hayes, of [St Giles in the Fields

Gorton, Mary, of the parish of St Giles in the Fields — licence dated July 1717 [—, Francis Stonestreet, of same

Gosford, Thomas, *widower*, of the parish of St Giles in the Fields — 13 Jan 1714-5 —, Esther Dovoy, *spin* of same.

Gosling, Francis, of St Dunstan's in the West — 12 Nov. 1742 —, Elisabeth [Midwinter, of St Bride's.

Gough, Charlotta, of St James', Westminster — 28 June, 1739 —, Sir William [Sanderson, bart, of Greenwich

Gould, Ann, of the parish of St Martin's in the Fields — 1 July, 1706 —, Thomas [Smith, of same

Gould, John, of St Martin's, Vintry — 8 May, 1745 —, Rachel Town, of same

Goulton, James, of the parish of St Leonard, Shoreditch — 15 Oct 1712 —, Ann [Handy, of same

Gover, Dorothy, of the parish of St Andrew's, Holborn — 20 Sept 1705 —, James Billington, gent of parish of St Giles in the Fields (married by Mr Billington of Dulwich College, — the man about [20, the woman 80)

Gower, Robert, of the parish of St Dunstan's in the West — 10 April, 1705 —, Hannah Hammond, of Chelmsford, [Essex

Grace, Isaac, clergyman in the parish of St Martin's in the Fields — 11 Nov. 1713 —, Barbara Case, of parish of St [Dunstan's in the West

Graham, Elizabeth, of the parish of St Bride's, London — 18 Nov 1706 —, [James Philpot, of same

Grainge, Margery, of the parish of St. Andrew, Holborn — 12 Sept 1714 —, [James Nottingham, of same

Gramer, Thomas, of St John, Zachary, London — 20 May, 1726 —, Elizabeth [Cooke, of St Mary, Islington.

Grandy, George, of Reading, Berks — 24 Dec 1750 —, Margaret Knight, of [same

Grant, David, gent of Brownlow Street — [13 April, 1701 —, Jane Lynn.

Grant, John, of Bread St — 1 Aug. 1734 —, Margaret Hooper, of St. Andrew's, [Holborn

Grantland, Shadrach, of the parish of St James, Westminster — 6 Jan 1713-4 [—, Ann Herd, of St Sepulchre's

Graves, Mary — 1 June, 1701 —, Thomas Ventum, poulterer in Stanmore Magna, [Middx

Graystock Sarah, of the parish of ——, by Sion College — 22 Oct 1713 —, Robert Fountain, of parish without [Bishopsgate

Green, Ann, of the parish of Great Coxwell, Berks — 15 Oct 1712 — John Ellon, [of parish of Lambourne, Berks

Green, John, servant to Thomas Mack Millon, gent in Drury Lane — 19 [Sept. 1695 —, Mary Benwell

Green, Mary, of the parish of St Giles in the Fields — 3 Sept 1710 —, Thomas [Watton, of same

Green, Matthew, wine cooper in Budge row [— 7 Sept 1700 —, Hannah Barnes

Green, Rebecca, of St Ann's, Aldersgate — 29 Oct. 1714 —, Simon Hopkins, of [same.

Green, Richard, a carpenter. — 23 June, [1700 —, Susanna Eiham.

Greenalgh   See Allen

Greenaway, Sara — 9 Jan 1696-7 —, James Foresyth, dealer in hair, near the [Black Bull, Holborn

Green , Thomas, yeoman, of the parish of Islington — 23 March, 1702-3 —, [Sarah Chambers of same

Greene, William, yeoman, of the parish of Abray (Albury), Herts — 21 April, 1703 —, Susanna Scott, of parish of St Ann s, [Westminster

Greenhill, Thomas, of St Nicholas Olaves — 31 Dec 1712 —, Margaret Donvile, [of parish of ——, Aldersgate

Greenup, Sarah, of St Andrew's, Holborn — 6 Aug 1724 —, Daniel Wilson, of [St James', Westminster

Greenwood, Elizabeth, of St Andrew's, Holborn — 4 Feb 1713-4 —, Josiah Gilder, of parish of St Clements Dane.

Greenwood, Elisabeth, of Chelsea — 7 Sept 1732 —, Ambrose Naish, of [same

Greenwood, Thomas, of the parish of St Giles Cripplegate — 16 Aug 1713 —, Mary Humphreys, of parish of Islington

Gregory, Mark, bat , of St Giles in the Fields — 10 May, 1720 —, Margaret [Mayhew, of same spin

Gretton, Thomas, of St. Dunstan's in the West — 5 April, 1726 — Elizabeth [Turner, of parish of Hampstead.

Grew, Robert, victualler in Newgate St — [16 April, 1697 —, Mary Normcott

Grey, Dorothy, of St Swithin, London Stone, spin — 5 Nov 1720 —, Henry Egleton, of St Stephen, Coleman St, [bat.

Grice, Joseph, of St Dunstan's in the West — 12 April, 1721 —, Jane Jones, of [Esher, Surrey.

Grice, Nicholas, gent of the parish of St Dunstan's in the West — 10 May, 1707 —, Sarah Pepys, of same (by [licence).

Griebe, Conrad, a soldier, near the Latine Coffee House, Warwick Lane — 7 Jan [1695-6 —, Mary Hammond.

Griffin, Anne, of Dingley, co Northampton — 26 Jan 1716-7 —, William Whitwell, [Esq , of Oundle in Northampton

Griffin, Edward, periwig maker near Ratcliffe Cross — 3 May, 1696 —, Anne [Frankling

Griffin, George, of the parish of Ewell, Surrey. — 16 June, 1737 —, Catharine [Wooder, of Gatton, Surrey.

Griffin, William, haberdasher, of Helmet Court, Strand. — 20 Jan 1701-2 —, [Margaret Edwards.

Griffis, Jane, of the parish of St James, Westminster — 2 Jan 1712-3 —, [William Thomas, of same

Grimes, Ann, of the parish of Hillington, Middx. — 3 Dec 1714 —, John Fig- [gings, of same.

Grinoway, Constantia, of the parish of St Sepulchre. — 7 Aug 1716 —, Jacob [Cooper, of same.

Groocock, William, of the parish of St
Alban's, Wood St — 23 June, 1713
[—, Sarah Allen, of Chelsea

Groom, Giles, of the parish of Watford,
Herts — 25 May, 1713 —, Mary Dod,
[of same

Groom, John, Vicar of Childerditch, Essex
— 28 June, 1712 —, Mary Moor, of
[parish of St James, Westminster

Gruban, Ann, of the parish of St James,
Clerkenwell — 9 Aug 1705 —, John
Fletcher, wire drawer in Distaff Lane,
[parish of St Nicholas, Cole Abbey

Grubb, William, of the parish of St. Lawrence — 21 July, 1709 —, Phebe
Parker, of parish of St. Saviour's, South-
[wark

Guidott, Priscilla, of the parish of St. Martin's in the Fields — 26 Nov 1713 —,
Thomas Rawston, of parish of St Giles
[in the Fields

Gullyford, William, of the parish of Christ
Church, Southwark — 6 July, 1712 —,
Mary Jones, of parish of St Giles in the
[Fields.

Gunter, Nathaniel, of the parish of St
Dunstan's in the West — 5 April, 1716
— Jane Leigh, of St Margaret's, West-
[minster

Gurdon, Mary — 7 Feb 1696-7 —, Edward
[Ryder, butcher in Clare Market

Gurney, Christian, of St Sepulchre, spin
—7 Dec 1721 —, John Love, bat, of
[Isleworth

Guy, Temperance, of parish of Wim-
bourne, co Dorset — 14 March, 1705-6
—, Richard Brown, of parish of St
[Andrew's, Holborn, organist

Guyon, Samuel, a joyner in St. Hellen's
[— 7 April, 1696 —, Isabella Parsons

Gwinnet, John, of the parish of St Clements
Dane — 19 May, 1711 —, Elizabeth
Coxe, of parish of St Martin's in the
[Fields

Gwynn, William, silk dyer near the Playhouse in Drury Lane — 16 Feb. 1696-7
[—, Jane Lucas

Gynes, Joseph, of the parish of St. Augus-
tine's, London — 3 Oct 1713 —,
Katherine Couch, of parish of All Saints,
[Broad St

Hackwood, Frances, spin, of the parish of
St Giles in the Fields — 21 March,
[1714-5 —, John Lobb, bat., of same

Haddock, Ann, of St Sepulchre. — 4 Jan
1735-6 —, Jonathan Copen, of St An-
[drew's, Holborn

Haddock, Elizabeth, of the parish of St
Margaret, Westminster — 12 Dec 1708
—, William Richardson, of parish of
[Hendon, Middx

Hagedorn, Henry, of the parish of St Martins in the Fields — 1 July, 1711 —,
[Mary Darrell, of Stepney.

Haggard, Mary, of St. Botolph without
Bishopsgate — 2 Feb 1724-5 —, John
[Burr, of same

Hailstone, Nicholas, of St Clements Dane
— 10 Aug 1727 —, Anne Archer, of
[of same

Hakewill, Catherine, of Weston, Bucks —
16 April, 1741 —, Richard Bates, of
[Chipping Wycomb, Bucks

Haldane, Robert (Esq), of St Mary le bone
— 29 Sept 1742 —, Elisabeth Holmes,
[of St Clements Dane

Hale, Elizabeth — 23 June, 1701 —,
Thomas Redferne, mason in Black-
[friars

Hale, Margaret, of the parish of St Giles in
the Fields — 21 Dec 1707 —, Edward
[Boswell, of same

Halfhide, Sarah, of the parish of St
Edmunds, in town of Cambridge —
28 July, 1711 - , Edward Chapman, of
[parish of Linton, co Cambridge.

Halham, John, surgeon in Hart St,
Covent Garden. — 9 Nov 1698 —,
[Isabella Lunt.

Hall, Bartholomew, of the parish of St Mar-
tin's in the Fields — 18 Oct. 1713 —,
Jane Sinck, of parish of St Giles in the
[Fields

Hall, Frances, of the parish of St. Bartholomew the Less. — 20 May, 1711 —,
[William Ball, of same

Hall, George, of the parish of St Bartholomew the Less — 26 Oct 1712 —,
[Esther Harris, of same

Hall, Hugh, periwig maker in Charles St,
Covent Garden — 23 April, 1702 —,
[Rachel Barnes

Hall, Isaac, a cooper against Chancey Lane
[—5 Oct 1697 —, Martha Elbrow

Hall, John, of the parish of St Clement's
Dane — 10 May, 1713 —, Elizabeth
Kikins, of parish of St Andrew, Hol-
[born

Hall, Manley, of the parish of St. Martin's
in the Fields — 7 Feb 1713-4 —,
[Susanna Moses, of same

Hall, Penelope — 24 May, 1704 —, Martin
Newport, merchant in Wandsworth,
Surrey (married by Mr. Edgeley, Vicar
[of Wandsworth)

Hall, Robert, gent, at the Holy Lamb, Long
Acre — 7 Sept 1697 —, Elizabeth
[Smith

Hall, Sarah, of St James' parish, Westminster
— 9 Sept 1705 —, Robert Austin,
[butcher, of same

Hall, Stephen, linen draper at Drury Lane
End — 27 April, 1697 —, Mary Good

Hall, William, of the parish of Mortlake,
Surrey — 21 Sept 1713 —, Anne Pole-
hampton, of parish of St Martin's in the
[Fields

Halsey, Richard, of the parish of St Andrews. — 29 Sept 1717 —, Margaret
[Meredith, of same

Halstead, Frances, of St Clements Dane
— 26 Jan 1722-3 —, Richard Carre, of
[parish of St Sepulchre

Hamersley, Hugh, of the Inner Temple
— 28 April, 1713 —, Elizabeth Hoole,
[of parish of St Martin's, Ludgate

Hamill, Mary, of the parish of St Clements
Dane — 19 Oct, 1707 —, Thomas
[Massey, of same

Hammond, Alice, of St Anne's, Black-
friars, *widow* — 30 Dec. 1719 —, Joseph
Allen, *widower*, of St Martin's in the
[Fields

Hammond, Anne, of Finchley — 26 April,
1750 —, John Manley, of the Middle
[Temple, Esq

Hammond, Hannah, of Chelmsford, Essex
— 10 April, 1705 —, Robert Gower, of
the parish of St Dunstan's in the West.

Hammond, John, of St Giles, Cripplegate
— 23 July, 1727 —, Rachel Dymmock,
[of same.

Hammond, Martha, of the parish of St.
Andrew, Holborn — 26 Aug 1710 —,
[Thomas Hull, of same

Hammond, Mary. — 7 Jan. 1695-6 —,
Conrad Griebe, a soldier, near the Latine
[Coffee house, Warwick Lane.

Hammond, Robert, of the parish of St.
Andrew, Holborn — 31 May, 1713 —,
[Mary Evans, of same.

Hammond, Samuel of St. Katherine, Coleman St — 18 April, 1714 —, Jane All-
[brooks, of Shoreditch.

Hamond, Mary, of St James', Westminster
— 5 July, 1716 —, Edward Gload, of
[Putney parish, Surrey

Hampson, Susanna, of the parish of Christ
Church, Southwark — 13 March, 1711-2
—, Joseph Gamble, of parish of St.
[Giles, Cripplegate.

Hanbury, Elisabeth, of St George the
Martyr, Queen Sq. — 6 April, 1734
[—, William Neale, of this society

Handy, Ann, of the parish of St Leonard,
Shoreditch. — 15 Oct 1712 —, James
[Goulton, of same

Hanmer, John, of the parish of St Giles in
the Fields — 10 Nov 1713 —, Susan
[Thompson, of same

Hannam, Mary, of the parish of St Andrew,
Holborn — 3 Aug 1710 —, Samuel
Baldwin, of the Inner Temple (married
by Mr Jackson, Reader of the Temple).

Hanscomb, Thomas, victualler in St
James' parish. — 8 April, 1697 —, Mary
[Kidd

Hanworth, Elizabeth, of the parish of St
Giles in the Fields — 6 April, 1707 —,
[Anthony Smith, carpenter, of same.

Harrison, Mary, of St Dunstan's in the West — 18 Dec 1740 —, Rev John [Howess, of St. Bride's

Harrison, Robert, haberdasher of small wares in Gerrard St, parish of St Ann's, Westminster. — 26 Jan 1704 5 [—, Elinor Wright

Hart, George, of Mitcham, Surrey — 3 Feb 1733-4 —, Elizabeth Turner, of Croydon, [Surrey

Hart, William, of the parish of St Katherine, Tower Hill — 21 Sept 1713 —, Elizabeth Peynter, of the parish of Richmond, [Surrey

Harte, Edward, of the parish of St Andrew, Holborn — 21 March, 1750-1 —, [Susanna Baty, of same

Hartley, Martha, of St Martin's in the Fields — 19 Nov 1713 —, George Elliot, of parish of Christ Church, [London

Harwood, Sarah, *widow*, of the parish of Christ Church — 9 Jan 1714-5 —, James Chamberlain, *widower*, of same

Haslewood, Mary, of Eltham, Kent — 5 May, 1730 —, George Worral, of [Long Sutton, co Lincoln

Hassell Abigail, of St Martin's in the Fields — 23 July, 1724 —, John Hutchins, of St. Paul's, Covent Garden

Hassell, John, of the parish of St Giles in the Fields — 21 Oct 1714 —, Ann Drot (blotted), of St. Olave's, Old [Jewry

Hassell, Ralph, of the parish of St Mary Magdalen, Milk St. — 1 July 1708 —, Martha Wyllymot, of parish of St Giles [in the Fields

Hassell, Rebecca, of St Bride's — 6 Feb 1724-5 —, John Arnold, of St Dunstan's [in the West

Hassel, Ruisshe, of St Giles in the Fields — 23 April, 1737 —, Jane Tynte, of [St James', Westminster

Hassel, Ruisshe, of St Giles in the Fields — 17 March, 1743-4 —, Charlotte [Mackeeily, of St Mary le bone

Haswell, John, of St Martin's in the Fields — 13 March, 1714-5 —, Anne Preven- [ter, *spr.*, of same

Hatley, Anne, of the parish of Hackney. — 14 July, 1753 —, Richard Nicholas, [Esq of same

Hatley, Richard, a Norwich factor in Ab- church Lane — 4 Sept 1698 —, [Martha Bray

Hatton, Jane, of the parish of St Martin's in the Fields — 9 Nov 1714 —, [William Barwick, of same

Havergill, Mary. — 17 Dec 1696 —, Ambrose Ash, tailor at New Inn gate, [in St Clements.

Hawkins, David, coachmaker in the parish of St Andrew's, Holborn — 6 July, [1705 —, Ann Manning (by licence).

Hawkins, Elizabeth, of St Bridget's, *spr* — 3 Jan 1720-1 —, Anthony Bristow, [of same *widower*

Hawkins, George, of St Botolph's Alders- gate — 17 July, 1728 —, Elisabeth [Richmond, of same

Hawkins, Helena, of St Ann's, Blackfriars — 9 Feb 1713-4 —, Robert Hutchin- [son, of St Dunstan's in the West.

Hawkins, John, of the parish of St. Mar- tin's in the Fields — 17 Dec 1713 —, Alice Whitell, of St. James, Westminster

Hawksford, Anne — 4 Oct 1696 —, [James Clarke, collier in Clerkenwell

Hawley, James (M D), of St Paul's, Covent Garden — 8 Nov 1744 —, Elisabeth [Banks, of St George's, Hanover Sq

Hawley, Thomas, of St Anne's, Westmin- ster — 22 Dec 1716 —, Mary Gillman, [of parish of St James, Westminster

Hawton, Judith — 26 Oct 1699 —, Charles Herbert, vintner at the Queen's Head, [Fleet St

Hayes, Elizabeth, of Wolverhampton, co. Stafford — 21 Sept 1752 —, George [Holyoake, of same

Hayes, James, of St Giles in the Fields — 27 Aug 1737 —, Anne Gorst, of St [Martin's in the Fields

Hayle, Elizabeth — 21 Oct 1701 — Nicholas Bunfoy, gent of Wellington, [Herts

Hayward, Mary, of St George, Southwark. — 10 May, 1705 —, John Archer, of [parish of St Botolph's, Billingsgate

Heacock, Thomas, of the parish of St Leonard's, Shoreditch — 26 Oct 1708 [—, Mary Bentley, of same

Heart, Richard, of St Sepulchre — 22 [Sept 1734 —, Mary Ellard, of same

Heath, Esther, of St Thomas the Apostle, London — 3 Aug. 1742 —, Robert Shippard, of St George's, Hanover sq

Heath, Francis, of the parish of St Andrew's, Holborn — 12 Sept 1708 —, Prudence [Jeynes, of same

Heathcote, Samuel, bat, of St John's, Hackney, Esq — 3 May, 1720 —, [Elizabeth Holworthy, of same, spin

Heaton, William, of the parish of St Botolph, Aldgate — 24 Jan. 1713-4 —, Sarah [Jollice, of same

Hedges, Mary, of St Anne's, Westminster — 29 March, 1741 —, Philip Tuten, of [St Giles in the Fields

Hemplock, Peter, of the parish of St Martin's in the Fields — 31 Oct 1714 [—, Ann Vean, of same

Henchman, Mary — 7 July, 1696 —, [Thomas Shepheard, wholesale glover.

Hendler, William (Esq), one of the masters of this society — 26 Feb 1733-4 —, Dorothea Singleton, of St [George's Bloomsbury

Hendley, Elizabeth, of Ottham, Kent — 4 June, 1726 —, Thomas Taylor, Vicar [of Hollingbourne, Kent.

Heneage, Phebe, of St. Andrew's, Holborn. — 8 April, 1716 —, Richard Brocas, [of All Saints' parish

Heneage, William, bat, of the parish of St James, Clerkenwell — 20 Feb 1714-5 —, Mary Hare, widow, of same.

Henley, John, of St Leonards, Shoreditch — 10 Oct 1714 —, Susanna Clay, of [Christ Church, Southwark

Henly, Jane, of St Clements Dane, spin. — 27 Sept 1720 —, Robert Thacker, of [same, bat.

Henman, William, coachman to the Lady in Hatton Garden — 1 June, 1698 —, [Elizabeth Puxty

Henn, Daniell, of the parish of St James. Westminster — 25 Nov. 1711 —, [Ann Frist, of same

Henning, Isaac, of the parish of St. Andrew, Holborn — 15 July, 1713 —, Eleanor [Hog, of Mark Lane.

Hent, John Eborchard, French schoolmaster in St James, Westminster — [12 Oct 1696 —, Mary Van-heck.

Henwood, Thomas, of St Mildred in the poultry — 14 July, 1739 —, Eleanor [Roles, of St Andrew's, Holborn.

Herbert, Alice — 22 Oct 1696 —, John Burrard, Esq, of Lymington, co, [Southampton

Herbert, Charles, vintner at the Queen's Head, Fleet St. — 26 Oct. 1699 —, [Judith Hawton.

Herbert, Robert, of the parish of St. Giles in the Fields — 17 Nov 1713 —, [Dorothy Bent, of same.

Herbert, Samuel, of the parish of St Andrew, Holborn — 22 June, 1714 —, Elizabeth Bryon, of parish of St Giles [in the Fields

Herbert, Thomas, victualler at the Windsor Castle in Charing Cross — 17 Feb [1701-2 —, Mary Hinton.

Herd, Ann, of St Sepulchre's — 6 Jan 1713-4 —, Shadrach Grantland, of parish [of St James, Westminster

Herdwix, John, of the parish of Battlesin, Colchester, bag maker — 13 May, 1703 —, Ann Turner, of parish of All Saints, Colchester (married by a reader of [Covent Garden Church).

Herne, Mary — 23 Dec 1699 —, Gilbert Edwards, a captain at the Nag's Head, [against Short's Gardens, Drury Lane

Herring, James, bat, of the parish of the Holy and undivided Trinity the Less — 1 Feb 1718-9 —, Martha Powel, of [parish of St Mary, Whitechapel, spin

Herring, Sare — 30 April, 1723 —, Christo-
[pher Toepken

Hewitt, Robert, of Ramsgate, Kent. — 13
Sept 1730 —, Jane Hewson, of St
[George's in the East

Hewson, Jane, of St George's in the East
— 13 Sept 1730 —, Robert Hewitt, of
[Ramsgate, Kent

Heysham, William, bat, of Greenwich,
Kent. — 1 Oct 1719 —, Sarah Perry,
[of St Catherine Cree Church

Hickman, William, of the parish of St
Sepulchre — 5 March, 1723 4 —,
Faith Cutting, of St Dunstan's in the
[West

Hicks, Benjamin, widower, of the parish of
St Andrew, Holborn — 27 Jan 1714-5
[—, Anna Maria ——, of same.

Hicks, John, joiner in Durham yard — 29
[Dec 1696 —, Dorothy Lee

Hide, Benjamin, bat, of the parish of St
Andrew, Holborn. — 15 Dec. 1714 —,
[Mary Smith, sing, of same

Higden, Edward, bat, of the parish of St
Mary, Savoy — 21 Jan 1714-5 —,
[Elizabeth Watts, widow, of same

Higgs, Thomas, of St. Andrew's, Holborn
— 24 Nov 1729 —, Jane White, of
[same.

Higham, Alice, of St Andrew's, Holborn.
— 17 April, 1737 —, Reynold New-
[stead, of Wakefield, co. York

Hildyard, Elizabeth — 15 Feb 1695-6 —,
Lockey Hill, of the Middle Temple,
[gent

Hiley, Elisabeth, of St Laurence Pountney,
London — 18 May, 1735 —, Thomas
[Woolley, of Edgar, Middx.

Hill, Ann, of St Giles, Cripplegate. — 2
March, 1712-3 —, Giles Watts, of parish
[of St. Mildred's, Poultry

Hill, Elizabeth, of the parish of St. Clements
Dane. — 27 Jan. 1712-3 —, John Bentley,
[of same

Hill, Elizabeth, of the parish of St Giles —
21 Feb. 1713-4 —, George Woddle, of
[same

Hill, Elizabeth, widow, of the parish of St.
Dunstan's in the West — 29 Jan 1714-5
[—, John Powel, widower, of same

Hill, Francis, of Whitby, co York, mariner
[— 25 July, 1695 —, Mary Ingledew.

Hill, John, of the parish of St. Giles in the
Fields. — 3 Oct 1713 —, Mary Seale,
[of same

Hill, Lockey, of the Middle Temple, gent. —
15 Feb 1695-6 —, Elizabeth Hildyard

Hill, Richard, of St George the Martyr —
26 Aug 1751 —, Elisabeth Burch, of
[St Catharine's, near the Tower

Hill, Robert, gent, of King St, Westminster — 16 April, 1698 — Mirabella
[Gainsford

Hill, Ruth, of Copland, Kent — 20 March
1718 —, Christopher Turner, of Tun-
[bridge, Kent

Hill, Samuel, of St Clements Danes. — 3
[Oct 1726 —, Hannah Rose, of same

Hill, Sarah, of St. Olave's, Southwark — 27
Oct 1713 —, Roger Osbadiston, of
[parish of St. Saviour, Southwark.

Hill, Sarah, of St Giles in the Fields, spin
— 25 Jan 1719 —, Edward Hughes,
[bat, of same.

Hill, Thomas, of the parish of St Andrew,
Holborn — 26 Aug 1710 —, Martha
[Hammond, of same

Hill, Thomas, of the parish of St Andrew,
Holborn — 29 July, 1711 —, Mary
Lilford, of same (married by Mr Shug-
[borow)

Hill, William, of the parish of St. Pancras
— 14 April, 1713 —, Deborah Purier (?),
[of same

Hillay, Sarah, of St Andrew, Holborn —
30 Nov. 1713 —, Peter Barton, of
[same

Hillon, Elizabeth, of St Sepulchre's parish
— 3 March, 1716-7 —, Arthur Crank,
[of St Stephen's, Coleman St.

Hillton, Sarah, of St. George the Martyr,
Queen Sq. — 28 Aug 1745 —, James
[Oswald, of same

Hinton, Mary — 17 Feb 1701-2 —, Thomas Herbert, victualler, at the Windsor [Castle, in Charing Cross

Hippisley, John, apothecary in St Martin's Lane — 28 Jan 1700-1 —, Theodosia [Bibbee

Hiron, Elizabeth, of Wandsworth, Surrey — 17 Feb 1725-6 —, John Barnard, of [Kensington

Hoar, Richard, of Deptford, Kent — 20 Dec 1730 —, Margaret Scapeland, of [same

Hoare, Patrick, of the parish of St Andrew, Holborn — 9 April, 1713 —, Jane Martin, of parish of St Giles in the [Fields.

Hobbs, Richard, of the parish of St Faiths — 4 Dec 1711 —, Jane Hodges, of parish [of St James, Clerkenwell

Hobbs, Sara — 22 April, 1697 —, John Moore, a broker, against the Great Turn- [stile, Holborn

Hobday Esther, of St Andrew's, Holborn, *spin* — 31 Dec 1719 —, James Young, [bat, of St Andrew's, Holborn

Hobson, Caleb, of the parish of Hampstead, Middx — 16 Dec 1707 —, Ann Cludley, [of same

Hockin, Thomas, of St Paul's, Covent Garden. — 30 Oct 1718 —, Elizabeth [Davies, of same

Hoden, Beatrice, of St Giles in the Fields — 5 March, 1727 8 —, Robert Smith, [of St Dunstan's in the West.

Hodge, Rebecca, of the parish of Hendon, Middx — 23 April, 1713 —, William Fisher, of parish of St Andrew, Hol [born

Hodge, Elizabeth, *spin*, of Hendon parish, Middx — 16 April, 1715 —, William [Downer, *bat*, of parish of Edgeworth

Hodges, Jane, of the parish of St James, Clerkenwell — 4 Dec 1711 —, Richard [Hobbs, of parish of St Faiths

Hodgkin, Elizabeth, of St Andrew's, Holborn — 16 May, 1703 —, Richard [Sowerby, of same

Hodgkin, Elizabeth, of Peterborough, co. Northampton, *spin* — 9 June, 1719 —, [William Raven, *bat* of Charing, Kent

Hodgson, James, of the parish of St Andrew, Holborn — 24 July, 1716 —, [Elizabeth Fowler, of same.

Hodgson, William, of St. Leonard's, Shore- ditch — 11 Nov. 1744 —, Elisabeth [Baston, of St Andrew, Holborn

Hoffman, Robert, of the parish of St. Alban, Wood St — 28 April, 1709 —, Elizabeth Lingard, of parish of St [Katherine Cree Church

Hog, Eleanor, of Mark Lane. — 15 July, 1713 —, Isaac Henning, of parish of [St Andrew, Holborn

Hoggins, Richard, victualler in Essex St — 24 May, 1702 —, Isabella Catfoss [(?)

Holbrook, John, husbandman in Deptford. [— 5 March, 1701-2 —, Mary Blabey

Holbrooke, Grace, of the parish of St Andrew, Holborn — 28 March, 1713 —, Francis Clerk, Esq, of North [Weston, co Oxford

Holcomb, Hannah, of the parish of St. Clements Dane — 14 July, 1713 —, [George Taylor, of same

Holdcraft, Isabella, of the parish of St. Andrew's, Holborn — 4 Nov 1714 —, [Edward Burrows, of same

Holden, Benjamin, of the parish of St Bridget — 24 Feb 1712-3 —, Dorothy Reynolds, of parish of St Dunstan's in [the West.

Holder, Cornelia — 13 Dec 1697 —, Francis Speke, saddler in Kentish [Town

Holding, Diana, of the parish of St Mar- tin's in the Fields — 4 May, 1718 —, [Simon Darby, of same.

Holland, Robert, twister in Allen St, Clerkenwell parish — 30 Jan 1699-1700 [—, Anne Franklin

Hollester, Thomas, *bat*, of the parish of St Martin's, Ludgate — 27 Jan 1714-5 —, Alice Ashworth, *spin* of St. Giles, [Cripplegate

Hollins, John, of the parish of St Andrew, Holborn — 1 Jan 1711-2 —, Elizabeth [Hovell, of same

Hollis, Elizabeth, of White Chapel — 12 Dec 1723 —, William Ashurst, of [Friday St

Hollon, Elizabeth Maria, of the parish of St Andrew's, Holborn — 13 Sept 1709 —, Anthony Phillips, of parish of [Deptford, Kent

Hollond, John, of the parish of St Mary Over, Southwark. — 12 April, 1714 —, [Elizabeth Shaw, of same

Holmby, Anne — 18 June, 1695 —, George Barker, of St Ann's, Aldersgate, [farmer

Holmes, Anne — 4 Sept 1700 —, John Sanders, a sedan man in Lester St , St [Anne's parish

Holmes, Elisabeth, of St. Clements Danes — 29 Sept 1742 —, Robert Haldane, [Esq of St Mary le bone

Holmes, Mary, of St James', Clerkenwell — 1 Aug 1733 —, Thomas Forrest, of [St James', Westminster

Holms, Elizabeth, of the parish of St Sepulchre — 6 Aug 1709 —, William [Gibson, of same

Holms, James (Eike), of the parish of St Margaret, Westminster — 19 Jan 1713-14, and 1 Dec. 1714 —, Mary Humes, [of St Brides', Fleet St.

Holms, Mary. — 19 May, 1704 —, Edward Woodford, bricklayer in Russell St., [Covent Garden

Holt, John, winner in Channel Row — 17 Jan 1698-9 —, Elizabeth Steele

Holworthy, Elizabeth, of St. John's, Hackney, spin. — 3 May, 1720 —, Samuel [Heathcote, Esq , of same, bat

Holyoake, George, of Wolverhampton, co Stafford — 21 Sept 1752 —, Elizabeth [Hayes, of same

Hon, Alice, of the parish of St Clement's Dane — 20 Oct 1705 —, Arthur Ingram, Esq of parish of St. Michael, [Basishaw (married by Dr Gascoign)

Hongest, Jacob, of the parish of St Giles, Cripplegate — 10 Dec 1713 —, [Katherine Pusey, of same

Honner, George, of the parish of Aldgate — 14 June, 1710 —, Katherine Watkins, [of same

Honnor, Frances, of St Dunstan's in the West. — 11 Aug 1706 —, John Blyth, [of same (by a licence)

Honour, Sarah, of St Andrew's, Holborn 12 July, 1748 —, George Flintham, of [same.

Hook, Elizabeth, of St George's, Southwark — 5 Nov 1710 —, Cornelius [Clarribus, of Bishopsgate parish

Hooke, Elizabeth, of St Andrew's, Holborn — 26 July, 1716 —, William Dicken. [of Shienton, Salop

Hooke, Sara — 30 Oct 1693 —, John [Harper, baker in Claor St

Hooke, Thomas, of St Giles in the Fields — 19 Jan 1730-1 —, Judith Wells, of [same

Hoole, Ann, of the parish of St Martin's, Ludgate — 9 July, 1711 —, Fletcher Powel, of parish of Whitney, co Oxford

Hoole, Elizabeth, of the parish of St Martin's, Ludgate — 28 April, 1713 —, Hugh Hamersley, of the Inner [Temple

Hooper, George, jun of Tunbridge, Kent — 14 July, 1722 —, Elizabeth Austen, [of Sevenoaks.

Hooper, Margaret, of St Andrew's, Holborn — 1 Aug 1734 —, John Grant, of [Bread St

Hooper, William, bat , of St James, Westminster — 5 Feb 1719 —, Anne [Wyat, of St Andrew's, Holborn, spin

Hope, Mary — 16 Jan 1699-1700 —, Robert Soper, chandler at the King's [Arms, near Newington Church

Hopkins, Anne — 13 Nov 1698 —, William Close, painter in King St , [Bloomsbury

Hopkins, Benjamin, bat , of the parish of St George, Southwark — 31 July, 1715 [—, Jane Booth, spin , of same

Hopkins Simon, of St Ann's, Aldersgate, — 29 Oct 1714 —, Rebecca Green, of [same

Hopkins, Thomas, parish clerk of Hampstead. — 17 Feb. 1701-2 —, Jane [Woodhouse

Hopley, Elisabeth, of St Andrew's, Holborn — 25 June, 1737 —, John Parran, [of St James', Westminster

Hopper, Mary, of Precinct of Whitefriars — 29 Feb 1707-8 —, Edward Lee, of [same

Horn, Edward, of St Clements Dane — [30 Dec 1706 —, Anne Cole

Horn, James, of St Andrew's, Holborn — 13 Jan 1731-2 —, Mary Kitchen, of [St Dunstan's in the West

Hornblower, Rebecca, of the parish of St Leonard's Shoreditch — 12 June, 1712 —, Francis Brookes, of parish of [St Giles, Cripplegate

Horne, Elisabeth, of Edmonton, Middx — 4 Jan 1753 —, James Hubbald, of [same

Horne, Jane. — 12 July, 1697 —, Henry Davis, a labourer at the Dolphin in [Shoreditch

Hornidge, William, bat , of the parish of St Andrew, Holborn — 30 March, 1715 —, Susannah Kingstone, spin , of Fors-[ter lane parish

Horseley, Marmaduke, lawyer in Fetter lane, St. Bride's parish. — 13 April, [1697 —, Judith Roberts

Horton, Margaret, of St. Giles, Cripplegate — 23 June, 1728 —, Peter Battershill, [of same

Horwood, Mary, of the parish of St Bride's — 1 Jan. 1711-2 —, John Beakley, of [same

Hotter, John, of the parish of St Alban's, Wood St — 8 June, 1714 —, Sarah [Shepard, of same

Hotwes, John, of the parish of Drayton, Middx — 6 June, 1714 —, Mary East, [of same

Houblon, Jacob (Esq), of Great Hallingberry, Essex. — 31 July, 1735 —, Mary [Cotton, of Madingley, co Cambridge

Houghton, Mary, widow, of the parish of St. Mary, Islington — 16 Jan 1714-5 [—, Samuel Nutt, bat , of same

Houlding, Samuel, of the parish of St Margaret, Westminster — 3 March, [1710-1, Sarah Morris, of same

House, William, of St Clement's Dane — licence dated Feb 1717-8 —, Jocose [Parker, of St Martin's in the Fields.

Hovell, Elizabeth, of the parish of St Andrew, Holborn. — 1 Jan 1711-2 —, [John Hollins, of same

Howard, Elizabeth — 23 June, 1714 —, Henry Neat, of parish of St Ann's, Westminster (the bride's father present)

Howard, John, of Clerkenwell, butcher — [28 Nov 1695 —, Elizabeth Munns

Howard, Mary, of St Martin's in the Fields. — licence dated July 1717 —, Henry [Crew, of St James', Westminster

Howard, Sarah, of the parish of St John, Hackney — 12 Jan 1712-3 —, Thomas [Read, of same

Howard, Thomas, bat , of the parish of St Margaret's, Westminster — 25 Dec 1714 —, Sarah Maybanke, spin , of St [Giles in the Fields.

Howard, William, of the parish of St Andrew, Holborn — 27 April, 1710 —, Isabella Cawsey, of parish of St James', [Westminster

Howell, Sinah, of the parish of St Giles in the Fields — 19 Nov 1710 —, Richard Morris, of parish of St Andrew, Hol-[born.

Howess, John (Rev), of St Bride's — 18 Dec. 1740 —, Mary Harrison, of St [Dunstan's in the West

Howse, Susanna, of St James', Clerkenwell — 30 March, 1730 —, Francis Cooper, [of All Hallows, Thames St

Hubbald, James, of Edmonton, Middx — 4 Jan 1753 —, Elisabeth Horne, of [same

Huddle, Joseph, poulterer in St James' Market — 27 Oct 1698 —, Margaret [Evans

Hudson, Martha Maria, of St Martin's in the Fields — 7 Sept 1741 —, Thomas [Wood, of St Giles in the Fields

Hudson, Rachel, of St. Clement Danes — 30 Sept 1712 —, John Nicholson, of [St Mary, Whitechapel

Hughes, Edward, *bat*, of St Giles in the Fields — 25 Jan 1719 —, Sarah Hill, [of same, *spin*

Hughes, Elizabeth, of the parish of St Andrew's, Holborn — 16 March, 1709-10 —, Michael Shaw, of parish [of St Mary le Bow.

Hughes, Hugh, of St Anne's, Westminster — 15 Jan 1732-3 —, Anne Taylor, of [St. Giles in the Fields

Hughes, Jane (Hewes) — 29 June, 1701 —, Samuel Harris, printer in Red Lion [Court, Drury Lane

Hughes, William, of Staple Inn. — 19 May, 1730 —, Mary Tushingam, of St. An- [drew, Holborn

Hulcap, Edward, of the parish of Kensington. — 24 May, 1713 —, Dorothy [Martin, of same.

Hulings, Hannah, of the parish of St Giles in the Fields. — 24 May, 1714 —, [William Canham, of same.

Hulse, Edward, of the parish of St. Alban, Wood St. — 15 Jan. 1712-3 —, [Elizabeth Levett, of same

Hulse, Elizabeth — 16 Dec. 1704 —, Thomas Taylour, gent of Broad St, [parish of St Peter Poor

Hulton, Jane, of St Steplong, Kent — 31 March, 1718 —, Xn William Kirschoff, of parish of St Clements, East- [cheap

Humes, Mary, of St Bride's, London. — 19 Jan 1713-4, and 1 Dec. 1714—, James Holmes (Like), of parish of St Margaret, [Westminster

Humfrey, William, *bat*, of St Bartholomew the Great — 9 June, 1715 —, Ruth James, *spin*, of parish of St Andrew, [Holborn

Humphreys, Ann — 27 April, 1710 —, Laurence Brodrick, D D (married by [Mr. Humphreys)

Humphreys, John, of St Paul's, Covent Garden — 6 May, 1714 —, Hannah [Taylor, of St. Giles in the Fields

Humphreys, Mary, of the parish of Islington — 16 Aug. 1713 —, Thomas Greenwood, of parish of St Giles, [Cripplegate

Humphreys, Susan — 23 Dec 1704—, Jonathan Ackers, watchmaker in parish [of St James, Clerkenwell.

Humphreys, Thomas, of St Gregory's — 12 Aug 1740 —, Letitia Nash, of St [Leonards, Foster Lane.

Humphrys. Arthur, rector of Barton, Beds — 9 May, 1704 —, Jane Robinson (married by Mr. Humprys, then [living in Hatton Garden)

Humphrys, Humphry, periwig maker in Holborn, St Giles parish — 24 July, [1696 —, Elizabeth Kent

Humphrys, Thomas, upholsterer at Mr. Raby's, in Lumley's Court, Strand. — [6 Oct 1700 —, Mary Beecher.

Hunt, John, of the parish of St. James, Clerkenwell. — 3 Sept. 1713 —, Ann [Barker, of same.

Hunt, John, of the parish of St. Botolph, Aldersgate — 23 Sept 1714 —, Mag- [dalen Bury, of same.

Hunt, Judith, of the parish of St. Antholin. — 18 July, 1734 —, Robert Innes, Dr [in physic, of same

Hunt, Leonard, of the parish of St Clement Dane. — 9 Feb 1713-4 —, Sarah [Morgan, of same.

Hunt, Nicholas, of Watford, Herts. — 26 Aug 1725 —, Elizabeth Sams, of Pirton, [Herts

Hunter, Elizabeth — 5 Dec 1700 —, George Aylworth, grocer in Milk Street

Hunter, Elizabeth, of St Ann's, Soho — 12 May, 1743 —, John Barras, of St [Clements Dane

Huntly, Stephen, of St Bartholomew, near the Royal Exchange — 1 June, 1736 —, Mary Wells, of St Michael, Crooked [Lane

Hurley, Jone, of St. George the Martyr, Queen Sq — 28 Jan. 1732-3 —, Hugh [Simpson, of same.

Hurlock, George, of the parish of Hayes, Middx. — 8 April, 1714 —, Elizabeth [East, of same

Husley, Ester, of St John's, Wapping, *spin.* — 29 March, 1720 —, Charles Morton, of St Giles without Cripplegate, [*widower*

Huslington, Mary, of St Andrew, Holborn. — 17 Dec 1713 —, Randolph Jenkins, [of parish of Islington.

Hussy, Henry, of the parish of St. John, Wapping — 24 June, 1714 —, Elizabeth Williamson, of St Katherine by the [Tower

Hussy, John, servant to Squire Montague in Lincoln's Inn Fields. — 28 Sept. 1702 —, Constance West, servant to [same gent.

Hutchins, John of St Paul's, Covent Garden — 23 July, 1724 —, Abigail [Hassell, of St. Martin's in the Fields.

Hutchins, Thomas, of Deptford, Kent. — 8 Jan 1729-30 —, Catharine Copland, [of same

Hutchinson, Henry, of St George's, Hanover Sq — 6 July, 1740 —, Betty [Reed, of same.

Hutchinson, Robert, of St Dunstans in the West — 9 Feb 1713-4 —, Helena [Hawkins, of St Ann's, Blackfriars

Hutton, Lydia, of the parish of St James, Clerkenwell. — 23 Feb 1711-2 —, Robert Kingston, of parish of St. An- [drew, Holborn.

Iliff, Elizabeth, of St. Giles in the Fields, *spin.* — 25 Jan. 1718-9 —, James Cooke, of parish of St Paul's, Covent [Garden, *bat.*

Iliffe, William, of Stevenage, Herts. — 20 Dec 1711 —, Mary Johnson, of parish [of St Giles, Cripplegate.

Ingledew, Mary. — 25 July, 1695 —, Francis Hill, of Whitby, co. York, [mariner

Inglesby, Elizabeth, of the parish of St. Andrew, Holborn. — 8 April, 1714 —, [John Jones, of same,

Ingoldesby, Magdalene, of the parish of St Giles in the Fields — 20 Aug 1710 —, St. John Baker, of St Andrew's, [Holborn

Ingram, Arthur (Esq.), of the parish of St. Michael Basishaw — 20 Oct. 1705 —, Alice Hon, of parish of St Clements [Dane (married by Dr Gascoign).

Innes, Robert, doctor in physic, of the parish of St. Antholins — 18 July, 1734 [—, Judith Hunt, of same.

Ireland, Bloomer, of St Martins le Grand. — 14 Nov 1731 —, Elizabeth Way, of [St. Dunstan's in the West.

Ireland, Francis, of Horton Kirby, Kent, clerk. — 15 Nov 1753 —, Elizabeth [Wade, of New Shoreham, Sussex.

Irving, Anthony, *bat*, of St Michaels, Crook Lane — 21 Nov 1721 —, Arundell [Ryves, of St Andrew, Holborn, *spin.*

Ives, John, of St Olave, Southwark. — 22 [Nov 1753 —, Sarah Palmer, of same.

Ivie, Margaret, of St Martins in the Fields. — 8 Jan 1727-8 —, Charles Fabre, of [St Paul's, Covent Garden

Izard, Mary, of St Andrew, Holborn. — 28 May, 1726 —, William Lewis, of [same

Jacket, Mary. — 30 Oct. 1699 —, Richard [Oates, grocer in Pinner, Middx.

Jackson, Elizabeth, of St. Gregory. — 20 June, 1725 —, Richard Croft, of St [Vedast, Foster Lane.

Jackson, James, gent of the parish of St. Andrew's, Holborn. — 20 July, 1704 [—, Susan Willson

Jackson, Mary, of the parish of St Paul's, Covent Garden. — 6 April, 1713 —, Thomas Kegg, of parish of St Andrew's, [Holborn.

Jackson, Thomas, of the parish of St
Bartholomew, behind the Exchange —
17 July, 1712 —, Elizabeth Harrison,
[of parish of St Peters Cheap

James, Elizabeth — 11 April, 1699 —,
Edward Jenkins, labourer in Turnmill
[St

James, Elizabeth, of the parish of St. Giles
in the Fields — 8 March, 1710-1 —,
Joseph Ash, of the Inner Temple, Esq.
(married by Mr. Barnes, at midnight.

James, John, of St Clements Danes — 24
June, 1724 —, Sarah Spensley, of St
[George the Martyr.

James, Ruth, spin., of the parish of St.
Andrew, Holborn. — 9 June, 1715 —,
William Humfrey, bat, of St Bartholo-
[mew the Great

Jeaks, Mark, of Tottenham, Middx. — 22
July, 1736 —, Elizabeth Turner, of
[same

Jeanes, Thomas, of St Paul's, Covent Garden. — 28 April, 1728 —, Mary Wors-
[wick, of St. George the Martyr.

Jefferson, Jane, of Trinity parish, Queenhithe. — 26 Sept 1714 —, James
[Burrows, of St. Sepulchres

Jefferson, Sara. — 8 Oct 1696 —, Robert
Rutland, yeoman of Hempsted, Essex.

Jeffery, Dorothy, of the parish of All Saints,
Lombard St — 9 April, 1712 —, John
[Saxston, of same

Jefferys, Hester. — 24 Sept. 1696 —,
James Wilson, a weaver near to Bishops-
[gate.

Jefferys, Rachel, of St Martin's in the
Fields, spin — 23 Oct 1721 —, Thomas
Vernon, of Ashley, co Worcester, bat

Jeffes, Robert, bat, of Mortlake, Surrey —
18 Feb. 1720-1 —, Martha Malyn, of
[St Saviour's, Southwark, spin.

Jeffries, Mary, of St. Andrew's, Holborn
6— April, 1731 —, Francis Wilks, of
[St. Dionis Backchurch.

Jenings, John, a keeper under Sir Basil
Firebrace in South Mimms parish. -- 9
[Jan. 1695-6 —, Anne Austin

Jenkins, Edward, labourer in Turnmill St.
— 11 April, 1699 —, Elizabeth James.

Jenkins, Martha. — 24 Feb 1697-8 —,
John Attwood, fruiterer in Thames St

Jenkins, Randolph, of the parish of Islington. — 17 Dec. 1713 —, Mary Hus-
[lington, of St Andrew, Holborn.

Jennings, Henrietta Maria, of St Paul's,
Covent Garden. — 20 March, 1711-2
—, Edward Spackman, of parish of St.
[Austin's.

Jenour, Lancelot, bat, of St Sepulchre. —
26 Feb 1719 —, Sarah Shaw, of St.
[Andrew, Holborn, spin.

Jephson, William, of St Paul's, Covent
Garden. — license dated Aug 1717
—, Hannah Chase, of St Giles in the
[Fields.

Jeynes, Prudence, of the parish of St.
Andrew, Holborn — 12 Sept. 1708 —,
[Francis Heath, of same.

Johnson, Anne — 8 Jan 1695-6 —,
Thomas Cator, journeyman baker in
[Greenwich.

Johnson, Charles, of the parish of St Anne
Westminster — 14 Dec 1708 —,
[Mary Bradbury, of same.

Johnson, Hannah, of St Giles in the Fields.
— 7 March, 1705-6 —, Robert Whitchurch, tailor in Russell Court, parish of
[St. Martins in the Fields.

Johnson, John, of the parish of St Martins
in the Fields — 10 Feb. 1712-3 —,
[Catherine Pearson, of same.

Johnson, John, of East Greenwich, bat. —
29 Dec 1720 —, Alice (?) Skifling, of
[same, spin.

Johnson, John. — 8 June, 1723 —, Mary
[Teasdle.

Johnson, Mary — 7 May, 1693 —, Edward
Chambre, silver wire drawer in Maul's
[Court, near Moorgate.

Johnson, Mary, of the parish of St. Giles,
Cripplegate — 20 Dec 1711 —, William
[Iliffe, of Stevenage, Herts.

Johnson, Mary, of St Andrew's, Holborn — 26 March, 1734 —, David Brown, [of St. Martin's le Grand

Johnson, Samuel, of St. Giles in the Fields. — 24 May, 1743 —, Jane Draper, of [St. Michael's, Basishaw.

Johnson, Sarah, of St. Andrew's, Holborn — 10 Feb. 1744-5 —, William Raven, [of St Giles in the Fields

Johnson, Thomas, of the parish of St James, Westminster — 7 May, 1714 —, Susanna [Ford, of Henley on Thames.

Johnson, William, of St. Andrew, Holborn — 21 Jan 1753 —, Elisabeth Short, of [same

Johnston, William (Esq.), of St. James', Westminster. — 21 Nov 1742 —, [Charlotte Parry, of Oakfield, Berks

Jolleme, Susanna, of the parish of St Giles in the Fields — 3 June, 1713 —, Henry [Simpson, of same.

Jollice, Sarah, of the parish of St Botolph, Aldgate. — 24 Jan 1713-4 —, William [Heaton, of same.

Jolly, Katherine, of St Brides — 25 April, 1706 —, Frederick Kremar, of parish of St. Giles in the Fields, periwig maker [in Great Turnstile, Holborn

Jonathan, Foun——, of the parish of St Giles' Cripplegate — 12 Nov. 1710 —, Mary Willson, of parish of St Martin's [in the Fields

Jones, Alice, of St Andrew's, Holborn — 12 Feb. 1742-3 —, John Thomas, of [St George's, Hanover Sq

Jones, Anne — 26 Oct 1701 —, Paul [Ludlow, apothecary in Broad St

Jones, Elizabeth. — 4 April, 1706 —, [John Read, of Enfield, Essex, gent.

Jones, Elizabeth, of the parish of St Margaret's, Westminster. — 26 May, 1718 —, Dr. John Dighton, of parish of St. [Mary's, Newmarket, Suffolk

Jones, Erasmus, bat, of the parish of St Brides — 25 Jan 1714-5 —, Anne [Newin, spin, of same.

Jones, Humphrey, of the parish of St. Clements Dane. — 28 July, 1713 —, Eliza-[beth Tatlam, of same.

Jones, Jane, of Esher, Surrey — 12 April, 1721 —, Joseph Grice, of St Dunstan's [in the West.

Jones, John, barber near Leadenhall — 11 [June, 1696 —, Elizabeth Ellis.

Jones, John, of the parish of St. Andrew, Holborn. — 8 April, 1714 —, Elizabeth [Inglesby, of same.

Jones, John, of Chelsea — 24 April, 1723 [—, Mary Wadsworth, of same

Jones, Joseph, of Chilton parish, Salop, lawyer — 20 May, 1697 —, Elizabeth [Burton.

Jones, Laurence, of St. Andrew's, Holborn. — 12 Aug. 1716 —, Hester Yeandell, [of St. Dunstans in the West.

Jones, Lucy, of the parish of St Sepulchre. — 27 June, 1703 —, Robert Rustal, in White Hart, New St, same parish, a [grocer.

Jones, Margaret, of Deptford — 7 May, 1711 —, William Pack, of parish of [St. Peter's, Paul's Wharf.

Jones, Marrice, of the parish of St. Giles in the Fields — 7 April, 1716 —, Eliza-[beth Lloyd, of same.

Jones, Mary, of the parish of St Giles in the Fields. — 6 July, 1712 —, William Gullyford, of parish of Christ Church, [Southwark

Jones, Mary, of St. James, Westminster. — — 9 May, 1714 —, Henry Burgis, of [St. Clements Dane.

Jones, Richard, bat, of the parish of St. Giles in the Fields. — 12 Jan. 1714-5 —, Mary Willmott, of St. Mary, White-[chapel, spin.

Jones, Robert, bat., of St Bartholomew, near the Royal Exchange. — 19 May, 1719 —, Elizabeth Falkener, of St. [Leonard's, Shoreditch, widow.

Jones, Sara. — 17 June, 1701 —, Edward Shilfox, clerk to Mr. Ayres of Lincoln's [Inn.

Jones, Thomas, vintner in St. Bride's. — 22 [Oct 1696 —, Elizabeth Sanders.

Jones, Thomas, waterman in Greenwich — [14 Feb 1698-9 —, Jane Tapley

Jones, Thomas, of the parish of St Giles in the Fields — 17 May, 1714 —, Jane [Leighton, of St. James, Westminster

Jones, William, gent of Swallow St , parish of St James, Westminster. — 20 Dec [1705 —, Sarah Stone, of same parish.

Jones, William, of St. Bartholomew the Great, Smithfield. — 30 Oct 1744 —, [Rachel Edwards, of same.

Jordon, Sarah, of the parish of St Giles in the Fields. — 16 Jan 1713-4 —, [Edward Cawley, of same

Joyner, Elizabeth — 15 Oct 1695 —, Charles Randall, haberdasher next the [White Hart Inn, Southwark

Joynes, John, of the parish of St James, Clerkenwell. — 14 Nov. 1714 —, Eliza- [beth Peck, of same.

Kanes, Edmund, of the parish of St Botolph, Aldersgate — 7 Aug 1712 —, [Sarah Butcher, of same

Kay, Edward, of St Andrew's, Holborn — 10 April, 1731 —, Catherine Gardiner, [of St George the Martyr.

Keat, William, of the parish of St Botolph, Aldgate. — 20 July, 1708 —, Ann [Garraway, of same

Keay, Samuel, of the parish of St. Andrew's, Holborn. — 12 Aug. 1708 —, Susan [Weston, of same.

Keell, Francis, of the parish of St. Bartholomew the Less, Smithfield. — 31 Dec [1706 —, Mary Bradly, of same

Keep, Mary, of the parish of St. Andrew's, Holborn. — 9 April, 1707 —, Robert [Cave, of same

Kegg, Thomas, of the parish of St Andrew's, Holborn. — 6 April, 1713 —, Mary Jackson, of parish of St. Paul's, Covent [Garden.

Keibman, Martha, *widow*, of St. Andrew, Holborn — 9 March, 1714-5 —, Jonas Peidham, *bat*, of parish of St. Mary, [Savoy

Kelly, John, of St. Giles in the Fields. — 7 March, 1731-2 —, Rachel Shorter, of [St. Martins in the Fields.

Kelly, Thomas, of the parish of St Clements Danes — 27 Nov. 1713 —, Judith Ren- [sin, of same.

Keme, Mary. — 18 Oct. 1701 —, Robert Needham, coachman at the Ball in [Kirby St.

Kenn, John, of the parish of St Andrew, Holborn — 10 Oct 1714 —, Elizabeth [Stafford, of same.

Kenn, Richard, of St Margaret's, Westminster. — 12 March, 1723-4 —, [Susanna Ross, of St. Mary le Bow.

Kennell, John, of the parish of St. James, Clerkenwell — 18 Nov 1714 —, Ann [Chaterton, of same.

Kent, Clement, of Goring, co Oxford, Esq. — 8 Jan. 1703-4 —, Barsheba Marsh, [of Stepney, Middx.

Kent, Elizabeth. — 24 July, 1696 —, Humphry Humphrys, periwig maker in St. [Giles parish Holborn.

Kent, Hannah, of the parish of St Andrew, Holborn — 21 March, 1712-3 —, [William Pierpoint, of same

Kent, Mary, of the parish of St. Andrew's, Holborn. — 27 April, 1710 —, William [Ororle, of same.

Kent, Mary, of Hampstead — 13 Sept. [1711 —, John Mann, of same.

Kent, Robert, brewer of Fulham. — 24 Aug. [1702 —, Mary Perry.

Kenyon, Jane. — 3 March, 1697-8 —, Joseph Duckett, wine cooper in Elbow [Lane.

Ker, Robert, of the parish of St. Mary, Whitechapel. — 30 April 1710 —, [Mary Bland, of same

Ker, Robert, of the parish of St Stephen, Coleman St. — 3 Aug 1710 —, Susan Bland, of parish of St. Mary, White- [chapel.

Kerington, Elizabeth, of St. Antholins, London — 6 Jan. 1725-6 —, Thomas [Knight, of same.

Kerrey, Barbara, of St. Clements Dane. —
6 April, 1731 —, Robert Milbourn, of
[St James', Clerkenwell

Kew, Ann — 15 June, 1698 —, Charles
Saunders, a servant in St. James', West-
[minster.

Key, Charles, victualler in Hampstead. — 10
[Feb 1697-8 —, Rebecca Treddwell

Key, Christopher, of St James', Westminster
— 30 Aug 1728 —, Mary Wildgoose,
[of same,

Kidd, Mary — 8 April, 1697 —, Thomas
Hanscomb, victualler in St James'
[parish

Kikins, Elizabeth, of the parish of St An-
drew, Holborn — 10 May, 1713 —,
John Hall, of parish of St Clements
[Dane

Kilborne, Mary. — 17 May, 1697 —, James
Weatherley, bricklayer in Clerkenwell
[parish

Killett, Stephen, of Paddington, *widower*
— 21 March, 1720-1 —, Martha Lead-
[beater, of same, *spin*

Killmain, David, of the parish of St Martins
in the Fields — 29 July, 1714 —, Mary
Evans, of parish of St James, West-
[minster

Kimber, Richard, of Fulham, victualler —
21 Jan. 1695-6 —, Margaret Harrison

King, Anne — 26 Nov 1695 —, Richard
Wright, of Hanwell parish, Middx , hus-
[bandman

King, Bartholomew, instrument maker in St
Clement's parish, — 23 Jan. 1695-6 —,
[Phillis Bower

King, Betty, of St. Clements Dane. — 5
Feb. 1742-3 —, Thomas Tilbury, of
[Ringwood, Hants.

King, John, of St Sepulchres. — 2 Sept
1714 —, Susanna Taylour, of St Giles,
[Cripplegate.

King, Nevile, of Ashby de la Laund. —
(12 April), 1717 —, Mary Midlemore, of
[Grantham, co Lincoln

King, Thomas, of the parish of St Giles in
the Fields, soldier. — 11 Oct. 1705 —,
[Ann Beveridge, of same

King, William, of the parish of St Nicholas
Acrons London. — 13 Jan. 1707-8
—, Mary Williams, of parish of St Ed-
[mund the King

Kingsley, John, *bat*, of the parish of St.
Clements Dane — 15 Dec 1714 —,
[Rebecca Nicholls, *spin.*, of same.

Kingston, Robert, of the parish of St. An-
drew, Holborn. — 23 Feb. 1711-2 —,
Lydia Hutton, of parish of St James,
[Clerkenwell.

Kingstone, Susannah, *spin* of Forster lane
parish — 30 March, 1715 —, William
Hornidge, *bat*, of parish of St Andrew,
[Holborn.

Kinneir, George, of St Paul's, Covent Garden. — 21 Dec. 1723 —, Ann Cooke,
[of the Poultry

Kirby, Edward, of the parish of St. Andrew,
Holborn — 25 Feb. 1710-1 —, Sarah
Tinwell, of parish of St Clements Dane
[(they had five certificates).

Kirby, Edward, of the parish of Borden,
Kent — 28 Oct. 1713 —, Katherine
[Dennis, of same.

Kirke, George, husbandman of Putney,
Surrey — 10 May, 1698 —, Sara
[Moore.

Kirshhoff, Christian William, of the parish
of St. Clements, East Cheap. — 31
March, 1718 —, Jane Hulton, of St.
[Stephen, Kent.

Kitchen, Mary, of St Dunstan's in the West
— 13 Jan 1731-2 —, James Horn, of
[St. Andrew's, Holborn

Kitching, Elizabeth — 4 July, 1695 —,
Robert Wilson, coachman, Lincoln's Inn
[Fields.

Kitching, Priscilla, of St Andrew's, Holborn. — 14 Oct. 1732 —, John Dawson,
[of Islington

Kitchingham, Grace, of St Andrew, Holborn. — 12 Oct. 1722 —, John Martin,
[of St. Dunstan's in the West

Kitchingham, Hannah, of St. Martins in the Fields. — 11 April, 1748 —, Richard [Beauchamp, of same.

Knapper, Charles, tailor in Tuttle St — [6 Jan 1696-7 —, Anne Burke.

Knapton, Mary — 15 June, 1698 —, Charles Nendick, Indian gown seller at [the Three Crowns in Fleet St

Knight, Henrietta (Hon), of St James', Westminster — 28 May, 1748 —, Charles Wymondesold, of Wanstead, [Essex.

Knight, John, of St Saviour's, Southwark — 26 June, 1732 —, Mary Drewett, of [St. Olave's, Southwark.

Knight, Margaret, of Reading, Berks. — 24 Dec. 1750 —, George Grandy, of [same

Knight, Thomas, of St. Antholins, London. — 6 Jan 1725-6 —, Elizabeth Kering- [ton, of same

Knight, Thomas, of St Trinity's — 23 Dec 1732 —, Rebecca Powell, of St Mary [le Bow

Knowles, Henry, of St. Anne's, West-minster. — 5 March, 1727-8 —, Alice Batson, of St. Margaret's, Westminster

Kremar, Frederick, of the parish of St. Giles in the Fields, a periwig maker in Great Turnstile, Holborn — 25 April, 1706 —, Katherine Jolly, of St. Brides.

Lacey, Samuel, tallow chandler in Drury Lane — 2 Nov. 1699 —, Elizabeth [Brookes.

Lake, Mary, of the parish of Tring, Herts — 23 June, 1713 —, Richard Man, of [parish of Leighton Buzzard, Beds.

Lalham, Mary, of the parish of St Andrew, Holborn. — 13 Oct 1705 —, William Manning, of parish of St. Clements [Dane, tailor

Lamb, Abigail. — 29 May, 1701 —, James [Ellis.

Lamb, Mary, of the parish of Hatfield, Herts — 16 June, 1713 —, John [Palmer, of same.

Lambert, Mary, of the parish of St Botolph, Bishopsgate. — 4 Sept 1712 —, John [Worgan, of same.

Lambley, Edward, of St. Sepulchres — 5 Dec 1750 —, Jane Nevill, of Hemp- [stead, Herts.

Lambton, William, of St Dunstans in the West — 14 Feb 1715-6 —, Elizabeth [Fawcett, of St Anne's, Westminster

Lamley, Alexander, of the parish of St Peter's, nr St. Paul's Wharf. — 22 June, [1712 —, Joyce Frances, of same.

Lancaster, Isaac, of the parish of St Andrew's, Holborn — 13 Jan 1707-8 —, Jane Cordall, of parish of St Giles [in the Fields.

Lancaster, John, servant to Madam Parrot in Leadenhall St. — 29 May, 1706 —, Mary Wood, of parish of Epsom (by [license).

Lancaster, John, of St. James' Westmin-ster — 9 June, 1726 —, Margaret [Barker, of St. Paul's, Covent Garden.

Lane, Elizabeth, of the parish of St Paul's, Covent Garden — 2 Dec 1714 —, [William Gorham, of same.

Lane, Mary, of the parish of St. Botolph, Aldgate — 1 Sept. 1713 —, William [Benson, of same.

Lane, Mary, of the parish of St. Paul's, Covent Garden. — 29 Oct. 1713 —, [Samuel Goodall, of same.

Lane, William, of Hampstead, Middx, *widower*. — 8 Oct 1722 —, Joan Brown, of Clapham parish, Surrey, [*widow*.

Langford, Susan, of the parish of St. Dun-stan's in the East. — 30 May, 1710 —, William Barlin, of parish of St. James, [Westminster.

Langhorne, Susanna, of St. Andrew, Hol-born, *spin* — 23 Jan 1721-2 —, Robert Norwood, of Stanmore the Great, [*widower*.

Langley, Richard, chairman in German St, St Anne's parish, Westminster — 4 [Oct 1698 —, Elizabeth Carter

Langmore, Mary, of the parish of St Peter's, Cornhill — 20 Aug 1713 —, Abel Shepeard, of parish of St Chads, Salop. (Married by Mr Skerret, chap-[lain to the Duke of Ormond)

Langton, Elizabeth, of the parish of St Giles in the Fields — 20 April, 1712 —, John Carter, of parish of St Olave's, [Southwark

Langton, Henry, of St. Botolph, Aldgate — 21 Sept 1749 —, Mary Harling, of [St Andrew, Holborn

Langton, Mary, of St. Andrew, Holborn — 12 Jan. 1723-4 —, John Lassells, of [St. Dunstans in the West.

Langworth, Dorothy — 8 Jan. 1700-1 —, Thomas Bennet, surgeon in Greenwich.

Lannoy, Leonora, of Baddow, Essex — 16 Aug 1748 —, Henry Godsalve, of [same

Lanton, Mary, of the parish of St. Giles in the Fields. — 3 Oct 1714 —, William [Mudge, of same

Lapper, James, of St Catherine, Coleman St. — 24 April, 1726 —, Mary Clay, of [St. Giles, Cripplegate.

Lascelles, Christian, of Enfield, Middx — 3 Sept 1747 —, Josiah Osborne, of [So Mims, Middx

Lasdick, Henry, victualler at the Crown in Burlington St — 4 Jan 1701-2 —, [Mary Everson

Lasenby, Anne — 22 April, 1701 —, Thomas Crump, apothecary in Shoe [Lane

Lasenby, Samuel, bat, of the parish of St Clements Dane — 28 March, 1715 —, Elizabeth Rooke, spin, of St Mary, [Savoy

Lassells, John, of St Dunstans in the West — 12 Jan 1723-4 —, Mary Langton, of [St Andrew, Holborn

Late, Margaret. — 18 Feb 1699-1700 —, John Adams, tripeman in St Clement's [parish, Clements Danes.

Latham, Francis, of the parish of St. Clements Dane — 22 April, 1708 —, [Honor Fowkes, of same

Latton, Letitia, of Esher, Surrey — 22 Nov 1715 —, Thomas Cox, of Normanton, [Rutland.

Law, Elizabeth, of the parish of St. James, Westminster — 21 Feb 1712-3 —, [Robert Smith, of same.

Law, Jane — 19 June, 1695 —, Nicholas Munday, of Southaker, Norfolk, [labourer.

Law, Thomas, of Hertford — 3 Nov. 1723 —, Martha Young, of St Martin's [Vintry

Lawley (als Allen), Mary — 1 Feb 1699-1700 —, Thomas Simkin, cheese-factor [(of Stone), co Stafford.

Lawrence, Elizabeth, of the parish of St. Anne, Westminster — 27 Sept 1710 —, Robert Stewart, Esq, of parish of [St. Margaret, Westminster.

Lawson, George, butcher in Clare Market. [—5 June, 1698 —, Mary Suffield.

Lawson, John, turner in Jewin St — 1 Dec. [1698 —, Alice Gay

Lawton, Dorothy, of Highgate parish. — 6 May, 1717 —, Robert Dawley, of [same

Lay, Gifford, of St Brides — 4 Nov. 1714 —, Mary Toune (?), of St Martin's in [the Fields.

Layton, Richard, of the parish of St. Andrew, Holborn. — 27 April, 1714 [—, Elizabeth Allstroope, of same.

Leadbeater, Martha, of Paddington, spin. — 21 March, 1720-1 —, Stephen [Killett, of same, widower.

Leadbetter, Edward, of St. Clements Danes, journeyman tailor — 17 June, [1695 —, Mary Ffanch.

Leafe, Margaret, of St Andrew, Holborn, spin — 30 May, 1715 —, George Tay-[lor, bat., of Westbury, Wilts.

Lee, Ann (Hon), dau of Earl of Lichfield. — 30 Dec 1709 —, Thomas Morgan, gent of parish of St. Mary, Alder Mary.

Lee, Dorothy — 29 Dec 1696 —, John
[Hicks, joiner in Durham Yard

Lee, Edward, of Precincts of Whitefriars
— 29 Feb 1707-8 —, Mary Hopper, of
[same.

Lee, James, of St Payts, Shadwell. — 23
April, 1714 —, Elizabeth Turner, of
[St Giles in the Fields

Lee, John, of Oaking (Woking) Surrey —
30 Oct 1730 —, Esther Tichborne, of
[Ash, Surrey

Lee, Mary, of the parish of St George the
Martyr, Queen sq — 17 Feb 1727-8
[—, George Duckar, of Enfield

Lee, Samuel, fruterer, of the parish of St
Botolph's, Aldersgate. — 28 Jan 1702-3
[—, Sarah Attly, of same

Lee, Thomas, chamberlain at Chequer Inn,
Holborn — 24 Feb 1703-4 —, Deborah
Evans, of parish of St Andrew's, Hol-
[born

Lee, Thomas, of St Andrew's, Holborn —
16 May, 1714 —, Elizabeth Corbet, of
[St Giles in the fields

Leech, Catherine, of St John's, Westminster — 3 Jan 1748-9 —, Joseph
[Reading, of St. Clements Dane.

Lefeuer, Ister, of St Dunstan's, Stepney
— 22 Nov 1714 —, Elizabeth Willson,
[of St Peter Poer, Wood St

Legard, Mirabella, of the parish of St
Andrew's, Holborn — 22 Jan 1707-8
—, James Smyth, Esq , of parish of St
[Margaret's, Westminster

Leigh, Jane, of St Margaret's, Westminster
— 5 April, 1716 —, Nathaniel Gunter,
[of parish of St Dunstans in the West

Leighton, Jane, of St James, Westminster
— 17 May, 1714 —, Thomas Jones, of
[parish of St Giles in the Fields

Leman, Abigail, of St Martins in the
Fields. — 10 Jan. 1713-4 —, Edward
Press, of parish of St Andrew, Holborn

Lens, Bernard, of the parish of St. Paul's,
Covent Carden — 30 Nov 1706 —,
[Katherine Woods (by license)

Lenton, William, of Finchley parish — 11
Sept. 1716 —, Elizabeth Westward, of
[Edmonton parish.

Levett, Elizabeth, of the parish of St Alban,
Wood St — 15 Jan 1712-3 —, Edward
[Hulse, of same

Levett, Elisabeth, of St Sepulchres. — 6
May, 1729 —, Andrew Tock, of the
[Charter House.

Lewis, Catherine, of St Andrew's, Holborn.
— 26 Oct 1752 —, John Potts, of St.
[Sepulchre's.

Lewis, Elizabeth, of Hackney. Middx ,
spin — 15 Oct 1720 —, Joseph
[Chitty, of St Olave, Hart St., *bat*

Lewis, Elizabeth, of St Anne's, Westminster — 26 Aug 1753 —, William
[Trott, of St Saviour's, Southwark.

Lewis, John, of the parish of St Sepulchre
— 25 July, 1714 —, Elizabeth Read, of
[same

Lewis, John, of St Pancras in the Fields
— 16 Nov 1728 —, Mary Fry, of
[Hornsey

Lewis, Martha, of St Sepulchre. — 16 Nov.
1714 —, George Milson, of St James',
[Westminster.

Lewis, Mary, of St Pancras, *spin*. — 11
Oct 1720 —, John Stringer, of All
[Saints the Greater, *bat*.

Lewis, Mary, of Chelsea, *spin* — 7 Dec.
1721 —, Robert Thurkill, *bat*, of same

Lewis, Susana — 16 May, 1695 —, Joseph
Waddingham, of St Martin's in the
[Fields, journeyman shoe maker

Lewis, William, of St. Andrew, Holborn
— 28 May, 1726 —, Mary Izard, of
[same

Leyne, John D , of the parish of St Andrew, Holborn — 10 Oct 1714 —,
[Elizabeth Mash, of same

Libanns, Mary, of St Margaret's, Westminster — 1 Dec. 1714 —, John
[Perry, of St Martins in the Fields

License, Mary, of the parish of St Giles in
the Fields — 13 Feb 1715-6 —,
[Robert Merryfield, of same

Lilford, Mary, of the parish of St. Andrew,
Holborn — 29 July, 1711 —, Thomas
Hill, of same. (Married by Mr Shuck
[burgh)

Lillise, Catherine, of St. Giles in the Fields —16 Dec 1716 —, Robert Carlile, of [parish of St. Brides.

Lindesay, James, of the parish of St. James, Westminster — 22 March, 1710-1 —, [Katherine Whitehurst, of same.

Lindsey, Tirrill, of the parish of St. Ann's, Westminster — 11 Nov 1713 —, [Elizabeth Gairdon, of same.

Lingard, Elizabeth, of the parish of St Katherine Cree Church — 28 April, 1709 —, Robert Hoffman, of parish St [Alban's, Wood St

Linn, John, of the parish of St. James', Westminster. — 23 June, 1710 —, Luce [Gamble, of same.

Linnet, Anne, of High Holborn, parish of St. Giles in the Fields — 8 May, 1705 —, Timothy Budworth, coachmaker, of [same

Linter, John. — 5 June, 1723 —, Mary [Bosley.

Linton, Hannah, of the parish of St Giles, Cripplegate — 8 Aug 1714 —, John [Fuller, of same

Litchfield, Elizabeth, of Esher, Surrey — 28 April, 1726 —, John Moore, of [same

Littell, John Eden, of the parish of Allhallows the Less — 4 Dec. 1716 —, [Elizabeth Blake, of same

Littell, Susanna, of Stoke upon Aland, Suffolk, *widow* — 29 Dec 1720 —, Edward Foster, of St Mary le Bow, *bat*

Littleton, Catherine, of Isleworth, Middx — 12 Nov 1752 —, John Shutter, of [St. Paul's, Shadwell, Middx

Living, Elizabeth, of the parish of Harefield, Middx — 14 April, 1714 —, [Richard Watson, of same

Lloyd, Elizabeth, of the parish of St Giles in the Fields — 7 April, 1716 —, [Marrice Jones, of same

Lloyd, George, gent of the parish of Aberdeene, co Carmarthen — 3 April, 1703 —, Mary Pitts, of parish of St Sepulchre.

Lloyd, John, of Aston, Salop — 6 April, 1736 —, Sarah Savage, of St Andrew, [Holborn.

Lloyd, Richard, of St. George's, Bloomsbury — 16 April, 1740 —, Catharine [Ellis, of St. Martin's in the Fields.

Lobb, Anne — 13 Jan 1697-8 —, Henry [Winder, coachman at Kensington.

Lobb, John, *bat*, of the parish of St. Giles in the Fields — 21 March, 1714-5 —, [Frances Hackwood, *spin*, of same

Lock, John, of Kensington — 20 Dec 1733 —, Elisabeth Coleman, of Pad- [dington

Lock, Thomas, a mariner in Parker's Lane [— 30 Dec 1698 —, Mary Tomkin.

Lockett, Anne, of St Giles in the Fields — 11 Feb 1737-8 —, James Shonk, [of same.

Lockwood, Sarah, of the parish of St. Sepulchre. — 24 June, 1707 —, An- [drew Denton, of same.

Lodley, Ralph, of the parish of St Andrew, Holborn. — 2 Dec. 1712 —, Susanna [Boswell, of same.

Loft, John, of the parish of St. Botolph, without Aldersgate — 26 Aug. 1708 —, Elizabeth Boddington, of parish of [St Bartholomew the Less

Loftus, Mary — 29 Dec 1697 —, William Southall, of Vine St., St Giles, mariner.

Lohaire, John, of the parish of St Giles in the Fields — 23 Oct 1713 —, Sarah Wood, of parish of Littleton, Middle- [ton.

Lone, William, farmer, of Lee, Essex. — 4 [July, 1701 —, Mary Rules.

Long, Grace, of the parish of Deptford — 28 Aug. 1711 —, William Weaving, [of parish of St Dunstan's in the East.

Long, Margaret, of Albury, Herts — 9 May, 1734 —, Edward Chester, of [Bygrave, Herts.

Longdon, Alice, of St Luke's, Middx — 17 Jan 1736-7 —, Benjamin Ramsey, [of St Anne's, Blackfriars

Longdon, Alice, of St Edmund the King — 6 Sept 1748 —, Gilbert Gibson Mackmurdo, of parish of St Mary at [Hill

Longdon, Edward — 18 April, 1723 —,
[Isabel Dennis.

Longford, Henrietta Frances, of the parish
of Highgate, Middx. — 5 May, 1722
[—, William Thatcher, *bat*, of same

Longston, Moses, of the parish of St. James,
Westminster. — 15 July, 1713 —, Mary
[Freeman, of same.

Longworth, James, of St Stephen's, Coleman St — 29 July, 1728 —, Dorothy
[Forrester, of St Andrew's, Holborn

Loomes, Edward, *bat*, of the parish of St.
Andrew, Holborn. — 20 Feb. 1714-5
[—, Sarah Saunders, *spin*, of same

Lord, William, *bat*, of the parish of St.
Margaret's Westminster. — 6 Jan
1714-5 —, Mary Somner, *spin*, of
[Tring, Herts.

Loudor, Katherine, of the parish of St
Botolph, Aldgate — 12 May, 1714 —,
Joseph Brooks, of parish of St Giles in
[the Fields

Love. John, *bat*, of Isleworth. — 17 Dec.
1721 —, Christian Gurney, of St Sepul-
[chre, *spin*.

Love, Thomas, of the parish of St Andrew's,
Holborn. — 31 Dec 1706 —, Ann
[Cunningham

Lovelidge, Sarah, of St Andrew's, Holborn
— 25 June, 1743 —, George Clarke, of
[same

Lovell, Susan. of the parish of St Sepulchre
— 14 Oct 1708 —, William Cawthorne,
of parish of Gamlingay, co Cambridge

Lovesuch, Edward, *bat*, of the parish of
St Andrew, Holborn — 16 Aug 1715
[—, Mary Tailor, of same

Low, Mary, of the parish of St Andrew,
Holborn — 2 Feb 1713-4 —, William
[Shefford, of same

Lowe, Mary, of Whitechapel — 11 Sept
1714 —, Samuel Fenwick, of Stepney
[parish

Lowe, Mary, of Kew Green, Surrey — 16
May, 1741 —, William Plaistow, of
[same

Lowray, Margaret, of St Andrew's, Holborn
— 21 Oct. 1732 —, William Sparharke,
of Baldock, Herts (By Richard Low-
[ray, minister of Bilbrough, Yorks)

Lowry, William, of Chelsea College — 26
July, 1713 —, Anna Gillson, of parish
[of Whitechapel

Lowsley, Isaac, of Hampstead Parish —
license dated Sept 1717 —, Elizabeth
[Young, of St. Martin's in the Fields.

Loyd, John, *bat*, of St Giles in the Fields
— 27 May, 1720 —, Anne Gill, of
[same, *spin*

Lucas, Ann, of the parish of St Brides —
— 2 Nov 1714 —, John Ford, of
[parish of Islington.

Lucas, Jane — 16 Feb 1696-7 —, William
Gwynn, silk dyer near the Playhouse in
[Drury Lane

Lucke, James, of the parish of Cheshunt,
Herts. — 17 Nov 1714 —, Anne
[Austin (Oston), of same

Ludford, Jane — 31 March, 1699 —,
Joseph Smith, pewterer at Long Lane
[End, St Botolph's.

Ludlow, Paul, apothecary in Broad Street —
[26 Oct 1701 —, Anne Jones.

Lunt, Isabella. — 9 Nov 1698 —, John
Halham, surgeon in Hart St. Covent
[Garden.

Lydford, Margaret of the parish of St Giles
in the Fields — 20 Sept 1713 —,
[Matthias Brindisdon, of same.

Lyne, Alice, of the parish of St Giles in the
Fields — 3 Nov 1716 —, William
Compton, of Sheevington, co Gloucester

Lynn, Jane — 13 April, 1701 —, David
[Grant, gent. of Brownlow Street.

Mabis, Christian, of St. Andrew's, Holborn
— 18 Feb. 1728-9 —, Mary Stonestreet,
[of St Martin's in the Fields

Maccarty, Phillis, of St George the Martyr
— 20 Feb 1730-1 —, Edward Ewer, of
[Luton, Beds.

Maccoon, Kathrine, of the parish of St Giles in the Fields. — 24 Nov 1714 —, [William Cook, of same

Macgie, Robert, of St. Martins in the Fields — 1 Jan. 1727-8 —, Mary Whitehead, [of St Clements Danes.

Macgregor, Ann, of the parish of St Andrew, Holborn. — 19 Oct. 1715 —, [Robert Farlie, of same.

Machin, Samuel, bat, of the parish of St Botolph, Bishopsgate — 2 Jan 1714-5 —, Margaret Rumney, spin, of St Mary, [Whitechapel

Mackeerly, Charlotte, of St. Mary le bone. — 17 March, 1743-4—, Ruisshe Hassell, [of St. Giles in the Fields

Mackenzie, George, of St Martins in the Fields — 21 Aug 1735 —, Elisabeth [Robinson, of St. Andrew's, Holborn.

Mackmurdo, Gilbert Gibson, of the parish of St. Mary at Hill — 6 Sept 1748 —, Alice [Longdon, of St. Edmund the King.

Madbury, Thomas, of the parish of St James' — 21 May, 1711 —, Rebecca [Barber, of the same

Maddox, Roger, of the parish of St Pancras where the banns were published. — 22 March, 1710-1 —, Hannah Black, of [same.

Magew, Thomas, of the parish of St Dunstans in the West. — 23 May, 1714 —, [Margaret Bayly, of same.

Maiden, Ester, of the parish of St Giles in the Fields. — 14 Oct 1714 —, John [Dyson, of same.

Major, Grace, of St Clements Dane. — 1 July, 1730 —, Richard Davis, of same.

Makennis, Mary, of the parish of St. James, Westminster. — 8 Sept 1707 —, William [Child, of same

Malard, Elizabeth, of the parish of Barking, Essex. — 28 Oct. 1714 —, George Stil- [ing, of same.

Malchar, John, bat, of the parish of St Andrew's, Holborn — 28 Dec 1714 —, [Margaret Willets, spin, of same.

Males, Joseph, butcher in Clare Market — [23 July, 1699 —, Mary Freeman.

Malins, Elizabeth — 26 Aug 1697 —, Thomas Pasmore, gent of St Alban's [Street.

Mallard, Elisabeth, of St Martins in the Fields — 8 Jan 1735 6 —, John Bradly, [of St. Giles in the Fields.

Mallard, Lennard, of St Giles in the Fields — 27 Oct. 1723 —, Elizabeth Cutler, of [same.

Mallary, Philip, of St Bridget's, als. Bride's parish — license dated Dec. 1717 —, Elizabeth Crundall, of St Lawrence, [Jewry.

Malyn, Martha, of St. Saviour's, Southwark, spin — 18 Feb 1720-1 —, Robert Jeffes, [bat, of Mortlake, Surrey.

Man, Edward, of the parish of St Alban's, Wood St — 23 Aug 1713 —, Elizabeth Man, of parish of St. Stephen's, Coleman [St.

Man, Elizabeth, of the parish of St. Stephen's, Coleman St — 23 Aug. 1713 —, Edward Man, of parish of St. Alban's, Wood St.

Man, Richard, of the parish of Leighton Buzzard, Beds — 23 June, 1713 —, Mary [Lake, of parish of Tring, Herts.

Man, Samuel, of the parish of All Hallows, Bishopsgate St. — 6 Feb. 1713-4 —, [Mary Corbin, of same.

Mandrell, Mary. — 11 March, 1695-6 —, William Wilmore, a broker in Drury- [Lane

Manley, John, of the Middle Temple, Esq — 26 April, 1750 —, Anne Hammond, [of Finchley.

Mann, John, of Hampstead — 13 Sept. 1711 [—, Mary Kent, of same.

Manning, Ann — 6 July, 1705 —, David Hawkins, coachmaker in parish of St. [Andrew's, Holborn.

Manning, Gilbert, bat., of St James, Westminster. — 21 Dec. 1714 —, Margaret [Deekings, widow, of same.

Manning, William, of the parish of St Clements Danes, tailor — 13 Oct 1705 —, Mary Lalham, of parish of St Andrew's,
[Holborn

Maple, Ralph, baker in White's Alley, Chancery Lane, within the liberty of the Rolls — 20 April, 1704 —, Elizabeth Parris, of
[parish of St. Dunstan's in the West

March, Richard, of the parish of Mortlake, Surrey. — 8 Oct. 1713 —, Mary White,
[of same

March, Sarah, of Enfield, Middx — 5 Oct. 1731 —, Richard Darby, Esq , one
[of the Masters of this Society

March, Thomas, of St. Clements Dane — 18 April, 1730 —, Sarah Price, of St
[Giles in the Fields.

March, William, baker against Smock Alley, Spittlefields — 14 April, 1700 —, Eliza-
[beth Walker

Marjoram, Cassandra, *widow*, of St. Paul's, Covent Garden — 12 Dec 1714 —, Charles Eccleston, *bat*, of parish of St
[Giles in the Fields

Marlow, John, of the Tower liberty — 12 [May, 1725 —, Alice Cox of same

Marple, Francis, a servant — 9 Aug. 1699 [—, Anne Pyke.

Marr, Peter, of the parish of St Gregory, London — 18 Oct 1745 —, Mary
[Watts, of same

Marriot, Sarah, of St. Vedast, Foster Lane. — 6 Oct. 1747 —, John Bamborough, of
[St Clements Dane

Mars, Margaret, of St Paul's, Covent Garden — 3 Sept. 1729 —, Thomas Taylor, of
[St Giles in the Fields

Marsh, Barsheba, of Stepney, Middx — 8 Jan. 1703-4 —, Clement Kent, of Gor-
[ing, co Oxford, Esq.

Marter, Isaac, of the parish of Islington — 1 May, 1714 —, Elizabeth Simes, of
[same.

Martin, Anne, of St. George's, Hanover sq. — 1 July, 1736 —, George Sexty, or
[Sexly, of St Giles in the Fields.

Martin, Dorothy, of the parish of Kensington — 24 May, 1713 —, Edward Huleap,
[of same

Martin, Edward, of Stepney parish. — 11 June, 1728 —, Ann Dangerfield, of St.
[Giles, Cripplegate.

Martin, Elizabeth, of the parish of St. Martin in the Fields. — 16 July, 1713 —,
[Joseph Aldertor, of same.

Martin, Jane, of the parish of St Giles in the Fields — 9 April, 1713 —, Patrick Hoare
[of parish of St Andrew, Holborn.

Martin, John, baker in St. Giles in the Fields [— 20 Aug. 1696 —, Elizabeth Barber.

Martin, John, of the parish of St Giles in the Fields — 22 June, 1711 —, Mary Thompson, of parish of St Clements
[Dane

Martin, John, of St. Dunstans in the West — 12 Oct. 1722 —, Grace Kitchingham,
[of St Andrew, Holborn

Martin, John, of St Martins in the Fields — 3 Oct 1731 —, Elizabeth Smith, of
[St James', Westminster.

Martin, Lydia, of the parish of St. Giles, Cripplegate. — 11 March, 1713-4
[Arthur Richbell, of same —

Martin, Seth, fishmonger at Smithfield bars. — 17 Nov. 1700 —, Elizabeth Welden.

Marton, Mary, of St. Andrew, Holborn — 8 Feb. 1738-9 —, Rigby Molyneux, of
[Preston, co Lanc.

Mash, Elizabeth, of the parish of St. Andrew, Holborn — 10 Oct 1714 —, John D
[Leyne, of same

Massey, Pearse, servant to Squire Randall in Leicester St, St. Anne's parish, Westminster — 12 Feb 1701-2 —, Rebecca
[Rayner.

Massey, Thomas, of the parish of St Clements Dane. — 19 Oct. 1707 —, Mary
[Hamill, of same,

Masters, Anne, of the parish of St James Westminster. — 28 Aug 1715 —, Paul
[Wiggins, of same.

Matthews, Dorothy, of St. Andrew's, Holborn — 12 Sept 1714 —, William Steed, [of St. James', Clerkenwell.

Matthews, Jane, of St. Mary le Bow — 26 April, 1733 —, Richard Matthews, of the [Inner Temple

Matthews, Mary, of St Martins — 28 Feb 1703-4 —, John Norman, fishmonger in King St , parish of St Margaret's, West-[minster

Matthews, Richard, of the Inner Temple — 26 April, 1733 —, Jane Matthews, of [St Mary le Bow

Maund, Ann, of St. Andrew's, Holborn — 31 Jan 1727-8 —, Joseph Thackthet, of [Iver, Bucks.

Maxwell, Bridget, of St Brides — 3 June, 1705 —, Thomas Singleton joiner, of Old Fish St , parish of St Mary Magda-[len

May, Margaret, of the parish of St James, Westminster — 25 Feb. 1717-8 —, [William Austen, widower, of same

May, Thomas, of Godmersham, Kent — 11 July, 1729 —, Jane Monk, of Sevenoaks, [Kent

Maybanke, Sarah, spin , of St Giles in the Fields — 25 Dec. 1714 —, Thomas Howard, bat., of parish of St Margarets, [Westminster

Mayhew, Margaret, of St Giles in the Fields, spin — 10 May, 1720 —, Mark Gregory, [bat , of same

Maynard, John, of the parish of St. Dunstan, Stepney — 23 Oct 1711 —, Mary [Monk, of parish of St Pancras

Maynard, Martha, of St Martin's Vintry. — 2 Oct. 1736 —, John Scattergood, of [St. Dunstan's in the East.

Maynard, Rachel, of St James', Garlick Hill. — 22 Oct. 1730 —, Daniel Town, [of St. Martin's Vintry.

Mayo, John, of St Martins in the Fields — 9 April, 1730 —, Mary Wynn, of same

Mayse, William, of the parish of St Andrew's, Holborn. — 16 June, 1708 —, Mary Col-[lins, of same.

Maysey, Joseph, of the parish of St Sepulchre. — 21 Sept. 1710 —, Mary Nichol-[son, of same.

Meacham, Anne. — 6 Oct 1698 —, Robert Wheeler, gingerbread baker at Cow [Cross.

Mead, John, of the parish of St Giles in the Fields, labourer — 7 Jan 1702-3 —, Elizabeth Gaskell, of parish of St Law-[rence.

Meade, Robert, coachman of St. Andrew's, Holborn. — 9 May, 1695 —, Sara Wil-[ford.

Meads, Thomas (Esq), widower, of St Andrew, Holborn — 8 Feb 1718-9 —, [Anne Baker, of Bucks, spin.

Meal, Mary — 30 Dec 1696 —, Samuel [Smith, baker in New St , Shoe lane

Medcalf, Martha. — 26 Dec. 1695 —, Thomas Wright, hostler at the Star in [New Fish St.

Meers, Elizabeth, spin., of Newington Butts. — 22 Dec. 1714 —, Joseph Pearson [widower, of St Giles in the Fields,

Meeson, Hannah — 5 May, 1698 —, Thomas [Nevin, periwig maker in Chandos St

Meller, Thomas, of St Alban's, Wood St. — 7 Jan 1750-1 —, Margaret Parkes, [of St George's, Bloomsbury

Mellish, Jacob, of St Margaret's, Westminster. — 10 Sept 1714 —, Mary Aish, [of St. Sepulchre.

Meredith, Margaret, of the parish of St. Andrews — 29 Sept 1717 —, Richard [Halsey, of same.

Meredith, Mary, of St James', Westminster. — 10 Nov. 1722 —, Charles Sims, of same, "ye duck of Shandos running [footman "

Merigeot, Daniel, of the parish of St James, Westminster — 26 Oct 1708 —, Mary [Partridge, of parish of Kensington

Merrifield, William, of St Bride's, Fleet St. — 13 Aug. 1752 —, Anne Chowse, of [same

Merryfield, Robert, of St. Giles parish in the Fields — 13 Feb. 1715-6 —, Mary [License, of same.

Metcalf, James, of St Andrew's, Holborn.
— 30 Oct. 1735 —, Susannah Pepper,
[of St. George's, Hanover Sq

Meynell, Godfrey, of Bradley, co Derby,
Esq — 23 April, 1752 —, Frances
[Dealtry, of Owston, co Lincoln

Meyrick, Owen (Esq), of Lincoln's Inn —
12 Dec. 1749 —, Hester Putland, of
[St. Margaret's, Westminster

Micklewright, Anne, of St Andrew's,
Holborn — 23 April, 1739 —, Edward
[Coles, of Richmond, Surrey.

Middleton, Elizabeth, of St Giles, Cripplegate. — 20 Sept 1712 —, Thomas
[Dalton, of parish of St Magnus

Midhurst, Sara, *spin*, of the parish of
Battle, Sussex — 5 Jan 1714-5 —,
[John Vidler, *bat*, of same

Midlemore, Mary, of Grantham, co Lincoln — (12 April), 1717 —, Nevile King,
[of Ashby de la Laund.

Midwinter, Elisabeth, of St. Brides — 12
Nov 1742 —, Francis Gosling, of St
[Dunstans in the West

Milborne, Catherine. — 27 Sept 1696 —,
Robert Thorp, upholsterer in Greek St

Milbourn, Robert, of St. James, Clerkenwell
— 6 April, 1731 —, Barbara Kerrey, of
[St Clements Dane

Miles, Eustace, of the parish of St. James,
Clerkenwell — 28 Jan. 1713-4 —,
[Dorothy Appleby, of same

Miles, Grace, of the parish of St. Andrew's,
Holborn — 15 June, 1704 —, John
Friend, coachman, of same parish (by
[license)

Millborne, Dorothy, of the parish of St
Clements Dane. — 18 July, 1713 —,
Edward Stanley, of parish of St. Andrew,
[Holborn.

Millbourn, Alexander, of the parish of
Twickenham, Middx — 7 July, 1709
—, Eleanor Gillot, of parish of
[Leatherhead, Surrey

Miller, Thomas, of Croydon, Surrey, *bat*. —
10 April, 1721 —, Margaret Richardson,
[of same, *spin*

Miller, William, of St James', Westminster.
— 13 Jan. 1742-3 —, Margaret Corn-
[wall, of St George's, Hanover Sq.

Millington, Elizabeth, of St. Olave's, Silver
St. — 23 April, 1730 —, Humphrey
[Chadwick, of same

Mills, Bryan, of the parish of St Sepulchre.
— 17 July, 1707 —, Elizabeth Wytt, of
[St James', Clerkenwell.

Mills, Elizabeth, of the parish of St Andrew,
Holborn. — 17 Jan 1712-3 —, Thomas
[Furnis, of same

Mills, Frances, of St Mary le Savoy. — 7
[Jan. 1724-5 —, John Currer, of same.

Mills, Jane, of St. Michael's, Queenhithe.
— 18 Dec. 1729 —, Edward Dare, of
[same.

Mills, Mary — 25 June, 1697 —, Joseph
[Ward, butcher in Newport Market

Mills, Mary. — 24 Aug 1700 —, John
Thornton, labourer, in Red Lion Yard,
[Holborn

Mills, Thomas, of the parish of Henfield,
Sussex — 31 Jan 1706-7 —, Prudence
Pelcome, of St Leonard, Shoreditch
(married by the Bishop of Chichester)

Milner, Edward, of the parish of Christ
Church, Southwark. — 28 Aug 1713
—, Audry White, of same [Mr. Nevil,
[an apothecary in King St, present).

Milner, Thomas, gent, of Christ Church
parish, London — 12 Jan. 1701-2 —,
Mary Furley, of St James', Westminster

Milson, George, of St James', Westminster
— 16 Nov 1714 —, Martha Lewis, of
[St Sepulchre

Milton, Anthony, bargeman in Richmond,
Surrey — 9 April, 1702 —, Mary Cox

Mionet, Elizabeth, of St. Bennet Fink, *spin*.
— 5 Dec. 1720 —, Isaiah Bertlet, of
[Ann's, Westminster, *bat*.

Misson, Eleanor, of Ealing the Great, *spin*
— 21 Dec 1721 —, John Moody, *bat*.,
[of St. Martins in the Fields.

Mist, John, of the parish of St Anne, Westminster. — 2 Oct 1711 —, Elizabeth
[Carter, of St. Alban's, Herts.

Mist, Sarah, of St Andrew's, Holborn —
2 May, 1717 —, Charles Bridgeman, of
[parish of Kensington.

Mitchell, Elizabeth, of the parish of South
Mims, Middx — 18 April, 1710 —,
[Benjamin Nicoll, of same

Mitchell, John, a butcher in Chiswell St.
[— 15 April, 1696 —, Mary Rosser

Mitchell, Mary — 13 Jan. 1697-8 —,
Philip Townsend, shoemaker in Pearpo-
[lane

Mitchell, Thomas, of the parish of Sunderland, co Durham, mariner — 18 Dec
1705 —, Elizabeth Atkinson, of parish
[of St Andrew, Holborn (by license)

Mitchell, William, printer at the Crown
Lion, in Russell St., Covent Garden. —
[22 Sept. 1701 —, Deborah Sprat

Molyneux, Rigby, of Preston, co. Lanc —
8 Feb 1738-9 —, Mary Maiton, of St.
[Andrew, Holborn

Money, Elizabeth, of St Paul's, Covent
Garden — 26 Dec 1737 —, James
[Barker, of same.

Monger, Susanna. — 3 Nov 1696 —,
William Ellis, surgeon in Dartford,
[Kent

Monk, Jane, of Sevenoaks, Kent — 11 July,
1729 —, Thomas May, of Godmersham,
[Kent

Monk, Mary, of the parish of St Pancras. —
23 Oct. 1711 —, John Maynard, of
[parish of St Dunstan, Stepney

Moody, John, *bat*, of St Martins in the
Fields — 21 Dec 1721 —, Eleanor
[Misson, of Ealing the Great, *spin.*

Moon, Mary, of the parish of St James,
Clerkenwell. — 19 Jan 1713-4 —,
[Richard Elley, of same

Moor, George, of the parish of St James,
Clerkenwell — 7 Feb 1713-4 —, Mar-
[garet Taylour, of same

Moor, John, of the parish of St Marylebone.
— 9 Feb 1713-4 —, Elizabeth Pritchard,
[of same

Moor, Mary, of the parish of St. James,
Westminster. — 28 June, 1712 —, John
[Groom, vicar of Childerditch, Essex.

Moor, Thomas, of the parish of All Hallows,
Staining — 20 Aug. 1713 —, Ann
[Penry, of same.

Moore, John, a broker against Great Turnstile, Holborn — 22 April, 1697 —,
[Sara Hobbs.

Moore, John, of the parish of St. Dunstans
in the East. — 15 July, 1716 —, Hannah
Roberts, of St Catherine Cree Church.

Moore, John, of Esher, Surrey — 28 April,
1726 —, Elizabeth Litchfield, of same

Moore, Mary, *spin*, of St Andrew, Holborn
— 27 Feb 1714-5 —, Henry Rutter.
widower, of parish of St James, Clerken-
[well

Moore, Sara — 10 May, 1698 —, George
Kirke, husbandman in Putney, Surrey

Moors, Anne. — 14 Jan 1696-7 —, Thomas
Parker, yeoman, of Marsh Gibbon, Bucks

Mophet, Mary, of Tottenham, Middx. —
17 Nov 1711 —, Thomas Robins, of
[Enfield.

More, Elizabeth, of the parish of St. Matthew, Friday St — 28 Oct 1712 —,
[Nathaniel Oldfield, of St Lawrence.

More, Rebecca, of the parish of St Clements
Dane — 4 March, 1710-1 —, William
Beaching, of parish of St Andrew, Hol-
[born.

Morgan, Anne, of St. Andrew's, Holborn.
— 14 Feb. 1727-8 —, William Eckels,
[of St. Giles in the Fields

Morgan, Anthony, *bat*, of St Martins in
the Fields. — 19 Jan 1719 —, Eleanor
[Cole, of same, *spin*

Morgan, Sarah, of the parish of St Clement
Dane — 9 Feb 1713-4 —, Leonard
[Hunt, of same.

Morgan, Susan, of St. Clements Dane —
21 May, 1738 —, William Shaw, of St.
[Ethelburghs.

Morgan, Thomas, gent of the parish of St.
Mary, Alder Mary. — 30 Dec 1709 —,
Hon. Ann Lee, dau of Earl of Lichfield.

Morgan, William, of St Andrew's, Holborn.
— 13 Oct. 1735 —, Eleanor Evans, of
[St. Michael, Cornhill

Morley, Jane, of St. George's, Bloomsbury.
27 July, 1743 ——, Thomas Williamson,
[of same

Morphew, Richard, *bat*, of the parish of
St Sepulchre. — 27 Jan 1714-5 —,
Sarah Weston, *widow*, of St Andrew,
[Holborn.

Morris, Bridget, of Camberwell — 1 April,
1703 —, Robert Ball, of parish of St
Giles in the Fields (married by Mr.
[Fettiplace)

Morris, David, of the parish of St Martins
in the Fields — 26 Jan 1713-4, Eliza-
[beth Godard, of same

Morris Henry, of St. Michael's, Wood St
— 10 Sept. 1723 —, Martha Peters, of
[St. Bartholomew, in the Minories

Morris, John, of St Giles, Cripplegate —
26 Aug 1712 —, Ann Arkwright, of
[St James, Clerkenwell

Morris, Martha, of the parish of St Martins
in the Fields. — license dated July 1717
[—, John Segerin, of same.

Morris, Martin, of St. George the Martyr.
— 17 Jan 1732-3 —, Mercy Rogers, of
[St Paul's, Covent Garden.

Morris, Richard, of the parish of St Andrew,
Holborn. — 19 Nov 1710 —, Sinah
Howell, of parish of St Giles in the
[Fields

Morris, Richard, *bat*, of St Martins in the
Fields. — 4 Jan 1718-9 —, Ann Price,
[of same.

Morris, Sarah, of the parish of St Margaret,
Westminster. — 3 March, 1710-1 —,
[Samuel Houlding, of same

Morris, Sarah, of the parish of St Sepulchre — 28 Feb. 1713-4 —, Samuel
[Broughton, of same.

Mors, Rose. — 21 June, 1705 —, Edward
Scott, mercer in Round Court, Covent
[Garden, (by license)

Morten, Hannah, of St. Dunstans in the
West — 17 May, 1714 —, Edward
[Folkes, of St. Giles in the Fields

Mortimer, Edward, of the parish of St
Clare, Hart St — 20 May, 1712 —,
[Ann Crook, of Henley on Thames

Morton, Charles, of St Giles without
Cripplegate, *widower*. — 29 March,
1720 —, Ester Husley, of St John's,
[Wapping, *spin*

Moses, Susanna, of the parish of St.
Martins in the Fields — 7 Feb. 1713-4
[—, Manley Hall, of same

Moss, Martha. — 26 Sept 1690 —, John
Poile, vintner at the Red Lion, Red
[Lion St.

Motteux, John, of St Mary le Bow. —
23 March, 1724-5 —, Sarah Rayner, of
[same.

Moulden, Thomas, journeyman shoemaker
in Baldwin's Gardens — 10 Jan. 1698-9
[—, Susanna Comine.

Mountsteevens, Katherine, of the parish
of St Martin's in the Fields — 4 May,
1714 —, Henry Birchman, of parish of
[St Giles in the Fields.

Mowbray, John, of St. Giles in the Fields
— 21 Nov. 1747 —, Anne Buxton, of
[Royston, co. Cambridge.

Moxon, Elizabeth, of the parish of Greenwich, Kent — 6 May, 1712 —, William
[Thomas, of parish of St Mary, Savoy.

Moxon, Samuel, of the parish of St Andrew,
Holborn. — 7 Oct 1711 —, Mary
[Witton, of same

Moy, Mary, of the parish of St. Martins in
the Fields. — 6 Dec 1710 —, Francis
[Blayow, of same

Moyser, James, of St Paul's, Covent Garden.
— 5 May, 1716 —, Sarah Peirson, of
[St Andrews, Holborn.

Mudge, William, of the parish of St Giles
in the Fields — 3 Oct. 1714 —, Mary
[Lanton, of same.

Mugge, Emanuel, gent. of Inkbarrough,
co. Worcester. — 5 June, 1698 —, Jane
[Reek.

Munday, Nicholas, of Southaker, Norfolk,
labourer. — 19 June, 1695 —, Jane Law.

Munns, Elizabeth. — 28 Nov 1695 —, John
[Howard, of Clerkenwell, butcher.

Munslo, Anne — 18 May, 1695 —, Phineas
Robbins, of St Giles in the Fields, coach-
[man.

Murray, Mary, of St. Leonard's, Foster Lane.
— 12 Aug. 1740 —, Thomas Harriman,
[of same

Mushin, Samuel, of the parish of Barnes,
Surrey. — 10 Sept 1712 —, Elizabeth
[Odal, of St George's

Musket, Susanna, of Enfield, Middx — 13
Sept 1722 —, John Freeman, of St
[Mary, Aldermanbury

Muslers, Francis, of the parish of St. Michael.
— 14 March, 1709 10 —, Elizabeth
Peter, of Southgate within parish of
[Edmonton

Naish, Ambrose, of Chelsea. — 7 Sept 1732
[—, Elisabeth Greenwood, of same

Napier, John, of St. Margaret's, Westminster
— 1 Aug. 1731 —, Elisabeth Brown, of
[St. Clements Dane.

Nash, John, of the parish of St Andrew,
Holborn. — 23 April, 1713 —, Margaret
Sherrard, of parish of St. Ann's, West-
[minster

Nash, Letitia, of St. Leonard's, Foster Lane
— 12 Aug 1740 —, Thomas Humphreys,
[of St Gregory's.

Nash, Mary, of the parish of St Clements
Dane. -- 1 Oct. 1704 —, Elias Allington,
[salesman, of same.

Nash, Mary, of St Paul's. Covent Garden. —
15 April, 1733 —, John Parsons, of St.
[Giles in the Fields

Nash, Samuel, of the parish of St James,
Westminster. — 19 Jan. 1713-4 —, Ann
Arnold, of parish of St. Martin's, Iron-
[monger lane.

Nash, Thomas, bat, of the parish of St Botolph, Bishopsgate — 9 June, 1715 —,
Elizabeth Smallwood, spin of St An-
[drew, Holborn.

Neale, Hannah — 31 Oct. 1701 —, Edmund
[Oddy, shoemaker at Holborn Bridge

Neale, John, of Iver, Bucks, maltster — 14
[June, 1696 —, Elizabeth Steward.

Neale, William, of this Society — 6 April,
1734 —, Elisabeth Hanbury, of St
[George the Martyr, Queen sq.

Neat, Henry, of the parish of St. Anns,
Westminster — 23 June, 1714 —, Eliza-
[beth Howard (her father present).

Needham, Robert, coachman at the Ball in
Kirby St — 18 Oct 1701 —, Mary
[Keme

Nelson, Thomas, of the parish of St Martins
le Grand — 21 May, 1713 —, Margaret
[Binnyon, of same

Nendick, Charles, Indian gown seller at the
Three Crowns, Fleet St — 15 June, 1698
[—, Mary Knapton

Neve, John, salesman in Monmouth St,
parish of St Giles in the Fields —
2 Nov. 1703 —, Ann Boan, of parish of
[St. Andrew's, Holborn.

Nevile, Hester, of the parish of St. Martin in
the Fields, spin — 6 July, 1718 —, Robert
[Arthur, of same, bat

Nevill, Jane, of Hempstead, Herts — 5 Dec
1750 —, Edward Lambley, of St Sepul-
[chres

Nevin, Thomas, periwig maker in Chandos
St — 5 May, 1698 —, Hannah Meeson.

Newbold, John, attorner in Middle row —
[22 Oct 1696 —, Jane Walker

Newbould, William, of the parish of St.
Botolph, Aldersgate — 6 June, 1714 —,
Elizabeth Stockdald, of St Martins in
[the Fields

Newby, Elizabeth, of St. Dunstan's, Stepney,
spin. — 27 June, 1720 —, Robert Wan-
[mer, bat, of St. Martins in the Fields.

Newin, Anne, of the parish of St. Bride's,
spin. — 25 Jan 1714-5 —, Erasmus
[Jones, bat., of same

Newitt, Jane, of St Faith's, London. — 16
June, 1726 —, Richard Steele, of same

Newman, Phœbe, of St. Botolph's, Aldersgate. — 26 Oct. 1732 —, Richard Poul-
[ton, of same.

Newnham, Mary, of the parish of St
George's, Southwark — 12 July, 1712 —,
Arthur Savage, of parish of St Saviour's,
[Southwark.

k

Newport, Martin, merchant in Wandsworth, Surrey. — 24 May, 1704 —, Penelope Hall (married by Mr. Edgeley, Vicar of [Wandsworth)

Newsham, Richard, of Finchley, Middx — 19 Oct. 1744 —, Grace Bowring, of [same.

Newsom Anne — 8 Dec. 1698 —, Henry [Figgins, periwig maker in Gray's Inn

Newstead, Reynold, of Wakefield, co York — 17 April, 1737 —, Alice Higham, of [St. Andrew, Holborn

Nicholas, Elisabeth, of St. Bride's, Fleet St — 30 Nov. 1727 —, Solomon Wheatley, [of same

Nicholas, Richard (Esq), of the parish of Hackney — 14 July, 1753 —, Anne [Hatley, of same

Nicholls, Daniel, of the parish of Shenley Herts. — 24 Feb 1707-8 —, Martha [Barnes, of same.

Nicholls, John, of the parish of St Pancras — 5 May, 1713 —, Mary Warren, of [same

Nicholls, Mary — 28 Feb. 1695-6 —, Lewis Royeand, a soldier in Fountaine Court, [next the Savoy

Nicholls, Rebecca, spin. of the parish of St. Clements Dane. — 15 Dec 1714 —, [John Kingsley, bat., of same

Nichols, Sarah, of the parish of Hendon, Middx — 15 April, 1704 —, Edward Tew, yeoman, of parish of St Pancras [(by license).

Nicholson, John, of St Mary, Whitechapel — 30 Sept 1712 —, Rachel Hudson, of [St Clement Danes

Nicholson, Mary, of the parish of St Sepulchre. — 21 Sept 1710 —, Joseph [Maysey, of same

Nicholson, Mary, of the parish of St Giles in the Fields. — 3 Nov. 1714 —, John [Fish, of same

Nicolas, Margaret, of the parish of St. Andrew, Holborn — 27 March, 1712 —, [Henry Carpenter, of same

Nicoll, Benjamin, of the parish of South Mims, Middx — 18 April, 1710 —, [Elizabeth Mitchell, of same

Nicolls, Sarah, of Finchley. — 13 Feb. 1734-5 —, William Arlidge, of St. Andrew, Holborn.

Nightingale, Peter, of the parish of St. Mary, Savoy. — 1 Sept 1712 —, Ann [Campbell, of St. Clements Dane.

Nixson, Mary — 19 Nov 1697 —, William Thornton, gardener in Richmond parish, [Surrey

Noak, Letitia — 29 Sept 1700 —, Henry Bourne, mercer in King's Clere parish, [co. Southampton

Noble, William (junr), of Gray's Inn — 26 Feb 1739-40 —, Susanna Braithwaite, [of St Mary Islington.

Nokes, Anne — 12 Jan 1695-6 —, Edward Cook, journeyman shoe maker in Middle [Row, Holborn.

Noone, Hannah, of St. Alban's, Wood St. — 18 Dec 1740 —, George Cape, of [St Michael's, Wood St.

Norcutt, Elizabeth — 29 Sept. 1698 —, Peter Rulean, surgeon, near Bedford [House, Strand.

Norish (?), Trevor, bat , of the parish of St. Swithin. — 26 April, 1715 —, Elizabeth Somers, spin., of St Dunstans in the [West.

Norket, George, saddler, near the Greyhound in the Strand by Charing Cross — 21 [May, 1696 —, Judith Fluellin

Norman, John, fishmonger in King's St, parish of St. Margaret, Westminster. — 28 Feb. 1703-4 —, Mary Matthews, of [St. Martins.

Normcott, Mary. — 16 April, 1697 —, Robert Grew, victualler in Newgate St.

Norminger, William, of the parish of St. Pancras.—15 Nov 1713—, Alice Cotterell, [of St Andrew, Holborn.

Norris, Ann, of the parish of St. Ann, Westminster. — 18 Nov 1708 — John Tuke, [of parish of St. Andrew, Holborn.

Norris, George, gardener, of Chelsea — 8
Oct 1702 —, Elizabeth Tipping, of same

North, Anne. — 11 June, 1696 —, Silvester
Russell, shoemaker in Bridges St., Covent
[Garden

North, Johanna, of St. Mary Over, Southwark. — 31 Oct 1714 —, Thomas
[Williams, of St. James', Garlick Hill

Northcutt, Elizabeth, of the parish of St.
Andrew, Holborn. — 31 Oct. 1713 —,
[Edward Arnold, of same.

Norton, Jane, of the parish of St James,
Westminster. — 29 Dec 1712 —, John
[Soux, parish of St Giles in the Fields.

Norwood, Robert, of Stanmore the Great,
widower. — 23 Jan. 1721-2 —, Susanna
Langhorne, of St. Andrew, Holborn,
[*spin*

Nottingham, James, of the parish of St
Andrew, Holborn — 12 Sept 1714 —,
[Margery Grainge, of same

Nugent, Thomas, of Fulham. — 14 Nov
[1723 —, Margaret Parker, of same

Nutling, Thomas, poulterer in Bloomsbury
Market, parish of St Giles in the Fields.
— 25 Nov 1705 —, Mary Boswell, of same
[parish

Nutt, Samuel, *bat*, of the parish of St Mary,
Islington — 16 Jan 1714-5 —, Mary
[Houghton, *widow*, of same

Nutter, James, of St Luke's parish, Middx
— 12 April, 1743 —, Theodosia Fawkes,
[of same

Nutter, James, of St. Luke's, Old St —
27 Oct. 1750 —, Sarah Swift, of Ed-
[monton

Oates, Richard, grocer in Pinner, Middx —
[30 Oct 1699 —, Mary Jacket

Odal, Elizabeth, of St George's — 10 Sept
1712 —, Samuel Mushin, of parish of
[Barnes, Surrey

Oddie, Henry, of St. Anne's, Soho — 4
Sept. 1739 —, Margaret Bristow, of
[Reigate, Surrey

Oddy, Edmund, shoemaker of Holborn
Bridge. — 31 Oct 1701 —, Hannah
[Neale

Odson, William, of Arundel St., Strand,
waterman. — 12 Dec 1695 —, Jane
[Blackston.

Okey, Sarah, of St. Andrew, Holborn. — 16
May, 1728 —, Richard Ashley, of St
[Mary le Strand

Oldacker, Richard, of the parish of St.
Sepulchre — 4 April, 1714 —, Jane
[Snelling, of same.

Oldfield, Nathaniel, of St Lawrence — 28
Oct 1712 —, Elizabeth More, of parish
[of St. Matthew, Friday St.

Oliver, John, of St. Martin's in the Fields.
— 28 Oct 1734 —, Mary Walton, of
[St. George's, Hanover Sq.

Oliver, Mary, of the parish of St Andrew's,
Holborn — 17 July, 1707 —, Edward
Boldock, of parish of St James, Clerken-
[well.

Olliver, William, of St Andrew's, Holborn.
— 26 April, 1736 —, Mary Albon, of
[same.

Ororie, William, of the parish of St Andrew's,
Holborn. — 27 April, 1710 —, Mary
[Kent, of same.

Orpin, Edward, of St. Martin's in the Fields.
— 3 Feb. 1740-1 —, Frances Chandler,
[of same.

Osbaldiston, Roger, of the parish of St.
Saviour, Southwark. — 27 Oct 1713 —,
[Sarah Hill, of St. Olave's, Southwark.

Osborn, Thomas, *bat*, of the parish of
Epping, Essex — 25 Jan 1714-5 —,
[Anne Turner, *widow*, of same.

Osborne, Ann, of Hackney, Middx. — 31
March, 1734 —, Rev James Croker, of
[West Chiltington, Sussex.

Osborne, Josiah, of So Mims, Middx —
3 Sept 1747 —, Christian Lascelles, of
[Enfield, Middx.

Oswald, James, of St George the Martyr,
Queen Sq — 28 Aug 1746 —, Sarah
[Hillton, of same

Overston, Robert, gent. of the parish of St.
Paul's, Covent Garden. — 1 Jan. 1711-2
[—, Mary Chamberlain, of same.

Owen, Elizabeth, of St Clements Danes — 10 Feb 1729-30 —, Richard Perry, [of same.

Owen, Ellen, of St. Botolph's, Bishopsgate — 11 Jan 1731-2 —, Richard Evans, [of St. Andrew's, Holborn

Owogan, Henry, *bat.*, of the parish of St. Bridgets — 15 June, 1721 —, Mary [Robinson, of Christ Church, *spin*

Oxley, Elizabeth — 19 Aug 1697 —, Thomas Gardiner, carpenter, between [the turnstiles in Holborn.

Pace, John, coachman in St. Ann's, Westminster — 21 May, 1695 —, Anne [Bromwich.

Pack, Penelope, of St Giles in the Fields, *widow* — 12 Feb 1719 —, James Pendlebury, Esq , *bat*, of St Anne's, [Westminster

Pack, William, of the parish of St Peters, Paul's wharf — 7 May, 1711 —, Mar- [garet Jones, of Deptford

Page, George, *bat*, of Amesbury, Wilts — 25 Feb 1719 —, Mary Shaw, of same, [*spin*

Page, John, of St Andrew's Holborn — 1 Nov 1744 —, Mary Bolland, of St [Botolph's, Bishopsgate.

Page, Mary —3 Feb 1699-1700 —, Richard [Borsley, turner, at the Ditch-side.

Paget, Thomas Catesby, commonly called Lord. — 6 May, 1718 —, Lady Elizabeth [Egerton.

Paine, Anne, of St James', Westminster. — 22 Nov. 1719 —, Samuel Beaver, of [Covent Garden

Paine, George, coachman to Squire Middleton in Soho sq. — 31 March, 1698 —, [Anne Buckle.

Paine, Joseph, apothecary in New Brentford. [— 22 July, 1697 —, Jane Bruce

Paley, Henry, a case maker in Chancery Lane — 27 Sept 1696 —, Elizabeth [Canning.

Palgrave, William, of Pullham, Norfolk — 4 Sept. 1727 —, Elisabeth Burton, of [St. James, Westminster

Palmer, Clement, cutler in Gray's Inn passage, parish of St. Andrew's, Holborn. — 7 March, 1702-3 —, Warbro Palmer, of [same parish.

Palmer, Jane, of St. Paul's, Covent Garden. —29 Nov 1716 — John Stone of parish [of Braybrooke, co. Northampton.

Palmer, John, of the parish of Hatfield Herts — 16 June, 1713 —, Mary Lamb, [of same.

Palmer, Warbro, of the parish of St Andrew's, Holborn. — 7 March, 1702-3 —, Clement Palmer, cutler in Gray's Inn [passage, same parish.

Palmer, Samuel, of the parish of St. Paul's, Covent-Garden. — 2 Oct 1716 —, Mary [Barradell, of same.

Palmer, Sarah, of St Olave, Southwark — [22 Nov 1753 —, John Ives, of same

Palmer, William, mason in Hart St , Bloomsbury — 19 Nov. 1696 —, Elizabeth [Simpson.

Palphrey, Ann, of the parish of St. James, Westminster. — 10 July, 1709 —, John [Adam, of same.

Pantalini, Mary, of the parish of St Botolph without Aldgate. — 5 Nov 1710 —, [Charles Willson, of same

Pantalini, Richard, of the parish of St Mary le Bow — 22 Aug. 1713 —, Elizabeth Peterson, of parish of St. Thomas, South- [wark.

Pardee, Robert, of St Giles in the Fields, *widower* — 5 Aug 1722 —, Mary Gad- [ler, of St Andrew's, Holborn.

Parfitt, Mary, of Wycombe, Bucks. — 18 Dec 1729 —, Joseph Cawthorp, of St [Vedast, Foster Lane.

Parker, Charles (Esq), of Peterboro', co. Northampton. — 1 March, 1711-2 —, Katherine Wilson, of Leithorpe, co [Leicester.

Parker, Dorothy, *widow*, of St Mary, Savoy — 1 March, 1714-5 —, Richard Wainwright, *bat.*, of parish of St Clements
[Dane

Parker, Hugh (Esq.), in St Bride's parish
[— 24 June, 1701 —, Anne Smith

Parker, Jocose, of St Martins in the Fields — license dated Feb 1717-8 —, William
[House, of St Clements Dane

Parker, John, of St Mary, Savoy, yeoman — 28 May, 1695 —, Sara Allen, of
[same

Parker, John, husbandman, of Wyrardisbury, near Windsor — 28 Sept 1702 —, Fortune Store, of same.
[tune Store, of same.

Parker, John, of the parish of St Martins in the Fields — 2 Dec 1714 —, Jane
[Samson, of same

Parker, John, of St Andrew's, Holborn — 14 March, 1741-2 —, Anne Wilson, of
[Newcastle upon Tyne

Parker, Margaret, of Fulham. — 14 Nov.
[1723 —, Thomas Nugent, of same

Parker, Phœbe, of the parish of St Saviour, Southwark. — 21 July, 1709 —, William
[Grubb, of parish of St. Lawrence.

Parker, Sarah, of St George the Martyr, Queen sq — 6 Dec 1750 —, James
[Fleming, of St Alban's, Wood St

Parker, Thomas, yeoman, of Marsh Gibbon, Bucks. — 14 Jan. 1696-7 —, Anne
[Moors

Parker, William, of St. Faith's — 24 June, 1729 —, Mary Davis, of St. Anne's, West-
[minster.

Parker, William, of St Michael's, Cornhill — 10 March, 1749-50 —, Anne Black-
[noe, of Christ Church parish, London

Parkes, Margaret, of St. George's, Bloomsbury. — 7 Jan. 1750-1 —, Thomas
[Meller, of St. Alban's, Wood St

Parkins, Alice — 19 July, 1702 —, Samuel
[Hardy, apothecary in Hampstead.

Parkis, Abraham, of the parish of St. Andrew's, Holborn, servant to Mr. Shales, at the Vine, Lombard St — 27 Jan. 1703-4 —, Frances Gitles, of same
[parish.

Parkyns, Thomas, of Deptford — 14 Sept 1728 —, Elizabeth Woodroffe, of St
[Martins in the Fields.

Parr, Edward, of St Vedast's, Foster lane — 6 April, 1731 —, Sarah Dennis, of
[St Botolph's, Aldersgate

Parran, John, of St. James', Westminster — 25 June, 1737 —, Elisabeth Hopley, of
[St Andrew's, Holborn

Parris, Elizabeth, of the parish of St Dunstans in the West — 20 April, 1704 —, Ralph Maple, baker in White's Alley, Chancery Lane, within the liberty of the
[Rolls

Parrot, Thomas, of St Sepulchres — 10 Aug. 1740 —, Mary Deale, of St Luke's,
[old st

Parrott, Abraham, of the parish of St Martin's, Ongars — 30 Oct. 1711 —, Mary Gerrard, of parish of St. Nicholas Acrons,
[London.

Parrott, Simon, founder in West Cross St.
[— 14 Aug 1701 —, Anne Godfry.

Parry, Charlotte, of Oakfield, Berks — 21 Nov. 1742 —, William Johnston, Esq
[of St James', Westminster.

Parsons, Ann, of St Dunstans in the West. — 17 Jan. 1727-8 —, John Fuller, of
[Bushey, Herts.

Parsons, Isabella — 7 April, 1696 —, Samuel
[Guyon, a joiner in St. Hellens.

Parsons, John, of St Giles in the Fields. — 15 April, 1733 —, Mary Nash, of St.
[Paul's, Covent Garden.

Parsons, Richard, of St. Bartholomew — 13 Jan 1722-3 —, Christian Sergant,
[of St Andrew, Holborn.

Partridge, Mary, of the parish of Kensington — 26 Oct 1708 —, Daniel Merigeot, of parish of St James,
[Westminster.

Partridge, Robert, mariner in Strutton ground, Westminster. — 21 Feb. 1698-9
[—, Margaret Rawlins.

Paschall, Mary, of Great Baddow, Essex, *spin* — 21 Aug 1718 —, John Stone, esq., *bat.*, of parish of Brightwell, co.
[Oxford.

Pasmore, Thomas, gent. of St. Alban's Street. — 26 Aug. 1697 —, Elizabeth
[Malins

Patridge, Sarah, of the parish of St Giles in the Fields — 25 Dec 1703 —, William Beale, fishmonger in Newport Market, parish of St Ann's, West-
[minster

Paul, Samuel, of St James, Westminster — license dated May 1717 —, Hannah Tayleure, of parish of St. Giles,
[Cripplegate.

Pavillard, John, servant to Squire Popham in St. James' Square — 30 Sept 1695
[—, Elizabeth Chapman.

Pawlett, Mary, of the parish of St James, Westminster — 25 June, 1714 —, Hon Richard Parsons, Lord Ross, of Ireland

Payne, Joseph, of Hammersmith — 11 Aug. 1748 —, Hannah White, of St. Paul's,
[Covent Garden.

Peacock, George, of the parish of St. Dunstans — 13 Feb. 1709-10 —, Ann
[Tasker, of St Andrew's, Holborn

Peak. John, of the parish of St Ann's within Aldersgate. — 14 May, 1713 —, Mary
[Powel, of same.

Pearce, Elizabeth — 12 Nov 1701 —, Robert Tuite, merchant at Mr Brumig-
[ham's, a barber in Finch Lane.

Pearce, Moses, of St. Andrew's, Holborn — 7 Sept. 1714 —, Elizabeth Tyre, of
[Stepney parish

Pearce, William, upholsterer next the Dog tavern in Drury Lane. — 21 Jan 1700-1
[—, Mary Browne.

Pearch, Richard, of Keston, near Bromley, Kent, gent — 3 March, 1695-6 —, Mary
[Tutall

Pearles, Edward, innholder at the King's Arms in St Martin's Lane — 4 Aug
[1698 —, Mary Emes.

Pearse, Ellinor — 14 July, 1696 —, Thomas Renolds, felmonger, of Chinck-
[ford, Essex.

Pearson, Catherine, of the parish of St. Martin's in the Fields — 10 Feb 1712-3
[—, John Johnson, of same.

Pearson, Christian — 26 Feb 1722-3 —,
[Francis Boycott.

Pearson, John, a seaman, near the Ship in Salisbury Court. — 4 Nov. 1701 —,
[Sara Broggrove.

Pearson, Joseph, widower, of St. Giles in the Fields. — 22 Dec 1714 —, Eliza-
[beth Meers, spin. of Newington Butts.

Peart, Martha. — 19 Aug 1697 —, Henry Cook, victualler in Bloomsbury, St Giles.

Peat, Edmund, periwig maker against St Dunstan's Church — 5 Jan 1696-7 —,
[Sara Bly.

Peate, Elizabeth — 6 Dec 1696 —, John
[Bingley, firkin man in Lay-stall Street.

Peck, Elizabeth, of the parish of St James, Clerkenwell — 14 Nov 1714 —, John
[Joynes, of same

Peck, William (esq), of Santford Hall, Essex. — 11 June, 1700 —, Bridget Randyll (married by B Bramston, minister of
[Woodham Water, Essex).

Peckham, Susanna, of St Margaret's, Westminster. — 30 June, 1741 —, Thomas
[Williams, of same.

Peckleton, Gerard, of St George's, Bloomsbury — 10 Nov 1751 —, Anne Pick,
[of same,

Pee, Margaret, of the parish of St Giles in the Fields — license dated Dec 1717
[—, Nicholas Ritherden, of same.

Peidham, Jonas, bat of the parish of St. Mary, Savoy — 9 March, 1714-5 —, Martha Keibman, widow, of St Andrew,
[Holborn.

Peirson, Sarah, of St Andrew's, Holborn — 5 May, 1716 —, James Moyser, of
[St Paul's, Covent Garden.

Peirson, William, of the parish of Kensington — 2 Sept 1715 —, Susannah
[Alchorne, of same.

Pelcome, Prudence, of St Leonard's, Shoreditch. — 31 Jan. 1706-7 —, Thomas Mills, of parish of Henfield, Sussex (married by the Bishop of Chichester).

Pember, James, of the parish of St Clements Dane, gent. — 26 Oct 1707 —, Sarah de Bert, of parish of St Andrew's, Hol-
[born (by license).

Pemberton, Ann, of St Mary Magdalen, Milk St — 6 Aug 1724 —, William [Garsden, of St. James', Westminster

Pendlebury, James (esq), *bat* , of St Anne's, Westminster — 12 Feb 1719 —, Penelope Pack, of St Giles in the [Fields, *widow*

Pendridge (*als* Pendred), Jeremiah, of St Stephen's, Coleman St. — 6 May, 1732 —, Mary Cross, of St. Andrew's, Holborn.

Penry, Ann, of the parish of All Hallows, Staining. — 20 Aug 1713 —, Thomas [Moor, of same

Pepper, Susannah, of St George's, Hanover sq — 30 Oct 1735 —, James Metcalf, [of St Andrew's, Holborn

Pepys, Sarah, of the parish of St Dunstan's in the West — 10 May, 1707 —, Nicho- [las Grice, of same, gent , by license

Perkins, Matthias, surgeon in Swithin Lane — 24 Feb 1698-9 —, Elizabeth Aspley

Perkins, William, of St Andrew's parish, Holborn. — 23 June, 1737 —, Sarah [White, of same

Perrey, James, mercer in Chandos St — 4 March, 1696-7 —, Lydia Goodwin (by [Mr Elborough of the Fleet)

Perrin, Thomas, labourer. — 7 Sept. 1697 [—, Jane Preist.

Perry, Elisabeth, of St. Catherine Cree Church. — 18 Jan 1732-3 —, Salusbury [Cade, of Greenwich

Perry, Jane, of St. Andrew's, Holborn. — 9 Feb 1702-3 —, James Strodwick, of [St Dunstans in the West, yeoman

Perry, John, of St. Martins in the Fields — 1 Dec. 1714 —, Mary Libanns, of [St Margaret's, Westminster.

Perry, Mary — 24 Aug 1702 —, Robert [Kent, brewer, of Fulham

Perry, Richard, of St. Clements Danes. — 10 Feb. 1729-30 —, Elizabeth Owen, [of same

Perry, Richard (Esq), of the Inner Temple. — 30 Nov 1752 —, Mary Browne, of [St Giles in the Fields.

Perry, Sarah, of St Catherine Cree Church — 1 Oct 1719 —, William Heysham, [*bat.*, of Greenwich, Kent

Perry, Thomas, of the parish of St. Andrew, Holborn — 4 Feb. 1715-6 —, Elizabeth [Anger, of same

Pervill, Oliver, mariner, in St Peter's St , Bloomsbury. — 16 Feb 1696 7 —, Mary [Burden

Peter, Elizabeth, of Southgate within the parish of Edmonton — 14 March, 1709-10 —, Francis Muslers, of parish [of St. Michael.

Peter, Richard of Ealing, Middx , *bat* — 22 Dec. 1718 —, Martha Faulkner, of same, [*spin.*

Peters, Frances, of the parish of St Mary le Bow — 5 July, 1709 —, George Dixson, of parish of St Andrew, Hol- [born.

Peters, Martha, of St Bartholomew, in the Minories. — 10 Sept. 1723 —, Henry [Morris, of St Michael's, Wood St.

Peterson, Elizabeth, of the parish of St. Thomas, Southwark — 22 Aug 1713 —, Richard Pantalini, of parish of St [Mary le Bow.

Petit, Sarah, of the parish of St Giles in the Fields — 9 Feb 1713-4 —, Robert [Adams, of same.

Petty, Anne, of the parish of St. Margaret Westminster — 15 Dec. 1716—, Thomas [Coxe, of same.

Petty, Anne, of Sunbury, Middx. — 24 June, 1731 —, Thomas Rapley, of [same

Petty, John, *bat* , of St Giles in the Fields. — 1 June, 1720 —, Jane Townsend, of [St Marylebone, *spin.*

Pew, David, of the parish of St Andrew, Holborn. — 14 Sept 1714 —, Elizabeth Ston, of parish of St. Dunstans in the [West.

Peynter, Elizabeth, of the parish of Rich- mond, Surrey — 21 Sept 1713 —, William Hart, of parish of St. Katherine, [Tower Hill.

Philipps, Jane, of St. Giles in the Fields — 9 Sept. 1731 —, Robert Courtney, of [same

Philips, Catharine, of St Sepulchre, *spin* — 25 April, 1719 —, Edward Clark, [*bat*, of the Inner Temple

Philips, Mary, of the parish of St. Giles in the Fields — 30 Oct. 1714 —, Charles [Willson, of same

Phillibrown, Anne, of St Martin's, Vintry — 22 Aug 1753 —, William Richards, [of same.

Phillips, Anthony, of the parish of Deptford, Kent. — 13 Sept 1709—, Elizabeth Maria Hollon, of parish of St Andrew, [Holborn

Phillips, Catharine — 3 Sept. 1696 —, Job Bailey, victualler near Temple Bar

Phyllips, Sarah, of the parish of St Giles in the Fields — 21 Sept 1713 —, Joseph [Rice, of same

Philpot, George, of Sevenoaks, Kent — 8 [Oct 1751 —, Sarah Allen, of same

Philpot, James, of the parish of St. Bride's, London. — 18 Nov. 1706 —, Elizabeth [Graham, of same

Pick, Anne of St. George's, Bloomsbury. — 10 Nov. 1751 —, Gerard Peckleton, of [same

Pick, Richard, of St Giles in the Fields — 22 May, 1726 —, Elizabeth Scarborough, [of Chelsea

Pickersgill, John, a joiner, Pearpolane. — [22 April, 1697 —, Elinor Chancellor

Pickford, Mary, of St. Dunstans in the West — 5 Nov. 1714 —, John Eaton, of St. [Giles, Cripplegate.

Pierce, Mary, of the parish of St. James, Westminster. — license dated July [1717 —, Roger Farrell, of same.

Pierpoint, John, of the parish of St. Andrew, Holborn — 14 Aug. 1712 —, Percks [Shaw, of same.

Pierpoint, William, of the parish of St. Andrew, Holborn. — 21 March, 1712-3 [—, Hannah Kent, of same.

Pierson, Sara, of St. Anne's, Westminster. — 6 Jan 1718-9 —, John Boreman, *bat.*, [of same

Pigeon, Mary, of St Brides. — 21 Aug. 1736 —, Ralph Day, of Clifford's Inn.

Piggot, Thomas, of the parish of Lingfield, Surrey — 18 June, 1708 —, Ann Turner, [of same.

Pile, Richard, apothecary in Candleford, Cornwall. — 5 June, 1696 —, Mary [Fowler

Pinckney, Henry, vintner in Fetter lane. — [23 Aug 1696 —, Rebecca Cooper.

Pinfold, Elizabeth — 15 May, 1701 —, Thomas Crofts, upholsterer at the Royal Oak, near Somerset House, [Strand.

Pinkney, William, of the parish of St Margarets. — 26 June, 1711 — Elizabeth Finch, of parish of St James', Westminster.

Piper, Mary, *widow*, of the parish of Chiswick, Middx. — 6 Jan. 1714-5 —, [Samuel Snelson, *bat*, of same

Pitcher, Susan, of St. Andrew's, Holborn — 2 Feb 1706-7 —, Russell Reed, of parish of St. Dunstan's in the West.

Pitfield, William — 7 Jan 1696-7 —, [Dorothy Allen.

Pitt, Penelope, of St. Andrew's, Holborn. — 26 Dec. 1752 —, Bernard Stead, of St [Matthew's, Friday St

Pitt, Stephen (Esq), of Kensington — 1 Jan 1753 —, Dorothy Arthington, of [same.

Pitts, Mary, of the parish of St. Sepulchre. — 3 April, 1703 —, George Lloyd, gent., of parish of Aberdeene, co. Carmarthen.

Place, Thomas, of St. Andrew's, Holborn. — 19 Feb 1744-5 —, Elizabeth Frost, [of St. Giles in the Fields.

Plaistow, William, of Kew Green, Surrey. — 16 May, 1741 —, Mary Lowe, of same.

Platt, Elizabeth, of St Andrew's, Holborn. — 23 Aug. 1724 —, Bartholomew Gisbitzby, of St Mary Monthaw, London.

Player, Elizabeth — 7 May, 1706 —, William Brage, Esq of Hatfeild Peverill, [Essex

Playters, Francis, *widower*, of parish of St Brides — 24 Feb 1714-5 —, Margaret Barnes, *widow*, of St. Clements Dane

Plimloy, Elizabeth, of Highgate, Middx. — 14 Sept. 1723 —, William Wilkes, of [Whitefriars

Plyford, Lucie — 30 June, 1698 —, Vere Harcourt, a gent in St Anne, by Dr. [Wall

Poile, John, vintner at the Red Lion, Red Lion St. — 26 Sept 1699 —, Martha [Moss.

Pole, Anne, of Nottingham — 31 May 1753 —, Valentine Stead, of Halifax, co [York.

Polehampton, Anne, of the parish of St Martins in the Fields — 21 Sept 1713 —, William Hall, of parish of Mortlake, [Surrey.

Pollett, Elizabeth, of St Sepulchre's parish — license dated Dec 1717 —, John [Bent, of the Society of Lincoln's Inn

Pond, Gilbert, of Christ Church, Newgate St. — 8 Aug 1751 —, Mary Chasselup, [of St Andrew, Holborn

Poole, John, of the parish of St Nicholas Coole Abbey — 1 Aug 1714 —, Ruth [Abbott, of same

Pooley, Mary — 29 Jan. 1698-9 —, John Bird, a labourer against Chancery Lane, [Holborn.

Poplewell, Ruth, of St Andrew's, Holborn. — 28 Jan 1715-6 —, Thomas Goodgame, [of parish of Edmonton Middx.

Pott, Thomas Henry, of St James' Westminster — 5 July, 1744 —, Elizabeth [Shepherd, of same

Potter Mary, of the parish of St. Paul, Shadwell — 7 Feb 1713-4 —, John [Coombs, of same

Potter, Sarah (*æt* 34), of the parish of St James, Clerkenwell — 13 June, 1714 —, [Peter Bilbo (*æt* 60), of same

Potts, John, of St Sepulchre s — 26 Oct. 1752 —, Catherine Lewis, of St Andrew's, [Holborn.

Poulton, Richard, of St Botolph's, Aldgate — 26 Oct. 1732 —, Phoebe Newman, of [same

Pounceby, Mary, of the parish of St Clement Danes — 12 June, 1709 —, Thomas Baxter, of parish of St. Andrew's, Holborn [born

Powel, Fletcher, of the parish of Whitney, co Oxford — 9 July, 1711 —, Ann Hoole, of parish of St Martin's, Ludgate [gate

Powel, John, *widower*, of the parish of St Dunstans in the West — 29 Jan 1714-5 [—, Elizabeth Hill, *widow*, of same

Powel, Martha, of the parish of St. Mary, Whitechapel, *spin* — 1 Feb 1718-9 —, James Herring, *bat*, of parish of the Holy and Undivided Trinity the Less, [London

Powel, Mary, of the parish of St Ann's within Aldersgate — 14 May, 1713 —, [John Peak, of same.

Powell, Rebecca, of St. Mary le Bow — 23 Dec 1732 —, Thomas Knight, of St. [Trinity's

Prastring, Sarah, of the parish of St Andrew, Holborn. *spin* — 25 March, 1721-2 —, Caleb Colchester, *bat.*, of [same

Praynald, Mary, of St Andrew's, Holborn — 27 March, 1735 —, Henry White, of [the parish of Chelsea

Preist, Jane — 7 Sept 1697 —, Thomas [Perrin, labourer.

Prescott, Margaret, of St Botolph's, Aldersgate — 11 Nov. 1729 —, James Farrer, [of St Mary le Strand

Press, Edward, of the parish of St Andrew, Holborn — 10 Jan 1713-4 —. Abigail [Leman, of St Martin's in the Fields.

Preston, Roger, of the parish of St Giles in the Fields — 11 Nov 1713 —, Ann, [Steers, of same.

Pretor, Samuel, of St Olave's, Southwark — 15 April, 1741 —, Elisabeth Smith, of [same.

Preventer, Anne, of St Martins in the Fields, *spin* — 13 March, 1714-5 —, [John Haswell, of same

Price, Ann, of St Martin's in the Fields — 4 Jan 1718-9 —, Richard Morris, *bat*, [of same

Price, Elizabeth, of Christ Church parish, London, *spin* — 26 Feb 1719 —, William Harris, of St Andrew, Holborn, *bat*

Price, Jane, of St James', Westminster, *spin* — 30 Sept 1721 —, Gabriel Frith, of St [Giles in the Fields, *bat*

Price, Joseph, silk stocking weaver in Sherborne lane. — 8 Aug 1697 —, Sibil [Tarlton.

Price, Lewis, shoemaker in St Giles. — 2 [Sept. 1697 —, Elizabeth Watson

Price, Mary, of St Giles in the Fields — 16 Feb 1728-9 —, William Thomas, of [St Botolph's, Aldgate

Price, Morgan, of the parish of St. Olave, Southwark. — 11 Feb 1712-3 —. Eliza- [beth Brown, of parish of St Sepulchre

Price, Sarah, of West Barnet, *spin* — 19 Oct. 1721 —, Thomas Denton, *bat* of [Furnival's Inn.

Price, Sarah, of St. Giles in the Fields — 18 April, 1730 —, Thomas March, of St. [Clements Dane.

Price, Thomas, of St. Andrew's, Holborn — 14 Nov 1730 —, Elizabeth Sutton, [of same

Prichard, Catherine — 30 May, 1699 —, Edward Clarke, yeoman in Hog Lane, [near Soho

Prince, William, of the parish of St Giles in the Fields — 28 March, 1714 —, Mary [——, of same

Printon, William, victualler, of Edmonton, Middx. — 28 Jan 1702-3 —, Joice Wheeler, of St. James, or St Ann's, [Westminster.

Prior, Benjamin, of St Ann's, Blackfriars — 12 March, 1754 —, Ann Sankey, of St. [Andrew's, Westminster.

Pritchard, Elizabeth, of the parish of St. Marylebone. — 9 Feb. 1713-4 —, John [Moor, of same.

Pritchard, Mary, of St Martins in the Fields. — 9 Sept. 1722 —, William Walton, of [same.

Procter, Richard, of the parish of St. Andrew's, Holborn — 13 Aug 1710 —, [Elizabeth Gardiner, of same

Prowse, Ambrose, of South Petherton, co. Somerset — 15 Aug 1730 —, Philadel- [phia Way, of St Andrew's, Holborn.

Riches-Puckle, Katherine, of the parish of St Andrew, Holborn. — 6 April, 1713 [—, Francis Tolson, of same.

Pugh, Hugh, gent. in Church lane alley, Fetter lane — 3 Aug. 1697 —, Mary [Futerill.

Pugh, Mary, of the parish of St. Andrews, Holborn — 10 Oct. 1713 —, Edward [Clark, of parish of St Bride's.

Pulleyn, Elizabeth — 25 May, 1697 —, William Row, a brewer's servant in [Cripplegate parish.

Pullin, Edward, of the parish of St. Martins in the Fields. — 4 July, 1711 —, Edith [Callaway, of St James', Westminster

Pullin, John, of the parish of St Magnus, London — 16 Sept. 1711 —, Elizabeth [Fretwell, of Totteridge, Herts.

Purdon, William, *bat*, of the parish of St. Giles in the Fields — 31 Jan. 1714-5 [—, Martha Rowney, *spin* of same.

Purior (?), Deborah, of the parish of St. Pancras — 14 April, 1713 —, William [Hill, of same.

Pusey, Ann, of the parish of St Martins in the Fields. — 27 July, 1707 —, Thomas [Bass, of same

Pusey, Katherine, of the parish of St Giles, Cripplegate — 10 Dec 1713 —, Jacob [Hongest, of same.

Pusey, Thomas, of the parish of Marcham, Berks — 19 June, 1709 —, Mary Barugh, of parish of St. Bride's, London.

Putland, Hester, of St Margaret's, Westminster — 12 Dec. 1749 —, Owen [Meyrick, Esq of Lincoln's Inn

Puxty, Elizabeth. — 1 June, 1698 —, William Henman, coachman to the [Lady in Hatton Garden.

Pye, Anna, of St Luke's, Old St — 2 Jan 1748-9 —, John Crook, of St Giles in [the Fields.

Pyke, Anne — 9 Aug 1699 —, Francis
[Marple, a servant

Quixey, Elizabeth, of the parish of St.
Andrew, Holborn — 27 Sept 1713 —,
[William Carruthers, of same

Rabbuts, Agatha, of the precinct of Norton
Folgate — 18 Aug. 1736 —, Thomas
Weaver, of St Dunstan's in the West

Rabbuts, Edward, of St Mary Magdalen,
Bermondsey. — 6 April, 1731 —, Agatha
[Dennis, of St Botolph, Aldersgate.

Rainsford, Mary, of the parish of St. Martins in the Fields — 18 Feb 1706-7 —,
[Daniel Suker, of same.

Ramsden, William (Esq), of the parish of
St. Andrew, Holborn — 19 June, 1711
[—, Mary Robinson, of same.

Ramsey, Benjamin, of St Anne's, Blackfriars — 17 Jan 1736-7 —, Alice
[Longdon, of St Luke's, Middx

Ramsey, Betsey, of Romford, Essex —
2 Nov 1753 —, William Willett, of
[St. Andrew's, Holborn

Rance, Anne. — 30 Oct. 1698 —, Lucas
Shrimpton, cheesemonger without
[Bishopsgate.

Randall, Charles, haberdasher next the
White Hart Inn, Southwark. — 15 Oct
[1695 —, Elizabeth Joyner

Randyll, Bridget. — 11 June, 1700 —,
William Peck, Esq. of Santford Hall,
Essex. (Married by B Bramston,
minister of Woodham Water, Essex)

Rapley Thomas, of Sunbury, Middx. — 24
[June, 1731 —, Anne Petty, of same.

Raven, William, bat , of Charing, Kent —
9 June, 1719 —, Elizabeth Hodgkin,
of Peterborough, co Northampton, spin

Raven, William, of St Giles in the Fields.
— 10 Feb. 1744-5 —, Sarah Johnson,
[of St Andrew's, Holborn.

Rawlet, Mary — 18 Aug. 1698 —, John
Andrewes, weaver in Bishopsgate St ,
[St. Botolph's

Rawlins, Margaret — 21 Feb 1698-9 —,
Robert Partridge, mariner in Strutton
[ground, Westminster.

Rawlins, Thomas, of St. Andrew's, Holborn.
— 3 Feb. 1732-3 —, Sarah Clum, of
[Finchley, Middx

Rawston, Thomas, of the parish of St Giles
in the Fields — 26 Nov. 1713 —, Priscilla Guidott, of parish of St Martin in
[the Fields

Ray, Ann, of the parish of St Botolph,
Aldersgate —16 Feb 1713-4 —, Charles
[Walker, of same

Rayner, Rebecca. — 12 Feb 1701-2 —,
Pearse Massey, servant to Squire Ran-
dall in Leicester St , St Anne's parish,
[Westminster.

Rayner, Sarah, of St. Mary le Bow — 23
March, 1724-5 —, John Motteux, of
[same.

Read, Elizabeth, of the parish of St Sepulchre. — 25 July, 1714 —, John Lewis,
[of same.

Read, John, of Enfield, Essex, gent. — 4
[April, 1706 —, Elizabeth Jones.

Read, Thomas, of the parish of St. John,
Hackney. — 12 Jan 1712 3 —, Sarah
[Howard, of same.

Reading, Joseph, of St Clements Dane. —
3 Jan 1748-9 —, Catherine Leech, of
[St John's, Westminster.

Redferne, Thomas, mason in Blackfriars
[— 23 June, 1701 —, Elizabeth Hale.

Redhead, Nathaniel, of St. Andrew, Holborn — 25 Aug. 1752 —, Olive Sands,
[of St James', Westminster.

Redman, John, of the parish of St. Andrew,
Holborn. — 12 June, 1722 —, Jane
Seyhard, of parish of Blechingley, Surrey,
[spin.

Reed, Andrew, a cook in Abchurch Lane.
— 8 April, 1697 —, Rebecca Barrabay.

Reed, Betty, of St. George's, Hanover-sq
— 6 July, 1740 —, Henry Hutchinson,
[of same

Reed, Mary, of St Sepulchres. — 9 Aug.
1727 —, Robert Thorowgood, of same.

Reed, Russell, of the parish of St. Dunstan's
in the West — 2 Feb 1706-7 —, Susan
[Pitcher, of St. Andrew's, Holborn.

Reek, Jane — 5 June, 1698 —, Emanuel Mugge, gent. of Inkbarrough, co Wor-
[cester.

Reeve, Thomas, gent of the parish of St Brides — 14 Feb. 1709-10 —, Elizabeth
[Berkley, of same

Reeves, Henry, coachman to ——, in Soho Sq. — 11 Feb. 1695-6 —, Elizabeth
[Scot

Reeves, Katherine, of the parish of St. James, Westminster — 11 Aug. 1713 —, John
[Wright, of same

Renolds, Thomas, felmonger, of Chinckford, Essex. — 14 July, 1696 —, Ellinor
[Pearse

Rensin, Judith, of the parish of St. Clements Dane. — 27 Nov 1713 —, Thomas Kelly,
[of same

Renwood, Isaac, of the parish of St Martins in the Fields — 1 Jan 1713-4 —,
[Rebecca Schooler, of same.

Revell, Andrew, a brewer's clerk near Cripplegate — 23 May, 1697 —,
[Catherine Cocker.

Rewalling James, of St. Giles, Cripplegate. — 21 April, 1712 —, Judith Freeman, .
[of same.

Reynolds Dorothy, of the parish of St Dunstan's in the West. — 24 Feb 1712-3 —, Benjamin Holden, of parish of St
[Bridget.

Reynolds, John, bat, of the parish of St Giles in the Fields. — 26 Feb. 1714-5 —, Elizabeth Willson, widow, of same

Reynolds, Sarah, of Peckham, Surrey — 13 June, 1738 —, Joseph Wright, of All Hallows, Bread St. (by Rev Daniel
[Bentley)

Rice, Elizabeth, of the parish of St Giles in the Fields — 21 Sept 1707 —, Richard
[Warburton, of same (by license)

Rice, Elizabeth, of St George's, Hanover sq. — 22 Sept 1737 —, Rice Davies,
[of St. Paul's, Deptford

Rice, Joseph, of the parish of St. Giles in the Fields. — 21 Sept 1713 —, Sarah
[Phyllips, of same

Richards, Evan, of the parish of St Andrew, Holborn. — 13 July, 1711 —,
[Honor Bone, of same.

Richards, Jane — 23 Feb 1695-6 —, Robert Smith, clockmaker in Long
[Acre.

Richards, John, of Owsdon, Suffolk — 13 Oct. 1748 —, Anne Wood, of Culford,
[Suffolk

Richards, Margaret — 17 Feb 1701-2 —,
[Thomas Bramston

Richards, William, of St Martin's Vintry — 22 Aug. 1753 —, Anne Phillibrown,
[of same.

Richardson, Ann, of the parish of St Catherine Cree Church, widow — 5 March, 1718 —, Edward Brownjohn, bat, of parish of St Michael, Cornhill.

Richardson. Henry, of Cheshunt, Herts. — 26 May, 1737 —, Eleanor Drew, of
[same.

Richardson, Margaret, of Croydon, Surrey, spin — 10 April, 1721 —, Thomas
[Miller, bat, of same.

Richardson, Sarah, of the parish of Wrotham, Essex — 10 Feb 1703-4 —, Lancelot Atkinson, of parish of St Andrew's, Holborn, in Leather lane, coachman.

Richardson, Thomas, bat, of the parish of St. Andrew, Holborn — 9 June, 1715
[—, Barbara ——, of same.

Richardson, William, of the parish of Hendon, Middx — 12 Dec 1708 —, Elizabeth Haddock, of parish of St.
[Margaret's, Westminster

Richbell, Arthur, of the parish of St Giles, Cripplegate. — 11 March 1713-4 —,
[Lydia Martin, of same.

Richbell, Rebecca, of St. George's, Queen sq — 22 June, 1736 —, James Shirley,
[of St Andrews.

Richboll, John, of the parish of St Andrew, Holborn. — 29 Nov 1713 —, Mary
[Booker, of same.

Richmond, Elisabeth, of St Botolph's, Aldersgate. — 17 July, 1728 —, George
[Hawkins, of same.

Rickstone, Joseph — 14 Jan 1695-6 —,
[Rebecca Velley

Ridley, Ann, of the parish of St Clements
Dane. — 20 April, 1708 —, John Tay-
[lour, of same

Riley, George of St. James', Westminster
— 24 Oct 1723 —, Margaret Washford,
[of same

Rimon, Anne, *spin* of Barking parish —
24 Feb 1714-5 —, John Todd, *bat*, of
[parish of Bishopsgate

Ritherdon, Nicholas, of the parish of St.
Giles in the Fields — license dated
Dec 1717 —, Margaret Pee, of same.

Robbins, Phineas, of St. Giles in the Fields,
coachman — 18 May, 1695 —, Anne
[Munslo.

Robe, Anne, of St James, Clerkenwell, *spin*
— 19 April, 1720 —, Edward Smith,
[*bat*, of Holkham, Norfolk

Roberts, Ann, of the parish of St Giles in
the Fields — 9 Dec 1703 —, Joseph
Brotherton, of same parish, butcher in
[Hart St, Bloomsbury

Roberts, Ann — 19 Oct 1704 —, Jonathan Charllon, of St. Botolph's, Aldgate

Roberts, Anne, of St James', Westminster
— 14 Dec 1732 —, George Adams, of
[St Brides

Roberts, Hannah, of St Catherine Cree
Church. — 15 July, 1716 —, John
Moore, of parish of St. Dunstans in the
[East.

Roberts, Judith — 13 April, 1697 —, Marmaduke Horseley, a lawyer in Fetter
[lane, St. Bride's parish

Roberts, Margaret. — 4 Nov. 1697 —,
George Atkinson, vintner in St Martins
[le Grand

Roberts, Mary, of the parish of St James,
Clerkenwell — 20 Nov 1713 —,
[William Wynn, of same

Robins, Thomas, of Enfield, Middx. — 17
Nov. 1711 —, Mary Mophet, of Totten-
[ham.

Robinson, Amie — 6 Aug 1699 —, Andrew Welch, merchant in Mark Lane

Robinson, Ann, of St. Michael, Cornhill
— 3 Sept 1723 —, Matthew Warren,
[junr, of St. Mary Abchurch.

Robinson, Elizabeth, of the parish of St.
Giles in the Fields. — 17 Feb 1707-8
—, John Dixon, of parish of Stepney,
[Middx.

Robinson, Elizabeth, of the parish of St.
Andrew, Holborn. — 13 June, 1711 —,
Henry Brearcy, clerk of parish of Box-
[worth, co Cambridge.

Robinson, Elizabeth, of the parish of St
Sepulchre — 4 Oct. 1712 —, Walter
[Chambers, of Chelsea College

Robinson, Elisabeth, of St Andrew's, Holborn — 21 Aug. 1735 —, George
Mackenzie, of St. Martin's in the Fields

Robinson, James, of the parish of St Andrew, Holborn — 17 Oct. 1714 —,
[Sybil Barmley, of same

Robinson, Jane. — 9 May, 1704 —,
Arthur Humphrys, rector of Barton,
Beds (Married by Mr Humphrys,
[then living in Hatton Garden)

Robinson, Mary, of the parish of St. Andrew, Holborn — 19 June, 1711 —,
[William Ramsden, esq. of same.

Robinson, Mary, of the parish of St James,
Westminster — 11 Oct 1715 —, James
[Uridge, of same.

Robinson, Mary, of Christ Church, *spin.*
— 15 June, 1721 —, Henry Owogan,
[*bat*, of parish of St Bridgets.

Robinson, Sary, *widow.* — 2 Sept. 1722
—, Henry Harper, of parish of St.
[Sepulchre

Robinson, Thomas, of St Andrew's, Holborn — 29 Jan. 1745-6 —, Anne
[Croshold, of St Olave, Hart St.

Rogers, Benjamin, of the parish of St.
James, Westminster — 3 May, 1714
—, Margaret Faithly, of St Giles in
[the Fields.

Rogers, Daniel, soldier at the gentlom
porter — 3 Jan 1698-9 —, Mary
[Douglas.

Rogers, Daniel, *bat* of St. Andrew's, Holborn. — 5 Feb. 1719 —, Mary Everet,
[of same.

Rogers, Elizabeth, of Buckingham, co Bucks — 2 Sept. 1708 —, William Streatfeild, of parish of St. Lawrence, [London

Rogers, James, *bat*, of the parish of St. Giles in the Fields. — 12 Dec. 1714 [—, Mary Eaton, *spin.*, of same.

Rogers, Mercy, of St. Paul's, Covent Garden — 17 Jan. 1732-3 —, Martin [Morris, of St George the Martyr

Rogers, Robert, of St. Sepulchre. — 29 Oct. 1713 —, Katherine Brainsby, of [same

Roles, Eleanor, of St. Andrew's, Holborn — 14 July, 1739 —, Thomas Henwood, [of St Mildred in the Poultry

Rolfe, John, of the parish of St. John's, Wapping — 17 June, 1712 —, Mary [Allen, of same

Rooke, Elizabeth, *spin*, of St. Mary, Savoy. — 28 March, 1715 —, Samuel Lasenby, [*bat*, of parish of St Clements Dane

Rose, Hannah, of St. Clements Danes — 3 [Oct. 1726 —, Samuel Hill, of same

Rose, Samuel, cook in Mutton Lane, parish of St James, Clerkenwell. — 24 June, 1704 —, Armanel Abraham, of parish [of St Andrew's, Holborn

Ross, Elizabeth, of St Mary le bone. — 24 Aug 1749 —, Hugh Ross, of St. An- [drew Undershaft, London

Ross, Hugh, of St. Andrew, Undershaft, London. — 24 Aug. 1749 —, Elizabeth [Ross, of St. Mary le bone.

Ross, Richard Parsons, Lord, of Ireland — 25 June, 1714 —, Mary Pawlett, of [parish of St. James, Westminster

Ross, Susanna, of St. Mary le Bow. — 12 March, 1723-4 —, Richard Kenn, of [St. Margaret's, Westminster

Rossam, Jacob, of the parish of St. Andrews, Holborn — 27 Oct. 1716 —, Sarah [Weston, of same

Rossell, Ann, of the parish of Alderman-bury — 1 Jan. 1713-4 —, Pascho [Wills, of parish of Hornsey, Middx

Rosser, Mary — 15 April, 1696 —, John Mitchell, a butcher in Chiswell St.

Roswell, Mary, of the parish of St Giles, Cripplegate — 7 March, 1710-1 —, Thomas Brown, of parish of St. Antho- [nies

Rouse, John, of St James in the Fields, surgeon — 20 Aug 1696 —, Elizabeth [Taylor.

Row, William, a brewer's servant in Cripple-gate parish. — 25 May, 1697 —, Eliza- [beth Pulleyn.

Rowe, James, of St Margaret's, Westminster — 30 Nov 1725 —, Susanna Wheeler, [of St Sepulchre.

Rowe, Thomas, of St Botolph's, Alders-gate — 9 May, 1728 —, Rebecca [Dennis, of same.

Rowel, Henry, *widower*, of the parish of St. Brides — 19 March, 1718 —, Eliza-beth Harding, *spin* of parish of St. [Giles in the Fields.

Rowley, John, gardener, Isleworth — 27 [Nov 1697 —, Anne Saunders

Rowney, Martha, of the parish of St. Giles in the Fields, *spin* — 31 Jan 1714-5 —, [William Purdon, *bat.*, of same

Royeand, Lewis, a soldier in Fountaine Court, next the Savoy — 28 Feb. 1695-6 [—, Mary Nicholls.

Royse (*als* Rouse), Mary, of St Clements in the Strand — 30 Jan. 1732-3 —, Hugh Blake, of St Giles in the Fields.

Royston, Ann, of the parish of St Sepul-chre. — 1 June, 1712 —, Edward [Cumber, of same.

Ruff, William, *bat*, of the parish of St.Andrew, Holborn — 13 March, 1714-5 —, [Mary Williams, *spin*, of same

Rulean, Peter, surgeon, near Bedford House, Strand. — 29 Sept. 1698 —, [Elizabeth Norcutt.

Rules, Mary — 4 July, 1701 —, William [Lone, farmer, of Lee, Essex.

Rumney, Margaret, *spin*, of St Mary, Whitechapel. — 2 Jan 1714-5 —, Samuel Machin, *bat*, of parish of St. [Botolph, Bishopsgate.

Rush, Hannah, of St Ann's, Westminster — 13 May, 1712 —, Thomas Wright, [of parish of St James, Westminster

Russell, Silvester, shoemaker in Bridges St, Covent Garden — 11 June, 1696 [—, Anne North.

Russett, Elizabeth, of St. George's parish, Southwark — 25 Sept 1715 —, Edward [Brown, of Withersfield, Suffolk

Rustal, Tobias, of the Close, near the City of Lincoln. — 3 July, 1735 —, Mary [Barkham, of same.

Rustat, Robert, of White Hart, New St, parish of St Sepulchre, a grocer — 27 June, 1703 —, Lucy Jones, of same [parish.

Rutland, Robert, yeoman, of Hempsted, Essex. — 8 Oct 1696 —, Sara Jefferson

Rutter, Dorothy, of Hackney. — 16 Sept 1736 —, William Atkinson, of this Inn

Rutter, Henry, widower, of the parish of St. James, Clerkenwell — 27 Feb 1714-5 —, Mary Moore, spin of St [Andrew, Holborn

Ryder, Edward, butcher in Clare Market [— 7 Feb 1696-7 —, Mary Gurdon

Ryland, George, of St. Andrew, Holborn — 18 April, 1714 —, Charity Folwell, [of same

Ryley, Sarah, of the parish of St. Andrew, Holborn — 2 Dec. 1714 —, John [Smith, of same

Rymer, Mathew, joiner in White's Alley — [10 Dec 1699 —, Sara Busher

Ryves, Arundell, of St. Andrew, Holborn, spin — 21 Nov 1721 —, Anthony Irving, bat, of St. Michael's, Crook [Lane

Ryves, Susanna, of the parish of St. Mary le bone — 24 Feb 1752 —, William [Girdler, Esq of parish of Fulham

Sabberton, Jane, of St Margaret's, Lothbury. — 5 May, 1748 —, Richard Walter, [clerk, M A. of Portsmouth, Hants.

Saer, Elizabeth, of the parish of Harrow on the Hill, Middx. — 8 May, 1711 —, John Friend, of parish of Great Stan- [more

Sale, Grace, of the parish of Bolney, Sussex. — 17 Aug. 1714 —, John Dalton, of [same

Salesbury, Margaret, of Hampstead, widow — 1 Dec. 1720 —, Thomas Dance, of [St Paul's, Covent Garden

Salisbury, Rt Hon. James, Earl of — 12 Feb 1708-9 —. Hon Lady Ann Tufton, dau of Earl of Thanet (Married by [Dr Savage

Salley, Katherine, of the parish of St Giles in the Fields — 6 Oct 1709 —, Edward [Bond, of St Andrew's, Holborn.

Sams, Elizabeth, of Pirton, Herts — 26 Aug. 1725 —, Nicholas Hunt, of Wat- [ford, Herts.

Samson, Jane, of the parish of St Martins in the Fields — 2 Dec. 1714 —, John [Parker, of same

Samwell, Ann, of Watton, Norfolk, spin. — 3 Jan 1720-1 —, William Henry Fleming, bat, of St Andrew's, Holborn.

Sancroft, Elizabeth, of St James', Westminster — 8 May, 1735 —, John [Wogan, of Gaudy Hall, Norfolk.

Sancroft, William (esq), of Fressingfield, Suffolk — 9 June, 1710 —, Katherine [Cotton, of Madingley, co Cambridge

Sanders, Elizabeth — 22 Oct 1696 —, [Thomas Jones, vintner in St Bride's

Sanders, John sedan man in Lester St, St Anne's parish — 4 Sept 1700 —, [Anne Holmes

Sanderson, Bartholomew, of the parish of St Mary Wolnoth — 3 Aug 1713 —, [Judith Droyner, of same

Sanderson, Sir William (bart), of Greenwich. — 28 June, 1739 —, Charlotta [Gough, of St James', Westminster

Sandilands, Alexander, of the parish of St Martins — 17 Jan 1711-2 —, Mary [Tombs, of same.

Sands, Olive, of St James', Westminster. — 25 Aug. 1752 —, Nathaniel Red- [head, of St. Andrew, Holborn.

Sandwich, Thomas, of the parish of Christ Church, Southwark — 12 Sept 1714 —, Ann Young, of parish of St Andrew, [Holborn.

Sankey, Ann, of St Andrew's, Westminster
— 12 March, 1754 —, Benjamin Prior,
[of St. Ann's, Blackfriars

Sare, Joseph, of Hungerford, Berks — 26
Feb 1708-9 —, Mary Warker, of same

Saunders, Anne — 27 Nov 1697 —,
[John Rowley, gardener, Isleworth

Saunders, Charles, a servant in St James',
Westminster — 15 June, 1698 —, Ann
[Kew

Saunders, Jane — 28 Nov 1704 —,
Richard Brothers, wheelwright in Brew-
ers St, parish of St James, Westmin-
[ster

Saunders, John, of the parish of St Sepulchre — 9 Nov. 1714 —, Mary Crafford,
[of same

Saunders, Mary, of the parish of St Mary,
Abchurch. — 26 Oct. 1735 —, Samuel
[Adderley, of same.

Saunders, Sarah, spin, of the parish of St.
Andrew, Holborn — 20 Feb 1714-5
[—, Edward Loomes, bat, of same

Saunderson, Dorothy, of St Benet's,
near Paul's ditch. — 5 Feb 1718-9 —,
Benjamin Field, bat., of St. Andrew's,
[Holborn

Saunderson, Frances — 15 Oct 1696 —,
[Thomas Dyson, of Greenwich, gent

Savage, Ann, of St. Andrew's, Holborn.
— 19 May, 1731 —, James Winter, of
[St. Bartholomew the Great

Savage, Arthur, of the parish of St Saviour,
Southwark — 12 July, 1712 —, Mary
Newnham, of parish of St. George's,
[Southwark

Savage, Sarah, of St Andrew, Holborn —
6 April, 1736 —, John Lloyd, of Aston,
[Salop

Saxston, John, of the parish of All Saints,
Lombard St. — 9 April, 1712 —,
[Dorothy Jeffery, of same

Scaife, Edward, bat, late of Hampstead,
Middx. — 8 April, 1720 —, Mary
[Brown, of same, spin

Scapeland, Margaret, Deptford, Kent. —
20 Dec. 1730 —, Richard Hoar, of
[same

Scarborough, Elizabeth, of Chelsea —
22 May, 1726 —, Richard Pick, of St
[Giles in the Fields.

Scarbourgh, Elizabeth, 'of Richmond,
Surrey — 5 March, 1736-7 —, Richard
[Fitzwater, of same

Scattergood, John, of St Dunstan's in
the East — 2 Oct 1736 —, Martha
[Maynard, of St. Martin's Vintry.

Scawen, Anthony, linendraper of the parish
of St. Michael, Cornhill — 22 May,
1708 —, Prudentia Evans, of parish of
[St. Andrew's, Holborn (by license).

Scholefield, Sarah, of the parish of St
Antholins — 16 May, 1714 —, ——
[Batch (sic) of same

Scholler, Thomas, hatter in Fetter Lane
[— 20 June, 1697 —, Anne Darling.

Schooler, Rebecca, of the parish of St.
Martins in the Fields — 1 Jan 1713-4
[—, Isaac Renwood, of same.

Scot, Elizabeth. — 11 Feb 1695-6 —,
Henry Reeves, coachman to ——, in
[Soho Sq.

Scott, Edward, mercer, in Round Court,
Covent Garden — 21 June, 1705 —,
[Rose Mors (by license)

Scott, Mary, of St. Botolphs, Aldersgate.
— 14 June, 1736 —, Thomas Whitford,
of St. Bartholomew's, near the Royal
[Exchange

Scott, Susanna, of the parish of St Ann's,
Westminster — 21 April, 1703 —,
William Greene, yeoman, of parish of
[Abray, Herts

Scott, Valentine, of St Dunstan's in the
West — 29 March, 1725 —, Mary
[Dineley, of same.

Scott, William, bat., of St. Andrew, Holborn.
— 4 Aug 1720 —, Dorothy Bentham,
[of same, spin.

Scrafton, William, clerk at Mr Barrett's,
in Doctor's Commons — 19 May, 1702
[—, Frances Barrett.

Scrivener, Richard, of the parish of St.
Martin's in the Fields — 12 Feb. 1708-9
[—, Elizabeth Bach, of same.

Seaborn, John, of the parish of St Andrew, Holborn. — 4 Feb. 1713-4 —, Ann [Combe, of same.

Seale, Mary of the parish of St Giles in the Fields — 3 Oct 1713 —, John [Hill, of same

Seears, John, butcher of Gt. Stanmore, Middx — 2 June, 1701 —, Mary [Waller.

Segerin, John, of the parish of St Martins in the Fields — license dated July [1717 —, Martha Morris, of same.

Selby, Mary, of the parish of St. Paul's, Covent Garden — 30 Dec 1712 —, Amos Welden, of parish of St Giles in [the Fields

Sells, Edward, of St Saviour's, Southwark — 24 Dec 1749 —, Martha [Burnham, of St Andrew's, Holborn

Seol, Mary, of St. Martins in the Fields. — 23 March, 1717-8 —, William Bean, of [same.

Sergant, Anne — 7 July, 1696 —, John Cock, vintner in Black Bull Court, [against Iveybridge, in the Strand

Sergant, Christian, of St. Andrew, Holborn. — 13 Jan. 1722-3 —, Richard [Parsons, of St. Bartholomew.

Serjeant, Jane, of Dinton, Bucks. — 6 Feb 1727-8 —, John Harrington, of [St Martins in the Fields.

Serjent, John, a disbanded soldier, of Drury Lane — 12 Nov 1698 —, Eliza-[beth Woodcock

Sexly, George, of St Giles in the Fields. — 1 July, 1736 —, Anne Martin, of St [George's, Hanover sq.

Seyliard, Jane, of the parish of Blechingley, Surrey, spin. — 12 June, 1722 —, John Redman, of parish of St Andrew, Hol-[born

Shadd, Thomas, of St James, Clerkenwell — 5 Feb. 1729-30 —, Martha Bristow, [of St. Andrew's, Holborn

Sharpe, Mary, of Thetford, Norfolk — 17 Dec. 1724 —, Thomas Hare, of Harg-[ham, Norfolk.

Sharpe, Sarah, of the parish of Clements Dane. — 23 May, 1711 —, Francis [Stanly, of same.

Sharples, John, barber-surgeon in Chancery Lane End, Holborn. — 30 Aug. 1696 [—, Elizabeth Taylor

Sharratt, Abraham, of St Giles in the Fields. — 19 Feb 1725-6 —, Susanna Cawdron, of St. Margaret's, Westminster

Shaw, Elizabeth, of the parish of St Mary Over, Southwark. — 12 April, 1714 —, [John Ffollond, of same.

Shaw, Mary, of Amesbury, Wilts, spin — 25 Feb 1719 —, George Page, bat., [of same

Shaw, Michael, of the parish of St Mary le Bow — 16 March, 1709-10 —, Eliza-beth Hughes, of parish of St. Andrew's, [Holborn

Shaw, Percks, of the parish of St. Andrew, Holborn. — 14 Aug 1712 —, John [Pierpoint, of same.

Shaw, Sarah, of St. Andrew, Holborn, spin — 26 Feb. 1719 —, Lancelot Jenour, [bat., of St. Sepulchre.

Shaw, Ursula. — 25 Oct. 1696 —, Thomas [Cook, gent. of Whittingslow, Salop.

Shaw, William, of St. Ethelburghs — 21 May, 1738 —, Susan Morgan, of St [Clements Dane.

Shefford, William, of the parish of St Andrew, Holborn. — 2 Feb 1713-4 —, [Mary Low, of same.

Shepard, Sarah, of the parish of St Albans, Wood St — 8 June, 1714 —, John [Hotter, of same

Shepeard, Abel, of the parish of St Chads, Salop — 20 Aug 1713 —, Mary Lang-more, of parish of St Peter's, Cornhill (married by Mr Skerret, chaplain to the [Duke of Ormond)

Sheperd, Edeth, of the parish of Kensing-ton — 13 May, 1714 —, John Thomas, [of same.

Shepheard, Thomas, wholesale glover. — [7 July, 1696 —, Mary Henchman

Shepherd, Elizabeth, of St. James', West-minster. — 5 July, 1744 —, Thomas [Henry Pott, of same

m

Sheppard, Philip, of the parish of St
Sepulchre — 1 April, 1711 —, Hannah
Banbury, of parish of St. Bennet, Grace-
[church St.

Sheppard, Richard, of St Paul's, Covent
Garden. — 29 May, 1712 —, Diana
[Stacey, of same.

Sherborne, Ann, of St Giles in the Fields.
— 26 Jan. 1727-8 —, George Allison,
[of St Clements Danes

Sherlocke, Katherine, of the parish of St
Gregory — 20 Jan. 1708-9 —, Edward
Eslon, of parish of St Martin's, Lud-
[gate

Sherman, Mary, of the parish of St
Clements Dane. — 25 May, 1718 —,
[William Chandler, of same

Sherrard, Margaret, of the parish of St.
Ann's, Westminster — 23 April, 1713
—, John Nash, of parish of St Andrew,
[Holborn

Sherwood, Elizabeth. — 20 July, 1704 —,
[Thomas Walder, gent of Lothbury.

Shilfox, Edward, clerk to Mr Ayres of
Lincoln's Inn — 17 June, 1701 —,
[Sara Jones

Shipley, Hannah, of the parish of St. James,
Clerkenwell. — 19 Nov 1714 —, John
[Harrington, of same

Shippard, Robert, of St George's, Han-
over sq — 3 Aug. 1742 —, Esther
Heath, of St Thomas the Apostle,
[London.

Shippey, Charles, of St. Andrew's, Holborn. — 18 June, 1732 —, Henrietta
[Gibbs, of St. James, Clerkenwell.

Shippin, Margaret, of the parish of St
Andrew, Holborn — 22 Aug 1714 —,
Rice Wright, of parish of St. Giles in
[the Fields.

Shipward, Thomas, corn chandler in Middle row, Holborn — 18 April, 1698
[—, Bridget Wheelwright

Shirley, James, of St. Andrew's. — 22
June, 1736 —, Rebecca Richbell, of
[St George's, Queen sq

Shitlle (or Shillito?), Katherine, of the parish
of St James, Clerkenwell — 4 March,
1711-2 —, Nathaniel Simmes, of same

Shonk, James, of St. Giles in the Fields.
— 11 Feb 1737-8 —, Anne Lockett,
[of same

Short, Elisabeth, of St. Andrew, Holborn.
— 21 Jan 1753 —, William Johnson,
[of same

Shorter, Rachel, of St. Martin's in the
Fields — 7 March, 1731-2 —, John
[Kelly, of St. Giles in the Fields

Shower, Ann, of the parish of Clerkenwell. — 8 Feb. 1706-7 —, John Warner,
of parish of St Martin's, Ironmonger
[lane.

Showwell, William, of the parish of St.
James, Westminster — 17 June, 1714
[—, Mary Bundy, of same.

Shrimpton, Lucas, cheesemonger, without
Bishopsgate. — 30 Oct 1698 —, Anne
[Rance

Shuckburgh, Lettice, of St Paul's, Covent
Garden — 31 Dec. 1724 —, William
[Wotton, of St Clements Danes

Shutter, John, of St Paul's, Shadwell,
Middx — 12 Nov 1752 —. Catherine
[Littleton, of Isleworth, Middx

Siddall, Mary, of St James, Westminster,
— license dated Jan 1717-8 —, Henry.
Tinney, of parish of St. Martin's in the
[Fields

Side, William, of the parish of St Saviour's,
Southwark — 14 Feb 1712-3 —, Ann
[Collier, of St. Giles, Cripplegate.

Simes, Elizabeth, of the parish of Islington.
— 1 May, 1714, —, Isaac Marter, of
[same.

Simkin, Thomas, cheesefactor (of Stone),
co. Stafford — 1 Feb 1699-1700 —,
[Mary Lawley [als Allen)

Simmes, Nathaniel, of the parish of St
James, Clerkenwell. — 4 March, 1711-2
—, Katherine Shitle (or Shillito?), of
[same

Simons, John, of the parish of St Andrew,
Holborn — 6 Aug 1714 —, Bridget
Acklon, of parish of St Giles, Cripple-
[gate

Simpkin, Sarah, of St. John's, Clerkenwell.
— 15 Feb 1728-9 —, Robert Taylor, of
[St James', Clerkenwell

Simpson, Alexander, of Leake, co. Lincoln — 4 May, 1741 —, Mary Godfrey, of [Chipping Barnet, Middx

Simpson, Elizabeth. — 19 Nov. 1696 —, William Palmer, mason in Hart St, [Bloomsbury

Simpson, Henry, of the parish of St. Giles in the Fields. — 3 June, 1713 —, [Susanna Jolleme, of same.

Simpson, Hugh, of St. George the Martyr, Queen Sq. — 28 Jan 1732-3 —, Jane [Hurley, of same.

Sims, Charles, of St. James', Westminster, "ye duck of Shandos running footman." — 10 Nov. 1722 —, Mary Meredith, of [same parish.

Sinck, Jane, of the parish of St Giles in the Fields — 18 Oct 1713 —, Bartholomew Hall, of parish of St. Martins [in the Fields.

Sing, Robert, of the parish of St Martins in the Fields — 29 March, 1714 —, Ann [Thomson, of same.

Singleman, Thomas, bat, of the parish of St James, Westminster. — 26 Feb 1714-5 [—, Anne Allin, spin. of same

Singleton, Dorothea, of St. George's, Bloomsbury — 26 Feb 1733-4 —, William Hendler, Esq, one of the [Masters of this Society

Singleton, Eleanor, of the parish of Islington — 6 Dec 1713 —, Abraham [Tuncks, of same.

Singleton, John, of the parish of St. Ann, Westminster — 15 Jan 1711-2 —, [Ann Ellis, of same.

Singleton, Thomas, joiner, of the parish of St Mary Magdalen, in Old Fish st — 3 June, 1705 —, Bridget Maxwell, of [St. Brides.

Sissons, Robert, of St Giles, Cripplegate. — 13 June, 1714 —, Sarah Crosly, of St [Michael's, Wood St

Skeeles, Thomas, of St Ives, Hunts — 19 July, 1753 —, Cordelia Corney, of [Bobinger, Essex.

Skeen, George (Esq), of the parish of St James, Westminster — 7 Feb 1713-4 —, [Elizabeth White, of same

Skeltor, Hester, of St Paul's, Covent Garden — 26 Oct 1723 —, John Witt, of St [James, Westminster

Skifling, Al——, of East Greenwich, spin — 29 Dec 1720 —, John Johnson, of [same, bat.

Skrymsher, Charles, of Barnard's Inn 6 June, 1730 —, Mary Fryer, of St [Martin's in the Fields

Slade, Philippa, of St. Nicholas, Deptford — 28 Feb. 1730-1 —, Antony Fisher, [of same,

Slann, Andrew, of the parish of St Paul's, Covent Garden — 9 April, 1713 —, Sarah Goodall, of same (married by Mr Goodall, fellow of Peter House [Coll, Cambridge)

Slenn, Ann, of the parish of St. Giles, Cripplegate — 3 March, 1716-7 —, [Nathaniel Stafford, of same

Slinte, Thomas, of Cabbage Lane, St Margaret's, Westminster — 19 Nov 1704 —, Elizabeth Warner (by a parson from [the Fleet).

Smallwood, Elizabeth, single woman, of St. Andrew, Holborn. — 9 June, 1715 —, Thomas Nash, bat, of parish of St. [Botolph, Bishopsgate

Smalwell, Joseph, of Maidstone, Kent, widower — 24 Nov 1719 , Elizabeth [Thatcher, of St Martin's, Ludgate

Smart, Dorothy, of the parish of St. Clements Dane — 22 March 1710-1 —, John Wright, of Kentish Town, Middx.

Smart, Elizabeth, of St Giles in the Fields — 22 May, 1739 —, William Bedford, [M D of St Nicholas Olaves

Smart, John, of the parish of St James, Westminster, — 7 April, 1713 —, Eleanor [Alsop, of same

Smart, Robert, of the parish of St. Dunstan's in the East. — 12 Oct 1707 —, Sarah Clarke, of parish of St. Botolph, Billings- [gate

Smart, William, of Maldon, Essex. — 4 Oct. [1748 —, Elisabeth Standish, of same

Smedley, George, of the parish of All Hallows the Less, Thames St — 17 Nov 1737 —, Ellis Williams, of same.

Smith, Alice. — 24 Feb 1697-8 —, John
Broadgate, farrier in St Giles in the
[Fields.

Smith, Anne — 24 June, 1701 —, Hugh
[Parker, Esq in St. Bride's parish

Smith, Anthony, carpenter, of the parish of
St Giles in the Fields — 6 April, 1707
[—, Elizabeth Hanworth, of same.

Smith, Edward, *bat*, of Holkham, Norfolk
— 19 April, 1720 —, Anne Robe, of
[St James', Clerkenwell, *spin*

Smith, Elizabeth — 7 Sept. 1697 —,
Robert Hall, *gent.*, at the Holy Lamb,
[Long Acre.

Smith, Elizabeth, of the parish of St An
drew, Holborn — 8 May, 1711 —, John
[Collins, of same.

Smith, Elizabeth, of the parish of St. Kath
erine Cree Church — 5 Oct. 1713 —,
William Dobar, of parish of Christ
[Church

Smith, Elizabeth, of the parish of Hornsey,
Middx. — 20 Oct. 1714 —, John
[Weaver, of same

Smith, Elisabeth, of St. Magnus the Martyr
— 6 March, 1728-9 —, William Wilkin-
[son, of St Mary's, Aldermanbury

Smith, Elisabeth, of St. James', Westminster
— 3 Oct. 1731 —, John Martin, of
[St. Martin's in the Fields.

Smith, Elizabeth, of St Pancras, Soper Lane
— 4 Nov 1732 —, John Waldron, of
[same.

Smith, Elisabeth, of St. Olave's, Southwark
— 15 April, 1741 —, Samuel Pretor, of
[same

Smith, Esther of St Andrew's, Holborn —
20 April, 1732 —, Joseph Dethendge, of
[St John the Evangelist, Westminster

Smith, George, of St. James', Westminster
— 11 May, 1725 —, Mary Colthurst,
[of same.

Smith, Henry, of St. Ethelberg's, London
— 8 Nov. 1729 —, Mary Chance, of
[Charlton Kent

Smith, James, a brewer's servant. — 20 Nov.
[1698 —, Elizabeth Bayly.

Smith, John, of the parish of St Andrew's,
Holborn. — 2 Dec 1714 —, Sarah
[Ryley, of same.

Smith, John, *bat*, of the parish of St Paul's,
Covent Garden — 1 March, 1714-5 —.
Anne Cale, *widow*, of St James, Clerk-
[enwell.

Smith, Joseph, pewterer at Long Lane End,
St Botolph's. — 31 March, 1699 —,
[Jane Ludford

Smith, Joseph, of the parish of St. Andrew,
Holborn — 20 March, 1710-1 —, Hester
Bucknall, of parish of St Giles in the
[Fields.

Smith, Judith. — 25 Feb. 1700-1 —,
Thomas Francknell, husbandman of
[Weston on the green, co Oxford.

Smith, Lydia, of Ashton, Salop. — 25 Nov
1729 —, Thomas Bryan, of White
[Friars.

Smith, Mary, of parish of St Andrew, Hol-
born — 10 May, 1713 —, Thomas
Smith, of parish of St Dunstan's in the
[West.

Smith, Mary, *sing.* of the parish of St.
Andrew, Holborn. — 15 Dec 1714 —,
[Benjamin Hide, *bat*, of same

Smith, Mary, of Holkham, Norfolk. — 20
April, 1720 —, John Francis, *bat*, of
[North Elmham, Norfolk, clerk.

Smith, Mary, of St Andrew, Holborn —
15 Sept 1722 —, John Cuel, of St.
[Dunstan's in the West, *widower.*

Smith, Richard, of Turnmill Street — 10
[Dec 1695 —, Alice Steward

Smith, Robert, clockmaker in Long Acre —
[23 Feb 1695-6 —, Jane Richards

Smith, Robert, of the parish of St. James,
Westminster — 21 Feb 1712-3 —,
[Elizabeth Law, of same.

Smith, Robert, of St Dunstan's in the West
— 5 March, 1727-8 —, Beatrice Hoden,
[of St. Giles in the Fields

Smith, Samuel, baker in New St., Shoe Lane
[— 30 Dec. 1696 —, Mary Meal.

Smith, Thomas, of the parish of St Martin's
in the Fields. — 1 July, 1706 —, Ann
[Gould, of the same

Smith, Thomas, of the parish of St. Peter's, Cheap — 15 Nov. 1707 —, Elizabeth Blare, of parish of St Magnus the [Martyr

Smith, Thomas, of the parish of St Dunstans in the West — 10 May, 1713 —, Mary Smith, of parish of St Andrew, Holborn

Smith, William, of the parish of St Andrew, Holborn. —23 Feb. 1710-1 —, Elizabeth Turner, of parish of St. Dunstan's in the [West.

Smyth, James (Esq), of the parish of St Margaret, Westminster —22 Jan 1707-8 —, Mirabella Legard, of parish of St [Andrew's, Holborn

Snath, Henry, of Covent Garden, fringe maker. — 7 May, 1695 —, Martha [Sylverton, of same

Snelling, Jane, of the parish of St Sepulchre — 4 April, 1714 —, Richard Oldacker, [of same

Snelson, Samuel, *bat*, of the parish of Chiswick, Middx — 6 Jan 1714-5 — [Mary Piper, *widow*, of same

Somers, Elizabeth, *sing* of St Dunstans in the West — 26 April, 1715 —, Trevor Norish (?), *bat.*, of parish of St Swithin

Somner, Mary, *sing* of Tring, Herts — 6 Jan. 1714-5 —, William Lord, *bat.*, of [parish of St Margaret, Westminsetr

Soper, Robert, chandler at the King's Arms, near Newington Church —16 Jan 1699- [1700 —, Mary Hope

Soper, Thomas, of the parish of St Clements Danes, woollen draper. — 10 Jan 1702-3 —, Dorothy Chaplyn, of Sutton, Isle [of Ely

Sorsby, Deborah, of St. Luke's, old st — 9 June, 1745 —, Thomas Coleby, of [same

Sorsby, Samuel, of St Sepulchre's. — 12 Jan. 1752 —, Elisabeth Turbutt, of St [Giles in the Fields.

Soulby, John, of St. Giles in the Fields — 16 Aug 1743 —, Mary Bedford, of St [Nicholas Olave.

Southall, William, mariner in Vine St , St Giles. — 29 Dec 1697 —, Mary [Loftus

Soux (?), John, of the parish of St. Giles in the Fields — 29 Dec 1712 —, Jane Norton, of parish of St. James, [Westminster.

Sowerby, Richard, of St Andrew's, Holborn — 16 May, 1703 —, Elizabeth [Hodgkin, of same

Spackman, Edward, of the parish of St. Austin's, London. — 20 March, 1711-2 —, Henrietta Maria Jennings, of St [Paul's, Covent Garden.

Sparhanke, William, of Baldock, Herts — 21 Oct 1732 —, Margaret Lowray, of St Andrew's, Holborn (by Richard Lowray, minister of Bilbrough, Yorks)

Sparrow, Bodychen, of Kensington, Esq. — 6 March, 1749-50 —, Frances Arthington, of St Margaret's, West- [minster

Speakman, John, watchmaker near Hatton Wall, parish of St Andrew's, Holborn. — 17 Feb 1703-4 —, Honor Barry, of same [parish.

Spearing, Robert, of St. Martins in the Fields. — 13 Oct 1726 —, Alice Tiener, [of St Andrew, Holborn.

Speke, Francis, saddler in Kentish Town. — [13 Dec. 1697 —, Cornelia Holder.

Spencer, Beckwith, of the parish of South- well, Notts. — 15 May, 1707 —, Susan Ward, of parish of St. Ann, Westminster

Spencer, John, servant to Judge Hook in Lincoln's Inn Fields — 16 June, 1698 [—, Sara Emley

Spencer, John, of St. Bartholomew behind the Change. — 25 July, 1749 —, Mar- garet Wells, of St. Margaret's, West- [minster

Spencer, Samewell, of the parish of St. Giles, Cripplegate. — 11 April 1714 —, [Mary Evans, of same

Spensley, Sarah, of St. George the Martyr — 24 June, 1724 —, John James, of [St Clements Dane.

Spicer, Thomas, of St. Dunstan's in the West. — 25 Sept 1733 —, Sarah [Egerton, of same.

Spier, Matthew, of the parish of St Andrew, Holborn — 13 Feb. 1715-6 —, Mary [Wilford, of same

Stephenson, Sophia. — 19 Oct. 1695 —,
James Collins, journeyman tallow
[chandler in the Old Bailey

Stevens, Bridget — 2 May, 1699 —,
Theophilus Duchesne, Soldier, in Guillard
[Street, St. Anne's parish, Soho.

Stevens, William, gent. of the parish of St
Ann, Westminster. — 13 Oct 1703 —,
Susanna Symonds, of same (by a license).

Stevens, William, of St. Catherine Coleman
— 5 Dec. 1708 —, Elizabeth Brown, of
[parish of St. Ann's, Westminster

Steward, Alice —10 Dec. 1695 —, Richard
[Smith, of Turnmill Street

Steward, Elizabeth — 14 June, 1696 —,
[John Neale, of Iver, Bucks, Maltster

Stewart, Robert (Esq.), of the parish of St
Margaret, Westminster. — 27 Sept 1710
—, Elizabeth Lawrence, of parish of St
[Anne, Westminster

Stewart, Sarah, of the parish of St Andrew,
Holborn. — 22 Jan 1712-3 —, Henry
Elmes, of parish of St. Clements Dane.

Stiling, George, of the parish of Barking,
Essex. — 28 Oct. 1714 —, Elizabeth
[Malard, of same

Stoakes, John, farmer, of High Ongar,
Essex. — 20 May, 1701 —, Joan
[Boons

Stockdald, Elizabeth, of St. Martins in the
Fields — 6 June, 1714 —, William
Newbould, of parish of St. Botolph, Al-
[dersgate

Stocken, Richard, of the parish of St. Andrew, Holborn. — 16 April, 1712 —,
Mary Walkees, of parish of St. Martin's
[in the Fields

Ston, Elizabeth, of the parish of St. Dun-
stans in the West — 14 Sept 1714 —,
David Pew, of parish of St. Andrew,
[Holborn.

Stone, John, of the parish of Braybrooke,
co Northampton. — 29 Nov. 1716 —,
Jane Palmer, of St. Paul's, Covent Gar-
[den.

Stone, John (Esq). bat., of the parish of
Brightwell, co Oxford — 21 Aug 1718
—, Mary Paschall, of Baddow the Great,
[Essex, spin.

Stone, Mary, sing., of the parish of St Giles,
Cripplegate — 5 Dec. 1714 —, Thomas
[Abbot, widower, of same

Stone, Mary, of Battersea, Surrey, spin. —
10 Feb. 1718 —, Edward Clark, bat., of
[St. Andrew's, Holborn.

Stone, Sarah, of the parish of St James,
Westminster. — 20 Dec 1705 —, William Jones, gent , of Swallow St , same
[parish.

Stonestreet, Francis, of the parish of St
Giles in the Fields. — license dated
July 1717 —, Mary Gorton, of same

Stonestreet, Mary, of St Martins in the
Fields — 18 Feb. 1728-9 —, Christian
[Mabis, of St Andrew's, Holborn.

Stop, Sara — 2 June, 1698 —, Robert
Cooper, mercer in the Royal Exchange

Store, Fortune, of Rasbury, near Windsor.
— 28 Sept. 1702 —, John Parker, hus-
[bandman, of same.

Strathan (?), John, of the parish of St.
James, Clerkenwell — 1 Dec 1713 —,
[Mary Sweler (?), of same

Streatfeild, William, of the parish of St
Lawrence, London — 2 Sept 1708 —,
Elizabeth Rogers, of Buckingham, co
[Bucks

Street, Richard, of the parish of St Dunstan's — 14 Oct. 1708 —, Agnes Bed-
[ford, of St. Paul's, Covent Garden

Stringer, John, of All Saints the Greater,
bat — 11 Oct 1720 —, Mary Lewis, of
[St Pancras, spin.

Stringer, Mary, spin , of Sevenoaks, Kent
— 15 April, 1722 —, John Austin, bat ,
[of same

Stringer, Mary, of Orsett, Essex. — 26
May, 1735 —, Thomas Butler, of Horn-
[don, Essex.

Strodwick, James, of St. Dunstans in the
West, yeoman — 9 Feb. 1702-3 —, Jane
[Perry, of St Andrew's, Holborn

Stronovins, Tobias, of St Giles, bat — 25
Jan 1718-9 —, Elizabeth Boydany, of
[same, spin.

Strut, George, apothecary, of the parish of Uggly, Essex. — 13 July, 1703 —, Mary Denn, *widow*, of parish of St [Andrew's, Holborn (by a license)

Stuart, Robert, of the parish of St Andrew, Holborn. — 15 Sept 1715 —, Margaret Denison, of St. Dunstan's in the West.

Stuart, Thomas, of St Martins in the Fields, *bat* — 10 June, 1722 —, Mary Withrell, [of St. Giles in the Fields, *widow*.

Stukeley William (D D), rector of All Saints, Stamford, co. Lincoln — 9 Jan 1738 9 —, Elisabeth Gale, of St. An- [drew, Holborn

Sturgeon, Thomas, labourer in Dean St, St Ann's, Westminster — 2 July, 1695 [—, Susanna Evans

Stydwell, John, mariner, next the Golden Mortar in Berry's St , near St. Germans [— 14 Sept 1699 —, Mary Sutton

Styles, Elizabeth, of the parish of St. Andrew, Holborn — 16 April, 1713 —, Joseph Fisher, of parish of St. Michaels, [Cornwall.

Sudbury, William, of St Paul's, Covent Garden. — 5 Sept. 1716 —, Arrabella [Boswell, of St Giles in the Fields

Suffield, Mary. — 5 June, 1698 —, George [Lawson, butcher in Clare Market

Suker, Daniel, of the parish of St Martins in the Fields — 18 Feb. 1706-7 —, [Mary Rainsford, of same

Surnerfield, John, of the parish of St. Martins in the Fields — 24 Aug 1710 —, Rachel Dyer, of parish of St Giles [in the Fields

Sunderland, Mary, of St George the Martyr. — 16 Nov. 1724 —, John [Atwood, of St. Martin's, Vintry

Sutton, Elizabeth, of St Andrew's, Holborn — 14 Nov 1730 —, Thomas [Price, of same

Sutton, Jane, of St Andrew's, Holborn — 21 June, 1734 —, Thomas Coote, of [Rotherhithe, Surrey

Sutton, Mary. — 14 Sept 1699 —, John Stydwell, mariner, next the Golden Mor- [tar, in Berry's St., near St. Germans

Sutton, Mary, of St Edmundsbury, Suffolk, *widow*. — 20 Oct 1718 —, Bartholo- mew Young, Esq. of Broadfield, Suffolk, [bat

Sweler (?), Mary, of the parish of St James, Clerkenwell. — 1 Dec. 1713 —, John [Strathan (?), of same

Swift, Sarah, of Edmonton — 27 Oct 1750 —, James Nutter, of St Luke's, Old St

Sylverton, Martha, of Covent Garden — 7 May, 1695 —, Henry Snath, fringe [maker of same

Symms, Prudence. — 30 April, 1699 —, William Symms, goldsmith in Peasecoed [St , Whitechapel

Symms, William, goldsmith in Peasecoed St , Whitchapel — 30 April, 1699 —, [Prudence Symms.

Symonds, Mary, of St Ann's, Westminster. — 1 Oct 1705 —, William Hare, of [the parish of Kensington, yeoman.

Symonds, Susanna, of the parish of St Ann, Westminster. — 13 Oct. 1703 —, William Stevens, gent. of same (by a license).

Tailor, Mary, of the parish of St Andrew, Holborn — 16 Aug 1715 —, Edward [Lovesuch, *bat*, of same

Tale, Joseph, of the parish of St. Giles in the Fields. — 10 Jan. 1711-2 —, Susan [Austin, of same.

Tapley, Jane. — 14 Feb 1698-9 —, Thomas [Jones, waterman in Greenwich.

Tarlton, Sibill — 8 Aug 169? —, Joseph Price, silk stocking weaver in Sherborne [lane.

Tasker, Ann, of St. Andrew's, Holborn — 13 Feb 1709-10 —, George Peacock, of [parish of St. Dunstans.

Tate, Katherine, of St. Giles, Cripplegate. — 13 May, 1714 —, Giles Barwell, of [parish of St James, Clerkenwell.

Tatlam, Elizabeth, of the parish of St. Clements Dane — 28 July, 1713 —, [Humphrey Jones, of same

Tayler, Grace, of the parish of St. Dunstan's in the West. — 5 Dec. 1724 —, William [Turner, of St. James', Westminster.

Tayler, Mary, of the parish of St. Anne's, Westminster — 20 March, 1715 6 —, [John Tyus, of same

Tayleure, Hannah, of the parish of St. Giles, Cripplegate. — license dated May 1717 —, Samuel Paul, of St [James', Westminster

Taylor, Anne, of St Giles in the Fields. — 1 June, 1732 —, James Brookes, of [St. Andrew's, Holborn

Taylor, Anne, of St. Giles in the Fields — 15 Jan. 1732-3 —, Hugh Hughes, of [St Anne's, Westminster

Taylor, Benjamin, tailor in Nelson's Court, Drury Lane — 20 Jan 1697-8 —, Sara [Browne.

Taylor, Elizabeth — 20 Aug 1696 —, John Rouse, of St James in the Fields, [surgeon

Taylor, Elizabeth — 30 Aug. 1696 —, John Sharples, barber-surgeon in Chan-[cery Lane end, Holborn

Taylor, George, bat, of Westbury, Wilts — 30 May, 1715 —, Margaret Leafe, of [St. Andrew, Holborn, spin

Taylor, Hannah, of St. Giles in the Fields — 6 May, 1714 —, John Humphreys, of [St Paul's, Covent Garden

Taylor, Isaac, bat, of Hammersmith — 29 April, 1719 —, Mary Waller, of St [Stephen's, Coleman St

Taylor, John (Rev), of Swanscomb, Kent — 26 May, 1748 —, Frances Birch, of [Writtle, Essex

Taylor, Robert, of St. James', Clerkenwell — 15 Feb. 1728-9 —, Sarah Simpkin, [of St. John's, Clerkenwell

Taylor, Thomas, Vicar of Hollingbourne, Kent — 4 June, 1726 —, Elizabeth [Hendley, of Ottham, Kent

Taylor, Thomas, of St. Giles in the Fields. — 3 Sept. 1729 —, Margaret Mars, of [St. Paul's, Covent Garden

Taylour, Elizabeth, of the parish of St Mildred, Bread St. — 11 May, 1707 —, Thomas Winckworth, of parish of St [Mary Magdalen, Old Fish St.

Taylour, George, of the parish of St. Clements Dane — 14 July, 1713 —, [Hannah Holcomb, of same

Taylour, John, of the parish of St Clements Dane, Middx — 20 April, 1708 —, Ann [Ridley, of same.

Taylour, Margaret, of the parish of St James, Clerkenwell — 7 Feb. 1713 4 [—, George Moor, of same

Taylour, Richard, of the parish of St. Mary Hill, London. — 9 Oct. 1711 —, Mary [Whitby, of same

Taylour, Susanna, of St Giles, Cripplegate — 2 Sept. 1714 —, John King, of St. [Sepulchres

Taylour, Thomas, gent , of Broad St., parish of St Peter poor. — 16 Dec 1704 —, [Elizabeth Hulse

Taylour, Thomas, of the parish of St Andrew, Holborn, mason in Red Lion St — 26 May, 1706 —, Ann Farmer, of [same (by license)

Teasdle, Mary. — 8 June, 1723 —, John [Johnson

Temple, Elizabeth. — 26 Oct 1699 —, Thomas White, tallow chandler in White [Hart Yd , Drury Lane

Terry, William, of Stroud, Kent — 31 Dec 1751 —, Damaris Wyatt, of Woolwich, [Kent

Tew, Edward, yeoman, of the parish of St. Pancras. — 15 April, 1704 —, Sarah Nichols, of parish of Hendon, Middx. [(by license)

Thacker, Mary — 5 Aug 1701 —, Matthew Bramly, butcher in Little Lincoln's Inn [Fields.

Thacker, Robert, of St. Clements Dane, bat. — 27 Sept. 1720 —, Jane Henly, [of same, spin

Thackeray, William, of St Mary Monthaw, London — 12 Sept. 1734 —, Elisabeth [Burr, of Hocliff, Beds

Thackthet, Joseph, of Iver, Bucks — 31 Jan 1727-8 —, Ann Maund, of St [Andrew's, Holborn

Thatcher, Elizabeth, of St. Martin's, Ludgate. — 24 Nov 1719 —, Joseph Smal-[well, of Maidstone, Kent, widower.

Thatcher, William, of the parish of Highgate, Middx., bat. — 5 May, 1722 —, [Henrietta Frances Longford, of same

Thirly, Sarah, of St. James', Clerkenwell — 7 Sept 1731 —, William Harris, of [same

Thomas, John, of the parish of Kensington — 13 May, 1714 —, Edeth Sheperd, of [same.

Thomas, John, of St George's, Hanover-sq — 12 Feb 1742-3 —, Alice Jones, of [St Andrew's, Holborn

Thomas, Noah, of the Tower of London, M D — 23 April, 1750 —, Susanna [Day, of same.

Thomas, Ursula, of St Andrew's, Holborn — 25 Dec 1736 —, James Cooke, of [St. Dunstan's in the West

Thomas, William, of the parish of St. Mary, Savoy — 6 May, 1712 —, Elizabeth [Moxon, of parish of Greenwich, Kent

Thomas, William, of the parish of St. James, Westminster. — 2 Jan 1712-3 —, Jane [Griffis, of same

Thomas, William, of St Botolph's, Aldgate. — 16 Feb. 1728-9 —, Mary Price, of [St. Giles in the Fields.

Thompson, Jane. —1 May, 1698 —, John Harris, a mariner, near the Lee-Hoy, [St Katharine's.

Thompson, Mary, of the parish of St. Clements Dane. — 22 June, 1711 —, John Martin, of parish of St Giles in [the Fields

Thompson, Susan, of the parish of St Giles in the Fields — 10 Nov. 1713 —, [John Hanmer, of same

Thompson, Susanna — 19 Oct 1701 —, Zechariah Else, brewer's clerk in Hock- [ley Hole.

Thompson, William, vintner in Lime St. [— 7 Dec. 1701 —, Catherine Bamford

Thomson, Ann, of the parish of St. Martin's in the Fields. — 29 March, 1714 —, [Robert Sing, of same.

Thorne, Mary. — 18 Sept. 1706 —, John Wooldridge, cabinet maker in Red Cross [St., parish of St. Giles, Cripplegate.

Thorne, Ruperlia, of the parish of St. Stephen, Walbrook — 7 Dec 1708 —, Richard Collins, of parish of St Andrew's, [Holborn

Thornton, John, labourer in Red Lion Yard, Holborn. — 24 Aug. 1700 —, [Mary Mills.

Thornton, William, gardener, in Richmond parish, Surrey — 19 Nov. 1697 —, [Mary Nixson

Thorold, John, of Lea, co. Lincoln. — 6 Aug. 1730 —, Elisabeth Ayton, of [West Herrington, Northumberland

Thorold, Prudence, of Covent Garden, spin — 5 Feb 1721-2 —, Sir George Brown, [bart, of same

Thorowgood, Robert, of St Sepulchre — [9 Aug 1727 —, Mary Reed, of same

Thorp, Robert, upholsterer in Greek St — [27 Sept. 1696 —, Catherine Milborne.

Thory, William, of St. Brides, Fleet St — 16 Feb 1734-5 —, Elisabeth Burrough, [of St Andrew's, Holborn.

Thurkill, Robert, of Chelsea, bat — 7 Dec [1721 —, Mary Lewis, of same, spin

Thurkill, Susanna, of St. Giles, Cripplegate. — 2 Nov 1713 —, William Boisler, of [parish of Islington.

Thurston, Jones, of the parish of St Giles in the Fields — 1 July, 1712 —, Hannah Davis, of parish of St Andrew's, Hol- [born

Tichborne, Esther, of Ash, Surrey — 30 Oct. 1730 —, John Lee, of Oaking [(Woking), Surrey.

Tiener, Alice, of St. Andrew's, Holborn — 13 Oct 1726 —, Robert Spearing, [of St Martins in the Fields

Tilbury, Thomas, of Ringwood, Hants. — 5 Feb 1742-3 —, Betty King, of St. [Clements Dane.

Tillbury, William, of St. Mary Axe — 10 April, 1729 —, Mary Young, of same

Tinney, Henry, of the parish of St Martins in the Fields —licensed dated Jan 1717-8 —, Mary Siddall, of St. James', West- [minster.

Tinsley, Daniel, *bat*, of Greenwich parish — about 31 Jan. 1714-5 —, Elizabeth [Standwell, *spin.* of same.

Tinwell, Sarah, of the parish of St. Clements Dane — 25 Feb. 1710-1 —, Edward Kirby, of parish of St. Andrew, [Holborn (they had five certificates).

Tipping, Elizabeth, of Chelsea — 8 Oct. 1702 —, George Norris, gardiner, of [same

Todd, Jane, of Wickham, Essex. — 11 June, 1733 —, Marmaduke Allanson, of Yarm, [co. York.

Todd, John, *bat*, of the parish of Bishopsgate — 24 Feb 1714-5 —, Anne Rimon, [*spin* of Barking parish

Todd, John, of St Andrew's, Holborn — 30 April, 1737 —, Elisabeth Bolton, of [same

Todd, Mary, of Edmonton, Middx — 4 May, 1736 —, Henry Harper, of same.

Toepken, Christopher — 30 April, 1723 [—, Sare Herring.

Tolson, Francis, of the parish of St. Andrew, Holborn — 6 April, 1713 —, [Katherine Riches-Puckle, of same

Tombs, Mary, of the parish of St. Martin's. — 17 Jan 1711-2 —, Alexander Sandi- [lands, of same

Tomkin, Mary — 30 Dec. 1698 —, Thomas [Lock, a mariner in Parker's Lane.

Tomlinson, Elizabeth, of the parish of St. Andrew, Holborn — 2 Dec 1714 —, [Thomas Abbitt, of same

Tomlinson, Playdell, of St. Olave's, Southwark — 29 April, 1703 —, James Ash, [gent, of the Inner Temple

Took, Andrew, of the Charter House. — 6 May, 1729 —, Elisabeth Levett, of St [Sepulchres

Toovey, Caleb, of St. Botolph's, Aldersgate — 30 March, 1729 —, Elisabeth [Tresham, of same

Topp, Thomas, of St Giles in the Fields — 13 Feb 1734-5 —, Tamar Allison, [of St. Paul's, Covent Garden

Torver, John, of the parish of St. Bride's. — 2 April, 1711 —, Mary Brabben, of [same

Toune, Mary, of St. Martins in the Fields. — 4 Nov. 1714 —, Gifford Lay, of [St Bride's

Town, Daniel, of St. Martin's, Vintry — 22 Oct. 1730 —, Rachel Maynard, of [St. James', Garlick Hill

Town, Rachel, of St. Martin, Vintry. — 8 [May, 1745 —, John Gould, of same.

Townley, Charles, of the parish of St Dunstan's in the East — 9 June, 1712 —, [Sarah Wild, of Edmonton, Middx

Townsend, Jane, of St Marylebone, *spin* — 1 June, 1720 —, John Petty, *bat*, of [St. Giles in the Fields

Townsend, Philip, shoe maker in Pearpolane — 13 Jan. 1697-8 —, Mary Mit- [chell.

Trappat, James, of the parish of Boreham, Essex. — 8 May, 1709 —, Katherine Wallis, of parish of St. Giles in the [Fields.

Treddwell, Rebecca — 10 Feb 1697-8 —, Charles Key, victualler in Hampstead.

Treegood, Elizabeth, of St. Andrew's, Holborn — 29 March, 1740 —, Raymond Blackmore, esq of parish of [Heathfield, Sussex.

Tresham, Elisabeth, of St. Botolph's, Aldersgate — 30 March, 1729 —, Caleb [Toovey, of same.

Trevor, John, of the parish of St Nicholas, Rochester, Kent. — 18 Feb. 1713-4 —, Mary Gibbon, of St Gabriel, Fenchurch [St.

Trewin, Susanna, of the parish of St. Andrew, Holborn. — 21-26 Oct 1714 —, [Richard Underhill, of same.

Trigg, Mary, *sing* of the parish of St. James, Westminster — 24 Feb. 1714-5 [—, Edward Williams, *bat*, of same.

Trott, William, of St. Saviour's, Southwark. — 26 Aug 1753 —, Elizabeth Lewis, [of St Anne's, Westminster.

Tower, Elizabeth, of St Martin's in the Fields — 20 June, 1719 —, John [Barnes, of same

Trunly, Samuel, of the parish of St Dunstans in the West. — 18 Nov 1716 —, [Elizabeth Tuthill, of same

Trustfield, Martha, of St Brides — 10 Oct. 1714 —, Frederick Bentley, of [St George's, Southwark

Trye, Mary — 26 March, 1701 —, John [Abson, butcher in Clare Market

Tucker, Alice, of Redriffe. — 4 Oct 1711 —, John Cronk, of Bishopsgate parish

Tucker, Benjamin, of St Martins in the Fields — 2 May, 1743 —, Sarah An-[sell, of St Clements Dane

Tufton, Ann, dau of Rt Hon the Earl of Thanet — 12 Feb. 1708-9 —, Rt Hon James, Earl of Salisbury (married by Dr [Savage)

Tuite, Robert, merchant at Mr. Brumigham's, a barber in Finch Lane. — 12 April, [1701 —, Elizabeth Pearce

Tuke, John, of the parish of St Andrew's, Holborn — 18 Nov 1708 —, Ann Norris, of parish of St Ann, Westmin-[ster

Tull, Francis, of Edgware, Middx — 31 Oct. 1714 —, Susanna Walker, of Whitchurch, [Middx.

Tumersid, Jane, *sing.* of the parish of St James in the Fields. — 19 April, 1715 [—, Daniel Brock, *bat*. of same

Tuncks, Abraham, of the parish of Islington — 6 Dec 1713 —, Eleanor Single-[ton, of same.

Turbutt, Elisabeth, of St Giles in the Fields — 12 Jan 1752 —, Samuel [Sorsby, of St. Sepulchre.

Turner, Ann, of the parish of All Saints, Colchester — 13 May, 1703 —, John Herdwix, of parish of Battlesin, Colchester, bag maker (married by a reader [of Covent Garden Church)

Turner, Ann, of the parish of Lingfield, Surrey — 18 June, 1708 —, Thomas [Piggot, of same

Turner, Anne, *widow* of the parish of Epping, Essex — 25 Jan 1714-5 —, [Thomas Osborn, *bat*, of same

Turner, Christopher, of Tunbridge, Kent. — 20 March, 1718 —, Ruth Hill, of [Copland, Kent

Turner, Elizabeth, of the parish of St Dunstans in the West — 23 Feb 1710-1 —, William Smith, of parish of St. An-[drew, Holborn.

Turner, Elizabeth, of St Giles in the Fields. — 23 April, 1714 —, James Lee, of St. [Payts, Shadwell.

Turner, Elizabeth, of the parish of Hampstead — 5 April, 1726 —, Thomas [Gretton, of St. Dunstan's in the West.

Turner, Elizabeth, of Croydon, Surrey — 3 Feb 1733-4 —, George Hart of [Mitcham, Surrey

Turner, Elizabeth, of Tottenham, Middx. — 22 July, 1736 —, Mark Jeaks, of [same

Turner, George, of St Paul's, Covent Garden. — 13 Nov 1729 —, Sibella [D'Oyley, of same

Turner, John, of the parish of St George's, Southwark — 6 April, 1713 —, Ann [Whale, of same

Turner, Martha, of the parish of St. Andrews — 7 July, 1713 —, Thomas Frewin, esq. of parish of Northyam, [Sussex (married by Mr Frewin)

Turner, May — 24 June, 1723 —, William Steele

Turner, Robert, of St Ann's, Westminster — 26 Aug. 1716 —, Jane Willmore, of [St. Dunstan's in the West.

Turner, Roberts, of the parish of St. Dunstans in the East. — 6 Nov. 1707 —, Ann Blake, of parish of All Hallows the [Great

Turner, Sarah, of St. John's parish, Southwark — 6 Feb 1748-9 —, Robert [Watford, of same.

Turner, William, of St James, Westminster. — 5 Dec. 1714 —, Grace Tayler, of [parish of St Dunstans in the West.

Turner, William, of St Bartholomew the Great. — 8 Aug. 1716 — Sarah Wixon, [of Hampstead parish.

Turst, Elisabeth, of St. Mary le bone. — 2 June, 1739 —, Robert Burker, of [Paddington

Tushingham, Mary, of St Andrew, Holborn. — 19 May, 1730 —, William [Hughes, of Staple Inn.

Tutall, Mary. — 3 March, 1695 6 —, Richard Pearch, of Keston, near Bromley, Kent, gent

Tuten, Philip, of St Giles in the Fields — 29 March, 1741 —, Mary Hedges, of [St Anne's, Westminster

Tuthill, Elizabeth, of the parish of St Dunstan's in the West — 18 Nov. 1716 —, [Samuel Trunly, of same.

Tynte, Jane, of St James', Westminster — 23 April, 1737 —, Russhe Hassel, of [St. Giles in the Fields

Tyre, Elizabeth, of Stepney parish — 7 Sept 1714 —, Moses Pearce, of [St. Andrew's, Holborn

Tyrrill, Anne — 2 Dec 1699 —, Thomas Fry, glover, near Iveybridge in the [Strand

Tyus, John, of the parish of St Anne's, Westminster — 20 March, 1715-6 —, [Mary Tayler, of same

Underhill, Richard, of the parish of St Andrew, Holborn — 21-26 Oct 1714 —, [Susanna Trewin, of same

Underwood, Francis, of the parish of St Michael, Cornhill — 7 Sept. 1710 —, Elizabeth Ambrose, of parish of St [Mary Woolnoth

Underwood, Richard, of Ross, co Hereford. —15 Sept 1715 —, Martha Bigg, [of same

Underwood, William (Esq.), of Enfield, Middx — 31 Jan 1737-8 —, Sarah [Darby, of same

Uphallfence, Hannah, of the parish of St. Andrew's, Holborn — 1 Jan 1703-4 —, Thomas Bosworth, of parish of St. Sepulchre, pewterer near Holborn Conduit. [duit.

Uridge, James, of the parish of St James, Westminster — 11 Oct 1715 —, Mary [Robinson, of same

Vale, John, of the parish of St James, Westminster. — 26 Dec. 1716 —, Mary [Weston, of same

Vanmore, Bridget, of the parish of St Andrew, Holborn — 18 Feb 1704-5 —, William Emerson, servant to Squire [Strafford, of same parish.

Varden, Margaret, of St Andrew's, Holborn — 21 March, 1750-1 —, John [Craik, of St. Clements Dane.

Vaughan, Rachel, of St Giles in the Fields — 5 Sept 1716 —, Thomas Boswell, of [same

Vaughan, Thomas, of Stepney parish — 16 Dec 1713 —, Sarah Barton, of [St Katherine's, Tower Hill.

Vean, Ann, of the parish of St Martins in the Fields — 31 Oct 1714 —, Polcer [Hemplock, of same

Velley, Rebecca — 14 Jan 1695-6 —, [Joseph Rickstone.

Ventum, Thomas, poulterer in Great Stanmore, Middx — 1 June, 1701 —, [Mary Graves

Vere, Mary, of St Martin's, Ludgate — 23 Jan 1727-8 —, Nathaniel Adams, of [same.

Vernon, Thomas, of Ashley, co Worcester, bat — 23 Oct. 1721 —, Rachel Jefferys, [of St Martins in the Fields, spin.

Vidler, John, bat., of the parish of Battle, Sussex — 5 Jan 1714-5 —, Sarah Midhurst, sing. of same [hurst, sing. of same

Waddingham, Joseph, of St Martin's in the Fields, journeyman shoe maker — [16 May, 1695 —, Susana Lewis

Wade, Alexander, of the parish of St Andrew, Holborn. — 22 April, 1714 —, Elizabeth [Woodhouse, of same

Wade, Elizabeth, of New Shoreham, Sussex. — 15 Nov 1753 —, Francis Ireland, of [Horton Kirby, Kent clerk.

Wadley, Manasses, of the parish of St. Andrew, Holborn. — 1 May, 1714 —, [Sarah Dolphin, of same.

Wadsworth, Mary, of Chelsea — 24 April, [1723 —, John Jones, of same.

Wainwright, Richard, *bat*, of the parish of
St Clements Dane — 1 March, 1714-5
—, Dorothy Parker, *widow*, of St Mary,
[Savoy

Walden, Mary. — 3 Dec. 1697 —, Job
Dean, hatter in Popping Alley, St.
[Bride's parish.

Walder, Thomas, gent. of Lothbury, London.
— 20 July, 1704 —, Elizabeth Sherwood

Waldron, John, of St. Pancras, Soper Lane
— 4 Nov 1732 —, Elizabeth Smith, of
[same.

Walford, Robert, of St. John's, Southwark.
— 6 Feb. 1748-9 —, Sarah Turner, of
[same.

Walkees, Mary, of the parish of St Martin
in the Fields. — 16 April, 1712 —,
Richard Stocken, of parish of St An-
[drew, Holborn.

Walker, Charles, of the parish of St. Botolph,
Aldersgate — 16 Feb 1713-4 —, Ann
[Ray, of same

Walker, Elizabeth — 14 April, 1700 —,
William March, baker against Smock
[Alley, Spittlefields

Walker, Jane — 22 Oct 1696 —, John
[Newbold, attorner in Middle row.

Walker, Jennet, of St Michaels, Bassishaw.
— 10 April, 1740 —, Bellamy Banyer,
[of parish of St Gregory

Walker, Martha, of St Andrew's, Holborn
— 13 Sept. 1748 —, George Wheeler,
[of same

Walker, Mary, of the parish of St. Clements
Dane — 2 Sept 1711 —, Daniel
[Stephens, of same.

Walker, Sarah, of St Gabriel, Fenchurch
St — license dated Dec. 1717 —,
William Clifford, of St Giles in the
[Fields

Walker, Susanna, of Whitchurch, Middx. —
31 Oct 1714 —, Francis Tull, of Edg-
[ware, Middx.

Walker, Thomas, of the parish of St. Martins, Ludgate — 28 March, 1714 —,
[Dinah Cottle, of St Giles in the Fields

Waller, Anne, of St Helen's, London —
14 Feb 1733-4 —, John Ducker, of
[Limber, co Lincoln

Waller, Mary — 2 June, 1701 —, John
Seears, butcher of Great Stanmore,
[Middx

Waller, Mary, of St. Stephen's, Coleman St.
— 29 April, 1719 —, Isaac Taylor, *bat*,
[of Hammersmith

Walley, John, corn chandler in King St.,
near Bloomsbury, parish of St. Giles in
the Fields — 14 Sept 1704 —, Mar-
[garet Burgen (by license).

Wallis, Elizabeth, of the parish of St
Sepulchre — 12 April, 1714 —, Richard
[Gill, of same.

Wallis, Jacob, of Edmonton, *widower* —
15 Dec. 1720 —, Hanna Brightwell, of
[St. Andrew's, Holborn, *widow*

Wallis, Katherine, of the parish of St Giles
in the Fields — 8 May, 1709 —, James
[Trappat, of parish of Boreham, Essex

Wallis, William, of Detchworth, Herts. —
17 June, 1726 —, Hannah Evans, of
[Tewin, Herts.

Wallman, John, *bat*, of the parish of St
Martin's in the Fields. — 28 Feb 1714-5
[—, Elizabeth Collins, *spin.*, of same

Walter, John, of St Andrew's, Holborn —
3 Oct. 1728 —, Catharine Bradshaw,
[of same.

Walter, Richard (clerk, M A.), of Portsmouth, Hants. — 5 May, 1748 —, Jane
Sabberton, of St Margaret's, Lothbury.

Walton, Mary, of St George's, Hanover-sq
— 28 Oct 1734 —, John Oliver, of St.
[Martins in the Fields

Walton, William, of St Martins in the Fields
— 9 Sept 1722 —, Mary Pritchard, of
[same.

Wane, Mary — 21 Dec 1697 —, Richard
[Stanton, carpenter in Fetter Lane.

Wankford, Henry, of the parish of Rick-
mansworth, Herts — 28 Jan 1724-5
—, Sarah Eve, of parish of Watford,
[Herts.

Wanmer, Robert, *bat*, of St. Martins in the
Fields. — 27 June, 1720 —, Elizabeth
Newby, *spin* of St Dunstan's, Stepney,
[spin

Warburton, Richard, of the parish of St Giles in the Fields. — 21 Sept 1707 —, [Elizabeth Rice, of same (by license).

Ward, Joseph, butcher in Newport Market. [— 25 June, 1697 —, Mary Mills

Ward, Susan, of the parish of St Ann, Westminster — 15 May, 1707 —, Beckwith [Spencer, of parish of Southwell, Notts

Ward, Theophilus, of St. Paul's, Covent Garden. — 20 Sept 1724 —, Hannah [Denton, of same.

Ward, Thomas, bat , of the parish of St Andrew, Holborn — 1 March, 1714-5 —, Mary Williams, sing of St. James, [Clerkenwell.

Wardour, Anne — 29 Sept. 1698 —, Gideon Bonnivert, soldier, in Panton [Street

Warker, Mary, of Hungerford, Berks — 26 Feb 1708-9 —, Joseph Sare, of same

Warner, Elizabeth — 19 Nov. 1704 —, Thomas Slinte, of Cabbage Lane, St Margaret's, Westminster, by a parson [from the fleet

Warner, John, of the parish of St Martin's, Ironmonger lane — 8 Feb 1706-7 —, [Ann Shower, of parish of Clerkenwell

Warren, Mary, of the parish of St. Pancras — 5 May, 1713 —, John Nicholls, of [same

Warren, Matthew, jun , of St. Mary, Abchurch — 3 Sept. 1723 —, Ann [Robinson, of St Michael, Cornhill.

Wasdell, Anne — 17 Feb. 1701-2 —, Daniel Davis, servant to Mr Littlebury, [in Hendon.

Washford, Margaret, of St. James', Westminster — 24 Oct 1723 —, George [Riley, of same

Waterland, Theodore, rector of Long Stanton, co Cambridge. — 9 June, 1726 —, Mary Yate, of parish of St. Michael [Royal, London

Watkins, Elizabeth, of the parish of St. Andrew, Holborn — 4 Dec. 1712 —, Thomas Duffin, of parish of St Mar[garet More

Watkins, Katherine, of the parish of Aldgate, London. — 14 June, 1710 —, [George Honner, of same.

Watson, Elizabeth — 2 Sept 1697 —, Lodowick, als Lewis Price, shoe maker [in St Giles.

Watson, Grace — 2 Jan. 1699-1770 —, Thomas ffallitt, farmer in Chicheley [parish, Bucks.

Watson, Richard, of the parish of Harefield, Middx — 14 April, 1714 —, Elizabeth [Living, of same.

Watson, Thomas, of this Society. — 9 Sept 1736 —, Jane Cray, of St Dunstan's in [the West

Watton, Thomas, of the parish of St Giles in the Fields — 3 Sept. 1710 —, Mary [Green, of same

Watts, Dennis, or Denins. — 3 Feb 1697 8 —, Matthew Bunce, clock maker in Pear[pool lane

Watts, Elizabeth, widow, of the parish of St. Mary, Savoy — 21 Jan 1714-5 —, [Edward Higden, sing , of same.

Watts, Giles, of the parish of St. Mildred, Poultry — 2 March, 1712-3 —, Ann [Hill, of St. Giles, Cripplegate.

Watts, Hannah — 5 June, 1701 —, Peter Bazire, barber, in Dean St., St An[drews.

Watts, Mary, of the parish of St. Gregory. London — 18 Oct 1745 —, Peter [Marr, of same

Way, Elizabeth, of St Dunstan's in the West. — 14 Nov. 1731 —, Bloomer Ireland, [of St. Martin's le grand.

Way, Philadelphia, of St Andrew's, Holborn — 15 Aug. 1730 —, Ambrose Prowse, [of South Petherton, Somerset.

Weatherall, Mary, of the parish of St Martins in the Fields — 22 July, 1714 [—, John Whitny, of same

Weatherley, James, bricklayer in Clerkenwell parish — 17 May, 1697 —, Mary [Kilborne

Weaver, John, of the parish of Hornsey, Middx. — 20 Oct 1714 —, Elizabeth [Smith, of same.

Weaver, Thomas, of St. Dunstan's in the West — 18 Aug. 1736 —, Agatha Rabbuts, of the precinct of Norton Folgate

Weaving, William, of the parish of St Dunstans in the East — 28 Aug 1711 —, Grace Long, of parish of Deptford

Webb, Augustin, *bat*, of the parish of St. Sepulchre — 9 Jan 1714-5 —, Eliza-[beth Buck, *widow*, of same

Webb, John, of Greenwich. — 12 June, [1729 —, Sarah Fendale, of Deptford

Webb, Mary, of Maidstone, Kent — 21 April, 1712 —, Robert Cooke, of Tot-[tenham High Cross.

Webb, Sara, of Hillydon, *spin* — 9 Jan [1720-1 —, John Davies, *bat.*, of same.

Webel, Grace, of St Giles in the Fields, *spin* — 23 April, 1719 —, Benjamin Broadhead, *bat*, of St Andrew's, Holborn.

Wedale, Upton, of St Lawrence, old Jewry, *spin* — 22 Dec 1718 —, William Wood, [*bat*, of St Mary's, Aldermanbury

Weekes, Catherine. — 26 Dec. 1700 —, Archibald Cahoun (Colquhoun?), chandler against the New Chapel, Westmin-[ster

Weeks, John, of the parish of St Ann's, Westminster — 15 April, 1710 —, Elizabeth Denew, of parish of St James', [Westminster

Welch, Andrew, merchant in Mark Lane [— 6 Aug 1699 —, Anne Robinson

Welden, Amos, of the parish of St Giles in the Fields — 30 Dec 1712 —, Mary Selby, of parish of St Paul's, Covent [Garden

Welden, Elizabeth — 17 Nov 1700 —, Seth Martin, fishmonger at Smithfield [bars

Welles, Daniel, of St Clement's, Eastcheap — 29 June, 1730 —, Mary Dennis, of [St Botolph's, Aldersgate

Wells, Judith, of St Giles in the Fields — 19 Jan 1730-1 —, Thomas Hooke, of [same

Wells, Luke, *widower*, of the parish of St. Giles, Cripplegate. — 25 March, 1715 [—, Mary Delarus, *spin*. of same

Wells, Margaret, of St. Margaret's, Westminster — 25 July, 1749 —, John Spencer, of St. Bartholomew's, behind [the Change.

Wells, Mary, *sing*, of the parish of St Giles in the Fields — 17 Dec 1744 —, John [Barrett, *bat*, of same.

Wells, Mary, of St Michael, Crooked Lane, — 1 June, 1736 —, Stephen Huntly, of St Bartholomew, near the Royal Ex-[change.

Wesson, Carolina — 12 Jan 1698-9 —, William Bibbey, journeyman tailor at [the White Hart, Bloomsbury

West, Charles, gent, in Nagshead Court, Fenchurch St. — 5 Nov 1700 —, Mary [Canby.

West, Constance, servant to Squire Montague in Lincoln's Inn Fields — 28 Sept 1702 —, John Hussy, servant to [same gent

West, Henry, coachman in Swallow St., parish of St. James, Westminster. — 24 Aug 1704 —, Frances Winch, of [St. Andrew's, Holborn

West, Mary, of St Andrew's, Holborn. — 8 Feb 1753 —, Peter Davies, of same.

Westbrooke, Richard, of Deptford, Kent — 3 Feb 1729-30 —, Margaret Easton, [of same.

Westland, Mary, of the parish of St Luke's, Old St — 13 Nov 1737 —, Robert [Willis, of same.

Westmore, John, of Parivale (*sic.*) parish, Middx, husbandman — 30 April, 1696 [—, Susana White

Weston, John, of St Dunstan's in the West — 12 April, 1724 —, Elizabeth Young, [of St Sepulchres.

Weston, Mary, of the parish of St. James, Westminster — 26 Dec 1716 —, John [Vale, of same.

Weston, Sarah, *widow*, of St Andrew, Holborn. — 27 Jan. 1714-5 —, Richard Morphew, *bat*, of parish of St Sepul-[chre

Weston, Sarah, of the parish of St. Andrew, Holborn — 27 Oct 1716 —, Jacob [Rossam, of same.

Weston, Susan, of the parish of St Andrew's, Holborn — 12 Aug 1708 —, Samuel [Keay, of same.

Weston, Thomas, of St Sepulchre — 19 [Dec 1713 —, Sarah Asher, of same.

Westward, Elizabeth, of Edmonton parish — 11 Sept. 1716 —, William Lenton, [of Finchley parish

Wetenhall, Thomas, a gent of Peckham, Kent. — 16 June, 1697 —, Elizabeth [Butler

Wetherley, Judith. — 14 May, 1699 —, Vincent Engham

Whale, Ann, of the parish of St. George's, Southwark. — 6 April, 1713 —, John [Turner, of same

Wheatley, Solomon, of St Bride's, Fleet St. — 30 Nov 1727 —, Elisabeth [Nicholas, of same

Wheeler, George, of St Andrew's, Holborn — 13 Sept 1748 —, Martha Walker, of [same.

Wheeler, John, tailor near Drury Lane End, St Giles — 6 July, 1701 —, Mary [Batchelor

Wheeler, Joice, of St James, or St. Ann's, Westminster. — 28 Jan 1702-3 —, William Printon, victualler of Edmonton, [Middx

Wheeler, Robert, gingerbread baker at Cow Cross — 6 Oct 1698 —, Anne [Meacham

Wheeler, Susanna, of St Sepulchre — 30 Nov 1725 —, James Rowe, of St. Mar-[garet's, Westminster

Wheelwright, Bridget. — 18 April, 1698 —, Thomas Shipward, corn chandler in [Middle Row, Holborn

Whetton, Mary, of St Anne's, Soho — 23 June, 1751 —, Benjamin Allen, of St [Clements Dane.

Whitby, Mary, of the parish of St Mary Hill, London — 9 Oct 1711 —, [Richard Taylour, of same

Whitchurch, Elizabeth, of Salisbury, Wilts. — 15 April, 1732 —, John Whitchurch, of Symond's Inn (married by Mr Whit-[church, curate of Chiselhurst, Kent)

Whitchurch, John, of Symond's Inn. — 15 April, 1732 —, Elizabeth Whitchurch, of Salisbury, Wilts (married by Mr Whitchurch, curate of Chiselhurst, Kent)

Whitchurch, Mary, of St Andrew, Holborn — 10 Jan 1727-8 —, Richard [Cooke, of same

Whitchurch, Robert, tailor in Russell Court, parish of St Martins in the Fields — 7 March, 1705-6 —, Hannah Johnson, of [St Giles in the Fields

White, Audry, of the parish of Christ Church, Southwark. — 28 Aug 1713 —, Edward Milner, of same (Mr Nevil, an [apothecary in King St present).

White, Elizabeth — 25 Nov 1699 —, [Joseph Brooke, servant.

White, Elizabeth, of the parish of St James, Westminster — 7 Feb. 1713-4 —, [George Skeen, Esq of same

White, Hannah, of St Paul's, Covent Garden. — 11 Aug 1748 —, Joseph Payne, [of Hammersmith

White, Henry, of the parish of Chelsea — 27 March, 1735 —, Mary Praynald, of [St Andrew's, Holborn.

White, Jane, of St Andrew's, Holborn — 24 Nov 1729 —, Thomas Higgs, of [same

White, Mary, of the parish of Mortlake, Surrey — 8 Oct 1713 —, Richard [March, of same.

White, Mary, of Whitefriars Precinct — 5 Feb 1727-8 —, Thomas Bryan, of St [James', Westminster

White, Samuel, linen draper in Winchester, Hants — 18 Aug 1702 —, Joan Darby, [of Wimborne Minster, Dorset.

White, Sarah, of St Andrew's parish, Holborn — 23 June, 1737 —, William [Perkins, of same

White, Susana. — 30 April, 1696 —, John Westmore, of Parivaile (sic) parish, [Middx, husbandman.

White, Thomas, tallow chandler in White Hart Yard, Savoy parish. — 30 June, [1696 —, Elizabeth, Chester

o

White, Thomas, tallow chandler in White Hart Yd , Drury Lane — 26 Oct 1699 [—, Elizabeth Temple

White, Thomas, of the parish of Stevens, Coleman St. — 22 June, 1714 —, Mary Dasnett, of parish of St. Giles, Cripple- [gate.

Whitehall, Joseph, of Kentish Town, Pancras parish. — 28 Nov 1719 —, Eliza- [beth Bocker, of same

Whitehead, Mary, of St. Clements Danes — 1 Jan 1727-8 —, Robert Macgie, of [St Martins in the Fields

Whitehurst, Katherine, of the parish of St James, Westminster — 22 March, [1710-1 —, James Lindesay, of same

Whiteing, John, of the parish of St Katherine, near the Tower of London — 27 May, 1707 —, Elizabeth Beaumont, of [parish of St Bride's

Whitell, Alice, of St James', Westminster. — 17 Dec 1713 —, John Hawkins, of [parish of St Martins in the Fields.

Whitford, Thomas, of St Bartholomews, near the Royal Exchange — 14 June, 1736 —, Mary Scott, of St Botolph, [Aldersgate

Whiting, Anne — 18 May, 1700 —, George Crump, surgeon, against Villiers St , [Strand

Whitlow, Hannah, of Wycombe, Bucks — 23 April, 1704 —, Edward Foot, woolcomber, of parish of St. Martin's, near [Salisbury, Wilts

Whitmore, Isabella, of the parish of St Sepulchre — 6 Dec 1712 —, George [Bishop, of same

Whitny, John, of the parish of St. Martins in the Fields — 22 July, 1714 —, Mary [Weatherall, of same.

Whitwell, William (Esq), of Oundle in Northampton. — 26 Jan. 1716-7 —, Anne Griffin, of Dingley, co Northamp- [ton.

Whitworth, Elisabeth, of St John's, Southwark — 12 June, 1750 —, Thomas Bradshaw, of St Mary Magdalen, Ber- [mondsea

Wichehallse, John, of St Andrew's, Holborn — 7 Feb 1735-6 —, Mary Bar- [rington, of same

Wiggins, Paul, of the parish of St James, Westminster — 28 Aug 1715 —, Anne [Masters of same

Wightman, Cuthbert, late of Morpeth, Northumberland — 13 Sept 1715 —, [Dorothy Young, late of same

Wild, Sarah, of Edmonton, Middx — 9 June, 1712 —, Charles Townley, of parish of [St Dunstan's in the East

Wildgoose, Mary, of St James, Westminster — 30 Aug 1728 —, Christopher Key, [of same

Wilds, Judith, of the parish of St Andrews, Holborn — 13 April, 1710 —, Joseph [Birch, of same

Wilford, Mary, of the parish of St Andrew, Holborn — 13 Feb. 1715-6 —, Matthew [Speer, of same.

Wildford, Sara — 9 May, 1695 —, Robert Meade, coachman, of St Andrew's, Hol- [born.

Wilkes, William, of Whitefriars. — 14 Sept 1723 —, Elizabeth Plimloy, of Highgate, [Middx.

Wilkin, Mary, of the parish of St Andrew — 21 May, 1738 —, William Baxter, of [same

Wilkins, Catherine, of St. Olave's, Southwark. — license dated June 1717 —, Richard Beaser, of parish of St Mar- [garet's Westminster

Wilkinson, Richard, of the parish of St. Anns, Westminster. — 20 Jan. 1707-8 —, Elizabeth Boone, of parish of St. [Martins in the Fields.

Wilkinson, William, of St. Mary's, Aldermanbury — 6 March, 1728-9 —, Elisa- [beth Smith, of St Magnus the Martyr

Wilks, Francis, of St. Dionis, Backchurch. — 6 April, 1731 —, Mary Jeffries, of [St. Andrew's, Holborn.

Wilks, Joan — 8 Aug 1697 —, William [Wrench, a sedan man in St James'

Willets, Margaret, spin of the parish of St Andrew, Holborn — 28 Dec 1714 [—, John Malchar, bat , of same

Willett, William, of St Andrew's, Holborn — 2 Nov. 1753 —, Betsey Ramsey, of [Rumford, Essex.

Williams, Edward, *bat*, of the parish of St James', Westminster — 24 Feb [1714-5 —, Mary Trigg, *sing* of same

Williams, Ellis, of the parish of All Hallows the Less, Thames St — 17 Nov. 1737 [—, George Smedley, of same.

Williams, Jane, of the parish of St Andrew's, Holborn — license dated Nov 1717 [—, William Carter, of same

Williams, John, victualler, Newton St, St Giles — 19 May, 1698 —, Ruth Exall

Williams, Margaret — 6 June, 1695 —, John Belson, of St Giles Fields, yeo-[man

Williams, Mary, of the parish of St Edmund the King — 13 Jan 1707-8 —, William King, of parish of St Nicholas [Acrons.

Williams, Mary, *sing*, of St James, Clerkenwell. — 1 March, 1714-5 —, Thomas Ward, *bat*, of parish of St Andrew, [Holborn

Williams, Mary, *sing*. of the parish of St. Andrew, Holborn. — 13 March, 1714-5 [—, William Ruff, *bat*, of same

Williams, Mary, of St George the Martyr — 4 Oct 1726 —, Samuel Brown, of [same.

Williams, Moses, of Dyfynoly, co Brecon. — license dated Jan 1717-8 —, Elizabeth Battell, of St Margaret's, Westminster

Williams, Richard (Esq), of the Middle Temple. — 22 Dec 1738 —, Sarah [Bishop, of Manningtree, Essex.

Williams, Thomas, of St. James', Garlick Hill — 31 Oct 1714 —, Johanna [North, of St. Mary Over, Southwark.

Williams, Thomas, of St. Margaret's, Westminster — 30 June, 1741 —, Susanna [Peckham, of same.

Williams, William, of Finchley, Middx — 5 March, 1711-2 —, Elizabeth Blake, of [St Botolph's, Aldersgate

Williamson, Elizabeth, of St Katherine by the Tower — 24 June, 1714 —, Henry Hurry, of parish of St John, Wapping

Williamson, Isabella — 9 Feb. 1696-7 —, John Denins, haberdasher of small wares [in Paul's Alley

Williamson, Thomas, of St. George's, Bloomsbury — 27 July, 1743 —, Jane [Morley, of same

Willimott, Isabella — 29 Aug 1697 —, William Dobbs, a powtherer next Temple [Bar

Willis, Robert, of the parish of St Luke, Old St — 13 Nov 1737 —, Mary West-[land, of same

Willmore, Jane, of St. Dunstan's in the West — 26 Aug 1716 —, Robert Tur-[ner, of St Ann's, Westminster

Willmott, Mary, of St Mary, Whitechapel, *sing* — 12 Jan. 1714-5 —, Richard Jones, *sing*, of parish of St Giles in the ·[Fields

Wills, Joshua, of Yeterton, co. Northampton — 19 Aug. 1714 —, Elizabeth Gibbs, of [St James, Clerkenwell

Wills, Pascho, of the parish of Hornsey, Middx. — 1 Jan 1713-4 —, Ann Ros-sell, of parish of Aldermanbury, London

Willson, Charles, of the parish of St Botolph without Aldgate — 5 Nov 1710 —, [Mary Pantalini, of same.

Willson, Charles, of the parish of St. Giles in the Fields — 30 Oct. 1714 —, Mary [Philips, of same

Willson, Elizabeth, of St. Peter Poor, Wood St — 22 Nov 1714 —, Ister Lefeuer, [of St Dunstans, Stepney

Willson, Elizabeth, *widow*, of the parish of St Giles in the Fields — 26 Feb. 1714-5 [—, John Reynolds, *bat*, of same

Willson, Mary, of the parish of St. Martin's in the Fields — 12 Nov 1710 —, Jonathan Foun——, of parish of St. [Giles, Cripplegate

Willson, Susan. — 20 July, 1704 —, James Jackson, gent of the parish of St An-[drew's, Holborn

Wilmore, William, a broker in Drury Lane — 11 March, 1695-6 —, Mary Man-[drell.

Wilson, Anne, of Newcastle upon Tyne — 14 March, 1741-2 —, John Parker, of [St. Andrew's, Holborn

Wilson, Daniel, of St James', Westminster — 6 Aug 1724 —, Sarah Greenup, of [St Andrew's, Holborn

Wilson, Edward, of the parish of St Ann's, Blackfriars. — 1 June, 1712 —, Elizabeth Ellond, of parish of St Giles in the [Fields

Wilson, Edward, of St Andrew's, Holborn — 10 July, 1731 —, Mary Atkinson, [of St Magnus, near the Bridge.

Wilson, James, weaver, near to Bishopsgate [— 24 Sept 1696 —, Hester Jefferys

Wilson, Katherine, of Leithorpe, co Leicester — 1 March, 1711-2 —, Charles Parker, Esq. of Peterboro', co North-[ampton.

Wilson, Robert, coachman, Lincoln's Inn Fields — 4 July, 1695 —, Elizabeth [Kitching.

Wiltshire, Henry, dyer at Lambeth — 11 [Nov 1697 —, Mary Starman

Winch, Frances, of St. Andrew's, Holborn — 24 Aug 1704 —, Henry West, coachman in Swallow St, parish of St James, [Westminster

Winckworth, Thomas, of the parish of St Mary Magdalen in Old Fish St. — 11 May, 1707 —, Elizabeth Taylour, of [parish of St Mildred, Bread St

Winder, Henry, coachman at Kensington [— 13 Jan 1697-8 —, Anne Lobb

Winder, Thomas, of parish of Rotherwick, co Southampton. — 19 May, 1709 —, [Mary Dobson, of City of Oxford

Windsor, George, of St Andrew's, Holborn — 4 Nov 1714 —, Elizabeth Dennis, of [St Alphage.

Wingfield, Anne, of St Andrew's, Holborn — 23 Nov 1718 —, William Chase, of [St Michael, Cornhill.

Winne, Alice, of the parish of St. Giles. — 7 Sept. 1703 —, Thomas Smith Cowell, [printer in Plumtree St, same parish

Winter, James, of St Bartholomew the Great — 19 May, 1731 —, Ann Savage, of [St Andrew's, Holborn.

Wintle, Durley, of St James', Westminster — 17 Feb 1749-50 —, Mary Berners, [of Hampstead.

Withrell, Mary, of St Giles in the Fields, *widow*. — 10 June, 1722 —, Thomas Stuart, *bat.*, of St. Martin's in the [Fields

Witt, John, of St James', Westminster — 26 Oct. 1723 —, Hester Skelton, of [St. Paul's, Covent Garden.

Witton, Mary, of the parish of St Andrew, Holborn. — 7 Oct. 1711 —, Samuel [Moxon, of same

Wixon, Sarah, of Hampstead parish — 8 Aug 1716 —, William Turner, of [St. Bartholomew the Great

Woddle, George, of the parish of St Giles — 21 Feb 1713-4 —, Elizabeth Hill, of [same

Wogan, John, of Gaudy Hall, Norfolk — 8 May, 1735 —, Elizabeth Sancroft, of [St. James', Westminster

Wolfrys, Sarah — 24 Jan, 1704-5 —, Joseph Cooper, cheesemonger, of parish [of St Stephen's, Coleman St.

Wollfrys, St. John, farrier without Bishopsgate. — 31 Aug 1699 —, Elizabeth [Burchell

Wood, Anne, of Culford, Suffolk — 13 Oct. 1748 —, John Richards of Cwsdon, [Suffolk

Wood, Lionel, of the parish of St Giles, Cripplegate — 6 Nov 1712 —, Sarah Dickinson, of parish of St. Olave's, [Silver St

Wood, Mary. — 26 May, 1696 —, Thomas Croutch, a tailor lodging in Gray's Inn [passage

Wood, Mary, of the parish of Epsom. — 29 May, 1706 —, John Lancaster, servant to Madam Parrot, in Leadenhall St

Wood, Mary, of the parish of St Sepulchre. — 3 Nov 1713 —, Robert Gardiner, of [same

Wood, Sarah, of the parish of Littleton, Middleton. — 23 Oct. 1713 —, John Lohaire, of parish of St Giles in the [Fields.

Wood, Sarah, of the parish of Mortlake, Surrey — 28 Jan 1713-4 —, John [Betton, of same

Wood, Sarah, sing (æt about 47), of the parish of St. Martins in the Fields — 29 March, 1714 —, John Holland, [widower (about 50), of same.

Wood, Thomas, of St Giles in the Fields — 7 Sept 1741 —, Martha Maria Hud- [son, of St Martins in the Fields

Wood, William, bat , of St Mary's, Alder- manbury — 22 Dec 1718 —, Upton Wedale, of St Lawrence, Old Jewry, spin

Woodcock, Elizabeth — 12 Nov 1698 —, John Serjent, a disbanded soldier in [Drury Lane.

Wooder, Catharine, of Gatton, Surrey — 16 June, 1737 —, George Griffin, of [parish of Ewell, Surrey.

Woodfield, John, of St. Martins in the Fields — 6 May, 1714 —, Mary Day, of parish of St. Mary Magdalen, Ber- mondsey.

Woodford, Edward, bricklayer in Russell St , Covent Garden — 19 May, 1704 —, [Mary Holms

Woodhouse, Elizabeth, of the parish of St Andrew, Holborn — 22 April, 1714 —, [Alexander Wade, of same.

Woodhouse, Jane. — 17 Feb 1701-2 —, Thomas Hopkins, parish clerk of Hamp- [stead.

Woodroffe, Elizabeth, of St Martins in the Fields — 14 Sept 1728 —, Thomas [Parkyns, of Deptford

Woods, Katherine. — 30 Nov 1706 —, Bernard Lens, of parish of St Paul's, [Covent Garden (by license).

Wooldridge, John, cabinet maker in Red Cross St , parish of St Giles, Cripple- gate — 18 Sept 1706 —, Mary Thorne

Woollard, Elizabeth, of the parish of St James', Clerkenwell — 25 May, 1742 [—, Henry Frith, of same

Woollaston, Michael, of Highgate. — 29 Jan. 1727-8 —, Sarah Anderson, of [same.

Woolley, Elizabeth, of St George's, Blooms- bury — 23 Aug. 1739 —, William [Staverton, of same.

Woolley, Judith — 21 May, 1723 —, [Robert Ashurst

Woolley, Thomas, of Edgar, Middx. — 18 May, 1735 —, Elisabeth Hiley, of St [Laurence Pountney, London.

Worgan, John, of the parish of St Botolph, Bishopsgate — 4 Sept 1711 —, Mary [Lambert, of same

Worral, George, of Long Sutton, co Lin- coln. — 5 May, 1730 —, Mary Hasle- [wood, of Eltham, Kent

Worrall, Penelope, of the parish of St An- drew's, Holborn. — 22 Aug. 1703 —, Samuel Francomb, victualler in Fetter [lane, same parish.

Worswick, Mary, of St George the Martyr — 28 April, 1728 —, Thomas Jeanes, [of St. Paul's, Covent Garden.

Wotton, William, of St Clements Danes. — 31 Dec 1724 —, Lettice Shuckburgh, [of St Paul's, Covent Garden

Wren, John, of the parish of Maidstone, Kent — 2 July, 1707 —, Mary Cum- [bridge, of same

Wrench, William, a sedan-man in St James' [— 8 Aug 1697 —, Joan Wilks.

Wright, Elinor — 26 Jan 1704-5 —, Robert Harrison, haberdasher of small wares in Gerrard St , parish of St Ann's, [Westminster

Wright, James, bat , of the parish of South Mimms, Middx. — 24 Feb 1714-5 —, [Mary Day, spin of same.

Wright, John, of Kentish Town — 22 March, 1710-1 —, Dorothy Smart, of [parish of St Clements Dane

Wright, John, of the parish of St James, Westminster — 11 Aug 1713 —, [Katherine Reeves, of same

Wright, John, of the parish of St Martins in the Fields — 22 Sept 1715 —, [Martha Church, widow, of same

Wright, Joseph, of All Hallows, Bread St. — 13 June, 1738 —, Sarah Reynolds, of Peckham, Surrey (by Rev Daniel Bentley).

Wright, Rice, of the parish of St. Giles in the Fields. — 22 Aug. 1714 —, Margaret Shippin, of parish of St Andrew, [Holborn.

Wright, Richard, of Hanwell parish, Middx., husbandman — 26 Nov. 1695 —, Anne [King.

Wright, Thomas, hostler at the Star, in New Fish St. — 26 Dec. 1695 —, Martha [Medcalf.

Wright, Thomas, of the parish of St James, Westminster — 13 May, 1712 —, Hannah Rush, of St Ann's, Westminster

Wyat, Anne, of St. Andrew's, Holborn, *spin.* — 5 Feb. 1719 —, William Hooper, [*bat*., of St James, Westminster

Wyatt, Damaris, of Woolwich, Kent — 31 Dec. 1751 —, William Terry, of Stroud, [Kent.

Wybergh, Elizabeth. — 11 Nov 1697 —, John Bennit, woolcomber in Plough St, [Whitechapel.

Wyllymot, Martha, of the parish of St. Giles in the Fields — 1 July, 1708 —, Ralph Hassell, of parish of St Mary Magdalen, [Milk St

Wymondesold, Charles, of Wanstead, Essex — 28 May, 1748 —, Hon Miss Henrietta Knight, of St. James', West- [minster

Wynde, William, *bat.*, of St Giles, Cripple-gate. — 9 Jan. 1714 5 —, Mary Dagger, [*sing.* of St. Andrew's, Holborn

Wynn, Mary, of St Martins in the Fields — 9 April, 1730 —, John Mayo, of same.

Wynn, William, of the parish of St. James, Clerkenwell — 20 Nov 1713 —, Mary [Roberts, of same

Wyse, Thomas (Esq.), of this Inn — 16 Jan. 1738-9 —, Hester Edwards, of [St James, Westminster

Wytt, Elizabeth, of St James', Clerkenwell. — 17 July, 1707 —, Bryan Mills, of [parish of St. Sepulchre.

Yate, Mary, of the parish of St. Michael Royal, London — 9 June, 1726 —, Theodore Waterland, rector of Long [Stanton, co Cambridge.

Yates, Elizabeth, *sing* of the parish of St Anne's, Westminster — 14 Dec 1714 [—, Thomas Cooke, *bat*, of same

Yates, Hannah, of Charterhouse Yard. — 8 Oct. 1719 —, Humphrey Cooper, *bat*, [of Barnet, Herts.

Yeandell, Hester, of St. Dunstan's in the West. — 12 Aug 1716 —, Laurence [Jones, of St. Andrew's, Holborn

Yexly, Francis, of the parish of Cheshunt, Herts — 30 Aug. 1711 —, Jane Combs, [of same

Young, Ann, of the parish of St Andrew, Holborn — 12 Sept 1714 —, Thomas Sandwich, of parish of Christ Church, [Southwark

Young, Bartholomew (Esq.), of Broadfield Suffolk, *bat* — 20 Oct. 1718 —, Mary Sutton, of St Edmunsbury, Suffolk, [*widow.*

Young, Charity, of the parish of St Magdalen, Bermondsea — 18 April, 1714 [—, Richard Young, of same

Young, Dorothy — 13 Sept 1715 —, Cuthbert Wightman, late of Morpeth, [Northumberland

Young, Elizabeth, of St. Martins in the Fields. — license dated Sept. 1717 —, [Isaac Lowsley, of Hampstead parish.

Young, Elizabeth, of St Sepulchres — 12 April, 1724 —, John Weston, of St [Dunstans in the West.

Young, James, *bat*, of St Andrew's, Holborn — 31 Dec 1719 —, Esther Hob- [day, of same, *spin*

Young, John, of the parish of St Andrew, Holborn. — 7 Feb 1711-2 —, Mary [Bird, of same.

Young, Martha, of St. Martin's, Vintry — 3 Nov. 1723 —, Thomas Law, of [Hertford

Young, Mary, of St Mary Axe. — 10 April, [1729 —, William Tilbury, of same.

Young, Rachel, of St. Martin, Vintry. — 12 April, 1724 —, Edward Bickerton, of [St. Stephen's, Coleman St

Young, Richard, of the parish of St. Magdalen, Bermondsea. — 18 April, 1714 [—, Charity Young, of same

Young, William, of the parish of St Michael Basishaw — 6 March, 1708-9 —, Emblyn Brown, of parish of Rotherhithe, [Surrey.

ADDENDA.

Egerton, Lady Elizabeth. — 6 May, 1718 —, Lord Thomas Catesby
[Paget

Hulton, Jane, of St. Stephens, Kent. — 31 March, 1718 —, Christian
[William Kirshhoff, of parish of St Clements, East Cheap

Holland, John, *widower* (aged about 50), of the parish of St Martins in the
[Fields. — 29 March, 1714 —, Sarah Wood, *sing.* (about 47), of same.

CPSIA information can be obtained at www.ICGtesting.com
235040LV00003B/8/P